THE MANAGEMENT CHALLENGE

An Introduction to Management

THE MANAGEMENT CHALLENGE

An Introduction to Management

JAMES M. HIGGINS
Crummer School
ROLLINS COLLEGE

MACMILLAN PUBLISHING COMPANY
New York
COLLIER MACMILLAN CANADA
Toronto

Acquisitions Editor: Charles E. Stewart, Jr.
Developmental Editor: Lee M. Marcott
Production Supervisor: J. Edward Neve
Production Manager: Richard C. Fischer
Text & Cover Designer: Sheree L. Goodman
Photo Researchers: Vicki Bonomo, Chris Migdol
Art Buyer: Anna Yip
Illustrations: York Graphic Services, Inc.

Cover Illustration: This three-dimensional paper sculpture was created expressly for **The Management Challenge** *by illustrator, Pat Allen. The international aspects of the current management environment, which are a key focus of the text, are deftly captured in this illustration.*

This book was set in Sabon by Waldman Graphics, Inc., printed and bound by Von Hoffmann Press, Inc. The cover was printed by Lehigh Press, Inc.

Macmillan Publishing Company
866 Third Avenue, New York, New York 10022

Collier Macmillan Canada, Inc.
1200 Eglinton Avenue East
Suite 200
Don Mills, Ontario M3C 3N1

Library of Congress Cataloging-in-Publication Data

Higgins, James M.
    The management challenge : an introduction to management / James
M. Higgins.
        p.   cm.
    Includes bibliographical references.
    ISBN 0-02-354471-6
    1. Management. I. Title.
HD31.H48823   1991
658—dc20

89-78468 CIP

Printing: 2 3 4 5 6 7 8   Year: 1 2 3 4 5 6 7 8 9

*This book is dedicated to Charles Stewart
and Lee Marcott, colleagues in this adventure.*

Preface

The decade of the 1990s will be more challenging to managers than any decade that has preceded it. Only by being prepared for the challenges they will face can managers hope to manage effectively.

When I first began this project in the fall of 1986, there were several very good introductory management texts in the market. Several more have come into the marketplace since then. But now, as in 1986, these books generally have three major weaknesses: they do not focus on the changing nature of management; they do not take a creative problem-solving perspective; and their chapters present collections of theories rather than an integrated approach to the subject in question. **The Management Challenge** was written to address these perceived weaknesses in the available textbooks.

The five key features of this book are:

1. Its focus on the changing nature of management in response to ten management challenges in the internal and external managerial environments.
2. The problem-solving aspect of the managerial process, both for the individual manager and as a part of his or her role in aiding the creative problem-solving efforts of others.
3. The integration of various theories into models for the major subject areas helps students to understand how different approaches to management fit together.
4. The pedagogical elements of each chapter were chosen to support the learning process and include such features as learning objectives, boxed **Management Challenges** and **Global Management Challenges**, summaries, discussion questions, and cases.
5. The instructor's task is facilitated by the availability of an outstanding Supplements Package including an **Annotated Instructor's Edition**, which has a wealth of teaching notes in the margin and also indicates when audiovisual materials are available for use with the text. These instructional aids include overhead transparencies and one video segment per chapter.

I believe that this text stands alone among management books for what it can offer the student and the instructor. It provides the student with a means to understand the changing nature of management in the hectic decade we are in. It offers the instructor the added dimension of improving his or her teaching effectiveness. A brief look at the end-of-book References will convince the reader of the currency and academic soundness of the material presented here. In addition, the book has been praised by reviewers for its clarity, interesting themes, and overall success in conveying the wealth of information that comprises the study of management. Every effort was made to design and illustrate the book to encourage the reader to read further. Both the drawings and the photographs were carefully chosen to closely complement the text and to make the book inviting to look at.

In the following sections we will take a closer look at the five key features listed above and the benefits they provide teacher and student alike.

The Changing Nature
of Management

Ten challenges facing management are identified in the first chapter and reappear as themes throughout the text.

1. As they occur in each chapter, they are identified by a symbol in the text margin to indicate that one of these ten challenges has relevance to the point being made. Traditional theories and approaches to management are presented, but how they are changing and will have to change in future are identified.

2. At the end of each chapter the challenges that are discussed and possible solutions to these challenges are listed.

3. Focusing on these challenges, the student not only learns the basics of management but how management is changing, and can be expected to change further in the future.

The Focus on the
Problem-Solving
(Decision-Making) Processes

Research and experience clearly show that the primary function of a manager is to creatively solve problems and/or facilitate the creative problem-solving efforts of others, principally subordinates. This text demonstrates that concept in several different ways:

1. Each chapter on the functions of management is presented from the viewpoint of how a manager would make decisions.

2. Problem solving is covered early in the text in Chapter Three so that the student understands how the decision process occurs and how the presentations of the following chapters are related to the basic model of decision making.

3. At the end of most chapters, especially those discussing the functions of management—planning, leading, organizing, and controlling—the standard decision-making model presented in Chapter Three is displayed with the contents from each chapter as they relate to the basic decision-making model. This helps the student understand how the material from that chapter relates to problem solving.

4. Each chapter contains two to five **Management Challenges** and one **Global Management Challenge**. These boxes describe a company's problem situation and the efforts they undertook to solve that problem. In most cases these are well-known companies such as General Motors, IBM, Apple Computer, Xerox, Toyota, and Philips, among others.

Integrative Models of the
Management Functions

In many of the chapters, for example those on problem solving, strategy, motivation, communication, leadership, human resource management group processes, organizing and operations management, integrative models of those processes are presented. These models reveal how the major theories and approaches discussed in that chapter fit together so that the student will achieve a higher level of understanding than might otherwise be possible. The chapters are not merely collections of theories, but rather offer an integration of theories in that subject area.

Chapter Pedagogy

Each chapter has been carefully designed to provide students with a maximum number of learning experiences.

1. Each chapter opens with a set of **Chapter Objectives** and a **Chapter Outline**.

2. This is followed by a boxed opening **vignette** on some well-known company and its efforts to solve a management problem.

3. Two opening **quotations** from well-known people help focus attention on the content or importance of the chapter.

4. Each chapter contains two to five **Management Challenges** and one **Global Management Challenge**, which highlight problem-solving efforts by managers at companies both domestic and international.

5. Most chapters are constructed around a **model** so that students understand how the various theories and approaches work in an integrated way.

6. Marginal notes refer back to the boxed opening vignettes and demonstrate how that opening case can be related to the points under discussion.

7. Each chapter closes with:

a. A **Summary** that provides a brief review of the chapter organized to reflect the list of **Chapter Objectives**.

b. A list of **discussion questions** called **Thinking About Management**.

c. Two **cases**: The **Case** describes well-known companies' attempts to resolve typical problems encountered by modern managers and organizations. The second case— **Managers at Work**—features individual managers on the job and encourages students to consider their own course of action, given the same situation.

d. Finally, an **exercise**, called **Manage Yourself**, helps students understand how the chapter contents may apply to them personally.

8. **Marginal symbols** are used to identify when a management challenge is being discussed in the chapter.

The Supplements Package

The supplements package has been carefully prepared to aid the instructor teaching the course and the student in mastering the material. All of the supplements have been written and carefully reviewed to ensure consistency with the text and to conform to the highest standards of quality. A description of each of the student supplements in the package follows. A list of the instructor supplements is also provided.

Student Supplements

The **Study Guide** was prepared by Marcia Kurzynski of Cleveland State University. For each of the 23 chapters and 7 parts there are introductions, chapter objectives, outlines, and summaries. Key terms and concepts are highlighted. A variety of test questions allow students to test their understanding of the material. These include fill-in, true/false, multiple-choice, matching, and discussion questions. An Answer Key is provided.

The **Experiential Exercises** were prepared by Daniel James Rowley, University of Northern Colorado. At least four experiential exercises have been created for each chapter that help students develop problem-solving skills in real-life scenarios. Each activity includes the amount of time needed to complete the activity, the type of experience (group or individual), materials needed, an exercise objective, and discussion questions. An **Experiential Exercise Instructor's Manual** has been prepared by Daniel Rowley, which contains objectives and possible answers for each activity.

The **Software Cluster** has been created by Eugene Calvasina and Lee Barton, Auburn University at Montgomery, Alabama. This software program was designed to take a managerial problem-solving simulation and divide it into steps so that students are introduced slowly to concepts and do not become overwhelmed. It walks students through the decision-making process and demonstrates how one decision interrelates to another. The **Software Cluster** consists of the **Management Simulation**; the **Student Manual**, which contains exercises and the learning objectives covered; and the **Instructor's Manual**, which includes teaching objectives and solutions.

Instructor Supplements

An integrated **Annotated Instructor's Edition** (AIE) has been prepared for instructors' use. It includes many marginal annotations in each chapter that are designed to aid the instructor in preparing for class presentations. In addition, whenever overhead transparencies or videotapes are available to accompany the text, they are pointed out in the AIE. A small pink video symbol indicates that a video segment is linked to the chapter, challenge, or case. A pink notation for "Transparency Overhead" indicates that this figure or table is available as an overhead.

The **Instructor's Lecture Manual/Resource Guide** was prepared by Gene Burton, California State University, Fresno. Sample course outlines are provided as well as chapter-by-chapter lecture outlines and teaching notes. Teaching resources include chapter objectives, overviews, key terms, lecture outlines, chapter summaries, discussion questions and answers, case summaries, and suggested term paper topics. Selected audiovisual materials and software are recommended. All the material in this Guide has been written specifically for it and is in addition to the teaching annotations in the AIE.

The **Test Bank** was prepared by Garth Coombs, University of Colorado at Boulder and Gene Burton, California State University, Fresno. It contains over 4,000 test questions with a minimum of 170 questions per chapter. There are three types of questions: multiple-choice, true/false, and essay. One-half of the questions are terminology/concept-oriented and one-half are applied/comprehensive/integrative. The **Test Bank** has been critically reviewed to ensure accuracy and is offered in two forms—a printed **Test Bank** and **MTS** (Macmillan Testing Software).

MTS Computerized Testing System enables you to create, build, edit, style, and print flawlessly structured tests for your individual classes. **MTS** is available for IBM-PC, XT, AT, PS/2, or compatibles.

Macmillan Grader is a computerized grading system that can assist in managing student grades and reports. Convenient and time-saving print-outs can be produced for important recordkeeping.

A **Transparency Pack** of 150 overheads is available that reproduces many of the figures from the text. They were selected for their importance in complementing lecture content and are sequenced as they appear in the book. A number of transparencies were created specifically for this pack and provide additional teaching resources. The **Transparency Pack** is available free to adopters of the book.

A **Slide Package** of 150 color slides have been prepared to accompany the text. The slide set is available free to adopters of the book.

The educational **Video Package** has been edited and a **Video Guide** prepared by Trudy Verser, Western Michigan University. Each chapter of the book is accompanied by a seven- to ten-minute videotape that has been chosen, in most cases, to match one of the boxed opening vignettes, **Management Challenges**, **Global Management Challenges**, or cases described in that chapter. The companies featured in the videos are all well-known companies or organizations, such as 3M, Exxon, Chrysler, NASA, Volvo, Toyota, Xerox, McDonnell Douglas, Milliken, NCR, Federal Express, and many others. These videos are introduced by John McVay, Vice President for Football Operations of the San Francisco 49ers, arguably the best-managed of all the professional football franchises. McVay provides keen insight into the changing nature of management in general, and with respect to the 49ers, in his brief introductions to the videos.

Here is a complete listing by chapter of the videos available for **The Management Challenge**:

1. Apple Computer: MacWorld '88 Expo
2. 3M: Practical Dreamers
3. Fort Wayne, Indiana
4. Exxon: Cleaning Up the Valdez Oil Spill
5. Manufacturers Hanover: Geoserve
6. Baldor: The New Baldor Story
7. Intel: The Microcomputer Company
8. Chrysler: The Turnaround
9. NASA: Return to Space
10. Volvo: At the Torsland and Kalmar Plants
11. Toyota: Quality People
12. Eaton: The Eaton Philosophy
13. Xerox: The Malcolm Baldrige Award
14. AAL: Self-managing Work Teams
15. Morehouse College
16. McDonnell Douglas: The Chairman's Quarterly Report
17. Milliken: The Malcolm Baldrige Award
18. NCR: Awareness Program
19. Federal Express: Setting the Pace for the '90s
20. Allen Bradley: Computer Integrated Manufacturing
21. GE: Serving the World
22. Speech by Stew Leonard: Entrepreneur
23. 3M: Our World Tomorrow

Acknowledgments

No book is produced solely by the author. A book project, especially one as complex as this one, is a product of many minds. The many reviewers, most of whom reviewed most of the book, provided in-depth analyses of the manuscript. Several of them reviewed drafts at different stages of development. Their thoughtful insights are greatly appreciated. The reviewers on the project were:

Benjamin L. Abramowitz
University of Central Florida

Larry G. Bailey
San Antonio College

Steven Barr
Oklahoma State University

Daniel J. Brass
Pennsylvania State University

Gene E. Burton
California State University, Fresno

Thomas M. Calero
Illinois Institute of Technology

Alan Chmura
Portland State University

Garth Coombs, Jr.
University of Colorado, Boulder

Joan G. Dahl
California State University, Northridge

Leon A. Dale
California State Polytechnic University

C. W. Dane
Oregon State University

Theodore Dumstorf
East Tennessee State University

Stanley W. Elsea
Kansas State University

Douglas Elvers
University of North Carolina, Chapel Hill

James E. Estes
University of South Carolina

Janice M. Feldbauer
Macomb Community College

Lloyd Fernald
University of Central Florida

James A. Fitzsimmons
University of Texas, Austin

David A. Gray
University of Texas, Arlington

David Grigsby
Clemson University

Gene K. Groff
Georgia State University

Eileen B. Hewitt
University of Scranton

Marvin Karlins
University of South Florida

Ann Maddox
Angelo State University

Jane MacKay
Texas Christian University

Solon D. Morgan
Drexel University

Daniel James Rowley
University of Northern Colorado

John Vassar
Louisiana State University, Shreveport

Trudy G. Verser
Western Michigan University

Douglas Vogel
University of Arizona

Louis P. White
University of Houston, Clear Lake

My special thanks go to Susan Crabill, who has word processed this manuscript through numerous drafts and shown an amazing amount of patience over these four years.

Marty Schatz, Dean of the Crummer School, Rollins College, is to be commended for providing an environment in which authoring textbooks is encouraged and supported with the finest in electronic hardware and software.

I also want to thank Susan Lamp, who has provided encouragement during the past several and very hectic months of the project.

The Macmillan team is to be commended for an outstanding effort. I especially want to thank Charles Stewart, Senior Editor, and Lee Marcott, Developmental Editor, for truly, without them it would never have reached fruition.

The contributions of Bill Oldsey, former Executive Editor, and David Boelio, currently the Editor in Chief for Business and Economics, are very much appreciated. Their faith in the book and financial backing made it possible to realize my vision.

I would like to thank the design and production team for their outstanding effort: Rick Fischer, Production Manager; Sheree Goodman, Senior Designer; Edward Neve, Production Supervisor; and Anna Yip, Art Buyer. The following members of the project team are also to be congratulated: Michelle Byron, Supplements Editor; Kevin Flanagan, Senior Marketing Manager; Randi Goldsmith, Media Editor; Diane Kraut, Assistant Photo Editor; Chris Migdol, Photo Editor; Tom Nixon, Business and Economics Sales Specialist. Freelance photoresearcher Vicki Bonomo supplied all the photographs that appear herein.

Many companies, individual managers, and students have served as examples throughout the book. Most have been shown striving to be better managers, and thereby serve as role models for other aspiring managers. Their efforts are to be noted and commended.

James M. Higgins
Winter Park, Florida
August 1990

Brief Contents

Part One
Introduction

CHAPTER ONE

The Changing Management Process   3

CHAPTER TWO

Learning from Management History   33

Part Two
Problem Solving

CHAPTER THREE

The Manager as a Decision Maker
and Creative Problem Solver   67

CHAPTER FOUR

The Managerial Environment: Social
Responsibility and Ethics   103

Part Three
Planning

CHAPTER FIVE

The Planning Process and
Organizational Purpose   137

CHAPTER SIX

Strategy Formulation and Implementation   173

CHAPTER SEVEN

Quantitative Methods for Problem Solving
and Planning   209

Part Four
Organizing

CHAPTER EIGHT

The Organizing Process   245

CHAPTER NINE

Organizational Design   283

CHAPTER TEN

Job Design   313

CHAPTER ELEVEN

Staffing and Human Resource Management   347

CHAPTER TWELVE

Managing Culture and Organizational Change   385

Part Five
Leading

CHAPTER THIRTEEN

Motivation and Performance   421

CHAPTER FOURTEEN

Group Dynamics   459

CHAPTER FIFTEEN

Leadership   495

CHAPTER SIXTEEN

Managing Communication   531

Part Six
Controlling

CHAPTER SEVENTEEN

Controlling Performance: Strategic, Tactical,
and Operational Control   565

CHAPTER EIGHTEEN

Management Control Systems   597

CHAPTER NINETEEN

Management Information Systems and Control   629

Part Seven
Contemporary Issues
in Management

CHAPTER TWENTY

Operations Management   659

CHAPTER TWENTY-ONE

Managing in an Ever-Changing Global
Environment   697

CHAPTER TWENTY-TWO

Entrepreneurship, Small Business Management,
and Innovation   729

CHAPTER TWENTY-THREE

Careers and Management   755

Glossary   G-1

References   R-1

Company Index   I-1

Name Index   I-4

Subject Index   I-8

Contents

Part One Introduction

CHAPTER ONE

The Changing Management Process   3

Ford Changes the Way It Manages   4

Approaches to the Study of Management   6
> Management as a Functional Process 6 • Management as the Enactment of Roles 10 • Management as the Utilization of Certain Skills 11

Global Management Challenge:
Korea Exports Its Management Style   12

Organizations and Managers   12
> Types of Managers 13

The Universality of Management   17
> Management in For-Profits and in Not-for-Profits 18

The Managerial Environment   19

Management Challenge 1.1: Does Management
Make a Difference?—You Bet It Does   20
> The External Environment 20 • The Internal Environment 20

Management: An Art or a Science, or Both?   21
> Developing Management 21

The Management Matrix   22

The Changing Managerial Process—The Management Challenges   23
> Changing Employee Expectations as to How They Should Be Managed 24 • The Global Economy 24 • The Shift from an Industrially Based Economy to an Information-Based Economy 24 • Accelerated Rates of Change 25 • Increased Levels of Competition 25 • The Impact of Changing Technology, Especially Computers 25 • Finding a More Creative Approach to Improve Problem Solving 26 • Emphasis on Managing Organizational Culture 26 • The Increasing Demands of Constituents 26 • Changing Demographics: The Cultural Diversity of the Work Force 26

Management Challenge 1.2: Turning Employees On   27

Management Challenges and the Following Chapters   27

The Changing Face of Management—Is Everyone a Manager?   28

The Management Challenge   28

Summary   29

Thinking About Management   30

Case: Xerox Struggles to Cope   30

Managers at Work: Motivating Employees at General Mills   31

Manage Yourself: Should You Be a Manager?   31

CHAPTER TWO

Learning from Management History   33

General Motors Strategic Woes   34
Precursors of Modern Management Theory   36
    Management Reflects Society 36
The Classical Approaches to Management   37
    Scientific Management 37 • Administration and
    Organization 41 • Legacy of the Classical Approaches to
    Management 45
The Behavioral Approach to Management   45
    The Hawthorne Studies 46
Management Challenge 2.1: The Changing Business Curriculum   48
The Management-Science Approach to Management   48
    Models and Techniques 48
The Systems Approach to Management   49
Global Management Challenge:
Daimler-Benz Automaker! Conglomerate?   52
The Contingency Approach to Management   53
Management Challenge 2.2: Procter & Gamble Alters
Historically Ingrained Management Practices   54
Contemporary Management—A Synthesis   55
    Obtaining a Synthesis 55 • Japanese Management
    Approaches 56 • The Excellence Approach to Management 57
Management in the Future   60
The Management Challenges Identified   60
Some Solutions Noted in the Chapter   61
Summary   61
Thinking About Management   62
Case: IBM: Prisoners of What They Know?   63
Managers at Work: Florida Informanagement Services   64
Manage Yourself: The Management History Crossword Puzzle   65

Part Two Problem Solving

CHAPTER THREE

The Manager as a Decision Maker
and Creative Problem Solver   67

Fort Wayne Makes a Comeback   68
The Core Management Function   69
    Creative Problem Solving Versus Decision Making 70
The Creative Problem-Solving Process   73
Global Management Challenge: Porsche Takes Stock
of Its Situation, Makes Critical Decisions   73
    Constant Environmental Analysis 73 • Recognition of Problems
    or Opportunities 75 • Problem Identification 76
Management Challenge 3.1:
American Home's Costly Conservatism   76
    Making Assumptions About the Future 77 • Alternative
    Generation 78 • Evaluating and Choosing Among
    Alternatives 78

Management Challenge 3.2:
Revitalizing the Harvard Business Review   78
    Implementing the Choice 80 • Control 80
Conditions Under Which Decisions Are Made   80
    Problem Solving Under Conditions of Certainty 80 • Problem
    Solving Under Conditions of Risk 81 • Problem Solving in
    Uncertain Environments 81
Types of Problems and Decisions   82
    Structured Versus Unstructured Problems 82 • Anticipated
    Problems Versus Surprises 83
Management Challenge 3.3: Kodak Unleashes Its Creative Juices   84
Individual Versus Group Decision Making   84
    Major Types of Decision-Making Groups 84 • Advantages and
    Disadvantages of Group Decision Making 87
Behavioral Aspects of the Decision Process   87
    The Economic Model of Decision Making 88 • The
    Administrative Model of Decision Making 88
Problem-Solving Styles and Tendencies   89
    Problem-Solving Styles 90
How Much Participation, and When?   90
    Revisions: The Vroom-Yago Model 93
The Manager as a Creative Problem Solver   94
Management Challenge 3.4: 3M—Masters of Innovation   94
The Management Challenges Identified   97
Some Solutions Noted in the Chapter   97
Summary   97
Thinking About Management   98
Case: What's Teaching Excellence?   99
Managers at Work: Sun Equity   100
Manage Yourself: The Farley Test for Risk Takers   101

CHAPTER FOUR

The Managerial Environment, Social
Responsibility, and Ethics   103

The Valdez Oil Spill   104
The Nature of the Business Environment   107
    The Competitive Environment 109 • The General
    Environment 110
Management Challenge 4.1: Cracks in the Ivory Tower   112
External Organizational Environments: Stability and Complexity   113
The Organization/Environment Interface   114
    Adapting to the Environment 114 • Changing the
    Environment 114
Social Power and Social Responsibility   116
    Contrasting Views of Social Responsibility 116 • Levels of
    Responsibility 119
Management Challenge 4.2: Uncommon Decency:
Pacific Bell Responds to AIDS   122
    Identifying the Issues 122 • The Philosophy of
    Responsiveness 123
Management Challenge 4.3: Florida Power & Light Company
Shows Innovative Ways of Coexisting with the Environment   124
Improving Social Responsiveness   125

Corporate Social Policy Process 126 • The Social Audit 127 •
The Litigation Audit 127

Corporate Social Responsibility and Profitability — 127
Mechanisms of Social Control with Which
Managers Must Contend — 128
Ethics — 129
How the Individual Manager Should Decide 130 • How
Companies Can Improve Ethical Performance 130

Global Management Challenge: Good Neighbors — 131
Social Responsibility, Ethics, and Problem Solving — 132
The Management Challenges Identified — 132
Some Solutions Noted in the Chapter — 132
Summary — 133
Thinking About Management — 133
Case: Animal Torture or Research? — 134
Managers at Work: A Question of Ethics — 135
Manage Yourself: Grappling with Controversial Issues — 135

Part Three Planning

CHAPTER FIVE

The Planning Process
and Organizational Purpose — 137

Barnett Banks: Planning for Success — 138
Plans and Planning — 141
Management Challenge 5.1: Downsizing at AT&T — 141
The Importance of Planning 142 • Levels of Planning in the
Organization 142 • Standing, or Single-Use, Plans 144

Management Challenge 5.2: Barnett Is a Creative Planner — 149
Management Challenge 5.3: Wells Fargo and Strategic Response — 150
Planning and Control 150 • The Planning Situational, or SWOT,
Analysis 151 • The Limitations of Planning 151

*Global Management Challenge: Planning Is More
Than Difficult in the Soviet Union* — 152
Why People Fail at Planning 154 • Establishing an Environment
Conducive to Planning 154

Organizational Purpose — 155
Vision and Mission 155
*Management Challenge 5.4:
Jeff Campbell's Vision for Burger King* — 156
Goals and Objectives 159 • Managing by Objectives 161
*Management Challenge 5.5:
Competing in the Silicon Death Valley* — 000
Management by Objectives, Results, and Rewards 164 •
Alternatives to Objective-Based Systems 164 • Setting
Personal Objectives 165

Planning as a Problem-Solving Exercise — 165
The Management Challenges Identified — 167
Some Solutions Noted in the Chapter — 167
Summary — 167
Thinking About Management — 169

Case: Holiday Inns—Finding the Trip
a Bit More Difficult in the 80s   170
Managers at Work: An Information Services Division   171
Manage Yourself: Learning About MBORR   171

CHAPTER SIX

Strategy Formulation and Implementation   **173**

Sears: Getting Competitive   174
Strategic Planning, Strategic Management, Strategic Thinking   176
    The Strategic Management Perspective 177 • Strategic
    Thinking 178
Strategy Formulation   178
SWOT Analysis   179
    Planning Premises 179
Strategy Formulation at the Corporate Level   180
    Single Business Corporate Strategy 180
Management Challenge 6.1: The Zenith PC Strategy   182
    Multiple Business Corporate Strategy 184 • Strategy and the
    Industry Life Cycle 186
Strategy Formulation at the Business Level   187
    Generic Strategies—The Porter Competitive Strategies 187
Management Challenge 6.2: Milliken Uses Creativity
to Overcome Foreign Competition   189
    Hall's Competitiveness Model 190 • Other Generic
    Strategies 191 • Creating a Competitive Advantage 192 •
    Concern with the Product/Industry Life Cycle 192
Strategy Formulation at the Functional Level   193
The Strategists   193
Management Challenge 6.3: Baldor's Success Depends on
Functional Strategies   194
Human Behavior and Strategy   194
Strategic Planning and Different Types of Organizations   195
    Small Business 196 • Not-for-Profits 196 • International
    Business 196
Global Management Challenge: Thomson Wants
to Be Number One in Consumer Electronics   198
    Regulated Businesses 198
Strategy Implementation   198
    Organizational Structure 198 • Management Systems 199
Management Challenge 6.4: Boeing—Can It Live with Success?   200
    Leadership Style 200 • Management of Organizational
    Culture 201
Strategic Management in Increasingly Complex and Turbulent
Environments   202
Strategic Management as a Creative Problem-Solving Endeavor   202
The Management Challenges Identified   202
Some Solutions Noted in the Chapter   204
Summary   204
Thinking About Management   204
Case: Coca-Cola Is Shaken Up   205
Managers at Work: Apple MacIntosh for the Year 2000   206
Manage Yourself: Strategy Formulation   207

CHAPTER SEVEN

Quantitative Methods for Problem Solving and Planning   209

Citgo Embraces Management Science   210
Foundations of Quantitative Methods   212
     The Advantages of Quantitative Methods 213 • Disadvantages of Quantitative Methods 214
Fundamental Quantitative Decision-Making Techniques   214
Global Management Challenge: Statistics Assist Energy Policy
Decision Making in the Parliament of Finland   216
     Statistical Analysis 217 • Decision Theory: Decision Trees and Expected Value 218
Additional Quantitative Techniques for Problem Solving   221
     Inventory Models 221 • Queueing Models 221 • Distribution Models 222
Management Challenge 7.1: Marshall's Distribution System   222
Quantitative Techniques for Planning   223
     Forecasting 223
Management Challenge 7.2: GE Finds Sales Forecasting
Difficult in the Locomotive Industry   224
     Forecasting Techniques 225
Management Challenge 7.3: Polishing the Big Apple   227
     Qualitative Methods 228 • The Limits of Forecasting 228 • Forecasts: A Summary 228
Additional Quantitative Planning Techniques   229
     Break-even Analysis 229 • Linear Programming 231
Management Challenge 7.4: Linear Programming of Defense
Budget Decisions in the Air Force   232
     Network Models PERT/CPM 232
The Uses of Computers in Decision Making and Planning   235
     Simulations 236
Management Challenge 7.5: Computer Simulation
Redesigns the Factory Floor   236
Management Science as Decision Support for Problem Solving   238
The Management Challenges Identified   240
Some Solutions Noted in the Chapter   240
Summary   240
Thinking About Management   241
Case: Chrysler Corporation Must Cut Its Break-even Point   242
Manage Yourself: Using PERT/CAM to Build a Custom
Sports Car   243

Part Four Organizing

CHAPTER EIGHT

The Organizing Process   245

IBM Restructures to Meet the Challenges
of a Changing Environment   246
Organizing   247

Division of Labor—The Job   248
    Division of Labor 248 • Specialization of Labor 248 •
    Differentiation 249 • The Organization Chart 249

Management Challenge 8.1: Slimming Down at Chevron   250
    What the Organization Doesn't Show 251

Delegation of Authority   253
    Authority 253 • Delegating Authority 253 • The Scalar Chain
    of Command 253 • The Acceptance Theory of Authority 254 •
    Parity: Delegated Authority Must Equal Responsibility 254 •
    Centralization Versus Decentralization 255 • Line and Staff
    Authority 256 • Functional Authority 258

Departmentation   258
    Departmentation by Economic Function of the Organization 259 •
    Departmentation by Product 260

Management Challenge 8.2:
Apple Computers Reverses Its Structure   261
    Departmentation by Strategic Business Unit 262 •
    Departmentation by Geography 263 • Departmentation by Task
    Specialty 264 • Departmentation Based on Time 265 •
    Departmentation by Client or Customer 265 • The Complexities
    of Pyramidal Structural Possibilities 265

The Managerial Span of Control   265

Management Challenge 8.3: General Motors
Structure Is Too "Tall"   267

Coordination   268
    Formalization 268

Global Management Challenge: Rousing a Sleeping Giant   268
    Complexity 269 • Integration and Differentiation 270 •
    The Manager as a Linking Pin 270 • Additional Coordination
    Devices 271

Additional Structures   272
    Project Structure 272 • The Team 272 • The Matrix
    Organization 273 • Joint Ventures and Strategic Alliances 274 •
    Informal Structure 275

Organization as Problem Solving   276
The Management Challenges Identified   278
Some Solutions Noted in the Chapter   278
Summary   278
Thinking About Management   279
Case: Restructuring at BankAmerica   279
Managers at Work: Coping with Overgrowth   280
Manage Yourself: Designing a New Organizational Structure   280

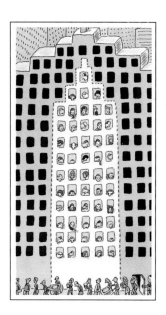

CHAPTER NINE

Organizational Design   283

Eastman Kodak Restructures in Order to Compete   284
Organizational Design   286
Strategy, the External Environment, and Organizational Design   287
    Strategies and Structures 287

Management Challenge 9.1: Bethlehem Steel
Restructures to Survive   288

Mechanistic and Organic Structures—Varying Responses to
External Environments 288 • Mintzberg's Five Types of
Organizational Design 290

Management Challenge 9.2: NASA's Challenge:
Overcoming the Challenger Catastrophe 294
Global Management Challenge: Honda and Adhocracy? 296
    The Lawrence and Lorsch Studies on Differentiation and
    Integration 297
Size, Age, Growth, and Organizational Design 298
    Growth Theories of the Firm 299 • Mintzberg's Five
    Configurations Theory 300 • Growth Theories in Review 301
Management Philosophy 301
Technology 301
    The Woodward Studies 302
Geographic Dispersion 304
Choosing the Appropriate Structure 304
The Shape of Things to Come 305
Organizational Design as a Problem-Solving Process 306
The Management Challenges Identified 308
Some Solutions Noted in the Chapter 308
Thinking About Management 309
Case: Managing After Restructuring 310
Managers at Work: Somebody Has to Be Let Go 311
Manage Yourself: Understanding Structural Related Factors 311

CHAPTER TEN

Job Design 313

Work Redesign at Volvo 314
A Situational Model of Job Design 316
Structural Elements at the Micro Level 317
Management Challenge 10.1:
General Motors' Problems in Job Design 319
Job Design and the Quality of Work Life 319
Job Redesign Effort 320
    Job Enlargement and Job Enrichment 320 •
    Work Simplification 321 • Job Rotatation 322
Job Redesign at the Group Level 322
    Autonomous Work Teams 322 • Quality Circles 322
How Job Redesign Works 324
    Reflections on Job Enrichment 326 • Matching Job Design to
    Individual Growth Needs 327
Management Challenge 10.2: Bethlehem Steel's
Efforts to Become More Competitive 330
    The Effects of Job Redesign on Other Jobs 331
Technology and Job Design 331
    Robotics 331
Global Management Challenge: The Apple Orchard 332
    Office Automation 334 • Work at Home 334 • Worker
    Expectations 334
Management Challenge 10.3: Citibank's Job Enrichment Program 336
Time Also Influences Work Design 336

Management Challenge 10.4: Creativity in Job Design 338
    Part-Time Workers 339 • Compressed Work Week 339 •
    Job Sharing 339
Job Design as a Problem-Solving Process 339
Management Challenges Identified 341
Some Solutions Noted in the Chapter 341
Summary 342
Thinking About Management 342
Case: Work Redesign at Motorola 343
Managers at Work: The Customer Should Be the Focal Point 343
Manage Yourself: The Eight Primary Job Dimensions 344

CHAPTER ELEVEN

Staffing and Human Resource Management 347

Honeywell's Systems and Research Centers'
Human Resource Practices 348
Human Resource Management Practices 350
Equal Employment Opportunities (EEO) 350
Management Challenge 11.1: IBM's Commitment
to Equal Employment Opportunity 352
Placing the Employee 353
Human Resource Planning 353
    Human Resource Planning Process 354 • Job Analysis and
    Design 357 • Forecasting the Need for Human Resources 358 •
    EEO Considerations of Job Specifications 359
Recruitment 360
    Factors Affecting the Ability to Recruit 360 • Matching the
    Recruit with the Organization 360 • Who Recruits? 361 •
    Sources of Job Applicants 361 • The Job Application 361 •
    EEO Considerations 361
Global Management Challenge: Toyota, An Exacting Employer 362
Selection 363
    The Application Blank 363 • Interviews 364
Management Challenge 11.2: Increased Use of Personality Tests
for Entry-Level Blue-Collar Jobs 364
    Employment Testing 365 • Reference Checks 367 • Physical
    Exams 367 • Employment Decisions 368 • Assessment Centers:
    Selecting Managers 368 • Realistic Job Previews 368
Orientation 368
Training and Development 369
Management Challenge 11.3:
Aetna's Institute for Corporate Education 370
    Ongoing HRM Practices 370
Continuing Employee Development and Training 371
Compensation and Benefits/Motivation 372
    EEO Considerations 373
Employee Health and Safety 373
Employee Relations 375
Managing Change 375
Employee Evaluation and Control 376
    Performance Appraisal 376 • Grievance Procedures 377
Employee Transitions 378

HRM and Organizational Strategy 378
Recent EEO Developments 378
HRM and Staffing as Problem Solving 378
The Management Challenges Identified 380
Some Solutions Noted in the Chapter 380
Summary 380
Thinking About Management 381
Case: First Service Bank 382
Managers at Work: Managing the Work Force of the 1990s 382
Manage Yourself: Lawful or Unlawful? 382

CHAPTER TWELVE

Managing Culture and Organizational Change 385
John Sculley Redefines the Culture at Apple Computers 386
The Management of Organizational Culture 387
    Culture as Revealed in Artifacts 388
Management Challenge 12.1: Eaton Corporation 392
Culture and Strategy 393
    Tough-Guy, Macho Culture 393 • Bet-Your-Company
    Culture 393 • Work Hard/Play Hard Culture 395 •
    Process Culture 395
Shared Values That Organizations Espouse 396
Management Challenge 12.2: The Creative Organizational Culture 398
Fitting Employees into the Company Culture 398
Management Challenge 12.3: Providing Important
Culture at General Electric 400
    Managing Culture 401 • Multiple Cultures 402
Management Challenge 12.4: Pillsbury: A Clash of Cultures 403
Organizational Climate 403
    Assessing Organizational Climate 404
Managing Change 406
Organizational Development 407
    Resistance to Change 409
Management Challenge 12.5: Harley-Davidson
Changes Culture to Survive 410
Global Management Challenge: Moments of Truth 414
Managing Culture and Change as Problem Solving 414
The Management Challenges Identified 415
Some Solutions Noted in the Chapter 415
Summary 417
Thinking About Management 417
Case: A Du Pont Division's Need to Transform Its Culture 418
Managers At Work: Hughes Supply Company 419
Manage Yourself: What Kind of Manager Are You? 419

Part Five Leading

CHAPTER THIRTEEN

Motivation and Performance 421
Jim Johnson: Master Salesman and Motivator 422

The Motivation Cycle   424
Global Management Challenge: Motivation According to
New Rules   424
    Content and Process Theories   427
Stage 1 of the MPC: Needs   427
    The Hierarchy of Needs   427   •   The Nature and Strength of
    Current Needs   430
Management Challenge 13.1: A&P Shares
Profits to Increase Them   430
    Managerial Implications   431   •   Achievement Motivation   432   •
    Additional Categories of Needs   433   •   Manager and Employee
    Needs   435
Stage 2: The Manager Must Recognize and Be Able
and Willing to Satisfy Needs   435
Stage 3: Offering Extrinsic and Intrinsic Need Satisfiers   436
    Herzberg's Theory   436
Stage 4: The Individual Searches for Alternative, Evaluates the
Consequences of Possible Action, and Makes a Decision   438
    Expectancy Theory   438   •   Equity Theory   440
Management Challenge 13.2: American Airlines Struggles
with the Two-Tier Pay System   442
Stage 5: Motivation to Expend Effort   442
Stage 6: Factors That Turn Motivation into Performance   442
    Goal (Objective) Setting   443
Stage 7: Performance   444
Stage 8: The Individual Obtains the Need Satisfiers or Not   444
    Reinforcement of Effort   445   •   Types of Reinforcement   446   •
    How Effective Is It?   448
Management Challenge 13.3: Using Reinforcement
Approaches to Change Employee Health Habits   449
Stage 9: The Individual Reassesses the Situation or Not   450
Stage 10: Will the Individual Continue to Be Motivated in the
Same Way or Not?   450
Influencing Motivation as Creative Problem Solving   451
The Management Challenges Identified   453
Some Solutions Noted in the Chapter   453
Summary: Guidelines for Using the Motivation/Performance Cycle   453
The Guidelines   454
Thinking About Management   454
Case: Nucor Steel   455
Managers at Work: Motivating the Difficult Employee   455
Manage Yourself: How Important Are Various Needs on the Job?   456

CHAPTER FOURTEEN

Group Dynamics   459

Teamwork at General Foods: New & Improved   460
Why Examine Groups?   461
The Context of Groups   463
    Types of Groups: Formal and Informal   464
Management Challenge 14.1: Improving Productivity
in the Service Sector Through Work Teams   464

Organizational Purpose, Strategies, Structure, Systems, and
Environment 467

How Groups Function   467
The Stages of Group Development 467

*Global Management Challenge: IBM Europe Uses Process
Quality Management Teams to Get Things Done*   470
Group Roles 470 • Group Structure 472 • Group Size 474 •
Group Norms 475 • Group Think: The Problem of
Conformity 476 • Group Cohesiveness 478

Management Challenge 14.2: Groupware: Software for the Team   480
Leadership in Groups 479 • Decision Making 479 •
Composition of Groups 480

The Results of Group Activity   480

*Management Challenge 14.3: How to Turn an Intimidating
Government Bureaucracy into a Partner and Ally*   482

A Comprehensive Look at Groups   482

Some Major Types of Groups   483
Teams and Task Forces 484

Management Challenge 14.4: Using Task Forces and Teams   484
Quality Circles 485

Leading Groups as Problem Solving   487

Conflict Management   487
The Consequences of Conflict 488 • Resolving Conflict 488

The Management Challenges Identified   490

Some Solutions Noted in the Chapter   491

Summary   491

Thinking About Management   491

Case: Honeywell Managers and Group Leadership   492

Managers at Work: Groups May Be the Answer   492

Manage Yourself: Team Building Checklist   493

CHAPTER FIFTEEN

Leadership   495

Jim Robinson's Management Style   496

Management Does Not Equal Leadership   498

*Management Challenge 15.1: Morehouse College Trains
Middle-Class Blacks to Lead*   498

Leadership, Power, and Influence   500

Approaches to Leadership   502

Trait Approaches   503
Douglas MacGregor's Theory X and Theory Y 504

Behavioral Approaches   505
The Ohio State and Michigan Leadership Studies 505 • The Yukl
Studies 506

Management Challenge 15.2: What Leaders Do to Be Leaders   506
The Managerial Grid 508

Contingency Approaches   509
Tannenbaum and Schmidt's Continuum of Leadership
Behavior 510 • Fiedler's Contingency Model 510 • Path-Goal
Theory 512 • The Hersey-Blanchard Contingency Model 514 •
Vroom-Yetton-Yago 516 • The Muczyk-Reimann Model 517

Leaders as Communicators   517

Management Challenge 15.3: International Management:
Gorbachev's Style Is Markedly Different from His Predecessors' 518
Leadership as a Problem-Solving Process 518
Leadership at the Top: Transformational Leadership 524
The Management Challenges Identified 525
Some Solutions Noted in the Chapter 526
Summary 526
Thinking About Management 526
Case: Federal Express's Leadership Development Program 527
Managers At Work: Transforming a Law Firm 527
Manage Yourself: Self-assessment of Managerial Style 528

CHAPTER SIXTEEN

Managing Communication 531

Monday Morning Management 532
The Functions of Communication 534
   The Emotive Function 534 • The Motivation Function 534 •
   The Information Function 535 • The Control Function 535 •
   Achieving These Functions 535
The Communication Process 535
   Ideation 536 • Encoding 536 • Transmission 538 •
   Communication Channels 538 • Receiving 539 •
   Decoding 540 • Understanding and Action 540 •
   Feedback 540
The Sender and Receiver: Perception and Other Issues 540
Forms of Communication 541
   Verbal Communication 541
Management Challenge 16.1:
Improving Managers' Communication Skills 542
   Listening 544
Global Management Challenge: Problems of Succeeding in Japan 545
   Nonverbal Communication 546
Communicating in Organizations 549
   Formal Communication 549 • Informal Communication 551
Common Barriers to Communication 551
   Language Limitations 551 • Speaking and Listening
   Habits 552 • Physical and Social Differences 552 •
   Timing 552 • Wordiness 552 • Characteristics of the Sender
   and Receiver: Personality, Role, Status, Perception, and
   Self-image 552 • Overload 553 • Coping with Barriers to
   Communication 553
Organizational Communication 554
   Structural Approaches 555
Management Challenge 16.2: Casino Hits It Big
with Employee Hot Line 556
   Informational Approaches 557
The Portable Manager: Technology Changes Communication 559
Management Challenge 16.3: At Westinghouse
Electronic Mail Is the Answer 559
Communication as a Problem-Solving Exercise 560
The Management Challenges Identified 560
Some Solutions Noted in the Chapter 560
Summary 560

Thinking About Management   561
Case: Communicating with Employees at McDonnell Douglas   561
Managers at Work: Deciphering Communication   562
Manage Yourself: Listening   563

Part Six Controlling

CHAPTER SEVENTEEN

Controlling Performance: Strategic, Tactical, and Operational Control   565

The Challenger Tragedy   566
Control   568
     The Importance of Control 569
Steps in the Control Process   569
     Establishing Performance Standards and Methods for Measuring
     Performance 570 • Measuring Actual Performance 570 •
     Comparing the Actual Performance Against the Standard 571 •
     Taking Necessary Action 571
Management Challenge 17.1: Drexel Burnham Lambert
Failed to Control Its Operations Adequately   572
Characteristics of the Control Process   572
The Interrelationships of Planning and Control   574
Management Styles of Control   575
     Market Control 576 • Bureaucratic Control 577 •
     Clan Control 577
Choosing a Management Style   578
Designing Effective Control Systems   578
Management Challenge 17.2:
Overcoming the Problems at Kennedy   580
Dysfunctional Consequences of Control   581
Global Management Challenge: Moscow's Problems
with Control at Chernobyl   582
Types of Control   583
     Control by Timing Relative to the Transformation Process 584
Management Challenge 17.3: Concurrent Control at S-K-I   585
     Controls by Level of Plan 586 • Control of Economic
     Functions 587
Management Challenge 17.4: Turning Griping Customers
into Loyal Customers   588
     Control of the Management Functions 589
Control and the Changing Environment   590
Control as a Problem-Solving Endeavor   591
The Management Challenges Identified   591
Some Solutions Noted in the Chapter   591
Summary   593
Thinking About Management   593
Case: E. F. Hutton Loses Money the Old-Fashioned Way—
They Don't Control It   594
Managers at Work: Controlling Paperwork Reveals
Other Areas in Need of Control   595
Manage Yourself: What Is Cheating?   595

CHAPTER EIGHTEEN

Management Control Systems — 597

Universal Studios: "Deep Pockets" No More — 598
Core Control Systems — 600
Global Management Challenge:
Creativity Stifled in Japan by Overcontrol — 602
Strategic Control Systems — 602
    Financial Analysis 604 • Ratio Analysis 605 • Return on
    Investment (ROI) 607 • Shareholder Value 609 • Cost
    Accounting 609
Management Challenge 18.1: Waterford Shows a Few Cracks — 610
    Financial Audits 611
Tactical, or Middle-Management, Control Systems — 611
    Budgets 611 • Responsibility Center Management 612 • Types
    of Budgets 612 • The Budgeting Process 614 • Departmental
    Budgets 614 • Zero-Based Budgeting 616 • Strengths and
    Weaknesses of Budgeting 616 • Performance Appraisals 617
Management Challenge 18.2: When Performance Appraisal
Criteria Are Inadequate, Trouble Follows — 618
Management Challenge 18.3: Photo Circuits' Reverse Review — 620
Operational Control — 620
    Disciplinary Systems 621 • Operations Management Control
    Mechanisms 621
Management Challenge 18.4:
Difficulty in Detecting Health Care Scams — 622
Control in a Changing Environment — 622
Control Systems as Part of the Problem-Solving Process — 623
The Management Challenge Identified — 624
Some Solutions Noted in the Chapter — 624
Summary — 624
Thinking About Management — 625
Case: Solving Cyanamid's Problems with Performance Appraisals — 625
Managers at Work: Getting A Grasp on a New Business — 626
Manage Yourself: Computing Financial Ratios — 627

CHAPTER NINETEEN

Management Information Systems and Control — 629

Mrs. Fields' Secret Ingredient — 630
Management Information Systems (MISs) — 633
    Characteristics of Quality Information 633 • The Information
    Needed by Managers 633 • MISs Defined 635 • The Evolution
    of MISs 636 • MIS Components 637
MIS Design — 638
Using an MIS — 639
Management Challenge 19.1: Tuscaloosa Steel Corporation — 640
    The Internal and External Environmental Information
    Needed 641 • Information Requirements in a Rapidly Changing
    World 641
Global Management Challenge: Managing Information
Systems at Multinationals — 643
    Strategic Use of Information 643

*Management Challenge 19.2: Excellence in Information
Management*   644
The MIS Director   646
   The Role of the CIO 646
The Changing Role of the MIS Function   646
Telecommunications and the MIS   647
Decision Support Systems (DSSs) and Expert Systems (ESs)   649
   DSSs 649 • ESs and Artificial Intelligence 650
*Management Challenge 19.3: United Uses Expert
Systems to Reduce Delays at Hubs*   651
   Executive Information Systems 651
Protecting the Information System   652
How an MIS Affects the Organization   653
Knowledge-Based Organizations and Their Management   654
Managing Information as a Problem-Solving Process   654
The Management Challenges Identified   655
Some Solutions Noted in the Chapter   655
Summary   655
Thinking About Management   656
Case: Northern Telecom Changes Its Strategy   656
Managers at Work: Gathering Competitive Information   657
Manage Yourself: Developing an Executive Information System   657

Part Seven Contemporary Issues in Management

CHAPTER TWENTY

Operations Management   659

*Westinghouse Expects to Grow on the Basis of Productivity Gains
in the Factory and in the Office*   660
Operations Management in Manufacturing and Service
Organizations   662
   Operations Managements as Decision Making 666
Operations' Strategic Importance   666
Global Management Challenge: Federal Express Goes Global   668
Strategic Operations Decisions   668
   Positioning the Operations System 668 • Focused
   Factories 669 • Product/Service Design and Process Planning 670
*Management Challenge 20.1: IBM Simplifies
and Automates to Beat Asian Rivals*   671
   Allocation of Resources to Strategic Alternatives 671 • Facility
   Capacity, Location, and Plant Layout 672 • Production
   Technology 675 • Work Force Management 677 • Total
   Quality Strategy 677
*Management Challenge 20.2: Hewlett-Packard's
Total Quality Control Program*   678
Tactical Operations Decisions: Planning Production to Meet
Demands   678

Production Planning Systems 679 • The Control of Inventory and
the Planning Process 681 • Material Requirements Planning 683

*Management Challenge 20.3: Having a Hard Time
with JIT*   684
Materials Management and Purchasing 684

Planning and Controlling Day-to-Day Operations   684
Scheduling and Shop Floor Planning and Control 684

*Management Challenge 20.4: American Airlines'
Fixer of Broken Schedules*   685
Workers and Productivity 686 • Quality Control 686 • Quality
According to W. Edwards Deming 687 • Project Management:
Planning and Controlling Projects 687 • Maintenance
Management and Reliability 687

The Factory of the Future   687
Productivity Management   689
How to Improve Productivity 689

Management Challenge 20.5: Allen Bradley's Factory of the Future 690
Operations Management as Problem Solving   691
The Management Challenges Identified   692
Some Solutions Noted in the Chapter   692
Summary   692
Thinking About Management   693
Case: Quality Control at Spectrum Control, Inc.   694
Managers at Work: Groups May Be the Answer   694
Manage Yourself: Deming's 14 Points   695

CHAPTER TWENTY-ONE

Managing in an Ever-Changing Global Environment

Global Environment   697

GE Moves to Become a Global Competitor   698
The Globalization of Business   699
The Triad of Key Markets   703
Japan 704 • Europe—Europe 1992, East-West Economic
Integration 706

Management Challenge 21.1: Cat Acts Like a Tiger   710
North America 710 • Potential for Other Global Change 711

Management and the Global Environment   712
The Four Environmental Factors and the Global
Environment 713 • Impacts of the Factors on the Management
Functions 715

*Management Challenge 21.2: H.J. Heinz'
Approach to Joint Ventures in Developing Nations*   718
Global Competitiveness 718 • Impacts on Economic
Functions 718

Applying Management Practices Internationally   721
Applying Japanese Management Practices Abroad 722

Unique Problems for Multinational Corporations   722
Political Instability 723 • Terrorism 723 • Host Government
Conflicts 723 • Monetary Transactions 723 • Human
Rights 723

The Management Challenges Identified   724
Some Solutions Noted in the Chapter   725

Summary   725
Thinking About Management   726
Case: To Invest or Not to Invest   726
Managers at Work: Skopbank   727
Manage Yourself: Factors to Consider   727

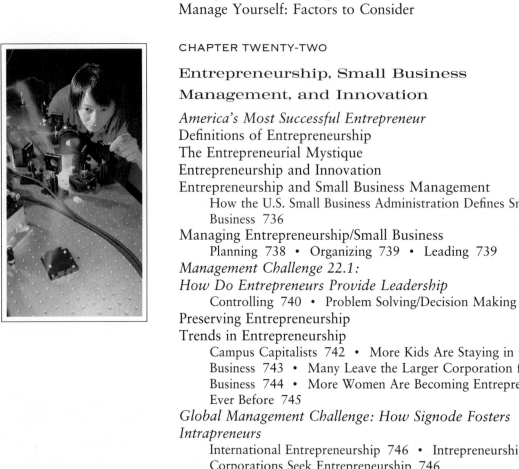

CHAPTER TWENTY-TWO

Entrepreneurship, Small Business Management, and Innovation   729

America's Most Successful Entrepreneur   730
Definitions of Entrepreneurship   732
The Entrepreneurial Mystique   733
Entrepreneurship and Innovation   736
Entrepreneurship and Small Business Management   736
    How the U.S. Small Business Administration Defines Small
    Business 736
Managing Entrepreneurship/Small Business   737
    Planning 738 • Organizing 739 • Leading 739
Management Challenge 22.1:
How Do Entrepreneurs Provide Leadership   740
    Controlling 740 • Problem Solving/Decision Making 741
Preserving Entrepreneurship   741
Trends in Entrepreneurship   741
    Campus Capitalists 742 • More Kids Are Staying in the Family
    Business 743 • Many Leave the Larger Corporation for the Small
    Business 744 • More Women Are Becoming Entrepreneurs than
    Ever Before 745
Global Management Challenge: How Signode Fosters
Intrapreneurs   746
    International Entrepreneurship 746 • Intrepreneurship: Major
    Corporations Seek Entrepreneurship 746
Management Challenge 22.2: David D. Glass
Becomes CEO of Walmart   748
Succession   749
The Management of Innovation   749
The Management Challenges Identified   749
Some Solutions Noted in the Chapter   750
Summary   750
Thinking About Management   750
Case: Stew's Dairy   751
Managers at Work: Why Work for Someone Else?   751
Manage Yourself: Entrepreneurial Profile   752

CHAPTER TWENTY-THREE

Careers and Management   755

Thirty Something   756
Managing Your Career   757
Management Challenge 23.1: Blue Cross and Blue Shield
Improve Career Planning   761
    Life's Stages 762 • Major Career Choices 762 • The Interview
    and You 764 • Special Issues in Career Planning 767

Careers in Management   768
Global Management Challenge: Career Plateauing in a Japanese
Firm   769
    Stages in Management Careers 769
Management Challenge 23.2: GE's New Managers Program   770
    Management Development Programs 772 • Stress and the
    Manager 772
The Manager in the Twenty-first Century   777
The Management Challenges Identified   779
Some Solutions Noted in the Chapter   779
Summary   779
Thinking About Management   780
Case: Squibb Pharmaceuticals   780
Managers at Work: Todd & Associates   781
Manage Yourself: Formulating a Career Plan   781

Glossary   G-1

References   R-1

Company Index   I-1

Name Index   I-4

Subject Index   I-8

THE MANAGEMENT CHALLENGE

An Introduction to Management

CHAPTER ONE

The Changing Management Process

CHAPTER OBJECTIVES

By the time you complete this chapter you should be able to

1. Describe the management process in organizations.
2. Indicate why management and management styles are changing.
3. Identify the three primary approaches to the study of management and describe each.
4. Indicate the types of managers that exist.
5. Discuss the universality of management.
6. List the major factors involved in both the internal and external managerial environments.
7. Discuss whether management is an art or a science, or both.
8. Describe the management matrix.
9. Characterize the changing management process, including why it will change and how it will change.

CHAPTER OUTLINE

Approaches to the Study
of Management
    Management as a Functional Process
    Management as the Enactment of
      Roles
    Management as the Utilization of
      Certain Skills

Organizations and Managers
    Types of Managers
The Universality of Management
    Management in For-Profits
      and in Not-for-Profits
The Managerial Environment
    The External Environment
    The Internal Environment
Management: An Art or a Science,
or Both?
    Developing Management
The Management Matrix
The Changing Managerial Process—
The Management Challenges
    Changing Employee Expectations as
      to How They Should be Managed
    The Global Economy
    The Shift from an Industrially Based
      Economy to an Information-Based
      Economy
    Accelerated Rates of Change
    Increased Levels of Competition
    The Impact of Changing Technology,
      Especially Computers
    Finding a More Creative Approach
      to Improve Problem Solving
    Emphasis on Managing
      Organizational Culture
    Increasing Demands of Constituents
    Changing Demographics: The
      Cultural Diversity of the
      Work Force
Management Challenges and the
Following Chapters
The Changing Face of Management—
Is Everyone a Manager?
The Management Challenge

3

Ford Changes the Way It Manages

Besieged by quality problems, morale problems, declining market share, and overcapacity, Ford Motor Company entered the 1980s bloodied but not beaten. Many of its plants were "war zones" between managers and their unionized subordinates. Angry shouts often typified communication. Employees were "zombies" responding aimlessly to their work, while increasing competition, especially from Japan, demanded more of them than ever before. Ford believed that if it were to remain profitable, it had to take action. It began a major overhaul of the way it managed.

Ford took several strategic actions, which in the short term meant losses, but in the long term would mean increased profitability. The actions were unique for Ford, for the auto industry, and indeed for most American firms, which tend to emphasize the short term. Among these actions were plant closings, which resulted in losses on the books, and an effort to improve the nature of management-labor relations. This latter strategy meant changing managerial style for most of Ford's management staff. The new style came partly through an employee-involvement program. Employees were given the right to stop the assembly line to improve quality and were urged during group meetings to contribute ways to improve the operation. Ford managers then had to learn to operate in this environment.

Tom Rivers is typical of the Ford managers who have made the transition from the old to the new style of management. Tom is a supervisor on the line at Ford's Louisville Assembly Plant. Tom comments, "It's like night and day. Before, largely because of constant confrontation between the managers and the workers, we couldn't get anything done, or at least not done right. No one cared. Now we all work together to get the job done right."

Perhaps no one, however, illustrates the change at Louisville more than "Red Dog" Hamilton. He used to feel sick as he approached the plant. "I'd sit in the parking lot and think of some excuse I could tell my wife for not working that day." He was often absent two or three days a week. Hamilton is now an enthusiastic supporter of the company, and one who likes his new authority as a line worker. Since the switch in management styles was made, he is seldom absent and never without good reason. In the old days, he relates, "If something wasn't right, we'd let it go and hope the inspector caught it. We didn't care a lot. If I hollered too often, I'd be taken to labor relations for not doing my job. Now we are supposed to holler."

Ford's chairman, Donald E. Petersen, believes that it is Ford's employee-involvement program which will sustain Ford's competitive advantage in the 1990s. He views Ford's human resources as pivotal in fending off Japanese competition. Ford has established a strategic human resources plan for the 1990s based on teamwork to ensure that people like "Red Dog" have a chance to increase their contribution to Ford's success while growing personally.

SOURCES: Donald E. Petersen, Speech to the Academy of Management, August 14, 1989, Washington, D.C.; Beverly Geber, "The Resurrection of Ford," Training, April 1989, pp. 23–32; Paul A. Banas and Raymond Sauers, "The Ford Transformation," (Detroit: Ford Motor Company, February, 1989); "What's Creating an 'Industrial Miracle' at Ford," Business Week (July 30, 1984), pp. 80–81; Jeremy Main, "Ford's Drive for Quality," Fortune (April 18, 1983), pp. 62–66; Phillip Caldwell, "Cultivating Human Potential at Ford," Journal of Business Strategy (Spring 1984), pp. 74–77; and Michael Smith, "Employee Involvement Fuels Dramatic Turnaround at Ford's Louisville Assembly Plant," Labor–Management Brief, Washington, D.C.: U.S. Dept. of Labor (November 1986), pp. 1–6.

New competitors, new technologies and new lifestyles demand a new breed of American management.

John A. Young
President and CEO, Hewlett-Packard

90% of all problems in the organization are caused by bad management.

William Edwards Deming
Noted Quality Consultant

Management is the creative problem-solving process of planning, organizing, leading, and controlling an organization's resources to achieve its mission and objectives. And although we've been managing reasonably successfully for hundreds of years, managers today are changing the way they manage. The world of work is changing so dramatically that managers and the management process must also change.

People are changing; our society is changing; competitors are changing; government is changing; technology is changing. Management must change. Now, more than at any time before, managers are being challenged to improve the way they manage.[1]

Management and managers underwent a barrage of criticism in the 1980s. Thomas J. Peters, coauthor of *In Search of Excellence* and *Passion for Excellence,* and author of *Thriving on Chaos,*[2] is typical of the critics. He declares, "The state of American management practice, it is my duty to say, is deplorable. We have lost sight of the basics. We have been trapped by complexity and the complex techniques we have invented to deal with complexity. We have forgotten the people who make the product, that deliver the service. We have forgotten the customer and the clients, and we have forgotten the basic nature of the service itself."[3] Carl Icahn, the noted corporate-takeover specialist, blasts, "The U.S. corporation is in crisis. We cannot compete with foreign producers in our basic industries, and balance-of-payments problems get worse each year. One cause of these problems is bad management—not everywhere, but at too many big corporations. The directors who choose these chief executives seem to study from a primer titled *In Search of Mediocrity*. Bureaucracy has produced a corporate welfare state, an army of nonproductive workers."[4] Many others have sounded the same alarm, an alarm that is sending a clear message: **the way we manage in many of our organizations is not accomplishing our missions and objectives.** Much of this criticism of American business practice is leveled at the management process itself, especially at how managers solve problems. The criticism is also aimed at how managers abuse the process.[5]

Tom Rivers at the Ford plant in Louisville is an example of a manager who has changed the way he manages. Ford is a company that exemplifies the management transition we are going through. Ford's top management recognized the need to change how the company was managed. Foreign competitors, principally the Japanese, were eroding Ford's market share and lessening its profits, and some say even threatening its long-term viability.

One of the key factors in Ford Motor Company's successful turnaround in the 1980s, and of its strategy for the 1990s is its employee-involvement program in which line employees, singly and in groups, make decisions. (SOURCE © Robert Reichert)

Tom Rivers doesn't manage the way he did a few years ago and neither do most other Ford managers. They and thousands of other managers in the United States, Canada, and Western Europe are being forced to reexamine the way they solve problems when they plan, organize, lead, and control. Tom and his fellow managers, as part of the development of the Ford organization, have become more participative. They not only allow, but also encourage, their subordinates, such as "Red Dog" Hamilton, to participate in the problem-solving process whether in planning, organizing, leading, or controlling. Increasingly, authority and responsibility are shared. Managers today are also using more creativity in the problem-solving process than ever before. Old ways of doing things just don't suffice. Management will continue to evolve. Much of the change will occur in the way managers solve problems, much of it will continue to focus on participation in problem solving and decision making by all members of the organization, and much of it will involve continuing to increase creativity. However, other forces are at work in the managerial environment that might reduce participation and creativity. **Management's challenge** is to be able to change in the right direction at the right time to meet the demands of the situation.

In this chapter you will learn about the management process—creative problem solving in planning, organizing, leading, and controlling; the roles and behaviors expected of managers; and the skills required to be a successful manager. You will learn about the types of managers that exist, whether they perform a specific function or are general managers, and at what levels of the organization they may perform. You will also learn whether the functions and principles of management are universal. You will explore the nature of the managerial environment, both inside and outside the organization. You will discover whether management is an art or a science, or both. You will then examine the relationship of the management functions to the economic functions of a business and to each other as revealed in the management matrix. Finally, you will discover how ten challenges are changing the managerial process.

Approaches to the Study of Management

Historically, three themes have dominated the study of management: management as a functional process, as a series of roles, and as a series of skills.[6] The functional process approach suggests that managers engage in certain functions or activities to accomplish their jobs. The roles approach is similar but focuses on a different set of actions. Finally, the skills approach suggests that managers are supposed to be capable of certain actions to be successful. All three approaches focus on behaviors, but each defines the set of necessary actions in a different, yet related way.

Management as a Functional Process

The management process consists of several **management functions** or activities in which managers engage much of the time in order to achieve organizational objectives effectively and efficiently.[7] Figure 1.1 portrays two principal types of management functions. The first is the **mission functions,** the activities directly associated with accomplishing an organization's mission. They include planning,

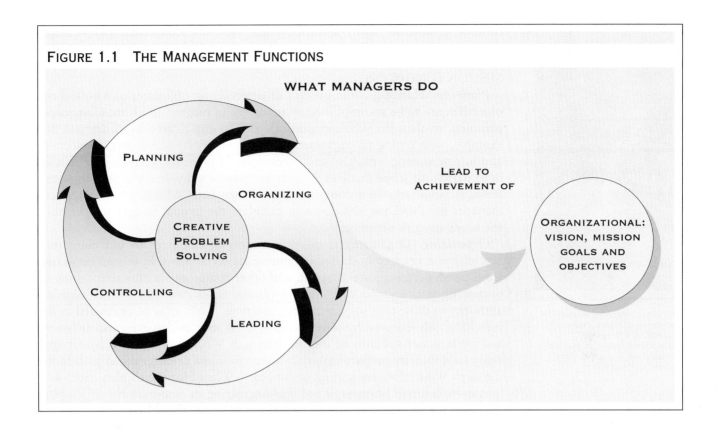

FIGURE 1.1 THE MANAGEMENT FUNCTIONS

WHAT MANAGERS DO

PLANNING

ORGANIZING

CREATIVE PROBLEM SOLVING

CONTROLLING

LEADING

LEAD TO ACHIEVEMENT OF

ORGANIZATIONAL: VISION, MISSION GOALS AND OBJECTIVES

organizing, leading, and controlling. These functions occur in a cycle, as shown by the arrows in the figure. This cycle may be interrupted at any point. The second type of function shown in the figure is the **core function of management:** creative problem solving.

THE CORE FUNCTION: CREATIVE PROBLEM SOLVING

Creative problem solving is the process of practicing ongoing environmental analysis, recognizing and identifying a problem, making assumptions about the decision environment, generating creative alternatives to solve the identified problem, deciding among those alternatives, acting to implement the chosen alternative(s), and controlling for results. In this text problem solving is also referred to as decision making. An increasingly vital part of this process is the sharing of authority, the power to make decisions given to a jobholder by the formal organization. Managers are sharing this authority primarily with subordinates. In many instances the manager's primary function in creative problem solving is becoming the facilitation of the creative problem-solving efforts of others.

Creative problem solving is the core function of management because it occurs during and is used in every other function of management to achieve those functions. Only recently has problem solving been recognized as the core function of management.

THE ETHICAL NATURE OF PROBLEM SOLVING

All of the manager's decisions should occur in an ethical manner. Managers are responsible for their decisions and held accountable for them by peers, friends, family, the organization, and society. In recent years, as unethical decisions have

AT FORD: *Tom Rivers and his subordinates meet periodically in groups known as quality circles to solve jointly their work unit's problems. In these group meetings, Tom acts as a facilitator of his subordinates' creative problem-solving efforts.*

Problem solving, often in groups, is the very core of management. The manager, and increasingly, subordinates, must learn problem-solving skills. (SOURCE © Gabe Palmer/Stock Market)

resulted in notable negative consequences for those concerned and affected, more stress has been placed on improving business ethics.[8]

MISSION FUNCTIONS

Planning. **Planning** is the process of determining objectives and how those objectives are to be accomplished in an uncertain future.[9] In its broadest scope, planning involves the whole organization. Planning is broadly concerned, for example, with setting an organization's mission, goals, and strategic objectives and in determining strategies and other types of plans to reach them. Planning in its narrowest scope involves the development of individual job objectives and the associated tasks to accomplish them. When Betty Mizek, a health services manager for Pru-Care, sits down to calculate the annual budget for her unit, she is engaging in planning.[10]

Organizing. **Organizing** is the preparation of resources to put plans into action. It is a key step in the final implementation of plans. In this process tasks are defined, personnel are assigned, and other resources are allocated. Much of organizing is concerned with turning specific tasks into jobs and distributing authority to those jobs to accomplish objectives. Tasks may be organized at the individual job level, or by jobs and groups of jobs in departments, divisions, and other major subunits of the organization. When workers at a Nucor specialty steel foundry prepare materials inventories in a predetermined pattern for the day's work, they are getting organized.[11] When Honeywell eliminated 400 jobs in its controls business, it too was organizing its resources.[12]

Leading. **Leading** is the process of making decisions about how to treat people and then carrying out those decisions to influence behavior. This function is also often referred to as influencing, motivating, or directing. The purpose of leading or influencing individuals is to channel their behavior to accomplish organizational objectives. When a manager for Hewlett-Packard walks from person to person, counseling, facilitating, and building relationships, he or she is practicing leading.[13]

Controlling. **Controlling** is the process of ascertaining whether organizational objectives have been achieved; if not, why not; and determining what actions should then be taken to achieve objectives better in the future. It involves the following steps: establishing standards that are more specific definitions of objectives; obtaining information on performance in pursuit of those objectives; comparing the two; and taking corrective or preventive action, or none at all. Controlling is an ongoing process. In 1986, when the Reagan administration proposed a worldwide ban on freon and other ozone-destroying chemicals, it was trying to exercise a form of control. The ban was aimed at saving the ozone layer around the earth, in order, for example, to reduce skin cancer levels, which are expected to increase as ozone levels diminish.[14]

OTHER FUNCTIONS OF MANAGEMENT

Some functions of management are typically minor for most managers but may be major for others. For example, representing is often a major function of the organization's chief executive officer (CEO) but is a minor function for most managers. A variety of distinct functions of management other than the five principal functions described thus far have been identified. In several cases in this book, they are considered part of one of the preceding five functions, as noted in the following paragraphs. Other functions of management can include the following:

1. Communicating: Transferring information from one communicator to another. A major function of all managers. Viewed in this text as part of leading.

2. Representing: Interacting with external constituents, often referred to as stakeholders. Stakeholders are groups or individuals who have a "stake" in decisions made by the organization.

3. Staffing: Recruiting, selecting, training, evaluating, and performing other functions relative to utilizing human resources. Viewed as part of organizing in this book.

4. Negotiating: Bargaining with various parties to reach agreement. A type of conflict management approach.

5. Coordinating: Acting to ensure understanding. Viewed as part of organizing in this book.

6. Supervising: Close monitoring of employee activities across all functions of management. Viewed as a specialized form of management for managing operative-level employees.

THE MAHONEY, JERDEE, AND CARROLL STUDIES OF MANAGEMENT FUNCTIONS

T. A. Mahoney, T. H. Jerdee, and S. J. Carroll performed the landmark study of how much time managers spend on various management functions. They examined 452 managers from 13 companies, ranging in size from 100 to over 4,000 employees.[15] They studied several different industries, including wholesale trade, manufacturing, insurance, agriculture, public utilities, and finance. The managers in the study ranged from first-level supervisors to chief executives.

Managers were asked how much time they spent on eight management functions. Table 1.1 summarizes their responses. Note that we have integrated these eight functions into those we just discussed. Investigating, for example, is part of problem solving, and problem solving as defined here would occur in all eight functions. The numbers shown in the table are averages. A wide variance was found to exist among respondents. The level of the manager, the industry, the stage of the relevant industry or product cycle, and other factors affect how much time is spent on each function. It is important to note that managers may be performing several functions simultaneously with the same actions.

Table 1.1 Percentage of Workday Spent by Managers on Eight Management Functions

Management Function		Percentage of Workday
Functions in the Study	Closely Related to These Functions in This Book	
Planning	Planning	19.5
Investigating	Problem solving	12.6
Coordinating	Organizing	15.0
Evaluating	Controlling	12.7
Supervising	Leading	28.4
Staffing	Organizing	4.1
Negotiating	Leading	6.0
Representing	Leading	1.8

SOURCE: Adapted from T. A. Mahoney, T. H. Jerdee, and S. J. Carroll, "The Job(s) of Management," *Industrial Relations,* vol. 4, no. 2 (February 1965), p. 103.

Management as the Enactment of Roles

The second approach to studying management examines the roles managers are expected to play. Henry A. Mintzberg developed the major articulation of this perspective in 1973 in *The Nature of Managerial Work,* which has become a classic of management research.

MINTZBERG'S MANAGERIAL ROLES

Mintzberg's study of top managers and duplicate studies, or replications, by others suggest that the following principal roles characterize managerial work, especially that of chief executives:[16]

Table 1.2 Mintzberg's Ten Management Roles

Role	Description	Identifiable Activities
Interpersonal		
Figurehead	Symbolic head; obliged to perform a number of routine duties of a legal or social nature	Ceremony, status, requests, solicitations
Leader	Responsible for the motivation and activation of subordinates; responsible for staffing, training, and associated duties	Virtually all managerial activities involving subordinates
Liaison	Maintains self-developed network of outside contacts and informers who provide favors and information	Acknowledgements of mail, external board work, other activities involving outsiders
Informational		
Monitor	Seeks and receives a wide variety of special information (much of it current) to develop a thorough understanding of the organization and environment; emerges as nerve center of the organization's internal and external information	Handling all mail and contacts categorized as concerned primarily with receiving information (e.g., periodical news, observational tours)
Disseminator	Transmits information received from outsiders or from subordinates to members of the organization; some information factual, some involving interpretation and integration	Forwarding mail into the organization for informational purposes, verbal contacts involving information flow to subordinates (e.g., review sessions, instant communication flows)
Spokesperson	Transmits information to outsiders on the organization's plans, policies, actions, results, and so forth; serves as expert on organization's industry	Board meetings, handling mail and contacts involving transmission of information to outsiders
Decisional		
Entrepreneur	Searches organization and its environment for opportunities and initiates "improvement projects" to bring about change; supervises design of certain projects as well	Strategy and review sessions involving initiation or design of improvement projects
Disturbance Handler	Responsible for corrective action when organization faces important, unexpected disturbances	Strategy and review involving disturbances and crises
Resource Allocator	Responsible for the allocation of organizational resources of all kinds—in effect the making or approving of all significant organizational decisions	Scheduling, requests for authorization, any activity involving budgeting and the programming of subordinates' work
Negotiator	Responsible for representing the organization at major negotiations	Negotiation

Adapted from Henry A. Mintzberg, *The Nature of Managerial Work* (Englewood Cliffs, N.J.: Prentice Hall, 1980), pp. 91–92.

1. **Interpersonal Relationships:** Most of the manager's time is spent interacting with others through three often ceremonial, but also often critical roles: figurehead, leader, and liaison. (Table 1.2 contains a description of each of these roles.)

2. **Information Processing:** Virtually all managers must process information—they give it, receive it, and analyze it. Mintzberg suggests that receiving and communicating information is the most important aspect of a manager's job. Information is vital to decision making and problem solving. The three informational roles include monitor, disseminator, and spokesperson.

3. **Decision Making:** Managers ultimately must use the information they process to make decisions that solve problems. Mintzberg found four decision making roles: entrepreneur, disturbance handler, resource allocator, and negotiator.[17]

The essence of Mintzberg's theory is that the manager's activities divide into these three categories, which further subdivide into a number of roles managers must play (Table 1.2). Mintzberg's work is useful when studying top managers but is not necessarily applicable to all levels of management, as will be discussed shortly.

Management as the Utilization of Certain Skills

The third major perspective on managerial activity is that of **managerial skills.** A skill is an ability to translate action into results. Managers must possess skills. Skills can be innate, but managers must also be able to translate experience and learning into action. Robert L. Katz has classified the essential skills of managers into three categories: technical, human, and conceptual.[18] These are described in Table 1.3 along with examples of each.

Table 1.3 Essential Managerial Skills

Skill	Description	Examples
Technical	Ability to use tools, techniques, and specialized knowledge	Accountant doing an audit; engineer designing a machine
Human	Ability to work effectively in interpersonal relationships	Accounting manager supervising a group of accountants during an audit; manufacturing manager resolving conflict with a design engineer
Conceptual	Ability to see the organization as a whole and solve problems to benefit the total system	Analysis of a possible merger with another firm; analysis of employee absenteeism and turnover

SOURCE: Adapted from Robert L. Katz, "Skills of an Effective Administrator," *Harvard Business Review* (September–October 1974), p. 94.

Technical skill is the ability to use tools, techniques, and specialized knowledge as related to a method, process, or procedure. Accountants, engineers, and professors, for example, acquire technical skills through their education. Almost all jobs have technical skill components. Not all require preparatory education, but virtually all require some preparatory training or job experience. For example, a salesperson must learn how to close a sale.

Korea Exports Its Management Style

We're being invaded. Global competition is rampant. Our competitors are very good. Can we, or have we learned from them? Yes, and yes.

First we learned from the Japanese that the proper management of human resources could substantially improve productivity. Their lessons for us included the increased use of group decision making, viewing the employee as a human being, and building commitment. Now the Koreans are beginning to teach American managers additional lessons.

Hai Min Lee, president of Samsung USA Inc., eats lunch in the employee cafeteria, wears a blue Samsung uniform as would a line worker, and works out of a spartan office. He practices an egalitarian management style more pronounced even than that of the Japanese—whom we often feel invented the practice. The Koreans are apparently more flexible than the Japanese and more willing to listen to others' views. They too emphasize workers' consensus in decision making: "The person who knows the factory process best should not be left out," observes Lee.

Americans seem to like the Korean style. Myrtel Sanders, a Samsung employee comments, "I used to work at an RCA plant, and they took the employees for granted. You can voice your opinion here. I once spoke up to a manager. I would have been fired anywhere else, but it was O.K. There's no union here, but we get all the benefits we need."

Employee benefits are numerous. "If a worker is buying a house or getting a

---

Human skill is the ability to work effectively in interpersonal relationships. As you can probably tell by now, interpersonal skills are critical to being a successful manager. The functional approach describes this in terms of leadership. Mintzberg's relevant role is the interpersonal one. Thus, all three perspectives on management identify the interpersonal function/role/skill as important. People with high human skills build trust and cooperation as they motivate, influence, or lead. The importance of this skill is becoming ever clearer, largely because several of our international competitors have used it so effectively to compete with us, as this chapter's Global Management Challenge reveals. The human skill is a difficult one to master. Emotionally sound managers perform this skill better than those who are not.

Conceptual skill is the ability to see the organization as a whole and to solve problems to benefit the total system. While it draws heavily on analytical and rational abilities to solve problems, it also depends on the more creative and intuitive talents of the individual manager for problem-solving purposes.

> AT FORD: *When Ford moved to a new strategy to cut costs and produce high-quality cars, its managers had to learn new skills, especially people skills, to be effective.*

Organizations and Managers

Managers do their work in organizations. An **organization** is a collection of people working in a coordinated manner to achieve a common purpose. There are many types of organizations, which may, for example, be classified as either for-profit or not-for-profit (nonprofit). Ford Motor Company and IBM are for-divorce, we get the company lawyer," Lee commented. The Koreans openly celebrate events important to employees, such as birthdays. Employees are kept informed and are often actively involved in creative problem solving. Views are openly exchanged.

SOURCE: Laurie Baum, "Korea's Newest Export: Management Style," *Business Week* (January 19, 1987).

Hai Min Lee of Samsung, helps foster team spirit, a feeling of company loyalty, and the importance of the individual, by wearing a blue front-line worker's uniform and eating in the company cafeteria with the line employees. (SOURCE © Ken Kerbs)

profit organizations, the federal government and the United Steel Workers Union are not-for-profit organizations. Many other classifications of organizations are possible, such as large or small, from gigantic IBM to your local ice-cream parlor.

Historically, organizations have used managers to direct the efforts of others to achieve organizational objectives effectively and efficiently. **Effectiveness** describes whether objectives are accomplished. **Efficiency** describes the relative amount of resources used in obtaining effectiveness. The cost of effectiveness must be considered. If the cost of achieving objectives is too high, they may be abandoned. Managers have been responsible for solving problems in planning, organizing, leading, and controlling to ensure that objectives are accomplished efficiently.

A major change is occurring in organizations, however. Increasingly, management is becoming the responsibility of every individual in the organization, not just of designated formal managers. In many organizations all members are beginning to manage themselves more than they have in the past. They are beginning to perform the functions of management, not simply the tasks they have been assigned routinely as part of the organizing process.

Types of Managers

In any organization managers may be identified by whether they are general managers or functional managers. In addition, managers are often designated by their level in the organization.

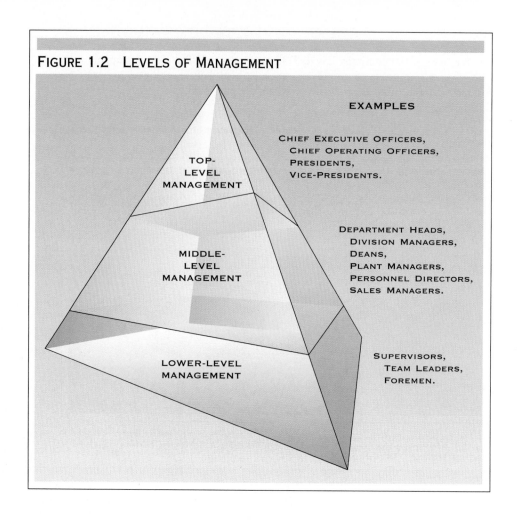

FIGURE 1.2 LEVELS OF MANAGEMENT

EXAMPLES

TOP-LEVEL MANAGEMENT

CHIEF EXECUTIVE OFFICERS,
CHIEF OPERATING OFFICERS,
PRESIDENTS,
VICE-PRESIDENTS.

MIDDLE-LEVEL MANAGEMENT

DEPARTMENT HEADS,
DIVISION MANAGERS,
DEANS,
PLANT MANAGERS,
PERSONNEL DIRECTORS,
SALES MANAGERS.

LOWER-LEVEL MANAGEMENT

SUPERVISORS,
TEAM LEADERS,
FOREMEN.

GENERAL VERSUS FUNCTIONAL MANAGEMENT

Functional managers are responsible for an economic function of the organization or some part thereof. They therefore are concerned singly with some aspect of marketing, finance, operations, human resources, or information systems. Most managers are functional managers. The responsibilities of general managers cover more than one function and often all of them. General managers are normally product or divisional managers, or CEOs.

The general manager's role is considerably different from that of a functional manager. Functional managers need principally to understand their job situation within a broader environmental context. The general manager's task is to take a total organizational viewpoint, a task made more difficult because most general managers were formerly functional managers and are often predisposed to a functional viewpoint when they make decisions.[19]

LEVELS OF MANAGEMENT

Virtually all organizations, except the very smallest, have three levels of management: top, middle, and lower level, as portrayed in Figure 1.2. There may be several sublayers within each of these major levels of management in large organizations.

Top Managers. Top managers include CEOs, chief operating officers, presidents, and vice-presidents. Such managers direct their attention to the major issues affecting the organization, such as setting goals and objectives and devising strategies to meet them. Their principal job is to scan the environment and make certain the organization is reaching its objectives. John Sculley, president of Apple Computer, Inc., for example, continually monitors the environment of that firm to make certain that their products, their prices, their distribution system, and so on meet the challenges of the competitive environment. He must make sure that the firm can compete with IBM, Compaq, and other major personal computer manufacturers.[20]

Middle Managers. Middle managers include department heads, division managers, deans, plant managers, personnel directors, sales managers, and so on. They occupy the second and often third, fourth, fifth, sixth, or seventh layers of management in a large organization.

Middle-level managers traditionally have been thought of as critical to organizations because they translate top management's directives for use by lower-level management and first-level employees. They have also been viewed as critical in providing information for upper-level management's problem-solving endeavors. Top managers are selected from middle management. Sometimes managers are top managers of one part of an organization, but middle managers from a total organization perspective. The dean of your business school is the top manager of that school but is a middle-level manager of the college or university. The dean leads the business school but serves as a middle manager in implementing the directives of the president and/or provost of the college or university. Thus, a manager's level depends on the unit of the organization being analyzed. As very large organizations attempt to become more competitive, many are reducing the number of middle managers they employ.

Lower-Level Managers. Supervisors, team leaders, and foremen are common titles in lower-level management. In most organizations operating employees report to front-line management. This first line of management implements the plans and directives of middle or upper management.[21]

This is the entry level of management. An operating employee is normally promoted to the first line of management before moving further upward. Supervision is a pivotal level. Performance here makes or breaks a managerial career. Normally a person who is exceptionally good at his or her first operating position will be promoted to this first level of management. Very early in his career, Roger B. Smith, president of General Motors, for example, was a first-line supervisor. He eventually worked his way through several middle- and top-management positions, finally becoming president.[22]

MANAGEMENT FUNCTIONS BY LEVEL[23]

Based on the studies by Mahoney, Jerdee, and Carroll and others,[24] as shown in Figure 1.3, it appears that each mission function is practiced in varying degrees throughout the levels of management. Planning occupies much more time of the upper-level manager than the lower-level one. Organizing seems to occur to about the same degree in each level. Leading and controlling are performed more in lower levels than in higher levels. Creative problem solving occurs in all these functions. Naturally, how much time and effort managers spend on each of the mission functions depends on the situation. If the management functions are increasingly assumed by all employees, the balance between the various functions that managers perform will begin to change. Planning and leadership will begin to require more time.

The studies noted here also indicate that the degree to which the management functions are practiced varies by industry. This variance might be the result of the degree of change in the industrial environment. Environments that frequently

AT FORD: *Tom Rivers from Ford is a good example of a manager managing in a world of change. He is doing more planning now than he used to, and his subordinates are more self-controlled. He also spends more time leading through facilitating and assisting than he used to. He walks around. He builds teamwork.*

FIGURE 1.3 MANAGEMENT FUNCTIONS BY LEVEL

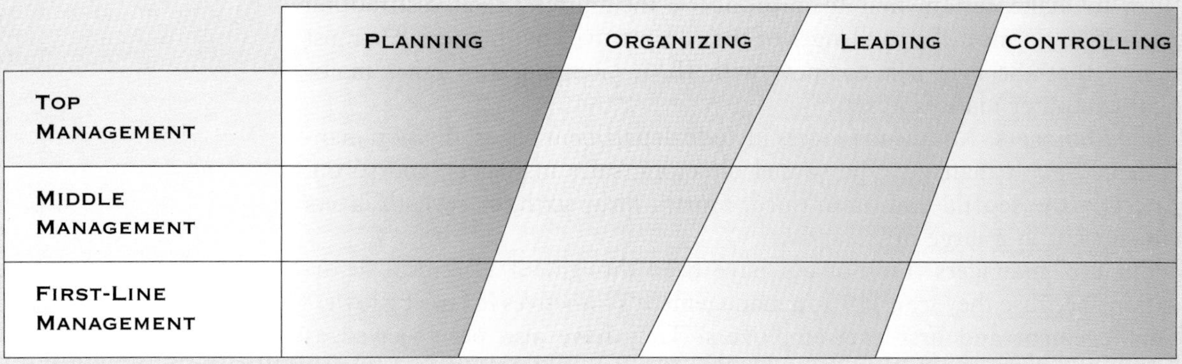

	PLANNING	ORGANIZING	LEADING	CONTROLLING
TOP MANAGEMENT				
MIDDLE MANAGEMENT				
FIRST-LINE MANAGEMENT				

change require more planning, for example, than do very stable ones. Some industries center on tasks that require close supervision—for example, diamond cutting. Others do not—such as food processing. Leadership practices would vary greatly in these two industries.

MANAGEMENT ROLES BY LEVEL

Mintzberg's conceptualization of the three major sets of roles that managers engage in is based on studies of chief executives in a small number of organizations. Although the study was replicated by others with similar results,[25] it was still accomplished at the CEO level. Related studies of similar roles at other levels of the organization don't support Mintzberg's classifications.[26] One explanation might be that the roles of managers might vary by level. At other levels, for example, certain "executive" roles have little meaning.

MANAGEMENT SKILLS BY LEVEL

As portrayed in Figure 1.4, the skills required of managers are also believed to vary according to an individual's level in the organization. Technical skills are much more important at the lowest management levels, but some technical skill is still important in the upper levels. In the upper levels of management, conceptual skills are extremely important because general managers have to make many broad, complex, unstructured decisions. Furthermore, they are dealing not with just one economic function, but with all the organization's economic functions. They must also have an overall understanding of how the organization operates in its environments. Human relations skills seem to be important throughout the various levels of management, as Figure 1.4 suggests. Researcher Virginia Boehm examined a similar set of skills by management level among managers at SOHIO. She found distinct differences among skills required in the three levels.[27]

LINE MANAGERS VERSUS STAFF MANAGERS

Line managers are those directly concerned with accomplishing the goals of a particular organization. **Staff managers** are in charge of units that provide support to the line units. From a total organization perspective, marketing, operations, and finance have always been viewed as line functions, and virtually everything else as staff functions. That view has changed somewhat as the human resource management function, which has traditionally been considered a staff function, has come to be viewed as critical to organizational success. Var-

FIGURE 1.4 MANAGEMENT SKILLS BY LEVEL

	CONCEPTUAL	HUMAN	TECHNICAL
TOP			
MIDDLE			
LOWER			

ious companies may view certain economic functions as being so important as to be line functions, when normally they might be considered staff functions. For example, research and development (R&D) might be considered to be a line function in a high-tech computer firm.

The Universality of Management

When John Sculley became the president and chairman of the board of Apple Computers in 1983, Steven Jobs and the other members of the Apple board, assumed that management was universal and that Sculley's excellent performance record as president of PepsiCo of America could be duplicated at Apple, with a different product, in a different market, and using different technologies. They felt that Sculley could manage Apple as well as he had PepsiCo. Sculley himself was wise enough, however, to realize that he had to learn the specifics of the new industry before he made many major changes. He immersed himself in the technology, in the product design, and in all other facets of the business before he made major decisions, other than those that resolved the most obvious problems. Among these were the need for reorganization, the need for making members of the company much more profit-oriented than they had been in the past, and the need for making employees aware of competition. But until he had a chance to study the situation, he made no major product or major marketing decisions.[28]

The **universality of management**—the belief that management practices are applicable to all organizations—has long been argued. Management probably is universal, but only after a manager has become familiar with the specific situation in which it must be applied. In contrast to Sculley, Archie R. McCardell, who had been a successful executive at Xerox for years, proceeded to make many decisions on the same basis as he would have at Xerox when he assumed the presidency of International Harvester. However, he failed to allow for the specifics of the situation. Having left a nonunionized environment for a unionized one, he opted to hold out and let the United Auto Workers remain on a long strike against the firm. The consequence of this "problem-solving action" was bankruptcy for International Harvester.[29]

John Sculley realized that management was universal, but only so long as the manager thoroughly understands the factors in each management situation. (SOURCE © Chuck Nacke/Picture Group)

Management in For-Profits
and in Not-for-Profits

Recently a client from a division of a city management team explained to a management consultant that several people in his division were opposed to the particular management system about to be introduced because, "It may work everywhere else, but it won't work here because we're unique."[30] Management is universal whether the organization is for-profit or not-for-profit, but the management process must be tailored to fit each unique situation. It was possible to provide that organization with some specific applicable modifications of a basic concept. Many people question the applicability to not-for-profits of many of the typical techniques and processes of management in the for-profit environment;[31] however, transference of the functions, roles, and skills is possible.

Make no mistake, there are significant differences between the environments faced by managers in for-profit organizations and those that challenge managers in not-for-profits. The for-profit organization operates in a market-dominated economic situation. Customers influence incentives, constraints, and values in this environment. Not-for-profits, on the other hand, operate in more politically influenced environments, where clients are often not the source of funds. Instead, different external sources, be they resource contributors, legislators, or other political or activist groups, greatly influence incentives, constraints, and values. Even within each of these classifications, there are major differences. For example, conditions vary in the for-profit sector by industry and by firm. The environment of USX differs substantially from that of McDonald's.

Similarly, the situation confronting the private not-for-profit varies significantly from that of the public not-for-profit.[32] The Easter Seal Society competes with other charities for voluntary contributions, while the Federal Communications Commission (FCC) competes with other federal agencies for mandated funds. The Easter Seal Society must appeal to the general population; by contrast the FCC must, while serving the needs of the general population, function within a highly political and bureaucratic arena. The real question is whether the resulting differences in management practices between classifications are greater than those within them.[33] The answer seems to be no. The management process is transferable from for-profits to not-for-profits, but you must modify for the specifics of the situation when going from for-profits to not-for-profits, just as you would when going between industries or companies in the for-profit sector.

In fact many of the great success stories in management in recent years have occurred in the not-for-profit sector. For example, states and cities have become known for their ability to adapt business-based systems successfully. Profit is not the issue, but cost savings are. In North Carolina, for example, quality circles—a participative group-decision process for improving quality and saving money—have been employed successfully in state agencies as part of the governor's Program for Productivity. Their introduction in the Department of Motor Vehicles resulted in annual savings of more than $50,000.[34] The early successes of quality circles have led to their widespread usage.[35]

In another example, the city of Houston found that by applying the management principles one of its new administrators had learned while completing a master of business administration (MBA) degree, they could save hundreds of thousands of dollars a year. In one instance they used part-time labor instead of full-time employees who weren't working all the time. Savings were especially noticeable for labor involved in setting up and taking down hundreds of exhibits that Houston had each year at its convention center. Similarly, New York's Metropolitan Museum of Art reports that once it began treating its operation like a business, it began to be much more successful and much less in need of donations. It sells hundreds of thousands of reproductions annually, for which it earns many millions of dollars.[36] Just because an organization is not-for-profit doesn't mean it can't be managed like a profit-making organization.

The Managerial Environment

Managers operate in extremely complex environments. They face both **external and internal environmental factors** that they must manage, as portrayed in Figure 1.5. The specifics of the environment vary with a manager's level in an organization and area of economic function, as well as other contextual factors such as whether the organization is for-profit or not-for-profit. But, in general, managers face the same external and internal factors, regardless of contextual situations.

The scope of the factors that the manager confronts is more limited at lower levels of the organization than at upper levels and in general management. Nonetheless, all managers must cope with both internal and external factors. For example, the manager in charge of work-in-process inventories for a modular home manufacturer, such as Cardinal Industries, must balance the demands of the market against the demands of the production line; against the demands of the accounting department, which looks for lower inventories to save costs; against the demands of the sales department, which seeks higher inventories to ensure delivery of the sale, to sell more; and so on.

When New York City's Metropolitan Museum of Art began treating its operation as a business, its financial requirements from donations lessened considerably, and it became better managed. (SOURCE © Jimmy Rudnick/Stock Market)

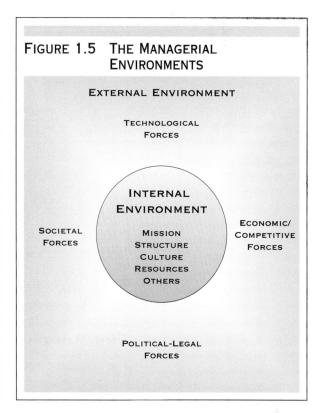

FIGURE 1.5   THE MANAGERIAL ENVIRONMENTS

EXTERNAL ENVIRONMENT

TECHNOLOGICAL FORCES

SOCIETAL FORCES

INTERNAL ENVIRONMENT

MISSION
STRUCTURE
CULTURE
RESOURCES
OTHERS

ECONOMIC/ COMPETITIVE FORCES

POLITICAL-LEGAL FORCES

Managers are pulled in many directions by many different forces. They must always be cognizant not only of the fact that managerial decisions are greatly affected by the environment, but that these decisions affect the environment, as well.

The External Environment

As shown in Figure 1.6, the manager confronts four principal external forces: economic, competitive, technological, political-legal, and societal. Each of these forces is made up of components that have vested interests in the actions of the organization's management. In fact these components often anticipate and demand certain actions by management. The federal government, a political-legal force, for example, has passed numerous laws to protect the environment, to provide equal employment opportunity, to protect consumers, to regulate the use of energy, to stabilize the economy, to define relationships between business and organized labor, to tax businesses, and to govern many other facets of doing business.

Many other examples of the actions of government and other organizational stakeholders can be seen every day in the life of any major organization. The competitive environment is especially critical, being comprised of current competitors, buyers, suppliers, substitutes, and the threat of new entrants.[37] Managers must manage the factors in the external environment in some way, either by changing the environment or adapting to it, or they will suffer the consequences. Management Challenge 1.1 portrays how two managers accepted this challenge.

AT FORD: *Ford was forced by competition, principally from the Japanese, to change its strategies. Hence, it had to change its leadership style, as well.*

The Internal Environment

The manager must consider many factors within the organization that will affect his or her management decisions. These factors include people—owners, board members, general management, organized labor, nonorganized workers, informal leaders, and so on. The manager's role is also governed by such factors as the organization's rules, policies, procedures, management systems, structure,

(slides, waves, and rides) and movie tour attractions in Florida to take advantage of demand, futuristic rides at Disneyland to take advantage of new technologies, real estate development and hotel ventures in Florida, the syndication of certain Disney movie and TV properties, the return to main market television, and opening EuroDisneyland, a new Disneyland in Europe, a project the previous administration had begun but that the new management team completed.

Frank Wells, on the other hand, saw the need not only to raise profits to satisfy stockholders, but also to finance Eisner's new ventures. A combination of actions ensued in which prices were raised at Disney theme parks, adding millions immediately to the bottom line; costs were cut by trimming staff and reducing some functions; and special financial arrangements for funding projects were sought.

Their predecessors had begun to move in some of these directions, but had failed to do so quickly enough to avert the takeover attempts that eventually led to their downfall. Eisner and Wells moved swiftly, and with much more momentum, to overcome their management challenges. They read the changes in their external and internal environments and acted to manage them.

Andrea Gabor and Steve L. Hawkins, "Of Mice and Money in the Magic Kingdom," *U.S. News & World Report* (December 22, 1986), pp. 44–46.

Epcot Center and Spaceship Earth at Disney World in Orlando, Florida are Disney ventures that have been affected by the management decisions of Michael Eisner and Frank Wells. (SOURCE © Philip Hayson/Photo Researchers)

strategy, and resources. The manager must be able to balance the needs and requirements of all of these factors against each other and against the demands of the external environment.

Management: An Art or a Science, or Both?

Is management an art or a science? The answer by now is probably obvious: both. Some people seem to be able to manage skillfully simply as a natural extension of their personalities. But for most of us, management is a skill that we must learn. Many organizations fail to recognize the need to develop this skill in their managers, assuming that because they are made managers they also know how to manage. A student in one of my evening classes recently complained about the problems this thinking can cause. She indicated that her company, a large regional commercial banking institution with several billion dollars in assets, assumed that by making her a manager she would automatically know what to do as a manager. They had not trained her in interpersonal or conceptual skills, and had given her only limited training in the relevant technical skills. She also had had no training in management functions, or in the roles a manager must play. Unfortunately, this is a common situation. Management skills and abilities can be developed. People can learn how to manage, but most don't know how to manage without development.[38] Thomas Mulligan further argues that currently most management education focuses on the science of management and not enough on the art of management.[39]

Developing Management

Managers in major Japanese firms spend an average of at least one day a month, every month, every year of their careers learning how to manage better. In

AT FORD: *Ford Motor Company evidently felt that managers could be developed and that management was a skill that could be learned. The company adopted a new culture, a new series of values, to which organizational members were expected to adhere. To manage better in this new culture, Ford managers had to acquire different skills and attend extensive training programs to acquire them. This series of strategies has succeeded for Ford.*

Japanese managers endure intense, samurai-like training in order to improve their management skills. Leadership is believed to be heightened by demanding assertive, even aggressive behavior. Participants receive ribbons of shame which they must "work off" during this training. Ribbons may denote the acquisition of self-confidence, reading ability, manners, positive thinking, and so on. (SOURCE © Greg Davis/Black Star)

addition, at the beginning of their careers and periodically thereafter they participate in exhausting two- or three-week, or longer, sessions of intense management training. Japanese firms believe managers *must* be developed, that the personalities and leadership style of managers cannot be changed through a one-day course, but only over time and with considerable effort. They believe that this can and must be done. Many large American firms, those that have been extremely successful, practice a similar approach to management development. Firms such as IBM, Hewlett-Packard, Ford, and others, train their managers in a fashion not unlike the Japanese, although not usually as extensively. However, they still train them repetitively and often throughout their careers. The training their managers receive depends on the function they perform and their level of managment, as well as on their perceived career development needs.

The Management Matrix

The management functions of creative problem solving, planning, organizing, leading, and controlling are applicable to each of the economic functions of an organization, which include marketing, finance, operations, human resources, information management, and R&D. But as you can see in Figure 1.6, managers must also manage each of the management functions. They have to plan planning, organize planning, lead planning, control planning, and so on, for all of the management functions. The **management matrix** shows that managers manage both economic and management functions. Thus, when AT&T Information Systems recently reorganized its entire management structure, it had first of all to plan how it was going to reorganize, then organize that reorganization effort, then have its managers lead the implementation of the reorganization, and finally practice control by checking to see if the structural change had achieved the desired results.[40] It's been my experience as a consultant that most managers understand the need to manage the economic functions but often fail to manage the management functions. Both must occur.

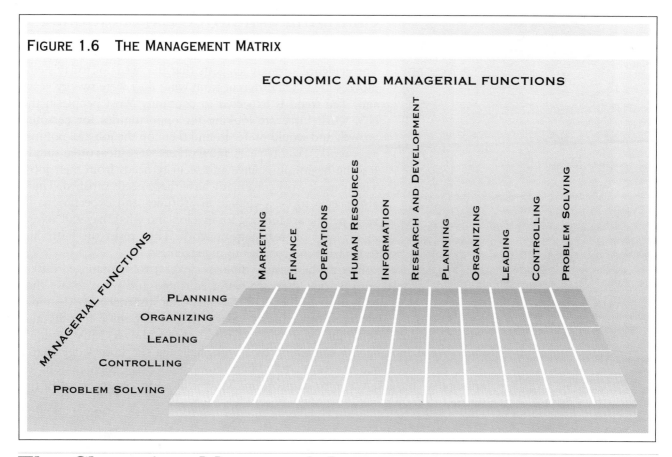

FIGURE 1.6   THE MANAGEMENT MATRIX

The Changing Managerial Process—The Management Challenges[41]

Many forces for change greatly affect managers and the management process, as you can see in Table 1.4. These forces, these management challenges, are **changing** the nature of the **management process** functions, the skills required of managers, and the roles that are necessary. They are also changing the relative mix of management functions, as well as how they are performed.[42] Both from within and from outside the organization, **forces for change** are constantly pressuring managers just as they always have, but the forces are stronger and less familiar than at any time in recent history. The forces are constantly changing and the actions required to meet successfully the demands of these forces are changing. First we will discuss the principal forces for change affecting managers and the management process and then the major impacts of these forces.

Table 1.4 Why Management Will Change: The Major Management Challenges

1. Changing employee expectations of how they should be managed
2. The global economy
3. Shift from an industrially based economy to an information-based economy
4. Accelerated rates of change
5. Increased levels of competition
6. Changing technology, especially computers
7. Finding a more creative approach to improve problem solving
8. Emphasis on managing organizational culture
9. Increasing demands of constituents
10. Changing demographics: the cultural diversity of the work force

Changing Employee Expectations as to How They Should Be Managed

Those graduating from colleges today, exemplify the new employee—they have expectations far exceeding those of most of their predecessors. Managers must find ways of accommodating these expectations while influencing these employees with these different expectations, to assist in the achievement of organizational objectives. (SOURCE © Robert Reichert)

The evidence strongly suggests that the needs of today's employees are much different from what they were twenty years ago. The trend is expected to continue. Most people in the U.S. work force are looking for opportunities for personal growth and would prefer to find them on the job and not just after work. Twenty years ago workers were most often simply seeking basic subsistence and security needs from their jobs. Today most workers already have those needs satisfied. There also seems to be a change in attitudes and expectations in what people are looking for in a job and what they will accept in the way of treatment at work. They resist the more authoritarian approaches to management.[43]

Part of the reason employees expect to be managed differently is that they are better educated and want to use that education on the job.[44] As one of my students said, "I simply couldn't take it. I worked on a factory assembly line for three months and just had to quit—doing the same thing over and over and over, I just couldn't take it. I'm looking for something that will challenge the knowledge that I have, the experience that I have." Many companies are designing jobs to attempt to alleviate this type of problem. More will be forced to do so in the future.

The Global Economy

When the price of gasoline rose so dramatically in the 1970s, we began to realize that we were operating in a global economy—what happens elsewhere greatly affects North America. Today, three primary trading zones exist: Europe, North America, and the Pacific Rim. To be successful on a large scale means that you have to be able to compete in all three zones. To be successful in North America, the world's largest consumer and industrial market, you have to be able to compete against firms from all over the world. You have to be able to offset the various competitive advantages that firms from various nations enjoy—technology, low-cost labor, and capital.[45] This global perspective is so essential to understanding the management situation that a whole chapter in this book is devoted to the global management challenge, and each chapter contains a global management challenge discussion.

The Shift from an Industrially Based Economy to an Information-Based Economy

A number of authorities have pointed out that we are shifting from an industrially based to an information-based economy.[46] The general belief is that how companies are managed, how managers manage, and the nature of the management process itself must all change as a consequence of this shift. What worked for managing workers in highly repetitive, automated jobs, when the workers had much less education than they do now, will simply not succeed for workers whose jobs are constantly changing, whose educational levels and expectations are higher, and who must frequently make decisions on the job.[47]

Accelerated Rates of Change

In 1970 Alvin Toffler, in his book *Future Shock*,[48] predicted that as we approach the end of this century, all members of our society will face increasing rates of change—socially, politically, economically, and technologically. His predictions have come true. All the evidence indicates that the rate of change in our society is accelerating. Product life cycles, which used to last ten years, are now lasting a year and a half. The personal-computer industry is a good example of this. Most computer products have a very short life cycle. Thomas J. Peters, noted management consultant and author, in his recent book *Thriving on Chaos*, predicts a revolution in management at least partly because of this accelerated rate of change. He feels that because managers must cope with so much change, they must manage differently.[49]

Increased Levels of Competition

On an international basis, we face increased levels of competition. Japanese companies, companies in Brazil, and companies on the Pacific Rim—Taiwan, Hong Kong, Singapore, and Korea—are formidable competitors, especially in the basic industries in which their low labor costs offer them strategic cost advantages. Many of them are also formidable competitors on the quality issue, as are many European firms. The Japanese, and to a great extent European automobile companies, have beaten the American automobile companies in the marketplace on the basis of quality. Unfortunately, we seem to be losing ground in many ways to foreign competition; one reason is that we are losing our innovative edge over this competition. For that edge to be regained requires new management approaches.[50]

Other factors are also at work. Deregulation in banking and transportation have clearly increased competition. Federal government regulations are forcing health care firms to cut costs. Overbuilding in the hospitality industry, especially hotels, has helped increase competition there. In virtually all high-tech segments of the economy, competition has increased tremendously: computer chips, personal computers, and copiers, for example. Combine this competition with the movement from an industrially based to an information-based economy, an anticipated shortage of labor as we enter the 1990s[51] (when the demand for labor will increase in a service-dominated economy), and it becomes quite clear that we will need to continue to change the way we manage people. In a labor-intensive economy in which labor is in short supply, people's expectations will require more attention from management. Yet, to survive, companies must eliminate many staff positions and strive to justify financially all positions. Managers must "add value" to the product or service of the organization to be retained.[52]

The Impact of Changing Technology, Especially Computers

The increased use of technology, especially computers, has given managers more ability to obtain information both about their unit and their entire organization.

This increased use of technology carries with it the necessity for changing the way managers make decisions.[53] Previously neither this information nor the capacity to turn raw data into usable information was available. Today a tremendous amount of software does "the number crunching" that was formerly done by hand. Now managers have more time to do something meaningful with those numbers. In fact there is considerable evidence that we really need to be more creative. Michael Naylor, executive in charge of strategic planning for General Motors, cautions that everyone can now crunch the numbers, that every competitor has virtually the same information. To gain the competitive advantage, he suggests, means being creative in response to those numbers.[54]

Finding a More Creative Approach to Improve Problem Solving

There is strong evidence that the person who is intuitive as well as rational is a far superior decision maker than one who is simply rational and analytical. Studies by Arthur Reberg and Henry Mintzberg indicate that, especially in more complex jobs, such as CEO, intuition is a necessity, not merely an advantage.[55] Management Challenge 1.2 reveals just how important creative problem solving can be.

Emphasis on Managing Organizational Culture

Studies of successful organizations provide evidence that managing culture, the organization's shared values, is a way of improving productivity and employee job satisfaction.[56] The key to managing culture is managers' leadership ability. Increasingly they must facilitate, counsel, increase participation in problem solving, and work with teams. But it is not just leadership. How managers plan, organize, and control is also critical.

The Increasing Demands of Constituents

The 1990s will be an era of constituent advocacy of their needs.[57] **Constituents** are major groups affected by an organization's decisions including stockholders, customers, suppliers, the general public, and competitors. Preserving the natural physical environment is expected to be a major issue. Air and water pollution, the depleting ozone layer, and protection of animal rights will be focal points.

Changing Demographics: The Cultural Diversity of the Work Force

In the next few years, virtually all women under the age of thirty will be employed in the work force. Most are already. Reduced birth rates mean that fewer people will be entering the work force and that it will contain more older workers. There will also be an influx of foreign workers, especially from Mexico. Most of the work force, with some exceptions, will be better educated. Only 15 percent of the new workers added to the work force between 1990 and the year 2000 will be native-born white males. Most of the rest of the additions will be females and minorities, creating a very culturally diverse work force. Both these factors and other trends indicate a need to change the way we manage.[58]

Management Challenges and the Following Chapters

While this is an introductory text in management and must therefore focus on the basic theories and applications of management, the pervasiveness and importance of the management challenges listed in Table 1.4 dictate that they be integrated into the discussions of basic theories and applications in the following chapters of this book. Each time a relevant discussion of one or more of them appears, you will see the icon to the side of this paragraph in the margin, as it is here. And, at the end of each chapter, the management challenges noted in the chapter and their suggested solutions are listed to remind you of their impact on the management process.

The Changing Face of Management—Is Everyone to Become a Manager?

Because of the preceding management challenges, and others, each management function will change dramatically.[59] Details of these challenges and the required changes will be covered in the relevant chapters, but the following are some of the major ways that management is expected to change.

In problem solving it is expected that more creativity will be necessary, and that employee participation in decision making will increase. Every employee may become a manager. They may be asked to solve problems in a complex environment where they will plan, organize, lead, and control their own efforts to a much greater degree than is common today. They will act almost as an independent business.

In planning there probably will be more participation in setting goals; more efforts to encourage individual entrepreneurship in the company (intrapreneurship); more strategic, yet short-range planning; and more computer simulations of actual and anticipated situations.

In organizing, delegation of authority is expected to increase. Jobs will repeatedly be redesigned to accommodate new technologies and to make them more meaningful. The organization itself will be redesigned to give more autonomy to major subunits and to eliminate layers of middle management. Teamwork will increase.

In leading, the increasing acceptance of the concept that management is a service to the rest of the company will result in more managing by wandering around (MBWA)—facilitating, coaching, encouraging.

In controlling there will be both increased emphasis on self-control and increased control by computers. Costs will also be more closely watched as competition intensifies.

The Management Challenge

The management challenge is enjoyed by those who experience it. Management *is* challenging. It is ever changing. It is constantly in need of fine tuning. And in many companies, it needs to be completely revamped. Good managers are seldom bored.

This book is based on the belief that you should not only learn about management, but also try to learn how managers think and solve problems. You will also learn how management is going to change and thus how to prepare yourself to become a better manager.

If you were to ask managers at Ford's Louisville plant whether they enjoy managing more now than they did in the early 1980s, they would answer strongly in the affirmative. Perhaps more importantly, their subordinates feel they are being well managed and now have opportunities for self-management that were not available to them several years ago.

Summary

1. Management is the creative problem-solving process of planning, organizing, leading, and controlling an organization's resources to achieve its mission and objectives effectively and efficiently. It is complex, it varies by level, and it is not easy, but it can be fun.

2. Management and managers have come under tremendous criticism in the 1980s. Results simply aren't being achieved. As a consequence, there are changes in the way managers manage and in the management process itself.

3. There are three primary approaches to the study of management:

   a. As a functional process: creative problem solving in planning, organizing, leading, and controlling.

   b. As a series of roles: interpersonal, informational, and decisional.

   c. As a series of skills: technical, human, and conceptual.

   All are interrelated. This book focuses on the functional approach but integrates the other perspectives.

4. There are several types of managers: general, or functional, managers; top, middle, and lower managers; line and staff managers.

5. Management is universal but must be adapted to the specifics of a situation whether it is for private/for-profit, public/not-for-profit, or private/not-for-profit.

6. All managers function in both external and internal environments. Externally managers confront government, technology, competition, other members of the industry, new entrants, customers, clients, substitute products, suppliers, creditors, society as a whole and its constituent groups, the economy, natural resources situations, international variables, various pressure groups, organized labor, and a host of other potential factors. Internally the manager is concerned with general management; others who direct the organization, such as board members; members of management throughout the organization; various informal leaders; nonorganized employees; culture; the organization's rules, policies, and procedures; the organization's strategy and structure; management systems; and organizational performance.

7. Management is both an art and a science. Management skill can be developed.

8. The management process occurs not only in each of the economic functions—that is, marketing, finance, operations, and human resources management—but also in the management functions themselves. Management occurs in planning, organizing, leading, controlling, and problem solving, as shown in the management matrix.

9. The management process is changing because of several major factors in the environment. There are ten key reasons why management will change:

   a. Changing employee expectations of how they should be managed

   b. The global economy

   c. The shift from an industrially based economy to one based on an informational paradigm

   d. Accelerated rates of change

   e. Increased competition

   f. The impact of changing technology, especially computers

   g. The growing evidence that improved problem solving results from a more creative approach

   h. A new emphasis on managing organizational culture

   i. Increased demands of constituents

   j. Changing demographics: The cultural diversity of the work force.

Management is becoming more participative, and to some extent more creative. Numerous other aspects of management are changing as the rest of this book will reveal.

Thinking About Management

1. What is a manager? What is an organization? What does a manager do?

2. Why do organizations need managers? Why do organizations need everyone to manage themselves better?

3. Describe each of the functions of management, each of the roles of management, and each of the skills the manager should have. Now describe how these might differ for a manager working in a line position as a nursing supervisor of 50 beds in a 500-bed hospital; the president of the Women's Junior League of 50 women in a 400,000-person city (the Junior League is a volunteer service organization); the production manager in an automobile assembly plant; and the president of a 100-employee software firm.

4. Describe the management challenge facing the president of your college or university.

5. Describe the internal and external forces confronting the marketing manager for Apple Computers.

6. Describe how each of the factors listed in Table 1.4 is probably affecting the product-development manager in charge of creating new cars for the Pontiac Motors Division of General Motors. Now describe how these same ten factors would affect the manager of a McDonald's hamburger franchise.

CASE

Xerox Struggles to Cope

Xerox Corporation is typical of many U.S. corporations in the late 1980s. It found itself, in 1989, struggling to raise a low return on equity and to improve profits. Its stock, in December 1989, languished in the high $50s, with breakup value estimated at almost twice the stock price. It faces a Japanese attack on its core business—high performance copiers. Its R&D efforts, $3 billion in recent years, have had mixed results, as have its diversification efforts. A major gamble is under way to leapfrog photocopying and move to digital copying in which a computer takes the original document image apart dot by dot and reassembles it in a copy, for faxing, or for use in some other form. But technology is moving rapidly in all aspects of its businesses, and where it's headed is anybody's guess. And, Xerox has experienced problems with a mixing of corporate cultures reflecting the backgrounds of various top managers.

But Xerox has not been standing still. It has cut costs to the bone and increased quality significantly, winning the label of "American Samurai" for its Japanese-style results. It has reduced its overhead considerably, slashing the number of white-collar workers. It has closed its inefficient plants and modernized the others. It has written off several expensive diversification efforts. It has invested more time and money in improving its main products. Yet, in the 1980s, price competition held its profits to virtually no gain.

It has improved customer relations and is developing a program for listening to customers. It has attempted to improve its ability to move new products from research into production. It has increased the authority of those in its sixty divisions. And CEO David T. Kearns insists on creative solutions from his managers. Yet, Kearns wonders if all this is enough. So do stock analysts.

DISCUSSION QUESTIONS

1. What management challenges does Xerox face?

2. What more could a company be expected to do than Xerox has already done?

3. How does the number of challenges, and their interrelationships, make the problem even more severe?

SOURCE: "Xerox Rethinks Itself and This Could Be the Last Time," *Business Week* (February 13, 1989), pp. 90–93.

Motivating Employees at General Mills

Linda Sampieri, vice-president for employee relations for General Mills Restaurants (Red Lobster, the Olive Garden, and others), contemplated the changing nature of the work force. Motivation had become a major issue for the firm. She pondered what the company could do to improve the motivation of operative employees—cooks, waitresses, hostesses, hosts, dish washers, and so on. The 42,000 employees of the firm were, on average, better educated than ever before, although many were less well educated. They all had much higher expectations from work than the work force did ten years ago. There were fewer potential employees to choose from because of the changing demographics in the labor market, which further compounded her problems.

Additional training for first-level supervisors was an obvious need, but Sampieri was looking for something special, innovative, in the way of a motivation system.

DISCUSSION QUESTIONS
1. What kinds of unique compensation programs might be tried?
2. What kinds of other motivation programs might be attempted?

Should You Be a Manager?

Based on what you have read so far, and what you know from other sources, what do you think the requirements are to be a good manager? Do you have, for example, good interpersonal skills and good conceptual skills? List below what else is required.

		Low	High
1. Interpersonal skills			
2. Conceptual skills			
3. Technical skills			
4. Planning skills			
5. Organizing skills			
6. Leadership ability			
7. Controlling skills			
8. Problem-solving skills			
9.			
10.			
11.			
12.			
13.			
14.			
15.			

Now rate yourself as either High or Low on that factor by placing a check under High or Low. So, should you be a manager? Obviously it's too soon to tell, but you're beginning to get the idea of what is required.

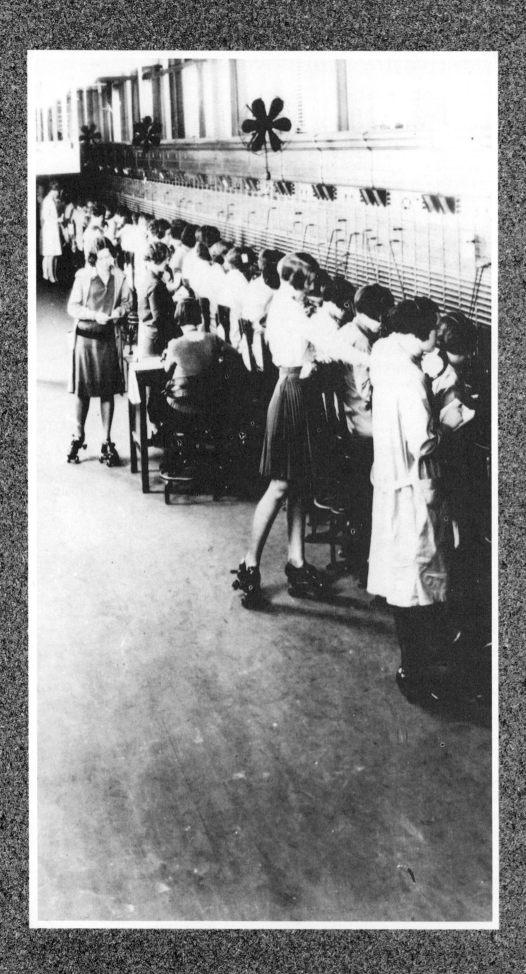

CHAPTER TWO

Learning from Management History

CHAPTER OBJECTIVES

By the time you complete this chapter, you should be able to

1. Discuss the relevance to management of the two quotations on page 35.
2. Identify the five forerunners of contemporary management.
3. List some of the early contributors to management thought and their contributions.
4. Indicate the principal concerns of the scientific management theorists and the administrative theorists regarding the classical approaches to management.
5. Discuss the major concerns of the behavioral approach to management.
6. Describe how the management-science approach attempts to aid the management problem-solving process.
7. Identify the principal contributions of the systems approach to management.
8. Describe how the contingency approach functions.
9. Define the contemporary management approach.
10. Review how the Japanese have contributed to contemporary management.
11. Describe how Tom Peters and other critics of management have influenced management.

CHAPTER OUTLINE

Precursors of Modern Management Theory
    Management Reflects Society
The Classical Approaches to Management
    Scientific Management
    Administration and Organization
    Legacy of the Classical Approaches to Management
The Behavioral Approach to Management
    The Hawthorne Studies
The Management-Science Approach to Management
    Models and Techniques
The Systems Approach to Management
The Contingency Approach to Management
Contemporary Management— A Synthesis
    Obtaining a Synthesis
    Japanese Management Approaches
    The Excellence Approach to Management
    Common Themes
Management in the Future
Management Challenges Identified
Some Solutions Noted in the Chapter

General Motors' Strategic Woes

In early 1987, Roger B. Smith, chairman of General Motors, realized that GM was in a precarious strategic position. While it was selling millions of cars, and had in 1986 made more than $3 billion in profit, it had also, for the first time since 1921, made less profit than Ford Motor Company. Worse, Ford made more profit than GM on half the sales, and GM's market share had dropped from 48 percent in 1979 to 36 percent in early 1987.

In 1979 Chairman of the Board Thomas A. Murphy and CEO Elliott M. Estes, after examining the strategic environment, had assumed that it would be the same in the future as it had been in the past:

1. Energy problems, which had begun to plague the country, would continue.
2. Therefore, consumers would continue to purchase small cars with high fuel efficiency.
3. Quality would be important to compete with the growing Japanese market penetration.
4. Technology would drive the automobile industry both in terms of manufacturing and product content.

Acting on these assumptions, they moved to downsize their cars. The subsequent redesigning involved a major change in plant and equipment. General Motors thus embarked upon a proposed $40 billion—but ultimately $60 billion—program of technology improvement. GM also sought to lower costs through product design but especially through state-of-the-art technologically based manufacturing. One of the major results of these strategies was common body parts for the various models, both within and among the various automobile divisions—Cadillac, Buick, Oldsmobile, and Pontiac and Chevrolet. This decision to employ common body parts was one of the major reasons for GM's precipitous drop in market share. It led many Buicks to look like Cadillacs and Oldsmobiles, and many Pontiacs to look like Chevrolets. Furthermore, GM became so engrossed in implementing its strategy it ignored the fact that the strategy wasn't succeeding. General Motors was creating cars that were high tech, downsized, and fuel efficient for a market that no longer existed. GM was manufacturing cars and then looking for a market for them, rather than first finding out what the customer wanted and then making the cars.

Unfortunately for GM, technological improvements did not prove to be the successful cornerstone strategy for which it had hoped. The $40 billion invested in technology as of 1987 did not allow GM to produce any more or better automobiles than it had produced without the massive investment. Furthermore, the joint venture with Toyota Motor Corporation in GM's Fremont, California, plant, NUMMI, New United Motors Manufacturing, Inc., had revealed that proper management of human resources combined with reasonable technological improvement could be more efficient and effective than a fully robotized plant. The NUMMI plant, which had been GM's least productive plant, became its most productive and highest-quality plant within three years after the introduction of Japanese management techniques to the same work force that had been there previously.

In 1987 GM believed that it would again sell cars at its previous rate. Therefore it continued operating at 70 percent of plant capacity, which was far above what was necessary for current sales. This caused profits to plunge drastically. As a consequence, GM announced in mid-1987 that it would close 16 plants throughout the United States and Canada and would lay off 25,000–50,000 white-collar workers in the near future.

SOURCES: William J. Hampton and James R. Norman, "General Motors: What Went Wrong?" *Business Week* (March 16, 1987), pp. 103–110; "GM Chairman Smith Finds Lots of Critics at Meeting," *Wall Street Journal*, 26 May, 1987, p. 18; "Perot's War with GM Ends in $743 Million Goodbye," *U.S. News & World Report* (December 15, 1986), p. 53; and David E. Whiteside, "Roger Smith's Campaign to Change the GM Culture," *Business Week* (April 7, 1986), p. 84.

Those who cannot remember the past are condemned to repeat it.

George Santayana

We are the prisoners of what we know.

Walter B. Wriston,
Former CEO, Citicorp

General Motors forgot what it already knew. It had introduced stylistic choice to the automobile industry in 1921, but in the 1980s it failed to provide its customers with stylistic choices. It offered look-alike cars to meet strategic cost and quality objectives, but this caused the company to fail to meet strategic market-share objectives. General Motors repeated Henry Ford's classic error of selling a car in "any color as long as it was black" because it failed to remember its own past success. Its thorough study of the 1970s oil crisis made it a prisoner of what it knew about it, and it made strategic assumptions that failed to materialize. GM's executives extrapolated from recent history to forecast the future, without adequately examining their assumptions about the future. When they forecasted the demand for automobiles, they assumed that yesterday would continue to repeat itself tomorrow. It did not.

NUMMI factory workers are involved in decision making, and thereby help improve productivity more than total robotization could. (SOURCE © Lawrence Migdale/Photo Researchers)

The opening vignette on General Motors, when taken in the context of the opening quotations for this chapter, gives you a perspective for studying materials in this chapter, relative to history in general, or any specific problem: You need to know history and you need to learn from it, but you don't want to be bound by it. You need to understand what it tells you and also what it doesn't tell you. You need to know how to use it, but you also need to know what its limitations are.

Managers should be concerned with historical perspectives. They need to know the facts about what has happened in a similar situation and to relate them to other experiences and other knowledge. Only when they understand the problem environment and how it developed can they fully understand the problem they are trying to solve. Managers search for patterns in the problems they face, and they tend to use learned solutions when those patterns recur. Experienced managers have more experiences to draw on than less experienced managers, but all managers can benefit from the history discussed in management books or cases. No manager has enough personal experience to deal with every problem he or she faces.

As the rate of change in our society continues to accelerate, more and more new situations will occur that are likely to resemble others that occurred in the past. This allows effective solutions to be repeated and ineffective solutions to be avoided across all of an organization's economic functions: marketing, finance, operations, human resources management, and information management. A successful manager needs to know what worked before, what didn't, and why.

You will benefit from knowing the history of management because, as a practicing manager, you don't have to make the same mistakes that your predecessors made. You will be able to consult the appropriate sources to discover what worked and what didn't. You can then decide the best ways of managing for yourself. Understanding history also gives you a basis for acting with your future coworkers and with others who are practicing and studying management now, or who will be in the future. History also helps you recognize when to act and when not to.[1] Knowing history helps you identify the common themes that seem to recur. By knowing how issues have been handled in the past, you should also know better how to act now.

This chapter explores five forerunners of current approaches to management: the classical, behavioral, management-science, systems, and contingency approaches.[2] We will review the contributions of leading experts in each of these approaches and show how these approaches are still applied today. The chapter concludes with a review of current issues, two contemporary approaches to management, and a discussion of how management may change in the future.[3]

Precursors of Modern Management Theory

Historian Daniel A. Wren observed that "management is as old as man."[4] But, as he also points out, only recently has there been scientific interest in the process. This is probably because we have only recently realized that how we manage our resources affects what we get from them and because large business organizations have only existed since the early nineteenth century. However, early civilizations did practice management—and in a way not very different from how it was done until the late nineteenth and early twentieth centuries. Table 2.1 lists the major contributions to the practice of management from approximately 5000 B.C. to the late nineteenth century. To appreciate each of these contributions, remember that not until 1776, when Adam Smith described the benefits of the division of labor in *The Wealth of Nations,* did mass production, which is the foundation of our current economic success, become recognized as possible and desirable. Until the 1800s, there really was no systematic development of management theory, and perhaps only in the mid-1900s did it become useful to the average manager.

Management Reflects Society

Management philosophy and its related practices reflect the society within which they exist—its culture, its values, its needs. The technological, social, political, and economic forces at work in society change, and therefore management has changed and must continue to change.[5] Before the twentieth century, for example, the practice of management was largely authoritarian and was based on hierarchical organizational structures similar to those developed by the early military forces of the Egyptians, Romans, and other ancient societies. The decentralized organizational structure of the Roman Catholic church slightly modified these structures.[6] As Western society became less agriculturally and more industrially based, its leaders and scholars began to realize that traditional management approaches were unsatisfactory. Entering the twentieth century, some 150 years after the beginning of the industrial revolution, and some 35 years after the U.S. economy became industrially based (1865),[7] managers began to ponder all the factors that should be considered in managing and in alternative ways of managing. It is from this point that we pursue the history of management in detail.

The remainder of this section reviews the five major approaches to modern management theory that characterized the twentieth century before the contemporary approaches were developed: classical, behavioral, management science, systems, and contingency.

Table 2.1 The Early Evolution of Management Thought

Time Period	Contributor	Major Contributions
5000 B.C.	Sumerians	Established written records for both government and commercial use
4000–2000 B.C.	Egyptians	Employed inventory practices, sales ledgers, taxes; developed an elaborate bureaucracy for agriculture and large-scale construction, e.g., pyramids; employed full-time administrators; used forecasting and planning
4000 B.C.	Hebrews	Exception principle, departmentation; Ten Commandments; long-range planning; span of control
2000–1700 B.C.	Babylonians	Enforced law for conducting business, including standards for wages and obligations of contractors
500–200 B.C.	Greeks	Developed the work ethic; Socrates' universality of management, the beginning of the scientific method for problem solving
200 B.C.–A.D. 400	Romans	Developed a factory system for manufacturing armaments, pottery, and textiles; built roads for distribution; organized joint stock companies; used specialized labor; formed guilds; employed an authoritarian organizational structure based on function
A.D. 300–20th century	Catholic church	Decentralized hierarchical structure with centralized strategic control and policies
1300	Venetians	Established a legal framework for business and commerce
1494	Luca Pacioli	Developed the first system of double-entry bookkeeping
1776	Adam Smith	Focused on division of labor and mass production as the key to prosperity
1800	Eli Whitney	First to use interchangeable parts for mass production
1850s	Robert Owen	One of the first to recognize the importance of human resources; improved working conditions, reduced hours of work, raised minimum age of work for children
1860s–70s	Charles Babbage	Improved the efficiencies of production using mathematical problem-solving techniques; emphasized human resources

SOURCE: Based primarily on Daniel A. Wren, *The Evolution of Management Thought,* 2nd ed. (New York: Wiley, 1979), chap. 2. By permission of John Wiley & Sons, Inc.

The Classical Approaches to Management

The **classical approaches** to management were developed early in the twentieth century. There were two primary thrusts, scientific management and organization and administration. They focused primarily on improving work methods and formulating principles to understand how to administer and structure organizations, respectively.

Scientific Management

Scientific management sought to find "the one best way" to do the job. Its leading proponent was Frederick W. Taylor, an industrial engineer, who, in

(a) Frederick W. Taylor

(b) Rolling mills at the Steubenville Works of Bethlehem Steel. (SOURCE © Bettmann)

AT GM: *General Motors invested heavily in technology, attempting to improve productivity. Their experience at their Fremont, California, plant suggests they should have spent more time on improving each worker's productivity.*

publishing *The Scientific Principles of Management* in 1911, revolutionized the practice of management. Other major early contributors to the practice of scientific management were Henry R. Gantt and Frank and Lillian Gilbreth.

FREDERICK W. TAYLOR (1856–1915): SCIENTIFIC MANAGEMENT[8]
Frederick W. Taylor was interested in prosperity both for the employer and for the employee. Working principally with heavy manufacturing and steel workers, he showed that work could be redesigned so that workers could do more. He also redesigned their compensation systems, so that they wanted to do more. Using scientific management approaches, a company and its workers would both make more money. He also believed that the workers would be happier as a result. Taylor's **scientific management** had four underlying principles:

1. The development of a true science of management
2. The scientific selection of the individual to fill each job
3. The scientific education and development of each employee, so that he or she would be able to do his or her job properly
4. Cooperation between management and workers[9]

Taylor emphasized that all four of these elements in combination, not any one of them singly, were responsible for improved productivity and increased worker satisfaction. He believed that managers should use science, not rules of thumb; that they should seek harmony, not discord; that organizations should have cooperation, not individualism; that managers should seek maximum output, not restricted output; that each person should be developed to his or her greatest level of efficiency and prosperity.[10]

A major part of Taylor's scientific management system was an incentive compensation plan that paid people a piece rate for a specified amount of work and a bonus for anything beyond that.[11] At the time the idea of paying people for what they did rather than for the time they spent on the job was not only innovative but suspect. In fact Taylor was called to testify before Congress to defend his ideas. Unions and others with vested interests in maintaining the status quo denounced many of his concepts and called for an investigation, which proved inconsequential. Taylor believed that by scientifically redesigning work to make it more efficient—for example, by reducing the number of motions to perform a job—and by providing proper incentives, he could eliminate the underachievement of the work force.

How far have we come since Taylor's time? Think of the jobs that you have had. Were you paid for what you did or for showing up? How productive were you? Managers who want to get the most they can from their people must reward performance. They must also seek harmony and cooperation and develop their subordinates to the fullest if they expect to solve the productivity problem. It is amazing that we face the same problems we faced eighty years ago and that they still seem to require many of the same solutions. Have we learned from history?

HENRY L. GANTT (1861–1919)

One of Taylor's leading disciples, perhaps *the* leading disciple, was Henry L. Gantt. Gantt had worked with Taylor on several of his major projects. Thus, Gantt's scientific management approaches naturally reflect Taylor's four principles of scientific management. Gantt is perhaps best known for the **Gantt chart,** a simple, yet effective way to allow managers to schedule work forces across a series of tasks. An example is shown in Figure 2.1 for a bank planning to open a new branch. Gantt charts were the forerunners of today's program evaluation review technique (PERT), a technique we will discuss in detail in Chapter 7.[12]

Other key contributions by Gantt included a task-and-bonus system and what he labeled "the habits of industry." Gantt felt that instead of simply developing an employee's skills, foremen should instill positive characteristics, such as industriousness and cooperation. He modified Taylor's incentive system to give workers base pay plus bonuses. Gantt was also one of the first managers to be concerned about the social responsibility of businesspeople. "The business system must accept its social responsibility and devote itself primarily to service or the community will ultimately make the attempt to take it over in order to operate it at its own interest."[13] Business philosophers and critics in the 1960s, 70s, and 80s have repeated these words many times.

AT GM: *One of the problems GM and other American automobile manufacturers face is that they are not paying the majority of their workers for what the workers accomplish, but for the time they spend on the job. This is at least partly the result of a unionized labor force and of management's attitudes toward it. Further compounding management's problem are such historical factors as animosity, not harmony; an environment of confrontation, not cooperation; restricted levels of output; and underdeveloped worker potentials, all factors Taylor tried to overcome in his principles of scientific management.*

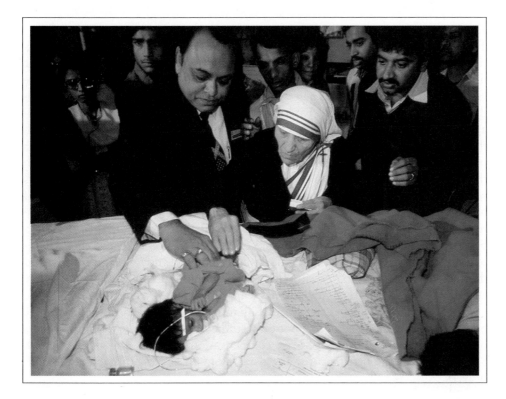

Mother Theresa is shown here comforting victims of the Bhopal, India gas leak tragedy which killed over 2,000 people. This tragedy raised concerns about corporate social responsibility. Henry Gantt foresaw the need to identify such responsibilities. (SOURCE © Morvan/SIPA)

FIGURE 2.1 GANTT CHART FOR BANK EXAMPLE

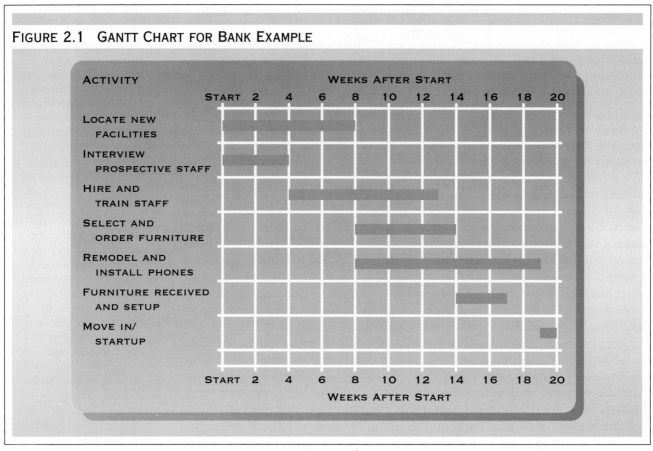

SOURCE: WILLIAM J. STEVENSON, PRODUCTION-OPERATIONS MANAGEMENT, 2ND ED. (HOMEWOOD, IL: IRWIN, 1986), P. 629.

FRANK (1868–1924) AND LILLIAN (1878–1972) GILBRETH

This husband-and-wife team is perhaps best known for their child-rearing practices as revealed in the book *Cheaper by the Dozen,* which referred to the number of children they had, written by Frank B. Gilbreth, Jr. and Ernestine Gilbreth Carrie.[14] However, their contributions to management outside the family also are significant. While Taylor was known as the father of scientific management, the Gilbreths' forte was the study of work itself, especially through the use of motion and time studies. Their careful studies of the work motions of various types of employees and their analysis of the time it took to perform those motions, always led to increased employee productivity. The Gilbreths constantly searched for "the one best way." One of Frank's motion studies of bricklayers found that the number of motions necessary to lay bricks could be reduced from 18½ to 4. This reduction tripled the number of bricks that a bricklayer could lay with no additional effort. The Gilbreths were the first researchers to use motion picture cameras and lights to study work motions, and they also were the first to describe elementary human micromotions, which they labeled therbligs (Gilbreth spelled backward, with the *th* transposed).[15]

After Frank Gilbreth's early death, Lillian became more concerned with the psychology of management. She not only studied work efficiency, but the effects on the worker of efficiency efforts, compensation systems, and other factors. She was one of the first to study the psychology of successfully managing employees.[16]

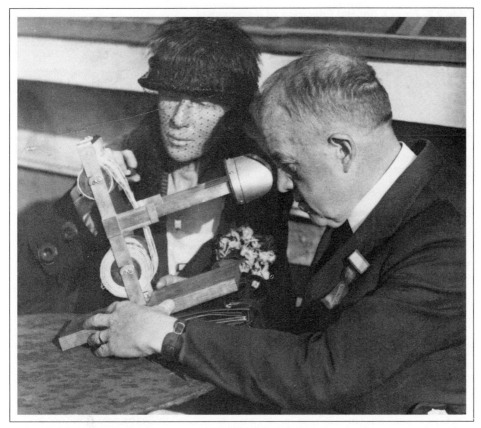

Frank and Lillian Gilbreth utilizing a motion study device invented by Lillian.
(SOURCE © Bettmann)

Bricklayers today employ several of the motion reduction efforts first recommended by Frank Gilbreth. (SOURCE © Junebug Clark/Photo Researchers)

Administration and Organization

Concurrent with the efforts to study job design that characterized scientific management were those that examined how managers managed and how organizations were structured. Key contributors were the French executive Henri Fayol; the German sociologist Max Weber, who was interested in the structure of organizations; and the Americans Mary Parker Follett, a political theorist turned business philosopher, and Chester Barnard, president of New Jersey Bell.

HENRI FAYOL (1841–1925):
FUNCTIONS AND GENERAL PRINCIPLES OF MANAGEMENT
In 1916 Fayol, the father of modern management, published *Administration Industrielle et Generale,* in which he described what he had found to be the proper way to manage organizations and their members. Fayol's major contributions were to define the functions and list the general principles of management. He defined management as consisting of planning, organizing, commanding, coordinating, and controlling. Commanding and coordinating, when combined, are what we define as leadership. So in this book, as in most others, we are essentially following Fayol's functions: planning, organizing, leading, and controlling. Problem solving occurs in each of these functions.

Table 2.2 lists Fayol's second major contribution, his 14 general principles of management. These 14 **principles of management** specify rules for successfully managing and structuring an organization.

Table 2.2. Fayol's General Principles of Management

1. Division of work: This is the classic division of labor prescribed by Adam Smith. Division of labor reduces the number of tasks performed by a job unit to as few as possible. This improves efficiency and effectiveness because it allows for the simple but rapid repetition of effort.
2. Authority and responsibility: Authority is the right to give orders and the power to exact obedience. Responsibility accrues to those who have authority. If you have responsibility, you must also have commensurate authority. (This is the "parity principle.")
3. Discipline: There must be obedience and respect between a firm and its employees. For Fayol, discipline is based on respect rather than fear. Poor discipline results from poor leadership. Good discipline results from good leadership. Management and labor must agree. Management must judiciously use sanctions to ensure discipline.
4. Unity of command: A person should have only one manager and receive orders from only one manager.
5. Unity of direction: The organization, or any subunit thereof that has a single objective or purpose, should be unified by one plan and one leader.
6. Subordination of individual interest to the general interest: The interests of the organization as a whole should take priority over the interest of any individual or group of individuals within the organization.
7. Remuneration of personnel: Workers should be motivated by proper remuneration. Remuneration levels are the function of many variables, including supply of labor, condition of the economy, and so on.
8. Centralization: Centralization means that the manager makes the decisions. Decentralization means that subordinates help make the decisions. The degree of centralization or decentralization depends on the organization's circumstances.
9. Scalar chain: Managers in hierarchical organizations are part of a chain of superiors ranging from the highest authority to the lowest. Communication flows up and down the chain, but Fayol also allowed for a communication "bridge" between persons not on various dimensions of the scalar chain. The "bridge" would allow subordinates in different divisions to communicate with each other—although formally they were supposed to communicate through their bosses and through the chain of command.
10. Order: There is a place for everything, and everything must be in its place—people, materials, cleanliness. All factors of production must be in an appropriate structure.
11. Equity: Equity results from kindliness and justice and is a principle to guide employee relations.
12. Stability of tenure for personnel: Retaining personnel, orderly personnel planning, and timely recruitment and selection are critical to success.
13. Initiative: Individuals should display zeal and energy in all their efforts. Management should encourage initiative.
14. Esprit de corps: Esprit de corps builds harmony and unity within the firm. This harmony or high morale will be more productive than discord, which would weaken it.

SOURCE: Daniel A. Wren, *The Evolution of Management Thought* (New York: Wiley, 1979), pp. 218–221. By permission of John Wiley & Sons, Inc.

The importance of Fayol's contributions to the practice of management cannot be overemphasized. Most of Fayol's observations are relevant to most organizations today. For example, virtually all organizations are still arranged according to the division of work using highly specialized labor, whether they are making the B-1 bomber or microchips or providing health care services. All organizations use the principle of authority; virtually all employ the unity of command concept; and all use some degree of centralization versus decentralization, and the scalar chain.

Moreover, we are beginning to learn that most of the other principles—equity, order, stability of tenure for personnel, initiative, esprit de corps, remuneration, and discipline—can contribute to successful organizational management. Managers looking to solve structuring problems would do well to use many, if not most, of Fayol's basic concepts.

MAX WEBER (1864–1920)

Weber's major contribution to the study of management was the concept of "bureaucracy," and he is often referred to as the father of organization theory. Weber defined **bureaucracy** as "the ideal or pure form of organization." He was interested in improving organizational structures used in large-scale organizations and in designing a blueprint of a structure that would help large organizations achieve their objectives.[17]

Weber's concept of bureaucracy is conceptually close to Fayol's view of structure. Its basic elements are revealed in Table 2.3.

Table 2.3. Characteristics of Weber's Bureaucracy

1. A division of labor in which authority and responsibility are clearly defined and legitimized.
2. A hierarchy of authority resulting in a chain of command.
3. Organizational members who are selected on the basis of their qualifications, either by examination or because of their training or education.
4. The appointment of managers and not their election (as might occur in government).
5. Managers to be paid for fixed hours and to be career oriented.
6. Managers who do not own the unit they administer.
7. Manager's conduct subject to strict rules and procedures, disciplinary actions, and controls.

SOURCE: Adapted with permission of The Free Press, a Division of Macmillan, Inc., from Max Weber, *The Theory of Social and Economic Organizations*, ed. and trans. by A. M. Henderson and Talcott Parsons, pp. 329–333. Copyright 1947, renewed 1975 by Talcott Parsons.

Max Weber, German sociologist, coiner of the term bureaucracy, conversing with colleagues. (SOURCE © Culver Pictures)

Weber envisioned three types of legitimate authority that formed the basis of any organizational structure: (1) rational, legal authority; (2) traditional authority; and (3) charismatic authority. Rational, legal authority depended on position, traditional authority on the legitimacy of the person in command, and charismatic authority on the follower's personal trust and belief in the leader.[18]

The importance of Weber's contributions became evident when organizations around the world began to grow in size and complexity in the 1940s and 1950s. As leaders began to search for ways to improve these organizations' structures, Weber's "ideal bureaucracy" became the model. His formalized structures then led to the examination of informal organizations, human relations, organizational behavior, and other factors that influence the formal blueprint of an organization.

AT GM: *General Motors is a bureaucracy, but perhaps not an "ideal" one. It has experienced difficulty in making the right decisions, partly because its members were prisoners of what they already knew.*

MARY PARKER FOLLETT (1868–1933)

Mary Parker Follett focused on relationships within an organization and on the power of the group. Instead of basing administration on the idea of power over people, she suggested that authority resided in the situation. To her, responsibility was inherent in the functions a person performed and not in his or her authority. She was instrumental in helping managers recognize the importance of the group.[19]

Another of her major contributions was to refine the concept of coordination. For Follett coordination involved the sharing of responsibility by all people involved in an organization and was a means of relating all factors in a situation to each other. She felt that coordination was critical in the early stages of an enterprise and was an ongoing process.[20] She believed that coordination achieved control because it achieved unity, which was control.

Finally, Follett was also one of the first to point out that leaders had to have followers to be leaders, and that reciprocal influence occurred between leaders and their followers. Leadership to her, however, was not just a situation in which leaders had followers, but rather one in which leaders had the ability to influence their followers.[21] This was an important distinction because it broke with the military model on which the theory of the business hierarchy had hitherto been based. A business manager does not have the absolute authority that a military officer has.

CHESTER IRVING BARNARD (1886–1961)

Chester Irving Barnard was a Horatio Alger success story. Barnard was a poor farm boy who attended Harvard on scholarship and later became president of New Jersey Bell and student and teacher of the sociology of the organization.

AT GM: *Echoing Barnard's words, GM has instituted a program designed to improve cohesiveness, cooperation, and self-respect for its employees. GM's "partnership" program is also an attempt to enable it to overcome Japanese competition. Its NUMMI (New United Motor Manufacturing, Inc.) plant in Fremont, California, is a model for the rest of the company. It employs Japanese management techniques in combination with modern technology, making it the most effective and efficient plant the company has. Barnard would have been proud of these actions.*

Barnard's *Functions of the Executive,* published in 1938, was many years ahead of its time. It contains many doctrines whose importance is only beginning to be fully understood today. For example, he identified three goals of an organization:

1. "The maintenance of an equilibrium of complex character (modifying a complex and ever-changing organization) in a continuously fluctuating environment of physical, biological, and social materials, elements, and forces
2. To examine the external environment and adapt to it
3. To examine and understand the functions of executives at all levels"[22]

Barnard's external focus in points 1 and 2 foreshadowed the current view of the importance of strategic planning that most organizations adopted in the 1970s. **Strategic planning** involves formulating major plans (strategies) that guide the organization in the pursuit of its major (strategic) objectives. It involves adapting the organization to its environment or changing that environment.

Barnard's focus on the building of a cooperative system to make individuals work for the good of the organization revealed similar advanced thinking. He helped define the meaning of an organization as "cooperation among men which is conscious, deliberate, and purposeful."[23] He was concerned with how groups as well as individuals affected this system and how the overall organization could be maintained. He recognized that organizations were comprised of subsystems, all of which contained three universal elements: (1) a willingness to cooperate, (2) a purpose, and (3) communication.[24] Barnard believed that without the willingness to cooperate, organizations would fail. He was also one of the first to discuss the informal organization—those informal relationships existing apart from, but within the formal organization. He felt that it helped to maintain communication, cohesiveness, and feelings of integrity and self-respect.[25]

Barnard is perhaps best known for his **acceptance theory of authority.** His view is essentially opposed to the views of those who had written previously on the subject, except for Mary Parker Follett. Where Weber, for example, saw authority principally as a top-down function in an organization, Barnard saw it as deriving from the acceptance or rejection of authority by the subordinate—a bottom-up approach.[26] Barnard suggested that there was a "zone of indifference" within which each person would obey orders without questioning the authority of those who gave them. Once an order exceeded that zone of indifference, however, the person would have to choose whether to accept or reject that authority. In organizations today, people will often question and disobey their manager's orders. This happens when a union member refuses to obey a manager's order because "it's not in the contract, and therefore you can't make me do it." Such disobedience was also common among the American military in Vietnam in the late 1960s and early 1970s. Many, if not most, people today sometimes quietly disobey orders to some extent because the orders have exceeded their zones of indifference.

Finally, Barnard postulated three executive functions: (1) to provide a system of communication for the organization; (2) to influence people to perform at high levels in acceptance effort; and (3) to formulate and define the organization's purpose.[27] To Barnard, the creative force of the organization was its mission. He believed executives must have a vision and should lead by example, creating cooperation where none previously existed. Barnard was one of the first to recognize that organizations must not only be **effective**—achieve their organizational objectives—but also **efficient**—use the least amount of resources to achieve those objectives. He recognized the possible dichotomy of attempting to achieve both effectiveness and efficiency at the same time. It might, for example, be necessary to spend massive amounts of money for advertising to increase market development and reduce efficiency, in order to be effective—to sell the product.

Legacy of the Classical Approaches to Management

The concerns of the classical management approaches still provide insight into many of the problems managers face today. The scientific management approach showed that job design was critical to job efficiency and effectiveness. Managers should not assume that the way a job is being done is the best way. Performance can always be improved. Another insight was that managers must reward performance.

The administrative concerns of the classical management approaches also have relevance today. Weber's rules for bureaucracy, for example, help define most organization structures. Fayol's guidelines are followed by almost all modern organizations. Barnard's view of cooperation has recently become accepted practice. Accomplishing both effectiveness and efficiency is still an issue confronting most organizations. The acceptance of authority as related by both Follett and Barnard is something managers are learning that they must strive to achieve. Managers would be wise when making decisions to listen to Barnard's concerns about cooperation, strategic planning, external and internal analysis, and the need for developing systems of communication.

The classical approaches do have limitations. The one most generally cited is that they do not take human matters into account—that is, how people would fulfill the work roles given to them. Instead they tend to treat worker efficiency from a mechanical viewpoint. These shortcomings were addressed to some extent by Follett and Barnard. In fact, Follett was so concerned with the human resource, she is sometimes considered the founder of this movement. Barnard, too, is often viewed as part of the behavioral approach. Human concerns were addressed in the behavioral approach to management, which is the second of our five forerunners to management to be considered. Barnard and Follett help bridge the gap between the two approaches.

The Behavioral Approach to Management

While Weber and Barnard were defining the concept of the organization, another approach to management was being developed—the behavioral approach. The behavioral approach was concerned with increasing productivity by focusing on understanding the human element of an organization—individuals and groups and how they can be combined, both effectively and efficiently, in a larger organization.

Concern for the human being in the productivity equation began with a series of studies performed at the Western Electric Plant in Hawthorne (Chicago) from 1924 to 1932. The original purpose of these studies was to provide support for an advertising campaign claiming that increased electric lighting would increase productivity. Their findings in the first phase of these studies, called the illumination experiments, led investigators to examine social relationships and the work group.

The Hawthorne Studies

The Hawthorne studies consisted of three parts: the illumination experiments, experiments in the relay-assembly test room, and experiments in the bank wiring observation room.

THE ILLUMINATION EXPERIMENTS (1924–1927)

The illumination experiments were based on the belief that such factors as fatigue and monotony were functions of improper job design and environmental conditions—lighting, temperature, and materials flow. In 1924 a study of these factors was commissioned by the National Academy of Sciences (NAS) at the Hawthorne Works of the Western Electric Company near Cicero, on Chicago's west side. Two groups of workers were examined: a control group, whose illumination would not be varied, and a test group, whose illumination would be varied. The results were surprising. Regardless of the level of light, which in one case equaled moonlight, productivity increased in both the control and test groups. Unable to explain the results, researchers began looking for other key variables, including pay, rest periods, and refreshments. Yet, no matter how they manipulated the variables, productivity increased. Even after canceling all the privileges that workers had recently earned, productivity still increased. Reinstating rest pauses and refreshments led to yet another increase. Researchers were at a loss to explain the results. During the studies, which lasted until 1927, output increased from 2,400 relays to 3,000 relays per week per worker.

THE RELAY-ASSEMBLY TEST ROOM EXPERIMENTS

In 1927, just as researchers were considering abandoning their efforts, Elton Mayo, a Harvard professor, began to consult on the studies. Mayo believed strongly that "a remarkable change of mental attitude in the group" explained the Hawthorne situation.[28] In a sense, Mayo simply rediscovered what Robert Owen (see Table 2.1), the nineteenth-century industrialist, had already written about: Workers would perform at higher levels if managers seemed more concerned about them. The classical theorists assumed that people always reacted rationally and were motivated principally by money. Environmental factors

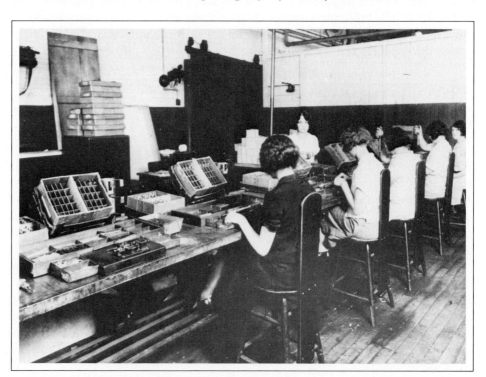

These five women were part of the relay assembly room experiments at the Hawthorne plant of Western Electric. (SOURCE © AT&T Archives)

were also believed to influence productivity, but virtually no attention had been paid to the behavioral aspects of managing. In the Hawthorne studies, the special attention given to the group by the leader of the experiment, who was not viewed as "a boss" and who also gave special attention to the workers' sentiments and motives, created a special relationship that led to higher productivity.[29] As a result of these studies, when a secondary factor, such as the attention given the workers in these experiments, produces a result that could have come from the phenomenon being studied—here the level of lighting—this result is known as the **Hawthorne effect.**

After the experiments in the relay-assembly test room, lengthy interviews revealed that the supervisor should show concern, should establish open communication with employees, and should be willing to listen to employees. These experiments also uncovered the existence of informal groups—groups not officially designated as part of the formal organization. These informal groups were discovered as researchers sought to explain productivity levels. Interviews revealed informal group norms to which most workers adhered.

THE BANK WIRING OBSERVATION ROOM EXPERIMENT

The third phase of the research effort at Western Electric was designed to study the informal group. The bank wiring room experiments showed clearly that informal group norms affected productivity levels. The study revealed that the work group had a clear idea of what constituted a fair day's work, and it was less than what management thought it should be. However, the work group also considered that a certain amount of work was the minimum that should be done. The group expected its members to do the minimum but condemned them for doing more than the maximum (fair day's) amount. Those who violated the maximum levels were known as rate busters; those who violated minimum levels were known as chiselers. While the researcher had been an active participant in the relay-assembly test room experiment, he merely observed the bank wiring room group at work. As a result, group productivity there tended not to change.

The primary contribution of the Hawthorne studies was to reveal the effect of behavioral factors on productivity—specifically social systems within a work group. The studies clearly showed that sentiments were as important as any formal requirements for the individual or group. The Hawthorne studies called for a "new mix of managerial skills—these skills were ones which were crucial to handling human situations: first, diagnostic skills and understanding new behavior; and second, interpersonal skills and counseling, motivating, leading, and communicating with workers. Technical skills alone were not enough to cope with the problems discovered at the Hawthorne works."[30] The Hawthorne studies helped balance management thought and style from its narrow, one-sided classical view. Many believed that if people's social needs were satisfied, they would perform better. Unfortunately, manipulation became a common influencing technique. Managers might go out of their way to be "nice" to employees, for example, providing coffee and donuts, in order to try to increase productivity. But employees soon caught on, so manipulation often failed. The search for a better explanation of human motivation continued.

Additional issues have been discussed over time as part of the behavioral approach. These are covered in this text principally in the chapters on motivation, group dynamics, and leadership. Contemporary with the behavioral approach, another group of scholars was developing quantitative techniques to improve the managerial problem-solving process. These researchers initiated the management-science approach to management, the third of our management forerunners to be considered.

AT GM: *The Fremont, California, plant clearly indicates the importance of behavioral factors on productivity. GM forgot the lessons of history and was therefore doomed to repeat them.*

The Changing Business Curriculum

The top managers of the future will need to be able to speak a foreign language and be familiar with a foreign culture—preferably Japanese or European—know how to negotiate, be a skilled communicator, possess the proper social graces, be a sound leader and a visionary, be innovative and entrepreneurial, understand the global marketplace and the role of technology, and behave in an ethical manner. All of these talents are in addition to understanding one's functional discipline, those of the rest of the organization, and strategic planning. To accommodate these needs, MBA programs across the United States are changing, some dramatically.

For example, the University of Virginia will "fundamentally alter" its curriculum in the fall of 1989, according to Dean John Rosenblum, adding more political

The Management-Science Approach to Management

Like the scientific management approach, the management-science approach attempted to make management decision making more rational. The **management-science approach** has four primary characteristics:

1. A focus on problem solving
2. A rational orientation
3. The use of mathematical models and techniques to solve problems
4. An emphasis on computers in decision support systems

Models and Techniques

Management science, often called **operations research,** or **quantitative analysis,** employs mathematical techniques to solve problems. The management-science approach sprang from efforts to cope with the numerous complex problems encountered in World War II. As it turned out, the models and techniques used to solve those problems later had wide application in other business situations. Operations researchers believed that the more scientifically they could approach a problem and the more information they could use to analyze and solve it, the more likely they would be to reach a satisfactory solution. The decision would be more rational and less based on a "gut reaction." Until recently, management science has focused largely on production and planning, but now mathematical models and techniques and computers are being used more frequently in financial analysis, market research, personnel selection, and other decision support systems.[31] They are least successful when applied to interpersonal relations or individual human problems.

Two men, Robert A. Gordon and James E. Howe, were responsible for the general belief that more rigor was needed in managerial problem solving. Gordon and Howe prepared a report in 1959, entitled "Higher Education for Business," in which they criticized business schools for not being rigorous enough.[32]

orientation and global coursework in the first year and more electives in the second year. Perhaps no school is changing more than the University of Denver, where Chancellor Dwight Smith reports that a "total restructuring" is under way. At Denver, the whole experience of MBA education is becoming more experiential, more global, more applied, thanks largely in part to a $10 million endowment by businessman Bill Daniels. At Denver, for example, the faculty and students are required to donate ten days a year to community service. The school is trying various new experiences, such as a weekend "Outward Bound" excursion for faculty and students in the Rocky Mountains. Daniels wants to provide a separate institute, a sort of finishing school, at the end of the MBA program to teach "what goes on in the real business world." The University of Denver is also making a major thrust to include ethical issues throughout its curriculum.

These and other changes may soon be appearing in undergraduate programs as well, as business schools wrestle with the changing needs of students and businesses.

SOURCES: Jeremy Main, "Business Schools Get a Global Vision," *Fortune* (July 17, 1989), pp. 78–86; and Lyman W. Porter and Lawrence E. McKilbin, *Management Education and Development, Drift or Thrust Into the 21st Century* (New York: McGraw-Hill, 1988).

Denver University Business School participants scaling a wall at Outward Bound, demonstrating the importance of teamwork. (SOURCE Courtesy Tom Watkins of the Denver School of Business Administration)

Business schools responded by employing more of the management-science techniques, or operations research techniques, that had been developed during and after World War II. Gordon and Howe's report reinforced the growing belief that these approaches should be used in business, and therefore more managers also began to employ them. Ironically, business schools are now being criticized for focusing too much on quantitative issues and not enough on issues such as leadership, communication, and global competition, as Management Challenge 2.1 suggests.

Herbert Simon, Nobel laureate for economics in 1978, researched at great length, from a quantitative, rational analytic viewpoint, how individuals make decisions in organizations. He discovered that decision making was not as rational as had been proposed. He provided several observations about decision making in organizations that will be discussed in Chapter 3. Simon was an important bridge between the management science and behavioral approaches.[33]

In Chapter 7, on quantitative tools for planning and problem solving, and in Chapter 20, on operations management, we will highlight many of the models and techniques embodied in the management-science approach. Managers have a host of tools available to help make the problem-solving process more rational: simulations, inventory control models, and statistical decision theory, for example. These tools are especially useful in recognizing and identifying a problem and in helping choose among alternatives. The entire focus of the management-science orientation is on decision making. Managers should learn to use the appropriate techniques. Personal computer software programs that use management-science techniques are becoming increasingly available.

AT GM: *GM has attempted to overcome some of its problems partly by having both the most scientific and complete information systems and the software packages to use them. These include simulations, forecasting models, statistical sampling theory—virtually all of the quantitative methods discussed in Chapter 7.*

The Systems Approach
to Management

The **systems approach** views the organization as a system that is interdependent with other systems in its environment. The environment of an organization includes the social, political, technological, and economic forces that affect it.

Management was affected by systems theory as a consequence of several circumstances. First, in the 1960s and 1970s, managers were bombarded by external environmental influences. The Sierra Club and other public interest groups, for example, put significant pressure on managers to become more accountable for the impacts of their decisions on those in their environments. Managers became especially concerned with the impact of business decisions and actions on the physical environment, equal employment opportunity, employee health and safety, and consumer protection. Echoing the words of Chester Barnard on social responsibility, business critics, management scholars, and many executives themselves began to recognize the tremendous influence that business decisions had on a wide range of people outside the organization. Paralleling the realization of these concerns was the development of systems theory. Simply stated, **systems theory** maintains that everything is related to everything else. At a time when business and its critics were experiencing difficulty identifying its role in society, the systems perspective offered some insight into the situation.

In business the interconnectedness of systems to one another became a focal point for examining business effects on others. For example, DDT, a pesticide that had been widely used to protect crops, was eventually banned because of its deleterious effect on the food chain and ultimately on humankind at the top of that chain. The business organization that produced DDT served as an example to others to consider the impacts of decisions on other systems—for example, the physical environmental system, the economic system, the political system, the consumer system, and the educational system.

Systems theory also affected management by allowing for the conceptualization of business as an input, transformation process and output system (operating in an external environment), as shown in Figure 2.2. Businesses take certain inputs—financial, human, material, informational, and technological—and transform them through operations, management, the efforts of labor, and the use of technology into outputs—product/services and financial, human, and societal consequences. Inputs often come to the organization from outside sources—materials and finances—but may also be internally generated—labor and finances. Transformation occurs in many ways—for example, manufacturing or service provision. Outputs are varied, and while products and services are the principal concerns, the others should not be ignored. One of the perspectives realized by using a systems approach, is that business operates in a societal system, and that there are societal consequences from a business—for example, wastes. From this perspective, businesses' relationships to certain entities become more apparent—for example, suppliers and creditors provide certain inputs; employees make certain transformations by performing certain processes—for example, assembling parts or processing a check. And consumers receive certain outputs—for example, products and services.

Systems Characteristics. All systems have subsystems. A subsystem is a part of the whole system. A department, for example, is part of a company. Most subsystems have their own subsystems. The marketing system, for example, may have sales, product development, and distribution subsystems.

Systems are open or closed. An open system interacts with its environment. A closed system does not. All forms of organizations—businesses, government and other nonprofit organizations—operated for many years as if in a vacuum, as if they were closed systems, failing to recognize their impacts on their stakeholders and the impacts of stakeholders on them. Today managers increasingly recognize that businesses are open systems. When solving problems and making decisions, managers must take into account how their decisions and solutions will affect various stakeholders. This is probably the greatest lesson of general

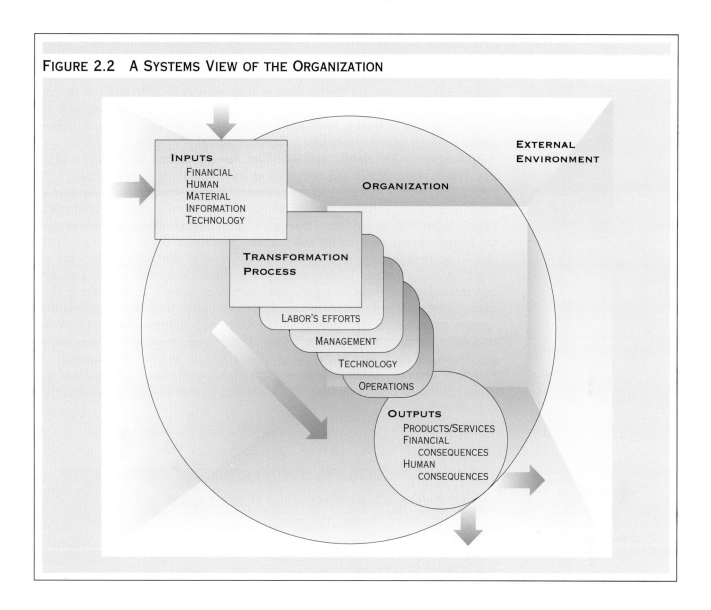

FIGURE 2.2   A SYSTEMS VIEW OF THE ORGANIZATION

INPUTS
FINANCIAL
HUMAN
MATERIAL
INFORMATION
TECHNOLOGY

EXTERNAL
ENVIRONMENT

ORGANIZATION

TRANSFORMATION
PROCESS

LABOR'S EFFORTS

MANAGEMENT

TECHNOLOGY

OPERATIONS

OUTPUTS
PRODUCTS/SERVICES
FINANCIAL
    CONSEQUENCES
HUMAN
    CONSEQUENCES

systems theory for managers. Whatever managers decide, whatever their solutions are, whatever they implement, will affect others, and those effects must be taken into account before making or implementing a decision. Businesses are interdependent with many other systems in society. Furthermore, they must realize how their decisions affect others in their own organizations. Finally, they must realize how their environment affects them.

Systems, to survive and prosper, must have synergy.[34] **Synergy** means that the combined and coordinated actions of the parts (subsystems) achieve more than all of the parts acting independently could have achieved. Suppose, for example, that all of the employees of Kroger food stores went into the one-person independent food store business. They could not achieve singly what they did collectively because of the advantages of specialization of services, size, professional knowledge, and so on. As an organization though, these individuals can do much more through synergy.

The best known of the systems theorists is probably Ludwig von Bertalanffy.[35] His general systems theory helped to explain how organizational systems function. Von Bertalanffy was a biologist who attempted to find a general systems theory that would fit all sciences. While he failed to do that, his concept of steady-state equilibrium in the environment and the openness of systems to the environment were cornerstones in the systems theory of management. Economist Kenneth Boulding built directly on von Bertalanffy's theory in an attempt to build a general model that people in various fields—economics, the sciences, and management—could use to discuss their respective specialities with each other.[36] Boulding's model met with considerable fanfare but has not been applied beyond its role as a basis for a discussion of systems. It has, however, served to point others toward an integrative model.[37]

Although von Bertalanffy and Boulding developed their ideas in the 1930s and 1950s, management did not develop a systems theory approach until the 1960s and 1970s. It was then that systems theory was viewed as a way of explaining the organization and its relationship to its environment. Fremont E. Kast and James E. Rosenzweig, management researchers and authors, extended the systems perspective to the internal functioning of the organization. They viewed an organization as a system consisting of several subsystems—for example, a social system. Understanding how these subsystems work, and how they interrelate, can help managers make better decisions.[38] Today management information system designers use the systems concept to model organizations' internal and external environments in order to help managers make better decisions, especially strategic ones.[39] One of the major systems concerns of organizations in the future has to be to understand the impact of technology on how they function. Daimler-Benz, makers of Mercedes Benz automobiles, understands that systems aspect, as the following Global Management Challenge suggests.

GLOBAL MANAGEMENT CHALLENGE

Daimler-Benz Automaker! Conglomerate?

Many companies choose to stick with what they know. Daimler-Benz, the extraordinarily successful German automaker, has historically found "sticking to the knitting" quite to its liking. But, uncharacteristically, in 1985 it chose to diversify significantly. It acquired three firms—Dornier (aerospace), MTU (engine manufacturing), and AEG (diversified consumer products)—which added substantially to the company's revenues but virtually nothing to its bottom line. These companies all had a strong technological base, and the company's chairman, Werner Breitschwerdt, felt compelled to bring that technology to Germany's second largest corporation. Breitschwerdt believed that this market's consumers will demand ever more sophisticated automobiles, the kind that only technological supremacy can deliver. He felt that cars had to be intelligent, be able to "see" through fog and be able to "talk" to each other. He also felt that increased levels of competition in Daimler-Benz's luxury auto markets dictated diversification. He also believed that the new subsidiaries will provide ways for getting the costs of auto production down, to better enable the company to prosper in the future.

Note how similar Daimler-Benz's strategies are to those of General Motors, discussed in the opening vignette. Did Werner Breitschwerdt makes the right decisions? Should he have gone against the company's history? Only time will tell.

SOURCE: Louis S. Richman, "Daimler-Benz Conglomerates," *Fortune* (October 27, 1986), pp. 84–88.

The Contingency Approach to Management

Fayol and other early theorists searched for general principles of management that might be applied to all situations. But while many of these principles worked in most situations, none functioned appropriately in all situations. Therefore, in the 1970s it became evident that a manager's actions should be contingent on the condition of various key elements in a given situation—**the contingency approach.**

The first major research on contingency theory was undertaken by Fred E. Fiedler, management researcher (1967), who attempted to determine what style of leadership a manager should use in a given situation. Leadership styles have been characterized most commonly as either production oriented or people oriented.[40] Depending on the degree to which leader-member relations are good, a task is well defined, and a manager has position power (authority of the job itself), Fiedler found that managers should exhibit varying degrees of concern for production and for people.

Paul Hersey and Kenneth H. Blanchard, management researchers and authors, have identified different factors on which a manager's leadership style should depend.[41] They believe that the maturity level of the subordinate work group is the key factor and that leadership style should change according to whether subordinates have low, medium, or high levels of maturity. In this context maturity is defined as a combination of job skills and psychological maturity. Spurred on by research in leadership, research on contingency theory followed in strategic planning, personnel, and marketing.

Thus, it became evident in the 1970s that virtually all management functioning is contingent on the elements of a situation.[42] A series of contingency approaches for each major function of management and for several subfunctions has subsequently been worked out. In future chapters, when you study planning, organizing, leading, controlling, and even the problem-solving process itself, you will be shown various contingency models to help make decisions. For example:

1. In strategic planning recommended actions are often based on the particular stage of the product or industry life cycle.
2. The design of organization structure must match growth, size, environment, technological conditions, the requirements of strategy, and the philosophy of top management.
3. In choosing leadership style, managers should first determine the condition of several key factors, such as their personality, the personality of a particular subordinate, the dynamics of the subordinate's work group, the nature of the subordinate's job, organizational culture and structure, and other situationally important variables.
4. In controlling performance the manager must recognize the who, what, when, where, how, and why of the situation.

Procter & Gamble, for example, failed to comprehend fully the changing nature of its environment. As a consequence it was forced to change management practices it had used for years, as Management Challenge 2.2 suggests.

While true contingency theory would attempt to define the factors and prescribe behavior for a specified set of these factors and their conditions, this becomes virtually impossible when the number of the potential combination of elements in any given situation is considered. Charles Hofer, researcher of management strategy, for example, has determined that some 186,000,000 combinations of the 50+ key strategic planning variables exist.[43] Hence, contingency

Procter & Gamble Alters Historically Ingrained Management Practices

Procter & Gamble had a rich, historically founded organizational culture. There was the P&G way, and that was it. Well, that *was* it. Now there is the new P&G way. P&G, and more importantly its employees, lived by the rules. Among them was the one that said that brand managers have offices that are exactly 12 ceiling tiles by 12 ceiling tiles. Walls were moved to make certain that offices were the right size. When P&G built its new headquarters building, it did away with ceiling tiles, just one signal among many that the culture was changing. History, discipline, and rules are one thing, beating the competition is another. P&G discovered in the early 1980s that its traditional way of proceeding, its long-established discipline, and its rules were impeding the company in its market situations.

So it changed the rules. The company that did not lay off a single worker in the Depression has asked employees to retire early and has even laid off some. It has been adamant about cutting costs. It cut the work force by 4 percent overall in a matter of months by requesting early retirement, by reduced hiring, and by firing people. Perhaps of most symbolic importance, the traditional one-page memo, which could spell success or failure for the new manager, is declining in importance. These one-page memos were used for almost everything, but especially to move ideas upward for a decision. P&G became a bureaucracy in the worst sense of the word. When it came time to choose the color of the cap for a Folger's coffee can, the options were green or gold. The decision went all the way to CEO John Smale. He chose gold. Now there are even interdivisional project teams making decisions about issues that once were made secretly by only those with the primary responsibility for the product or project. The company has added a new "super" brand manager, the category manager, taking power from the traditionally focal brand manager. Finally, CEO John Smale, having overseen years of gut-wrenching change, in late 1989, turned over the reins to Edwin Artzt. This move signaled a new global focus for P&G. Artzt was responsible for turning around the fortunes of the firm's international division, and promises to make the company more global.

History is what you make of it.

SOURCES: Brian Dumaine, "P&G Rewrites the Marketing Rules," *Fortune,* November 6, 1989, pp. 34–48; Jolie B. Solomon and John Bussey, "Cultural Change: Pressed by Its Rivals, Procter & Gamble Company Is Altering Its Ways," *Wall Street Journal,* 20 May, 1985, pp. 1, 22.

theory for most managers has evolved into situational management. Situational management suggests that the manager must review the key factors in a situation and then determine what action to take based on past experience and knowledge. Good managers recognize that in most situations behavior cannot be prescribed. They also recognize that some limited prescriptive models can be used to help solve problems.

The contingency theory is a problem-solving approach. It dictates that managers should consider the major elements in a situation before making a decision, determining what management style to use, determining how to structure an organization, or determining a plan or a budget. They then base their decision on experience and knowledge and any prescribed models of actions that happen to exist for the situation.

Contemporary Management—
A Synthesis

Contemporary management is a synthesis of the seven approaches to management discussed in this chapter and any other approaches that may contribute to the improvement of management, as shown in Figure 2.3. The contemporary management approach recognizes that management is dynamic and that it must change with the organizational environment.

Obtaining a Synthesis

As Harold Koontz, one of the co-authors of the first major text on management observed, considered separately these different approaches may seem "like the

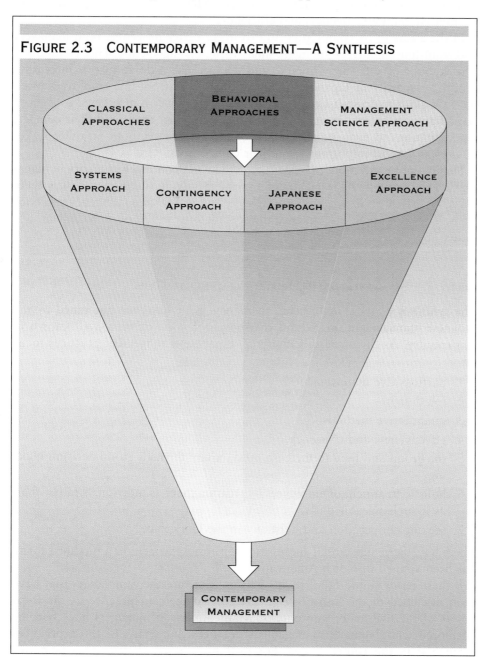

FIGURE 2.3   CONTEMPORARY MANAGEMENT—A SYNTHESIS

CLASSICAL APPROACHES

BEHAVIORAL APPROACHES

MANAGEMENT SCIENCE APPROACH

SYSTEMS APPROACH

CONTINGENCY APPROACH

JAPANESE APPROACH

EXCELLENCE APPROACH

CONTEMPORARY MANAGEMENT

proverbial blind men from Hindustan (trying to figure out what an elephant is like with each touching a uniquely different part). Some specialists were describing management only through the perceptions of their specialties."[44] When these five approaches to management are combined, they provide a synthesized approach, with each in some way contributing to our view of management.

For example, scientific management provides the means of beating Japanese and other competitors who have made major inroads in many of our industries and have taken total control of others, such as the television industry. We are reemphasizing job design, making products simpler, scientifically examining the workplace to improve work functions, and so on. We often automate and robotize to achieve the same ends that Frederick Taylor sought at the beginning of this century.

International competition has also resulted in the institutionalization of many actions proposed by the behavioralists, such as Chester Barnard's concern for communication and cooperation and Douglas McGregor's belief in participation to improve both effectiveness and efficiency.

In the effort to be competitive and to make better decisions, both managers and front-line employees are increasingly using management-science techniques. The amount of software available and being used to do so also is increasing rapidly, especially in Japanese organizations where front-line employees often have the skills to do statistical sampling. Systems theory is also being used more now than ever before, as organizations build complex models of their competitive situations to evaluate the impact of their decisions, both on other stakeholders and, most importantly, on their competitors.

Finally, more and more managers are practicing contingency theory management. They examine the variables in a problem-solving situation and then make decisions based on experience, knowledge, and available contingency prescriptions. They no longer just practice the so-called principles of management, but rather apply concepts to situations.

Japanese Management Approaches

The synthesis of these approaches to management has been fine-tuned by the **Japanese management** procedures that have become extremely well known in this country. As discussed in Chapter 1, Japanese management practices focus on

1. participative management.
2. job design.
3. quantitative methods.
4. effectiveness and efficiency.
5. the group and how to increase productivity through group decision making.
6. holistic treatment of employees by treating them as individuals rather than as interchangeable parts.
7. seeking cooperation and harmony in the workplace.[45]

There have been substantial successes when this approach, in a modified form, has been applied in North American firms.[46]

If these terms sound familiar, it's because they are the same issues that have been discussed in the history of American management practice as the focal points of the five major approaches. Many American managers have become enamored with Japanese management practices, but many of those practices originated in the United States. For example, the emphasis on participative management was first articulated by Douglas McGregor, and the concern with job design by Taylor. American consultants, principally William Edwards Deming and Joseph Juran, brought quantitative methods to the Japanese. The group orientation of the Japanese, however, evolves naturally from Japanese culture, which was one reason they were so quick to adopt it. Barnard, Follett, and Robert Owen expressed holistic concern for the employee in the nineteenth century. The Japanese management system, style, or philosophy, if you will, mirrors many of the aspects of the five approaches to management. The Japanese have imitated many of the more desirable aspects of our management philosophy and practices, just as they have often imitated our products. They have refined them and pursued some that we chose not to pursue, recognizing their applicability to their own culture and needs. We must recognize that Japanese management is not totally transferable to our culture; it must be adapted to be used in our society.[47]

The Excellence Approach to Management

Thomas J. Peters and Robert H. Waterman, Jr., have added "excellence" to the management vocabulary. Their 1982 book, *In Search of Excellence,* the best-selling business book ever, has had a profound effect on many managers and many organizations.[48] Peters and Waterman suggest that financially successful companies possess certain common characteristics of excellence, as defined in Table 2.4. They derived those characteristics from information gathered from interviews, questionnaires, and secondary data obtained principally from thirty-three leading U.S. companies, including McDonald's, Hewlett-Packard, NCR, Eastman Kodak, IBM, 3M, Delta Airlines, and Boeing. Their research finds fault with management-science approaches and supports "softer" issues, such as "closeness to the customer" and the importance of innovation.[49]

Table 2.4. The Excellence Characteristics

1. A bias for action: They make decisions quickly; they don't suffer from "analysis-paralysis."
2. Closeness to the customer: They know what the customer wants, and they provide it.
3. Autonomy and entrepreneurship (innovation): Innovation is encouraged and the authority to innovate and take risks is given to key players.
4. Productivity through people: The rank and file are viewed as the root source of quality and productivity and are managed accordingly.
5. Hands-on and value driven: A basic philosophy of business drives the company.
6. Sticking to the knitting: The excellent companies are not highly diversified, they stick to one primary business.
7. Simple form and lean staff: Excellent companies don't have much middle management, or much support staff.
8. Simultaneous loose-tight properties: Excellent companies use formal control mechanisms, but individuals are expected to be very responsible, and often self-managing.
9. Leadership—management by wandering around (MBWA): Managers should coach, facilitate, assist, and be with their employees.

SOURCE: Thomas J. Peters and Robert H. Waterman, Jr., *In Search of Excellence* (New York: Knopf, 1985), pp. 14–16; and Thomas J. Peters and Nancy K. Austin, *Passion for Excellence* (New York: Knopf, 1985), pp. 4–7.

Three years after *In Search of Excellence,* Peters coauthored with Nancy K. Austin, *Passion for Excellence.* Additional findings, they claimed, indicated that there were really three characteristics from the list in Table 2.4 and a management style that made for excellence, as Figure 2.4 indicates.

In 1987 Thomas J. Peters wrote *Thriving on Chaos: Handbook for a Man-*

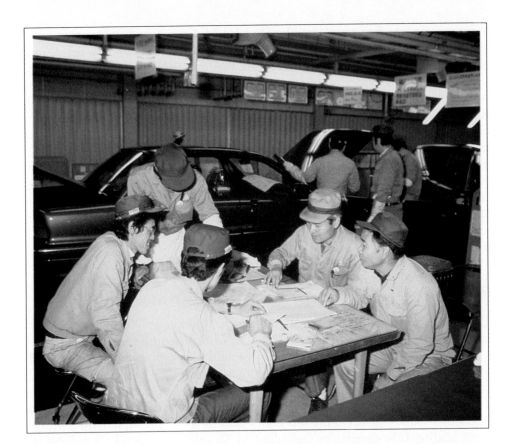

These Mitsubishi workers are using quantitative methods through a group participative management process in order to improve effectiveness and efficiency of operations. (SOURCE © Rene Dorel/SIPA)

agement Revolution in which he identified five prescriptions for managing in the complex and turbulent environment of the future. To the four schemes identified in *Passion for Excellence,* he added "control of the right stuff," suggesting that management should pay more attention to strategic control and self-control and spend less time controlling unimportant factors such as minute costs. Peters also suggested that to remain excellent companies would have to change and improve constantly.[50] These "excellence" characteristics have often been touted as *the* way to manage. Indeed, they address, in one way or another, creative problem solving in planning, organizing, leading, and controlling. Millions have read these books. However, the characteristics are not panaceas; they have their critics, as well. The Peters and Waterman study is criticized for not being very systematic because only successful companies are studied. It is possible that unsuccessful companies may have had similar characteristics. Several of the firms cited as excellent subsequently experienced financial or marketplace difficulties, and Peters himself admits later in *Chaos* that the environment is changing so rapidly that what is excellent is uncertain.[51] But the "excellence" phenomenon has changed management. It's too soon to tell how much.

All seven of the following approaches attempt to improve management problem solving.

1. Classical Management: The three goals were rational decision making, better job design, and improved productivity.
2. Behavioral Management: Key concerns were how better to motivate, lead, communicate, achieve cooperation, and raise productivity through participative management.
3. Scientific Management: The goal was to make decision making more logical and analytical.
4. Systems Management: The major issue was to ensure that managerial de-

FIGURE 2.4 THE SIMPLE SCHEME OF EXCELLENCE

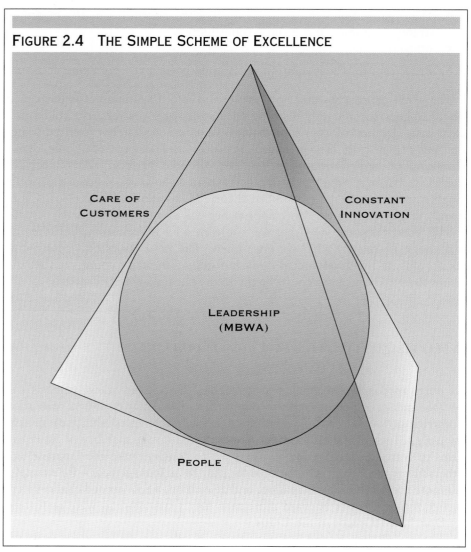

CARE OF
CUSTOMERS

CONSTANT
INNOVATION

LEADERSHIP
(MBWA)

PEOPLE

SOURCE: THOMAS J. PETERS AND NANCY K. AUSTIN, PASSION FOR EXCELLENCE.
(NEW YORK: KNOPF, 1985) P.5.

cisions take into account the environment in terms of inputs, processes, and outputs.

5. **Contingency Management:** The manager needs to consider all the major elements before making a decision.

6. **Japanese Management:** Major concerns include employee participation in problem solving, group problem solving, and the use of quantitative methods in problem solving.

7. **Excellence Management:** The principal focus of excellence management is how to improve management, how to make companies more "excellent." One of the key ways it suggests to do so is to increase participation in decision making.

Several **common themes in management** are found in the seven approaches:

1. Improving the rationality of decision making

2. Achieving effectiveness and efficiency, especially through job design and rewards

3. Proper use of the human resource, especially in terms of manager-subordinate relationships

4. The organization's interaction with its environment, especially regarding strategic planning and social responsibility

5. Which factors to consider in making decisions

6. The extent to which subordinates should participate in making decisions

The seven approaches and how they blend into a **synthesis of management** are analogous to randomly distributing marbles of seven different colors in a clear vase. Distinct colors are noticeable on close inspection, but from a distance one sees a single color. The management process as described in this book draws from each of the various approaches. You will note the focal points of each of the seven, but over time they will blend. There is, however, no consensus on a single system, nor is there a unified theory. In addition, management is constantly changing. It must. More approaches will eventually evolve.

This book takes the view that we can learn a lot from history, but often do not and must relearn what we once knew. The same issues that emerged as focal points in the development of each of the seven major approaches remain issues today. The issues seem to be the same, but the answers change.

Management in the Future

As other approaches to management emerge, the contemporary synthesis will be fine tuned, and perhaps even revolutionized. There may even be a revolution occurring now. Many people continue to criticize managers' ability to manage properly. Much of the criticism has concentrated on the inability of American firms to compete internationally. The need to compete with the Japanese and others has in turn reaffirmed the need for changes in management—for example, for more cooperation, participation, and delegation. These needed changes were recognized by Chester Barnard more than fifty years ago and were reaffirmed by Douglas McGregor in the 1950s.

Thomas J. Peters is fond of saying that virtually any management approach would have been successful for U.S. business organizations after World War II because of the huge, pent-up demand resulting from the war, even though we tended to attribute our success to our management techniques and styles. Peters believes that the true test of management problem solving is meeting competition. Increased competition has revealed that our old management practices are inappropriate. Peters points out in *Thriving on Chaos: Handbook for a Management Revolution* that managers must now learn to thrive on the massive changes coming in our society. He leads what may be yet another revolution in the way managers manage, in the way management is practiced. Only time will tell.[52]

AT GM: *General Motors is now moving toward a synthesis of management approaches. It is adapting the applicable Japanese techniques and becoming more customer focused.*

Management Challenges
Identified

1. Constant change in the management environment

2. The Japanese as competitors

3. Recognition of shortcomings in management as practiced in the United States

Some Solutions Noted
in the Chapter

1. Changing management to fit the demands of the situation
2. Recognition that basic issues are often the same, but the solutions to the problems change
3. Willingness to employ new and different management styles and practices.
4. New approaches to management, for example, the Japanese and excellence approaches.

Summary

1. Managers need to learn from the past, but they shouldn't be imprisoned by it. General Motors is a good example of not approaching history correctly. It failed to learn from history and let history dictate its actions. A manager should be able to consult the appropriate sources about the past, about what worked and what didn't, combine this with experience and knowledge, and make a better decision for having examined the history of the situation.
2. There are five principal approaches to management thought: classical, behavioral, management science, systems, and contingency.
3. Table 2.1 lists some of the principal early contributors to management thought and their contributions.
4. The scientific management theorists of the classical approach may be described as searching for "the one best way." The administrative theorists of the classical approach were attempting to determine universal rules for structuring the organization and for engaging in the management process.
5. The behavioral approach focuses on the human element: individuals and groups and their interactions in organizations. Communication, cooperation, trust, and delegation of authority are all critical components of this approach.
6. The management-science approach attempts to use certain quantitative techniques, most recently with computers, to improve the analytical nature and rationality of the decision-making/problem-solving process.
7. The systems approach focuses on the interdependency of the business organization with stakeholders in the external environment and within the organization. It helped make managers aware of the impact of their decisions and of the viewpoint of the organization as a transformer of inputs into outputs.
8. The contingency theory suggests that a manager must consider all elements in any situation and arrive at a decision that balances all of their requirements.
9. Contemporary management views management as a dynamic synthesis of the five approaches to management—as well as any others that may add to our ability to manage, such as Japanese management systems and philosophy.
10. The Japanese have, in many ways, synthesized the five approaches.
11. Thomas Peters and other critics of the management process have caused managers to examine their management practices. Many organizations and their many managers are questioning past practice and changing how they manage. They are using the prescriptions set forth by Peters and others.

Thinking About Management

1. Show how each of the seven approaches to management discussed in this chapter have contributed to the following six common themes: (Not all approaches have been described as contributing to each theme. What position do you think theorists in each approach might have taken on each theme?)
   a. Increasing rationality in decision making
   b. Effectiveness and efficiency
   c. Using the human resource
   d. The relationship of the organization to its environment
   e. The factors to consider in problem solving in any managerial situation
   f. The extent to which subordinates should participate in making decisions
2. Identify the contributions to management of each of the following individuals: Frederick W. Taylor, Henry Gantt, Frank and Lillian Gilbreth, Henri Fayol, Mary Parker Follett, Max Weber, Chester Barnard, Elton Mayo, Herbert Simon, Ludwig von Bertalanffy, Kenneth Boulding, Thomas J. Peters, and Robert H. Waterman, Jr.
3. Is scientific management applicable today? Why?
4. Is Weber's ideal of bureaucracy still valid? What are its strengths and weaknesses?
5. Relate Fayol's 14 principles and functions of management to a college and how it functions and to the dean of a college and how he or she functions.
6. If you were the manager of a grocery store, how could you use management-science techniques?
7. Describe your class as an open system.
8. Describe your instructor or professor in this class as a contingency manager—i.e., how well does he or she use the contingency approach to manage the class?
9. Draw a model that represents a synthesis of the five major approaches to management. It can be any shape or form and can contain any number of components, but it must show how the five major approaches blend into one.

CASE

IBM: Prisoners of What They Know?

In late 1989 IBM is struggling to compete in a world that is rapidly changing. Its biggest moneymaker, a mainframe computer, is growing old and has become vulnerable to minicomputers. It has no entrant in the laptop market, the computer industry's hottest market. It has only 2 percent of the workstation market, a $4.5 billion market growing at only 30 percent a year. Its software development is behind schedule. Its minicomputers' sales have stalled after a very successful 1988. It has experienced technical problems in several new products. And most analysts agree that it has way too many employees. It has been forced into slashing prices on mainframes in order to maintain market share, something IBM has never done before.

IBM has been the world leader in computers for many years. But the market is changing, and it has been slow to capitalize on those changes. It has stuck with mainframes, with the exception of its highly successful PC. It has thus lost out on critical minicomputer, workstation, and laptop markets. As minicomputers have grown in power, they have become competitive with IBM's mainframes for much of

These employees of the customer service department have an increasingly important role as IBM becomes more customer driven. (© Sepp Seitz/Woodfin Camp & Associates)

the work needed by many customers. IBM has long had a policy of not laying off people, but analysts feel the employer of 387,000 has about 50,000 too many people.

It has taken some action and does appear to be shedding some traditions and attitudes that have been blocking its progress. For example, it has established early retirement programs. In 1988 it restructured into seven autonomous business units in an attempt to make the company more customer driven. It has begun a program to change IBM's organizational culture, its shared values, to attempt to overcome its shortcomings. It has also moved rapidly to improve its technological strengths. It has cut red tape, reduced bureaucracy, and changed its old way of making strategic decisions, allowing division managers to make more of their own decisions rather than having the corporate management board make them. It has developed new programs to bring new products to the market faster. Yet, Chairman and CEO John Akers, architect of virtually all of these changes, recognizes that even more changes are necessary.

DISCUSSION QUESTIONS
1. How has IBM been trapped by its history?
2. How has IBM attempted to overcome related problems?
3. What remains to be done?

SOURCES: "What's Ailing IBM? More than this Year's Earnings," *Business Week,* October 16, 1989, pp. 75–86; "Big Changes at Big Blue," *Business Week,* February 15, 1988, pp. 92–98; Paul B. Carroll, "IBM to Cut U.S. Work Force by 3000 to 4000, Part B; Second Period Change," *Wall Street Journal,* June 30, 1988, p. 3.

Florida Informanagement Services

FIS is a data-transaction, information-processing company servicing numerous savings banks throughout the state of Florida and adjoining states. It is in the unique position of being owned by most of its users, who created the organization for the purpose of supplying information-processing services. Competitive forces in the industry are pressuring the firm to look to diversification, but its owners are very reluctant to give their approval to anything that would increase their data costs, even for a short period of time.

In the spring of 1986, the company held its annual strategic planning conference. The top nine managers of the company and an outside facilitator spent two exhausting days formulating six or seven major strategic issues the organization was to work on during the next year. Among them were studies to be performed on possible acquisition candidates and analyses of other businesses that the firm might wish to enter. Several operational issues had also resulted from their meeting. About three months after the session, the group met once again with the planning facilitator to discuss progress on the strategic plans. At that point, not much had happened, but the group agreed to meet once a month from that point forward to determine progress on their strategic efforts, to assign responsibilities, to prioritize, and so forth.

Harry Shuman, president of FIS, and Bob LaHair, his chief operations officer, pondered the situation with which they were confronted. It was then the spring of 1987, and they had really failed to do much about their strategic plans. As had historically been true, they had completed the operational aspects deriving from their planning session quite readily, but somehow they never quite got around to the strategy. They both felt that they needed to take the initiative and get the ball rolling, but they were not quite sure how to proceed to instill a more strategically oriented approach to planning in the organization.

DISCUSSION QUESTIONS

1. How is this firm trapped by what it already knows?
2. Why is operations easy for a firm like this but strategy more difficult?
3. How should Harry solve this problem?

The Management History
Crossword Puzzle

How well do you remember the contributions of each of the major contributors
to early management? Complete the following puzzle to find out.

SOURCE: Adapted from Arthur G. Bedeian, *Management,* 2nd ed. (Chicago: Dryden, 1989), p. 63.

THE MANAGEMENT HISTORY CROSSWORD PUZZLE

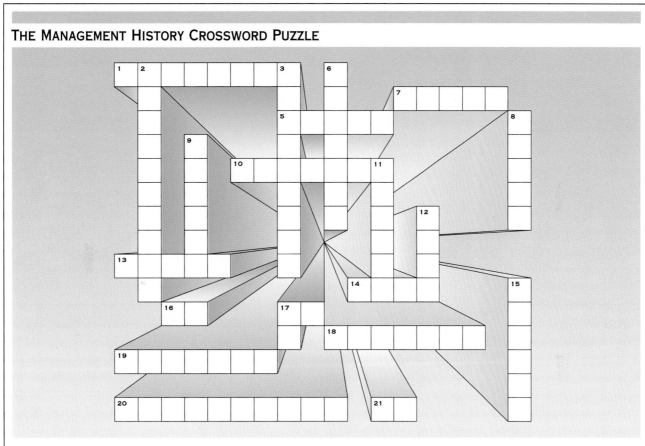

ACROSS

1. PIONEERED MOTION STUDY
5. DESCRIBED BUREAUCRACY
7. FATHER OF MODERN MANAGEMENT
10. FIRST CLASS MAN (ASK YOUR INSTRUCTOR)
13. A PLANNING AND CONTROL CHART IS NAMED AFTER HIM
14. AUTHOR OF MANAGEMENT HISTORY BOOK
16. 19—, THE YEAR OF FRANK GILBRETH'S DEATH
17. NUMBER OF CHILDREN IN THE GILBRETH FAMILY
18. POINTED OUT IMPORTANCE OF "RECIPROCAL INFLUENCE"
19. ACCEPTANCE THEORY
20. DO MORE THAN A FAIR DAY'S WORK
21. NUMBER OF FAYOL'S PRINCIPLES

DOWN

2. 18TH CENTURY REVOLUTION
3. SERIES OF STUDIES CONDUCTED FROM 1924 TO 1932
6. EARLY USERS OF DEPARTMENTATION (MISP INTL)
8. ITEM (SINGULAR) PRODUCED BY ASSEMBLY OPERATORS IN STUDIES REFERENCED IN #4 ABOVE
9. FAYOL'S _____ DE CORPS
11. FATHER OF SCIENTIFIC MANAGEMENT
12. RAISED MINIMUM AGE OF WORK FOR CHILDREN (IN A TABLE)
15. A MODERN APPROACH TO MANAGEMENT (SINGULAR)
17. 19—, THE YEAR OF FRED TAYLOR'S DEATH

SOURCE: ADAPTATION OF "THE MANAGEMENT HISTORY CROSSWORD PUZZLE" FROM <u>MANAGEMENT</u>,
SECOND EDITION, BY ARTHUR G. BEDEIAN, COPYRIGHT © 1989 BY THE DRYDEN PRESS, A DIVISION OF
HOLT, RINEHART AND WINSTON, INC., REPRINTED BY PERMISSION OF THE PUBLISHER.

CHAPTER THREE

The Manager as a Decision Maker and Creative Problem Solver

CHAPTER OBJECTIVES

By the time you complete this chapter you should be able to

1. Define problem solving/decision making and describe the stages of this process.

2. List and describe the conditions under which decision making and creative problem solving may occur.

3. Distinguish between the characteristics and requirements of structured versus unstructured decisions.

4. Describe the advantages of individual and group decision-making processes.

5. Discuss the behavioral factors involved in decision making and creative problem solving in an organization.

6. Recognize individual decision preferences and styles and their impacts on decision making and problem solving.

7. Discuss when and why a manager should engage in participative problem solving.

8. Indicate the pros and cons of rational and intuitive problem solving.

9. Discuss creative problem solving and decision making across all management functions.

CHAPTER OUTLINE

The Core Management Function
  Creative Problem Solving Versus
    Decision Making
The Creative Problem-Solving Process
  Constant Environmental Analysis
  Recognition of Problems
    or Opportunities
  Problem Identification
  Criteria
  Determining Key Situational Factors
  Making Assumptions About
    the Future
  Alternative Generation
  Evaluating and Choosing Among
    the Alternatives
  Implementing the Choice
  Control
Conditions Under Which Decisions
Are Made
  Problem Solving Under Conditions
    of Certainty
  Problem Solving Under Conditions
    of Risk
  Problem Solving in Uncertain
    Environments
Types of Problems and Decisions
  Structured Versus Unstructured
    Problems
  Anticipated Problems Versus
    Surprises
Individual Versus Group Decision
Making
  Major Types of Decision-Making
    Groups

Advantages and Disadvantages
  of Group Decision Making
Behavioral Aspects of the Decision
Process
    The Economic Model of Decision
    Making
    The Administrative Model
    of Decision Making

Problem-Solving Styles and Tendencies
    Problem-Solving Styles
How Much Participation, and When?
Revisions: The Vroom-Yago Model
The Manager as a Creative Problem
Solver
Management Challenges Identified
Some Solutions Noted in the Chapter

Fort Wayne Makes a Comeback

In February 1983 unemployment in Fort Wayne, Indiana, reached 14.5 percent, 3.2 percentage points above the national average. The St. Mary's Catholic Church soup kitchen was serving 1,100 meals a day in a city of 170,000. International Harvester, the city's major employer, had closed its truck plant, and the city had recently been swept by a flood. It was a gloomy town, with little promise for the future.

In November 1986 unemployment stood at 5.7 percent, 1.3 percentage points below the national average. A new General Motors plant was scheduled to open in December 1986. Burlington Express, the nation's second largest air express service had made Fort Wayne its national hub in late 1985. Firms such as GE, ITT, and Magnavox had been persuaded to expand their work forces in the city, as opposed to leaving or cutting back. The city had gotten 35,400 jobs to replace the 27,600 it had lost in the early 1980s. What made for the change? Fort Wayne succeeded when other cities had failed because of the way it managed its problems.

The city solved its problems via the combined effort of all its constituents. Spearheading the effort were Mayor Winfield Moses, Jr., and two business leaders—Ian M. Rolland, president of Lincoln National Corporation, a diversified financial company, and Richard K. Doermer, president of Summit Bank. Politicians, philanthropists, business leaders, and other citizens cooperated to avert what seemed a bleak future. The chamber of commerce raised almost $10 million to finance the city's strategy for turning around its fortunes. A council of the city's top forty corporate leaders was formed to attract business and make the city a better place to live.

Fort Wayne first identified its underlying problems and then determined, often creatively, how to solve them. It devised unique solutions for each set of problems. The city tried to attract new businesses that wouldn't be lost to Korea and Japan, and it came up with huge incentives to attract them. For example, almost $70 million in tax breaks and municipal improvements were offered for the GM plant. The city also set out to attract businesses with its cultural assets, as well as its labor force. To do this it developed a $5 million botanical garden, a $4 million performing arts center, and a new art museum. Nor were the little details overlooked. Callers to city hall are put on hold to the sound of Vivaldi.

Fort Wayne used team work and creative problem solving to succeed where others had failed.

SOURCE: Jeremy Main, "A Rust Belt City Takes on a Shine," *Fortune* (November 10, 1986), pp. 116–128.

All decision is compromise.

Herbert Simon
Nobel Laureate in Economics for the
examination of problem solving

I have a philosophy that no man should come in to his immediate supervisor for a decision. He should come in with a decision.

Lee S. Bickmore, former chairman
of the board of NABISCO

The **manager's primary function** is to solve problems creatively.[1] In the changing management environment, the manager's creative problem-solving role is also changing. The role of facilitator of the problem-solving efforts of subordinates and others is expanding. As individuals seek more control of the decisions that affect their jobs and their lives, this trend will continue. Mayor Win Moses' successful efforts to turn around the fortunes of Fort Wayne, Indiana, a typical rust-belt city, exemplify these changes. Faced with a crisis that would have doomed most cities, Moses and Fort Wayne business leaders brought together politicians, businessmen, labor leaders, philanthropists, and ordinary citizens in a concerted, collaborative effort to deal with it. When the mayor and citizens of Fort Wayne, who shared in the decisions and actions, solved their problems, they did so as a team.

In addition to being more of a facilitator and team leader than in the past, managers and other problem solvers are finding it necessary to be more creative in their problem-solving efforts. Mayor Moses and the other members of the Fort Wayne team sought new solutions as well as innovative versions of old ones. They didn't give up, the way others had. They kept trying until they found solutions that would work. Their success came from many hours of searching for new ways to solve problems.

In this chapter we will explore creative problem solving: its stages; the conditions under which decisions are made; structured versus unstructured decisions; individual versus group problem solving; the behavioral aspects of decision making; problem-solver styles and preferences; intuitive and rational thinking; and when to be participative in problem solving and when not to be. These key concerns are shown in Figure 3.1.

Mayor Win Moses opens an exhibit of houses built to meet a growing market in Ft. Wayne, a town that feared there would never be any more ribbon cutting ceremonies until Mayor Moses and his community problem-solving teams took action. (SOURCE © Ron Geibert)

The Core Management Function

The single action that makes or breaks the individual, the group, or the organization is creative problem solving. Creative problem solving is the core function of management. As portrayed in Figure 3.1, whether planning, organizing, leading, or controlling, managers must seek out and solve problems. They must be aware that a problem exists; they must be certain they know what the

FIGURE 3.1   KEY ISSUES IN THE CREATIVE PROBLEM-SOLVING PROCESS (CPS)

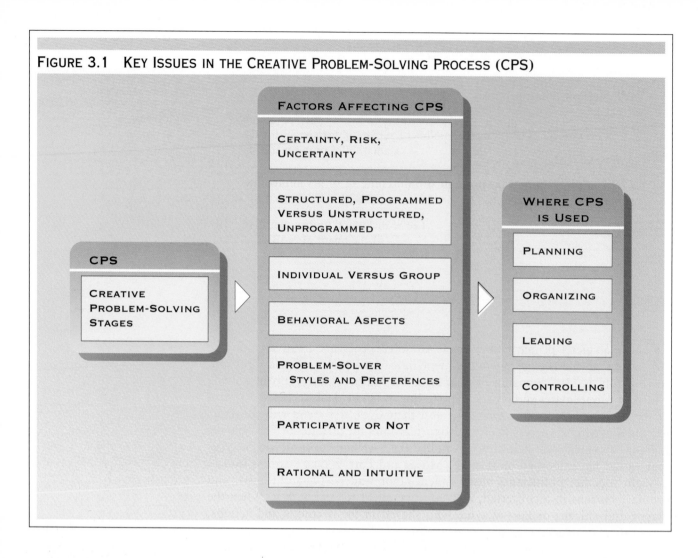

real problem is; they must make assumptions; they must develop alternative solutions; they must choose among those solutions; they must implement their choices; and they must check to see that they have solved the problem.

Situations calling for problem-solving skills can come in the form of problems or opportunities. A *problem* exists when a level of performance is less than the established objectives. This can result from an organization's internal weakness or from an external threat. An *opportunity* exists when there is potential for exceeding the established objectives. Opportunities result from the internal strengths of an organization or a favorable external environment. Typical problems and opportunities that managers may face in each of the management functions are listed in Table 3.1. The weaknesses of one organization may create an opportunity for another, as occurred when Digital Equipment Company began to dominate the minicomputer market in the 1980s because IBM did not have a highly competitive product in that market segment.

Creative Problem Solving Versus Decision Making

As shown in Figure 3.2, **creative problem solving** includes eight key steps: constant environmental analysis; recognizing the problem; identifying the problem; making assumptions about the future; generating alternatives; choosing from

Table 3.1 Typical Creative Problem-Solving Decisions Faced by Managers

Planning
What is the mission of the organization?
What are our objectives?
What are the objectives of our work unit?
What are our strengths, weaknesses, opportunities, and threats?
What actions are our competitors taking and how should we react to them?
What are the relevant needs of our customers that we aren't meeting?
What should our strategies be?
How can we carry out our strategies?

Organizing
What specific tasks are needed?
How should we combine jobs into departments?
How much authority should be delegated?
What staffing needs are there within the organization?
How can we best train people to perform their jobs?

Leading
How do we achieve productivity?
How do I influence my subordinates to make them more effective and efficient?
What are the needs of my subordinates?
What are the key group dynamics of my subordinates' work group?
What other factors affect my leadership choices?

Controlling
What are our standards?
What is the level of performance against those standards?
How often should we measure level of performance?
What control systems are needed?
If we haven't achieved our objectives why not?
How can we increase performance in the future?

Problem Solving
How can I improve my problem solving?
Are there new, creative ways to make decisions?

among your alternatives; implementing your choices; and controlling your actions to see whether your objectives were achieved. A **decision** is a choice among alternatives. Therefore, technically, **decision making** encompasses only the third through the sixth parts of that model: problem identification, making assumptions, alternative generation, and choice.[2] In problem solving, as opposed to decision making, you would find problems, you would also see the decision through to its fruition; you would implement your choice; and you would determine whether your decision was a good one based on the results it achieved. While it is important to recognize that there is a difference between solving a problem and making a decision, in this text, these terms are treated throughout as describing the same sets of actions and they are used interchangeably.

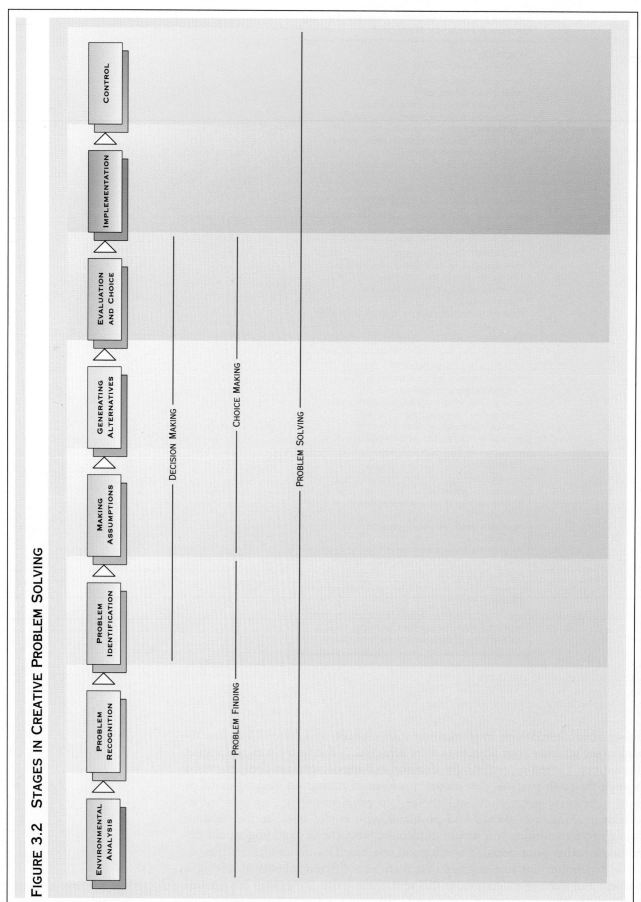

FIGURE 3.2 STAGES IN CREATIVE PROBLEM SOLVING

SOURCE: ADAPTED FROM GEORGE P. HUBER, MANAGERIAL DECISION MAKING (CHICAGO: SCOTT, FORESMAN, 1980), P. 8.

The Creative
Problem-Solving Process

The **creative problem-solving process** consists of the eight **stages** identified in Figure 3.2 and further identified in Figure 3.3. In Figure 3.3 three substeps have been added: determining criteria to select alternatives, determining the primary factors in the situation, determining the outcomes of various alternatives to aid in the choice process. Throughout the discussion of this model, Porsche's 1989 decision to cut prices on several models as portrayed in the Global Management Challenge will be used as a basis for discussion.

GLOBAL MANAGEMENT CHALLENGE

Porsche Takes Stock of Its Situation, Makes Critical Decisions

Porsche had seen sales decline by 40 percent from 1986 to 1988. Much of the decline had resulted from the perceived extremely high cost of the product compared to other foreign sports cars in the American market. As the dollar lost its value, Porsche's prices had skyrocketed, while Japanese automakers had chosen to cut costs to retain market share. Porsche chose to remain the choice of the elite. But that market proved too small. Porsche sales were further hurt by the October 1987 stock crash. Thus, in April 1989 Porsche cut the price of models sold in America by 6 percent to 9 percent and sold as many Porsches in the following two months in the United States as it had in the three previous months. (Additional details of the Porsche decision will be provided throughout this section as Figure 3.3 is discussed.)

SOURCES: Thomas F. O'Boyle, "Porsche Succeeds in Revving Up U.S. Sales by Throttling Down Prices of Some Cars," *Wall Street Journal*, 3 July 1989, p. 9; and "Jaguar and Porsche Try to Pull Out of the Slow Lane," *Business Week* (December 12, 1988), pp. 84–85.

AT PORSCHE, A.G.: *Porsche's environment was changing, especially in the United States—the declining dollar, the stock crash, the Japanese and U.S. entries into the luxury market, and their cost and pricing strategies. It appears that at Porsche, A.G. no one was monitoring these closely, especially early on in their sales decline.*

Constant Environmental Analysis

Problem solvers must be constantly scanning their ever-changing environments for signs of problems. They must also refer to the environment and their analysis of it during all other stages of the decision process. The environment is usually thought of as having two components: one external to the organization, and one internal to the organization. Firms such as Anheuser-Busch have sophisticated environment analysis systems to assist their managers. While the analysis of the environment tends to be a very rational process, interpreting the meaning of the information obtained often requires the use of intuition. As you will see later in this chapter, people have preferences for how they gather and evaluate information, which can greatly affect their decisions.

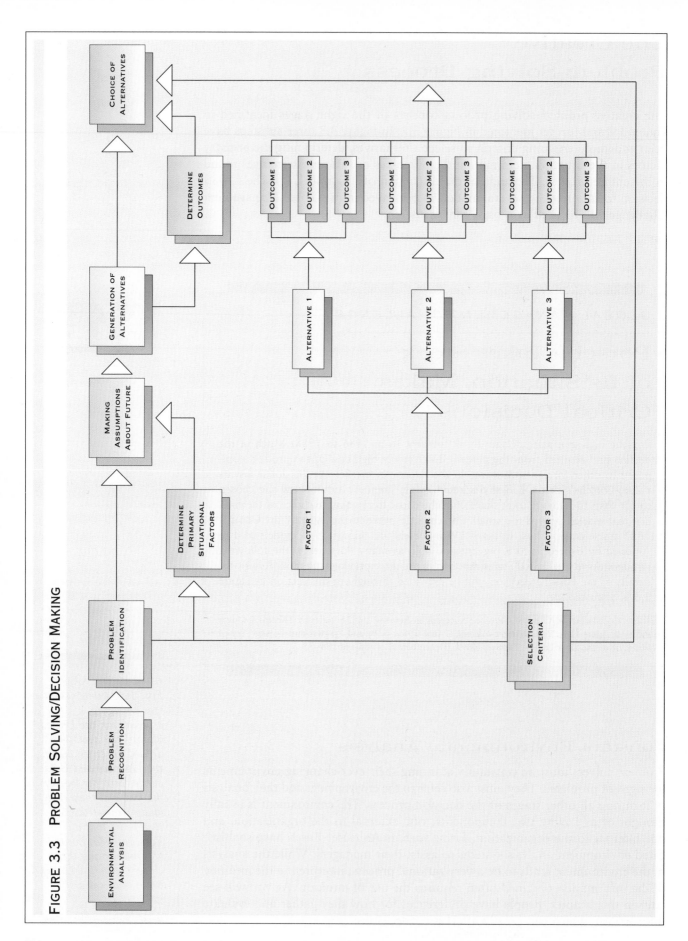

FIGURE 3.3 PROBLEM SOLVING/DECISION MAKING

Recognition of Problems
or Opportunities[3]

A problem solver is concerned with either problems or opportunities. In the recognition stage, problem solvers depend on formal and informal information systems, and often on their intuition, to alert them to a possible problem. In the recognition stage, problems are not precisely defined. Rather, the problem solver often has a vague feeling that something is amiss or that a tremendous opportunity exists.

Research by W. F. Pounds reveals that most managers simply do not ask themselves often enough, "How do we know that we have a problem?"[4] Problem recognition tends to be informal and intuitive. Pounds indicates that managers might be able to find problems in four ways:

1. Comparing a current with a past experience
2. Comparing a current experience with current objectives or plans
3. Through discussions
4. Comparing performance with that of other organizations or subunits

The most preferred of these, based on a planning orientation, would be the second method because managers should be striving to achieve current objectives. But typically Pounds found the first method is most often used, whereas the third and fourth are seldom used. Pounds's studies reveal that business managers do not usually use current objectives to compare against current performance; rather they rely on other benchmarks, such as last year's performance, as a comparison. He suggests that "consequently they may be defining the wrong problem or may not recognize one when it exists."

Later research by Marjorie A. Lyles and Ian I. Mitroff confirmed that problem recognition is informal and intuitive. They collected case histories from top managers in major organizations. Eighty percent of the managers reported that they had recognized the existence of a problem before being told of it by subordinates or supervisors or before it appeared in some type of formal information system, such as a financial statement. When asked how they knew of those problems, they replied, "informal communication and intuition."[5]

Too often managers fail to recognize problems at all.[6] When International Harvester continued to hold out against the strike demands made by the United Auto Workers in 1979–1980, its managers, principally its chairman and CEO, Archie McCardell, failed to recognize that the union simply wasn't going to give in either. The company not only lost nearly $400 million that year as a result, but also lost most of its market share. McCardell remained optimistic too long.[7] Once he became locked into holding out against the strike and refused to budge, he had set in motion the forces that would eventually result in the company's declaring bankruptcy after his termination.[8]

Finding problems or opportunities depends on constant environmental scanning and analysis. Successful managers are continually alert, always monitoring, always watching. They recognize weak signals as well as obvious ones. In *Innovation and Entrepreneurship*, Peter Drucker observes that many managers fail to recognize opportunities and hence fail to take advantage of them.[9] Apparently very few managers actively seek opportunities.[10] The entrepreneurial manager, one who would act much like an independent business person, however, is constantly aware of opportunities and takes advantage of them. Some companies encourage entrepreneurship among their managers: most do not. But more top-level managers are beginning to do just that.[11]

AT PORSCHE, A.G.: *Sales were declining. It wasn't clear to then president Peter Schultz, who had been in charge during the go-go years of booming sales in the early 1980s, what actions to take. He wasn't quite sure of the problem, but he knew something was wrong.*

Problem Identification[12]

IN FORT WAYNE:
Mayor Win Moses could have reacted to the problem and said, "What we need is new business. We lost jobs, we need businesses." Instead, he identified the problem as not just losing jobs but jobs in a basic industry. So he sought replacement businesses that wouldn't be lost to Korea and Japan again.

The creative problem solver seeks to determine what the real problem is or the real problems are. In recognition you learn that a problem or problems exist, but you are not quite sure what it is or they are. In identification you attempt to get at the roots of the problem—the causal factors, the causal problem or problems. In most organizations there is a complex series of problems, but many times one or a few seem to cause most of the others. For example, lower profits may have resulted from lower sales, which may have resulted from lessened advertising as part of a cost-cutting program. The question is to determine which problem or problems are the causal ones. For example, workers' poor performance may result from poor leadership, inadequate training and knowledge, change in quality of materials, improper procedures, members who are bored by their work or overwhelmed by it, pay that doesn't seem fair to members, lack of penalties for poor performance and lack of rewards for excellent performance, to name a few.[13] Identification of the problem is fraught with likely errors, many having to do with perception and self-image.[14]

Charles Kepner and Benjamin Tregoe, management consultants, suggest that asking a few questions often helps to identify the problem better. Table 3.2 lists their questions.

A company's managers would do well to ask themselves these questions, as Management Challenge 3.1 suggests.

CRITERIA

As part of the identification stage, problem solvers must establish criteria for a successful solution. They must determine and specify, preferably both quantitatively and qualitatively, what makes a "good" decision. They must decide what the solution to the problem must do before they choose that alternative. They also need to identify desirable, but not necessarily critical, criteria. In the choice stage, they then compare each alternative to these criteria in order to make their choice. (See Figure 3.3.) A. M. Castle, one of the nation's largest suppliers of metal products, has formed virtually all of its strategic decisions on one critical criterion: Does it improve customer service? As a consequence, A. M.

AT PORSCHE, A.G.:
New president Heinz Branitzki felt Schultz had overlooked the basics and traditional Porsche values. He felt Schultz had not identified the causes of sales decline—costs, prices, changing market, and the dollar's value.

MANAGEMENT CHALLENGE **3.1**

American Home's Costly Conservatism

In late 1986 American Home, a diversified drug company that had regularly recorded a return on equity of more than 30 percent and that had an income of about $780 million in 1986 on sales of $5 billion, was beginning to show signs of fatigue. Pretax income, which had previously grown at double-digit rates, was increasing by only 3 percent. Several obvious problems existed, but the question top management had to answer was, "What is the underlying causal problem." Some people blamed the low increase in pretax income on the company's failure to develop new products. Further analysis revealed other problems, as well. Key patents were expiring on two critical prescription drugs. One of those drugs had grossed $423 million in 1985 but showed a loss in sales of 30 percent in 1986.

Table 3.2 The Kepner-Tregoe Problem Definition Worksheet

Problem Symptoms
Describe, as specifically as possible, the nature of the symptoms.
Describe where the symptoms occurred.
Describe when the symptoms occurred.
Describe the extent of the symptoms.
Describe any changes that occurred.
Do the changes explain the symptoms?
If not, examine other changes.

SOURCE: Adapted from Charles H. Kepner and Benjamin B. Tregoe, *The Rational Manager.* Copyright © 1965, McGraw-Hill Book Company. Reprinted with permission of McGraw-Hill, Inc.

Castle has developed numerous innovative programs to assist customers, including designing specific products for them, helping them assess their needs, and showing them how they can improve their profitably. A. M. Castle's market share and profits have increased dramatically.[15]

DETERMINING KEY SITUATIONAL FACTORS

Before making assumptions, before generating alternatives, the key situational variables must be identified. These are the factors that are prominent parts of the problem, will influence your ability to solve the problem, and will be included in the solution. In making leadership choices (how to influence others' motivations), for example, the key factors are usually a manager, a subordinate, the work group, the task, the organization's structure and culture, and other situationally critical variables.[16]

> AT PORSCHE, A.G.:
> *Heinz Branitzki established the criteria that decisions must meet traditional Porsche values and that, in the short term, competitiveness must be restored.*

> AT PORSCHE, A.G.:
> *Branitzki believed that the key situational factors were changes in the U.S. market and determining at which end of the high-priced market the firm would concentrate its products.*

Other products were in the mature or late stages of their product life cycles, and consequently their gross incomes were near zero. The company had also followed a policy of extremely conservative development, such as taking on little new debt and not making acquisitions. All of these were problems, but further analysis indicated that none was the causal problem. Most analysis felt that the root problem was that the company had been cost conscious for too long, in order to improve its operating results, income statements, and balance sheets. It had become risk averse and was therefore experiencing false economies—trying to save money by cutting back on new-product development and thereby stifling profits in the long term. As a consequence, it had not invested in new-product research or acquired new products. Compounding the problem was the fact that American Home expected a too rapid performance from the few new products it had. It expected profits from new products within a year and a half, whereas most companies give their new products three years to turn a profit.

SOURCE: Christopher Power, "Too Much Penny Pinching at American Home," *Business Week* (December 22, 1986), pp. 64–65.

Making Assumptions About the Future

Decision makers, after analyzing the environment and recognizing and identifying the problem or problems, must make assumptions about the future, assumptions about the conditions of various elements in the decision situation. In planning, an assumption is required, for example, as to whether the competition will continue to compete in the same way. An assumption might be required in organizing as to the probable effectiveness of giving someone more work to do. In leading, an assumption might be necessary about how someone would react to a particular type of treatment from a manager. Based on these assumptions, problem solvers generate and evaluate alternatives. They make choices based on these assumptions.

Alternative Generation

Once a manager has recognized a problem, identified the underlying cause, or causes, and made assumptions, he or she must generate alternatives to solve it and related problems. Realistically, unless the problem is extremely simple, alternative solutions are actually being generated for a model of the situation. The search for alternatives can be time consuming and complicated—sometimes too long and too complicated. Herman Miller, probably the nation's most innovative furniture design company, encourages its employees to generate lots of alternatives, even wild and crazy ones, in hopes of uncovering something special. It has even designed its office areas to provide plenty of informal gathering spaces to encourage interchanges of ideas.[17]

Evaluating and Choosing Among the Alternatives

After generating a series of alternative solutions, the manager must then choose one or more alternatives that will meet the criteria for a successful solution. Determining the outcomes of these various alternatives allows for better comparison to the criteria and improves the choice eventually made. Choosing an alternative seems rational, but it is often intuitive, involving social and political relationships. Even a rational decision-making process may involve many complex variables, sometimes making the situation controversial and almost untenable, as Management Challenge 3.2 suggests.

MANAGEMENT CHALLENGE **3.2**

Revitalizing the *Harvard Business Review*

In 1985 Theodore Levitt became the editor of the *Harvard Business Review*. He inherited a magazine that, while still earning $500,000 a year, had seen circulation fall from 242,000 to 200,000 in recent months and ad pages decline from 460 in 1985 to 440 in 1986. Levitt decided that one of the major underlying problems was that the magazine was "intimidating and uninviting." "People work all day, they shouldn't have to work after hours to get through our magazine." Levitt

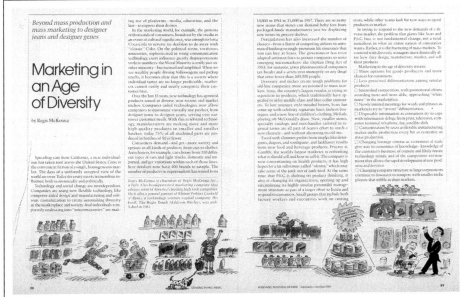

Note the contrasting styles of the *Harvard Business Review* before and after changes made by Theodore Levitt. (SOURCE Courtesy *Harvard Business Review*)

introduced cartoons; shortened the average article by 25 percent; added short summaries, graphics, color photos, and illustrations; and in 1987 redesigned the cover. He also lured well-known business and political figures to contribute articles instead of just traditional Harvard academics and other authors whose prose had historically filled the magazine. He had other alternatives available, several which the Harvard faculty might have preferred. For example, he could have opted to increase the academic rigor of the magazine. He could have left out the cartoons. He could have chosen a lower cost strategy and printed the magazine on cheaper paper and deleted features, attempting to sell more subscriptions with a lower price. What do you suppose some of his criteria for making his choices were?

SOURCE: Alex Beam, "Dusting Off the *Harvard Business Review*," *Business Week*, (December 15, 1986), p. 58.

AT FORT WAYNE:
Mayor Win Moses and his team had to implement the choice they made to save their town. This meant tough negotiations with prospective and current employers, changing various laws and regulations, and putting together attractive tax packages for prospective employers. Their implementation effort included many long, hard hours of personal selling, dead ends, and frustration. But they made it.

One factor greatly affecting choices of alternatives is the problem solver's **risk propensity**, the willingness to undertake risk for possible gain. Some individuals are willing to take high risks, others are not. The relative amount of risk affects the choice that a manager or other decision maker may make. Research by Danny Miller reveals that top managers with a high risk propensity often make choices that leave their organizations in dire straits.[18] Are you willing to take risks? Take the Manage Yourself test at the end of the chapter to find out.

Implementing the Choice

Implementation is the action taken to carry out a decision. Once managers have made a choice, they must implement it. Managers should consider the difficulty of implementation when they choose among alternatives. Many choices seem appropriate on the surface, but if they are difficult to implement, they are not good choices. Factors such as an absence of resources and a negative political situation in an organization could influence a manager to choose one alternative over another. Whatever choice is made, implementation requires mustering resources, gaining support for the project, and then taking the series of actions necessary to carry out that choice.

AT PORSCHE, A.G.:
Porsche's 1989 financial results were improved over 1988. They made $27 million as opposed to $13 million.

Control

Once the decision has been implemented, its success must be evaluated. During the control stage, you find out if you have a continuing problem, or one you haven't yet discovered, or if you have solved the problem. Returning to the American Home example from Management Challenge 3.2, when profit growth dropped to 3 percent, top management knew they had a problem, so the creative problem-solving cycle began again. Apparently their choice to be extremely cost-oriented had failed to produce the expected results.

Conditions Under Which Decisions Are Made

The conditions under which managers make decisions have a tremendous impact on their choices of alternatives. Figure 3.4 shows the three possible degrees of certainty that exist about the outcome of decisions. The less routine, the less anticipated the problem, the more complex the problem, the more uncertain the environment usually is.

AT PORSCHE, A.G.: *An 8 percent to 9 percent price cut on U.S. models was made. The lowest-priced model in Porsche's line was chopped. A new, very expensive car was added to the U.S. lineup. Costs were cut significantly at the Stuttgart headquarters and in the production process.*

Problem Solving Under Conditions of Certainty

Certainty exists in a problem-solving environment when a decision maker can predict the results of implementing each of the alternatives with 100 percent certainty. For example, when a city's treasurer leaves the city's money in a bank overnight, he knows exactly how much interest that account will generate. He also knows with certainty what other alternatives, such as not leaving the money in the overnight account, will generate for the city. Seldom do managers know with 100 percent certainty the results of their decisions. Many times, however, they act as if they did.

FIGURE 3.4 CONDITIONS UNDER WHICH DECISIONS ARE MADE

DECISION MAKING UNDER CERTAINTY

PROBLEM	ALTERNATIVE 1	100%	OUTCOME 1	ALTERNATIVES ARE KNOWN, CONDITIONS SURROUNDING EACH ARE KNOWN. OUTCOMES ARE CERTAIN.
	ALTERNATIVE 2	100%	OUTCOME 2	
	ALTERNATIVE 3	100%	OUTCOME 3	

DECISION MAKING UNDER RISK

PROBLEM	ALTERNATIVE 1	70%	OUTCOME 1	ALTERNATIVES AND RELATED CONDITIONS ARE NOT KNOWN, BUT PROBABILITIES ARE ESTIMABLE. OUTCOMES ARE UNKNOWN.
	ALTERNATIVE 2	20%	OUTCOME 2	
	ALTERNATIVE 3	10%	OUTCOME 3	
		100%		

DECISION MAKING UNDER UNCERTAINTY

PROBLEM	ALTERNATIVE 1	UNKNOWN	OUTCOME 1	ALTERNATIVES, NUMBER OF ALTERNATIVES, RELATED CONDITIONS, AND PROBABILITIES ARE UNKNOWN.
	ALTERNATIVE 2	UNKNOWN	OUTCOME 2	
	ALTERNATIVE 3	UNKNOWN	OUTCOME 3	
	ALTERNATIVE N	UNKNOWN	OUTCOME N	

Problem Solving Under Conditions of Risk

Under conditions of **risk,** problem solvers do not have complete certainty about the outcomes of their actions, but neither are they completely uncertain about what might result. Rather, they can assign a probability to the outcome of each alternative, if it were to be implemented. Probabilities are usually expressed as a percentage—for example, a 10 percent chance of occurrence.

Risk is probably the most frequent situation confronting a manager. When a manager believes that there is a one-in-ten chance that the new pay procedure will fail, but a nine-in-ten chance that it will succeed, he or she is making a decision under conditions of risk.

Problem Solving in Uncertain Environments

Uncertainty exists when managers cannot assign even a probability to the outcomes of the various alternatives that the problem-solving process generates. Managers may not even know all of the alternatives. Uncertainty forces managers to rely on hunches, or intuition, or creativity, or "gut feel." It is not that the numbers are not analyzed, they usually are. But the manager must also rely on such nonrational decision processes. Unstructured, complex, unanticipated situations almost always occur in uncertain environments. When the Cabbage

Owners of Cabbage Patch Dolls can even send their "kids" to summer camp. At Dr. Sanford Stein's "Camp Small Fry," participants can engage in all sorts of summer fun. (SOURCE © P. Tatiner/Black Star)

Patch doll was launched, its makers had no idea how successful it would be. They could not even assign probabilities to demand levels. They were working in an uncertain environment.

Types of Problems and Decisions

Two principal types of problems exist:

1. Structured or unstructured
2. Anticipated or surprise

Structured Versus Unstructured Problems

Structured problems are those that occur on a routine basis and have readily identifiable attributes—the factors involved and their interrelationships. They have standard, almost automatic solutions, often referred to as **programmed decisions**. When students' grade point averages reach a certain level, they may be dismissed from school. Whether to dismiss them is a routine problem. When a computer signals a malfunction, a maintenance person is dispatched to fix it. This, too, is an example of a recurring routine event that triggered a structured response.

Unstructured problems are nonroutine, complex problems with difficult-to-identify attributes. They lead to **unprogrammed decisions**. Normally, unstructured problems have not been faced before. One of the most complex unstructured problems ever analyzed is how to rid Los Angeles of smog. Biology, earth sciences, chemistry, and physics are all involved. Industry, automobiles, and even drive-through hamburger stands are major issues. A 500,000-equation computer simulation has been developed to help solve the problem, but its developer admits that the model is only as good as the assumptions it's based on, many of which themselves result from complex, often intuitive thought processes.[19] Because structured responses cannot be employed, nonroutine prob-

Solving the L.A. smog problem may just be the most complex task ever undertaken. (SOURCE © T. Spiegel/ Black Star)

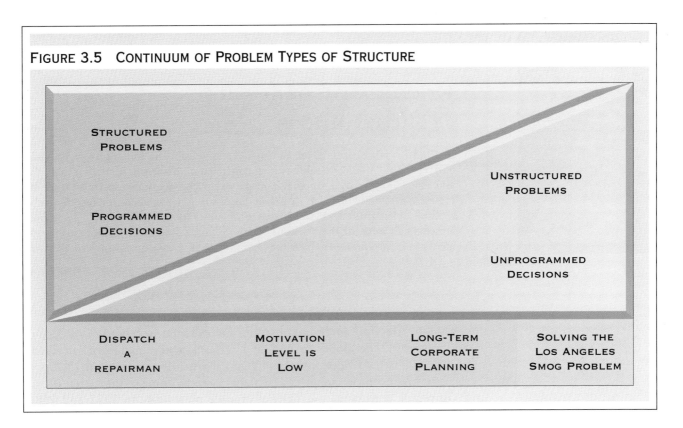

FIGURE 3.5 CONTINUUM OF PROBLEM TYPES OF STRUCTURE

STRUCTURED PROBLEMS

PROGRAMMED DECISIONS

UNSTRUCTURED PROBLEMS

UNPROGRAMMED DECISIONS

| DISPATCH A REPAIRMAN | MOTIVATION LEVEL IS LOW | LONG-TERM CORPORATE PLANNING | SOLVING THE LOS ANGELES SMOG PROBLEM |

lems demand that the manager engage in creative problem solving. Solving these types of problems requires intuition, creativity, and heuristics—rules of thumb. Figure 3.5 reveals that a continuum of structuredness exists among problems. Some problems are clearly structured, some clearly unstructured. Most problems, however, vary in the degree to which the factors involved are readily identifiable and relatable to each other. Solving an employee's problem of low motivation is more structured than long-term planning for companies, which tends to be more unstructured, for example.

Anticipated Problems Versus Surprises

Another way of looking at managerial problems is whether they were anticipated or were surprises. Good managers anticipate the problems that may occur as a result of most, if not all, of their actions and decisions. They should anticipate the potential problems of any situation in which they find themselves, regardless of whose decisions brought them there. Such monitoring prepares them to anticipate a diverse range of problems relating to productivity, motivation, concerns about pay, concerns about not being promoted, the failure of an advertising campaign, or failing to gain a certain market share.

Some problems are surprises. Equipment breakdowns, power failures, a competitor's strategy in the marketplace, or a sudden loss of market share may all take a manager by surprise. The less complex of these surprises may be handled by routine solutions. Good managers will recognize that over time certain events may occur. These surprises can thus be anticipated to some extent. Absenteeism, tardiness, and similar personnel problems, for example, may be handled through various policies and rules. While the exact timing of this type of event is unknown, its occurrence is almost assured.

On the other hand, any manager may face a crisis. A crisis is the most extreme form of unanticipated problem. It often requires quick problem-solving actions

IN FORT WAYNE:
When Mayor Win Moses and his colleagues in Fort Wayne began to deal with the high unemployment in the city, they faced a complex problem that they had not faced before. There were no ready-made solutions. They had to invent them. Each different employer they sought to attract posed a unique, unstructured problem.

IN FORT WAYNE:
Although some could argue that Fort Wayne decision makers should have seen their problems coming, the closing of the International Harvester plant was a surprise.

Johnson & Johnson, makers of Tylenol, could never have anticipated the Tylenol cyanide poisonings. Their response to the tragedy and the potential for more poisonings was to remove all bottles of the product from store shelves and destroy them. (SOURCE © Brad Bower/Picture Group)

under highly stressful conditions. It often involves the expenditure of considerable resources. The ability to handle a crisis is a key managerial problem-solving skill. There is evidence that managers frequently, especially in the upper levels of an organization, are forced to manage crises. Some of the better-known crises in recent years were the Tylenol cyanide poisonings in 1982 and 1986, the Delta 1011 crash in Dallas in 1985, and the Iranscam affair in 1987, the next to last year in the Reagan administration. Organizations must frequently manage less spectacular crises, such as the one discussed in Management Challenge 3.3.

Individual Versus Group Decision Making

So far we have spoken of the decision maker as an individual, but groups already make many decisions in many organizations. If trends continue, they will be making even more decisions in the future. Managers must first choose whether to use individual or group problem-solving processes. If groups are used, managers must next choose the type of group that fits the situation best. They must be able to pick not just the type of group, but the specific techniques to be used by it. Criteria for choosing an individual or group decision-making process will be described later in the chapter.

Major Types of Decision-Making Groups

Group processes can raise the level of creativity in problem solving because more people will generate more ideas and people can build on the ideas of others. Three major types of problem-solving groups exist: the **interacting group**, the **nominal group**, and the **Delphi group**. These groups are similar, but yet distinct. Most groups are simple interactive groups. The nominal and Delphi groups are designed to overcome some of the problems interactive groups encounter. Generally speaking, there are many types of interactive group techniques, but only one major nominal and one major Delphi technique.

its one-product orientation by diversifying into a related field. It acquired Texas-based Fox Photo for $96 million, making Kodak the country's largest wholesale photo finisher. Perhaps more importantly, this acquisition provided a major customer for its photographic paper and chemical products. In another crisis move, Kodak laid off 12,900 workers, about 10 percent of the work force in 1985–1986. This cost-cutting action almost doubled earnings in 1986. Along more traditional creative lines, Kodak has established an Innovation Department for developing new products. Members of the department are specially trained to meet the challenges of their job.

SOURCES: Leslie Helm and James Hurlock, "Kicking the Single-Product Habit at Kodak," *Business Week* (December 1, 1986), pp. 36–37; and Leslie Helm, "Why Kodak Is Starting to Click Again," *Business Week* (February 23, 1987), pp. 134–139.

INTERACTING GROUPS

Interacting groups meet face-to-face with open interchange. They are usually unstructured, although many have an agenda and objectives. In creative problem-solving situations, interactive group meetings usually begin with the group leader stating the problem. Open, unstructured discussion follows. Problem recognition, identification, the generation of alternatives, and choice processes are focal points of such groups. A simple majority usually controls the eventual result. Two highly productive, interactive, creative group processes are brainstorming and storyboarding.

This group is honing its group skills by playing the "Innovation" game, a practice exercise designed to improve innovation and group interaction. (SOURCE © John Colletti/Stock Boston)

Brainstorming. **Brainstorming** is a group creative problem-solving process that focuses on the following procedures:

1. No negative feedback is allowed on any suggested alternative until all alternatives have been generated.
2. Piggybacking on others' ideas is encouraged.
3. Quantity of ideas, not quality, is the key. Evaluation comes later.
4. Freethinking is pursued. Let the "wild and crazy" ideas flow.

These sessions have a leader and a recorder; the latter writes the ideas, usually on a board, where all participants can see them. Sessions last about thirty minutes. There are usually six to ten participants. Ideas are evaluated after brainstorming. Brainstorming is especially useful for generating alternative solutions. It is often used in advertising but can be used to solve any well-defined problem.

Storyboarding. **Storyboarding** is a structured, but flexible brainstorming process that focuses on identifying major issues and then brainstorming each of them. Storyboarding allows for a complete picture (story) of the problem to be placed before participants, usually on some type of wallboard. Storyboards have two thinking sessions—one creative, the other critical. Basic brainstorming rules are followed in the creative thinking session. In the critical session, ideas are evaluated and the list of ideas is reduced. Storyboarding is good for analyzing a problem as well as generating alternatives. Implementation may also be an issue for a storyboard. A leader and recorder are used in a group that ranges from six to ten participants. Each thinking session lasts about thirty minutes. Storyboarding is used to solve complex, less well-defined problems in almost all industries. PepsiCo, Disney Companies, and Sun-Trust Banks are just a few of the hundreds of major firms that use storyboarding.

NOMINAL GROUPS

André L. Delbecq and Andrew H. Van de Ven originated the **nominal group technique** in 1968, partly as a consequence of their dissatisfaction with interactive group processes. A nominal group is more structured than an interactive one. It intentionally eliminates much of the interpersonal exchange of the interacting group. The primary purpose of this process is to eliminate dominance by one or a few people in the choice process.[20] It follows these four steps:

1. Group members independently write down their ideas on the group's problem.
2. Each group member then presents each of his or her ideas to the group in round-robin fashion, one at a time. Each idea is summarized on a chalkboard, or on some other media device, so that all members can see them. No ideas are discussed until all are presented and recorded.
3. An open group discussion of ideas follows, but only to clarify those ideas that group members do not understand. No attack or defense of ideas is allowed.
4. Next, a secret ballot occurs. Group members list their top ideas in order of priority. The ballots are tallied, and then a second round of voting usually occurs. The eventual decision of the nominal group is a pooled outcome of this vote.

DELPHI GROUPS

Norman Dalkey and his associates at the RAND Corporation developed the **Delphi technique**. It utilizes a series of questionnaires administered by a central individual to experts who never meet face-to-face. As the respondents reply, their questionnaires are summarized, and a new questionnaire, based on their responses to the first, is developed and sent to them. This repeating process continues until a group consensus on the problem is reached. **Normally** only two repetitions are necessary. This technique has four principal uses:

1. Generating alternatives, alternative futures (forecasts)
2. Examining a situation for underlying assumptions or to gain additional information

3. Discovering information that might lead to a decision consensus among participants

4. Combining expert opinions from different disciplines

Advantages and Disadvantages of Group Decision Making

Groups offer six **advantages** over individual decision making:

1. The group can provide a superior solution to that of an individual. Groups collectively have more knowledge than an individual. Interactive groups not only combine this knowledge, but create a knowledge base greater than the sum of its parts, as individuals build upon each other's inputs.

2. There is an increased acceptance of the final decision when those who will be affected by it or who must implement it have a say in making it.

3. Group participation leads to a better understanding of the decision.

4. Groups help ensure a broader search effort.

5. Risk propensity is balanced. Individuals who are high-risk takers often fail. Groups moderate this desire. Groups also encourage the risk avoider to take more risks.

6. There is usually a better collective judgment.[21]

On the other hand there are **liabilities** to employing **group decision making**.

1. In interactive groups, there is pressure to conform. Sometimes these groups become guilty of what is known as "group think," where people begin to think alike and where new ideas or ideas contrary to the group's ideas are not tolerated.

2. One individual may dominate the interactive group, so his or her opinions and not the group's may result. Nominal groups are designed to overcome this problem. Delphi groups usually do not have this problem because the participants never meet.

3. Groups typically require more time to come to decisions than individuals do.

4. Groups usually make better decisions than the average individual, but seldom better ones than the superior individual. In fact, a group's superior performance may result from the efforts of one superior group member.

5. The total time spent solving problems by a group may negate the advantages of its superior choice.

6. Groups often make more risky decisions than they should. This propensity of groups to endorse a riskier position is known as **risky shift**.[22,23]

IN FORT WAYNE: *Mayor Win Moses, Ian Rolland, Richard Doermer, and others formed a team, many teams, that accomplished objectives that none of them individually could have accomplished. More ideas, more resources, and more efforts were brought to bear on the problems Fort Wayne faced. Participants were more accepting of solutions. The city was often at odds with the county, for example, but when it came to creating jobs, they worked together.*

Behavioral Aspects of the Decision Process

Decision making in an organization seems to occur according to two principal behavior models: the economic and the administrative. The economic revolves around the rational systematic perspective discussed earlier, whereas the administrative focuses on the psychological, interpersonal aspects of decision making. The economic model was for many years believed to be the way decisions were actually made. We now know from studies of decision making that the administrative approach is the more realistic of the two. People simply do not make decisions in a strictly rational manner. Rather, various types of psychological and interpersonal factors greatly affect the process.

The Economic Model of Decision Making

The eight-part model of decision making provided earlier—environmental analysis, recognition, identify the problem, making assumptions, alternative generation, choice, implementation, and control—follows the rational economic perspective. It describes how decisions are made from a conceptual, analytical viewpoint. The assumptions of the **classical**, or **economic**, model follow:

1. Objectives are known and agreed upon.
2. The existence of the problem is recognized and its nature has been identified.
3. The consequences of implementing each alternative are certain, or a probability may be assigned to each.
4. Criteria for the best decision are known and agreed upon. Decision makers will seek to maximize their situation by choosing the "best alternative" indicated by these criteria.
5. Managers are rational. They can assign values, order preferences, and make the decision that will optimize the attainment of the decision's objectives.
6. Managers have complete knowledge of the situation.

The Administrative Model of Decision Making

Research by Herbert A. Simon, Nobel laureate, management researcher James G. March, and others reveals that decision making is often dominated by nonrational social and political processes.[24] Furthermore, these researchers found that the assumptions under which decisions are made according to the economic model do not conform to reality. As a consequence of their combined efforts, the **administrative model** of decision making has been constructed. This model is based on the concept identified by Simon as "bounded rationality." It suggests that decision makers are restricted in the decision process and must settle for something less than an ideal solution. The administrative model is based on the following assumptions:

1. Objectives of the decision are often vague, conflicting, and not agreed upon.[25]
2. Often managers do not recognize that a problem exists.[26]
3. Managers often do not go through the identification process and therefore solve the wrong conceptualization of the problem (what academician Ian Mitroff calls "making an error of the third kind").[27]
4. Decision makers and problem solvers solve models of their world. These models never encompass all the variables, facts, or relationships involved in the actual problem. Therefore, if and when rationality is applied, it is applied only to a part of the total problem. Recent research at the Center for Decision Research at the University of Chicago reveals several biases in the construction of such models: poor framing, the availability of evidence, and anchoring on a piece of information associating a solution with

a past success. For example, managers make decisions based on the most available evidence, which may not be the best evidence. They also often anchor on a dollar amount—some financial hurdle, if achieved by an alternative, may bias the manager to choose that alternative, even if "better" ones exist.[28]

5. Only a few of the possible alternatives are considered. The decision maker's knowledge of the situation is usually limited.

6. As a core part of bounded rationality, few managers search to find the best possible alternative. Most will settle for the first alternative that minimally satisfies minimally considered objectives, what Simon calls "satisficing" criteria. Managers often do not seek the best decision, but only the decision that improves, or satisfies, their situation, and one that the time constraints will allow them to make.

7. Managers base decisions on rules of thumb and frequently won't even evaluate alternatives according to criteria. Past experience is often the basis for making decisions.

8. The decision-making process, especially in the higher levels of the organization, is greatly affected by social relationships. Coalitions of decision makers are formed, which vie for power. Problem solvers must gain the support of powerful individuals and various coalitions to ensure that their solutions are chosen and implemented.

9. Decisions often occur in a series of small steps. There are few "great leaps," especially in large organizations.

While the rational economic model is certainly the basis for decision making in organizations, the process is often anything but rational. It is also political, social, and satisficing, not maximizing. What makes for "the best decision" is not always apparent. All decision makers must anticipate their own limitations and the constraints of the situation. They must also anticipate the political and social realities of not only the decision process but the implementation and control processes as well. This often requires participation, or "selling" their decision to those of importance. Managers must recognize these constraints and work within them. They should also seek to improve the decision process, to reduce its limitations.

IN FORT WAYNE: *The decisions made clearly involved the administrative model, not the economic model. The decision makers were constrained and faced a complex, unstructured, uncertain set of decisions.*

Problem-Solving Styles and Tendencies

Managers have historically tended to deal with problems in three primary ways: avoiding them, solving them, and seeking them out.[29]

Some managers avoid problems by burying their heads in the sand and refusing to recognize that a problem or an opportunity exists. Some say that the Bush administration has avoided the federal budget deficit issue rather than faced it head on.

Other managers solve problems as they surface. IBM's PCjr was totally redesigned after it failed to penetrate the market. Although it was ultimately scrapped because it apparently was trying to meet the demands of a market that didn't exist, IBM personnel met the problem head on.[30]

Problem-seeking managers actively search for potential problems or opportunities. These problem solvers are proactive in anticipating problems before they occur. Royal Dutch Shell is a company well known for its strategic-planning simulation systems, which actively monitor all the signals from its internal and external environments. Royal Dutch Shell has developed an ability to recognize even weak signals of potentially dangerous situations.[31]

Problem-Solving Styles

According to James L. McKenney and Peter G. W. Keen, managers develop preferences for one of two primary styles for approaching problem solving: systematic or intuitive.[32] Systematic thinkers approach a problem in a logical and rational manner. They divide the problem into smaller parts, analyze each of them, reassemble the problem, and apply various complex analytical techniques. **Systematic thinkers** tend to "look for a method, make a plan for problem solving, be very conscious of their approach, defend the quality of the solution largely in terms of the method, define specific constraints of the problem early in the process, discard alternatives quickly, move through a process of increasing refinement of analysis, conduct an orderly search for additional information, and complete any discrete analysis that they begin."[33]

Intuitive thinkers, on the other hand, are especially good at keeping track of many variables, which may defy ordinary analytical techniques. The term **intuitive** implies that positions are reached without rational and analytical thought. The solution or the observation simply "comes to the individual" via insight. **Intuitive thinkers** tend to "keep the overall problem continuously in mind, redefine the problem frequently as they proceed, rely on verbalized guesses, even hunches, to find a solution, consider a number of alternatives and options simultaneously, jump from one step of analysis research and back again, and explore and abandon alternatives quickly."[34] Intuitive thinkers are very good at handling extremely complex problems in a spontaneous fashion. They seem to be able to view the entire situation much better than a person who is strictly rational and analytical. Despite the advice of his attorney, Ray Kroc purchased a small hamburger chain because he had a feeling that the chain had tremendous potential. He was right, and McDonald's was born. These individual preferences in problem-solving style probably stem from, or are at least partly related to, preferences for gathering and processing information.[35]

How Much Participation, and When?

IN FORT WAYNE:
Mayor Moses had to determine whether he could succeed in bringing Fort Wayne back from the brink by himself or would have to involve numerous others. Full participation by all involved was the obvious solution for Fort Wayne.

Managers need some way to determine when members of their work groups, individually or collectively, should participate in managerial decisions and when they should not—and how much they should participate if they do. These are not easy decisions to make. We gave some guidelines in the previous section, when we focused on individual versus group decision making, but the factors involved affect more than just the superiority of the decision.

Victor Vroom and P. W. Yetton have constructed a **model** (Figure 3.6) that uses a decision tree to help answer the questions of when and how to allow participation in decision making. They suggest that by following their decision tree, which includes the major factors critical to each decision point, a manager will be able to make an appropriate decision with respect to whether and how much participation should occur. Five management decision styles are described in Table 3.3—AI, AII, CI, CII, and GII. These are offered as possible solutions to the fourteen possible problem types shown in Table 3.3. Those problem types result from decisions related to seven primary decision variables, A, B, D, E, F, G, and H, characterized in Figure 3.6. For several problems, more than one participative style may be appropriate, as is indicated in Table 3.3.

Table 3.3. Decision Methods for Group Problems

AI.	You solve the problem or make the decision yourself, using information available to you at the time.
AII.	You obtain the necessary information from your subordinates, then decide the solution to the problem yourself. You may or may not tell your subordinates what the problem is in getting the information from them. The role played by your subordinates in making the decision is clearly one of providing the necessary information to you, rather than generating or evaluating alternative solutions.
CI.	You share the problem with the relevant subordinates individually, getting their ideas and suggestions without bringing them together as a group. Then *you* make the decision, which may or may not reflect your subordinates' influence.
CII.	You share the problem with your subordinates as a group, obtaining their collective ideas and suggestions. Then you make the decision, which may or may not reflect your subordinates' influence.
GII.	You share the problem with your subordinates as a group. Together you generate and evaluate alternatives and attempt to reach agreement (consensus) on a solution. Your role is much like that of chairman. You do not try to influence the group to adopt "your" solution, and you are willing to accept and implement any solution which has the support of the entire group.

SOURCE: Reprinted from Victor Vroom and P. W. Yetton, *Leadership and Decision Making* by permission of the University of Pittsburgh Press. © 1973 by the University of Pittsburgh Press.

FIGURE 3.6   DECISION-PROCESS FLOW CHART

A.   IS THERE A QUALITY REQUIREMENT SUCH THAT ONE SOLUTION IS LIKELY TO BE MORE RATIONAL THAN ANOTHER?

B.   DO I HAVE SUFFICIENT INFO TO MAKE A HIGH QUALITY DECISION?

D.   IS THE PROBLEM STRUCTURED?

E.   IS ACCEPTANCE OF DECISION BY SUBORDINATES CRITICAL TO EFFECTIVE IMPLEMENTATION?

F.   IF I WERE TO MAKE THE DECISION BY MYSELF, IS IT REASONABLY CERTAIN THAT IT WOULD BE ACCEPTED BY MY SUBORDINATES?

G.   DO SUBORDINATES SHARE THE ORGANIZATIONAL GOALS TO BE ATTAINED IN SOLVING THIS PROBLEM?

H.   IS CONFLICT AMONG SUBORDINATES LIKELY IN PREFERRED SOLUTIONS?

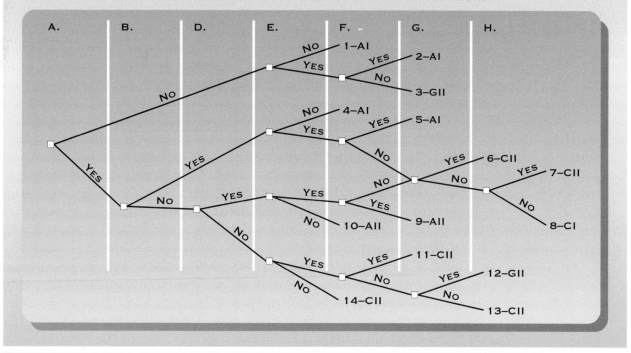

SOURCE: REPRINTED FROM VICTOR VROOM AND P.W. YETTON, LEADERSHIP AND DECISION MAKING BY PERMISSION OF THE UNIVERSITY OF PITTSBURGH PRESS ©1973 BY THE UNIVERSITY OF PITTSBURGH PRESS.

These styles range from the authoritarian, in which subordinates have no inputs in decisions, to the highly participative, in which subordinates essentially make the decisions. The A types of decisions are authoritarian; AI decisions are more authoritarian than AII. The C types are consultative, with CII more consultative than CI. In consultative decision making, subordinates serve as advisors to the manager. The G type of decision is group oriented. Here subordinates make the decision in conjunction with the manager. The Vroom-Yetton model gives managers a practical means of determining which of these styles they should choose.[36]

To use the model, managers state the problem and then answer questions A, B, D, E, F, G, and H in sequential order. Each question can be answered with a yes or a no, so that managers follow one branch or another of the decision tree as a consequence of their answer, proceeding onward to the next relevant question. Managers work through the decision tree until they reach an optimal decision point. Figure 3.6 and Table 3.4 indicate the most preferred and the possible decision styles for each decision point. This decision tree is an important step forward in the management problem-solving process because it identifies the major contingency variables for a set of common decisions used in problem solving and prescribes what to do about them.

Table 3.4. Problem Types and the Feasible Set of Decision Methods

Problem Type	Acceptable Methods
1	AI, AII, CI, CII, GII
2	AI, AII, CI, CII, GII
3	GII
4	AI, AII, CI, CII, GII*
5	AI, AII, CI, CII, GII*
6	GII
7	CII
8	CI, CII
9	AII, CI, CII, GII*
10	AII, CI, CII, GII*
11	CII, GII*
12	GII
13	CII
14	CII, GII*

*Within the feasible set only when the answer to question G is yes.

SOURCE: Reprinted from Victor Vroom and P. W. Yetton, *Leadership and Decision Making* by permission of the University of Pittsburgh Press, © 1973 by the University of Pittsburgh Press.

USING THE MODEL

Suppose you were the professor in a typical Introduction to Management class. Your problem is to choose a book for the class. Think through each of the questions from a professor's perspective.

QUESTION A: Is one book likely to be of better quality than another? The answer is yes. This places the professor at B.

QUESTION B: Does the professor have sufficient information to choose the best book? The answer is yes. If you are following Figure 3.6, this places the professor at E.

QUESTION E: Is the students' acceptance of the book critical to using it successfully? The answer is yes. This places the professor at F.

QUESTION F: If the professor chooses a book, will his students use it? The answer is yes. This yields under G, 5AI as a solution. An AI decision means the manager solves the problem and makes the decision using information available at the time.

Suppose, on the other hand, you were the sales manager for a software manufacturer, and you were faced with developing a new sales promotion technique. Let's go through the questions again.

QUESTION A: Is one technique likely to be better than another? Yes. This places you at B.

QUESTION B: Do you as sales manager have sufficient information to make a high-quality decision? The answer could be yes or no. If you suppose it to be no—because you are not familiar enough with the requirements of the territory to decide yourself—then you would move to D.

QUESTION D: Is the problem structured? The answer is no. This problem is seldom faced, and there are no obvious or easy answers. You then move to E.

QUESTION E: Is acceptance of the solution by subordinates critical? The answer is yes. You move to F.

QUESTION F: If you make the decision yourself, is the decision likely to be accepted by your subordinates. The answer could be yes or no. Suppose, however, that because of the subordinates' past independence the answer is no. You must move to G.

QUESTION G: Do subordinates share the organizational goals to be attained in solving this problem? The answer is yes. The solution is 12GII, which is a highly participative solution to this problem. You made some assumptions that could just as easily have been different, so your solution could have been different.

Revisions: The Vroom-Yago Model

In 1988 Vroom and Arthur G. Yago proposed that an additional factor needed to be considered in the basic model itself: whether the subordinate has sufficient information to make the decision. They also suggested that two versions of the model exist: one based on whether time is an overriding factor—that is, the amount of time available to make decisions—and the other on whether the manager is driven to develop subordinates' decision-making skills. Vroom and Yago provide a decision-process flowchart similar to Figure 3.6 for each of these two models. They also refine, in considerable detail, when and when not to use the various decision methods. They do so for groups and for individuals. Time and space do not permit us to review these here in detail. But it is important for you to grasp the underlying concepts of how to make choices using the basic model. You must also realize that insufficient time may override the choices that would normally be made, as might the desire to improve the decision skills of the subordinates.[37]

The Manager as a Creative Problem Solver

The increased complexity of the decision environment, the changing personalities and expectations of organizational members, and all the other factors noted in Chapter 1 are changing the way that problems must be solved. Managers are not only moving toward increased participation, but are also responding to the increased need for the decision maker, the problem solver, to be more creative. Most individuals in our organizations are confronted with an environment that demands increased levels of problem-solving creativity for four key reasons:

1. An accelerated rate of change
2. Increased levels of competition
3. The requirements of decision making in the computer age

MANAGEMENT CHALLENGE 3.4

3M— Masters of Innovation

Spencer Silver, 3M innovator of the Post-it note pads, displays their line of products. (SOURCE © Mitch Kezar)

Like most U.S. firms, 3M found itself in competitive difficulty in the mid-1980s. To improve its situation, 3M turned to what it knew best, innovation—not just innovation in product development, where it had always been strong, but also in process innovation, in cutting costs. Chairman and CEO Allen (Jake) Jacobson

4. The edge that those who are intuitive as well as rational have over those who use only rational approaches to decision making[38]

As our society changes technologically, socially, economically, and politically, creative solutions are necessary to solve problems. As we become more competitive, as product life cycles shorten, as more and more new entrants supply products and services in all market areas, creativity is needed. William P. Hewlett, cofounder of Hewlett-Packard, speaking at the 1986 graduation ceremony at the Massachusetts Institute of Technology, proclaimed, "Creativity is the only American competitive advantage left."[39]

Today the computer does the number crunching. Problem solvers need to learn how to use that information to make better decisions. Finally, we know from a series of studies, that the intuitive individual who also uses rational analytical approaches has an advantage over the person who is simply rational and analytical.[40] The intuitive person, especially in complex problem-solving situations, generates better decisions than those of the singlemindedly rational person.

commenced his J-35 program in 1985, J for Jake, 35 for 35 percent cuts in labor and manufacturing costs by 1990. It worked.

3M's penchant for innovation translates to a 32 percent share of its $10.6 billion in 1988 sales coming from products introduced since 1983. This has propelled the firm to a record $1.15 billion profit, up 25 percent from 1987. How does it do it? It has paid close attention to cultivating a culture that incorporates the ingredients leading both to creativity and innovation. It

1. tolerates creative people and their ideas.
2. believes in the long-term potential of creativity.
3. encourages entrepreneurial spirit and activity.
4. allows people to make mistakes, looking for a good batting average, rather than a home run every time at bat.
5. ties salaries and promotions to innovation.
6. allows innovation champions with good products to run their own businesses.
7. lets nothing, especially politics, get in the way of innovation.
8. keeps divisions small, usually under $200 million in sales.
9. encourages information-sharing meetings among employees.
10. has specific financial hurdles for new products.
11. forms new-product teams.
12. uses a 25 percent rule: 25 percent of a division's profits must come from products that didn't exist five years before.
13. uses a 15 percent rule: 15 percent of an employee's time may be spent on anything, as long as it leads to new-product development.
14. uses objectives to elicit process innovations.
15. encourages front-line employees to contribute.
16. stays close to the customer.
17. provides seed money to develop a product through project Genesis.
18. formally spreads technology to all divisions.
19. keeps corporate rules to a minimum.
20. allows virtually unfettered creative thinking.

SOURCE: "Masters of Innovation—How 3M Keeps Its New Products Coming," *Business Week* (April 11, 1989), pp. 58–63.

Creativity is extremely important in all stages of successful problem solving/decision making. While we tend to think of creativity as being principally concerned with generating alternatives, it also takes creativity to analyze the environment, search out problems and separate them from symptoms, choose good solutions and implement them in an effective way, and develop effective control systems.

Achieving creativity in problem solving revolves around the **four Ps of creativity:** product, processes, possibilities, and the person. The creativity process produces creative services, physical products, or ideas. These result from using the other three Ps. Individuals or groups may use some fifty or so process techniques to improve creativity, including two we have already discussed, brainstorming and storyboarding.

The possibilities for creativity include a certain type of organizational culture, a supportive management style, and the right combination of societal characteristics. Rewards must be provided, creativity must be encouraged, and open communication and trust should dominate. Innovative companies such as 3M, Hewlett-Packard, and Merck, possess such organizational cultures.[41] Milliken even has an "Innovator's Hall of Fame."[42] The 3M Company, widely regarded as the most innovative large company in the United States, if not the world, is discussed in Management Challenge 3.4. It provides possibilities for creativity.

Personal creativity can be raised in two principal ways. First, most people have been socialized against being creative. Overly burdensome rules, regulations, procedures, and attitudes against new ideas dominate most organizations. Therefore you need to resocialize yourself to overcome negative attitudes, and noncreative habits.[43] Second, you can use several techniques to develop your intuition and improve your creativity.[44] Research by professor Weston H. Agor reveals that many top executives emphasize the importance of intuition to successful problem solving. They also emphasize, however, that intuition is only one way of approaching a problem and that rational analysis must come first.[45]

Visitors to Milliken Company's Hall of Fame review the awards the employees have received for their various innovations. This Hall of Fame helps instill in employees the belief that innovation is important. (SOURCE Courtesy Milliken Company)

The title of this chapter "The Manager as a Decision Maker and Creative Problem Solver" is intended to convey the importance of using intuition and feeling in problem solving. Unfortunately most of our educational processes develop only systematic thinking. While some decisions lend themselves readily to systematic thinking, others do not. The more complex, unstructured, and less frequent the decision, the more likely it is that intuition and feeling will be necessary. It has been shown, for example, that chief executives' jobs require intuition for them to be effective at strategic planning because some of the problems they face are so complex they almost defy rational approaches.[46]

Management Challenges Identified

1. Decision making/problem solving in a rapidly changing environment
2. Decision making/problem solving for all of the management functions, all of the management challenges

Some Solutions Noted in the Chapter

1. Learning to solve problems by using each of the stages of the problem-solving/decision-making process
2. Learning to solve problems by using more creativity as well as rationality
3. Learning when to allow participation

Summary

1. Creative problem solving is the core function of management. For our purposes, problem solving and decision making are viewed as being the same process. Problem solving consists of eight stages: environmental analysis, problem recognition, problem identification, making assumptions, alternative generation, evaluation and choice, implementation, and control.
2. Decisions are made under three principal conditions:
   Certainty: Alternatives, conditions, probabilities are known. Outcomes are certain.
   Risk: Alternatives and conditions are known, probabilities are estimable. Outcomes are unknown.
   Uncertainty: Alternatives, number of alternatives, conditions, probabilities, and outcomes are all unknown.
3. Decisions exist along a continuum from highly structured, or programmed, to highly unstructured, or unprogrammed. Structured problems are routine and simple and lead to routine decisions. Unstructured problems are unique and complex and require

one-of-a-kind solutions. Top managers tend to face more unstructured problems, whereas lower-level managers tend to face more structured problems.

4. The advantages of group problem solving include potentially superior solutions, an increase in decision acceptance, improved understanding, broader information base, balanced risk propensities, and better collective judgment. The disadvantages of group problem solving include conformity, domination by one person, more time needed, superior people still making better decisions, amount of time it takes to make a decision, risky shift.

5. While much of the theoretical explanation for decision making follows the economic model, the administrative model, which takes into account the behavioral aspects of decision making, portrays the process more accurately. Individual psychological, social, and political forces often enter into the process.

6. Managers can be classified as either intuitive or systematic in their problem-solving styles.

7. The Vroom-Yetton model provides guidelines about when and how much participation in decision making a manager should allow.

8. Most organizations and many people, especially managers, will have to become more creative in the near future. Being creative requires learning creative techniques and developing both sides of the brain. To be creative in an organization requires the right type of organizational culture.

9. Table 3.1 discusses typical problem-solving issues that might arise in the economic functions.

Thinking About Management

1. Why is creative problem solving management's primary responsibility?

2. Describe a decision you have been part of or have witnessed as a member of an organization, in terms of the stages of the creative problem-solving process— environmental analysis, problem recognition, identification, making assumptions, alternative generation, choice, implementation, and control.

3. Review the major decisions you have made in the last month. Which of these were structured, and which were unstructured? Were they made under conditions of risk, uncertainty, or certainty?

4. Think of an organization to which you have belonged. Describe its typical problem-solving action in terms of the classical and administrative models of decision making. Which was it most similar to?

5. Describe the politics of decision making in organizations. Use personal examples.

6. Do you use rules of thumb in decision making? Describe them.

7. Review the pros and cons of both individual and group problem solving.

8. What is your probable problem-solving style, your preference?

9. Describe each of the three major types of problem-solving groups and how each might be used.

10. Why do we need more creativity in problem solving, especially in complex situations?

What's Teaching Excellence?

The five faculty members examined the documents in front of them carefully. As members of Roger Warren's tenure committee, they had to determine whether Roger met the school's standards for tenure. Tenure would normally be granted if the committee determined that the candidate had successfully achieved the preestablished levels of performance for the school's tenure criteria. Determining whether a colleague should be awarded tenure is a serious responsibility, not one to be taken lightly. The approval of the dean, the university president, and the board of trustees was also necessary but was usually given if the committee recommended it. These were the five criteria for tenure:

1. Teaching excellence
2. Publications
3. University service
4. Community service
5. Professional development

Roger had satisfied the last four without question. He had written a sufficient number of articles in the proper journals and one book. He was on a major committee at the university. He provided community seminars. And, he had attended several professional meetings. But teaching excellence was another matter. The business school, of which he was a member, had recently defined teaching excellence as "consistently at or above the mean score for all school faculty on student evaluations." Unfortunately for Roger, the faculty average for the business school was 7.5 on a 9-point scale for virtually all 26 items rated. This was the highest in the university, and it made it difficult for Roger, or for anyone, to achieve the desired standard on this criterion item. Obviously someone had to be below average for an average to exist, unless everyone scored the same. Roger taught three different undergraduate classes. His student evaluation averages for two of his classes were 6.2 and for the other one 7.4. The lower averages were in difficult, required accounting classes. The higher-average course was an elective accounting course for accounting majors. Over the last two years for which they were available, the averages for the two introductory courses had changed substantially each fall. Roger's ratings seemed to go up slightly in the spring.

The committee had discussed the definition of the standard of teaching excellence, the impact of the change in the content of those courses on evaluations, the impact of the nature of the courses on evaluations, and the previously determined policy of using supplementary materials to show teaching effectiveness in addition to the student evaluations. But the issue had not been settled after an hour of calm, but emphatic discussion. The committee largely favored granting tenure, but felt it needed additional information, provided perhaps by the candidate, to substantiate their position. The committee chairperson agreed to obtain such information before the following Friday, when the committee would meet again. Committee members returned to their offices to be alone with their thoughts. One member, Carlos Alvarez, a tenured, full professor of finance, was particularly bothered by what had just transpired. He felt Roger had made a solid contribution to the school. Yet Roger's approach to teaching was very boring in what many consider to be a very boring discipline. And Carlos had heard many students complain about the way Roger taught. Still, other students liked Roger. Carlos thought back to one committee member's argument that because the total faculty averages were so close to Roger's, you could not say that Roger was not at the average. He also recalled a recent presentation on student evaluations and performance appraisals by Kate Stanford of the management department. She indicated that student evaluations often measured their perceptions of teaching style, especially liveliness, humor, and wit; teaching enthusiasm;

and rigor. Actual performance, in terms of changing student behaviors, was not measured by those evaluations. Ultimate performance would be determined by what students did once they left the college. Carlos wondered how you measured that. Finally, his thoughts turned to Roger's other contributions, which he felt were certainly worthwhile to the university. Carlos was not sure if Roger was an excellent teacher, but some decision had to be made.

DISCUSSION QUESTIONS
1. Show how Carlos and the members of his committee are attempting to use the rational approach to decision making. What role should intuition play here?
2. Indicate how Carlos and the committee may be using an administrative approach to decision making.
3. Describe this problem in terms of the stages of the problem-solving process.
4. What would your decision be if you were Carlos and the additional data provided by Roger simply substantiated what you already knew? Why?
5. Put yourself in Roger's place. What kinds of comments could you make to substantiate your role as an excellent teacher?

Sun Equity

Sue Simon had been contemplating how to differentiate Sun Bank's equity loan program from all of the other home mortgage programs offered by its competitors. As vice-president in charge of product development, she and her staff were constantly generating marketing strategies, often basing them on market research, sometimes on their intimate knowledge of the marketplace. They needed something really creative this time because research had revealed that virtually none of the equity loan packages from the various banks seemed to stick out in the customer's mind, and they all seemed to have the same features. Her staff and the other half of the product-planning division had recently been through a creativity training program, and she was anxious to try some of the individual and group techniques to arrive at a differentiated product strategy.

DISCUSSION QUESTIONS
1. What types of processes might Sue use to create this differentiated product?
2. What ideas do you have for differentiating the product?

The Farley Test for Risk Takers

Answer yes or no to each item as it applies to you (check your answer).

1. I would take the risk of starting my own business rather than work for someone else. ☐ YES ☐ NO

2. I would never take a job that requires lots of traveling. ☐ YES ☐ NO

3. If I were to gamble, I would never make small bets. ☐ YES ☐ NO

4. I like to improve on ideas. ☐ YES ☐ NO

5. I would never give up my job before I was certain I had another one. ☐ YES ☐ NO

6. I would never invest in highly speculative stocks. ☐ YES ☐ NO

7. To broaden my horizons, I would be willing to take risks. ☐ YES ☐ NO

8. Thinking of investing in stocks does not excite me. ☐ YES ☐ NO

9. I would consider working strictly on a commission basis. ☐ YES ☐ NO

10. Knowing that any particular new business can fail, I would avoid investing in one even if the potential payoff was high. ☐ YES ☐ NO

11. I would like to experience as much of life as possible. ☐ YES ☐ NO

12. I don't feel that I have a strong need for excitement. ☐ YES ☐ NO

13. I am high in energy. ☐ YES ☐ NO

14. I can easily generate lots of money-making ideas. ☐ YES ☐ NO

15. I would never bet more money than I had at the time. ☐ YES ☐ NO

16. I enjoy proposing new ideas or concepts when the reactions of others—my boss, for example—are unknown or uncertain. ☐ YES ☐ NO

17. I have never written checks without having sufficient funds in the bank to cover them. ☐ YES ☐ NO

18. Business deals that are relatively certain are the only ones I would engage in. ☐ YES ☐ NO

19. A less secure job with a large income is more to my liking than a more secure job with an average income. ☐ YES ☐ NO

20. I am not very independent-minded. ☐ YES ☐ NO

If you answered yes on the Farley Fisc-Risk Scale to questions 1, 3, 4, 7, 9, 11, 13, 14, 16, 19, give 1 point for each answer. If you answered no to items 2, 5, 6, 8, 10, 12, 15, 17, 18, 20, give 1 point for each answer.

If your total score was 17 or 18 or higher, this might suggest financial-risk-taking potential and Type-T tendencies. However, this questionnaire is a sample and is not definitive. Scores may vary from person to person and from time to time because of many factors. To help with research, clip and send your results along with your age, sex and occupation to Frank Farley, 1025 West Johnson Street, University of Wisconsin, Madison, Wis. 53706.

Test used with permission of Frank Farley.

SOURCE: Frank Farley

CHAPTER FOUR

The Managerial Environment, Social Responsibility, and Ethics

CHAPTER OBJECTIVES

By the time you complete studying this chapter you should be able to

1. Describe the major components of the internal, competitive, and general environments of the business organization.
2. Define the stakeholder concept.
3. Identify the changing nature of the organizational environment and describe the organization in terms of the complexity of the environment in which it operates and how that environment is changing.
4. Identify the four principal components of social responsibility for a business.
5. Describe the major issues.
6. List and discuss the possible philosophies of response.
7. Define and discuss ethics.
8. Identify the factors to be considered in making decisions.

CHAPTER OUTLINE

The Nature of the Business Environment

The Competitive Environment
The General Environment
External Organizational Environments: Stability and Complexity
The Organization/Environment Interface
  Adapting to the Environment
  Changing the Environment
Social Power and Social Responsibility
  Contrasting Views of Social Responsibility
  Levels of Responsibility
  Identifying the Issues
  The Philosophy of Responsiveness
Improving Social Responsiveness
  The Corporate Social Policy Process
  The Social Audit
  The Litigation Audit
Corporate Social Responsibility and Profitability
Mechanisms of Social Control with Which Managers Must Contend
Ethics
  How the Individual Manager Should Decide
  How Companies Can Improve Ethical Performance
Social Responsibility, Ethics, and Problem Solving
Management Challenges Identified
Some Solutions Noted in the Chapter

The Valdez Oil Spill

Not every management decision is a sound one. Far from it. One of the worst series of management decisions imaginable accompanied the worst oil disaster to occur in North American waters when 240,000 barrels (10 million gallons) of oil leaked from the Exxon Valdez in March 1989, covering much of Alaska's Prince William Sound. The spill covered more than 900 square miles, taking a catastrophic toll on animals—sea otters, birds, whales, walruses, herring, and salmon. More salmon spawn in the waters around the town of Valdez, than anywhere else on earth. Several of the fisheries were protected, but many fishermen saw their livelihoods and way of life destroyed by the spill. One consequence of the spill was that at least four lawsuits were filed against Exxon and Alyeska, the pipeline company formed by the seven firms who share in the oil field.

On Friday, March 24, 1989, at 12:04 A.M., third-mate Gregory T. Cousins, who was illegally in command while Captain Joseph Hazelwood reportedly was asleep in his cabin, ordered the Exxon Valdez to execute a strange series of right turns in an attempt to dodge floating ice. The ship ran aground and the oil spilled. At 12:30 A.M. Alyeska Pipeline dispatched an observation team to the scene, but it did not have any containment equipment. Alyeska was meanwhile attempting to put together a containment operation, but its people were in total disarray. By 3:23 A.M. the Coast Guard was aboard the Exxon Valdez and found that it had already lost 138,000 barrels. According to the government-approved containment plan, Alyeska should by then have arrived with containment equipment, but it had not. And, when the containment barge was first loaded with equipment, it was loaded with the wrong equipment. It had to be reloaded, delaying the response further.

Ironically the Alyeska containment operation was understaffed. It should have had fifteen crew members on hand, but there were only eleven. Until 1981 Alyeska had an around-the-clock containment team, but it was cut from the budget to save money. State officials had permitted it.

At 6:00 A.M. Exxon officials flew over the spill for the first time.

At 9:00 A.M. the Coast Guard tested Captain Hazelwood for alcohol consumption. It had been reported that he had had alcohol on his breath at the time of the spill. Apparently the Valdez's captain had a history of alcoholism but had been retained nonetheless by Exxon. At 2:30 P.M. the Alyeska crew finally arrived with containment equipment. At 11:00 A.M. the Exxon Valdez was finally encircled by an Alyeska containment boom, but the oil spill now covered 12 square miles. The spill was out of control.

It is estimated that it may take as many as ten years for the Sound to recover fully. Early on in the pipeline project, Alyeska officials had promised that state-of-the-art equipment would be used for any tankers passing through the Sound. A few of the ships in the Valdez fleet employed them, but the Exxon Valdez did not.

Lee Raymond, president of Exxon Corporation, made excuses for the company claiming that it was in a situation beyond its control. He blamed "ultimately the Coast Guard" for prohibiting it from moving as quickly as it could. But the evidence clearly indicated otherwise. For example, Michelle Hahn-O'Leary, spokeswoman for local fishermen, asserts that the community was ready to respond immediately and had called on Exxon to tell officials they would help. In fact, the entire fishing fleet of Valdez was ready to take action, but Exxon did not respond for days.

From an environmentalist's viewpoint, the toll at Prince William Sound was extremely high for the most innocent of victims, the animals. Most of those exposed suffered painful deaths. From the viewpoint of local fishermen, their livelihoods at first appeared jeopardized, but Exxon made substantial efforts, mostly financial, to ensure their security, . . . and silence.

SOURCES: Kim Wells and Charles McCoy, "Out of Control: How Unpreparedness Turned the Alaska Spill into an Ecological Debacle," *Wall Street Journal* 3 April, 1989, pp. A1, A4; Ken Wells and Marilyn Chase, "Paradise Lost: Heartbreaking Scenes of Beauty Disfigured Follow Alaska Oil Spill," *Wall Street Journal* 31, March 1989, pp. A1, A4; "Smothering the Water," *Newsweek* (April 10, 1989), pp. 54–57; "Environmental Politics," *Newsweek* (April 17, 1989), pp. 18–19; and Meg Greenfield, "In Defense of the Animals," *Newsweek* (April 17, 1989), p. 78.

Change is the order of the day, either choose it or chase it. Adapt or die.

Theodore Levitt
Editor, *Harvard Business Review*

We have become far too careless, self-indulgent, and cruel in the pain we inflict on these creatures (laboratory test animals) for the most frivolous, unworthy purposes.

Meg Greenfield, *Newsweek* editorialist

The Valdez oil spill incident represents the worst in management decision making, negligence, and unpreparedness. The results were devastating. Such decisions, unfortunately, are not isolated incidents. Rather, thousands of similar events occur every day in all types of businesses and governments. Most of these decisions lack the impact of a Valdez, but many are leading collectively to problems even more devastating than that witnessed at Valdez.[1] The mid-1980s, for example, brought a realization that the "greenhouse effect" is a fact. The earth is getting warmer, as record temperatures, drought, and forest fires caused by dryness helped prove.[2] The ozone layer is being depleted and the incidence of skin cancer and other cancers is bound to increase in the future as a consequence of actions already taken.[3] Acid rain is deforesting much of the United States, Canada, and Europe, destroying fish in lakes and rivers.[4] The world's oceans are dying as a consequence of industrial pollution dumped into rivers or directly into the ocean. Developers are using up all the nation's shore-lines, preventing natural cleansing as well as fish breeding.[5] The world's rivers, especially those in the United States, and the world's water supply is becoming polluted.[6] Plastic is choking the world's oceans and rivers, killing millions of innocent animals, destroying beaches, and disintegrating into lethal chemicals.[7] About 40,000 square miles of tropical forests are destroyed every year, mostly

The Amazon jungle, before and after the tree removal process known as clear-cutting. Notice how the entire mountain top has been laid bare. (SOURCE © Laif/SIPA)

by burning, which adds to the carbon dioxide already in the atmosphere and, more importantly, decreases the amount taken out of the atmosphere by trees.[8] In the summer of 1988, record levels of smog occurred in major cities throughout the United States.[9] All of these examples relate to just one of numerous organizational-societal interface areas: the physical environment. A business must also still be concerned about customers, competitors, and suppliers,

Table 4.1. Categories of Social Responsibility

Product Line

Internal standards for products
Average product life
Product performance
Packaging impacts

Marketing Practices

Sales practices
Credit practices against legal standards
Accuracy of advertising claims—specific government complaints
Consumer complaints about marketing practices
Provision of adequate consumer information
Fair pricing
Packaging

Employee Education and Training

Policy on leaves of absence
Dollars spent on training
Special training program results (systematic evaluations)
Plans for future programs
Career training and counseling
Failure rates
Personnel understanding

Corporate Philanthropy

Contribution performance
Selection criteria for contributions
Procedures for performance tracking of recipient institutions or groups
Programs to permit and encourage employee involvement in social projects
Extent of employee involvement in philanthropy decision making

Environmental Control

Measurable pollution
Violations of government (federal, state, local) standards
Cost estimates to correct current deficiencies
Extent to which various plants exceed current legal standards (e.g., particulate matter discharged)
Resources devoted to pollution control
Competitive company performance (e.g., capital expenditures)
Effort to monitor new standards as proposed
Programs to keep employees alert to spills and other pollution-related accidents
Procedures for evaluating environmental impact of new packaging of products

External Relations

Community development
Support of minority and community enterprises
Investment practices
Government relations
Specific input to public policy through research and analysis
Participation and development of business/government programs
Political contributions

External Relations con't.

Disclosure of information (communications)
Extent of public disclosure of performance by activity category
Measure of employee understanding of programs (relations/communications with stockholders, fund managers, major customers, etc.)
International relations
Comparisons of policy and performance with those of other countries and against local standards

Employee Relations, Benefits, and Satisfaction with Work

Comparison of wage and other policies with competition and/or national averages
Comparison of operating units on promotions, terminations, hires
Performance review system and procedures for communication with employees whose performance is below average
Promotion policy—equitable and understood
Transfer policy
Termination policy (e.g., how early is notice given?)
General work environment and conditions
Fringe benefits as percentage of salary at various salary levels
Evaluation of employee benefit preferences (questions can be posed as choices)
Evaluation of employee understanding of current fringe benefits
Union/industrial relations
Confidentiality and security of personnel data

Employment and Advancement and Minorities and Women

Current hiring policies in relation to requirements of affirmative action programs
Company versus local, industry, and national performance
Percent minorities and women employed in major facilities in relation to minority labor force available locally
Number of minorities and women in positions of high responsibility
Promotion performance of minorities and women
Specific hiring and job upgrading goals established for minorities and women
Programs to ease integration of minorities and women into company operations (e.g., awareness efforts)
Specialized career counseling for minorities and women
Special recruiting efforts for minorities and women
Opportunities for the physically handicapped

Employee Safety and Health

Work environment measures
Safety performance
Services provided (and cost of programs and human resources) for safety equipment, instruction, special safety programs
Comparisons of health and safety performance with competition and industry in general
Developments/innovations in health and safety
Employee health measures (e.g., sick days, examinations)
Food facilities
AIDS policies

SOURCE: Adapted from *Business and Society Review,* Summer 1973, Copyright © 1973, Business and Society Review. Reprinted with permission.

changes in technology, and threats to its domain from government, special-interest groups, and the overall society. Additional issues that arise may be related to equal employment opportunity; consumerism; the use of energy, economics, and markets; labor relations; corporate philanthropy; and employee health, education, and welfare. These issues are identified in more detail in Table 4.1. This chapter discusses how business management can bring its many talents and resources to bear on these problem and opportunity areas.

Ethics is also of major importance. In the 1980s accepted standards of business ethics were violated by numerous firms. The role call of firms and/or individuals involved in unethical business practices reads like a who's who: Anheuser-Busch for improper payments and kickbacks;[10] Northrup Corporation for substantial improper charges made to the U.S. Air Force on contracts;[11] Raytheon for its kickback scheme;[12] E. F. Hutton for a check-floating scheme aimed at defrauding banks of interest payments;[13] General Electric and General Dynamics for overcharging the U.S. government on defense contracts;[14] much of the construction industry in New York City for its apparent ties to organized crime and its use of extortion and bribery in securing contracts;[15] the U.S. Postal Service and other major U.S. government agencies for bribery and kickback schemes involving the purchase of computers;[16] Shearson and Lehman Brothers for laundering gambling funds;[17] Ivan Boesky for insider trading on Wall Street, just to name a few.

Business has moved rapidly from a simple environment to a complex one, with a large number of groups in the environment demanding action by business to satisfy their needs. Furthermore, business is confronted with a much more changeful environment than it was a few years ago. Theodore Levitt, editor of the *Harvard Business Review,* suggests that "Change is the order of the day, either choose it or chase it. 'Adapt or die' is the tag mark that covers almost every business and organization."[18] Only those businesses that adapt to the myriad problems and opportunities will be successful. Business cannot operate in isolation. Neither can the United States. Cooperation between all countries in the world will be necessary to solve many of the problems confronting businesses.

This chapter explores the nature of the business environment, examining the internal and external environments. The two main external environments are the competitive environment and the general environment. The general environment has four main components: economic/competitive, political/legal, social/cultural, and technological. The chapter then discusses the social responsibility of businesses, defining the issues and noting the range of responses possible in the light of society's needs. Ethics, a vital topic in today's society, is integrated into the discussion of social responsibility. This chapter focuses principally on social responsibility and ethics. Subsequent chapters will focus on other aspects of the internal and external environments.

The Nature of the Business Environment

As discussed in Chapter 2, most organizations are open systems. They have interactions across their boundaries with other elements of the society. A closed system, on the other hand, does not have interactions with other elements. Managers who act as if their organizations are closed systems, except for interactions with customers and suppliers, will suffer severely, as the opening vignette on the Valdez oil spill revealed. As shown in Figure 4.1, the organization has two principal environments: an external environment and an internal environment. The organization's **external environment** consists of all those elements outside the boundaries of the organization that have the potential to affect the organization.[19] The external environment has two principal parts: its competitive environment and the general environment.[20] The **competitive environment** is comprised of those elements that form its competitive situation. Its major components include customers, competitors, suppliers, substitutes, and new entrants. The **general environment** includes those elements—such as society, technology, the economy, and legal/political factors—that have less daily contact with the organization, but which occasionally influence it or can be influenced by it in a significant way. The increasing use of personal computers and the changing value of the dollar are just two of thousands of specific examples of such factors. The **internal environment** includes all of the elements within the

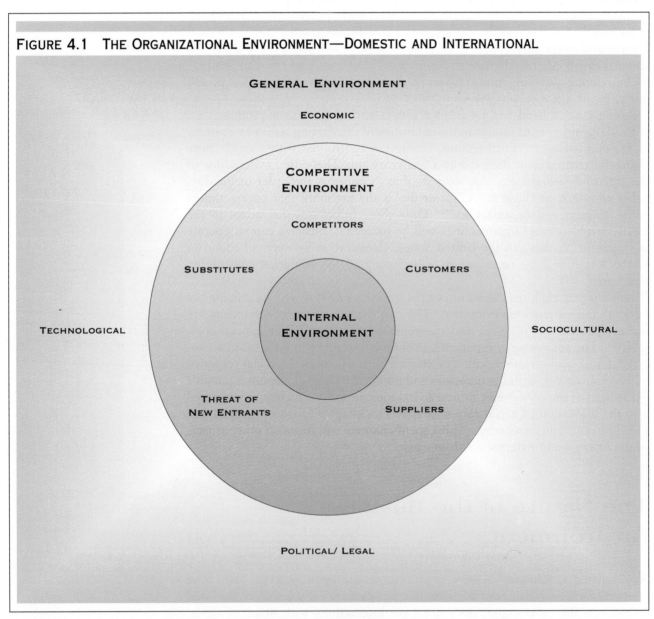

FIGURE 4.1   THE ORGANIZATIONAL ENVIRONMENT—DOMESTIC AND INTERNATIONAL

SOURCES: ADAPTED FROM L. J. BOURGEOIS, "STRATEGY AND THE ENVIRONMENT: A CONCEPTUAL INTEGRATION," ACADEMY OF MANAGEMENT REVIEW JANUARY (1980), PP. 25–39, BY SUBSTITUTING MICHAEL PORTER'S COMPETITIVE FACTORS FOR THOSE IN BOURGEOIS'S TASK ENVIRONMENT; AND MICHAEL E. PORTER, COMPETITIVE STRATEGY (NEW YORK: FREE PRESS, 1986).

More than one stock brokerage firm has been found guilty of unethical business practices in recent years. (SOURCE © John Abbott)

organization's boundaries—corporate culture, current employees, stockholders, management, leadership style, organizational structure, and other similar factors.

An organization may operate both within and across national boundaries. Thus, both its competitive environment and its general environment may be performed either locally or globally. There may be many local national environments within which the organization operates if it is a global firm.

The Competitive Environment

The competitive environment consists of those elements that have a direct, ongoing relationship with, or an effect on, the organization as it transacts its business. It includes customers, competitors, suppliers, substitutes, and potential new entrants. It is part of the economic situation that firms face, but it is so important it is discussed as a separate environment. Changes in these factors are occurring at a rapid rate for most organizations.

CUSTOMERS
Customers consume the organization's products or services and include people or organizations. Thanks to management critics such as Thomas J. Peters and Robert H. Waterman, Jr.,[21] organizations have begun to focus their attention on the importance of the customer. The customer is becoming a focal point of organizational competitive efforts, instead of being viewed as a problem. Phy-

Dunkin Donuts is typical of most businesses—it has many competitors—other donut chains, mom and pop bakeries, and the in-store bakeries in grocery stores, to name a few. (SOURCE © John Abbott)

sicians and hospitals are providing better service to their patients, colleges are more concerned about their students' welfare, and many airlines are taking better care of their passengers.

COMPETITORS

Competitors are other organizations that market similar products or services to the same set of customers. For example, in the personal computer industry, Apple Computer with its unique, user-friendly Macintosh PC, competes with IBM, Compaq, and others. IBM competes on the strength of its name and reputation. Compaq competes on the basis of power, speed, and features.

SUPPLIERS

Suppliers provide the organization with the materials it uses to produce outputs. These may be raw materials, subassemblies, labor, computer programs, energy, or a host of other factors the organization takes in as inputs and transforms into outputs. In the manufacturing process, relationships with suppliers have become extremely critical in recent years, as organizations attempt to improve product quality. One of the major suppliers is labor. Every organization has to have the right people with the right skills at the right time to perform the necessary jobs to achieve organizational objectives. Numerous factors affect the labor supply—unions, demographics, competitors, wages, and the growth of the economy. In coping with this myriad of factors, various strategies must be used. Tupperware, for example, has made increasing use of benefits to entice more women into their work force in recent years because women have begun to seek employment in other than part-time jobs.[22]

SUBSTITUTES

Substitutes include those products that have a similar function to a company's products. Automobiles are substitutes for airplanes, for example. Firms are concerned about substitutes because they may reduce the sales of its products.

THREAT OF NEW ENTRANTS

Firms must be concerned about the threat of new entrants into the industry because these often greatly affect its ability to compete successfully. When Wendy's entered the fast-food market in 1969, they took market share from McDonald's, Burger King, Kentucky Fried Chicken, and others.

The General Environment

The **general environment** tends to affect business on a less than day-to-day basis and is not directly a competitive factor, although technology greatly affects a firm's ability to compete. Its dimensions include technology, society and culture, the economy, and the law and politics. Organizations must constantly scan this general environment, as well as the competitive environment, for signals of threats and opportunities. Companies that operate in more than one country are confronted with many, usually different, general environments. Even in the same country, different environments may exist.

TECHNOLOGY

The **technology** element includes existing technology as well as advances in technology. One of the principal means by which organizations compete is by differentiating their products or services from those of other firms. This means somehow improving upon current products or creating new ones. One of the main ways this may occur is through the employment of new technology. Radial

Society and culture are becoming more similar in countries throughout the world as this presence of vending machines and Coca-Cola in Japan suggests. (SOURCE © Frilet/SIPA)

tires replaced standard ply tires. The digital watch replaced the pin-lever watch. Xerox machines replaced carbon copies. The laser is replacing the high-speed drill in dentistry. According to one study, once a major technological advancement has been introduced in an industry, the formerly dominant firms find it almost impossible to recover.[23] Thus, it behooves an organization not only to stay current with technology, but to be on the technological edge, and/or have the ability to bring a product to market very rapidly, using its own technology or that of others.[24]

SOCIETY AND CULTURE

The **societal/cultural** element of the general environment includes the social, cultural, and demographic characteristics of the society(ies) within which an organization operates. If, for example, a society becomes more concerned about environmental pollution, as was discussed in the opening management challenge, organizations will be forced to respond to society's values in that area. These will often be expressed in laws involving the legal/political element. Such events were occurring in the late 1980s as a new wave of social activism is rising. Americans, and others around the globe, have begun a new war on pollution.[25] Other values that might affect business include such factors as the perceived importance of health care in an aging population, the importance of education, and the importance of equal employment opportunity. Demographic trends include an aging population, a baby boom segment, and a geographic shift of populations in the United States and Europe from north to south.

> AT EXXON: *Top management had apparently failed to modify Exxon's values to be more compatible with society's, relative to environmental pollution. Alyeska had also failed in this regard.*

THE ECONOMY

The **economy** element includes the general economic condition of the country or countries, region or regions, in which the organization functions. Factors such as the rate of inflation, the level of interest rates, the value of currencies, consumer purchasing power, the level of employment, the amount of budget deficit, the trade deficit with foreign countries, and numerous other factors must be analyzed for their impact upon the organization. In the late 1980s, the decline of the value of the dollar, for example, made many U.S. firms more competitive globally, resulting in additional exports, which helped offset record imports.

One firm which has rebounded from an early 1980s slump to compel successfully in the global marketplace is Caterpillar. This Caterpillar product is being shipped to a foreign market. To achieve such ends, Caterpillar had to greatly increase its productivity, especially by cutting costs. (SOURCE © Robert Holmgren)

Similarly, unemployment rates of 2 percent or less in the Boston area caused wages to skyrocket there. Boston's employers experienced great difficulty in finding sufficient numbers of qualified personnel. Low-level service jobs were especially affected. Hamburger chains offered as much as $9.50 per hour in 1988 for front-line service employees. One final example is that, as interest rates rise, invariably the housing market declines, affecting not only builders and resellers, but building supply companies, real estate agents, and the overall economy.

LEGAL-POLITICAL

The **legal-political** segment includes laws and regulations at local, state, federal, and international levels, as well as those individuals and organizations that

MANAGEMENT CHALLENGE 4.1

Cracks in the Ivory Tower

Oxford University, famed for its ancient architecture adorned with Gothic spires, and the beneficiary of eight centuries of benevolent patronage from a host of notaries, including Henry VIII, Cardinal Wolsey, and Cecil Rhodes, found itself confronted with major budget cuts by Prime Minister Margaret Thatcher. Thatcher has been determined to make England's universities more self-sufficient and businesslike in their operations. The government was cutting Oxford's $185 million operating budget by 11 percent over a four-year period. Government funds, which at one time paid two-thirds of Oxford's operating budget, paid only 45 percent in 1988. A hundred academic posts were vacant during 1988, due to a lack of funds. An estimated total of 2,000 positions were vacant in various British universities, including six senior historians from Oxford who had accepted much higher paying positions in the United States.

One of the major consequences of the "brain drain" at Oxford was a change in the time-honored tradition of the tutorial, the one-on-one instruction of under-

attempt to influence the legal environment, such as lobbyists and numerous protest groups. Federal and state governments have issued numerous laws related to the treatment of unionized workers, occupational safety and health, equal employment opportunity, protection of the physical environment, protection of the consumer, and honesty in business practices. Ironically the impact of state regulations has increased in the 1980s, at a time when the federal government seemed to be decreasing its tendency to influence business.[26]

Numerous groups attempt to influence government at various levels in their efforts to regulate business and other organizations. The National Association for the Advancement of Colored People (NAACP), for example, historically lobbies heavily for civil rights legislation and the enforcement of equal opportunity laws. The Sierra Club has similarly pursued increased protection for the physical environment. Organizations such as MADD (Mothers Against Drunk Drivers) have initiated legislation that may affect companies that sell alcoholic beverages. On the other hand, business organizations themselves may attempt to influence laws that affect their political situations through lobbyists and PACs (Political Action Committees).

The legal-political environment is subject to constant change. Changes are occurring everywhere on the globe for organizations of all kinds, as Management Challenge 4.1 indicates.

External Organizational Environments: Stability and Complexity

Tom Burns and G. M. Stalker, British researchers, first brought our attention to two types of organizational environments: stable and unstable. Stable environments have little change. Unstable environments are full of change. Burns and Stalker also identified organizational design responses to these external environments: mechanistic and organic.[27] The mechanistic model focuses on

graduates. Tutorials in the future are expected to be at least two-on-one. One of Oxford's major problems is that it is extremely rich in assets that do not produce any income. The library's books are being held together in many cases by ribbons. It will take ten years to computerize the card catalogue. Purchases of books and periodicals have been cut back. The library's hours have been shortened, and research opportunities have all but dried up.

Faced with such dire straits, Oxford's staid management decided to take up the ungentlemanly art of fund raising. Thus, in 1988 it launched a $400 million American-style fund-raising campaign to improve Oxford's library, laboratories, and staff. They hired Henry Drucker, an American political scientist, to be its first fund-raising director, recognizing that magnificent buildings and art collections don't pay salaries. A major target of the endowment campaign will be Oxford's 8,000 American graduates, corporations, and charitable foundations. Oxford hopes to raise 30 percent of the total needed from these sources. It is even setting up a three-person fund-raising office in Japan because its reputation there is legendary.

SOURCE: Peter Schmeisser and Wendy Anderson, "Cracks in the Ivory Tower," *U.S. News & World Report* (December 5, 1988), pp. 65–66.

hierarchical relationships and tends to be rigid in the worst sense of the word "bureaucratic." Organic organizations are characterized essentially by openness, responsiveness, and a lack of hierarchy of authority.[28]

Their study indicated that firms operating in stable environments tend to use mechanistic organizational designs, whereas firms operating in unstable environments tend to use organic organizational designs. The necessity for employing these particular designs in those types of situations has been demonstrated over and over. As mechanistic firms encounter changeful environments, they find the transition difficult, if not impossible. Those organizations that are able to make the transition to an organic structure will survive, those that don't will fail. Contrast, for example, Eastern Airlines and American Airlines. American Airlines was able to adapt to changes in its environment. It became more organic. Eastern Airlines remained mechanistic and bureaucratic.[29] Burns and Stalker were quick to recognize that no organization is purely mechanistic or organic, both will continue to exist in some form. Burns and Stalker do not indicate that either design is superior. Rather, each design best fits a particular environmental situation. But as organizations begin to face more unstable environments, the organic structure is going to be the more preferred design.

Robert B. Duncan, academician, later conceptualized the environment as not just an issue of stability, but also one of complexity.[30] Simple environments have few products, few competitors, few locations, and simple technology. Complex environments usually have a large number of products, a large number of geographic locations, a change in consumers or their nature, and they often involve complex technology. Figure 4.2 suggests the possible combinations of these factors—environmental complexity and environmental change—indicating the resulting degree of uncertainty in each situation. Environments of increasing levels of instability and complexity exist now and are forecasted for most organizations in the future. Thus, Figure 4.2 shows relative degrees of these factors, as few firms exist as largely simple or unstable environments anymore. This rapidly changing and more complex environment has caused CEOs to need broader-based experience and to spend more time on the external environment than ever before.[31]

AT EXXON: *Exxon's competitive environment is rather stable, but it is also complex. Exxon appears to be treating it as if it were simple. Their response to an environmental catastrophe was slow and measured, as it might have been in response to a competitor's action. Their response should have better recognized the complexity and gravity of the situation.*

The Organization/Environment Interface

Organizations can interface with their environments in either of two ways: they can adapt to them or change them.

Adapting to the Environment

Organizations adapt to their environments primarily through the strategic planning process, in which they assess the situation, establish major objectives, and establish strategic plans accordingly. To be adaptive, an organization needs a structure that is flexible and responsive—organic. Normally this means allowing for decision making by the managers directly involved in a situation, as opposed to all major decisions being made by top management.

Changing the Environment

Companies have several strategic and tactical options for changing their environments: public relations, politics, trade associations, and illegal activities.

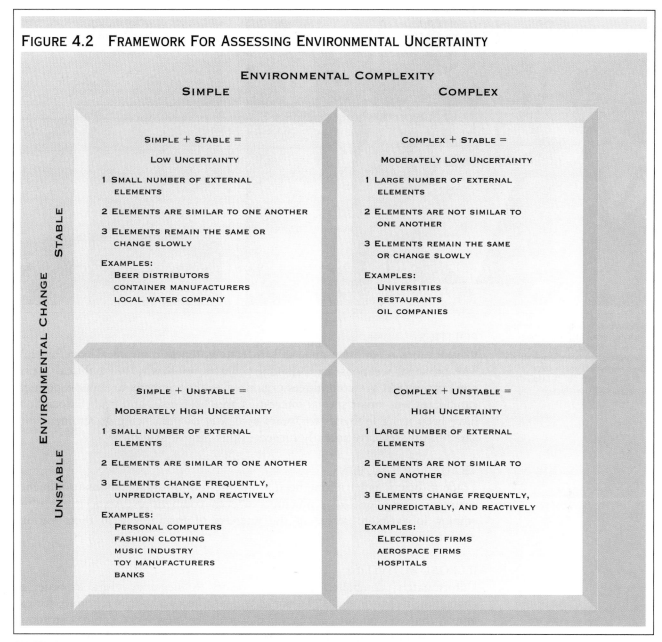

FIGURE 4.2 FRAMEWORK FOR ASSESSING ENVIRONMENTAL UNCERTAINTY

ENVIRONMENTAL COMPLEXITY

SIMPLE   COMPLEX

STABLE

SIMPLE + STABLE =

LOW UNCERTAINTY

1 SMALL NUMBER OF EXTERNAL
  ELEMENTS

2 ELEMENTS ARE SIMILAR TO ONE ANOTHER

3 ELEMENTS REMAIN THE SAME OR
  CHANGE SLOWLY

EXAMPLES:
  BEER DISTRIBUTORS
  CONTAINER MANUFACTURERS
  LOCAL WATER COMPANY

COMPLEX + STABLE =

MODERATELY LOW UNCERTAINTY

1 LARGE NUMBER OF EXTERNAL
  ELEMENTS

2 ELEMENTS ARE NOT SIMILAR TO
  ONE ANOTHER

3 ELEMENTS REMAIN THE SAME
  OR CHANGE SLOWLY

EXAMPLES:
  UNIVERSITIES
  RESTAURANTS
  OIL COMPANIES

UNSTABLE

SIMPLE + UNSTABLE =

MODERATELY HIGH UNCERTAINTY

1 SMALL NUMBER OF EXTERNAL
  ELEMENTS

2 ELEMENTS ARE SIMILAR TO ONE ANOTHER

3 ELEMENTS CHANGE FREQUENTLY,
  UNPREDICTABLY, AND REACTIVELY

EXAMPLES:
  PERSONAL COMPUTERS
  FASHION CLOTHING
  MUSIC INDUSTRY
  TOY MANUFACTURERS
  BANKS

COMPLEX + UNSTABLE =

HIGH UNCERTAINTY

1 LARGE NUMBER OF EXTERNAL
  ELEMENTS

2 ELEMENTS ARE NOT SIMILAR TO
  ONE ANOTHER

3 ELEMENTS CHANGE FREQUENTLY,
  UNPREDICTABLY, AND REACTIVELY

EXAMPLES:
  ELECTRONICS FIRMS
  AEROSPACE FIRMS
  HOSPITALS

ENVIRONMENTAL CHANGE

SOURCE: ADAPTED AND REPRINTED FROM "CHARACTERISTICS OF PERCEIVED ENVIRONMENTS AND PERCEIVED ENVIRONMENTAL UNCERTAINTY" BY ROBERT B. DUNCAN, PUBLISHED IN ADMINISTRATIVE SCIENCE QUARTERLY 17(3) (1972): 313-327 BY PERMISSION OF THE ADMINISTRATIVE SCIENCE QUARTERLY COPYRIGHT © 1972 BY CORNELL UNIVERSITY. EXAMPLES ABOVE WERE EDITED FOR THE 1990 ENVIRONMENT.

PUBLIC RELATIONS

Through the media, and often through advertising, firms may influence various conditions within their environments. Advertising is most often used to stimulate demand, but it can also be used to influence public opinion for other reasons. For example, probably the group of firms most concerned in the late 1980s and early 1990s about their ability to be socially responsible are members of the chemical industry. They are frankly running scared. And so they have become more socially responsive. DuPont, for example, has vowed to stop making chlorofluorocarbons by the end of the 1990s, in order to help protect the earth's ozone layer. Monsanto Company has promised to reduce its hazardous air emissions by 90 percent by 1992.[32]

These Du Pont scientists are searching for a solution to the fluorocarbon problem which has led to the hole in the world's ozone layer, shown in this artistic representation. (SOURCE (a) © John Abbott; (b) © Michael Gilbert/Photo Researchers)

POLITICS

Corporations often attempt to influence state, federal, and local governments. The principal weapons are personal contacts, lobbyists, and **political action committees (PACs)**—committees organized by the company to support political candidates who favor special interests. Large businesses and trade associations have been using lobbyists for years as a way of influencing government, but small businesses have recently turned to this means, as well.[33]

TRADE ASSOCIATIONS

Trade associations have long been a favorite tool of organizations to influence customers, suppliers, government, and even competition. Associations often employ lobbyists to represent the interests of members with these various constituencies.

ILLEGAL ACTIVITIES

Unfortunately, companies sometimes resort to illegal activities in order to change their environments. To some, it seems necessary. It is reported, for example, that you cannot be a major player in the New York City construction industry without paying bribes, often to organized crime.[34] Many times firms simply yield to the pressures of competition and commit such acts to beat out competition. Such was the case with the Anheuser-Busch and General Dynamics executives noted in the beginning of the chapter.

Social Power and Social Responsibility

The organization interacts with a large number of constituents in its environments, each of which may be impacted on by actions that the organization takes. These constituents may in turn take actions that will affect the organization. Because of its tremendous amount of social power—the power to influence various constituents—business is perceived by many components of society as inheriting a commensurate level of social responsibility.[35] **Social responsibility** may be defined as the obligation of an organization to solve problems and take actions that further the best interests of both society and the company.[36]

While this definition seems relatively straightforward, what constitutes social responsibility in practice is much more difficult to discern. For example, if a company dumps certain pollutants into a river that have been approved for dumping by state and federal law, thereby contaminating the water supply for a city, is this socially responsible? Or when Japanese firms flood the American market with products, selling them below cost in order to gain market share, though the consumer may benefit, is this act socially responsible? Numerous reasons for and against corporate social responsibility have been identified. These are revealed in Table 4.2.

Table 4.2. Summary of Major Arguments For and Against Business Social Responsibility

For Social Responsibility
1. It is in the best interest of a business to promote and improve the communities where it does business.
2. Social actions can be profitable.
3. It is the ethical thing to do.
4. It improves the public image of the firm.
5. It increases the viability of the business system. Business exists because it gives society benefits. Society can amend or take away its charter. This is the "iron law of responsibility."
6. It is necessary to avoid government regulation.
7. Sociocultural norms require it.
8. Laws cannot be passed for all circumstances. Thus, business must assume responsibility to maintain an orderly legal society.
9. It is in the stockholders' best interest. It will improve the price of stock in the long run because the stock market will view the company as less risky and open to public attack and therefore award it a higher price-earnings ratio.
10. Society should give business a chance to solve social problems that government has failed to solve.
11. Business, by some groups, is considered to be the institution with the financial and human resources to solve social problems.
12. Prevention of problems is better than cures—so let business solve problems before they become too great.

Against Social Responsibility
1. It might be illegal.
2. Business plus government equals monolith.
3. Social actions cannot be measured.
4. It violates profit maximization.
5. The cost of social responsibility is too great and would increase prices too much.
6. Business lacks the social skills to solve societal problems.
7. It would dilute business's primary purposes.
8. It would weaken the U.S. balance of payments because the price of goods will have to go up to pay for social programs.
9. Business already has too much power. Such involvement would make business too powerful.
10. Business lacks accountability to the public. Thus, the public would have no control over its social environment.
11. Such business involvement lacks broad public support.

SOURCE: R. Joseph Mansen, Jr., "The Social Attitudes of Management," in Joseph W. McGuire, ed., *Contemporary Management* (Englewood Cliffs, N.J.: Prentice-Hall, 1974), p. 616.

Contrasting Views of Social Responsibility

There are varying views on what constitutes social responsibility. Social responsibility is both an issue of obedience to the law and of ethics—the adherence to society's norms and values.[37] (What is ethical varies with the values and norms that society expresses.)[38] There are at least three major contrasting views of social responsibility—the profit concept, the stakeholder concept, and social power/social responsibility concept.

THE PROFIT CONCEPT

Milton Friedman, Nobel laureate in economics, the primary proponent of the profit concept, takes a narrow view of the corporation's social responsibility. He believes that the sole social responsibility of an organization is to make a profit. The **profit concept** embodies his belief that the single purpose of a business is "To use its resources and energy and activities to increase its profits, so long as it stays within the rules of the game."[39] Friedman has expressed the viewpoint of the traditional economist—the free market system is the best system for regulating the conduct of a business, and it is up to society to establish the rules within which it operates.

STAKEHOLDER CONCEPT

Stakeholders are all those who are directly or indirectly affected by the decisions of the organization. The **stakeholder concept** suggests that management must account for its impact on its stakeholders when it makes decisions, and it must take their interests into account.[40] Just determining what is socially responsible depends upon the values placed upon the leading interests of each of the stakeholder groups. Some may be in conflict—for example, stockholders versus suppliers versus consumers versus special-interest groups. The organization must balance all these successfully if it is to be a truly socially responsible corporate citizen.

SOCIAL POWER/SOCIAL RESPONSIBILITY CONCEPT

The **social power/social responsibility concept** suggests that business has a certain social responsibility because of the power that it wields. If it fails to adhere to those social responsibilities, the business will find itself at the mercy of societal constraints upon its operations. This is the "Iron Law of Social Responsibility."[41] This clearly happened in the 1960s and 1970s. Numerous laws were passed to make business adhere to society's interests in the areas of equal employment opportunity, water pollution, air pollution, occupational safety and health, and consumerism. Because companies had not adhered to society's norms, society took action and created laws to force them to do so.

These three contrasting perspectives are summarized as follows:

1. Organizations should seek a profit but play within the rules of the game. If businesses don't play within the rules of the game, they may be punished.
2. Organizations should administer to the needs of their stakeholders.
3. With social power comes social responsibility.

Recognizing these differing viewpoints, Archie Carroll, management researcher and author, has developed a model of social responsibility to incorporate them. More fundamentally, in reviewing the literature on social responsibility, he detected three fundamental perspectives regarding social responsibility:

1. Defining it. (The perspective discussed thus far.)
2. Enumerating the issues for which social responsibility exists—pollution control, equal employment opportunity, consumerism, occupational safety and health, and so on.
3. Determining the philosophy of social response.

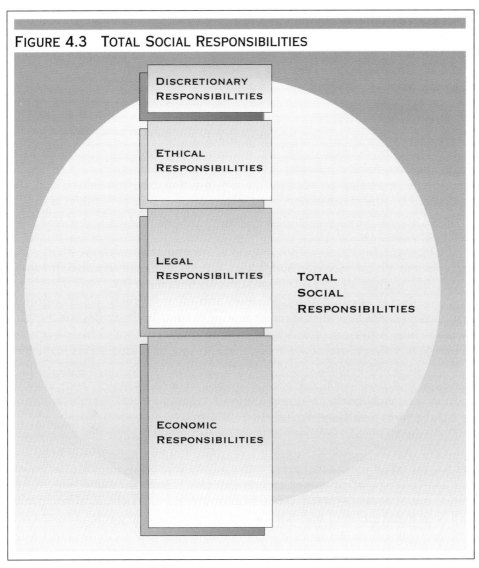

FIGURE 4.3 TOTAL SOCIAL RESPONSIBILITIES

DISCRETIONARY RESPONSIBILITIES

ETHICAL RESPONSIBILITIES

LEGAL RESPONSIBILITIES

TOTAL SOCIAL RESPONSIBILITIES

ECONOMIC RESPONSIBILITIES

SOURCE: ARCHIE CARROLL, "A THREE DIMENSIONAL CONCEPTUAL MODEL OF CORPORATE PERFORMANCE," ACADEMY OF MANAGEMENT REVIEW, 1979, P. 500.

Levels of Responsibility

Carroll's model of the levels of responsibility consists of four principal components: economic, legal, ethical, and discretionary responsibility, as revealed in Figure 4.3.[42] The four levels encompass the three principal perspectives: profit, stakeholder, and social power.

ECONOMIC RESPONSIBILITIES
A business is first of all an economic unit in society. Its economic responsibility is to make a profit. "All other business rules are predicated on this fundamental assumption."[43]

LEGAL RESPONSIBILITY
Business must also play within the rules. No one would view it as socially responsible if it broke the law to obtain profits. Society has laid out laws, rules, and regulations, thousands of which exist at the international, federal, state, and local government levels to regulate all types of businesses. Government can

affect business through legislation, judicial actions, agency administration (bureaucracy), or executive actions, as Figure 4.4. reveals. Some legitimate businesses break laws or rules, as the "Pentagate Scandal" of the late 1980s revealed. But such behavior is not condoned by society, and so firms have not only an economic responsibility, but also a legal one.

ETHICAL RESPONSIBILITY

Ethical responsibility includes behaviors that fit within the norms of society, the organization, the individual, and the profession that have not necessarily been made into law. **Ethical behavior** is behavior that is acceptable and considered appropriate according to society, the organization, the individual, and the profession.[44] **Unethical behavior** is outside the norms of society.[44] **Ethics** is simply the rules that say what is right and wrong, as defined by a particular reference group or individual.[45]

The manager functions within a society. **Societal ethics** defines what is acceptable and ethical behavior within that society. The manager also functions within an organization. **Organizational ethics** defines those behaviors considered ethical within an organization. Managers also often function within a profession, and many believe management is a profession itself. **Professional ethics** includes those behaviors prescribed by professional associations as appropriate to members of that profession. Finally, managers are individuals. **Personal ethics** is behavior the individual considers to be appropriate and is derived from a variety of sources: societal, organizational, professional, as well as from religious institutions, family norms, and peer groups. A crisis can reveal our ethical values, as Management Challenge 4.2 reveals.

The complexity of corporate ethics becomes clearer when one examines a company like W. R. Grace. Grace is nationally known for its efforts to reduce the federal deficit by running provocative ads on television, showing the potential consequences of continued federal excesses. Yet at the same time, it has settled out of court for water contamination by one of its chemical companies and been found guilty of fraudulently obtaining an oil and gas loan from Continental Illinois National Bank & Trust Company, for which it was fined $100 million.[46]

In our global society, what is perceived to be ethical in one society is not ethical in another. This often poses a problem for businesses. Multinational corporations find, for example, that in most Third World countries, bribery is a way of doing business. However, it is illegal in the United States, and it is illegal for U.S. businesses to commit bribery, even in countries where it is considered to be legal.[47] Despite the apparent need to do so, some companies, such as Ford Motor Company, have refused to pay bribes in order to do business in foreign countries.[48]

DISCRETIONARY RESPONSIBILITIES

Discretionary responsibilities are those for which there are no societal laws, rules, or ethical statements, but for which expectations might exist. These are matters of personal choice. Discretionary responsibilities are the highest form of social responsibility because they are voluntary. This is not just charitable giving, although that plays an important part. Dayton-Hudson department stores, for example, have given 5 percent of their taxable income to charitable institutions since 1945 and urge other corporations to do so, as well.[49] Another example of discretionary social responsibility, one which also assisted the company, was John Hancock's sponsorship of the Boston Marathon. Hancock's sponsorship of the marathon benefited the community because it attracted star runners for its field. The company benefited because it received free exposure.[50]

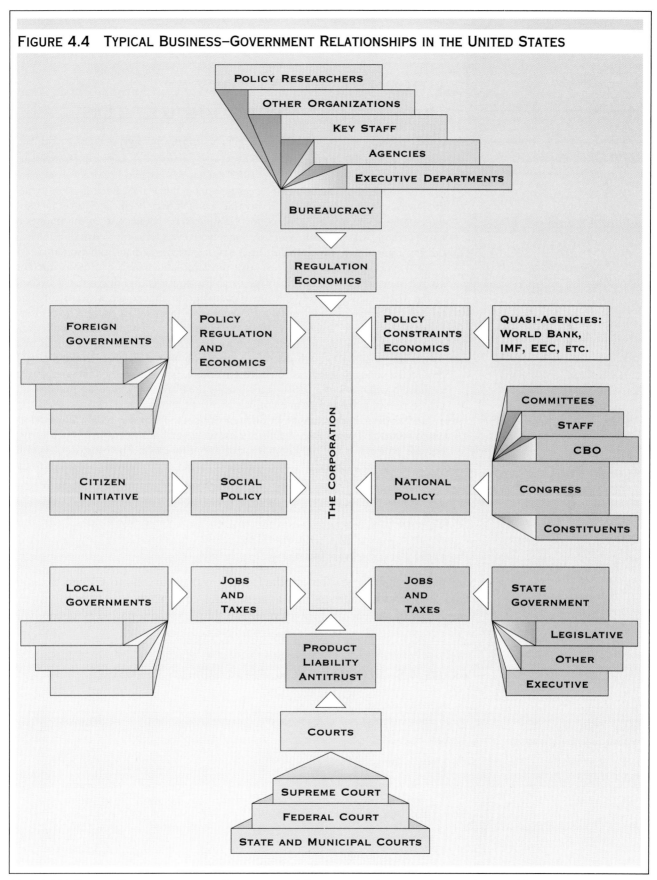

FIGURE 4.4   TYPICAL BUSINESS–GOVERNMENT RELATIONSHIPS IN THE UNITED STATES

POLICY RESEARCHERS

OTHER ORGANIZATIONS

KEY STAFF

AGENCIES

EXECUTIVE DEPARTMENTS

BUREAUCRACY

REGULATION ECONOMICS

FOREIGN GOVERNMENTS

POLICY REGULATION AND ECONOMICS

POLICY CONSTRAINTS ECONOMICS

QUASI-AGENCIES: WORLD BANK, IMF, EEC, ETC.

COMMITTEES

STAFF

CBO

THE CORPORATION

CITIZEN INITIATIVE

SOCIAL POLICY

NATIONAL POLICY

CONGRESS

CONSTITUENTS

LOCAL GOVERNMENTS

JOBS AND TAXES

JOBS AND TAXES

STATE GOVERNMENT

LEGISLATIVE

OTHER

EXECUTIVE

PRODUCT LIABILITY ANTITRUST

COURTS

SUPREME COURT

FEDERAL COURT

STATE AND MUNICIPAL COURTS

SOURCE: R. EDWARD FREEMAN, STRATEGIC MANAGEMENT: A STAKEHOLDER APPROACH (BOSTON: PITMAN, 1984), P. 15.
COPYRIGHT © 1984 BY R. EDWARD FREEMAN.

Uncommon Decency: Pacific Bell Responds to AIDS

Pacific Bell was headquartered in San Francisco, with 70,000 of its employees concentrated in San Francisco and Los Angeles, two cities with a high incidence of AIDS cases. It was estimated in 1989 that as few as two hundred or as many as two thousand of Pacific's employees may have had AIDS. Back in 1984, when little was known about AIDS, it became evident that Pacific Bell was facing a difficult situation. Some installers, for example, were refusing to install phones in houses where AIDS patients resided. Some were even refusing to install phones in the gay community, which makes up a major part of the San Francisco area.

Michael Eriksen, Pacific's preventive medicine and health education director, became concerned with Pacific's lack of ability to function operationally because of the AIDS crisis. In 1984 he began a campaign to change the way the company treated AIDS patients and to educate employees in order to prevent widespread havoc among them. When fewer than one business in ten had an AIDS policy and even fewer had AIDS education programs, Pacific determined that it would treat its workers with AIDS as they would anyone else with a life-threatening illness. It provided a series of seminars to educate workers. It was also the first company to produce a video about AIDS, a hard-hitting program that pulled no punches but helped reduce fears and calm emotions.

Jim Henderson, the company's director of human resources policy and services, noted bluntly, "People with AIDS are sick, we don't fire sick people." As it turned out this policy was not only humane, but also affordable. The company began to reexamine totally its health-care packages for long-term terminal patients. It found that by using hospices and other home-care programs, patients got better-quality

Identifying the Issues

Society has generally spelled out the issues it wants business to address through laws, rules, and regulations. But as new issues emerge, such as how to prevent destruction of the earth's protective ozone shield, often a period of debate will

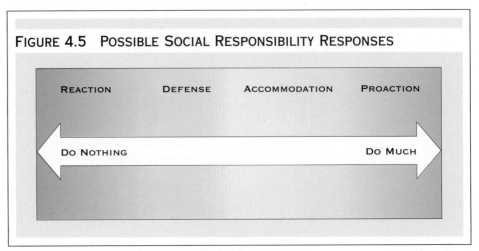

FIGURE 4.5 POSSIBLE SOCIAL RESPONSIBILITY RESPONSES

REACTION   DEFENSE   ACCOMMODATION   PROACTION

DO NOTHING   DO MUCH

SOURCE: ARCHIE CARROLL, "A THREE-DIMENSIONAL CONCEPTUAL MODEL OF CORPORATE PERFORMANCE," ACADEMY OF MANAGEMENT REVIEW, 1979, P. 502.

care than they would receive in a hospital. In addition, the company saved literally millions of dollars. They found that using this system, the average AIDS patient cost no more to treat than was to be expected with other terminal illnesses, such as cancer. At the urging of Eriksen, the company also published information about AIDS in their corporate newspaper "Update." The first article appeared on July 22, 1985, the same day Rock Hudson revealed publicly that he had AIDS.

Pacific Bell has historically been a conservative company and a great deal of persuasion was necessary to adopt this approach. It was Steve Poulter, Pacific's director of consumer affairs, who pushed hard to reduce the skepticism of top management. He was able to convince them that the company's competitive situation could be improved if the company adopted an AIDS policy and education program, especially because the company had been perceived as a negative force in the very dominantly gay parts of San Francisco. The company had the opportunity to do good and at the same time do good for itself.

One Pacific Bell manager, a Mormon with eight children and twenty grandchildren, whose heroes were John Wayne and George Patton, was totally transformed by the AIDS crisis, when one of his repair men, Dave Goodenough, contracted AIDS. Chuck Woodman had been very negative about homosexuals, but the whole process of working with Goodenough and keeping him employed changed his whole attitude. He commented that it was the toughest managerial challenge in his four years with Pacific, "When I look at where I was and where I am now, AIDS has had a bigger impact on my thinking about people than anything I have come up against." Woodman educated himself about AIDS and became somewhat of an advocate for helping AIDS patients. Now twenty-five of his 750 employees have been diagnosed with AIDS. Chuck juggles his schedule so that all can work when they are able to.

SOURCE: David Kirp, "Uncommon Decency: Pacific Bell Responds to AIDS," *Harvard Business Review* (May–June 1989), pp. 140–151.

ensue before, or even if, response to such issues becomes mandated by law. Businesses must scan their environments not just for competitive factors, but for social responsibility issues, as well.

The Philosophy of Responsiveness

When confronted with social demands, an organization may respond in four principal ways, ranging from very uncooperative to extremely cooperative: reactive, defensive, accommodative, and proactive.[51] These postures are highlighted in Figure 4.5.

REACTIVE

Reactive social responsibility activities means that the organization "fights all the way" against taking responsibility for its actions.[52] It might typically deny involvement, it might deny the evidence against it, and it would probably attempt to obstruct those who would show it was irresponsible. The company might accept its economic responsibility but deny its legal and ethical responsibilities.

DEFENSIVE

Defensive social responsibility response occurs when the company admits that it made a mistake but defends its position as having been caught up in circumstances beyond its control; it may even take minor actions to attempt to offset

AT EXXON: *In the oil spill at Valdez, Exxon followed a reactive strategy to some degree. Lee Raymond, Exxon's president, told ABC News that he blamed "ultimately the Coast Guard" for delaying use of dispersants. His position was contradicted by the available evidence. Alyeska, the pipeline service company, also followed this strategy, claiming that its unit "did an excellent job" of responding to the spill, again contradicted by available evidence: its equipment was not prepared to take those actions it said it could.*

its errors. When General Dynamics, the nation's number one defense contractor, came under target of military auditors, congressional committees, and the Justice Department in 1985, Chairman and CEO David S. Lewis testified, "I'm not here to say that our company is perfect, but I refuse to accept any portrayal of our company or its people as being dishonest or lacking integrity in our dealings with the United States Government. . . ." He complained that General Dynamics was being "badly maligned by forces beyond our control."[53] This statement was made despite substantial evidence of wrongdoing by the company.

ACCOMMODATIVE

The **accommodative social response** means that the company has accepted its economic, legal, and ethical responsibilities, although sometimes it does so under pressure. The company is willing to take action to adhere to society's demands in those three areas. General Electric Company has provided a mobile laboratory to test for chemical pollutants in Connecticut's soil. The Olin Corporation is underwriting environmental law enforcement in Louisiana. Bethlehem Steel Corporation is helping to clean up the Chesapeake Bay. These corporate actions weren't voluntary. They were the consequence of "citizens suits," a popular weapon in the fight against industrial polluters. Companies are being sued more frequently than ever before by citizens seeking redress for damages to society. An estimated six hundred such suits occurred from 1980 to 1987, and many more are expected in the near future. As social activism becomes more prominent, companies are more and more likely voluntarily to take action, or at least to settle out of court and agree to take action in order to avoid stiffer penalties.[54] Dow Chemical Company and the Sierra Club have joined together to endorse a proposed federal law to reduce sharply hazardous waste production. These actions are all taken principally because firms recognize that they must be socially responsible. They are doing these things voluntarily because they recognize that if they don't, citizen pressure groups may force them into even more stringent situations.[55]

AT EXXON: *Lee Raymond indicated that Exxon was victimized by factors beyond their control—yet Exxon failed, despite pleas from fishermen, to mobilize squads of private fishing boats ready to rush to the disaster scene.*

MANAGEMENT CHALLENGE 4.3

Florida Power & Light Company Shows Innovative Ways of Coexisting with the Environment

For years power companies have been perceived as rampant destroyers of the environment, moving in and laying waste to many species of animals and plants. Florida Power & Light Company (FPL), along with many other utilities, has come to recognize that living with the environment is a requirement of doing business. Ross Wilcox, the company's chief ecologist, takes numerous actions to help preserve the state's fragile ecology. For example, he has lobbied plant managers at the Turkey Point, Florida, nuclear plant to seek their assistance in creating buffer zones around crocodile nests in the company's cooling canals, thus protecting one of only three preserves where crocodiles are known to have nesting areas. (The others are in the Everglades National Park and in a wildlife refuge in north Key Largo.)

PROACTIVE

In pursuing **proactive social response,** a firm goes beyond what is legally and ethically required. It leads the industry, seeking ways to improve communities. Typical of this approach is that taken by American Express. "At American Express, we measure performance by profitability and return on investment. There is, however, another significant measure: how we fulfill our responsibility to the communities from which our profits are derived. Public responsibility is a fundamental corporate value at American Express."[56] American Express has long been a leader in many areas of social responsibility: equal employment of minorities and women in businesses, philanthropy, employing and marketing to the disabled, protecting the interests of consumers, assisting worthy causes, practicing corporate ethics, and serving customers in times of crisis. American Express made one of the first postearthquake telex connections between Mexico and the outside world almost immediately after Mexico City's earthquake in 1985. It has recently increased its goals for hiring minorities, including four top management positions, and it has made a commitment to double its corporate contributions to the United Way for 1988 through 1991.[57]

Some other companies also have been innovative or proactively carrying out their social responsibilities, as the following Management Challenge 4.3 reveals.

Improving Social Responsiveness

There are two principal ways through which corporate social responsiveness can be improved: institutionalizing social responsibility through a social policy process (planning) and the social audit (control). The organization must also be concerned with its potential legal liabilities, and therefore consider a litigation audit.

FPL is protecting one of the nation's most fragile environments partly because it does business in that area. State and federal laws, such as the endangered species act, require it to work to retain as much of the natural ecology as possible. But FPL has gone beyond that. It has taken several innovative actions to protect manatees (sea cows), crocodiles, and Florida's sea turtles. FPL won the Florida Audubon Society award for innovation in 1986. It has gone to especially great lengths to protect manatees. Almost 900 of the state's 1,200 manatees have been spotted in the waters near five of FPL's plants. The manatees seek out the warm waters near power plants during colder weather, and the power company must be careful to protect them. In January 1985, under pressure from Florida's governor's office, FPL went to great lengths to protect manatees by keeping its Fort Myers plant running for eleven days when economics justified closing it down. This was done to keep the water warm for nearly 100 manatees gathered there. The company agreed to do it only on the condition it would not be asked to do it again. But subsequently FPL voluntarily drilled three underground wells, which cost it nearly half a million dollars, to tap the warmer groundwater to help the manatees in the future. Florida Power & Light started its environmental affairs office in 1972, and since then has been serious about its charge to protect and restore the environment.

SOURCE: Eric Morgenthaller, "Ecology Effort: A Florida Utility Earns Naturalists' Praise for Guarding Wildlife," *Wall Street Journal* 7 May, 1987, pp. 1, 19.

FIGURE 4.6 CONTRIBUTIONS OF BUSINESS ETHICS, CORPORATE SOCIAL RESPONSIBILITY, AND CORPORATE SOCIAL RESPONSIVENESS TO THE CORPORATE SOCIAL POLICY PROCESS

BUSINESS ETHICS

VALUE-BASED REFLECTION AND CHOICE CONCERNING THE MORAL SIGNIFICANCE OF INDIVIDUAL AND ORGANIZATIONAL ACTION BY BUSINESS DECISION MAKERS. THIS REFLECTION AND CHOICE EMANATES FROM AND PERTAINS TO CRITICAL ISSUES AND PROBLEMS CONFRONTING THE ORGANIZATION AND ITS LEADERS.

+

CORPORATE SOCIAL POLICY PROCESS

INSTITUTIONALIZATION WITHIN THE CORPORATION OF PROCESSES FACILITATING VALUE-BASED INDIVIDUAL AND ORGANIZATIONAL REFLECTION AND CHOICE REGARDING THE MORAL SIGNIFICANCE OF PERSONAL AND CORPORATE ACTION. INDIVIDUAL AND COLLECTIVE EXAMINATION OF THE LIKELY OVERALL CONSEQUENCES OF SUCH ACTIONS, THEREBY ENABLING THE FIRM'S LEADERS BOTH INDIVIDUALLY AND COLLECTIVELY WITHIN THE ORGANIZATIONAL SETTING TO ANTICIPATE. RESPOND TO AND MANAGE DYNAMICALLY EVOLVING CLAIMS AND EXPECTATIONS OF INTERNAL AND EXTERNAL STAKEHOLDERS CONCERNING THE PRODUCTS (SPECIFIC ISSUES OR PROBLEM-RELATED CONSEQUENCES) OF ORGANIZATIONAL POLICIES AND BEHAVIOR.

=

CORPORATE SOCIAL RESPONSIBILITY

DISCERNMENT OF SPECIFIC ISSUES, PROBLEMS, EXPECTATIONS AND CLAIMS UPON BUSINESS ORGANIZATIONS AND THEIR LEADERS REGARDING THE CONSEQUENCES OF ORGANIZATIONAL POLICIES AND BEHAVIOR ON BOTH INTERNAL AND EXTERNAL STAKEHOLDERS. THE FOCUS IS UPON THE PRODUCTS OF CORPORATE ACTION.

+

CORPORATE SOCIAL RESPONSIVENESS

DEVELOPMENT OF INDIVIDUAL AND ORGANIZATIONAL PROCESSES FOR DETERMINING, IMPLEMENTING, AND EVALUATING THE FIRM'S CAPACITY TO ANTICIPATE, RESPOND AND MANAGE THE ISSUES AND PROBLEMS ARISING FROM THE DIVERSE CLAIMS AND EXPECTATIONS OF INTERNAL AND EXTERNAL STAKEHOLDERS.

SOURCE: EDWIN M. EPSTEIN, "THE CORPORATE SOCIAL POLICY PROCESS: BEYOND BUSINESS ETHICS, CORPORATE SOCIAL RESPONSIBILITY, AND CORPORATE SOCIAL RESPONSIVENESS." <u>CALIFORNIA MANAGEMENT REVIEW</u> (SPRING 1987), P. 107. COPYRIGHT 1987 BY THE REGENTS OF THE UNIVERSITY OF CALIFORNIA. REPRINTED FROM THE <u>CALIFORNIA MANAGEMENT REVIEW</u>, VOL. 29, NO. 3. BY PERMISSION OF THE REGENTS.

Corporate Social Policy Process

In the corporate social policy process, the organization institutionalizes the social responsibility needs and wants of society within the policy framework of the organization.[58] As reflected in Figure 4.6, the corporate social policy process is viewed as an all-encompassing way of institutionalizing the three key components discussed thus far in this chapter: business ethics, corporate social responsibility, and corporate social responsiveness. Without the institutionalization envisioned by this model, it is unlikely that the type of performance sought will be forthcoming. Kathleen Black, publisher of *USA Today,* offers an important insight into this process. She comments that the CEO must "make it happen." Al Neuharth, CEO of *USA Today*'s partner company, Gannett Company, Inc., made it happen with regard to equal employment opportunity. Neuharth tied bonuses and promotions to EEO goals. Gannett, and specifically *USA*

Today, have excellent statistics for hiring and promoting women and minorities. Black believes it was Neuharth's policies that made it happen. For example, middle management at *USA Today* was 34 percent female and 11 percent minority in 1989.[59]

The Social Audit

The second principal way in which organizations can improve social responsiveness is through management control. While the corporate social policy process attempts to use planning—goals, objectives, strategies, policies, rules, and procedures—to achieve corporate social responsiveness, it is necessary also to measure the performance of organizations in order to ascertain whether they have achieved corporate social responsiveness. The idea of an audit of an organization's social performance dates back to at least 1940.[60] Since that time the social audit has evolved not so much in concept but as to the particulars of what is audited and with respect to the recognition of what organizations ought to be accomplishing in social goals.[61] Social audits have been performed in a number of companies and for a number of issues—for example, for environmental pollution and equal employment opportunity.[62] In the 1980s interest in the social audit seems to have waned somewhat, but renewed interest should occur. Increased social activism seems to be gaining momentum in the early 1990s. Table 4.3 provides an example of how a company might "keep score" with its various stakeholders.

The Litigation Audit

David Silverstein, attorney, suggests that companies periodically perform a litigation audit to determine potential corporate exposure to litigation. This audit requires management first to recognize an evolving legal issue; second, to forecast its direction of movement; and third, to decide how best to respond. Many companies suffering from legal problems, such as Johns Manville, which knowingly exposed workers and customers to the hazards of asbestos, failed to follow this process and suffered financial loss.[63] Such an audit at least keeps firms moving toward society's requirements.

In a process repeated thousands of times across the nation, these workers are removing asbestos from building ceilings in order to eliminate the high probability of increased levels of cancer among those with offices or classrooms in these buildings. (SOURCE © P. Goudvis/Picture Group)

Corporate Social Responsibility and Profitability

There seem to be three principal views regarding the relationships between a company's social responsibility and its financial performance:

1. The first of these holds the view that firms incur costs from being socially responsible and that these will put them at an economic disadvantage compared to other firms.
2. The second perspective is that firms actually invest very little in corporate social responsibility and that firms actually benefit from socially responsible actions because they increase productivity or morale.
3. The last view is that the costs of social responsibility may be significant, but they may be offset by a reduction in other firm costs.[64]

A number of research studies have been performed attempting to analyze relationships between corporate responsibilities and financial performance

Table 4.3. A Sample Scorecard for "Keeping Score with Stakeholders"

Stakeholder Category	Possible Near-Term Measures	Possible Long-Term Measures
Customers	Sales ($ and volume) New customers Number of new customer needs met ("tries")	Growth in sales Turnover of customer base Ability to control price

Suppliers	Cost of raw material
	Delivery time
	Inventory
	Availability of raw material
		Growth rates of
		  Raw material costs
		  Delivery time
		  Inventory
		New ideas from suppliers

Financial Community	EPS (Earnings per share) Stock price Number of "buy" lists ROE (Return on equity)	Ability to convince Wall Street of strategy Growth in ROE
Employees	Number of suggestions Productivity Number of grievances	Number of internal promotions Turnover
Congress	Number of new pieces of legislation that affect the firm Access to key members and staff	Number of new regulations that affect industry Ratio of "cooperative" vs. "competitive" encounters
Consumer Advocate (CA)	Number of meetings Number of "hostile" encounters Number of times coalitions formed Number of legal actions	Number of changes in policy due to CA Number of CA initiated "calls for help"
Environmentalists	Number of meetings Number of hostile encounters Number of times coalitions formed Number of EPA complaints (Environmental Protection Agency) Number of legal actions	Number of changes in policy due to environmentalists Number of environmentalist "calls for help"

SOURCE: R. E. Freeman, *Strategic Management* (Boston: Pitman Publishing, Inc., 1984), p. 179. Copyright © 1984 by R. E. Freeman. Reprinted by permission.

(through stock market values and financial accounting measures). Reviews of these studies by Kenneth E. Aupperle, Archie B. Carroll, and John D. Hatfield; Philip L. Cochrane and Robert A. Wood; and A. Ullman, have revealed mixed results.

Thus, in some cases, there was a correlation between social responsibility and future performance, but not in others.[65] A study by Jean B. McGuire, Alison Sundgren, and Thomas Schneeweis revealed that past performance is more closely correlated with social responsibility than is future performance. These authors surmise that one possible explanation for this might be that firms with high levels of financial success may act more socially responsibly than firms that are not financially successful. They also found that firms that were socially responsible tended to take lower levels of risk than did firms that were not socially responsible.[66]

Mechanisms of Social Control with Which Managers Must Contend

Managers must contend with external social controls at several different levels of an organization or industry:

1. Those that focus on the individual firm or industry

2. Those that focus on the specific practices or business functions

3. Those that are systematic and apply to all firms in the industry or society[67]

Several different models or philosophies of control exist and may be used in each of three levels. For example, the government may attempt to let the market have more control over the company, perhaps bringing antitrust actions. Or, government may initiate regulations. Pressure groups may call for social audits. Stockholders may bring lawsuits against a company. Managers must formulate strategies for coping with these and other methods of social control.

Ethics

It is debatable whether anyone can really teach you ethics at this point in your life. What someone else can do is teach you how to think through an ethical dilemma, a situation in which there is a conflict between the firm's economic performance and its social performance. In most ethical dilemmas the ethical answer is obvious, but in many there are multiple alternatives, the consequences extend beyond the immediate decision, there are uncertain consequences, there are usually personal implications for the manager, and the available choices typically have mixed outcomes (positive and negative).[68] Your professor can help you identify what your values are and what some of the values of society are. When you are faced with an ethical dilemma in an organization, you will then be better able to know what to look for and how to think about the problem.[69]

The disconcerting reality about ethics is that often the "ethical signpost does not always point in the same direction."[70] There may be information indicating that opposite courses of action are equally appropriate. Furthermore, managers often have not only to resolve their own personal ethical dilemmas, but also make decisions for others, weighing numerous variables. Business ethics is "applied ethics." Managers have to come up with real answers. It isn't an academic debate; a manager must make decisions, as Table 4.4 suggests.

Table 4.4. Dimensions and Boundaries of Ethical Conduct

1. Business ethics is "applied" ethics. It has to come up with an answer, not just a debate. It relates to specific patterns of conduct, not eliminating but going beyond such generalized attributes as honesty or fairness.
2. Business ethics deals with relationships. It must be accepted as well as asserted; its validity depends upon mutual acceptance.
3. Business ethics can often be institutionalized, with systematic procedures and rules for administering and implementing them.
4. Business ethics is designed to provide a common denominator of understanding and communication between parties to a transaction or relationship, vastly simplifying the negotiation process by providing predictability and dependability in the conduct of affairs.
5. A business ethic (or pattern of conduct) is valid only for the area of common acceptance by the parties affected by the transaction involved.

SOURCE: Henry B. Arthur, "Making Business Ethics Useful," *Strategic Management Journal* (October–December 1984), pp. 319–332.

A corporate culture establishes its own values. There is a tremendous pressure to perform in an organization, and it often compromises personal principles. People tend to lose sight of their personal values because of the demands corporations have placed upon them.[71]

How the Individual Manager Should Decide

The issues are complex. Many variables often intervene in important decisions for managers. There are few guidelines, but academician Laura L. Nash has provided a list of twelve questions that managers should ask themselves when making a business decision, in order to make it ethically:

1. Have you defined the problem correctly?
2. How would you define the problem if you stood on the other side of the fence?
3. How did this situation occur in the first place?
4. To whom and to what do you give your loyalty as a person and as an employee?
5. What is your intention in making this decision?
6. How does this intention compare with the probable result?
7. Whom could your decision or action injure?
8. Can you discuss the problem with the affected parties before you make your decision?
9. Are you confident your decision will be as valid over a long period of time as it seems now?
10. Could you disclose without qualm your decision or action to your supervisor, your CEO, your board of directors, your family, and society as a whole?
11. What is the symbolic potential of your action if understood? If misunderstood?
12. Under what conditions would you allow exceptions to your stand?[72]

Arthur Bedeian, a management author, suggests that the toughest question the manager must answer is, "How willing are you to discuss your decision on national television with Mike Wallace on '60 Minutes' next Sunday evening?" He suggests that if your decision will really enhance the corporation's image when it gets national television exposure, it probably is an ethical decision.[73]

Among the firms in the most tenuous ethical positions are chemical companies and the waste disposal companies that represent them. The following Global Management Challenge discusses the problem of global ethics and global social responsibility for such firms.

How Companies Can Improve Ethical Performance

Companies have a variety of ways to improve ethical performance: codes of ethics, whistleblowing, ombudsmen, corporate committees, task forces, and inculturation programs.

CODE OF ETHICS

To help improve ethical conduct, more and more corporations are installing a code of ethics. A survey of a large number of U.S. firms conducted by the

Good Neighbors?

Firms in the industrialized West, especially those in plastics, chemicals, and similar industries, find themselves faced with an increasingly small number of places where they can dispose of industrial waste. More and more they are turning to waste management firms to dispose of their hazardous waste. This would seem simple enough, but does their responsibility end there?

Increasingly, waste management firms are exporting toxic shipments to Third World countries. At least 2.2 million tons of hazardous waste from the United States and other countries cross international borders every year, most of it perfectly legally. For example, the United States exports waste to Haiti, South Africa, Mexico, the Dominican Republic, Zimbabwe, Honduras, New Guinea, Costa Rica, the Philippines, Tonga, American Samoa, Venezuela, and Guyana. Many of these deals are made with top people in the governments of those countries.

Companies are not alone in such disposal actions. Some cities also hire waste management groups to dispose of garbage. The impact on some Third World countries has been horrendous. Environmental groups such as Greenpeace International question whether such practices, though legal, are really ethical. One must wonder whether firms could be considered socially responsible who knowingly hire waste management companies, realizing that the hazardous waste may be dumped on unknowing, unsuspecting citizens of Third World countries.

SOURCES: "Dirty Jobs, Sweet Profits," *U.S. News & World Report* (November 21, 1988), pp. 54–55; "Waste: A Stinking Mess," *Time* (January 2, 1989), pp. 44–47; and "The Global Poison Trade: How Toxic Waste Is Dumped on the Third World," *Newsweek* (November 7, 1988), pp. 66–67.

This Chem Dyne worker is sampling the contents of drums containing hazardous waste in preparation for their shipment to dumping sites. (SOURCE © Fred Nard/Black Star)

Conference Board, an independent, non-profit, business research organization, determined that 52 percent of them had such a code.[74] Companies such as Chemical Bank, Xerox, General Mills, and Johnson & Johnson have fired people for violating their credo. Most of these firms take their codes seriously, holding seminars to inform employees of what they expect.[75] How valuable are such codes? They have to help, but they are not a guarantee.[76] Part of the problem with codes of ethics is that they often don't match managers' personal values. In 1988 Hertz Car Rental Company admitted to overcharging motorists and insurance companies $13 million for repairs on their cars. Hertz had a code of ethics and required employees to sign a compliance statement, but neither of these made a difference. Most of the problem resulted from charging retail prices for repairs for which Hertz received a volume discount because of its size. Allen Blicker, the company's national accident control manager, five management levels below the chief executive, was viewed as the "architect" of several fraudulent practices that eventually led to a grand jury probe. Hertz' CEO, Frank D. Olson, fired Blicker and eighteen others in centralized control. The company refunded more than $3 million to customers and insurers, but the damage had been done—all despite a code of ethics and a compliance agreement.[77]

WHISTLEBLOWING

Another way to improve corporate social responsibility is not only to allow whistleblowing, but to encourage it.[78] **Whistleblowing** occurs when an employee discloses an illegal, immoral, or unethical practice by members of an organization.[79] Unfortunately the evidence suggests that most firms not only discourage, but punish whistleblowing. For example, after Allan J. McDonald, senior engineer on the shuttle rocket for Morton Thiokol, Inc., and another engineer, Roger Boisjoly, graphically demonstrated the problems with the infamous "O-ring," and testified about their objections to the launch of the Challenger, they were pressured by the company to take lower-level positions. They were stripped of their responsibilities and transferred to lesser jobs. Fortunately, their original positions were restored after pressure was applied to the company.[80]

OMBUDSMEN, CORPORATE COMMITTEES, AND TASK FORCES
Additional techniques employed by organizations to improve their social responsibility performance include ombudsmen, committees, and task forces. These individuals or groups of individuals oversee programs for encouraging ethical behavior, for reviewing violations of codes of ethics, and for being recipients of whistleblowers' observations of illegal, immoral, or unethical acts.

INCULTURATION PROGRAMS
Organizations must provide training to managers, professionals, and other staff—sometimes employees at all levels and especially those in sensitive positions such as purchasing, waste disposal, personnel, research and development, sales, and manufacturing, where various social responsibility issues might be involved. Examples of such issues are equal employment opportunity hiring, treatment of animals in research and development, bribery in purchasing, pollution as a result of manufacturing, and so on. This training must be aimed at improving the social performance of the individuals involved. It should be aimed at understanding ethical dilemmas, possible consequences, and company policies on such issues.

Social Responsibility, Ethics, and Problem Solving

Social responsibility issues are problems. They are solved using the problem-solving model discussed in the previous chapter. When ethical dilemmas are encountered, they too are problems and are solved by the standard problem-solving model.

Management Challenges Identified

1. Rapid change in all elements of the task and general environments
2. Problem solving in social responsibility areas and ethical dilemmas

Some Solutions Noted in the Chapter

1. Employ an organic organization structure.
2. Adapt to or change the environment.
3. Institute flexible rules, policies, and procedures.
4. Learn about ethics.

Summary

1. The environment of the organization has two principal components: internal and external. The external environment similarly has two principal components: the competitive environment and the general environment. The external environment affects the organization at both domestic and international levels. Organizations often face many competitive and general environments if they function in different countries.

2. The stakeholder concept requires that firms take into account the impact of their decisions on stakeholders.

3. Organizations are confronted with much more complex and unstable environments than they have been in the past. They must learn to adapt to or change their environments in order to survive.

4. Social responsibility—corporate social performance—has been shown to have four principal components: economic, legal, ethical, and discretionary.

5. Key issues include environmental pollution, equal employment opportunity, employee health and safety, consumerism, the quality of the work life, product safety, and business ethics.

6. The four philosophies of response are reactive, defensive, accommodative, and proactive.

7. Ethics is the rules of the game. It is the norms and values defining conduct. It may be societal, organizational, professional, or personal.

8. Twelve questions have been provided that managers can ask themselves to determine whether a decision is ethical.

Thinking About Management

1. What is an ethical dilemma and why is it so difficult to make decisions in such situations?

2. What causes Milton Friedman to say that the only responsibility of a business is to make a profit? How would you argue against this decision, or would you? Why or why not?

3. Think of four different companies, each of which fits one of these descriptions of levels of social responsibility: economic, legal, ethical, and discretionary.

4. Describe several different companies' social responsibility performance across several different issue areas—for example, air pollution, water pollution, equal employment opportunity, consumerism, employee safety and health, and product safety. Try to find companies that encompass each of the four major philosophical positions: reaction, defense, accommodation, and proaction.

5. If you were to construct a social audit of equal employment opportunity for your college, what questions would you ask of the college to determine whether it is socially responsible in this area?

6. Air and water pollution are two of the major problems facing the world in the next twenty years. If you are a major chemical producer, what kind of actions can you expect to have to take in the next fifteen years in order to avert increased legal activity on the part of citizens or higher levels of federal law?

7. To what reasons would you attribute the ethics crisis that seems to have peaked in the late 1980s?

8. Devise some typical strategies for coping with two or three of the various types of potential sources of control over business—for example, federal legislation or consumer pressure groups.

9. Discuss what should be done to prevent another Valdez oil spill anywhere in the world.

CASE

Animal Torture or Research?

Michiko Okamoto received nothing but praise for her fourteen years of experimentation in drug abuse using live animals as subjects. She showed, for example, why the medicines that physicians prescribe may become as addictive as a typical street drug. She also showed why some people die from an overdose, even though they have developed a tolerance for the particular drug. She won numerous grants from the National Institute on Drug Abuse (NIDA), and her findings are cited in numerous medical texts. Keith Killiam, professor of pharmacology at the University of California, Davis, describes her work as a "shining, crystal example of how to do science."

Steve Seigel of Trans-Species Unlimited, an animal rights group based in Pennsylvania, calls her experiments "the worst of the worst." In 1987 Seigel's group launched an all-out effort to stop Okamoto's experiments. They picketed her laboratory for months, barraging her office with phone calls. Cornell University, where Okamoto worked, received more than ten thousand letters protesting her experiments. The Trans-Species Unlimited organization printed brochures using her words describing the horrendous ways in which the cats she used died or suffered during her experiments. Eventually Okamoto capitulated, returning her latest grant, worth $530,000, to the NIDA. Depending on your perspective, it was either a great victory for abused and innocent animals, or a defeat for science and medicine.

At least 17 million animals are used in laboratory experiments each year. About 85 percent are rats and mice. In 1987 the nation's 1,260 registered research centers used 180,000 dogs, 50,000 cats, 61,000 nonhuman primates, 540,000 guinea pigs, and 555,000 rabbits. Ten federal agencies sponsored or conducted tests with animals. And while science may be involved in many of these tests, some of them are simple pharmacological experiments that have been repeated literally thousands of times for seemingly unimportant issues such as whether soapsuds hurt your eyes or some degree of a chemical in a soap will hurt a customer's eyes. A potent force is emerging in the American animal rights activist movement, and its power is much greater than most laboratories have anticipated. Bomb threats and actual bomb attempts, break-ins, and burglaries at various laboratories have prompted managers to take a second look at their practices.

DISCUSSION QUESTIONS

1. If you are president of a company in nonmedical research, employing large numbers of laboratory animals, what kinds of ethical dilemmas do you face?

2. What kinds of actions do you need to prepare to take for the future?

3. If you are the manager of a medical research laboratory, performing what is generally considered to be important scientific work but using large numbers of laboratory animals for experimentation, what kinds of actions must you consider in the future and what dilemmas do you face?

SOURCES: "Of Pain and Progress," *Newsweek* (December 26, 1988), pp. 50–59; Meg Greenfield, "In Defense of the Animals," *Newsweek* (April 17, 1989), p. 78; "A Serious Case of Puppy Love," *Time* (November 28, 1988), p. 24; and "Saving Creatures Great and Small," *U.S. News & World Report* (December 5, 1988), p. 13.

A Question of Ethics

Sue was an administrator of special projects in a large health care organization located in the southern United States. She supervised the work of specialty project teams, and a staff of six professionals and two secretaries. Previously, she had managed the work of from eight to ten supervisors, each of whom in turn had eight to ten subordinates.

Both Sue and her boss, Mike, were enrolled in MBA programs. She was attending a local college evening program. He was enrolled in a correspondence program with a "Big Ten" university. Sue's boss approached her one day about letting him look at one of her papers. She said sure, thinking he was interested in her work. A few weeks later, he showed her a paper he had mailed in to his faculty advisor in his MBA program. Seventy-five percent of it was a verbatim plagiarism of her paper. She couldn't believe it. She vowed to herself not to let him have any more of her papers. She started to tell him that he was wrong in doing this when he interrupted her and said, "Have you ever had the statistics course in your school yet? I need another paper for my course."

She spoke bluntly, "You can't do that. It's unethical."

"As a manager, I can get my subordinates to do my work here, so why not for school?" he replied flippantly.

"Well, for one reason, because that's not how it works in school. You are supposed to do your own work," she retorted.

"Well, if you are going to be uncooperative with your boss, that could cause you serious problems," he threatened.

"If you want to dance, we will," she said angrily, implying that he could not threaten her.

The conversation continued for several minutes. She left knowing that he knew that she thought he was a cheater, and that she would not help him cheat. If he caused her problems with the administration, she felt she would be forced to go right to the president.

DISCUSSION QUESTIONS
1. Is this an ethical dilemma for Sue? Why or why not?
2. If you were Sue, what would you have said to Mike in addition to what she said?
3. What would you say to Mike's boss if such a conversation became necessary?

Grappling with Controversial Issues

Students will break into small groups to discuss the following questions. Each group is to arrive at a consensus and report their findings to the class as a whole. Further discussion may occur at that point.

1. Contrast "situational ethics" to the requirements of morality and the belief in absolute right and wrong. Discuss which view is correct and why.
2. Discuss the issue of abortion and right to choice as an ethical issue, a moral issue.

CHAPTER FIVE

The Planning Process and Organizational Purpose

CHAPTER OBJECTIVES

By the time you complete this chapter, you should be able to

1. Describe the planning process and its two principal parts: its purpose—what you intend to accomplish—and the plan—who, how, where, and when you intend to accomplish your purpose. Be able to distinguish the major types of each of these two principal parts.

2. Indicate how planning is "problem solving for the future."

3. Identify the relationships between planning and the other functions of management.

4. List ten factors that reveal the importance of planning.

5. Identify differences in the planning problems that confront different levels of management.

6. Discuss the key issues in the scope and characteristics of plans and planning.

7. Enumerate the limitations of planning and the reasons people fail at planning.

8. Indicate the relationships between organizational purposes and the planning process.

9. Describe the relationships between vision, mission, goals, and objectives.

10. Indicate the importance of goals and objectives.

11. List the characteristics of sound objectives.

12. Describe the MBO process and the MBORR process, and specify their differences.

13. Describe setting objectives and planning as problem-solving processes.

CHAPTER OUTLINE

Plans and Planning
   The Importance of Planning
   Levels of Planning
     in the Organization
   Standing, or Single-Use, Plans
   Planning and Control
   The Planning Situational,
     or SWOT, Analysis
   The Limitations of Planning
   Why People Fail at Planning
   Establishing an Environment
     Conducive to Planning
Organizational Purpose
   Mission and Vision
   Goals and Objectives
   Managing by Objectives
   Management by Objectives, Results,
     and Rewards (MBORR)
   Alternatives to Objective-Based Systems
   Setting Personal Objectives
Planning as a Problem-Solving Exercise
Management Challenges Identified
Some Solutions Noted in the Chapter

Barnett Banks: Planning for Success

In 1990, Barnett Banks is the 23rd largest bank holding company in the United States. In the late 1970s, it found itself facing a rapidly changing environment and many opportunities in the growing state of Florida and in the southeastern United States. It is the darling of Wall Street because of its successful performance in this situation. Underlying its success are its strategy, its structure, its systems, and its culture. Barnett's strategy began with actions to dominate Florida. It expanded from 75 offices in 1977, to 457 in 1987, and had a 20.2 percent market share of deposits at the end of 1986, compared to a 8.2 percent market share at the end of 1976. It had also begun to move to position itself regionally, examining various acquisition possibilities outside of Florida. Finally, Barnett provides what customers demand—service. Its chief financial officer, Steven Hansell, suggests that if you want to succeed in banking today, you shouldn't think of yourself as a banker, but as a retailer of services. Barnett does just that. It pays careful attention not only to corporatewide service programs, but to tailoring to the needs of each individual banking unit's customers. It offers a very different program for retiree deposits in rich Naples, Florida, for example, than it does in much less affluent parts of the state.

To support this strategy, it has divided its 475 banks into 35 regional banks. Each division's regional president has his or her own board of directors, and more importantly, considerable autonomy to do what is necessary to carry out the company's growth strategy and to meet other objectives, such as profit. Each bank's objectives for market share, net income, and profitability are set with the holding company. After that, it's up to each bank's managers to achieve those objectives in the ways that they see fit, within company policies. To make the system work, these regional presidents set objectives with and delegate similar high-level authority to each of their branch unit managers and other key officers. Barnett's culture—its shared values—focuses on performance. So do its systems. Hundreds of top managers receive a 36-page report every month analyzing the operations of each of the 35 regional banks. Bank managers are expected to perform. "If you foul up, the consequences won't be good," comments Charles Rice, Barnett's chairman. "If you do well, the performance bonuses will be very good."

Barnett stresses success over politics. You don't find many turf battles. It keeps its corporate staff to just 350 people, and it encourages risk taking and innovation. It does have its critics, who believe that it cannot survive in a cost-conscious market. Barnett retorts that it provides services that people are willing to pay for. So far, they are.

SOURCES: "Bank Scoreboard," *Business Week*, April 2, 1990, p. 98; Thomas E. Ricks, "Branching Out: Attentive to Service, Barnett Banks Grows Fast, Keeps Profit Up," *Wall Street Journal* 3 April, 1987, pp. 1, 27; and an interview with a Barnett Bank branch manager.

If you don't know where you are going, you'll probably end up somewhere else.

David P. Campbell
Author of the book by the same name.

Management's job is to see the company not as it is . . . but as it can become.

John W. Teets, chairman
The Greyhound Corporation

Barnett Banks is one of those unique companies that plans at every level of the organization. Barnett has positioned itself in a number of lucrative markets and has restructured its composition of services to meet the demands of the marketplace. Consequently, it has required its managers at all levels of the organization to align their performance expectations with these changes.

Planning is problem solving for the future in a changing environment.[1] As the external business environment becomes more changeful, planning becomes more important and more difficult. The planning process is divided into two principal parts. The first is the determination of **purpose**, what you intend to accomplish: vision, mission, goals, and objectives. The second part is the expression of who, how, where, and when you intend to accomplish what you intend to accomplish, as expressed in a plan. A **plan** is the intended set of actions to achieve an objective, goal, mission, or vision. Typical plans include strategies, intermediate plans, operating plans, budgets, policies, procedures, and rules.

One of Barnett's major strengths is its ability to segment its markets. In some locations, for example, the bank specializes in meeting the needs of the elderly. (SOURCE Courtesy of Barnett Banks)

At the total organizational level, what you intend to accomplish—your purpose—is defined first in terms of a directional vision, then a general mission, and then more definitively in terms of goals. Goals are then stated in terms of specific objectives. These guide the subunits of the organization and, more importantly, each individual in the organization. How the organization intends to accomplish its vision, mission, goals, or objectives is described in plans. The major plans of action to achieve vision, mission, goals, and major objectives are called strategies. These are the concerns of the top level of the organization. Intermediate (tactical) plans and operational plans, which are aimed at achieving less encompassing objectives, are the concerns of middle and lower levels of management.

Planning is the organization's best course of action for achieving its common purpose, for gaining support for that purpose, and for assuring individuals that they have a stake in what the organization seeks to accomplish. The organization's planning process is an opportunity for individuals to see beyond their own department, share a common vision, and solve their own problems. It requires the highest level of human endeavor, both rational and creative, to plan successfully an organization's, a department's, a group's, or an individual's future.

This chapter first examines the basic planning process: plans and planning; the importance of planning; the scope of planning in an organization; the char-

The zoning board for the City of Miami must routinely plan for changes in the use of real estate within city limits. In a city where growth is rampant, and real estate in low supply relative to demand, such planning becomes critical. (SOURCE © Michal Heron/Woodfin Camp & Associates)

acteristics of plans and planning; the limitations of planning; and why people fail at planning. The purposes of planning—vision, mission, goals, and objectives—and the general processes by which they are determined are then examined. Finally, planning and objective setting as problem-solving processes are discussed. Chapter 6 reviews the critically important strategic planning process. Chapter 7 describes the major quantitative techniques that may be used to improve decision making of all types, but especially planning decisions.

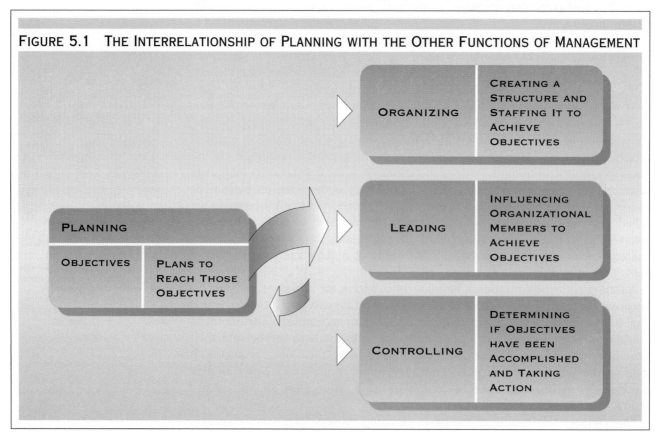

FIGURE 5.1 THE INTERRELATIONSHIP OF PLANNING WITH THE OTHER FUNCTIONS OF MANAGEMENT

PLANNING

OBJECTIVES | PLANS TO REACH THOSE OBJECTIVES

ORGANIZING | CREATING A STRUCTURE AND STAFFING IT TO ACHIEVE OBJECTIVES

LEADING | INFLUENCING ORGANIZATIONAL MEMBERS TO ACHIEVE OBJECTIVES

CONTROLLING | DETERMINING IF OBJECTIVES HAVE BEEN ACCOMPLISHED AND TAKING ACTION

Plans and Planning

Planning is not concerned with future decisions, but rather with the future impact of the decisions made today.[2] Planning involves assessing the future and preparing for it, or creating it. Planning is *the* fundamental function of management. Everything the organization attempts to accomplish, everything any manager attempts to achieve, and everything the individual employee attempts to bring about, depends on setting objectives and formulating plans to reach those objectives. Whether a manager is at the strategic, intermediate, or operational level, whether he or she is the chief executive officer or a front-line supervisor of a research lab, planning is the quintessential management function.

All management activity stems from planning, as revealed in Figure 5.1. Organizing and leading occur to achieve the objectives and accomplish the plans established. Controlling occurs to determine if the objectives established have been achieved and the related plans carried out. However, planning also depends on what happens in the other functions, as the smaller arrow pointing to planning in Figure 5.1 suggests. Throughout the planning process, the manager is making decisions and solving problems. Managers are focusing on current decisions that will lead to future results. The process is often difficult, not only in terms of solving the problems, but from an emotional perspective, as Management Challenge 5.1 illustrates.

MANAGEMENT CHALLENGE 5.1

Downsizing at AT&T

An upper-level manager in the AT&T Information System Division had to determine how to combine two data centers and eliminate fifty jobs. He knew what his objectives were, they had been given to him. But he had to establish a plan of action to achieve them. The complexities of that decision were immense. The entire company had been forced to downsize as a result of deregulation. He did not want to hurt anyone's future, but he knew that, somewhere along the line, many people would no longer be employed in the Bell systems. The fifty people were among those many. He had to take the best course of action within a six-month period to help those he could to find other jobs, to meet company objectives, to satisfy his own personal values, and to solve the problem. One of the ways he chose was to work with the fifty people who would be affected in a participative management problem-solving process to help him find ways to achieve his multiple, conflicting objectives. This was a unique solution in a company that, during its downsizing after deregulation, was often noted for less than careful attention to human concerns. To the manager's satisfaction, employees understood the problem, were appreciative of his willingness to share a difficult situation with them, and with all but a couple of exceptions, recognized and accepted that certain actions had to be taken. They were able to formulate a plan that would, over a six-month period, through attrition and outplacement, satisfy most of the job needs of most of the people involved. Two data centers were combined, and the manager involved felt that he had retained the best people.

SOURCE: Author's conversation with that manager.

The Importance of Planning

Planning is fundamental to the success of the organization for several reasons. It helps the organization, its groups, or individuals think about and prepare for the future, and especially for change. As the rate of change increases, planning becomes more important and more difficult. It results in the establishment of performance objectives for the organization, groups, and individuals that can be used to measure progress. It provides motivation to the organization, group, or individual. Planning is the primary basis for the other management functions of organizing, leading, and controlling. It initiates systematic proactive problem solving, as opposed to reactive decision making and provides for the integration of organizational, group, and individual effort.

Levels of Planning in the Organization

Planning occurs at the three major levels of the organization: top, middle, and lower. As shown in Figure 5.2, at the top level of the organization, the manager is concerned with strategic planning—the planning that has a major impact on the organization as a whole, and that usually involves a major commitment of resources. Middle- and lower-level managers are principally concerned with implementing these strategic plans. They are concerned with obtaining the most effective and efficient use of an organization's resources to achieve strategic plans through intermediate and operational planning.

As shown in Figure 5.2, the planning problems confronting top-level management are more complex, have a higher degree of uncertainty, are more unique and unstructured, and are longer term than those confronting middle- and front-line managers. This is not to say that complex, uncertain, unique/unstructured, and long-term problems do not occur except at top management levels. They do. Nor is it to say that top managers do not face some simple, certain, routine/structured, and short-term problems. They do. But normally the characteristics of the planning problems confronting these levels of management are as shown in Figure 5.2. Top-level managers usually face a myriad of interdepartmental environmental variables, such as resource allocations. They usually are uncertain about the likelihood of events transpiring and almost always face situations that are not likely to recur and for which no simple rule will work. Top managers usually plan one to three years in advance, with five-year, very general, visionary "strategic thinking"—simply thinking about the environment and making plans for coping with it.[3] Middle managers typically plan a few months to two years in advance. Lower-level managers would normally plan a few weeks to a year in advance. Finally, top-level managers also spend much more time planning than do managers at other levels.

Middle- and lower-level managers work within the policies and strategies created by top management. These two lower levels are concerned with implementing top-management strategies. These managers are often given their objectives but are usually allowed to develop plans to achieve them (sometimes they are also given the plans). Their principal concerns are not with what must be done but who should do it, where and when it should be accomplished, and how it should be achieved. Lower- and middle-level managers make significant inputs to the planning information systems used by top-level managers to develop strategic plans. Lower-level managers make similar inputs to the information system used by middle-level managers to make intermediate-level plans. Table 5.1 provides a list of plans that might typically be generated by selected managers in each of the three levels of the organization for an organization with only one major business.

AT BARNETT: *At Barnett, planning is integrated among all three levels of management. Top management is concerned with determining how the company will compete and where. Each manager of a regional bank is concerned with meeting objectives for competing, future growth, market share, income, and profitability. Each front-line branch manager or other officer is concerned with achieving his or her objectives that contribute to company and regional objectives. Performance against objectives is continuously reviewed at all levels.*

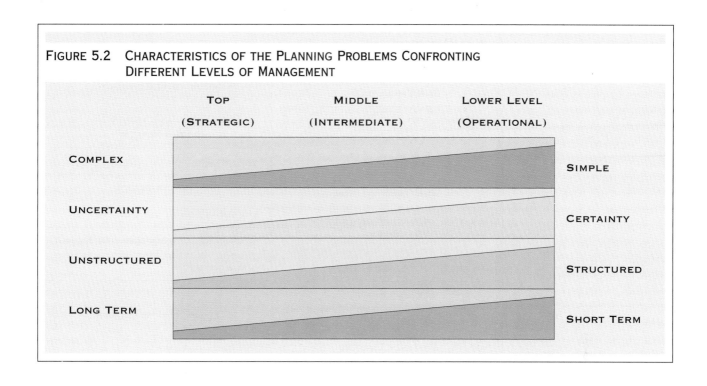

FIGURE 5.2 CHARACTERISTICS OF THE PLANNING PROBLEMS CONFRONTING DIFFERENT LEVELS OF MANAGEMENT

	TOP (STRATEGIC)	MIDDLE (INTERMEDIATE)	LOWER LEVEL (OPERATIONAL)	
COMPLEX				SIMPLE
UNCERTAINTY				CERTAINTY
UNSTRUCTURED				STRUCTURED
LONG TERM				SHORT TERM

John Reed, CEO of Citicorp, is known for his relaxed style, his creativity, and his ability to plan strategically. Citicorp has moved boldly ahead in global banking as a result of his vision for the firm.
(SOURCE © Mark Ferri)

Table 5.1. Selected Plans Created by Each Level of Management

Top-Level Management	Middle-Level Management
Chief Executive Officer	
5-year strategic vision	
3-year strategy for acquiring other businesses	**Sales Manager**
3-year strategy for developing an advantage over competition	1-year sales plan
Chief Operating Officer	**Financial Manager**
3-year capital budget for purchasing major items such as plant and equipment	1-year plan for providing cash to build facilities
2-year operating budget—revenues and expenses	**Human Resource Management Manager**
1-year plan for acquiring other businesses	1-year recruitment plan
Marketing Executive	**Lower-Level Management**
3-year marketing plan	
Production Executive	**Regional Sales Manager**
3-year plan for how many plants and how much equipment will be needed to sustain operations	1-year sales plan for Midwest region
Human Resource Management Executive	**Financial Investments Officer**
3-year staffing plan	1-year plan to achieve 20% return on investments
Chief Financial Officer	**Human Resource Management Manager of Training and Development**
3-year plan describing how much cash will be needed by the company	1-year plan to train 220 managers in organizational culture management
1-year operating budget	

Standing, or Single-Use, Plans

Plans may be classified as either standing plans or single-use plans. Both types are used to pursue organizational goals and objectives, but in very different ways, as Figure 5.3. suggests. Standing plans offer guidance to the mainstream single-use planning activity.

STANDING PLANS

Standing plans are used to guide activities that recur over a period of time. There are three principal types of standing plans: policies, procedures, and rules and regulations.

Policies are plans that provide general guidance to action. Policies vary from organization to organization, both in which subjects are covered by policies and how the issues relating to a subject will be treated. For instance, many companies have policies permitting managers to allow subordinates time off to go to college, but how much time they can take and how frequently are issues likely to be treated differently by each business.

Procedures are plans that describe the exact series of actions to be taken in a given situation. Companies have hundreds, if not thousands, of procedures—for example, telling how to perform a job. Many companies have a policy of at least partially reimbursing their employees for educational expenses. When this occurs the employee will have to follow a set procedure in order to be

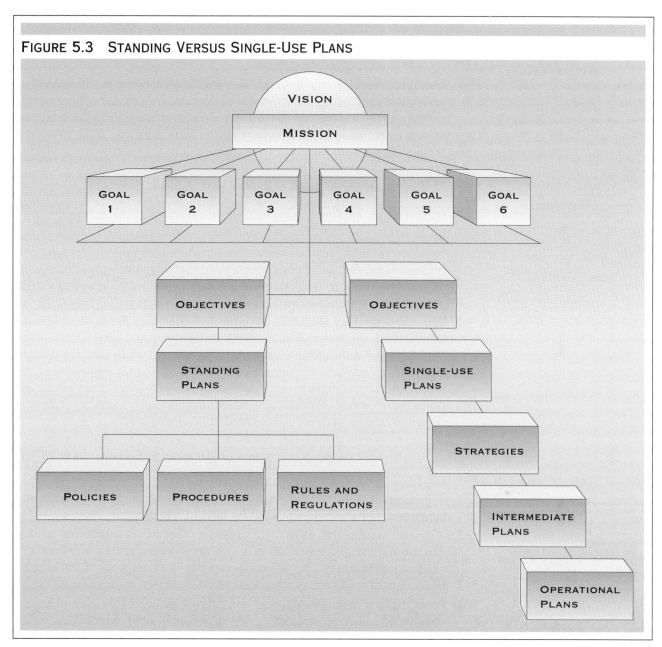

FIGURE 5.3 STANDING VERSUS SINGLE-USE PLANS

reimbursed. He or she may have to fill out company Form 1063, attach a copy of his or her grades, take both documents to the personnel office for processing, and wait for the check in the mail.

Rules and regulations are plans that describe exactly how one particular situation is to be handled. "No smoking" is a rule.

Whereas policies guide decision making, procedures and rules and regulations make the decision for you. Procedures are different from rules and regulations primarily in what they apply to. Procedures describe a series of steps to accomplish a particular objective. Rules state an action to be taken in response to a certain situation.

SINGLE-USE PLANS

Single-use plans are plans that are used once, and then discarded. In some cases it may take ten years to finish using such a plan. In other situations this type of plan could be used for one day only. There are three types of single-use plans: strategies, intermediate plans, and operational or operating plans.

Strategies are major plans committing extensive resources to proposed actions to achieve an organization's major goals and objectives. Managers are often concerned with three levels of strategy:[4]

1. **Corporate strategy** is a strategic plan that identifies the business or businesses in which an organization will engage and how it will fundamentally conduct that business or those businesses. United Airlines at one time owned Hertz and the Westin and Hilton hotel chains, but it decided it really didn't belong in those businesses. It decided to rededicate itself to the airlines business.[5] Thus it changed its corporate strategy.

2. **Business strategy** is a strategic plan that indicates how an organization competes in a particular business. Each business is referred to as a **strategic business unit** (SBU). Each SBU serves a particular set of customers with a group of products or services distinct from each of those served and offered by other SBUs in the same organization. Most companies are single SBU organizations. Georgia-Pacific, having determined that it wanted to expand its paper business, moved rapidly to add many new products and to market them in a more sophisticated way—a business strategy.[6]

3. **Functional strategy** is a strategic plan that addresses the issue of how an organization can use its resources most effectively and efficiently to carry out corporate and business strategy. Typical areas addressed are marketing, finance, operations, human resources, information management, research and development, and management. Wal-Mart emphasizes low prices, cost cutting, and service—functional strategies aimed at making it the number one retailer in the United States.[7]

Intermediate plans are plans that help translate strategy into operations. These plans normally commit far fewer resources than do strategies.

1. A **program** covers a large set of activities. The development of the 486 computer chip was accomplished by Intel in a program.

2. A **project** is usually a subset of a program; the term is sometimes used as a substitute for *program*. When British Airways undertook a program of recapturing business by providing superior service, one of its integral projects was developing its business class lounge—a huge success.[8]

3. **Product plans** cover the activities related to a product for some set period of time, often a year. As part of its product plan for Coors Light, Coors, for example, spends more on advertising than Miller's and Busch spend on their light beers.[9]

4. **Divisional plans** are plans for the major divisions of an organization—for example, the marketing plan for the year, or the plan for one of the product divisions for the year. General Mills's Red Lobster, a major division of the company, must develop strategic plans for its operations.

Operating plans are plans that deal with day-to-day operations, typically for a time frame of less than one year. They commit far fewer resources than strategies or intermediate plans.

1. The **annual operating plan** is the one-year plan of action to implement strategy. This particular plan is corporatewide, but commits resources for only one year. At Mrs. Fields's Cookies, for example, the annual operating plan is input into a computer. Progress against that plan is checked daily.[10]

2. The **budget** is the annual operating plan, with revenues and expenses determined for the actions necessary according to the annual operating plan.

Parker-Hannefin pays very close attention to its budget as a way of making operating decisions.[11]

3. **Departmental plans** are typically, but not necessarily, a department's annual operating plan. They may include longer- or shorter-term plans that are departmentwide. In a large law firm, for example, the litigation department will have an annual operating plan detailing expected billings and expenses.

4. **Group plans** are plans for a work group—typically, but not necessarily, the group's intended actions as their part in the annual operating plan. Work groups at General Foods develop plans to help achieve corporate objectives.[12]

5. **Individual plans** are plans by an individual to contribute to the organization's accomplishment of objectives—typically, but not necessarily, his or her contribution to achievement of the annual operating plan. At Cypress Semiconductor individuals have weekly plans for achieving weekly objectives, all aimed at achieving longer-term corporate objectives.[13]

CRITERIA FOR PLANS

When planning, the manager must test his or her plans against these criteria:

1. Appropriate level of complexity and coverage
2. How comprehensive it is
3. Realization of the impact of its importance
4. Proper quantitative and qualitative content
5. Strategic or operational perspectives
6. Whether it can be publicly revealed or should remain confidential
7. What parts of the plan are written, unwritten
8. Whether it is formal or informal
9. Its ease of implementation
10. Its balance of rationality and creativity
11. Its flexibility
12. Its cost

Complex Versus Simple. The strategic decision by General Motors to spend $60 billion to upgrade technology, to make it cost and technologically competitive, was a complex plan. It led to thousands of strategic, intermediate, and operational ramifications. It required a tremendous amount of integration and hundreds of millions of man hours to implement.[14] In contrast, a simple plan might be the daily work schedule for one of the work groups seeking to achieve some minor part of that complex plan.

Comprehensive Versus Narrow Coverage. Comprehensive plans have broader coverage than do narrow ones; they affect a broader scope of the organization; and they tend to be more concerned with corporate, business, or functional strategies, as opposed to departmental, group, or individual plans. An example of a comprehensive plan would be John Hancock's strategy to enter into several businesses within the financial services industry.[15] A narrower plan would be that in which a division of that insurance company chose to employ a lower price and intensive personal selling over a two-month period to increase sales by 20 percent.

Major Versus Minor Importance. Strategic plans have a major importance; operational plans are less important. Chevron's merger with Gulf was a result of a major plan. The decision to change office-furnishing requirements when the merger was complete was a more minor plan to managers at Chevron.

However, it ended up having a major negative impact on employee morale at Gulf because furnishings were made quite austere, in contrast to what they had been.[16]

Qualitative Versus Quantitative. Most business plans are not completely quantitative. Many involve complex, qualitative judgments. When Microsoft decided to go public, for example, a range of the selling value for the stock was chosen that would be acceptable. The plan was instituted to achieve a stock offering price within that range based on a quantitative examination of the organization. But some qualitative forecasts of the organization's future helped raise that price above expected levels.[17]

Strategic Versus Operational. Strategic plans involve significant commitments of resources. Operational plans involve the employment of resources to a much less substantial degree. When the United States Department of Defense decided to seek a Star Wars Defense Initiative (SDI) and commit $30 billion, at a minimum, to the project, that was a strategic decision. That the objective be achieved through a combination of detectors and multiple defense weapons systems was a strategic plan. Commitment of a few hundred thousand dollars for early research and development to a series of firms for research in laser weapons was an operational decision within the framework of that strategic plan.

Confidential Versus Public. Confidential plans are an organization's proprietary property. Most major companies make their strategic plans, at least in the general sense, available to the public. Almost all announce their strategic goals. These can often be found in their annual reports. IBM, for example, has consistently listed its four cornerstone goals as growth, product leadership, efficiency, and profitability.[18] Their vagueness and broadness are of little use to competitors wanting to counteract them. But the specifics of the numerous confidential plans intended to bring them to fruition would be. IBM is extremely concerned about its confidential plans because of industrial espionage; therefore, it has high levels of security in many of its facilities.[19]

Written Versus Unwritten. Many plans, especially those at lower levels, are unwritten. Much of an intended plan is unwritten but assumed. A supervisor for Bell Labs, for example, may read the strategic plan, the related policies, and the intermediate plans he or she is given and from them determine a work schedule to use in the upcoming year. The manager may, from time to time, make verbal changes in them. He or she may have several plans in mind that are never committed to writing but are passed on verbally to subordinates.

Formal Versus Informal. Most smaller organizations, such as your local print shop, manufacturing company, or record store, will have informal plans. Most of the plans of entrepreneurial organizations are carried in the head of the owner/entrepreneur. Many times these are not really even plans but simply reactions to events. Most larger organizations—such as IBM, Hewlett-Packard, General Motors, General Electric, American Airlines, the U.S. Department of Agriculture, the Teamsters Union, and others—have formal written plans that were drawn up as a consequence of an established series of procedures—a plan to plan.

Easy or Difficult to Implement. Some plans are very easy to implement. Others are not. It is the manager's responsibility to assure that a plan is implementable, and that in the planning process, he or she has considered the ease of implementation. Japanese firms spend significantly more time on procedures to implement a plan than do American firms.[20]

Rational Versus Creative. Plans must be both rationally and creatively derived. As reviewed in Chapter 3, creativity is a part of any problem-solving process, but as discussed in Chapter 1, the changing nature of the organization environment makes creativity much more important to planning today than it

Apple's Macintosh development team takes great pride in their accomplishments. Working 90-hour weeks, they developed a personal computer which revolutionized the industry. Planning at Apple was characterized in the early 1980s by wild abandon and creativity which led to this innovation. (SOURCE © Robert Holmgren)

ever was. This increased rate of change, the increasing level of competition, the nature of decision making in the computer age, and the edge that intuitive managers have in making decisions demand more creativity from an organization. It is for such reasons that companies such as Apple Computer create whole cultures to enable them to instill creativity throughout their organization to meet the challenges of the four preceding demands. Even the way that Apple names its conference rooms—after the human sins of lust, envy, greed, and so on—is designed to promote a different feeling, a creative feeling.[21]

Management Challenge 5.2 reveals how important creativity is to Barnett Banks.

Flexible Versus Inflexible. In the changing management environment, the manager must create more flexible plans than he or she has historically. A plan must be adjustable, smoothly and quickly, to the requirements of these changing conditions.[22] IBM knows that for years it has made a considerable portion of its revenues from service contracts. Personal computers (PCs)—the largest-growing segment of the information market—do not typically require service contracts. As a consequence, IBM established a compensation plan to encourage its sales force to sell more PC service contracts.[23] IBM realized it had to be flexible to remain in the marketplace. In contrast though, IBM has had difficulty becoming sufficiently flexible to meet Digital Equipment Company's thrust into its minicomputer market because it has been primarily a mainframe company for so long.[24] The importance of flexibility cannot be overstated. Any number of major organizations have publicly characterized their environments as rapidly changing and requiring planning flexibility, as well as shortened strategic time horizons. The executives in charge of strategic planning at General Electric and Olivetti, a leading European office automation company, for example, suggest that to forecast beyond three years is folly. Even over a three-year period, situations change so rapidly that strategic planning in their organizations provides direction, not hard-and-fast plans.[25] Management Challenge 5.3 tells how flexible you must be to take advantage of opportunities in fast-moving situations.

Economical Versus Excessively Costly. Plans are one thing. Implementable plans are another. One of the key factors involved in implementing plans is their cost. The numbers must be put to plans in order that their cost be held below an excessive level.

Planning and Control

Planning and control are inseparably linked. Planning provides the criteria with which to control—the standards established in planning are used as the companion items to determine whether performance achieved results.[26] A plan is not likely to be successfully implemented unless control of progress on the plan occurs. In most organizations the budget is the most frequently used device for controlling performance. A well-thought-out budget is critical to successful plan-

AT BARNETT BANKS:
At Barnett authority is decentralized. Regional and branch managers are allowed to set their own plans of action to achieve objectives. But the bank controls performance very closely through its 36-page report on performance in its 35 regional banks. This report is scrutinized by hundreds of managers. Performance is expected and rewarded.

ning and control. A well-thought-out budget integrates an organization's strategy, structure, management, resources, and the tasks it must accomplish.[27] Across all economic functions of the organization—marketing, finance, operations, and human resources—the objectives and plan established provide the basis for control. Planning and control are linked by the objective-setting process, as well as by the plans that result. Participation in objective setting and planning by those who must implement the plans often assists the control process.

The Planning Situational, or SWOT, Analysis

As in any problem-solving situation, the decision maker performs a situational analysis. The contents of the situational analysis depend upon the level of the manager in the organization—top, middle, or lower. In virtually any planning situation, the manager is looking for problems to solve, and in many cases the problems are opportunities to take advantage of. An **opportunity** is a chance to improve your situation significantly. The problems encountered may also be threats or weaknesses. **Threats** are external environmental situations that may keep you from achieving your objectives. **Weaknesses** are internal situations that might keep you from achieving your objectives. In achieving your objectives you are are interested in relying upon your **strengths**—internal situations that will help you achieve your objectives, to overcome threats, to overcome weaknesses, and to take advantage of opportunities. Examining these four factors—Strengths, Weaknesses, Opportunities, and Threats, or SWOT, is a situational analysis.[28]

At the upper levels of the organization, the manager's focus is largely external. In a single business organization, the manager is principally concerned with competing in the marketplace. In organizations composed of several business units, upper-level managers are concerned with managing the portfolio of businesses the company has. The top-level manager of each business unit remains concerned with competing in his or her business. Further down in the organizational hierarchy, managers are more concerned with functional perspectives. These managers usually have a more internal focus in their planning process, unless they are in areas such as sales or purchasing. Goals and objectives, required responses to strategies, policies, procedures, and rules are already defined for middle- and operational-level managers. It is within these constraints and guidelines that their planning must occur, while upper-level managers might look to mission and goals and some policies in formulating the strategies and key results expected of others.

As in any problem-solving situation, in planning the manager is searching for the key set of factors that will help identify the real problem. For a middle-level or operational-level manager, that manager's manager may be one of the most important factors in the situation. Similarly, at upper levels, many times a board of directors or a chairman of the board or a chief executive officer will be an executive's key factor in the situation. Additional information on the SWOT analysis is provided in Chapter 6.

The Limitations of Planning

Several limitations to planning exist. Managers must be aware of them and take action to overcome them:

Environmental events cannot always be controlled.

Internal resistance.

Planning is expensive.

Current crises.

Failure to understand the weaknesses of the planning premises.

Planning is difficult.[29]

ENVIRONMENTAL EVENTS CANNOT ALWAYS BE CONTROLLED

In the mid-1980s, many graduate programs in business noticed that the number of people taking the Graduate Management Aptitude Test was down. MBA program executives—deans, assistant deans, and program directors—also listened to business executives talking about the high salaries of MBAs and the increasing difficulty in placing people with MBAs in sufficiently challenging jobs. They read the numerous articles about how too many MBAs were being graduated and an oversupply was occurring in the marketplace. They saw the demographic studies suggesting that fewer students would be available in the future. Many of those MBA program executives, like most other executives, lowered their expectations for future enrollments. They didn't increase their faculty sizes and they didn't expand facilities. Thus, in 1987, when they were faced with an unprecedented demand, many programs were unprepared to take advantage of the opportunity.

INTERNAL RESISTANCE

Invariably, without the proper levels of participation and without careful planning for implementation, proposed plans and objectives will be resisted by organizational members. Within a major entertainment company's information system division, for example, a new, systematic approach to planning for that division was resisted by the employees primarily as the result of fear. People were uncertain about many changes occurring within the division. Some of these involved changing the critical skills needed in the division, and thus many wondered whether their jobs would exist in a few weeks. They were not trying to sabotage the program, but they were sufficiently concerned about their self-interest that they did not devote as much time to supporting the program as top management might have liked.[30]

GLOBAL MANAGEMENT CHALLENGE

Planning Is More Than Difficult in the Soviet Union

Konveyer is a Ukrainian manufacturer of conveyor systems and automated production equipment. Konveyer is on the cutting edge of "perestroika," the restructuring of the Soviet economy to make it more capitalistic. The rules of the economy change virtually every day, and planning for those changes is more than difficult. Plus, factory director Valentin Vologzhin, fifty-one, must also remain true to the Socialist movement, which requires him to provide cradle-to-grave care for his workers. Vologzhin must plan for his employees' needs. One spinoff operation is building five hundred homes to be sold to workers with company-sponsored loans.

PLANNING IS EXPENSIVE

Effective planning requires a lot of time and energy. The more committed to planning an organization is, the more such resources are utilized. As the environment requires more flexibility in planning, it is more probable that plans will have to be updated constantly to take advantage of, and to react to, changing environmental situations. The cost of planning will rise, but the cost of being unprepared will be still greater.

CURRENT CRISES

There is always a need to solve current crises. Crisis management abounds in U.S. organizations. Many crises occur because of poor or no planning. Many others occur because of uncontrollable environmental circumstances, such as governmental policy actions, technological change, or a competitor's new marketing strategy. A plan of anticipated reaction must be available, especially for changing environmental circumstances. New ways of planning must evolve.

FAILURE TO UNDERSTAND THE WEAKNESSES
OF THE PLANNING PREMISES

Premises, assumptions about a situation and the future condition of factors in a situation, must be made, but they should not be made without thorough consideration.[31] In 1987 Rule Industries, Inc., a Massachusetts marine products maker with $60 million in sales, dropped Peat Marwick as its auditor when it merged with KMG Main Henderson to become KPMG, the world's biggest accounting firm, and a global competitor. John Geishecker, a Rule executive, cited as the primary reason the inability of a huge firm to provide the same kind of service that the smaller Peat Marwick had provided. Two years later, Rule's new auditor, Deloitte, Haskins, & Sells, merged with Touche Ross & Company to give them global size. In 1989 Rule was worried again but reluctant to change auditors a second time. The assumption that Deloitte would not do just as Peat had done was incorrect.[32]

PLANNING IS DIFFICULT

Nobody said planning was easy. It requires a tremendous amount of creativity, and it requires a great deal of rational and analytical capability. Many variables must be considered and plans are often based on uncertain assumptions. It is

Numerous other divisions produce an array of products from honey to mushrooms. Most employees prefer to shop at the well-stocked company store, avoiding the poorly stocked local shops.

But Vologzhin has managed well. Under perestroika, he has taken a faltering plant and made it profitable. He studied Western business methodologies and created a distribution network and tailored products to customer needs. He has even issued stock that pays a 20 percent dividend to employees. He has raised 10 percent of his operating capital by issuing this stock. Employees have the right to sell the stock back to the company. "What we are doing is consistent with the ideals of socialism," states Vologzhin. But what he is doing to remain consistent with "socialism" changes every day, as perestroika changes "socialism" into capitalism.

SOURCE: "The Ukraine: The Critical Republic," *Business Week* (April 3, 1989), p. 49.

often very time consuming. Two or three hundred pages of documentation may be necessary for major capital budgeting purchases or major programs and hundreds or even thousands of hours of manpower may be required to accomplish them. Meanwhile, the world changes. And while we recognize that tremendous change is occurring in North America, Europe, and the Pacific Rim, perhaps nowhere is change greater nor planning more difficult than in the Soviet Union of 1989, as the Global Management Challenge reveals.

Why People Fail at Planning

Planning fails for a number of reasons. Managers must be prepared to overcome or anticipate and therefore mitigate problems such as the following:

Lack of commitment to planning
Failure to develop and implement sound strategies
Lack of meaningful objectives or goals
Failure to see planning as both a rational and creative process
Excessive reliance on experience
Failure to identify the most critical factor for success
Lack of clear delegation
Lack of adequate control techniques and information on results
Resistance to change[33]

Establishing an Environment
Conducive to Planning

Planning must be planned, organized, led, and controlled if it is to be successful. There must be a planning system, and it must be adhered to. The organization should establish a culture that is receptive to planning—that not only encourages

While other airlines kept flying, Braniff found itself parked due to bankruptcy. Poor planning, and poor implementation led to its demise. (SOURCE © W. Johnson/Picture Group)

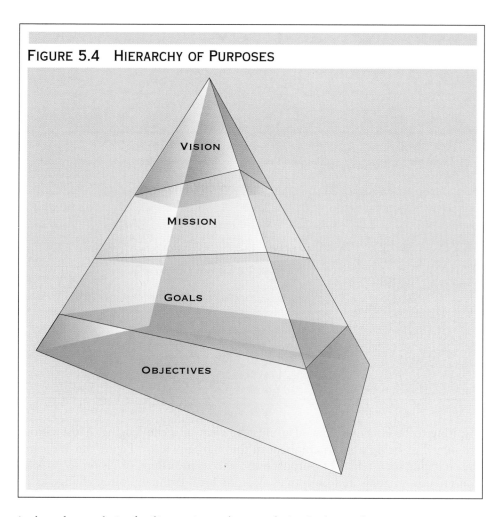

FIGURE 5.4 HIERARCHY OF PURPOSES

VISION

MISSION

GOALS

OBJECTIVES

it, but demands it, facilitates it, and rewards it. Such a culture encourages top managers to review the plans of their subordinates, who in turn review the plans of those working under them. Individuals should be recognized and rewarded when they reach planned goals and encouraged, through delegated authority and an emphasis on risk taking, to participate in the process.

Organizational Purpose

A number of organizational purposes exist. A hierarchy, from the most general and greatest scope, to the most specific and narrowest scope, would include vision, mission, goals, and objectives, as seen in Figure 5.4.

Vision and Mission

Increasingly it is being recognized that the strategic managers in an organization must have a "vision" of what the organization is to become.[34] **Vision** is non-specific directional guidance normally provided to an organization by its CEO. It describes where the company is going conceptually in the most general of terms, but it must also provide emotional direction.[35] Father Theodore Hezberg, former president of Notre Dame University, comments: "The very essence of leadership is that you have a vision. It has got to be a vision you articulate clearly; unfortunately you can't blow an uncertain trumpet."[36] Visions must be

FIGURE 5.5   CHANGING HIERARCHY OF PURPOSES

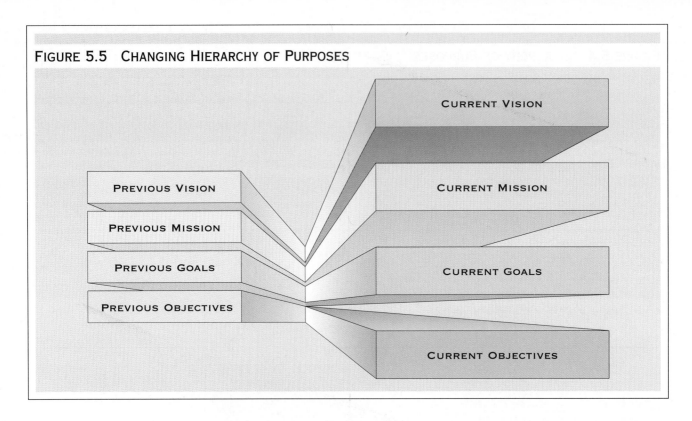

inspiring to be effective; they also must be clear and challenging. Most visions are aimed at being able to compete in the marketplace.[37] Figure 5.5 indicates the changing hierarchies of purposes and the relationships of vision to mission and mission to goals and objectives. Visions for a company often change as its CEO changes, as organizations are acquired or merged, as the environment changes, or as management challenges are encountered. Creating vision is not easy, as Management Challenge 5.4 reveals.

MANAGEMENT CHALLENGE 5.4

Jeff Campbell's Vision for Burger King

How do you mobilize an organization's energy? How do you get people moving? Sometimes you have to be creative. Jeff Campbell, chairman of Burger King, relates how he brought vision to Burger King.

"While I was running the New York region, I was complaining to the then-chairman about a number of things. He said, 'Why don't you put your thoughts on paper?' Well, I wrote a memo that must have been ten pages long. I said, 'Here's all the things I think are wrong and here's how I would attack them.' I never heard from him about any of it, but after I had been made president of Burger King, I said, 'Hey, I've been thinking about this for a long time. I know what we need to do short term,' but as I thought about what we were and where we might go, a vision took shape. About one year into the turnaround, I was made chairman. We had a meeting of all the officers at Marco Island, Florida. I was sitting in my den thinking about where we had to go and listening to a recording

Mission is the organization's "*raison d'être*"—its reason to be. It is easy to say that an organization's mission is to make money, or serve society. But these are really insufficient as mission statements. Rather, as Philip Kotler, noted author on marketing, and John A. Pearce, II, author on strategies, suggest, an organization's mission is its widely stated definition of basic business scope and operations, which distinguishes it from other organizations of a similar type.[38] The primary thrust of an organization's mission statement is external: it focuses on customers, markets, and fields of endeavor. The exact nature of mission statements varies from organization to organization. Some mission statements include descriptions of such basic corporate concerns as product quality, location of a facility, important aspects of perceived strategic advantage, and so forth. Many mission statements reveal not simply purpose, but philosophy. Research by John A. Pearce, II, and Fred David suggests that the more comprehensive the mission statement, the more likely the firm is to make a profit.[39] Mission statements vary greatly in scope and length. Conceptually, every objective, every plan, and every action of every individual and group in the organization should be in pursuit of achieving the organizational mission. Table 5.2 contains representative portions of organization mission statements.

Bill Gates, thirty-one-year-old billionaire whiz-kid founder of Microsoft, runs his company according to his "vision" of what he wants to happen—computing for the masses. Microsoft will bring it to them.[40]

Periodically, organizations redefine their mission, their purpose. Probably no organization has had to change its mission more dramatically in the last twenty years than AT&T once deregulation became effective in 1984. Subsequently, the goals and the objectives of the organization—its strategies, its plans, its culture, its whole way of life—were changed. All of those changes were embodied in its **planning** process: the process of establishing vision, missions, goals, and objectives and the plans to reach them. As Management Challenge 5.1 revealed, these changes had a profound impact on thousands of lives.

While the process of establishing a mission statement might seem to be a simple one, careful consideration must be given to delineating the critical fea-

---

of the theme from *Chariots of Fire* and I got an idea of making a speech about where we needed to go and punctuating it with music just to get the guys thinking about it. I know that sounds corny, but sometimes corny things work and I decided to go with my gut on this one.

"So I talked about us becoming not only the best company in the portfolio, but the best convenience restaurant in America by 1992. I talked about what kind of a company we would be and the kinds of careers we would build for people. At the end I said, 'I'm going to put on one more piece of music and I want you to think about everything we've talked about. Don't talk to your friend or look at anybody else. Just sit there a second and listen to the music and ask yourself if it's something you really think you can do and—if you really want to do it. Then, when the music is over, get up and I will be waiting at the back door to shake your hand.'

"I was pretty nervous, but when the music ended guys in their early sixties—not just the younger people—started coming back. You know it was a corny thing to do, but what happened was magic. We had a 76 percent increase in earnings."

SOURCE: As reported in Noel M. Tichy and Mary Anne DeVanna, *The Transformational Leader* (New York: Wiley, 1986), pp. 122, 123.

Bill Gates, founder of Microsoft, had a vision of providing "computing for the masses." He formulated a strategy for achieving that end. His firm wound up dominating the PC software industry. His strategy worked. (SOURCE © N. Alexanian/Woodfin Camp & Associates)

Table 5.2. Mission Statement Components

1.	Customer Market	We believe our first responsibility is to the doctors, nurses, and patients, to mothers and all others who use our products and services. (Johnson & Johnson)
2.	Product/Service	AMAX's principal products are molybdenum, coal, iron ore, copper, lead, zinc, petroleum and natural gas, potash, phosphates, nickel, tungsten, silver, gold, and magnesium. (AMAX)
3.	Geographic Domain	We are dedicated to the total success of Corning Glass Works as a worldwide competitor. (Corning Glass)
4.	Technology	Control Data is in the business of applying microelectronics and computer technology in two general areas: computer-related hardware and computing-enhancing services, which include computation, information, education, and finance. (Control Data)
5.	Concern for Survival	In this respect, the company will conduct its operations prudently and will provide the profits and growth which will assure Hoover's ultimate success. (Hoover Universal)
6.	Philosophy	We believe human development to be the worthiest of the goals of civilization and independence to be the superior condition for nurturing growth in the capabilities of people. (Sun Company)
7.	Self-concept	Hoover Universal is a diversified, multi-industry corporation with strong manufacturing capabilities, entrepreneurial policies, and individual business unit autonomy. (Hoover Universal)
8.	Concern for Public Image	Also, we must be responsive to the broader concerns of the public, including especially the general desire for improvement in the quality of life, equal opportunity for all, and the constructive use of natural resources. (Sun Company)

SOURCE: J. A. Pearce, II, and F. R. David, "Corporate Mission Statements: The Bottom Line," *Academy of Management Executive* (May 1987), vol. 1, no. 2, pp. 109–116.

tures upon which the organization will be based. As John A. Pearce, II, notes, "the critical role of the company mission as the basis of orchestrating managerial actions is repeatedly demonstrated by failing firms whose short-run actions are ultimately found to be counterproductive to the long-run purpose."[41] W. T. Grant, a retail chain of almost $2 billion in sales and one thousand stores went bankrupt in 1975 because it couldn't decide what it wanted to be. It didn't know whether it wanted to be a Sears, Roebuck or a K Mart, and so became neither. It landed somewhere in between. Consequently, customers could not determine what it was and who was supposed to shop there. It didn't know its mission, and neither did the customer.[42]

This Hewlett-Packard team is working on various stages of a software package. Functioning within policies, they are operationalizing the plans of others. They are helping achieve the goals of the company. Note the openness of the environment, and the apparent friendliness of the work situation. These factors help accomplish the "people goal." (SOURCE © Robert Holmgren)

Goals and Objectives

Goals are broadly stated, further refinements of organizational mission. They are more specific than mission and address key issues within the organization, such as market standing, innovation, productivity, physical and financial resources, profitability, management performance and development, worker performance and attitude, public responsibility,[43] treatment of employees, growth, efficiency, treatment of customers, returns to owners, and so on.[44] But they are not as specific as objectives. They are open-ended statements of purpose to be used when you do not want to be entangled in specifics.[45] Goals help describe an organization's philosophy—its philosophical purposes and the types of general ends it would like to achieve. **Objectives** are specific statements of results anticipated. They further define the organization's goals. Typically, each goal will be subdivided into a set of very specific objectives.

THE IMPORTANCE OF GOALS AND OBJECTIVES

Goals are important because they provide a first stage of refinement for an organizational mission that allows the organization to explain philosophically the areas in which it intends to proceed. Sample goals for Hewlett-Packard are presented in Table 5.3.

AT BARNETT: *Barnett Bank develops very general goals, such as service, growth, and profit. Then several specific objectives are derived for each. Growth, for example, might mean three acquisitions, an increase in market share of 10 percent, and a regional banking acquisition.*

Table 5.3. Hewlett-Packard's Goals

The following is a brief description of the Hewlett-Packard goals in 1989:

1. Profit Objective: To achieve sufficient profit to finance company growth and to provide the resources we need to achieve our other corporate objectives.
2. Customer Objective: To provide products and services of the highest quality and the greatest possible value to our customers, thereby gaining and holding their respect and loyalty.
3. Fields of Interest Objective: To participate in those fields of interest that build upon our technology and customer base, that offer opportunities for continuing growth, and that enable us to make a needed and profitable contribution.
4. Growth Objective: To let growth be limited only by our profits and our ability to develop and produce innovative products that satisfy real customer needs.
5. Our People Objective: To help Hewlett-Packard people share in the company's success, which they make possible; to provide employment security based on their performance; to ensure them a safe and pleasant work environment; to recognize individual achievements; and to help them gain a sense of satisfaction and accomplishment from their work.
6. Management Objective: To foster initiative and creativity by allowing the individual great freedom of action in attaining well-defined objectives.
7. Citizenship Objective: To honor our obligations to society by being an economic, intellectual, and social asset to each nation and each community in which we operate.

SOURCE: Hewlett-Packard Company, Inc., Corporate Objectives, 1989.

Objectives are important to the organization for eight principal reasons:[46]

1. They provide specific direction.
2. They provide integration of employee actions by causing those efforts to be accomplished for common reasons.
3. They provide mechanisms for control. Objectives are typically further broken down at the individual work level into standards of performance. Workers are held accountable for their performance against these standards.[47]
4. They provide motivation to those who are assigned the task of accomplishing them. People are goal-striving animals, they seek to accomplish objectives; therefore, having objectives available helps to channel their particular motivations.
5. They help relieve boredom. They provide a way of keeping score.
6. Feedback on attainment can help provide recognition.
7. Achievement of objectives helps raise self-esteem.
8. Achievement of objectives, when combined with feedback, can lead to increased liking for the task and increased satisfaction with performance.

CHARACTERISTICS OF SOUND OBJECTIVES
Effective objectives possess four common characteristics:

1. The goal area or attribute sought
2. An index for matching progress toward the attribute
3. A target to be achieved or hurdle to be overcome
4. A time frame within which the target or hurdle is to be achieved[48]

A sample for each of these characteristics is given in Table 5.4. These characteristics are relevant whether the objectives are set by top-level managers or by a front-line manager. They are also relevant for objectives anyone might set for personal planning purposes.

Table 5.4. Characteristics of Effective Objectives

Possible Attributes	Possible Indices	Targets and Time Frame		
		Year 1	Year 2	Year 3
Growth	Dollar sales	$100 million	$120 million	$140 million
	Unit sales	1.00 × units	1.10 × units	1.20 × units
Efficiency	Dollar profits	$10 million	$12 million	$15 million
	Profits/sales	0.10	0.10	0.11
Utilization of resources	ROI	0.15	0.15	0.16
	ROE	0.25	0.26	0.27
Contributions to owners	Dividends per share	$1	$1.10	$1.30
	Earnings per share	$2	$2.40	$2.80
Contributions to customers	Price Quality Reliability	Equal to or better than competition	Equal to or better than competition	Equal to or better than competition
Contributions to employees	Wage rate	$3.50/hour	$3.75/hour	$4.00/hour
	Employment stability	<5% turnover	<4% turnover	<4% turnover
Contributions to society	Taxes paid	$10 million	$12 million	$16 million
	Scholarships awarded, etc.	$100,000	$120,000	$120,000

SOURCE C. W. Hofer, "A Conceptual Scheme for Formulating a Total Business Strategy," no. BP-0040 (Dover, Mass.: Case Teacher's Association, 1976), p. 2. Copyright 1976 by C. W. Hofer. Reproduced by permission.

Managing by Objectives

Managing by objectives was first employed by General Motors in a system known as Managing for Results, as reported to us by management author and consultant Peter Drucker.[49] It was popularized by management consultant and author George Odiorne as management by objectives (MBO), in the 1960s.[50] At one time about half of the Fortune 500 industrial firms employed some form of the system.[51] More recently Heinz Weihrich has comprehensively examined MBO systems as a way of instilling managerial excellence. One of his major contentions is that MBO must be integrated thoroughly in the other major organizational systems—strategic management, organizational development, and human resource development—in order for it to be effective.[52]

The process is a relatively simple one, consisting of just a few steps at each level of management:

1. Objectives are determined. Objectives are then distributed to the next level of management.
2. Action plans are formulated.
3. Some degree of participation occurs in the setting of objectives and the formation of plans.
4. Implementation occurs.

DETERMINING OBJECTIVES

Mission is defined in terms of goals. Goals are further defined in terms of more specific objectives. Related subobjectives are established for each major function or other division of the organization. Objectives are then distributed down the hierarchy. This process occurs until each and every manager in the organization, and each and every other person in the organization who has control of the contents of his or her job, have some share of each of the top-level objectives established to achieve organizational goals. Examination of numerous studies on MBO and goal setting by researchers Gary P. Latham and Gary Yukl indicate that

1. The more specific the objective, the more likely the performance will increase.
2. Difficult objectives, if they are accepted by the subordinate, stimulate higher levels of performance than do easier goals.
3. Setting objectives works well at both management and operative levels.
4. Whether objectives are assigned or set participatively, they help improve performance.[53]

The number of objectives that can be practically considered by a manager or other employee ranges from six to twelve. If there are any more than that, a person would have a difficult time giving all of them his or her full consideration. Objectives should be established that stretch each individual, but they should not be so demanding as to frighten, discourage, or create fear of failure. Research suggests that specific objectives are more effective than "do the best you can" objectives.[54]

DEVELOPING ACTION PLANS

Once objectives are determined at each level of the organization, plans must be formulated to accomplish them. Normally most managers formulate their own action plans and seek approval for them from above in the hierarchy.

PARTICIPATION

One of the major issues in any MBO type management system is the degree to which the subordinate gets involved in establishing objectives and what plans should be made to achieve those objectives. In most organizations objectives are negotiable but generally are directed from above. Normally top management suggests objectives to the next level of management, which in turn suggests objectives to the succeeding level of management, and so on until operational managers or other employees involved in the system have received their objectives. There is usually some room for negotiation. On the other hand, in most organizations the individual manager is allowed to determine how to achieve the objectives. There is often a high level of participation in the total planning process but not in that segment devoted to the establishment of objectives. The more you would want to develop your subordinates, the more you would probably allow them to help participate in setting objectives.[55] The more and faster you need to respond to environmental changes, the more likely you will use participation.

IMPLEMENTATION OF ACTION PLANS

Once the plans necessary to achieve objectives have been determined, it is necessary to implement them. Although this may seem like a simple process, actually it is one of the most complex processes at all levels of the organization. It involves leadership, communication, motivation, staffing, human resource management, culture management, systems management, and information management.

MBO systems have both positive and negative aspects.[56] The positive aspects of MBO include

1. Increases in quantity and quality of performance.
2. Improvement in communication and understanding.
3. Raised job satisfaction for the individual.
4. Enhancement of individual growth.

MANAGEMENT CHALLENGE **5.5**

Competing in the Silicon Death Valley

How do you make money in a business that everybody else is losing money in? One way is by using Turbo MBO. Cypress Semiconductor Company of San Jose, California, made $13.4 million on sales of $40.9 million in 1986, with third-quarter, 1987 sales already exceeding $52 million. Almost every other firm in the industry was losing money. Cypress's president, T. J. Rodgers, swears by his MBO system. He knows every day, by reading a computer printout, what every one of his six hundred employees is doing, how close they are to achieving their goals, and if they are failing to achieve their goals. Every Wednesday at noon on the dot, T. J. Rodgers assembles his top people for a status report on goals for each of the departments in the company. There is no escape; the computer knows all. The large screen containing computer-generated graphics and performance charts details the status of each executive's weekly goals.

Rodgers likes to call his system "Turbo MBO." He begins every Monday morning with project leaders sitting down with their staffs and assigning the jobs that

5. Clarification of role prescriptions—this is a highly beneficial effect, as people know what is expected of them.

6. Motivation provided by objectives.

The negative aspects of MBO include

1. Various problems with objective setting, such as objectives being set too high or too low, objectives being rejected, objectives being inflexible, and it being difficult to set objectives for nonquantifiable areas such as employee morale.

2. Managers become more critical when using MBO systems than under previous systems.

3. Objectives are often used as whips.

4. Rewards are often not tied to performance, or are nonexistent altogether.

5. MBO is a very time-consuming process.

6. Group dynamics are usually not taken into consideration.

7. Each individual has physical and mental limitations that many MBO systems attempt to expand.

8. The goals established often set the upper limit of performance even if they could be exceeded.

9. MBO has historically worked best in a slowly changing environment—something we are going to see less and less of in the future.

Although the negatives listed here outnumber the positives, the importance of the positives and their strengths should not be overlooked. Virtually all of the research indicates that MBO programs tend to fail most commonly because results are not evaluated; rewards are not tied to performance; and there has been some failure to implement the program properly—for example, too little or too much participation.[57]

The benefits and liabilities of MBO are well illustrated in Management Challenge 5.5.

need attention that week. Everyone's new goals are put into a DEC minicomputer, which is linked to executives and managers via personal computers. Lotus 1-2-3® spreadsheets are used to display goals. On Tuesday prioritization of individual objectives occur. On Wednesday any manager with 35 percent of his or her goals delinquent has some serious explaining to do. The computer alerts the president when his executives are delinquent on 20 percent of their goals.

Rodgers's Turbo MBO and MBO in general have their critics. One engineer who left the firm said he was self-motivating and professional and did not need someone looking over his shoulder all the time. Others such as Julian Philips, a San Francisco principal at McKinsey and Company, indicates that MBO is not able to keep up with a changing environment. Rodgers disagrees. He feels that the Turbo MBO system allows managers to change quickly. The important thing is to have frequent meetings about achieving objectives and not to put them away and wait for six months to find out whether you have reached them. This is one reason he has weekly major performance reviews and daily performance reviews on the computer. As Rodgers says, his competitors may surprise him, but he wants no surprises from his organization.

SOURCE: Steve Kaufman, "Going for the Goals," *Success* (January–February 1988), pp. 38–41.

T. J. Rogers of Cypress Semiconductor examines the computer printout of his firm's MBO program. Rogers believes strongly in this program and its contribution to the company's profitability. (SOURCE © Robert Holmgren)

Management by Objectives, Results, and Rewards (MBORR)

Failure at measuring results and rewards has led this author to believe that the proper type of MBO program is an MBORR program, where *results* and *rewards* are integral components of this system.

As is indicated elsewhere, the evidence suggests that MBO does not always produce the desired results unless actual results are measured and considered in performance appraisals and rewards are given for the successful attainment of objectives. Using MBO in combination with checking for results and rewarding performance is mangement by objectives, results, and rewards, or MBORR.[58] One outstanding example of a successful MBORR-type program is used by the Cypress Semiconductor Company of San Jose, California, discussed in Management Challenge 5.5.

PRIORITIZING OBJECTIVES

Every manager faces a conflict regarding the priorities of the multiple objectives he or she has established. At the strategic level, for example, what does the chief executive sacrifice in efficiency to achieve market share objectives? Or, a front-line manager may have personal development objectives for each subordinate but to achieve those objectives he may temporarily have to sacrifice productivity by sending an employee to a developmental seminar, thus taking him or her out of the operation. There are almost always conflicts betwen long-term and short-term objectives at any level of the organization. And an individual's personal objectives may be in conflict with organizational priorities. The problem is made more complex by the fact that objectives are often interdependent.

How then does the manager prioritize objectives? First there are few proven rules of thumb for determining appropriate priorities. As in any problem-solving situation, the manager must look to the alternatives—in this case alternative objectives—and then evaluate them according to criteria. Thus, the important factor would be to develop criteria for prioritizing the needs of customers, bosses, or subordinates; for balancing resources, time frames, and impact on the company. All of these factors and others may be used to determine priorities.

Alternatives to Objective-Based Systems

Fundamental to any objective-based system is the belief that the individual's job can be narrowly separated from other's efforts. It is easy to see how MBORR-type systems would work in sales and in manufacturing, where each person clearly affects the bottom line. It is even possible to identify contribution for many jobs in service industries or service functions in manufacturing or sales. Accounts payable clerks, for example, can be required to process so many pieces of paper in a certain period, or a hospital nurse can be required to receive a 98 percent positive patient evaluation. But many jobs in many organizations are difficult to describe in terms of the specific objectives each is to achieve. For example, what does a trainer in the personnel department accomplish—is it the number of people trained, is it how they are trained or is there some productivity measure that can be evaluated as increasing as a result of the training given? Or take, for example, the financial manager for the company—what factors are under his or her control? What can he or she accomplish? Can the president of the company actually increase profits? If so, to what identifiable degree?

It is sometimes necessary to provide behavioral descriptions of what is expected, rather than objective accomplishments, and hold people accountable for applying the description of the behavior. A technique known as the **behaviorally**

anchored rating scale (BARS) does just that. It lists a series of behavioral activities that should be undertaken in any one job. It then provides verbal descriptions of several levels of performance for each behavioral activity. BARS are expensive to create and time consuming to use as a method of planning and control, but they are very useful in those situations described here.[59] Managers and human resource management experts are still attempting to objectify further what it is that people are supposed to accomplish in many jobs. BARS are very useful where this has not been accomplished.

Another problem facing organizations more and more today is the increasing complexity and changefulness of their external environments. MBORR systems, which function very well in many organizations, must be made more flexible to meet tomorrow's challenges. Target zones for accomplishment, rather than specific standards for accomplishments, appear to be one change that's necessary. More frequent review of more flexible objectives and of performance are also occurring, as we saw with Turbo MBO. Ten years ago banks, for example, readily fit the mold of companies that could use an MBORR system. And while banks now need an objective/performance-driven system more than ever, their environments are changing quite rapidly. They need to be able to respond to those changes rapidly, but still, in some way, objectively describe that anticipated performance. What appears to be occurring are two approaches. On the one hand, rather broad statements of objectives with acceptable ranges of performance are being established; and on the other hand, frequent reviews of very specific, but flexible, objectives are being used in many companies.

Setting Personal Objectives

Part of a manager's responsibility is to set personal objectives—not just those related to the organization, but objectives he or she personally must achieve for self-development and growth in order to be a more productive member of the organization (and of society).[60] While most of a manager's objectives should be tied directly to the organization's mission, goals, and objectives, he or she should, and probably always will, be alert to the need to develop and grow within and beyond a particular job's objectives. One's mental, physical, psychological, social responsibility, achievement, interpersonal, leadership, and related family objectives must be considered. Many of these stem directly from achieving organizational objectives, but some may be in conflict with them. For example, working overtime can conflict with family objectives.

Planning as a Problem-Solving Exercise

Figure 5.6 reveals just how clearly planning is a problem-solving exercise. In fact the only major difference between problem solving and general planning is the time horizon. While most problems are solved for the immediate future, most planning is expected to bring results over an extended length of time. The key in planning, perhaps more than in any other type of problem solving, is to search the environment for important pieces of information. In organizing, leading, and controlling, much more of the information necessary to make the choice to solve the problem is usually readily available. Problem solving in planning often deals much more with unknown and forecasted factors than do the other three management functions. The manager must search for this information in a much more organized fashion.

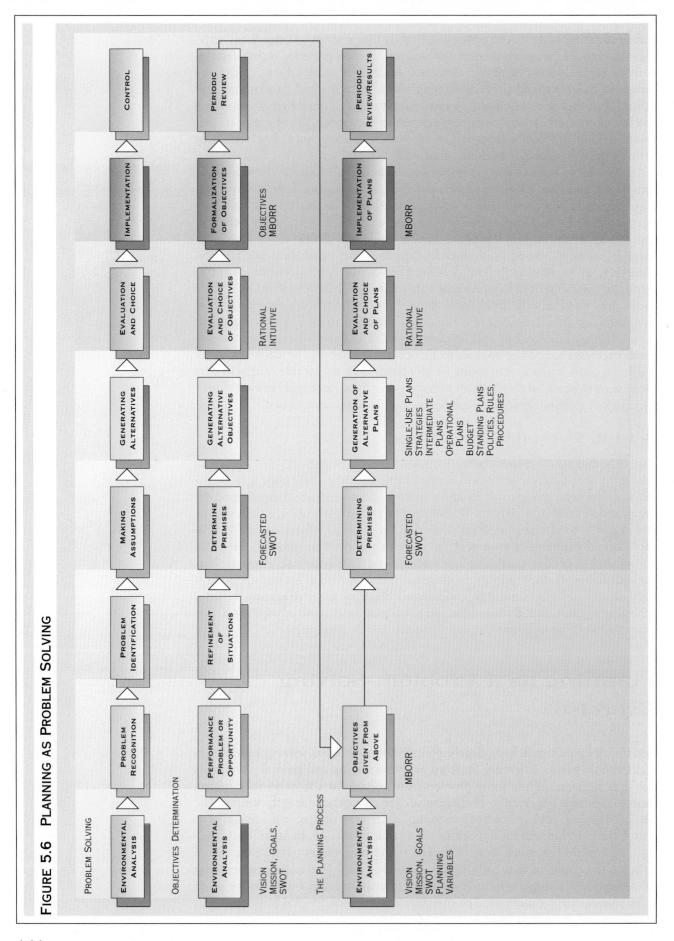

FIGURE 5.6 PLANNING AS PROBLEM SOLVING

PROBLEM SOLVING

| ENVIRONMENTAL ANALYSIS | PROBLEM RECOGNITION | PROBLEM IDENTIFICATION | MAKING ASSUMPTIONS | GENERATING ALTERNATIVES | EVALUATION AND CHOICE | IMPLEMENTATION | CONTROL |

OBJECTIVES DETERMINATION

| ENVIRONMENTAL ANALYSIS | PERFORMANCE PROBLEM OR OPPORTUNITY | REFINEMENT OF SITUATIONS | DETERMINE PREMISES | GENERATING ALTERNATIVE OBJECTIVES | EVALUATION AND CHOICE OF OBJECTIVES | FORMALIZATION OF OBJECTIVES | PERIODIC REVIEW |

VISION
MISSION, GOALS,
SWOT

FORECASTED
SWOT

RATIONAL
INTUITIVE

OBJECTIVES
MBORR

THE PLANNING PROCESS

| ENVIRONMENTAL ANALYSIS | OBJECTIVES GIVEN FROM ABOVE | DETERMINING PREMISES | GENERATION OF ALTERNATIVE PLANS | EVALUATION AND CHOICE OF PLANS | IMPLEMENTATION OF PLANS | PERIODIC REVIEW/RESULTS |

VISION
MISSION, GOALS
SWOT
PLANNING
VARIABLES

MBORR

FORECASTED
SWOT

SINGLE-USE PLANS
STRATEGIES
INTERMEDIATE
PLANS
OPERATIONAL
PLANS
BUDGET
STANDING PLANS
POLICIES, RULES,
PROCEDURES

RATIONAL
INTUITIVE

MBORR

The manager goes through the problem-solving process at least twice for each plan derived. The first time is to determine objectives, and the second time is to formulate the plans to achieve those objectives. Figure 5.6 expands these two processes by showing how the key terms and concepts introduced in this chapter fit into the process. Many times the manager is given objectives to achieve. Going through the problem-solving process for each objective is simply a matter of making certain that other factors don't warrant a change in that objective. A manager, for example, may have been given an objective of reducing scheduled work hours of employees in the program or service area by 10 percent. However, if he or she is aware that sales are expected to increase beyond what top management could have known when determining this objective, this manager must provide feedback to top management and indicate the inappropriateness of the objective. Additionally, as seen in the figure, certain planning assumptions known as premises exist at any level of the planning process. The manager must always be as certain as possible about the validity of these premises.

Management Challenges Identified

1. External environmental factors—for example, competition
2. Internal environmental factors—for example, management philosophy
3. Accelerated rates of change
4. The need for a myriad of plans and ways to integrate them

Some Solutions Noted in the Chapter

1. Different types of planning
2. Turbo MBO-type systems
3. Flexibility, willingness to change vision, mission, goals, objectives, plans
4. Participation

Summary

1. The planning process consists of two parts: determining objectives and planning formulation. Both of these subcomponents follow the basic problem-solving model. Determining objectives consists of the following steps: environmental analysis, performance/opportunity analysis, the refinement of the situation, generating alternative objectives, evaluating objectives, formalizing objectives, and periodic review. These objectives then become part of the planning formulation process which consists of the following steps: environmental analysis, objectives, generating alternative plans, identifying premises, evaluating alternative plans, choosing plans, implementing plans, and periodically reviewing the results of plans.

2. Planning is problem solving for the future, in the sense that the future's concerns are typically more long term than problem solving for organizing, leading, or controlling might be. All management is problem solving for the future; the issue is how far into the future you plan. Most organizational leadership and control concerns are solved with knowledge of the immediate situation; forecasting is not necessary.

3. Planning leads to the other three functions of management. Planning provides the objectives and plans of action that organization structure is designed to achieve. Leadership is used to influence individuals in that structure to accomplish those objectives and goals. Control determines if the objectives of planning are achieved, if the plans were carried out.

4. Planning is important because it:
   a. prepares people for the future.
   b. provides motivation.
   c. initiates proactive problem solving, not reactive decision making.
   d. is a basis for the functions.
   e. provides communication.
   f. leads to the establishment of performance objectives.
   g. limits emotional decision making.
   h. anticipates that changes are going to happen—why not plan for them?
   i. builds confidence in the organization and management.
   j. provides definition of the organization

5. Planning is more complex, more uncertain, more unique, more unstructured, and more long term at top levels of management than it is at middle or lower levels. At lower levels there are few factors involved, there is more certainty, many of the decisions are routine/structured and planning typically is for the short term.

6. a. The scope of an organization is concerned with how much of its resources—how much of the organization—the plan is concerned with. Is it a corporate, business, or functional strategy or an intermediate or operational plan?
   b. What are the plan's characteristics? Is it complex or simple? Comprehensive or narrow? Of major or minor importance? Quantitative or qualitative? Strategic or operational? Confidential or public? Written or unwritten? Informal or formal? Easy or difficult to implement? Rational or creative? Flexible or inflexible?

7. Reasons people fail at planning:
   a. Lack of commitment
   b. Failure to implement sound strategies
   c. Lack of meaningful objectives and goals
   d. Failure to see planning as rational and creative
   e. Excessive reliance on experience
   f. Lack of clear delegation

8. The planning process begins with organizational purposes, whether they be vision, mission, goals, or objectives. Plans are formulated to achieve purposes.

9. Vision is a broad general direction for the organization to move in. Mission describes an organization's line of business and how it basically chooses to proceed in that business. Other concerns include target market, some key product feature, geographical location, and often an organization's philosophy. Goals are broad statements that further define an organization's mission. Objectives provide exact, specific definitions of goals.

10. Goals are important because
    a. they provide further definition of the mission.
    b. they define the areas in which the organization will proceed.
    Objectives are important because they provide
    a. direction.
    b. integration.
    c. mechanisms for control.
    d. motivation.
    e. release from boredom.
    f. recognition through attainment.
    g. self-esteem through accomplishment.
    h. increased liking for the task.

11. Sound objectives have the following characteristics:
    a. Goals and attributes are sought.
    b. They are an index for measuring progress toward the attribute.
    c. They are a target to be achieved.
    d. They are a time frame in which the target is to be achieved.

12. MBO consists of these steps:
    a. Determination and distribution of objectives
    b. Formulation of action plans
    c. Some degree of participation
    d. Implementation
    e. Determining results and giving rewards on the basis of those results via MBORR

13. Point number 1 above indicated how objective setting and planning are problem-solving processes.

Thinking About Management

1. Describe the objective setting and planning processes for an organization with which you are familiar.
2. Discuss planning for a not-for-profit organization such as the United Way or the American Heart Association and indicate how it might differ from that in a for-profit organization.
3. What is the relationship between standing plans and single-use plans.
4. Given what you know about management and given the changing and complex external environment for most companies, what do you think is the future for intermediate planning? How might planning be improved in such environments?
5. Discuss each of the characteristics of plans for an organization with which you are familiar.
6. Will planning increase or decrease in importance in the future? Why?
7. With respect to your own personal planning, are you a short-term or long-term planner? Or do you plan your life at all? Write down five success-oriented goals for yourself for the next year and the next three to five years.
8. Are there any conflicts in the objectives you have set for number 7? How would you prioritize those objectives?
9. How would you integrate the objectives and plans of each business for a multi-business unit firm such as General Electric?
10. The chapter lists the reasons people fail at planning. How would you try to overcome each of them?

Holiday Inns—Finding the Trip a Bit More Difficult in the 80s

Kemmons Wilson founded Holiday Inns with the vision that car travelers should have affordable accommodations. He had plans drawn up for the motels, he established a strategy for expansion, and rapidly built the world's largest motel chain. (SOURCE © Will McIntyre/Photo Researchers)

Kemmons Wilson took a vacation with his wife and five children in the summer of 1951, driving from Memphis to Washington, D.C. and back. A series of unpleasant experiences, not the least of which was paying an extra $2 per child at motels, convinced him that he could do better. Mr. Wilson, than a successful thirty-eight-year-old home builder, ordered up plans. They came back labeled Holiday Inns—his architect had seen a Bing Crosby movie the night before. Two years later he had four Holiday Inns, one covering each approach to Memphis. By 1956 he had entered motel franchising, and the rest is history. He opened his 1,000th Holiday Inn in 1968. In the 1970s the firm attempted to diversify but did not fare well. In the 1980s the demographics that had fostered the company's spectacular growth in the 1960s turned against it. Fewer and fewer people were available in the age groups that traveled and used Holiday Inns. Furthermore, increased levels of competition in Holiday Inn's niche have created severe problems for the company. In 1979 Kemmons Wilson, after the board of directors purchased Perkins Cake and Steak restaurant chain against his better judgment, resigned from Holiday Inns.

The market is fragmented by price with luxury hotels and middle-range and budget motels. Holiday Inn, a middle-priced firm, is moving into both the high-priced and budget segments with its Holiday Crown Plazas, Plaza Suites, the budget Hampton Inns, and the extended-stay Residence Inns. The company seems to have lost the vision Kemmons Wilson had for it. The company makes money, but less than analysts say they should. Earnings declined 20 percent in 1986. "The sharks smelled blood." Takeovers were rumored. Holiday Inns, now managed by professionals, created a complex, special dividend program, with an increased number of shares for top management, that helped ensure that the company remained in its current manager's hands. The company seems more concerned with protecting itself from buyouts than it does about managing.

SOURCE: John Helyar, "Altered Landscape: The Holiday Inns Trip for Decades in the 80s," *Wall Street Journal* 11 February 1987, pp. 1, 18.

DISCUSSION QUESTIONS
1. Discuss the impact of vision on this company's successes through the 1970s.
2. How might planning have prevented concerns about takeovers?
3. How might planning help this company now?
4. What evidence of planning do you find in the history of this company?

An Information Services Division

Lou Follett, head of the East Coast department of a large information systems division, pondered the situation with which he was faced. His boss, Bob, had instituted a management by objectives (MBO) program for the division, as part of their changing approach to management—increased authority was given to various divisions, making them more autonomous. Consequently, the information division, which before had been a cost center providing service to captive clientele, would function as a profit center and compete against market service companies for clientele. The company had only begun formalized, corporatewide strategic planning in 1984, and three years later, the information systems division had adapted MBO as a way of implementing that effort. Lou decided that his human resources people needed to be involved and could provide him with guidance about which actions to take. He called a meeting with Karen Stone, his personnel manager, and her assistant, Marian Matthew, to solicit ideas. As a result of the meeting, he asked Karen to draw up a plan of action. She was to use the forms and limited information on MBO provided by the West Coast human resource department. Furthermore, she would arrange for Bob to talk with all of the East Coast managers about MBO. Beyond that, she was on her own and could move forward as she saw fit, with Lou reserving the right to final approval of any plans she and Marian might make.

DISCUSSION QUESTIONS
1. If you were Karen and Marian, what actions should you propose to Lou?
2. How might an MBO system best be used in this situation—for planning, for control, and for employee development?

Learning About MBORR

How well do you understand the MBORR system? Let's find out. Your instructor has established objectives for you for the semester and surely you have, too. It is time to formalize those objectives. Your MBORR system is at this point only partly participatory. You have been assigned objectives, but there are also some objectives you are determining for yourself. You have the ability to choose a plan of action to achieve your objectives. In the space below, indicate your instructor's objectives for you, your objectives, and the plans of action that you intend to use to achieve both sets of objectives. When the course is over, write the results and the rewards you received.

Your Instructor's Objectives
for You in This Course

Your Objectives for Yourself
in This Course

Your Plans of Actions to Reach Those Objectives

1. Instructor's Objectives
2. Your Objectives

Results

Rewards

CHAPTER SIX

Strategy Formulation and Implementation

CHAPTER OBJECTIVES

By the time you complete this chapter you should be able to

1. Describe the strategic management process in organizations.
2. Identify the major levels of strategy and describe each briefly.
3. Describe the major steps in the strategic planning process.
4. List and describe the major types of corporate strategies.
5. State the three questions that strategic planning answers.
6. Identify the various strategists.
7. Relate the role of human behavior in the strategic management process.
8. Discuss strategic planning in different types of organizations.
9. Discuss strategy implementation.

CHAPTER OUTLINE

Strategic Planning, Strategic Management, Strategic Thinking
  The Strategic Management Perspective
  Strategic Thinking
Strategy Formulation
  SWOT Analysis
  Planning Premises
Strategy Formulation at the Corporate Level
  Single Business Corporate Strategy
  Multiple Business Corporate Strategy
  Strategy and the Industry Life Cycle
Strategy Formulation at the Business Level
  Generic Strategies—The Porter Competitive Strategies
  Hall's Competitiveness Model
  Other Generic Strategies
  Creating a Competitive Advantage
  Concern with the Product/Industry Life Cycle
Strategy Formulation at the Functional Level
The Strategists
Human Behavior and Strategy
Strategic Planning and Different Types of Organizations
  Small Business
  Not-for-Profits
  International Business
  Regulated Businesses
Strategy Implementation
  Organizational Structure
  Management Systems
  Leadership Style
  Management of Organizational Culture
Strategic Management in Increasingly Complex and Turbulent Environments
Strategic Management as a Creative Problem-Solving Endeavor
Management Challenges Identified
Some Solutions Noted in the Chapter

Sears: Getting Competitive

In the fall of 1988, Sears, Roebuck & Company was faced with a possible takeover attempt. Its stock was significantly underpriced, relative to what its breakup value would be after a successful takeover. Rumors swirled that Revlon Group Chairman Ronald O. Perelman was preparing a bid for the $50.2 billion company. Sears Chairman Edward A. Brennan announced plans to move his six-thousand-member corporate headquarters out of the Sears Tower in Chicago, possibly, rumors said, to Dallas, Atlanta, or some other sunbelt city. Eventually he moved the headquarters into a Chicago suburb, but the move was just the beginning of a huge change for Sears's 520,000 employees.

Sears was under tremendous pressure from K Mart Corporation and Wal-Mart Stores, Inc.; traditional big-store retailers such as Macy's and Rich's; the major discount stores, such as those that dominate electronics; and niche players, such as Toys "R" Us. The number of employees in Sears's merchandising arm was nearly twice that of rivals Wal-Mart and K Mart. Not only did Brennan determine that he would move the headquarters and maybe sell the Sears Tower, he also decided that Sears would sell its Allstate Insurance Group and the Coldwell Banker Real Estate Group. His actions indicated a return from a multiple business unit firm to principally a single business unit firm, a consumer merchandising company.

On March 1, 1989, Sears announced its one-price strategy, indicating that it would try to compete with K Mart and Wal-Mart with "everyday low prices." It would discontinue its constant sales and always have the same low prices. This strategy was designed to reverse a drop in earnings of 7.7 percent for the last five years—1984–1988. But to support the low-price program, Sears had to cut costs. Brennan planned to cut excessive layers of management and, apparently, a large number of employees from the retail sales staff in order to attempt to bring the company in line with the staffing levels of competitors. Sears's selling and administrative expenses gobbled up an estimated $.30 of every sales dollar in 1988, compared with an estimated $.23 at K Mart and $.20 at hardware superstore Home Depot. And despite all the belt-tightening Sears had done in recent years, overhead grew faster than sales from 1984 to 1988. Bernard F. Brennan, Montgomery Ward chairman and the brother of Sears's chairman, Edward A. Brennan, notes, "The cost issue is the most significant one in a one-priced strategy." Montgomery Ward and Company had reduced costs by 5 percent from 1986 to 1988, before it introduced its everyday low-price strategy in February 1989.

Other strategic actions had to be taken. Sears decided to sell more name-brand products in order to attract more middle-class and upper-middle-class customers. Sears moved quickly, for example, to sign a special deal with McDonald's to create a line of McKids clothing. And Reebok, L.A. Gear, and even G.E. washing machines (which compete with Sears's own Kenmore brand) are appearing in Sears's stores. Sears also tried to change the way it competes in the marketplace by ridding itself of drab-looking stores and making more efficient use of space. It cut inventories and cut back on certain brands. Will it all work? It is too soon to tell, but the critical element is cutting costs by cutting employees. This strategy already has begun, and morale at Sears is at an all-time low. This may hamper turnaround efforts.

SOURCES: "The Big Stores' Big Trauma," *Business Week* (July 10, 1989), pp. 50–56; "Shakeup at Sears," *Newsweek* (November 14, 1988), pp. 51–52; "Will the Big Markdown Get the Big Store Moving Again?" *Business Week* (March 13, 1989), pp. 110–114; and Patricia Sellers, "Why Bigger Is Badder at Sears," *Fortune* (December 5, 1988), pp. 80–84.

> We are not managing this company for the next quarter. We are building it for the next generation.
>
> Sam Johnson, chairman and CEO,
> S. C. Johnson & Son, Inc. (Johnson's Wax)

> Of all the contrasts between the successful and the unsuccessful business, or between the corporate leader and its followers, the single, most important differentiating factor is strategy.
>
> J. Thomas Cannon
> Strategic Management Author

Among the most important actions that top managers take are those associated with the formulation and implementation of strategies.[1] As described in the opening vignette, strategy formulation and implementation occur in a hierarchical fashion at the corporate, business, and functional levels of an organization, as shown in Figure 6.1.[2]

There are two types of corporate strategies—those for multiple business organizations, and those for single business organizations. Sears is a multibusiness organization, operating in several business areas—each offering major different products to major different markets. Sears had formulated a multibusiness corporate strategy that included acquiring firms, both for their own sake and to improve synergy with customers. Each of its businesses also had a corporate strategy indicating how it would fundamentally conduct itself in that business.

Being perceived as low priced wasn't enough for Sears. Its top managers believed that they had to offer more popular brands, not just traditional Sears items. For example, they sell L. A. Gear, Reebok, and McKids apparel. (SOURCE © Andy Freeberg)

Each major business that an organization engages in must function competitively in its own marketplace. To do so, it formulates a business strategy. In the retail merchandising business for example, Sears has lowered prices and subsequently attempted to cut costs. It also has changed its product offerings to make it more competitive with K Mart, Wal-Mart, and others. Most organizations, such as Wendy's, Kroger's grocery stores, and Mrs. Field's cookies, operate only in one business area, although they may have many products.

Within any business, there are two types of functional strategies—economic functional strategies such as operations, finance, and human resources management and management functional strategies such as leading. Functional strategies must support the business' corporate and business strategies. Sears's decision to cut retail-store prices meant it had to cut costs. It had to eliminate a significant part of its labor force to do so. This is an example of a supportive human resource strategy. Its decision to cut back on some brands and reduce inventories is an example of an operations strategy aimed at supporting Sears's price and related cost-cutting strategies used to compete in the marketplace.

Finally, every business has a **grand strategy,** the strategy from which virtually all other strategies and plans derive. This is the driving force of an organization. It may be growth, diversification, or any number of factors.[3] Grand strategies may be corporate, business, or functional. At Sears, at this point in time, it is the "one-price" strategy.

The purpose of strategy formulation is to achieve the strategic objectives established earlier in the strategic management process. Strategy formulation is a complex problem-solving process. It not only involves different types of strategies for each of the three distinct levels of strategy, but it also involves a number of additional interrelated strategic factors. Each set of strategic objectives established, each strategy formulated, follows the planning/problem-solving model portrayed in Figure 3.2.[4]

This chapter explores the three levels of strategy and various other factors involved in the complex strategic decision process.[5] Included are discussions of environmental analyses; planning premises; basic action strategies; Porter's competitive strategies; Hall's competitive analysis; the relationships between product or industry life cycle and strategy; the various types of strategists; the role of human behavior in strategy formulation; strategic planning in different types of business, and environments; and strategy implementation. The chapter concludes by exploring the evolving nature of strategic management in increasingly complex and turbulent environments.

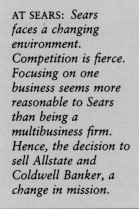

AT SEARS: *Sears's decision to cut prices drastically came suddenly, but it was clearly strategic, perhaps forever altering Sears's image in the marketplace.*

AT SEARS: *Sears faces a changing environment. Competition is fierce. Focusing on one business seems more reasonable to Sears than being a multibusiness firm. Hence, the decision to sell Allstate and Coldwell Banker, a change in mission.*

Strategic Planning, Strategic Management, Strategic Thinking

Strategic planning is the problem-solving process of establishing strategic objectives and formulating strategic plans to accomplish those objectives. Strategic planning may occur in any major area of an organization, but the central focus is most often the marketplace. It is principally concerned with long-term actions to achieve objectives, but it could also be concerned with major short-term

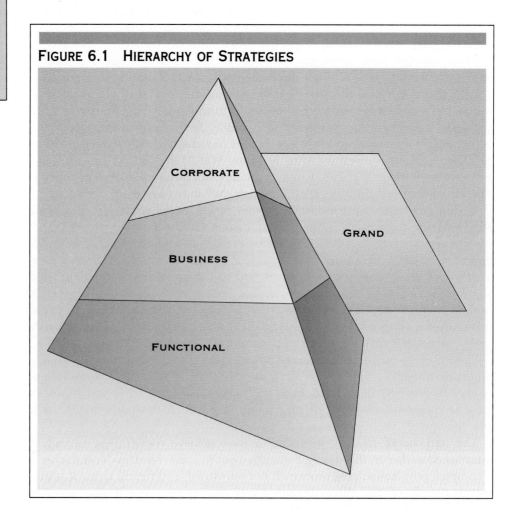

FIGURE 6.1   HIERARCHY OF STRATEGIES

CORPORATE

GRAND

BUSINESS

FUNCTIONAL

actions. Objective setting was discussed in Chapter 5. Strategy formulation is discussed in this chapter.

Any strategic plan is based on answering these three questions:

1. Where are we now?
2. Where do we want to be?
3. How do we get there?

The Strategic Management Perspective

Strategic management is the process of managing the pursuit of organizational mission while managing the relationship of an organization to its environment.[6] As environments continue to change, practicing strategic management becomes more important. Strategic management is more encompassing than strategic planning. Strategic planning is part of strategic management. All of an organization's strategic plans, at all levels and for all functional activities, are included. The strategic management process follows the series of five steps shown in Figure 6.2. Each step is a problem-solving exercise in and of itself.

1. Formulation of vision and mission statements, and goals (see Chapter 5)
2. Determination of strategic objectives (see Chapter 5)
3. Formulation of strategies (discussed in this chapter)
4. Implementation of strategies (discussed in this chapter)
5. Evaluation and control of strategies (discussed in Chapters 17 and 18)

Organizational and managerial concern with strategy has evolved through a series of stages.[7] Historically, much of the concern with strategy in business organizations has been to beat the competition in the marketplace. But in the 1960s and 1970s, strategic planners also became concerned with many non-traditional aspects of the total environment. Managers began to recognize that strategy was not simply a competitive process, but involved virtually any major aspect of running an organization. Of special concern during this period were stakeholders, those who had a stake in an organization's strategic decisions, but would not normally have been considered when those decisions were made. Among those concerned were environmental groups, minorities, and consumer groups. During this same period, a way of strategizing for multiple business organizations also became a major concern. Functional strategies for the management functions, such as planning, organizing, leading, and controlling, also became more formalized.

Although strategic management has received considerable attention, even the

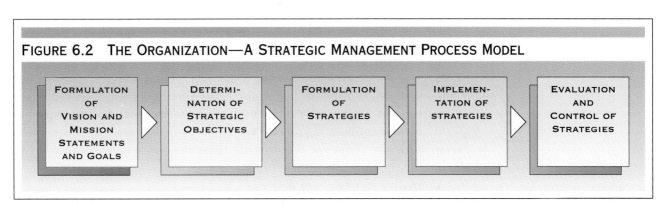

FIGURE 6.2 THE ORGANIZATION—A STRATEGIC MANAGEMENT PROCESS MODEL

| FORMULATION OF VISION AND MISSION STATEMENTS AND GOALS | DETERMINATION OF STRATEGIC OBJECTIVES | FORMULATION OF STRATEGIES | IMPLEMENTATION OF STRATEGIES | EVALUATION AND CONTROL OF STRATEGIES |

SOURCE: FIGURE FROM STRATEGIC MANAGEMENT, TEXT AND CASES BY J. HIGGINS AND J. VINCZE, COPYRIGHT © 1989 BY THE DRYDEN PRESS, INC., A DIVISION OF HOLT, RINEHART AND WINSTON, INC., REPRINTED BY PERMISSION OF THE PUBLISHER.

largest organizations have only recently become concerned with an integrated approach to strategic management. Michael E. Naylor, the executive in charge of corporate strategic planning for General Motors, reports that it was not until the late 1970s that General Motors began to take an integrated strategic management approach to its corporate strategy. It, too, had focused narrowly on the marketing and financial perspectives of individual businesses, not formulating a total corporate strategy or fully considering the various environmental stakeholders affected by its strategies.[8] Walt Disney Companies did not begin corporatewide strategic planning until 1984.[9] Furthermore, only recently has research begun to recognize fully the various aspects and impacts of strategic management.[10]

Strategic Thinking

A number of companies have begun to recognize that strategic planning is becoming more difficult because of the inability to forecast accurately beyond three years—perhaps even beyond two. Among these are GE, Royal Dutch Shell, and Olivetti.[11] So they have begun the practice of **strategic thinking**.[12] This means that they "think" through the strategic planning process. They recognize that they are doing so principally for providing direction, and that at any moment, their objectives and strategies may have to change. Because circumstances change, organizations develop **contingency plans**—here contingency strategies— to put into effect if the plan chosen becomes inappropriate. Shell often generates multiple scenarios of events so they have alternative contingency strategies ready to be implemented when circumstances change. For example, Shell developed several scenarios for the 1981 oil supply situation. When one of them began to materialize, Shell was able to sell off excess oil before the glut came.[13] While Shell prepares scenarios of possible futures, they do not formalize contingency plans—rather, they determine approximately what they should do. When the oil glut scenario began to occur, Shell already had a contingency plan formulated and implemented it quickly.

Strategy Formulation

Strategy formulation, whether corporate, business, or functional, follows the steps outlined in Figure 6.3.

1. It commences with a review of organizational vision, mission, and goals.

2. Next, strategists perform an internal and external environmental analysis.

3. These analyses are used to determine strengths, weaknesses, opportunities, and threats—**SWOT**. This SWOT analysis helps answer the strategic question "Where are we now?"

4. Next, planning premises must be developed. Premises are the assumptions upon which strategic objectives and related strategies will be based. Forecasts of the future states of both internal and external environments are involved in formulating premises.

5. Strategic objectives are determined. These define "Where do we want to be?"

6. Alternative strategies are derived.

7. Choices among those alternatives must be made. These answer the question "How do we get there?"

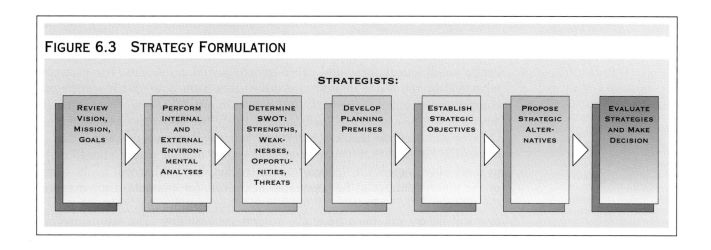

FIGURE 6.3 STRATEGY FORMULATION

STRATEGISTS:

REVIEW VISION, MISSION, GOALS → PERFORM INTERNAL AND EXTERNAL ENVIRONMENTAL ANALYSES → DETERMINE SWOT: STRENGTHS, WEAKNESSES, OPPORTUNITIES, THREATS → DEVELOP PLANNING PREMISES → ESTABLISH STRATEGIC OBJECTIVES → PROPOSE STRATEGIC ALTERNATIVES → EVALUATE STRATEGIES AND MAKE DECISION

Two steps of fundamental importance to this strategic process are the SWOT analysis and the planning premises.

SWOT Analysis

Determining alternative solutions depends greatly upon both an internal and external environmental analysis, the purpose of which is to determine the strengths, weaknesses, opportunities, and threats of an organization relative to another.[14] This process becomes more complex as the environment becomes more turbulent.

THE EXTERNAL ENVIRONMENTAL ANALYSIS
As discussed in Chapters 1, 4, and 5, the manager is confronted with **four principal sets of external factors:** technological, economic/competitive, political/legal, and social. These in turn include numerous subfactors. The competitive environment is so important that it is analyzed separately. Each of the **organization's stakeholders**—those with a vested interest in the actions of an organization's management—anticipate and often demand certain actions by management. Top management must manage these elements as part of strategy formulation.

INTERNAL ENVIRONMENTAL ANALYSIS
Within the organization the strategic manager, depending on his or her function and level, is confronted with a host of **internal environmental factors,** including the other functions of the organization; the general management; the owners—usually stockholders; others who direct the organization for example, in non-profits, the trustees; members of management throughout the organization; various management systems; a host of nonorganized employees; the organizational culture; the organization's rules, policies, and procedures; and the organization's strategy and structure. The manager must be able to balance the needs and requirements of all of these factors against each other, as well as against the demands of the external environment.

Planning Premises[15]

Once current SWOT have been determined, forecasted SWOT must also be. The same or updated SWOT used to determine objectives will be used in establishing premises and strategic alternatives. The strategist seeks to use current

AT SEARS: *The formulation of strategy in a complex organization such as Sears involves redefining the purpose of many organizational components. When Sears desired to change its pricing strategy and cut costs, for example, some of those who decided that those prices and costs should exist in the first place were still part of the management team. They had vested interests in choosing the actions to be taken. But, on the other hand, stockholders were concerned about the decreasing value of Sears's stock and were demanding that changes in strategy be made. Furthermore, organizational culture may not have been receptive to change.*

and predicted strengths to overcome weaknesses and threats and to take advantage of opportunities in achieving strategic objectives. In order to determine future SWOT, strategists must make *premises*—certain assumptions about the future condition of these and other environmental conditions. For example, what will be the prime interest rate three years from now? What will be our competitors' product strategy two years from now? What major technological advances will be made in the next three years? What major social/demographic changes will occur in the next five years? What will the future composition of ownership be? Will that new management system that we want to install make us more able to meet the demands of the marketplace? What will be the terms of the union contract to be negotiated next year, for example, and what will the labor rates be? These and hundreds of other assumptions, although only a few will be critical, must be made in strategic planning. The results are not always what is sought. GE engaged in a $500 million modernization of its assembly line for locomotives, in an attempt to obtain more market share, on the premise that demand would hold. It didn't. The program began to limp along at 30 percent of capacity after the huge investment.[16]

Strategy Formulation at the Corporate Level

The conceptual steps that the manager goes through in strategic management at the corporate level are essentially the same as they are at the business and functional levels. They involve three major stages: strategy formulation, implementation, and control.

However, the specifics of the strategic planning process at the corporate level differ from those at the business or functional levels. The focus of **corporate strategy** is to determine what business(es) we are in or should be in and how we fundamentally operate that business or businesses. The focus of **business strategy** is to determine how we obtain a strategic competitive advantage and how we should use that advantage to beat the competition. The focus of **functional strategies** is to determine how best to use our resources to support the competitive efforts of the business strategy.

Single Business Corporate Strategy

The underlying question in formulating any corporate strategy is "What business(es) are we in or should we be in?" At the single strategic business unit (SBU) level, as shown in Figure 6.4, the firm begins by asking itself:

1. Is there some business in which the organization has a natural strategic advantage or an innate interest, and if already in that business, does that advantage or interest still exist?
2. Does the company want to compete directly or find a niche where there isn't any head-on competition?
3. Does the company want or need to concentrate in one specific business line or in multiple product lines (or multiple businesses)?
4. Once the company has answered these questions, its basic action-strategy choices are to grow, stabilize, engage in investment reduction, defend against a takeover or seek one, turn around company fortunes, or some combination of these.

FIGURE 6.4   SINGLE BUSINESS CORPORATE STRATEGY

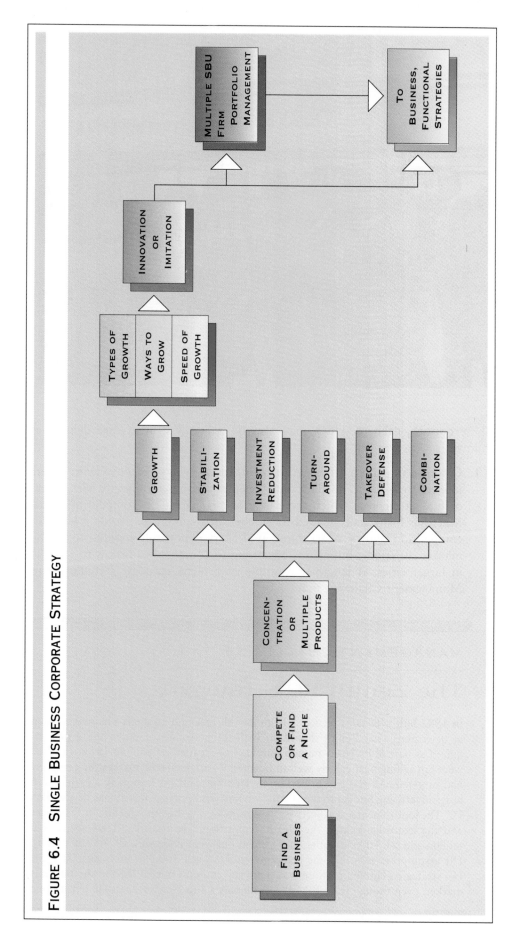

Sam Walton is a shrewd strategist. First he found a niche. As his firm gained strength, he mounted a direct campaign against K Mart. Here he opens a new store, something he will do often in the 1990s. (SOURCE © Jim Knowles/Picture Group)

These options, each of which may also be a grand strategy, are defined as follows:

1. **Compete or Find a Niche:** An organization always competes with others in a general sense. The question is whether it competes directly with others or finds a niche in which there isn't any real head-on competition. Wal-Mart has historically tended to "niche" in small cities, avoiding head-on competition with K Mart. Now Wal-Mart is not only looking for niche market situations, but also is beginning to compete head-on with K Mart in larger cities. A lengthier example of a niche strategy is contained in Management Challenge 6.1.

MANAGEMENT CHALLENGE 6.1

The Zenith PC Strategy

In 1982 half a dozen executives from Zenith met in a strategic planning session to determine what Zenith should do with the personal computer line it had acquired as part of its $64.5 million purchase of Heath Company in 1979. The PCs were not selling particularly well to business customers—the market the company had targeted. All the executives except one felt that the company should use a large advertising budget to wrestle its way into computer stores alongside the IBM PC. The lone dissenter was Jerry K. Perwin, who was then the chief financial officer and the executive behind the Heath acquisition. He argued, "If we spend $10 million and sell 100,000 units, that's great, but what if we only sell 10,000 units?" His assumption was that the company couldn't sell 100,000 units against IBM. His strategic planning premise was that they couldn't outsell IBM in the business market, even though their IBM PC clone was a superior product. He felt no one

2. **Concentration or Multiple Products:** Organizations may concentrate on a single product or product line. Random House publishes books and does nothing else. Conversely, an organization can seek multiple products or product lines, such as Procter & Gamble, which has hundreds of products across numerous segments of many markets.

3. **Growth:** Organizations can choose to grow or not. They may grow larger in sales and/or profits by employing any number of strategies. For example, they may seek new markets for existing products, as McDonald's did in going to Europe and Japan, or develop new products for old markets, as McDonald's did when it introduced salads to its menu. Organizations may innovate or imitate. They may follow numerous additional options.

4. **Stabilization:** Firms may choose to stabilize, perhaps to consolidate, until further growth is advisable. When Burroughs acquired Sperry Corporation to form Unisys, for example, CEO Michael Blumenthal chose to consolidate the firms and stabilize strategies and operations before pursuing growth.

5. **Investment Reduction:** Organizations may choose to cut costs and/or sell off assets. Multiple SBU organizations may divest whole firms. Organizations may even liquidate, sell out, or choose to extract profits from a cash-generating operation.

6. **Turnaround:** Organizations in dire straits must seek to turn around their situations. When Frank Mancuso became chairman of Paramount Studios in September 1984, the company situation was bleak. Former Paramount president, Michael Eisner, had accepted an offer to become chairman of Disney, there were few promising movies in the offing, and the financial situation was weak. But Mancuso succeeded in turning Paramount around because he was a shrewd marketer and was able to convince top stars to work with the company. In 1986 his efforts resulted in such hits as "Top Gun," "Crocodile Dundee," and "Star Trek IV."[17] These were followed by "Crocodile Dundee II" and "Star Trek V."

7. **Defending Against a Takeover or Seeking One:** Some organizations, because of their particular financial condition or because of the inabilities of management, or both, make particularly attractive targets for takeover by other firms. Firms must prepare a defense against takeovers or find them-

"Top Gun" helped Frank Mancuso turn around the fortunes of Paramount Studios. His strategy was simple—get top stars, such as Tom Cruise, to work on sound projects, such as "Top Gun." This turnaround strategy was extremely successful. (SOURCE © Kobal Collection, SuperStock International)

would buy it at a competitive price. Perwin argued successfully that the company would be better off cutting prices and going after niches that IBM and others would not be going after. This again is an assumption, a premise. The company decided to follow his strategy. All his premises turned out to be correct. Selling to customers such as universities and government agencies has proven to be extremely profitable for Zenith. These markets require only limited advertising and have received little attention from major competitors. In 1986 the company sold some $500 million in PCs, making it the second largest producer of IBM PC clones in the world. While competitors suffered from a glut of IBM PC compatibles in the business market, Zenith could not meet the demands of its niche markets. Among its clients are the U.S. Air Force, the Internal Revenue Service, and students, alumni, and faculty of several hundred colleges and universities, where the firm heavily discounts the list price of the product.

SOURCE: Kenneth Dryfack, "Zenith's Side Road to Success in Personal Computers," *Business Week* (December 8, 1986), pp. 100–101.

AT SEARS: *Sears is in the insurance business and the investment business, as well as the retail business. In order to achieve several of the following objectives, for example balancing cash flows, synergistic marketing, and increased profits. But ironically, it feels it can't stay in these businesses because it isn't achieving all of these objectives.*

selves in a crisis management situation, as Disney did in 1984. Unprepared, its top managers were ready only to "do dangerous and stupid things" to prevent a takeover.[18] Conversely, some organizations benefit greatly by seeking out organizations to acquire them.

8. **Combination:** Often, organizations invoke some combination of the preceding strategies. For example, Apple Computer, during the 1984–1986 period, first employed a turnaround strategy to overcome its degenerating market situation. Cost-cutting measures were used to shore up profits, while new products were created. After the financial situation stabilized, new products were introduced to enable the firm to grow successfully.

Multiple Business Corporate Strategy

Organizations that function in more than one business approach corporate strategy formulation in much the same series of steps as those formulating corporate strategy for a single business. They review vision, mission, and goals; examine the internal and external environments; determine SWOT; develop planning premises; establish strategic objectives; propose strategic alternatives; and finally evaluate the alternatives and make a decision. But the objectives and strategies are very different from those found at the business level. Managing a series of businesses strategically is principally concerned with **portfolio management.**[19] The objectives of portfolio strategies, strategies for managing a group (portfolio) of SBUs are several: to balance the shape, size, and risk of cash flows; to keep new business/products moving to the marketplace, to ensure the long-term viability of the organization; to provide synergistic marketing, production, financial, human resource, or research and development effects; to increase returns on investment; and to increase profits.[20] Sometimes the analysis of what is best for a multiple business organization, in terms of what businesses to retain, can have some rather ironic endings. For example, Singer no longer makes sewing machines, and Greyhound no longer runs a bus company.[21]

To achieve the preceding objectives, firms acquire and divest other firms, and they invest in varying amounts in those firms that are currently in their portfolios. Three basic strategies emerge: invest and grow (includes acquisition); use very selective investment and watch earnings; and harvest (cash flows and profits) and divest.

A number of techniques are employed to make these strategic choices. One of the more popular ones is the portfolio matrix. Characteristics of market and industry are plotted against the characteristics of the firm, forming a matrix. Various locations on the matrix call for one of the three primary strategies. An example of such a matrix is shown in Figure 6.5. This matrix, developed by the Boston Counsulting Group (BCG), is used by strategists to plot each business' relative competitive position (horizontal axis) as expressed by relative market share against the business' growth rate (vertical axis), the industry growth rate. Each business is represented by a circle on the matrix; the circle's size represents the business size—usually total sales. The matrix is divided into four cells, according to the relative desirability of combinations of competitive position and growth. These four cells are symbolized by stars, question marks, cash cows, and dogs. Once a business has been positioned in the matrix, the appropriate portfolio strategy can be identified. The assumptions underlying the matrix—and thus the strategies to be used—are that higher market share in growth markets leads to profitability, but that in slow growth markets, obtaining high market share takes too much cash.[22]

Stars represent the best profit potential, dogs the least. Stars are invested in. Dogs are usually divested, sold off. Question marks have poor cash flows and

FIGURE 6.5 THE BCG BUSINESS MATRIX

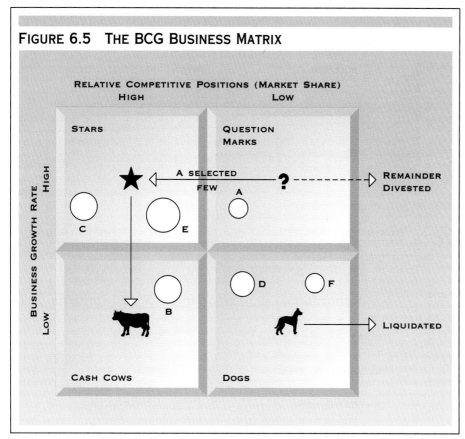

SOURCE: ADAPTED FROM BARRY HEDLEY, "STRATEGY AND THE BUSINESS PORTFOLIO," LONG RANGE PLANNING, FEBRUARY 1977, P. 10. REPRINTED BY PERMISSION OF PERGAMON PRESS LTD., OXFORD, ENGLAND.

must be monitored. Some will continue to be invested in. Some will be sold. Cash cows have the best cash flows, as they require little or no investment and give off high levels of profit and cash.

The BCG matrix has been criticized for its oversimplicity. For example, depending on how the terms are defined, 60 percent to 70 percent of firms could be classified as dogs, when they really do not warrant that description.[23]

Another matrix, the GE portfolio matrix, is shown in Figure 6.6. This particular matrix was developed by General Electric. More sophisticated financial models and simulations support their business screen, but the basic model has served them and many others well over the years.

THE GE STOPLIGHT PORTFOLIO MATRIX

The General Electric Company pioneered the development of the portfolio matrix to determine which strategic business units (SBUs) or major products it wished to retain in its portfolio, which it wished to divest, and how it wanted to treat those that it retained. With minor adjustments in the criteria employed, this matrix can also be used to evaluate potential acquisitions, mergers, or new-product developments. The GE Strategic Business Planning Grid, or "stoplight strategy" as it is known, employs the use of different colored cells in a nine-cell matrix to indicate which strategies it should follow for various businesses. SBUs or products are located on the grid based on an evaluation of the attractiveness of the industry in which they are found and upon GE's strengths in that business. Both industry attractiveness and GE business strength are rated either as high, medium, or low, according to differing criteria.

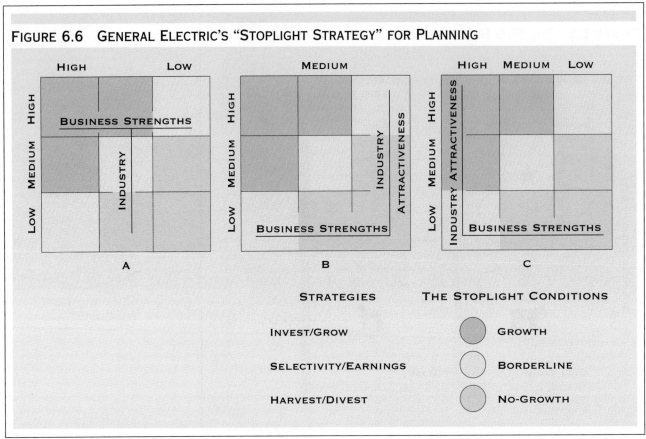

FIGURE 6.6 GENERAL ELECTRIC'S "STOPLIGHT STRATEGY" FOR PLANNING

The term *stoplight strategy* is applied to this matrix because of the green, yellow, and red color coding employed to identify various classifications of businesses or products according to their desirability. Those firms that turn up in the green are to be invested in and will employ growth strategies. Those SBUs that turn up in the red will no longer be invested in and may become cash cows and/or divested. Those that end up in the yellow are monitored for progress, for change in either industry attractiveness or business strengths. Large SBUs may have products that fall into each of these three categories.

In Figure 6.6 stoplight grid A indicates that the subject organization has medium business strengths but high industry attractiveness. Because the evaluations intersect in a green box, the business would receive an invest-and-grow strategy treatment. Stoplight matrix B portrays a business in which business strength and industry attractiveness are low. As a result, the business is in a red zone, and will be harvested and ultimately divested, with reduced or no investment occurring and with cash extraction occurring where possible before divestment. Stoplight grid C characterizes a firm with low business strengths but high industry attractiveness. Consequently, the firm lands in a yellow cell of the matrix and will thus be monitored for progress. Those firms that prove worthwhile from a potential earnings standpoint will be selected for invest-and-grow strategies. Those that do not will be divested. This matrix is backed by a significant amount of analysis, and is used only as a guide, not as an iron-fast procedure.

Strategy and the Industry Life Cycle

Product and industry life cycles are important to strategy formulation at the multiple business level. There are four primary stages to these cycles: introduction, growth, maturity, and decline. Because balance among life cycles, cash flows, and synergies is critical, a number of techniques for evaluating these factors have evolved. Firms attempt to have several businesses in each life-cycle stage—a "balanced" growth portfolio. There must always be new products/ businesses to replace older, less profitable ones. For example, General Electric has, in its portfolio, firms with mature products, such as lightbulbs; firms with growth products, such as certain types of electronic components; and firms with introductory products, such as certain consumer products.

Strategy Formulation at the Business Level

Corporate strategy focuses on choosing a business or businesses and their fundamental conduct. Corporate strategy prepares the firm for engaging in competition. Business strategy states how the firm will compete in the marketplace. The major issues are how to compete using generic strategies to create a competitive advantage (a strength that allows you to compete successfully) and the role of strategy over the product life cycle.

Generic Strategies—The Porter Competitive Strategies

Some experts believe that organizations should follow very specific strategies at the business level in order to be successful. Michael E. Porter, the nation's leading expert on strategy, argues that there are three **generic competitive strategies** that organizations should choose from in order to compete successfully:[24]

1. **Cost Leadership:** Having the lowest cost possible. Hyundai, the Korean automobile manufacturer, clearly followed that strategy with the introduction of the Hyundai XL in 1986 for $4,999. This low-price strategy was clearly based on a low-cost capability.
2. **Differentiation:**[25] Requires somehow distinguishing the product or service from others. Miller Beer follows that strategy with its "Tastes Better, Less Filling," advertising. Providing more service to customers than your competitors was a major differentiation strategy in the 1980s. A major differentiation strategy employed in 1989 was speed—providing customers with new products or service quickly. Hewlett-Packard and Brunswick, for example, developed special teams to get products to customers faster.[26] Many times it takes real creativity to differentiate your organization from another, as Management Challenge 6.2 reveals.
3. **Focus:** The firm serves a particular target market extremely well. The underlying assumption is that by so doing it can serve it better than the competition. As they say at Kentucky Fried Chicken, "We do chicken right."

Table 6.1 indicates some of the requirements for these generic competitive strategies. There is only limited research evidence to support the appropriateness of these generic strategies, but intuitively they are appealing.[27] Growth is the assumed basic action strategy for these generic strategies. The choice of which of Porter's strategies to use is based upon the conditions of the five factors shown in Figure 6.7: the strength and nature of existing competition; potential

FIGURE 6.7   FORCES DRIVING INDUSTRY COMPETITION

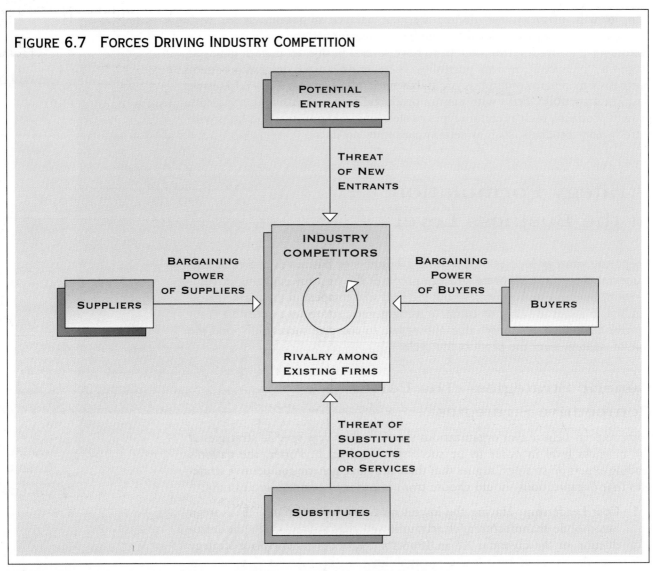

POTENTIAL
ENTRANTS

THREAT
OF NEW
ENTRANTS

INDUSTRY
COMPETITORS

RIVALRY AMONG
EXISTING FIRMS

BARGAINING
POWER
OF SUPPLIERS

SUPPLIERS

BARGAINING
POWER
OF BUYERS

BUYERS

THREAT OF
SUBSTITUTE
PRODUCTS
OR SERVICES

SUBSTITUTES

SOURCE: REPRINTED WITH PERMISSION OF THE FREE PRESS, A DIVISION OF MACMILLAN, INC.,
FROM COMPETITIVE STRATEGY: TECHNIQUES FOR ANALYZING INDUSTRIES AND COMPETITORS
BY MICHAEL E. PORTER, P. 378. COPYRIGHT© 1980 BY THE FREE PRESS.

This Levi Strauss factory has become much more efficient because of the creative "partners for profit" program developed by Milliken. For example, Strauss can now concentrate on finished products rather than on the management of raw material inventories. (SOURCE © Robert Holmgren)

Milliken Uses Creativity to Overcome Foreign Competition

Textile manufacturer Milliken and Company, Inc., with sales of over $2 billion, found itself facing extremely stiff foreign competition, especially based on price. Recognizing that it was physically closer to the customer, and that it therefore should be closer to the customer marketwise, as well, Milliken initiated a series of innovative programs to do just that. These followed on the heels of an all-out effort to increase product quality. Tom Peters describes their actions:

A "total customer responsiveness" effort added in 1984, cut development and delivery times up to 90 percent in the firm's forty business units. Typical is Milliken's carpet unit, where a six-week delivery cycle was cut to just five days.

Milliken's first step was to establish more than one thousand customer action teams (CATs) to unearth new market opportunities in partnership with an existing customer. To launch a CAT, the customer joins with representatives of the Milliken factory and sales, finance, and marketing staff to seek creative ways to serve current or new markets. Well over a hundred such projects were implemented last year, adding many millions to Milliken's bottom line.

For instance, a year-long "partners for profit" program with apparel maker Levi Strauss has revolutionized the way the two organizations do business together. Close cooperation enabled Milliken to produce fabric to Levi's exacting color standards and in sizes that enable Levi's to exploit every square inch of material. Milliken's quality and reliable delivery record convinced Levi's to omit its inspection of Milliken-supplied goods. That allows Milliken to ship directly to Levi's factory, making it unnecessary for Levi's to warehouse the material.

Next, state-of-the-art data and telecommunications linkups save Levi's sorting and storing steps at the plant. Milliken loads material into its trucks in the order that Levi's will need them, making them meticulously stocked warehouses on wheels. The trucks are unloaded in the exact order that the computers, interacting between the two firms, determine the fabric that will be needed at Levi's factory. With exact, time-coded order information, the truck brings exactly what Levi's needs to the plant, and the fabric is carried directly to the machine where the garment is cut and sewn.

In another maneuver, Levi's makes tags at a remote location for each bolt of fabric manufactured. Via another electronic hookup, the appropriate tags arrive at the Levi's finishing plant just as the Milliken truck pulls up; they are attached as the truck is unloaded. The result is a monumental savings of cost and delivery time for Levi Strauss, plus previously unheard-of flexibility in responding to today's lightning-fast fashion trends. Milliken shares the financial benefit. More important, it keeps an order onshore that might otherwise be lost to Hong Kong.

Another landmark Milliken program involves the mundane "shop towel" business, where cloths are made for industrial purposes. Milliken products are sold to industrial launderers, who rent towels to customers such as carwashes, garages, cafeterias, and factories. Milliken not only provides cloth to the industrial launderers, it also conducts extensive training for the launderers' sales force, manages their convention exhibits and promotions, and sends Milliken salespeople out with the launderers' representatives on joint sales calls 80 percent of the time. This partnership enables Milliken to serve its fragmented customer base better, charge a 40 percent premium for an otherwise commodity product, and gain more than a 50 percent return on its investment in the business.

SOURCE: Summarized from Tom Peters, "The Home Team Advantage," *U.S. News & World Report* (March 31, 1986), p. 49.

Table 6.1. Requirements for Generic Competitive Strategies

Generic Strategy	Commonly Required Skills and Resources	Common Organizational Requirements
Overall cost leadership	Sustained capital investment and access to capital Process-engineering skills Intense supervision of labor Products designed for ease in manufacture Low-cost distribution system	Tight cost control Frequent, detailed control reports Structured organization and responsibilities Incentives based on meeting strict quantitative targets
Differentiation	Strong marketing abilities Product engineering Creative flair Strong capability in basic research Corporate reputation for quality or technological leadership Long tradition in the industry or unique combination of skills drawn from other businesses Strong cooperation from channels	Strong coordination among functions in R&D product development and marketing Subjective measurement and incentives instead of quantitative measures Amenities to attract highly skilled labor, scientists, or creative people

SOURCE: M. E. Porter, *Competitive Strategy* (New York: Free Press, 1980), pp. 40, 41. Reprinted with permission of The Free Press, a Division of Macmillan, Inc.

entrants; the threat of substitutes; the bargaining power of suppliers; and the bargaining power of buyers. Together these five elements form an industry's structure. Under the topic of existing competition, the strategist might be concerned with industry growth, industry capacity, loss of capital, and the strength of each competitor. Concerns for the other four factors are also shown in the figure.

Hall's Competitiveness Model

Professor William K. Hall, after researching a number of firms, concluded that there were really two primary generic strategies—high differentiation relative to your competition, and a low cost position relative to your competition. His

The Mazda Miata is one of those rare products which is in the "Garden of Eden." It has been significantly differentiated from its competition, and it also has a low cost structure. (SOURCE © Courtesy Mazda)

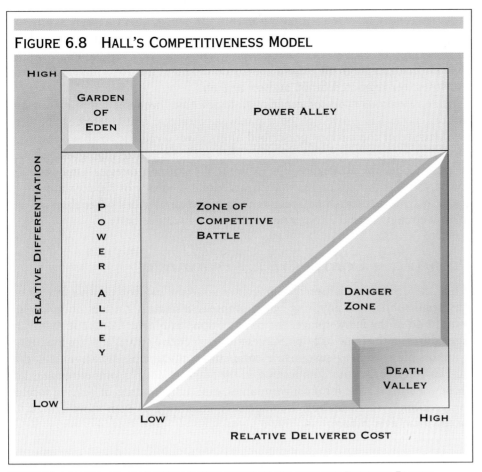

FIGURE 6.8   HALL'S COMPETITIVENESS MODEL

model is portrayed in Figure 6.8. Those firms that have a relatively low cost position or a very high degree of relative differentiation possess power alleys in the marketplace. Hyundai and Mercedes are examples of each. The firm that has both is in heaven, the firm with neither is in Death Valley. Mazda's Miata is an example of a product in heaven, whereas most of the firms in the U.S. steel industry in the 1970s were examples of firms in Death Valley. There are varying degrees of ability to compete, or not, according to the combinations of these two strategies.[28] Unlike Porter, Hall does not see differentiation and low cost as mutually exclusive.[29]

Other Generic Strategies

A host of other generic strategies exists. For example, Professors Raymond E. Miles and Charles C. Snow[30] propose that organizations should act in one of four basic ways: as defenders, prospectors, analyzers, and reactors. Defenders seek stability. Prospectors look for new opportunities. Analyzers are somewhere between the defenders and prospectors. Reactors react and really don't have a strategy and thus usually fail. Various portions of the firm may use one of these strategies or another. The problem then becomes integrating them.

Additional research reveals that firms seeking high market share emphasize product or service quality, spend considerable amounts of money on marketing, and invest heavily, which usually—eventually—gives them a high return on investment.[31] Other researchers have found strategies that best suit firms seeking intensive growth, as well as strategies for low market share companies, for those 154competing in stagnant industries, for dominant firms, for firms in declining industries, for regulated firms, and on and on.[32]

While numerous types of generic strategies have been suggested by various authors, none has proven to be a panacea. Strategic managers must be very much aware of the various prescribed alternatives available to them, but they must also recognize their limitations. They must recognize that many of prescriptive or generic strategies—for example the Porter strategies—may or may not be valid. Although there is much anecdotal evidence of their validity, it is not clear from a research perspective that any of them work other than in very narrow circumstances. These strategies are for guidance only.

Creating a Competitive Advantage[33]

While the distinction between competitive strategy and competitive advantage may seem subtle, it is anything but. Competitive strategy focuses on what you want to do in the marketplace, the basic options available. Competitive advantage addresses the issue of how. Successful competitive strategy in the long term is impossible without a sustainable **competitive advantage**—whatever it is that enables you to beat your competition in the marketplace.[34] Competitiveness has become a critical issue for most companies, especially in terms of beating foreign competition.[35] Thus, finding a competitive advantage is even more critical to success than ever before.

Concern with the Product/Industry Life Cycle

Many strategic options are dictated somewhat, if not extensively, by the **stage of the product or industry life cycle** in which the organization finds itself with a particular product line or perhaps a whole business.[36] Strategic managers must be concerned with the stage of the product or industry life cycle in which they find their product. They must be cognizant of desirable strategies in each of those stages. Strategies for all of the economic functions for each stage of the life cycle have been identified but are too numerous to discuss here.[37]

The classic example of how product life cycle affects strategy is the pricing strategy followed by IBM for its personal computer line. In 1982, 1983, and early 1984, when it had a unique position in the business market, with its only major competitor being Apple, IBM was able to charge an extremely high price for its products. As that segment of the computer industry grew, additional competitors with IBM PC clones entered the market at lower prices. IBM was forced to lower its price on its original computers, although not down to the prices of the clones because IBM could use its name and reputation to charge a higher price. As the product reached its maturity stage, IBM was forced to charge even lower prices. However, it continued to introduce new versions of the product, first with the IBM XT and then the IBM AT. These are more powerful PCs and again initially had few competitors, so IBM was able to charge higher prices. Their prices came down as clones and competitors entered the marketplace for each of the computers. In fact, IBM not only lowered prices to meet those of competitors, but lowered them to force competitors out of the market because IBM could produce PCs at lower costs than could many of their competitors.[38]

AT SEARS: *Divisions are continually changing product mixes, cutting costs, etc. Sears contemplated selling its tower in Chicago, a financial strategy to raise cash.*

Strategy Formulation at the Functional Level

The principal concern of functional strategy is the efficient use of organizational resources. Functional strategies support corporate- and business-level strategies. Functional strategies include those related to the economic functions of the organization: marketing, finance, operations, human resources, research and development, and logistics. They also include those related to managing: planning, organizing, leading, controlling, and creative problem solving. A typical financial strategy might be to sell and lease back crucial real estate or plant and equipment. The pricing of the various IBM PCs, which was discussed earlier, is an example of a marketing strategy. The major concerns of the economic functional strategies are shown in Table 6.2. Management Challenge 6.3 reveals how one firm used functional strategies to trigger its success.

Table 6.2. Economic Functional Strategies

Economic Functions	Major Concerns
Marketing	Marketing Mix—the combination of the following four factors
	Product Mix—the types and number of products or services
	Pricing
	Promotional Efforts—Image
	Distribution Channels—How, where, and when the products are distributed to customer
	Target Market Identification
Finance	Debt
	Dividends, Returns
	Capitalization Structure—how the firm is financed
	Asset Management—especially cash
	Liability Management
Operations	Production Technology
	Layout and Design of Physical Plant
	Productivity
	Quality Location
Human Resources and Human Resource Practices	Organizational Design and Development
	Culture Management
	Labor Relations
	Government Regulations
R&D and Product Development	Funds Utilization

The Strategists

There are **four principal types of strategists** in any organization: the single entrepreneurial-type leader who makes most or all of the strategic decisions; a coalition (informal group) of top managers; the professional planner; and, in an emerging role of importance, the division manager.

Lee Iacocca epitomizes the entrepreneurial-type manager. While these types of individuals are usually found in smaller firms, you occasionally find them in larger ones. These individuals make almost all, if not all, of the organization's strategic decisions.

In larger organizations strategic planning decisions are often made by an informal group of upper-level managers known as a **coalition**.[39] In most organizations there are several coalitions vying for power. In organizations dominated by a coalition, the decision process is often an incremental one as opposed to a sweeping decision process. Incremental strategic decision making involves a series of small steps as the decision moves from group to group up and down the hierarchy.

In a very limited number of organizations, the professional strategic planner has a tremendous impact upon organizational strategic actions. The professional planner is an advisor whose recommendations may become—because he or she often best knows the strategic situation—in effect, strategic decisions. The professional planners' role has been reduced in recent years in many organizations as they have restructured and reduced the level of staff support. This has forced strategic decision making farther down in the organization, placing it in the hands of division managers.

As organizations have decentralized they have sought to have division managers become entrepreneurs within the organization—hence, **intrapreneurs**. This decentralization occurred because the evidence suggests that those closest to the market can make the decision better than the very top managers; and that having a financial interest, and thereby an achievement interest, will result in much more successful strategic planning.[40]

Human Behavior and Strategy

Regardless of whether the strategist is an entrepreneurial chief executive, a coalition, a professional planner, a division manager, or someone else—such as a

deliver a high-quality motor in six weeks. Using a home-grown version of just-in-time manufacturing called "flexible flow," in which inventories were reduced to the amount needed essentially for that production run, Baldor cut its batch-order product-manufacturing process from four weeks to five days.

New products were developed, and innovation in both their design and manufacturing was stressed. In flexible flow, for example, progressive assembly was eliminated. Each worker assembles an entire motor based on directions from a computer printout. A worker may assemble as many as twenty different motors a day. This helps reduce worker boredom and increase autonomy and pride. More than three hundred new motors were listed in Baldor's last catalogue, and it has developed some new products no one has successfully done before, such as a motor that can work well in the very damp environments necessary for growing mushrooms. Several motivational programs were instituted—for example, having employees sign their work. And, Baldor has not laid off an employee in Fort Smith since 1962, which increases employee loyalty.

Baldor's decision not to go offshore turned out to be the right one, but they were criticized heavily by analysts when they made it. Baldor's sales jumped 40 percent between 1985 and 1988, hitting an all-time high of $243 million, despite increased foreign competition. Baldor even managed to penetrate the Japanese market with one of its motors. CEO Boreham observes, "Pride takes you one direction, short-term profit another. Pride usually wins out, if you're a confident person."

SOURCE: Alan Farnham, "Baldor's Success: Made in the U.S.A.," *Fortune* (July 17, 1989), pp. 101–106.

member of the board of directors (who are active in strategic planning, in only a very few firms)—the strategist's values, needs, perceptions, and personality will greatly affect his or her, or their strategic decisions. Where a group dominates the formulation of strategy, the dynamics of that group are going to affect greatly the resulting strategic choices. Even if there isn't a dominant group, strategic choices will be influenced by groups. Even Lee Iacocca delegates some strategic decisions and certainly listens to his subordinates in making the choices among the alternatives he has available.[41]

Furthermore, there are political processes that occur in any organizational decision situation. These are especially prevalent in not-for-profit organizations, which are highly politically influenced and often politically based. Major federal government decisions, for example, are often politically based, rather than based on strictly rational "what would be best for the taxpayer"-type criteria. Because the missions of not-for-profits are not founded on profits, their objectives differ, and hence their strategies often differ.[42]

AT SEARS: *Imagine the human variables involved in moving to the "one-price" strategy or in selling the Sears Tower. Those who had formulated previous strategies would have very mixed emotions. Some people would feel that selling the Tower would be like selling a part of the company and mean a lowering of the Sears image.*

Strategic Planning and Different Types of Organizations

Several special organizational situations exist apart from those of the medium- and larger-sized business organizations in the preceding discussion. Strategic planning may differ in some ways in each of them: small business, not-for-profits, international business, and regulated businesses.

Small Business[43]

Small business provides a unique case in strategic planning for several reasons. First, the owner/manager is often so absorbed with the everyday operation, he or she fails to see the importance of long-term strategic planning. Concentration is on now and not tomorrow. Any organization can survive and prosper in the short run without strategic planning—even for several years—as long as it has a product that has a strategic advantage. But for any organization, as competition changes, as products change, as demands change, as the economy changes, as technology changes, as the society changes, there will be a day of reckoning. Then the organization must be able not only to adapt to its environment, but proactively to create a strategic advantage. It must formulate strategic plans and implement them. Small business managers often lack the professional skill to plan strategically but must do so anyway. They often lack the information systems to do so, but they must plan anyway. They may also lack the time, but they must find it.

Some suggest that the rigorous type of strategic planning envisioned by the models presented in this and similar books are inappropriate for the small business manager. It is suggested that what this person really needs to do is simply think through the process—think through the stages—but not meticulously analyze or meticulously write down every facet of it. Perhaps the small business person doesn't even need to develop a written business plan. What he or she does need to do is develop objectives and plans. There are pros and cons to both views. The small businessperson can get bogged down in a very formalized strategic planning session. So, he or she must keep strategic planning simple, to receive the greatest benefit from it.

Not-for-Profits[44]

Strategic planning in not-for-profits is often dominated by the absence of a clearly defined mission and an absence of clearly defined objectives, partially at least because of the political nature of many of these organizations. Strategic policies are often vague, and the strategists are not of the same type found in a business organization—they may be contributors, top managers, board members, staff, clients, or members of various external coalition groups. Further compounding the problem, information systems in not-for-profits are often less adequate than those used in businesses. On the other hand, competition still exists and because most not-for-profits have one major service they provide to one major group of clients, they often have to compete with others for funding. For example, the United Way competes with the Heart Fund and the American Cancer Society for funds from the same target groups.

Another key difference in strategic planning for and in managing not-for-profits is that the provider of funds is often not the client or customer, as it is in business. Because of this, the strategic plan must not only create a service/product sales and delivery mechanism, but it must also create a separate strategy for obtaining payment to provide those services/products.[45] Not-for-profits face changing environments just like all businesses. In the face of reduced support at big firms, United Way, for example, developed a strategy for fund raising in small businesses.[46]

International Business

As with all management functions, strategic planning varies greatly in the international arena. There are at least four major problems:

The European Economic Community's goal of becoming a true common market by 1992 is having a major impact on global business relationships. The EEC Commission is establishing the rules by which the game of business will be played in Europe. (SOURCE © P. Alix/SIPA)

1. The international marketplace is highly competitive. For example, U.S. firms, in industries such as autos and PCs, receive tremendous competition from firms in Hong Kong, Germany, Brazil, Japan, Korea, Taiwan, Canada, and Great Britain.

2. Operations are conducted in widely varying economic, legal, political, social, and cultural environments. People are different in other countries, they have different needs, wants, desires, and capabilities.

3. The values of currencies vary frequently, and currency translations can turn a profit into a loss.

4. The governments in foreign countries often can make life extremely difficult for foreign companies.[47]

From a strategic management perspective, organizational missions are often more governmentally influenced outside the United States than in it. Strategists may sometimes be more influenced by the government. In much of Europe, for example, unions are required to sit on the board of directors. Information gathering is often much more difficult and the information needed is often quite different, as are the marketplaces. How others view time, the aspirations of the people in a particular country and their perspectives on authority, how rank and social status are determined, the roles of women, and the meaning of nonverbal communications are all different. These and other factors influence the ability of an organization to plan strategically and internationally, especially when doing business in several countries.

There is clearly a trend toward a global marketplace. Michael E. Naylor, executive in charge of strategic planning for General Motors,[48] has observed that the key characteristic of business through much of the rest of this century will be global competition. The European Economic Community's (EEC's) initiative to become a true single European market by 1992 has significant strategic implications for firms doing business in Europe and for European firms, as well, as the Global Management Challenge reveals.[49] The emerging economic freedom in Eastern Europe also has substantial significance.

Thomson Wants to be Number One in Consumer Electronics

In 1982 Alain Gomez was appointed CEO of Thomson, the huge state-controlled French electronics group. He found a company overstaffed and undermanaged. He quickly restructured, cutting costs and cutting jobs. His aggressive management style quickly helped turn the company around, but not without ruffling a lot of feathers. He justifiably axed numerous senior executives and nonperforming operations, but often without the face-saving actions that typically occur in these

Regulated Businesses

The constraints within which regulated businesses, such as utilities, must function often limit their overall management flexibility. This is especially true with regard to strategic planning. Regulated businesses are usually allowed to operate only within certain industries, so multiple industry activity is generally prohibited. This was true for banks and other financial service industry participants such as insurance companies until just recently. After deregulation members of the financial service industry have actively entered numerous other businesses because of the strategic opportunities that exist. Regulated firms are also often prohibited from geographic expansion. Most utilities are governed by state bodies with interstate facility ownership prohibited. Much of the strategic thrust of regulated firms is in competition against substitutes or established competitors in existing markets.

Strategy Implementation[50]

Once strategy is formulated, it must be implemented. In fact strategy should be formulated with implementation considered as one of the SWOT factors. There are four key ingredients in successful **implementation**: proper organizational structure, suitable management systems, leadership style, and astute management of organizational culture.[51]

Organizational Structure

"Strategy follows structure."[52] Matching the organizational structure to the strategy is an extremely important part of the strategic implementation process. Without the proper structure—jobs, departmentalizations of jobs, and distribution of authority—an organization cannot successfully carry out its chosen strategies. Managers have six or seven major ways to choose from to structure the whole organization. (These are discussed in Chapter 8.)

Various factors affect the choice of structure. An organization's structure and strategies should match the company's growth stage. In the early stages, an organization typically has a different structure than it will have later. And firms in certain industries, such as aerospace, often have structures different from

situations in France. "I didn't have to shake them out of the trees. Most of them were already senile and fell out on their own," he once said.

In 1989 Gomez faces a new challenge, preparing Thomson for Europe 1992. To do so, he has sought to acquire operations in markets in which he feels Thomson can become a world leader—consumer and defense electronics. For example, Thomson has aggressively pursued television, acquiring GE's RCA unit in the United States in late 1987. Gomez has moved swiftly to change RCA's stodgy, walnut-cabinet image and is moving ahead in research to be ready for the high-definition models expected in the mid-1990s. And, in a period of high profits, Gomez is still restructuring, cutting jobs and costs to prepare for the more competitive environment expected in 1992, but leaving the company vulnerable to strong union opposition and the possibility of strikes. When asked if he is making the right strategic moves, Gomez replies, "I'll know in ten years."

SOURCE: "Alain Gomez, France's High-Tech Warrior," *Business Week* (May 15, 1989), pp. 100–106.

those in other industries because of the magnitude of the projects involved and the fact that these change frequently.

These structures are not static. They are dynamic. One of the major structural changes that occurred in many firms in the 1980s was the elimination of many staff positions and many middle-management positions. It was part of an effort to cut costs and distribute authority farther down the chain of command, so that line managers could make more decisions. This increased decision-making authority allows managers to respond to local conditions and local situations better than upper-level managers probably would. One of the major strategic structural choices today is how much authority to delegate.

Management Systems

Operational planning systems; integrated planning and control systems; organization leadership, motivation, and communication systems; and the management of human resources from a system perspective are all critical to successful implementation. It is not enough simply to have strategic objectives and strategic plans; there must be operational and sometimes intermediate planning programs to carry them out. There must be budgets—annual or eighteen-month to two-year financial operating plans. There must be programs developed by the organization to provide leadership, to form a certain style of managing throughout the company. There must be compensation systems and other reward motivation systems, to encourage implementation. There must be communication systems such as attitude surveys, policies, rules, procedures, bulletin boards, meetings, and so on, so that people know what to do and how, when, where, and why to do it. There must be human resource management systems. To ensure proper utilization of this resource, the human resource management department must actively engage in personnel planning, recruiting and attracting, selecting, training and developing, orienting, providing compensation, insuring employee health and safety, helping group relationships, evaluating employees, controlling the performance of individuals, managing change, equal employment opportunity, and improving organizational communication. Management must develop systems of control and numerous other management systems to ensure the successful implementation of strategy. Selling the product is never enough. Management Challenge 6.4 details some of the strains that success brought to bear on Boeing's organization.

Boeing—Can It Live with Success?

Orders for new airplanes are at an all-time high worldwide, and industry sales of $500 billion are expected in the next fifteen years. Boeing has $80 billion in orders on the books, with, as yet, only modest competition in McDonnell Douglas and the European Airbus Industrie consortium. Boeing should be ecstatic, and it is, but not everything in the picture is rosy. McDonnell Douglas has the potential to be a strong competitor, if its restructuring efforts are successful and its new plane measures up to expectations. Furthermore, Airbus is heavily subsidized by the British, French, and West German governments, which allows it to compete on the basis of cost. Additionally, its work force is more experienced than Boeing's. And because no one manufacturer can supply the demand, competitors will get their fair share.

Boeing's strategy of innovation—providing leading edge technology and of providing a quality product, has worked. Now the question is, can they gear up to meet heavy demand. (SOURCE © R. Frishman/Picture Group)

But more importantly, Boeing has internal management problems trying to meet this tremendous demand. Symptoms include the fact that Boeing is six months behind in delivery on its jumbo 747–400 airplanes—the first time in twenty years the company has been behind in delivery. Design problems have arisen in the new planes and production lags because of an inexperienced work force. Furthermore, the company must determine whether to produce an even newer model, the 767-X, a long-range 350-seat jet smaller than the 747.

Analysts believe that Boeing's problems will lessen as the work force gets more experienced and management systems have time to be further fine tuned. Boeing has taken some short-range steps to help alleviate its problems, such as "borrowing" 650 workers with ten or more years experience from Lockheed, paying generous wages and housing allotments. However, the complexity of its situation can probably only be solved with systems designed to meet the needs of the situation, and with time.

SOURCE; Anthony Ramirez, "Boeing's Happy, Harrowing Times," *Fortune* (July 1989), pp. 40–45.

Leadership Style

Successful implementation of a strategic plan requires that the individual manager at all levels of an organization be cognizant of, and have skill in, communication and leadership. He or she must be aware of how individuals are motivated and be able to influence that motivation. He or she must develop a satisfactory leadership style, a pattern of leading subordinates. A manager must be skilled in interpersonal relationships. A manager must sell the strategy to those who will implement it, those who must approve it, and other key parties.[53]

Management of Organizational Culture[54]

As shown in Figure 6.9, organizational culture—an organization's shared values—is the focus and central point of the entire strategic process. McKinsey & Company developed this framework, known as the Seven Elements of Strategic Fit, or the Seven S's. The Seven S's are defined briefly in Table 6.3. The basic

Table 6.3. A Summary of the Seven S's

1. *Strategy:* A coherent set of actions aimed at gaining a sustainable advantage over competition, improving position vis-à-vis customers, or allocating resources.
2. *Structure:* The organization chart and accompanying baggage that show who reports to whom and how tasks are both divided up and integrated.
3. *Systems:* The processes and flows that show how an organization gets things done from day to day (information systems, capital budgeting systems, manufacturing processes, quality-control systems, performance measurement systems).
4. *Style:* Tangible evidence of what management considers important by the way it collectively spends time and attention and uses symbolic behavior. What managers say is less important than the way they behave.
5. *Staff:* The people in the organization. Here it is very useful to think not about individual personalities but about corporate demographics.
6. *Shared values (or superordinate goals):* The values that go beyond, but might well include, simple goal statements in determining corporate destiny. To fit the concept, these values must be shared by most people in an organization.
7. *Skills:* A derivative of the rest. Skills are those capabilities that are possessed by an organization as a whole, as opposed to the people in it. (The concept of corporate skill as something different from the skills of the people in it seems difficult for many people to grasp; yet some organizations that hire only the best and the brightest cannot get seemingly simple things done, while others perform extraordinary feats with ordinary people.)

SOURCE: Robert H. Waterman, Jr., "The Seven Elements of Strategic Fit." Reprinted by permission from *Journal of Business Strategy*, Winter 1982, p. 71. Copyright © 1982, Warren, Gorham & Lamont, Inc., 210 South Street, Boston, Mass. All rights reserved.

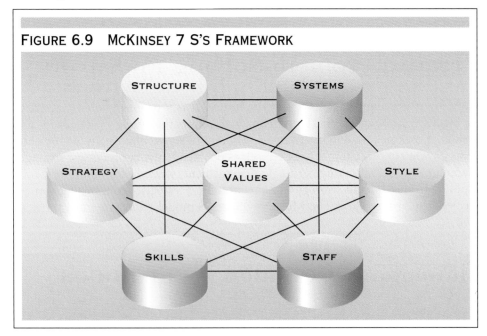

FIGURE 6.9   MCKINSEY 7 S'S FRAMEWORK

underlying concept of the Seven S's is that the efforts of the organization in each of the areas must be coordinated, aimed at the same objectives, and moved in the same direction in order for synergism to exist in the organization. "The whole is greater than the sum of its parts" is the conceptual belief of the Seven-S framework, as long as all Seven S's are working together. The Seven-S framework embodies the same major concepts of implementation introduced here: strategy, structure, systems, managerial/leadership style, and culture, or shared values. Their "staff" is a demographic consideration, and their "skills" is the synergistic competitive edge the organization receives if the other six S's are in concert.

Strategic Management in Increasingly Complex and Turbulent Environments[55]

The environments confronting strategists are increasingly complex and turbulent. Internal and external environments, especially the competitive environment, are posing significant challenges to top management. Consequently firms are moving to a series of actions to improve their strategy formulation. Among them are: strategic thinking; flexible strategic plans; resource-based strategies, that is, improving resources to cope with potential environments; scenario forecasting; improving information systems; better scanning of the environment; increasing capacity for change; speed strategies, that is, getting the product to the market faster; frequent reviews of plans; contingency plans; alliances; and simulations. At a time when strategic planning is most needed, it unfortunately has become more difficult. Innovative strategic planning is becoming more and more necessary. New approaches will evolve.[56]

Strategic Management as a Creative Problem-Solving Endeavor[57]

Planning is making decisions about the future. It is a problem-solving activity, as Figure 6.10 suggests. It stems from a situation that must be resolved and results in a choice among alternatives. The figure shows that many of the concepts covered in this chapter are themselves problem-solving processes: strategic planning, strategic thinking, strategic management, strategy formulation for all types of strategies, and strategy implementation. Strategists could engage in all parts of the process, and The McKinsey Seven-S model relates to all of them as well.

Management Challenges Identified

1. Rapid change results in planning environments
2. A need to link strategy formulation, implementation, and control
3. A requirement to construct a satisfactory strategic management program in an organization

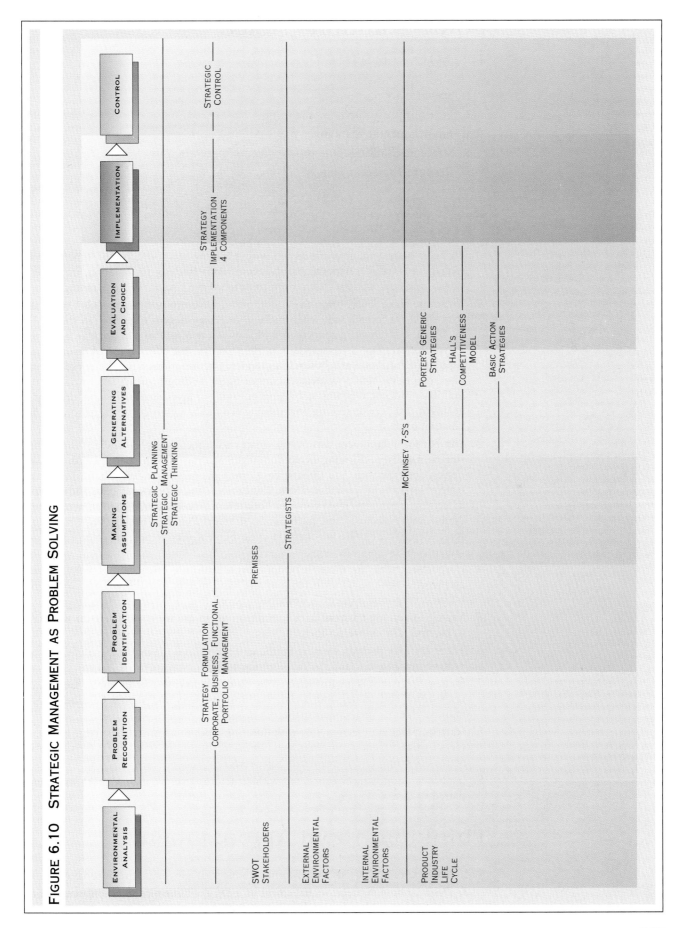

FIGURE 6.10 STRATEGIC MANAGEMENT AS PROBLEM SOLVING

Some Solutions Noted in the Chapter

1. Scenario forecasting
2. Flexibility, contingency planning
3. Environmental scanning
4. Strategic thinking
5. Resource based strategies

Summary

1. Strategic management is concerned with pursuing mission accomplishment while managing external relationships. It encompasses strategy formulation, implementation, and control. It is much more comprehensive than strategic planning.

2. There are three levels of strategy: corporate, business, and functional. Corporate strategy is concerned with what business or businesses an organization should be in. Business strategy is concerned with how to compete in a particular business. Functional strategy is concerned with the effective and efficient use of resources in support of corporate and business strategies. Organizations have choices of several basic corporate action strategies: competing or finding a niche, concentrating on multiple products, growing, stabilizing, engaging in investment reduction, defending against a takeover or seeking one, turning around company fortunes, or some combination of these.

3. Strategy formulation consists of strategists taking these steps: reviewing vision, mission, and goals; performing an environmental analysis; determining strengths, weaknesses, opportunities, and threats; developing planning premises; establishing strategic objectives; proposing strategic alternatives; evaluating strategies; and making a decision. Strategists must consider both internal and external environments when establishing objectives and formulating strategy. Planning premises are based on forecasted SWOT. The product life cycle plays a very important role in the formulation of business strategy.

4. Corporate strategy for multiple business organizations is essentially a portfolio management exercise using such tools as the BCG matrix and the GE matrix. Single business corporate strategy is described above.

5. Strategic planning answers three questions: where are we now, where do we want to be, and how do we get there?

6. There are four primary strategists: the entrepreneurial manager, the coalition, the professional planner, and the division manager.

7. Strategic planning is greatly affected by human behavior—for example, the strategist's needs and values and social relationships. It is and should be much more intuitive than is often conceptualized.

8. Strategic planning varies widely with differing types of organizations: large business versus small business, international versus domestic, not-for-profits versus businesses for profit, and in regulated businesses.

9. Implementation is most concerned with structure, systems, management style, and shared values.

Thinking About Management

1. Why are organizations so concerned about strategic management today?
2. Describe how strategic management at a Du Pont chemical division would vary from strategic planning at the same division.

3. Take a company with which you are familiar, or a well-known company such as Coca-Cola, and indicate how that company would accomplish each of the stages in the strategy formulation process, including what it should consider, and how it would go about setting premises, and so on.

4. Describe the major concerns for AT&T at the corporate level; at the business level; and at the functional level.

5. Describe a company's strategies using each of the basic action strategies.

6. Describe a nonprofit's potential strategy using each of Porter's generic strategies.

7. Describe an organization that uses each of the Miles and Snow typologies.

8. Why do multiple business organizations seek to have businesses in each of the three areas of the GE business screen? In each of the stages of the product, market, and industry cycle?

9. Describe what you think the major concerns of strategies for the management functions might be.

10. Describe how the processes of strategy formulation and implementation might differ for each of these environments: large businesses, small businesses, international businesses, not-for-profits, regulated businesses.

11. Relate both a successful and an unsuccessful example of implementation using the Seven-S model.

CASE

Coca-Cola Is Shaken Up

Not every strategy, no matter how well conceived, researched, and planned, is successful. The new Coke was conceived according to the book on planning and market research. Unfortunately, the customer hadn't read the book. (SOURCE © R. Frishman/Picture Group)

In 1980, when Roberto Goizueta took over as chairman of Coca-Cola, he commented, "the product and the brand had a declining share in a shrinking segment of the market. The value for Coca-Cola's trademark was going downhill." In order to preserve Coca-Cola's market share and the value of its trademark, Goizueta was forced to jeopardize the image that Coca-Cola had worked nearly a century to build. Goizueta and his team broke old taboos against taking on debt and extended the company's trademark to include entertainment; frozen, processed food; and even clothing.

In addition to diversification into these industries, Goizueta has been responsible for increasing Coca-Cola's product line. In 1982 Diet Coke was introduced and was an immediate success. The 1985 introduction of reformulated Coke did not have as favorable a reaction from consumers. In fact, it had been referred to as the "biggest fiasco in the company's history." Goizueta doesn't see it that way. In 1986 Coca-Cola and Coca-Cola Classic together outsold Pepsi, Coca-Cola's closest competitor.

Goizueta's changes have yielded very favorable results for the company. The number of shares of stock outstanding are decreasing through share repurchases financed by debt. Stock prices rose from $35 in 1980 to more than $117 in 1986. Also, overall profits for the company are steadily rising. Goizueta shook up Coca-Cola's corporate culture and disregarded some long-standing business practices, but most Coca-Cola managers and business associates agree, "the benefit was worth the risk." Goizueta came to Coca-Cola at a time when something drastic needed to be done to extend the company's life cycle. He did just that. He took the risk, and everyone agrees that the resulting benefits were great.

SOURCE: "Coke's Future: Profoundly Changed, Coca-Cola Company Strives to Keep on Bubbling Under Goizueta Team," *Wall Street Journal* 24 April, 1986, p. 22.

DISCUSSION QUESTIONS
1. What corporate strategy actions did Goizueta take to improve Coke's future?
2. What business strategy action did Goizueta take to improve Coke's future?
3. How did the "biggest fiasco in the company's history" turn into a plus for the company?

Apple Macintosh for the Year 2000

In 1989, John Sculley, CEO of Apple Computers, Inc., and his top staff members, pondered the future of the company. They successfully had begun to penetrate the business market, having reached a 15 percent share of PC sales in that market in 1988. Sales were at an all-time high. The firm had been reorganized in March 1989 into four major divisions: one to develop products and three geographic divisions covering Europe, North America, and Asia to position the company for an objective of $10 billion in sales by the mid-1990s. Sculley had established the vision of the company as one of providing evolutionary products building on existing technologies, but adding innovative features. But, Scully and his top staff members all recognized that the company could not continue simply to add features to the Macintosh and Apple II forever.

Competition was fierce in this market, and technologies were moving forward rapidly. Competitor intelligence revealed that Microsoft was working on a soft-ware program that would duplicate Macintosh's features for the IBM PC II. Advances in communication linkages, the power of computer chips, voice-activated commands for computers, and database availability and management all pointed toward an exciting potential for a new Macintosh for the year 2000—to be named the Mariner because of the independence it would bring its user. Now they had to determine just what that machine could and should do. Partly for that purpose and other R&D, they purchased a Cray supercomputer to run simulations of new computer designs.

DISCUSSION QUESTIONS
1. If you were Sculley and his top staff, how would you determine what the Mariner should be able to do?
2. What planning premises would you have to make?
3. How can you know what technologies will be available?
4. What would you want in a PC for the year 2000?

Strategy Formulation

Select a well-known national company and list below its current strengths, weaknesses, opportunities, and threats. Then identify its probable opportunities and threats for five years from now.

Company: _____

Current Strengths

Current Weaknesses

Current Opportunities

Current Threats

Future Opportunities

Future Threats

Now formulate a corporate strategy for the whole organization and a grand strategy for at least one of the organization's businesses.

Corporate Strategy

Business Strategy

Functional Strategy

Grand Strategy

CHAPTER SEVEN

Quantitative Methods for Problem Solving and Planning

CHAPTER OBJECTIVES

By the time you complete this chapter, you should be able to

1. Describe how quantitative methods/management-science techniques might be used to assist in problem solving.

2. Indicate the advantages and disadvantages of quantitative methods in problem solving.

3. Discuss the quantitative and qualitative aspects of decision making.

4. Discuss the importance of various decision science techniques to problem solving, based on surveys of their usage or familiarity.

5. Define and describe how you would use the following fundamental quantitative decision-making techniques: statistical analysis and decision theory, including decision trees and expected value.

6. Define and describe how you would use sales forecasts.

7. Define and describe how you would use the following forecasting techniques: time series

and such causal techniques as regression analysis.

8. Define and describe how you would use the qualitative methods of forecasting.

9. List the five basic steps in the forecasting process.

10. Define and describe when you would use the following additional planning techniques: break-even analysis, linear programming, networking models—PERT and CPM, and project management.

11. Indicate the uses of computers in decision making.

12. Describe the use and importance of simulation in problem solving.

13. Describe how quantitative methods aid in the problem-solving process.

CHAPTER OUTLINE

Foundations of Quantitative Methods
  Advantages of Quantitative Methods
  Disadvantages of Quantitative Methods
Fundamental Quantitative Decision-Making Techniques
  Statistical Analysis

Decision Theory: Decision Trees
  and Expected Value
Additional Quantitative Techniques
for Problem Solving
  Inventory Models
  Queueing Models
  Distribution Models
Quantitative Techniques for Planning
  Forecasting
  Forecasting Techniques
  Qualitative Methods
  The Limits of Forecasting
  Forecasts: A Summary

Additional Quantitative Planning
Techniques
  Break-Even Analysis
  Linear Programming
  Network Models PERT/CPM
The Uses of Computers in Decision
Making and Planning
  Simulations
Management Science as Decision
Support for Problem Solving
Management Challenges Identified
Some Solutions Noted in the Chapter

Citgo Embraces Management Science

Citgo Petroleum Corporation was purchased by the Southland Corporation in 1983, in order to make it into a profitable refining and marketing petroleum business, and to provide its 7-Eleven stores with quality motor fuels. Southland was faced with a problem: the organizational culture at Citgo was perceived as weak and noncompetitive. Citgo had been the oil-refining and marketing arm of Occidental Petroleum. It had to be transformed into an independent refiner and marketer of petroleum. This meant that management had to learn how to make decisions better and become market responsive and less driven by the refining aspects of its business.

Southland made two strategic decisions: it made Citgo into a wholly owned subsidiary with its own debt (rather than have the debt held by Southland), and it created a task force composed of Southland and Citgo personnel and consultants, to explore ways to improve Citgo's profitability. Various strategies were developed to help it achieve its two goals. Many of them focused on the use of quantitative methods. Citgo, which had lost moneyfor several years, including a pretax loss of about $50 million in 1984, achieved a pretax profit of $70 million in 1985.

Citgo Petroleum Corporation adopted numerous management-science applications, involving techniques such as statistics, export systems, linear programming and fore-

casting, in various areas of the company.

Using these quantitative models has changed the way the company does business. Their investment in management science began in 1984. It was supported by both top-level and operational areas. It was first used in selected areas, such as acquisitions, but then became widespread. It has now been used in decision making in supply and distribution systems, market planning, accounts receivables and payables, operations management, inventory controls, and individual performance objectives. A key factor in the success of this program was the integration of all the company's information systems, and the creation of strategic and operational information systems.

For example, the company created computerized expert systems in which expert's advice on certain decisions were programmed into software. These systems advised Citgo managers on decisions related to planning and controlling operations, pricing, and supply and distribution, problems. Linear programming, a management science technique that searches for optional solutions when several variables and constraints are involved, was used to schedule refining.

SOURCE: Darwin Klingman, Nancy Phillips, David Stieger, and Warren Young, "The Successful Deployment of Management Science Throughout Citgo Petroleum Corporation," *Interfaces* (January–February, 1987), pp. 4–25.

It is apparent that practitioners are having difficulty in dealing with ill-defined problems. Therefore academic institutions need to provide more training in applying quantitative techniques to "nonstructured" situations.

Ronald L. Coccari
Management Researcher

There are three kinds of lies: lies, damned lies, and statistics.

Benjamin Disraeli

Because of the critical importance of becoming more competitive and more productive, and the other numerous challenges managers face, managers seek to make decision making more rational, to reduce the level of uncertainty of the alternatives they choose. To do so, they have increasingly turned to management science, using quantitative methods and other decision-assisting techniques. At Citgo, management science helped make the company competitive and profitable. Management science helped make the company more analytical in its approach to problem solving. Usage of management-science techniques, limited in the beginning to a few departments, eventually spread throughout the company. While quantitative techniques can be employed in any of the stages of problem solving, their principal usages have been in two stages in problem solving.

1. To cause the manager to perform the situation analysis in a more rational manner in order to recognize and identify problems better
2. To help problem solvers improve the actual choice they make

Management science as we know it today evolved from operations research (OR) efforts designed to improve production capabilities and the utilization of scarce resources in the military and supportive industry during World War II. But even prior to that time, people such as Frederick W. Taylor, Frank and Lillian Gilbreth, and Henry L. Gantt attempted to base the problem-solving process more on fact than intuition, as was discussed in Chapter 2. Management-science techniques did not change significantly from the early 1950s through the late 1970s, but their usage increased significantly. With the advent

This Citgo refinery is able to process substantially more petroleum products than formerly, thanks to the use of quantitative methods. For example, expert systems provided advice on scheduling and raw materials inventory management. (SOURCE © Courtesy Citgo)

This Merck analyst is plotting computer-generated control report information against a Gantt chart of expected performance. (SOURCE © Robert Reichert)

of the personal computer (PC) and minicomputers with substantial mainframe capability, their usage has increased even more. Spreadsheet analysis and computer simulations are available for virtually anyone's use. Numerous PC programs have been developed to aid the manager in making more rational decisions. And quantitatively based programs and decision support system programs have been developed that enable the manager to make more scientific decisions.

This chapter reviews the major quantitative techniques available in the decision process, focusing on the ones used most consistently. The chapter begins with a brief discussion of the foundation of quantitative methods, and their advantages and disadvantages. Quantitative problem-solving techniques are then reviewed, followed by a section on quantitative planning techniques, including forecasting. Finally, the chapter closes with a review of the role of the computer in problem solving. Included are discussions of spreadsheets, simulations, and database management.

Foundations of Quantitative Methods

Management science is an extremely broad term that encompasses virtually all the rational approaches to managerial problem solving that are based upon scientific methods. This chapter deals principally with quantitative methods that assist in decision making. A managerial problem may have either qualitative or quantitative aspects. The aspects that lend themselves to qualitative analysis include competitor intentions, the ability to motivate the work force, and customer style preferences, for example. The aspects that can be analyzed from a quantitative perspective include costs of raw materials, market share, and the history of customer purchase decisions, among others.

The primary focus of **quantitative methods** is improving problem solving by making it a more rational, analytical process. Most of the quantitative methods are based on economic decision criteria. Referring back to the discussion of decision making in Chapter 3, you will recall that there are two models of the process: the economic model and the administrative model. Quantitative methods attempt to improve your ability to complete better the economic model of decision making.[1] Quantitative approaches rely on mathematical models, and more recently they have come to rely on the use of computers to perform the calculations of the models.

A manager would use management-science and quantitative methods within the standard problem-solving model as follows. In formulating the problem, the manager identifies key elements as usual, but identifies the relationships among the key elements in mathematical terms. As part of the process, he or she must determine all the variables involved. These will be either controllable or uncontrollable variables. Decision criteria must also be identified. The result of this analysis will be a mathematical model based on formulas describing the relationships of objectives and variables. This model is then manipulated to determine possible alternative solutions, given various values of the variables and constraints. The implementation of quantitative methods often requires special effort, as managers sometimes fail to understand fully their importance. Some managers invariably resist quantitative methods—often because they don't understand them, often because they don't see their relevance.[2] Imagine the complex process of designing and manufacturing a space shuttle vehicle with hundreds of thousands of parts without some type of computer assistance. The task would be impossible.

While most quantitative techniques have been applied to operations management, financial management, and research and development, and to some extent to market research, even the seemingly simple act of approaching a boss or a subordinate about a problem can be examined quantitatively, to derive a more rational plan for doing so. Leading Edge Software of Palo Alto, California, has created a PC program entitled "Mind Prober" that provides recommended approaches to interacting with others, based on an assessment of your and their personality.[3] The world of the future appears to belong to those who can master the computer to enhance their problem solving.[4] Despite the obvious need to use them, quantitative methods have both advantages and disadvantages.

Advantages of Quantitative Methods[5]

Quantitative methods can assist the problem solver in a number of very useful ways.

1. They enhance the rationality of the problem solver. For many years managers have relied upon their intuition to make decisions. And while elsewhere in this text you will find the suggestion that intuition is a critical component of problem solving, and one that has until recently been neglected in many ways, intuition is best used after "you have crunched the numbers." The numbers are provided by quantitative methods. Typically, managers have relied on rules of thumb, general knowledge, or organizational policies and rules to guide them. Now they have available powerful quantitative tools to aid in the problem-solving process.

2. They can simplify and help a manager better organize complex problems. By breaking complex problems into parts, the manager will more readily understand them and be better able to solve them.

3. They provide a means to evaluate risk. Many of the models ask for some estimate of risk. This requirement helps the manager choose among alternatives.

4. The cost of information, the cost of computers, and the cost of software have all been dropping significantly. Many managers now have a portable desktop computer that, costing less than $3,000, enables them to perform calculations only possible fifteen years ago with a large mainframe which cost several hundred thousand dollars and filled a sizeable room. Managers could not afford to ask "what if" questions then. The cost was prohibitive. But now, virtually anyone using a spreadsheet program such as Lotus 1-2-3® or a relatively inexpensive simulation can ask those types of questions. The level of uncertainty in recognizing and identifying problems and in making choices among alternatives have therefore been reduced.

5. Improved software allows managers who have only limited knowledge of the computer to employ quantitative methods. The "user friendliness" of software improved substantially in the 1980s. Personal computers have become more and more powerful. A million bytes of information is now the industry standard, with twenty million easily added. Hence, more and more of the machine's memory can be used to provide user-friendly features such as easy-to-understand instructions; and with such large memories, the machine can perform more and more complicated tasks. The evidence suggests strongly that more and more software will be available in the future that will be readily usable by the average manager.

6. There is a general belief that using management-science techniques leads to greater profitability. This was certainly true at Citgo and has been shown to be true in a limited research study of Fortune 500 companies.[6]

AT CITGO: *Had Southland Corporation not forced Citgo into using quantitative methods, Citgo managers could not have made the sound decisions they did. The quantitative methods they used enabled them to understand their problems better and to assess related risk.*

AT CITGO: *The bottom line is that using quantitative methods can help improve profits, as they did at Citgo. Without scientific management, Citgo would not have been a profitable acquisition for Southland.*

Disadvantages of Quantitative Methods

Unfortunately, certain problems in using quantitative methods also exist.

1. Quantitative methods typically employ models of reality. Models are simplified versions of an actual situation. In many software programs, there is a trade-off between obtaining the user-friendliness necessary for acceptance by formulating an even simpler model. Some of the more complex and expensive simulations enable the manager to model virtually the entire system, but few can afford this type of model. It is therefore critical to make certain that a situation's key variables are not left out of the model.

2. All-encompassing simulations may be too expensive. A model of the U.S. economy costs literally hundreds of thousands, if not millions, of dollars to build. Few organizations can afford to construct their own model. Fortunately, at least three U.S. firms are willing to sell their models of the U.S. economy to others, but that is usually not an option in most complex situations.[7]

3. There is usually resistance to quantitative methods when they are first introduced. There may be resistance again subsequently, when new techniques are introduced. Many people have not overcome their fear of the computer. Many organizations fail to introduce their personnel to the programs sufficiently to help reduce resistance to change.

4. Not every problem can be modeled satisfactorily using quantitative methods. In many cases the decision is almost totally qualitative rather than quantitative. Furthermore, quantitative methods do not account for many of the social/psychological variables involved in problem solving. Interpersonal problems, for example, are difficult to quantify. Nor have many models been designed yet to aid in the creative aspects of problem solving.

5. A continuing, but decreasing problem, as software becomes more user-friendly, is the manager's level of understanding of quantitative methods. As software becomes more user-friendly, the manager becomes a semi-expert in using a quantitative method. Yet, he or she is often not fully conversant with the theory behind the quantitative technique. Managers must understand the meanings of the numbers the software gives them, not just how to derive those numbers.

6. When insufficient time is available to solve extremely complex problems, it limits the use or applicability of many quantitative methods. There may not be enough time to construct models, to scientifically analyze. If a decision must be made immediately, intuition often must suffice. On the other hand, quite complex problems can be modeled in a page or two, so many complex problems can be modeled, even if time is short. Additionally, though, the available research indicates that many strategic problems almost defy scientific analysis because of their complex interdependent relationships. In these cases intuition must be used.[8]

These advantages and disadvantages are summarized in Table 7.1.

Table 7.1. The Advantages and Disadvantages of Quantitative Methods for Problem Solving and Planning

Advantages
1. The rationality of the problem solver is enhanced.
2. Problems are simplified and managers helped to organize a problem better.
3. A means of risk evaluation is provided for various alternatives.
4. Nonprohibitive cost of computer usage for quantitative methods makes computation and analysis relatively inexpensive.
5. User-friendly software makes it possible for almost any manager to use quantitative methods.

Disadvantages
1. Models are simplified versions of reality.
2. All-encompassing simulations may be cost prohibitive.
3. Resistance to change, to computers, and to quantitative methods occurs initially in every situation.
4. Not every problem can be satisfactorily modeled.
5. A method can be used without fully understanding it.
6. The short amount of time available to spend on very complex problems may limit the use or applicability of many quantitative methods.

Fundamental Quantitative Decision-Making Techniques

A number of quantitative techniques exist and are described briefly here.

INVENTORY MODELS
Several models exist that can forecast how much to inventory order and when.

QUEUEING THEORY
The number of service units that will minimize both customer waiting time and cost of service can be forecasted.

NETWORK MODELS
Building upon the GANTT chart technique, large complex tasks are broken into smaller segments that can be managed independently. The two most prominent models are PERT (Program Evaluation Review Technique) and CPM (Critical Path Method).

FORECASTING
A number of techniques exist that enable a manager to make predictions about the future. They are made largely on the basis of past experience.

REGRESSION ANALYSIS
One method for forecasting is regression analysis. It helps indicate relationships among two or more variables. Once a relationship has been defined historically, projections of it for the future can be made.

SIMULATION
Simulation involves the modeling of a problem situation. A computer is then used to solve the problem in many different ways, altering several variables each time it is solved. Lotus 1-2-3® is an example of a software which can be used to create a computer simulation.

LINEAR PROGRAMMING (LP)
How to allocate resources among potentially competing uses can be determined through LP. For example, LP can help you determine what relative amounts,

Table 7.2.
Quantitative Methods Used by Corporations

Method	Percent Using
Statistical Analysis	93
Simulation	84
Linear Programming	79
PERT/CPM	70
Inventory Theory	57
Queueing Theory	45
Nonlinear Programming	36
Heuristic Programming	34

SOURCE: Adapted from G. Thomas and J. DaCosta, "A Sample Survey of Corporate Operational Research," *Interfaces* (1979), no. 4, pp. 102–111.

Table 7.3. Areas in Which Management Science Studies Are Applied

Area of Application	Percentage of Companies Reporting Applications in that Area
Forecasting	88
Production Scheduling	70
Inventory Control	70
Capital Budgeting	56
Transportation	51
Plant Location	42
Quality Control	40
Advertising and Sales Research	35
Equipment Replacement	33
Maintenance and Repair	28
Accounting Procedures	27
Packaging	09

SOURCE: W. Ledbetter and J. Cox, "Are OR Techniques Being Used?" Reprinted from *Industrial Engineering* magazine, Volume 9, No. 2. Copyright Institute of Industrial Engineers, 25 Technology Park/Atlanta, Norcross, GA 30092.

Table 7.4. Areas in Which Chief Financial Officers Indicate OR Techniques Are Being Used

Technique	Percent of Firms Indicating Frequent/ Regular Use
Sales Forecasting Models	76
Project/Product Models	61
Inventory Management Models	60
Break-Even Analysis	47
Simulation	29
Linear Programming	24

SOURCE: Adapted from James S. Moore, "A Multivariate Study of Firm Performance and the Use of Modern Analytical Tools and Financial Techniques," *Interfaces* (May–June 1987), p. 81.

within acceptable tolerances, of wheat, barley, and malt to allocate to beer production, given spot prices on the commodities markets.

SAMPLING THEORY
Samples of populations to be used for a number of processes, such as quality control and marketing research, can be statistically determined through sampling theory.

STATISTICAL DECISION THEORY
Characteristics in models, based on probabilities, can be determined through statistical decision theory.

Quantitative techniques/management science are applied in numerous areas. In 1979 G. Thomas and J. DaCosta surveyed large corporations to determine which areas of application used management-science studies most frequently.[9] Their results are summarized in Table 7.2.

An earlier survey by Norm Gaither in 1979 indicates three principal areas in manufacturing in which quantitative techniques are employed: production planning and control, project planning and control, and inventory analysis.[10] A survey by W. Ledbetter and J. Cox, shown in Table 7.3, reveals that several techniques are used quite often by business managers in arriving at decisions.[11] A recent survey of the chief financial officers of Fortune 500 firms by James S. Moore and Alan K. Reichert reports that such techniques are being used selectively, but significantly, as shown in Table 7.4. (Note the differences in responses in Table 7.4 compared to those in Table 7.2. These differences are obviously caused by having different respondents to the two questionnaires.)

There are literally hundreds of quantitative methods techniques employed throughout organizations today. This chapter focuses on some of the more fundamental of these—statistical analysis, decision theory, and decision trees—and then reviews the vital planning aids of forecasting—linear programming, PERT/CPM, decision support software, and simulations. Techniques generic to production and operations management are discussed in Chapter 20.

GLOBAL MANAGEMENT CHALLENGE

Statistics Assist Energy Policy Decision Making in the Parliament of Finland

The Finnish Parliament was confronted with a complex issue: how to provide power for the future. Forecasts had shown varying levels of need, but clearly, additional power was needed. A number of extremely complex and interdependent variables were involved. Legislators asked for assistance. With a grant from the Academy of Finland, Raimo P. Hamalainen, of the Helsinki University of Technology, devised a statistically based model to assist them. More specifically, the model focused on the issue of whether an additional nuclear power plant should be constructed. If the answer was yes, construction needed to begin right away, as eight to ten years were required to construct a nuclear power plant. A 1983 poll had shown that less than 50 percent of the Finnish population supported

Statistical Analysis

Statistical analysis is the technique most frequently cited as used in business. **Statistics** are data that are assembled and clarified in some meaningful way. They are divided into two principal types: descriptive and inferential (predictive). **Descriptive statistics** describe a situation as it exists currently. **Inferential, or predictive, statistics** are used by managers to attempt to predict what will happen in a situation in the future. The two are strongly related. Most often, statistics about current situations are used to predict future situations. Marketing researchers, for example, often take samples of selected market populations to determine their characteristics. These are then used to suggest whether new products might be successful in that marketplace and what the characteristics of a successful product might be. Marriott, for example, used a particular type of statistical analysis in designing the features of its Courtyard Motels. It analyzed the interactive effects of numerous factors on the various design possibilities.[12] Production personnel, especially those in quality control, often sample products to determine how many errors there are in the larger population. Interestingly, many Japanese firms do not use sampling approaches when it comes to quality control. They test every single product.

For the average manager, descriptive statistics are more important than predictive ones. Managers use statistics in the preparation of charts, graphs, tables, indexes, and the like and use them to understand trends and perhaps even make some inferences about the future. Most managers are involved frequently in presentations to upper-level managers or to their subordinates or fellow managers and will most often employ descriptive statistics. They may, for example, combine information from software packages, such as spreadsheet analysis of production costs, with a professional presentation package such as Video Show®. Managers need to understand the data they are involved with, more than being concerned with how statistics can be used to predict future situations. For example, the Finnish Parliament found statistics to be extremely useful in making critical energy policy decisions, as the following Global Management Challenge shows.

nuclear power. Interviews by the Finnish Parliament revealed that one-third were for, one-third against, and one-third uncertain. All sides in the debate had vested interests. For example, Finnish power companies feared that a no vote would for many years eliminate nuclear power as an alternative. Those opposed feared the obvious problems associated with nuclear power, for example, atomic and nuclear accidents.

Hamalainen chose a personal computer-based statistical model to incorporate the values of those involved. Society's overall benefit, an elusive goal indeed, was the criterion used as the basis for decision making in the model. As revealed in Figure 7.1, numerous key variables were involved.

Interview sessions with members of Parliament were used to determine the values (preferences) associated with each of the major variables, and statistics were generated. The technique formed the decision as one of nuclear power versus coal-fired plants. As debate continued, the Chernobyl nuclear accident occurred (1987) and the power companies withdrew their application for a nuclear power plant license.

SOURCE: Raimo P. Hamalainen, "Computer Assisted Policy Analysis in the Parliament of Finland," *Interfaces* (July–August 1988), pp. 12–23.

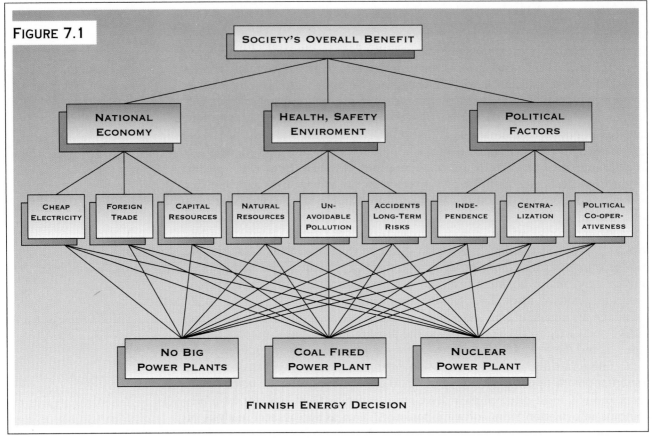

FIGURE 7.1

SOCIETY'S OVERALL BENEFIT

NATIONAL ECONOMY

HEALTH, SAFETY ENVIROMENT

POLITICAL FACTORS

CHEAP ELECTRICITY

FOREIGN TRADE

CAPITAL RESOURCES

NATURAL RESOURCES

UN-AVOIDABLE POLLUTION

ACCIDENTS LONG-TERM RISKS

INDE-PENDENCE

CENTRA-LIZATION

POLITICAL CO-OPER-ATIVENESS

NO BIG POWER PLANTS

COAL FIRED POWER PLANT

NUCLEAR POWER PLANT

FINNISH ENERGY DECISION

SOURCE: RAIMO P. HAMALAINEN, "COMPUTER-ASSISTED POLICY ANALYSIS IN THE PARLIAMENT OF FINLAND," _INTERFACES_ (JULY–AUGUST 1988), PP. 12–23.

The manager, however, does use some inferential statistics. For example, he or she may use regression or correlation to describe certain situations. He or she may then use these, assuming the underlying situation described will not change, to make predictions about the future. A pure statistician would almost never use them in that way. He or she would be more concerned about the existing relationships between variables than their future ones. But a manager can determine whether a relationship that existed historically will have any meaning in the future. He or she then can make decisions based on how useful that relationship is to predict the future. Judgment is vital. If it were demonstrated, for example, that a strong correlation exists between the birth rate in New York City and the number of storks that nest in Canada, would you see them as related? A manager of a Gerber's Baby Food division could possibly say that an increase in stork nesting in Canada would mean that the company should produce more baby food. It is not likely, however, that a production manager would make such a decision because it seems clear that, while a rise in the birth rate might be accompanied by a rise in the number of nesting storks, there is probably not a cause-and-effect relationship between them. Managers must make such determinations carefully.

Decision Theory: Decision Trees and Expected Value

Techniques such as decision trees and concepts such as expected value can be used to aid the decision maker in derermining optimal choices when confronted with several alternatives and a condition of uncertainty or risk associated with those alternatives.

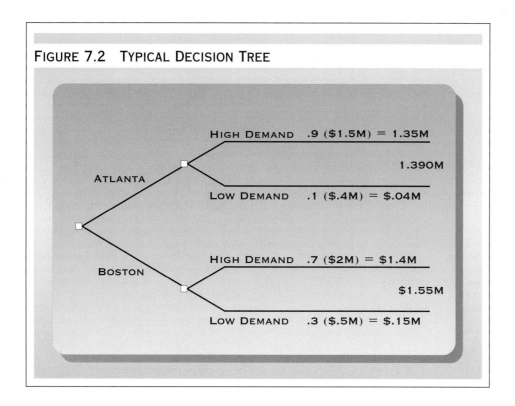

FIGURE 7.2 TYPICAL DECISION TREE

HIGH DEMAND   .9 ($1.5M) = 1.35M

1.390M

ATLANTA

LOW DEMAND   .1 ($.4M) = $.04M

HIGH DEMAND   .7 ($2M) = $1.4M

$1.55M

BOSTON

LOW DEMAND   .3 ($.5M) = $.15M

DECISION TREES

When BeniHana of Tokyo launched its new frozen-food dinners for sales in supermarkets, it was faced with a large number of possible production levels. To determine which of those levels to follow, BeniHana could have used a decision tree. A decision tree is used to describe the interrelationships of more complex problems involving a series of sequential choices.[13]

A **decision tree** is a visual representation of the decision alternatives available to the decision maker, their interconnectedness in the environment—events (the states of nature)—and their consequences. Figure 7.2 illustrates a typical decision tree. The organization portrayed in this figure is attempting to determine whether to sell its consulting services in Atlanta or Boston. In either city, services may have a high level of demand or a low level of demand. In Boston there is a 70 percent chance of high demand. The conditional payoff (from choosing the condition—i.e., Boston) would be $2 million. The low demand probability is 30 percent. The conditional payoff is $.5 million. The **expected value** is the sum of the conditional payoffs times the conditional probabilities: ($2,000,000 × .7) + ($500,000 × .3) = $1,400,000 + $150,000 for a total of $1,550,000. Consulting services in Atlanta have a high demand probability of .9. The conditional payoff is $1.5 million. The low demand probability is .10. The conditional payoff is $.4 million. The expected value is ($1,500,000 × .9) + ($.4 million × .1) = $1,350,000 + $40,000 for a total of $1,390,000. The expected value of establishing consulting services in Boston is higher than establishing services in Atlanta. All other things being equal, the decision maker would probably choose to begin selling consulting services in Boston.

While this information could have been portrayed using other techniques, the real utility of decision trees is that they can be used to model decisions that are sequential. For example, as illustrated in Figure 7.2, the second set of decision alternatives for the path chosen (a high demand in Boston) might be to determine what actions the company should take, or not take, until it made the Boston decision. It could wait until it offered services there and until a high demand

FIGURE 7.3   SEQUENTIAL DECISIONS SHOWN ON A DECISION TREE

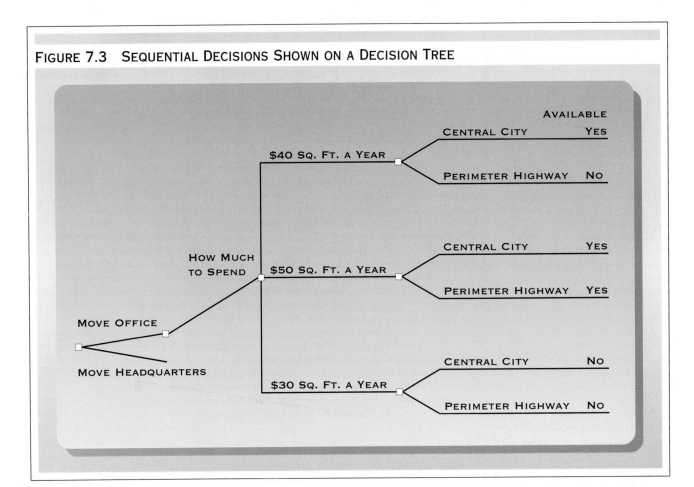

This fire in Yellowstone National Park might have been even more devastating if firefighters had not used quantitative methods to plot a plan of attack. (SOURCE © Stan Osolinski/ Stock Market)

occurred and then make certain decisions. But the decision tree allows the problem solver to see the results of a second decision, assuming the first is made. The decisions to be made about Boston might include locating just an office there or moving its headquarters there—because the Boston market is perceived to be more lucrative than where the firm is presently headquartered. If they choose just to open an office, key questions are where in Boston—a central city location versus a perimeter highway location—and how much to spend. An additional alternative might be to go ahead and begin to do some consulting in Atlanta because the difference in the expected values of the two original decision alternatives is not that large. One of the real advantages of using decision trees is their flexibility, as Figure 7.3 suggests. You can adjust them to suit your needs.

Decision analysis is being used in more organizations as its utility is recognized. A division of Eaton Corporation, for example, used the decision-tree technique to determine whether to acquire the rights to a night safety device. Honeywell, in another example, uses expected values to aid in growth planning in its defense industry segment.[14] The U.S. Forest Service uses decision-tree analysis to guide its decisions to control burn certain areas in order to prevent forest fires from covering much larger areas.[15] Decision-tree analysis has been used to help people choose which mortgage is best for them and to determine where to drill for oil.[16] Decision trees probably will be used more and more to make decisions as software to guide us through the process becomes available.

When substantial amounts of money are involved, decision makers will use these decision analysis tools, but they must be extra careful to apply judgment and intuition to the numbers derived from those tools.

Additional Quantitative Techniques for Problem Solving

In addition to statistics and decision trees, several other quantitative methods are available to facilitate decision making. Among them are inventory models, queueing models, and distribution models.

Inventory Models

Inventory models provide guidance to a manager in managing inventory, most often in determining how much inventory to maintain at a point in time. Inventory modeling is limited to those in production situations. Inventory models can be used with raw materials, work-in-process, and finished-goods inventories. There are costs associated with having too few or too much of each of these inventories. Too little inventory of raw materials or work-in-process goods may halt the production process while additional inventory is acquired. Too little inventory of finished goods may upset customers because of stockouts. Too much inventory for all three types means excessive carrying charges, costs of maintaining inventory levels, and money tied up in goods that have not yet been sold. Additionally there are costs associated with the ordering of raw material inventories and supplies inventories. Inventory holding costs must be counterbalanced in the manufacturing operation against the costs of continually changing production runs. Normally the longer the production run, the cheaper the per unit cost because start-up costs can be averaged out over a larger number of products.

One of the more recent innovations in inventory management is just-in-time inventory, where only enough inventory for one day's manufacturing is kept in work-in-process inventories and raw materials inventories. Suppliers have to meet production requirements or lose the contract.[17] In an example from Chapter 6, Milliken supplies Levi's with exactly one day's requirement for its manufacturing facilities.[18] The advantage of just-in-time inventory is that all of the holding costs are kept to virtually zero, production runs are at maximum for the plant's capacity for the day, and as finished goods are completed, they can be shipped to the customer. Two of the disadvantages are in maintaining control of the quality of the inputs and in making sure that needed materials are there in time. Because inventory models are so critical to the production situation, they are discussed in more detail in Chapter 20.

> AT CITGO: *Citgo used inventory modeling to help reduce its costs.*

Queueing Models

Queueing models are those that assist the manager in making choices about waiting-line problems. We have all experienced waiting in line at the bank, grocery store, or airline ticket counter.[19] The number of tellers or clerks available to service needs has in all probability been determined on the basis of some waiting-line model. As with the inventory model, there are both costs and benefits to various levels of "inventory"—in this case those waiting. Customers don't like to wait, so organizations may lose customers over the long or even short term if they have to wait very long. On the other hand, if a company has enough personnel to make sure a customer doesn't have to wait, personnel costs are very high. So the organization must balance the two factors. Personnel costs are readily known. The effect of waiting on customer revenues must be estimated. Queueing models are constructed that describe the system's operating charac-

The length of the lines at both the grocery store and the bank can be scientifically analyzed and thereby kept to a minimum at a minimal level of cost. Many stores settle for a less scientific approach and move clerks in and out of checking positions and stocking positions, as needed. (SOURCE © Mike Clemmer/Picture Group)

teristics—the percentage of time the service facilities are not being used; the anticipated number of those in the waiting line at any point in time; the average time that the organization would like each person to spend in the waiting line; and so on. Such models are quite versatile. The City of New York, for example, used a queueing model to determine whether to change the location of service areas for its police patrol cars. The travel time of the cars to their patrol areas was used as the "waiting-line time."[20]

Distribution Models

Logistics managers and marketing managers are particularly concerned with the effective and efficient distribution of an organization's products. To understand their distribution systems better, they employ distribution models, sometimes referred to as transportation models. **Distribution models** help a manager determine where the products are to go and how they are to be shipped. Each type of transportation—air, truck, railroads, cars, bicycles, and ships—has associated shipping costs. A manager must determine the optimum routes and the optimum means of transportation. Most firms today attempt to return to the point of origination with goods, as well as having vehicles full when they leave—whether the vehicles are the company's or are leased. Hughes Supply Company,

---

MANAGEMENT CHALLENGE **7.1**

Marshall's Distribution System

Marshall's, an off-price retail clothing chain, had been experiencing rapid growth at a compound annual rate of 30 percent. This growth was coming primarily from the addition of outlets. The pattern of clothing inventory flows from warehouses to stores was changing constantly, thereby straining existing corporate logistics models.

a $300 million + wholesale/retail commercial construction supply firm has the goal "no truck returns empty" translated into an objective of at least 60 percent full.[21] Most distribution models are formed using linear programming, a technique to be described shortly. However, they may also be the subject of more extensive computer simulation models, as Management Challenge 7.1 suggests.

Quantitative Techniques for Planning

Those involved in planning have several approaches available that will aid their problem solving. To begin with, most plans are based on premises, which in turn are based on forecasts of future situations. **Forecasts** are predictions of the future. These are often expressed in financial terms in business.[22] They become more difficult as change in the environment accelerates. Additional quantitative techniques available for planning include linear programming, break-even analysis, network analyses, and simulations.

AT CITGO: *Citgo used quantitative methods, including expert systems, to help it forecast demand, and to thereby help it schedule production.*

Forecasting

The principal strategic planning forecast that organizations must make is the sales forecast. Other types of forecasts that might be necessary include those for utilizing material resources and cash. In addition, there are several techniques that can be employed to forecast. Among them are the quantitative techniques of time series analyses and causal analyses—including regression and correlation—and the qualitative techniques of executive opinion, sales force opinion, expert opinion, and consumer surveys.

SALES FORECASTING
Sales forecasting is the process of predicting future sales. All organizations depend on inflowing financial resources for current and future operations, so predicting their level is an important task. For the nonprofit organization, revenue forecasting, tax forecasting, and other processes are equally relevant and are similar in nature. Your local school authority, for example, must make a forecast of tax funds to determine whether it can give its teachers a 7.5 percent raise this year.

Marshall's put together a team of consultants augmented by logistics software specialists. They chose to use an IBM PC AT as their hardware. The model actually consisted of three submodels analyzing inflows, inventories, and outflows. There are as many as 20,000 links in the system, but the package is surprisingly fast. Marshall's solved its distribution management problem by using this simulation because the model enables distribution managers to satisfy better their store managers' inventory requirements. It does so because, through the model, distribution managers can see how all of the stores and warehouses are interrelated.

SOURCE: David P. Carlisle, Kenneth S. Nickerson, Steven B. Probst, Denise Rudolph, Yosef Scheffi, and Warren B. Pal, "A Turnkey Computer Based Logistics Planning System," *Interfaces* (July–August 1987), pp. 16–23.

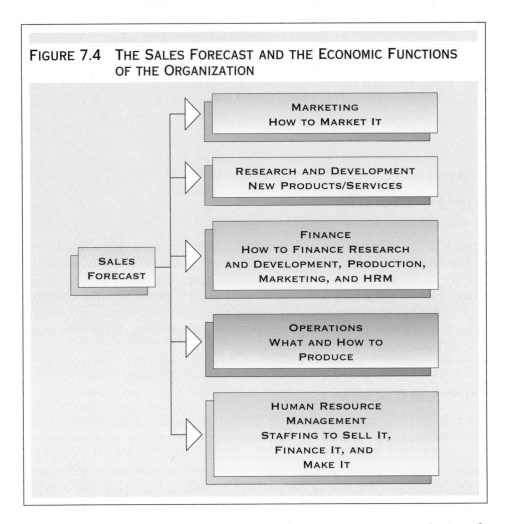

FIGURE 7.4   THE SALES FORECAST AND THE ECONOMIC FUNCTIONS OF THE ORGANIZATION

MARKETING
HOW TO MARKET IT

RESEARCH AND DEVELOPMENT
NEW PRODUCTS/SERVICES

SALES FORECAST

FINANCE
HOW TO FINANCE RESEARCH AND DEVELOPMENT, PRODUCTION, MARKETING, AND HRM

OPERATIONS
WHAT AND HOW TO PRODUCE

HUMAN RESOURCE MANAGEMENT
STAFFING TO SELL IT, FINANCE IT, AND MAKE IT

The four principal economic functions of an organization—marketing, finance, operations, and human resources—all depend on the sales forecast to some degree for the completion of their jobs, as seen in Figure 7.4. Because so much depends on the sales forecast, it is usually one of the very first steps in strategic planning. Virtually all an organization's expenses are based upon some assumption about the amount of sales for the forthcoming year. Marketing responds with promotion, pricing, and distribution efforts in response to the

MANAGEMENT CHALLENGE 7.2

GE Finds Sales Forecasting Difficult in the Locomotive Industry

In the early 1980s, General Electric committed $300 million to refurbish its locomotive engine plant in Erie, Pennsylvania, on the basis of a forecast for increased demand for the product in the coming years. Unfortunately for General Electric, those large sums may very well have been wasted, as demand for the product has failed to materialize. Accurate sales forecasting is critical to the future of most

sales forecast. R&D must determine the need for new products. Finance must determine how to finance related expenses such as compensation, which must be calculated and planned for based upon the availability of funds. These funds are estimated through the sales forecast. Operations management works in conjunction with marketing to determine how much product or service to create and then decides which jobs are necessary to do so. The human resources management department decides how to staff operations, as well as a company's other functions.

Sales forecasts typically cover a range of possibilities—a growth rate, for example, of 8 percent–15 percent. Managers must be prepared to operate within that range. Different actions will be possible at 15 percent that are not possible at 8 percent. Staffing levels, supply budgets, and travel budgets, for example, all depend on the sales forecast. An MBA program in a small college might concern itself with the accuracy of sales forecasts (number of incoming students) made by the dean. Just a few students more or less can cause a 10 percent variance in such a program's full-time operating budget. No one wants to be "under budget." And make no mistake, as Management Challenge 7.2 suggests, sales forecasting is not easy.

Forecasting Techniques

Forecasting techniques are either quantitative or qualitative. Quantitative techniques are either time series or causal.

TIME SERIES TECHNIQUES

Data that occur over a period of time can be analyzed using **time series analyses** in which the variable under study is plotted against time, as is shown in Figure 7.5. Time series analyses are very commonly used in sales forecasting. One of the key assumptions of forecasting is that the past is a good predictor of the future. This is often true with sales. The assumption of time series analyses is that there are four separate components that affect time series data: trend, cyclical, seasonal, and irregular or random.

Most time series data exhibit some sort of trend over a long period of time. In Figure 7.4 a hand-estimated best "fit" line is used. More precise mathematical computations can be used to determine that trend. Once a trend is determined, the line can then be extended past the current database to predict future points on that line, here future sales, and so on.

organizations. It is certainly critical to the future of any specific strategy to which it is linked.

From the corporate perspective, General Electric was not severely damaged by its locomotive investment because it has a large portfolio of businesses from which cash flows; profits can be used to balance the investment in the locomotive division. But from that division's perspective, the inaccurate sales forecast will affect profits for many years. Had that division been a single business not under the GE umbrella, it might very well have been bankrupted by the inaccuracy of that forecast. GE's locomotive division managers accepted the challenge presented by those dire circumstances, however, and found new markets for their product, principally mainland China.

SOURCE: Peter Petre, "What Welch Has Wrought at GE," *Fortune* (July 7, 1986), p. 45.

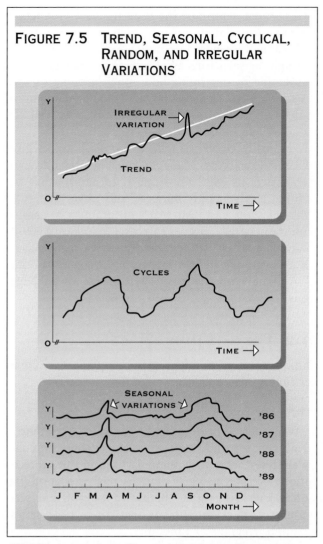

FIGURE 7.5   TREND, SEASONAL, CYCLICAL, RANDOM, AND IRREGULAR VARIATIONS

SOURCE: ADAPTED FROM WILLIAM J. STEVENSON, PRODUCTION-OPERATIONS MANAGEMENT, 3RD ED. (HOMEWOOD, IL: IRWIN, 1986). FIGURE 3–1, P. 136.

It is extremely important for any manager to adjust for seasonal and cyclical effects. The nation's economic cycle, for example, impacts heavily on forecasts for housing starts. Seasonal data are not too difficult to adjust for because a four-quarter or 12-month analysis will usually reveal the seasonal impact. The Walt Disney World theme parks, which include the Magic Kingdom and Epcot Center, for example, report that their attendance is lowest in May, September, and January and extremely high in June, July, August, December, February, March, and April. Knowing this allows them to staff at appropriate levels to keep "waiting lines," to a minimum.[23] Cyclical effects are more difficult to predict because economic cycles, industrial cycles, and product-technology cycles vary significantly, with often unpredictable factors in the economy, industry, or technology.

CAUSAL TECHNIQUES

The other principal type of quantitative forecasting technique is the causal technique. **Causal techniques** suggest causes for behavior of dependent variables and often use them to predict events. The two principal types of causal models are regression analysis and the econometric model. **Regression Analysis** is a statistical technique that develops relationships between two or more variables. One is the dependent variable and the other one (or more) is the independent variable. Regression techniques are descriptive per se but—again assuming that in the future relationships among the variables will be the same as in the past—the manager will often extend the regression line to some future date.

A typical regression equation might be as follows:

$$Y = AX_1 + BX_2 + C$$

where

Y = the dependent variable (sales of hamburgers, in this case)

X_1, X_2 = independent variables (businesses having more than 50 employees; and the number of high school students in the area)

A, B = weights for the independent variables calculated according to an analysis of past data

C = a constant derived from the same data

In this case hamburger sales are highly dependent upon business and student populations in the area. The formula could be used to estimate sales for a new store or to predict the amount of increased sales resulting from increased business or student populations in the area. The manager could substitute various values for X_1 and X_2 in the equation and determine increased sales. New York City used regression analysis to help it determine the most efficient way to clean the streets, as Management Challenge 7.3 reveals.

MANAGEMENT CHALLENGE 7.3

Polishing the Big Apple

In a city the size of New York, street cleaning is almost an endless problem. There are currently 12,000 employees in the sanitation department. It expends about half a billion dollars per year. How do you determine optimal manpower levels, and how do you determine the relationship between the number of street cleaners required and factors such as illegally parked cars?

In 1980 the sanitation department was faced with several major problems, including dirtier streets, 1,500 fewer cleaners than it had in 1965, and low morale among workers. Furthermore, it had no knowledge base to make decisions upon, little or no coordination with other city agencies, low support from top management, and no support from the city council.

To answer their questions and help solve their problems, New York City's Department of Sanitation initiated a regression-model analysis aimed at improving the conditions of the streets and the efficiency of the work force. A project team built a database that was then regressed to determine the relationship between manpower levels and their cleanliness score from the city. Different models were used for analyzing the effects of other factors. The program achieved both of its major goals, and it is estimated that it will save the city $12 million per year. The city has achieved five consecutive years of improved cleanliness ratings. Its 1986 rating was 68.7 percent, compared to a low of 53 percent, using seven hundred fewer cleaners. There was a cut of about $12 million a year in reduced salary and benefit costs.

SOURCE: Lucius C. Riccio, Joseph Miller, and Ann Litke, "Polishing the Big Apple: How Management Science Has Helped Make New York Streets Cleaner," *Interfaces* (January–February 1986), pp. 83–88.

Quantitative methods not only improved service, but also cut costs in New York City's Department of Sanitation. (SOURCE © Lisa Quinones/Black Star)

Econometric models use a complex series of interdependent regression equations, combining both theory and applied research, to predict the performance of some dependent variable, often the national economy. Corporate strategists usually buy econometric forecasts, which are costly to create, to use in their strategic planning programs rather than develop them themselves. Such forecasts are available not just for the total economy, but by industry segment. These forecasts are available from a number of services, such as Data Resources, Chase Econometrics, The Wharton Econometric Forecasting Associates, and the Evan's Group. These forecasts will offer different predictions, although presumably working with the same basic information, because of the beliefs, values, perceptions, and assumptions of their chief forecaster.[24]

Qualitative Methods

Qualitative forecasting methods are judgments and opinions used in forecasting. Many times when a forecast must be prepared quickly, there simply isn't enough time to gather and analyze quantitative data. At other times, when perceived environmental variables are changing rapidly, the past may not be a good predictor of the future. Furthermore, when seeking to determine the impact of new events, such as technological forecasting might seek to do, or for example, when attempting to determine how to launch new products, judgment or opinion may be advisable. Several techniques are commonly used in such situations: executive opinion, sales force composites, expert opinion (including the Delphi Technique), and consumer surveys. Another important technique is the technological forecast, used principally to keep the organization abreast of changes in technology.

The Limits of Forecasting

A wide variety of forecasting techniques exists; however, several limitations are common to all.

1. Forecasting techniques generally assume that the factors affecting the past will continue to exist in the future.
2. Forecasts are rarely perfect; actual results usually differ from predicted values.
3. Forecasts for groups of items such as products or services tend to be more accurate than forecasts for individual items because forecasting errors among items in a group usually have a canceling effect.
4. Forecasts are more accurate for the short term.[25]

Forecasts: A Summary

Similarly there seem to be five basic steps in the forecasting process:

1. Determine the purpose of the forecast and when it will be needed.
2. Establish a time horizon that the forecast must cover.
3. Select a forecasting technique.
4. Gather and analyze the appropriate data and then prepare the forecast. Identify any assumptions that are made in conjunction with preparing and using the forecast.
5. Monitor the forecast to see if it is performing in a satisfactory manner.[26]

Finally, knowing which forecasting technique to use is often a troublesome decision in itself, involving numerous issues: the length of the forecast, the availability of computer software, the changefulness of the external environment, and the need for accuracy.

Additional Quantitative Planning Techniques

In addition to forecasting techniques, a number of additional quantitative techniques are available to aid a manager in planning problem solving. Four of the most widely used include break-even analysis, linear programming, network models (PERT/CPM), and simulations.

Break-Even Analysis

Whenever new products or services are launched, whenever any projects are engaged in, whenever managers consider enacting an annual operating plan, in most cases, the plan will involve a point at which the revenue generated from the project, product, or service, from the year's efforts, is going to equal the cost of generating that revenue—the **break-even point.** Managers perform **break-even analysis** to determine the point at which revenues equal costs and to determine related information. The principal reason for determining this point is to make certain the organization isn't going to engage in a plan that won't result in a profit. Break-even analysis compares forecasted demand for the product and resulting income from the project, against costs of the project. If demand is less than the break-even point, the project should not be undertaken. Managers may also use break-even analysis to examine the effects on profits of different prices for a product or service, or the effects of different operational output levels. It is also a very sound technique for comparing production capacity alternatives.

As shown in Figure 7.5, all projects or products incur certain levels of **fixed costs**—costs that tend to remain constant regardless of volume of output. These include factors such as depreciation of plant and equipment, overhead items such as managerial salaries, and insurance costs. **Variable costs** are those that vary according to the volume of output. Normally these include direct labor and materials costs. Variable costs per unit typically remain the same regardless of the volume of output, whereas fixed costs per unit decrease as volume increases. The total cost of any product or service is equal to the fixed cost plus the variable cost per unit times the number of units.

These relationships are shown graphically in Figure 7.6. Also shown in Figure 7.5 is the fact that revenue varies with volume. It varies per unit as does variable cost. Hence, the total revenue line will have a linear relationship with output—that is, a change of a certain magnitude in the independent variable causes a change in the dependent variable of a directly related amount, regardless of the value of the independent variable.[27] At some point total revenue will equal total cost. This is the break-even point. Figure 7.6 calculates this point. It may also be calculated algebraically. Assuming a fixed cost of $3 million, variable costs of $400 per unit, and revenues of $700 per unit, the volume necessary to break even turns out to be 10,000 units.

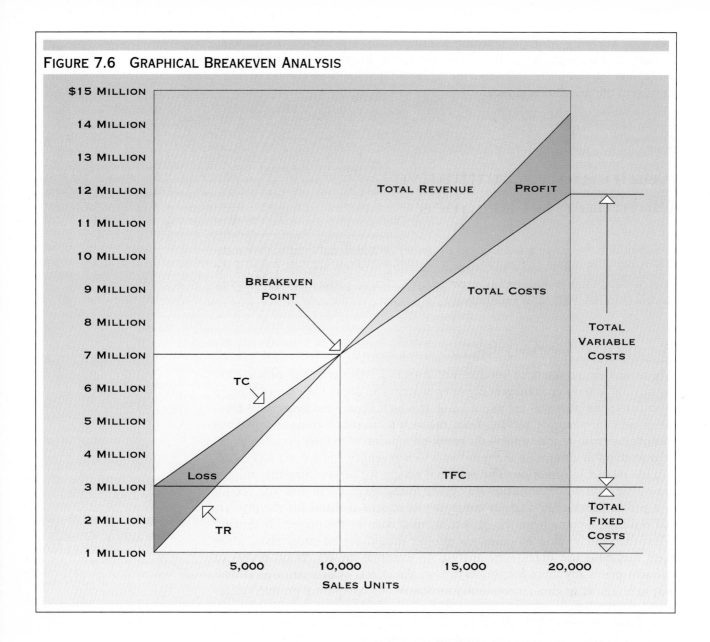

FIGURE 7.6 GRAPHICAL BREAKEVEN ANALYSIS

Let TFC = Total Fixed Costs
VC = Variable Cost Per Unit
P = Price Per Unit
BEP = Break-even Point

The formula for calculating the break-even point is

$$BEP = \frac{TFC}{P - VC}$$

In the preceding example, the formula would be calculated as follows:

$$BEP = \frac{\$3\ million}{700 - 400} = \frac{\$3\ million}{300} = 10,000\ units$$

Break-even analysis is very good for determining the answers to "what if" questions: What if we wanted a profit of so much, what if we raised prices by so much, what if we could cut costs by so much . . . what would be the results?

In order to determine the required volume (V) to generate a desired profit (DP) the formula would be (V is actually just a higher break-even point)

$$V = \frac{DP + TFC}{P - VC}$$

Suppose the company wanted to make $7 million. The required volume to do so would be calculated as follows:

$$V = \frac{\$3,000,000 + \$3,000,000}{700 - 400}$$

$$V = \frac{\$6,000,000}{300} = 20,000 \text{ units}$$

This use of break-even analysis can be extremely critical in profit planning. One version of this approach developed by Armco, Inc., uses an expanded break-even analysis to relate return on investment (ROI) targets to various volume levels. This is especially useful in capital intensive markets, where ROI is very sensitive to sales volume.[28]

The key underlying assumptions of break-even analysis are

1. One product is involved.
2. Everything that is produced can be sold.
3. Variable cost per unit is the same regardless of the volume.
4. Fixed costs do not change when the volume changes.[29]

Linear Programming

Linear programming (LP) is a technique that uses a sequence of steps leading to an optimum solution in a problem characterized by a single goal and objectives, a number of constraints, a number of variables, and a linear relationship among the variables.[30] It is a means of allocating resources or facilities on a project in an optimum way, given the selected constraints of the situation — perhaps price and the availability of resources. When Ralston Purina makes "Dog Chow" or "Fit and Trim" or "Puppy Chow" or any other similar product, it is confronted with combining a variety of grains with varying prices. It seeks to offer a dog food that satisfies its constraints for the cheapest market prices of grains and meets the advertised contents on the package. To solve this problem, it would typically use a linear programming model.

Most LP problems are solved on the computer because the equations involved require a large number of calculations. LP problems are solved in a series of steps. The model literally "closes in" on the optimal combination of variables. (You can solve a very basic problem in linear programming, one involving only one possible product and two variables, by hand, graphically.) LP is an extremely valuable tool. It can be used in a number of situations but is probably most frequently used as a production scheduling device or in cost determination situations. United Airlines, for example, uses it to schedule four thousand workers.[31] It can also be used in such diverse areas as allocating sales representatives to territories or selecting an optimal portfolio of investments.[32] One of the advantages of LP is that it allows the manager to perform sensitivity analysis examining the effects of changes in variables, similar to what was done with "what ifs" in break-even analysis. A recent version of LP is capable of performing extremely complex problems with numerous variables and solution possibilities.[33] LP is used in a wide variety of organizations to solve a multitude of problems, as Management Challenge 7.4 suggests.

Linear Programming of Defense Budget Decisions in the Air Force

How do you allocate billions of dollars for aircraft systems and munitions procurement for a large number of complex aircraft such as the F16, the A10, the F111, and the F15E; munitions such as the Maverick, the MK82, the MK84, and the LLGB; for various targets such as tanks; and for facilities?

Network Models PERT/CPM

PERT (**Program Evaluation and Review Technique**) and CPM (**Critical Path Method**) are networking models used to plan and coordinate large-scale projects. PERT and CPM

1. graphically display a project's activities.
2. give an estimate of how long the project and its subcomponent activities will take.
3. provide an indication of which activities are the most critical at the time of project completion.
4. suggest how long an activity within the project can be delayed without delaying the total project.[34]

Although PERT and CPM were developed separately, and although there were many differences between the two originally, these project planning techniques have come to be essentially identical over time.[35] PERT was originally developed through the joint efforts of Lockheed Aircraft, the U.S. Navy Special Projects Office, and the consulting firm of Booz, Allen & Hamilton, in an effort to speed up the Polaris missile submarine project. Critical Path Method was developed by J. A. Kelley of the Rand Corporation, for the Du Pont Corporation's use in planning and coordinating maintenance projects in chemical plants.[36] This text uses PERT as the example, although substantially the same discussion could be made about CPM.

Both PERT and CPM use network models to portray major project components—activities and the sequential relationships among them.[37] An example of a Gantt chart for the activities of a bank opening a new branch is shown in Figure 2.1 on p. 40. Figure 7.7 portrays these same activities in terms of a single-project network diagram. As seen in Figure 7.7, the PERT network, in its most fundamental sense, consists of circles, indicating the beginning or ending of an activity, and lines, with arrows indicating an activity. The network is drawn with activities arranged sequentially from left to right as you move through the network. This network diagram is superior to the Gantt chart in terms of portraying a sequence of activities. Activities occurring at the same time are represented by dual or multiple paths. You will notice that certain activities need to be done at the same time as others, or before others, but that some can also be accomplished independently.

An LP model was constructed using existing data and estimates on

1. aircraft and munition effectiveness.
2. target value—the value of the targets to be destroyed by the weapon system.
3. attrition of the aircraft used.
4. aircraft and munition costs.
5. existing aircraft and munitions inventories.

The program has proven successful in changing the way the Air Force procures munitions and targets. It has enabled them to save substantial amounts of money.

SOURCE: Robert J. Might, "Decision Support in Aircraft and Munitions Procurement" (September–October 1987), pp. 55–63.

One of the principal concerns of the manager is to determine the **critical path** through the model. The critical path is the sequence of activities that leads from the starting circle to the finishing circle, in terms of the longest amount of time. The manager is interested in determining the longest path through the network because that determines how long it will take to complete the project. The activities on the critical path are called the critical activities. The paths that are shorter than the critical path can experience delays and still not effect the completion date of the project. Delays in activities on the critical path will affect the completion of the project.[38] In Figure 7.7, the critical path takes twenty weeks—from the beginning point, locating facilities (eight weeks), through remodeling (eleven weeks) and moving in.

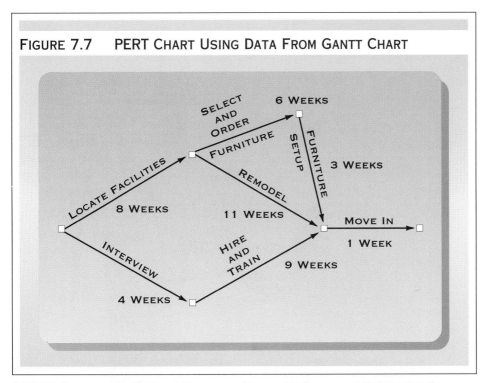

FIGURE 7.7   PERT CHART USING DATA FROM GANTT CHART

SELECT AND ORDER FURNITURE

6 WEEKS

FURNITURE SETUP

FURNITURE

3 WEEKS

LOCATE FACILITIES

8 WEEKS

REMODEL

11 WEEKS

MOVE IN

1 WEEK

INTERVIEW

4 WEEKS

HIRE AND TRAIN

9 WEEKS

SOURCE: ADAPTED FROM WILLIAM J. STEVENSON, PRODUCTION-OPERATIONS MANAGEMENT, 3RD ED. (HOMEWOOD, IL: IRWIN, 1986), P. 701.

ADVANTAGES AND DISADVANTAGES OF PERT

The following are the advantages of PERT.

1. The manager is forced to organize and quantify his or her plans and obtain information that is not readily available.
2. PERT provides a visual display of the project and its major activities. Visual displays usually aid the planning process.
3. PERT identifies activities that should be closely monitored, the critical path activities that might delay the project. It also indicates those activities that would have slack time and can be delayed without delaying the project.
4. Resources may be reallocated, if by doing so the length of time of the entire project would be shortened.

The following are PERT's disadvantages.

1. An important activity may be overlooked in the network.
2. Sequential relationships may not be correct as shown.
3. Time estimates are just that—estimates—and are therefore subject to the problems associated with estimation.
4. A computer is necessary to use PERT for large projects.[39]

Some three thousand contractors and subcontractors were involved with various segments of the Polaris project for which PERT was developed. Coordination might have been impossible without PERT. At the very least, the Navy estimates that it saved two years in completing the project as a consequence. PERT is used in almost all major construction projects. Blount Brothers Construction Company employed PERT when it constructed the Superdome in New Orleans.[40] PERT and CPM are used in virtually every major management situation today.

PERT enables contractors to provide the Navy with highly complex projects, such as this nuclear submarine, on time and at lower cost than if other project management systems were used. (SOURCE © Fred Ward/Black Star)

The Uses of Computers in Decision Making and Planning

The uses of computers in problem solving is increasing rapidly. Mainframes, minicomputers, and PCs all have expanded power, reduced costs, and widespread applications.[41] Perhaps most importantly, with the advent of powerful personal computers, most of the techniques portrayed in this chapter are available in relatively inexpensive computer software packages, well within the price range of most small businesses. **Decision support systems** (DSS) software packages that aid the decision-making process are becoming widely available. Most businesses can certainly afford them;[42] there are more complex ones for larger businesses. Increased quantitative analyses of problems at all levels of an organization are anticipated as a result of these DSS programs.

There are even programs, such as "Idea Generator," that help a manager structure any decision.[43] PERT and CPM, financial planning, LP, spreadsheets, break-even analysis, inventory planning and control, and numerous other programs are readily available for PCs. Bayard Wynne suggests that DSS software will become even more useful as artificial intelligence (where computers attempt to emulate the human decision process) expands capabilities and expert systems provide additional information to managers to aid them in making decisions.[44] But perhaps the most important use of the computer, with respect to planning and other problem-solving situations, is for simulations.

The use of databases, large computer-stored deposits of information from which needed information can be extracted, is another area of vital concern to managers. New York City, for example, placed all of its personnel records on a database management system, PRISE—Personnel Reporting and Information System for Employers—and significantly improved its ability to service its 200,000 employees, speed up personnel actions, and control personnel decision making. The program also allowed the city to decentralize more of its personnel decisions and thereby reduce its bureaucracy.[45]

These employees are consulting a decision support system about a management problem they have encountered in managing the information system itself. The computer will provide advice about how to solve that problem. (SOURCE © Robert Reichert)

Simulations

A **simulation** is a model of a real-world situation that can be altered to understand how changes in its various components affect other parts of the model. Typically managers simulate company operations or external environments to learn what changes in input production levels, processes or other changes, or sales might affect the total operation or some specific part thereof.

In America's war of competitiveness, computers have long been touted as one means by which this management challenge can be met. Until recently there seemed to be little hard evidence for this belief. Office automation didn't prove itself at first, although that situation is changing. The use of robotics, a very applied use of computers, was being reevaluated. General Motors's inability to reap full benefits from its robotized, highly computerized plants, for example, revealed flaws in the basic concept.[46] But there is growing evidence from a number of sources that computers—and more specifically computer simulations for a host of such production situations as inventory modeling and plant facilities layouts—are improving America's productivity. One of the keys to this change is the receptivity to simulations by managers. Animation has aided this receptivity. Graphic displays take the mathematician's simulation rationale and put it into readily understandable pictorial languages the average manager can understand. Another key factor in managerial receptivity is the growing number of programs for PCs that bring simulation within the capabilities of many small manufacturers, most of whom will benefit substantially from using the programs, as Management Challenge 7.5 suggests.

Simulations can be used very effectively in a number of situations, such as in training. They are often used in pilot training, for example. Weyerhaeuser has developed a simulation that greatly assists in the better use of raw materials. It trains its log cutters to make better decisions to improve the yield of usable lumber from a tree.[47]

Simulations are extremely useful for examining complex situations. Historically, simulations have been expensive and have been employed only by very large organizations with significant financial resources. More recently, relatively

---

MANAGEMENT CHALLENGE **7.5**

Computer Simulation Redesigns the Factory Floor

Engineers at Northern Research and Engineering Corporation, a subsidiary of Ingersoll Rand, saved one of their clients, the Torrington Company, $750,000 when they simulated the production-line facility Northern was designing for Torrington. Originally seventy-seven machines were considered necessary, but a simulation of the operation indicated that they could get by with only seventy-three. Numerous smaller firms are finding that simulations allow them to improve their just-in-time inventory scheduling, a requirement that is being laid on many of these firms by the larger manufacturers for whom they are vendors.

When GM subsidiary Electronic Data Systems simulated its intended plan to use automatic guided vehicles (AGVs) to transport parts and other materials to a proposed auto assembly line, it found that the AGV could handle only a limited level of production—certainly not as high as that planned for three or four years

This General Motors plant has been totally reconceived due to the output of computer simulations. Work was redesigned, and additional automation incorporated. (SOURCE © Lawrence Migdale/Photo Researchers)

inexpensive simulation software has become available, such as in the production area for the PC and minicomputers. Plus, minicomputers now do the work of the much more expensive mainframes of just a few years ago, which helps bring down the cost of simulation. PC simulation users must sacrifice complexity for ease of operation, but even with their limitations such simulations can be valuable to small organizations.

Spreadsheet programs such as Lotus 1-2-3® and more complex financial planning models such as EPS (Environmental Planning Systems) and IFPS (Interactive Financial Planning Systems) allow a company to model its financial situation and change various inputs, such as projected sales, to determine their effects on total income, expenses, assets, liabilities, and equity.

down the road. General Motors was forced to develop a new control logic for the system as a consequence. But the simulation saved General Motors millions of dollars and numerous headaches in its future operations.

Polaroid Corporation uses simulation to study production lines. Polaroid still employs inventories between segments of its production lines in order to keep a line from going down for lack of parts. But, simulation of these inventory buffers indicated that 25 percent of the inventories could be eliminated. This saved the company thousands of dollars, as well as substantial floor space. Polaroid also uses simulations to study its capital investment decisions and staffing policies.

Expectations are high for a new software program to be released soon that will allow on-line troubleshooting of production operations within minutes. The simulation will provide a series of alternatives to managers as courses of action necessary to correct the problems indicated. This and a host of other predicted software packages coming on line in the next few years will enable managers to make better decisions to solve problems more effectively and efficiently.

SOURCE: William G. Wild, Jr., and Otis Port, "This Video Game Is Saving Manufacturers Millions," *Business Week* (August 17, 1987), pp. 82–84.

The break-even point, for example, can also be determined using a computer spreadsheet. It can be viewed as a series of "what if" questions. (What if some event happens, what will be the result?) The computer can also be asked to indicate what the volume must be for profit to be zero. Some spreadsheets have a "Goal Seek" feature that calculates break-even point automatically.

One of the most important features of spreadsheets to emerge is "optimization" analysis. It is an extension of what-if questions. You change decision variables to get your objective—profit—as large as possible, without violating any of your constraints. Only a few spreadsheets have this feature, but more and more are adding it. A major gas company has used this approach and made substantial profits as a result.[48]

Bethlehem Steel Corporation uses a microcomputer for production planning and cost analysis. It is an optimization model of steel flows through the plant, based on the Lotus 1-2-3® software package and run on an IBM PC XT. It assesses the impact in changes on product demands on facilities, capacities, and costs. It allows the user to ask what-if questions. For example, how many eight-hour shifts will the plate mill require if this year's demand for steel plate products is 500,000 tons? Or, how much will the cost of products be raised if the price of natural gas goes up 20 percent? All five of Bethlehem's plants use the model.[49]

Just as with the decision-making techniques discussed in the early part of this chapter, planning techniques are most often found to be specialized or employed in only certain areas of an organization. You should become familiar with those that could be applied to your work. Computer software packages can and should be used wherever possible. It would be worthwhile to purchase one of the general problem-solving packages to improve your decision techniques. If you haven't searched for software decision support packages to help you in solving problems, you should.

Management Science as Decision Support for Problem Solving

Management science was designed to enhance problem solving. Its very purpose is to improve the rationality of the process. Increased computer use and user-friendly software have increased its utilization dramatically in recent years. Managers now find it much easier to employ the techniques described in this chapter and other managment-science quantitative techniques, as well. One of the most important considerations is that managers must learn to rely upon these techniques and must consider them as part of the normal decision-making process. To implement management science effectively means that managers must learn to rely upon it, trust it, embrace it.[50] But, they must use it as decision support, not as a substitute for making a decision. Judgment must be applied to the quantitative results derived from quantitative methods techniques. As was mentioned in Chapter 3, some managers are more rational than others, tend to use a more scientific approach, and tend to think rather then intuit. Others tend to avoid the use of rational and analytical approaches. What is sought is a balance between the two. We know that, especially in more complex decisions, both are vital. Figure 7.8 provides additional insight into how various key terms and concepts discussed in this chapter might be used in problem solving. Note that while only a few are identified as important in more than one stage of the process, many can be used in some way in more than one stage.

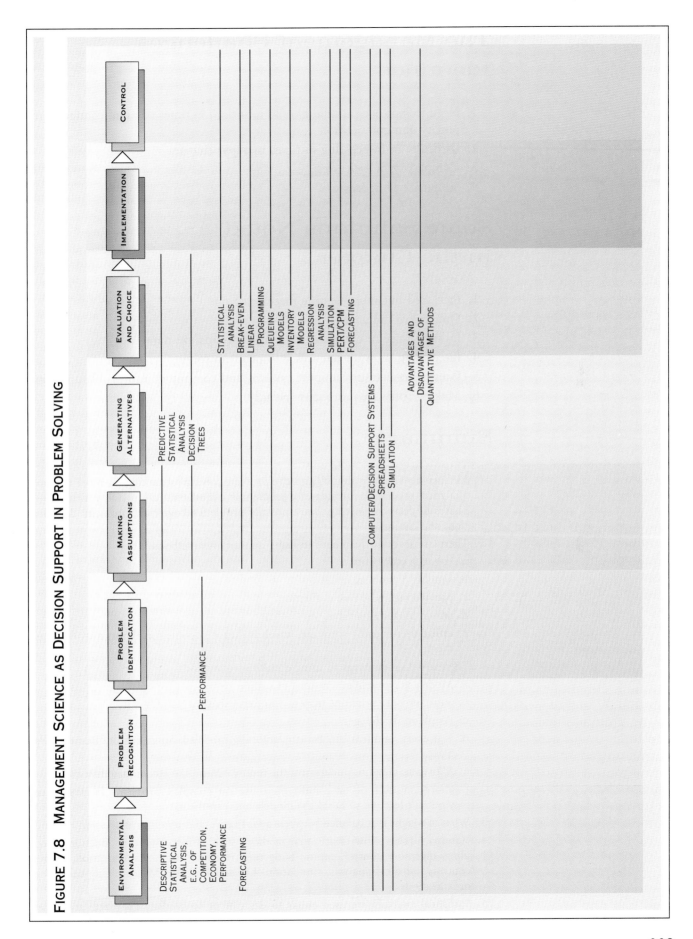

FIGURE 7.8 MANAGEMENT SCIENCE AS DECISION SUPPORT IN PROBLEM SOLVING

The Management Challenges
Identified

1. Need to increase rationality (and intuition) in times of rapid change, complexity and competition
2. Difficulty in forecasting in times of rapid change
3. Complexity of processes
4. Simplicity of processes

Some Solutions Noted
in the Chapter

1. Increased but more flexible forecasting
2. Qualitative judgment
3. Increased use of computer simulation to analyze data
4. Integrating decision sciences into problem solving
5. Integrating decision support systems and computers into problem solving
6. Making software more user-friendly

Summary

1. Management science aims to improve problem solving by making it a more rational/analytical process. It formulates a problem in a mathematical model, which aids all phases of decision making, but especially problem recognition, problem identification, and choice.
2. There are several advantages to using quantitative methods. They
   a. enhance rationality.
   b. simplify a problem.
   c. provide means of risk evaluation.
   d. are no longer expensive.
   e. utilize user-friendly software, which makes it possible for almost anyone to use them.

   There are disadvantages to using quantitative methods:
   a. Models are simplified versions of reality.
   b. Substantive simulations may be too expensive.
   c. People resist change.
   d. Not every problem can be satisfactorally modeled. Some require human judgment.
   e. Managers may not understand the theory behind the techniques they use.
   f. Short amounts of time limit their use on complex problems because there wouldn't be time to build the models and run them.
3. What is sought is a balance between quantitative and qualitative decision making.
4. Various surveys show clearly that methods such as forecasting, production scheduling, inventory control, capital budgeting, transportation, plant location, quality control, statistical analysis, simulation, LP, and PERT/CPM are highly utilized in organizations.
5. Statistical analyses are used either to describe or to predict. They are most often used by managers to describe current situations—often in presentations, often in

problem solving. They may be used also to predict and to forecast. Decision theory assists greatly in understanding a problem. Payoff tables are not frequently used, but decision trees are and may be used for any problem in which sequential decisions occur and modeling them is beneficial. The concept of expected value is critical and allows managers to choose between alternatives in risk situations.

6. Forecasting is critical to an organization, especially in the strategic planning area. There are two principal types: sales forecasts and technological forecasts. Sales forecasting is the basis for an organization's budget and for all of its economic functions. Marketing, finance, operations, and human resources all depend upon the anticipated revenues.

7. Forecasting techniques are either quantitative or qualitative. Quantitative techniques include time-series and causal techniques. Time-series techniques help you identify the effects of trend, seasonal, cyclical, and random variation from a set of data. Causal techniques describe the relationships between independent and dependent variables. The formulas derived are often extrapolated to predict future events.

8. Qualitative methods include executive opinions, sales force composites, expert opinion, and consumer surveys. Each of these can be used at the appropriate time and place to forecast. Technological forecasts help an organization remain competitive. Without proper understanding of the environment, organizations usually fail to respond successfully to competitors' actions.

9. The five basic steps to the forecasting process are to
   a. determine the purpose of the forecast and when it will be needed.
   b. establish the time horizons that the forecast must cover.
   c. select the forecasting technique.
   d. gather and analyze the appropriate data and then prepare the forecast.
   e. monitor the forecast to see if it is performing satisfactorily.

10. Break-even analysis is used to determine the point at which revenues equal costs. It is especially important to use break-even analysis to determine if the projected project, product, or service will make a profit, and at the desired level. It can also be used for what-if questioning—for example, changing costs or prices. Linear programming is especially useful in situations of known goals, multiple variables, and multiple constraints. Network models, PERT/CPM, are especially useful for showing the relationships among activities within large-scale projects. They are good for the scheduling of various activities. They reveal the criticality of each project.

11. Computers are being used more and more in problem solving. Decision-support software abounds.

12. Simulation is being used more and more in problem solving to show the impact of choosing various alternatives.

13. Computer programs, including simulation, assist in decision making by making it more rational.

Thinking About Management

1. What is the purpose of management-science/quantitative methods?
2. Why should managers be familiar with management-science techniques?
3. What are the key differences between the standard problem-solving model and the model used in quantitative methods?
4. Describe ways in which you might personally be able to use some of the scientific-management/quantitative methods described in this text.
5. Describe how management-science/quantitative methods can help managers in various management situations.
6. Describe the likely scenario relative to increased usage of computers and management science and the potential for more widespread use of management science by managers.

7. How do you think forecasting could be improved?

8. As the environment changes more rapidly, how do you think you might go about improving forecasting?

9. Give examples of quantitative and qualitative forecasting.

10. How could you improve the implementation of management-science techniques by all managers?

11. Where do intuition and qualitative decision making fit in with management science?

CASE

Chrysler Corporation Must Cut Its Break-Even Point

Many auto industry experts feel it was Lee Iacocca's ability to get his company's break-even point down to 1.1 million units in 1981 that helped save Chrysler. (Chrysler had had to make government-secured loans in 1979 in order to avoid bankruptcy.) Chrysler had had too many workers, and too few new ideas. Product quality was also quite low. Iacocca focused on cutting costs—labor and inventory, for example. He also hired a new-products manager to help improve quality and cut costs. New compensation programs were worked out with the unions to help reduce wages. Chrysler also sought increased levels of outside parts supplies in order to cut costs. Management and staff positions were cut to reduce overhead.

Iacocca was still very much concerned about breaking even in 1988. It had slipped back to 1.4 million units in early 1987, and he wanted to be back to 1.3 million units by early 1988.[51]

DISCUSSION QUESTIONS

1. If you were on Chrysler's management staff, how might you use the following management-science techniques in determining how to carry out that reduction?
   a. Break-even analysis
   b. Decision trees
   c. Simulation
   d. Statistics
   e. Regression analysis
   f. Linear programming

MANAGERS AT WORK

Forecasting at Perfumery on Park

David Currie, co-owner with his wife Anna, of Perfumery on Park (avenue), pondered the best way to forecast the next year's sales. Since opening the store in 1985, the perfumery had experienced steady growth of about 10 percent each year, over the previous year's sales. In 1989, however, sales during the two biggest sales months of November and December had seen increases of 30 percent, causing 1989's sales to average an increase of 22 percent.

David wondered whether to assume that the sales would continue to increase at a 10 percent rate, the recently experienced 22 percent rate, or somewhere in between. The consequences of the forecast were important. David and Anna had been considering hiring a full time clerk, Anna could free her time to pursue the company's new mail order perfume business.

Furthermore, inventories had to be ordered, and the problems resulting from not having a customer's perfume in stock, could have an impact on future sales. 1989 had not been a strong year for the U.S. economy, but neither had it been a down year. David wasn't quite sure what had caused the increase in sales.

DISCUSSION QUESTIONS

1. How does a small business forecast? Is it really any different than how a large buisness might forecast?

2. Breakeven could be used in this case to factor in the salary of the full time clerk. How?

3. How would you go about forecasting for 1990?

Using PERT/CAM to Build a Custom Sports Car

MANAGE YOURSELF

How well do you understand the PERT/CPM methodology? The following is a PERT/CPM chart problem. Please complete as per the instructions in order to "test yourself."

The Maser is a new custom-designed sports car. An analysis of the task of building the Maser reveals the following list of relevant activities, their immediate predecessors, and their duration.

Job Letter	Description	Immediate Predecessors	Normal Time (Days)
A	Start		0
B	Design	A	8
C	Order special accessories	B	0.1
D	Build frame	B	1
E	Build doors	B	1
F	Attach axles, wheels, gas tank	D	1
G	Build body shell	B	2
H	Build transmission and drive train	B	3
I	Fit doors to body shell	G, E	1
J	Build engine	B	4
K	Bench-test engine	J	2
L	Assemble chassis	F, H, K	1
M	Road-test chassis	L	0.5
N	Paint body	I	2
O	Install wiring	N	1
P	Install interior	N	1.5
Q	Accept delivery of special accessories	C	5
R	Mount body and accessories on chassis	M, O, P, Q	1
S	Road-test car	R	0.5
T	Attach exterior trim	S	1
U	Finish	T	0

CASE QUESTIONS

1. Draw an arrow diagram of the project "Building the Maser."

2. Mark the critical path and state its length.

3. If the Maser had to be completed two days earlier, would it help to:
   a. Buy preassembled transmissions and drive trains?
   b. Install robots to halve engine-building time?
   c. Speed delivery of special accessories by three days?

4. How might resources be borrowed from activities on the subcritical paths to speed activities on the critical path?

SOURCE: James A. F. Stoner and Charles Wankel, *Management*, 3rd ed. (Englewood Cliffs., N.J.: Prentice-Hall, 1986), p. 195. Reprinted by permission of Prentice-Hall, Inc. The authors are indebted to Peter L. Pfister for the material on which this case is based.

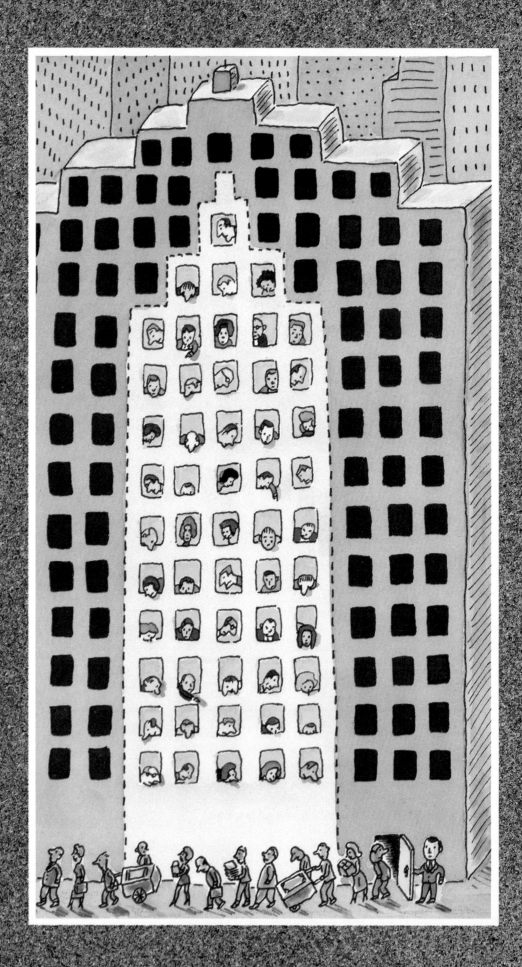

CHAPTER EIGHT

The Organizing Process

CHAPTER OBJECTIVES

By the time you complete this chapter you should be able to

1. Describe the organizing function in terms of the choices managers must make as to how to structure an organization.
2. Define an organization.
3. Indicate the differences between formal and informal organizations.
4. Interpret an organization chart.
5. Describe the organizing process and its relationship to the planning function.
6. Discuss how the combinations of jobs and the authority to perform those jobs, departmentation, span of control, and coordination result in organizational structure.
7. Identify each of the elements of organizational structure and describe their roles in structure and in accomplishing an organization's mission.
8. Indicate how resources, other than human resources, are organized.

CHAPTER OUTLINE

Organizing
Division of Labor — The Job
  Division of Labor
  Specialization of Labor
  Differentiation
  The Organization Chart
  What the Organization Chart
    Doesn't Show
  Delegation of Authority

  Authority
  Delegating Authority
  The Scalar Chain of Command
  The Acceptance Theory of Authority
  Parity: Delegated Authority Must
    Equal Responsibility
  Centralization Versus
    Decentralization
  Line and Staff Authority
  Functional Authority
Departmentation
  Departmentation by Economic
    Function of the Organization
  Departmentation by Product
  Departmentation by Strategic
    Business Unit
  Departmentation by Geography
  Departmentation by Task Specialty
  Departmentation Based on Time
  Departmentation by Client
    or Customer
  The Complexities of Pyramidal
    Structural Possibilities
The Managerial Span of Control
Coordination
  Formalization
  Complexity
  Integration and Differentiation
  The Manager as a Linking Pin
  Additional Coordination Devices
Additional Structures
  Project Structure
  The Team
  The Matrix Organization
  Joint Ventures and Strategic
    Alliances
  Informal Structure
Organizing as Problem Solving
The Management Challenges Identified
Some Solutions Noted in the Chapter

IBM Restructures to Meet the Challenges of a Changing Environment

More and more organizations are restructuring, which often means cutting out job positions and, hence, eliminating the employees that fill them. Organizations are seeking to become "leaner and meaner." The objectives of a business organization focus on profit. Historically, as business organizations have increased their sales, they have tended to increase the number of their employees. Staff and middle-management positions are often increased to levels that are unnecessarily high. The costs of these staffing levels may prevent organizations from achieving their profit objectives. But there are pros and cons to reducing staffing levels. Some of the obvious advantages are cost reductions, the increased ability of lower-level managers to make decisions, and the speed with which decisions can be made. Some of the possible disadvantages are loss of experience, haphazard decision making, and being stretched too thin.

John Akers, chairman of IBM, had experienced three very frustrating years of disappointing company results. Profits were there, but they weren't as great as he had anticipated. And while IBM was still king of the mainframe market, its market shares in minicomputers and personal computers had slipped significantly. Furthermore, in 1987 IBM's U.S. revenues fell slightly, at a time when many other computer companies were seeing tremendous increases in their revenues. IBM itself had long been criticized for having a structure too unwieldy to take advantage of market niches and develop new products quickly.

Akers recognized the problem. He took steps to remove much of the responsibility and authority from the six-man management committee and delegate it to six separate product (strategic business unit) and marketing groups. A position was created to control all six groups. Personal computers and typewriters were merged in the same group and the troubled mid-range computers were moved into the same group with the more successful mainframe. Akers comments, "This is a major delegation of authority; in many ways we now have several IBM companies." Akers describes the restructuring as the most significant in the decade and perhaps the most significant in thirty years. As part of the restructuring, jobs were eliminated, some layers of management disappeared, and considerable autonomy was provided to those down the hierarchy, especially in sales and research and development. "Just say yes" to customers became a slogan that drove the sales force.

Customer reactions to the restructuring appeared to be favorable. There are many IBM customers who can tell war stories from the days before the decentralization. For example, problems got lost in the many layers of IBM bureaucracy, and product developments that customers needed were never passed on to IBM inventors. John Rogers, the technology chief of The Bank of Boston, comments, "You had the feeling the guy you were talking to had to talk to 4,673 other people before he got the best answer he could come up with, which may not have been straight." Calvin Raider, a Delta Airlines computer manager, adds, "To get to the decision makers who could make things happen, you had to go up two or three different avenues."

Whether IBM's restructuring will solve its problems remains to be seen. It is not clear, for example, that the overburdening layers of management will be removed; it is hoped, however, certainly by IBM, that making the groups more autonomous will bring them closer to the customer.

SOURCES: Joel Dreyfuss, "Reinventing IBM," *Fortune* (August 14, 1989), pp. 36–39; Paul B. Carroll, "IBM to Cut U.S. Work Force by 3,000 to 4,000, Post Big 2nd Period Charge," *Wall Street Journal* 30 June, 1988, p. 3; Michael W. Miller, "IBM's Customers Know About Problems: Akers Is Dealing with a Reorganization," *Wall Street Journal* 1 February, 1988, p. 14; and Michael W. Miller and Paul B. Carroll, "IBM Unveils a Sweeping Restructuring and Bid to Decentralize Decision Making," *Wall Street Journal* 29 January, 1988, p. 3.

The typical large business twenty years hence will have fewer than half the levels of management of its counterpart today, and no more than a third of the managers.

Peter Drucker
Harvard Business Review, 1988

One of the most frequent organizing efforts of the 1980s, and one expected to continue throughout the 1990s, is downsizing. The number of people remaining to do the same amount of work is drastically reduced, as this artwork suggests. The building is still there, but many of the people are gone. (p. 244) (SOURCE © Marc Rosenthal)

Understanding one individual's behavior is challenging in and of itself; understanding a group that's made up of different individuals and comprehending the many relationships among those individuals is even more complex. Imagine, then, the mind-boggling complexity of a large organization, made up of thousands of individuals and hundreds of work groups with myriad relationships among these individuals and groups.

David A. Nadler and Michael L. Tushman
Management researchers and authors

What happened at IBM is happening in thousands of companies across the United States, including Eastman-Kodak, AT&T, TRW, Eastern Airlines, Du Pont, General Electric, and General Motors. Organizations are restructuring, reorganizing. They are changing the contents of jobs, often combining tasks and eliminating jobs. They are changing how jobs are grouped; the size of work groups; the amount of authority that has been delegated to individuals and groups to accomplish their jobs; and the manner in which the whole organization is coordinated.[1] The changing management environment, discussed in Chapters 1 and 4, is expected to show increased levels of competition, a need for faster new-product development, a quest for lower costs, demands for higher quality, and the potential for lower profit margins across virtually all industries. Consequently, the need to reorganize is likely to be pervasive.[2] Nonprofits find themselves in similar "lean" times and are also restructuring.[3] Never before in the history of American industry has the organizing function been so critical. Appropriate organizing is now, more than ever, viewed as a prerequisite for success.[4]

John Akers was faced with the unpleasant task of downsizing IBM in order to ensure its future competitiveness. The restructuring worked, however, making IBM customers much happier about IBM's responses to their needs. (SOURCE © Andrew Popper/Picture Group)

Organizing

Organizing is the process of determining how resources are allocated and prepared for accomplishing an organization's mission. The organization process results in an organization structure. **Structure** defines

1. The relationships between tasks and authority for individuals and departments.
2. Formal reporting relationships, the number of levels in the hierarchy of the organization, and the span of control.
3. The groupings of individuals into departments and departments into organizations.

4. The systems to effect coordination of effort in both vertical (authority) and horizontal (tasks) directions.[5]

There are two types of structures in an organization: formal and informal. **Formal structure** consists of that structure sanctioned by the organization. It is designed to achieve organizational objectives. **Informal structure** is whatever structure exists that has not been prescribed by the formal organization. For example, someone may meet someone else for other than organization mission-accomplishment reasons while at work. This is the most common form of informal structure: people interacting informally.

Most of this chapter acquaints you with the nature of structure. Chapters 9 and 10 offer more specific guidance for structuring at the total organization (macro) and individual job or group (micro) levels.

Managers structure organizations. An **organization** is a group of people working together to achieve a common purpose.[6] And while it had always been believed that structure had to be matched to strategy for the strategy to succeed, there is increasing research evidence for this belief.[7] The principal concerns of the manager with regard to structuring an organization are

1. Division of labor: determining the scope of work and how it is combined in a job.
2. Delegation of authority: determining how much authority should be granted to individuals and groups to do their jobs.
3. Departmentation: grouping jobs into work units or departments, on some rational basis.
4. Span of control: determining how many subordinates each manager should have.
5. Coordination: of the individuals, groups, and departments as they perform these jobs.[8]

Division of Labor—The Job

A **job** is a collection of tasks assigned to one individual; it is designed to achieve specific objectives and carry out related plans. A job is designed on the basis of the division of labor, the principle of the specialization of labor, and the need to differentiate organizational subunits in response to external factors.

Division of Labor

Division of labor is the subdivision of objectives and plans into smaller and smaller units until they reach the task level. Work is so divided based on the principle of specialization of labor.

Specialization of Labor

Specialization of labor dictates that work be divided into smaller and smaller subunits until it can be repeated easily and successfully by an individual or group of individuals. Specialization of labor is one of Fayol's fourteen principles. It was introduced into management and made a prominent component of organization structure design, especially job design, by Adam Smith. Specialization allows an individual to work on one part of a larger project. No one individual could build a space shuttle, but specialization allows many to construct specific

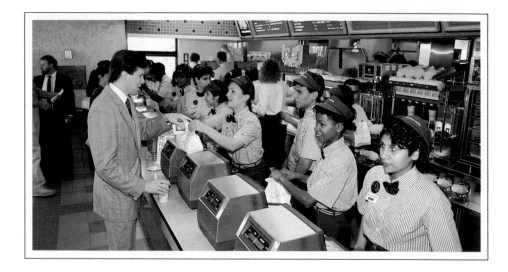

These McDonald's employees have highly specialized jobs. Their physical movements have been calculated over and over to provide the fastest, most economical service possible.
(SOURCE © Janice Rubin/Black Star)

parts that are then assembled and result in a space shuttle. Specialization causes an individual's work to be highly repetitive and, hence, less prone to errors. But there is a negative side to the ability to repeat a job numerous consecutive times without error. A person will get bored. What literally happens is that the analytical part of the person's brain falls asleep and he or she begins to daydream. Errors are the eventual result.

Division of labor is the fundamental element of almost all organizations. McDonald's, Wendy's, Burger King, and other hamburger chains, for example, are noted for their ability to routinize the handling of customers' requests, the filling of customers' orders in a fashion that gives credence to the term "fast food." They could not do this without specializing labor. They have continually studied and examined the number of specialized tasks necessary to perform their hamburger "manufacturing" jobs. Sometimes, however, too many jobs are created. Work that is not necessary becomes part of the organizational process. That is a major reason for restructuring, as Management Challenge 8.1 suggests.

Differentiation

Each organization, and each department of that organization, adapts its subcomponents, including structure, processes, and member behaviors, to meet the constraints of its respective, specific environment. This process of adaptation to the environment is known as **differentiation**.[9]

A marketing research department, for example, would be expected to have a more freewheeling structure—a more autonomous structure, in which more authority is delegated, than would be found in highly routinized manufacturing assembly lines. Similarly, the spans of control in a March of Dimes campaign, where volunteer fund collectors are largely self-supervising, would be expected to be larger than those in a complex computer-programming environment where projects are closely supervised by project leaders. In both cases, each of the fundamental elements of structure described—jobs, delegation of authority, departmentation, span of control, and coordination—is differentiated to its environmental circumstances.

The Organization Chart

The relationships between tasks and the authority to do those tasks are best represented in an **organization chart,** a pictorial representation of an organization's formal structure. Figure 8.1 is an illustrative organization chart that

Slimming Down at Chevron

In 1986 Chevron Corporation completed a gut-wrenching 8.7 percent reduction of its work force to boost profits. The subsequent reduction in paperwork saved money. Major budget proposals, for example, were 30–40 percent smaller than in preceding years. In some divisions meetings that had previously been held weekly began to be held monthly, to save time and so that those employees who remained could accomplish more. Unnecessary, or too highly detailed reports, which often crop up in times of plenty, were eliminated. One such report projected heating oil use in the Netherlands in 1995, information Chevron executives found they could do without. When there were plenty of people and plenty of funds at Chevron, engineers and managers could spend the time to justify their every move, their every proposed plan of action, in great detail. Now they had to plan more succinctly and more quickly.

Chevron's actions were the result of environmental factors affecting its strategic plans and operating income. In 1979, when it began to add layers of management and staff, it had more cash flow than it knew what to do with. But in 1986 oil firms were facing cash flow problems because oil prices had recently dropped significantly. With competition increasing, and with the temporary inability of

provides extremely useful information. By looking at Figure 8.1, you can determine the following relationships:

1. The division of labor: Each box on a typical organization chart represents a job position combining a certain number of tasks.

2. Specialization of labor: An organization chart typically indicates the type of work that is being performed by the various positions.

3. Relative authority: Normally the position higher up on the chart has more authority than the position below it. This is not always true, as some charts are designed in a somewhat complex fashion; however, normally those positions on the same level have the same amount of authority, and they have more authority than those below them on the chart.

4. Departmentation: Organization charts normally depict groupings of positions in what are known as departments.

5. Span of control: Visual scanning of the chart readily indicates the number of subordinates a manager has.

6. The levels of management: By looking quickly down an organization chart, you can see the number of levels of management in the organization.

7. Coordination centers: By observing an organization chart, you can see who would most likely be expected to coordinate the activities of various organizational subunits. The president, for example, would be expected to coordinate the activities of the vice-presidents; the vice-presidents would coordinate the actions of their reporting divisions; and the division chiefs would coordinate the actions of managers of reporting subunits.

8. Communication channels: Communication channels through which coordination would occur are most clearly indicated on the organization chart. However, as was discussed in Chapter 2, communication may occur

OPEC to maintain high prices, oil companies had to learn to work with smaller staffs. Chevron was by no means profligate—it had already reduced its total work force from 79,000 in 1984 to 61,000 in 1986. Many of those jobs were eliminated when Chevron acquired Gulf Oil. Nonetheless, Chevron executives felt they still had too many people, so they cut, cut, cut.

SOURCE: Amanda Bennett, "Slimming Down: Chevron Corporation Has Big Challenge Coming with Worker Cutback, *Wall Street Journal* 8 November, 1986, pp. 1, 27.

There used to be six people performing the work that these four now perform at Chevron. One consequence of Chevron's slimming down exercise was that work had to be prioritized, and some work simply not done. As often turns out, Chevron discovered that a lot of unnecessary work was being done and could be done away with. (SOURCE © Robert Holmgren)

diagonally or horizontally between positions, not just vertically. And, day-to-day operational communication involves complex interactions not revealed on the chart.

9. Decision responsibility: By observing the preceding factors, one can usually determine who will be responsible for making a decision relative to certain matters. However, exactly how much authority is delegated to each position is not apparent on an organization chart, so decision authority may vary somewhat from what might seem to be the case as shown on the chart.

Organization charts are typically presented on a piece of paper from top to bottom. Most organization charts depict structures as pyramids. The top of the pyramid represents top management, the bottom, the operational employees. Various levels of management and staff are shown in between. In Chapter 12, on organizational culture, you will be shown an organization chart that has been intentionally inverted from the norm, to emphasize the importance of serving the customer.[10]

What the Organization Chart Doesn't Show

While the organization chart provides a significant amount of information, it doesn't reveal several important organizational concerns. For example, in the informal organization, the day-to-day relationships not formally specified by the organization are missing. The real decision centers, for example, based on a charismatic leader, are also not clear. Finally, the day-to-day communication patterns, which don't always follow the formal chain of command, are also not obvious from this chart.

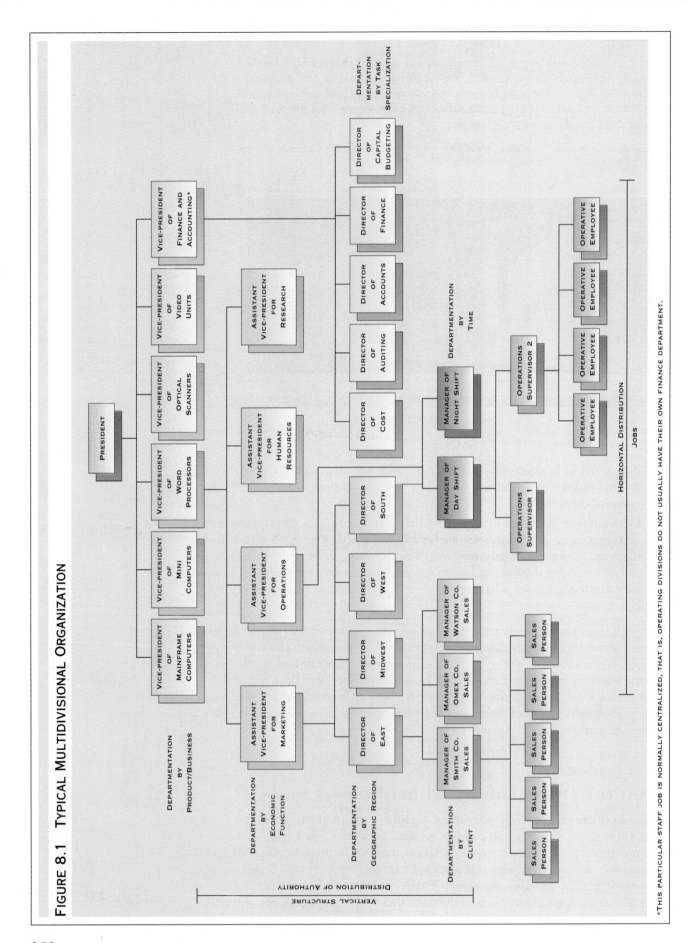

FIGURE 8.1 TYPICAL MULTIDIVISIONAL ORGANIZATION

PRESIDENT

DEPARTMENTATION BY PRODUCT/BUSINESS

VICE-PRESIDENT OF MAINFRAME COMPUTERS

VICE-PRESIDENT OF MINI COMPUTERS

VICE-PRESIDENT OF WORD PROCESSORS

VICE-PRESIDENT OF OPTICAL SCANNERS

VICE-PRESIDENT OF VIDEO UNITS

VICE-PRESIDENT OF FINANCE AND ACCOUNTING*

DEPARTMENTATION BY ECONOMIC FUNCTION

ASSISTANT VICE-PRESIDENT FOR MARKETING

ASSISTANT VICE-PRESIDENT FOR OPERATIONS

ASSISTANT VICE-PRESIDENT FOR HUMAN RESOURCES

ASSISTANT VICE-PRESIDENT FOR RESEARCH

DEPART-MENTATION BY TASK SPECIALIZATION

DIRECTOR OF COST

DIRECTOR OF AUDITING

DIRECTOR OF ACCOUNTS

DIRECTOR OF FINANCE

DIRECTOR OF CAPITAL BUDGETING

DEPARTMENTATION BY GEOGRAPHIC REGION

DIRECTOR OF EAST

DIRECTOR OF MIDWEST

DIRECTOR OF WEST

DIRECTOR OF SOUTH

DEPARTMENTATION BY TIME

MANAGER OF DAY SHIFT

MANAGER OF NIGHT SHIFT

OPERATIONS SUPERVISOR 1

OPERATIONS SUPERVISOR 2

DEPARTMENTATION BY CLIENT

MANAGER OF SMITH CO. SALES

MANAGER OF OMEX CO. SALES

MANAGER OF WATSON CO. SALES

SALES PERSON

SALES PERSON

SALES PERSON

SALES PERSON

SALES PERSON

OPERATIVE EMPLOYEE

OPERATIVE EMPLOYEE

OPERATIVE EMPLOYEE

OPERATIVE EMPLOYEE

VERTICAL STRUCTURE

DISTRIBUTION OF AUTHORITY

HORIZONTAL DISTRIBUTION

JOBS

*THIS PARTICULAR STAFF JOB IS NORMALLY CENTRALIZED, THAT IS, OPERATING DIVISIONS DO NOT USUALLY HAVE THEIR OWN FINANCE DEPARTMENT.

Delegation of Authority

Seven key issues are involved with authority and its distribution within the organization: the concept of authority itself and its delegation, the scalar chain of command, the acceptance of authority, the parity principle, centralization versus decentralization, and functional authority.

Authority

Authority is legitimized power. **Power** is the ability to influence others to carry out orders or to do something they would not have done otherwise, in order to achieve desired outcomes.[11] Organizations exist within the framework of a set amount of legitimate power. Authority is granted to managers of the organization, its owners, or other parties in control, such as the members of an association or by a government body, and by the society within which it operates. Total organizational authority is said to rest with the major position in each organization. Thus, whether the top position is the director of a United Way agency, the chairperson of the board of directors of Digital Equipment Company, the president of a local bridge club, or the president of the International Brotherhood of Electrical Workers, that position has the greatest amount of authority in the organization.

Delegating Authority

The person in authority is then able to **delegate**—to distribute authority to subordinate positions, within the constraints of the available authority of the organization and that person's position, to achieve objectives, to act to make decisions. Similarly, each person whose position has been delegated authority may delegate authority to subordinate positions within similar constraints. Some people have difficulty delegating because they like to be in control, or they may feel uncomfortable letting other people do a job they know how to do well. Entrepreneurs and most managers share this trait. Unfortunately, failure to delegate often means dissatisfied subordinates, overworked managers, and decreased productivity.

The distribution of authority allows managers not to have to supervise the work of all organizational members within their jurisdiction. It also allows organizational members to determine the nature of their behavior within prescribed limits. Authority to perform one's job is an essential ingredient in its completion, and the exact amount of authority that should be delegated to each position is a controversial issue. Many individuals can achieve more power in a situation than they are delegated through authority. Others fail to use fully the authority given them and, hence, lose power. Delegating authority, however, does not mean that the manager is not responsible. He or she is still held accountable for what subordinates do.

The Scalar Chain of Command

The **scalar chain of command** is the formal distribution of organizational authority in a hierarchical fashion. The scalar chain simply defines the relationships of authority from one level of the organization to another. In the scalar chain, individuals higher up on the chain have more authority than those below them. This is true of all succeeding levels of management from top management to

AT IBM: *If you had examined the organization chart at IBM after it restructured, you would have noticed that*
—*Many positions had disappeared.*
—*Specialization of labor had decreased.*
—*Authority would have changed for many managers.*
—*Departmentation would be different.*
—*Spans of control would in most cases be larger.*
—*Some levels of management had disappeared.*
—*Coordination centers and communication channels were different.*
—*Decision responsibilities had changed.*

These Communication Workers of America, on strike against their employer, the New York Telephone Company, are demonstrating quite clearly that management does not have authority unless the employees are willing to recognize it. (SOURCE © Robert McElroy/Woodfin, Camp & Associates)

the first-line employee. The scalar chain helps define authority and responsibility and, thus, accountability. If you will observe Figures 8.1 and 8.3–8.7, you will see examples of the scalar chain as portrayed in organizational charts.

The Acceptance Theory of Authority

Chester Barnard's **acceptance theory of authority** states that a manager's authority is authority only if the subordinate chooses to accept the manager's formal authority as real authority.[12] Otherwise, authority does not truly exist. In the 1970s, for example, the workers at General Motors' Lordstown assembly plant refused to produce more than 65 cars per hour, even though the ultra-modern plant was capable of producing 100 cars per hour.[13] They did not accept management's authority. Unions typically form a countervailing force with which management must contend. They are often able to influence their members not to accept management's authority. Millions of employees from all types of organizations have not always performed quite to their peak levels because they just did not accept the authority of their managers. Often they don't directly disobey; they just don't fully cooperate.

Parity: Delegated Authority Must Equal Responsibility

The **parity principle** states that if you assign someone the responsibility for achieving an objective, you should also give that person the authority to achieve it. This seems obvious, but the rule is often violated. Typical problems arise when a manager is assigned a task outside the normal chain of command. He or she may be required to lead several people to whom this person's authority has not been made clear, or who feel this person has no authority over them. When heading a committee or a task team, managers will often need to supervise and get cooperation from employees over whom they have no formal authority. For example, a project team leader on the space shuttle booster rocket program

These America West Airline mechanics are receiving cross training on different airplane systems in order to improve the efficiency of the organization. (SOURCE © Louie Psihoyos)

works with people from many technical disciplines, yet that leader has only limited formal authority over any of them. It is easy for team members to disregard this manager's authority and instructions, especially in deference to the orders of their normal functional manager, who in most cases will still complete the team member's performance appraisal.

Centralization Versus Decentralization

In a **centralized** organization authority is not widely delegated. Hence, virtually all important decisions—and in some cases, virtually all decisions—are made by the organization's top management. This is often dysfunctional. Take, for example, a U.S. Air Force missile wing commander, a colonel, who simply wouldn't delegate. With an annual operating budget of almost $100 million, the Colonel demanded that he personally approve all purchase orders over fifty dollars. He eventually came under the scrutiny of his boss, a three-star general, for failure to achieve objectives because of his lack of delegation.[14] Although the military is used as an example here, numerous similar examples of the inability to delegate abound in business, as well.

In a **decentralized** organization authority is widely delegated to subordinates. There is a broad range in the amount of authority that may be delegated, as Figure 8.2 reveals. The decentralized organization is characterized as delegating authority to managers to make decisions relevant to their departments, within organizational guidelines. At Xerox Corporation, headquarters staff, especially middle management, was trimmed significantly (25 percent) in the 1980s. District managers suddenly found themselves with the authority to adjust prices or extend credit and the power to further delegate to managers in the field.[15] The substantively decentralized organization carries the delegation process one step farther and delegates authority to subordinates to make decisions that their bosses would usually make.[16] At America West Airlines, the United States' eleventh largest airline, with some $800 million in sales in 1988, front-line supervisors manage their own units and delegate heavily to subordinates. Support personnel are cross-trained in numerous jobs and periodically may be called

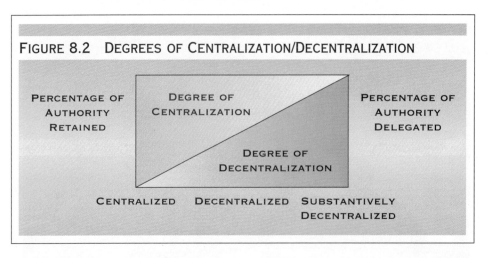

FIGURE 8.2   DEGREES OF CENTRALIZATION/DECENTRALIZATION

PERCENTAGE OF AUTHORITY RETAINED

DEGREE OF CENTRALIZATION

DEGREE OF DECENTRALIZATION

PERCENTAGE OF AUTHORITY DELEGATED

CENTRALIZED   DECENTRALIZED   SUBSTANTIVELY DECENTRALIZED

AT IBM: *One of the main reasons IBM restructured was to adapt better to a changing environment. By restructuring, it was able to get closer to its customers. Authority was delegated as IBM became more decentralized.*

on to perform as a baggage handler, reservation clerk, ticket taker, or flight attendant. They are given the authority to make decisions in their jobs.[17]

Managers must decide how much decentralization is appropriate to their organization or subunit. The issue is complex. Research studies have shown that the decentralized organization is better able to adapt to the demands of a changing environment.[18] Yet, as information systems provide more external environmental information to top management, these findings could change as top management becomes able to respond faster. Furthermore, subunits will vary in the degree of their decentralization. It is possible to have a centralized organization with some decentralized subunits and vice versa.

There has been renewed interest in recent years in decentralizing many organizations. Much of the momentum for this trend is the result of Japan's positive experiences with worker participation in decision making. The decentralized organization is not necessarily more productive, but it is more productive in many, if not the majority, of situations when all factors are considered. Business firms operating in stable external environments, for example, can prosper using centralized-organization structures. But firms operating in dynamic external environments, as most will be in the future, need decentralized structures in order for various departments to respond more readily to their environmental demands.

Virtually all personal computer firms, for example, attempt to have decentralized decision units, in order to respond to the unpredictability of the marketplace. The pace of change is so rapid in personal computers that, without decentralization, a firm could not survive. Decentralization allows the organizational members with the most knowledge about the problem at hand to make the necessary decisions to solve that problem. There are disadvantages to uncontrolled decentralization, however. Hewlett-Packard has been characterized as the epitome of the decentralized organization for years, and for years it has responded superbly to the marketplace. But in the mid-1980s, it found itself in a computer hardware market calling for machines that could communicate—that is, interface to each other. Theirs couldn't because they had all been designed by separate, decentralized units.[19] The advantages and disadvantages of decentralization are indicated in Table 8.1.

Line and Staff Authority

Most organizations have historically employed what is known as the **line and staff concept** in their organization structures. This concept evolves from the military use of line and staff. Line officers made battle-related decisions. Staff

These Hewlett-Packard employees operate almost totally autonomously. Their manager serves more as a facilitator than as a boss. (SOURCE © Robert Holmgren)

Table 8.1. Advantages and Disadvantages of Authority Decentralization

Advantages of Decentralization	Disadvantages of Decentralization
1. Efficiency: Decentralization spreads the management load and reduces red tape and bottlenecks. If management at lower levels can make on-the-spot decisions, less time is lost in getting approvals up the line.	1. Control: When managers have great latitude in making decisions, coordinating overall activities is more difficult.
2. Flexibility: Managers who can make decisions have the ability to cope with changing conditions and adjust for unexpected circumstances.	2. Duplication: If all department managers are autonomous, there is a greater danger of duplicating efforts. Several offices might be keeping identical records on customers, shipments, inventory, and so on.
3. Initiative: It is very challenging and motivating for managers to make decisions regarding problems and solutions in their own departments.	3. Centralized Expertise: Managers with a lot of decision-making latitude may tend to overlook home-office expertise.
4. Development: The best training for management development is to encourage managers at lower levels to run their own departments.	4. Competency: Additional decision making by lower-level managers strains the organization to produce competent managers at all levels.

SOURCE: Gerald H. Graham, *Understanding Human Relations: The Individual, Organization, and Management* (Chicago, Il.: Science Research Associates, 1982), p. 137. Copyright Science Research Associates Inc. 1982; reprinted by permission of the publisher.

officers advised in this decision process but could not make the decisions. **Line authority** is authority within the chain of command of a given unit. **Staff authority** is advisory and comes from outside the chain of command of that unit. The **line** has, over time, come to be defined in a macro sense as that which the organization cannot do without.[20] Marketing, operations (production or service operations), and finance have traditionally been considered to be the three major functions without which an organization could not survive. The basic idea is that, regardless of the service or product, you have to be able to sell it, make it, and finance the selling and making of it before you have an organization. All in the organization that is not line would be designated as **staff**. Staff functions are generally advisory, or provide assistance to the line functions. Thus, human resources management (personnel), logistics, research, corporate planning, and other similar functions have usually been considered to be staff functions. Line

AT IBM: *IBM's restructuring meant that the line, especially sales, was given more authority.*

authority is now being defined as the relationship between a manager and a subordinate. This is its more commonly accepted definition, but the older perspective survives.

Classically only line managers have authority over line operations. More recently, line authority has meant that only managers have authority over their subordinates. Staff persons advise but do not normally have authority over line activities. Thus, members of the personnel department can advise the production department that it needs to improve its hiring procedures or face absenteeism problems, but personnel cannot make production follow this advice if the organization uses only a line and staff authority approach.

Although the line and staff concept still governs the delegation of authority in most organizations, the distinction between the two types of authority is continually diminishing. Research by Henry Mintzberg suggests that the line and staff concept should be replaced by a more comprehensive five-part model that will be discussed in Chapter 9.

Under the concept of **concurrent authority**, the organization may require that all decisions be concurred with by the staff. This initialing, or signing off process, by staff members, on line members' proposals, gives staff substantially more power in an organization than if it is not used. For example, in most organizations, the strategic planning department (staff) must concur with divisional plans (functional or business strategies) before top corporate management will agree to them. In addition to concurrent authority, occasionally, for certain matters, staff positions are granted what is known as functional authority.

Functional Authority

Functional authority gives a person, work group, or department line authority over decisions related to their areas of expertise in other departments. This allows them to intervene within normal line chains of command. Thus, in the case just noted, the personnel department could order production to comply with changes in hiring practices if it possessed functional authority. In many organizations today, the entire organization operates under a functional authority concept, in which functional managers make all decisions related to their areas of expertise regardless of where the problem is. Organizations may encounter problems when using this approach because many decisions overlap. Line and staff are often in conflict in organizations. Accounting, for example, may say that costs can be reduced by cutting inventory, but marketing may say that sales will be hurt by such a practice. A joint decision must be arrived at. Giving either department functional authority to determine inventory levels could prove disastrous. Because staff is advisory and line has command authority, the two often disagree on what actions the line should take.

Departmentation

Division of labor occurs to fulfill the process of specialization. Tasks that comprise a job are identified. These jobs will then be grouped according to departments. **Departmentation** is the grouping of jobs under the authority of (usually) a single manager, according to some common, rational basis, for the purposes of planning, coordination, and control. The work group is the basic unit of departmentation. These work groups will then be grouped in larger departments, the largest of which are known as divisions, to form the organization.

There are seven principal bases for departmentation: economic function,

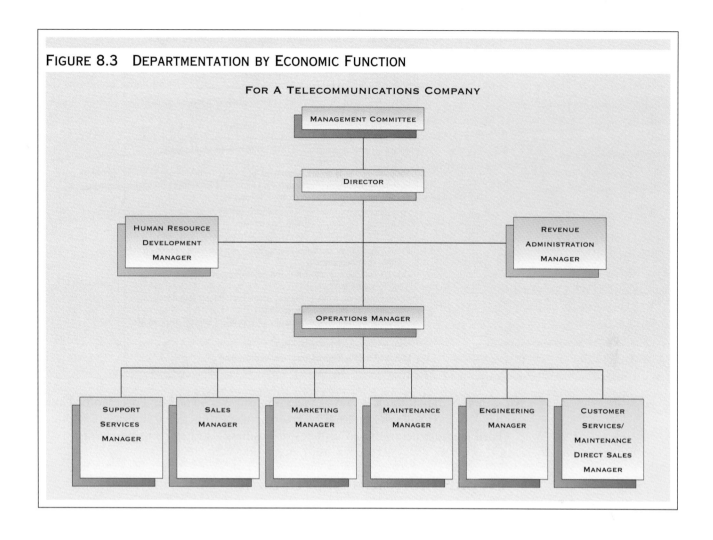

FIGURE 8.3   DEPARTMENTATION BY ECONOMIC FUNCTION

FOR A TELECOMMUNICATIONS COMPANY

MANAGEMENT COMMITTEE

DIRECTOR

HUMAN RESOURCE DEVELOPMENT MANAGER

REVENUE ADMINISTRATION MANAGER

OPERATIONS MANAGER

SUPPORT SERVICES MANAGER

SALES MANAGER

MARKETING MANAGER

MAINTENANCE MANAGER

ENGINEERING MANAGER

CUSTOMER SERVICES/ MAINTENANCE DIRECT SALES MANAGER

product, strategic business unit, geography, task specialization, time, and client or customer. Figure 8.1 provided an example of each of these. The first four—functional, product, strategic business unit, and geography—are often the first level beneath the CEO. The other three—task specialty, time, and client—are usually subdivisions of the others.

Departmentation by Economic Function of the Organization

Departmentation by economic function is the most common basis for the overall organization structure—its "macro structure." The reason for this is that most organizations are small and not complex, sell only one or a few products, and are therefore best organized along a functional basis, in which major economic functions of the organization report directly to the company president or other senior executive. Typically, marketing, operations, finance, and human resources report to the CEO. Figure 8.3 shows one example of functional departmentation modified to the needs of a company. Table 8.2 indicates the possible advantages and disadvantages of functional departmentation. Functional departmentation often occurs as a subpart of a more complex organizational environment with multiple products or multiple businesses.

Table 8.2. Possible Advantages and Disadvantages of Departmentation by Economic Function

Advantages
Suited to smaller, less complex organizations, with few products or services
Allows coordination from a holistic perspective
Staffing consistent with technical training
Allows for total organizational reaction to market situations, if coordinated properly
Reduces demands on the supervisor for technical knowledge
Fosters development of specialization in areas of expertise
Fosters more expert-based problem solving

Disadvantages
Often results in a "functional orientation," with divisions competing rather than cooperating
Overspecialized management, and other employees (They can't see the forest for the trees.)
Slowed response times to market situations in larger organizations, especially those with many products
Problems referred up the hierarchy when they should be decided at lower levels
General managers not developed
Can lead to problems of functional coordination

First National Bank is one of several businesses owned by Ford Motor Company, for example. Its internal macrostructure is functional, but it fits within a Ford macrostructure based on lines of business—strategic business units.

Departmentation by Product

At some point in time, an organization will have a sufficient number of products in its product line so that it becomes necessary to change from a functional structure to a product structure. The choice is not an easy one and the criteria are not easy to define. The advantages and disadvantages of both structures must be weighed. Management Challenge 8.2 describes Apple Computer's struggle to make the choice related to moving to a product structure and the eventual reversing of its choice. A typical product structure (in this case, services) is

Table 8.3. Advantages and Disadvantages of Product Structure

Advantages
Responsiveness to market
Facilitates interfunctional coordination
Enhances product visibility, product development
Develops general managers
Possible synergies between products, distribution, and so on

Disadvantages
Specialization and related expertise may wane.
Competition is fostered between product managers—a different but similar type of problem to that experienced in functional structure between functional managers.
Holistic perspective is limited.
Functions are still critical, but often have little power.
Functional efficiencies may decline.
Functional efforts may be duplicated.
Costs are duplicated.

Apple Computers Reverses Its Structure

How do you get a grasp on the corporate market? How big should you be to be a product-structured company? How many products and what revenues should each have? When do you change to a global structure? How do you cut costs, besides closing plants and laying off workers? The answers to all of these questions were related for Apple Computer. When John Sculley became CEO in 1983, he soon merged Lisa and Macintosh product lines, giving the company two product divisions instead of three. In 1985 he merged Apple II and Macintosh divisions, returning the company essentially to a functional structure. This move revealed that Sculley didn't think the company was big enough for a product structure. It cut costs by eliminating duplicate staffs, and it streamlined marketing efforts. Apple did not abandon the personal computer market, where cheap products abound, but did focus instead on the office market. Then in 1988, Sculley reorganized once again, changing from a functional structure to a global-based SBU structure with functional support. Three geographic SBU's report directly to Sculley: North America, Europe and Africa, and Asia, along with an R&D division. This structure was chosen due to increased revenues in Europe and the potential revenues in Asia.

SOURCE: Brenton R. Schlender, "Apple Sets Plan to Reorganize into 4 Divisions," *Wall Street Journal*, August 23, 1988, p. 2; Katherine M. Hafner, "The World According to John Sculley," *Business Week* (September 28, 1987), pp. 71–73; Peter Divorkin, "After a Long Diet, Apple Bites Back," *U.S. News & World Report* (January 26, 1987), pp. 47–48; and Joel Dreyfuss, "John Sculley Rises in the West," *Fortune* (July 9, 1987), pp. 180–183.

AT IBM: *IBM is structured principally by SBUs. The restructuring meant more autonomy for these SBU groups.*

Table 8.4. Advantages and Disadvantages of SBU Structure

Advantages
Only structure that satisfactorily suits a multibusiness organization
Enhances flexibility of response to marketplace
Retains business orientation to market
Retention of advantages of functional (or other) structures noted earlier for each business
Conceptually evens revenue flows and risks among businesses

Disadvantages
The complex structure is often subject to overstaffing at corporate levels.
Intense coordination is required.
Each business unit possesses certain disadvantages of the functional (or other) structures noted in this text.
There is mixed evidence that the multiple business structure offers any profit advantages over SBUs—that is, why not operate as separate companies rather than as SBUs of the same company.[a]
This structure may reduce innovation. It clearly causes a short-term focus, as opposed to a long-term focus.[b] Profits are viewed as the critical measure of SBU performance. Top management turns over frequently, and their compensation is almost always based on short-term profit, thus causing them to reduce long-term investment, for example, for R&D.

Table 8.5 Advantages and Disadvantages of Geographic Structure

Advantages
A company can adapt marketing and other functions to the needs of identified geographic markets.
Independent operations are allowed as profit centers for what essentially amount to independent companies.
Functional coordination should be improved within each specified geographic market.
A firm is allowed to take advantage of local market conditions, for example, cheaper labor or demand for the product.

Disadvantages
Sometimes it becomes difficult to know where all of the functions fit—for example, all under each geographic division or some divisions and some under headquarters.
Functions may be duplicated.
There may be difficulties in maintaining consistency of image in various regions.
Problems involving how much authority to delegate and how much autonomy and diversity to allow may arise.

[a]For a brief review of the evidence, see James M. Higgins and Julian W. Vincze, *Strategic Management: Text and Cases*, 4th ed. (Hinsdale, Ill.: Dryden, 1989) pp. 221–224.
[b]Charles W. Hill, Michael A. Hitt, and Robert E. Horkison, "Declining U.S. Competitiveness: Reflections on a Crisis," *Academy of Management Executive* (February 1988), pp. 51–60.

FIGURE 8.4 DEPARTMENTATION BY PRODUCT FOR A HOSPITAL

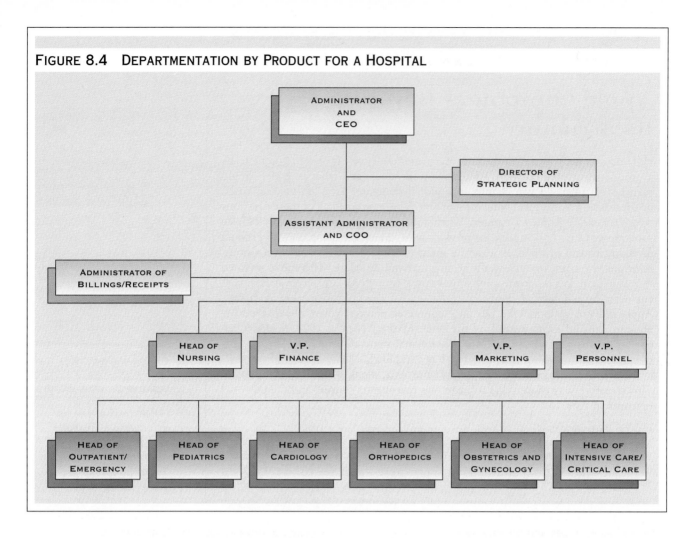

shown in Figure 8.4. Perhaps the best-known product structure is that of Procter & Gamble, with more than seven hundred product departments as decision points. Table 8.3 identifies the advantages and disadvantages of this structure.

Departmentation by Strategic Business Unit

For 500 to 1,000 U.S. businesses, and 100 or so very sizeable U.S. not-for-profits, the primary macrostructure is that of the **strategic business unit** (SBU). An SBU is a sizeable division within a multibusiness organization that operates much like an independent company and offers a set of distinct products to a distinct market. Disney Companies' theme parks—Disneyland and Walt Disney World—comprised one of six Walt Disney Companies' SBUs in 1990; the others included movies, consumer products, cable television, real estate development, and imagineering (a consulting department to improve corporate engineering by using imagination). When a company has a large number of SBUs, it creates group divisions to reduce spans of control and increase coordination. GenCorp, a diversified conglomerate, has four such divisions: Aerojet General, Diversitech General, General Tire, and RKO General. Figure 8.5 indicates the four group divisions and their principal SBUs and products. It is also an example of a horizontal organization chart. The advantages and disadvantages of the SBU structure, the multibusiness, multidivisional, or "M-form" structure, are listed in Table 8.4.

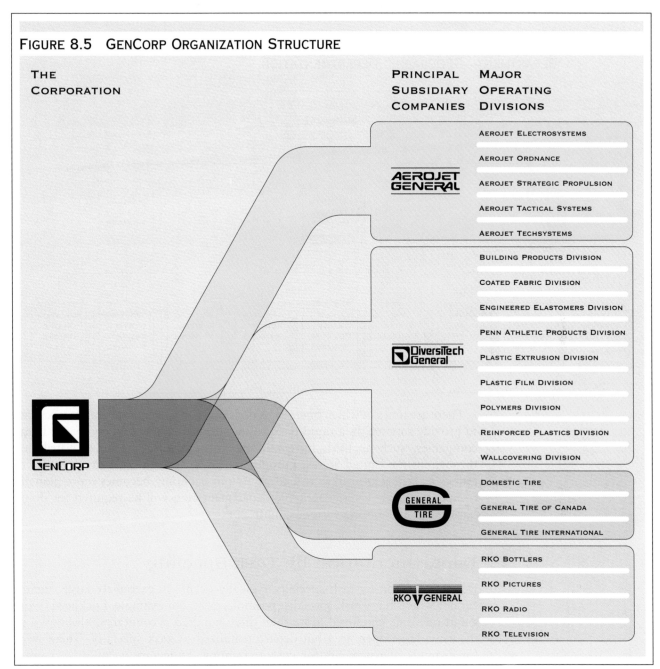

FIGURE 8.5 GENCORP ORGANIZATION STRUCTURE

THE CORPORATION

PRINCIPAL SUBSIDIARY COMPANIES

MAJOR OPERATING DIVISIONS

GenCorp

AEROJET GENERAL
- AEROJET ELECTROSYSTEMS
- AEROJET ORDNANCE
- AEROJET STRATEGIC PROPULSION
- AEROJET TACTICAL SYSTEMS
- AEROJET TECHSYSTEMS

DiversiTech General
- BUILDING PRODUCTS DIVISION
- COATED FABRIC DIVISION
- ENGINEERED ELASTOMERS DIVISION
- PENN ATHLETIC PRODUCTS DIVISION
- PLASTIC EXTRUSION DIVISION
- PLASTIC FILM DIVISION
- POLYMERS DIVISION
- REINFORCED PLASTICS DIVISION
- WALLCOVERING DIVISION

GENERAL TIRE
- DOMESTIC TIRE
- GENERAL TIRE OF CANADA
- GENERAL TIRE INTERNATIONAL

RKO GENERAL
- RKO BOTTLERS
- RKO PICTURES
- RKO RADIO
- RKO TELEVISION

SOURCE: REPRINTED FROM "THE CORPORATION," GENCORP ANNUAL REPORT, 1985.

Departmentation by Geography

As part of customer orientation, it is desirable to be near customers geographically, especially in the marketing and direct sales functions. Sales organizations, if not broken into client or customer departments, are typically broken into geographic territories, such as the St. Louis and Chicago offices, or the Midwest or Northeast sales territory, and so on. The general belief of geographic departmentation is that by being physically closer to customers, the organization can serve them better. Figure 8.6 contains an organization chart for the Macmillan Sales Department. It is based on geographic departmentation. Table 8.5 enumerates the advantages and disadvantages of departmentation by a geographic base.

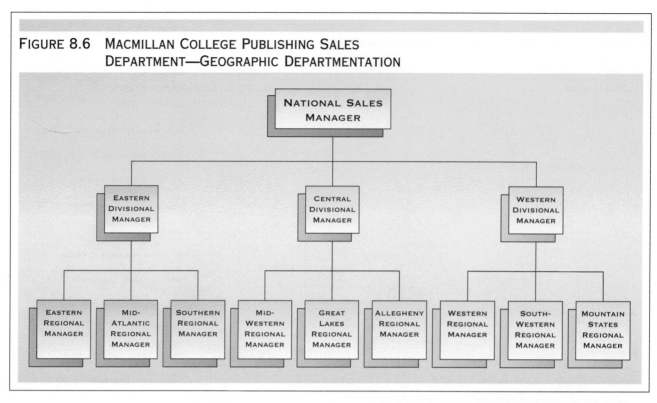

FIGURE 8.6 MACMILLAN COLLEGE PUBLISHING SALES
DEPARTMENT—GEOGRAPHIC DEPARTMENTATION

There are times in which operations divisions will be geographically structured to provide support on a rapid basis to the marketing arm of a company. Large companies, such as IBM, have multiple manufacturing facilities distributed throughout the United States, Europe, and other foreign countries in order to reduce transportation time and costs. As our economy becomes more globally competitive, increasing geographic departmentation will be required for doing business in and among various countries.

Departmentation by Task Specialty

Departmentation by task specialty typically occurs in extremely large organizations where many task-specialist positions exist. For example, Lockheed Georgia at one time employed more than three hundred accountants, all housed in the same large open area but departmentalized by task specialty. There were for example, departments for cost accounting, budgetary accounting, capital asset accounting, and a host of project accounts—C130, C141, C5-A, and Jet Star, all major types of airplanes. Even within some of these task specialties there were subdepartments based on task specializations. Cost accounting, for example, was broken into journal ledger and contract departments. Those in the journal ledger department were responsible for keeping the costs entered into the ledger by making various voucher entries; those in the contract area helped work up cost information on some of the various airplane contract proposals.[21] Figure 8.1 portrays task specialization in a typical accounting department.

One very interesting phenomenon occurring in several U.S. manufacturing industries is a move to departmentation on a micro basis, according to task specialization. This is being done to cut costs and improve quality in order to compete better with the Japanese. Outboard Marine, for example, no longer has sprawling plants with thousands of workers on an assembly line producing outboard motors. The project was just too great for a single manager to plan, organize, and control. Plants were automated and reduced to five hundred people in each of five plants, with each plant having one specific set of specialized tasks to achieve. This eliminates errors, raises quality, and cuts costs. Engine blocks are cast at their Spruce Pine, North Carolina, plant, using a rare "lost form" technique that produces smaller but more powerful engines at less cost. The blocks are trucked to Burmanth, North Carolina, for pistons, fuel systems, and other equipment and then on to either Rutherfordton, North Carolina, or Calhoun, Georgia, for transmissions.[22]

Departmentation Based on Time

A most obvious departmentation occurs with respect to time—day shift, night shift, and swing shift. In hospitals, for example, the day shift usually runs from 7:00 A.M. to 3:00 P.M.; the swing shift from 3:00 P.M. to 11:00 P.M.; and the night shift from 11:00 P.M. to 7:00 A.M. More complex time arrangements might be found, for example, in the Air Force, where crews on a Minuteman missile launch might be on duty for twenty-four hours, two or three days a week. Some bomber and fighter crews might be "on alert" for a week, living in an alert shack, waiting for possible scrambles of the airplanes. Figure 8.1 portrays this type of departmentation.

Departmentation by Client or Customer

One of the main reasons that organizations departmentalize is to ensure that decisions are made by the individuals most familiar with the situation. A client or customer orientation significantly aids success.[23] Client departments are usually found in sales. Figure 8.1 shows this type of departmentation for a sales division.

The Complexities of Pyramidal Structural Possibilities

Pyramidal structures are even more complex than the preceding discussion of the seven primary bases for structure suggest because combinations exist. Researchers and authors Ian C. MacMillan and Patricia E. Jones suggest that several major combinations exist for functional, product, geographic, and customer departmentations and cite several strengths and weaknesses for each configuration.[24] Furthermore, an SBU structure could be overlaid on each of the combinations, increasing the complexity immensely. Managers must decide which departmentations are necessary and at what point in the growth of the company. Some choices are obvious; others are not. Chapter 9 contains some guidelines for helping managers choose structural configurations, in a very general sense.

The Managerial Span of Control

The **managerial span of control** is the number of people a manager directs. Of critical concern to managers is determining the appropriate size of the span of control—that is, how many subordinates a manager can effectively direct. V. A. Graicunas, in studying the span-of-control concept, postulated that, as the number of subordinates increased arithmetically, there was an exponential increase in the number of possible relationships. This is known as **Graicunas'**

theory. He devised the following formula to be used in calculating the number of possible relationships:

$$R = n(2^{n-1} + n - 1)$$

where R = number of relationships

n = number of persons supervised

Thus, if the number of subordinates is 3, the number of relationships is $R = 3(2^2 + 3 - 1) = 18$; as n increases, the number of relationships increases rapidly, geometrically. Suppose $n = 5$; then $R = 5(2^4 + 5 - 1)$; and $R = 100$.

This formula reveals that the number of possible relationships increases geometrically with the number of people a manager has in his or her span of control.

For most jobs, the span of control should not exceed a certain number of subordinates. That number, however, varies with contingency factors within the specific situation: the nature of the job itself—is the work stable and routine or dynamic and changing?; the manager's leadership style; the time the manager has for managing; the manager's abilities; the subordinates' abilities—training, skill, and so on; the organizational culture; the nature of organizational management systems; the availability of rules and procedures; whether subordinates are concentrated in one location or not; and the performance objectives of the organization. In one large manufacturing organization, one department manager had seventy-five people reporting directly to him, and things went well—Maintenance Engineering.[25] Assembly-line managers typically have large spans of control, and managers of professional groups, such as engineers, typically have much smaller ones—at least partly because of the more frequent need to confer over problems, seek advice, and so forth. Most top managers have few direct subordinates because of the complexity and changing nature of their tasks and the limited time they have to supervise others directly. There is no absolute span of control that applies to all jobs, but a good rule of thumb is five to nine people.[26]

The size of a manager's span of control implies that certain management styles will be or are being utilized. A style of management that emphasizes relationships is more difficult to utilize where large spans of control are employed. Large spans of control also seem to suggest that the employee will work in the particular job with little supervision. There is usually a high level of delegation of authority. A large span of control often results in managers spending less time rewarding and controlling subordinates' performance than they might otherwise. Conversely, smaller spans of control imply closer relationships between manager and subordinates, less authority being delegated, more controlling, and more time for rewarding behavior.

Spans of control may be adjusted to encourage certain types of management styles. Some firms may want subordinates to make decisions, so they develop a structure with larger spans of control. The span of control in amusement parks, where managers may supervise as many as forty people, reflects both the desire to cut costs and the fact that the jobs are easy to learn and are essentially self-directed.[27] Naturally, larger spans of control foster more informal groups within the formal groups. Typically, managers of such groups must depend heavily on their cooperation; a manager who only had five subordinates could work with them to assure their cooperation with organizational efforts for success.[28] In addition to management philosophy, other factors shown to influence the span of control include the similarity of functions supervised and their complexity and geographic contiguity, the direction and control needed by subordinates, the amount of coordination necessary, the planning required of the manager, and how much assistance the manager receives from the organization.[29]

In this complex computer programming environment, a small span of control is necessary because managers must provide frequent assistance and facilitate the worker's efforts. (SOURCE © Robert Reichert)

The choices made about how an organization structures itself will result in its becoming "tall"—reflecting smaller spans of control, more levels in the chain of command, and centralization—or "flat"—reflecting large spans of control, fewer levels in the chain of command, and decentralization. Management Challenge 8.3 describes some of the consequences of such choices.

MANAGEMENT CHALLENGE **8.3**

General Motors Structure Is Too "Tall"

General Motors saw its U.S. market share plummet from 48 percent in 1979 to 36 percent in 1987. An evaluation of its strategic situation revealed a number of problems, including its structure. GM realized that with eleven layers of management, compared to Toyota's five, and a more centralized structure than Toyota's, it had become less responsive to the marketplace than its competition. Customer needs were blurred and decisions took far too long to make. For example, GM might take seven years to launch a new product from conception to showroom, whereas Toyota would take only four years. These additional layers in the scalar chain also meant that it was saddled with more management costs than Toyota. The following figure characterizes the situation: The more centralized organization is "taller" than the "flatter" decentralized organization.

GM moved to reduce its layers of management. It made a series of severe cuts in its managerial and professional staff levels in an effort to become more competitive.

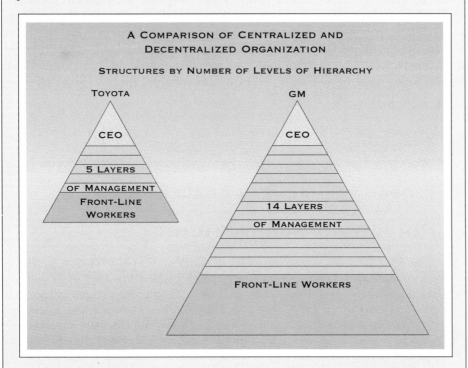

A COMPARISON OF CENTRALIZED AND DECENTRALIZED ORGANIZATION STRUCTURES BY NUMBER OF LEVELS OF HIERARCHY

TOYOTA
CEO
5 LAYERS OF MANAGEMENT
FRONT-LINE WORKERS

GM
CEO
14 LAYERS OF MANAGEMENT
FRONT-LINE WORKERS

SOURCES: William J. Hampton and James R. Norman, "General Motors: What Went Wrong?" *Business Week* (March 16, 1987), pp. 102–110; and Jack A. Seamonds and Kenneth R. Sheets, "GM's November Massacre," *U.S. News and World Report* (November 17, 1987), p. 56.

Coordination

Coordination is the process of integrating the efforts of individuals and departments in the organization to achieve organizational purpose.[30] From a coordinating viewpoint, several structural issues arise: formalization, complexity, integration and differentiation, and the linking-pin concept.

Formalization

Formalization is the extent to which written documentation occurs within an organization. It focuses on objectives and related job descriptions but also includes policies, strategies, procedures, and systems manuals, for example. A highly formalized organization structure would have policies and strategies; detailed job descriptions, objectives, and procedures; and detailed sets of rules, all in writing. Normally, smaller, more cohesive, family-type organizations are not very formalized. But as an organization grows, it eventually becomes necessary to formalize the structure, to eliminate confusion, clarify roles, and eliminate ambiguity. A typical example is Philip Crosby and Associates, Inc., one of the nation's leading quality consultants. When the firm had 105 employees, it was still as informal as it had been when it was founded three years earlier. Rapid growth left people uncertain of their job responsibilities and the firm's expectations. A massive formalization effort led to an easing of this problem and a recognition of overlapping job responsibilities.[31]

There is evidence that even though formalization occurs in an organization, employees may not feel that the detailed objectives and job descriptions have much relevance to them. Thus, there is not only the need to formalize the structure as the organization grows, but also to make certain that the resultant written statements are accepted as valid and necessary by employees.

Some organizations strive to be "informal." Electronic Data Systems founder and former CEO H. Ross Perot has always prided himself on having no written memos in his huge time-sharing company. The reality, though, was that a lot

AT IBM: *One of the major problems IBM had was that it had become too bureaucratic, too formalized, too inflexible, too complex, and too slow to respond to customer needs. The restructuring is intended to change that situation.*

Rousing a Sleepy Giant

From April 27, 1990 to June 29, 1990, the stock price of N.V. Philips, the Dutch electronics giant, plunged from 40 Netherlands guilders per share to 31 guilders per share on the Amsterdam Stock Exchange. The company's performance had been lackluster in the 1980s, and it had suffered heavy losses in computers and semiconductors in 1989, and in the first quarter of 1990. Despite efforts by CEO Cornelis van der Klugt to trim fat from the company, and to deal with the impacts of European market unification in 1992, Philips still plodded along. On July 1, van der Klugt stepped down a year ahead of schedule. He was succeeded by Jan Timmer, successful head of the firm's consumer products division.

Analysts cited the need to do major surgery on the bloated employment levels

One of the advantages that H. Ross Perot had in not writing memos when he was CEO of EDS was that he had a lot more free time to enjoy himself. (SOURCE © Barbara Laing/Black Star)

of his company's rules, regulations, policies, procedures, and job descriptions were highly formalized in what has been labeled as a "militaristic"—centralized and rule bound—culture.[32]

Complexity

The **complexity** of an organization refers to the number of different jobs and different departments it possesses. An organization's structure is said to be complex if it has a large number of differing jobs and differing departments. The issue of complexity is of concern because normally the more complex the structure, the greater the number and the more difficult the problems encountered

of the firm, and to sell off the computer and semiconductor businesses in order to improve profitability significantly. But Timmer reported that he would not sell off the two losers, and that he would eliminate only 10,000 jobs, not the 50,000 that some analysts believe are necessary for this firm of 293,000 employees. He did, however, promise major cost cutting in the computer division, and signaled a retreat from the minicomputer market. Timmer's task to overhaul the bureaucratic giant won't be an easy one. The culture is strong and not always with the CEO. For example, national divisions resisted van der Klugt's efforts to give product managers the power to chart global strategies. Timmer's strategies may meet with similar reactions. Morale is low, and the thought of more reorganizations is likely to drive it even lower. Yet, Timmer must take major actions if he is to turn the company around.

SOURCE: Bob Hagerty, "Philips' Timmer Faces Challenge Rousing Sleepy Electronics Giant," *Wall Street Journal,* June 29, 1990, p. A10.

in managing it. Complex organizations such as General Motors, for example, tend to have slower communications and tend to make decisions more slowly (unless they are highly decentralized) than less complex organizations.

Complex organizations often tend to be too tightly controlled. People frequently feel that they are about to drown in "red tape" in the complex bureaucracy. Organizations such as the U.S. Army and the Department of Agriculture are so complex and formalized that decisions on many issues can take virtually forever. In addition to formalization, one of the reasons that complex organizations are slow in decision making is that so many of their internal units must be considered in the choice process. As with most of the structural elements, a host of potential behavioral results must be considered as the organization grows more complex. Ways of overcoming the negative consequences of complexity must be developed. Behaviors must be changed. It may be necessary, for example, to increase the level of participation by subordinates in decision making. Organizations may also become mired in bureaucracy. This may necessitate serious restructuring. Some organizations are reluctant to take the necessary actions as The Global Management Challenge reveals.

Integration and Differentiation

Organizations, and more specifically, their subunits, **differentiate** their structures, processes, and member behaviors according to the requirements of their environments. For example, the accounting department is structured differently from the sales department because they operate in different environments. There are numerous other structural ramifications resulting from this adaptation—for example, those cited previously, relating to the creation of client departmentation and product departmentation in order to better relate to the environment. Spans of control may grow smaller in response to a highly unstable external environment.

Paul R. Lawrence and Jay W. Lorsch (and Henri Fayol before them) suggest that differentiated subunits tend to view the organization's purpose from a biased "differentiated" perspective.[33] That is, because subunits become different, they have a tendency to be parochial in their views and lose sight of organizational purpose. As a result of this differentiation, organizations must be integrated. **Integration** (coordination) is the directing of differentiated subunit efforts toward the fulfillment of an organization's central purpose, or mission. Typically, objective setting and planning systems are used as a major part of this integration activity. Research suggests that the most successful organizations are those that are both highly differentiated and highly integrated.[34] The implication is that the organization must plan to accomplish both differentiation and integration—that structure must be altered to meet the environment of each subunit and then coordinated to achieve mission. Differentiation and integration, including related research, will be discussed in more detail, from another perspective, in the following chapter—adapting to the organizational environment.

The Manager as a Linking Pin

The manager of each work unit is a **linking pin** between at least three groups: the group that he or she leads and manages (A), the group of which he or she is a subordinate peer manager (B), and the group of managers higher in the organizational hierarchy (C), of which the manager's boss is a member, as shown in Figure 8.7.[35] Modern organization structure theory and practice tell

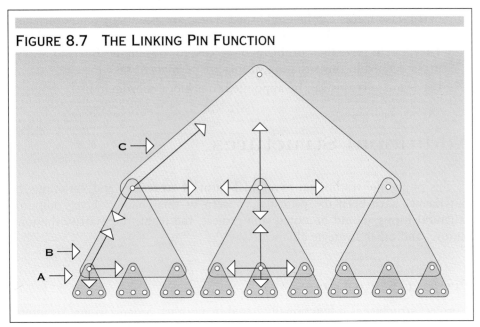

FIGURE 8.7   THE LINKING PIN FUNCTION

SOURCE: RENISSIS LIKERT, NEW PATTERNS OF MANAGEMENT, NEW YORK: MCGRAW-HILL, P. 165. REPRODUCED WITH PERMISSION.

us that organizations are formed around groups of people—departments. The function of the linking pin is critical to the success of the organization. The manager is the link among the basic work groups, which are assigned the objectives and tasks necessary for accomplishing mission with other groups. The manager is the vital connecting point for many of the elements of structure discussed previously: span of control, departmentation, delegation, decentralization, formalization, acceptance of authority, and parity. Most linking-pin managers are primarily responsible for implementation. This requires the coordination and communication of the organizational objectives that come from above in the hierarchy with individual objectives that come from below. Influencing motivation is also an essential task. Coordination with the peer-level managers facilitates these processes.

Additional Coordination Devices

Richard L. Daft identifies several ways in addition to objectives and planning in which organizations can coordinate better:

1. Add levels of positions to the hierarchy—If the manager is overworked, adding positions may aid in improving coordination.
2. Use information systems better—By improving periodic reports with information, especially from computer database summaries, managers may coordinate better.
3. Exchange paperwork—Managers may improve coordination by exchanging information.
4. Increase personal contact—Have more direct contact on a personal level.
5. Use liaisons—Liaison roles may be created for the sole purpose of better coordinating individuals, groups, and departments. There may be a need to appoint a full-time integrator.
6. Employ task forces—Direct contact with liaison roles usually serve to coordinate two departments. When more departments need to be coordi-

nated, task forces can be established. These are essentially temporary task groups of representatives from each department affected by a problem. They join to solve their problem, or at least to coordinate efforts to resolve it. As defined in this situation, teams are permanent task forces.

7. Use teams—Teams can be appointed to achieve coordination.[36]

Additional Structures

To this point, the traditional pyramidal form of structure, and variations on that theme, have been the principal concern of this chapter. Five additional structural forms should be noted: the project, the team, the matrix, the joint venture, and other strategic alliances.

Project Structure

A **project structure** is a functionally based, temporary organizational structure. It is disassembled in parts as each stage of the project is completed. The project structure is used principally in the construction industry but was used until the 1970s in the aerospace industry. One difficulty with the project structure is that employees are retained only for so long as their part of the project endures. In the construction business, this is not a great problem, as there is usually an available labor pool that moves from project to project in any given city. But in aerospace, engineers typically do not have that many projects to choose from in a given city; hence, they resist termination. The project structure closely resembles the product structure, except that groups of products are essentially ongoing for a substantial period of time, whereas projects endure only from a few months to a few years.

The Team

The **team structure** describes an egalitarian, highly cooperative, close-knit work group striving to achieve a set of mutually desirable objectives. Just as the pyramid best represents authority distribution in classical organization structure, the circle best represents authority distribution in team management situations. Each member of the team is conceptually equal in his or her level of authority. In true teams, managers participate as members of the team. They do not impose their decisions on others but in most cases, facilitate the group's efforts, rather than actually directing it. But in the broader sense, team management applies to building cohesive work groups. Authority may be shared up to some high level, but in many teams, the manager still retains ultimate authority. Team building is engaged in to help the team be more effective at performance and at the same time to help satisfy more member needs. It has been used extensively, for example, in the federal government to increase productivity and collaborative problem solving and in numerous businesses.[37]

Quality circles—formal groups of employees that meet periodically during work hours to solve company problems—are an example of the team concept in its purest form. The manager facilitates, coaches, counsels, and provides resources but does not intervene in the group's problem-solving process.

Team management is usually found not as a macro organization structure but as a micro one. Teams will be found throughout the pyramid and throughout the other principal forms of structure, for example, the matrix. It is very difficult

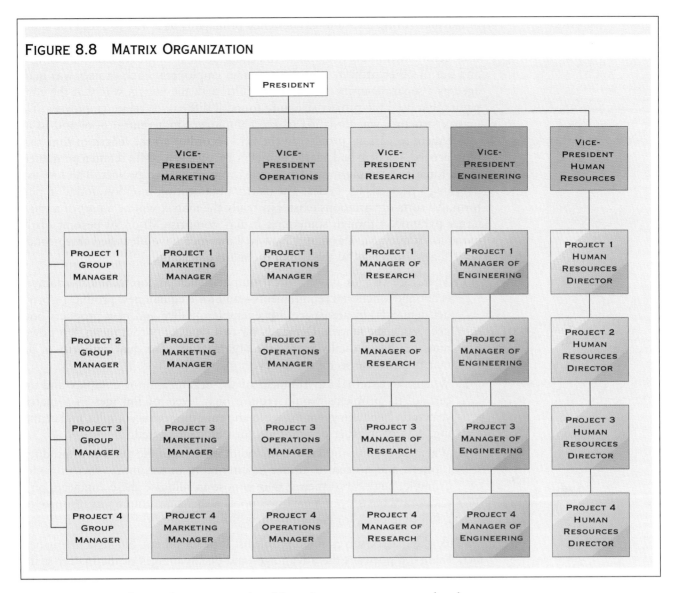

FIGURE 8.8   MATRIX ORGANIZATION

to imagine a team larger than ten people, although team management has been applied in industrial situations in organizations with sizes of up to about two hundred people. One effort in a milk processing plant worked quite successfully for a period of years. Twenty teams with ten members each, representing various levels of the organization, were successful in increasing productivity from an old hierarchical management system.[38] Cross-functional teams, where representatives from different departments—marketing, finance, operations—meet to solve a problem, are especially useful in improving customer need satisfaction. They also help overcome divided loyalties and speed project development.

The Matrix Organization

The **matrix structure** is characterized by simultaneous authority over line and/ or staff by project and by economic functional managers. As a pyramid represents hierarchical authority and the circle represents the equal authority of the team, the rectangle represents authority distribution in the matrix organization. An example of the matrix form of management is displayed in Figure 8.8. The matrix form of management is found principally in two industries: in aerospace, such as Lockheed or Martin Marietta, and banking, such as Sun Trust Bank.

The matrix organization was designed principally as a way to avoid the short-comings of project management. When a project was completed, employees were terminated. New projects were begun, often without regard to phasing in and out of other projects in order to retain employees. Each project was managed as a separate entity. A major difficulty with the matrix was that the companies that used the project structure found it difficult to rehire employees. The matrix structure was designed to keep employees in a central pool and to allocate them to various projects in the firm according to the length of time they were needed. If a firm had a large number of projects, it could retain a permanent labor force and simply move employees from project to project. The key was in timing a project's life cycles. The matrix organization is seldom found in pure form. All sorts of variations exist. Normally the matrix will be a part of a much larger pyramid, although sometimes it may comprise 80 or 90 percent of the pyramid. Stanley M. Davis and Paul R. Lawrence have identified three conditions that should lead to the use of the matrix structure.

1. There are two or more critical outputs, such as for technical quality—economic functional requirements—and for frequent new products—product demands. In aerospace, for example, quality and new products both necessitate the matrix. Demands for two types of output mean that power must be shared dually within the organization. The dual authority of the matrix structure seems necessary.
2. Where the external environment of the organization is complex and uncertain, its problems would require high levels of linkages in a matrix structure. In banking, for example, the environment is complex and changing. A large number of branches must be coordinated.
3. When the organization is at a midpoint in terms of the number of products it offers, and it needs to utilize its internal resources more efficiently—for example, engineers—then it may choose to allocate these engineers on a temporary basis from a common pool, rather than employ its resource on a full-time basis for those products.[39]

While the matrix solves some problems, it poses others. No structure is perfect. Table 8.6 portrays the advantages and disadvantages of the matrix structure. Of special concern is the fact that the matrix violates a principle adhered to in hierarchical structures: the unity of command. The **unity of command** states that an individual should have only one boss. With the matrix system he has two or more by definition: a functional boss and a project boss. If he works on enough projects in a year, he can have as many as five or six bosses. For the unity of command principle to be violated successfully, the managers must agree on how their joint subordinates are to be managed. Otherwise, near chaos ensues. Furthermore, while the project manager is the individual who works with the employee on a day-to-day basis, in many cases it is the economic functional manager who fills out the employee's performance appraisal.[40]

Joint Ventures and Strategic Alliances

Joint ventures are essentially partnerships between corporations. **Strategic alliances** are agreements to cooperate between two corporations. The joint venture is the most frequently used strategic alliance. In December 1983, for example, AT&T and Olivetti formed an alliance in which each would sell the other's products. This joint venture was solidified by the purchase of 25 percent of Olivetti's shares by AT&T. AT&T gained access to the personal computer industry, while Olivetti gained access to selling AT&T communications equipment in Europe, as well as the U.S. personal computer markets.[41]

Table 8.6 Advantages and Disadvantages of Matrix Organizational Structure

Advantages
Provides coordination necessary to satisfy dual environmental demands Flexible use of human resources Suited to complex and changeful environments Leads to functional and integration skill development

Disadvantages
Organizational members experience dual authority, which leads to role ambiguity, frustration, and confusion. Managers and other participants need sound interpersonal skills. Extensive training is required. It is time consuming to resolve conflicts and to reach agreement on objectives and actions. Without cooperation the matrix will not work.

SOURCE: Adapted from Robert Duncan, "What Is the Right Organizational Structure: Decision Tree Analysis Provides the Answer." Reprinted by permission of publisher, from *Organizational Dynamics,* Winter/1979, p. 429, © 1979. American Management Association, New York. All rights reserved.

Even Sears and IBM have joined in a venture, Prodigy, aimed at providing videotech services for shopping, banking, electronic mail information, and education. These services would provide home subscribers with video/computer capabilities to transact business in each of these areas. Through late 1987 they jointly invested $250 million. Their belief is that if every home has a computer, it can be linked to multiple information services by telephone.[42]

Informal Structure

Informal relationships develop among individuals while they are working, and when they get together away from work. Such groups develop on the basis of friendships or common interests.[43] These relationships are not typically sanc-

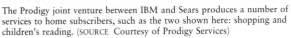

The Prodigy joint venture between IBM and Sears produces a number of services to home subscribers, such as the two shown here: shopping and children's reading. (SOURCE Courtesy of Prodigy Services)

tioned by the formal organization, although it is usually aware of them. There are times when such relationships are encouraged in order to maintain work group cohesiveness. You have probably been in a situation in which an informal organization existed. When, for example, a secretary has tremendous informal power, because she has access to the boss, she will develop followers who attempt to gain access to the boss through her. Or when someone knows more than anyone else about how to use Lotus 1-2-3, he or she has tremendous power to influence others in the organization, although granted no formal authority. Remember that even though individuals may report to a manager, they may not recognize his or her authority and may go to someone else for needed opinions or technical information.

Informal groups are often quite positive for an organization. Many times they are responsible for maintaining work group cohesiveness—that is, the desirability of remaining in and participating actively in the group. Cohesiveness many times assists the manager in keeping a group working toward its objectives. The informal group often provides quite important and often quite accurate information to those in the informal communication network. Informal structure helps satisfy the social needs of individuals and can often provide a sense of satisfaction of higher-level needs, such as esteem. On the other hand, informal groups that are extremely cohesive, but not aligned with organizational objectives, can be detrimental to the accomplishment of those objectives. The information provided may be inaccurate, there may be rumors, and there may be resistance to change resulting from informal groups. The manager must learn to manage informal groups. Chapter 14 provides more insight into how this may be accomplished.

Organizing as Problem Solving

This chapter has introduced you to various organization structures and their advantages and disadvantages. Chapters 9 and 10 will provide more information about the factors that influence your choices. Each of the key elements of structure, each of the types of departmentation, each of the concepts introduced in this chapter could be worked through this model. Figure 8.9 examines structure from a broad-based problem-solving perspective, assessing key terms and concepts to stages in the process, for the purpose of example.[44]

A manager, in using Figure 8.9, would proceed as follows. Environmental information would be continuously analyzed for signals of a need to change structure. Those factors shown in the figure are the major factors, but only a few of the total factors to be considered. Top management would be concerned mainly with overall macro structure—division and department structures; lower levels with micro structures—small departments, work groups, and individual jobs. At lower levels, managers recognize and identify structural problems, often in response to dictates from upper-level managers. For example, when Hewlett-Packard restructured in the mid-1980s, lower-level managers followed upper management's guidelines in restructuring their work groups and the jobs of subordinates. In essence, the problem was already recognized and identified for them. Conversely, top management at Hewlett-Packard was responding to market conditions. Wanting to be more responsive to customers, they changed strategy and moved to enable their computers to communicate with each other.[45] To do so, they had to change the corporation's overall structure, which allowed each of their separate businesses to operate totally independently. In the problem-identification stage, they determined that they needed more integration.

FIGURE 8.9 ORGANIZING AS PROBLEM SOLVING

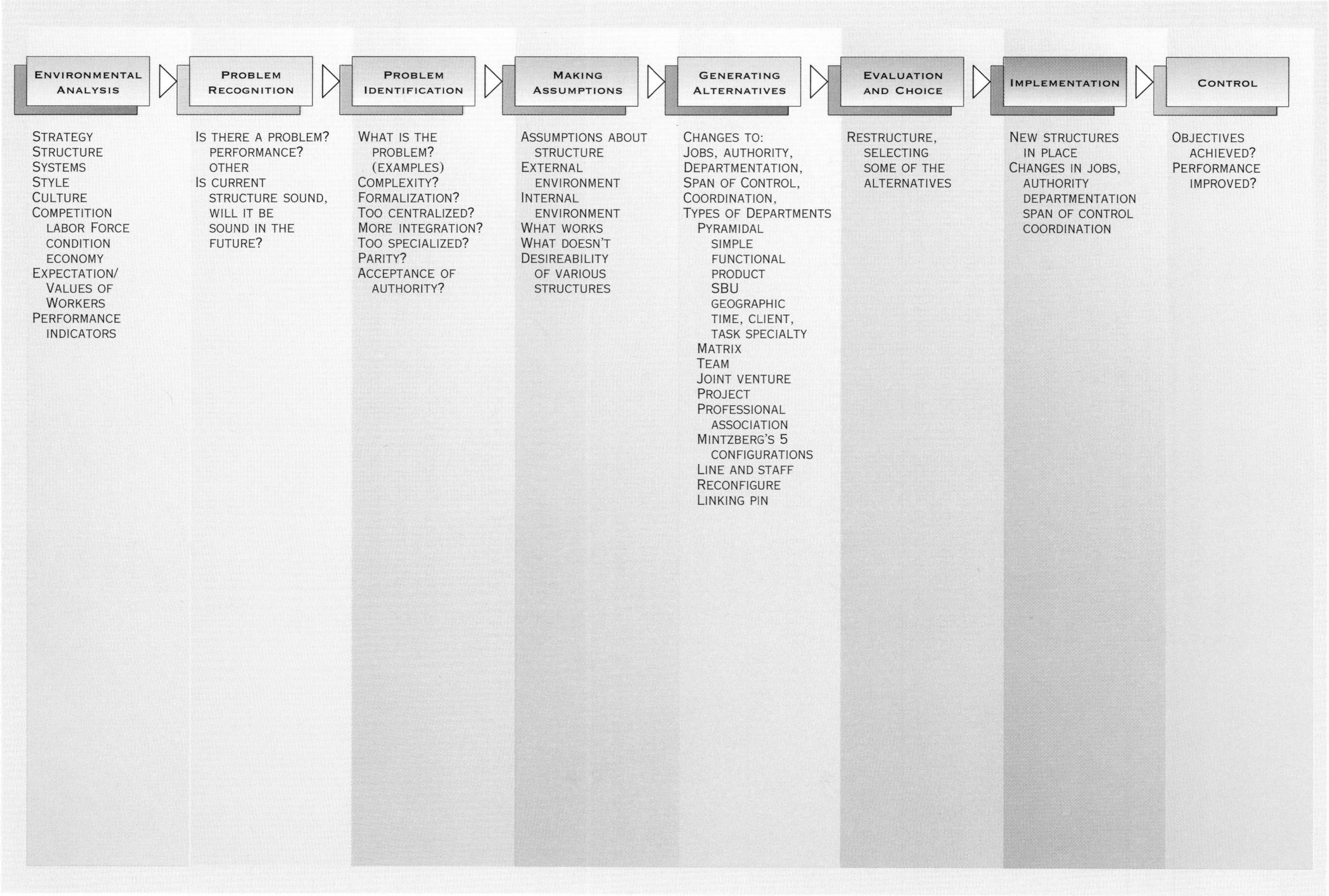

ENVIRONMENTAL ANALYSIS	PROBLEM RECOGNITION	PROBLEM IDENTIFICATION	MAKING ASSUMPTIONS	GENERATING ALTERNATIVES	EVALUATION AND CHOICE	IMPLEMENTATION	CONTROL
STRATEGY STRUCTURE SYSTEMS STYLE CULTURE COMPETITION LABOR FORCE CONDITION ECONOMY EXPECTATION/ VALUES OF WORKERS PERFORMANCE INDICATORS	IS THERE A PROBLEM? PERFORMANCE? OTHER IS CURRENT STRUCTURE SOUND, WILL IT BE SOUND IN THE FUTURE?	WHAT IS THE PROBLEM? (EXAMPLES) COMPLEXITY? FORMALIZATION? TOO CENTRALIZED? MORE INTEGRATION? TOO SPECIALIZED? PARITY? ACCEPTANCE OF AUTHORITY?	ASSUMPTIONS ABOUT STRUCTURE EXTERNAL ENVIRONMENT INTERNAL ENVIRONMENT WHAT WORKS WHAT DOESN'T DESIREABILITY OF VARIOUS STRUCTURES	CHANGES TO: JOBS, AUTHORITY, DEPARTMENTATION, SPAN OF CONTROL, COORDINATION, TYPES OF DEPARTMENTS PYRAMIDAL SIMPLE FUNCTIONAL PRODUCT SBU GEOGRAPHIC TIME, CLIENT, TASK SPECIALTY MATRIX TEAM JOINT VENTURE PROJECT PROFESSIONAL ASSOCIATION MINTZBERG'S 5 CONFIGURATIONS LINE AND STAFF RECONFIGURE LINKING PIN	RESTRUCTURE, SELECTING SOME OF THE ALTERNATIVES	NEW STRUCTURES IN PLACE CHANGES IN JOBS, AUTHORITY DEPARTMENTATION SPAN OF CONTROL COORDINATION	OBJECTIVES ACHIEVED? PERFORMANCE IMPROVED?

Hewlett-Packard's top management assumed that the competitive environment of the future would dictate this change in strategy and, hence, structure. They also assumed that their basic structure was all right, and needed modification, not wholesale change. Based on this, they generated a number of alternatives related to redefining division chiefs' jobs and authority, and on improving coordination. Lower-level managers had to make assumptions about such issues as continuing most aspects of the structure, rewards for change, and how best to use their people in the new structure. They would then generate alternatives based on their perceived situation.

Both top management and lower-level management would choose the various means for restructuring that best fit their circumstances. Top management chose, for example, to stick with an SBU structure and to increase coordination; they also chose, in one or two situations, to change significantly the amount of autonomy particular division chiefs had. Management at all levels then took the necessary actions to implement these structural changes, in one case physically removing an entire division. Finally, management analyzed changes in performance to see if the changes in structure had been effective.

The Management Challenges Identified

1. Increasing levels of competition resulting in the need to change structure
2. Increasingly complex sociotechnical situations requiring change in structure
3. Constant change, increasing levels of change requiring modifications of structure

Some Solutions Noted in the Chapter

1. Increased decentralization
2. Adjustments in the division of labor, delegation of authority, span of control, departmentation, and coordination

Summary

1. Managers must make decisions about how to structure the organization relative to these five fundamental elements of structure:
   a. The division of labor: determining a scope of work and how it is combined in a job
   b. Delegation of authority: determining how much authority should be granted to individuals and groups to do their jobs
   c. Departmentation: grouping jobs into work units and departments on some rational basis
   d. Spans of control: determining how many subordinates each manager should have
   e. Coordination of the individuals, groups, and departments as they perform
2. An organization is a group of people working together to achieve a common purpose.

3. Formal organization consists of that structure sanctioned by the organization. Informal structure is all other structure.

4. By examining an organizational chart you can determine the following relationships: horizontal divisions of labor, specializations of labor, relative authority, departmentation, spans of control, number of levels of management, coordination centers, communication channels, and decision responsibility.

5. The organizing process consists of the preparation and allocation of resources to achieve objectives and carry out the plans established in the planning process.

6. It is the combination of those five elements and their subcomponents that ultimately results in some organizational structure. It is the interaction of the content of the individual job based on specialization of labor; the amount of authority delegated; the groupings of individuals, groups, and departments; the sizes of the spans of control; the types of departmentation—task specialization, time, customer, geography, product, economic function, or strategic business unit; and the amount of complexity, formalization, integration, and coordination that lead to the structure you see on organizational charts.

7. The detailed definition of each element of structure, and its role in structure were provided in the chapter.

8. Resources other than human are organized in the broader meaning of that term essentially through planning and scheduling.

Thinking About Management

1. Describe an organization you know in terms of each of the five fundamental elements and each of their respective component parts; for example, is the principal macro departmentation based on product, economic function, or SBU? Do you see evidence of task-specialization departmentation? What are the spans of control?

2. Draw a simple organization chart for the organization you described for question number 1. Explain how its major structural elements relate to the change.

3. What would be your guess as to differences in structure between for-profit and not-for-profit organizations?

4. Describe the difference between formal and informal structure within organizations and describe how the informal structure actually alters the authority of the formal structure.

5. Discuss the advantages and disadvantages of the following forms of structure: economic function, product, strategic business unit, and matrix.

6. Why is organizing important?

7. Describe the relationship of authority to job performance.

8. Why is there no ideal span of control?

9. Is your college centralized or decentralized, relative to the degree of authority the professor has been delegated?

10. How would you go about delegating authority in an organization?

CASE

Restructuring at BankAmerica

In the 1970s, BankAmerica epitomized the successful American bank. Its returns were sound, it was a socially responsible and aggressive bank, making loans to Third World countries. It had domestic loans in exciting business-opportunity areas. A. W. Clausen, CEO, was a highly respected wizard of international banking. But in the 1980s, his plan, later carried out by his successor while Clausen was serving as head of the World Bank, began to collapse. Clausen had not moved rapidly enough to provide technology for the bank. At one time in the early 1980s, it only had a single ATM

machine, while its competitors had an ATM on every street corner. And many of its foreign and domestic loans appeared likely to be defaulted upon. It wrote off $1 billion in bad debts in 1984, $1.6 billion in 1985, and $1.4 billion in 1986. In 1987 it lost a whopping $995 million.

Part of its strategy to overcome its financial difficulty included selling off various divisions in order to raise funds. It also restructured, especially in terms of downsizing in the main bank. The original plan eliminated 10,000 positions in 1986 and 1987. Several hundred more were eliminated in 1987. The problem was whom to eliminate and upon what basis. A number of variables had to be considered.

DISCUSSION QUESTIONS
1. How would you go about choosing which macro structural changes to make?
2. How would you choose whom to terminate?
3. What are the likely problems resulting from restructuring?
4. What are the likely impacts on morale of restructuring, regardless of who is let go and on what basis?

SOURCE: Julian W. Vincze, "BankAmerica," 1987, in James M. Higgins and Julian W. Vincze, *Strategic Management: Text and Cases,* 4th ed., copyright © 1989 by The Dryden Press, Inc., a division of Holt, Rinehart and Winston, Inc., reprinted by permission of the publisher.

Coping with Overgrowth

Rita was the new president of a small service company, with 345 employees. She began examining various departments throughout the organization. She was concerned about cost and about having too many people. The company's sales had not grown after adjustment for inflation, for 10 years. Yet, the number of employees had grown from 285 to 345. She wondered why.

In 1985, the personnel department had only three people—an administrator and two secretaries. Now, the department had six people, and if you counted the affirmative action director, there were really seven people. Rita discovered that a new director, appointed in 1985, had added the additional staff. The affirmative action director had been appointed by the recently retired president in an effort to improve the company's hiring and promotion of minorities and women.

Rita wondered how many people the personnel department, and other departments in the organization really needed?

DISCUSSION QUESTIONS
1. What could account for the growth in employees throughout the company?
2. What might account for the growth of employees in personnel?
3. Recognizing that the company suffered a 15% attrition each year in the salaried positions—about half of the work force, the other half, the hourly work force, experienced only 5% attrition, what kinds of action could Rita take to reduce staffing back to old levels in two years?

MANAGE YOURSELF

Designing a New Organizational Structure

Yesterday Tom Andrews was officially promoted to his new job as hospital administrator for Cobb General Hospital. Cobb General is a 600-bed hospital located in a suburban area of New Orleans. Tom is extremely excited about the promotion; at the same time, he has some serious doubts about it.

Tom has worked at Cobb General for three years as its associate administrator. Although that was his official job title, he was really more of a "gofer" for the former administrator, Bill Collins. Because of his educational background (which includes a master of hospital administration degree) and his enthusiasm, Tom was offered the administrator's job last week, after the hospital's board of directors had asked for Bill Collins' resignation.

Tom was not looking at the organization chart for the hospital, which Collins had pieced together over the years (see Exhibit 1). In reality, each time a new unit had been added or a new function started, Bill merely had the person report directly to him. Tom is worried about his ability to handle all of the people that are currently reporting to him in his new position.

QUESTIONS
1. Do you agree with Tom's concern? Why?
2. How would you redraw the organization chart?

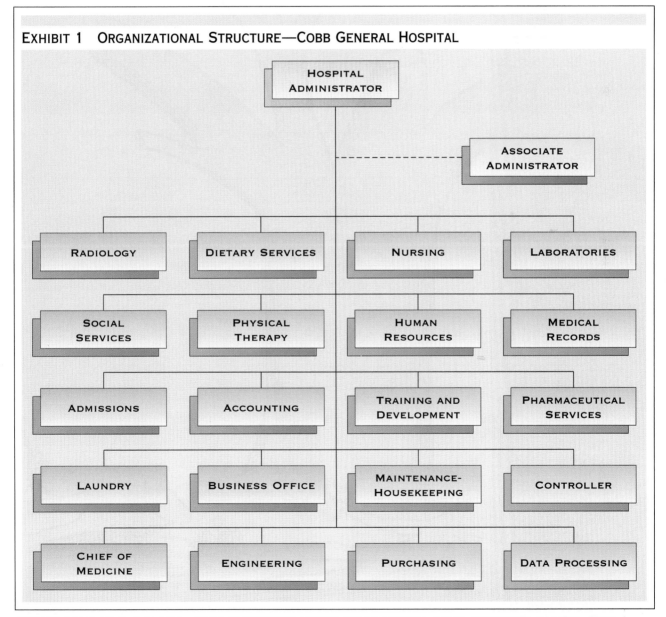

EXHIBIT 1 ORGANIZATIONAL STRUCTURE—COBB GENERAL HOSPITAL

SOURCE: LESLIE W. RUE, LLOYD L. BYARS, MANAGEMENT: THEORY AND APPLICATION, 4TH ED. (HOMEWOOD, IL: IRWIN, 1986), PP. 256, 257.

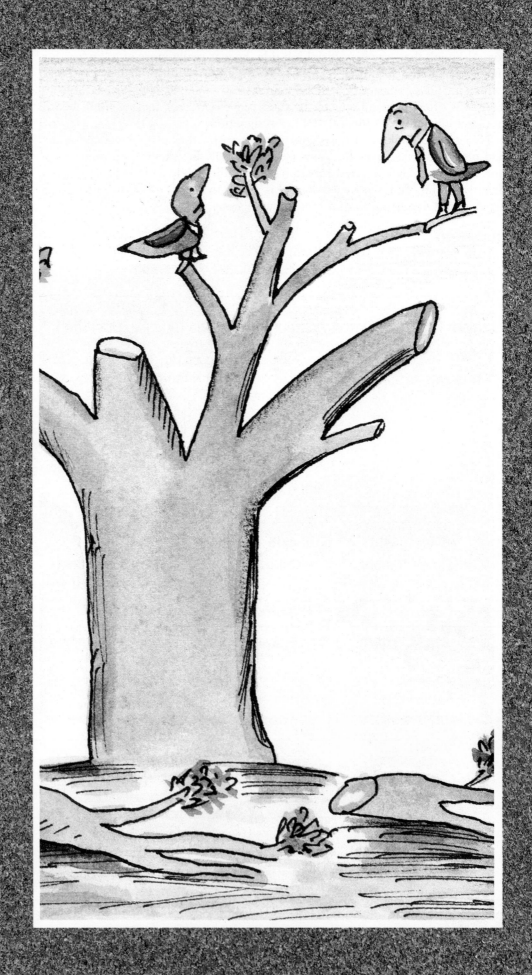

CHAPTER NINE

Organizational Design

CHAPTER OBJECTIVES

By the time you complete this chapter you should be able to

1. Describe the organizational design process.
2. Describe how each of the following affects organizational design: strategy, management philosophy, environment, geographical dispersion, technology, and size.
3. Distinguish between the characteristics of mechanistic and organic organizations.
4. Distinguish among the simple structure, professional bureaucracy, machine bureaucracy, divisionalized form, and adhocracy.
5. Indicate the importance of the Woodward studies of technology to organizational design
6. Describe the "shape of things to come."

CHAPTER OUTLINE

Organizational Design
Strategy, the External Environment, and Organizational Design
   Strategies and Structures
   Mechanistic and Organic Structures—Varying Responses to External Environments
   Mintzberg's Five Types of Organizational Design
   The Lawrence and Lorsch Studies on Differentiation and Integration
Size, Age, Growth, and Organizational Design
   Growth Theories of the Firm
   Mintzberg's Five Configurations Theory
   Growth Theories in Review
Management Philosophy
Technology
   The Woodward Studies
Geographic Dispersion
Choosing the Appropriate Structure
The Shape of Things to Come
Organizational Design as a Problem-Solving Process
The Management Challenges Identified
Some Solutions Noted in the Chapter

Eastman Kodak Restructures
in Order to Compete

In 1982 Kodak's then chairman, Walter A. Fallon, observed, "It's time to make this elephant dance." The elephant was Kodak, overweight and an underachiever. It was losing market share in its film business to its chief competitor, Fuji Photofilm Company. It had grown soft and lost its innovative edge. Fuji was fighting its way into the marketplace with new products, as well as by underpricing Kodak on existing products. One long-term Kodak customer indicated that Kodak used to be like God, but not anymore.

To make the elephant dance, Fallon changed the company's mix of businesses, acquiring compatible companies, and embarked on a program of restructuring. He encouraged the use of small entrepreneurial business units to develop new products, a practice begun several years before, but not pursued extensively. Fallon decentralized, establishing independent groups of products, and allowed the product managers to make decisions—something that had never been done before. Previously, even though Kodak had 50,000 products, the chairman often had gotten involved in nickel-and-dime decisions, but not anymore. Front-line supervisors were being encouraged to make decisions. The transition came slowly because most supervisors had never been allowed to make decisions. It was a skill they had to learn.

In 1986, Colby H. Chandler, who had become chairman in 1983, began slashing 10 percent of Kodak's work force, but many said that this would not be enough. In 1987, Chandler continued the restructuring. One

of his big challenges was to change the organizational culture and make it more market driven. This was not an easy task because Kodak's values had been instilled over a long period of time. But changes are being made. Kodak has, for example, decided to link some manager's salaries to company performance, something that most other companies have been doing for some time, but an action that Kodak had been reluctant to carry out. In a promising scenario, Vice-Chairman J. Phillip Samper relates the events of a recent trip to a Kodak plant. While he was touring the plant, bells started ringing and the entire production line was shut down because a technician had found a problem with quality control. "In the past," Mr. Samper notes, "it would have taken some part of a day for someone to make that decision."

In 1989 Kodak found it necessary to restructure once again, its fourth restructuring since 1983. Increased competition, higher costs, and reduced profits led to the effort. This restructuring continued the types of changes made earlier. The work force was cut another one percent or 1,500 jobs and marginal businesses, such as videocassette tapes and specialty films, were pared. Additional cuts of strategic business units were expected in 1990.

SOURCES: Peter Pae, "Kodak to Again Restructure Operations," *Wall Street Journal* 18 August, 1989, p. B-2; and Clare Ansberry, "Uphill Battle: Eastman Kodak Company Has Arduous Struggle to Regain Lost Edge," *Wall Street Journal* 2 April, 1987, pp. 1, 20.

> The challenge is not to design organizational structures that are perfect, but to design structures that are better than those of competitors.
>
> Ian C. MacMillan and Patricia E. Jones
> Management researchers on structural design

> The surge in restructuring is profoundly altering much of U.S. industry.
>
> *Wall Street Journal*

Kodak had to cut the number of employees, and find labor saving mechanisms in order to be more competitive with Fuji. This employee now has power to make decisions that he could not make before. (SOURCE © Phil Matt)

When Walter A. Fallon, Kodak's chairman, analyzed his company's situation, he found that it needed a dramatic change in both strategy and structure. To make these changes, he added to Kodak's basic mix of businesses, cut the work force to save costs, decentralized and delegated substantial power to existing product groups, began to rely more on front-line managers for decisions, and added entrepreneurial units to make the company more competitive. He changed the organization's design to enable it to be more competitive. Kodak is typical of many U.S. companies that in the 1980s found it necessary to undergo restructuring.[1]

While top managers perform most of the organization-design activities, lower-level managers must implement them. Therefore, lower-level managers must be able to understand the purposes and options and how their efforts can be used in making the designs work. Furthermore, they must be able to explain the issues to subordinates if they are to support the changes. They must also understand how these designs affect the design of their own jobs and those of their subordinates. All employees must understand these issues if changes in organizational design are to succeed.

Top managers have three basic organizational structures to choose from, whether they manage a large department, division, or the entire organization: the hierarchical pyramid, the matrix, and the team. (The team and the pyramid are the primary options of lower-level managers.) In 99.99 percent of the cases, managers will choose the pyramid, which, of course, comes in several variations. They may also choose to incorporate the matrix and team approaches within that pyramid; however, virtually all organizations are pyramidal in nature and designed according to the concepts discussed in the previous chapter. Thus, the key problem-solving issue in organizational design is how to structure the pyramid. Managers must decide on the best variations and combinations of division of labor, delegation of authority, departmentation, span of control, and coordination, in order to accomplish objectives, in order to carry out plans.

To this point, you know that the external environment affects virtually all decisions in an organization to some degree; strategy (planning) leads to structure (organizing); and the existing structure affects the choices of future structures, and so do other factors. What you will learn in this chapter is how several specific factors affect the macrostructure of the organization, and how the conditions of these factors in a particular situation can affect top management's choice of structural design.

AT KODAK: *When Kodak restructured, it did so to satisfy the demands of virtually all of these six primary variables. For example, to meet the requirements of competition (external environment), it reduced layers of management and operating employees in order to cut costs. More authority was delegated. New departmentation occurred. Spans of control were altered. Coordination became more collaborative.*

FIGURE 9.1   MACRO LEVEL STRUCTURE—MANAGERIAL AND CONTEXTUAL FACTORS

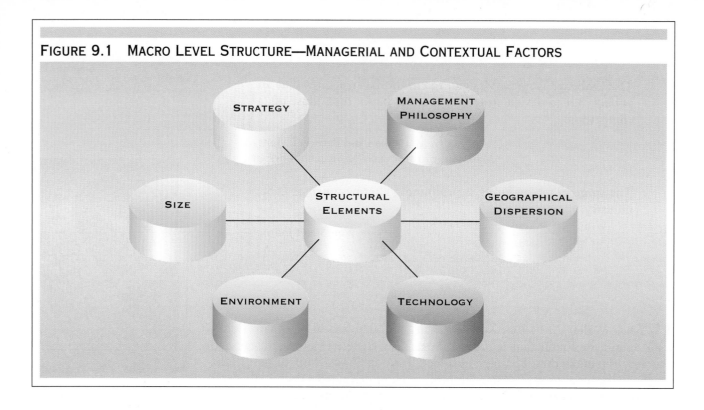

As Alfred D. Chandler, Jr., discovered after studying Sears, General Motors, Du Pont, and Standard Oil of New Jersey, macro structure should follow strategy.[2] But structure is also a function of five other key variables: organizational size, the technology employed, the external environment, management philosophy, and the geographical dispersion of subunits, as revealed in Figure 9.1.[3] Additional influential variables might include management systems, management style, organizational culture,[4] the characteristics of employees,[5] and the informal organization.

This chapter explores how each of the six factors identified in Figure 9.1 affect organizational design. Where possible, the related changes in specific structural elements are noted. A discussion of the changing nature of structure follows. The chapter concludes with a discussion of organizational design as a problem-solving process. It is important to recognize that no macro structure is ever perfect, and that constant fine tuning and occasional major restructurings are to be expected in most organizations. Restructuring, to some degree, is occurring almost all the time.

Organizational Design

Organizational design is the process of determining the best overall, macro organizational structure for the organization and its major subcomponents, and the subsequent characteristics of the structural elements. The concept of organizational design has evolved over time. It began with the classical approach to structure, drawn largely from military models, those of government, and that of the Catholic church. The classical approach reflected the belief that job design leads to organizational design. This approach resulted mostly from the belief that jobs were designed to carry out strategy and that collecting jobs in some logical fashion resulted in a macro organizational structure. Research supports this view but also notes that other situational variables affect the optimal organization design as well, such as those shown in Figure 9.1.[6] With the advent of increasingly complex situations, a situationally based approach to organization design is evolving.

It appears that **job design** resulting from strategy—determining the contents of individual jobs to implement strategy—while still an important factor, no longer dominates the organizational design process. Rather, the other factors identified in Figure 9.1, in addition to strategy, play very important roles in the organization design process.[7] The six factors identified in Figure 9.1 are of two principal types. The managerial factors are strategy and management philosophy, with regard to structure. The contextual variables are the external environment, the technology employed, the organization's size, and the geographical dispersion of the organization's subunits. Strategy is very closely linked to one of the contextual factors—environment. It is usually factors in the external environment that lead to changes in strategy, which then lead to changes in structure. Therefore, these two factors are discussed together here.

Strategy, the External Environment, and Organizational Design

The purpose of organizing is to prepare resources to carry out the plans established in the planning function. It follows that the purpose of structure is to carry out strategy. Strategy, as determined by top management, would naturally be expected to have a tremendous impact on structure. If the structure is inappropriate, strategy often fails. Management Challenge 9.1 reveals just how important having the appropriate organizational design can be, and also how important leadership can be to successfully changing strategy and structure.

However, researcher David J. Hall and Maurice A. Saias have clearly substantiated the fact that structure does not always follow strategy, but in fact that sometimes strategy follows structure.[8] Typical of companies whose strategy was dictated to some extent by their structure were the North American utility companies in the 1970s. They were extremely bureaucratic and structurally inflexible. Suddenly they had to change strategy in response to external environment changes, but were not able to respond strategically as quickly as they would have liked.

Strategies and Structures

In Chapter 6 various strategies that organizations can employ were reviewed, such as differentiation and cost leadership. An organization that focuses on innovation as a way of differentiating itself from its competitors would choose a macro organizational structure that was highly decentralized and that encouraged innovation.[9] Similarly, an organization that chooses to be a diversified conglomerate typically would be highly decentralized, allowing each strategic business unit to manage in its own right. TransAmerica, a financial services company serving the financial and insurance industries, for example, has fewer than one hundred people on its corporate staff to manage the numerous diversified businesses in its portfolio.[10] Each business functions independently. Conversely, an organization that chooses Michael Porter's cost leadership strategy would typically be extremely centralized, in order to control tightly all the functions of the organization in order to cut costs.[11] In such cases it can be clearly demonstrated that strategy leads to structure.

Sometimes it is difficult to tell where the impacts of the environment on strategy and strategy on structure leave off. Henry Mintzberg defines strategy as "the long-term adaptation of the organization to its environment."[12] In that context, and one with which most strategists would agree, strategy is a direct function of the environment, and structure is a direct function of strategy. It is therefore true that structure is most often an indirect function of the environment.

Mechanistic and Organic Structures—Varying Responses to External Environments

As discussed in Chapter 4, Tom Burns and G. M. Stalker first brought our attention to two types of organizational design responses to external environments.[13] One of these responses they labeled mechanistic, the other organic. The **mechanistic** model embodies the concepts of classic bureaucracy. It focuses on hierarchical relationships and tends to be rigid in the worst sense of "bureaucratic." **Organic** organizations are characterized essentially by openness, responsiveness, and a lack of hierarchy of authority.[14] Table 9.1 indicates the differences between these two structures.

the work force. Bethlehem's plants are now more efficient than those of their Japanese competition. Unlike Trautlein, who preceded him, Williams provided guidance to his managers and employees. He offered a folksy, friendly, but demanding management style, often visiting with employees in the plants, preaching his doctrines of productivity and quality.

Teams of hourly and salaried employees now meet periodically with customers to resolve quality issues. Incentives are tied to profits. Williams made decentralization work by making strategic decisions himself and by letting the work force implement them under his constant guidance.

SOURCES: "Forging the New Bethlehem," *Business Week* (June 5, 1989), pp. 108–110; and J. Ernest Beazley and Carol Hymowitz, "Steel Target: Critics Fault Trautlein for Failure to Revive an Ailing Bethlehem," *Wall Street Journal* 27 May, 1986, pp. 1, 20.

Walter Williams listens to what his employees have to say. Here he discusses operations with a manager and a front-line worker. Williams has made decentralization work. (SOURCE © Andy Freeberg)

Burns and Stalker identified environments as either stable or unstable, based on the amount of change in the environment. Their study indicated that firms operating in stable environments tended to use mechanistic organizational design, whereas firms operating in a dynamic unstable environment tended to use organic organizational design. The necessity for employing these particular designs in those types of situations has been demonstrated over and over. As mechanistic firms encounter changeful environments, they find the transition difficult, if not impossible. Those organizations that are able to make the transition to an organic structure will survive; those who don't will fail.

Contrast, for example, Eastern Airlines and American Airlines. American Airlines was able to adapt to changes in its environment. It became more organic. It adapted two-tier wage systems, for senior employees and new employees. New employees received much lower wages than senior employees, enabling American to compete in a very cost-conscious market. Similarly, American created the first "frequent flyer" program, which gave them a competitive edge for a while. Eastern Airlines remained more mechanistic and bureaucratic, failed to adapt, and met with serious problems. For example, it could not gain wage concessions from the machinists union, thereby causing it to be less competitive on a cost basis than other airlines.[15] And while American Airlines is more organic than Eastern, it isn't nearly as organic as Honda and William L. Gore and Associates. (Gore was discussed in Chapter 8, and Honda is discussed in Management Challenge 9.3.)

Burns and Stalker were quick to recognize that no organization is purely mechanistic or organic. Both designs will continue to exist. Burns and Stalker

Table 9.1. Mechanistic Versus Organic Organizational Design

Mechanistic	Organic
1. Tasks are highly fractionated and specialized; little regard is paid to clarifying the relationship between tasks and organizational objectives.	1. Tasks are more interdependent; there is an emphasis on the relevance of tasks and organizational objectives.
2. Tasks tend to remain rigidly defined, unless altered formally by top management.	2. Tasks are continually adjusted and redefined through the interaction of organizational members.
3. Specific role definition (rights, obligations, and technical methods) is prescribed for each member.	3. Role definition is generalized (members accept general responsibility for task accomplishment beyond individual role definition).
4. Hierarchic structure of control, authority, and communication exist. Sanctions derive from an employment contract between employee and organization.	4. There is a network structure of control, authority, and communication. Sanctions derive more from community of interest than from contractual relationship.
5. Information relevant to the situation and the organization's operations is formally assumed to rest with the chief executive.	5. The leader is not assumed to be omniscient; knowledge centers are identified where they are located throughout the organization.
6. Communication is primarily vertical, between superior and subordinate.	6. Communication is both vertical and horizontal, depending upon where information resides.
7. Communications primarily take the form of instructions and decisions issued by superiors. Information and requests for decisions are supplied by inferiors.	7. Communications primarily take the form of information and advice.
8. Loyalty to organization and obedience to superiors are insisted on.	8. Commitment to the organization's tasks and goals is more highly valued than loyalty or obedience.
9. Importance and prestige are attached to identification with the organization and its members.	9. Importance and prestige are attached to affiliations and expertise in the external environment.

SOURCE: Richard M. Steers, *Organizational Effectiveness: A Behavioral View* (Santa Monica, Calif.: Goodyear, 1977), p. 90. Adapted from Tom Burns and George M. Stalker, *The Management of Innovation* (London: Tavistock, 1961), pp. 119–122. Used by permission of Tavistock Publications Ltd.

do not indicate that either design is superior. Rather, each design fits a particular environmental situation best. However, because those situations to which mechanistic organizations are best suited are rapidly declining in number, and those to which organic organizations are best suited are increasing in number, organic organizations should dominate future organizational designs.

Robert B. Duncan later conceptualized the environment as not just an issue of stability, but also one of complexity.[16] Simple environments have few products, few competitors, few locations, and simple technology. Complex environments have a larger number of products, a large number of geographic locations, many different consumers, and they may employ complex technology. Figure 9.2 suggests the possible combinations of these factors (environmental complexity and environmental change), indicating the resulting degree of uncertainty in each situation. Henry A. Mintzberg has suggested the conditions under which the desired structure should be centralized or decentralized, mechanistic or organic, according to the degree of environmental complexity and change, as shown in Figure 9.2.

Mintzberg's Five Types of Organizational Design

Henry Mintzberg has also determined that there are five parts in an organization: the strategic apex, the operating core, the middle line, the technostructure, and the support staff. These are shown independently and in combination as a

Eastern failed to gain concessions from its machinist union members. The fight became very bitter. Eastern was eventually absorbed into the Frank Lorenzo airline empire. Eastern's mechanistic structure helped lead to its decline. (SOURCE © James Kamp/ Black Star)

FIGURE 9.2 ORGANIZATIONAL DESIGNS IN FOUR TYPES OF ENVIRONMENTS ACCORDING TO UNCERTAINTY

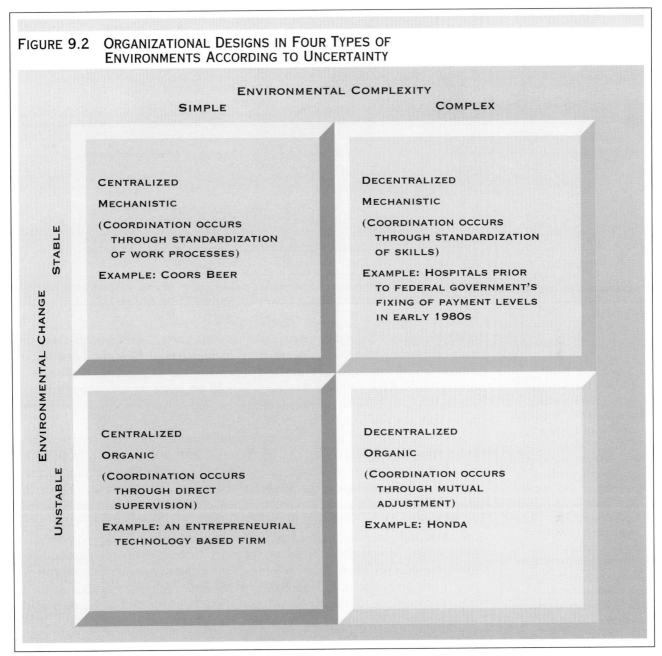

SOURCE: Adapted from Henry Mintzberg, STRUCTURE IN FIVES: DESIGNING EFFECTIVE ORGANIZATIONS (Englewood Cliffs, NJ: Prentice Hall, 1983) p.144.

simple structure in Figure 9.3. The strategic apex is at the top of the organization and consists of the organization's strategists. In a university, this would include the president, the provost, the board of trustees, and the vice-presidents. The **operating core** is comprised of those who perform the basic work functions. In a university, this is the faculty. The **middle line** is that group of management between the executives in the strategic apex and the operating core. These would be the deans and department chairpersons in most universities. The **techno-structure** consists of the staff analysts, who design systems for the planning and control of work. Curriculum committees are examples of this function in a university. The **support staff** provide indirect services to the rest of the organization. An example would be the university personnel department. In his model Mintzberg has taken the traditional line and staff structural elements and iden-

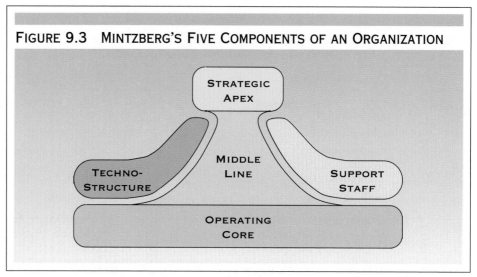

FIGURE 9.3   MINTZBERG'S FIVE COMPONENTS OF AN ORGANIZATION

SOURCE: ADAPTED FROM HENRY MINTZBERG, "ORGANIZATION DESIGN: FASHION OR FIT?" HARVARD BUSINESS REVIEW (JANUARY-FEBRUARY 1981), PP.103–117.

AT KODAK: *Kodak was the epitome of a centralized, mechanistic organization. It ruled its industry. Then Kodak's environment changed. The once simple, stable situation deteriorated into a more complex, unstable environment. Competition entered the picture. Fuji made significant inroads into Kodak's markets. The elephant had to learn how to dance. The company had to learn how to become organic and decentralized. Kodak has made many changes to move in that direction.*

AT KODAK: *Kodak was predominantly a machine bureaucracy. It still is, but it is changing. It is reducing the size of both its middle line and its operating core. It is emphasizing more of a divisionalized form. It is delegating more authority to the operating core.*

tified five parts—three line parts and two staff parts.[17] He believes these distinctions are necessary if you are truly to understand how the organization functions and how structure affects that functioning. Depending on the type of organization, each of these five parts would be more or less important. For example, the technostructure—engineers—would be very important in an aerospace firm but not in a university.

Based on these five macro structure components. Mintzberg suggested that most organization structures can be classified into five natural configurations based on the classic pyramid: the simple structure, the professional bureaucracy, the machine bureaucracy, the divisionalized form, and adhocracy. Figure 9.4 graphically portrays these structures. Each configuration consists of various combinations of the five components identified in Figure 9.3: the strategic apex, the operating core, the middle line, the technostructure, and the support staff. In his system Mintzberg identifies two primary differences in organization structures: the means of coordination and which of the five organizational component parts plays the most dominant, or key, role. As organizations adapt to their external environments, he believes these two dimensions change, as do subsequently the nature of the structural and situational elements.[18]

THE SIMPLE STRUCTURE

The **simple structure** is, in a word, simple. It has virtually no support staff, no technostructure, and almost no middle line. It consists principally of managers, normally an entrepreneur, and a group of subordinates. Almost all coordination comes from the strategic apex. There is little formalization, little planning, and little training. It is how Apple Computers began. It is even how GE began many, many years ago. This organization is lean and flexible. It has to be because it operates in a simple but dynamic environment. Simple structures are usually found in young and small organizations. Power is retained by the chief executive and normally is centralized. Growth is usually the key strategy. The company's flexibility and maneuverability in dynamic environments allow it to have a competitive edge against larger competitors with more bureaucratic structures. Typical organizations with simple structures include small high-tech firms; your local MacDonald's franchise; new but small governmental organizations, such as a state high-speed train commission; local clubs; and the huge majority of

FIGURE 9.4 THE FIVE CONFIGURATIONS

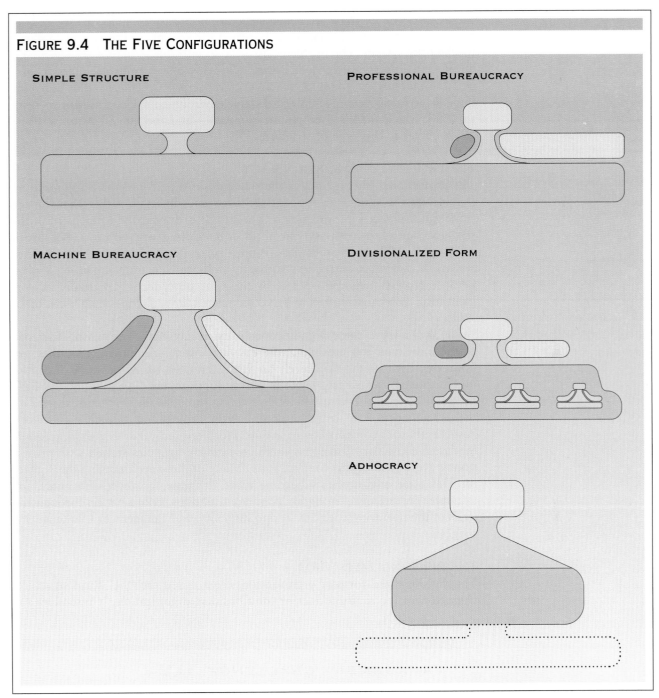

SIMPLE STRUCTURE

PROFESSIONAL BUREAUCRACY

MACHINE BUREAUCRACY

DIVISIONALIZED FORM

ADHOCRACY

SOURCE: HENRY MINTZBERG, "ORGANIZATION DESIGN: FASHION OR FIT?" HARVARD BUSINESS REVIEW, (JANUARY/FEBRUARY 1981), P. 107.

owner-managed firms. The simple form is probably the most prevalent form, simply because most small organizations employ it and most organizations in the world are small.

MACHINE BUREAUCRACY

The **machine bureaucracy** is the configuration most used in mass-production industries. The key means of coordination is the standardization of work; its operating core is characterized by low-skilled, highly specialized jobs. The middle line grows in size in order to coordinate the huge operating core. A large support staff exists to help create stability for the organization. The key part of the organization is the large technostructure necessary to support the needs of the operating core. The machine bureaucracy resembles Burns and Stalker's mechanistic system. The problems associated with this structure are legendary: an alienated work force; dull, boring work; excessive controls; massive size; and the inability to adapt. A machine bureaucracy is typically old and quite large. It performs best in simple and stable environments. General Motors prior to 1987, MacDonald's—the parent company—and the United Auto Workers all characterize this type of structure.

THE PROFESSIONAL BUREAUCRACY

The **professional bureaucracy** is the structure of the professional organization. It relies on the standardization of skills for coordination, rather than on the standardization of job processes or outputs. It is drastically different from the machine bureaucracy. It is typically a decentralized organization. Because it relies on the skills of its members, it must surrender authority to those professionals. It also often surrenders authority to those who train the professionals. Because professionals can operate by the same procedures in virtually any organization, coordination has to be accomplished through the standardization of skills.

The skill level in these organizations is extremely high. The depth and range of the individual job are high, whereas in the machine bureaucracy they are both low. Because the skill levels are high, the need for managers is less than in a machine bureaucracy. There is a large support staff, but there is very little need for the technostructure because training provides the professional with all the technological knowledge he or she needs. Professional bureaucracies work best in stable but complex environments. Hospitals, universities, public accounting firms, consulting firms, and small government agencies staffed with professionals are typical of this configuration. Many of these are changing their structures as their environments become more dynamic, however—hospitals, for example. Furthermore, in highly complex situations, coordination through the skills of the operating core can lead to difficulty, as Management Challenge 9.2 suggests.

THE DIVISONALIZED FORM

The **divisionalized form** of organization, often called the "M" form structure, characterizes the multiproduct or multibusiness organization. It resembles the

---

MANAGEMENT CHALLENGE **9.2**

NASA's Challenge: Overcoming the Challenger Catastrophe

After the Challenger disaster in 1986, NASA began an exhaustive self-examination, aided by external investigators and spurred by numerous pressure groups. The picture that emerged was one of unsound management in many areas, especially control. Structural problems existed, as well. Many felt those problems had contributed to the Challenger disaster. Lines of authority were fuzzy. Rivalries existed between divisions in the organization. Communications suffered and resulted in

professional bureaucracy in that it is a group of independent units joined by a loose administrative overlay; however, the independent units are either product divisions or business divisions. Divisions are typically autonomous, but not always. The key means of coordination are control systems focusing on outputs of the organization, usually profits or costs. The organizations tend to be old and quite large. The environment that this organization is best suited to is relatively simple and stable, with diversified markets and products. IBM is a divisionalized form of business, as are extremely large state governments, the U.S. Federal Government, and the AFL-CIO. Again, as environments become more dynamic, organizations such as IBM are changing their structures.

ADHOCRACY

Adhocracy is both a complex and nonstandardized organization. It is coordinated through mutual adjustment and informal interaction and decision making by expert job holders; it best suits the complex, dynamic environment. Support staff plays the most vital role. Adhocracy is almost a free-form structure, with frequently changing job descriptions and/or ill-defined definitions of authority. While typical of Burns and Stalker's organic design, adhocracy is "even more so." The matrix is often used in such organizations—as is the pyramid, with a large number of team structures. The company is generally young, and selective amounts of decentralization are employed. Honda Motor Company is a very good example of the adhocracy, as the Global Management Challenge reveals.

Table 9.2 shows the dimensions of the five configurations and the related means of coordination, the key part of the organization, the condition of the structural elements, and the condition of situational elements. Note how Table 9.2 identifies, under the situational elements section, the effects of factors such as age and size, technology, and the environment. Note also how each of the five configurations fits a different environment, according to its degree of complexity and stability.

MINTZBERG'S FIVE CONFIGURATIONS RECONSIDERED

No one form of organization structure is best. Each form suits a particular environment better than the other four; however, as environments continue to become more complex and more dynamic, adhocracy and some version of the simple form of structure for larger organizations seem to be called for. Mintzberg's configurations are only one of several perspectives on the effect of environment upon structure.

ineffectiveness and inefficiency. NASA's unwieldy structure caused confusion, as did the informal internal bickering. The role of technology in NASA's structure was also critical. No one knew quite how to manage it. The operating core simply could not coordinate through the use of its skills. It needed better structure, better control.

To overcome these problems, NASA restructured. NASA is typical of organizations in the North American economy in the late 1980s and early 1990s. Many are restructuring. Few major concerns will escape this process. NASA revised its chain of command and clarified authority relationships. It set about stopping internal bickering and redefined responsibilities. Its concern for managing technology also caused a redesign in structure, to incorporate more concern for quality and safety.

SOURCE: "Shifting Strategies: Surge of Restructurings Are Profoundly Altering Much of U.S. Industry," *Wall Street Journal* 12, August 1985, pp. 1, 12–13.

This 3M scientist is performing research designed to improve NASA's space hardware. NASA managers also had to find ways to improve NASA's management structure. How NASA had been managed helped lead to its hardware problems. (SOURCE © Mitch Kezar)

Honda and Adhocracy?

In 1971 Honda entered the U.S. market and sold only 9,500 cars. Its top management contemplated how it could become a major force not only in the United States, but in the world. Its top management determined that it should be productive, yet be innovative. Honda thrived on a number of firsts. Its Civic hit the market just when the market was clamoring for economy. Its later models, luxurious and "yuppie-ish," have also hit the market at the proper time. It was the first Japanese car company to enter the high-priced luxury market with its Legend. It was the first Japanese car firm to build a plant in the United States. One of the key factors in its success has been its structure: free wheeling, decentralized, and continually being modified.

President Tadashi Kume delegates heavily to his immediate subordinate managers, but Honda's culture goes beyond delegation. Honda continually reorganizes. Richard T. Pascale, who has examined Honda at great length, suggests that there is a constant dramatic "tension" within the organization.

According to Pascale, Honda has mastered both innovation and managing a business that is cost efficient. He feels it can do both because of the nature of its culture and structure. Both are strategic and opportunistic. Analysts believe Honda will be more of a force in the future. It is already the fourth-largest producer of automobiles in the United States and has long been known for its high productivity. Its president's goal in 1987 was to triple productivity in the next few years, an unbelievable goal many say, but a goal he claims they are moving toward rapidly. Honda has managed to get its product-development cycle in the automobile industry down to three years. Ford, the best of the American big three, has its down to seven years. Honda makes exciting preemptive moves because it understands the marketplace. Honda claims that its strategic advantage is that it learns quickly. Honda employs many innovative techniques. One they use is to place many individuals who have no knowledge of a problem in a room to solve that problem. This helps overcome the biases that people too close to a problem may have.

SOURCE: Richard T. Pascale, presentation to the Strategic Management Society, Boston, October 14, 1987; Frederick Hiroshi Katayama, "Plan: Hands On at Honda," *Fortune* (November 9, 1987), p. 88; Richard T. Pascale, "Perspectives on Strategy: The Real Story Behind Honda's Success," *California Management Review* (Spring 1984), pp. 47–73; and Stephen Koepp, "Honda in a Hurry," *Time* (September 8, 1986), pp. 48–49.

Honda's adhocracy enables it to be the most successful Japanese automobile company in the 1980s if growth and ability to react to changing environmental factors are the criteria.
(SOURCE © Andy Snow/Picture Group)

Table 9.2. Dimensions of the Five Configurations

	Simple Structure	Machine Bureaucracy	Professional Bureaucracy	Divisionalized Form	Adhocracy
Key means of coordination	Direct supervision	Standardization of work	Standardization of skills	Standardization of outputs	Mutual adjustment
Key part of organization	Strategic apex	Technostructure	Operating core	Middle line	Support staff (with operating core in operating adhocracy)
Specialization of jobs*	Little specialization	Much horizontal and vertical specialization	Much horizontal specialization	Some horizontal and vertical specialization (between divisions and headquarters)	Much horizontal specialization
Formalization of behavior—bureaucratic/ organic	Little formalization— organic	Much formalization— bureaucratic	Little formalization— bureaucratic	Much formalization (within divisions)— bureaucratic	Little formalization— organic
Decentralization**	Centralization	Limited horizontal decentralization	Horizontal and vertical decentralization	Limited vertical decentralization	Selective decentralization
Environment	Simple and dynamic; sometimes hostile	Simple and stable	Complex and stable	Relatively simple and stable; diversified markets (especially products and services)	Complex and dynamic; sometimes disparate (in administrative adhocracy)

*According to Mintzberg, a job has a high level of horizontal specialization if the work has a few narrowly defined tasks. Similarly, there is a high level of vertical specialization if the worker has little control over those tasks.
**According to Mintzberg, vertical decentralization describes how much decision making is delegated down the middle line, while horizontal decentralization describes how much decision making is delegated to nonmanagers. Decentralization is selective if it involves only certain kinds of decisions.
SOURCE: Adapted from Henry A. Mintzberg, "Organization Design: Fashion or Fit?" *Harvard Business Review* (January–February 1981), p. 107.

The Lawrence and Lorsch Studies on Differentiation and Integration

Chapter 8 discussed coordinating (integrating) the objectives and efforts of differentiated subunits of the organization. This chapter examines the *why* behind that differentiation process. Paul R. Lawrence and J. W. Lorsch examined firms in the plastics, food, and container industries and discovered that the degree of adaptation to the environment, or differentiation, that firms made to their environments, and the degree of integration of those differentiations, were related to their success.[19] Differentiation was seen as occurring within the organization to meet the particular subenvironments that each subunit of the organization encountered. Lawrence and Lorsch analyzed these companies in order to answer questions such as the following:

1. How are organizational factors confronting the various organizations different, and how do they affect the design of successful organizations?

2. Do organizations operating in stable environments rely more on centralized authority? If so, why?

3. Is there some variance in the degree of specialization and orientation among individuals and groups in organizations in different industrial environments?

4. If there are differences in specialization and perspectives among individuals and groups in different industries, how do those differences influence the coordination of the organization's subcomponents—the integration of those subcomponents?[20]

In their study Lawrence and Lorsch defined **differentiation** as the tendency of organizational subunits to become structurally different from each other because their structures resulted from adapting to different environments.[21] Although this definition may make differentiation sound like another term for specialization of labor, it is broader than that and includes departmentation and behavior. Lawrence and Lorsch classified subunits of the organizations they studied on a continuum from mechanistic to organic. They also examined integration, the "process of achieving unity of effort among various subsystems and the accomplishment of the organization's task."[22]

Lawrence and Lorsch were concerned with the degree to which the external environment affected differentiation and also integration, especially for firms in rapidly changing environments. The environment to them was divided into three key subunits: the market subenvironment made up of customers, competitors, distribution systems, and advertising agencies; the technical/economic subenvironment comprised of labor, raw materials, and equipment; and the science subenvironment, made up of rapidly changing developments in products and technologies, research centers, professional associations, and the study of science. These three subenvironments correspond to the marketing, production, and R&D economic functions within a typical organization. They found that each subunit will differentiate differently from each other subunit, and that mechanisms for integrating subsystems will vary from organization to organization. The most important finding of their study was that organizations must both differentiate and integrate in order to be highly successful. Another important finding was that the higher the level of uncertainty, the more differentiation occurred and, hence, the more integration was required.

In the broadest sense, environmental factors are adapted to through strategy. A firm's strategy is interdependent with its environment. The strategist must carefully review the environment when determining whether the structure should be mechanistic or organic, centralized or decentralized. The environment must also be considered when choosing one of Mintzberg's five configurations. Finally, the Lawrence and Lorsch studies clearly indicate that the manager must be concerned about both differentiation and integration in relationship to the environment. A manager must realize that there is no one best structure, but rather that there is a better structure for a particular set of environmental circumstances. Furthermore, the manager must recognize that no structure is perfect, and that all structures are compromises. The manager must also recognize that as environments continue to move toward less stable conditions, and as they move from simple to complex or complex to simple, the manager must be able to modify the structure to fit the environment. Interdependent with strategy and environment is the effect of size on structure. Most strategies seek growth, and changes in size usually require changes in structure.

Size, Age, Growth, and Organizational Design

Two principal theories of growth explain how organization size, age, and growth influence structure. These are the growth theories of the firm and Mintzberg's five configurations as growth models.

Growth Theories of the Firm

Organizations pass through a series of life cycle stages as they grow and as they become older.[23] Most business organizations begin as entrepreneurial endeavors, with a simple structure of owner and employees. At some point, the firm becomes large enough that it reaches a second stage of development—it departmentalizes on the basis of economic function. The first set of divisions beneath the chief executive on the organization chart are marketing, finance, operations, human resources, and information management. In the third stage, firms move from a functional structure to a product structure. The divisions reporting to the chief executive are product divisions—product 1, product 2, product 3. Each of these will usually have economic-function departments reporting to them—marketing, finance, operations, and so on. The fourth stage of development is from the product structure to the SBU structure, with the SBU being the first level of departmentation beneath the chief executive on the organization chart. The next level may be either product or function.[24]

Project structures and matrix structures are characteristic of late stages of growth in certain industries. Geographic-, client-, and task-specialization departmentations may occur under any of these structures, although normally geographic and client departmentations occur only after functional structure has been reached.

The major issue in this historical transition process is determining the points at which the organization should change structures from simple to functional, functional to product, and product to SBU. The other departmentations—geographic, client, and task specialization—although important, typically do not significantly affect the macro structure of the organization. These choices are made essentially on the basis of the ability of the organization to effectively meet the demands of its customer groups and its other constituents. As a simple structural organization grows, the complexity of performing numerous different economic functions becomes too great for the various job holders. Specializing by function becomes a necessity for achieving both effectiveness and efficiency. As a function-based organization grows, it begins to acquire a large number of product offerings. At some point, its ability to satisfy customer needs is taxed. Knowing that point is critical, but difficult to determine. At some point, it will become obvious; as the organization moves through the product-based stage, it eventually loses momentum again. And again managers should be monitoring the environment for signs of problems. The move from a product-based to an SBU structure occurs as the organization's managers recognize that there is the need to group products according to categories or markets. It becomes more efficient to run these groups of products as separate businesses. These structures and relevant considerations are indicated in Figure 9.5.

Another critical issue is that organizations proceed through a complete series of stages known as a firm's life cycle. Firms are born, and all eventually die, if renewal of the organization does not occur. Renewal of firms is discussed in Chapter 12.[25]

Mintzberg's Five Configurations Theory

Mintzberg's five configurations approach also suggests that there is a growth perspective to organizational configurations.[26] The organization typically starts with the strategic apex and an operating core. As it grows, it adds middle line and, to some extent, support staff and technostructure. As it continues to grow, all of these components may become larger. Observing Mintzberg's five configurations, however, there is also the distinct possibility that organizations pass through the five configurations in stages, just as they do from simple to func-

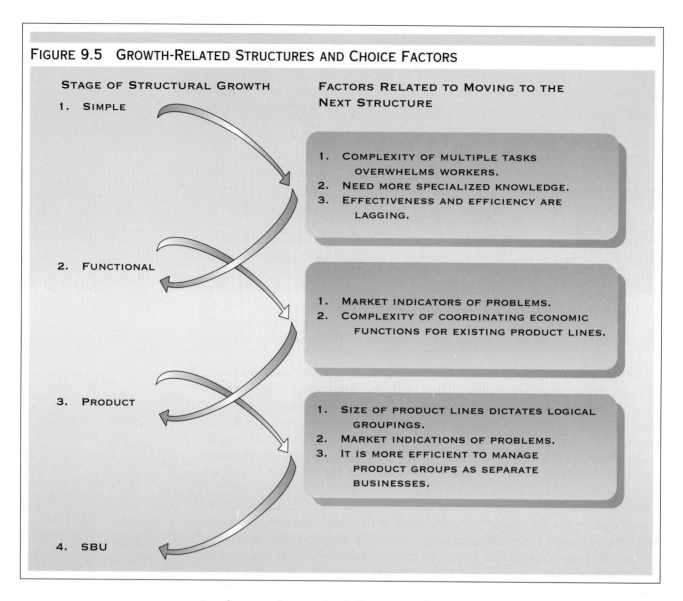

FIGURE 9.5   GROWTH-RELATED STRUCTURES AND CHOICE FACTORS

STAGE OF STRUCTURAL GROWTH

1. SIMPLE

2. FUNCTIONAL

3. PRODUCT

4. SBU

FACTORS RELATED TO MOVING TO THE NEXT STRUCTURE

1. COMPLEXITY OF MULTIPLE TASKS OVERWHELMS WORKERS.
2. NEED MORE SPECIALIZED KNOWLEDGE.
3. EFFECTIVENESS AND EFFICIENCY ARE LAGGING.

1. MARKET INDICATORS OF PROBLEMS.
2. COMPLEXITY OF COORDINATING ECONOMIC FUNCTIONS FOR EXISTING PRODUCT LINES.

1. SIZE OF PRODUCT LINES DICTATES LOGICAL GROUPINGS.
2. MARKET INDICATIONS OF PROBLEMS.
3. IT IS MORE EFFICIENT TO MANAGE PRODUCT GROUPS AS SEPARATE BUSINESSES.

tional to product to SBU. For example, an organization typically starts as a simple structure: it might then either become a professional bureaucracy or a machine bureaucracy, depending upon its mission and its environment. Both of these could then become divisionalized forms, and ultimately all organizations might become adhocracies, as environments tend to become more complex and dynamic. Any adhocracy that did not go through the other stages certainly progresses at least from a simple structure to the adhocracy structure.

Growth Theories in Review

These two theories provide a different perspective on how growth affects structure. The growth theories of a firm are concerned with types of departmentation.[27] Mintzberg's approach is concerned with configurations. Organizations could be going through both types of growth situations at the same time. A firm could be moving from a functional structure to a product structure and from a simple structure to a machine bureaucracy.

The manager must be keenly aware not only of environmental and strategic concerns, but also of the impact of the organization's size and growth on determining structure. The manager must balance the impacts of these factors

AT KODAK: *For a firm as old and as large as Kodak, it is amazing that it never delegated authority. It had rigid controls. It was bureaucratic. It had "red tape." Centralization worked fine in a simple, stable environment, but not in a complex dynamic one. It had to change.*

against each other, keeping in mind that organizations must be responsive to their environments while managing their size and growth.

It became fashionable in the late 1980s to suggest that effective organizations do not allow subunits to grow beyond certain size limits—for example, five hundred persons per location. Furthermore, most consultants suggest that these units should be allowed significant autonomy and, where possible, be run as profit centers.[28] The general belief is that employee contribution is more readily identifiable and employees are more satisfied, and more manageable, under such circumstances. Hewlett-Packard, for example, with one exception, has no units larger than one thousand people. There are many reasons for this. For example, it is easier to identify the contribution to success of individuals in smaller organizations. Overhead is less there than in large, more complex organizations. And, the organization is less bureaucratic. One study of the relationships between size, bureaucracy, and performance suggests that smaller, less bureaucratic organizations outperform smaller more bureaucratic organizations, but that for larger organizations the more bureaucratic outperform the less bureaucratic ones.[29]

Management Philosophy

Management may at any time, and at any level of the organization, determine that it wants a particular type of structure to achieve some chosen end or express its philosophy about management. If, for example, one of the company's strategies was to cut costs, this could be done by reducing the numer of managerial positions not directly involved with customers. Whatever the intent, it is clear that management philosophy does affect structure. Henry Ford, Lee Iacocca, Ronald Reagan, John Sculley, and Christie Hefner, for example, each put their personal stamp on their organizations. Their organizations reflected their individual needs, expectations, and personalities. Indeed the history of many organizations reflects their top managers.

Technology[30]

Technology, in its broadest sense, refers to the equipment, knowledge, materials, and experience employed performing tasks in an organization.[31] Technology affects any type of job and any type of organization, whether you are a college professor teaching English, a front-line employee on a robotized assembly line, a person selling computers, someone waiting on tables, or a nurse serving patients in a hospital.

Technology affects macro organizational design through its impact on the design of jobs, departmentation, spans of control, the delegation of authority, and coordination. While environment and size tend to dictate the total macro organizational structure, technology has more of an effect on departments and individual jobs.[32] It is easy, for example, to see how the design of each brewery at Anheuser-Busch would be greatly affected by technology, but that the corporation's overall size would probably determine its macro structure. Technology's impact on structure has only recently been well understood. And there are many types of technologies affecting the whole organization and/or specific departments, information technologies, PC's for example.[33]

The Woodward Studies

Much of the significant research on the relationship between technology and organization structure was carried out in the 1950s by Joan Woodward, a British industrial sociologist, and her colleagues.[34] They collected data from one hundred manufacturing firms from the county of Essex in southern England. Information regarding the firms' histories, objectives, manufacturing processes, structural elements, and performance were gathered. The researchers were principally concerned with a narrower definition of technology than was used above. They were concerned with equipment and related processes of production—"the methods and processes of manufacture," as opposed to the broader-based definition, which focuses on knowledge and experience.[35]

Woodward's group described three types of technology in manufacturing situations: as unit, or small batch; mass production; and process production. **Unit, or small batch,** production refers to the manufacture of a product or small number of products according to specific and unique customer requirements. The volume is low and the employee skill level is usually high. Stamos Yachts and Gulfstream corporate jet planes are examples of unit, or small batch, production situations. **Mass production** is production in large quantities on assembly lines, with standardized parts and high specialization of labor. Kenwood uses mass production technology to manufacture amplifiers, CD players, speakers, and other electronic components. **Process production** refers to the production of materials or goods in a continuous flow. Petroleum production is a process production technology. So is the brewing and bottling of beer. Woodward's classification of the one hundred firms her group studied is shown in Figure 9.6.

Woodward and her associates discovered that technology, organizational design, and performance are highly related. Successful small batch and process production organizations were simpler, less formalized, and more decentralized than less successful organizations. They were "organic" organizations. The successful mass production technology organizations were more complex, more formalized, and more centralized than less successful organizations of this type. They were "mechanistic" organizations. Some of Woodward's research findings appear in Figure 9.7. The findings tell us that each type of technology is characterized by different structural arrangements for the successful firm in that type of technology. For example, in successful mass production technology organi-

This winery makes small batches of different types of wine according to customer requirements. (SOURCE © Michael Greenlar/Picture Group)

AT KODAK: *Kodak is basically a mass-production firm. Its manufacturing facilities would clearly reflect the impact of this type of technology on the five key elements of structure. But if you analyzed its R&D department, its marketing department, and others using different technologies, you would find that they had a different set of key structural element characteristics from those in manufacturing operations because they are adapting to the technology used in that one department.*

This Glenfiddich Scotch plant in Scotland produces its product using continuous process technology. (SOURCE © Ron Sanford/Black Star)

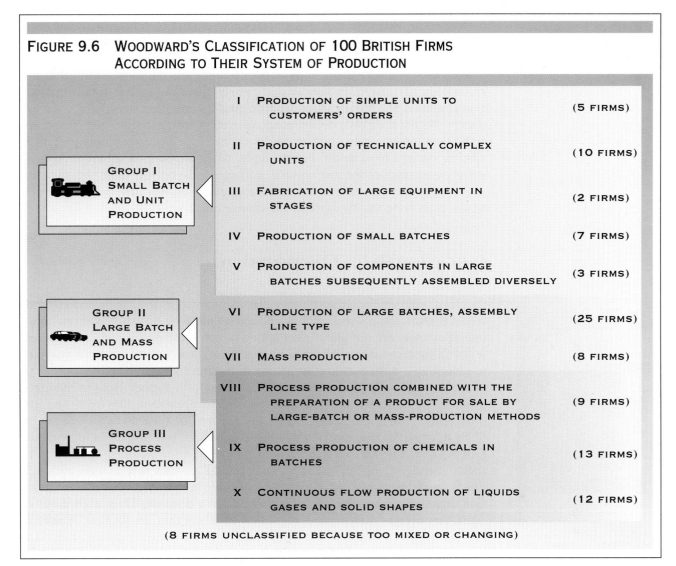

FIGURE 9.6   WOODWARD'S CLASSIFICATION OF 100 BRITISH FIRMS
ACCORDING TO THEIR SYSTEM OF PRODUCTION

GROUP I SMALL BATCH AND UNIT PRODUCTION	I PRODUCTION OF SIMPLE UNITS TO CUSTOMERS' ORDERS	(5 FIRMS)
	II PRODUCTION OF TECHNICALLY COMPLEX UNITS	(10 FIRMS)
	III FABRICATION OF LARGE EQUIPMENT IN STAGES	(2 FIRMS)
	IV PRODUCTION OF SMALL BATCHES	(7 FIRMS)
	V PRODUCTION OF COMPONENTS IN LARGE BATCHES SUBSEQUENTLY ASSEMBLED DIVERSELY	(3 FIRMS)
GROUP II LARGE BATCH AND MASS PRODUCTION	VI PRODUCTION OF LARGE BATCHES, ASSEMBLY LINE TYPE	(25 FIRMS)
	VII MASS PRODUCTION	(8 FIRMS)
GROUP III PROCESS PRODUCTION	VIII PROCESS PRODUCTION COMBINED WITH THE PREPARATION OF A PRODUCT FOR SALE BY LARGE-BATCH OR MASS-PRODUCTION METHODS	(9 FIRMS)
	IX PROCESS PRODUCTION OF CHEMICALS IN BATCHES	(13 FIRMS)
	X CONTINUOUS FLOW PRODUCTION OF LIQUIDS GASES AND SOLID SHAPES	(12 FIRMS)

(8 FIRMS UNCLASSIFIED BECAUSE TOO MIXED OR CHANGING)

SOURCE: J. WOODWARD, MANAGEMENT AND TECHNOLOGY (LONDON: HER MAJESTY'S STATIONERY OFFICE, 1958), P.11. DIAGRAM IS REPRODUCED WITH THE PERMISSION OF THE CONTROLLER OF HER BRITANNIC MAJESTY'S STATIONERY OFFICE.

zations, a supervisor would have a very large span of control. The span of control would be smaller in the successful unit, or small batch, technology firm, and smaller still in the successful process technology organization. The sizes of these spans of control reflect the need to differentiate structure to the technology involved.

Mass production technologies create job designs with low range (variety of tasks) and low depth (amount of decision authority). These types of jobs are best organized in the classical way. Conversely, unit and process technologies lead to job designs with high range and high depth, which lead to the "lean," highly decentralized structure. With unit and process technologies, employees need considerable latitude in performing their jobs, but with mass production the employees need very little.

Additional research has been performed on the technology/structure issue and it has generally been supported. However, there are technology structure research issues that limit the ability to generalize from the findings.[36] The research does show that technology does have a distinctive impact upon organizational structure—at least on certain features of the structure.[37] A series of studies performed at the University of Aston in England, and by others following their methodology, revealed a complex interdependent relationship between strategy, environment, size, and technology.[38]

Technology affects small units of an organization the most, those that are technologically driven. It doesn't particularly affect the macro, total organization structure, but it does affect departmental organization structures to a great degree. Within their own departments, managers must recognize the impacts of technology on structure and the need to adapt structure to technology. This is easy to say and hard to do. For example, when introducing different types of software to support the professional staff of a university, it might be advantageous to adopt a participative structure arrangement because the cooperation of the users is necessary to make the change effective.

Geographic Dispersion

Debbi Fields and other administrators at Mrs. Fields Cookies, keep in touch with over 500 shops via a computer network. This computer system helps them overcome problems often associated with geographic dispersion. (SOURCE © N. Alexanian/Woodfin, Camp & Associates)

As global competition emerges as a dominant force in the 1990s and beyond, structures for coping with global operations must be established. Even those operations that are not global, but within which subunits are widely dispersed, will find their structures modified by this separation. Eventually firms will find it advisable, if not necessary, somehow to organize geographically, in order to adapt properly to local environments. In general, the farther apart individuals, groups, departments, and major divisions are geographically from one another—and more importantly, from headquarters, or their manager—the more likely it is that the organization will be decentralized and that those individuals, groups, departments, and subdivisions will have more authority delegated to them. The old saying "out of sight, out of mind" applies here as well, although this is changing somewhat as computers enable management to have information that allows it to control performance from a distance. Thus, even if out of sight, they are not out of mind, regardless of where they are located. However, top management does not want to overburden itself with decisions. Even if it has the information, which it might have had before, it still may not have the time, or the expertise, to make the decisions.

Choosing the Appropriate Structure

Any structure chosen must match strategy, management philosophy, environment, size, technology, and geographic dispersion. Other factors also must be considered: organizational culture, management systems, management style, characteristics of employees, and the informal organization. In addition, Peter Drucker suggests that the structural options should be evaluated in light of the following criteria.

- Clarity, as opposed to simplicity. The Gothic cathedral is not a simple design, but your position inside it is clear; you know where to stand and where to go. A modern office building is exceedingly simple in design, but it is very easy to get lost in one; it is not clear.
- Economy of effort to maintain control and minimize friction.

FIGURE 9.7 THE RELATIONSHIPS BETWEEN CERTAIN ORGANIZATIONAL CHARACTERISTICS AND TECHNOLOGY

	UNIT OR SMALL BATCH	MASS PRODUCTION	PROCESS MANUFACTURING
MEDIAN LEVELS OF MANAGEMENT	3	4	6
MEDIAN EXECUTIVE SPAN OF CONTROL	4	7	10
MEDIAN SUPERVISORY GAIN OF CONTROL	23	48	15
MEDIAN DIRECT TO INDIRECT LABOR RATIO	9:1	4:1	1:1
MEDIAN INDUSTRIAL TO STAFF WORKER RATIO	8:1	5.5:1	2:1

SOURCE: JOAN WOODWARD, INDUSTRIAL ORGANIZATION: THEORY AND PRACTICE (LONDON: OXFORD UNIVERSITY PRESS, 1965), PP. 52–62. BY PERMISSION OF THE OXFORD UNIVERSITY PRESS.

- Direction of vision toward the product rather than the process, the result rather than the effort.
- Understanding by each individual of his or her own task, as well as that of the organization as a whole.
- Decision making that focuses on the right issues, is action oriented, and is carried out at the lowest possible level of management.
- Stability, as opposed to rigidity, to survive turmoil, and adaptability to learn from it.
- Perpetuation and self-renewal, which require that an organization be able to produce tomorrow's leaders from within, helping each person develop continuously; the structure must also be open to new ideas.[39]

It is important in designing structures for the macro organization, and in designing work groups and individual tasks at lower levels of the organization, to realize that results are often slow in coming. Westinghouse's redesign effort, discussed previously, required ten years to show a significant financial return.[40]

The Shape of Things to Come

We are in a time of structural change. Organizations are seeking ways to manage their resources better. Environments are changing. The structures that will dominate organizations in the future are uncertain. They may not even exist yet, but trends are identifiable.

As organizations face increasingly dynamic and complex environments, with increased levels of competition, they must create structures that are more responsive to the market. At the same time, they must be able to cut costs. Restructuring to the lean look is one way of accomplishing both objectives.[41]

These laboratory researchers operate almost independently of supervision. In the organization of the future, workers, knowledge workers especially, will operate autonomously. More and more jobs can be expected to become knowledge-based jobs. (SOURCE © Robert Reichert)

Decentralization must occur also. This reduces the need for middle management, and in many cases for support staff. Decentralization makes a configuration responsive to the environment: cutting the middle-management and support staff makes it cost effective. Decentralization also helps satisfy increasing worker expectations for decision-making authority. The implications of this for the U.S. work force are discussed in more detail in Chapter 11.

Organizations of the future may become more like professional bureaucracies, even though they may produce what machine bureaucracies do now. As operating core employees become more expert and make more decisions on their own, the need for technostructure decreases. On the other hand, one recurring theme is the SBU type of organization, with a small corporate staff, with small, usually functional, independent businesses as the primary form of organizational effort. Adhocracy may also be used more because of its flexibility. Honda employs a version of this very successfully, as noted earlier.[42] In another view of the adhocracy, Peter Drucker suggests that the symphony orchestra may be a useful model: a conductor and everybody else. He allows for "first chair" type positions, for coordination. His major point is that the organization is going to get a lot flatter and have far fewer managers.[43]

One very important final factor is that the organization must be developing its structure for the anticipated future environment and in anticipation of future strategy. It should not wait until the strategy is in place to think about structure. It should be changing structure to meet the requirements of the new strategy.[44]

Organizational Design as a Problem-Solving Process

The situational/contingency approach to organizational design is a complex problem-solving process involving a larger number of interdependent variables.[45] Examining Figure 8.13 in conjunction with Figure 9.8 will help you understand the issues involved and the complexity of the process. Most of the key terms and concepts examined in this chapter could be placed under more than one stage of problem solving in Figure 9.8. They have been placed under the stage(s) where they are significant factors.

FIGURE 9.8 ORGANIZATION DESIGN AS A PROBLEM-SOLVING PROCESS

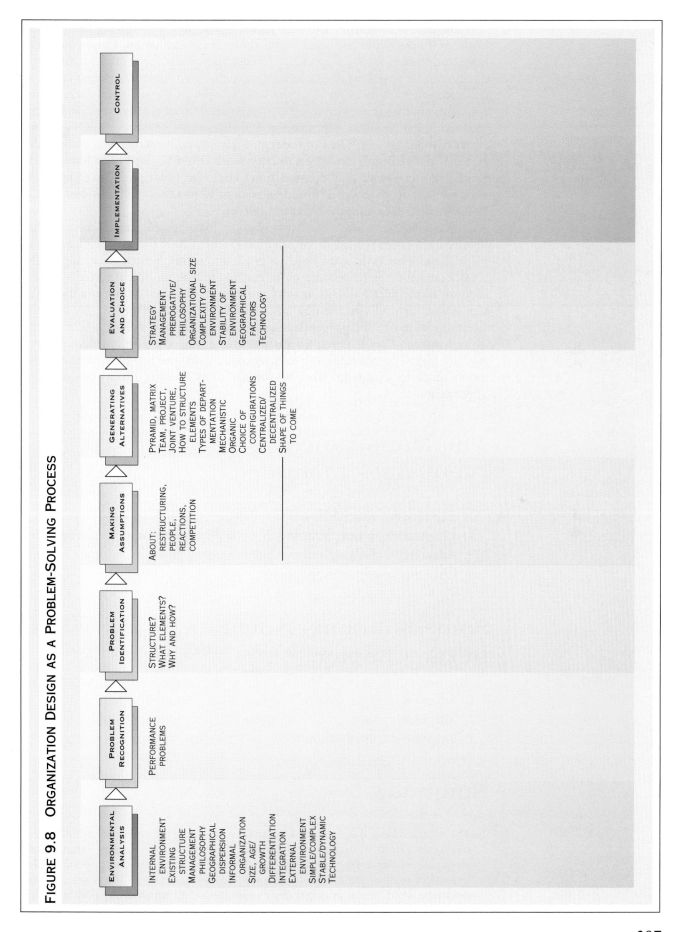

ENVIRONMENTAL ANALYSIS

INTERNAL
ENVIRONMENT
EXISTING
STRUCTURE
MANAGEMENT
PHILOSOPHY
GEOGRAPHICAL
DISPERSION
INFORMAL
ORGANIZATION
SIZE, AGE/
GROWTH
DIFFERENTIATION
INTEGRATION
EXTERNAL
ENVIRONMENT
SIMPLE/COMPLEX
STABLE/DYNAMIC
TECHNOLOGY

PROBLEM RECOGNITION

PERFORMANCE
PROBLEMS

PROBLEM IDENTIFICATION

STRUCTURE?
WHAT ELEMENTS?
WHY AND HOW?

MAKING ASSUMPTIONS

ABOUT:
RESTRUCTURING,
PEOPLE,
REACTIONS,
COMPETITION

GENERATING ALTERNATIVES

PYRAMID, MATRIX
TEAM, PROJECT,
JOINT VENTURE,
HOW TO STRUCTURE
ELEMENTS
TYPES OF DEPART-
MENTATION
MECHANISTIC
ORGANIC
CHOICE OF
CONFIGURATIONS
CENTRALIZED/
DECENTRALIZED
SHAPE OF THINGS
TO COME

EVALUATION AND CHOICE

STRATEGY
MANAGEMENT
PREROGATIVE/
PHILOSOPHY
ORGANIZATIONAL SIZE
COMPLEXITY OF
ENVIRONMENT
STABILITY OF
ENVIRONMENT
GEOGRAPHICAL
FACTORS
TECHNOLOGY

IMPLEMENTATION

CONTROL

A manager would work through Figure 9.9 as in the following example. A problem is detected in performance for the entire organization. Competitors are making decisions faster, responding to customer needs more quickly, and producing products at lower cost. In analyzing the environment, top management concludes that the existing structure worked well in a simple and stable environment, but that the environment has become complex and dynamic. In further identifying the problem, top management determines that there are too many layers of management. Some of the typical assumptions made might include the fact that the same amount of productive work could be done with fewer managers being involved, that decision times could be faster with fewer levels of management, that customers could be responded to faster, and that cost would be lowered by lessening the overhead burden.

Several alternative ways of cutting middle management are discussed. Also involved are issues related to information systems, how the work will continue to be done, what tasks must be reassigned, and so on. Several decisions result. The organization is to become more organic and more decentralized—flatter, in terms of the pyramid. During implementation, an improved information system is installed to assist the flow of information because there are fewer managers to summarize and process it. A significant number of managers (20 percent of all managers) are either given early retirement or are terminated with three months' pay. Top management follows costs, customer reaction time, and decision times to determine whether the decisions to alter macro design were appropriate.

The Management Challenges Identified

1. The need for restructuring
2. Choosing the proper structure in a complex organizational environment
3. Adapting to changing external environments
4. Changing employee expectations

Some Solutions Noted in the Chapter

1. Adhocracy
2. Adapt (or die)
3. Increased decentralization

Summary

1. The organizational design process consists of analyzing the environment and determining the effects of each of the following major factors on strategy: strategy, environment, management philosophy, size, technology, and geographic dispersion. The impacts of each of these must be balanced against each other. The manager must determine which of the principal departmentations and which of the principal configurations to use and how the structural elements should be characterized.

2. **a.** Strategy: Strategy leads to structure, but sometimes structure leads to strategy. It is clear that certain strategies must have certain structures in order for them to be successful.

   b. Environment: Environment and strategy are closely related. Environment affects structure because it impacts on strategy. It also affects structure in the following ways: subunits of the organizations must differentiate to their specific subsections of the environment; organization and environment are characterized in four ways as combinations of simple and complex, stable and dynamic. The resulting four types of environments call for specific types of organizational structures relative to combinations of mechanistic and organic structures, centralized and decentralized structures.

   c. Management philosophy: Managers may choose to structure at any time according to their beliefs about how structure will affect their ability to manage.

   d. Size: As organizations grow, they typically pass through a series of stages from simple to functional to product to SBU structures. Similarly, they may move from simple to either machine bureaucracy or professional structures to professional bureaucracies to divisionalized forms, to adhocracies. They pass through stages of evolutionary and revolutionary growth affecting centralization and decentralization, control, formalization, and complexity.

   e. Technology: Technology principally affects small units of an organization—those that are technologically driven—but can have an effect on any part of the organization and on any position.

   f. Geographic dispersion: As organizations continue to become global, or for those geographically dispersed domestically, organization structures follow certain patterns. They are normally decentralized.

3. Mechanistic organizations are highly specialized, task oriented, rigidly defined, hierarchical, highly controlled, usually centralized, and top-down communicators in nature. Organic organizations are continually defining tasks, generalized in their role definitions, characterized by vertical communication in both directions, collaborative, and knowledge based.

4. The simple structure is simple: owner and subordinates. Professional bureaucracy depends on the knowledge of its operating core. Machine bureaucracy is highly task oriented. The divisional form is that which is used for multiple business or division organizations. An adhocracy might be described as an organization that continually reorganizes or as an organization that has no structure.

5. Woodward provided the first scientific evidence that technology affects the design of structure and that matching types of structure to technology would result in higher levels of performance.

6. The shape of things to come is uncertain but seems to be moving in the direction of a return to smaller organizations with simpler structures, to adhocracies, and to large organizations with very little middle line. Organizations in the future may resemble professional bureaucracies, even though they may be machine bureaucracies in terms of operational functioning.

Thinking About Management

1. Think of an organization with which you are familiar. Describe that organization in terms of its structural design and the factors that should create this structure.

2. Describe this organization in terms of Mintzberg's five structural configurations.

3. Describe the type of technology used and its impact on structure.

4. Describe the environment and its impact on structure.

5. Describe the characteristics of the environment and its effects on strategy and structure.

6. Discuss the interrelationships of managerial and contextual factors in determining the organizational structure at General Motors.

Managing After Restructuring

Bradford Oelman is the vice-president of public affairs for Owens-Corning Fiberglas Corporation. He has a spacious corner office overlooking the Maumee River in the company's Toledo, Ohio, headquarters, as befits a vice-president. Mr. Oelman's office is responsible for sending out press releases, lobbying, talking with journalists, and communicating with employees, shareholders, and investment analysts. Until last year, these functions were handled by thirty-one people, but now Mr. Oelman has only one associate and two secretaries.

Faced with the potential of a hostile takeover if it did not raise the value of its stock, Owens-Corning chose to cut costs drastically as one way of raising stock prices. To do so, it restructured, cutting numerous personnel. When the restructuring came, Mr. Oelman had to make several decisions. The first was to determine the priorities of those tasks that had previously been accomplished. The second was to decide which of those tasks should be done in the future. The third was to assess whether his department could perform the tasks, and if they couldn't do them, who could?

Some of the functions clearly had to be accomplished. External public affairs had to be handled, but, the company had always prided itself on its internal communications, as well. For example, it had had six different newsletters to employees, each with its own editor. Monthly videos were made for employees, to keep them informed about what was going on. And the office had formerly taken on such functions as providing clippings of important news events for executives. There was even an individual whose single responsibility it had been to ride herd on the annual report.

Mr. Oelman considered his options.

DISCUSSION QUESTIONS

1. Of those functions noted, which are likely to stay and which go? Why?
2. How could former employees be utilized while the company saved money?
3. If the company, in fact, hired numerous outside firms to do most of the work that had been done internally and at essentially the same cost as former employees' combined salaries, what real benefit—that is, cost reduction—would accrue to the firm?
4. What are the disadvantages of having outside firms do such work as lobbying, public relations, and the preparation of testimonies for officials called to testify in court or before various legislative bodies, such as Congress?

SOURCE: "How a Manager Manages in Wake of Big Staff Cuts," *Wall Street Journal* 4 May, 1987, p. 12.

Fiberglas Tower, the headquarters of Owens/Corning Fiberglas Corporation, is located in Toledo, Ohio. (Courtesy Owens/Corning Fiberglas Corporation)

Somebody Has to Be Let Go

Ken was a senior vice-president of one of the nation's leading quality consulting firms. In four years the makeup of the company had expanded from the founder, a secretary, two full-time trainers, and four part-time trainers, to 125 full-time employees. Fifteen of these were full-time "account executives," trainers with limited sales responsibility, and with limited customer-service responsibility. About 70 percent of the company's revenues came from offering training courses on quality management to clients. Revenues and profits had grown by leaps and bounds. But in the summer of the fourth year, the last academic quarter of this largely training-course firm, revenues dropped drastically as the economy hit a mild recession and expected sales from the company's biggest client, IBM, failed to materialize.

Ken was assigned the task of determining what to do structurally. Losses were projected for this quarter, and the president and chairman of the board—the founder—had decreed that as many of the work force as were not productive had to be let go. A target of twenty-five people had been set. Ken had been placed in charge of a three-person task force, and given one week to develop a plan, including the names of those to be released and the timing of their releases. All releases had to be completed within three weeks.

The company had grown so rapidly that it had not had time to complete job descriptions for any of the jobs in the company. It was common knowledge that a lot of people, including some account executives, were sitting around doing nothing a lot of the day. There had never been any evaluations of employees, other than those of the training staff.

At the end of the briefing session in which Ken was assigned this task, the president commented: "Good luck, you are going to need it."

DISCUSSION QUESTIONS
1. If you were Ken, where would you start? How would you proceed?
2. The obvious temptation is to do what?
3. How can you rationally make these choices?

Understanding Structural Related Factors

MANAGE YOURSELF

Either individually or in small groups, review or discuss an organization with which you are familiar, one you work for, have worked for, or have belonged to, in terms of how its structure is or was affected by each of the following factors:

STRATEGY   GEOGRAPHICAL DISPERSION

MANAGEMENT PHILOSOPHY   TECHNOLOGY

ENVIRONMENT   SIZE

Was there any impact on structure due to:

THE INFORMAL GROUP?

Once individuals or groups have completed their review of discussion, observations should be shared with the class.

CHAPTER TEN

Job Design

CHAPTER OBJECTIVES

By the time you complete this chapter, you should be able to

1. Describe the situational model of job design and its component parts.
2. List and define each of the five core job dimensions and the three contextual dimensions that help define a job.
3. Describe each of the following job design programs: work simplification, job rotation, job enlargement, job enrichment, autonomous work teams, and quality circles.
4. Describe a typical job-enrichment program in terms of the core job dimensions model, including the critical psychological states, the related implementation concepts, and the personal and work outcomes.
5. Indicate how the growth need is a moderating factor in job enrichment.
6. Indicate how technology, especially robotics and personal computers, affect job design.
7. Indicate how the changing nature of the work force and its expectations and values affect job design.
8. Describe job design as a problem-solving process.

CHAPTER OUTLINE

A Situational Model of Job Design
Structural Elements at the Micro Level
Job Design and the Quality of Work Life
Job Redesign Efforts
    Job Enlargement and Job Enrichment
    Work Simplification
    Job Rotation
Job Redesign at the Group Level
    Autonomous Work Teams
    Quality Circles
How Job Redesign Works
    Reflections on Job Enrichment
    Matching Job Design to Individual Growth Needs
    The Effects of Job Redesign on Other Jobs
Technology and Job Design
    Robotics
    Office Automation
    Work at Home
    Worker Expectations
Time Also Influences Work Design
    Part-Time Workers
    Compressed Work Week
    Job Sharing
Job Design as a Problem-Solving Process
The Management Challenges Identified
Some Solutions Noted in the Chapter

Work Redesign at Volvo

In the late 1960s and early 1970s, Saab and Volvo, two of Sweden's major automobile companies, faced a series of complex personnel problems. Sweden has a small, homogeneous population and a very stable government with a high level of state-supported services (cradle to grave). Swedes tend to be highly educated and have high levels of personal expectation. Consequently, in most of these firms' facilities, turnover was 50 percent or higher annually, with absenteeism approaching 20 percent. Because very few students graduating from Swedish high schools wanted to take factory jobs, the firms had a 58 percent foreign work force. Both Saab and Volvo engaged in work redesign efforts incorporating work-group teams. Efforts were made both to increase the number of tasks each worker would perform and to allow each worker—as an individual or as a member of a group—to make more decisions. Job enlargement and job enrichment were the respective goals. Saab's efforts met with both positive and negative consequences. It was forced to abandon one project but found others to be successful. Volvo's efforts also met with mixed results—one effort was successful, one was largely unsuccessful.

Despite the mixed results, Volvo committed itself to a major organizational design and job redesign effort. Its new automobile plant at Kalmar was built from the ground up to incorporate job enlargement, job enrichment, job rotation, and autonomous work teams. The Kalmar plant is noted for the following characteristics:

1. Unique physical plant.
2. Large windows on the exterior of the plant.
3. The team approach.
4. The use of computers to help teams manage.
5. The job design to give each worker a maximum number of tasks and authority to do those tasks.

The plant is not without criticism. It costs 10 to 30 percent more than a conventional plant to produce the same automobile, and its production capacities are extremely limited, as compared to U.S. plants because of the reduced levels of specialized labor, and the increase in decision making by employees. However, the results have been satisfactory, according to Volvo executives: improved quality, improved worker attitudes, lower absenteeism and turnover, and reduced numbers of supervisory personnel. Even fifteen years after its inception, the Kalmar Volvo plant was performing well, beyond expectations.

Confronted with similar problems in the mid-1980s—a 24 percent absenteeism rate at one plant, for example—Volvo moved even further into work redesign with its Uddevalla plant. In fact, Volvo claims that this plant has totally abandoned the assembly line. Work teams of from eight to ten people totally assemble a car in one location. Each car is attached to a "tilt," which lifts and rotates the car body as workers assemble it. Parts appear as if by magic in this industrial Disneyland, arriving on carts guided by magnetic strips in the floor.

The plant is essentially run by the workers. Weekly production goals are set by assembly teams in consultation with management. Ten thousand units a year are assembled in this 85,000-square-foot facility, but Volvo officials promise that 40,000 units will be produced annually by 1991. Assembly teams are 57 percent male, 43 percent female. Some teams report having difficulties coping with management responsibilities.

Although friction occurs occasionally between top management and the work teams and within the work teams, few wish to return to the old ways with management making all of the decisions.

SOURCES: Berth Jonsson and Alden G. Lank, "Volvo: A Report on the Workshop on Production Technology and Quality of Working Life," *Human Resource Management* (Winter 1985), pp. 455–465; "Kalmar, Ten Years Later," *Via Volvo* (Spring–Summer), 1984, pp. 14–19; "Auto Plant in Sweden Scores Some Success with Worker Teams," *Wall Street Journal* 1 March, 1977, p. 1; Peter G. Gyllenhammar, *People at Work* (Reading, Mass.: Addison-Wesley, 1977); A. Mikalachki, "The Effects of Job Design in Turnover, Absenteeism and Health," *Industrial Relations* (August 1975), pp. 377–388; G. H. Gibson, "Volvo Increases Productivity Through Job Enrichment," *California Management Review* (Summer 1973), pp. 64–66; and William F. Dowling, "Job Design and the Assembly Line: Farewell to the Blue-Collar Blues?" *Organizational Dynamics* (Spring 1973), pp. 51–67.

CHAPTER OPENING PHOTO

For many employees, jobs in the future will involve more decision making and more creativity. Their contents may even rival that of some of today's more exciting jobs such as the automobile design team shown here. Furthermore, the teamwork involved in these jobs will be similar to that necessary in this design team. (p. 312) (© Michael L. Abramson/ Woodfin Camp & Associates)

Without work, all life goes rotten. But when work is soulless, life stifles and dies.

Albert Camus

Today, more and more individuals view their work life as one part of a broader life experience which involves not only job, but family, community, social responsibilities, and the concern for political and economic issues.

Robert A. Sutermeister
Author and expert on productivity

When Volvo managers revised traditional job contents for jobs at their Kalmar and Uddevalla plants, they were practicing job design. Job design is the process that determines the contents of a job, including the associated authority. Volvo's job design efforts were part of a larger organizational design initiative. Two of the most important tasks in which any manager can engage are job and organizational design. While few managers have the opportunity to design a total organization, as did Volvo executives at Kalmar and Uddevalla, most have the ongoing opportunity to redesign the work of those who report to them. Managers most frequently redefine individual jobs and the relationships among them within the work group.

As was portrayed in Figure 1.1, planning leads to organizing. The strategy developed in the organizational strategic planning process or the operational plans formulated by an individual line or staff manager or group of such managers for their departments must be put into place. Job and organizational design are important because they define how the organization will achieve the ends of these strategic and operational plans. Job and organizational design must work in concert.

One of the primary management challenges of the 1990s is to make organizations more competitive. It is increasingly apparent that organizational and job design are major ways of improving competitiveness by increasing productivity. Japanese business organizations have successfully designed work to make it more productive, and a growing list of North American firms has also. Most organizations worldwide will be forced into doing so soon, in order to be competitive. Furthermore, employees are demanding more participation in decision making. To successfully delegate authority requires redesigning the job. Thus, most managers will become very familiar with job design in the next few years, whether they want to or not. As with other management functions, managers are solving problems when they design jobs. This chapter focuses on actions that companies and managers can take to redesign work to meet the management challenges of the 1990s. Unfortunately, not all, perhaps not even most, will choose to employ these advanced ideas.

Job design is situational. Environmental factors, organizational factors, and individual characteristics impact on the contents of any job—its primary dimensions—and on performance and other outcomes expected from its satisfactory completion, as shown in Figure 10.1. The components of the job and its

Two members of an autonomous work team at the Kalmar Volvo plant are shown working on a car attached to the special platform which allows them to control the cars progress through the plant, even allowing for side trips to specialty shop areas where unique items can be assembled into the car. (SOURCE Courtesy Volvo)

AT VOLVO: *Volvo redesigned jobs at Kalmar and Uddevalla according to these four job-design factors. For example, environment: In Sweden, few high-school graduates wanted to work in an automobile factory. Absenteeism in the mid-1980s reached 28 percent at one plant. The job had to be made more attractive in order to recruit more Swedes into the factory. Organizational: The work groups became the focal point for job design. Individual characteristics: Swedes expected to have a satisfying job, so the job had to be designed to make it more satisfying. Primary job dimensions: Authority was one of the elements that was designed at the job level.*

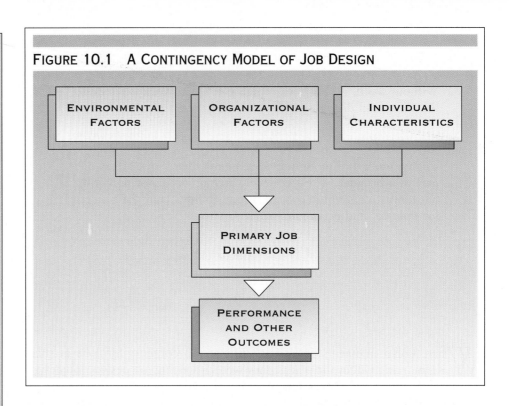

FIGURE 10.1 A CONTINGENCY MODEL OF JOB DESIGN

primary dimensions will be defined following this discussion. Next the contextual factors of the job—the environment, the organization, and the individual— are discussed in greater detail. Such job redesign efforts as job enlargement, job enrichment, and job rotation are then reviewed. The impact of technology on job design is discussed, with an emphasis on the impacts of computers and robotics, and the quality of work life (QWL) and related issues are explained. Finally, job design is portrayed in more depth as a problem-solving process.

A Situational Model of Job Design

During your life, you will spend more time at your job than you will at any other activity, including sleeping. A **job** is a collection of tasks designed to achieve an organization's objectives. A job can be exciting, glamorous, and rewarding, or dull, monotonous, and unsatisfying. A job can satisfy your basic needs by supplying money to provide food, clothing, shelter, and security. It can satisfy your social needs by providing friends and a chance for interpersonal relations. It can provide esteem, and it may even provide opportunities for self-fulfillment, achievement, and the attainment of power.[1] But a job may also do none of these. Jobs for some people don't even provide enough money to cover the basic necessities of life, much less satisfy those other needs. Furthermore, jobs that may seem glamorous or satisfying to some are not glamorous or satisfying to others. But managers and management researchers are learning that certain job contents lead to more productivity and/or more satisfaction than do others. Managers must design these contents into a job if they are to meet the management challenges of the 1990s.[2]

Figure 10.1 is a situational model of job design. **Job design** is the process of allocating work-related tasks to individual and work-group positions. The outcomes of a job, such as performance and satisfaction, are a function of four major factors:

1. Environmental factors: The economy, the marketplace, society, government, employees and potential employees, unions, and technology are key environmental factors.
2. Organizational factors: Mission, goals, objectives, strategy, operational plans, macro structure, management systems, leadership style, organizational culture, and group dynamics all affect the design of individual jobs.
3. Individual characteristics of the job holder: Personality, needs, self-image, attitudes and values, modes of perception and learning, motivation, and aspirations cause job holders to behave in certain ways in a job.
4. The primary job dimensions: The elements that constitute a job naturally affect its outcomes.[3] There are five core job dimensions and three contextual dimensions, all to be defined shortly.

When designing or redesigning a job, the manager must take into account not only the five elements that constitute a job, but the other three sets of factors that will affect the design of a job and how an individual performs in that job.

Structural Elements at the Micro Level

A job is comprised of tasks, which is its horizontal component, and the authority to accomplish those tasks, which is its vertical component. Each job has varying amounts of these components, known respectively as range and depth. **Range** indicates the variation and number of tasks in a job. **Depth** indicates the amount of decision-making authority available to the holder of that job. Figure 10.2 reveals how a cross section of jobs would contain varying amounts of range and depth. For example, an anesthesiologist has a limited number of tasks to perform but has a lot of authority; a surgical nurse also has a limited number of tasks but has a low level of authority.

Horizontal and vertical structure may be further analyzed in terms of various component dimensions. Five core job dimensions and three contextual dimensions comprise a job. The **core job dimensions,** as identified by management researchers J. Richard Hackman and Greg R. Oldham, follow.

1. Skill variety: the degree to which a job requires employees to perform a wide range of operations or to use a variety of procedures in their work
2. Task identity: the extent to which employees do a complete piece of work and can clearly identify the results of their efforts
3. Task significance: the extent to which employees perceive a significant impact upon others as a result of their efforts
4. Autonomy: the extent to which employees have substantial freedom and independence and a major say in scheduling their work, selecting the equipment they will use, and deciding on procedures to be followed
5. Feedback: the degree to which employees receive, in the course of their work, information that reveals how well they are performing the job[4]

Three additional **contextual dimensions** that help define a job include

1. Interpersonal relations: The extent to which the individual engages in meaningful human interactions on the job with peers, subordinates, and superiors

FIGURE 10.2 TYPICAL RANGES AND DEPTHS OF SELECTED JOBS

| | | RANGE | | | | |
		LOW				HIGH
DEPTH	**HIGH**	ASSEMBLY LINE WORKER AT A FORD MOTOR CO. PLANT	ANESTHESIOLOGIST	COLLEGE PROFESSOR	ASSEMBLY LINE WORKER AT KALMAR	DOCTOR	COMPANY PRESIDENT
	LOW	TYPICAL ASSEMBLY LINE WORKER	SURGICAL NURSE	GRADUATE ASSISTANT	ASSEMBLY LINE WORKER WITH "ENLARGED" JOB	NURSE IN A HOSPITAL WARD	MANAGER OF ACCOUNTS PAYABLE
	TYPE OF ORGANIZATION	BUSINESS	NON-PROFIT	NON-PROFIT	BUSINESS	NON-PROFIT	BUSINESS

SOURCE: ADAPTED FROM JAMES L. GIBSON, JOHN M. IVANCEVICH, JAMES H. DONNELLY, JR., ORGANIZATIONS: BEHAVIOR, STRUCTURE, PROCESSES, 6TH ED. (PLANO, TEX: BPI, 1988), FIGURE 13.2, P. 466.

2. Authority and responsibility for goal setting: The degree of authority and responsibility delegated to and inherent in a position—particularly the amount of latitude an individual has in setting objectives

3. Communication patterns: Formal and informal communications associated with a job[5]

You will observe that skill variety deals principally with the primary structural element of range. Autonomy, feedback, and authority and responsibility for goal setting deal primarily with depth. Task identity and task significance relate to the degree of need satisfaction an individual might have, relative to self-esteem. Interpersonal relationships and communication patterns relate to satisfying social needs on the job. While much attention has been given to the five core job dimensions, the three contextual dimensions should not be overlooked, as Management Challenge 10.1 reveals.

These eight dimensions affect both the design of the job and the outcomes of the job holder's efforts—the consequences of work to the individual, the organization, and the society. North American business organizations have become extremely interested in how all of these dimensions fit together in the design of a job. Many have begun to redesign work in an attempt to beat Japanese and other Pacific Rim competitors, who have natural cost advantages because of lower labor rates, as well as advantages resulting from their better utilization of human resources and technology, as the Global Management Challenge for this chapter suggests.[6] General Electric, for example, has adopted a worker-paced assembly line in its Louisville, Kentucky, dishwasher plant. Why? Because GE needed the increased quality, the resulting lower cost of warranty repairs, the associated reduced level of customer complaints, and an overall lower cost of the product—all of which have enabled them to compete better. Traditionally GE and other appliance manufacturers have employed continuous assembly lines without worker control. This GE line, however, moves faster than a continuous line would, and yet workers don't object and quality is still better. Units with problems are placed aside for repair at a later time.[7]

These eight factors are what constitute a job. When a manager, the individual job holder, a personnel specialist, or a consultant attempts to design or redesign a job, the eight factors are the building blocks they use. When a job is designed

General Motors' Problems in Job Design

As discussed in Chapter 8, General Motors experienced a number of difficulties at its Lordstown, Ohio, plant. Despite the fact that the plant was capable of assemblying one-hundred cars per hour, workers refused to assemble more than sixty-five. Much of the problem lay in the design of work, especially in the related perceived dehumanizing of the work situation with the use of so much technology. Other GM plants began experiencing similar complaints by workers. GM examined the situation carefully and came to several conclusions about the design of work. One of them was that some effort had to be made to improve morale by increasing the amount of allowed human interaction.

As a result of this examination, and of extensive negotiations between the union and the company, GM finally instituted two breaks on each shift at Lordstown, so that workers could interact with friends. Morale improved significantly in the plant. GM recognized that, although it is desirable from a productivity viewpoint to keep interaction to a minimum, there must be some interaction, or workers will feel so alienated they may rebel.

SOURCE: J. H. Foegen, "Job Socializing: 'Endangered Species'?" *Industrial Management* (July–August, 1984), pp. 10–12.

for a salesperson, secretary, company president, director of purchasing, carpenter, airline pilot, or for any other job, it will consist of varying contents from each of these eight dimensions. A job can have more or less task variety, identity, significance, autonomy, feedback, interpersonal relations, goal setting or communication. It is the job designer's responsibility to ensure that the appropriate levels of each of the factors are designed into the job.

When these dimensions are combined in appropriate levels and conditions, they may provide job satisfaction for the individual job holder. Satisfaction is important inasmuch as it is often related to levels of productivity—although not necessarily on a one-for-one basis. Normally, however, individuals who are satisfied in their work tend to perform at higher levels than those who are not.[8]

Job Design and the Quality of Work Life

Believing that job satisfaction leads to higher levels of performance, and that providing a satisfying workplace is an important goal for an organization, many organizations have become concerned with the **quality of work life** (QWL).[9] The term has come to be defined in several ways but essentially means improving the satisfaction of individual needs in the workplace. Richard E. Kopelman suggests that QWL is now generally accepted as "a philosophy of management that enhances the dignity of all workers; introduces changes in a organization's culture; and improves the physical and emotional well-being of employees."[10] Richard E. Walton suggests that an assessment of an organization's quality of work life should review the following eight criteria:

1. Adequate and fair compensation
2. Safe and healthy working conditions
3. Immediate opportunity to use and develop human capacities
4. Future opportunity for continued growth and security
5. Social integration in the work force
6. Employee rights to privacy, speech, equity, and due process
7. The balance between one's role as work related and the rest of one's life
8. A socially responsible work organization[11]

Criteria numbers 2, 3, 4, 5, and 7 are directly concerned with job design. This is not surprising because QWL is about work, and most of work is concerned with the job itself. The content of the job, which is the condition of the primary job dimensions, must eventually be matched with the needs and personality and other characteristics of that job's occupant. Many companies have taken actions to improve the quality of work life, including General Motors, Westinghouse, General Electric, and Volvo, by focusing on this match of individuals to their jobs.

Job Redesign Efforts

The primary QWL job redesign program options are

1. Job enlargement: Increasing the range of a job
2. Job enrichment: Increasing the depth of a job
3. Job rotation: Rotating someone from job to job
4. Work simplification: Reducing the range and usually depth of a job
5. Quality circles: Increasing the range and depth of a group of jobs
6. Autonomous work teams: Significantly increasing the range and depth of a group of jobs

Most redesign programs focus primarily on job enlargement and job enrichment.

Job Enlargement and Job Enrichment

It became evident in the 1960s that several factors—including increased employee expectations about work, especially in highly specialized jobs—were leading to unacceptable conditions of absenteeism, inferior performance, and even sabotage.[12] It had become evident that we had reached a point of diminishing returns with specialization. Chris Argyris spoke early (in 1957) and often of the incongruity between the needs of human beings and the needs of the organization. According to Argyris, an individual's drive toward maturity is frustrated by organizational rules, procedures, hierarchy, and specialized division of labor. These thwarted needs result in boredom, daydreaming, absenteeism, apathy, negativism, and lowered productivity.[13] Douglas McGregor addressed the same issue, but from the perspective of how managers' leadership style thwarted the needs of their subordinates. McGregor observed that managers who assumed that employees were lazy, unmotivated, and controllable (Theory X assumption) treated them that way, and the results were as predicted. Similarly, managers who assumed subordinates were mature, self-motivated, and self-controlled (Theory Y assumption) treated them that way, and the results were as predicted. Management style, then, leads to self-fulfilling prophecies about the performance of subordinates.[14]

These Texas Instrument employees are part of a project development team, just one of many job enrichment programs at the firm.
(SOURCE Courtesy Texas Instruments)

Frederick W. Herzberg, in 1971, was one of the first people to advocate that organizations increase the range of jobs—**job enlargement**—and/or the depth of jobs—**job enrichment**—as a means of changing these conditions, but especially as a way of improving employees' motivation. By "motivating," Herzberg meant influencing employees to do more on the job or to do a better job than they had been doing. His definition of motivating conflicts with the more traditional view that would accept simply doing the job as assigned—not doing more or better work. (Chapter 13 reviews his views of motivation in more detail.) Job enlargement was not viewed by Herzberg as a way of improving motivation, but rather as a way of slowing the eventual problems associated with specialization of labor. Herzberg viewed motivation primarily as a consequence of providing satisfiers that are intrinsic to the job itself. He stresses working on "motivators"—such factors as autonomy, feedback, and the authority and responsibility for goal setting. His concern is that individuals have a sense of achievement, that they receive recognition, that their efforts produce opportunities for advancement and that they grow as individuals. He thinks that factors that are extrinsic to the job, "hygiene factors," such as salary, relationships with others, company rules, and policies and procedures, do not "motivate." Herzberg comments, "If I kick my dog . . . , he will move. And when I want him to move again what must I do? I must kick him again. . . . It is only when [a person] has his own generator that we can talk about motivation. He then needs no outside stimulation. He wants to do it."[15] Among the many companies that have used job enrichment are Texas Instruments, IBM, and General Foods.[16]

Work Simplification

In **work simplification** the job is reduced to a very narrow set of tasks, involving standardized procedures with little or no latitude for making decisions. Work simplification is the classic result of the specialization of labor. Work simplification goes against the current trend in job design. It might be followed where the job could be done better this way and where workers were willing to tolerate highly specialized jobs—because of lower expectations of a job, as is often the case with foreign workers. Or it might be used in those firms that hire the mentally handicapped in order to provide them with the right amount of challenge in a task.

Job Rotation

In **job rotation** an employee moves from one job to another. It is very effective in a training setting. Bank management training programs typically employ job rotation. Such programs, often lasting as long as two years, give trainees an opportunity to learn how all major bank functions contribute to the accomplishment of the bank's mission. Hospitals are beginning to use this technique, as well, rotating their management trainees through a series of positions over a one- or two-year period. The individual who completes a job rotation program is presumed to be prepared to manage one part of the total system while better understanding the total system. Job rotation can be effective as a means of improving job design and can help improve the quality of work life. Swissair has found job rotation of its managers to be especially beneficial—for example, in improving employees' interest in their jobs. Managers are moved from department to department several times during their careers, often to areas totally unfamiliar to them. The company feels it benefits because managers have a strategic view, not a narrow one; managers are loyal because they appreciate the growth opportunities; and managers learn to work more closely with those in other departments.[17] Some rotation programs, however, prove frustrating because the employee has multiple dull, boring jobs, instead of just one.

Job Redesign at the Group Level

Two very important job redesign efforts at the group level are autonomous work teams and quality circles. Although work simplification, job rotation, job enlargement, and job enrichment are concepts usually applied to individuals, the principles involved can be applied to groups just as easily.

Autonomous Work Teams

Applying job enrichment to groups, in the sense of increasing depth—autonomy in decision making—creates what are known as autonomous work teams. **Autonomous work teams** are self-managed work teams that have the authority to accomplish work-group objectives. Because much of the work is performed in groups, the group is a natural unit around which to design jobs. Jobs are designed interdependently, rather than separately. Autonomous work groups may establish the pace of control, the distribution of tasks among members, the group's membership, training and development of members, and perhaps even their own compensation.

Many, if not most, QWL efforts are based on the use of work teams and improving teamwork within work groups. M&M Mars recently opened a new plant in Waco, Texas, that is run by self-managing work teams. Similarly, the Skippy Peanut Butter plant in Little Rock, Arkansas, has no fixed jobs, no fixed job descriptions, no inspectors, and no supervisors. A general manager, a human resources manager, and a quality manager act as advisors to the one hundred or so employees, who, through the process of consensus, arrive at decisions. Numerous other such programs are being experimented with today.[18]

Quality Circles

Quality circles are another group-based job redesign program. Lori Fitzgerald and Joseph Murphy describe quality circles as groups that "consist of three to twelve employees who perform the same work or share the work area. They

These Skippy Peanut Butter employees do not have fixed jobs. They rotate among the work stations as necessary according to group-derived decisions. (SOURCE © Ken Kerbs)

functionally meet on a regular basis, normally one hour per week on company time, in order to apply specific techniques and tools, learned in extensive training, to problems affecting their work and work area. Subsequently, they present solutions and recommendations to their management for the authorization of these solutions."[19] To a much lesser degree than autonomous work teams, quality circles offer limited job enrichment. Their principal concern is solving problems related to their work but, in a sense, quality circles provide task variety, identity, significance, autonomy, and feedback, even if only to a limited degree. They also provide increased levels of interpersonal behavior and communication. Hence, they satisfy all eight job dimensions to some degree.

Most Fortune 500 firms have at least investigated quality circles, and a large number of them have tried them. Quality circles are usually introduced in manufacturing and in highly competitive clerical areas such as claim processing in insurance companies. Although not traditionally thought of as a job design technique, quality circles effectively produce some of the same results: high levels of internal work motivation, high-quality performance, and increased levels of satisfaction.[20] Quality circles are discussed in more detail in Chapter 14.

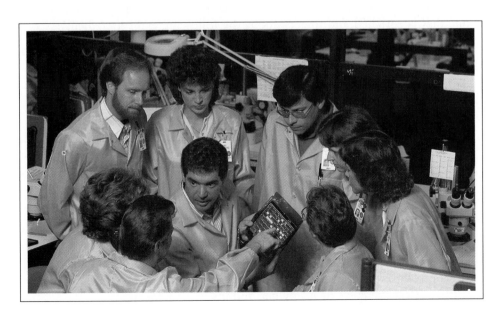

This Westinghouse quality circle is examining an electronic device to determine how to better manufacture it. (SOURCE © Dan Ford Connolly/ Picture Group)

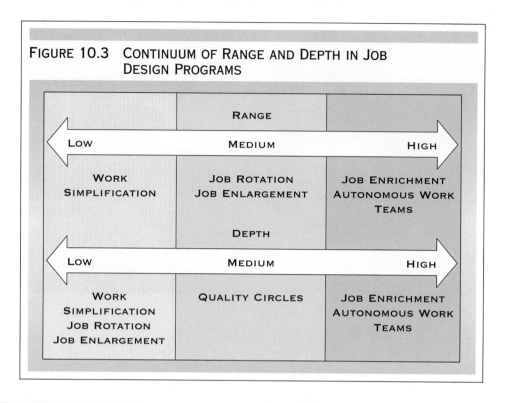

FIGURE 10.3   CONTINUUM OF RANGE AND DEPTH IN JOB DESIGN PROGRAMS

	RANGE	
LOW	MEDIUM	HIGH
WORK SIMPLIFICATION	JOB ROTATION JOB ENLARGEMENT	JOB ENRICHMENT AUTONOMOUS WORK TEAMS
	DEPTH	
LOW	MEDIUM	HIGH
WORK SIMPLIFICATION JOB ROTATION JOB ENLARGEMENT	QUALITY CIRCLES	JOB ENRICHMENT AUTONOMOUS WORK TEAMS

How Job Redesign Works

In any job design effort, the designer works with range and depth. A continuum of both is involved in the major types of job design efforts: work simplification, job rotation, job enlargement, job enrichment, quality circles, and autonomous work teams, as Figure 10.3 reveals. Most simplified jobs involve no depth and little range. Job rotation and enlargement mean increased range, but little if any more depth. Quality circles result in more range and more depth. Job enrichment and autonomous work teams result in substantially more depth.

In Herzberg's view the key to successful job design is job enrichment, the "loading" of a job with the intrinsic satisfiers that add depth to a job. He believes the manager must allow the individual employee to develop, to use his or her abilities in order to want to do the job. According to Herzberg, a "good" job is one that is enriched and thus contains the following eight ingredients:

1. Direct feedback: Information about a person's performance should be made available directly to that person, in a timely and nonevaluative manner. Such feedback is best delivered by a report on the result itself, not through the supervisor.

2. Client relationship: The employee who is responsible to someone who is a client for his or her output, either within or outside of the organization, is more likely to be motivated. There must be someone who depends on him or her.

3. New learning: The employee must have an opportunity to grow psychologically.

4. Scheduling: One should have the opportunity to schedule one's own work.

5. Unique expertise: The employee should have a unit of work with which he or she can identify and which has personal significance.

6. Control over resources: The worker should have control over those factors that affect the costs of his or her outputs.

7. Direct communications authority: A worker should be able to talk with the person who is able to solve a problem, whoever that may be, rather than be forced to run through a lengthy chain of command.

8. Personal accountability: People should feel their job is meaningful and be willing to account for their performance.[21]

Numerous researchers examined Herzberg's job enrichment theories. The large amount of information available resulted in some confusion as to just what *job enrichment* meant. Furthermore, another term, job enlargement, had been introduced and was being used to describe portions of what Herzberg and others had labeled as "enrichment."

Kae H. Chung and Monica F. Ross reviewed the principal treatises of job enlargement and job enrichment in order to identify common characteristics. Their research provides us with a better understanding of the differences between the two concepts, as well as their similarities. Job enlargement "involves reversing the work simplification or specialization process somewhat."[22] In their view job enlargement embodies five basic concepts, any one or several of which might constitute job enlargement:

1. Task variety: More and different tasks are performed.

2. A meaningful work module: By working on the complete unit of work, the employee gains an appreciation of his or her contribution to the entire product or project.

3. Performance feedback: Performance feedback is increased when a larger number of tasks involved in producing a more complete work unit are performed.

4. Ability utilization: Satisfaction (and, therefore, according to Herzberg, motivation) is increased where the work unit is enlarged to permit the use of a wider variety of skills and abilities.

5. Worker-paced control: When work activity is no longer paced by a machine, the employee's desire to control some part of his or her environment is satisfied; again, motivation results.[23]

Chung and Ross define **job enrichment** (labeled *vertical job loading* by Herzberg) as the provision for nonmanagerial employees to perform those functions previously restricted to managerial and supervisory personnel (in essence, increased depth). They view job enrichment as encompassing:

1. Employee participation: Employees participate in the decision process (but only at the level of the job, not at the management level, as with worker councils, junior boards, and so on); thus they feel personally responsible for carrying out their tasks.

2. Goal internalization: Workers set goals for their own jobs.

3. Autonomy: Workers need a high degree of control over the means they will use to achieve the objectives they have set; thus they evaluate their own performance, take risks, and learn from their mistakes.

4. Group management: Because most employees whose jobs are appropriate for enrichment work in groups, assignments and job redesign are often subject to team consensus.[24]

Most authorities on the subject would probably agree that job enlargement is concerned with range and is less motivating than job enrichment, which is concerned with depth. However, most would also agree that job enlargement does reduce boredom, and so in that sense does encourage employees to perform at minimally satisfactory levels. Organizations often pursue both paths. Sometown, Inc., for example, a fairly large, privately held manufacturing firm, redesigned its accounting department so that its junior accountants became product accountants. These people had previously been glorified bookkeepers, but after their jobs were redesigned, they became an integral part of the information management team. Becoming management accountants, they were "motivated" to assume responsibility for managing at least two clerical subordinates. Both job range and job depth were increased, as were task identity and feedback. To a limited extent, autonomy was increased, as well.[25]

Reflections on Job Enrichment

Job enrichment requires a transition in management philosophy for most organizations. It requires more delegation of authority than most firms have historically employed. It requires participative, rather than authoritarian, behavior. The management profession tends to attract people who have a high need for power, a need to control others. This need for control in people who manage others and/or in entrepreneurs was researched by David C. McClelland and will be discussed in more detail in Chapter 13.[26] Job enrichment is not very compatible with this type of personality. Furthermore, in the United States and Canada, unions have generally opposed job enrichment/enlargement programs, or at best have failed to support them. This situation is changing, however.[27] European unions, in contrast, have supported enrichment and participation programs.

And, although the vast majority of workers readily accept job enrichment, job enrichment is not for everyone.[28] Employees who do not want responsibility, who do not share the belief that work should be fulfilling, and who want to do just enough to get by are not going to adapt well to job enrichment or enlargement. Finally, employees who find themselves doing increased amounts of work with no corresponding increase in extrinsic rewards are not likely to be satisfied and, hence, will not be motivated. Thus, managers who initiate enrichment programs must be prepared to reward increased levels of performance. One front-line supervisor told me how he had merged "typists" and "word processing personnel" into the same "word processing pool." Several of the typists quit, partly because they were fearful of the more complicated work; however, one can surmise, that is was also because they had enriched jobs but were not being paid any additional money. After the firm increased compensation, the remaining typists adjusted satisfactorily to their enriched jobs.

Management cannot embrace a single technique and expect it to work for everyone. People are different. But job enrichment works for many people. It is important, though, to keep Herzberg's "hygiene" factors at acceptable levels; otherwise people will be dissatisfied. For example, if pay is perceived as too low, or supervision perceived as too authoritarian, "dissatisfied" employees may be the result.

Imagine the boredom of doing the same thing over and over, year after year. Imagine how your attention might wane. A young worker at GM's Lordstown plant, commented: "There's a lot of variety in the paint shop. You clip on the color hose, bleed out the old color, and squirt. Clip, bleed, squirt, think; clip, bleed, squirt, yawn; clip, bleed, squirt, scratch your nose."[29] This job could be enriched by providing more decision authority to the worker.

Not every job can be enriched—at least not in a manner that pays off at the bottom line. Trade-offs are involved in virtually every situation. Costs must be weighed against benefits. Absenteeism and turnover may be reduced by job enlargement or enrichment, but productivity may decline when jobs become less specialized. Workers may be discontented for any number of reasons. The problem may not be the job at all. Managers must attempt to uncover other possible

AT VOLVO: *Even with Volvo's tremendous success with job enrichment, there are problems. At Uddevalla, for example, workers had trouble coping with the additional responsibility. And there is friction between the work teams and management.*

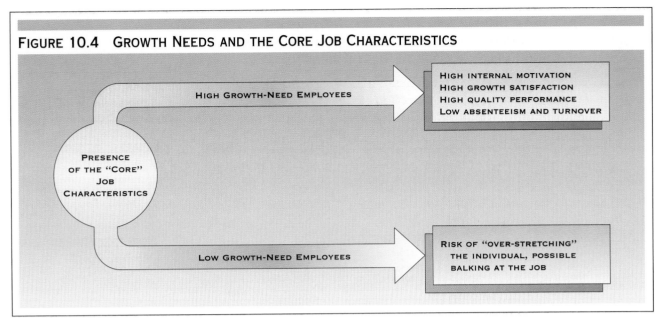

FIGURE 10.4   GROWTH NEEDS AND THE CORE JOB CHARACTERISTICS

HIGH GROWTH-NEED EMPLOYEES

HIGH INTERNAL MOTIVATION
HIGH GROWTH SATISFACTION
HIGH QUALITY PERFORMANCE
LOW ABSENTEEISM AND TURNOVER

PRESENCE OF THE "CORE" JOB CHARACTERISTICS

LOW GROWTH-NEED EMPLOYEES

RISK OF "OVER-STRETCHING" THE INDIVIDUAL, POSSIBLE BALKING AT THE JOB

SOURCE: FROM J. RICHARD HACKMAN, GREG OLDHAM, ROBERT JANSON, AND KENNETH PURDY, "A NEW STRATEGY FOR JOB ENRICHMENT." COPYRIGHT 1975 BY THE REGENTS OF THE UNIVERSITY OF CALIFORNIA. (REPRINTED FROM CALIFORNIA MANAGEMENT REVIEW, VOL. 17, P. 60 BY PERMISSION OF THE REGENTS.)

problems. Bernard J. White analyzed the responses of 1,500 workers who were asked to rank various factors, both internal and external to the job, according to their importance. He concluded that managers could ignore neither hygiene factors nor motivators.[30]

Job enrichment is just one more tool that you can use if you are a manager, or an arrangement that you can request as a subordinate, to improve productivity and the nature of work. It is a form of participative management that functions primarily at the level of the individual employee and his or her supervisor.

Matching Job Design to Individual Growth Needs

J. Richard Hackman, Greg R. Oldham, Robert Janson, and Kenneth Purdy have developed the model shown in Figure 10.5, which relates to the five core job dimensions discussed previously: skill variety, task identity, task significance, task autonomy, and feedback. They also identify the associated critical psychological states that result from the existence of various core job characteristic dimensions. For example, task variety, identity, and significance lead to the critical psychological state of experiencing the meaningfulness of the work. Task autonomy leads to experienced responsibility for the outcomes of the work. Feedback will lead to knowledge of the actual results of the work activities. The authors indicate that these three critical psychological states must be realized in order for people to develop the intrinsic work motivation Herzberg suggests is necessary. Their model is extremely important because it introduces the concept that individuals will not respond to the presence of the five core job characteristics in the same way. Thus, some will reach the critical psychological states and some will not. The moderating variable portrayed in Figure 10.5 is employee growth-need strength. Those employees who have a high need for growth, who want to develop as human beings, will respond favorably to intrinsic job satisfaction. Those who have lower levels of growth need will respond negatively,

FIGURE 10.5 RELATIONSHIP BETWEEN JOB DESIGN DIMENSIONS AND EMPLOYEE GROWTH-NEED STRENGTH

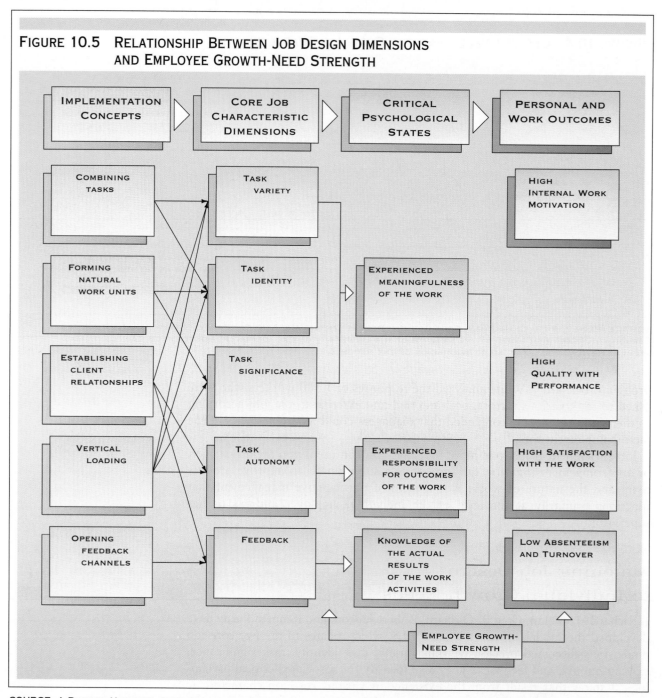

SOURCE: J. RICHARD HACKMAN, GREG OLDHAM, ROBERT JANSON, AND KENNETH PURDY, "A NEW STRATEGY FOR JOB ENRICHMENT." COPYRIGHT 1975 BY THE REGENTS OF THE UNIVERSITY OF CALIFORNIA. REPRINTED FROM THE CALIFORNIA MANAGEMENT REVIEW, VOL. 17, NO. 4. BY PERMISSION OF THE REGENTS.

or at least in a neutral manner, to attempts to incorporate the core job characteristic in a job's design. The relationship between those employees who have a high growth need and those employees who possess a low growth need and the consequences of the presence of the core job characteristics is portrayed in Figure 10.4. As you see, the combination of the core job characteristics and high growth needs results in high levels of motivation, satisfaction, and performance; the combination of core job characteristics and low growth needs results in potentials of reduced motivation, satisfaction, and performance.

In Figure 10.5 the authors provide five implementation concepts that can be used to include core job characteristic dimensions in a job's design: combining tasks, forming natural work units, establishing client relationships, vertical loading, and opening feedback channels. These are important because managers would use these concepts to include the actual core job dimensions in a job. With the exception of opening feedback channels, each of these implementation concepts affects more than one core job dimension. The implementation concepts are defined as follows:

1. Combining tasks: This implementation tactic is the reversal of the trend toward high task specialization resulting from the scientific management approach so commonly used. A variety of tasks are combined into the job, affecting both task variety and task identity.

2. Forming natural work units: The feeling of ownership of the job is increased when an employee is given responsibility for an identifiable unit of work. For example, employees might assemble an entire motor, as opposed to simply attaching the piston to the crankshaft. Forming natural work units affects both task identity and task significance.

3. Establishing client relationships: Allowing workers to become familiar with clients by developing ongoing relationships with them allows employees to gain a new perspective on their work. Establishing client relationships affects task variety, task autonomy, and feedback. How do you establish client relationships in an actual situation? Management Challenge 10.2 provides some insight.

4. Vertical loading: Vertical loading aims to give the employee responsibility for the outcome of the work. It includes such decisions as setting schedules, choosing work methods, quality control, development of other workers, establishing the work pace, and overall problem solving. It affects four of the five core job dimensions: task variety, task identity, task significance, and task autonomy.

5. Opening feedback channels: Providing employees feedback is extremely important to the satisfaction of their needs and to their understanding of their level of job performance. Feedback channels may be either external or built in as part of the job.

The experience of Volvo at the Kalmar and Uddevalla plants exemplifies the implementation concepts shown in Figure 10.5:

1. Combining tasks: Individuals perform more than one task. They can exchange jobs as often as they like.

2. Forming natural work units: A team of workers handles a general area, such as upholstery fitting, door assembly, or electric wiring.

3. Establishing client relationships: The emphasis has been on quality for the client, but distinct relationships have not been created.

4. Vertical loading: Workers are allowed to vary the pace of the work as long as they keep up with the general flow of production. Workers are allowed to solve problems. Workers can switch jobs at a time of their choosing. Workers are in charge of quality control.

5. Opening feedback channels: The workers' quality control mechanism is an internal computerized report for each team indicating the progress, problems, and quality issues.

AT VOLVO: *Volvo accomplished all five of the implementation concepts: combining tasks, forming natural work units, establishing client relationships, vertical loading, and opening feedback channels.*

The Kalmar and Uddevalla plants incorporate all the job enrichment implementation concepts that affect the core job dimensions. The critical psychological states have been reached. Workers experience meaningfulness of work and responsibility for outcomes and attain knowledge of the actual results. Consequently they have increased levels of internal work motivation, they produce a

Bethlehem Steel has been able to improve its productivity significantly and become more competitive by involving its employees in issues of quality, inventory management, customer need satisfaction, and other vital operations management issues. Employees' jobs became much more enlarged and enriched. (SOURCE © Ken Kerbs)

high-quality product with reasonably high levels of performance, they are highly satisfied with the work, and there is lower absenteeism and turnover.

Fortunately, the experience at the Kalmar plant, combined with that of GM's joint venture with Toyota—NUMMI—in Fremont, California, reveals that we don't have to design a plant with a small workshop orientation to obtain the same ends as at Kalmar.[31] We can redesign work using job enrichment, autonomous work teams, and quality circles. Such actions reduce the high overhead cost of a specially designed assembly line but yield the benefits of work redesign.

The Effects of Job Redesign on Other Jobs

Pragmatically speaking, there are only so many tasks and so much authority to go around. If a job is redesigned, an increase in tasks or authority must come from another job or jobs. Similarly, a decrease in tasks or authority means that these must be transferred elsewhere. Tasks may be taken from or given to

1. Prejobs—jobs that occur before the job in question.
2. Postjobs—jobs that occur after the job in question. For example, in order to give an assembler of small motors an additional task, it might be necessary to remove the task of putting the housing on the motor from the next stage in the manufacturing process and give it to the assembler of motors.
3. Other jobs.

Authority may be taken from or given to

1. Those above in the hierarchy.
2. Those below in the hierarchy.
3. Peers in the hierarchy.[32]

Technology and Job Design

Just as technology affects the macro organization structure, as discussed in Chapter 9, it has a major impact upon the structure of the individual job and a group of jobs. Probably no other factor has had as dramatic an effect on job design as the basic element of specialization. Technology, in one form or another, affects everyone's job, whether you are a manager, manufacturing employee, clerk, or an accountant. Many people tend to think of **technology** as machinery and equipment based.[33] But it is more broadly defined as "tools in a general sense"—not only including machines, but also such intellectual tools as computer languages and contemporary analytical and mathematical techniques. In its broadest interpretation, it is the organization of knowledge for the achievement of practical purposes.[34] Most research, especially at the macro level, has been done using the narrower definition of equipment and machinery. But for our purposes, we will consider any form of tools used in any job. Of special interest is the sociotechnical interface—the point at which people work with technology. As technology grows by leaps and bounds, its impact on human beings increases in significance. Two such technological developments are reshaping job design. First, robotics has been introduced into manufacturing facilities at a significant rate. Second, office automation, especially the personal computer, has the potential to reshape nearly everyone's job. One future scenario is almost a certainty: more and more manufacturing jobs will be automated and robotized. This doesn't seem compatible in many ways with increased worker demands for participation. Most jobs in highly automated situations and most jobs left after robotization are rather mundane and routine, often monotonous.[35]

Robotics

Most of the push to increase the use of robots comes from concerns over the ability of the United States to compete, especially with firms from Pacific Rim countries. David Packard, former chairman of Hewlett-Packard, observes, "We

This Mazak automated machinery works 24 hours a day, virtually unattended. Necessary repairs are handled by a day time maintenance crew. While jobs were eliminated by the introduction of such automated equipment, those jobs that remained were much more interesting and required more decision making on the part of jobholders. (SOURCE Courtesy Mazak)

have no choice but to automate because foreign competitors are doing so."[36] Robots have enabled many manufacturing firms to achieve extremely high levels of effectiveness and efficiency. Many jobs that formerly were held by human beings in steel and automobile plants and in virtually any major manufacturing facility are now performed by robots. In some contexts robots have replaced human beings altogether. For example, in the Mazak Corporation's plant in northern Kentucky, from midnight to 8:00 A.M. there is not a single person on the assembly line. The totally automated third shift is busy making parts for the Ford Motor Company and for General Electric Company appliances. If a problem occurs, the machines will shut down and will be repaired the next day. Normally the plant operates all night long without anyone there.[37]

But another scenario is also a certainty: the future will not hold as much robotization as was once predicted. One reason is that experience has taught managers that total robotization is usually less productive than a combination of well-managed individuals and automated machinery working together. The GM joint venture with Toyota to manufacture Chevy Novas—NUMMI—at GM's Fremont, California, plant, has shown quite clearly that this combination strategy works. The Fremont plant, which was once notorious for its inefficient and unproductive work force, became the most efficient and most productive plant in the GM system in a matter of months. The "new" operation uses automation with some robotization but stresses management of the work force as a key factor. Japanese management style, featuring participative management, proved to be a key factor in turning around the plant.[38]

Similarly, Briggs and Stratton, the world's leading producer of low-cost small engines, generally relies more heavily on humans than on technology. The company is semiautomated, but it believes that, through the proper incentives, it can maintain a work force that will be more efficient than a totally robotized work force could possibly be. The company employs a piecework incentive system, and its workers are extremely intense at performing their jobs well. "They even run to and from the bathrooms." Company executives believe that the human being is the most flexible of manufacturing systems, but they are also investing heavily in a new, more flexible, automated manufacturing system. Executives note that the company considers automation whenever possible, but that you will never see them totally robotized. Briggs and Stratton believes that robots cannot improve the system, but human beings can.[39]

Millions of unionized workers are horrified at the thought of robotization. Thousands of unionized jobs disappear every year, and while the major setbacks in the automobile industry seem to be over, there is evidence that technological change may be reshaping our economy. There is great fear that the economy may become segmented into a large number of low-paying service jobs and a few high-paying high-technology jobs. Some fear the middle class may disappear.[40]

A major concern of many is that highly automated, robotized work often reduces the chance for self-management. Not only is the number of available jobs reduced, but those that are left are often reduced in both range and depth. It becomes more difficult under such circumstances, for example, to pace your own work. One of the major concerns for managers in the future will be to reconcile the increased expectations of individuals for participation and for more exciting jobs with the apparently decreasing number of opportunities caused by increasing levels of robotization and automation of all types. Even where managers subscribe to a growth philosophy for employees, their ability to provide growth opportunities may be limited in such cases.[41] Additionally, some people fear change, fear robots, fear a loss of control, and have difficulty working in an environment where there are few people. On the other hand, Apple Computers' experience with robotization has been very favorable, as the Global Management Challenge indicates.

GLOBAL MANAGEMENT CHALLENGE

The Apple Orchard

If you were the chairman of Apple Computer in 1983, you would have wondered how you were to compete in the personal computer industry with low-cost, high-quality Japanese, Korean, and other Pacific Rim personal computer manufacturers. You would have recognized that you had a technological lead with the Macintosh personal computer, but that it could be mitigated by cost factors and the PC duplicated in a matter of months. Steven Jobs, founder and then chairman of Apple Computers, traveled to Japan to learn the reasons for their successful, low-cost manufacturing. He decided that automation/robotization was the appropriate manufacturing strategy.

Apple's Macintosh manufacturing facility in Fremont, California, produces 80,000 Macintosh's per month, one every 23 seconds, with fewer than 300 people, most of whom are not involved directly in manufacturing, but in quality control and distribution. These jobs tend to be more enriched than might have otherwise occurred if it had not been for robotization. The mundane work has been automated, leaving time and the capacity for decision making. The plant was built with the belief that it would be obsolete in as few as two years, with more automation and robotization being required to stay competitive. Peter Baron, the plant manager comments, "We have to be the lowest-cost producer in the world by the time the Japanese figure out how to make a good computer."

SOURCE: Victor Lazzano, "The Automated Apple Orchard," *Discover* (September 1985), pp. 80–81.

Office Automation

The trend toward office automation continues. The power of the personal computer is only beginning to be realized, with the increased availability of user-friendly software.[42] It seems inevitable that every manager, every professional, perhaps even every staff member and operational employee will have a PC on their desk or at their work station before the year 2000. Many firms, such as Travelers Insurance Company, have already computerized their organization, with almost every manager having a computer.[43] The PC is a form of technology that affects almost everyone's job design.[44] PCs allow their users not only to make more and faster decisions, but better decisions. Because the PC handles number crunching, the individual problem solver has the time to be more creative. In fact the PC makes it imperative for an individual to be more creative in his or her problem-solving efforts.[45]

In every phase of the problem-solving process, the manager can be aided by the computer. It can monitor the environment and it can analyze environmental factors with various software packages to indicate potential problem areas or opportunities. It can help, therefore, both recognize and identify problems. The computer can also help generate solutions through what-if scenarios. In evaluating alternatives, in implementation and control, and in monitoring the progress of action plans, the computer can also be of assistance.[46]

One of the consequences to the organization of the increased use of computers and related information systems is the flattening of the traditional pyramid. As more and more computers are networked, the need ceases for middle-level managers and staff to process information up and down the hierarchy. Computers can do that. Hercules, Inc., a diversified company engaged in construction, chemicals, aerospace, and defense, has reduced its levels in management from 12 to 6, trimming about 1,800 jobs (about 7 percent of its work force) with the introduction of a high-speed information network system.[47]

Work at Home

One of the implications of personal computers is that many people can perform their jobs at home. Individuals whose jobs consist largely of data analysis or data processing, such as an insurance claim processor would do, can perform much of their work at home, receiving and transmitting data over telephone lines. The desirability of working at home has been mentioned for many years, especially for people who have low-paying jobs or who have children. Working at home would not be possible for those engaged in typical assembly-line situations, or for those who have to interact with others in order to perform their functions. There are other kinds of problems associated with working at home. People tend to overeat when they work at home, and there is no particular evidence that productivity is increased by working at home.[48]

Worker Expectations

Another important factor affecting job design is the expectation of the average employee with respect to his or her job. While conceptually a job is designed and then an organization seeks an occupant to fill that job, a scientific approach to management does not recognize the realities of the individual job holder's characteristics and their influence on his or her willingness to do the job. It is evident that workers' need levels have risen in Canada and the United States in the last fifty years. Basic physiological and security needs are satisfied by most jobs; if they are not satisfied on the job, they will usually be satisfied by federal government economic support programs. Hence, workers tend to have social,

AT VOLVO: *Several of the conditions that existed in Sweden and caused Volvo and Saab to enrich jobs do not exist, as yet, in North America. We haven't had to import foreign workers to work on automobile assembly lines, and absenteeism levels are not nearly as high. Nor is there nearly as much opposition to being an assembly-line worker as there was in Sweden. But we have had similar problems.*

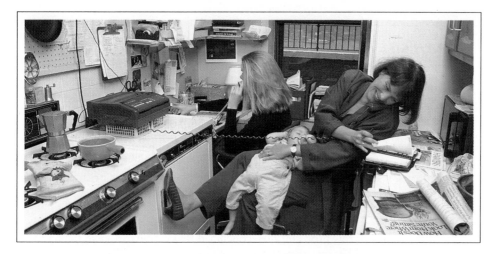

Sunny Bates, shown with her daughter Lola and assistant Ann Turnbull, runs a headhunting firm out of her Manhattan apartment. For people with young children these can be particularly satisfying arrangements, but not all jobs lend themselves to being done away from the office or factory. (SOURCE © Peter Freed)

esteem, or self-fulfillment needs.[49] Because of their higher-level needs, workers want to participate more in the organization's decision-making processes.[50] Workers' life-styles are changing, and consequently they want their work to fit better into the pattern of that life-style. Six of every ten mothers with children under eighteen years of age participated in the work force in 1984, for example, compared with only four in ten in 1970.[51] Furthermore, two-thirds of the jobs created from 1974 to 1984 were filled by women.[52] From 1990 to the year 2000, only 15 percent of the net new workers will be native white males. The remainder will primarily be women and male minorities.[53] Such changes in the content of the work force are generating different worker expectations about what a job should bring. Most of these factors have resulted in a greater concern for the quality of work life, which most often translates into a need for greater job enrichment. Table 10.1 reveals how important various job experiences are to workers. These desired experiences need to be matched to job design.

Table 10.1. The Importance of Various Job Experiences

Rank Order of Importance
1. Chance to do something that makes you feel good about yourself.
2. Chances to accomplish something worthwhile.
3. Chances to learn new things.
4. Opportunity to develop your skills and abilities.
5. The amount of freedom you have on your job.
6. Chances you have to do things you do best.
7. Resources that you have to do your job.
8. Respect you receive from people you work with.
9. The amount of information you get about your job performance.
10. Your chances for taking part and making decisions.
11. The amount of job security you have.
12. The amount of pay you get.
13. The way you are treated by the people you work with.
14. The friendliness with people you work with.
15. The amount of praise you get for a job well done.
16. The amount of fringe benefits you get.
17. Chances for getting a promotion.
18. Physical surroundings of your job.

SOURCE: Patricia Winwick, "What You Really Want from Your Job," *Psychology Today* (May 1978). Reprinted with permission from *Psychology Today* Magazine, copyright © 1978 (PT Partners, L.P.).

Citibank's Job Enrichment Program

Citibank sought to achieve greater consumer market penetration. To do so, it wanted superb front-line employee/customer relations. But when it surveyed its customers, it learned that its employees were not very customer oriented, at least not as perceived by the customer. Citibank recognized that it had a serious management challenge.

According to bank Vice-president George E. Segers, when management examined the causes of this problem, they concluded that employees were failing to be customer oriented because they "didn't feel like somebody." The employees were very dissatisfied with their mundane jobs, and one would have to assume that they therefore reacted in an unenthusiastic manner to the customer. Keeping in mind that everybody wants to "feel like somebody," bank management redesigned many of the front-line and other positions in the bank. The changes included

The reality remains that the workers in virtually all manufacturing situations today have greater expectations than did their predecessors. They want more from the job, just as workers at Volvo did. To accomplish this, more and more firms have moved to job enrichment. Much of these concerns exist in the service industry, as well. Citibank, for example, attempted to provide job enrichment for very pragmatic reasons, as Management Challenge 10.3 suggests.

Another factor to consider in workers' changing expectations is the dual wage earner family, sometimes called DINKS—"double income, no kids." But many double income families do have kids. People in this group expect more from their work than do others. The work force is also aging. The median age in the United States in 1970 was twenty-eight, in 1980 it was thirty, and by the 2000 it should be about thirty-five.[54] Much of this has to do with the aging of the baby boom generation as it moves through the total population, plus the fact that birth rates have decreased and then stabilized over the last few years. Daniel L. Yankelovich, a major surveyor of societal values, talks about the new values of the work force. He sees three key values of increasing importance: the need for leisure, the symbolic significance of having a paid job, and the insistence that jobs become less depersonalized.[55] Yankelovich asserts, "Throughout history, and certainly during the last century, American individualism stopped at the workplace door. Now it is knocking that door down, demanding entrance."[56]

Time Also Influences Work Design

Jobs vary not only by their contents, but also according to when they are performed. In an effort to solve a variety of problems, including worker absenteeism, tardiness, turnover, and the cost of benefits—plus factors such as the desire

1. Delegating more authority so that one individual could handle an entire transaction from the time it came into the bank until the time it was completed.
2. Allowing the employee more customer contact and more computer contact relative to performing his job.
3. Encouraging communications between the various functional departments, marketing, services, and operations.
4. Polling employees as to what was dull and routine about their job before the bank automated those positions.
5. Engaging in substantial training and development for the entire work force.

Considerable training was required because new attitudes had to be formed by managers and workers, and the actual skills involved had to be trained and developed in those who would use them. Citibank has found its program to be quite successful.

SOURCE: Roy W. Walters, "Citibank Project: Improving Productivity Through Work Design," in Donald L. Kirkpatrick, ed., *How to Manage Change Effectively* (San Francisco: Jossey-Bass, 1985), pp. 195–208.

Peter Reformat found himself doing the same job for a lot less money when he was laid off by USX Corporation in 1984. By subcontracting the work to a smaller company USX was able not only to save on Peter's hourly wage but also had no responsibility for Peter's benefit package. (SOURCE © Gwendolen Cates)

by employees to spend more time with their families and to have more personal time—employers have focused on making changes in the hours of work. Among these are flexi-time, part-time, the compressed work week, and job sharing.[57]

Many jobs now incorporate **flexi-time,** a process in which a worker is allowed to set his or her own hours within common ranges, as long as the total is forty hours a week. The individual may choose to come in at 10:00, for example, and leave at 6:00, as opposed to coming in at 9:00 and leaving at 5:00. In a truly flexible time system, the individual could conceivably come in and leave at different times each day and maybe different segments of the day during the week.

Part-Time Workers

An increasing number of jobs that were formerly full time are now being taken over by part-time employees. One of the key reasons is that this helps reduce the costs of employees to the organization. Benefit packages are typically nonexistent for part-time employees, and basic pay rates are usually lower as well. For example, when Pete Reformat was laid off in 1984, he made $13 per hour plus a tremendous benefit package at USX Corporation's Gary, Indiana, steel plant. A few weeks later he went back to work at the Gary works for a small company that had subcontracted the work he had been doing previously. He was paid $5 per hour and had no benefits for doing the same work. Subcontractors employ an equivalent of 7.5 percent of the industry's work force, up from 3 percent in the mid-1970s. Involuntary part-time workers made up a total of 17 percent of all workers in 1986, a figure that had doubled since 1980. When employees who choose to work part-time are included, fully 25 percent of the work force, or 25,000,000 people, are part-time workers.[58] The I & R Company uses job enrichment coupled with techniques to redesign work along varying hours, as discussed in Management Challenge 10.4.

Compressed Work Week

Another variety of work schedule is the **compressed work week**, in which forty hours of work are scheduled to be completed in fewer than the traditional five days. Organizations that have adopted this program include Atlantic Richfield, R. J. Reynolds, John Hancock, and General Dynamics. It is generally believed that the compressed work week offers employees the advantage of an extra day off and offers employers who use the program a means of cutting absenteeism and tardiness. Most compressed work schedules are done on a four-day-week basis.[59] However, the level of fatigue encountered usually increases with the end of each work day, especially on a three-day shift. Companies seem to be dropping out of these programs, although one clothing manufacturing plant has successfully used the compressed work week.[60] The plant improved its productivity in an industry in which a large number of the job holders are single parents who need the additional time for family responsibilities. No lowered productivity at the end of the day was in evidence. They were, however, paid by the piece rate, which may help explain the continuing levels of productivity.

Job Sharing

Job sharing is another form of alternative work scheduling. Typically, two individuals split the day in half, although the sharing could be done on alternating days, as well. Job sharing is excellent for those who have children and don't want to spend the whole day at work, who are retired or semiretired, or who simply don't want to work all day. The employer gains the expertise of two people on the job, and if someone is sick, only a half day of work is lost.[61] Since job sharing is a new technique, it is too soon to determine how effective this program will be.

Job Design as a Problem-Solving Process

As can be seen in Figure 10.6, a considerable amount is known about job design as a problem-solving process. This chapter has indicated the factors to be analyzed in the external environment and the organization, along with the relevant employee characteristics. The key issues identified were technology, computers, and the changing nature of work-force demographics, values, and expectations. To recognize and identify problems, these and other factors must be considered, as must the job's existing design. Generating alternatives for changing a job's design focuses on changing the job's eight key dimensions. Some of the typical alternatives include work simplification, job rotation, job enlargement, job enrichment, autonomous work teams, quality circles, and other participative programs.

Figure 10.6 Job Design as a Problem-Solving Process

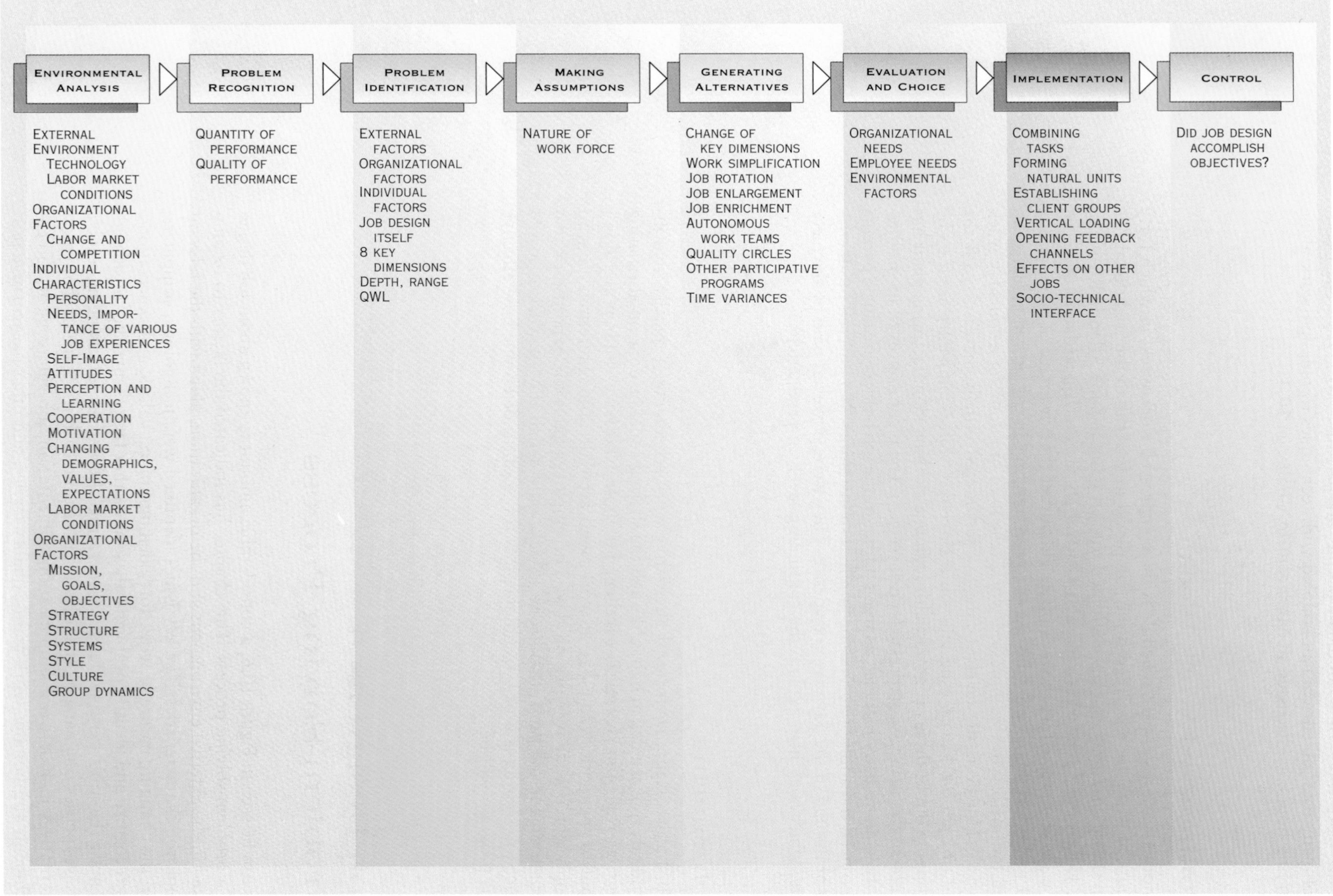

Environmental Analysis

External Environment
Technology
Labor Market Conditions
Organizational Factors
Change and Competition
Individual Characteristics
Personality
Needs, Importance of Various Job Experiences
Self-Image
Attitudes
Perception and Learning
Cooperation
Motivation
Changing Demographics, Values, Expectations
Labor Market Conditions
Organizational Factors
Mission, Goals, Objectives
Strategy
Structure
Systems
Style
Culture
Group Dynamics

Problem Recognition

Quantity of Performance
Quality of Performance

Problem Identification

External Factors
Organizational Factors
Individual Factors
Job Design Itself
8 Key Dimensions
Depth, Range
QWL

Making Assumptions

Nature of Work Force

Generating Alternatives

Change of Key Dimensions
Work Simplification
Job Rotation
Job Enlargement
Job Enrichment
Autonomous Work Teams
Quality Circles
Other Participative Programs
Time Variances

Evaluation and Choice

Organizational Needs
Employee Needs
Environmental Factors

Implementation

Combining Tasks
Forming Natural Units
Establishing Client Groups
Vertical Loading
Opening Feedback Channels
Effects on Other Jobs
Socio-Technical Interface

Control

Did Job Design Accomplish Objectives?

In observing Figure 10.6, a manager might approach a job design problem in this way: Suppose a control report indicates some performance problem and the manager suspects that an employee might be unmotivated. The manager might identify the cause of the problem as job design. Or higher-level management might direct a manager to change a job's design as part of the company's strategy to become more cost competitive in the marketplace. The manager would analyze the situation, for example, the unmotivated employee's characteristics and organizational objectives. In that way he or she could determine what to do with the eight key job dimensions to make the job in question more motivating or more efficient. The manager would have to make certain assumptions about the nature of the individual in the job to be redesigned. The manager would then choose among the available alternative solutions—job enrichment, for example. The solution would be implemented, perhaps through forming more natural work units, or vertical loading. The manager might choose to allow the employee to participate in redesigning his or her job. After a period of time, the manager would then evaluate the effectiveness of such an action.

The Management Challenges Identified

1. Increasing levels of competition in the marketplace
2. Increasing levels of employee expectation
3. Increasing robotization (high tech) in the workplace
4. The changing nature of the work force, in terms of values, expectations, and so on, leading to a need to change job design
5. Other forces, primarily technological, leading to a need to change job design, often in a different direction
6. Competitive pressures demanding increased productivity, leading to a need to change job design
7. The drastic change in the demographics of the available labor pool leading to a need to modify job design
8. The perceived need for an improved quality of work life leading to a need to modify job design

Some Solutions Noted in the Chapter

1. Job redesign, especially job enlargement and job enrichment
2. Quality circles and autonomous work teams
3. Improvement of the quality of work life
4. The use of part-time workers, a compressed work week, or job sharing
5. High touch—increased managerial concern for employees
6. Job enrichment, job enlargement, job rotation, and job sharing
7. Changing macro organization structures
8. More people working at home

Summary

1. The design of a job according to a situational model is dependent upon recognition of the impact of environmental and organizational factors, the individual characteristics of the job holder, and the primary job dimensions. The consequences of the interactions of these four factors are performance and job satisfaction.

2. The core job dimensions are task variety, task identity, task significance, autonomy, and feedback. The three contextual dimensions that help define a job include interpersonal relations, authority and responsibility for goal setting, and communication patterns.

3. The key job design programs include work simplification, job rotation, job enlargement, job enrichment, autonomous work teams, and quality circles. Work simplification involves reducing the job to as narrow a set of tasks as possible. Job rotation means moving a person from one job to another. Job enlargement means increasing the number of tasks in an individual's job, or raising the levels of job range. Job enrichment essentially means increasing the individual's decision-making authority, or raising the levels of job depth. Autonomous work teams serve at the group level to increase individual's decision making, as do quality circles.

4. Figure 10.5 portrays the relationship between job design dimensions and the strength of employee growth need. Generally, by taking one of the five implementation actions, you affect one or more of the five core job characteristics. One of three critical psychological states will be reached, depending on the employee growth need and its strength. If these states are reached, the desired personal and work outcomes will occur.

5. The individual who has a high need level for growth will respond more favorably to the inclusion of the core job characteristics than will one with a low growth-need level.

6. Technology affects job design by changing the tasks necessary in a job. Robotics often eliminates jobs and drains enrichment from those that remain. Computers aid the manager in every stage of problem solving and free him or her to be more creative.

7. Workers expect more from the job in terms of higher-level need satisfaction—participation in decision making.

8. Figure 10.6 describes job design as a problem-solving process in detail.

Thinking About Management

1. Why are so many employers concerned about the quality of work life?

2. Which would you consider to be a "superior" form of job redesign, one that works on range or one that works on depth? Why?

3. Think of several jobs with which you are familiar. Do these jobs need enlarging? Enriching? Could they be performed better by autonomous work teams? What advantages might quality circles have for these jobs? Can you think of jobs that could not be enriched, at least not on a cost-benefit basis?

4. Why do you think so many union leaders typically oppose job enrichment and job enlargement?

5. Indicate how technology affects the design of a job you have held.

6. How has the personal computer changed the design of the job of the college student?

7. Select a typical job and describe how you would use the core job dimension characteristics to enrich it.

Work Redesign at Motorola

Motorola is a major manufacturer of electronic products. It employs 55,000 individuals in the United States. In the mid-1980s it found itself under considerable competitive attack from Japanese firms. The strategic plan called for Motorola to become more cost-effective—in order to meet the challenge of Japanese firms' low prices—and to produce high-quality products—in order to meet the challenge of the high quality of Japanese products. The company's executives, in examining their products, felt that neither productivity nor quality were as high as was needed to compete effectively against the Japanese. To carry out their strategy, they determined to develop a program that would increase employee participation.

DISCUSSION QUESTIONS
1. If you were to design such a program for Motorola, what might its contents be?
2. What types of goals would you set?
3. What types of participation would you include?
4. What would you do to encourage employees to continue to improve productivity and quality?

The Customer Should Be the Focal Point

One of the first actions David O'Neal took when he became director of the Orange County Convention Center was to give his subordinates an interaction survey. This survey asked respondents to indicate the importance of their interpersonal activities on the job. Such a survey is used to determine the need to have certain peoples' offices in proximity to each other, to determine if the right patterns of communication exist, and to determine who or what activity is the focal point of the organization. The results were surprising. The operations manager turned out to be the hub of the wheel in the organization. (See the organization chart.) Interviews with subordinates revealed that, consequently, there were communication road blocks, and that staging the shows and physically supporting them (the operations function) were receiving more attention than the customer. Furthermore, there was really no one in charge of bookings, and there were only two evening coordinators, whose function was principally as a liaison with the client groups (exhibitors at conventions held in the facility). The coordinators were not really spending much time on customer service. David contemplated how to redesign certain jobs and whether to create new jobs.

DISCUSSION QUESTIONS
1. What job(s) would you create if you were David?
2. How would you restructure existing jobs?

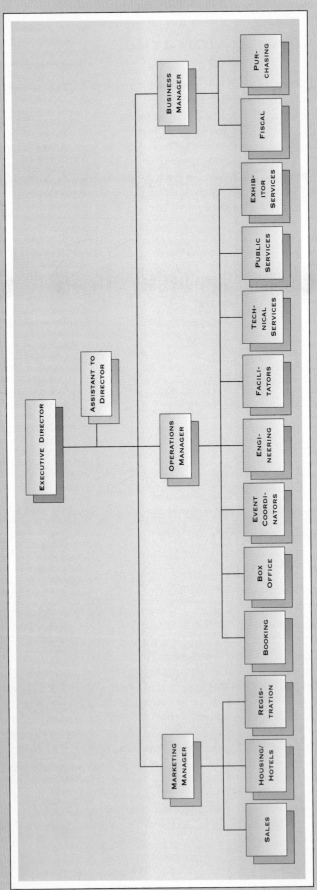

The Eight Primary Job Dimensions

Think about the jobs you have had or the job you would like to have when you graduate. How important have the various primary job dimensions been to you? How important are they to you now? How important will they be in future jobs? What are you looking for in the job you will get upon completion of this course? In the space provided, rank the eight dimensions in accordance with their importance to you, from 1 (most important) to 8 (least important).

Primary Job Dimensions	Rank in Current or Last Job, or Job upon Graduation	Rank in Next Job After That
Task Variety	_____	_____
Task Identity	_____	_____
Task Significance	_____	_____
Autonomy	_____	_____
Feedback	_____	_____
Interpersonal Relationships	_____	_____
Authority and Responsibility for Goal Setting	_____	_____
Communication	_____	_____

Why did you rank these items as you did? What will be different in your future job than in your current job? What do the rankings tell you about your needs previously, now, and in the future?

CHAPTER ELEVEN

Staffing and Human Resource Management

CHAPTER OBJECTIVE

By the time you complete this chapter you should be able to

1. Describe the major trends in human resource management.
2. Describe human resource management practices and their purposes.
3. Discuss the effects of equal employment opportunity laws upon human resource management practices.

CHAPTER OUTLINE

Human Resource Management
   Practices
Equal Employment Opportunity (EEO)
Placing the Employee
Human Resource Planning
   The Human Resource
      Planning Process
   Job Analysis and Design
   Forecasting the Need
      for Human Resources
   EEO Considerations of Job
      Specifications
Recruitment
   Factors Affecting the Ability
      to Recruit
   Matching the Recruit
      with the Organization

Who Recruits?
   Sources of Job Applicants
   The Job Application
   EEO Considerations
Selection
   The Application Blank
   Interviews
   Employment Testing
   Reference Checks
   Physical Exams
   Employment Decisions
   Assessment Centers: Selecting
      Managers
   Realistic Job Previews
Orientation
Training and Development
   Ongoing HRM Practices
Continuing Employee Development
   and Training
Compensation and Benefits/Motivation
   EEO Considerations
Employee Health and Safety
Employee Relations
Managing Change
Employee Evaluation and Control
   Performance Appraisal
   Grievance Procedures
Employee Transitions
HRM and Staffing as Problem Solving
The Management Challenges Identified
Some Solutions Noted in the Chapter

Honeywell's Systems and Research Centers' Human Resource Practices

How does a major, diversified corporation prepare its human resources for the future it foresees? How does it staff better for a competitive scenario? Honeywell was faced with just such a situation. It instituted a "winning edge" program aimed at making its human resource management program more effective. Honeywell believed that management style had to become more humanistic. Consequently, the company has attempted to increase managers' concerns for the long-term aspects of managing human resources. Many participative management techniques—for example, quality circles—were introduced. Jim Renier, president of the control system division of Honeywell, comments: "If people know you are really interested in them, they will respond. Most people want to do a good job, be recognized as intelligent. Interested workers receive information so that they can make informed decisions, derive a sense of self-fulfillment on the job, and experience self-esteem."

The program varies from division to division at Honeywell, but one division that has worked hard to improve its human resource management practices is the Systems and Research Center, the SRC. Tolly Kizilos and Roger P. Heinisch describe SRC's participative human resource management (HRM) approach as one that has become a guide to the rest of Honeywell because the approach worked so well at SRC. Kizilos and Heinisch observe, "We are convinced that a team effort yields better decisions, protects us from arbitrary or careless actions, and above all strengthens team members' commitment to our goals. In our view a boss cannot obtain by decree the creativity, initiative, and dedication needed to do a job properly; such allegiance can come freely only from people who have a sense of 'ownership' of the organization's goals."

The team managers of the center make decisions by consensus in virtually every functional area—for example, resource allocation, facility design, budgeting, funds distribution, and human resource management.

Managers are hired by a team of managers. They may be hired from outside the center or from within, but to achieve a management position, a candidate must be passed by the center's management team. Candidates for the position of section chief are evaluated according to eight criteria which include:

> Past performance at technical jobs; responsiveness to the job requirements of a section chief; interpersonal relations; judgment; creativity; innovation; management values in action; motivation, energy, ambition, and leadership.

The committee evaluates each candidate on the basis of these criteria and his or her relative strengths and weaknesses. Eventually an agreed upon candidate is recommended to top management for approval.

Honeywell's changing human resource management is reflected in its statement of group leadership: Kizilos and Heinisch continue, "Leadership should be the ability of those leading work units (managers, supervisors, engineers, technical support, and group leaders) to create an atmosphere of acceptance, openness, and trust that will properly motivate members of the work units." In Honeywell's view, leadership essentially consists of two parts: interpersonal competencies and administrative competencies. Interpersonally, leaders should care, should be able to communicate skillfully, and should be able to guide and inspire. Administratively the leader should understand his or her job, understand employees' jobs, and be able to take immediate action when necessary.

SOURCES: William H. Wagel, "A Team Approach to Selecting Managers," *Personnel* (April 1987), pp. 4–6; Tolly Kizilos and Roger P. Heinisch, *Harvard Business Review* (September–October 1986), pp. 5–9; Perry Pascarella, "Management at Honeywell," *Industry Week* (July 27, 1982), pp. 23–24; William L. VanHorn and William D. Dimmett, "The Ideal Work Environment: Total Employee Involvement," *SAM Advanced Management Journal* (Autumn 1984), pp. 43–45.

Only 15 percent of the net growth in the work force—those entering minus those leaving—will be comprised of white males by the year 2000.

Hudson Institute's "Work Force 2000" report

Traditional ways of managing a work force don't work anymore.

Donna Taylor
Manager, Valuing Differences Program
Digital Equipment Company

This chapter discusses the topics of staffing and human resource management. **Human resource management** (HRM) is the process of first placing employees in jobs determined in the planning and organizing processes, and then managing those employees, from an organizational point of view, once they are placed. HRM is the process of putting the right people with the right skills in the right place at the right time with the right motivation in order to accomplish strategy.[1] **Staffing** describes the individual manager's role in the HRM process. Honeywell is representative of a number of companies taking a different approach to staffing and HRM. This approach differs from that of most firms of a few years ago in several ways:[2]

- It is more strategic in nature.[3]
- The human resource is now considered to be more critical to mission accomplishment.
- There is a greater concern with the overall governance of the work force, as opposed to just simple labor relations.
- The approach emphasizes managing the culture of an organization.
- There is a trend away from individual job concerns toward a renewed interest in teamwork.
- There is more concern with the outcomes of the process.
- There is a movement from specific skills training to broader development of the employee on a long-term basis.

This Honeywell Systems Research Center researcher is investigating materials for fabricating circuits. His boss reached consensus with others regarding the details of this research effort. (SOURCE Courtesy Honeywell)

At Honeywell, for example, there is an increased emphasis on team management. The employee is viewed as strategic and important, and resource programs have been developed to attempt to improve the utilization of human resources in the organization. There is long-term employee development and a sense of overall management of the human resource, as opposed to simply administering to traditional personnel problems. Results are important and culture is being managed.

In most organizations with one hundred or more employees, there is a "human resource management" or "personnel" department. As an organization grows, as its commitment to human resource management grows, the size, strength, power, and importance of the human resource management department also increase. As the human resource management department grows, the role of the individual manager in the staffing process also changes—normally his or her role decreases. HRM is managed as would be any other function of the organization or as would be any other management problem situation. Planning, organizing, leading, and controlling occur across the human resource management function. As with any other management function, staffing and HRM are problem-solving processes.

Human Resource Management Practices

HRM practices, whether they are part of the individual manager's staffing activities or performed by the HRM department, can be broken into two principal types: those concerned with placing the employee in the job position, and those concerned with the organizational/employee relationship once the individual assumes that position. The two groups of HRM practices are shown in Figure 11.1. The first series of practices occurs sequentially, whereas the second series occurs during the same time period on an ongoing basis. These practices are described in more detail in the remainder of this chapter. Each of the descriptions of these practices is usually divided into three parts. In the first part, HRM practices are described from the perspective of the HRM department. In the second part of the discussion, the individual manager's role in that practice is noted. Finally, because EEO affects each of these practices, observations on relevant implications are noted. Most of these sections conclude with a paragraph describing the manager's role in managing that HRM practice at the individual manager level. This three-part process will help you better understand the setting within which the individual manager operates and what is expected of him or her.

Equal Employment Opportunity (EEO)

As you can see in Figure 11.1, equal employment opportunity (EEO) is an externally imposed requirement that affects each and every HRM practice in virtually all organizations (those with fifteen or more employees, in most cases). Equal employment opportunity laws prohibit the making of human resource management practice decisions on the basis of race, color, sex, religion, national origin, physical and mental handicap, pregnancy, age, or veteran status. Equal employment opportunity is enforced principally by the Equal Employment Opportunity Commission (EEOC) of the federal government. It is also enforced by various state EEO agencies. A number of laws, as shown in Table 11.1, define the principal concerns to which employers must adhere. These laws are refined in great detail in guidelines issued by various federal EEO enforcement agencies, principally the EEOC. These guidelines define what is acceptable and what is not acceptable EEO behavior. Many times, the courts further define what is acceptable personnel practice and what is not. Major issues often end up in the U.S. Supreme Court.[4] Employers must also adhere to state EEO laws and guidelines. These vary from state to state, and in some cases are more stringent than federal laws and guidelines. Every single HRM practice is affected by EEO laws for most organizations. Historically, access to employment was the major thrust

FIGURE 11.1 HUMAN RESOURCE MANAGEMENT PRACTICES

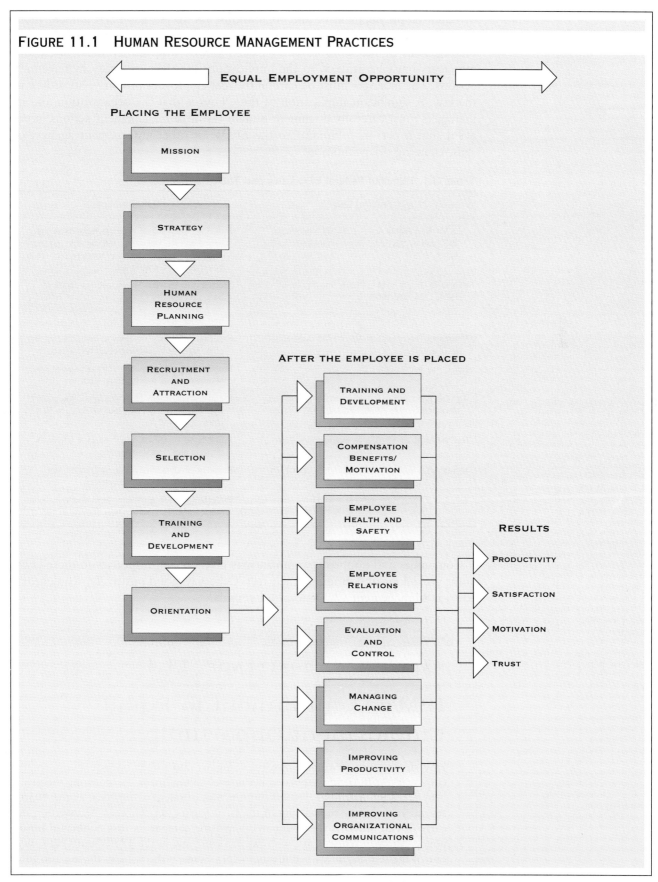

SOURCE: ADAPTED FROM JAMES M. HIGGINS, <u>HUMAN RELATIONS: CONCEPTS AND SKILLS</u> (NEW YORK: RANDOM HOUSE, 1982), P. 328.

of equal employment laws and regulations. As access has been gained, more attention is being given to how employees are treated while employed. Daily management of the work force has been greatly affected by these laws, and managers must be attuned to the implications for their everyday management actions. The manager must be careful to treat employees properly, according to the law. A significant implication of these laws is that the organization and its managers must carefully document human resource management actions in the event that a person complains to the EEOC or other enforcement agency, or sues, claiming discrimination.

Table 11.1. Principal Federal EEO Laws and Their Requirements

Federal Law	Requirements
Title VII, Civil Rights Act of 1964, as amended in 1972 and by the Equal Employment Opportunity Act of 1978	Prohibits discrimination in employment decisions based on race, color, sex, religion, and national origin, for employers of 15 or more employees in both public and private sectors.
Executive Orders 11141, 11246, and 11375, of 1964, 1965, and 1967	Prohibit discrimination in employment decisions based on age, race, color, sex, religion, and national origin, for federal government contractors and subcontractors.
Pregnancy Discrimination Act of 1978 (amendment to Title VII)	Requires pregnancy/maternity to be treated as any other significant disability would be treated.
Equal Pay Act of 1963	Prohibits wage discrimination on the basis of sex. Mandates equal pay for equal work.
Age Discrimination in Employment Act of 1967 as amended in 1978, 1986, and 1988	Prohbits employment discrimination on the basis of age. Specifically protects individuals ages 40 and older.
Rehabilitation Act of 1973 as amended in 1986	Prohibits discrimination on the basis of employee physical and mental handicaps.
Vietnam-Era Veteran's Readjustment Act of 1974	Provides for affirmative action for Vietnam-era Veterans and for disabled veterans.
Americans with Disabilities Act of 1989	Protects 43 million Americans from discrimination in employment. (Legislation was pending in 1989.)

Companies and nonprofit organizations give varying responses to these laws. Some go kicking and dragging their feet. Others respond positively, wholeheartedly, as Management Challenge 11.1 reveals.

MANAGEMENT CHALLENGE **11.1**

IBM's Commitment to Equal Employment Opportunity

How do you turn a virtually all-white company into a bona fide equal opportunity employer? At IBM, it's happened because of commitment. Recognizing the problems faced by minorities, recognizing the loss of talent as far back as the 1950s, several years before the passing of the Civil Rights Act, Thomas Watson, Sr., the early driving force of the company, issued the company's first nonbiased hiring policy. Thomas Watson, Jr., who ran the company in the 1950s and 1960s, was one of the few corporate presidents to speak out on the issue in those days. IBM began recruiting at Black colleges in the 1950s, and it wasn't easy. Blacks were

Placing the Employee

Placing employees in jobs involves all the practices that occur up to the point where the employee is able to carry out assigned tasks on the job. Thus, the practices of human resource planning, recruitment, selection, orientation, and training and development are components of placement.

Human Resource Planning

Historically, the HRM department has been responsible for human resource planning. Human resource planning, often referred to as personnel planning, is the process of determining the staffing requirements necessary to carry out an organization's strategy in order to achieve its strategic objectives. It is part of implementing strategy, as Figure 11.2 reveals. There was very little human resource planning in most organizations until recently. The U.S. military services have, for years, possessed the most advanced forms of personnel planning systems of any U.S. organization. The military has always been a "people business." The armed services have understood the importance of employee planning because they have understood the importance of people to the accomplishment of their missions. Furthermore, because of pressures from time to time to cut budgets, plus the tremendously high levels of turnover and job rotation, the armed services have found it necessary to be able to determine their needs. Their sheer size has also dictated more planning than smaller organizations might need. They have always faced the problem of having enough people with the right skills at the right place at the right time to do the job—the essence of employee planning.

A fuller recognition of the strategic importance of human resources has occurred in recent years. Structuring occurs to carry out strategy. The employment planning function is involved with refining the specifics of the macro organizational structure discussed in Chapters 8 and 9. The job design activity discussed in Chapter 10 is usually considered to be a human resource planning practice and is normally carried out by the HRM department in conjunction with individual managers managing specific job situations. The recordkeeping

often uncertain about going to work in all-white cities where many IBM plants and offices were located. But IBM pursued them, and convinced them to move.

IBM continues to work hard at EEO. Current chairman John Aker's first official policy memo in 1985 was a reaffirming of IBM's EEO position. In 1987 Blacks made up 9.1 percent of all employees and 7.2 percent of the managers at IBM, compared to 8.2 percent of all employees and 5.0 percent of all managers in 1977. Managers must review the company's EEO position each year. Grievance procedures are well defined, and Aker's door is open to anyone with a complaint. People have been fired for discrimination, although, the company notes, it is difficult to police every action. The company also backs its workers. When several Black employees could not get mortgages, IBM threatened to withdraw its money from the bank involved. The employees got their mortgages.

SOURCE: Barbara Kantrowitz and Karen Springen, "A Tenuous Bond from 9 to 5," *Newsweek* (March 7, 1988), pp. 24–25.

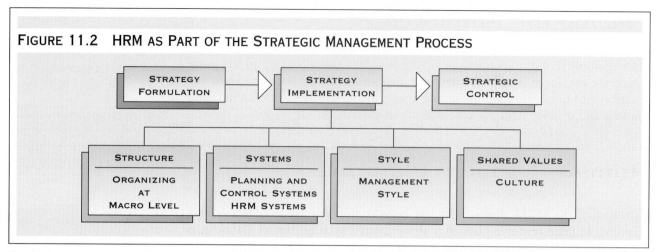

FIGURE 11.2 HRM AS PART OF THE STRATEGIC MANAGEMENT PROCESS

```
STRATEGY          STRATEGY          STRATEGIC
FORMULATION   →   IMPLEMENTATION →  CONTROL
```

STRUCTURE	SYSTEMS	STYLE	SHARED VALUES
ORGANIZING AT MACRO LEVEL	PLANNING AND CONTROL SYSTEMS HRM SYSTEMS	MANAGEMENT STYLE	CULTURE

SOURCE: ADAPTED FROM FIGURE 7.2, STRATEGIC MANAGEMENT, TEXT AND CASES BY J. HIGGINS AND J. VINCZE, COPYRIGHT © 1989 BY THE DRYDEN PRESS, INC., A DIVISION OF HOLT, RINEHART AND WINSTON, INC., REPRINTED BY PERMISSION OF THE PUBLISHER.

and management requirements imposed by external bodies, especially the EEOC, have grown significantly in recent years. Consequently, organizations are creating sophisticated central personnel files and in so doing have found that they can use this information for employment planning purposes, not just for reporting purposes. Additionally, as business organizations have grown, with several now having 100,000 or more employees, and hundreds having 5,000 or more in diverse locations, human resource planning has required more attention.

The Human Resource Planning Process

Figure 11.3 is a comprehensive diagram of the human resource planning process. The process begins with an organization's strategic objectives and plans. The requirements to meet these are then compared with the human resource supply available in the marketplace. Human resource supply and demand depend, re-

The U.S. military must have thousands of personnel available in the right place at the right time. These Marines are undergoing jungle training school in Panama, an effort made possible by a sophisticated personnel planning program. (SOURCE © Wesley Bocxe/ Photo Researchers)

FIGURE 11.3 THE HUMAN RESOURCE PLANNING PROCESS

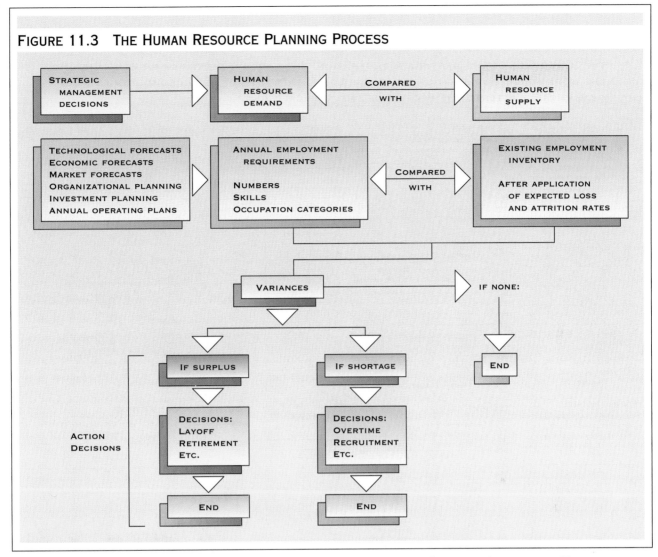

SOURCE: L. JAMES HARVEY, "EFFECTIVE PLANNING FOR HUMAN RESOURCE DEVELOPMENT," PERSONNEL ADMINISTRATOR (OCTOBER 1983), PP. 45–52, 112. REPRINTED WITH PERMISSION FROM HR MAGAZINE (FORMERLY PERSONNEL ADMINISTRATOR) PUBLISHED BY THE SOCIETY FOR HUMAN RESOURCE MANAGEMENT, ALEXANDRIA, VA.

spectively, upon the organization's ability to forecast requirements and upon existing inventories of employees. Variances between demand and supply are then accounted for and decisions made. If a surplus exists, decisions may be made to lay off or retire workers, for example. If a shortage exists, decisions might be made to use overtime, to recruit, and so on.

CURRENT TRENDS

One trend in human resource planning is the "disposable employee." Contingent workers make up about 25 percent of the labor force now. The benefits to the corporation are obvious. By having individuals only work part-time, or for short periods of time, wages are usually less, benefit packages can be scaled way down, and the cost of the worker to the employer is significantly less. An individual might rather keep a job at some lowered total compensation rate than lose it. Another trend in employment planning is a consequence of the shortages of unskilled labor. Because of the change in population mix, a reduced number of people in the eighteen- to twenty-five-year-old age group exists. Therefore, many employers are hiring more older workers. Many employers, McDonald's, for

FIGURE 11.4 THE CHANGING AMERICAN WORKER

THE SHEER SIZE OF THE BABY-BOOM GENERATION, THE LARGE NUMBERS OF WOMEN ENTERING THE WORK FORCE, AND SUCH OTHER FACTORS AS THE GROWTH OF SERVICE INDUSTRIES HAVE DRAMATICALLY ALTERED THE PROFILE OF THE "TYPICAL" AMERICAN WORKER.

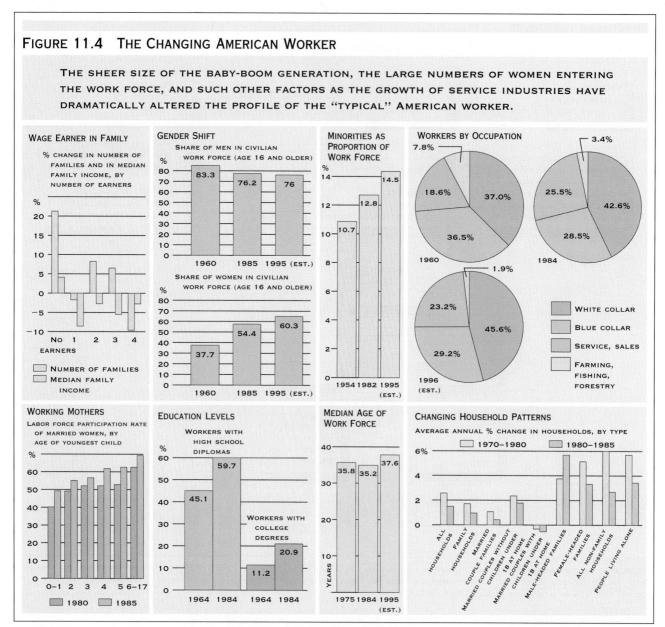

SOURCE: DAVID J. RACHMAN AND MICHAEL H. MESCON, BUSINESS TODAY, 5TH ED. (NEW YORK: RANDOM HOUSE, 1987), P. 193.

example, are finding them excellent employees when placed in the right job. Plus, benefits are often less, especially if they are part-time and already receiving social security.[5] Figure 11.4 details several changes in the demographics of the U.S. work force. Each of these changes will require the modification of HRM practices in the next few years.

The individual manager works within the HRM practice policies established by the total organization, whether those are made by an HRM department or by the president of a small company. The manager may help design job descriptions and specifications but often is involved only to a minor extent in human resource planning. Most managers are not involved in the strategic planning aspects of employment planning, but rather in determining certain aspects of individual job designs and individual job descriptions. Often it is the manager who must hire or terminate people according to the strategic HRM plan. Managers tend to be more responsive and reactive rather than proactive in staffing. The manager's role is portrayed in Figure 11.5.

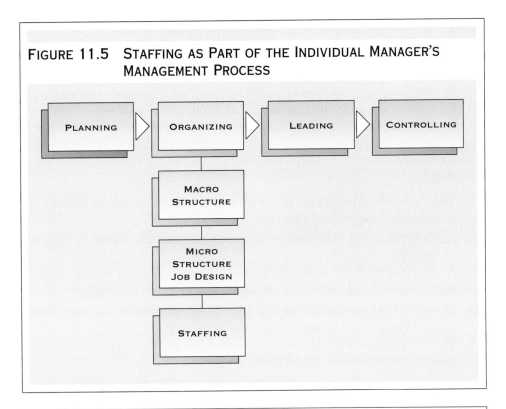

FIGURE 11.5 STAFFING AS PART OF THE INDIVIDUAL MANAGER'S MANAGEMENT PROCESS

PLANNING → ORGANIZING → LEADING → CONTROLLING

ORGANIZING
↓
MACRO STRUCTURE
↓
MICRO STRUCTURE JOB DESIGN
↓
STAFFING

Publix is one of many employers who have found that hiring retired workers for part-time jobs really pays off. With a shortage of available teenage labor due to changing demographics, retired personnel make an excellent source of labor for service industries.
(SOURCE © Walt Johnson/Picture Group)

Job Analysis and Design

Job analysis is a major part of the human resource planning process and ultimately leads to job design. This process helps create the demand portion of Figure 11.3. Existing jobs and potential jobs must be analyzed or reanalyzed, designed or redesigned, respectively, to ensure that they help fulfill the company's mission. Job analysis consists of several steps leading to the job design process. Job analysis begins with an examination of the job and its fit in the organization. It continues with an in-depth analysis of the job using standard techniques. Job analysis concludes by producing a **job description,** which describes the job and its responsibilities and duties, and a **job specification,** which indicates the kind of person needed to perform the job depicted in the job description, in terms of skills, knowledge, and abilities. This job specification is the basis of recruitment and selection. Most job analyses are performed by professional job analysts, but supervisors, the job holder, or some combination of these may perform the analysis.

Job analysis may be performed through observation; through interviews with job incumbents or supervisors or others; through questionnaires; or through the use of a diary or log used to describe the individual's performance of the job.

There is no standard format for job descriptions but they usually include the following:[6]

1. The job's title: More than twenty thousand titles are available in the *Dictionary of Occupational Titles.*[7]
2. A job summary: A brief one- or two-sentence statement as to the contents of the job.
3. A description of job activities: Descriptions of the tasks performed and materials used and the extent of supervision given or received.
4. Relevant working conditions and physical environment: Lighting, noise levels, heat, hazardous and other conditions.
5. The job's social environment: Information on the work group and interpersonal relationships required to perform the job.

JOB DESIGN

Job design, discussed in Chapter 10, can be accomplished through the rational approach, introduced to us as part of scientific management, or the behavioral approach of Frederick W. Herzberg.[8] The rational approach emphasizes the scientific study of a series of tasks and the design of jobs such that it includes as few tasks as possible, so that any worker can efficiently perform the job. The behavioral approach emphasizes looking at the core dimensions of a job—those that lead to meaningful work, responsibility for outcomes, or knowledge of results—and building the job around them.[9] The five core dimensions include task variety, task identity, task significance, autonomy, and feedback. The three contextual dimensions include interpersonal relations, authority and responsibility for goal setting, and communication patterns.

Often the individual manager is supervising individuals in jobs designed by others, principally job analysts and personnel specialists or engineers. Nonetheless, the manager must be attuned and should look for opportunities to improve the job design not only scientifically, but also in terms of the key job core dimensions. Managers must also be able to help identify those candidates who would match the job specifications that result from job analysis. Managers can also ensure that the job descriptions that result are accurate and timely.

Forecasting the Need for Human Resources

The organization must predict its future needs and compare them with its current supply of individual job holders. Forecasting future human resource requirements depends heavily upon the existing and potential demand for the organization's products or services. Managers must staff to meet the anticipated labor demands. Because the labor force will undergo dramatic demographic changes from 1990 to 2000, human resources planning is now even more critical.[10]

As we approach the year 2000, human resource data bases, such as the one being processed here, are becoming more and more critical. The supply of labor is changing significantly, as are many of the jobs and necessary skills for which employees must be chosen. Making the match will become more and more difficult without such databases. (SOURCE © Robert Reichert)

In either growth or staff-reduction situations, an important consideration is the mix of current employees. A human resource audit—a systematic inventory of personnel—and the strengths and weaknesses it reveals, can be used to provide this information. A human resource inventory database results from this audit, and obtaining this database is in many organizations an ongoing process, updated periodically. The database provides information on promotability, the need for training and development, and the need for replacement where weaknesses continue to exist. Such databases can be extracted from the overall human resource information system.

The need for such a database would appear obvious. In fact, relatively few organizations maintain one, although more are recognizing the need to do so.[11] However, organizations such as IBM, RCA, and the U.S. Civil Service Commission have databases that do allow them to plan for their employees' careers and to match individuals to the jobs for which they are suited.[12] Not all organizations have been as attentive to such issues as they should have been. Prior to the 1984 replacement of top management in the Disney companies that resulted from a "friendly nontakeover" (one the management agreed to) by the Bass brothers, the Disney companies had no human resource database. Within a few months, Michael Eisner and Frank Wells, who had assumed the positions of CEO and COO, respectively, initiated a human resource database for Disney, seeking to improve the company's ability to manage its most important resource. The company was confronted with high levels of demand for employees in Florida. The company's operations there were expected to grow significantly from 1984 through 1989, with only a limited supply of workers in the local area. In order to make the situation more manageable, Eisner and Wells began the database.[13]

EEO Considerations of Job Specifications

Job specifications must not be set beyond what are truly necessary to perform in the job. (This subject is discussed subsequently in more detail under "Selection.") Job designs should take into account their potential occupants. To do otherwise would possibly eliminate certain applicants protected by EEO laws, and thus specifications could be used to discriminate.

Recruitment

Recruitment consists of a series of activities intended to attract a qualified pool of job applicants. The recruitment stage of placing the employee involves the HRM practice actions taken from job design up to the time the first physical contact is made with a prospective employee after the application blank has been filed. Once that contact is made, the selection process is invoked. Those recruited are sought for their abilities to match the job specifications determined in the employment planning process. Once a qualified pool of applicants is obtained, selection will determine which of them is hired to perform the actual job.

Recruitment can occur either internally or externally to the firm. Current employees have a legal right under EEO laws to apply for other jobs in the company. Similarly, the company must notify current employees of available positions. This normally takes place through "posting" of job availabilities on bulletin boards, or through memos. Most firms try to mix hiring—promoting from within and hiring from without. If promotions occur only from within, the company does not benefit from new ideas from outside experiences; if it doesn't promote at least some from within, morale suffers.

Recruitment can also occur either actively or passively. Active recruitment involves placing advertisements in various media—newspapers, radio, TV, trade journals, and the like; visiting high schools, colleges, and other places where applicants may be found; and making contacts with people who seek applicants for the organization—for example, employment agencies, or union hiring agents. Passive recruitment means that the organization simply waits for applicants to walk in and apply for the available jobs. Passive recruitment is quite common in many industries, such as in banking. Banking attracts numerous suitable applicants because of its positive image as a place of employment (although not because of high salaries). Banks seldom have to recruit for any positions except those that are low-paying front-line, such as tellers, and certain highly specialized or top-management positions. In contrast, most organizations must actively recruit employees. Location, specialization, low pay, the condition of the economy, competition for employees, or poor working conditions are some reasons that active recruitment may be necessary. EEO is another. Were you recruited for your current or most recent job, or did you just walk in?

Factors Affecting the Ability to Recruit

Government, unions, labor market conditions, composition of the work force, location of the organization, job applicant preferences, and resources affect an organization's ability to recruit satisfactory applicants. Because the work force is changing demographically and in terms of expectations, recruitment practices will be changing as well.

Matching the Recruit with the Organization

AT HONEYWELL: *A team of managers makes the final selection of the new manager for the SRC division.*

Once job descriptions and specifications have been determined, the organization advertises the job and has contact with applicants; a preliminary screening process will usually disqualify some of the applicants because they will fail immediately to meet certain of the job specifications. Once the initial pool of applicants is determined, line managers become involved and the selection process begins. Typically, personnel sends applicants to line managers for their inputs. Often the line manager makes the final decisions. The evidence strongly indicates that where the employer attempts to make an accurate match of the job to the applicant, both employer and employee will be more satisfied than if less of an effort is made.[14]

Who Recruits?

Most recruiters are internal, but some are external. In very large organizations, the human resource management department normally does the recruiting. In the largest organizations, a whole staff of professional interviewers and recruiters may be found. The individual manager need only know how the organization's recruitment process is supposed to work for him or her, and how to make it work. In smaller organizations the individual manager or a personnel or staff specialist may do the recruiting and needs to know the entire process. Recruiters need to be trained in how to provide a positive image of the firm as well as a realistic one.

The initial treatment of potential applicants is extremely important, regardless of who is doing the recruiting. Applicants form a negative impression of the organization if they are treated with a lack of concern.[15] The recruiter is usually the first person the applicant meets. It is important that he or she give a positive impression of the company. Think about a job that you have had. What kind of an impression did you get in your initial recruiting situation? Was it positive or negative? Why?

External recruiters can include employment agencies, unions, or "head hunters," the latter being employment agencies that place professional or managerial candidates. These organizations serve a vital function for employers: They help internal recruiters in areas with which they may be unfamiliar—such as a national search for an engineer—or in which they have no jurisdiction—such as might occur when a company has, in effect, turned over the recruitment process to a union.

Sources of Job Applicants

Job posting (advertising job openings in company media, usually bulletin boards), friends of present employees, and those who appear on human resource databases as having needed skills are all internal sources of job applicants. External sources include walk-ins, various agencies, educational institutions, and unions (through their hiring halls).

The Job Application

The cornerstone document for both recruitment and selection is the job application itself. The application blank may be given to all applicants, or it may be given only to those who pass a preliminary screening process. Because of federal and state EEO laws, many employers have increased their levels of preliminary screening, taking an application from every person who inquires about a job.

EEO Considerations

Recruitment is a human resource management practice that has been greatly affected by EEO laws. The recruitment process, especially if application forms are part of this process, may be investigated for discriminatory content or im-

Toyota, An Exacting Employer

When you invest $800 million dollars in a plant in Georgetown, Kentucky, as a spearhead for your sales operation in the United States, you want to be doubly sure that you hire the right three thousand people to run it. And when you compete on the basis of quality, manage by teamwork, seek flexibility in your work force, and also want its loyalty, you want to be quadruply sure you have the right people. How do you ensure you hire the right workers?

If you are Toyota, you run them through twenty-five hours of tests, including a grueling final interview. You probe not just for educational levels, but personality factors. You test people with paper and pencil and with job simulations. Applicants are even put through job-situation simulations for positions they are not applying for. Their interpersonal skills are noted, as are their responses to questions. There are mock production lines where applicants must actually assemble something. The company is looking for people who can keep to a fast pace and endure tedious work, yet remain alert.

Only one applicant in twenty makes it to the interview, which is conducted by a team comprised of members from various Toyota departments. Some say this "fussiness" is aimed at keeping out prounion people. Others say it's done because the Japanese fear that American workers' work habits are not that good. Some officials feared it could be potentially traced to racial discrimination. At Toyota there are fewer minorities in management positions than as a percentage of those who apply, and there are fewer women being hired as well. Regardless of the reasons, Toyota is taking great pains to select the proper people. There is no

pacts. Furthermore, EEO laws require employers to give careful attention to the matching of applicant qualifications to job descriptions and job specifications. Although technically this may be part of the selection process, initial screening often occurs during the recruitment phase.

The EEO guidelines prohibit questions about race, color, age, sex, national origin, veteran status, religion, and mental or physical handicaps, unless a bona fide occupational qualification (BFOQ) is allowed for a particular job. That is extremely rare but does occur. A church-affiliated college, for example, might be allowed to hire for certain positions on the basis of religion and could therefore inquire about an individual's religious preference. Inquiries related to information on race, color, sex, and so on may be asked once an individual has been hired so that the organization can provide employee insurance. The information may not be used to discriminate in any way in the administration of the employment practices.

As a consequence of equal employment opportunity laws, employers who fail to show an appropriate percentage of minorities or females in various job classifications must make an extra special effort to recruit them. This may mean going to minority or women's colleges, into various minority housing areas, or advertising in minority newspapers or women's magazines. This would be part of an affirmative action program, meaning that the organization took extra actions to fulfill their EEO **obligations** in an organized way. The requirements for such programs, and the identification of those who must have them, are spelled out in federal (and in some state) regulations.

shortage of applicants either for the 2,700 production jobs or the 300 office jobs. A labor pool of more than 40,000 has applied for the 2,700 production jobs, so Toyota can afford to be choosy.

SOURCE: Richard Koenig, "Exacting Employer: Toyota Takes Pains, and Time Filling Jobs at Its Kentucky Plant," *Wall Street Journal* 1 December, 1987, pp. 1, 31.

These prospective employees are taking just a few of the numerous tests that they must pass if they are to become Toyota employees at Toyota's Georgetown, Kentucky plant. (SOURCE © Andy Freeberg)

Selection

When a pool of applicants has been chosen, the organization must decide who best matches the job specification—that is, who is most qualified to fill the position. This process is known as **selection** and consists of the following steps:

1. Completion of the application blank or some biographical data form
2. An employment interview/ongoing interviews
3. Testing
4. Reference checks/recommendations
5. A physical exam
6. Choice/selection

Some companies are extremely rigorous in their selection process. Major Japanese firms are particularly so, as Management Challenge 11.2 suggests. Firms will need to be very concerned with selection in the future as a result of the changing skill levels in the future potential work force.

The Application Blank

The application blank is part of recruitment and selection. Once the organization begins to use it to make choices among candidates, it is part of the selection process. Application blanks have been subject to close scrutiny for compliance with EEO legislation because of the questions that employers ask.

Interviews

AT HONEYWELL'S SRC:
This team of managers must be careful not to bias their selections from an EEO perspective. Much of the selecting occurs through interviews that probe for the satisfaction of specific criteria.

The interview is perhaps the weakest link in the applicant selection process, but it often is the most critical. Vital information may be exchanged in the interview, but research has clearly shown it is susceptible to a number of problems. Unless each candidate is asked the same questions, for example, the same information is not gathered for each. When a manager or group of managers goes to evaluate candidates, they may be comparing apples and oranges.[16] Interviews are also subject to personal bias, such as the effects of one's appearance.[17] Yet the interview is still widely used. One major reason is the apparent belief that face-to-face interaction provides information about the interviewee's personality and sociability that other techniques do not. As an individual conducting the interview, you need to be alert to the following guidelines for interviewing:

1. Plan for the interview; review the job description and specification.
2. Create a good climate.
3. Allow sufficient time for an uninterrupted interview.
4. Conduct a goal-oriented interview.
5. Screen questions beforehand to avoid those that might constitute discrimination.
6. Press for answers to all questions and check for inconsistencies.
7. Write notes about the interview immediately upon its completion.[18]

MANAGEMENT CHALLENGE **11.2**

Increased Use of Personality Tests for Entry-Level Blue-Collar Jobs

With employees needing more interpersonal skills than ever before, and with front-line employees costing more than ever before, how can organizations ensure that their selection process produces the "right" person? One increasingly popular way is to use tests that check for personality factors. Robert Goehing, manager of human resources development for Kimberly Clark Corporation, a manufacturer of disposable personal and health care products and paper and specialty products, comments: "Ten years ago we didn't expect as much from people. Now we have participative organizations that foster a high degree of responsibility even at the operator level." At Kimberly Clark's newest plant, for example, applicants for nonunion machine operator jobs must qualify by taking "leadership simulation" exercises. A typical exercise might include having an applicant play a supervisor who has to direct a seasoned employee to switch to a more demanding job. An actual supervisor would play the worker's role. Mr. Goehing adds, "We are looking for people who can assume work-group leadership even if they wouldn't have that responsibility initially."

Criticism of such tests abounds. Some claim that such sought-after traits are not necessary for all people and therefore may violate EEO laws. Others, such as union leaders, are concerned that companies are using these personality inventories to weed out people who might be prounion. Furthermore, critics also charge that

As a job candidate in an interview situation, you need to be alert to the following:

1. Be prepared: Find out about the potential employer.
2. First impressions are critical: It is absolutely vital that you create a positive image.
3. Prepare answers for typical interview questions.
4. Probe for information about the company.

Chapter 23 provides an indepth look at these and other issues involved in the interview.

The manager is often involved in interviewing candidates and must therefore know what he or she can legally ask. The manager must also be able to structure interviews, use probing questions effectively, and learn not to be subject to the weaknesses of the process. To the extent that the manager helps make up tests and application blanks, he should know the ins and outs of the process. Finally, in making choices, the manager must be able to balance criteria for hiring.

Employment Testing

Some companies use testing devices to help them make employment decisions. Typical tests include those for job skills, such as typing. Psychological tests are given for people in certain occupations, such as sales and management. Testing may also include such devices as performance appraisals, where promotions are

> AT HONEYWELL'S SRC:
> *At Honeywell's SRC, managers are chosen by a team of managers.*

simulations are only as good as the people judging them. Nonetheless, more and more companies are employing testing as a way of trying to predict those who will be successful on the job.

One of the most popular personality tests is the Myers-Briggs Type Indicator, or MBTI as it is most commonly known. Responses to over one hundred questions are used to indicate why an individual would be classified more at one or the other end of four dimensions:

1. Social interaction—introvert or extrovert
2. Preference for gathering data—intuitive or sensor
3. Preference for decision making—feeling or thinking
4. Style of making decisions—perceptive or judgmental

Combinations of these preferences for psychological dimensions result in the sixteen personality types shown in Figure 11.6. Users of the MBTI believe that it is important to identify these types because these preferences affect the way that people interact and solve problems. Knowledge about personality types, if identified and acted upon, can allow bosses, subordinates, and peers to interact and solve problems more meaningfully. If your boss is a sensor and you are an intuitor, for example, you will be gathering information in different ways. A sensor would like facts; an intuitor would like gut reactions. If you must work with your boss, you must be giving him facts, not gut reactions, if you want to work well together. Furthermore, people of various types perform better in different jobs. If you want the most from your selection process, you should only be placing certain "types" in certain jobs.

SOURCES: Larry Reibstein, "More Firms Use Personality Tests for Entry-Level, Blue-Collar Jobs," *Wall Street Journal* 16 January, 1986, p. 31; and Thomas Moore, "Personality Tests Are Back," *Fortune* (March 30, 1987), pp. 74–82.

FIGURE 11.6 THE 16 DIFFERENT PERSONALITY TYPES

		SENSING TYPES S		INTUITIVE TYPES N	
		THINKING T	FEELING F	FEELING F	THINKING T
INTROVERTS I	JUDGING J	ISTJ SERIOUS, QUIET, EARN SUCCESS BY CONCENTRATION AND THOROUGHNESS. PRACTICAL, ORDERLY, MATTER-OF-FACT, LOGICAL, REALISTIC, AND DEPENDABLE. TAKE RESPONSIBIL-ITY.	ISFJ QUIET, FRIENDLY, RESPONSI-BLE, AND CONSCIEN-TIOUS. WORK DEVOTEDLY TO MEET THEIR OBLIGATIONS. THOROUGH, PAINS-TAKING, ACCURATE. LOYAL, CONSIDERATE.	INFJ SUCCEED BY PER-SEVERANCE, ORIGINAL-ITY, AND DESIRE TO DO WHATEVER IS NEEDED OR WANTED. QUIETLY FORCEFUL, CONSCIEN-TIOUS, CONCERNED FOR OTHERS. RESPECTED FOR THEIR FIRM PRINCIPLES.	INTJ USUALLY HAVE ORIGINAL MINDS AND GREAT DRIVE FOR THEIR OWN IDEAS AND PURPOSES. SKEPTICAL, CRITICAL, INDEPEN-DENT, DETERMINED, OFTEN STUBBORN.
INTROVERTS I	PERCEIVING P	ISTP COOL ONLOOKERS—QUIET, RESERVED, AND ANALYTICAL. USU-ALLY INTERESTED IN IMPERSONAL PRINCI-PLES, HOW AND WHY MECHANICAL THINGS WORK. FLASHES OF ORIGINAL HUMOR.	ISFP RETIRING, QUIETLY FRIENDLY, SENSITIVE, KIND, MODEST ABOUT THEIR ABILITIES. SHUN DIS-AGREEMENTS. LOYAL FOLLOWERS. OFTEN RELAXED ABOUT GET-TING THINGS DONE.	INFP CARE ABOUT LEARNING, IDEAS, LANGUAGE, AND INDE-PENDENT PROJECTS OF THEIR OWN. TEND TO UNDERTAKE TOO MUCH, THEN SOME-HOW GET IT DONE. FRIENDLY, BUT OFTEN TOO ABSORBED.	INTP QUIET, RESERVED, IMPER-SONAL. ENJOY THEO-RETICAL OR SCIENTIFIC SUBJECTS. USUALLY INTERESTED MAINLY IN IDEAS, LITTLE LIKING FOR PARTIES OR SMALL TALK. SHARPLY DEFINED INTERESTS.
EXTROVERTS E	PERCEIVING P	ESTP MATTER-OF-FACT, DO NOT WORRY OR HURRY, ENJOY WHATEVER COMES ALONG. MAY BE A BIT BLUNT OR INSENSI-TIVE. BEST WITH REAL THINGS THAT CAN BE TAKEN APART OR PUT TOGETHER.	ESFP OUTGOING, EASYGOING, ACCEPTING, FRIENDLY, MAKE THINGS MORE FUN FOR OTHERS BY THEIR ENJOYMENT. LIKE SPORTS AND MAKING THINGS. FIND REMEMBERING FACTS EASIER THAN MASTERING THEORIES.	ENFP WARMLY ENTHU-SIASTIC, HIGH-SPIRITED, INGENIOUS, IMAGINATIVE. ABLE TO DO ALMOST ANYTHING THAT INTERESTS THEM. QUICK WITH A SOLU-TION AND TO HELP WITH A PROBLEM.	ENTP QUICK, INGE-NIOUS, GOOD AT MANY THINGS. MAY ARGUE EITHER SIDE OF A QUESTION FOR FUN. RESOURCEFUL IN SOLVING CHALLENGING PROBLEMS, BUT MAY NEGLECT ROUTINE ASSIGNMENTS.
EXTROVERTS E	JUDGING J	ESTJ PRACTICAL, REALISTIC, MATTER-OF-FACT, WITH A NATU-RAL HEAD FOR BUSINESS OR MECHAN-ICS. NOT INTERESTED IN SUBJECTS THEY SEE NO USE FOR. LIKE TO ORGANIZE AND RUN ACTIVITIES.	ESFJ WARM-HEARTED, TALKATIVE, POPULAR, CONSCIENTIOUS, BORN COOPERATORS. NEED HARMONY. WORK BEST WITH ENCOURAGE-MENT. LITTLE INTER-EST IN ABSTRACT THINKING OR TECHNI-CAL SUBJECTS.	ENFJ RESPONSIVE AND RESPONSIBLE. GENERALLY FEEL REAL CONCERN FOR WHAT OTHERS THINK OR WANT. SOCIABLE, POPULAR. SENSITIVE TO PRAISE AND CRITICISM.	ENTJ HEARTY, FRANK, DECISIVE, LEADERS. USUALLY GOOD IN ANY-THING THAT REQUIRES REASONING AND INTEL-LIGENT TALK. MAY SOMETIMES BE MORE POSITIVE THAN THEIR EXPERIENCE IN AN AREA WARRANTS.

SOURCE: INTRODUCTION TO TYPE BY ISABEL BRIGGS MYERS

being considered. More commonly, tests are concerned with preemployment situations. To be used legally, a test (or any other selection device) must have **validity**—it must actually discern who will be successful in a job versus who will not.[19] It must also have **reliability**—it must give the same results over time if taken more than once by the same person or if various forms of the same test are taken by the same person.[20]

EEO CONSIDERATIONS
Historically, the EEOC has required a validity demonstration in order for an organization to be able to use a test—or any selection device. Interviews and performance appraisals are both considered to be tests by the EEOC. Further-

One of the ways to be prepared for an interview is to videotape a mock interview and have an expert in the field critique it. This candidate's performance in the real situation was greatly improved by doing just that. (SOURCE © John Abbott)

more, tests cannot be used that have an adverse impact on a group protected by EEO laws—that is, if it disqualifies a significantly larger percentage of minorities than nonminorities.

Many organizations have used some type of test to ascertain who should have certain jobs. However, because of the difficulty and cost of validating that a test actually predicts future job performance, many employers abandoned formal testing, except for the most critical jobs. They have instead settled for a first-come, first-hired, "hear thunder, see lightning" approach. However, as the cost and skill level of front-line employees have increased, more and more firms are returning to testing as part of the selection process, as Management Challenge 11.2 suggests.

Reference Checks

One of the best ways to verify the desirability of hiring an individual has always been to check his or her references. Lately, however, this has proven to be difficult. Former employers are afraid to talk about ex-workers, even in a positive fashion, for fear of potential lawsuits.[21] International Multi-Foods Corporation, for example, won't say anything about former workers without their written consent.[22]

Physical Exams

Many organizations ask an individual to pass a physical exam before he or she is hired. This makes sense where the ability to do certain physical actions is part of the job. In a related matter, testing for drug usage is becoming more common in the workplace, both before and after employees are placed. AIDS is also a major concern of employers. Both drugs and AIDS are discussed later in the chapter.

EEO CONSIDERATIONS
Government contractors and subcontractors are prohibited from discriminating against people with mental or physical handicaps unless they would directly interfere with performance on a job. Such handicaps must reasonably be accommodated. Employers might, for example, intentionally screen out individuals with the potential for heart attack in order to keep their insurance rates low, when such a predisposition might have nothing to do with the ability to

perform on the job.[23] As a consequence of potential difficulties with EEO law, most employers make the physical exam the last step in the process. Many have abandoned it altogether.

Employment Decisions

In most organizations the final decision as to whether someone is to be hired rests with the individual line manager. In some organizations the personnel department may make the decision with respect to lower-level jobs, but current trends are away from this practice. Another current trend is in the direction of work-group decisions about whom to hire.

Harvey MacKay, president of MacKay Envelope Corporation, suggests that there is one acid-test question about a potential employee. After you've gone through all of the standard process, you ask yourself "How would you feel if he (or she) worked for your competition?"[24] If you wouldn't want that, then hire the individual. It is important to remember that the employment decision is a two-way street. The prospective employee must be sufficiently convinced by an organization and a manager of the merits of joining the organization. He or she must also consider issues such as centralization versus decentralization, job autonomy, the amount of travel, and employee promotion opportunities.

Assessment Centers: Selecting Managers

One of the most successful programs for selecting managers is known as an assessment center. It is usually a two- or three-day program consisting of simulation exercises, various tests, interviews, and problem-solving assignments that are used to measure the potential for promotion or assignment to some specific job for which the assessment center has been designed as a comprehensive test. Assessment centers provide very valid predictions of future success in management. Their primary drawback is their expense. A small number of candidates is usually supervised by a large number of administrators. Two reasons for the high validity of the assessment center are that several measures are used to evaluate a candidate, and the actual components of the job are used as part of the testing process.

Realistic Job Previews

In the recruitment process, both the employer and the potential employee should seek to make their presentations to each other as realistic as possible. The potential employee wants to get the job but doesn't want to exaggerate his or her abilities, as performance ultimately will be required for continued employment. Similarly, the firm needs to present a realistic job preview, clearly indicating expectations, requirements, culture, leadership style, and so on. Studies reveal that such previews help reduce turnover and increase employee satisfaction.[25]

Orientation

Orientation introduces the employee to the organization—to the requirements of the job, to the social situation in which he or she is about to be thrust, and to its norms and culture. Most organizations use some type of checklist to orient

More and more training and development will be necessary in the future to acquaint old and new employees with job responsibilities. The IBM seminar is just one of perhaps a hundred that a career employee might be expected to attend. (SOURCE ©Ken Kerbs)

the employee to the job situation. Key organization factors include an overview of the company, policies and procedures, compensation, benefits, safety and accident prevention, employee and union relations, physical facilities, and economic factors. Departmental and job-related issues include department functions; job duties and responsibilities; policies, rules, procedures, and regulations; the autonomy of the department; and socialization into the work group. A sound orientation process is vital.[26]

Managers are directly involved in orientation to the specific job situation. Socialization of the new employee is critical. Managers should treat it as such and do a professional job at orientation. Chapter 12 reviews the enculturation process in more detail.

Training and Development

Training helps the employee gain the specific job-related skills that ensure effective performance. **Development** is the process of helping the employee to grow, principally in his or her career, but perhaps also as a human being outside of work as well. It is a long-term investment.[27] Selection for training and development is part of the career planning process.

Training and development may occur on or off the job. On-the-job training occurs while the individual is actually performing in the work setting. Off-the-job training and development occur typically in classrooms or similar training situations. Training and development may also be done either internally or externally. Internally, the manager or human resource department may provide them. Externally, consultants, seminar leaders, and others may be hired, or employees may be sent to seminars away from the workplace. In 1988 U.S. businesses spent $30 billion to provide 17.6 million formal training and development courses for employees.[28]

Aetna's Institute for Corporate Education

Aetna Life & Casualty Company in Hartford, Connecticut, found itself with a shortage of qualified workers in entry-level positions. Those workers in the available pool were often woefully lacking basic reading and writing skills. The company's Institute for Corporate Education began working with local organizations to teach nineteen- to twenty-four-year-olds basic reading and writing. They work with them until they can read the materials they must work with at Aetna. Then Aetna will employ them. Aetna has hired more than one thousand people this way so far. Badi Foster, head of the institute, indicates that the company is "looking for a payoff from five to eight years" later. Many of the people being taught are minorities.

In a related action, Aetna has also developed a management of cultural diversity education program for its managers. At first people resisted because they say it as "fuzzy-headed, soft-hearted" kind of thinking, recounts Mr. Foster. But, he notes, "if you don't get the managers to see this as a business problem, no matter what you do for the entry level, it won't be enough."

SOURCE: Amanda Bennett, "Company School: As Pool of Skilled Help Tightens, Firms Move to Broaden Their Role," *Wall Street Journal* 8 May, 1989, pp. A-1, A-4.

Classroom instructional techniques include lecture and discussion, case studies, simulations, and role playing. Lecture and discussion tend to be more knowledge oriented, whereas case studies, simulations, and role playing are more skill oriented. Lecture and discussion are passive, whereas the latter three techniques are active.

One of the major trends in organizational training and development is the increased amount of activity in basic education by business. With a smaller labor pool than in the past, the educational level organizations require is often insufficient. This means that business must train more employees in basic skills.[29] Management Challenge 11.3 describes one firm's efforts in such training. A result of this shallow labor pool is that business is hiring more retarded workers.[30] Finally, business is also investing more in education in general in order to be more competitive. Workers' skills, for example, may be outdated as a result of rapid technological change.[31] The need for education has not been lost on the Japanese, who spend $1,000 more to recruit and train their new U.S. employees than do American firms for their new recruits.[32] More and more firms are turning to computers and interactive video to bring training to more people.[33]

Ongoing HRM Practices

Once an employee is placed in a job, a number of employment practices must be pursued: continuing employee development and training, compensation packages and benefits, employee health and safety, employee relations, managing change, employee evaluation and control, and employee transitions.

Aetna's Institute for Corporate Education offers a wide variety of training programs. In its Youth Training and Employment program, it trains high schools from the Hartford public schools in computer usage, oral and written communication, math skills and the world of work. These students may work part or full time for the firm during the school year, during the summer, or upon graduation. (SOURCE Courtesy Aetna)

Continuing Employee Development and Training

The manager's principal function is to make certain that the individual first receives adequate training to do the job, and later, to grow beyond the job. The manager must ascertain whether an employee needs more training and development. The manager should ensure that the employee is promotable in the long term. There are, of course, exceptions. If the manager does the training, he or she must learn to train effectively. Managers themselves often go through the development process. Many organizations have specific management development programs aimed at improving management skills and abilities for the long term, as well as for the current job in management. The manager should manage his or her own training and development, as well as that of others.

Employee development takes a longer-term approach and is not as job related as training.[34] It tends to provide more general skills and knowledge to be used both in the current job and later in organizational life, as the individual moves through his or her career. Development is a critical part of the strategic approach to the management of human resources. It is based on the recognition that more and more employees should be integrated into the organization and should be further developed for future strategic actions.[35] Development tends to occur after the individual has been on the job for a while. IBM and other companies, such as AT&T, GTE, Wang, Motorola, and Xerox, operate their own internal "universities," teaching a wide variety of technical and managerial subjects.[36] Finally, from time to time, employees will have to be trained for a specific new job.

Compensation and Benefits/Motivation

One of the primary functions of any manager or any organization is leadership—influencing the internal motivation of individuals. The HRM department plays a major role in enabling the organization and the manager to do so, by developing compensation and benefit programs aimed at influencing motivation. Such programs define the limits within which individual managers can influence motivation using compensation or benefits. The classic method of influencing employee motivation is to offer financial-need satisfiers. Direct compensation is generally based on time worked, performance, or some combination of the two. To be effective the HRM department should construct compensation programs to reward performance and such factors as seniority. It should also construct them in such a way that the manager can use them to influence the motivation of his or her subordinates.

The organization has numerous compensation options, including hourly wages, salaries, overtime, merit pay, bonuses, incentive plans, stock options, profit sharing, piece rates, commissions, and group incentives.[37] Benefits are part of total compensation and in 1986 constituted approximately 37 percent of the average employee's salary.[38] Benefits are increasing as a percentage of total compensation and could reach 40–45 percent, if current trends continue.[39] Typical benefits include life and health insurance, unemployment compensation, retirement benefits (including social security), paid vacations, paid holidays, and sick leave. Health care costs are skyrocketing, and so are health insurance costs.[40] It is difficult, if not impossible, to use benefits as a way of influencing motivation because they are given regardless of the level of employee performance. Confronted with rising costs, employers have pondered which actions to take.[41] This problem was further compounded in 1989 with the passage of the Technical and Miscellaneous Revenue Act of 1989 (TAMRA), which requires equality in benefits for virtually all employees with those of "highly compensated employees." In most cases, employers face increased costs and paperwork as a result.[42] Section 89, as it is called, is being reviewed by Congress in 1990, and changes, most likely a reduction in requirements, are expected.

Most organizations perform job evaluations in order to determine basic wages. **Job evaluation** is the systematic determination of the relative worth of a job in an organization. Job evaluation allows the organization to rank jobs and determine their hierarchy of importance across all jobs in the organization. A successful job evaluation depends upon up-to-date job descriptions and specifications. One of the methods used for job evaluation is the point method. It is used where jobs are readily segmented into identifiable parts. The point system uses several common factors for all the jobs being evaluated, and scales measure the degrees to which those factors occur in a given job. Such factors might include decision authority, skill level, or environmental hazards. The comparison method is more complicated. Here key jobs are evaluated and then other jobs are related to each key job based on their comparison factors, similar to those used in a point system. The third method is the classification method. Jobs are classified according to levels, grades, and so on, based on their job descriptions. Pay rates are established in ranges for each classification of job. Finally there is the ranking method. Evaluators simply rank all jobs relative to each other on some basis, such as the perceived degree of skill required. This latter method is not a very scientific one. Wages determined by these processes may be raised or lowered upon the evaluation of external market conditions.

Factors affecting the compensation and benefit structure and decisions related to these include the worth of the job and the employee; market compensation and benefit conditions; collective bargaining; the ability of the organization to pay; perceptions of employee equity relative to pay; and equal employment opportunity laws and guidelines.

The wages paid often result from wage, salary, and benefit surveys in the community where the organization is located. Most local personnel associations annually perform such surveys so that member employers' compensation and benefit packages are "in the same ballpark." Sometimes organizations simply will not be able to hire people and will be forced to raise their compensation and benefit packages in order to do so.

EEO Considerations

The Equal Pay Act of 1963 prohibits discrimination in wages for equal work on the basis of sex. Title VII of the Civil Rights Act of 1964 prohibits discrimination on the basis of sex in any employment practice. More recently the issue of comparable worth—the idea that jobs should be paid relative to the job's worth to the organization regardless of the sex of the job holder—has received significant attention. A number of lawsuits have been filed in both the public and private sectors of the economy claiming that organizations were not paying women on a comparable-worth basis.[43] Job evaluation systems used to determine the worth of a job are being revised substantially. At Bank of America, for example, physical labor as a factor in a job was redefined to include eye strain, allowing many female-dominated clerical jobs to be evaluated at a higher level of pay.[44]

Employee Health and Safety

Employee health and safety are major concerns of most employers. Medical insurance is part of most benefit packages. But much of management's concern is with the organizational work environment—including air, water, and noise pollution; other hazards to health; the safety of the work area; and the safety of the equipment. Actions required to provide safety in the work area and in equipment, as well as to reduce certain hazards to health, are defined in considerable detail in the United States through the provisions of the Occupational Safety and Health Act of 1970. This act requires employers to make their work areas safe and eliminate environmental hazards.

Accident-prevention programs are a critical part of employee health and safety programs. Extensive feedback and positive reinforcement of safe behavior have been shown to produce favorable results for bakers, bus drivers, paper mill employees, and farm machinery manufacturing employees.[45] Unfortunately, as employers have pushed for increased productivity, accident levels have increased significantly.[46]

In addition to accident prevention, eliminating illness and diseases caused by health hazards in the employee work environment is a key component in improving occupational health. A focal issue today is employee stress. A number of legal cases found employers guilty of providing too stressful an environment.[47] Consequently, many organizations are now developing wellness programs. For example, Metropolitan Life Insurance Company has such a program for its 9,500 headquarters employees. The concerns of this program include

These Southwestern Bell Telephone employees are engaged in a corporate wellness program. This aerobics class provides the heart-lung portion of their weekly exercise requirement. (SOURCE © Andy Freeberg)

blood pressure control, cholesterol reduction, weight training, stress management, and smoking prevention. Numerous other companies have physical fitness programs, in an attempt to keep employees healthier and more physically fit.[48]

Another critical issue in the work force today is the use of drugs, including alcohol. The use of both is widespread in many industries. More and more employers are using drug testing as part of the hiring process. Coors, the United States' fourth largest brewer of beer, headquartered just outside Denver, Colorado, dropped lie detector tests in favor of drug testing.[49] There is, of course, a controversy as to whether such testing is legal. The issue is not totally settled in early 1990.[50] More and more companies are providing counseling, but they are also testing for drugs among current workers and occasionally raiding worksites. Southern California Edison Company raided its Laughlin, Nevada, generating station, going through employee lockers and having employees empty their pockets. Employees found in possession of alcohol or drugs were terminated on the spot for violating company rules.[51] Again, the legality of such actions is a concern to many.

While the manager must manage within the occupational safety and health programs of the company, he or she nonetheless is responsible for the day-to-day occupational safety and health practices of subordinates. The manager typically must enforce rules, regulations, and procedures. Failure to do so endangers many. Failure to comply with the law is illegal, and stretching the "law" is unethical. Managers in such occupations as construction face many moral dilemmas because employers often ask or even demand they bend safety rules.[52]

Acquired Immune Deficiency Syndrome, AIDS, is a managerial problem in all large organizations and in many medium and small ones as well. Many employers have policies and programs related to the employment treatment of employees with AIDS. Most of these deal with shifting work schedules to accommodate periods of illness and similar issues. Making employment decisions—for example, termination—based on someone's having AIDS probably violates the Rehabilitation Act of 1973. With the exception of a few health-care organizations, employers are not testing for AIDS as an employment screening device. Managers must use their best interpersonal skills to assist not only those afflicted with AIDS, but to improve the understanding of those who work alongside AIDS victims.[53]

Employee Relations

Employee, or labor, relations is concerned with managing a unionized work force. An organization's relationship with organized labor is tremendously important to its success. A major part of the human resource department's efforts in unionized firms traditionally has been to manage that relationship; in nonunionized situations the effort has been to prevent the organizing of the work force. Many large organized firms have two departments within the human resource function, one to handle employee relations, and one to handle all other personnel functions. Employee relations activities are usually concerned with all HRM practices as they relate to the organized labor force.

Most of the employee relations department's concerns revolve around managing and administrating the union contract, grievances, compensation, work rules, and other issues that arise from time to time. The other principal concern of employee relations is the actual negotiation of the union contract. Almost invariably at negotiation time, unions want more money. Today most of them are seeking to protect existing jobs for current union members. They face difficult times; competition, especially foreign, has forced many givebacks in contracts and tougher management negotiating positions. Unions seek to gain new members, especially in service industries, to counter the effects of losses of jobs in such traditional unionized work forces as autos and steel.[54]

The manager in a unionized situation must administer according to the requirements of the union contract as well as company policies, rules, and procedures. His or her decision environment is highly defined, and the latitude of decision making is extremely limited. Normally, work rules, compensation, grievance, and disciplinary choices are all spelled out in very specific terms by the contract or company policy. As with EEO issues, the individual manager must make certain that recordkeeping is exact. The requirements of the contract must be met; otherwise disciplinary and similar efforts may fail or be disallowed by an arbitrator.

Managing Change

The HRM department, now more than ever, has been assigned the central responsibility for aiding the organization in planning for and managing change. Of special concern is the management of the organization's culture, or shared values. The HRM department typically establishes programs of planned change that individual managers will then be asked to implement. The human resources department also creates cultural indoctrination programs for use during orientation, taking raw recruits and molding them into employees who can live according to the culture of that organization.[55] Most cultural management programs come through part of an extensive organizational development effort. Organizational development "is a long-range (planned) effort to improve an organization's problem-solving and renewal processes, particularly through a more effective and collaborative management of organizational culture, with special emphasis on the culture of formal work teams, with the assistance of a change agent or a catalyst, and the use of theory and technology of applied behavior science including research."[56]

The normal cycle of an organizational development intervention begins with some type of survey or other diagnostic effort, such as a series of interviews, to determine what needs to be done. Next a plan is formulated to prepare for change, to make the changes, and to reinforce the changes. Anheuser-Busch uses extensive organizational development in moving its culture toward a more participative and team-oriented effort in many of its plants.[57] Managing change will be discussed in more detail in Chapter 12.

The manager must learn how to accept and manage change. He or she must learn to manage culture and be able to develop teamwork in the work group. He or she must learn to manage participatively.

Employee Evaluation and Control

The HRM department is concerned with establishing systems for employee evaluation and control. Among them are performance appraisals, disciplinary systems, and grievance procedures. A number of actions may take place subsequent to using these systems, such as promotion, bonuses, disciplinary actions, and even termination.

Performance Appraisal

Several types of performance appraisals exist.

1. **Graphic rating scales,** in which employees are rated on a scale, usually from 1 to 10, on traits and/or behavior such as intelligence, neatness, and quantity of work accomplished.
2. **Management by objectives, results, and rewards,** wherein objectives are established, plans determined, performance reviewed, and rewards given, as described in Chapter 5.
3. **Forced choice,** which requires the evaluator to choose among descriptions of employee behavior. These are then scored according to a key.
4. **Simple ranking,** wherein raters simply rank their subordinates from best to worst on their perceived performances.
5. **Critical incidents,** in which raters identify critical positive and negative employee performance.
6. **Essay,** in which raters describe employee performances in an essay format.

Each one is better for certain situations than others. None is the best for all situations.

A number of persons may do the evaluating: the employee himself, the immediate supervisor, a second-level supervisor, an external consultant, subordinates, peers, or a combination of these. Currently, the most frequently recommended system is one in which the employee and supervisor perform independent evaluations. They exchange their evaluations and then negotiate the differences.

Performance appraisals were originally instituted for the purpose of controlling performance, but they also greatly influence motivation and communicate and set goals as part of the planning process. A number of problems exist with performance appraisals—with the form used, the process used, and with the rater and ratee. For example, raters may have a tendency to rate too leniently, or too hard.

EEO CONSIDERATIONS

The performance appraisal is considered to be a test by the EEOC and must pass validity requirements if it is used to determine promotion—it must be objective and job related.[58] It may also be used as a basis for disciplining or terminating someone from the organization. Therefore, managers and the HRM department must be certain to document carefully the reasons and justifications for the evaluations given. A disgruntled employee might claim discrimination or unfairness, or insufficient justification for the actions taken.

With respect to the potential for promotion, many Anglo and Black employees feel that Japanese firms discriminate against them, saving upper-level jobs for Japanese employees. A number of significant lawsuits charging discrimination have been brought against Japanese firms such as Sumitomo, Honda, and C. Itoh & Company.[59]

DISCIPLINARY PROGRAMS

In conjunction with the labor agreement, if one exists, many organizations typically have a routine program of discipline normally consisting of a series of five steps:

1. Verbal warning: The manager talks with the subordinate about his or her problem.
2. Written warning: The manager presents a written warning notice to the employee, detailing the undesirable behavior. It has become necessary in many situations, especially in unionized organizations, to have the employee sign this notice or to have a witness present.
3. A one-day suspension: If the undesirable behavior is repeated after the written warning, a one-day absence without pay is usually prescribed.
4. A three-day suspension: If the undesirable behavior still continues, the employee is suspended for three days without pay.
5. Termination: If the employee's behavior is still not improved, the employee is terminated.

It is the individual manager's job normally to administer these steps on an individual employee basis.

Grievance Procedures

The organization often provides a system for employees to air their grievances. Such a system is almost always a part of a union contract. Normally a grievance system follows the chain of command, but special grievance committees, or grievance-handling staff personnel, are not uncommon.

The HRM department determines the systems, and then the individual manager must function within them. They provide policies, rules, and procedures for use in appraising performance, disciplining, and handling grievances.

Employee Transitions

A number of employee transitions must be managed for those who quit, receive promotions and demotions, are layed off or transferred, retire, die, or are fired. The HRM department designs the system. The manager administers his or her subordinates according to its requirements.

HRM and Organizational Strategy

All of the HRM practices are engaged in, in order to carry out the corporate, business, and functional strategies of the organization. Each organization faces its own unique set of environmental and organizational circumstances. Hence, these practices are conducted on a contingency basis. For example, in high-technology industries there has been an increase in incentive-type compensation programs because the organizations are simultaneously faced with a very competitive marketplace and a tight labor pool.[60] In another example, firms in light labor markets, such as Boston, as noted earlier, must often make special recruitment efforts to expand their labor pools, for example, to older workers. Walt Disney World in 1985 took only one in ten applicants. But as the relative labor pool shrank in the central Florida area, and the demand for labor increased, by early 1990 Disney was hiring one in three applicants.[61]

Recent EEO Developments

In 1989, the U.S. Supreme Court handed down three decisions indicating their dissatisfaction with some of the current practices in affirmative action programs. While their decisions supported the concept of affirmative action they indicated that some practices were unacceptable. It is too soon in May 1990 to assess the impact of these decisions. They may or may not impede progress in affirmative action.[62]

HRM and Staffing as Problem Solving

The environment within which HRM and staffing must be practiced is changing rapidly. HRM and staffing practices must change with this environment. This chapter essentially reviewed what the practices are. Space limitations prevent an in-depth probe of the environmental factors that demand changes in HRM practices and the changes themselves. Figure 11.7 therefore identifies only in broad terms how problem solving occurs. Each HRM/staffing practice would be processed through the problem-solving model in any specific situation.

For example, the human resources department might encounter a labor market shortage. After careful analysis of the environment, and making an assump-

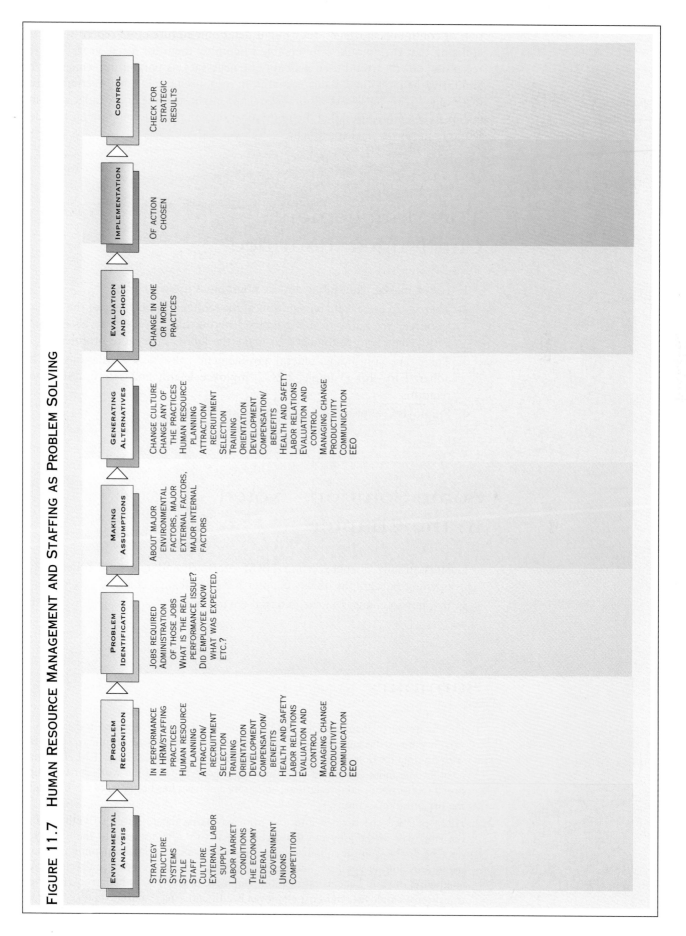

FIGURE 11.7 HUMAN RESOURCE MANAGEMENT AND STAFFING AS PROBLEM SOLVING

ENVIRONMENTAL ANALYSIS

STRATEGY
STRUCTURE
SYSTEMS
STYLE
STAFF
CULTURE
EXTERNAL LABOR
  SUPPLY
LABOR MARKET
  CONDITIONS
THE ECONOMY
FEDERAL
GOVERNMENT
UNIONS
COMPETITION

PROBLEM RECOGNITION

IN PERFORMANCE
IN HRM/STAFFING
  PRACTICES
HUMAN RESOURCE
  PLANNING
ATTRACTION/
  RECRUITMENT
SELECTION
TRAINING
ORIENTATION
DEVELOPMENT
COMPENSATION/
  BENEFITS
HEALTH AND SAFETY
LABOR RELATIONS
EVALUATION AND
  CONTROL
MANAGING CHANGE
PRODUCTIVITY
COMMUNICATION
EEO

PROBLEM IDENTIFICATION

JOBS REQUIRED
ADMINISTRATION
  OF THOSE JOBS
WHAT IS THE REAL
  PERFORMANCE ISSUE?
DID EMPLOYEE KNOW
  WHAT WAS EXPECTED,
  ETC.?

MAKING ASSUMPTIONS

ABOUT MAJOR
  ENVIRONMENTAL
  FACTORS, MAJOR
  EXTERNAL FACTORS,
  MAJOR INTERNAL
  FACTORS

GENERATING ALTERNATIVES

CHANGE CULTURE
CHANGE ANY OF
  THE PRACTICES
HUMAN RESOURCE
  PLANNING
ATTRACTION/
  RECRUITMENT
SELECTION
TRAINING
ORIENTATION
DEVELOPMENT
COMPENSATION/
  BENEFITS
HEALTH AND SAFETY
LABOR RELATIONS
EVALUATION AND
  CONTROL
MANAGING CHANGE
PRODUCTIVITY
COMMUNICATION
EEO

EVALUATION AND CHOICE

CHANGE IN ONE
  OR MORE
  PRACTICES

IMPLEMENTATION

OF ACTION
  CHOSEN

CONTROL

CHECK FOR
  STRATEGIC
  RESULTS

tion of continued shortages, they might determine to hire more retired workers, realizing that they would only be able to employ them for a few years. Special recruiting efforts would then probably be necessary as part of implementation. Similarly, the individual manager might, in response to personnel's actions, have to change his or her selection process. That might also mean a change in leadership style—motivational and communication—in order to employ more older workers in his or her department.

The Management Challenges Identified

1. Labor market conditions and demographics are changing.
2. There is an increasing recognition of the strategic importance of the human resource. We know from Chapters 5 and 6 that increasing levels of competitiveness lead to the need to make the labor force more productive.
3. There are continuing federal government rules and regulations to be adhered to—for example, EEO, employee health and safety, and labor relations.
4. Employees' expectations and values are changing.

Some Solutions Noted in the Chapter

1. Substantially change certain HRM practices and fine tune others. The opening paragraphs of this chapter list several such changes.
2. Be alert to changes in the external environment.

Summary

1. Human resource management (HRM) is more strategically oriented today than it was in the past because of the need to match the management of human resources with an organization's attempt to compete in the marketplace. The HRM effort has also become more concerned with the overall governance of the work force, as opposed to just simple labor relations; and more emphasis has been placed on managing the organization's culture.
2. HRM practices are divided into two principal parts: those concerned with placing the employee in the job; and those concerned with administering to the employee once he or she is in the job. The former include human resources planning, recruitment, selection, orientation, and training; the latter include employee development, compensation, and benefits/motivation; employee evaluation and control; employee transitions; employee relations; employee health and safety; and the management of

change. Many advances are being made in several of these transitions. For example, more and more firms are providing outplacement counseling for those laid off or terminated.

a. The principal concern of human resources planning is to make certain that the human resources necessary to carry out an organization's strategy have been identified and planned for.

b. Recruitment aims to provide the proper number of resources with the right types of skills at the right place at the right time, to carry out the organization's strategy.

c. Selection consists of a series of steps beginning with preliminary screening, interviewing, testing, reference checking, and a physical exam. The final decision is aimed at selecting the best applicants from the pool created by the recruitment effort.

d. Orientation is designed to socialize the individual into the organization, acquainting him or her with not only the job, but with general rules and procedures and the social aspects of the work situation.

e. Training prepares the individual with skills to do a specific job.

f. Development provides long-term career skills, abilities, and knowledge, as the individual makes various transitions within the organization.

g. Compensation and benefits/motivation systems must be developed by the organization. They will not only enable it to recruit employees, but will influence individual and group levels of motivation.

h. In companies with unions, the particular circumstances of employee relations must be administered to. Major concerns typically include the negotiation of the contract and the administration of the contract.

i. Management of change is believed by most authorities to be better than an unplanned reaction to it. As organizations face more and more change, management of the change in culture becomes more critical.

j. Evaluation and control are necessary to achieve satisfactory performance levels and develop personnel.

k. Managing transitions such as promotions, transfers, retirements, and terminations is critical to an organization's health.

3. Equal Employment Opportunity affects every employment practice, and several significantly—principally human resources planning, selection, benefits and compensation, evaluation, and control.

Thinking About Management

1. Describe briefly how HRM has changed in the last few years.

2. How have EEO and affirmative action generally affected employment practices?

3. How are human resources planning and strategy related?

4. How will the changing characteristics of the work force affect employment practices?

5. What is the advantage to the prospective employee and employer of the realistic job preview?

6. Generally speaking, what can't be asked on a job application or in a job interview, relative to EEO requirements?

7. Why should a test have validity, regardless of EEO requirements?

8. Why are firms having to do more fundamental education of new employees?

9. Discuss some of the problems related to drugs and alcohol and testing for them.

10. What is the role of HRM in implementing strategy?

CASE

First Service Bank

One of the challenges facing business is motivating employees over the long period of time that job-development programs require. In 1987 First Service Bank was a small thrift institution headquartered in Leominster, Massachusetts, with assets of $857 million and thirteen branches scattered throughout north-central Massachusetts. It was experiencing difficulty in motivating its tellers first of all to remain in the program, and second, to perform at high levels. The bank's task was made even more difficult by the low rate of unemployment in the Boston area, and the subsequent high wages being paid for service employees. For example, fast food chains were then paying over $7 an hour for beginning workers. Making matters worse, the types of employees the bank was seeking for these positions wanted more than just a typical teller job. They wanted challenges and growth in their jobs. The company felt that higher pay alone was not the answer because lots of higher-paying jobs were going begging in the area. The bank had to solve this problem because it had based its competitive strategy on providing superior service to its customers over what they might obtain with other financial institutions. The human resources department was asked to develop a plan of action to overcome the problems.

DISCUSSION QUESTIONS
1. What actions would you recommend, relative to the training program?
2. Assuming that job design might be part of the problem, what actions would you take there?
3. What motivational schemes might you employ?

SOURCE: Arnold H. Wensky and Robin J. Legendre, "Incentive Training at First Service Bank," *Personnel Journal* (April 1989), pp. 102–112.

MANAGERS AT WORK

Managing the Work Force of the 1990s

Linda Sampieri, director of employee relations for Red Lobster Restaurants, had been challenged by her boss, the vice-president for human resources, to develop appropriate HRM programs for the restaurant's first-line employees and their managers. It was her boss's belief that as the work force changed dramatically in the next few years, new programs would be necessary. In Chapter 1's "Managers at Work," you were asked to suggest a new motivational program for her to use with the new work force, but now, she, and you, must contemplate what other HRM issues need to be addressed and how to deal with them.

The firm has the standard series of personnel practices—benefit packages, grievance procedures, and compensation programs— that other major food-service companies, and major companies in general, would be expected to have for full-time employees. What is being asked of her, and you, is to determine what else must be done, or what could be done instead of what is being done now. Costs are critical, as the restaurant industry will experience little or no real growth, and competition is expected to increase in the 1990s.

DISCUSSION QUESTIONS
1. For the restaurant industry, what types of major changes in work-force composition and diversity would you expect?
2. What changes in typical HRM practices might be necessary as a consequence of such changes?

Lawful or Unlawful?

The following are common pre-employment questions and requests that show up on job application forms and in interviews. With an eye toward discrimination, test yourself on the below, circling "L" for lawful and "U" for unlawful.

1. What is your maiden name?	L	U
2. What was your previous married name?	L	U
3. Have you ever worked under another name?	L	U
4. What is your title—Mr., Miss, Mrs., or Ms.?	L	U
5. What is your marital status?	L	U
6. What is your birthplace?	L	U
7. What is the birthplace of parents, spouse, or other relatives?	L	U
8. Submit proof of age (birth certificate or baptismal record).	L	U
9. What is your religious denomination or affiliation? (or church, parish, pastor or religious holidays observed)	L	U
10. Are you available for Saturday or Sunday work?	L	U
11. Are you a citizen of the U.S.?	L	U
12. Are you a naturalized citizen?	L	U
13. On what date were you granted citizenship?	L	U
14. Submit naturalization papers or first papers.	L	U
15. List past work experience.	L	U
16. List organizations, clubs, societies and lodges to which you belong.	L	U
17. What is your wife's maiden name?	L	U
18. Submit names of persons willing to provide professional and/or character references.	L	U
19. Supply names of three relatives other than father, husband or wife, or minor-age dependent children.	L	U
20. What relative can we notify in case of accident or emergency (name and address)?	L	U
21. What foreign languages can you read, write or speak?	L	U
22. How did you acquire the ability to read, write or speak a foreign language?	L	U
23. Have you ever been arrested for any crime? If so, stipulate when and where.	L	U
24. List names of dependent children under the age of 18.	L	U
25. What arrangements have you made for the care of minor children?	L	U
26. What is the lowest salary you would accept?	L	U
27. What is your height and weight?	L	U
28. Have you ever had your wages garnished?	L	U
29. Have you ever been refused a fidelity bond?	L	U
30. Do you own a home? Car? Have charge accounts?	L	U
31. What kind of work does your spouse do?	L	U
32. Attach a photograph to the application form.	L	U
33. Please submit a photograph (optional).	L	U

SOURCE: Reproduced from an article entitled "The 1.5 Million Dollar Interview," by Dr. Suzanne H. Cook, published in the December 1977 issue of *Management World* with permission from the Administrative Management Society, Willow Grove, PA 19090.

Answers

The class will discuss why each of these questions is either lawful or unlawful.

Except for questions 11, 15, 18, and 21, the questions could reasonably be construed to be discriminatory unless the employer had a very good and statistically valid reason for asking them.

Your instructor has information to assist in this discussion.

CHAPTER TWELVE

Managing Organizational Culture and Change

CHAPTER OBJECTIVES

By the time you complete this chapter you should be able to

1. Define organizational culture and describe the importance of managing culture to increasing the levels of organizational performance.
2. Discuss how to manage culture in an organization.
3. Indicate the relationships between the McKinsey Seven S's and culture.
4. Describe how organizations instill culture in their members.
5. Define and describe organizational climate and its impact on culture.
6. Describe the Likert system of climate types.
7. Describe the process of change management.
8. Define organizational development and describe its purposes.
9. Discuss resistance to change and the various strategies for coping with resistance to change.

CHAPTER OUTLINE

The Management of
Organizational Culture
 Culture as Revealed in Artifacts
Culture and Strategy
 Touch-Guy, Macho Culture
 Bet-Your-Company Culture
 Work Hard/Play Hard Culture
 Process Culture
Shared Values That
 Organizations Espouse
Fitting Employees into
the Company Culture
 Managing Culture
 Multiple Cultures
Organizational Climate
 Assessing Organizational Climate
Managing Change
Organizational Development
 Resistance to Change
Managing Culture and Change as
Problem Solving
The Management Challenges Identified
Some Solutions Noted in the Chapter

John Sculley Redefines the Culture at Apple Computers

In 1983 John Sculley, then president of PepsiCo America, agreed to become the CEO of Apple Computers. To many observers, nothing seemed farther apart than selling soft drinks and personal computers. However, Steven Jobs, then chairman of the board at Apple, a co-founder with Stephen Wozniak, and the largest single stockholder of the company, believed that both were essentially consumer products. He saw the need to have a president who could sell consumer products in a highly competitive market, someone who was more marketing oriented than Jobs or his current staff. Hiring Sculley represented an important transition for Jobs, who previously had scoffed at the inability of professional managers to make it at Apple.

Once Sculley was on board, he delayed making major decisions for a few months, except for a few immediate personnel and structural changes, until he felt sufficiently familiar with the company, its products, and the industry. But then, slowly but surely, he began to make the changes that would turn the firm from a very undisciplined, entrepreneurial organization into a more competitive, professionally managed organization.

He sought to maintain the creative and entrepreneurial spirit that had made Apple so successful, while making the company more responsive to market demands and less responsive to the demands of the egos of its managers and staff. He reorganized the company from a functional structure into one based on the major product groups. He instilled in all employees an awareness of IBM and the knowledge that IBM was not just a competitor, but a competitor that could eradicate them from the market. Apple may have invented the personal computer, but others could duplicate their feat and market it more successfully than they had. The rapid market dominance of IBM in the PC market taught this lesson more quickly than if Apple had not faced a crisis. Sculley showed them the need to look for products that met consumer demands rather than simply to sell products they had created.

He also made them aware that they couldn't just announce that they were going into the business market without a product that met the needs of that market, as they had done with the Macintosh. He looked for accessory products to work with their newest computer, the Macintosh, in order to penetrate the business market. He formulated bold marketing campaigns, among them the back-to-back SuperBowl advertising campaigns that helped attract the attention of major prospective customers. He instilled performance, competitiveness, and market orientation as values, while preserving the entrepreneurial spirit.

But he also retained much of Apple's culture. He allowed employees to continue selecting members of their work teams. He joined in the ninety-hour work weeks, beer bouts, and frivolity. He quit wearing a coat and tie and adopted a casual look. He did not interfere with those aspects of culture that aided entrepreneurship but did not harm competitiveness.

However, his quest to manage change and culture was not without conflict. He met resistance to his proposed changes, first from the professional staff, and later from Jobs. Sculley caught some of the spirit at Apple to help reduce this resistance. He surprised the staff with his enthusiasm. He won them over. Jobs was another matter. Eventually, their visions for the company diverged and could not be reconciled. Jobs resigned in 1985, after the company's board of directors backed Sculley in a showdown between the two men.

SOURCES: Joel Dreyfuss, "John Sculley Rises in the West," *Fortune* (July 9, 1984), pp. 180–184; *In Search of Excellence*, the film; and Katherine M. Hafner, "Apple's Comeback," *Business Week* (January 19, 1987), pp. 84–89. Available from Tom Peters Group, Inc., Palo Alto, CA.

Many of the best-managed companies in the United States and around the world are skilled at getting new employees to adopt their corporate culture of shared values and practices as their own. They want their people to "fly in formation," pursuing their common goals and objectives. (p. 384) (© 1984 Mark Hess)

Loving change, tumult, even chaos is a prerequisite for survival, let alone success.

Thomas J. Peters, author

Companies start with a white cloth and dye it in the colors they like.

Noritake Kobayashi
Japanese executive

When John Sculley assumed the CEO position at Apple Computers, he knew that he would have to make substantial changes in that organization's culture in order to make it more competitive in the marketplace. The constantly changing environment of personal computers called for the effective management of change. Some would resist the changes. Eventually, even Jobs himself would resist those Sculley thought necessary. The events at Apple are not unique. Every time a new company president or other organizational leader assumes the top manager's position, he or she must manage these same circumstances: culture, change, and the resistance to change. Furthermore, culture and change must be managed well by virtually all top managers and to a great extent by all managers, not just those recently appointed to their positions. AT&T, for example, underwent tremendous change in the mid- to late 1980s, after deregulation of the industry eliminated thousands of jobs. Its culture was drastically redefined from noncompetitive to competitive, and a substantive amount of resistance occurred in the years following deregulation.[1] Managers in numerous other firms, such as General Electric, Xerox, Johnson & Johnson, and Eastern Airlines, have had to manage substantial change, have modified their cultures, and in most cases have had to manage resistance, as well.[2] This chapter explores the management of culture, change, and resistance to change.

One of Apple's major market niches has always been the education market. To perpetuate that relationship, Sculley himself will sometimes introduce kids to their Apple computers. By doing so, he is maintaining a cultural ritual begun by his predecessor, Steve Jobs. (SOURCE © Rob Kinmonth)

The Management of Organizational Culture

Just as strategic management was the major concern of top management in the 1970s, the management of organizational culture was one of the two major concerns of top management in the 1980s. (Restructuring was the other.) As was shown in Figure 6.9, the McKinsey Seven S's, culture (shared values) is at the core of the organizational framework. It influences and is influenced by strategy, structure, systems, staff, style, and skills. **Organizational culture** is that pattern of shared values and norms that distinguishes an organization from all others.[3] These values and norms define "what is important around here." They provide direction, meaning, and energy for organizational members as they pursue organizational success. Managing culture requires managing the McKinsey Seven S's, setting value goals, instilling those values in new and veteran em-

AT APPLE: *On joining Apple, John Sculley was faced with numerous problems, many of which involved Apple's culture. His efforts changed the culture at Apple from free-spirited entrepreneurial and increasingly uncompetitive to disciplined entrepreneurial and high spirited but under control, professionally managed, and increasingly competitive. Without this managed change of its culture, it is likely that Apple Computers today would be either bankrupt or only a minor force in its industry. Sculley instituted new values and norms, while maintaining the more successful and relevant of the older values and norms.*

ployees, integrating culture through the use of cultural artifacts, controlling climate, and changing culture as necessary. Culture and structure are highly interdependent. As structure is changed, culture must be also. If culture changes, structure must also.

The success of most Japanese firms in managing their organizational cultures to increase levels of productivity, and the success of many American firms to do likewise, have provoked interest in managing culture.[4] Not all Japanese and American efforts have been successful, especially where transferring cultures from one societal culture to another is involved. Europeans have begun to emulate both Japanese and U.S. cultural models in an attempt to improve productivity. Assimilation of different cultures must occur on a country-to-country basis in Europe if the twelve nations of the European Economic Community (EEC) are to become one true common market in 1992.

Culture as Revealed in Artifacts

An organization's culture is revealed in four common artifacts, as shown in Figure 12.1: its myths and sagas; its language systems and metaphors; its symbols, ceremonies, and rituals; and its identifiable value systems and behavioral norms.[5]

CORPORATE MYTHS AND SAGAS

Corporate myths and sagas tell us important historical facts about organizational behavior, including pioneer people and products; past triumphs and failures; and those visionaries who have transformed the company. Such stories help shape the values and norms, attitudes, and behavior of new employees, as well as continue to mold those of established employees. Myths and sagas focus organizational members' concerns upon shared values and norms and reinforce them.

Mary Kay Ash, founder of Mary Kay Cosmetics, believes strongly in the right of women to succeed. And she has a clear understanding of the women she is trying to motivate. She motivates them principally with money and symbols of success—mink coats, diamonds, and pink Cadillacs. She also motivates by providing recognition and opportunities for the success for other women. She often tells the story that she couldn't find opportunities for women in her career as a salesperson. She wanted to create some place where women could be successful. So she did. She started her own company with a $5,000 investment. Her success story is told over and over by those who work for her. Now her company is a multimillion-dollar, international company. Her concerns for people are also well known. She bakes cookies for each and every class of new recruits and serves them herself in her own home.[6] Such stories serve to promote the values and norms that Mary Kay seeks for her company: A place where women can succeed and gain self-esteem, a place where high levels of motivation are desired, a place where performance is rewarded, and a place where management cares about its people.

When top management changes, its culture often changes as well. For years General Electric's heroes thrived on innovation. The company slogan reminded all, "Progress is our most important product." It became a multinational conglomerate, with literally hundreds of businesses grouped into several major business divisions. But it became stagnant. Some of those businesses grew old and seemed incapable of innovating or performing well, such as the television division. Along came John F. Welch, Jr., in 1981. In five years he eliminated 100,000 employees, more than one-fourth of the work force, sold off the ailing businesses, and acquired others, including RCA. Welch himself claims that he has transformed the company into a lean and mean fighting machine. Others

FIGURE 12.1 CULTURAL ARTIFACTS

MYTHS AND SAGAS
MARY KAY, STANDING AT THE LEFT, HAS CAREFULLY FOSTERED MYTHS AND SAGAS ABOUT SUCCESS FOR HER EMPLOYEES. SHE HAS CREATED A PLACE WHERE WOMEN CAN SUCCEED AND GAIN SELF-ESTEEM. HER PERSONAL HISTORY OF SUCCESS, COMBINED WITH MANY OTHER ELEMENTS, SUCH AS THIS AWARDS CEREMONY, ENABLE HER TO HAVE HIGHLY MOTIVATED EMPLOYEES. (© TED MUNGER/COURTESY MARY KAY COSMETICS, INCORPORATED)

SYMBOLISM, CEREMONIES, AND RITUALS
EVERYONE AT DISNEY IS A MEMBER OF THE CAST. THIS USE OF LANGUAGE AND METAPHOR HAS HISTORICALLY LED TO A HIGH LEVEL OF EMPLOYEE LOYALTY, AND A HEIGHTENED LEVEL OF EMPLOYEE COMMITMENT. (COURTESY WALT DISNEY COMPANY)

LANGUAGE SYSTEM AND METAPHORS
AT FORD, THE "QUALITY IS JOB 1" MOTTO, COMPLETELY TRANSFORMED THE COMPANY, MAKING IT COMPETITIVE WITH THE JAPANESE. (© ROBERT REICHERT)

IDENTIFIABLE VALUE SYSTEMS AND BEHAVIORAL NORMS
ONE OF HEWLETT-PACKARD'S BEHAVIORAL NORMS IS THAT PEOPLE SHOULD NOT ONLY BE HEALTHY, BUT HAVE FUN. A LITTLE EXERCISE MAY ALSO HELP PEOPLE WORK BETTER. (© ED KASHI)

disagree. They see Welch as a cost cutter who doesn't understand strategy. "Neutron Jack," as he is known to some, has a habit of making a major impact like a nuclear weapon, without, many argue, being discriminating about the target area—everybody goes, but the building is left standing. While the vote is still out on Jack, it is clear that his actions have changed the company's culture. His changes lowered morale, especially in some of the core businesses, as the GE business portfolio moved more toward high tech and away from its core firms. Undeniably, he has made managers much more cost conscious, more concerned about the bottom line, and much more concerned about innovation, but not for its own sake, as was true early on at GE. Rather, innovation is important to keep the various businesses competitive.[7] GE's myths and sagas, rituals, and values and norms have all changed. "What's important around here," has changed.

LANGUAGE SYSTEMS AND METAPHORS

The language systems and metaphors used in organizations often indicate their shared values. Some companies focus on the competition—they must "do battle" or "capture" market share. Leaders talk about ambushes and shootouts with competitors.[8] Others focus on the technologies or processes that they use. Professors often speak of pedagogical devices, course content, and presentation techniques. A high-tech firm might be concerned with nuclear accelerators or photon lasers or working on "the project." Bureaucrats in Washington often speak in terms of acronyms, ever searching to contain the "bureaucratese" with which they are saddled: PUD—Planned Urban Development; DEA—Drug Enforcement Administration; DOD—Department of Defense. When people who work at Disney talk about the Magic Kingdom, an imaginary character is brought to life, such as Mickey or Donald. Everyone at Disney is a "member of the cast," not an employee. Everyone is constantly "on stage," referring back to the company's original core business—movies.

SYMBOLS, CEREMONIES, AND RITUALS OF ORGANIZATIONS

An organization's symbols, ceremonies, and rituals also tell what's important.[9] Its logo, flag, and slogans convey the importance it places on certain ideas or events. In business, celebrations of successful sales campaigns are often flamboyant. Versitek, a Xerox subsidiary that manufactures computer printers, celebrated one very successful year in a rather unique way. Robert Murray, director of corporate communication, describes the way the company announced the achievement of its financial objectives to employees with a special profit-sharing program. "We hired an elephant and the Stanford University marching band. It is quite a job to get eight hundred employees into a building without letting them know what was going on. We got them inside and the VPs announced this year's highlights and then got to the profit sharing. 'We can't say how big the numbers are,' one said, 'so let's see how big they really are.' Then we slid open the door and in marched the band, and they all thought it was fairly impressive."[10] No ceremony could have been noticed more than the movement of R. J. Reynold's corporate headquarters from Winston-Salem, North Carolina, to Atlanta, Georgia. In January 1987, less than a year and a half after the 1985 acquisition of Nabisco by R. J. Reynolds, Nabisco's former chief executive, F. Ross Johnson, became CEO of RJR. He immediately moved the company's headquarters to Atlanta to signal quite clearly to everyone involved that tobacco was no longer the company's central focus.[11] At Apple Computer, when Steven Jobs became angry over his reduced role in the company, he established the Macintosh division to develop the new PC. He and a group of followers established their own company within a company in a building separate from the rest of Apple. They proudly flew the "Jolly Roger" as a symbol of defiance in front of the building as a symbol of their independence.[12]

Organizational mottos are also important. Robert Hershey relates a story about the 1983 terrorist bombing of the U.S. Marine encampment in Beirut, which ended in the death of 142 Marines. General Paul S. Kelley, commandant of the U.S. Marine Corps, was visiting surviving servicemen in the hospital. One Marine, covered in bandages, unable to talk, and connected to every type of life-support system imaginable, upon seeing the General asked for a piece of paper and a pen. He wrote the words *Semper Fi,* an abbreviation for the Marine motto, *Semper Fidelis* or "Always Faithful" (Figure 12.2).

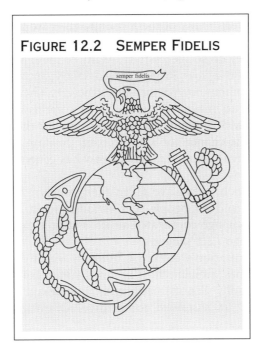

FIGURE 12.2   SEMPER FIDELIS

In that recounting of a motto, a young Marine told the world what he and the Marines stood for, the kind of people they were, the kind of person a Marine is. Other organizations receive similar, if not as dramatic, loyalty from many of their employees.[13]

A good motto should meet the following criteria:

1. It should convey and promote a core philosophy of the organization.
2. It should have an emotional appeal rather than a rational and intellectual appeal.
3. It should not be a direct exhortation for loyalty, productivity, quality, and any other organizational objective; otherwise, it will not have an emotional impact on the employee.
4. It should be mysterious to the public but not to organizational members. This allows insiders to understand it, but not others.[14]

"*Semper Fi*" meets all those characteristics; so does "*Je me souviens,*" French for "I Remember," the motto of the Canadian province of Quebec.[15] Ford Motor Company's "Quality is Job 1" is a motto that has helped transform the company into a manufacturer of high-quality automobiles. According to surveys, Ford was the producer of the highest-quality American automobiles for seven years in a row—1980–1987.[16] While the definition has an obvious meaning to outsiders, and exhorts quality, only its intensity is understood within the company.

IDENTIFIABLE VALUE SYSTEMS AND BEHAVIORAL NORMS

Identifiable value systems and behavioral norms are reflected in strategy, structure, systems, style, staffing, corporate skills, policies, rules, procedures, and what is rewarded and what is not. Very importantly, they are passed on in informal communications. How an organization is structured, for example, whether it allows individuals to participate or not, and how it allows individuals to participate are critical components of the value system. Even the size of an organization's corporate staff signals values. The recent concern for quality among automobile firms and other American manufacturers shows a trend in values toward increased competitiveness.[17]

At Trammel Crow Company, the global real estate development and management firm, employees, many of them young MBAs from major colleges (350 of the 1,900 employees are MBAs), are encouraged to take risks, and they are highly rewarded if they do so successfully. Many of these MBAs come to Trammel Crow for $18,000 a year in guaranteed salary, much below the market wage, but within a commission/partnership structure. They have an almost immediate opportunity to make very, very large commissions, although some might "starve." The MBAs come to Trammel Crow for the big commissions in the short term and the chance for a partnership position in the long term. By using this dual incentive system, Trammel Crow has generated the entrepreneurial spirit it needs.[18]

At Eaton Corporation, they have taken their concern for culture, for management philosophy, and for people very seriously for a long time. Reflecting the time required to change corporate culture, Eaton is proud of its results, as Management Challenge 12.1 suggests.

Managing an organization's culture is not easy. Even determining what the culture is, is sometimes difficult. It is becoming increasingly evident that organizations with a readily identifiable culture, that manage the culture properly, usually have a source of sustained competitive advantage. Conversely, those

---

MANAGEMENT CHALLENGE 12.1

Eaton Corporation

It has become a commonplace of management theory that the expectations of today's employees have changed and that a primary task of effective management is to create a system that meets modern employees' demands for more knowledge about, and more participation in, the decisions that affect their lives.

Eaton, in fact, began two decades ago the long, hard process of transforming its human resources management techniques through an experiment with an all-salaried plant. That experiment, and the results of similar approaches at some twenty Eaton facilities constructed since, convinced Eaton to pursue this management approach at all its facilities. They call it the Eaton Philosophy. Such an approach was very advanced when they began it.

Creating the atmosphere in which employees can and will give their full potential is a never-ending task, but one which Eaton has adopted as a companywide imperative. The practice of the Eaton Philosophy is an on-going priority for every Eaton manager. It requires periodic fertilization in order to keep up the momentum, but it is creating a work force whose dedication to excellence is the company's most valuable—and proudest—asset.

SOURCE: *Eaton Corporation: 1985 Annual Report*, Cleveland, Ohio, p. 25.

with less identifiable cultures and/or those who do not manage their culture very well are usually less successful.[19]

Ralph H. Kilmann found that norms play a very important part in establishing culture.[20] Typical norms include: Don't express your feelings. Tell the boss what he wants to hear. Don't be late. Don't be associated with a failure. Don't upstage the boss. Keep plenty of records to protect yourself. Norms, which are informally set standards of behavior, were found by Kilmann to be negative in connotation about 90 percent of the time. This finding suggests that, at least in the organizations he studied, people are survival oriented. Viewed in this light, culture, as expressed in norms, could become a negative influence on performance.

Culture and Strategy

Major influences on corporate culture are corporate and business strategies, as defined in Chapter 6, and as interrelated by the McKinsey Seven S's model, also discussed in that chapter. Terrence E. Deal and Allan A. Kennedy,[21] researchers of and consultants on corporate culture, suggest that the relationship between strategy and culture is very pronounced and results in the four readily identifiable cultural categories shown in Figure 12.3: tough-guy, macho culture; bet-your-company culture; work hard/play hard culture; and process culture. These are based on combinations of the speed of the feedback given on strategic performance and the degree of risk taken in the strategic decisions being made. Companies may change from one type to another over time, sometimes intentionally, sometimes as the consequence of changing circumstances.

Tough-Guy, Macho Culture

When strategic problem solvers commit large sums of money in highly competitive situations seeking a quick turnaround in sales, a **tough-guy, macho culture** dominates. Managerial problem solvers operating in a tough-guy, macho culture quickly learn the consequences of their high-risk strategic decisions. Such cultures are typical in venture-capital investments for high-tech manufacturers with short product life cycles, such as computer work stations or PCs; large construction projects such as the Taj Mahal casino in Atlantic City, New Jersey; or the chance to obtain a new client if you are an advertising company. Leaders in this culture tend to be individuals. They are also the heroes, the ones that pulled off the big deal. The stories that are told involve past risks that resulted in success. Slogans recount battle cries, and ceremonies focus on problem solving.

Bet-Your-Company Culture

The **bet-your-company** culture results from decisions where feedback is slow, but risks are high. Large financial investments are made in highly competitive environments where payoffs take a while to develop. This culture is common in capital-intensive industries (those requiring major investment in plants, equipment, or R&D), such as aerospace, defense, and petroleum. Boeing Aircraft, for example, is spending billions of dollars to develop its 7J7 airplane, but it won't know for several years whether it will pay off.[22] Genentech, the leading biotechnology company in the 1980s, invested hundreds of millions of dollars on R&D and hired a marketing staff before it had any products. It literally bet the

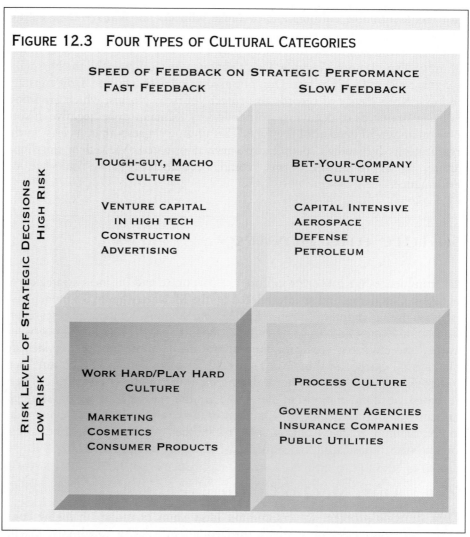

FIGURE 12.3 FOUR TYPES OF CULTURAL CATEGORIES

SPEED OF FEEDBACK ON STRATEGIC PERFORMANCE
FAST FEEDBACK   SLOW FEEDBACK

RISK LEVEL OF STRATEGIC DECISIONS

HIGH RISK

TOUGH-GUY, MACHO
CULTURE

VENTURE CAPITAL
IN HIGH TECH
CONSTRUCTION
ADVERTISING

BET-YOUR-COMPANY
CULTURE

CAPITAL INTENSIVE
AEROSPACE
DEFENSE
PETROLEUM

LOW RISK

WORK HARD/PLAY HARD
CULTURE

MARKETING
COSMETICS
CONSUMER PRODUCTS

PROCESS CULTURE

GOVERNMENT AGENCIES
INSURANCE COMPANIES
PUBLIC UTILITIES

SOURCE: TERRENCE E. DEAL AND ALLAN A. KENNEDY, CORPORATE CULTURES: RITES AND RITUALS OF CORPORATE LIFE (READING, MA: ADDISON-WESLEY, 1982), PP. 107–108. REPRINTED WITH PERMISSION OF THE PUBLISHER.

Donald Trump epitomizes the leader in the tough-guy macho culture. He rolls the dice often in major construction projects. Some win, some lose. (SOURCE © Bernard Gotfryd/ Woodfin Camp & Associates)

The success of a product depends partly on constant testing. In the work hard/play hard culture of Procter & Gamble, no facet of product development is left to chance. These professional laundresses at P&G's Cincinatti research center, test P&G detergents in waters and washing machines from such countries as Japan, Peru, and Mexico. (SOURCE © Louis Psihoyos/Matrix)

company and its investors' money on its ability to develop products that didn't exist when the company was born.[23]

The heroes in this culture are sage and experienced. They have survived the long haul and worked the ins and outs of betting the company. The culture's ceremonies typically call for formal meetings to reduce uncertainty, and it is businesslike when it comes to evaluating its successes and failures.

Work Hard/Play Hard Culture

The **work hard/play hard** culture merges the situation characterized by fast feedback but low risk. It is a fast-paced culture where fun is important and there is lots of action for everyone. This culture encourages creativity in problem solving.

This culture often occurs in marketing-oriented firms. Mary Kay Cosmetics, certain types of retail stores, consulting firms, and larger computer manufacturers possess this type of culture. Managers make many decisions, but most of them involve little risk. The new product either sells or it doesn't; the effect of its sales on total company sales is minimal, although for that particular manager it may be extremely consequential. A product manager's efforts at Procter & Gamble, a company with more than seven hundred products and product managers, will have little effect on the total company if he or she fails. But failure could mean he or she will be fired. The heroes are super salespeople, yet they are often team players. Sales conventions, meetings, contests, and parties, all reinforce the values of hard work, hard play. Mary Kay Cosmetics, for example, is well known for its extravagant annual convention.

Process Culture

The **process culture** evolves from situations in which the feedback is slow and the risk is low. Organizations with this culture typically include governmental

AT APPLE: The tough-guy, macho culture best characterizes the early days of Apple. Steven Jobs and Stephen Wozniak founded the company in 1977 and immediately dominated the industry with the Apple II. Over time, the company faced many challenges. Its strategy grew; the company began to look more like a bet-your-company culture. In many ways Apple also resembled a work hard/play hard culture, with its beer busts, practical jokes, and ninety-hour work weeks.

agencies, insurance companies, and public utilities. Note, however, that cultures in some of these organizations—for example, insurance companies—are now beginning to change because the environments they face are higher in risk than in the past. (In some cases there is also faster feedback.) The title "process" culture describes how problems are solved and how decisions are made. Because it is often difficult to tell what the results of decisions are, and because there is no particular risk in these organizations, the key value is the way in which one makes decisions—the process. They are not result-oriented organizational environments, but rather activity oriented. Typically these organizations are described as mechanistic. The Department of Health and Human Services of the federal government is a classic example.

Heroes in this culture are those who devise new processes and who serve in maintenance roles for the organization; they act to keep the company going, perhaps by providing recognition or passing on information. Ceremonies reward performance in processes. A thirty-year pin is a symbol of one's success in this organization.

Shared Values That Organizations Espouse

IBM has charted its course since 1924 with three key values originated by its founder Thomas J. Watson, Sr.

1. Respect for the individual—caring about the basic rights of each person in the organization and not just when it is convenient or expedient to do so.
2. Customer service—giving the best customer service of any company in the world, not some of the time but all of the time.
3. Excellence—believing that all job holders and products should perform in a superior way.[24]

This credo appears everywhere at IBM—on the walls, in manuals, in discussions among employees. If you ask any IBM employee, he or she will tell you the customer comes first, that IBM cares about the individual, and that everything must be done with a high level of quality. More and more organizations are beginning to recognize the importance of stating what is of value to them. Such a statement is contained in Figure 12.4.

If you want to know what an organization's culture is, just ask people there what is important. Have them describe their strategy, structure, systems, style, staff, skills, rules or policies, and procedures. Have them describe their heroes, their ceremonies, their symbols, their stories, their slogans. If they say the customer is important around there, what do they do to make it so? AM International, a worldwide sales and service firm serving the graphic arts industry, inverted its organization chart, with the customer at the top. The "players," who are the front-line employees, are next to the top. Then, in succeeding order, there are the "coaches" and "scorekeepers."[25] This unique organization chart is shown in Figure 12.5. Management's role changes dramatically in such a situation, from order giver to facilitator, counselor, and supporter. What about the creative organizational culture? What is it like? Management Challenge 12.2 provides some insight into those questions.

FIGURE 12.4 SAMPLE OF A CULTURAL STATEMENT

SECURITY PACIFIC CREDO—FINAL DRAFT

FULFILLING SIX COMMITMENTS

THIS SECURITY PACIFIC CREDO IS THE PRODUCT OF HUNDREDS OF EMPLOYEES WORKING TO ESTABLISH A SET OF IDEAS WHICH WOULD PROVIDE GUIDELINES FOR DECISION AND ACTION THROUGHOUT THE CORPORATION. IT IS CLEAR THAT AMONG THE EMPLOYEES OF SECURITY PACIFIC THERE ARE MANY DIFFERENT DEFINITIONS OF THE COMMITMENTS, OBLIGATIONS AND RESPONSIBILITIES OF THE FIRM AND ITS EMPLOYEES. THIS CREDO REPRESENTS MUCH OF THE COLLECTIVE COMMON GROUNDS WHICH EXISTS WITHIN THE MANY PARTICIPANTS FROM ALL LEVELS OF THE ORGANIZATION WHO HELPED BRING IT TO ITS PRESENT STAGE. IT DOES NOT REPRESENT PERFECTION TO ANY WHO HAVE PARTICIPATED, BUT IT DOES REPRESENT POINTS OF BROAD GENERAL AGREEMENT WITH REGARD TO A DESIRABLE COLLECTIVE CORPORATE ENVIRONMENT AND SET OF STANDARDS FOR ALL OF US.

COMMITMENTS

THE BASIC OBJECTIVE IN DEVELOPING THIS CREDO WAS TO SEEK A SET OF PRINCIPLES AND BELIEFS WHICH MIGHT PROVIDE GUIDANCE AND DIRECTION TO OUR WORK, AND TO CONTINUE TO BUILD ON WHAT WE ALREADY HAVE. CONFLICTING PRESSURES IN TODAY'S HIGHLY COMPETITIVE ENVIRONMENT PRODUCE DIFFERENT MEASUREMENTS OF SUCCESSES THAT CAN ACCOMPANY ECONOMIC SUCCESS. FOR THAT REASON, WE HAVE SHAPED THESE SIX EQUALLY IMPORTANT COMMITMENTS.

COMMITMENT TO CUSTOMER

THE FIRST COMMITMENT IS TO PROVIDE OUR CUSTOMERS WITH QUALITY PRODUCTS AND SERVICES WHICH ARE INNOVATIVE AND TECHNO-LOGICALLY RESPONSIVE TO THEIR CURRENT REQUIREMENTS, AT APPROPRIATE PRICES. TO PERFORM THESE TASKS WITH INTEGRITY REQUIRES THAT WE MAINTAIN CONFIDENTIALITY AND PROTECT CUSTOMER PRIVACY, PROMOTE CUSTOMER SATISFACTION AND SERVE CUSTOMER NEEDS. WE STRIVE TO SERVE QUALIFIED CUSTOMERS AND INDUSTRIES WHICH ARE SOCIALLY RESPONSIBLE ACCORDING TO BROADLY ACCEPTED COMMUNITY AND COMPANY STANDARDS.

COMMITMENT TO EMPLOYEE

THE SECOND COMMITMENT IS TO ESTABLISH AN ENVIRONMENT FOR OUR EMPLOYEES WHICH PROMOTES PROFESSIONAL GROWTH, ENCOUR-AGES EACH PERSON TO ACHIEVE HIS OR HER HIGHEST POTENTIAL, AND PROMOTES INDIVIDUAL CREATIVITY AND RESPONSIBILITY. SECURITY PACIFIC ACKNOWLEDGES OUR RESPONSIBILITY TO EMPLOYEES, INCLUDING PROVIDING FOR OPEN AND HONEST COMMUNICATION, STATED EXPECTATIONS, FAIR AND TIMELY ASSESSMENT OF PERFORMANCE AND EQUITABLE COMPENSATION WHICH REWARDS EMPLOYEE CONTRIBU-TIONS TO COMPANY OBJECTIVES WITHIN A FRAMEWORK OF EQUAL OPPORTUNITY AND AFFIRMATIVE ACTION.

COMMITMENT OF EMPLOYEE TO SECURITY PACIFIC

THE THIRD COMMITMENT IS THAT OF THE EMPLOYEE TO SECURITY PACIFIC. AS EMPLOYEES, WE STRIVE TO UNDERSTAND AND ADHERE TO THE CORPORATION'S POLICIES AND OBJECTIVES, ACT IN A PROFESSIONAL MANNER, AND GIVE OUR BEST EFFORT TO IMPROVE SECURITY PACIFIC. WE RECOGNIZE THE TRUST AND CONFIDENCE PLACED IN US BY OUR CUSTOMERS AND COMMUNITY AND ACT WITH INTEGRITY AND HONESTY IN ALL SITUATIONS TO PRESERVE THAT TRUST AND CONFIDENCE. WE ACT RESPONSIBLY TO AVOID CONFLICTS OF INTEREST AND OTHER SITUATIONS WHICH ARE POTENTIALLY HARMFUL TO THE CORPORATION.

COMMITMENT OF EMPLOYEE TO EMPLOYEE

THE FOURTH COMMITMENT IS THAT OF EMPLOYEES TO THEIR FELLOW EMPLOYEES. WE MUST BE COMMITTED TO PROMOTE A CLIMATE OF MUTUAL RESPECT, INTEGRITY, AND PROFESSIONAL RELATIONSHIPS, CHARACTERIZED BY OPEN AND HONEST COMMUNICATIONS WITHIN AND ACROSS ALL LEVELS OF THE ORGANIZATION. SUCH A CLIMATE WILL PROMOTE ATTAINMENT OF THE CORPORATION'S GOALS AND OBJECTIVES, WHILE LEAVING ROOM FOR INDIVIDUAL INITIATIVE WITHIN A COMPETITIVE ENVIRONMENT.

COMMITMENT TO COMMUNITIES

THE FIFTH COMMITMENT IS THAT OF SECURITY PACIFIC TO THE COMMUNITIES WHICH WE SERVE. WE MUST CONSTANTLY STRIVE TO IMPROVE THE QUALITY OF LIFE THROUGH OUR SUPPORT OF COMMUNITY ORGANIZATIONS AND PROJECTS, THROUGH ENCOURAGING SERVICE TO THE COMMUNITY BY EMPLOYEES, AND BY PROMOTING PARTICIPATION IN COMMUNITY SERVICES. BY THE APPROPRIATE USE OF OUR RESOURCES, WE WORK TO SUPPORT OR FURTHER ADVANCE THE INTERESTS OF THE COMMUNITY, PARTICULARLY IN TIMES OF CRISIS OR SOCIAL NEED. THE CORPORATION AND ITS EMPLOYEES ARE COMMITTED TO COMPLYING FULLY WITH EACH COMMUNITY'S LAWS AND REGULATIONS.

COMMITMENT TO STOCKHOLDER

THE SIXTH COMMITMENT OF SECURITY PACIFIC IS TO ITS STOCKHOLDERS. WE WILL STRIVE TO PROVIDE CONSISTENT GROWTH AND A SUPERIOR RATE OF RETURN ON THEIR INVESTMENT, TO MAINTAIN A POSITION AND REPUTATION AS A LEADING FINANCIAL INSTITUTION, TO PROTECT STOCKHOLDER INVESTMENTS, AND TO PROVIDE FULL AND TIMELY INFORMATION. ACHIEVEMENT OF THESE GOALS FOR SECURITY PACIFIC IS DEPENDENT UPON THE SUCCESSFUL DEVELOPMENT OF THE FIVE PREVIOUS SETS OF RELATIONSHIPS.

SOURCE: SECURITY PACIFIC CORPORATION

The Creative Organizational Culture

What are some of the characteristics of a creative organizational culture? They tolerate extremely creative people, they reward creative ideas, they have systems for advancing creative ideas upward in an organization, they train people to be creative, they celebrate creative successes, and they tend to be more democratic and less rules oriented. One company, Herman Miller, Inc., a highly innovative

Fitting Employees into the Company Culture

AT APPLE: *The organization inculturation process begins with a very rigorous selection process. Apple doesn't have the training indoctrination that others might, but they seem to follow the seven steps of socialization from there on. For a while, it wasn't clear, within the company, what the role models should be—innovator, manager, entrepreneur?*

Corporate culture is an expression of the shared values of an organization, but individual values vary. This implies that individual values must be changed to match those of the group and the organization or that, at the very least, the individual must adopt new values. If a three-piece blue suit, white shirt, dark tie, and wing-tip shoes constitute the IBM "uniform," then the individual had better dress that way. If, as is the case, the official doctrine of Electronic Data Systems is that you shall not wear shoes with tassels, then no one who intends to be with the company in the future will be wearing shoes with tassels.[26]

Richard T. Pascale, after examining numerous corporate cultures, proposed that organizations fit employees into the company culture through a seven-step process that he calls the "Seven Steps of Socialization."

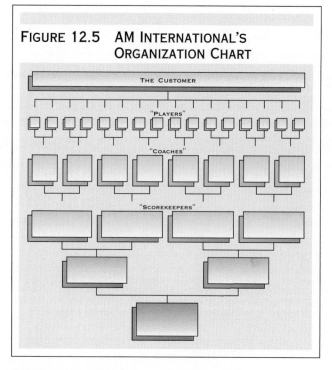

FIGURE 12.5 AM INTERNATIONAL'S ORGANIZATION CHART

THE CUSTOMER

"PLAYERS"

"COACHES"

"SCOREKEEPERS"

SOURCE: AM INTERNATIONAL INTERNAL DOCUMENTS.

office furniture design company, believes that the key to creativity is in eliminating the stress and inconveniences of the daily work routine. They have provided informal meeting areas throughout their offices. These give people a place to sit and chat whenever ideas occur. They let employees design their own offices, believing that different people need different types of work spaces. And they have located their research department far from the main office, giving them real, as well as symbolic, freedom.

SOURCES: James M. Higgins, "Increasing Organizational Innovation: A Seven S's Perspective," article in progress; Charles O'Reilly "Corporations, Culture, and Commitment: Motivation and Social Control in Organizations," *California Management Review*, Summer 1989, pp. 9–25 and "Eureka! New Ideas on Boosting Creativity," *Success* (December 1985), p. 27.

Step 1: **The company subjects candidates for employment to a selection process so rigorous that it often seemed designed to discourage individuals rather than encourage them to take the job.**

Companies with strong cultures—those that are clearly defined and well entrenched—employ numerous selection devices, including multiple interviews. Candidates are given a realistic picture of the organization, its pluses and minuses. Procter & Gamble, for example, conducts a series of at least two front-line manager interviews before candidates are flown to its headquarters in Cincinnati for an additional round of interviews. The New York investment banking firm Morgan Stanley carefully outlines the demands of a 100-hour work week, and suggests that those whose families would object need not apply.

Step 2: **The company subjects the newly hired individual to experiences calculated to induce humility and to make him question his prior behavior, beliefs, and values. By lessening his comfort with himself, the company hopes to promote openness toward its own norms and values.**

Morgan Stanley works its new recruits to a state of near exhaustion with fourteen-hour-a-day, seven-day-a-week schedules. At Xerox the process is designed to turn recruits into "Xeroids." A three-week-long, exhaustive indoctrination takes place.[27] Management Challenge 12.3 describes one such program in more detail.

Step 3: **The companies send the newly humbled recruits into the trenches, pushing them to master one of the disciplines of the core of the company's business. The newcomer's promotions are tied to how he does in that business.**

At Delta Airlines, Morgan Stanley, McKinsey and Company, IBM, and a host of others, new recruits must work their way up through the organization. It takes six years to become an IBM marketing representative. Advancement is slow and based on performance.

Step 4: **At every stage of the new manager's career, the company measures the operating results he has achieved and rewards him accordingly.**

At IBM, the company makes certain that managers and others adhere to the company's three credos. Especially important for the manager is the one about the treatment of other people. IBM has been known to punish managers who failed to treat subordinates properly by reassigning them to less desirable jobs.

At Procter & Gamble, the performance of new professionals is evaluated against three core factors: building volume, building profits, and conducting changes.

Step 5: All along the way the company promotes adherence to its transcendent values, those overarching purposes that rise way above the day-to-day imperative to make a buck.

At Delta Airlines, new recruits learn about "the family." All employees are members of the family, and the family works together through thick and thin. Members take paycuts to avoid laying off other members of the family. Or senior pilots may take reduced hours to avoid cutbacks. Sacrifices are necessary but "the family" survives.

Step 6: The company constantly harps on watershed events in the organization's history that reaffirm the importance of the firm's culture. Folklore reinforces a code of conduct—how we do things around here.

One of the stories frequently told at Procter & Gamble reveals its emphasis on honesty. A top-brand manager was fired because he overstated the product's features. At AT&T, stories focus on keeping the system working regardless of emergency situations. These stories not only carry a moral, but they encourage the continuation of such behavior by the recruit.

MANAGEMENT CHALLENGE **12.3**

Providing Important Culture at General Electric

How do you assimilate 2,500 new college graduates a year into a company? How do you assimilate acquisitions of corporations like RCA, Kidder, Peabody and Company, and others? How do you get thousands of new managers a year to manage the company way? How do you get everyone in the company to share a common vision? General Electric's answer is Crotonville—the Crotonville Management Development Institute in Ossining, New York.

The thirty-one-year-old Crotonville Institute spreads over fifty rolling acres near the Hudson River. It does much more than teach traditional business courses like accounting and finance. It spreads Chairman John Welch's vision of the company. It helps mold a common GE culture. Its success has caused several companies to emulate it, including Hitashi, Limited, which built a virtual replica of Crotonville in Japan. Others, such as Ford Motor Company and Life Insurance Company of America, have adopted some of its ideas for their own use. Courses at Crotonville vary. Each of the 2,500 new college graduates that GE hires every year spends approximately 2½ days there. At the other extreme, upper-level managers are expected to attend much longer programs. Lectures vary from in-house staff to ex-West Point officers to professors from leading business schools. The focus is on teamwork and learning from others. It is more than just classwork. River raft races help build camaraderie as well as leadership.

Crotonville's mission reads "to make GE managers more action-oriented, more risk-oriented, more people-oriented." "It's supposed to develop leaders, not just managers," Chairman Jack Welch observes, "Yesterday's idea of the boss, who became the boss because he or she knew one more fact than the person working for them, is yesterday's manager. Tomorrow's person needs to envision a shared set of values, a shared objective."

Step 7: The company supplies promising individuals with role models. These models are consistent—each exemplary manager displays the same traits.

These role models are winners, winners to be imitated. IBM, 3M, and AT&T all provide models for what is expected. They may be peers or supervisors. The protégé watches the role model make presentations, write memos, handle conflicts, or manage and then attempts to duplicate those efforts. The good companies provide these models intentionally. In some firms, they may not just happen by accident.[28]

Managing Culture

Probably the most talked about organizational phenomena for managers in the 1980s has been organizational culture. The effective manager must identify the existing culture and its impact upon organizational effectiveness and efficiency. He or she must then determine if it is the appropriate culture and, if it is not, must change it to the one that is. Each manager must learn to manage within the culture.

New managers are sent to Crotonville about six months after their promotion. They have had time to make mistakes as managers, and they come armed with performance appraisals noting successes and failures. They work in teams partly to help them realize that others are suffering similar problems.

Important critical company issues are addressed. Many of the exercises are focused on real GE problems—for example, becoming more competitive in a particular division in a global economy. One of many interesting tools used is "The New Manager's Starter Kit," which contains a guide to solving eighty-two problems, ranging from cutting a budget to handing disgruntled employees.

SOURCES: Janet Guyon, "Culture Class: GE's Management School Aims to Foster Unified Corporate Roles," *Wall Street Journal* 10 August, 1987, p. 29; and Judith H. Dobrzynski, "GE's Training Camp: An Outward Bound for Managers," *Business Week* (December 14, 1987), p. 98.

This professor at the Crotonville facility has just introduced his class to one of the practical rules of thumb that GE tries to teach its new managers. Using a case, he is discussing with students how to handle an employee whose motivation level has dropped. (SOURCE © John Abbott)

Culture has to be understood at two levels: the mythical side, which includes the myths, stories, heroes, symbols, slogans, and ceremonies; and "the way we do it around here."[29] "The way we do it around here" is indicated in strategy, structure, systems, style, staffing, skills, rules, procedures, policies, and norms. The manager, whether a department manager or CEO, must learn to manage both these shared values.

Multiple Cultures

Managing culture is further complicated by the fact that culture varies within the organization. There will be a common culture and a set of multiple subcultures. In addition, there will be varying degrees of acceptance or rejection of the key values of each culture.[30] A particular manager, a particular group of managers, a set of environmental circumstances, responses to corporate pressures or a lack thereof, disagreement with company policies and procedures, and even interpretations of meanings of values will lead to different behaviors within an organization.

Cultural diversity also exists within an organization because of the changing demographics of the U.S. work force. Historically, the American work force has been perceived as predominantly white and male with a wife at home. But that perception has been changing and will change even more drastically in the future. From 1989 to the year 2000, only 15 percent of the net new members of that work force will be native white males, compared to 48 percent of the total work force in 1988. The remainder of the new employees will be nonwhite males and females, immigrant males and females, and native white females (42 percent).[31] Furthermore, the number of married women working will continue to increase significantly. There are going to be more divorced people in the work force, and more single parents. The Black and Hispanic populations will increase disproportionately at a higher rate than whites, as well. A more diverse racial and ethnic work force will exist, along with one with fewer traditional male head-of-household wage earners.[32] Some companies—Digital Equipment Corporation (DEC), for example—have already initiated programs to work within such an environment. DEC's cultural diversity program—"valuing diversity"—cuts across all levels of the organization. Barbara Walker, its founder, labels it "good business," not just doing good.[33] For multinational firms, numerous cultures may exist. In such cases, a cultural integrator may be used. He or she functions to coordinate the diverse operations of various cultures and, hence, must be familiar with several.[34]

Multiple cultures naturally exist within an organization when two organizations merge.[35] When General Motors acquired Electronic Data Systems (EDS),

One of the principles of DEC's cultural diversity program is that cultural diversity is something that should be celebrated. Another is that cultural diversity can be managed. (SOURCE © Michael Carroll)

for example, the cultures of the two organizations clashed severely. H. Ross Perot, founder and CEO of EDS, ran a militaristic organization much thinner in the management ranks than the bloated bureaucracy at GM. The values the entrepreneurial Perot had were quite different from those of GM's CEO Roger Smith, a company man who began at GM as a clerk. Only when GM purchased all of Perot's shares did Perot cease his constant carping in the media about GM's low quality of management. Only then was GM able to begin to resolve the clash of cultures.[36] Pillsbury also suffered with the problems associated with two cultures, as Management Challenge 12.4 reveals.

MANAGEMENT CHALLENGE 12.4

Pillsbury: A Clash of Cultures

Then Chairman John M. Stafford of Pillsbury was confronted with a significant problem. At Pillsbury the company's two main divisions—packaged foods and the recently acquired restaurants—had distinctly different cultures. Complicating matters, their relative contributions to the company's income were changing rapidly. In 1981 packaged foods dropped from 45 percent of company income and then to only 40 percent in 1986. In 1981 restaurants rose from 38 percent of income to 60 percent in 1986. The company's restaurant group, headed up by Burger King, was anything but conservative, while the Pillsbury packaged foods group was totally conservative. Executives at Burger King, headquartered in Miami, favored brasher marketing approaches, flashier cars, and brighter clothes than their counterparts in the packaged foods group. Furthermore, some of the products offered by the packaged foods division were in competition with those offered by the restaurant chain. Godfather's Pizza restaurants, for example, compete with Jeno's and Totino's supermarket pizzas. The Beacon Street seafood chain vied with the VanDeKamp's packaged fish unit. The restaurants didn't always use Pillsbury's products either. Bennigan's and Steak and Ale sometimes used Gold Medal instead of Pillsbury flour. Nicknames have flowed easily: Miami Vice and Minneapolis Ice.

Pillsbury Chairman John Stafford recounted, "my job is to make sure the competition is constructive, not destructive. It is a balancing act."

SOURCE: Robert Johnson, "Cultural Clash: At Pillsbury Company Restaurants Have Up-Staged Packaged Food Group," *Wall Street Journal* 3 October, 1986, pp. 1, 29.

Organizational Climate

Organizational climate indicates the desirability of the work and social environment of an organization. How people communicate, make decisions, establish objectives, lead, and carry out control are all indications of this desirability. Climate is a function of many variables, including the manager's actions, the individual employee's behavior, work-group behavior, organizational factors, and factors external to the organization.[37] Climate is a critical component of organizational culture, but there are many more values in culture than just those related to the desirability of the work and social environment. Culture includes values about appropriate behavior—the do's and don'ts of getting along in the organization.

Assessing Organizational Climate

Every organization should assess its climate periodically. Several systems for measuring organizational climate have been developed, among them those of Rensis Likert, Keith Davis, George Litwin and Robert Stringer, Garlie Forehand and B. Von Haller Gilmer, and Andrew W. Halpin and D. B. Crofts.[38] The best known and most widely used of these is the Likert system. Rensis Likert stated that four essential types of climate exist: exploitive authoritative, benevolent authoritative, consultative, and participative group, referred to respectively as systems 1, 2, 3, and 4. Each of the systems is part of a continuum based on the degree of participation in each of several major issues involved in climate. Exploitive authoritative is the least participative; participative group is the most participative. In exploitive authoritative the manager makes the decision regardless of employee needs. In benevolent authoritative the manager makes the decision in a sort of parental way, having considered employee needs. In consultative authoritative the manager makes the decision but uses the inputs of subordinates. In group participative the group makes the decision. According to Likert, System 4 is the most appropriate style of management in most situations.

Likert and his associates at the Center for Social Research at the University of Michigan developed a questionnaire for employees. Four responses are provided for each question in a series of questions. Each response is a behavior representing one of the four systems. The questions are subdivided into issue areas: leadership, motivation, communication, decisions, objectives, and control. Figure 12.6 is a shortened version of the questionnaire. Why not complete it as directed, using your current or a past work situation as the organization in question? You may use either your immediate boss and work group or the total organization as a point of reference. Simply read the question on the left, and circle the answer to the right that best describes your situation.

Once you have answered the nineteen questions, score one point for each System 1 answer; two points for each System 2 answer; three points for each System 3 answer; and four points for each System 4 answer. Add the total points scored and divide by 19. The average score that you compute should be between one and four and should be compared with the descriptive titles for systems 1, 2, 3, and 4 to obtain a "rough" idea of your organization's climate. A score of 2.4, for example, would be about halfway between systems 2 and 3, halfway between being benevolently authoritative and communicative.

According to Likert and his associates, the higher the score, the better the management style. Allowance must be made for contingency actions, of course, because no management style prescription works for all situations. The national average on the Likert scale is about 2.4, but scores will vary between organizations and within the same organization at any one point in time, and over time. Those firms with scores below two have cause for concern. Such organizations will be less desirable places to work and probably less productive ones. Beginning in 1969 Likert demonstrated quite dramatically the correlation between scores and performance, using two GM plants in the same city. The one that scored lowest on the scale had low morale and low productivity. The plant that scored much higher had high morale and high productivity. Furthermore, when the lowest-scoring plant adopted the other's management practices, morale, productivity, and climate scores all improved dramatically.[39]

Likert's System 4 is highly group-oriented. There are individuals who would not benefit from this type of climate. More specifically, highly creative or highly achievement-oriented individuals may not desire to work in teams or groups. And, participation may not be employable where subordinates are not sufficiently mature or do not have the appropriate needs to support this climate. In

FIGURE 12.6 LIKERT'S 4 STYLES OF MANAGEMENT

	SYSTEM 1 EXPLOITIVE AUTHORITATIVE	SYSTEM 2 BENEVOLENT AUTHORITATIVE	SYSTEM 3 CONSULTATIVE	SYSTEM 4 PARTICIPATIVE GROUP
HOW MUCH CONFIDENCE IS SHOWN IN SUBORDINATES?	NONE	CONDESCENDING	SUBSTANTIAL	COMPLETE
HOW FREE DO THEY FEEL TO TALK TO SUPERIORS ABOUT JOB?	NOT AT ALL	NOT VERY	RATHER FREE	FULLY FREE
ARE SUBORDINATES' IDEAS SOUGHT AND USED, IF WORTHY?	SELDOM	SOMETIMES	USUALLY	ALWAYS
IS PREDOMINANT USE MADE OF 1 FEAR, 2 THREATS, 3 PUNISHMENT, 4 REWARDS, 5 INVOLVEMENT?	1, 2, 3, OCCASIONALLY 4	4, SOME 3	4, SOME 3 AND 5	5, 4 BASED ON GROUP SET GOALS
WHERE IS RESPONSIBILITY FELT FOR ACHIEVING ORGANIZATION'S GOALS?	MOSTLY AT TOP	TOP AND MIDDLE	FAIRLY GENERAL	AT ALL LEVELS
HOW MUCH COMMUNICATION IS AIMED AT ACHIEVING ORGANIZATION'S OBJECTIVES?	VERY LITTLE	LITTLE	QUITE A BIT	A GREAT DEAL
WHAT IS THE DIRECTION OF INFORMATION FLOW?	DOWNWARD	MOSTLY DOWNWARD	DOWN AND UP	DOWN, UP AND SIDEWAYS
HOW IS DOWNWARD COMMUNICATION ACCEPTED?	WITH SUSPICION	POSSIBLY WITH SUSPICION	WITH CAUTION	WITH AN OPEN MIND
HOW ACCURATE IS UPWARD COMMUNICATION?	OFTEN WRONG	CENSORED FOR THE BOSS	LIMITED ACCURACY	ACCURATE
HOW WELL DO SUPERIORS KNOW PROBLEMS FACED BY SUBORDINATES?	KNOW LITTLE	SOME KNOWLEDGE	QUITE WELL	VERY WELL
AT WHAT LEVEL ARE DECISIONS FORMALLY MADE?	MOSTLY AT TOP	POLICY AT TOP, SOME DELEGATION	BROAD POLICY AT TOP, MORE DELEGATION	THROUGHOUT BUT WELL INTEGRATED
WHAT IS THE ORIGIN OF TECHNICAL AND PROFESSIONAL KNOWLEDGE USED IN DECISION MAKING?	TOP MANAGEMENT	UPPER AND MIDDLE	TO A CERTAIN EXTENT, THROUGHOUT	TO A GREAT EXTENT THROUGHOUT
ARE SUBORDINATES INVOLVED IN DECISIONS RELATED TO THEIR WORK?	NOT AT ALL	OCCASIONALLY CONSULTED	GENERALLY CONSULTED	FULLY INVOLVED
WHAT DOES DECISION-MAKING PROCESS CONTRIBUTE TO MOTIVATION?	NOTHING: OFTEN WEAKENS IT	RELATIVELY LITTLE	SOME CONTRIBUTION	SUBSTANTIAL CONTRIBUTION
HOW ARE ORGANIZATIONAL GOALS ESTABLISHED?	ORDERS ISSUED	ORDERS, SOME COMMENT INVITED	AFTER DISCUSSION, BY ORDERS	BY GROUP ACTION (EXCEPT IN CRISIS)
HOW MUCH COVERT RESISTANCE TO GOALS IS PRESENT?	STRONG RESISTANCE	MODERATE RESISTANCE	SOME RESISTANCE AT TIMES	LITTLE OR MORE
HOW CONCENTRATED ARE REVIEW AND CONTROL FUNCTIONS?	HIGHLY AT TOP	RELATIVELY HIGHLY AT TOP	MODERATE DELEGATION TO LOWER LEVELS	QUITE WIDELY SHARED
IS THERE AN INFORMAL ORGANIZATION RESISTING THE FORMAL ONE?	YES	USUALLY	SOMETIMES	NO—SAME GOAL AS FORMAL
WHAT ARE COST, PRODUCTIVITY, AND OTHER CONTROL DATA USED FOR?	POLICING, PUNISHMENT	REWARD AND PUNISHMENT	REWARD, SOME SELF-GUIDANCE	SELF-GUIDANCE, PROBLEM SOLVING

SOURCE: D. FABUN, THE CORPORATION AS A CREATIVE ENVIRONMENT (NEW YORK: MACMILLAN, 1972). REPRINTED BY PERMISSION OF MCGRAW-HILL.

some situations, as may occur in many parts of a military organization, authoritarian management styles are necessary. Given the changes in employee expectations and educational levels today, it would seem that System 4 is probably more desirable than the others. Each system, however, may be appropriate in some situations.

Managing Change

Change is all around us and managing change is what this section is about. First, the issues of accelerating change and changes in the business environment are discussed. Next, organizational development, a program for managing change, is reviewed. **Managing change** means that the individual and organization develop plans to influence change, implement it, and control its effects, as opposed to just letting change happen. Finally, resistance to change and how to overcome it are discussed.

In 1970 Alvin Toffler's *Future Shock* sounded an alarm about our future: it would be dominated by change that would increase at an accelerating rate, as revealed in Figure 12.7.[40] As changes come faster and faster, the individual and organization find it more difficult to cope with them, and hence develop future shock. Imagine the difficulties of grocery stores trying to cope with an increasing number of new food product introductions each year.

Toffler's predictions have come true. Accelerating rates of change are occurring in science and technology, industrial competition, organizational structure, social relationships, the law, societal structure, and global events. In 1982 John Naisbitt identified the ten megatrends of change in our society he envisioned for the near future. They appear in Table 12.1.

Table 12.1. Megatrends

Changing from	Changing to
1. Industrial society	Information society
2. Forced technology	High tech/High touch: In a high-technology society, high levels of interpersonal relations are necessary to counterbalance the impersonalness of this technology.
3. National economy	World economy
4. Short-term perspective	Long-term perspective
5. Centralization (of organization and society)	Decentralization (of organization and society)
6. Institutional help	Self-help
7. Representative democracy (in society and organization)	Participation (of organization and society)
8. Hierarchies in structures of organizations	Networking
9. North (geographic migration in the United States)	South (geographic migration in the United States)
10. Either/or (personal choices)	Multiple options (personal choices)

SOURCE: John Naisbitt, *Megatrends* (New York: Warner Books, 1982). Reprinted by permission of Warner Books, Inc.

Echoing the alarm sounded by Toffler and Naisbitt, Thomas J. Peters warns that managers are going to have to learn to manage in a world of increasing change, a world of chaos. Managers are going to have to learn to thrive on this chaos.[41] Peters recognized that accelerated rates of change, megatrends, and

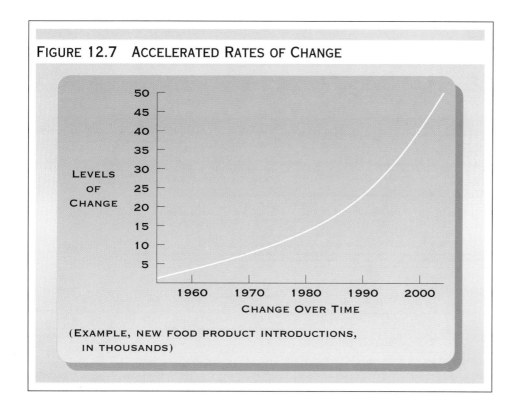

FIGURE 12.7   ACCELERATED RATES OF CHANGE

LEVELS
OF
CHANGE

50
45
40
35
30
25
20
15
10
5

1960   1970   1980   1990   2000

CHANGE OVER TIME

(EXAMPLE, NEW FOOD PRODUCT INTRODUCTIONS,
IN THOUSANDS)

other similar events directly impact organizational life and, hence, management. He suggests that the world is turning upside down. Ten major areas in which this is occurring are identified in Figure 12.8.

Throughout this book many management challenges are identified. Most are the consequence of change. Two of the principal ways in which managers can manage change in the organization are strategy and organizational development. Strategy was discussed in Chapter 6.

Organizational Development

In its broadest definition, organizational development is any planned program for managing change. It would in this view include strategies of all types.[42] It is more commonly construed, however, to be concerned with managing the change of organizational cultures. Wendell French and Cecil Bell have provided us with a very widely accepted definition of **organizational development** (OD)— "a long-range effort to improve an organization's problem-solving and renewal processes, particularly through a more effective and collaborative management of organizational culture, with special emphasis on the culture of formal work teams, with the assistance of a change agent or catalyst, and the use of the theory and technology of applied behavioral science, including action research."[43] In pragmatic terms this definition translates in the following way:

LONG-RANGE EFFORT
Most organizational development interventions—attempted programs of change—require from two to five years to complete the cycle of diagnosis, planning, implementation, stabilization, and evaluation that characterizes the OD process. Anheuser-Busch, in 1988, was engaged in several OD interventions to solve specific problems at its various facilities. For example, at one brewery

FIGURE 12.8 A WORLD TURNED UPSIDE DOWN

	WAS/IS	MUST BECOME
1. MARKETING	MASS MARKETS, MASS ADVERTISING, VIOLENT BATTLES TO SHIFT A SHARE POINT (MARKET SHARE), FUNCTIONAL INTEGRITY OF MARKETING PROS	MARKET CREATION, NICHE FOCUS, INNOVATION FROM BEING CLOSER TO MARKETS, THRIVING ON MARKET FRAGMENTATION, CEASELESS DIFFERENTIATION OF ANY PRODUCT (NO MATTER HOW MATURE)
2. INTERNATIONAL	"GLOBAL" BRANDS WHICH ARE MANAGED FROM THE U.S., INTERNATIONAL AS AN ADJUNCT ACTIVITY, FOR BIG FIRMS ONLY	FOCUS ON NEW MARKET CREATION, DEVELOPMENT DONE OFFSHORE FROM THE START, ESSENTIAL STRATEGY FOR FIRMS OF ALL SIZES.
3. MANUFACTURING	EMPHASIS ON VOLUME, COST, HARDWARE, FUNCTIONAL INTEGRITY	PRIMARY MARKETING TOOL (SOURCE OF QUALITY, RESPONSIVENESS, INNOVATION), PART OF PRODUCT DESIGN TEAM FROM THE START, SHORT RUNS, FLEXIBILITY, PEOPLE SUPPORTED BY AUTOMATION
4. SALES AND SERVICE	SECOND-CLASS CITIZENS, "MOVE THE PRODUCT" PREDOMINATES	HEROES, RELATIONSHIP MANAGERS (WITH EVERY CUSTOMER, EVEN IN RETAIL), MAJOR SOURCE OF VALUE ADDED, PRIME SOURCE OF NEW PRODUCT IDEAS
5. INNOVATION	DRIVEN BY CENTRAL R&D, BIG PROJECTS THE NORM, SCIENCE- RATHER THAN CUSTOMER-DRIVEN, CLEVERNESS OF DESIGN MORE IMPORTANT THAN FITS AND FINISHES, LIMITED TO NEW PRODUCTS	SMALL STARTS IN AUTONOMOUS AND DECENTRALIZED UNITS THE KEY, EVERYONE'S BUSINESS, DRIVEN BY DESIRE TO MAKE SMALL AND CUSTOMER-NOTICEABLE IMPROVEMENTS
6. PEOPLE	NEED TIGHT CONTROL, TRY TO SPECIALIZE AND DIMINISH ROLE	PEOPLE AS PRIME SOURCE OF VALUE ADDED, CAN NEVER TRAIN OR INVOLVE TOO MUCH, BIG FINANCIAL STAKE IN THE OUTCOME
7. STRUCTURE	HIERARCHICAL, FUNCTIONAL INTEGRITY MAINTAINED	FLAT, FUNCTIONAL BARRIERS BROKEN, FIRST-LINE SUPERVISORS GIVE WAY TO SELF-MANAGED TEAMS, MIDDLE MANAGERS AS FACILITATORS RATHER THAN TURF GUARDIANS
8. LEADERSHIP	DETACHED, ANALYTIC, CENTRALIZED STRATEGY PLANNING, DRIVEN BY CORPORATE STAFFS	LEADER AS LOVER OF CHANGE AND PREACHER OF VISION AND SHARED VALUES, STRATEGY DEVELOPMENT RADICALLY BOTTOM-UP, ALL STAFF FUNCTIONS SUPPORT THE LINE RATHER THAN VICE VERSA
9. MANAGEMENT INFORMATION SYSTEMS (MIS)	CENTRALIZED FOR THE SAKE OF CONSISTENCY, INTERNALLY AIMED	INFORMATION USE AND DIRECT CUSTOMER/SUPPLIER LINKUPS AS A STRATEGIC WEAPON MANAGED BY THE LINE, DECENTRALIZATION OF MIS A MUST
10. FINANCIAL MANAGEMENT AND CONTROL	CENTRALIZED, FINANCE STAFF AS COP	DECENTRALIZED, MOST FINANCE PEOPLE TO THE FIELD AS "BUSINESS TEAM MEMBERS," HIGH SPENDING AUTHORITY DOWN THE LINE

SOURCE: ADAPTED FROM THOMAS J. PETERS, THRIVING ON CHAOS: HANDBOOK FOR A MANAGEMENT REVOLUTION (NEW YORK: KNOPF, 1987), PP. 42, 43.

management styles were dramatically changed from authoritative to participative. Productivity increased substantially as a result. Expectations are that each of these will take at least several months to several years, depending upon circumstances.[44] The reason OD interventions require so much time is that the behavioral changes sought require fundamental changes in attitudes and values. To diagnose the organization sufficiently before deciding what actions to take also requires a significant amount of time. Typically, surveys, interviews, and performance analyses are employed in the diagnosis stage.

TO IMPROVE THE PROBLEM-SOLVING AND RENEWAL PROCESSES
The very purpose of OD is to improve the way problems are solved in an organization and to make the organization self-renewing. The central focus of such efforts is usually increased levels of participation in decision making—giving those involved in the situation at hand a chance to make decisions about how to improve that situation. Unfortunately, one of the most common characteristics of organizations is that as they age, they stagnate.[45] OD aims to remove that genetic defect.

COLLABORATIVE MANAGEMENT OF ORGANIZATIONAL CULTURE
At the core of OD is the management of shared values—values about strategy, structure, systems, style, staff, skills, and other key factors in the organization—and norms—the informal "do's" and "don'ts" of organizational life.

SPECIAL EMPHASIS ON THE CULTURE OF FORMAL WORK TEAMS
The emphasis almost always is on work groups and improving their effectiveness and efficiency. Team-building exercises are typically employed. The manager's role changes significantly from one of "boss," before OD, to one of counselor, coach, and facilitator, after OD.

ASSISTANCE OF A CHANGE AGENT OR CATALYST
A **change agent** is a consultant, sometimes internal but usually an external consultant to the organization, who helps initiate and then guides the OD intervention. A **catalyst** is any event, perhaps a decline in productivity or profits, that triggers the recognition of a need for an OD program. Organizational development is unique in the management consulting field because the consultant remains with the organization to help implement the plans he or she suggests rather than simply writing a report and then leaving for another assignment.

THE USE OF APPLIED BEHAVIORAL SCIENCE AND ACTION RESEARCH
OD relies on both theory and the results of research studies relative to that theory. The OD consultant diagnoses the situation and makes recommendations about the actions necessary, based on that diagnosis. If a particular behavior practice has been shown to be effective in one situation, it is usually transferred to another.

Harley-Davidson experienced a decline in market share that became the catalyst for an OD effort to regain its dominance in the U.S. market. It is described in Management Challenge 12.5.

Resistance to Change

OD is but one type of change management. Regardless of which program is used to manage change, the manager making the changes will invariably be faced with resistance to change. To better manage change, the problem solver

Harley-Davidson Changes Culture to Survive

In 1983 President Vaughn Beals of Harley-Davidson could envision a scenario in which his company would not exist in just a few years. The company had downsized significantly from its heyday of the 1960s, a downsizing forced by the inexpensive, high-quality Japanese motorcycles that devoured its market in the 1970s. Manufacturing for the U.S. motorcycle market, a market Harley-Davidson once held virtually all to itself, had moved across the Pacific. Harley's market share dropped to a low of 5 percent between 1960 and 1987. Harley decided that the best strategy for its survival would be to sell large bikes, but it sold only 26,000 in 1985, compared to 50,000 in 1979. Japanese manufacturers were "dumping" their bikes in the United States in order to gain market share. In 1983 the United States passed a law prohibiting the importation of large motorcycles for five years.

FIGURE 12.9 FORCE FIELD ANALYSIS

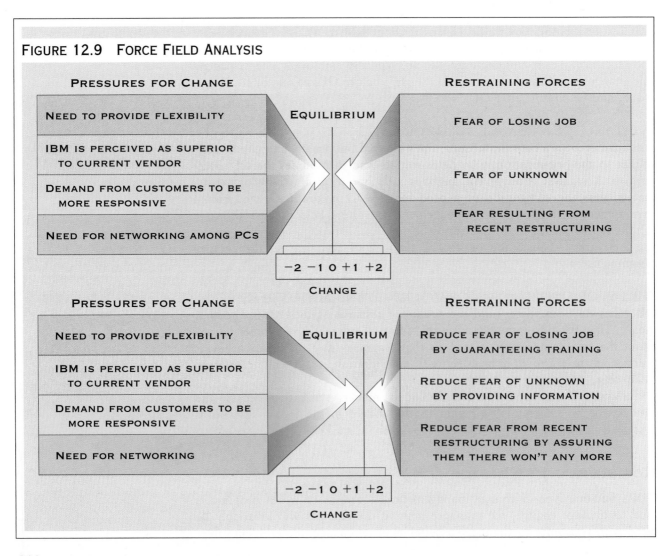

Beals recognized that the company had to change in order to survive. Their inefficient plants, outmoded technology, unmotivated work force, and low product quality all had to be changed if the company were to survive. Beals decided that to save Harley-Davidson he had to imitate his competitors. He took his whole top executive group to visit Japanese motorcycle factories. Subsequently the company adopted many Japanese management techniques. The culture of the organization was changed, their values were changed, work was structured around a series of small work groups, the vertical hierarchy was abolished. The small work groups created gave employees a sense of identity with the product. New equipment was purchased to make the plants more technologically efficient. Employees participated in making improvements in the manufacturing process. In return for accepting these changes, the company provided guarantees of job stability and security to employees. The new values of the organization focused on high quality, performance, motivation, concerns for the product, and concern for the customer. The company's strategy was so successful that by 1989, the company had captured 50% of the U.S. super-heavyweight motorcycle market.

SOURCE: "How Harley Beat Back the Japanese," *Fortune*, September 25, 1989, pp. 155–1104. Rod Willis, "Harley-Davidson Comes Roaring Back," *Management Review* (March 1986), pp. 20–27.

If Harley-Davidson had not changed its culture, it probably would not be in business today. Because of his own suggestions, it takes this worker many fewer minutes to perform his job than it used to. Such savings add up to competitiveness. (SOURCE © John Abbott)

needs to understand **force-field analysis,** a concept developed by Kurt Lewin, a pioneer in the study of change. It suggests that change results from the relative strengths of competing driving and restraining forces.[46] The driving forces push the organization toward change; the restraining forces push against change. The actual change that emerges is a consequence of the interaction of the two sets of forces. If you want change, you should push. But the natural tendency of those you are pushing is to resist the change, to push back. According to Lewin, the driving forces activate the restraining forces. He suggests that decreasing the restraining forces is a more effective way of encouraging change than increasing the driving forces.

Figure 12.9 portrays the use of force-field analysis to reduce resistance to change from using a single computer vendor, UNISYS, to multiple computer vendors—IBM, Digital Equipment Company (DEC), and UNISYS—for the information division of a major entertainment company. This is a partial analysis of the situation as viewed by that division's managers.[47] As you can see, the managers determined that the best way to move toward the change was to reduce employee fears by providing job guarantees and training and to provide open communication.

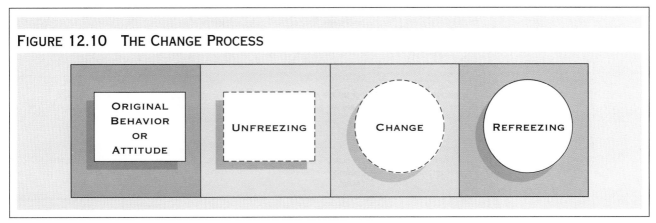

FIGURE 12.10 THE CHANGE PROCESS

| ORIGINAL BEHAVIOR OR ATTITUDE | UNFREEZING | CHANGE | REFREEZING |

ADAPTED FROM JAMES A.F. STONER AND CHARLES WANKEL, <u>MANAGEMENT</u>, 3RD ED. (ENGLEWOOD CLIFFS, NJ: PRENTICE-HALL, 1986), P. 35.

MAKING CHANGE EFFECTIVE

Lewin sought to improve the process by which change could be made effective. He discovered that there were two major obstacles to change. First, individuals were not willing (or were unable) to change behaviors and attitudes that they had had for some time. Second, almost any change in attitude and behaviors lasts only a short period of time. People may be willing to change for a little while, but they often revert to their original behavior. Lewin suggested that in order to overcome these two problems, a three-step process of unfreezing, changing, and refreezing was necessary (Figure 12.10). He and others further expounded on a model that is applicable to individuals, groups, or organizations.[48] In the unfreezing stage, present behavior must be shown as no longer desirable to the individual, group, or organization, and that fact must be accepted. In the changing phase, the behavior desired must be instilled in the individual, group, or organization. Finally, in the refreezing stage, behavioral changes must be reinforced in order for them to become part of individual, group, or organization behavior patterns in the long term.

REASONS FOR RESISTANCE TO CHANGE

People resist change for a number of reasons:
- Self-interests
- Fear
  Fear of failure
  Fear of change itself
  Fear of the loss of one's economic situation
  Fear of the loss of social relationships

Table 12.2. Approaches to Lessening Resistance to Change

Approach	Commonly Used When . . .	Advantages	Disadvantages
1 Education + communication	There is a lack of information or inaccurate information and analysis.	Once persuaded, people will often help implement the change.	Can be very time-consuming if many people are involved.
2 Participation + involvement	The initiators do not have all the information they need to design the change, and others have considerable power to resist.	People who participate will be committed to implementing change, and any relevant information they have will be integrated into the change plan.	Can be very time-consuming if participators design an inappropriate change.
3 Facilitation + support	People are resisting because of adjustment problems.	No other approach works as well with adjustment problems.	Can be time-consuming, expensive, and still fail.
4 Negotiation + agreement	Some person or group with considerable power to resist will clearly lose out in a change.	Sometimes it is a relatively easy way to avoid major resistance.	Can be too expensive if it alerts others to negotiate for compliance.
5 Manipulation + co-optation	Other tactics will not work, or are too expensive.	It can be a relatively quick and inexpensive solution to resistance problems.	Can lead to future problems if people feel manipulated.
6 Explicit + implicit coercion	Speed is essential, and the change initiators possess considerable power.	It is speedy and can overcome any kind of resistance.	Can be risky if it leaves people angry with the initiators.

SOURCE: Reprinted by permission of the *Harvard Business Review.* An exhibit from "Choosing Strategies for Change" by John P. Kotter and Leonard A. Schlesinger (March–April 1979). Copyright © 1979 by the President and Fellows of Harvard College. All rights reserved.

- General misunderstanding and lack of trust
- Different perceptions of the goals and objectives of the organization
- Lack of tolerance for change.[49]

Resistance in some cases is appropriate. Some changes are ill conceived or more trouble than they are worth, and people should resist them. Managers should therefore not always automatically discount resistance as negative.

OVERCOMING RESISTANCE TO CHANGE

Managers cannot allow resistance to change to thwart their efforts to achieve their objectives. They must develop satisfactory strategies for overcoming resistance to change. Each of the following strategies is commonly used in certain situations and has distinctive advantages and disadvantages, as summarized in Table 12.2.

EDUCATION AND COMMUNICATION

Many times employees simply need more information about a change. The absence of information often leads to fear. By providing logical and rational reasons for change, managers may help smooth the way for its acceptance and reduce the forces working against change.

PARTICIPATION AND INVOLVEMENT

Lester Coch and John French found that an approach to be favored in reducing resistance to change is the participation of those involved in determining how they will be affected by change.[50] Participation is a prominent characteristic of the very successful Japanese management systems. Those who participate by "buying into the project" don't have to be convinced later to do so.

FACILITATION AND SUPPORT

Managers who offer support to their subordinates, perhaps through retraining or maybe through emotional support, see resistance fade. By bringing in outside facilitators or acting as a facilitator to the process itself, managers may also help reduce resistance.

NEGOTIATION AND AGREEMENT

Sometimes negotiation is necessary between those who seek change and those who resist it. Companies, for example, often negotiate with unions to obtain work-rule changes. It may be necessary to negotiate with any number of powerful individuals or groups or their organizations in order to achieve change.

MANIPULATION AND CO-OPTATION

Though not recommended, manipulation and co-optation are possible means for reducing resistance to change. In co-optation managers may assign the worst resisters, for example, to key positions in the change process in order to elicit their support covertly. This can be done to individuals or by taking the leader of a group and assigning him or her a key role in the change process.

EXPLICIT AND IMPLICIT COERCION

Not infrequently managers threaten to punish resisters or lessen rewards as means to gain support for change. This strategy potentially increases resistance, especially in the long term. Once used, coercion may make future changes even more difficult.

Moments of Truth

In 1983 Jan Carlzon had just been made president of the floundering Scandinavian Airlines Systems (SAS). He had to turn the company around and overcome the resistance to change that inevitably accompanies change.

Carlzon turned around the fortunes of SAS, a consortium of the national airlines of Denmark, Norway, and Sweden, in one year. He did so principally by changing the organization's culture and by managing the resistance to change that he encountered. The major cultural change he made was to no longer focus internally but to focus externally. "Moments of truth" was Carlzon's way of portraying the first fifteen seconds of encounter between a passenger and a front-line employee. According to Carlzon, any service business succeeds or fails depending upon the results of these moments of truth. If the customer is not satisfied, loyalty to the company will not occur. At SAS these moments of truth happened 50,000 times a day, every day.

Carlzon achieved dramatic results by employing a strategy he previously had used in two other turnaround situations. His strategy with employees and customers was based on four beliefs about human nature:

How would a real top manager handle resistance to change? How could he or she change a culture steeped in failure and turn it into success in one year? The Global Management Challenge provides insight into managing change and resistance to change.

Managing Culture and Change as Problem Solving

Managing culture and change are interrelated with problem-solving issues, issues that are becoming increasingly important. Managers are going to be asked to enhance their skills at managing all three. Figure 12.11 provides insight into how each is a problem-solving situation, using the key issues raised in this chapter.

As an example of how managers would problem solve using the concepts from this chapter, suppose that top managers in examining the internal environment identify several organizationwide performance problems. In studying the external environment, they observe stronger competition in their markets. Further examination uncovers low morale among employees and a general belief that the company is mired in such a tough competitive situation that it is doomed to failure. The organization's culture must be changed drastically with respect to this issue. They embark on a major campaign, involving all top-, middle-, and lower-level managers in changing the company's vision, mission, goals, and objectives. Those who are successful in the new strategy are cast as heroes, and the manager creates opportunities for people to succeed. Those who are successful are rewarded. They develop teams of managers and workers at all levels to devise ways to make the new strategy work.

1. Everyone needs to know and feel that he is needed.
2. Everyone wants to be treated as an individual.
3. Giving someone the freedom to take responsibility releases resources that otherwise remain concealed.
4. An individual without information cannot take responsibility—and an individual who is given information cannot help but take responsibility.

Carlzon is a transformational leader. He transformed, dramatically changed, his organization's culture. He had a vision, he instilled it in those who worked for him, and he did so based on the four beliefs just noted. He placed the front-line employee at the top of the organizational pyramid and changed the role of the middle manager from a person who is a director to one who is a facilitator and supportive coach. Fearing he would encounter resistance to change, he involved the unions and various boards in the strategy-building process. Through education, the creation of a vision for the organization, participation, and showing support for his people, he overcame that resistance.

SOURCE: Jan Carlzon, *Moments of Truth* (Cambridge, Mass.: Ballinger, 1987).

The Management Challenges Identified

1. Competition, especially foreign, has led to the need to change corporate culture and management style.
2. Accelerating rates of change have led to the need to change corporate culture and management style. This includes concerns expressed in *Megatrends,* and *Thriving on Chaos.*
3. Culture can be better managed.
4. Change can be managed, especially cultural change.
5. Resistance to change can be managed.
6. Diverse cultures can be managed.

Some Solutions Noted in the Chapter

1. Learning about culture
2. Changing the ways we manage, as suggested in Figure 12.8, for example
3. Employing known strategies to overcome resistance to change
4. Organizational development (OD)
5. Cultural integrators, cultural diversity programs

FIGURE 12.11 MANAGEMENT OF CULTURE AND RESISTANCE TO CHANGE AS PROBLEM SOLVING

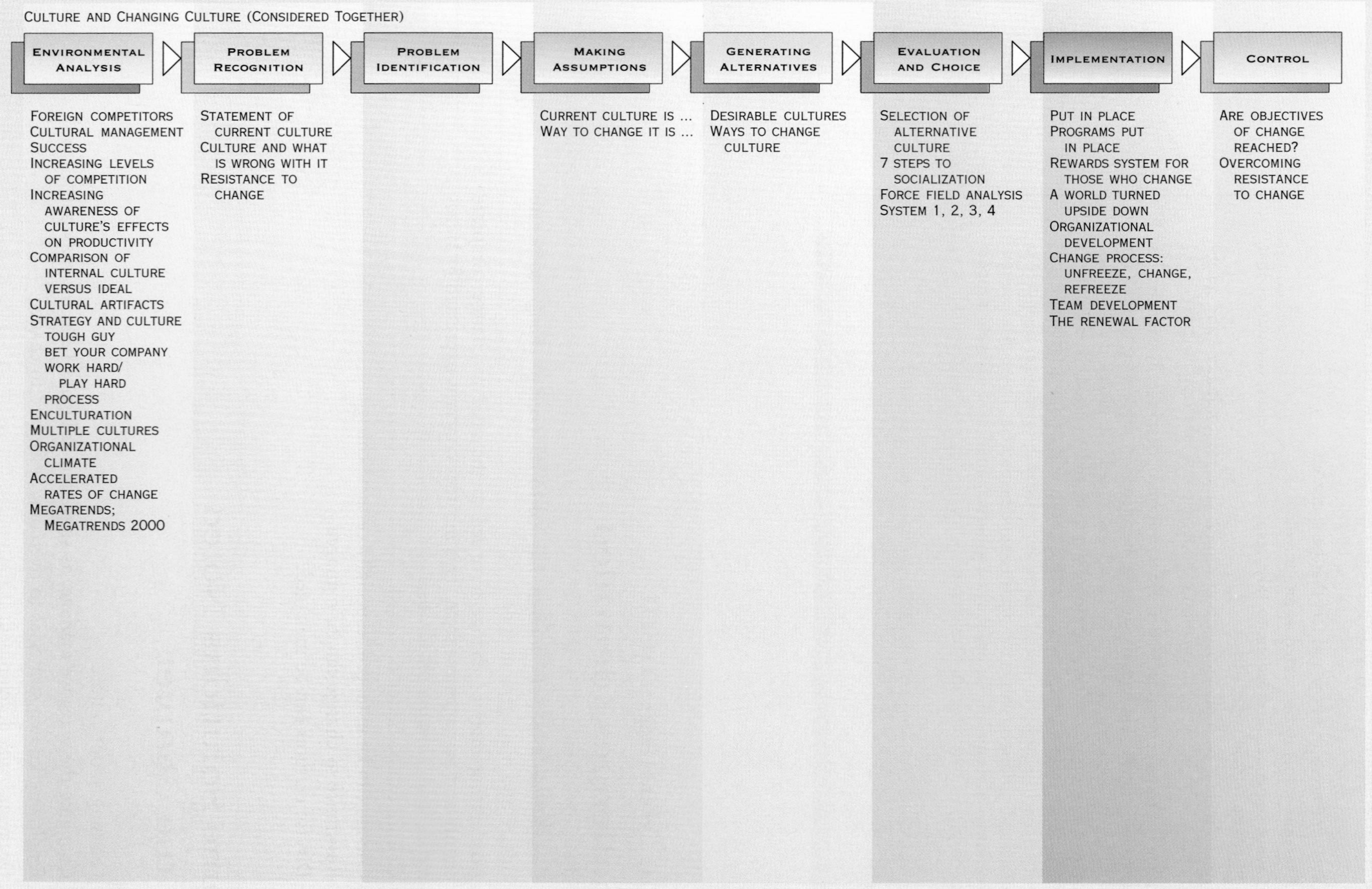

CULTURE AND CHANGING CULTURE (CONSIDERED TOGETHER)

ENVIRONMENTAL ANALYSIS	PROBLEM RECOGNITION	PROBLEM IDENTIFICATION	MAKING ASSUMPTIONS	GENERATING ALTERNATIVES	EVALUATION AND CHOICE	IMPLEMENTATION	CONTROL
FOREIGN COMPETITORS	STATEMENT OF		CURRENT CULTURE IS …	DESIRABLE CULTURES	SELECTION OF	PUT IN PLACE	ARE OBJECTIVES
CULTURAL MANAGEMENT	CURRENT CULTURE		WAY TO CHANGE IT IS …	WAYS TO CHANGE	ALTERNATIVE	PROGRAMS PUT	OF CHANGE
SUCCESS	CULTURE AND WHAT			CULTURE	CULTURE	IN PLACE	REACHED?
INCREASING LEVELS	IS WRONG WITH IT				7 STEPS TO	REWARDS SYSTEM FOR	OVERCOMING
OF COMPETITION	RESISTANCE TO				SOCIALIZATION	THOSE WHO CHANGE	RESISTANCE
INCREASING	CHANGE				FORCE FIELD ANALYSIS	A WORLD TURNED	TO CHANGE
AWARENESS OF					SYSTEM 1, 2, 3, 4	UPSIDE DOWN	
CULTURE'S EFFECTS						ORGANIZATIONAL	
ON PRODUCTIVITY						DEVELOPMENT	
COMPARISON OF						CHANGE PROCESS:	
INTERNAL CULTURE						UNFREEZE, CHANGE,	
VERSUS IDEAL						REFREEZE	
CULTURAL ARTIFACTS						TEAM DEVELOPMENT	
STRATEGY AND CULTURE						THE RENEWAL FACTOR	
TOUGH GUY							
BET YOUR COMPANY							
WORK HARD/							
PLAY HARD							
PROCESS							
ENCULTURATION							
MULTIPLE CULTURES							
ORGANIZATIONAL							
CLIMATE							
ACCELERATED							
RATES OF CHANGE							
MEGATRENDS;							
MEGATRENDS 2000							

Summary

1. Organizational culture is that set of shared values and norms that distinguishes one organization from others. It has two components, that which is somewhat mythical and that which talks about "the way we do it around here." The available research and anecdotal evidence suggest that a strong culture can be a long-term competitive advantage.

2. Managing culture requires managing the McKinsey Seven S's, setting value goals, instilling those values in new and current employees, integrating culture through the use of cultural artifacts, controlling climate, and changing culture as necessary.

3. McKinsey's Seven S's are strategy, structure, systems, style, staff, skills, and shared values. Each is reciprocally interdependent of the others, although the basis for all is conceptually strategy, and culture plays a major role in the formation of each. The strategy of the organization apparently results in four principal types of culture, as identified by Terrence E. Deal and Allan A. Kennedy.

4. Organizations instill culture in their members through a seven-step process outlined by Richard T. Pascale.

5. Organizational climate indicates the desirability of the work and social environment of an organization. Climate constitutes a major determinant of culture because it reflects the values relative to how people are managed, especially how much participation in problem solving the organization encourages.

6. The Likert system describes management style as being of four types relative to problem-solving authority on a continuum from very authoritative to highly participative: exploitive authoritative, benevolent authoritative, consultative, and group participative. The Likert system measures organizational climate with a survey.

7. Change may be either managed or reacted to. Managing change requires objectives and strategy. Managing cultural change usually requires an OD intervention.

8. OD is a long-range effort to improve an organization's problem-solving and renewal processes, particularly through a more effective and collaborative management of organizational culture. There is a special emphasis on the culture of formal work teams, with the assistance of a change agent or catalyst, and the use of the theory and technology of applied behavioral science, including action research. The stages include diagnosis, planning, implementation, and stabilization/control.

9. Any forces for change seem automatically to evoke forces against, or resistance to, change. Resistance to change occurs for a variety of reasons, most stemming from some type of fear. Resistance may be overcome by any one or a combination of six strategies: education and communication, participation and involvement, facilitation and support, negotiation and agreement, manipulation and co-optation, and explicit and implicit coercion.

Thinking About Management

1. Describe the culture of an organization with which you are familiar.
2. Discuss the interrelationship of the McKinsey Seven S's at some organization with which you are familiar.
3. Discuss myths and sagas; language systems and metaphors; symbolism, ceremonies and rituals; and the identifiable value systems and behavioral norms for some organization with which you are familiar.
4. In which one of the four Deal and Kennedy types does your organization fit?
5. How does your organization "socialize" its new recruits into the culture?
6. Why do you suppose that, according to Ralph H. Kilmann's research, most behavioral norms are negative in connotation—that is, don't do this, don't do that?

7. On the Likert scale where do you think the faculty of the school at which you are taking this course would rank their situation, on the average?

8. Describe a typical OD intervention.

9. Indicate how you would go about changing a mechanistic into an organic culture. How would you unfreeze, change, and refreeze the behavior of those who manage the organization?

10. Indicate the relationships between OD, culture, and planned change for some organization with which you are familiar.

11. What are the major changes taking place in society? In management?

12. Why do people resist change?

13. How can you overcome resistance to change?

CASE

A Du Pont Division's Need to Transform Its Culture

The Polymer Product Department of E. I. Du Pont de Nemours and Company faced a problem common to firms with mature products: how to rejuvenate sales and employee enthusiasm while cutting costs to increase profits. One of the first solutions chosen was to restructure the company, putting all mature products into one division—Industrial Polymers Division (IPD). This would allow for concentration of effort on similar products and a refocusing of strategy. Joe Miller was appointed director of the new division. He recognized several major problems immediately. Employees perceived that mature products were second-class citizens in the company. Morale was low. The division had high operating costs. There were few new products on line, and there was a dearth of marketing and advertising ideas. Finally, productivity was very low. The more Miller read and heard, the more convinced he was that a total overhaul of division purposes, strategies, and culture was necessary. He wanted to make this a participative effort as well, involving all levels of management, work teams, and front-line employees.

DISCUSSION QUESTIONS

1. Assuming Joe Miller allows his management team to develop a new vision and a new mission for the company, what might it be?

2. Describe how you would go about creating a new culture. What would this culture be like—that is, what would some of the key values be?

Du Pont was the first company to unlock the secrets of polymer chemistry that led to Neoprene, the first commercial synthetic rubber, over 50 years ago. Today, Neoprene has been joined by a broad family of polymer products. (SOURCE Courtesy Du Pont Company)

Hughes Supply Company

Stewart Hall, executive vice-president for Hughes Supply Company, pondered how he and the rest of the management team should go about changing the culture of Hughes Supply. Hughes had sixty-one branch outlets in three states. Each outlet sold construction supplies to contractors and real estate developers. Inventory accounts varied with the size of the store, which in turn depended on the size of the market in which each store was positioned. Sales in 1989 were $400 million.

Competition was increasing significantly in almost every market. Competition had always existed, but mainly from smaller independents. Now large discount retailers such as Home Depot cut into the Hughes markets, as did more traditional building supply companies such as Lowes.

Each branch manager in essence ran his or her own business, but most were ill prepared for the high-technology, highly sophisticated job of managing in the increasingly complex and dynamic environment. All branch managers had worked their way up from sales positions in the stores. Stewart was convinced that all sorts of training was needed, but that other options also existed. Somehow, he had to create a competitive environment.

DISCUSSION QUESTIONS
1. How would you change the culture of such a company?
2. How would you train managers?
3. What are your other options?

What Kind of Manager Are You?

MANAGE
YOURSELF

If you have not already done so, please take the self-test shown in Figure 12.6, "Likert's 4 Styles of Management."

CHAPTER THIRTEEN

Motivation and Performance

CHAPTER OBJECTIVES

By the time you complete this chapter you should be able to describe how you would use the motivation/performance cycle to motivate someone.

CHAPTER OUTLINE

The Motivation Cycle
   Content and Process Theories
Stage 1 of the MPC: Needs
   The Hierarchy of Needs
   The Nature and Strength
    of Current Needs
   Managerial Implications
   Achievement Motivation
   Additional Categories of Needs
   Manager and Employee Needs
Stage 2: The Manager Must
Recognize and Be Able and Willing
to Satisfy Needs
Stage 3: Offering Extrinsic
and Intrinsic Need Satisfiers
   Herzberg's Theory
Stage 4: The Individual Searches
for Alternatives, Evaluates the

Consequences of Possible Action,
and Makes a Decision
   Expectancy Theory
   Equity Theory
Stage 5: Motivation to Expend Effort
Stage 6: Factors That Turn Motivation
into Performance
   Goal (Objective) Setting
Stage 7: Performance
Stage 8: The Individual Obtains
the Need Satisfiers or Not
   Reinforcement of Effort
   Types of Reinforcement
   How Effective Is It?
Stage 9: The Individual Reassesses
the Situation or Not
Stage 10: Will the Individual Continue
to Be Motivated in the Same Way
or Not?
Influencing Motivation as Creative
Problem Solving
The Management Challenges Identified
Some Solutions Noted in the Chapter
Summary: Guidelines for Using the
Motivation/Performance Cycle

Jim Johnson, Master Salesman and Motivator

"You're going to charge in there and half of you will probably get killed." Those were Jim Johnson's opening words at a 1979 sales meeting designed to save his first company, Psych Systems. If the ten people he had assembled didn't come back with $30,000 each in cash orders from the computer show with which they had coordinated their sales meeting, the company would go under. James Chapman, former salesman, testifies that Johnson gave "the most incredible, rabble rousing, God-and-country sermon I've ever heard. When we left him we were so charged up and full of the flutters nothing could have stopped us." They went home with $500,000 in orders.

Johnson is a high achiever, with high goals for himself and those who work for him. Psych Systems was just the beginning. When the company went public with its stock in 1982, he sold his 10 percent and started Human Edge Software Corporation. Human Edge is one of several highly competitive firms selling management assistance software, principally in the business market for personal computers. Human Edge has been very successful from its inception. Much of its success depends on this former psychology professor's development of a sound product and his understanding of marketing. But much of the company's success also stems from his understanding of how to motivate a sales force.

Johnson has found two keys to motivating his people. First, he gives them very noticeable rewards. For example, at sales meetings he encourages people to talk about their goals, and the first one to talk wins a bonus. The best salesperson each day wins a bonus. He has initiated various sales promotions. One was "The Gucci Club" in which the winning salesman won Gucci shoes and six Brooks Brothers suits. The winning saleswoman won Gucci shoes and a mink coat. Cartier watches are frequent bonus items. Second, he shows them that he is genuinely interested in them. He also uses peer pressure via the noticeable rewards to get everybody earning them: "Everybody feels a kind of peer pressure to keep up. For example, to get a pair of Gucci shoes you have to work 45 hours a week. If 90 percent of the company is walking around in Gucci shoes, the other 10 percent is going to feel embarrassed." He talks at least once a day to each member of the field sales force, and he chats several times daily with each person in the office. "I do it so often I almost have to apologize and explain that I don't have a secret agenda; it's just I'm honestly curious. That's the best way to feel the pulse of the company."

SOURCE: Jill Neimark, "The Cutting Edge," *Success* (January 1985), pp. 24–29.

Successful companies address the human needs and give
them priority.

Thomas J. Peters and Robert H. Waterman, Jr.

The results of a twenty-year study are in. The answer to the
question "What really motivates people?" is "Go ask your
people."

Vincent S. Flowers and Charles L. Hughes
Management researchers

Motivation is the internal drive to satisfy an unsatisfied need. While motivation is internal to the individual, its strength and direction may be
influenced by forces outside the individual. One of the manager's most important jobs is to influence the motivation of others in the direction of achieving
organizational objectives in an effective and efficient manner.[1] The manager
must utilize his or her knowledge of individual motivation to turn someone's
efforts to satisfy personal needs into organizational performance. To lead, to
influence motivation, the manager must first of all understand motivation.

Jim Johnson, chief executive and owner of the Human Edge Software Corporation, understands how to influence motivation. He understands how to use
his knowledge of that process to influence someone's motivation to achieve
performance. He recognizes the needs of those who work for him and provides
them with need satisfiers—principally financial rewards. He also provides rewards for other needs they may have. He is especially attentive to the individual's need for recognition. These rewards are based on peer recognition as well
as his own efforts to build employees' self-esteem. He, for example, spends time
with each employee in order to satisfy his or her need for appreciation as a
human being.

This chapter first explores the motivation cycle an individual goes through in
an attempt to satisfy his or her needs. The cycle begins when someone becomes
consciously or subconsciously aware of personal needs. The person then pro-
ceeds through a series of steps aimed at satisfying those needs until the cycle
begins all over again. After learning about each stage in the individual motivation process, you will learn about the principles that allow managers and
organizations to attempt to influence an individual's motivation cycle. The two
issues, individual motivation and how it is influenced, are integrated into a ten-
stage model. Virtually all other introductory books on management review motivation as a collection of independent theories. In this book the model is used
to show the interdependencies of the various motivation theories along the lines
of the relationships suggested by academicians Lyman W. Porter and Edward
E. Lawler, III.[2] This model also provides a vehicle for understanding how motivation theories can be applied. Specific actions managers can take in each of
these stages to influence the strength and direction of that motivation are reviewed. However, it is important to realize that the model is just that, a simplification of a very complex set of processes. Furthermore, no set of actions
will always, maybe not even usually, influence someone else's motivation. Fi-

Jim Johnson displays a few of the
rewards which motivate his salespeople to perform at extraordinarily
high levels. While Cartier watches,
Gucci shoes and mink coats may not
motivate everyone, Johnson has used
them very successfully with his
personnel. (SOURCE © Roger
Ressmeyer)

nally, each theory integrated into this model can be used within its own framework, to study motivation. The model is used primarily so that their interdependencies will be accounted for and so that all parts of this complex puzzle will be considered.

The Motivation Cycle

The **motivation cycle** begins with unsatisfied needs. It ends after the individual assesses the consequences of attempting to satisfy those needs or the process is interrupted for some reason. Motivation is a cyclical process.[3] The six stages in this cyclical process follow:

1. An individual has an unsatisfied need.
2. Because the individual is driven to attempt to satisfy this need he or she searches for alternative need satisfiers.
3. The individual chooses the "best" way to satisfy the need.
4. The individual is motivated to take action to obtain the need satisfier.
5. The individual reexamines the situation, contemplating what has transpired.
6. Depending on the outcomes of these efforts, the individual may or may not be motivated again by the same type of need satisfiers.

The stages in this motivation cycle are presented in Figure 13.1. The manager's ability to employ his or her knowledge of this cycle is fundamental to the ability to manage. One of the manager's primary functions, perhaps *the* primary function, is to influence this motivation cycle in order to achieve organizational objectives.

As shown in Figure 13.2, at each stage of the motivation cycle, the manager (and the organization through its managers) must take certain actions in order to influence that process. You will notice that several related stages involving managerial and organizational actions to influence motivation have been added to the original motivation cycle. These are the actions that managers and the

Motivation According to New Rules

Imagine the plight of Claudia Sebastian, sales and marketing director for East German candy manufacturer, Elfe. "People here just aren't buying our chocolates. The quality is bad, and the packaging unattractive. We never had the capital to invest before, and now we don't have the financing to compete." She worries that her economics degree, grounded in Marxism, will be worthless if the company goes bankrupt. The popular uprising has unpleasant consequences for many.

Predictions are that there will be significant unemployment. Overstaffed and

FIGURE 13.1   THE INDIVIDUAL MOTIVATION PROCESS

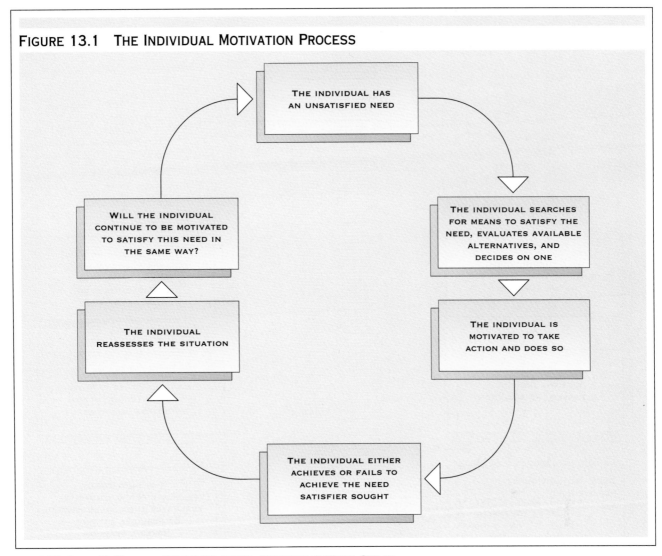

SOURCE: JAMES M. HIGGINS, <u>HUMAN RELATIONS: BEHAVIOR AT WORK</u>, 2ND ED.
(NEW YORK: RANDOM HOUSE, 1987), P. 51.

undertechnologied East German industry is simply not ready is simply not ready for competition with the West. East Germans now realize that there is much more to capitalism than working hard. You have to have a job first. And then, there are many who are not used to a full day's work. Workers often put in their time, but worked much less than a full day. What was the incentive? Now, they have to pay attention to quality, there are no guarantees, and how hard you work matters very much.

Then, there are the entrepreneurs among the East Germans who see tremendous opportunities. Christa Keller is among them. She plans on opening a food catering business for business clients. Motivation to succeed now means different things to different people in East Germany.

SOURCE: Frederick Kempe, "After the Euphoria: Specter of Capitalism Haunts East Germans Used to Certainties," *Wall Street Journal,* June 14, 1990, pp. A1, A8.

FIGURE 13.2 THE MOTIVATION/PERFORMANCE CYCLE (MPC)

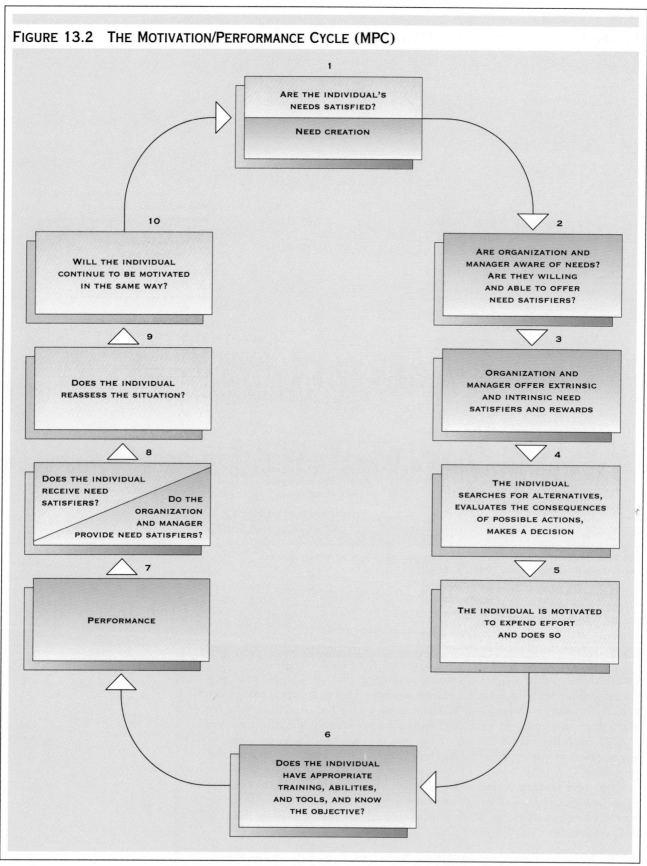

1
ARE THE INDIVIDUAL'S NEEDS SATISFIED?

NEED CREATION

2
ARE ORGANIZATION AND MANAGER AWARE OF NEEDS? ARE THEY WILLING AND ABLE TO OFFER NEED SATISFIERS?

3
ORGANIZATION AND MANAGER OFFER EXTRINSIC AND INTRINSIC NEED SATISFIERS AND REWARDS

4
THE INDIVIDUAL SEARCHES FOR ALTERNATIVES, EVALUATES THE CONSEQUENCES OF POSSIBLE ACTIONS, MAKES A DECISION

5
THE INDIVIDUAL IS MOTIVATED TO EXPEND EFFORT AND DOES SO

6
DOES THE INDIVIDUAL HAVE APPROPRIATE TRAINING, ABILITIES, AND TOOLS, AND KNOW THE OBJECTIVE?

7
PERFORMANCE

8
DOES THE INDIVIDUAL RECEIVE NEED SATISFIERS? DO THE ORGANIZATION AND MANAGER PROVIDE NEED SATISFIERS?

9
DOES THE INDIVIDUAL REASSESS THE SITUATION?

10
WILL THE INDIVIDUAL CONTINUE TO BE MOTIVATED IN THE SAME WAY?

SOURCE: JAMES M. HIGGINS, <u>HUMAN RELATIONS: BEHAVIOR AT WORK</u>, 2ND ED. (NEW YORK: RANDOM HOUSE, 1987), P. 53.

organization should take in order to use properly their knowledge of motivation to influence the strength and direction of motivation. By examining these stages, you can better relate the individual's motivation cycle to its enactment in an organizational context.

The manager's and the organization's principal concern is that the individual achieve organizational objectives in an effective and efficient way. This is **performance**. Performance is so important to the discussion of motivation within an organizational context that Figure 13.2 has been titled **The Motivation/Performance Cycle** (MPC). The following paragraphs examine the relationship between motivation and performance revealed in Figure 13.2 stage by stage. This model is used as the vehicle for reviewing the motivation theories. It is also used to show how these theories relate to each other and how a manager can use them in attempting to influence motivation. No one theory stands alone or explains motivation. Managers and companies must understand the basic components of this cycle if they are to be successful at influencing motivation. The Global Management Challenge illustrates how sudden change can highlight the difficulties of moving from a system with few incentives to one in which the worker's motivation and performance are critical.

Content and Process Theories

There are two principal types of theories that you will encounter in the motivational performance cycle model: content theories and process theories. **Content theories** are concerned with the internal individual factors that motivate people—needs and how needs may be satisfied. **Process theories** are concerned with how people are motivated—more specifically, with how people choose need satisfiers and how external factors affect the internal process. Content theories are examined in stages 1 and 3 of Figure 13.2. Process theories are examined in stages 2, 4, 6, 8, 9, and 10. Stages 5 and 7 are results stages of the cycle.

Stage 1 of the MPC: Needs

A **need** is something one must have or wants to have. Unsatisfied needs motivate. It is then the manager's responsibility to determine the need satisfiers that will lead people to attempt to achieve organizational objectives while satisfying their needs. There are a few general need satisfiers such as pay and recognition that are often used, but these do not work on everyone all the time. To the extent possible, the manager, within the framework of the organization's motivation system, attempts to help satisfy employee needs.

> AT HUMAN EDGE SOFTWARE: *Jim Johnson offers need satisfiers that satisfy employees' needs— bonuses, prizes, recognition.*

The Hierarchy of Needs

Most experts feel that needs are ordered in a hierarchy of importance. There are two principal hierarchy of needs theories. The first was formulated by psychologist Abraham Maslow, the second by C. P. Alderfer. Both theories suggest that human needs are ordered in a hierarchical fashion, but each has a different number of levels in the hierarchy and a different set of rules for how the hierarchy functions.

MASLOW'S HIERARCHY
Clinical psychologist Abraham Maslow, after a number of years researching the problems of his patients, concluded that people's needs are ordered in a hierarchy of prepotency.[4] As shown in Figure 13.3, *Maslow's hierarchy* theory

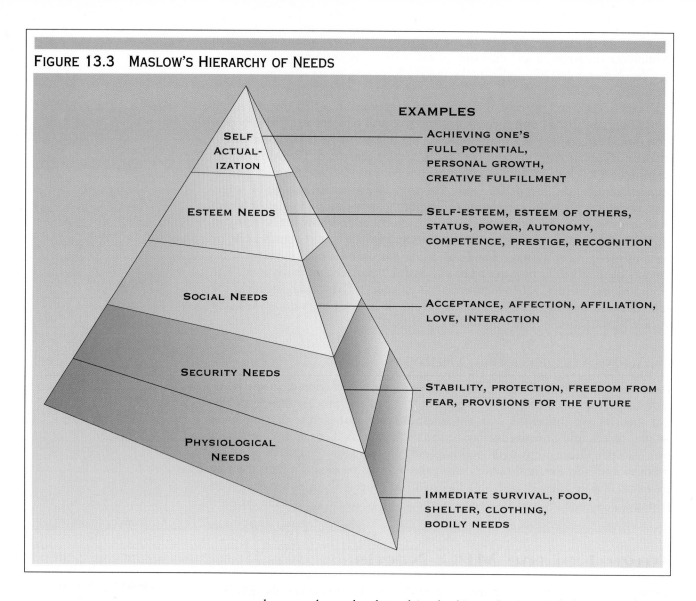

FIGURE 13.3   MASLOW'S HIERARCHY OF NEEDS

EXAMPLES

SELF ACTUAL-IZATION — ACHIEVING ONE'S FULL POTENTIAL, PERSONAL GROWTH, CREATIVE FULFILLMENT

ESTEEM NEEDS — SELF-ESTEEM, ESTEEM OF OTHERS, STATUS, POWER, AUTONOMY, COMPETENCE, PRESTIGE, RECOGNITION

SOCIAL NEEDS — ACCEPTANCE, AFFECTION, AFFILIATION, LOVE, INTERACTION

SECURITY NEEDS — STABILITY, PROTECTION, FREEDOM FROM FEAR, PROVISIONS FOR THE FUTURE

PHYSIOLOGICAL NEEDS — IMMEDIATE SURVIVAL, FOOD, SHELTER, CLOTHING, BODILY NEEDS

suggests that as a lower-level need in the hierarchy is satisfied, it is no longer the individual's primary motivator. The individual then becomes most motivated by the next need in the hierarchy. Thus, as physiological needs are satisfied, security needs become the most important. As these needs are satisfied, social needs become the most important, and so on. Maslow conceptualized that the journey up the hierarchy would take almost a lifetime for most people. In fact, some people might never reach the highest levels. Furthermore, if a formerly satisfied need were no longer satisfied, the individual would drop back down the hierarchy. If an individual who was predominantly motivated by social needs lost his or her job, for example, security might become the most important need. If he or she were unemployed long enough, physiological needs might become dominant.

Maslow also noted that some people might ignore lower-level needs because they were fixated on a higher-level need. Martyrs, for example, seem to be ignoring the need for security altogether. Teachers, nurses, and others in low-paying, but socially beneficial occupations are often satisfying higher-level needs at the expense of lower-level ones.

A number of research studies have been performed on Maslow's hierarchy. These strongly suggest that five levels are too many, that his findings are somewhat suspect because he used his patients as the basis for the theory, and that

FIGURE 13.4 A COMPARISON OF THE ALDERFER AND MASLOW HIERARCHIES

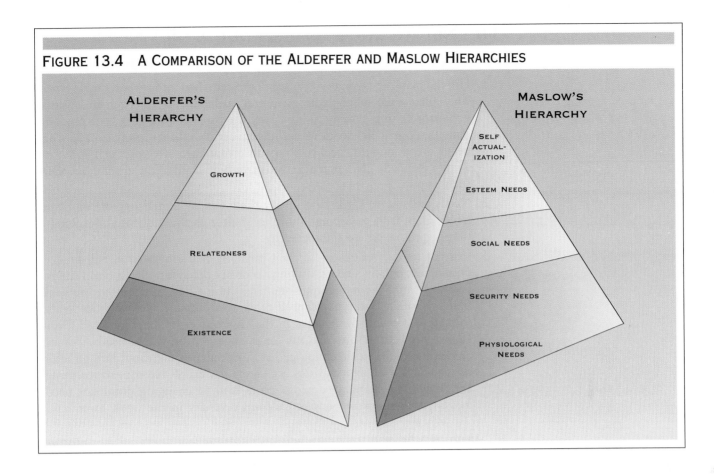

this hierarchy is bound by both cultural and economic factors.[5] Thus, the hierarchy may not be generalizable to all people. It is probably not the same in one country as it is in another, nor is it likely to be the same among different economic groups in the same country. Edwin C. Nevis, for example, finds that belonging is the first need level in China, followed by physiological needs, safety, and self-actualization in the service of society. The latter is different from our view of individual self-actualization. The sense of serving community is a very important need in China.[6] It is not even clear that a hierarchy exists, per se, but it is clear that there are major types of needs and that some are more important than others at a given time to any individual. And if you view the hierarchy as a lifelong process in terms of achieving self-actualization, as Maslow did, then the hierarchy concept is a reasonable conceptualization of how people's needs are ordered.

CLAYTON P. ALDERFER

Clayton P. Alderfer, after examining Maslow's approach and the related research, proposed that the hierarchy of needs was more accurately conceptualized as having only three levels, as indicated in Figure 13.4: existence needs, relatedness needs, and growth needs. There is some research support for this model as a more universally usable one.[7] Importantly, Alderfer's hierarchy does not contain the requirement of having lower-level needs satisfied before an upper-level need can be activated. His theory also allows for need frustration and subsequent regression to lower-level needs, as does Maslow's. For example, if a person's most dominant need is growth, but that person loses his or her job, the most dominant need might become existence. Under Alderfer's approach, growth might still continue to be important, however.

The Nature and Strength of Current Needs

Up to this point we can summarize what we know about needs as follows:

1. Human beings have many needs that are classified into several major types. This allows the manager in an organization to offer certain need satisfiers—for example, money—to satisfy the type of needs that seem to dominate that particular work force. Seldom can a manager know exactly what needs are dominant, and seldom can a manager offer precisely what an employee needs. The manager must, rather, depend on general satisfiers such as pay.

2. Needs and the rewards that satisfy them can be either tangible or intangible. They tend to become more intangible as the individual develops—that is, progresses up the hierarchy.

3. Current needs, regardless of their position in the hierarchy, will tend to dominate a person's goals, driving his or her behavior. Needs often change and there may be more than one need motivating someone at the same time, although one type of need tends to dominate. People's needs also change as a result of changes in the environment. Chapters 10, 11, and 12 explored numerous reasons for changes in individual needs. For example, high levels of technology lead to needs for increased human interaction. Employee expectations are changing. Employee educational levels are changing. Changing demographics lead to changing dominant needs for various groups of people. Cultural diversity in the work force has a

---

MANAGEMENT CHALLENGE 13.1

A&P Shares Profits to Increase Them

From 1974 to 1982, A&P food stores shrank in number from 3,468 to 1,016 stores. Its rivals called it the worst-run chain in the industry. It experienced four straight years of losses from 1978 to 1981. Managers were doubling as bagboys. Something had to be done. After examining the situation it faced and considering the needs of its employees, many of whom were worried about job security, the company decided on a risky move: share profits in return for increased productivity.

In a trial operation negotiated with the United Food & Commercial Workers (UFCW) for the sixty stores in the Philadelphia area, workers took a 25 percent pay cut in exchange for this agreement: If a store's workers could keep the store's labor costs to 10 percent of sales, they would get a cash bonus equal to 1 percent of the store's sales. Their bonus would drop to .5 percent of sales if labor rose to 11 percent of store sales, and they received a 1.5 percent bonus if labor dropped to 9 percent of store sales. The bonus could be obtained either by working more efficiently or by increasing sales. The two lowest-need levels—physiological and security needs—were being appealed to in this plan.

But the company also satisfied higher-level needs when it allowed employees to begin meeting twice a month to offer suggestions for improving their stores. They were motivated. The ideas poured in and so did the profits. "You'd be amazed at the willingness of people to participate when they can say anything without fear of reprisal," observes Thomas R. McNutt, president of UFCW Local 400 in Landover, Maryland.

major impact in such situations. Management Challenge 13.1 explores one company's approach to using its understanding of human needs to help achieve its objectives.

Managerial Implications

The hierarchy theories in and of themselves are interesting, but their importance to management lies principally in the ability of the manager and other users of the theories—for example, those in the human resources department—to identify dominant needs in individuals and groups. The manager, in order to influence the motivation process, must know or have a good estimate of what each person's or group's needs are, and then work to attempt to satisfy those needs for the benefit of the individual and the organization. With all of the changes occurring in subordinates' needs—for example, as a result of education levels and cultural diversity—managers will need training to identify needs better.

As shown in stage 1 of the motivation/performance cycle, another action the manager can take to use his or her knowledge of motivation is to create needs in the individual—or, more appropriately, to strengthen existing needs and make them dominant. For example, at Merrill-Lynch, a catalog of very expensive items is distributed to stockholders to strengthen existing needs for luxury items.[8]

AT HUMAN EDGE SOFTWARE: *Creating needs is really what Jim Johnson does at Human Edge Software. He strengthens his employees' existing needs for financially based rewards and recognition. When he was at Psych Systems, during the dramatic sales meeting to save the company, he brought out peoples' needs to contribute, to achieve goals.*

From 1982 to 1986, the plan spread to a total of 281 stores, with the rest to be included in the near future. Profits jumped 81 percent from 1984 to 1986, and much of the credit goes to this plan. Not only has labor efficiency been increased, but store sales volume has jumped 24 percent in those stores using the plan. The workers are happy too—they usually end up making more money under this plan than under the old contract.

SOURCE: Christopher S. Eklund, "How A&P Fattens Profits by Sharing Them," *Business Week*, (December 22, 1986), p. 44.

By sharing profits, A&P increased them. They may even have saved the company by doing so. Because it had old, inefficient and undersized stores, it had to rely on employee ingenuity for survival. (SOURCE © Allen Green/ Photo Researchers)

Achievement Motivation

Another major contribution to our understanding of human needs was made by researchers David C. McClelland and J. W. Atkinson.[9] They found that a small percentage of people have an unusually high **need for achievement** (principally economic achievement) or "nAch." These people tend to possess a consistent set of traits:

1. They prefer to set their own goals and pursue tasks for which the probability for success is moderately high.
2. They prefer to work at tasks that give them quick feedback—this feedback helps them gauge their success levels.
3. They prefer tasks in which their own efforts will have a significant impact on the accomplishment of the task. This gives them a feeling of achievement.
4. They constantly search for ways to improve their performance.

People with a high need for achievement typically choose certain occupations, for example, business management or sales. In addition to a high need for achievement, McClelland and Atkinson identified two other associated needs that complement the achievement need in their **achievement need** theory: the need for power (nPower)—control over others—and a need for affiliation (nAff)—social interaction. A successful business manager typically has a high need for achievement and power but a low need for affiliation. The successful entrepreneur is similarly motivated.[10]

An important underlying principle of this theory is that these needs are largely culturally derived. The family plays a very important role in developing them. Because environment plays such an important role in developing achievement, it is generally believed this need can be developed in someone through training. The high achiever develops most often under the following circumstances:

1. When the dominant belief system of a society or culture, for example religion or government, encourages and allows individuals to be successful, to achieve, and to make money, economic development will occur and high achievers will emerge. Some societies stress achievement in other areas. When the prevailing belief system is opposed to economic achievement, such as was true in Western civilization prior to the Protestant Reformation and in the Soviet Union prior to "perestroika," the high achiever will fail to materialize. In the Soviet Union, for example, the key to success is changing from political skills, and a high need for power, to, at least to some degree, a need for economic achievement.[11]

One of the underpinnings of the economic success of the United States has been those entrepreneurs who had a high need for achievement. Stephen Wozniak, cofounder of Apple computers, finds time to enjoy some of the fruits of his labors. (SOURCE © Ed Kashi)

2. When the stories that children learn and the television they watch point to economic achievement as being important, children will tend to emulate those role models.

3. The family plays an extremely important part in the development of high achievers. High achievers come from families that stress high levels of performance; give positive recognition for performance and take a problem-solving attitude toward failure; give continuous feedback; and are characterized by a more democratic than authoritarian decision-making process.

It is not clear exactly how, or even if, achievement fits into the hierarchy theory. Achievement could be a specific type of self-actualization need, or it might be one of several needs that don't fit nicely into the hierarchy.[12]

People with high achievement needs seem to be critical to organizational performance. The manager who understands achievement need theory can understand his or her own personal motivations and those of other managers, as well as the motivations of people who generally have a high need for achievement. In most business organizations, there are many such people. Understanding this need to achieve, the manager should create (or seek out) opportunities for that need to be satisfied.

People with a high need for achievement tend to gravitate to businesses, especially to positions in sales, management, and other areas where demonstrated performance is usually rewarded, where feedback is frequent, and where there is a chance to accomplish goals. Thus, it makes sense for organizations to seek out high achievers to fill positions of importance. Charles A. Garfield studied over 250 managers, salespeople, and entrepreneurs carefully selected through a peer-review process where fellow managers, salespeople, and entrepreneurs recommended those in the sample. He and his associates found that peak performers share ten common characteristics:

1. Vision and the ability to plan strategically.
2. The drive to surpass previous levels of performance.
3. High levels of self-confidence and self-esteem.
4. A high need for responsibility and control.
5. Strong communication and salesmanship skills.
6. The habit of mentally rehearsing before critical events.
7. Little need for outside praise or recognition. (This conflicts somewhat with the need for feedback McClelland found among high achievers.)
8. A willingness to take risks.
9. The ability to accept feedback and make self-corrections.
10. An ownership attitude toward their ideas and products.[13]

A major challenge confronting managers is how to manage such peak performers. The best answer seems to be to provide them with jobs that allow them to achieve, that allow them to decide, that provide feedback, and that give rewards.

Additional Categories of Needs

There are several additional types of needs that do not fit cleanly into the hierarchy approaches. Among them are role motivation; objectives as motivators; the need to be socially contributive; and the need for truth, beauty, and justice.

ROLE MOTIVATION

John Miner has formulated a very relevant theory of human needs known as **role motivation**.[14] His research indicates that certain individuals enjoy the managerial role and seek it out. He has principally examined the managerial role and has developed a set of characteristics of those who like to play that role. There is no reason to believe though, that others—teachers, lawyers, doctors, and dentists—do not also feel the need to fulfill their particular roles, as well.

The manager must identify the roles, if any, that people like to fill and then attempt to help them fulfill them, as long as doing so influences their motivation in the direction of achieving organizational objectives efficiently. Offering somebody a promotion into a higher level of management, for example, is one way of helping him or her fulfill that role. The manager must also be attuned to his or her own needs for role fulfillment.

OBJECTIVES AS MOTIVATORS

People are goal-striving animals, and therefore **objectives** may be used to **influence** their **motivation**. Both Maslow's and Alderfer's hierarchies are goal-striving needs hierarchies. They are based on levels of needs that are also goals to achieve. These goal-striving needs are in contrast to such nongoal striving needs as needs for truth and beauty, closure, or other, similar needs.[15] People want to satisfy needs. They therefore seek to achieve those objectives that enable them to do so. Sales quotas, for example, help motivate sales people. Some individuals become concerned with simply accomplishing objectives, regardless of their position on the hierarchy, or perhaps in addition to their interests in satisfying these other needs. Expectations of subordinate performance, especially if positive, do seem to have positive motivational force.[16]

The astute manager provides an environment in which the individual can accomplish objectives.[17] Earlier, in Chapter 5, you learned about a management system called management by objectives. Organizations and their managers use such systems as part of planning and control processes, but also as ways of influencing internal motivation. The setting of objectives, or goals, is discussed in more detail later in this chapter.

SOCIALLY CONTRIBUTIVE ACTIONS

Many people feel a great **need to contribute to society**. Many teachers, nurses, doctors, and others feel that they are giving themselves to society in their particular occupations. Environmentalists and those who support social causes have a similar need.

The manager of a socially contributive organization, such as a state child adoption agency, should seek out people with this type of dominant need. The manager in other types of organizations—in socially responsive organizations such as IBM—should select people with a high need to contribute to society for certain tasks, perhaps raising money within the organization for the United Way campaign, for example.

THE NEED FOR TRUTH, BEAUTY, AND JUSTICE

Maslow recognized certain needs that do not fit into his hierarchy: **truth, beauty, and justice**. These are not goal-striving needs, they are simply to be enjoyed. There are other types of needs outside the hierarchy, such as the need for symmetry and the need for closure.[18]

Manager and Employee Needs

The manager must be attuned to employee needs, both goal striving and the other needs. He must be alert to the impact of needs on performance. Managers must constantly seek to find out what their subordinates' needs are. Through constant interaction, the manager can learn most of them. He or she can find out by asking, either personally or through questionnaires, and through observation. The manager must then offer appropriate need satisfiers as described in stages 2 and 3 of the motivation/performance cycle. This job is made more difficult by the fact that needs are always changing.

Stage 2: The Manager Must Recognize and Be Able and Willing to Satisfy Needs

Once the individual becomes aware of certain needs, he or she then searches for ways to satisfy them. Managers should take action to identify these needs, but unfortunately, they often fail to recognize them. Managers often, for example, forget to recognize performance. Or worse, they may overlook the employee's need for recognition simply as a human being. But constant interaction with employees should help minimize such failures. The recognition process is further compounded by the fact that multiple needs may be driving the individual. Salespeople clearly seek recognition, especially financial. But they also need autonomy. Too often, the latter is ignored.[19] One survey of supervisors' perceptions of what employees want from their jobs reveals that managers often badly misjudge needs. For example, supervisors ranked "good wages" as the most important employee need. Employees ranked this as the fifth most important factor. Employees felt "interesting work" was most important; "full appreciation of work well done" was number two. Supervisors ranked these as being fifth and eighth in importance to workers.[20]

One example of changing employee needs is that for day care. With an increasing number of women with children entering the work force, employers are more frequently finding it necessary to provide on-site day care centers for the use of employees with small children. This group of children from one of Zales day care centers have just been on a nature hike. (SOURCE © Mark Perlstein/Black Star)

The manager must take the necessary actions to determine the needs of his or her subordinates. But the manager must also assess whether he or she is able or wants to satisfy those needs. Various constraints may prevent the manager from offering the satisfiers that employees need: the budget may not have the funds; there may be no promotion available; or he or she may have only limited time to spend with each subordinate.

Sometimes the manager may be able, but not willing to satisfy someone's needs. An employee with a high need for affiliation often tries to spend time at work talking to everybody around him or her. The manager will not be willing to satisfy that need because it conflicts with his or her need for performance. Sometimes managers do not offer need satisfiers for less legitimate reasons. They may not like someone, for example, and therefore would not reward that person, regardless of performance. As the impact of employees' personal needs on their performance is being better recognized, more and more companies are seeking to satisfy them—for example, through providing on-site child care centers.[21]

Stage 3: Offering Extrinsic and Intrinsic Need Satisfiers

Herzberg's Theory

Frederick A. Herzberg's[22] work on job design, which was discussed in Chapter 10, is just one part of his overall theory, which has been particularly helpful in our understanding of how to offer need satisfiers to influence motivation. According to Frederick **Herzberg**, there are two basic types of need satisfiers: **hygiene factors and motivators**. He views the hygiene factors as extrinsic to the job. They include pay and supervision. He views motivators as intrinsic to the job. They include achievement and recognition for performance. Figure 13.5 provides examples of Herzberg's factors and how they compare to Maslow's need hierarchy. As a consequence of his research, Herzberg believes that hygiene factors do not influence an individual's motivation level in an upward fashion, only motivators do. We must remember that by motivation, Herzberg means motivation to do a better job, not just an adequate job, and that he is concerned about motivation in the long term. These facts may help to explain some of the differences between his results and the results found in other research. Herzberg is concerned with raising motivational levels. The manager is often concerned with maintaining them, which supplying hygiene factors will usually do.

Therefore, he suggests that an organization and its managers should be providing opportunities for intrinsic job satisfaction and not just be concerned with extrinsic job satisfaction, as has so often been more typical. Hygiene factors are also often labeled dissatisfiers, meaning that if these items are absent, the individual will be dissatisfied and not perform, or not perform as well as if they were present. Motivators are also referred to as satisfiers. If the individual is intrinsically satisfied, Herzberg believes he or she will be motivated to perform at a higher level of effort. Herzberg is careful to point out that decreased levels of motivation are caused by extrinsic factors, but supplying them won't increase levels of motivation. Motivation levels just won't decline in their presence. Only a different set of factors, intrinsic satisfiers, leads to higher levels of motivation, according to his theory.

Herzberg's theory has been severely criticized for several reasons: It was formulated using a limited sample base of accountants and engineers—two groups whose lower-level needs are satisfied. The research methodology used provided

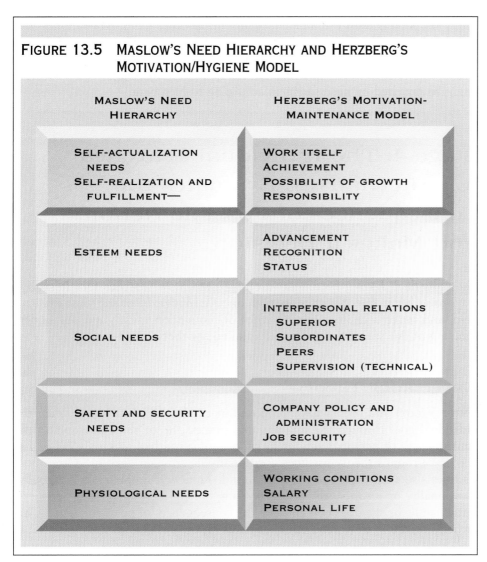

FIGURE 13.5   MASLOW'S NEED HIERARCHY AND HERZBERG'S
MOTIVATION/HYGIENE MODEL

MASLOW'S NEED HIERARCHY	HERZBERG'S MOTIVATION-MAINTENANCE MODEL
SELF-ACTUALIZATION NEEDS SELF-REALIZATION AND FULFILLMENT—	WORK ITSELF ACHIEVEMENT POSSIBILITY OF GROWTH RESPONSIBILITY
ESTEEM NEEDS	ADVANCEMENT RECOGNITION STATUS
SOCIAL NEEDS	INTERPERSONAL RELATIONS SUPERIOR SUBORDINATES PEERS SUPERVISION (TECHNICAL)
SAFETY AND SECURITY NEEDS	COMPANY POLICY AND ADMINISTRATION JOB SECURITY
PHYSIOLOGICAL NEEDS	WORKING CONDITIONS SALARY PERSONAL LIFE

SOURCE: JAMES M. HIGGINS, HUMAN RELATIONS: BEHAVIOR AT WORK,
2ND ED. (NEW YORK: RANDOM HOUSE, 1987) P. 69.

for individual story telling in response to questions and is highly subject to personal attribution biases—an individual attributing his or her motivation to factors that might not be the actual cause. He overlooked certain responses that didn't agree with his theory—for example, items that are satisfiers for some people are dissatisfiers for others. Finally, his principal belief that money does not lead to increased levels of motivation disagrees with about 95 percent of all other research.[23] It is clear, however, that job design is important to motivation as was discussed in Chapter 10.

Herzberg's observations are useful because they point managers to groups of satisfiers or types of satisfiers that can be offered to satisfy the different types of needs people have. An individual who is dominated by lower-level needs might still need to be provided with hygiene factors in order to influence his or her motivational levels, or at least to maintain them at satisfactory levels. On the other hand, the individual who has upper-level needs would probably require "motivators" to increase his or her motivation. As members of our society move upward in the Maslow or Alderfer hierarchy, in general they are going to have high-level expectations about what they expect from the job. This is one of the factors that is changing the nature of management, as discussed in Chapter 1.

Thus, job designs must often be changed. On the other hand, while money will motivate many, if not most workers in the short run, contrary to what Herzberg advises, compensation programs may need to be redesigned to make them effective. Figure 13.5 shows how the various types of needs suggested by Maslow might be matched by need satisfiers according to Herzberg.

Stage 4: The Individual Searches for Alternatives, Evaluates the Consequences of Possible Action, and Makes a Decision

The individual, having become aware of a need, now searches for alternative ways to satisfy it. Faced with more than one alternative, he or she must evaluate them and make a choice. Two theories of motivation greatly aid our understanding of this stage: the expectancy and equity theories.

Expectancy Theory

Victor Vroom and others have proposed in **expectancy theory** that when the individual goes through the motivational process, he or she contemplates the consequences of personal actions in choosing alternatives to satisfy his or her needs.[24] Vroom's theory assumes a rationally determined decision. Other possibilities also exist. Much of the time an individual will simply react habitually, emotionally, or instinctively when choosing among alternative need satisfiers. But when he or she does contemplate the consequences of personal actions, his or her motivation to expend effort depends on the answers to these questions:

1. Can I do the job?
2. If I do the job, what is the probability that I will receive the need satisfier?
3. If I get the need satisfier, what is it worth to me?

In the organizational context, this translates into the individual's perception of the situation. More formally, expectancy theory is based on the following assumptions.

1. A combination of forces within the individual and in the environment determine behavior.
2. People make decisions about their own behavior and that of organizations.
3. People have different types of needs, goals, and desires.
4. People make choices among alternative behaviors based on the extent to which they think a certain behavior will lead to a desired outcome.[25]

Figure 13.6 summarizes the expectancy model of employee motivation.[26] An **expectancy** is the probability that one action results in a certain consequence. Motivation in this model is believed to lead to effort, which leads to performance. Performance leads to various outcomes, each of which has some associated value known as a **valence.** Such values are unique to each individual. Most immediate outcomes, such as compensation, are associated with secondary outcomes, such as being able to make a car payment. Additional important considerations shown in the figure include

AT HUMAN EDGE SOFTWARE: *Jim Johnson's sales personnel, for example, examine the sales quotas that they must achieve in order to obtain the rewards he offers. If they feel they can make them, then they will probably take the actions necessary— but only as long as the mink coat, Gucci shoes, expensive suits, or cash or other rewards are worthwhile to them. If they already have two mink coats, a third would hardly be motivating. Thus, Jim Johnson, as any manager, would be forced over time to change the rewards he offers.*

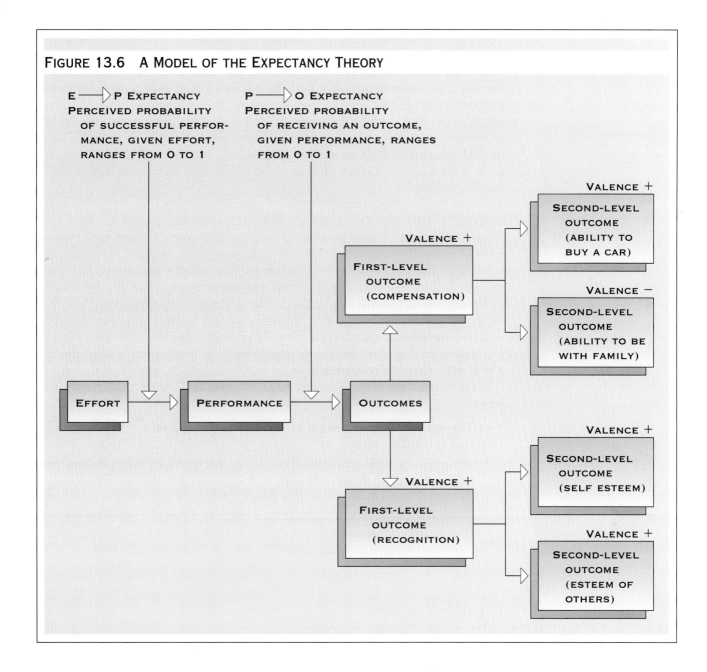

FIGURE 13.6 A MODEL OF THE EXPECTANCY THEORY

1. an effort-to-performance expectancy.
2. a performance-to-outcome expectancy.
3. degrees of relationship between outcomes and values.

THE EFFORT-TO-PERFORMANCE EXPECTANCY

The individual's perception of the probability that effort will lead to high performance is defined as having a value somewhere between 0 and 1. If the expectancy is high, the value is 1; if it is low, the value is near 0. When the individual asks him- or herself: "Can I perform the task?," if he or she thinks it possible, the expectancy will be 1. If he or she thinks the answer is no, or at best at a low level of performance regardless of the effort expended, then the expectancy is weak and close to 0. IBM sets its sales goals so that 80 percent of its salespeople can reach their goals. Expectancy is high. People sell.[27]

THE PERFORMANCE-TO-OUTCOME EXPECTANCY

When the individual asks him- or herself the question: "If I perform, will I receive the expected outcome?," if he or she thinks the answer is yes, or nearly yes, the expectancy approaches 1. If the individual feels that being a high performer may not have a bearing on the outcome, then a lower expectancy, somewhere between 1 and 0, would result. If he or she thinks there may be no relationship between performance and the outcome—the expectancy is 0. Those at IBM who make their goals automatically are members of the 100 Percent Club. This is an expectancy of 1, as is the probability of financial rewards for meeting quotas![28]

THE RELATIONSHIP BETWEEN OUTCOMES AND VALENCES

When the individual asks him- or herself the question: "If I get the reward, what is it worth to me?," he or she is attempting to estimate the value, or valence, of the outcome. A high performer may receive pay raises, fast promotions, substantial praise, and critical assignments but would also be subject to fatigue, stress, jealousy, and political manipulations. He or she may find, for example, that money, a first-level outcome, is not a motivating reward because it doesn't have much comparative value if its takes him or her away from family, a second-level outcome. Each outcome (reward) is being compared to the rewards that other behaviors result in.

For motivated behavior to occur, stage 5 of the MPC, three conditions must be met:

1. The individual must have a reasonably high expectancy that effort will lead to performance.
2. The individual must have a reasonably high expectancy that performance will lead to the desired outcome.
3. The desired outcomes, both first level and second, must have reasonably high valences, or values. Technically, as long as the expectancies are greater than 0, and the valences are stronger than those of other alternatives, some motivated behavior should result.[29]

Equity Theory

In concert with the decisions relative to expectancies and the valences of outcomes, the individual also assesses the degree to which the potential rewards will be equitably distributed. J. Stacy Adams contends in his **equity theory** that people will seek rewards only if they perceive that the rewards will be equitably distributed.[30] The term *equity* implies that a person is being treated equally or fairly when compared to the treatment of others who behave in a similar way.

As shown in Figure 13.7, employees compare their inputs and outcomes (rewards) with those of other employees, especially with those who are performing the same basic job. When they find inequity they must adjust their behavior to make the situation more tenable.[31] If they feel they are in a less than equitable situation, they can reduce their inputs—work effort, for example—or increase their outputs by trying to build psychological benefits for themselves: "I do better work than Jane," for example. They could also attempt to secure greater rewards, or leave the job. Conversely, if they feel they are in an overly equitable situation, they can increase their inputs or, in an unlikely scenario, seek to have their outcomes reduced.

A worker in a unionized situation, for example, may find him- or herself producing a higher-quality product, may be more diligent about serving his or

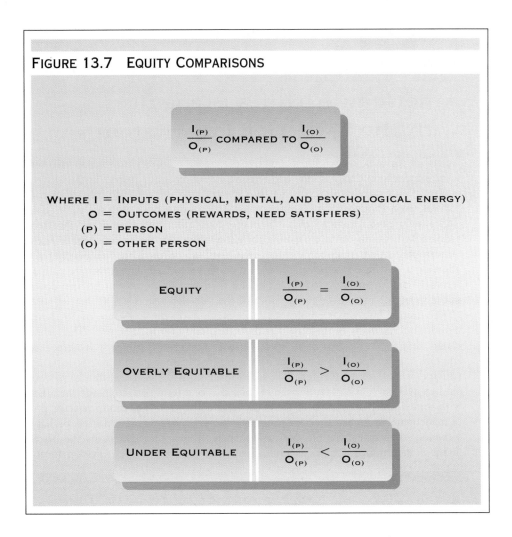

FIGURE 13.7 EQUITY COMPARISONS

$$\frac{I_{(P)}}{O_{(P)}} \text{ COMPARED TO } \frac{I_{(O)}}{O_{(O)}}$$

WHERE I = INPUTS (PHYSICAL, MENTAL, AND PSYCHOLOGICAL ENERGY)
O = OUTCOMES (REWARDS, NEED SATISFIERS)
(P) = PERSON
(O) = OTHER PERSON

EQUITY $\quad \dfrac{I_{(P)}}{O_{(P)}} = \dfrac{I_{(O)}}{O_{(O)}}$

OVERLY EQUITABLE $\quad \dfrac{I_{(P)}}{O_{(P)}} > \dfrac{I_{(O)}}{O_{(O)}}$

UNDER EQUITABLE $\quad \dfrac{I_{(P)}}{O_{(P)}} < \dfrac{I_{(O)}}{O_{(O)}}$

her employer, and may be paying more attention to details than a peer worker but receiving no more pay than that individual. When comparing his or her inputs and rewards to the other worker's an inequity is perceived and something must be done to correct it. He or she may make this adjustment by decreasing personal inputs or increasing rewards. If inputs are adjusted, he or she will have to lower effort. If rewards are to be increased, they will have to be rewards other than financial since income is fixed by the union contract. The worker might, for example, seek praise for his or her efforts or might "reward him- or herself" by talking about how enjoyable work is. He or she might even choose to quit. It has been proposed that people have varying degrees of sensitivity to the equity of a situation. This sensitivity varies along a continuum, ranging from those who prefer to have a lesser ratio than those they work with, to those who prefer an equal ratio, to those who prefer a higher ratio.[32] Management Challenge 13.2 highlights American Airline's attempt to enforce a two-tier wage system, something clearly violating the equity principle.[33] Generally, the manager should provide perceived equity among subordinates. This can be accomplished both by providing actual equity and by maintaining good communication, to ensure understanding of nonequitable outcome distributions.

Have you ever suffered inequities on the job? What did you do about them? How did you make your inputs/outcomes ratio equal to those of others? Have you ever felt that your ratio was higher than somebody else's? What did you do then?

Stage 5: Motivation to Expend Effort

If the individual has been able to work satisfactorily through the MPC up to this point, then he or she will be motivated to expend effort in the direction and to the strength level desired to accomplish organizational objectives. The degree to which he or she is willing to take action, and the strength of that motivation, depends on the answers to the questions asked up to this point, and/or upon his or her habitual, emotional, or reflexive actions and general personality. If, and only if, the answers are sufficiently positive, will the individual be motivated to take the actions desired by management.

Stage 6: Factors That Turn Motivation into Performance

The manager and the organization are not just concerned with motivation. They must ensure that motivated effort results in performance—the effective and efficient accomplishment of objectives. To ensure that motivated effort results in performance, managers and the organization must assure that the individual

one important thing. New workers quickly become old workers, and they question the pay inequity. While they might have been happy to have had the job to begin with, now they want what everybody else has: equal pay for equal work. American's managers will probably be glad to see the system go because they've had the task of motivating people despite obvious inequities.

SOURCE: Marj Charlier and Francis C. Brown, III, "American Air Attendants Seek to Topple Two-Tier Pay," *The Wall Street Journal* 25 March, 1987, p. 6; and Aaron Bernstein, "Why Two-Tier Wage Scales Are Starting to Self-Destruct," *Business Week* (March 16, 1987), p. 41.

Some of these American Airlines employees earn one wage for doing the job, while others, more senior employees, earn a higher wage. A manager's job is made more difficult in such circumstances, because equity is not present. (SOURCE © Larry Mulvehill/Photo Researchers)

knows the objectives that must be achieved, knows the tasks necessary to achieve the objectives, and has the abilities, skills, and tools to accomplish the necessary tasks. Training and development, and capital investment are obviously very important.

In 1970 Jim Marshall, one of the National Football League's premier linemen at that time, caught a fumble in midair and ran to the nearest end zone for what he thought was a touchdown. Unfortunately, it became a safety, as he had run to the wrong end zone. He was highly motivated, but he had failed to perform because in this particular instance he didn't know the objective. He didn't know to which end zone he had to carry the ball.

Goal (Objective) Setting

In recent years the importance of the manager's **goal-setting** actions (objective setting as defined in Chapter 5) has been recognized. Edwin A. Locke was the first to focus on their importance in 1968.[34] Since that time, considerable conceptualization and research have taken place. From the manager's perspective, a series of five steps encompasses the objective-setting process: diagnosis for objective-setting readiness, preparation for objective setting, implementation through focusing on objective-setting attributes, an intermediate review to adjust objectives, and a final review.[35]

These steps are largely self-explanatory, except for the implementation of step 3. Implementation indicates that the manager must set objectives in light of desirable objective-setting attributes. Objectives should be specific—that is, quantifiable and clear. Because the difficulty level affects performance, the manager must weigh carefully how hard to make the objective. The manager must treat objective setting in a way that reveals his or her concern, or intensity, for the outcomes of setting objectives and/or determining plans to reach those objectives. Commitment, the amount of effort used to achieve a goal, is really a behavioral demonstration of objective intensity. A manager shows his intensity by showing his commitment.

Research on objective setting reveals the following:

1. More specific objectives, like a 10 percent increase in annual sales, lead to higher levels of performance than general statements such as, "Do as much as you can."
2. The more difficult the objective, the higher the level of performance, assuming the individual is committed.
3. The actual process of setting objectives is full of problems, as discussed in Chapter 5.[36]

The importance of objective setting to successfully influencing motivation helps explain the results of the management-by-objective-type programs discussed in Chapter 5. These programs focus on the goal-setting process as a way of influencing motivation and thus take advantage of its integral impact on the motivation process. From the subordinate's perspective, commitment to an objective leads to performance. If an employee is not committed to an objective, he or she is not likely to reach it. The manager can influence to a significant degree the amount of commitment a subordinate has.[37] Designing programs to increase such commitment may be very necessary in the future.

Stage 7: Performance

If the individual is highly motivated and if a certain set of characteristics of the situation are met, the individual will perform. High levels of performance—the effective and efficient accomplishment of objectives—will occur if certain managerial actions have transpired. How performance is defined varies from organization to organization, from situation to situation. In some organizations performance is not well defined in advance. It should be. In large organizations especially, but in most organizations in general, an individual's performance results from numerous factors such as competition, organizational support, cooperation among departments, and so on. Achieving performance is being stressed more and more as competition increases.

Stage 8: The Individual Obtains the Need Satisfiers or Not

Need satisfiers are critical to influencing motivation successfully. The individual is originally motivated by unsatisfied needs. He or she is motivated to take action on the expectancies that effort leads to performance and performance leads to an outcome that has value; and upon the belief that the need satisfiers will be equitably distributed. If these conditions are not met by stage 8 of the cycle, the individual, when assessing the situation in stage 9, is not likely to continue, in stage 10, to be motivated in the same way again. Much of our understanding of this stage of the process results from reinforcement theories of motivation.

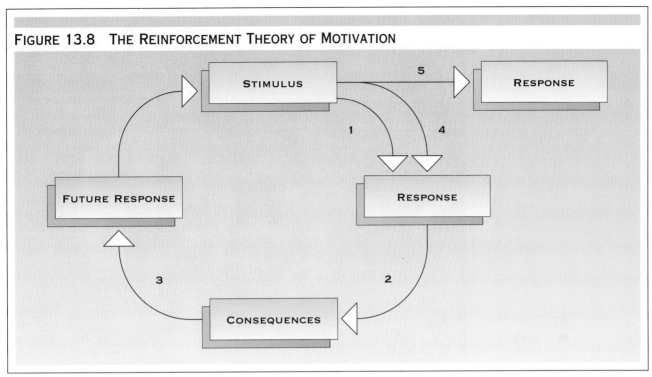

FIGURE 13.8 THE REINFORCEMENT THEORY OF MOTIVATION

SOURCE: B.F. SKINNER, <u>BEYOND FREEDOM AND DIGNITY</u> (NEW YORK: KNOPF, 1971).

Reinforcement of Effort

Based on research studies,, **reinforcement theory** suggests that behavior that results in rewarding consequences is likely to be repeated, whereas behavior that results in no rewards or in punishing consequences is less likely to be repeated. These are not absolutes. These are tendencies. Much of the original work in this area came from the efforts of psychological researcher E. L. Thorndike, who formulated what is known as the **law of effect** (1898): "Of several responses to the same situation, those that are accompanied or closely followed by satisfaction . . . will be more likely to recur; those which are accompanied or closely followed by discomfort . . . will be less likely to occur."[38]

Since the late 1930s, psychologist B. F. Skinner has been a major force in demonstrating how reinforcement works.[39] Figure 13.8 uses the language of reinforcement theory to explain human motivation. More recently, this phenomenon has come to be known in its applied form as **organizational behavior modification** (OBM).[40] Reinforcement theory works almost conversely to expectancy theory. In expectancy theory the individual focuses on expectations of success and associated values before the behavior or response, shown in Figure 13.8 as a path from stimulus to response indicated in circle number 1 before the box labeled "Response." Getting to the response is consistent with the processes of expectancy theory. The emphasis in reinforcement is more on what happens afterward. Following the response the individual experiences consequences. As a result of these consequences, future behavior—future responses—depend upon whether the consequences were desirable or undesirable. When encountering the same action choices again—for example, when offered a reward—the response depends upon whether the consequences were pleasant or not after previous responses. If consequences were pleasant, the individual is likely to return again to the same response, down path 4. If consequences were unpleasant, the individual is likely to go down path 5 seeking a new response.

AT HUMAN EDGE SOFTWARE: *How successful do you think Jim Johnson's company would be if he didn't reward with the Gucci shoes, the Brooks Brothers suits, and the mink coats he has promised? If he didn't recognize the efforts of his subordinates? "Not very" is the answer.*

The CEO of Black & Decker makes it a point to personally reward employees for their contributions to the firm. Such positive reinforcement does much to help continue motivation. (© Rob Kinmonth)

Types of Reinforcement

There are four types of reinforcement: positive, negative, punishment, and extinction. Positive and negative reinforcement strengthen or maintain behavior. Punishment and extinction weaken or decrease behavior.

Some examples of reinforcement in the organizational setting include the following:

1. Positive reinforcement: In positive reinforcement something positive is given after the behavior occurs. A very easy way of providing positive reinforcement is to give someone a raise. Another is to send a timely, personal, short, precise memo outlining a person's performance successes.[41] Or when a manager responds in a positive way to the friendly interpersonal actions of an individual, this is likely to encourage the individual to be friendly and sociable toward others.

2. Negative reinforcement: In negative reinforcement something negative is taken away when the desired behavior occurs. An employee may, for example, be motivated to perform at high levels in order to avoid a reprimand from a manager. New recruits in military training camp, for example, seek to perform at extremely high levels in order to avoid the shouts and physical punishment that might follow if they failed to perform. In this case the manager (drill sergeant) allows for avoidance, which motivates performance.

3. Punishment: Punishment is often used by managers to discourage undesirable behaviors. According to reinforcment research, if the consequence is unpleasant, the future response when facing the same choice again will be a different response than the previous one in order to avoid punishment. One of the manager's most unpleasant, but sometimes frequent chores is to discipline employees—for coming in late, for being absent, for low quality of work, or for low quantity of work. Managers often must counsel employees. They often invoke reprimands that may result in a loss of pay

or even in termination. The general belief is that if the consequence is sufficiently undesirable, the employee will not engage in the negative behavior again. There are many counterproductive side effects to punishment that have caused many managers and certainly most management authors to suggest that discipline be handled from a problem-solving perspective that encourages self-determined "discipline" and not punishment. The attitude taken is that the manager and the subordinate have a joint problem they must solve. The manager asks the subordinate's help in solving the problem, even when the subordinate's behavior is that problem. When the subordinate does the analysis, when he or she makes the determination as to what actions would be appropriate to solve the problem, the punishment aspects of the process are reduced. The solution is much more palatable, in most cases, to the individual who is "disciplined" because it is self-administered discipline.

4. Extinction: In extinction no positive or negative reinforcement is given. Behavior is ignored. Over time the unrewarded behavior should fail to be repeated. If an employee is absent but is not punished, for example, the belief is that the unrewarded behavior will cease. This type of approach can be used only so long as subordinates do not begin to take advantage of the manager's nonaction. Ignoring violations of policy can pose many problems. But if nothing happens after performance occurs, employees wonder if performance really matters.

THE SCHEDULE OF REINFORCEMENTS
The degree to which rewards are tied to performance is also critical. There are two fundamental types of reinforcement schedules: continuous and intermittent. In continuous reinforcement a reinforcement follows every behavior. In intermittent reinforcement a reinforcement follows some responses but not others. There are four types of intermittent reinforcement: fixed interval, variable interval, fixed ratio, and variable ratio. Each of the five types of schedules for reinforcement has varying impacts, as revealed in Table 13.1.

1. Continuous Schedule: Reinforcement follows every behavioral response. If a manager praises a subordinate every time he or she succeeds at a task, continuous reinforcement is being used. Emery Air Freight used continuous reinforcement (feedback on container usage) to significantly improve employee usage rates on the appropriate sized container. Appropriate usage levels rose from 45 to 95 percent, saving the company $650,000 in one year.[42]

2. Fixed-Interval (see Table 13.1): This reward is applied at some periodic interval. The best example of this is the weekly or monthly paycheck. There is very little, if any, correlation between rewards and performance. Thus, when the individual asks the question, "Is the outcome related to performance?" in stage 9, the answer is often no. This provides very little incentive for good work.

3. Variable-Interval Schedule: Time is again the basis for reinforcement, but the time interval varies from one reinforcement action to the next. Unfortunately, sometimes this provides little incentive to perform because reinforcement occurs regardless of behavior.

4. Fixed-Ratio Schedule: In this situation, regardless of time, after a fixed number of behaviors, the reinforcement is given. This typically results in a higher level of effort (performance is different from effort). For example, if a person working in a telephone "boiler room" (a high-pressure sales telephone activity) receives a bonus of $25 for every ten subscriptions that

Emery Air Freight has used applications of reinforcement approaches to improve employee utilization of freight containers. (SOURCE Courtesy Consolidated Freightways, Inc.)

Table 13.1. Reinforcement Schedules and Their Effects on Behavior

Schedule	Description	When Applied to Individual	When Removed by Manager	Organizational Example
Continuous	Reinforcer follows every response.	Fastest method for establishing new behavior	Fastest method to cause extinction of new behavior	Praise after every response, immediate recognition of every response
Fixed interval	Response after specific time period is reinforced.	Some inconsistency in response frequencies	Faster extinction of motivated behavior than variable schedules	Weekly, bimonthly, monthly paycheck
Variable interval	Response after varying period of time (an average) is reinforced.	Produces high rate of steady responses	Slower extinction of motivated behavior than fixed schedules	Transfers, promotions, recognition
Fixed ratio	A fixed number of responses must occur before reinforcement.	Some inconsistency in response frequencies	Faster extinction of motivated behavior than variable schedules	Piece rate, commission on units sold
Variable ratio	A varying number (average) of responses must occur before reinforcement.	Can produce high rate of response that is steady and resists extinction	Slower extinction of motivated behavior than fixed schedules	Bonus, award, time off

SOURCE: Adapted from O Behling, C. Schriesheim, and J. Tolliver, "Present Theories and New Directions in Theories of Work Effort," *Journal of Supplement Abstract Service of the American Psychological Association* (1974), p. 57.

he or she signs to a contract, motivation will be high to perform because there is a definite relationship between performance and outcomes.

5. Variable-Ratio Schedule: According to the research, the variable-ratio schedule is the most powerful reinforcement mechanism for maintaining desired behavior. Exactly why this is true is not clear. The manager who praises an individual lavishly after two or three successful performances and then later after the eighth or the tenth is using a variable-ratio schedule. This would be very difficult to use for formal rewards such as pay because of the difficulty of keeping track of what was current.

How Effective Is It?

A lengthy review of the few major applications of OBM indicates that it almost always has positive results. It has been used positively in separate situations to increase performance (several times), reduce absenteeism (several times), improve customer service, increase sales, reduce cash shortages, get employees to wear seat belts more often, set better goals, improve feedback, improve safety, improve cashier friendliness, raise beaver-trapping levels, reduce errors, improve the miles per gallon performance of truck drivers, increase efficiency, increase usage of earplugs, and reduce hazards.[43] Despite these successes, OBM is not widely used. Perhaps one reason is that OBM can be used to manipulate employees and is often perceived as manipulation whether or not that was the intent.

Reinforcement research clearly indicates that if desired performance is to be continued, the consequences of the individual's actions must have been pleasant. This means that management must give the reward promised as an incentive either on a fixed- or variable-ratio reinforcement schedule. Management Challenge 13.3 provides an interesting illustration of the use of the various types of reinforcement.

Using Reinforcement Approaches to Change Employee Health Habits

Health insurance costs continue to rise for most employers, but a few have found that positive reinforcements—some fixed interval, some variable interval—can help change employee health habits and thus reduce insurance costs. An added benefit is more healthy employees who miss fewer work days. Johnson & Johnson awards "live-for-life dollars" to those who quit smoking, attend health seminars, and exercise at least twenty minutes a day. These dollars can be cashed in for goodies such as clocks, sweat suits, and frisbees.

Intermatic Inc., a manufacturing company headquartered in Spring Grove, Illinois, rewards employees with a trip to Las Vegas if they stay off cigarettes for a year. The Hospital Corporation of America reinforces employees who exercise by paying 24 cents for every mile run or walked, each quarter-mile swum, or for every four miles cycled. Scherer Brothers Lumber Company rewards healthy employees with "well pay." If an employee is neither late nor ill for a month, he or she receives a bonus of two hours' pay. An employee who loses no more than three days a year due to on-the-job injury earns a bonus of $300.

Some of the reinforcement schemes are very complex. Coors pays a higher percentage of insurance as long as employees meet certain conditions, most revolving around a three-year period to "shape up." Bellevue, Washington, awards city workers points according to the cost of their health insurance. They are docked points for claims filed. At the Berol Corporation, an employee is given an extra $500 per year in a fund. This amount is reduced by the amount of insurance claims paid. At the end of the year, the employee gets to keep the difference.

The results are very impressive. Berol's program, for instance, saved them $125,000 in insurance premiums its first year. The Speedall Corporation in Hayward, California, found that after four years of its rewards for a not smoking program, health claims filed by former smokers had dropped 50 percent.

SOURCE: Anastasia Toufexis, "Giving Goodies to the Good," *Time* (November 18, 1985), p. 98.

Employees who receive positive reinforcement for working out, such as these employees of Xerox Corporation, are more likely to repeat the process. (SOURCE © Ken Kerbs)

But providing rewards for performance, although conceptually appealing, is pragmatically often difficult outside of sales and manufacturing, where direct contributions are readily identifiable. And even in these areas, there may be problems with worker jealousy or with managers who are, for one reason or another, reluctant to identify the performing subordinate. Unions usually object to such programs, as well. Poorly trained managers may not recognize performance, and some managers use inappropriate criteria. Performance appraisals often suffer from "grade inflation" and thus fail to differentiate performance really. Some jobs lend themselves to measurement and others do not. And sometimes, performance—such as measured by service calls handled per hour—may be in conflict with how well a customer was treated during a service call—another measure of performance.[44]

Stage 9: The Individual Reassesses the Situation or Not

At this point in the motivation cycle, the individual often will reassess the situation in a logical and rational manner. Individuals may simply continue to behave based on past experience or in a reactive, habitual, or emotional way. But when an individual reexamines the situation, he or she will ask essentially the same questions as in stage 4, except that instead of "Can I perform the task?" he or she asks, "Was the outcome related to performance?" The other questions asked include these: Was I rewarded? What is the valence (value) of the reward? Were the rewards equitably distributed? Depending on the individual's answers, he or she may or may not be motivated in the same way again. Management's actions already have been taken. The individual has reassessed the situation. Not much can be done to change what happens from this point forward, except perhaps to provide explanations for misperceptions or errors on management's administration of evaluations and rewards.

The implications for companies and managers can be enormous, and more and more companies seem to be realizing it. Du Pont, for example, has made the 20,000 workers in its fibers business eligible for up to 12 percent in bonus pay per year. And while Burlington Northern Railroad caps the pay of its 3,000 workers, it makes them eligible for bonuses tied to company success.[45]

Stage 10: Will the Individual Continue to Be Motivated in the Same Way or Not?

The answer to the question of whether an individual will continue to be motivated in the same way depends on all the factors that have come before. From a very broad perspective, whether the individual will continue in the same way depends on his or her satisfaction or dissatisfaction with the entire process and the results of that process.[46] This level of satisfaction not only depends on the results of what happens, but also on the environment and on the personality of the individual.

The answer to the question may also depend on the self-image of the individual and the impact of the process on that self-image. For example, a number of studies and conceptual theories indicate that if the impact strengthens the individual's self-image, the individual is likely to be motivated in the same way again.[47] Or he or she may move up a level in the hierarchy and consequently need different satisfiers. If the impact on the self-image is negative, the individual may not continue to be motivated in the same way because he or she moves down the hierarchy or rejects the process and satisfiers offered to stabilize his or her position on the hierarchy. A review of the research clearly shows that people with high self-esteem are likely to be more motivated, show higher job satisfaction, and have higher productivity than those with low self-esteem.[48] So it behooves managers and organizations to attempt to improve or maintain high levels of self-esteem in their employees. Low levels of self-esteem may also affect the workings of expectancy theory. Those with high self-esteem may see expectancies and values realistically, but those with low self-esteem may underestimate the probability of success.[49]

ATTRIBUTION THEORY

One of the most critical factors in determining future motivation is to whom the individual attributes success or failure, or to whom his or her manager attributes subordinate success or failure. In formulating his **attribution theory,** psychologist A. Bandura has shown that individuals **tend** to attribute success to themselves and failures to outside variables. Conversely, managers *tend* to attribute the failure of subordinates to the subordinate and successes to outside factors.[50] At this point the organization and manager can clarify the situation and make certain that the individual understands the process and results, and that the organization and manager have done the best that they can. If the needs couldn't be satisfied, someone must explain why to the individual. If there is a misperception of attribution, then it must also be clarified.

Influencing Motivation as Creative Problem Solving

Determining how to influence motivation requires a tremendous creative problem-solving effort. Figure 13.9 indicates how the key terms and concepts discussed in this chapter enter into the problem-solving process. The manager must first recognize that there is a problem with motivation and/or with performance. He or she must then identify the needs that are dominant, that require effort on his or her part to satisfy. Next the manager must determine those alternative satisfiers he or she has available to offer the individual in order to influence the direction of achieving organizational goals to the degree required. The manager must determine which, for him or for her, is the best alternative to offer and

FIGURE 13-9   INFLUENCING MOTIVATION AS PROBLEM SOLVING

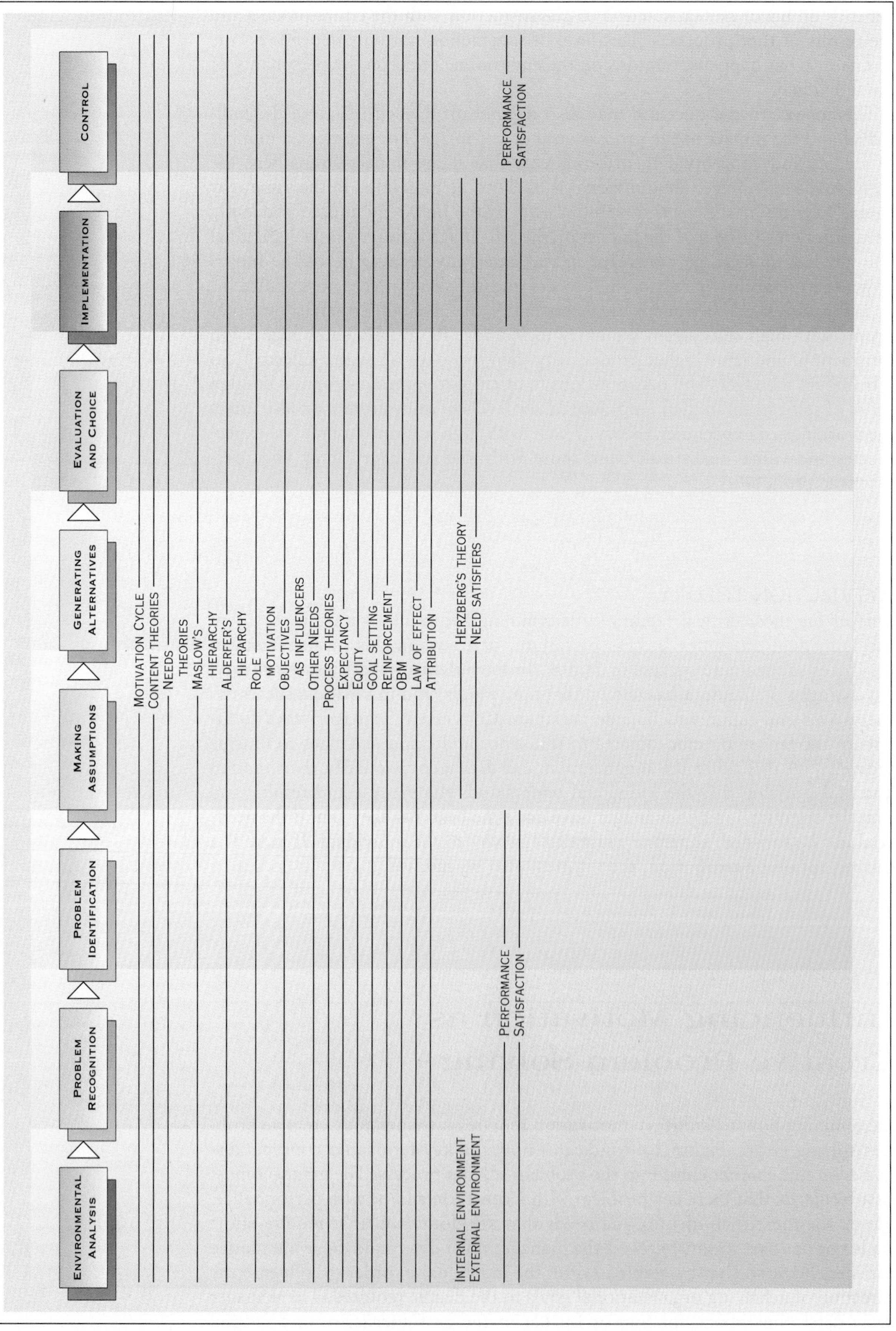

the best way to offer it. Getting the process right is another problem-solving effort in itself, as is making certain that all of the factors that allow motivation to become performance are in place. Then the manager must implement his or her decision by giving the satisfiers in an appropriate manner. Finally, the manager must ascertain whether the problem is solved. Many of the firms and managers discussed in this chapter have solved their problems very creatively: A&P, the top manager who awards medals, Johnson & Johnson, Berol, and Jostens.

The Management Challenges Identified

1. Recognizing needs
2. The changing nature of individual needs, expectations
3. The impact of cultural diversity on a manager's ability to recognize needs
4. Being able to choose the right satisfiers and then being able to obtain and offer them
5. Managing the process aspects of the cycle

Some Solutions Noted in the Chapter

1. Training to assist managers in recognizing employee needs
2. Job redesign
3. Redesign of evaluation/reward/compensation programs
4. Designing programs to increase employee commitment

Summary: Guidelines for Using the Motivation/Performance Cycle

Using the concepts taught in this chapter can be accomplished by working through the motivation/performance cycle. The manager can ask him- or herself a series of questions in using this cycle to solve virtually any motivation problem. The questions are presented here as **guidelines for using the motivation/performance cycle.** These questions can be used by anyone, not just managers, attempting to influence someone's motivation, including one's own. These guidelines are presented according to the stages of the motivation/performance cycle.

The Guidelines

1. What are the dominant needs of the individual?
2. Are there any other possible dominant needs? How do I know? Am I able to satisfy these needs? Am I willing to satisfy these needs?
   Will satisfying these needs lead to overcoming performance problems? What are the implications of my answers to these questions?
3. What need satisfiers do I have available to offer, both extrinsic and intrinsic? What satisfiers are there outside the normal reward system? Will offering these satisfiers lead to overcoming performance problems?
4. How is this person likely to react to the satisfiers offered: rationally, emtionally, habitually? Are these satisfiers contingent on performance? Are they likely to induce effort? Can the individual perform sufficiently to receive these? What is the probability of reward? Are these rewards worth the effort I'm asking? Are they going to be equitably distributed? How are these rewards likely to be perceived by the individual? What should I do as a result of the answers to these questions?
5. Has this person been motivated to expend mental or physical effort? Is this effort adequate? If not, why not?
6. Does this individual have sufficient ability and training to perform? Does he or she know the series of tasks necessary to accomplish the objectives? Does he know the specific objectives? Have I worked diligently enough at goal setting? Have I made the proper tools and technology available so that this person can perform well? Is the job designed to provide the right type of intrinsic satisfiers for this person?
7. Is there a satisfactory level of performance? If not, why not?
8. Have I now issued the need satisfier I promised? If not, why not? If not, have I explained why not?
9. Does the individual perceive the rewards as contingent on performance, of sufficient value, and to be equitably distributed? How do I know? What do the answers mean?
10. Will this individual continue to be motivated in the same way in the future, or will I have to offer him or her different need satisfiers because of the effects of the law of effect, the process on his or her self-image, his or her satisfaction or dissatisfaction with the overall process, his or her attribution of success and failure? What should I do now?

Thinking About Management

1. Define motivation and performance.
2. Describe each of the major motivational theories presented in this chapter and indicate how each integrates into the motivation/performance cycle.
3. Give examples of actions that would occur in each of the ten stages of the motivation/performance cycle.
4. What motivates you to perform really well?
5. Critique these theories using information from the text and from your intuitive reactions to the theory: Maslow's hierarchy; Herzberg's motivators and hygiene factors; achievement needs theory; goal setting; expectancy; equity; reinforcement; and attribution.
6. Think of creative reward systems you have seen, or design some yourself.
7. Why do most organizations pay people—reward people—on fixed intervals rather than on variable-ratio schedules, when the latter seem to be more effective?
8. Evaluate the grading system used in this class in terms of the motivation/performance cycle.

Nucor Steel

CASE

How do you compete with foreign steel makers with modern plant and equipment, with low wage rates, and with efficient distribution systems if you are a United States steel maker? Ken Iverson, chairman and CEO of Nucor Steel, headquartered in Charlotte, North Carolina, with sales of just over $1 billion in 1988, believes he knows how. First, he suggests you stick to small, highly automated steel mills. Nucor Steel has four such mills spread throughout the southeastern United States, producing various types of specialty steels. It also has six manufacturing plants that use a large portion of the steel produced in those mills to make metal products for the construction industry. These mini-mills require a smaller capital investment than do major mills. Second, he thinks you should employ modern technology yourself. Nucor does so, and Iverson is always looking for technology and labor-utilization systems that will help cut costs. Nucor's low capital investment, combined with high R&D, allows you to keep up with the Japanese, Koreans, and others, and perhaps even move ahead of them in some technological areas.

But Iverson believes that the real key is keeping a high level of productivity in the work force. To get that productivity, he believes you must not be hampered by burdensome work rules, which means you need to keep from being unionized. To do that, and to keep productivity high, Iverson suggests you provide an environment worth working in. You need worker/management cooperation. You need to focus on needs and reward performance. You also need to keep your top management staff lean.

DISCUSSION QUESTIONS

1. What type of motivation system would you recommend? Why?
2. Discuss Iverson's philosophy of how to compete.
3. Describe what you might expect in the way of a top management staff overseeing the ten plants described here.

SOURCE: Nucor Corporation Annual Report, 1988; Frank C. Barnes, "Nucor Corporation, 1987," case appearing in James M. Higgins and Julian W. Vincze, *Strategic Management: Text and Cases,* 4E, (Hinsdale, Ill.: Dryden Press, 1989) pp. 580–608; John J. Kendrick, "Productivity Pays at Nucor," *Quality,* February 1988, pp. 18, 20.

Motivating the Difficult Employee

MANAGERS AT WORK

Lynn had been a supervisor over eight programmers for just three weeks, and already she was having problems with two of them. Previously she had been a programmer herself. She knew, upon taking the job, that she would face a difficult task. She knew the personalities of the eight people all too well. Two of them, Mary and Arnold, were extremely difficult to work with. Both were primadonnas, believing that they had the true source of knowledge when it came to programming. Arnold was really good; Mary was not as good as she believed herself to be.

On Lynn's very first day on the job, a new change order had been received for one of the existing programs. Mary and Arnold had been assigned to the task. Both resented being taken off their current assignments, but Lynn had assured them that they were needed badly on the assignment, so they agreed to do it. Two weeks into the project, Mary complained that she couldn't work with Arnold any more. He was too immersed in his part of the project to cooperate with her as he should have. He

MANAGERS AT WORK (Cont.)

retorted that she simply didn't understand what was going on. Lynn had asked her boss for advice. He told her that her job was to manage the situation, and that he would stand behind her 100 percent, no matter what course of action she chose.

Lynn thought over her problem. Both Arnold and Mary made very high salaries and could get jobs anywhere they wanted at a moment's notice. They were both good at their work. Mary tended to be a whiner, and Arnold did like to tell you how good he was. He was also very intolerant of the inadequacies of others. Lynn herself had had a few run ins with him in the past, when she had worked with him as a programmer. The previous manager had let Arnold and Mary have their way. Lynn, however, was determined to make them both fit into the work group better.

DISCUSSION QUESTIONS
1. What needs seem to be driving these two people?
2. What options does Lynn have, with respect to attempting to get these people to cooperate?

MANAGE YOURSELF

How Important Are Various Needs on the Job?

One of the more widely used surveys of needs on the job is that designed by Lyman W. Porter. A portion of his survey is reproduced here. If you are currently employed, circle a number on the scale with regard to the importance of each of the items described to your job. If you are not employed, think of the job you would like upon graduation, or of some job you have had in the past. The scale goes from 1 to 7, with 1 being very unimportant and 7 very important.

1. The feeling of self-esteem a person gets from being in my job. 1 2 3 4 5 6 7
2. The opportunity for personal growth and development in my job. 1 2 3 4 5 6 7
3. The prestige of my job inside the company (that is, the regard received from others in the company). 1 2 3 4 5 6 7
4. The opportunity for independent thought and action in my job. 1 2 3 4 5 6 7
5. The feeling of security in my job. 1 2 3 4 5 6 7
6. The feeling of self-fulfillment a person gets from being in my job (that is, the feeling of being able to use one's unique capabilities, realizing one's potential). 1 2 3 4 5 6 7
7. The prestige of my job outside the company (that is, the regard received from others not in the company). 1 2 3 4 5 6 7
8. The feeling of worthwhile accomplishment in my job. 1 2 3 4 5 6 7
9. The opportunity in my job to give help to other people. 1 2 3 4 5 6 7
10. The opportunity in my job for participation in the setting of goals. 1 2 3 4 5 6 7
11. The opportunity in my job for participation in the determination of methods and procedures. 1 2 3 4 5 6 7

12. The authority connected with my job.　　1 2 3 4 5 6 7

13. The opportunity to develop close friendships in my
　　job.　　1 2 3 4 5 6 7

Now, score the results as follows for each of these Maslow or related needs:

Security:	List score for question 5	————
Social:	Add scores for questions 9 and 13 and divide by 2	————
Esteem:	Add scores for questions 1, 3, and 7 and divide by 3	————
Autonomy:	Add scores for questions 4, 10, 11, and 12 and divide by 4	————
Self-actualization:	Add scores for questions 2, 6, and 8 and divide by 3	————

Your instructor will provide you with some comparison scores.

SOURCE: Adapted from Lyman W. Porter, *Organizational Patterns of Managerial Job Attitudes* (New York: American Foundation for Management Research, 1964), pp. 17, 19.

CHAPTER FOURTEEN

Group Dynamics

CHAPTER OBJECTIVES

By the time you complete this chapter, you should be able to

1. With respect to how managers manage, understand why groups form, the types of groups, the role of groups in formal and informal organizations.

2. Understand how managers work with and through groups to achieve organizational objectives.

3. Describe the stages of group development, how groups function, and some of their more important characteristics, from the manager's perspective.

4. Depict the proper functioning of a quality circle.

5. Describe the essence of conflict management.

CHAPTER OUTLINE

Why Examine Groups?
The Context of Groups
 Types of Groups: Formal and Informal
 Organizational Purpose, Strategies, Structure, Systems, and Environment
How Groups Function
 The Stages of Group Development
 Group Roles
 Group Structure
 Group Size
 Group Norms
 Group Think: The Problem of Conformity
 Group Cohesiveness
 Leadership in Groups
 Decision Making
 Composition of Groups
The Results of Group Activity
A Comprehensive Look at Groups
Some Major Types of Groups
 Teams and Task Forces
 Quality Circles
Leading Groups as Problem Solving
Conflict Management
 The Consequences of Conflict
 Resolving Conflict
The Management Challenges Identified
Some Solutions Noted in the Chapter

Teamwork at General Foods:
New & Improved

General Foods believed that human beings were any company's primary asset. Yet, its managers felt that most large organizations, including their own, continued to organize their people in basic work patterns that inhibited or limited employee contributions. General Foods was searching for a way to increase employee contributions to the organization and decided to change the way it organized its people. The company established interfunctional work teams as a strategic way of maximizing the contributions of their human resources in a wide variety of settings. Individuals from marketing, manufacturing, finance, human resources, and other economic functional areas worked together to solve problems from a total company perspective. Thus, the finance member of the Minute Rice team would, for example, be expected to make contributions on packaging, advertising, and strategy, as well as on financial structure and status.

The company sought to create a work environment that would promote the achievement of peak performance, which it sought to achieve through group activity. Group peak performance was viewed as "a group's ability to sustain superior output, quality, and member satisfaction in terms of its principal goals." General Foods believed that the peak performance of work groups could be obtained, just as it is for superior athletes. "For the group, it's the unique synergy created by the integration of the various resources and capacities of its members, focused against a clearly understood and deeply valued goal, that makes extraordinary outputs possible." Increasing innovation was one of the major objectives of this program.

General Foods recognized that peak performance was not easily achieved. It found that interfunctional teams, relying on the principals of ownership, involvement, and responsibility for results by all team members, was the most effective use of groups to achieve productivity.

They felt that teams were effective because there was

- more sharing and integration of individual skills and resources.
- untapping and use of unknown member resources.
- more stimulation, energy, and endurance by members working jointly than is usual when individuals work alone.
- more emotional support among team members.
- better performance, in terms of quantity and quality, more wins, more innovation.
- more ideas for use in problem solving.
- more commitment and ownership by members around the team goals, i.e., higher motivation.
- more sustained effort directed at team goals.
- more team member satisfaction, higher motivation, and more fun.
- the sense of being a winner, greater confidence, and the ability to achieve more.

General Foods found that for a company to reach extraordinary levels of achievement, it had to establish, through its managers, certain characteristics. These included clear and concise, agreed-upon goals and objectives; well-defined roles; appropriate leadership; an open and trusting environment in which the team can function; and rewards and recognition for the team. Experience showed that it took from six months to a year for a team to establish identity, develop trust, work out its roles and procedures, and then effectively solve problems.

SOURCE: Marc Bassin, "Teamwork at General Foods: New & Improved," *Personnel Journal* (May 1988), pp. 62–70.

All for one, one for all.

Alexander Dumas
The Three Musketeers

Groups and individual factors are merely different aspects of
the same phenomena in constant interaction with each
other.

Kurt Lewin

One of the major changes in management in recent years has been the increasing use of the work group to improve productivity and quality. Organizations have always been structured around work groups, each led by a manager, but only recently have managers really begun to learn to work truly effectively with groups. General Foods' peak performance teams are but one of a myriad of examples of the use of teamwork in organizations.

Why are some groups more effective than others? Why are groups so important to organizations and to individuals? Why are so many organizations now concentrating on better management of the group as a means of becoming more productive and of raising quality, and why didn't they concentrate on groups before?

This chapter explores answers to those questions, first examining the types of groups that exist—both formal and informal—and why they are formed. Then the chapter explores a group's organizational context; how groups function; and the positive results of groups. Figure 14.1 shows these three aspects of groups and the topics to be covered in this chapter under each of them. The latter portion of the chapter focuses on what managers can do to work well with groups, especially how the manager can best manage four specific groups: the quality circle, the team and the task force. The chapter concludes with a discussion of conflict management.

This General Foods interfunctional work team is tackling an important product development issue. This problem will be solved quickly, but prior to the team concept, solving such problems might have taken months. (SOURCE © Robert Reichert)

Why Examine Groups?

Much of work is accomplished through group activity. Work is organized around groups. The organization is a system of overlapping groups. Tasks are usually assigned to groups before they are assigned to individuals. Groups naturally develop to satisfy individual needs. Groups dominate life both at and away from work. The family is a group. Friends meet in groups. A fraternity is a group. Athletic teams are groups.

Groups establish norms and influence their members to adhere to those norms. Sometimes the group's norms conflict with the organization's objectives. Some informal groups may countermand formal organizational authority. Within the organization, groups often make decisions. In the absence of an "expert," groups are believed by many to make better decisions than their individual

AT GENERAL FOODS:
Interfunctional task teams were used to improve productivity. Decision making was improved and innovation increased.

FIGURE 14.1   MANAGING GROUP EFFECTIVENESS: THE DYNAMICS OF FORMAL AND INFORMAL GROUPS

CONTEXT OF THE GROUP	HOW GROUPS FUNCTION	POSITIVE RESULTS OF GROUPS
TYPES OF GROUPS ORGANIZATIONAL PURPOSES, STRATEGIES ORGANIZATION STRUCTURE AND CULTURE ORGANIZATION SYSTEMS ENVIRONMENT	STAGES OF GROUP DEVELOPMENT ROLES STRUCTURE SIZE NORMS COHESIVENESS LEADERSHIP DECISION MAKING COMPOSITION	EFFECTIVENESS EFFICIENCY MOTIVATION TRUST EMPLOYEE SATISFACTION

members would normally arrive at singly. Yet a group probably does not arrive at any better decisions than a superior individual would make independently. Groups tend to take more risks than individuals, and this aids creativity and innovation. Where sharing information is important and division of labor useful, groups tend to make better decisions than individuals.[1]

In recent years considerable attention has been focused on the organization of work activity in groups, as opposed to individual specialization, partly to take advantage of this group decision synergy. Organizational culture depends greatly on the group, and on the leader's ability to discern the proper combinations of behaviors that will cause the group to follow him or her. General Foods, Ford, GM, Chrysler, Lockheed, Martin Marietta, Hyatt, Honeywell, Foremost-McKesson, and thousands of other organizations have turned to groups as a major means for improving productivity. Groups are the focal point of work in even more organizations. How do they function? To begin, there

This Digital Equipment Company marketing team is typical of groups in today's work environment. They make decisions together and work closely to achieve organizational objectives. (© Michael Carroll)

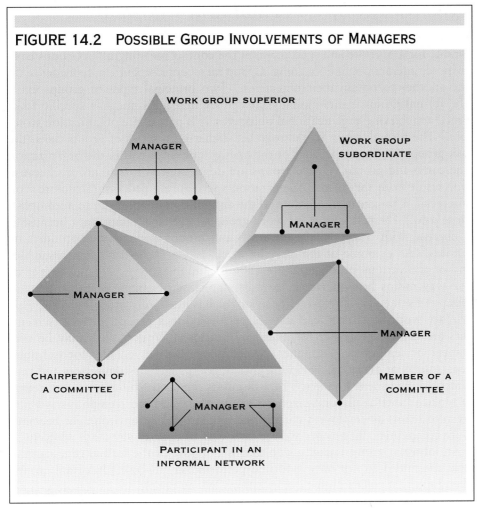

FIGURE 14.2 POSSIBLE GROUP INVOLVEMENTS OF MANAGERS

WORK GROUP SUPERIOR

MANAGER

WORK GROUP SUBORDINATE

MANAGER

MANAGER

MANAGER

CHAIRPERSON OF A COMMITTEE

MEMBER OF A COMMITTEE

MANAGER

PARTICIPANT IN AN INFORMAL NETWORK

SOURCE: JOHN R. SCHERMERHORN, JR., JAMES G. HUNT, AND RICHARD N. OSBORN, MANAGING ORGANIZATIONAL BEHAVIOR, 3RD ED. (NEW YORK: WILEY, 1988), P. 201. REPRINTED BY PERMISSION OF JOHN WILEY & SONS, INC.

are two primary groups within any organization: the formal and the informal. The manager must decide on the right combination of actions to cause the two to work in unison.

Groups have formal and informal leaders. One of the leader's primary tasks is to provide the formal group with task leadership. Leaders have followers, otherwise they would not be leaders. Sometimes managers find themselves without followers because they are not really leaders, just managers. Managers are members of many groups, as Figure 14.2 indicates, and must learn to function within each possible involvement.

The Context of Groups

Groups operate within an organizational context.[2] There are different types of groups—formal and informal—which are formed for various reasons. Regardless of the type of group, each operates within an organization that has purposes and strategies, structure, culture, and systems. The organization functions within an external environment.

Types of Groups: Formal and Informal

T. M. Mills suggests that a group is "two or more persons who come into contact for a purpose and who consider the contact meaningful."[3] Groups have purpose, interaction, and meaning. Group members also share a dependence on one another to obtain their objectives.[4] Two principal types of groups exist. The **formal group** is intentionally created by managers and has specific tasks aimed at achieving organizational objectives. It is part of the organization structure.[5] The formal group works together, either on a series of group tasks (the **task group**), or simply because of the lines of authority within the organization (the **command group**).[6] These groups are designated as formal groups because they result from the formal organization's structuring process. (Structure, you will recall, is the creation of jobs and the distribution of authority to accomplish those jobs.) The task group, or **work group**, is extremely important because it is charged with transforming materials and other resources into products or services.[7] An example of the task, or work, group is the team that assembles any of the various products at Recency Communications, a manufacturer of two-way radios headquartered in Indianapolis. An example of the command group is the faculty of a university school of business. Very little, if any, of their primary work function—teaching—is performed in a group, yet faculty members are grouped together for authority purposes. Work groups may be permanent or temporary. Permanent work groups would include, for example, departments or divisions. Temporary work groups include committees and task forces. Management Challenge 14.1 discusses the successful use of work teams to replace functionally organized divisions. More and more emphasis is being given to teams as employees change and as the external environment becomes more competitive. Teams are viewed as a way of coping with both problems.

An **informal group** is any group that is not part of the formal organization structure and does not have a formal performance purpose.[8] Informal groups play important roles in most organizations. Many people are by nature gregarious, and informal groups provide satisfaction of social needs. For example, there are informal groups that eat lunch together, that play bridge during break, and that discuss what's happening in the company as they meet at the water cooler. Informal groups also arise for other reasons. They may form to help

---

MANAGEMENT CHALLENGE **14.1**

Improving Productivity in the Service Sector Through Work Teams

Aid Association for Lutherans (AAL), an 84-year-old fraternal society that operates a huge insurance business, recognized the need to increase productivity in an industry being squeezed for profits, mostly by higher levels of competition. To achieve these ends, the company, on August 14, 1987, completely reorganized its 500-person insurance staff into largely self-managing work teams. Prior to the team arrangement, claims were sent to each of the functionally designed departments—health insurance, life insurance, and support services. Similarly, any one of the 1,900 field agents would have to contact the three departments, each of which had two major divisions. Where multiple, complex claims were involved,

overcome bureaucracy by providing faster communications. They may occur in a crisis situation to help solve problems. Table 14.1 summarizes the purposes, structures, and processes of formally and informally organized groups. Note that when the organizations of formal and informal groups do not match well, there are some serious consequences. By means of this table, you can compare the similarities and differences between formal and informal groups. For example, the process of the formal group primarily revolves around tasks, whereas the process of the informal group primarily revolves around interactions. Managers are very concerned with the informal group in organizations because it often serves as an alternative need satisfier and source of power for the individual who might have otherwise looked to the formal organization for them. Informal groups will also have leaders whose power may detract from the authority of the manager.

Table 14.1. The Purposes, Structures, and Processes of Formally and Informally Organized Groups

	Purpose	Structure	Process
Formal organization	Adequate financial return for effort, investment, and risk	Jobs, positions, organizational units; formal roles, relations, and rules; designated authority and accountability	Tasks, procedures, work-flow sequences, formal organizational policies
Informal organization	Satisfaction of personal, social, and psychological needs	Personal influence or power based on interpersonal and group skills, friendships, cliques, likes and dislikes, and ability to use job processes to advantage	Interpersonal processes, group processes, intergroup processes
Possible consequences of serious mismatch	Low productivity, low profitability, may fail	Management and supervision have authority but lack power to make things happen the way they should and lack respect of workers. Low productivity, low profitability, may fail.	Formal processes misused to satisfy personal needs. Production wasteful, inefficient; everything bogged down in red tape. Buck passing, finger pointing, game playing. Low productivity, low profitability, may fail.

SOURCE: From *Organizational Team Building* by Earl J. Ends and Curtis W. Page. Copyright © 1977. Reprinted by permission of Winthrop Publishers, Inc., Cambridge, Massachusetts.

the insured or the agent would be shuffled from department to department. An inquiry could take thirty days. Now, each team of twenty to thirty employees can handle all of the 167 procedures formerly split among the three functional departments.

The results of the reorganization have been dramatic. Employment has been cut by 10 percent, yet the remaining employees have processed 10 percent more work. Fifty-five management positions and three levels of management have been eliminated, as the teams have assumed most management tasks. Customers and agents receive responses in just a few days, and the agents are able to develop ongoing relationships with specific teams, improving customer service as a result. Employees are rewarded for their new responsibilities and no one has been laid off. Those people whose positions were eliminated were offered other jobs in the organization if they wanted them. The implications of AAL's success for other insurers, for banks, and other service firms is staggering.

SOURCE: "Work Teams Can Rev Up Paper-Pushers, Too," *Business Week* (November 28, 1988), pp. 64–72.

WHY GROUPS FORM

All groups form for the purpose of satisfying needs of some type. Formal groups are formed to satisfy formal organizational needs. Informal groups are formed to satisfy the needs of organization members that are not satisfied by the formal organization. Physical proximity also contributes to group development.

THE FORMATION OF FORMAL GROUPS

Formal groups are formed, at least conceptually, for the purpose of accomplishing the organization's mission, or more specifically, the organization's objectives. Examples include winning a football championship, putting together the most efficient hamburger products operations (an objective of Wendy's), or having the most productive sewing line in the shirt industry (an objective of Arrow Shirts). All organizational objectives are eventually parceled out to groups or individuals to accomplish. The logical grouping of these tasks and the distribution of authority to accomplish them are the bases of organizational structure. Think of an organization you have belonged to. (If you currently work, think of your work organization.) How was/is it structured? What roles did/do groups play?

THE FORMATION OF INFORMAL GROUPS

Informal groups form for one primary reason: to satisfy employee needs that the organization or manager does not satisfy. The organization and the manager should satisfy as many subordinate needs as is practical. Needs they do not satisfy will be satisfied elsewhere. Obviously no organization and no manager can satisfy all needs of all subordinates, nor should they; however, they should satisfy those they are capable of satisfying efficiently as long as satisfying them benefits both the organization and the individual. Otherwise, one of the informal groups that arises will often be counterproductive to the aims of the organization and the manager. Not all informal groups are negative from the organizational viewpoint. **Friendship groups,** those that exist to satisfy social needs, naturally arise from human interactions within the same and nearby work locations. But when major need satisfiers are not provided, informal groups of employees have

Table 14.2. How Informal Groups Satisfy Needs

Need	Example of How This Need is Satisfied by Informal Groups
Physiological	Groups may be able to negotiate for more compensation and other benefits.
Safety or Security	There is safety in numbers. Groups may counteract bad management.
Social Needs	Groups provide the opportunity to fulfill social needs through interaction.
Esteem Needs	Informal leadership positions or simple membership in a group may result in esteem satisfaction.
Self-actualization	Leadership and group accomplishment are important contributors.
Role Fulfillment	People contribute through the roles offered by the group, perhaps to lead or to follow, or to do what the group was formed to do.
Power	There is strength in numbers. Leadership allows for control over others. Groups control various situations.
Achieving Objectives	Informal groups come together for some purpose, whether it's to play poker, bowl, or counteract the company.
Truth, Beauty, and Justice	Some groups form to go to museums, to go hiking, to fish, to read, and so on.

a way of becoming formal groups that make demands instead of requests—unions. Using the Maslow hierarchy first, and then the other needs outlined in Chapter 13, Table 14.2 examines how the informal organization provides need satisfiers.

Informal groups offer the individual the opportunity to satisfy needs that are not satisfied by the organization. The important issues to the manager and the organization are why the needs are not being satisfied by the organization, and what can be done about them. If the manager and organization fail to satisfy needs they are capable of satisfying, then potential trouble exists. As the diversity of the work force increases, as businesses become more global, the potential for additional informal groups increases.

Informal groups are usually classified as interest or friendship groups. When social needs are fulfilled, they are **friendship groups. Interest groups** are those formed on the basis of other common interests. For example, groups may form to seek ways to satisfy grievances with the company. Sometimes such groups become formal groups—unions or groups seeking unionization.

Organizational Purpose, Strategies, Structure, Systems, and Environment

The organization's purposes—vision, mission, goals, and objectives—will lead to strategies that progressively will result in the tasks the group will be expected to perform and to the way in which those tasks are distributed. The organization's structure and culture largely determine the group's size and composition and how it will be structured, the preferred style of management, and other factors critical to functioning. The organization's systems, especially reward systems, will directly affect how group members will be influenced to perform. Other systems affecting behavior will include objective setting and control systems, each of which should be linked to reward systems. The environment of the organization will affect its strategies and, hence, work group objectives and tasks. The environment will also aid or detract from performance under certain conditions. For example, in a growth environment, with plenty of resources available for the group, the group would act much differently than in a recessionary economy or a cost cutting period of organizational history.

AT GENERAL FOODS: *At General Foods, the organization made a conscious effort to build work-group teams. It established a culture within which these groups could function properly. The groups were seen as mechanisms for achieving organizational goals. Rewards and recognition were provided for team successes.*

How Groups Function

All groups function in the same basic ways. How they function can greatly affect their results. A group's effectiveness is influenced by its stages of development; the roles people play within the group; its structure, size, norms, cohesiveness, and leadership; the decision process; and competition.

The Stages of Group Development

When a new group is formed, it passes through a series of stages of development.[9] Several studies have identified various stages of group development, but they are all essentially similar.[10] From a decision-making perspective, those stages identified by J. Steven Heinen and Eugene Jackson are most appropriate: forming, storming, initial integration, and total integration. A final stage of dissolution will also eventually occur.

FORMING

In the forming stage, a group becomes acquainted. Members learn about each other and about the objectives and tasks they are to accomplish. Members examine these issues in view of their own needs and the personal need satisfaction that may result from being in the group. During this stage, members learn to accept one another. Sometimes this process can be difficult if members have had past negative experiences with some others in the group.

STORMING

The storming stage is characterized as a period of high emotions. Cliques and coalitions of subgroups may occur and these are often accompanied by tension. Members learn further about their expected objectives and roles and about how their needs may be satisfied. Conflict may occur as each member seeks to have his or her agenda adopted by the group. The amount of storming varies considerably in groups, and in some cases may be almost nonexistent; in others it may be quite highly charged. Some decision making may occur here, but more often it deals with group dynamics, as opposed to accomplishing tasks.

INITIAL INTEGRATION

In this stage, the group begins to function cooperatively. This stage is sometimes referred to as the "norming" stage because members are establishing the rules of acceptable conduct, or norms, for the group. Most individual needs become less important than the good of the group, and most hostility ceases. Decision making occurs relative to the task, but maintenance of the group may be more important at this stage than is task accomplishment. A sense of closeness and group purpose emerges.

TOTAL INTEGRATION

At last, the group becomes fully functioning. Productive decisions are arrived at. Members are well organized, concerned about the group and its results, and are able to deal with task accomplishment and conflict in rational and creative ways. The primary concerns of the group at this stage are continuing to achieve results and adapting over time to changing conditions. A mature, totally integrated group will score high on the criteria for such groups, as shown in Figure 14.3.

> AT GENERAL FOODS:
> *It took from six months to a year for groups to become fully functioning. Cross-functional teams had to come together and go through each of these stages.*

DISSOLUTION

Eventually, all groups dissolve. Temporary groups do so when their task is accomplished. Permanent groups do so when work is restructured or, for some other reason, the work of the group is no longer necessary.

In the on-going group, the preceding stages would be similar when new members are admitted. The new members would have to be accepted and accept the group (forming), and they would have to learn to work out their needs and interpersonal relations with it (storming). The group would eventually begin to function in an integrated fashion as reconstituted (initial integration), and it would eventually mature once more (total integration).

Knowing these stages, the manager can take actions to ensure that the group progresses toward total integration. For example, he or she may be especially nurturing to those in forming and storming, who feel uncertain about their need satisfaction. Similarly, he or she may find it necessary to practice conflict resolution in these stages and to focus the attention of the group on objectives. Later, the manager may delegate more power to members or use other techniques to keep the group adapting and performing.

FIGURE 14.3 CRITERIA OF GROUP MATURITY

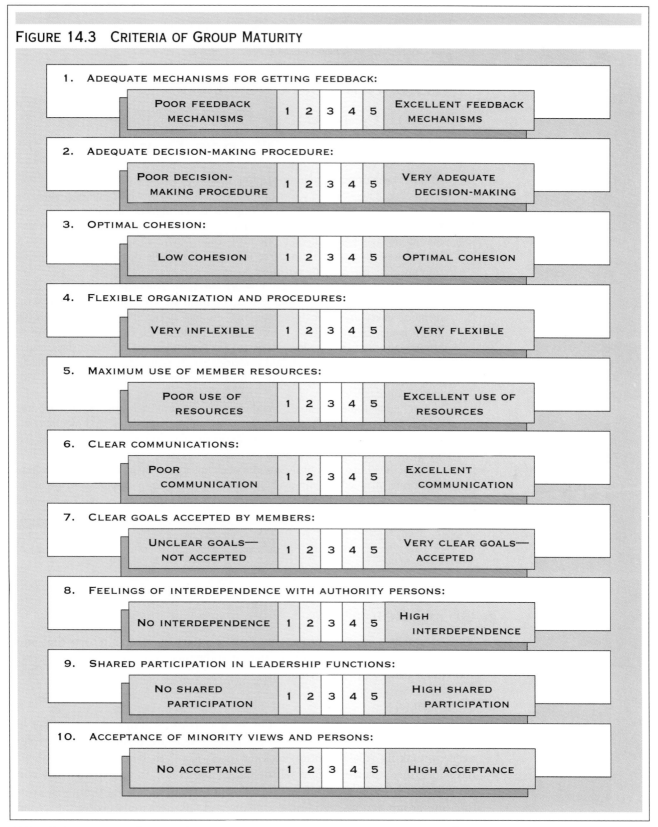

1. ADEQUATE MECHANISMS FOR GETTING FEEDBACK:

| POOR FEEDBACK MECHANISMS | 1 | 2 | 3 | 4 | 5 | EXCELLENT FEEDBACK MECHANISMS |

2. ADEQUATE DECISION-MAKING PROCEDURE:

| POOR DECISION-MAKING PROCEDURE | 1 | 2 | 3 | 4 | 5 | VERY ADEQUATE DECISION-MAKING |

3. OPTIMAL COHESION:

| LOW COHESION | 1 | 2 | 3 | 4 | 5 | OPTIMAL COHESION |

4. FLEXIBLE ORGANIZATION AND PROCEDURES:

| VERY INFLEXIBLE | 1 | 2 | 3 | 4 | 5 | VERY FLEXIBLE |

5. MAXIMUM USE OF MEMBER RESOURCES:

| POOR USE OF RESOURCES | 1 | 2 | 3 | 4 | 5 | EXCELLENT USE OF RESOURCES |

6. CLEAR COMMUNICATIONS:

| POOR COMMUNICATION | 1 | 2 | 3 | 4 | 5 | EXCELLENT COMMUNICATION |

7. CLEAR GOALS ACCEPTED BY MEMBERS:

| UNCLEAR GOALS— NOT ACCEPTED | 1 | 2 | 3 | 4 | 5 | VERY CLEAR GOALS— ACCEPTED |

8. FEELINGS OF INTERDEPENDENCE WITH AUTHORITY PERSONS:

| NO INTERDEPENDENCE | 1 | 2 | 3 | 4 | 5 | HIGH INTERDEPENDENCE |

9. SHARED PARTICIPATION IN LEADERSHIP FUNCTIONS:

| NO SHARED PARTICIPATION | 1 | 2 | 3 | 4 | 5 | HIGH SHARED PARTICIPATION |

10. ACCEPTANCE OF MINORITY VIEWS AND PERSONS:

| NO ACCEPTANCE | 1 | 2 | 3 | 4 | 5 | HIGH ACCEPTANCE |

SOURCE: ADAPTED FROM EDGAR H. SCHEIN, PROCESS CONSULTATION, 2ND ED., COPYRIGHT© , 1988, ADDISON-WESLEY PUBLISHING COMPANY INC., CHAPTER 6, PP. 81–82, FIGURE 6-1, "A MATURE GROUP PROCESS," REPRINTED WITH PERMISSION.

Formal and informal groups go through these same stages.[11] Imagine how the group described in the following Global Management Challenge might go through the five stages.

IBM Europe Uses Process Quality Management Teams to Get Things Done

IBM has been using the planning technique known as Process Quality Management (PQM) for many years. PQM requires that the group assembled establish objectives and the activities critical to achieving them. The group identifies specific performance measurement standards for the results of their actions. PQM requires that all key managers attend a one- or two-day intensive session. Before they can leave this session, they must agree upon what must be done and accept specific responsibility for carrying out those actions.

The process begins with team member selection. The team leader identifies the key people (up to twelve) and assembles them in a PQM session. The group members meet and quickly accept one another as members of the group. The group begins by collectively identifying its mission. This is the first decision the group makes as a group. Other decisions follow. Objectives are established, critical success factors are identified, and priorities are determined. Plans are established and responsibilities are agreed to. All of this must occur with unanimity of the participants.

Arriving at these decisions, members will motivate each other to achieve unanimity. Group norms of acceptable behavior will be established and members will make certain that all members adhere to them; thus, group control will occur. The group becomes totally integrated.

When IBM Europe launched a series of changes, including continuous-flow manufacturing, it relied heavily on PQM sessions. First, the vice-president for manufacturing and his team made sure they understood what their mission was—what

Group Roles

Both formal and informal groups have two primary membership roles that must be filled: task roles and building and maintenance roles. In addition, certain individual roles will be enacted.

TASK ROLES

Task roles relate to the task that the formal group is assigned or that the informal group has determined to undertake. These are problem-solving roles, decision-making roles, solution-seeking roles. Kenneth Benne and Paul Sheats have identified twelve largely self-defining task roles, among them roles concerned with offering new ideas, gathering information, giving opinions, coordinating group actions, refining problems and solutions, energizing the group, and record keeping.[12] It is assumed in the typical pyramidal organization that these roles are performed by the manager, but often, especially in a democratic/participative management situation, any group member may assume these roles. For example in the "GM Saturn Project, work teams will perform the functions on a fully participative basis. They will operate without foremen."[13] In the informal group, these roles are often filled by members, as well as by leaders.

the changes were designed to achieve. Then they focused on the major changes and their priorities for the company's materials-management process. The results were satisfying. There was a successful introduction of continuous-flow manufacturing to all fifteen of IBM Europe's plants. Manufacturing cycle times and inventory levels improved, costs dropped, quality rose, and the company became more flexible in meeting customer demands.

SOURCE: Maurice Hardaker and Bryan K. Ward, "How to Make a Team Work," *Harvard Business Review*, (November–December 1987), pp. 112–120.

Here at IBM's European headquarters in Paris, France, the company stresses teamwork to develop new products and to ensure their high quality. (Courtesy International Business Machines)

Earlier we noted the importance of the manager as a linking pin. Much of the manager's success as a linking pin depends on his or her ability to perform most of these roles successfully. As Chapter 3 emphasized, leaders should facilitate problem solving and task completion. They establish the "right climate." They help members to satisfy their individual needs, within reason. They represent the group, its values, and its objectives when the group interacts with other groups or other members of management. But most important, as the roles identified here suggest, they are also responsible for moving the organization forward, for achieving organizational objectives. The same comments apply to informal leaders. They, too, facilitate, represent, establish climates and help their groups achieve their objectives.

Think of a group to which you belong, formal or informal. How does the leader perform these roles? Is he or she a good task leader?

BUILDING AND MAINTENANCE ROLES

Members of groups must also build group-centeredness by performing actions that tend to maintain the group. There are seven major **building and maintenance roles** according to Kenneth D. Benne and Paul Sheats: roles devoted to encouraging members, mediating differences, compromising, communicating, setting standards, observing, and following passively.[14] These roles mean exactly what their names suggest.

Often some of these roles are performed by the manager. Many are not. Obviously no one can be all things to everyone. Thus, leaders need to draw others into performing some of these roles, but they also must be aware of how these roles affect their own leadership actions. Leaders must be prepared to recognize who is naturally performing these roles and use these persons and their abilities. Think of a group to which you belong. Who most often performs these roles? How does the leader facilitate the maintenance of the group?

INDIVIDUAL ROLES

Most groups have some members who are playing **individual roles** in the group setting, in an effort to satisfy their own needs rather than those of the group. Benne and Sheats identify the following as typical individual roles: aggressor/attacker, blocker/resister, recognition seeker, dominator, and special interest pleader.[15] Think of a group to which you belong. Who fills these roles?

If you will take a few minutes to reflect on groups to which you have belonged, you will identify people who fill several roles in each of the three major categories in the group. When you are a leader, you must make certain that group roles are carried out and that individual roles are minimized because they contribute nothing to the group's purposes. In certain cases some might be useful, however. For example, the blockers/resisters may prevent self-destructive change. You must learn to guard against individuals who would determine group efforts.

Group Structure

In the 1940s J. L. Moreno, a sociologist, developed an approach to the structure of groups known as **sociometry**.[16] Using his scheme, Figure 14.4 identifies group structure as consisting of a leader, a primary group, a fringe group, and an out-group.

The formal group leader/manager will usually not be a major informal group leader. After all, there are many informal groups based on many interests and friendships. It is not likely that any one leader/manager could be the leader of many informal groups, nor should any manager try to be. Again, what is necessary is to be alert to these groups and their potential meanings for the formal group.

The primary group, also popularly known as the in-group, consists of the group members of highest status—active members and members accorded all of the group's rights and responsibilities. In Figure 14.4, A, B, C, D, E, and F are members of the primary group. This group would share information, otherwise help each other, and establish rules for member behavior.

The fringe, or secondary, group consists of people who have lesser status and fewer group privileges but who still have greater acceptance than people the group does not recognize at all. G, H, I, and J are members of the fringe group. They might be "let in" on some group activities or knowledge, perhaps knowledge of how to do a job better.

The out-group consists of people who have no membership, no privileges, and no interests in the group under discussion. These people may belong to many other groups, but not to this one.

Communication tends to be highest among members of the primary group. They are on friendly, but more distant, terms with members of the fringe group. They do not communicate at all with the out-group. In the work organization, the manager must ensure communication among all group members and must also take steps to forestall, or at least to minimize, the exclusion of an out-group.

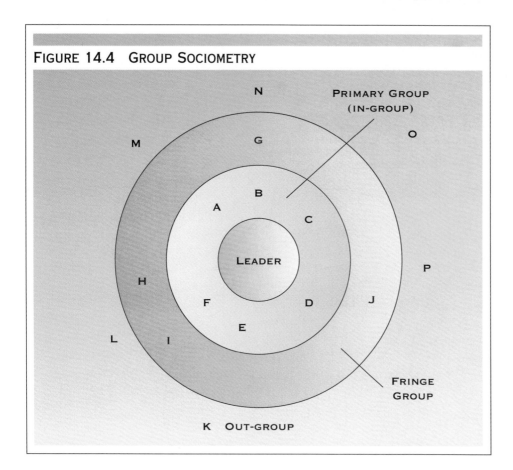

FIGURE 14.4 GROUP SOCIOMETRY

OVERLAPPING GROUP STRUCTURES

Secondary members of one group may be primary members of another group and vice versa. When members of these overlapping groups talk among themselves, they create a phenomenon called the grapevine—so named because its tendrils seem to reach everywhere. Much has been said and written about the grapevine. Just what is it? The **grapevine** is the path of communication within the organization that exists outside the formal channels. Some say such communication should be kept to a minimum. Some say managers should use it to their advantage. We do know that it is generally accurate and often faster than formal channels. Figure 14.5 depicts how the grapevine might function in a typical organization.

Keith Davis, human relations expert, has examined the organizational grapevine for more than thirty years. "With the rapidity of a burning powder train," Davis asserts, "information flows out of the woodwork, past the manager's door and the janitor's mop closet, through steel walls or construction-glass partitions." The messages are often "symbolic expressions of feelings." For example, if a rumor says the boss may quit, and he or she is not going to, it may very well be that the employees wish it were true. Among Davis's findings are the following:

1. Grapevines are accurate 75 to 95 percent of the time.
2. There are only a few sources that supply the entire formal network.
3. Admittedly, the grapevine does have some dramatic failures in accuracy.
4. The grapevine actually is a psychological reflection of employee interest in the organization or its members.

FIGURE 14.5   THE GRAPEVINE

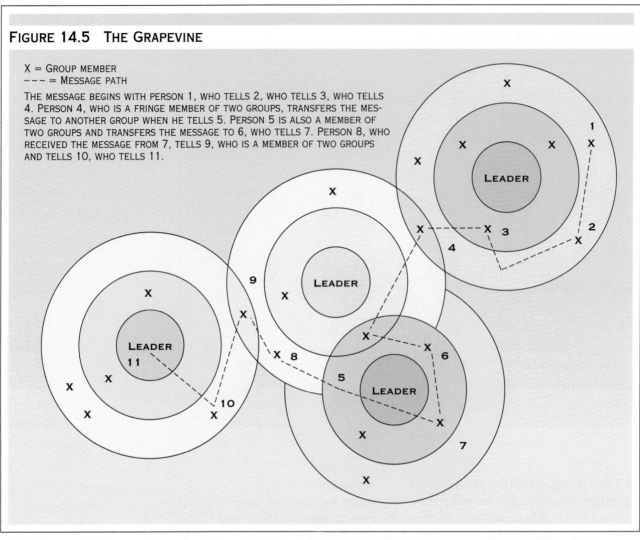

X = GROUP MEMBER
– – – = MESSAGE PATH

THE MESSAGE BEGINS WITH PERSON 1, WHO TELLS 2, WHO TELLS 3, WHO TELLS 4. PERSON 4, WHO IS A FRINGE MEMBER OF TWO GROUPS, TRANSFERS THE MESSAGE TO ANOTHER GROUP WHEN HE TELLS 5. PERSON 5 IS ALSO A MEMBER OF TWO GROUPS AND TRANSFERS THE MESSAGE TO 6, WHO TELLS 7. PERSON 8, WHO RECEIVED THE MESSAGE FROM 7, TELLS 9, WHO IS A MEMBER OF TWO GROUPS AND TELLS 10, WHO TELLS 11.

SOURCE: JAMES M. HIGGINS, HUMAN RELATIONS: BEHAVIOR AT WORK, 2ND ED. (NEW YORK: RANDOM HOUSE, 1987) P. 176.

5. Levels of activity in the informal network parallel those in the formal network.

6. Troublemakers sometimes use the grapevine. All untrue rumors, whether started by troublemakers or not, are best countered by truth, told directly by management to employees early in the situation in question.

Davis concludes that wise managers "feed, water, cultivate the grapevine" because it "cannot be abolished, rubbed out, hidden under a basket, chopped down, tied up, or stopped. It is as hard to kill as the mythical glass snake which, when struck, broke into fragments and grew a new snake out of each piece."[17] The grapevine can be nurtured by the manager by developing friendship relationships with key people in it, and by providing it with useful information from time to time. Ethically, the manager should not abuse it, but rather listen to it and keep it informed.

Group Size

Groups can function adequately in various **sizes,** but the optimum size appears to be between five and seven members when problem solving is involved and frequent small group communication must occur.[18] Various studies show different optimum sizes, and that different situations call for different sizes.[19] GM's Saturn Project work groups, for example, will have from six to fifteen members.[20] Increasing group size allows for more interaction, an important function of groups; more decision inputs, an important factor in achieving the decision synergy noted earlier; and greater division of labor.

At the same time, however, the larger the group, the less chance for discussion each individual has, and the less time the manager will have for each individual. Subgroups may emerge within large groups. Each of these subgroups may be attempting to achieve its own goals, rather than those of the main group. Communication becomes more difficult as the size of the group increases and openness among members appears to diminish. In addition, it is difficult to permit every member to be recognized every day, when the group numbers, say, sixty.[21] It is difficult even to know everyone in a large group, but the leader must make that effort. Furthermore, depending on the type of task, a larger group may actually reduce productivity because of the difficulties of coordination.

The desirable group size is a membership just large enough to serve the group's function. That size is determined by an examination of the major contingency variables in the situation—for example, group purpose. As groups grow in size, they tend to be less intimate, less homogeneous, offer less of a chance for individual participation, and tend to be less concerned with the group's focal interest or task. Thus, group tasks such as selection of personnel and problem solving emotionally charged topics are not as effectively performed in large groups as in small ones. Large groups tend to be more difficult to lead and to maintain because of the complex number of interrelationships—which multiply geometrically with size, thus reducing the quality of communication, or at least making it more difficult.[22] Realistically, a group much larger than twelve becomes difficult to manage, but there are cost trade-offs to be considered. Smaller group sizes will necessitate paying the salaries for the extra managers to manage the groups, unless the groups are self-managing.

Group Norms

Norms are standards of performance or other conduct established by a group. They are the behavior that group members "ought" to engage in.

J. R. Hackman has identified these five characteristics of norms:

1. They represent the structural characteristics of the group. They are its "personality."
2. They apply strictly to behavior and not to private thoughts and feelings.
3. They are developed only for behavior judged to be important by the majority of group members.
4. Although they usually develop slowly, norms can be developed rapidly if the need arises—for example, in a crisis.
5. Not all norms apply to all members. For example, productivity norms will be established for each job, and thus will differ by the member's job.[23]

Typical norms are shown in Table 14.3.

Group norms are followed in varying degrees by different members. But any norm that is particularly important to group members will usually be adhered to very strictly by most, if not all, members. Otherwise the deviant member may be subjected to disciplinary action and sanctions from group members or the leader.[24] In some groups such disciplinary actions might only be chastisement. In other groups physical punishment is possible. A union's members might physically abuse another member who crossed a picket line, for example. "Rate

AT GENERAL FOODS: *The norms were in agreement with company objectives. The groups therefore performed well.*

Table 14.3. Typical Norms

There are hundreds of norms in every organization, and maybe just as many in each work group. Norms can be positive or negative, productive or unproductive, healthy or unhealthy. Examine the following norms of one large company as perceived by more than 100 of its top managers. As you review them, put a check mark beside those you feel are productive and should be enforced. Put a minus mark beside those that are unproductive.

Do	Don't
—Dress conservatively	—Turn down promotions
—Be punctual	—Associate with lower-level employees
—Be frugal	—Discuss salaries
—Stress accepted values or be quiet	—Ask embarrassing questions
—Operate through a chain of command	—Admit weakness
—Eat with a work-defined group	—Use profanity
—Consider an invitation a command	—Cross departmental lines to handle a problem
—Be a self-starter	—Work late in the office
—Answer your own phone	—Disagree with immediate supervisor
—Be prompt in answering mail	—Go over boss's head
—Be available	—Grow a beard
—Be cooperative and diplomatic with other departments	—Socialize with your boss
—Be conservative with expenses	—Eat lunch with clerical employees
—Be accurate	—Leave the lunch table until the boss does, even if he or she arrives late
—Stay at your desk and look busy	
—Be discreet about goofing off	—Leave early
—Decorate your office conservatively	—Spread rumors
—Defer to superiors	—Moonlight
—Respond instantly to vice-presidents	—Lose your self-control
	—Close your office door
	—Call in sick on a long weekend

SOURCE: Adapted from Robert W. Goddard, "Everything Swings Off #1," *Manage,* (January 1984), p. 8.

busting" is a term used to describe high achievers who go beyond the group's productivity norms or the formal organization's standards in the workplace. Rate busters are often punished by their groups.

Group norms are more likely to be strongly enforced if they:

1. ensure group success or survival.
2. reflect the preferences of powerful group members—for example, supervisors or informal leaders.
3. simplify, or make predictable, what behavior is expected of group members.
4. reinforce member roles.
5. help the group avoid embarrassing interpersonal problems.[25]

Group Think: The Problem of Conformity

Because of their need to belong to groups and because of the control that groups have over members, people often conform to rather rigid and sometimes irrational behavior requirements. When self-esteem becomes extremely dependent on the group and when individualism is not highly regarded, the behavior of group members will be quite similar. The designer-jeans phenomenon is a classic example of conformity. If you didn't have a designer name on your clothing,

John Dean, here shown at the Watergate hearings, was a member of a Presidential advisory group where group think took over. The group had no dissenters, it perceived itself as invulnerable, it rationalized its actions, and morally justified breaking the law. (SOURCE © Fred Ward/Black Star)

you just were not "in." In the workplace the informal group may establish productivity norms less than, or even occasionally more than, company standards. To belong, and sometimes to avoid retribution, people will usually adhere to these norms.

GROUP THINK

Group think is a condition that exists in a group when "concurrence seeking becomes so dumb that in a cohesive 'in' group it tends to override realistic appraisal and alternative courses of action."[26] There is a definite tendency in groups that are extremely cohesive to attempt to have complete unity of opinion. This group-think phenomenon can become detrimental to decision making for both the group and the leader. Irving Janis cites Watergate as an example of group think, where a leader, President Nixon, was surrounded by "yes" men who did not challenge his assumptions and therefore did not act creatively or see alternative courses of action. The eight symptoms of group think identified by Janis include the following:

1. Illusions of invulnerability by the group: Members become overconfident and are willing to assume great risk.
2. Collective rationalization in the group: Problems with group thoughts or actions, or counterbeliefs in the group, are "rationalized" away.
3. Unquestioned belief in group morality: Decisions of the group become not overly sensible but morally correct.
4. Stereotyping the enemy: The targets of group decisions are stereotyped, as evil, weak, or stupid.
5. Direct pressure on deviate members in the group to conform: For example, at Lincoln Electric Company, the world's leading manufacturer of welding equipment, headquartered in Cleveland, Ohio, low-producing employees are pressured by peers to increase performance.

These Marine Corps recruits learn early on at Parris Island boot camp that the Corps is more important than any individual member. The Corps uses the group process to build teams of men willing to fight and die for the Corps. (SOURCE © Bob Krist/Black Star)

6. Self-censorship of deviant behavior by individual group members: Members convince themselves that it is inappropriate to voice opinions contrary to the group's.

7. An illusion of unanimity by the group: Members believe every decision is supported by every other group member.

8. Self-appointed "mind guards" arise: These are group members who feel it is necessary to protect the group from adverse information.

The dangers of group think can be lessened. Team building, organizational development, management development, education of leaders and group members, and structuring the creation of an organizational culture that honors and rewards original thinking, all can contribute to lessening group-think phenomena. We want groups to be cohesive, but we don't want them to be so cohesive that individuals lose their identity, including the leader. Nor do we want members of groups to become so immersed in group norms that they fail in their roles as decision makers—failing to see, for example, proper objectives, a number of viable alternatives, or their own biases in evaluating alternatives. There is a tendency for groups to take more risks than individuals acting alone might. Group think can contribute to this by lessening the sense of responsibility any one individual feels for a group decision.

If an organization is to be effective, what it must do is work through, not against, group norms. Organizational managers must, through their leadership ability, make certain that organizational objectives are congruent with group norms. Ideally, work groups should embrace organizational objectives as their goals. A very successful example of this is the U.S. Marine Corps. The welfare of the corps is far more important than the welfare of any individual marine. By applying group norms in support of the corps, the corps capitalizes on the group process rather than resisting it.

Group Cohesiveness

Cohesiveness is the tendency of members to want to belong to the group, as opposed to wanting to leave it.[27] Cohesiveness, productivity, and member satisfaction are usually positively correlated when the group agrees with its formal organizational objectives. Thus, if cohesiveness can be created within the group, productivity and member satisfaction will usually increase. How does the manager or the nonmanagerial leader promote cohesiveness? How can members contribute to cohesiveness? One way is by carrying out the task and building and maintenance roles; another is by providing proper leadership for groups and individuals.

Building conditions that foster cohesiveness include a friendly group atmosphere, similarity among members, interdependence among members, high status, a threatening environment, attractive group objectives, and small group size. Forces that diminish group cohesiveness include low public image, disagreement over group activities, membership in other groups, and unpleasant group demands.[28] Sometimes groups may become cohesive against the organization or against the manager. In such cases the organization's objectives are seldom achieved, at least not efficiently.

The manager needs to monitor cohesiveness and take appropriate leadership actions because research indicates that a strong correlation exists between group norms and productivity. Where norms are strongly in favor of productivity, the group will have high levels of output. Where the norms are strong and against productivity, there will be low levels of output.

One of the difficulties managers have in today's high-technology environment is assuring that groups will work together and remain cohesive. Much work is done today on personal computers, which, until now, have only had software for individual users. But that is changing, as Management Challenge 14.2 suggests.

Leadership in Groups

Within any group there are usually two leaders, the formal leader and the informal leader. The formal leader can employ a wide range of behaviors to influence employee motivation. These behaviors can be classified into four categories: task oriented and aimed at achieving organizational group objectives; relationship oriented and designed to build relationships and increase cohesiveness; the offering of intrinsic and extrinsic rewards; and management encouragement to subordinates to participate in decision making. The informal leader would use similar behaviors, but his or her power is more likely to be based on something other than authority—the basis of the formal leader's power. The formal leader must be aware of, and take into account, the informal leader's power in making management decisions. The leadership role is explained in more detail in Chapter 15.

Decision Making

Groups go through distinct processes as they attempt to make decisions. The satisfactory **group decision process** is characterized by a large number of inputs from each individual member upon which other members may build. The advantages of group decision making versus individual decision making are that often groups will be superior to individuals in terms of the quantity and quality of decisions to any given problem. The basis for the success of groups has typically been their closeness to the problem, the larger number of ideas generated because more people are working on them, and the group's ability to build upon a solution recommended by others. All of these factors contribute to the desirability of having group decision making.[29] Yet, there is no evidence to suggest that group decisions are necessarily better than those made by individuals, especially superior individuals.[30] Chapter 3 discussed these issues in detail.

Groupware: Software for the Team

"Groupware," software, which enables work groups and teams to tackle problems together through networked personal computers, is on its way. Groupware is especially effective for projects and task teams. Until now, workers would function independently when using their PCs and then meet to discuss results. But groupware allows problem solvers to share their results with others simultaneously. WordPerfect's® "Office" program and Lotus 1-2-3's® "Notes" program allow employees to schedule meetings jointly, share messages, and track project statuses.

"Coordinator" by Action Technologies bases its functioning on "categories" of conversations. The user composes his or her message, assigns it a category, and then transmits it over phone lines to other users. "Coordinator" reminds users of pending commitments, tracks users' conversations, and keeps a record of a project's status. "Coordinator" is used at General Motors's Dayton offices and at GTEL, a California retailer of telephone equipment, with twenty outlets. Broderbund has a program entitled "For Comment," which allows up to sixteen users to work jointly on up to a 236-page document simultaneously—for example, a business plan. Wilson Learning Corporation and Xerox have developed networked software to allow simultaneous brainstorming.

More "groupware" is in the offing, but most authorities believe products that really enable job-specific group problem solving won't be available until at least 1990–1991.

Composition of Groups

Group members have varying personalities, work styles and motivations, backgrounds, sexes, races, religions, and so on. The composition of a group can greatly affect its productivity.[31] One of the manager's greatest challenges will be managing the cultural diversity of the 1990s. Furthermore, the global nature of business will demand multicultural work teams. Finally, handicapped workers are expected to increase as a percentage of the work force. Managers will need to learn an entire set of new skills for selecting and managing such teams. The composition of a group can be very important, as Management Challenge 14.3 reveals.

The Results of Group Activity

There are six primary positive results of proper group functioning: effectiveness (achieving objectives) and efficiency (with the least amount of resources), which together lead to productivity, motivation, trust, and employee satisfaction. Motivation occurs if groups are led and rewarded properly. Trust develops when the leader's and members' behaviors are appropriate. The final positive result,

SOURCE: "New Software Helps PC Users Work as Groups," *Wall Street Journal* 24 February, 1988, p. 25; Louis S. Richman, "Software Catches the Team Spirit," *Fortune* (June 8, 1987), pp. 125–136; and a demonstration by Wilson Learning Corporation.

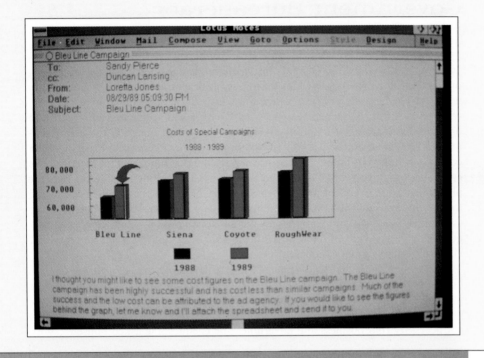

This is a sample screen from the Lotus 1-2-3® "Notes" groupware program. As shown, the program allows people to share information and track a project's status. (Courtesy Lotus Corporation)

employee satisfaction, is not necessarily contributive to the other five, but it usually is.[32] The proper leadership choices will promote the occurrence of all six results.

Groups can be effective, or they can choose to be counterproductive. Only if the manager functions properly, so that the group then functions properly, are organizational objectives likely to be achieved. An **effective work group** is one that achieves high levels of performance and also maintains good interpersonal relations.[33] Barry M. Staw summarizes the way to utilize groups to enhance both performance and member satisfaction:

1. Organize work around intact groups, as opposed to starting new ones.
2. Have groups select, train, and reward members.
3. Have groups enforce strong norms, with groups involved in on- and off-the-job activities.
4. Distribute resources on a group, rather than individual basis.
5. Allow, even promote, intergroup rivalry in order to build within-group solidarity.[34]

Other factors that play an important part in determining group effectiveness include task interdependence—how closely group members work together; outcome interdependence—whether, and how, group performance is rewarded; and potency—members' belief that the group can be effective.[35] Highly effective work groups possess the characteristics shown in Table 14.4.

Table 14.4. Characteristics of Effective Work Groups

1. The members of the group are attracted to it and are loyal to its members, including the leader.
2. The members and leaders have a high degree of confidence and trust in each other.
3. The values and goals of the group are an integration and expression of the relevant values and needs of its members.
4. All the interaction and problem-solving and decision-making activities of the group occur in a supportive atmosphere. Suggestions, comments, ideas, information, and criticisms are all offered with a helpful orientation.
5. The group is eager to help members develop to their full potential.
6. The group knows the value of "constructive" conformity and knows when to use it and for what purposes.
7. There is strong motivation on the part of each member to communicate fully and frankly to the group all the information that is relevant and of value to the group's activity.
8. Members feel secure in making decisions that seem appropriate to them.

SOURCE: Excerpted from Rensis Likert, *New Patterns of Management* (New York: McGraw-Hill, 1961), pp. 166–169. Copyright © 1961, McGraw-Hill. Used with the permission of McGraw-Hill Book Company.

A Comprehensive Look at Groups

Figure 14.1 presented a comprehensive model of the materials discussed thus far in this chapter.[36] As this model indicates, groups form for various reasons, but all of those reasons are related to needs. All groups develop through essen-

not turn government into an ally and partner?" Further, he thought, "Why not consider environmental activists as a fourth branch of government?" He decided to make government relations the primary business of his firm for the immediate future.

Henry believed deeply in what he was doing, and so apparently did others. For example, one of his company's probable products could significantly reduce the level of chemical fertilizers used each year, thus helping reduce fish and bird kills and potential food-chain problems for humans. He assembled a team of key former government officials to aid him in his quest. The team's members included:

William D. Ruckelshaus, twice former director of the EPA
Douglas M. Costle, head of the EPA during the Carter administration
Robert M. Teeter, a prominent Republican pollster who would eventually become co-chairman of the George Bush presidential transitional team
Elliot L. Richardson, former attorney general, who has held a number of other federal posts

The "team" met in brainstorming sessions for which participants received $1,000 per day plus certain stock options. These sessions produced a list of obstacles that Henry might face and strategies for overcoming them. The sessions also provided valuable insight into the workings of government and how a company could best work its way through the bureaucratic maze. The result? Crop Genetics became the first genetics firm to make it through the first round of regulator hoops without being delayed or stalled.

SOURCE: Jay Finnegan, "All the President's Men," *Inc.* (February 1989), pp. 44–54.

Co-founder and chief scientist, Peter Carlson of Crop Genetics International, had little trouble creating the plants, but getting them approved by regulatory agencies was another matter. Thus, CEO John Henry turned to a team of former government members to advise how to proceed. Their advice helped move approval forward faster than any of their predecessors had been able to move. (SOURCE © Greg Pease)

tially the same stages and function in approximately the same ways. The results of group activities are related to the reasons for the group's formation, though not always directly. The formal and informal reasons are not always the same, and the objectives for which a group was formed are not always achieved.

Managers' knowledge of groups can be used appropriately, or it can be misused. In one instance, for example, at a newspaper, a manager attempted to use the group to make himself look better. He knew that the organizational climate survey (a questionnaire administered by a company to assess organizational climate—this one included a large section evaluating each manager) would be given to all employees in another few weeks. He seemed to sense that he might not fare well. He knew that top management would be concerned about his ratings from his subordinates. Therefore, he took steps to ensure that his ratings were high. He began bringing in donuts for everyone each morning. He began "buddying" up to everyone. But he became too zealous, and too obvious. He failed to understand how groups really work. The group became cohesive against him rather than in support of him. His climate survey results were very negative. He then punished the group; through the grapevine, it succeeded, within a few months, in having him transferred to a nonmanagement position. The group had managed to make his boss's secretary aware of his actions. She made his boss aware. His boss made him aware.

> AT GENERAL FOODS: *Teams were formed expressly to achieve peak performance. In order to achieve the high level of performance, the company stressed clear and concise agreed-upon goals and objectives, well-defined roles; appropriate leadership; an open and trusting environment; rewards, and recognition.*

Some Major Types of Groups

In the work world, the manager works with groups every day, especially his or her group of subordinates. The manager will encounter other types of groups or may work with his or her subordinate group in special ways. The following sections review two special groups, the team or task force; and a special form of the work group—the quality circle.

Teams and Task Forces

Two very important uses of groups in today's organization are the team and the task force. The **team** is a group, normally within the same department, that is designed to work together to identify and solve group-related work problems. Special training is usually necessary in order to improve cohesiveness among members, and members' abilities to find, analyze, and solve problems. Teams typically are ongoing work units. The **task force** is a special type of temporary group that comes together to solve one specific problem or series of problems. It is normally interdepartmental or, at the very least, composed of numerous specialists.[37] Task forces are very useful where multidisciplinary problems exist—for example, in product design. Often, team-type training will be used with task forces, and in many organizations "team" and "task force" are synonymous. Management Challenge 14.4 contains interesting applications of both within a hospital setting.

Thomas J. Peters believes that self-managed work groups may be the most important tool there is to increase productivity.[38] Such groups are autonomous in making decisions related to their work. Systematic research on such groups

---

MANAGEMENT CHALLENGE **14.4**

Using Task Forces and Teams

When managers at United Hospitals, Inc., a multi-health-care system in the Philadelphia area are confronted with interdepartmental problems, they turn to task forces for solutions. At other times, when they want to solve problems, they often rely on competition between work teams.

In management's view task forces should be employed for very specific problems, encouraged to be creative, recommend solutions, be cross-representational—especially with respect to including the often forgotten second- and third-shift personnel—and be able to see that the results of their efforts are implemented. Task forces have been used to solve numerous problems, including the scheduling issues that crop up between departments, the coordination of tests for patients undergoing surgery, and the reduction in patient-care "downtime"—when the professional arrives to treat the patient but the patient is not there.

Similarly, the hospital has used a Team Competition Program to reduce costs, enhance morale, and improve patient satisfaction. For example, five medical/surgical units competed against each other to achieve levels of performance determined jointly by management and employees. Mixed shift representation made the teams quite unique from the typical hierarchical approach, where only one shift is represented. Over a 24-month period, the program saved the hospital $40,000 from reduced absenteeism, and performance levels exceeded previous ones. Side benefits included higher levels of group cohesiveness and the identification of work standards and specific work-group problems.

SOURCE: M. Michael Markowich, "Using Task Forces to Increase Efficiency and Reduce Stress," *Personnel* (August 1987), pp. 34–38.

---

indicates very positive results over a period of time.[39] Certainly one of the major organizational behavior trends of the 1970s was the effort to improve teamwork among group members. Several **team-building** approaches have been applied to improving **teamwork,** but each is essentially a planned series of steps, beginning with examining the functioning of a group and ending with implementing change to improve effectiveness.[40] Team building often means redesigning jobs and attempting to open up communication among members and between members and the rest of the organization. Teamwork and team building, already discussed in more detail in Chapter 12, are discussed to some extent in the following section, on quality circles.

In this General Foods Corporation exercise managers learn a lesson about letting lower-level managers work without interference. Above, the raft founders due to a barrage of instructions from those above, whereas below, each person has their job and is allowed to do it. (© Taro Yamasaki)

Quality Circles

Quality circles represent an application of knowledge about groups to business and other organizational environments. Specially formed groups known as **quality circles,** "consist of three to twelve employees who perform the same work or share the same work area and function and meet on a regular basis, normally one hour per week on company time, in order to apply specific techniques and tools learned in extensive training to problems affecting their work and work area; subsequently they present solutions and recommendations to their management for the authorization of these solutions."[41] Quality circles have been used in the United States to help companies compete with their Japanese and other competitors. In order to be successful, quality circles seem to need to possess four basic characteristics. First, there must be a sincere desire on the part of management to assist each employee's growth to the maximum of the individual's potential. Second, employees must be voluntary participants and not forced to participate. Third, there must be a structured process for problem solving. Individuals must be trained with and use certain tools and techniques. Fourth, management must support the program by creating time and space and support the results of the quality circles.[42]

Quality circles were first used in the United States by Lockheed's Space and Missile Unit in Sunnyvale, California, in 1974. There is no central source of information to indicate how many quality circles exist in the United States or how many firms have adopted them. But it is safe to say that most of the Fortune 500 manufacturing firms have looked at quality circles and that the majority have tried them, most of them successfully. It is also probably safe to say that thousands of other firms are using them as well. Quality circles are usually introduced only in selected areas and are not typically found throughout the whole organization. Experience has taught us that they work extremely well in manufacturing situations. They are less effective in service areas, but some effective quality circles have been developed. Historically they have more than paid for themselves, with figures as high as five to one payback being reported.[43]

The American quality circle is not exactly like its Japanese counterpart. For example, in Japan the foremen run their quality circles; in the United States, a facilitator, an external individual brought in to begin the circle, often manages the circle for several months. In many groups, after a period of time, the foreman, or someone who is elected to the position, may lead the quality circle. The role of the facilitator is to promote and help implement the quality-circle program; train quality-circle members; guide initial meetings; solve any problems that may arise; and serve as liaison between the group and staff personnel controlling the resources needed by the group.[44] In Japan the groups also meet on their own time, whereas in the United States they are paid for this time.

Finally, there is a quality-circle infrastructure that is created within the administrative system in the United States to provide support for the program because it may meet with internal resistance. This does not occur in Japan. For example, several quality-circle specialists may manage these programs for even a small company. The *Los Angeles Times* has three such specialists, even though it uses only forty teams among three hundred employees.[45]

Quality circles work for a variety of reasons. For example, they help improve the person-job relationships of those who become involved. They are a form of job enrichment—that is, individuals are given more decision power. The individual is taught new problem-solving skills and various decision-making tools. There is teamwork, and thus, to some extent, the individual's need to belong to a group is also satisfied. They also provide a mechanism for communication, both up, down, and side-to-side. Lastly, but perhaps most importantly, they provide for a way of improving self-esteem. American workers tend to believe that they are underutilized. Quality circles allow workers to show that they can perform at higher levels than a typical manufacturing job might provide the opportunity for.

Some failures have been reported. Quality circles may fail because they are introduced in the wrong context, there may be poor training, or there may be flaws in the technique. Often managers expect too much in the short term, and their expectations may fail to materialize. There may also be resistance to the quality-circle program from managers (who fear that they are losing their authority), as well as from employees and possibly from unions. Where workers are dissatisfied by aspects of their jobs that may not be improved by joining the quality circle, the quality circle may also fail.[46] Teams may become disheartened when their solutions fail, despite their best efforts. Quality-circle teams sometimes have difficulties accepting new members. There may be problems when management needs flexibility in work assignments. Quality circles need stability to function properly.[47] Teams may also fail where top management fails to support the program adequately.[48]

Quality circles are like any other management technique: they tend to be adopted as a fad and when they are successful they can be retained and where they are not, they are not retained. One must recognize that some cultures simply will not support quality circles—highly authoritative ones, for example. One must also recognize that the long-heralded Hawthorne effect (see Chapter 2) may be responsible for some of the success of these programs. Finally, one must also realize that, over time, any technique, if not renewed, will tend to lose its effectiveness, which may result in cancellation of the program.[49] For example, Toyota Auto Body in Japan found, in the late 1970s, that its major program of quality circles was losing momentum and was failing to provide the same kind of results it had earlier. Recognizing inherent problems, Toyota provided significant renewal by making quality circles responsible for new areas, such as customer complaints.[50]

Employees benefit from participating in quality circles in several ways. First, supervisors of quality circles seem to become more self-assured, knowledgeable, and poised.[51] Front-line employees benefit for the following reasons:

1. Communication improves: Trust is increased, people learn how to handle conflict, and interpersonal relations among group members improve.
2. Individual skills develop: Circle leaders are trained in valuable interpersonal skills, for example, and in turn teach them to other circle members. Creativity is fostered. Decision making is developed.[52]
3. Self-esteem rises: Participation, treatment as adults, and seeing the effects of their decisions raises member esteem.[53]

4. Employees become agents of change: Resistance to change reduces or disappears because employees choose the changes to be made.

Leading Groups as Problem Solving

The material so far in this chapter has examined groups and how they function to provide the necessary background to understand their role in the organization and, more specifically, how they can be managed. The manager must determine how best to lead the group. He or she has choices of ways to lead people in a group (discussed in Chapter 15) and bases these choices partly on the condition of the factors in Figure 14.1. Some of the choices leaders must make involve changes in the condition of these factors. Virtually all of the key points in this chapter could be involved in all stages of problem solving. For example, suppose a manager had problems with a product's quality, he or she would use the organizational contextual factors in determining whether to use a group and, if so, what type—task or command, permanent or temporary. Other choices the manager would have to make would include the size of the group, its composition, and how to deal with an informal group. Similarly, a manager might examine a group's cohesiveness, the strength of informal leadership, group norms and roles and the like before making changes in a permanent work group's individual job assignments.

A good manager is constantly attuned to his or her work group's contextual factors, to how the group is functioning, and to the group's results. Ongoing changes, most often small, occasionally significant, in all three of these group concerns will be necessary.

Conflict Management

Conflict is inevitable in any organization. Unless it is managed effectively, it can destroy both sides of the controversy. Conflict has historically been viewed as undesirable, something to be avoided. The contemporary view is that conflict cannot always be avoided, but it can be managed. All of the organization's individuals and groups have their own objectives and needs. No two of them can ever completely agree on everything because no two of them can ever perceive the same situation in precisely the same way. Engineers and production managers continually clash over the best way to construct an engine. Top management often clashes with personnel administrators over compensation programs. Supervisors clash with upper managers over operational procedures. Conflict is pervasive in the modern organization.

The potential for conflict exists between individuals, between individuals and groups, between groups, between the organization and the individual, between the organization and the group, and between organizations. Several **sources of conflict** have been identified: the aggressive or conflict-prone personality, ambiguous roles, conflicting roles, differences in objectives, differences in values, differences in perceptions, inadequate authority, oppressive management, status incongruence, interdependence, inadequate resources, and unsatisfactory communication.

The Consequences of Conflict

Conflict can have positive as well as negative consequences. Although many people would like to eliminate all conflict, it seems more realistic to try to keep it within bounds and make use of it.

POSITIVE CONSEQUENCES
Much of change depends on conflict. Competition tends to enhance the general welfare, if the conflict level is not too high. The offensive unit and the defensive unit of a football team may compete to see who does its job better, and in so doing overcome the common opponent. Branch A and branch B may compete, and in so doing may cause the whole bank to grow at a much faster rate than it would have otherwise. Conflict in the form of competition ordinarily increases group cohesiveness, which in turn usually increases the group's productivity. Loyalty normally increases when people unite against a common foe. If problems are recognized, solutions may be forthcoming. Change results. The organization survives and prospers.

NEGATIVE CONSEQUENCES
People stop talking to each other. Activities, not results, become important. Biased perceptions of "the other guys" are reinforced. Communication that does not support such stereotypes is blocked. Strong leaders are sought—and strong leaders often turn autocratic in conflict situations. The overall objectives of the organization are forgotten. Bitterness turns to hatred. The conflict may become a test of wills, a test of egos, a test of who can outlast the other person, group, or organization. At the very least, inappropriate types or levels of conflict have been shown to be counterproductive. Some of the very negative results of conflict occur because people attack the individual rather than the problem.

Resolving Conflict

The manager's role is to choose the correct **conflict-management** techniques and to keep conflict at an appropriate level. Unnecessary conflict is counterproductive. Many of the twelve sources of conflict identified earlier give rise to difficulties that could be avoided if appropriate steps are taken in time.

The common technique of simple dominance of the opponent will not suffice as a long-run method of conflict resolution, at least not in the business organization. The conflict situation should be viewed as a problem that should be solved in a rational manner, like any other problem.

MANAGING CONFLICT
As not all conflict can be eliminated and some is even desirable, managers must learn to manage conflict. Several conflict-management methods have been suggested. Kenneth W. Thomas has suggested that these approaches can be explained in terms of the degrees of cooperativeness and assertiveness of one of the contending parties with respect to intentions concerning the conflict. Figure 14.6 modifies his approach to include aggression. Thomas's approach can be used as a vehicle for discussing virtually all of the major conflict-resolution techniques:

1. Avoidance: no assertiveness, no cooperation. Most unpleasant realities can be avoided. The problem is not solved, it is only postponed, but in the short run this technique may work. It is not uncommon, for example, for

One of the most negative of possible consequences occurred to Eastern Airlines as a result of the inability of the airline and its machinists union to come to contract terms—the airline was taken over by Frank Lorenzo, shown on the left. (SOURCE © Rob Kinmonth)

FIGURE 14.6   A TWO-DIMENSIONAL MODEL OF CONFLICT INTENTIONS

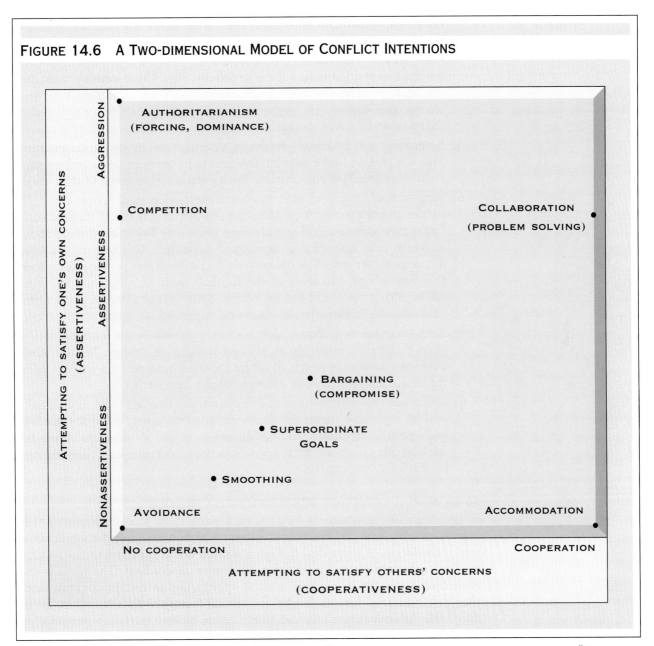

SOURCE: ADAPTED FROM KENNETH W. THOMAS, "INTRODUCTION" (TO A SERIES ON CONFLICT MANAGEMENT ENTITLED, "CONFLICT AND THE COLLABORATIVE ETHIC"), CALIFORNIA MANAGEMENT REVIEW, WINTER 1978, VOL. XXI, NO. 2, P. 57. © 1978 BY THE REGENTS OF THE UNIVERSITY OF CALIFORNIA. BY PERMISSION OF THE REGENTS.

people who do not have the strength to oppose their bosses on an issue to avoid them, perhaps in the hope of delaying a decision until they do gain strength.

2. Accommodation: no assertiveness, cooperation. One may also give in. Some people give in to others all the time. The win-lose situation must have a loser. Sometimes one must accommodate other people. Many people say that U.S. auto manufacturers have for years accommodated most union demands in the interest of labor harmony, to the detriment of their ability to compete effectively with foreign firms. In the economy of the 1980s, however, labor was more ready to accommodate management.

3. Smoothing: low assertion, low cooperation. Smoothing is a mild attempt at problem solving. It focuses on similarities, not differences, and seeks

resolution. The intent is to move the parties toward a common goal. Political parties must smooth over differences after a primary campaign.

4. Competition: assertiveness, no cooperation. This is a win-lose approach, but the competition must adhere to certain rules. The assertive person does not seek to harm the other's self-image, but competition does serve to change and improve the organization. Change and success are based on competition in a free-market economy.

5. Bargaining (compromise): moderate assertiveness, moderate cooperation. This is a give-and-take position. Negotiations between labor and management usually follow this pattern. Both parties satisfy some of their needs.

6. Superordinate goals: increasing assertiveness, increasing cooperation. The parties attempt to find a common set of objectives that will cause them to forget their differences. Superordinate goals may be imposed from above, in which case authoritarian forcing is the technique employed. Superordinate goals do not solve the underlying problem but provide more focus than smoothing. Members of the football team may fight among themselves during the week, but on Friday, Saturday, or Sunday, those differences should be forgotten because of a superordinate goal.

7. Authoritarianism (forcing, dominance): aggression, no cooperation. A party that feels it must win at any cost is using aggression. The unfriendly business takeover in which all of the previous managers are terminated by the new management is an example of this approach.

8. Collaboration: assertiveness and cooperation. This approach is characterized by a genuine attempt to find solutions that satisfy all of the needs of both parties. It differs from compromise in the participants' attitudes: while trying to obtain their own objectives (assertiveness), they become increasingly cooperative.

CHOOSING A CONFLICT-RESOLUTION TECHNIQUE
In deciding how to resolve a conflict, each party must assess the other's willingness to cooperate and the other's assertion level and factor the implications into the solution. A great deal has been written about the need to collaborate, as if it were the preferred mechanism to resolve all conflicts. The truth is that each conflict-resolution method is most appropriate in certain circumstances. Our task is to base our decision on the critical factors in each situation, beginning with the cooperativeness and assertiveness of both parties. Sometimes the conflict will be between equals; at other times one party will be dominant and the other subordinate. The same factors that should be considered in leadership decisions seem to apply here: the personality of the decision maker, the personalities of those involved, the nature of the groups involved, the organization's climate, the task, and other factors.

The Management
Challenges Identified

1. The cultural diversity of the work force, which affects, for example, group composition and the potential for informal groups
2. The globalization of business
3. Increased levels of competition

Some Solutions Noted in the Chapter

1. Increased level of group management skills
2. Quality circles
3. Task teams
4. Improved leadership
5. Managing the grapevine

Summary

1. Groups form to satisfy needs. Formal groups form to satisfy organizational needs. Informal groups form to satisfy their members' needs that are not satisfied by the formal group.
2. The organization's structure results from the grouping of jobs and the distribution of authority. Managers become important linking pins in this structure, linking various authority levels and job groups. Managers manage by leading groups.
3. All groups, whether formal or informal, go through approximately the same stages of development and have essentially the same functions. The stages of development include forming; storming initial integration, and total integration. Groups function according to the task, the building and maintenance roles that must be played, the individual roles that people choose to play, their structure (as identified by sociometry), the norms that define acceptable group conduct, cohesiveness, leadership, composition, decision processes and size. All groups within an organization expect their efforts to have three major results: effectiveness, efficiency, and their members' satisfaction; plus trust and motivation.
4. Quality circles represent applied knowledge of the group process. Quality circles meet to solve group problems.
5. Conflict management requires that managers understand that conflict can be managed. Secondly that this involves making choices among varying degrees of cooperativeness and assertiveness.

Thinking About Management

1. Think of groups to which you belong or to which you have belonged. Trace these groups through each of the parts of the model presented in Figure 14.1.
2. What sanctions can you think of that the group might impose against rate busters in various work situations: construction (carpenters, electricians, bricklayers); manufacturing (sewing-machine operators, tool and die makers, welders); clerical (accounts payable clerks, secretaries); and professionals (accountants, lawyers, college teachers)?
3. Think of a recent committee meeting you attended. Critique the performance of the leader. Then critique the effectiveness of various members in filling the task and maintenance roles. What were the results of this meeting? How good were those results?
4. Based on what you know about groups, explain how the informal group leader might be an aid or an obstacle to the formal group leader/manager. What can the formal group leader do to ensure the informal group leader's assistance?
5. If you were the leader of a formal work group and the informal group seemed always to be countermanding what you needed done, what strategies could you follow to change the situation?
6. Demonstrate your knowledge of group processes by showing how Figure 14.1 is used in quality circles.

Honeywell Managers and Group Leadership

Honeywell wanted to improve quality and productivity. It decided to focus on the work team and a "total employee involvement program" where workers make substantial work decisions to achieve those ends. Leadership was viewed as central to the success of these programs. To that end, managers were expected to develop interpersonal competence skills. As part of these skills, managers were expected to be linking pins, "linking management with employees, employees with management, and employees with each other." Honeywell provided the following guidelines to managers to help them improve their leadership.

> Leadership should be the ability of those leading work units (managers, supervisors, engineers, technical support, and group leaders) to create an atmosphere of acceptance, openness, and trust that will properly motivate members of the work units. Interpersonal competence should be the ability to relate to people in a considerate and effective way.

DISCUSSION QUESTIONS

1. If you were designing specific characteristics for leaders to define the general description provided by Honeywell, what would they be?
2. How would you prepare employees for "total involvement"?
3. How would you determine a manager's interpersonal skills?
4. What specific kind of support does top management need to provide?

SOURCE: William L. VanHorn and William D. Stimmett, "The Ideal Work Environment: Total Employee Involvement," *S.A.M. Advanced Management Journal* (Autumn 1984), pp. 43–45.

Groups May Be the Answer[1]

Martin Marietta's plant in Orlando, Florida, had landed major defense contracts through expert salesmanship. But as the company began to build the products, it discovered that it was not manufacturing as efficiently as it would have liked. Top operations managers, spearheaded by the efforts of Charles Hardin and Bob Jones, set out to determine ways in which to improve productivity.

Charles Hardin had been exposed to the quality-circle concept while obtaining his MBA. He knew the value of such groups, but the culture at Martin Marietta was too authoritarian to allow participative quality circles. Furthermore, the company wanted a solution that worked primarily to raise the levels of efficiency in production. Charles Hardin, Bob Jones, and others set out to examine all alternatives, but with the goal in mind of somehow using groups to improve productivity. Some 1,500 operations employees would be involved in any solution they derived.

DISCUSSION QUESTIONS

1. Design a group situation that would fit the needs of Martin Marietta.
2. What types of implementation problems would you foresee, given the authoritarian culture described?

[1]This case is to be used in conjunction with the Managers at Work case for Chapter 20, "Operations Management."

Team-Building Checklist

The following exercise is designed to reveal to you the type of questions that might be asked of actual managers and actual team members, to determine if a team-building program is necessary. After you have completed the form and scored it according to the instructions, your instructor will discuss the questionnaire with you.

Team-Building Checklist

Problem identification: To what extent is there evidence of the following problems in your work unit? (Use a previous one if you are not now employed, or use any other group to which you have belonged.) If you choose some school group as an example, you will need to interpret the questions in light of that group and its purposes.

	Low Evidence		Some Evidence		High Evidence
1. Loss of production or work-unit output.	1	2	3	4	5
2. Grievances or complaints within the work unit.	1	2	3	4	5
3. Conflicts or hostility between unit members.	1	2	3	4	5
4. Confusion about assignments or unclear relationships between people.	1	2	3	4	5
5. Lack of clear goals, or low commitment to goals.	1	2	3	4	5
6. Apathy or general lack of interest or involvement of unit members.	1	2	3	4	5
7. Lack of innovation, risk taking, imagination, or taking initiative.	1	2	3	4	5
8. Ineffective staff meetings.	1	2	3	4	5
9. Problems in working with the boss.	1	2	3	4	5
10. Poor communications: people are afraid to speak up, are not listening to each other, or are not talking together.	1	2	3	4	5
11. Lack of trust between boss and member or between members.	1	2	3	4	5
12. Decisions made that people do not understand or agree with.	1	2	3	4	5
13. People feel that good work is not recognized or rewarded.	1	2	3	4	5
14. People are not encouraged to work together in a better team effort.	1	2	3	4	5

Scoring: Add up the score for the fourteen items. If your score is between 14 and 28, there is little evidence your unit needs team building. If your score is between 29 and 41, there is some evidence, but no immediate pressure, unless two or three items are very high. If your score is between 43 and 56, you should think seriously about planning the team-building program. If your score is over 56, then building should be a top priority item for your work unit.

SOURCE: William Dyer, *Team Building: Issues and Alternatives,* © 1977, Addison-Wesley Publishing Company, Inc. Chapter 4, pp. 36–37. Reprinted with permission.

CHAPTER FIFTEEN

Leadership

CHAPTER OBJECTIVES

By the time you finish this chapter, you should be able to

1. Define leadership.
2. Distinguish between leaders and managers.
3. Describe the bases of power.
4. Explain how various theories and research have contributed to our understanding of this process.
5. Make leadership choices based on the various models of leadership.
6. Discuss transformational leadership.

CHAPTER OUTLINE

Management Does Not Equal Leadership
Leadership, Power, and Influence
Approaches to Leadership
Trait Approaches
   Douglas McGregor's Theory X and Theory Y
Behavioral Approaches
   The Ohio State and Michigan Leadership Studies
   The Yukl Studies
   The Managerial Grid
Contingency Approaches
   Tannenbaum and Schmidt's Continuum of Leadership Behavior
   Fiedler's Contingency Model
   Path-Goal Theory
   The Hersey-Blanchard Contingency Theory
   Vroom-Yetton-Yago
   The Muczyk-Reimann Model
Leaders as Communicators
Leadership as a Problem-Solving Process
Leadership at the Top: Transformational Leadership
The Management Challenges Identified
Some Solutions Noted in the Chapter

Jim Robinson's Management Style

Every leader has his or her own style. Jim Robinson, chairman of American Express, might be best characterized as demanding and unrelenting. He pounds and pounds until he gets what he wants. Ironically, he delegates a tremendous amount of authority to the managers of the company's operating subsidiaries. Within his guidelines, you can function rather autonomously. Therefore, much of the pounding relates to vision. He wanted a service-oriented service company, period. He got a service-oriented service company, despite numerous acquisitions of diverse financial institutions. He wanted a quality-oriented company. He got it. He pounds on the quality issue relentlessly in all of the company's discussions. One of his favorite sayings is, "Quality is the only patent protection we've got."

He is a stickler for detail, a consensus builder, and a man who likes to surround himself with capable people. He doesn't like to be caught by surprise. Subordinates had best keep him informed. He is not a political person and he doesn't manipulate, but he is indomitable when it comes to power. He sets his goals and expects subordinates to reach them. He is reasonable, deliberate, and almost too nice to be tough, but he is. For example, when AMEX acquired Shearson Loeb Rhoades and Trade Development Bank, Robinson found himself confronted with two very powerful, maverick types of leaders in Sanford Weill at Shearson and Edmond Safra at Trade Bank. Although many analysts predicted a downfall for Robinson, he simply persevered. Eventually both Weill and Safra moved on, not because Robinson played politics, but rather because the other two found themselves unable to mold themselves to the AMEX culture and situation.

Finally, Robinson is ever the member of the establishment, making this or that black tie dinner virtually every night of the work week. He is always impeccably groomed. He is extremely active in federal trade issues, "almost a member of the administration," according to an official.

Robinson is intense. Up at 5:30 A.M., he exercises for an hour or so, arriving at work at 7:00 A.M., leaving at 7:00 P.M. He uses exercise to help him through his tough schedule and through periods of tough times. An avid weight lifter, he uses that training regimen to give himself mental toughness. His approach to corporate quality in service reflects that regimen, always pushing to make it just a little bit better, a task especially difficult in the investment banking business.

After assuming control of AMEX in 1977, Robinson began slowly but surely to turn the stodgy old credit card company into the largest service company in the United States, largely through acquisitions of firms such as Shearson Loeb Rhoades, Inc.; Investors Diversified Services; Trade Development Bank; Lehman Brothers; and E. F. Hutton Group, Inc. Through his perseverance, the firm digested these giants, their cultures, and their leaders. He has molded a company whose culture allows risk taking, yet that might be described as conservative. Perhaps as testimony to his style, despite all of the potential for visibility, and all of his actions, few people really know who he is.

SOURCE: John Paul Newport, Jr., "American Express: Service That Sells," *Fortune* (November 20, 1989), pp. 80–97; and "Do You Know Me?" *Business Week* (January 25, 1988), pp. 72–82.

Transformational leadership is about change, innovation, and entrepreneurship. It is a leadership process that is systematic, consisting of purposeful and organized search for changes, systematic analysis, and the capacity to move resources from areas of losses to greater productivity. It is a behavior process capable of being learned and managed.

Noel M. Tichy and Mary Anne Devanna,
authors of *The Transformational Leader*

A business short on capital can borrow money, and one with a poor location can move. But a business short on leadership has little chance of survival.

Warren Bennis and Burt Nanus, authors of *Leaders*

Robert Leach, president of Genencor, the fourth largest genetic engineering firm in the world, is shown "cooking up a new batch" of products. The managers of the 1990s will similarly have to learn to "cook up" new ways of leading. (p. 494) (© Ed Kashi)

Everyone agrees that leadership is essential to organizational success. People such as Jim Robinson prove that. But while leadership is a pivotal force in organizational success—perhaps *the* most important factor in organizational success—precisely what it means is uncertain.[1] There are almost as many definitions as there are people using the term.[2] Most would agree, however, that leadership involves influencing others, and all would agree that a leader is a person who has followers. Most would also agree that leaders have followers because they take certain actions and behave in certain ways. **Leadership**, then, is the process of making choices about how to treat people in order to influence them and then translating those choices into actions.[3] Those choices and the actions based on them are designed to influence others to follow the leader. People at American Express follow Jim Robinson. If you look around and no one is following you, then you are not a leader. You have not made the right choices. You have not taken the right actions. Organizations are especially concerned that their managers be leaders. Managers are not necessarily leaders.[4]

Jim Robinson finds lifting weights provides the kind of self-discipline necessary to move ahead in the corporate world. His dogged pursuit of athletic achievement has been partly responsible for his dogged, demanding management style. (SOURCE © John Abbott)

They may be, but all too often they are not. Some organizations spend millions of dollars training their managers in leadership skills, hoping to turn more of them into leaders.[5]

If managers cannot influence people to become followers, managers will have nothing to manage. All organizations need people to carry out their work. Most successful managers are leaders who practice sound human relations and thus are able to influence others to carry out that work. A manager who has no followers soon finds that the work of the organization is just not getting done. Some managers, of course, try to do it all themselves. But that's not managing.

This chapter pursues the basic issues of organizational leadership: how it is defined, the factors that affect its success, the major leadership theories, and the practical approaches you can take to improve your leadership ability. There are many different approaches to leadership, ranging from the study of traits and behaviors shared by successful leaders, to the behaviors successful leaders should follow in very specific situations. The section of the chapter on approaches to leadership concludes with a model of leadership that suggests that, in any given situation, leadership choices should be based on consideration of certain major factors. The chapter concludes with a discussion of an important emerging issue in management: the need for managerial leaders, especially top managers, who can "transform" their organizations into entities to meet the demands of the highly competitive and changeful environments organizations will face in the 1990s.[6]

Management Does Not Equal Leadership

There are inherent differences between managers and leaders.[7] Generally, managers are rational problem solvers; leaders are more intuitive, more visionary.

MANAGEMENT CHALLENGE 15.1

Morehouse College Trains Middle-Class Blacks to Lead

Morehouse College administrators have for years asked themselves how best to train college students to make them into leaders. And each year, they reaffirm what began many years ago. The Morehouse College credo is simple, "Whatever you do in this hostile world, be the best." Little known among White Americans, Atlanta's Morehouse men's college has for decades played a prominent role in shaping the Black middle class, producing doctors, lawyers, teachers, and most notably civil rights activist Dr. Martin Luther King, Jr.

Morehouse's impact in the Black community and elsewhere far exceeds its limited number of graduates. Much of its success is attributed to its creation of the "Morehouse man." This phrase was first coined by Benjamin Mays, president of

Managers perform several administrative functions in addition to leadership, such as planning, organizing, controlling, decision making, and communicating. Leaders are primarily concerned with results. Managers must also be concerned with the efficiency of results. Managers must be primarily concerned with achieving an organization's objectives, but they must also represent their followers' objectives if they are to be leaders. Leaders obtain their power from below; managers obtain theirs from above. Some believe that managers and leaders are so different that managers cannot be made into leaders, but this is a narrow view.[8] As organizational environments change, it becomes clear that it is necessary to increase the leadership skills of managers. Noel M. Tichy and Mary Anne Devanna, authors of *The Transformational Leader*, see this type of development as critical in the future.[9] Thus managers must also be leaders. Managers who seek to be leaders must use their skills to balance the needs of their organization and their followers.

James M. Korzes and Barry Z. Posner, authors of *The Leadership Challenge*, after studying five hundred cases of managers who were also leaders, concluded that to be effective, (managerial) leaders rely on five principles of action:

1. Leaders challenge the process. They are pioneers and innovators. They encourage those with ideas.
2. Leaders inspire a shared vision. They are enthusiastic.
3. Leaders enable others to act. They are team players.
4. Leaders model the way. They show others how to behave as leaders.
5. Leaders "encourage the heart." They openly and often celebrate achievements.[10]

Think of managers that you have had either at work or in clubs and on athletic teams. Which ones did you follow? For which did you perform best? For which did you perform the worst? Why?

Management Challenge 15.1 discusses the approach of one organization that has been developing leaders for years.

AT AMEX: *Jim Robinson is both a leader and a manager.*

the college beginning in 1940, who dominated the institution for decades. The "Morehouse man" is expected to possess the essential qualities of self-discipline, self-confidence, and, above all, strength. Although this mission was conceived in a segregationist world, it is still believed to be relevant for today's environment, one perceived by many Blacks to be filled still with prejudice and discrimination.

How is the "Morehouse man" created? The process is complex, but most of all demanding. It begins with an indoctrination process similar to boot camp when the student first arrives on campus. The academic process itself is rigorous. On the average, only half of those from any given class finish the four years. But it is the twice-a-week lectures for freshmen, once a week for others, on subjects from Black history to etiquette, and the uncompromising attitude with respect to performance in the classroom, that seem to make the process so effective. Students do something until they get it right.

SOURCE: Linda Williams, "Molding Men: At Morehouse College, Middle Class Blacks Are Taught to Lead," *Wall Street Journal* 5 May, 1987, pp. 1, 25.

Dr. Martin Luther King, Jr., shown giving his "I Have a Dream" speech on August 28, 1963, is the most notable example of the heritage of black leadership nurtured at Morehouse College. (SOURCE © UPI/Bettmann)

Leadership, Power, and Influence

The ability to influence the direction and strength of other people's motivation is the most important quality of leadership. One may influence others in many ways, but all forms of influence are based on some type of power—the ability to control others by successfully influencing the strength and direction of their motivation. By exerting power, the leader influences motivation. Managers have power because of their position in an organization. Thus, they normally have more sources of power at their disposal than do leaders outside of formal organizations. However, the manager's power still must be accepted by followers if he or she is to be effective.

Chester Barnard recognized that unless followers accept a manager's power, the manager will have no influence.[11] For example, it is not uncommon for athletes to break training and go into town for a few beers, or a late-night date. They simply refuse to recognize the authority of their coaches. Workers often go on strike rather than recognize the authority of their bosses. Students sometimes question the authority of their professors and refuse unreasonable homework demands. When subordinates do not accept the authority of someone in a superior position, that person has no influence at that point with those subordinates.

It has been suggested that the only successful leadership is that which is dictated by the followers, in which case the followers become the leaders, and vice versa. Thus, if the leader fulfills certain expectations of the subordinates, the subordinates will reciprocate with performance and esteem for the leader.[12] The more conventional view is that leaders lead and followers follow. There is an element of truth in both views. The successful leader realizes these truths. A leader must accept responsibility for his or her power and influence if leadership is to be perpetuated. In order to have followers, a leader must accept those followers as human beings with needs that must be satisfied. As the work force changes in composition, these needs and employee expectations will also change.

People possess power for various reasons. John R. P. French and Bertram Raven, social researchers, have identified five key sources of power: legitimate, reward, coercion, expertise, and reference.[13] The first three of these are a consequence of the leader's position—position power. The latter two result from personal characteristics—personal power.

1. Legitimate power, or authority, results from a person's position in the organization. The leader who simply depends on this type of power for success may suffer in the long run. Ordinarily, followers will follow a leader only as long as their needs are reasonably well satisfied. Much of the ongoing process of the organization depends on this type of power.

2. Reward power depends on the leader's ability to control the rewards given to other people. Studies have shown that when leaders are no longer able to satisfy their followers' needs, the followers cease to follow.[14] A good leader is able to provide rewards.

3. Coercive power depends on the ability to punish others. Fear is a motivator, but fear does not highly motivate very many people for long. The Nazi work camps produced less and less, even though the punishment meted out to the people in them became greater and greater.[15] The thinking adult does not respond to fear in the same manner as the child. Leaders who expect their followers to submit to their authority like children will find themselves in trouble when they face assertive subordinates. When Robert Abboud was CEO of First Chicago Bank, he was an absolute tyrant. The bank's profits suffered enormously, hundreds of key managers

Robert Abboud didn't make many friends inside the bank, but did manage some outside the firm. Here he is shown shaking hands with then Japanese Prime Minister Masayoshi Ohira, right, as former U.S. Ambassador to Japan Robert Ingersoll looks on, at the premiere's official residence in Tokyo. (1979) (© AP/ Wide World Photos)

left, and, eventually, Abboud was forced out.[16] Yet, fear is often part of organizational leadership.

4. Expert power depends on special skill or knowledge. Think of someone where you work who is very good at what he or she does. Does this person have followers because of this skill? In most circumstances the answer will be yes. In many college business administration programs, student computer experts have many followers because people who are less skilled at computers need their help.[17]

5. Referent power is that which depends on appeal, magnetism, and charisma. John Kennedy and Martin Luther King, Jr., had this kind of power. Can you think of ways in which both of these men also used the other types of power at their disposal?

Managers determine the success of the organization through their leadership behavior. Unfortunately, our managers and our leaders of work organizations do not seem to be performing as well as we would like. One poll of the nonmanagerial work force reported that:

1. Less than 25 percent indicate they are working to their fullest potential.

2. Fully 50 percent report not putting any more effort into their job than they are required to.

3. Seventy-five percent feel they could be more effective than they are.

4. Nearly 60 percent say they "do not work as hard as they used to."[18]

In one of its frequent philosophical advertisements, United Technologies, a diversified conglomerate with core industries of defense and aerospace, has suggested that our organizations may need more "leaders" and fewer "managers," again emphasizing the need to develop leadership skills in managers.[19]

The two most important points for all managers to remember are that, first, they have choices as to the way they treat their subordinates (and other people within and without the organization). Second, it is how they carry out these choices that determines their and their organization's success or failure. Proper

These GM managers are learning more about managing, more about leading, and more about ensuring quality of products. These small group sessions help improve small group leadership. (© Peter Yates)

choices and actions result in followers and productivity. Wrong choices and actions result in few followers and little productivity. The manager may fail to be rewarded, as may his or her subordinates. The manager may also find that in extreme cases he or she may be punished from below. Employees retaliate in rather creative ways—for example, one person sent her boss anonymous get well cards after his tirades.[20] Managers can select the appropriate way to treat subordinates only after they have considered all of the major factors in a situation. Unfortunately, leadership behavior is often based either on learned authoritarian or emotional response or on current bad examples. Because most leadership behavior is learned from inappropriate role models, leadership development and training are not only necessary, but vital to the success of the organization. General Motors, following Ford's lead, spent over $3 million in the late 1980s to teach its managers how to be better leaders.[21]

Approaches to Leadership

From the dawn of time through the early twentieth century, most leaders led as they had been led in their families—by authoritarian methods. Early leadership was often charismatic and often coercive. The few managers during this time followed those same patterns. The influence of learned reactions and emotions on management/leadership style was great. During this time period, very few examples of the more effective rational, ethical, and assertive leadership can be found. There was little emphasis on objectives, little delegation of authority, little maintenance or building of subordinates' egos, little participation in management by subordinates, and very little knowledge of how to manage properly.

The large organizations that existed throughout most of this time period were primarily government and religious organizations, or state governments run by churchmen, especially up through the early nineteenth century. Almost all of these organizations had extremely authoritarian structures and climates. In the United States and Canada and in some European nations, governments, and to some extent businesses, were more democratic than elsewhere, and some better leadership practices were followed. But only as the business organization began to grow in size and influence did more modern and successful leadership styles begin to flourish and the role of the manager as leader develop and become important.

Many theories about what makes for successful leadership have been proposed. There are approaches based on the traits, abilities, or characteristics of successful managers; behavioral approaches, which suggest that successful leaders act in certain ways; and contingency, or situational, approaches, which propose that leadership actions should result from considering the major variables in a situation. This chapter reviews these approaches for the insight they shed on current recommended management practices. If you know how leadership has been practiced in the past, you will have a better understanding of why it is practiced as it is now. More importantly, you will understand why many leadership behaviors are inappropriate and what you can do to change them—both in yourself, if you are a leader, and in the people who lead you. (The latter task is often more challenging than the former.) Each of the preceding contributes in some way to a situational behavior-choice model of leadership, known as the Leadership TRRAP, which concludes this section.

Trait Approaches

Management was not examined as a science until the late nineteenth and early twentieth centuries, when Henri Fayol, Frederick Taylor, Frank and Lillian Gilbreth, and others initiated their studies. Leadership was not examined in depth as a discipline within this science until the 1940s. At that time, as earlier, leadership was approached from the perspective of traits. In **trait theories** successful leaders are considered to possess common traits. What are the traits that you feel a successful leader possesses? How tall are they? What color is their hair and their eyes? How intelligent are they?

Much of early trait research was directed toward inherited physical and mental traits. This research eventually examined intellectual, personal, emotional, social, and other traits. The leadership-trait studies focused not only on managers, but on political and religious leaders, as well. Apparently the trait approach came into existence partly because of the continuing dominance of certain families in power situations, such as the Hapsburgs, a family that ruled much of Europe for several centuries, and the Roosevelts, who dominated American politics and government for fifty years. People noted common traits in these families and assumed that all leaders possessed them. But when the various family traits were examined and compared, few common characteristics emerged. Early trait research failed to produce either a list of traits common to successful leaders, or one that would predict what leaders would actually do in a given situation. Those early efforts to formulate a trait theory were confusing and fraught with methodological problems in the research design and implementation. Most authorities agreed then that the trait approach was, at best, weak.[22] Later studies, using improved definitions and methodologies, proved more fruitful. Table 15.1 contains lists of traits and skills found most frequently to be characteristics of successful leaders.

Ralph Stogdill, author of *The Handbook of Leadership,* in reviewing the trait research suggests that the successful leader has the following profile: task-performance orientation, self-confidence, tolerance of interpersonal stress, and ability to influence others' behaviors (leadership).[23] But even these traits, or characteristics, are not accepted by everyone as being representative of successful leaders, and they are not effective in all leadership situations. And while these are identifiable traits of successful leaders, it is clear that all "leaders are not born," but rather they may develop these characteristics through experience. Thus, they may be trained to possess them. It is also clear that while leaders

AT AMEX: *Jim Robinson seems to possess most of the traits and skills listed in Table 15.1.*

Table 15.1. Traits and Skills Found Most Frequently to Be Characteristic of Successful Leaders

Traits	Skills
Adaptable to situations	Clever (intelligent)
Alert to social environment	Conceptually skilled
Ambitious and achievement oriented	Creative
Assertive	Diplomatic and tactful
Cooperative	Fluent in speaking
Decisive	Knowledgeable about the group task
Dependable	Organized (administrative ability)
Dominant (desire to influence others)	Persuasive
Energetic (high activity level)	Socially skilled
Persistent	
Self-confident	
Tolerant of stress	
Willing to assume responsibility	

SOURCE: Gary Yukl, *Leadership in Organizations* (Englewood Cliffs, N.J.: Prentice-Hall, 1981), p. 70.

may possess certain traits that may improve their leadership, the situation also influences their ability to be successful leaders. "Certain traits increase the likelihood that a leader will be effective, but they do not guarantee effectiveness, and the relative importance of different traits is dependent on the nature of the leadership situation."[24]

The trait approach, although limited in its applicability, contributes to our understanding of leadership by pointing out the need to consider one's own characteristics in making leadership choices and taking actions. These leader characteristics are related to leader personality and needs. Leaders respond to situations according to two factors: their personality and their needs.[25] One of the major components of personality is the leader's assumptions about people.

Douglas McGregor's Theory X and Theory Y

In his classic book *The Human Side of Enterprise* (1960), Douglas McGregor (1906–1964) postulated that managers tend to make two different assumptions about human nature. He called these views Theory X and Theory Y.[26] Their assumptions are shown in Table 15.2.

Theory X tended to lead to authoritative, perhaps even aggressive, managerial behavior, Theory Y to a participative style. McGregor insisted that Theory Y managers were just as concerned about productivity as Theory X managers. They just were more "adult" and less "parental" about achieving results than were Theory X managers.

Heavily influenced by Maslow's hierarchy of needs, McGregor recognized that social, esteem, and self-actualization needs were more dominant than they had been in the past. A management style based on Theory X was thus inappropriate. McGregor urged managers to base their behavior on the assumptions of Theory Y.

McGregor believed that the assumptions managers make about their employees will influence how they treat them. Theory X managers tell people what to do, are very directive, are very control oriented, and show little confidence in

Table 15.2. Theory X and Theory Y Assumptions

Theory X
1. The average human being has an inherent dislike of work and will avoid it if he or she can.
2. Because of this human characteristic of dislike of work, most people must be coerced, controlled, directed, and threatened with punishment to get them to put forth adequate effort toward the achievement of organizational objectives.
3. The average human being prefers to be directed, wishes to avoid responsibility, has relatively little ambition, and wants security above all.

Theory Y
1. The expenditure of physical and mental effort in work is as natural as play or rest.
2. External control and the threat of punishment are not the only means for bringing about effort toward organizational objectives. People will exercise self-direction and self-control in the service of objectives to which they are committed.
3. Commitment to objectives is a function of the rewards associated with their achievement.
4. The average human being learns, under proper conditions, not only to accept, but to seek responsibility.
5. The capacity to exercise a relatively high degree of imagination, ingenuity, and creativity in the solution of organizational problems is widely, not narrowly, distributed in the population.
6. Under the conditions of modern industrial life, the intellectual potentialities of the average human being are only partially utilized.

subordinates. They foster dependent, passive subordinates. Theory Y managers, on the other hand, would allow for more participation in making decisions, delegate more authority, and offer people more interesting jobs. If managers operate on the wrong assumptions, their management style is not very likely to help solve problems on the job.

Do you see that the assumptions one holds about people generally lead to a certain kind of behavior? Do you see the need to change some of those assumptions? How about your own assumptions and behavior—do they need changing? Not all people fit the assumptions of Theory Y, but most people probably do. McGregor made a tremendous contribution to leadership theory. His theories link assumptions to action. His contribution was made during the 1960s and antedates some of the work we will examine on leadership behavior and situational approaches.

Behavioral Approaches

After the early failure of the trait approach to discover common traits that could predict leadership success, a number of studies were carried out, in the 1950s and 1960s, in attempts to identify the **leadership behaviors** in which successful leaders engage. Thus, attention shifted from what leaders were like to what they did. Noteworthy studies were performed at both Ohio State University and the University of Michigan.

The Ohio State and Michigan Leadership Studies

A series of studies at Ohio State University indicated that two behavior dimensions proved significant in successful leadership:

1. **Consideration:** Behavior indicative of friendship, mutual trust, respect, and warmth.
2. **Initiating structure:** Behavior that organizes and defines relationships or

roles and establishes well-defined patterns of organization, channels of communication, and ways of getting jobs done.

Studies conducted at the University of Michigan revealed two similar concepts of leadership style that correlated with effectiveness:

1. **Employee orientation:** The human relations aspect of the leader's job, with employees considered to be human beings of intrinsic importance, with individual, personal needs.
2. **Production orientation:** Stress on production and the technical aspects of the job, with employees viewed as the means of getting the work done.[27]

As you can see, these are quite similar conceptualizations. More recently they have been referred to as relationship and task orientations (as noted in Chapter 14), but the underlying behaviors remain essentially the same. What these studies and others revealed was that successful leaders (success is defined in terms of productivity and employee satisfaction) engaged not in one or the other, but in both behaviors to varying degrees. Thus, to be successful most of the time, the leader must behave in a manner consistent with task orientation (initiating structure and concern for productivity) and also in a manner consistent with relationship orientation (consideration and concern for people). It is important to understand that in both the Ohio State and Michigan studies, numerous behaviors were statistically collapsed into the two very general descriptive categories expressed here.

The Yukl Studies

Gary M. Yukl, author of *Leadership in Action,* and his colleagues spent four years researching what they thought to be a void in the descriptions of leader behavior.[28] While the Ohio State and Michigan descriptors (and those of other studies they examined) were beneficial in terms of comprehensibility and relevance to many kinds of leaders, their brevity did not provide very specific be-

---

MANAGEMENT CHALLENGE 15.2

What Leaders Do to Be Leaders

Andrew Grove, CEO of Intel Corporation, the giant semiconductor company, relates one story of how a manager could have been a leader. He prefaces his story by stating that if a young manager is told that leaders and managers are not the same thing, this may be more discouraging than informative. What managers need to learn, he says, is how to convey their emotions to their subordinates—in the right way at the right time.

One young marketing manager Grove encountered confessed that he lacked leadership skills. A short time later, Grove, witnessing the manager make an important pitch to corporate sales managers, concluded that the young manager was right. The manager's task was a difficult one. His task was to ensure that his products would receive a healthy share of attention by the sales force. But the managers in the audience raised objections to which the marketing manager had few, if any, rebuttals. In fact, it was almost as if he agreed with them. The young man basically failed in his mission that day, leaving a group of disgruntled sales

haviors for varying situations. Their research efforts isolated nineteen behaviors, some of which are described in Table 15.3. Note, however, that although the choices of behaviors are well defined, the factors that would cause a manager to stress one behavior more than another have not been identified. As the nature of subordinates' needs and expectations change, some of these behaviors become more likely to be successful—for example, number 10, "coaching," and number 15, "work facilitation."

Table 15.3. Selected Items from Yukl's List of Leadership Behaviors

Performance Emphasis: The extent to which a leader emphasizes the importance of subordinate performance, tries to improve productivity and efficiency, tries to keep subordinates working up to their capacity, and checks on their performance.

Consideration: The extent to which a leader is friendly, supportive, and considerate in his or her behavior toward subordinates and tries to be fair and objective.

Praise-Recognition: The extent to which a leader provides praise and recognition to subordinates with effective performance, shows appreciation for their special efforts and contributions, and makes sure they get credit for their helpful ideas and suggestions.

Decision Participation: The extent to which a leader consults with subordinates and otherwise allows them to influence his or her decisions.

Training-Coaching: The extent to which a leader determines training needs for subordinates and provides any necessary training and coaching.

Problem Solving: The extent to which a leader takes the initiative in proposing solutions to serious work-related problems and acts decisively to deal with such problems when a prompt solution is needed.

Work Facilitation: The extent to which a leader obtains for subordinates any necessary supplies, equipment, support services, or other resources; eliminates problems in the work environment; and removes other obstacles that interfere with the work.

The other behaviors identified included inspiration, structuring reward contingencies, autonomy-delegation, role clarification, goal setting, information dissemination, planning, coordinating, representation, interaction facilitation, conflict management, and criticism-discipline.

SOURCE: Gary A. Yukl, *Leadership in Action* (Englewood Cliffs, N.J.: Prentice-Hall, 1981), adapted from pp. 121–125.

Management Challenge 15.2 reviews how one manager could have shown more "Inspiration"—item 3 on Yukl's list.

managers in that room. From Grove's viewpoint, "leaders are individuals who make ordinary people do extraordinary things in the face of adversity." It's easy to sell the perfect product, and salespeople don't like to have to make an extra effort to sell a product that is not perfect. Rather than answer the sales managers' objections, the marketing manager simply tried to appease them, leaving them dissatisfied.

The marketing manager simply did not rise to the occasion. Grove thought he should have said, "Here's our product line, we know it's not perfect and we will work to improve it continually, but, for now, this is what we—and you—have to work with, and what you must sell. I know it can be sold because I have sold it myself. You can call me any time, day or night—here's my home phone number. If you need help to work out an approach that is right for a customer, give me 24 hours and I will be there to go with your salespeople to call on any account that needs it."

Leaders must not only know what to say, but must be able to gauge the right moment to inject this type of emotion into a business situation. Grove believes that leaders don't learn this from a book. They learn it by watching other great leaders in action.

SOURCE: Andrew S. Grove, "Taking the Hype Out of Leadership," *Fortune* (March 28, 1988), pp. 167–168.

Andrew S. Grove, CEO of Intel, believes very strongly in the manager as a leader of a team of individuals, and that the manager's efforts to elicit the best performance from each of those members of the team is what management is all about. (SOURCE © Robert Holmgren)

FIGURE 15.1 THE MANAGERIAL GRID®

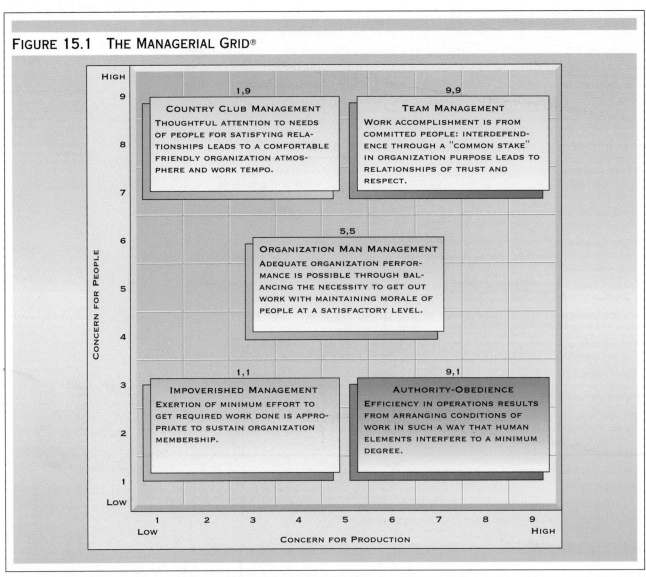

SOURCE: THE MANAGERIAL GRID® FIGURE FROM THE MANAGERIAL GRID III: THE KEY TO LEADERSHIP EXCELLENCE, BY ROBERT R. BLAKE AND JANE SRYGLEY MOUTON. HOUSTON: GULF PUBLISHING COMPANY, COPYRIGHT © 1985, PAGE 12. REPRODUCED BY PERMISSION.

The Managerial Grid

The fourth behavioral theory, the **Managerial Grid,**® contributes a great deal to our understanding of leadership because it portrays the leadership choice situation as having many possible styles.

Robert Blake and Jane Mouton developed a model that, like most leadership models, focused on the task of relationship orientations uncovered in the Ohio State and Michigan leadership-behavior studies. Blake and Mouton created a grid, based on managers' concern for both people (relationships) and production (tasks).[29] Figure 15.1 shows each of these concerns as one of the two axes of the grid, so that concerns for both people and productivity are combined in various management styles.

Like other behavioral theories, the Managerial Grid® proposes that there is a best way to manage people, the way used by the 9,9 manager, who has 9 units of concern for productivity and 9 for people. Four other major styles are indicated: the 1,1, the 9,1, the 1,9, and the 5,5. Typical characteristics of these five styles are presented in Table 15.4. The Grid is often used in organizational development programs, which are programs of planned change with a focus on organizational culture and climate. Before training, managerial style is measured by means of a self-assessment instrument and managers determine their Grid style—for example, as a 3,6. After training, in which they receive feedback and critique from colleagues, managers reevaluate their Grid style and determine what changes may be necessary to strengthen personal contributions. The desired objective is 9,9.

Table 15.4. The Major Managerial Grid® Styles

1,1	Impoverished management, often referred to as laissez-faire leadership. Leaders in this position have little concern for people or productivity, avoid taking sides, and stay out of conflicts. They do just enough to get by.
1,9	Country club management. Managers in this position have great concern for people and little concern for production. They try to avoid conflicts and concentrate on being well liked. To them the task is less important than good interpersonal relations. Their goal is to keep people happy. (This is a soft Theory X approach and not a sound human relations approach.)
9,1	Authority obedience. Managers in this position have great concern for production and little concern for people. They desire tight control in order to get tasks done efficiently. They consider creativity and human relations to be unnecessary.
5,5	Organization man management, often termed middle-of-the-road leadership. Leaders in this position have medium concern for people and production. They attempt to balance their concern for both people and production, but are not committed to either.
9,9	Team management. This style of leadership is considered to be ideal. Such managers have great concern for both people and production. They work to motivate employees to reach their highest levels of accomplishment. They are flexible and responsive to change, and they understand the need to change.

SOURCE: Robert R. Blake and Jane S. Mouton, *The Managerial Grid III* (Houston: Gulf Publishing Company, copyright © 1985), chaps. 1–7. Reproduced by permission.

The Managerial Grid® provides no indication when some other style might be more appropriate than 9,9–9,1, for example. According to this theory, 9,9 is always and everywhere best, and managers should strive to come as close to it as they can. If they develop high levels of concern for both production and people, their concerns will be translated into behavior.[30] The importance of this concern for both people and productivity has intuitive appeal and substantial research support.[31]

Contingency Approaches

The behavioral approaches to leadership contributed significantly to our understanding of leadership by identifying what it is that successful leaders do—what actions they take. But they did not identify when certain actions should be taken. The contingency approaches described here attempted to do that.

Contingency theories propose that for any given situation there is a best way to manage. Contingency theories go beyond the **situational approaches,** which observe that all factors must be considered when leadership decisions are to be made. Contingency theories attempt to isolate those key factors that must be considered and to indicate how to manage given the conditions of those key factors. Six such theories will be reviewed here: those developed by Robert Tannenbaum and Warren H. Schmidt, Fred Fiedler, Robert J. House and Terrence R. Mitchell, Paul Hersey and Kenneth Blanchard, Victor Vroom and P. W. Yetton, and Jan P. Muczyk and Bernard Reimann.

Tannenbaum and Schmidt's Continuum of Leadership Behavior

The first of these contingency models was **Robert Tannenbaum and Warren H. Schmidt's continuum of leadership behavior.**[32] Their model, Figure 15.2, presents seven alternative ways for managers to approach decision making, depending on how much participation they want to allow subordinates in the decision-making process. The actions shown at the left side of the continuum are boss centered and authoritarian. The behaviors at the right side of the continuum are employee centered and participative. The behaviors between the two extremes are gradations from authoritarian to participative approaches. The manager's choices, according to Tannenbaum and Schmidt, depend on three factors:

1. Forces in the manager: the manager's value system, confidence in subordinates, leadership inclinations, and feelings of security in an uncertain situation.
2. Forces in the subordinate: expectations, needs for independence, readiness to assume decision-making responsibility, tolerance for ambiguity in task definition, interest in the problem, ability to understand and identify with the goals of the organization, and knowledge and experience to deal with the problem.
3. Forces in the situation: type of organization, group effectiveness, the problem itself (the task), and the pressure of time.

This model was extremely important because it was the first to frame leadership in terms of the specific behavior choices that managers have. Later, in 1975, research by Jerome Franklin indicated that elements of point 3 of Tannenbaum and Schmidt's model, organizational structure and climate, are more important factors than that model indicates. Leaders must function in accordance with the "rules of the game" set forth by their organizations.[33]

Fiedler's Contingency Model

In **Fred Fiedler's contingency model,** leadership is effective when the leader's style is appropriate to the situation, as determined by three principal factors: the relations between leader and followers, the structure of the task, and the power inherent in the leader's position. These three factors enable the manager to influence (motivate) subordinates. After analyzing these three factors by means of selected questionnaires developed by Fiedler, the manager would choose between task and relationship leadership styles. These three variables are more precisely defined as follows:

1. Leader-member relations: the nature of the interpersonal relationship between the leader and the follower, expressed in terms of good through poor, with qualifying modifiers attached as necessary. Obviously the leader's personality and the personalities of subordinates play important roles in this variable.
2. Task structure: the nature of the subordinate's task, described as "structured" or "unstructured," associated with the amount of creative freedom allowed the subordinate to accomplish the task, and how the task is defined.
3. Position power: the degree to which the position itself enables the leader to get the group members to comply with and accept his or her direction and leadership.[34]

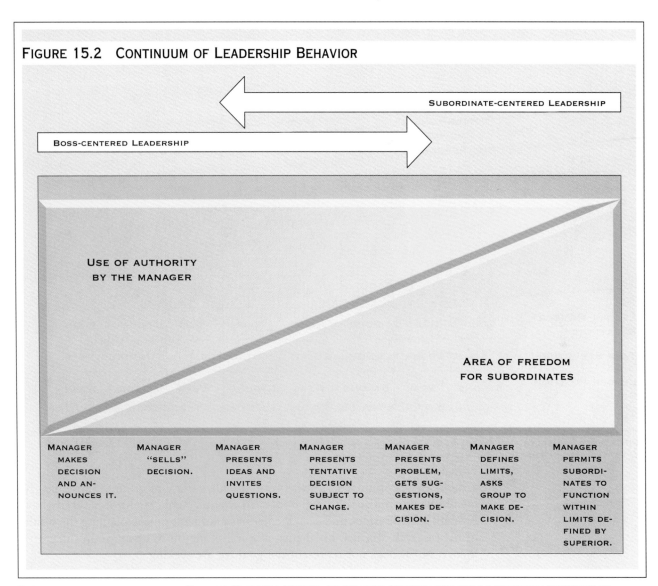

FIGURE 15.2   CONTINUUM OF LEADERSHIP BEHAVIOR

SUBORDINATE-CENTERED LEADERSHIP

BOSS-CENTERED LEADERSHIP

USE OF AUTHORITY
BY THE MANAGER

AREA OF FREEDOM
FOR SUBORDINATES

| MANAGER MAKES DECISION AND ANNOUNCES IT. | MANAGER "SELLS" DECISION. | MANAGER PRESENTS IDEAS AND INVITES QUESTIONS. | MANAGER PRESENTS TENTATIVE DECISION SUBJECT TO CHANGE. | MANAGER PRESENTS PROBLEM, GETS SUGGESTIONS, MAKES DECISION. | MANAGER DEFINES LIMITS, ASKS GROUP TO MAKE DECISION. | MANAGER PERMITS SUBORDINATES TO FUNCTION WITHIN LIMITS DEFINED BY SUPERIOR. |

Fiedler and his associates have compared productivity with the two leadership styles and combinations of the three prime variables. As Figure 15.3 shows, the leader who has good relations with members, a structured task, and strong position power should use a directive (task-oriented) management style because that is the style associated with high productivity under those conditions. Other combinations of "favorable" and "unfavorable" conditions call for the management styles indicated in the rest of the table. Put simplistically, when things are going your way as a manager, you can be task oriented. When they are not, people orientation is necessary, according to this theory. One of Fiedler's conclusions is that the manager should attempt to change the situation to match his or her style.

Fiedler's work, too, has contributed a great deal to leadership theory because it identifies some specific situational factors and the behaviors appropriate when these factors occur in certain combinations. As Robert Vecchio, management researcher and author, has indicated, however, not all of the variables in most managerial situations have been addressed by this research and subsequent theory, and Fiedler's methodology is fundamentally weak in some respects. His

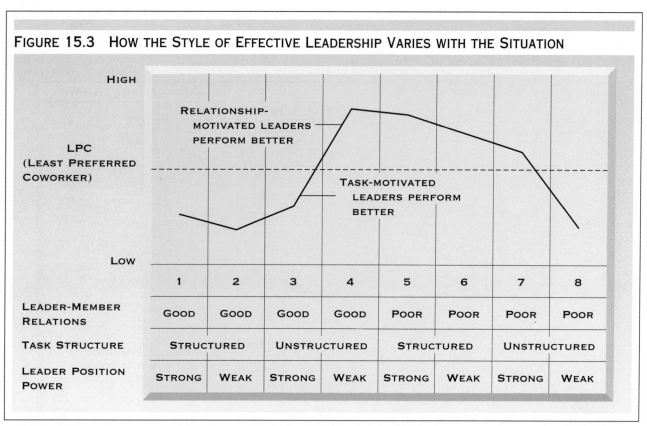

FIGURE 15.3   How the Style of Effective Leadership Varies with the Situation

	1	2	3	4	5	6	7	8
LEADER-MEMBER RELATIONS	GOOD	GOOD	GOOD	GOOD	POOR	POOR	POOR	POOR
TASK STRUCTURE	STRUCTURED		UNSTRUCTURED		STRUCTURED		UNSTRUCTURED	
LEADER POSITION POWER	STRONG	WEAK	STRONG	WEAK	STRONG	WEAK	STRONG	WEAK

SOURCE: FRED E. FIEDLER AND MARTIN M. CHEMERS, LEADERSHIP AND EFFECTIVE MANAGEMENT (GLENVIEW, IL: SCOTT, FORESMAN, 1974), P. 80. REPRINTED BY PERMISSION OF FRED E. FIEDLER.

sample for his original study was from a wide variety of groups. Subsequently, his results may reflect nothing more than chance. Replications of his study have brought mixed results, and even Fiedler has a difficult time explaining the results of his research.[35] Thus, his theory is a milestone on the way to an integrated theory, but it does not represent the goal we are seeking.

Path-Goal Theory

Robert J. House and Terrence R. Mitchell propose that leaders can be effective—that is, effect the satisfaction, motivation, and performance of group members in several ways.[36] The first is by making rewards contingent on the accomplishment of organizational goals—objectives as we have defined them in this text. Second, the leader can aid group members in attaining rewards that are valued by clarifying the paths to those goals and by removing obstacles to performance. This view of leadership depends greatly on the instrumentality-expectancy theory discussed in Chapter 13. In this theory the person to be influenced asks three questions: Can I do the job? If I do the job, will I get the reward? What is the reward worth to me? The leader's activity is designed to show subordinates that first of all a given action will produce a valued reward. Second, the manager must show subordinates that they can be successful at that particular kind of action. The leader's job, after all, is to influence behavior toward performance. According to the path-goal theory, the way to accomplish this is obvious from the instrumentality-expectancy theory. The rewards must be valued and the path to the goal must be clarified and made easier to follow.

According to path-goal theory, there are four primary types of leadership, as shown in Figure 15.4:

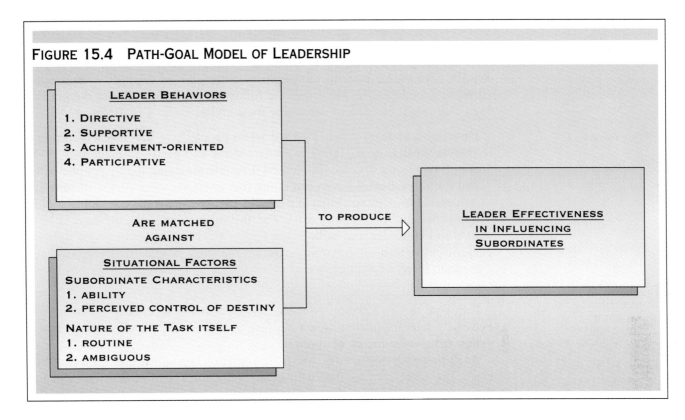

FIGURE 15.4 PATH-GOAL MODEL OF LEADERSHIP

LEADER BEHAVIORS

1. DIRECTIVE
2. SUPPORTIVE
3. ACHIEVEMENT-ORIENTED
4. PARTICIPATIVE

ARE MATCHED AGAINST

SITUATIONAL FACTORS

SUBORDINATE CHARACTERISTICS
1. ability
2. perceived control of destiny

NATURE OF THE TASK ITSELF
1. routine
2. ambiguous

TO PRODUCE

LEADER EFFECTIVENESS IN INFLUENCING SUBORDINATES

1. **Directive leadership:** The leader explains what the performance goal is and provides specific guidance rules and regulations.
2. **Supportive leadership:** The leader displays his or her personal concern for the subordinate. This includes being friendly to subordinates and sensitive to their needs.
3. **Achievement-oriented leadership:** The leader emphasizes the achievement of difficult tasks, emphasizes the importance of excellence of performance, and simultaneously shows confidence that subordinates will perform well. It entails setting challenging goals.
4. **Participative leadership:** In this style the leader consults with subordinates about work, task goals, and paths to resource goals. It involves sharing information, as well as consulting with subordinates before making decisions.

House believes that all four styles can be, should be, and often are used by any individual leader according to situational requirements. Which style is chosen depends on the situational variables, as shown in Figure 15.4.

SITUATIONAL DIFFERENCES

The leader attempts to match his or her style for the particulars of any situation. According to this theory, there are two major differences in leadership situations. The first is related to the nature of the people being led—subordinates. For example, what is their degree of ability and knowledge on this kind of task—is it high or do they need additional training? Furthermore, what is their internal feeling relative to the control of their destiny—do they feel they are in control or do they feel that they are at the mercy of an outside force? A second factor deals with the nature of the job itself. The job may be routine and subordinates may have dealt with the tasks many times and feel comfortable on the basis of task repetition. Or the task may be ambiguous in terms of its definition and their understanding of it, or it may be somewhat new, and it may therefore require the help of someone else, or inventiveness in order to master the task.

There are many different situations in which a manager may find him or herself. Each would have to be diagnosed completely in order to ascertain the correct leadership style. However, the following examples indicate the kind of logic that might be used to determine these styles.

Directive leadership would be used when people have low levels of training and the work they are doing is partly routine and partly ambiguous.

Supportive leadership would be used if people are doing highly routine work and the subordinates have been doing this work for some period of time.

Achievement-oriented leadership would be used if people are doing highly innovative and ambiguous work and the subordinates already have a high level of knowledge and skill.

Participative leadership would be used if the work people are doing possesses medium levels of ambiguity and subordinates have medium levels of experience doing it.

Path-goal theory attempts to merge motivation and leadership theories. It is extremely relevant in that aspect because it is, after all, the influence of motivation that leadership is all about.

Analyzing path-goal theory, one realizes that certain **substitutes for leadership** exist. These are systems that help define behavior and preclude the need for direct managerial actions. For example, if the leader's role is to clarify and make easier the path to the goal, organizational rules and plans, if clear and precise, would be substitutes for leadership, as would very good incentive systems for personal motivational effort. Subordinate ability and routine tasks, or tasks with intrinsic satisfaction, would also be substitutes.[37]

The Hersey-Blanchard Contingency Theory

Like most of the behavioral and contingency theories, the **Hersey-Blanchard contingency (life-cycle) theory** is based on task and relationship behaviors.[38] Each of these dimensions of leadership behavior is represented on an axis of a two-dimensional grid (see Figure 15.5).

The underlying assumption of this model is that the most important factor in determining appropriate leadership behavior is the subordinate's perceived level of maturity. The manager should match his or her style to this maturity level. Maturity has two components: (1) job skill and knowledge, and (2) psychological maturity.

The grid is broken into four quadrants, each quadrant representing a leadership style. The curvilinear subordinate's maturity line enables the manager to know when to use the styles indicated by the grid. The name may be a little misleading; the maturity line does not represent the actual maturity of a subordinate, but rather the amount or degree of task and relationship behaviors in which a manager should engage, given his or her perception of the subordinate's maturity.

For purposes of illustration, assume that a single subordinate begins with a low level of maturity. The manager looks to the subordinate's maturity line to determine what his or her own style should be. As the subordinate's maturity increases (or if it begins at a relatively high level), the emphasis shifts from a high-task, low-relationship orientation to one of high task and high relationship. As the subordinate further matures, the style shifts to one of low task and high

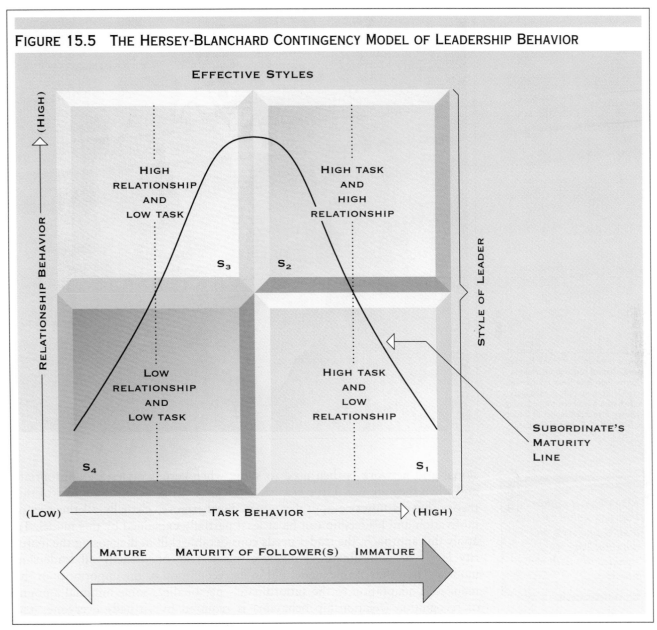

FIGURE 15.5   THE HERSEY-BLANCHARD CONTINGENCY MODEL OF LEADERSHIP BEHAVIOR

SOURCE: FROM PAUL HERSEY AND KENNETH R. BLANCHARD, MANAGEMENT OF ORGANIZATIONAL BEHAVIOR: UTILIZING HUMAN RESOURCES, 4TH ED. © 1982, P. 200. REPRINTED BY PERMISSION OF PRENTICE-HALL, INC., ENGLEWOOD CLIFFS, NEW JERSEY.

relationship. Finally, as the subordinate reaches full maturity, the style shifts to low relationship and low task. At this maturity point, the subordinate should be able to manage him- or herself. The intuitive appeal of this approach is great, and it seems to work in many areas.

There are numerous variations of task and relationship within each style. Ordinarily the changes in task or relationship orientation occur incrementally, in small steps. Few managers make sweeping changes in their styles.

A questionnaire, the Leader Effectiveness and Adaptability Description (LEAD), is administered to managers to determine, first, their most commonly used style; second, the range of this style; and third, the leader's adaptability to the situation—that is, will the leader indeed use the proper style, or continue to use the style he or she is accustomed to using? LEAD tests for the leader's ability to change styles according to subordinate maturity levels. A tridimen-

James Seeley Brown, vice-president of advanced research, and Frank Squires, vice-president of research operations, for Xerox Palo Alto Research Center, are typical of thousands of managers at Xerox who have been trained using the Hersey-Blanchard model of leadership. (SOURCE © Robert Holmgren)

AT AMEX: *It appears that Jim Robinson uses mainly one style and does not vary it significantly with the situation.*

sional grid network is then used to show when certain styles are appropriate and when they are not. Little empirical evidence exists as to the validity of this theory, but its intuitive appeal is great. Furthermore, virtually all theories of motivation and leadership can be at least partially explained by this model. To apply this approach, the leader needs considerable skill in diagnosing the maturity levels of subordinates. However, this is true of virtually all leadership models. The value of this model lies in its recognition of the importance of the manager's adaptation to the subordinate's personality. Some minimal amount of recognition (relationship behavior) is required by virtually everyone, and managers should take this need into account, whether they use the model or not. Most employees will not be productive without some minimal recognition.

This approach successfully identifies an important variable in successful leadership: the match between the characteristics of the manager/leader and those of the subordinate. Many organizations, including Holiday (Inns) Corporation and Xerox Corporation, have adopted this approach. But, like all other leadership approaches to date, it leaves out several important variables that need to be considered: position power, work group dynamics, and the nature of the task, as discussed by Fiedler.

Vroom-Yetton-Yago

In Chapter 3, the Vroom-Yetton-Yago decision-tree model for determining degrees of participative leadership was discussed. The focus in that chapter was on participation as part of basic problem solving. In this chapter the issue is participation from the leader's viewpoint.[39] When do you allow participation?

The Muczyk-Reimann Model[40]

Jan P. Muczyk and Bernard C. Reimann suggest that "participation" behavior is concerned with the degree to which subordinates are allowed to be involved in decision making. They separate this from "direction" which they view as the degree of supervision exercised in the execution of the tasks associated with carrying out the decision. Other authors either combine "direction" with "task," or with "participation." Muczyk and Reimann's distinction is an important one because it allows managers to adapt to different situations. They conclude, as I have, that managers should always emphasize task, relationships, and rewards.[41] Thus, the major issue in adapting style to the situation, they believe, is related to delegation, as applied in both participation and direction. In the Muczyk-Reimann model, the combination of high and low levels of participation and direction leads to four leadership styles that cope with the question of delegation—delegation of decision making and delegation of execution.

The directive autocrat makes decisions unilaterally and closely supervises the activities of subordinates.

The permissive autocrat makes decisions unilaterally but allows subordinates a great deal of latitude in execution.

The directive democrat wants full participation but closely supervises subordinate activity.

The permissive democrat allows high participation in decision making and in execution.

Muczyk and Reimann describe at length situations in which each of these styles might be used. For example, the directive autocrat would function well in situations where time was at a premium and subordinates were less mature in terms of job skills or psychological development. Conversely, with the permissive democrat, plenty of time must be available to make decisions, and subordinates must be very mature.

Perhaps no leadership style change has ever been so great as that attempted by Mikhail Gorbachev, the leader of the Soviet Union. Recognizing that changing situations called for new approaches to management and the need to bring these into the USSR, he boldly moved forward in the late 1980s, as the Global Management Challenge reports.

Leaders as Communicators

Not examined in substantive detail in the leadership literature, but studied a great deal as part of the communication literature, is the need of leaders to use certain communication styles to carry out appropriately their choice of leadership styles. For example, a leader may choose to be supportive but have a very aggressive communication style. In that case the supportive behavior would be totally mitigated by his or her style. Similarly, a leader may choose to be very directive but have a passive communication style that makes the leadership style ineffective. Within the leadership literature, a few studies on communication styles and their effect on leadership success have been performed and suggest the same results as do those in the communications literature. Both suggest that an assertive approach to communication is probably best in all leadership styles, although an aggressive style may be desirable often times for a more task-oriented leadership style.[42] Chapter 16 examines in more detail the manager/leader's role as a communicator.

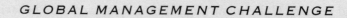

GLOBAL MANAGEMENT CHALLENGE

International Management Gorbachev's Style Is Markedly Different from His Predecessors'

Mikhail Gorbachev is attempting to reshape the entire Soviet economy in his bold campaign of *perestroika,* or "restructuring." To do so, he has adopted *glasnost,* or "openness." Glasnost has been necessary in order to move the economy toward the capitalistic approach for which Gorbachev aims. Soviet Premier Gorbachev's effort to promote glasnost is in direct contrast to the leadership styles of any of his predecessors. In a country known for its absence of openness, it is amazing to see the merit of virtually all major proposals being highly debated in the Soviet press, on television, and even in the streets. It is also amazing to see the various free markets coming into existence within the Soviet Union.

As a major part of perestroika, Gorbachev has reduced the power of formerly powerful central committees and given a great deal of autonomy to plant managers and industry managers throughout the Soviet Union. In 1990, perestroika has not yet met with as much success as Gorbachev had desired. He is, in turn, taking further steps to increase factory performance in order to improve the lot of the Soviet consumer and to improve productivity and the economy. Glasnost also aids him in improving his foreign relations situation relative to arms reduction and other major issues. It shows his willingness to be open on such issues within his own country, a first for a premier in the USSR.

Leadership as a Problem-Solving Process

Figure 15.6 indicates the chapter contents in terms of the standard problem-solving model. The figure shows that a manager's personality, needs, and characteristics would affect all stages of problem solving. For example, a manager with a need to control others might view his or her environment in terms of power struggles. Such a manager might perceive a problem if a subordinate attempts to solve a problem rather than asking for help. The manager's choice of leadership actions to solve problems would definitely be affected by his or her need for power. Similarly, the various management behaviors described in the text—for example, the nineteen identified in Table 15.3, or the more generic task and relationship behaviors—would affect all stages of the decision process, but mostly alternatives, choice, and implementation.

In examining all of the various studies mentioned in this chapter, it becomes clear that several important factors emerge that a manager must take into account in choosing a behavior to engage in: the subordinate's personality and needs, the dynamics of the subordinate's work group, the nature of the subordinate's job, and the overall organizational culture, climate, and structure. These would primarily affect the problems that arise and the choice process, but they

SOURCE: "Reform Is Risky Business," *U.S. News & World Report* (June 19, 1989), pp. 27–28; "The Vote Heard Round the World," *Business Week* (April 10, 1989), pp. 26–27; "The Altar of a Broken Idea," *U.S. News & World Report* (April 3, 1989), pp. 34–55; "Gorbachev Is Making a Bold Bid to Get His Reforms Moving," *Business Week* (June 29, 1987), p. 29; "Reforming the Soviet Economy," *Business Week* (December 7, 1987), pp. 76–88; and "The Risks of a New Revolution," *U.S. News & World Report* (October 19, 1988), pp. 31–58.

Mikhail Gorbachev has begun a transformation of the Soviet Union, using a leadership style never seen in that country before. Part of that style has included improving relationships with various world powers and forces. (SOURCE © Gamma Liaison)

could affect all stages of the process. For example, a manager faced with a problem subordinate, one difficult to motivate, should determine that person's needs and personality and see what impact he or she might have on the choice of leadership styles. He or she would also analyze the job to see if it was demotivating, and which leadership style choices would be best for that job. Finally, he or she would consider the culture and structure of the organization to see what values and rules existed relative to the leadership choices. Taking all of these factors into account simultaneously, the manager would then choose one or more of the available behaviors to influence the employee's motivation, perhaps a disciplinary action.

Drawing upon this figure and materials on motivation, group dynamics, culture, structuring, and climate as discussed elsewhere in this text, a situational model of leadership incorporating the major points of these issues then follows. This *Leadership-TRRAP model* (see Figure 15.7) is a situational model of leadership developed by this author and is based on the belief that leadership is a choice and an action process—a choice and enactment of how to treat people, especially subordinates. We know from the various studies and theories examined thus far in the chapter that there are three points to this process: determinants of behavior, behavioral choices, and the results of leadership behavior. These three issues are depicted in Figure 15.7, which rearranges and refines the

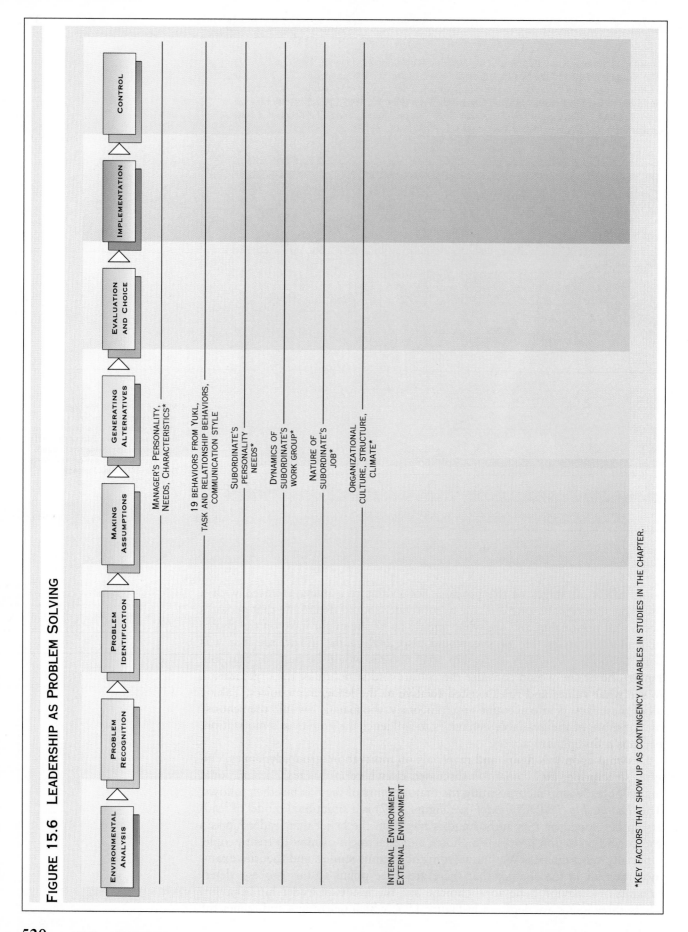

FIGURE 15.6 LEADERSHIP AS PROBLEM SOLVING

ENVIRONMENTAL ANALYSIS → PROBLEM RECOGNITION → PROBLEM IDENTIFICATION → MAKING ASSUMPTIONS → GENERATING ALTERNATIVES → EVALUATION AND CHOICE → IMPLEMENTATION → CONTROL

MANAGER'S PERSONALITY, NEEDS, CHARACTERISTICS*

19 BEHAVIORS FROM YUKL, TASK AND RELATIONSHIP BEHAVIORS, COMMUNICATION STYLE

SUBORDINATE'S PERSONALITY NEEDS*

DYNAMICS OF SUBORDINATE'S WORK GROUP*

NATURE OF SUBORDINATE'S JOB*

ORGANIZATIONAL CULTURE, STRUCTURE, CLIMATE*

INTERNAL ENVIRONMENT
EXTERNAL ENVIRONMENT

*KEY FACTORS THAT SHOW UP AS CONTINGENCY VARIABLES IN STUDIES IN THE CHAPTER.

FIGURE 15.7 THE TRRAP MODEL OF LEADERSHIP

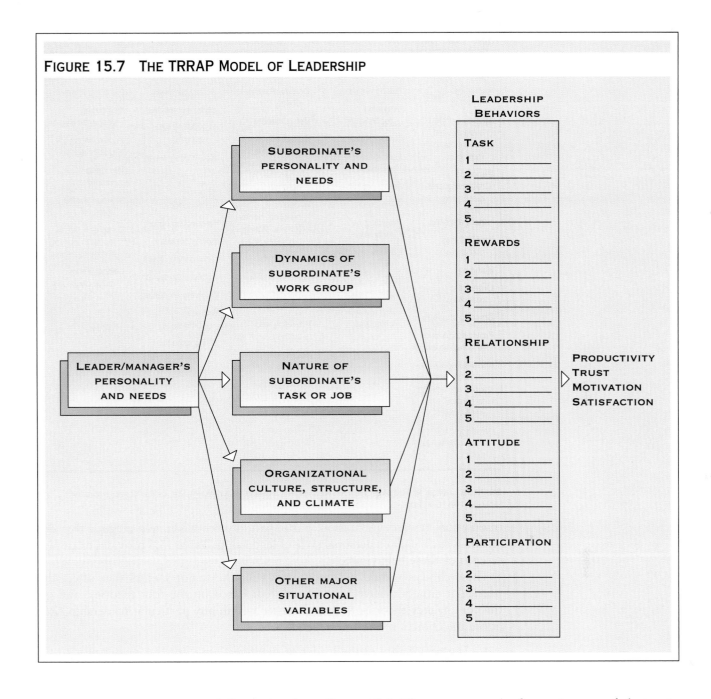

information from Figure 15.6. There appear to be five major sets of choices in behavior: how much and/or what kind of task, relationship, reward, attitude, and participation behaviors to employ or emphasize.

Figure 15.7 includes only five behaviors and not nineteen, as Yukl suggests, because most managers have difficulty keeping track of that many. The ones chosen reflect perceived key summary behaviors, plus an attitude component not addressed in other models. Yukl's nineteen behaviors can be summarized in the form indicated in TRRAP (Task, Reward, Relationship, Attitude and Participation). The attitude component refers to the leader's attitude while engaging in the other four types of behaviors. The attitude component is critical because "how you say it" is just as important, if not more important, than "what you say."[43]

These style choices occupy various positions on a continuum, as suggested by Figure 15.8. It is the consistent combination of task orientation, relationship

Table 15.5. Behaviors Associated with the Elements of the TRRAP Model

Task	Reward	Relationship	Attitude	Participation
Assigning objectives	Giving raises	Communicating openly	Acting passively	Deciding jointly
Making certain subordinates know how to do their jobs	Providing recognition	Being friendly	Being submissive	Delegating responsibility
	Giving praise	Supporting subordinates with top management when they're right	Not saying what you think	Implementing quality control
Periodically reviewing and discussing others' performances	Patting people on the back		Not making waves	Using job enrichment
	Being equitable	Attending to others' personal needs (family, illness, birthdays, etc.)	Acting assertively	Asking for others' opinions
Emphasizing objectives	Giving promotions		Showing impatience	
	Providing incentives	Building trust	Respecting others	Using others' inputs in making choices
Planning			Acting honestly	
Organizing resources	Publicly reporting successes	Working well with groups	Confronting others	Letting others make decisions
	Tying rewards to performance	Listening to others	Acting aggressively	
Creating structure		Providing ego support	Showing contempt	
Providing direction to achieve goals	Tying rewards to objectives		Showing indifference	
Knowing how to do subordinates' jobs well enough to correct performance		Representing values of group	Being deceitful	
		Working with informal group leader		
Developing subordinates' job skills				

SOURCE: JAMES M. HIGGINS, HUMAN RELATIONS BEHAVIOR AT WORK, 2E, (NEW YORK: RANDOM HOUSE, 1987), P. 209.

orientation, reward orientation, participation orientation, and attitude that determines each leader's personal style of leadership. Table 15.5 provides examples of each of these behaviors.

These choices should be made only after the major factors that affect the particular situation have been considered. Based on the trait theories, and on the contingency theories reviewed earlier within any particular leadership situation, the choices made will depend on

1. The personality of the leader or manager, especially his or her needs.
2. The personalities of the subordinates, especially their needs.
3. The dynamics of the group.
4. The particular task or job of the subordinate in which the leader or manager is concerned with influencing performance.
5. The organization's culture, structure, and climate.
6. Other major situational variables.

According to this model, the overall context of the situation provides an environment within which the manager must function. The manager's choices and rational or learned responses must be adapted to the environment created by the personalities of the people involved in the situation; the dynamics of the subordinate's work group; the nature of the task or job; the culture, structure, and climate of the organization; and all other major factors that affect the situation. Knowing just how much task, relationship, reward, and participation behaviors to use and what attitude to take while using them is critical to a manager's success.

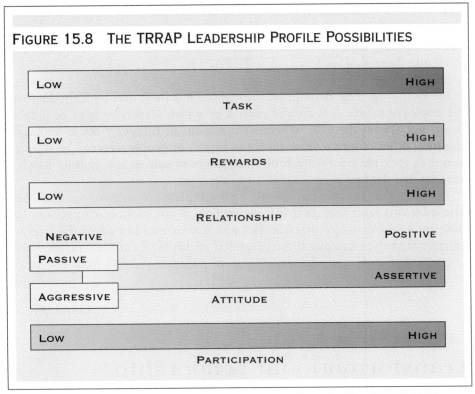

FIGURE 15.8 THE TRRAP LEADERSHIP PROFILE POSSIBILITIES

SOURCE: JAMES M. HIGGINS, HUMAN RELATIONS BEHAVIOR AT WORK, 2E, (NEW YORK: RANDOM HOUSE, 1987), P. 208.

The TRRAP model of leadership is based primarily on the following concepts:

1. Managers have choices in leadership behaviors. These choices are contingent on several factors.

2. The behaviors from which the leader may choose are many, but several have been shown to be appropriate most of the time.

3. The leader's personality and needs affect the choice process, and these factors need to be taken into account.

4. Probably the single most important factor to be considered in making these choices is the subordinate's or other person's personality and needs.

5. Several studies have pointed to the need to include the group's dynamics within the process because a leader, after all, leads a group, not just individuals.

6. The task or job of the subordinate is important to the leader's choice of behavior. Some tasks require closer supervision than others, for example.

7. Organizational culture, structure, and climate play important roles in the process because any manager's decisions must be made within the structure of the guidelines, rules, procedures, policies, and authority distributions of the organization.

8. Other variables may enter into the process: time, for example. The leader who has only a limited time to make a critical decision will probably find that a participative style is not a viable alternative, for example.

9. In the long run, those behaviors that increase or maintain subordinates' self-image are the types of behaviors in which managers should engage. In the short run, negative leadership behaviors will be effective, but the long-term consequences may be disastrous.

10. When the appropriate behaviors are chosen, motivation, productivity, satisfaction, and trust result.

11. Trust is an important ingredient in this process and is highly correlated with continued performance.[44]

12. Managers have five primary choices: task, reward, relationship, attitude, and degrees of participation—TRRAP.

One final note: The assumption throughout has been that both productivity and employee satisfaction are the criteria by which leadership is to be judged. This is not always the case. When organizations or followers desire managers who meet other criteria—yes-men, for example, or people who can be counted on not to rock the boat—much of what has been said in this chapter has less meaning than it should.

The successful manager today must be a complete leader/manager. The complete leader/manager realizes that there are few, if any, cookbook solutions. The complete leader/manager practices not just one or two but all of the relevant managerial skills, especially those presented in this book, and the management functions that are usually discussed in an introductory management course.

Leadership at the Top: Transformational Leadership[45]

In recent years the study of leadership has focused on leadership in small groups, which is applicable throughout the organization, and transformational leadership, which is principally applicable at the upper levels of an organization. James McGregor Burns, the formulator of the term *transactional leadership*, has identified two types of political leadership: transactional and transformational.[46] **Transactional leadership** occurs when one individual approaches others for the purpose of exchanging something that is valued. That is, the leader will exchange something he or she values for something that followers value. **Transformational leadership** involves shifting beliefs, needs, and values for followers. It is more than simply asking for the compliance of followers. According to Burns, "the result of transforming leadership is the result of mutual stimulation elevation that converts followers into leaders and may convert leaders into morale agents."[47]

Bernard Bass, management author and leadership researcher, has applied Burns's ideas to organizational management.[48] He notes that transactional leaders "look to consider how to marginally improve and maintain the quantity and quality of performance, how to substitute one goal for another, how to reduce resistance of particular actions, and how to implement decisions,"[49] This, then is typical of the type of small-group leadership this chapter has emphasized. However, Bass goes on to note that, in contrast, transformational leaders "attempt and succeed in raising colleagues, subordinates, followers, clients, or constituencies to a greater awareness about the issues of consequence. This heightening of awareness requires a leader with vision, self-confidence, and inner strength to argue successfully for what he [or she] sees as right or good, not for what is popular or acceptable according to established norms."[50] Bass notes that charisma is also an important part of transformational leadership. He identifies Lee Iaccocca as the premier example of a transformational leader with vision and charisma. He also argues that such leadership occurs not only at the top of organizations, but may occur anywhere throughout the organization if

Lee Iacocca transformed his company from one on the verge of bankruptcy, to one able to compete in the modern auto industry. To do so, he had to have a vision, and he had to convey that vision to his employees. He elicited their emotional commitment by making them believe that they could succeed, and by rewarding them for doing so. (SOURCE © Wally McNamee/Woodfin Camp & Associates)

the manager involved understands and seizes the opportunity to be transformational. He cites a case in which a military sergeant can transform his troops into extremely loyal followers.[51] As organizations face more change and increased levels of competition, it appears that transformational leadership will be vital to their success.

Noel M. Tichy and David O. Ulrich have identified three key programs of activities associated with transformational leadership. The first is the creation of a vision, the second is mobilization of commitment to that vision, and the third is institutionalization of change throughout the organization. Transformational leaders engage in these activities in order to transform their organizations and their subordinates into willing agents of change.[52] Tichy and Mary Anne Devanna have examined the case histories of numerous leaders who were transformational—the types of leaders who will be absolutely essential to success in the future as organizations go through changeful environments.[53] They concluded that organizations must train their leaders to be transformational and must promote managers to leadership positions who will transform the organization.

The Management Challenges Identified

1. The changing nature of employees, their needs, and expectations
2. Increased levels of change and competition

Some Solutions Noted
in the Chapter

1. Transformational leadership
2. Increased levels of participation
3. The changing emphasis on different types of leadership behavior

Summary

1. Leadership is the making of choices and the carrying out of those choices in order to influence people's motivation.
2. A manager is not necessarily a leader but should be. Leaders are concerned with effectiveness, managers with effectiveness and efficiency. Leaders receive their power from their followers, managers from the authority of the organization.
3. There are five bases of power: legitimate, reward, coercive, expert, and referent.
4. Existing contingency models point in certain directions, but none is totally predictive of appropriate managerial leadership behavior.
5. Certain managerial behaviors seem to lead to successful managerial leadership most of the time: high task, high relationship, high reward, positive and assertive attitude, and medium to high levels of participation.
6. Transformational leadership is becoming increasingly critical to successful organizational management in a rapidly changing world.

Thinking About Management

1. Indicate the major differences between leadership and management.
2. Describe leadership as a process of influence.
3. Describe leadership as a choice process.
4. Why did the trait theory not hold up? On the other hand, why does a skills approach seem to have some merit?
5. Are you a Theory X or a Theory Y person?
6. Which of Yukl's nineteen behaviors are more likely to be important in the future? Why?
7. Which of the management grid styles is best? Why?
8. How do you determine which style to use with the Hersey-Blanchard model?
9. What does path-goal theory contribute to leadership style?
10. Explain the contribution of the Muczyk-Reimann model.
11. Describe a leadership situation you have seen and indicate how the leader should have handled it, using the TRRAP model.

Federal Express's Leadership Development Program

Federal Express executives wanted managers to "experience" leadership, not just read about it. They wanted their managers to develop four qualities: the ability to understand others, to understand one's self, to learn from the feedback from others, and to calculate and take risks. They had a useful series of classroom exercises, but they wanted something where leadership really had to be used. They chose the "wilderness experience." They saw the wilderness as a metaphor for the corporate jungle. Participants would be faced with seemingly insurmountable problems that require quick and creative solutions and built teamwork. They chose to have a series of outdoor physical activities in a remote location that would have an immediate, tangible impact on people. Human resource department staff members set out to design a program to do just that.

DISCUSSION QUESTIONS
1. What approaches would you take?
2. Design such a program.

SOURCE: Based on William H. Wagel, "An Unorthodox Approach to Leadership Development," *Personnel* (July 1986), pp. 4–6; also see Jeremy Main, "Wanted: Leaders Who Can Make a Difference," *Fortune* (September 28, 1987), pp. 92–102.

Transforming a Law Firm

MANAGERS AT WORK

William C. Martin, managing partner and chairman of the board of Akerman, Senterfitt & Eidson, a thirty-partner, one hundred eighty-person law firm, pondered his firm's future. His firm, like all law firms, faced increasing levels of competition. New firms often used low price strategies in order to acquire business. Thus, the firm was vulnerable to losing some of its clients and some of the business with any client where no clear advantage could be demonstrated to justify the firm's higher fees.

The firm only hired law students in the top fifteen to twenty percent of their class from the various law schools at which they recruited, so it always had top talent. But attorneys were changing in terms of the needs that dominated their work habits. Associates simply were, in most cases, not willing to put in the same kind of hours as the existing partners. They were concerned about family, leisure, and other personal issues. Increasing billable hours was a major concern of the firm, and motivating associates to work longer hours was a primary concern of Bill's and the management committee.

The firm had been seeking a way to differentiate itself from others. It had settled on a full-service, high-quality approach, but somehow that didn't sit well with Bill. Most other large firms would be attempting a similar strategy, and he wasn't sure that his firm would be clearly differentiated.

The firm believed in participation and providing a high quality of life for its members. Yet, it needed a vision that probably only one partner, the managing partner, could provide. Bill was a studious, articulate, and rather quiet leader, not given to flamboyance. He was surrounded by many large egos and knew that he had to balance many needs and wants in shaping a vision for the firm, in transforming it to compete in the 1990s.

But shape a vision he must. He sat looking out over the city's skyline, contemplating how to go about transforming his law firm.

DISCUSSION QUESTIONS
1. How does transformation occur? What would it really mean in the case of this law firm?
2. What might be a suitable vision?
3. How might Bill go about being "the leader" in a participatory firm?

MANAGE YOURSELF

Self-Assessment of Managerial Style

A major challenge facing virtually all managers is how to solve their people-production problems. Grid OD provides managers with an opportunity to evaluate their managerial style and identify alternative ways of managing for increased enterprise effectiveness. To assess your own managerial style, respond to the following items according to how you would likely behave if you were a manager. Each item describes an aspect of managerial behavior. Circle whether you would probably behave in the way described: Always (A), Frequently (F), Occasionally (O), Seldom (S), or Never (N).

If I were a work group manager, . . .

1. I would act as group spokesperson	A	F	O	S	N
2. I would allow group members complete freedom in their work	A	F	O	S	N
3. I would encourage the use of uniform procedures	A	F	O	S	N
4. I would permit group members to use their own judgment in solving problems	A	F	O	S	N
5. I would needle group members for greater effort	A	F	O	S	N
6. I would let group members perform their jobs the way they think best	A	F	O	S	N
7. I would keep the work moving at a rapid pace	A	F	O	S	N
8. I would settle conflicts when they occur in the group	A	F	O	S	N
9. I would decide what should be done and how it should be done	A	F	O	S	N
10. I would turn group members loose on a job and let them go to it	A	F	O	S	N
11. I would be reluctant to allow group members any freedom of action	A	F	O	S	N
12. I would assign group members to particular jobs	A	F	O	S	N
13. I would push for increased production	A	F	O	S	N
14. I would be willing to make changes	A	F	O	S	N
15. I would schedule the work to be done	A	F	O	S	N
16. I would persuade others that my ideas are to their advantage	A	F	O	S	N
17. I would refuse to explain my actions	A	F	O	S	N
18. I would permit the group to set its own pace	A	F	O	S	N

Scoring

1. Underscore the item numbers for activities 1, 3, 5, 7, 9, 11, 13, 15, and 17.
2. Write a "1" next to the underscored items to which you responded A (Always) or F (Frequently).
3. Write a "1" next to the items *not* underscored to which you responded A (Always) or F (Frequently).
4. Circle the "1s" which you have written next to items 2, 4, 6, 8, 10, 12, 14, 16, and 18.
5. Count the circled "1s." This is your *concern for people* score.
6. Count the uncircled "1s." This is your *concern for production* score.

SOURCE: Adapted from Thomas J. Sergiovanni, Richard Metzcus, and Larry Burden, "Toward a Particularistic Approach to Leadership Style: Some Findings," *American Educational Research Journal* 6 (January 1969), 62–79. © 1969, American Educational Research Association, Washington, D.C. By permission of the publisher.

CHAPTER SIXTEEN

Managing Communication

CHAPTER OBJECTIVES

When you have completed this chapter, you should be able to

1. Describe the functions of communication in an organization.

2. List the seven steps in communication.

3. Indicate the importance of communication.

4. Discuss the various forms of verbal and nonverbal communication and paralanguage.

5. Identify the barriers to communicating effectively.

6. Explain how listening skills can be developed.

7. Discuss the use of organizational communication approaches.

8. Improve managerial communications.

9. Identify how electronics is changing communications.

CHAPTER OUTLINE

The Functions of Communication
  The Emotive Function
  The Motivation Function
  The Information Function
  The Control Function
  Achieving These Functions
The Communication Process
  Ideation
  Encoding
  Transmission
  Communication Channels
  Receiving
  Decoding
  Understanding and Action
  Feedback
The Sender and Receiver: Perception and Other Issues
Forms of Communication
  Verbal Communication
  Listening
  Nonverbal Communication
Communicating in Organizations
  Formal Communication
  Informal Communication
Common Barriers to Communication
  Language Limitations
  Speaking and Listening Habits
  Physical and Social Differences
  Timing
  Wordiness
  Characteristics of the Sender and Receiver: Personality, Role, Status, Perception, and Self-image
  Overload
Coping with Barriers to Communication
Organizational Communication
  Structural Approaches
  Informational Approaches
The Portable Manager: Technology Changes Communication
Communication as a Problem-Solving Exercise
The Management Challenges Identified
Some Solutions Noted in the Chapter

Monday Morning Management

Art Williams, CEO of the giant A. L. Williams Insurance Company, wondered how he could reach the members of some one thousand branches spread throughout the United States. He wanted to be able to talk to them and he wanted the people in those branches to be able to talk back to him. He wanted to be personal, but he couldn't talk to each employee individually. The solution was a program called "Monday Morning Management."

Television, says Williams, "is the most awesome thing in American business today." Each week Williams stars as the host of a Monday morning program sent to his one thousand branches. It is a combination revival hour and sales report. The program begins something like this:

"Live, from the Atlanta studios of the ALW-TV, the Common Sense Network, it's 'Monday Morning Management' with host Arthur L. Williams."

(Enter the balding emcee, wearing a red sport shirt.)

Williams: "Good morning everybody. My butt's on fire!"

(While the applause resounds from the studio audience.)

Williams: "We're not going to get fat and lazy like those other companies in America, right?"

Audience: "Right!"

"This ain't a dad-burned business, it's a dad-burned family, right?"

"Right!"

The A. L. Williams Company is by far the largest convert to the television show approach to communication. This media blitz seems to work. The A. L. Williams Company has the largest annual sales in the life insurance business. Williams actively involves members of his staff in his shows. The best salesmen are awarded with visits to the company's $5 million broadcast center to see tapings of the show. After the show Williams often convenes impromptu video conferences with vice-presidents around the country. Williams's success will obviously cause others to follow. On a lesser scale, firms such as J. C. Penney, Merrill Lynch, Ford, Domino's Pizza, and Federal Express have all ventured into periodic and often frequent television shows to their employees.

SOURCE: "Broadcast News, Inc.," *Newsweek* (January 4, 1988), pp. 34–35.

Perfect understanding between human beings is impossible. Grasp that concept.

James W. Newman
Communications expert

We rule men with words.

Napoleon Bonaparte

Communication is the transfer of information from one communicator to another through the use of symbols. For communication to be complete, both parties must understand what has been transferred. Every management function involves communication.[1] In fact, the second activity that all managers share in addition to problem solving is communication.[2] The understanding and proper use of communication are therefore essential to successful management. It may even be a manager's most important activity.[3] Most managers are more ineffective at communications than they would like to admit. Few actively practice the skill, they just engage in it. Most seem to take for granted that they know how to communicate. All too often, they don't. A. L. Williams recognizes the importance of letting people know about what is going on in their company. That's why he has turned to television to get his message across. He also recognizes the tremendous revolution that is occurring in communication as electronics—fax machines, television, cellular phones, and computers—makes instantaneous communication across vast distances a reality.

The average manager spends 50 to 70 percent of his or her time communicating in some way.[4] Professionals, staff, and first-line employees often communicate as much as or more than managers do. The coordination that is required to achieve organizational objectives depends on effective communication. Yet, few organization members really know how to communicate effectively. Perhaps that is why many organizations fail to achieve their objectives.

Sam Walton, CEO and owner of Wal-Mart, is so convinced of the importance of communication to achieve objectives that he personally visits the managers of each of the company's more than 750 stores at least once a year. At the company's annual meeting, he can call every manager by name and recall details of each store's operations. His concern for communication reflects his concern for people.[5]

This chapter first briefly examines the functions of communication and then explores the basic communication process by means of a two-communicator model. The various verbal and nonverbal forms of communication are then explored. You may be surprised to discover just how many ways of communicating exist and how they complement or detract from one another. It is just as important to know the meanings conveyed by finger pointing as it is the words that may accompany the gesture. The common problems associated with effective communication are noted, and some of the solutions to these problems are suggested. Systems to improve communication are reviewed. Finally, there is a brief discussion of the electronic revolution in communication. Chapter 19 covers these issues in more detail.

"Live from Atlanta, it's Monday Morning with Art Williams." It may not be "Saturday Night Live," but it is a dynamite show serving the needs of its listeners just as well. Television broadcasting offers many advantages to a geographically dispersed company attempting to keep its employees motivated. (SOURCE © Rob Nelson/Picture Group)

Sam Walton communicates with his people. He knows about them, and he participates with them in many activities. That management style, that open communication is one reason he has been so successful in business. (SOURCE © Eli Reichman)

The Functions of Communication

William G. Scott and Terrence R. Mitchell, management authors, have identified four major functions of communication within the organization: the emotive, motivation, information, and control functions.[6] A communication normally involves at least one of these functions, and often more than one.

The Emotive Function

It is people who communicate, even when one of the communicators is a group or organization. People have emotions. They express these emotions to others through communication. The emotive function is oriented toward feelings. Within the organizational framework, the organization's objective with this type of communication is to increase acceptance of organizational actions. But informally, satisfaction, dissatisfaction, happiness, bitterness, and the entire range of human emotions may be expressed.

Holiday Inns, Inc., is so concerned with the emotional side of its customer service business that it requires the managers of its hotels to train their employees to handle upset customers. A standardized program for dealing with various emotional issues is incorporated into its comprehensive customer satisfaction program, known as "The First Concern."[7]

AT A. L. WILLIAMS:
Art Williams uses his "Monday Morning Management" show not only to inform, but to motivate, partly through emotional pitches, but also by inviting top salespeople to see the show live as a reward.

The Motivation Function

Motivation, in this context, is **influence**, the ability or process of affecting the behavior of others. Communication concerned with motivation is designed to elicit commitment to the organization's objectives. Virtually all motivation (influence) approaches detailed in Chapter 13, plus the leadership approaches you read about in Chapter 15, are entailed in this type of communication. Leaders lead—that is, they make choices among ways to treat people in order to influence their motivation. Most of the major activities of leaders, especially those activities concerned with the implementation of plans, require communication. Instructing, rewarding, disciplining, informing subordinates about objectives, and defining roles all require communication. Outside the organization, we all engage in efforts to influence others, to influence their motivation. We do so by communicating.

The Information Function

Decision making depends on information. The organizational objective of this communication function is to provide the information necessary for decision making. The information involved is often technical. Financial information, for example, is the technical information necessary to make major purchase decisions—for example, about plant and equipment. Much of the communication involved in the information function takes place through the organization's formal management-information system. Anytime a manager wishes to make a decision about anything, he or she needs information—which meeting to go to, what to do when the plane arrives, where the lecture is to be given. A manager learns these bits of information through communication.

The Control Function

Reports, policies, and plans function to control the behaviors of an organization's members. They define roles; clarify duties, authority, and responsibilities; and provide organizational structure (defined as jobs and the authority to do them). By routinizing organizational activity, by providing a means of checking for achievement of objectives, these types of communication further the mission of an organization. In other contexts, with friends, parents, spouses, children, bankers, and waiters—for just about anyone whose behavior anyone wishes to influence—this effort requires some form of communication.

Achieving These Functions

Achieving these four functions of communication will become increasingly difficult as the cultural diversity, demographics, and expectations of the work force change, as business becomes more global, and as change in all phases of business accelerates. Yet, the need to achieve these will increase as competition accelerates and more expression of concern for people is needed in the face of an increasingly technological work place.

The Communication Process

The communication process, shown in Figure 16.1, begins when the sender, whether a person, a group, or an organization, has a thought, feeling, idea, or concept that the sender wishes to share with another entity, the receiver.[8] This message must be **encoded**, or put into symbols, in a form that the receiver can easily recognize. Transmission may be verbal or nonverbal. Communications can be transmitted in person, in print, in memos, on television, or by any medium. The message is received through the senses—hearing, sight, feeling, touch, smell—and by intuition.

Once the message has been transmitted, it must be **decoded**, or interpreted, by the receiver. The receiver transforms the message into thought and (ideally)

Figure 16.1 A Basic Model of Communication

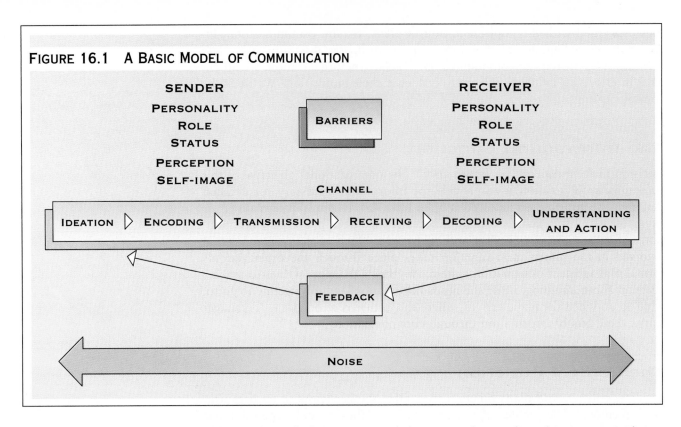

understands or finds its meaning. Are you understanding this message? If not, is it you or I—the receiver or the sender—who is at fault? Or is the message being interfered with by some external factor (noise) or by some internal factor pertaining to the sender or receiver or both? Such factors as personality, role, status, perception, and self-image have an impact on the process. They affect the sender's ideation, encoding, and transmission of the message, and they have an equal impact on the way the receiver receives, decodes, understands, and acts on that message. Finally, if communication is to be effective, the sender must receive feedback from the receiver during or after the communication process.

Ideation

The conception of an idea or a thought is known as **ideation**. Ideation is the first step in the communication process. Ideation encompasses all that occurs before the idea is encoded—that is, before it is placed in an understandable language for transmission. Consider an individual who has developed a new product, a social group that has established norms of acceptable behavior, or an organization that has established rules and procedures for achieving its objectives. The conceptions of the product, the norms, and the rules all occur as part of the ideation process. Before the product developer, the group, or the organization can convey a message, it must have formulated an idea.

Encoding

The person, group, or organization that wishes to communicate must place the message in some transmittable language, either verbal or nonverbal. The essence of **encoding** is to put ideas into symbols that others will understand. Verbal languages include not only oral encodings, but written language and silence, as well. Nonverbal languages may be as simple as body movements or as complex as a work of art that conveys many messages in a language all its own. The individual's personality, the personality of group members, and the personalities of organizational members who are given the task of encoding messages greatly affect the encoding process and the subsequent content of the message. Each person has his or her own perception of what a message should accomplish and how it should be symbolized. Encoding requires the careful selection of the appropriate verbal or nonverbal symbols to convey the exact idea that was originally conceived. Unfortunately, symbols can only represent and approximate the idea, thus complicating the process.[9]

If you have ever had to write rules, directives, policies, procedures, or the like for others to follow, you know the difficulty involved in the encoding process. We often must write and rewrite, practice and repractice our communications until the message is exactly as we would like it to be. And even then we sometimes fail to communicate. One example of the difficulties of the encoding process is the instructions for assembling bicycles, lawnmowers, barbecue grills, and fertilizer spreaders. If you have never tried to follow such directions you should. Manufacturers' encodings often leave a lot to be desired. For some incorrect encodings, see Table 16.1, "Say What You Mean."

Table 16.1. Say What You Mean

It is said that back in the 1940s, the following message was prominently displayed at the front of the main chemistry lecture hall at a major university.

"The English language is your most versatile scientific instrument. Learn to use it with precision."

In the intervening years, the teaching of proper grammar in the public elementary and high schools fell into disfavor. The inevitable result is that the manuscripts submitted to us are often full of grammatical errors, which their authors probably do not recognize (and often would not care about if they did).

We regard this state of affairs as deplorable, and we want to do something about it. For many years we have tried to correct the grammar of papers that we publish. This is toilsome at best, and sometimes entails rather substantial rephrasing. It would obviously be preferable to have authors use correct grammar in the first place. The problem is how to get them to do it.

One fairly effective way is to provide examples of what not to do; it is particularly helpful if the examples are humorous. We have recently seen several grammatical examples of this type. A few weeks ago we found, taped to a colleague's office door, the most complete one we have seen. (He tells us it was passed out in a class at Dartmouth—not in an English class—at the time a term paper was assigned.) We reproduce it here in the hope that it will have some effect. (Each sentence contains the error it describes.)

1. Make sure each pronoun agrees with their antecedent.
2. Just between you and I, the case of pronouns is important.
3. Watch out for irregular verbs which have crope into English.
4. Verbs have to agree in number with their subject.
5. Don't use no double negatives.
6. Being bad grammar, a writer should not use dangling modifiers.
7. Join clauses like a conjunction should.
8. A writer must not shift your point of view.
9. About sentence fragments.
10. Don't use run-on sentences you got to punctuate.
11. In letters essays and reports use commas to separate items in a series.
12. Don't use commas, which are not necessary.
13. Parenthetical words however should be enclosed in commas.
14. Its important to use apostrophes right in everybodys writing.
15. Don't abbrev.
16. Check and see if you any words out.
17. In the case of a report, check to see that jargon wise, it's A-OK.
18. As far as incomplete constructions, they are wrong.
19. About repetition, the repetition of a word might be real effective repetition—take, for instance the repetition of Abraham Lincoln.
20. In my opinion, I think that an author when he is writing should definitely not get into the habit of making use of too many un-necessary words that he does not really need in order to put in his message.
21. Use parallel construction not only to be concise but also to clarify.
22. It behooves us all to avoid archaic expressions.
23. Mixed metaphors are a pain in the neck and ought to be weeded out.
24. Consult the dictionary to avoid misspellings.
25. To ignorantly split an infinitive is a practice to religiously avoid.
26. Last but not least, lay off cliches.

SOURCE: "Grammar," *Physical Review Letters* (March 19, 1979), pp. 747–748. Reprinted by permission of George L. Trigg.

Transmission

Once the sender has determined the content of the message, it is transmitted across one or more of the available channels—the method of transmission. Channels may include the spoken word, body movements, the written word, television, radio, an artist's paint, electronic mail—anything through which a message is transmitted. Each medium has certain advantages over others; some may be used in certain situations but not in others. For example, organizations that communicate information to employees via television have found this medium to be superior in many ways to company newspapers. But not all organizations can afford television and must use company newsletters or newspapers. Speed of message delivery, cost effectiveness, and availability are important considerations when choosing a channel and a medium. After all, a picture is worth a thousand words. In fact, fax machines, which allow you to send pictures and other messages visually over telephone lines, are becoming so important to doing business today that not having one can pose major problems for small-business people. Mark Eisen, director of marketing for Retail Planning Associates of Columbus, Ohio, goes so far as to say that he wonders about firms without fax machines: "What's wrong—a gap in management sophistication?"[10]

Oral communication most often flows between individuals. A leader who talks to a group of followers may be speaking as an individual; but if the leader is speaking on behalf of an organization, it is the organization that is communicating with the group. Once the transmission is under way, the message is no longer under the sender's control. It is then up to the receiver to receive the message, decode it, and extract meaning. Feedback from receiver to sender may cause the sender to restate the message in order to improve the receiver's understanding.

Communication Channels

Managers may choose from a variety of channels over which to communicate to subordinates, managers, and others in the organization. Memos, telephone, face-to-face conversation, and interactive video programs are but a few choices available. Richard L. Daft and Robert H. Lengel discuss how managers choose among communication channels in order to enhance communication effectiveness.[11] They found that channels differ in their capacity for communicating information. This capacity is influenced by three principal characteristics:

1. The ability to handle multiple cues simultaneously—for example, eye, face, hand, and body-language indicators.
2. The ability to facilitate rapid feedback.
3. The ability to establish a personal focus for the communication.

The degree to which these three criteria can be satisfied is called **channel richness.** It is the amount of information that can be transmitted during a communication episode. The hierarchy of channel richness is illustrated in Figure 16.2. As you can see, face-to-face conversation involving physical presence is the richest channel and is best used for nonroutine, ambiguous, and difficult messages. At the other end of the hierarchy are impersonal static channels—those that do not allow for feedback—such as fliers, bulletins, and general reports; these are quite sufficient for routine, clear, and simple messages. Managers must be extremely careful in choosing a channel, to make sure that it has the right level of richness for the message. If it doesn't the message may not be understood and acted upon.[12]

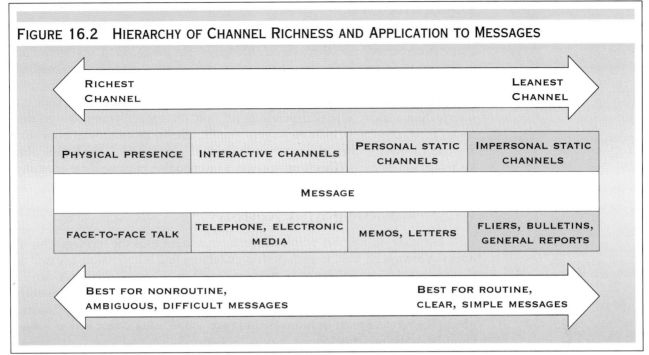

FIGURE 16.2   HIERARCHY OF CHANNEL RICHNESS AND APPLICATION TO MESSAGES

RICHEST CHANNEL

LEANEST CHANNEL

PHYSICAL PRESENCE	INTERACTIVE CHANNELS	PERSONAL STATIC CHANNELS	IMPERSONAL STATIC CHANNELS
MESSAGE			
FACE-TO-FACE TALK	TELEPHONE, ELECTRONIC MEDIA	MEMOS, LETTERS	FLIERS, BULLETINS, GENERAL REPORTS

BEST FOR NONROUTINE, AMBIGUOUS, DIFFICULT MESSAGES

BEST FOR ROUTINE, CLEAR, SIMPLE MESSAGES

SOURCE: FIGURE, "HIERARCHY OF CHANNEL RICHNESS AND APPLICATION TO MESSAGES" FROM MANAGEMENT BY RICHARD L. DAFT, COPYRIGHT © 1988 BY THE DRYDEN PRESS, A DIVISION OF HOLT, RINEHART AND WINSTON, INC., REPRINTED BY PERMISSION OF THE PUBLISHER.

Walter St. John, director of educational services and management development of National Food Associates, recommends the following guidelines for channel selection:

1. Important messages should be shared, both orally and in writing.
2. Face-to-face communication is usually best; don't rely too heavily on written communication.
3. Provide for feedback.
4. Use a variety of media.
5. Customize the medium—for example, create a television program (channel) just for the organization.
6. Be sure you understand the message and follow up on it.
7. Be cautious about using cost criterion in choosing channels.[13]

Choosing the best channel is a complex process, and there is not always a "best" channel. For example, two key issues are clarity and feedback. Memos, graphs, and reports provide clarity. Telephones, interactive videos, and face-to-face conversations allow for feedback.[14]

Receiving

The process of **receiving** a message is more complex than you might assume. The various senses must work in combination to detect the message and subsequently report it to the brain. There, the perceptual set, a person's remembered experiences, will be consulted and meaning will be given to the perceived message. Ideally, understanding and action will result. Numerous factors affect the receiving process, including the degree to which the senses and brain area already engaged in other activities, the individual's sensory and extrasensory capabilities (such as intuition), and one's current physical and mental capacities. External noise, interference of any type, also affects the receiving process. The ability to listen is a critical skill that is discussed later in more detail.

Decoding

The sensory information that arrives from the sender must undergo **decoding**—that is, interpretation by the receiver. Messages that are received are interpreted in light of all factors that affect the perceptual process: selectivity, stereotyping, the receiver's self-image, needs, and personality. If the sender is sending two contradictory messages at once, the task of decoding is made more difficult. Interpreting sensory inputs depends greatly on perception. Interpreting other visual messages—or written messages, sounds, smells, or emotional cues such as tone of voice—often depends on individual perceptions, which can alter meanings significantly. This is one reason why encoding must be done carefully.

Understanding and Action

If all has gone well at this point, the receiver understands the message. But all does not always go well. In fact, perfect understanding is impossible because no two communicators will perceive the same event in an identical fashion. So, we settle for a satisfactory level of understanding, which most of the time is sufficient. We should always be concerned that the message is understood and acted upon. The receiver must be motivated to take action, even if that action is only filing away the information.

Communication is subject to noise at any stage of the process. **Noise,** as defined in this model of communication, is any factor that interferes with communication. During ideation, noise may take the form of unclear conceptualization. During encoding, for example, the use of slang to communicate with someone who does not understand it will result in noise. If the message is garbled during transmission, as when a television signal breaks up, the result is noise. If a word, a symbol, or an event has a different meaning for the receiver than for the sender, their differing perceptions will cause noise during the decoding process. If the receiver does not link all parts of the message as the sender intended, the resulting noise will interfere with understanding. Many of these problems have to do with word meanings and individual personalities. The common problems or barriers to communication are discussed in more detail later in this chapter.

AT A. L. WILLIAMS:
Television does not provide the opportunity for feedback. The only way Williams really knows his show is working is by employee performance.

Feedback

Feedback is a message sent by the receiver to the sender during a communication. A frown on the receiver's face as the sender is talking, for example, may be interpreted as disagreement or incomprehension, and may cause the sender to alter the message. Such return messages facilitate understanding and increase the potential for appropriate action. Where the sender and receiver (in feedback) do not use the same encoding and decoding processes, miscommunication may result.[15]

The Sender and Receiver: Perception and Other Issues

Perception is our window to the world. Every decision, every action taken by anyone, including managers, hinges on the ability to perceive. **Perception** is the process of organizing and interpreting incoming sensory information in order to define oneself and one's surroundings.[16] Behavior is a result of this process.

It is important to realize that the senses do not give meaning to the environment; they merely extract raw data for processing by the brain. The brain provides the meaning. Through **selectivity** the brain sorts out what it believes to be the key stimuli from the thousands being received.

Once pieces of information are selected, they are evaluated by reference to what is known as the **perceptual set**—an information base that includes a self-image component. We all tend to give meaning to our perceptions according to our self-image. When new stimuli are encountered, they are interpreted by comparing them with similar ones stored in the information base. Reality for the individual consists of the meanings given to those stimuli. This is the process of **interpretation.** Once meanings have been assigned, the individual can and will act on those stimuli, even if that action is merely to dismiss them as unimportant.

Vital insight into the content of the perceptual set has been provided through the efforts of neurological research. One of the major early contributors to this field was Dr. Wilder Penfield. His research caused him to conclude that probably every single event that we have ever consciously experienced is stored in our brains. Most such events slip from our memory—we forget them. Most important to our understanding of the way the perceptual set is constructed is the fact that under external electrical stimulation of their brains, Penfield's patients remembered not only long-forgotten events, but the emotions that the events had aroused—no matter how unimportant the event, no matter how long ago it had "taken place."[17] Thus, the perceptual set influences emotional as well as factual interpretations. This knowledge of perceptual set helps us to understand why a seemingly unimportant event may trigger a highly emotional reaction: the mind associates it with a similar, remembered piece of information that is highly charged with emotion.

OTHER ISSUES

Part of the issue of perceptual set are factors related to people's self-image, their status, their personality, and their backgrounds—for example, their cultural backgrounds. Managers must be attuned to the impacts of these factors on the communication process. For example, a timid employee might not communicate upward, even though a manager encouraged it. Similarly, a manager must be attuned to such key issues as cultural differences—communicating with foreign-born employees or with members of our culturally diverse work force.[18] More and more organizations are beginning to recognize the need for communication skills training, especially of their managers.[19] One such training program is described in Management Challenge 16.1

Forms of Communication

There are two major forms of communication: verbal and nonverbal. **Verbal communication** is either speech (oral communication) or writing. **Nonverbal communication** is body language and the use of time, space, touch, clothing, appearance, and aesthetic elements to convey a message.

Verbal Communication

Verbal communications are transmitted by means of two primary channels, hearing (for oral communication) and sight (for written communication). Oral communication frequently involves other channels, as well. For example, we see another communicator's body movements, facial expression, eye contact, and gestures. But written communication usually depends solely on what is written down. No other clues, such as voice tones, can be given or received to help us encode or decode the message. Feeling, smell, hearing, and touch normally do not come into play.

ORAL COMMUNICATION

We probably spend more time in **oral communication**—speaking and listening—than we do in any other activity except sleeping. Speech involves ideation, encoding, and transmission of messages through language and through **paralanguage**—voice tone, inflection, speed, volume, and silence. Variation of any elements may give the message an entirely different meaning.

LANGUAGE

Language is communication by manipulation of recognizable symbols. It varies by country, culture, social class, age, sex, and other factors. Even when two people have all these factors in common, they may not agree on the meanings of all words. There are always slang and colloquial definitions as well. In much of Georgia, for example, people will say "fixing to get ready," meaning preparing, not repairing, which is the more common definition for the term *fixing*. No two persons have exactly the same perceptions of a word's meaning because no two persons have identical life experiences on which to base their definitions. If we are to be effective speakers, we must be alert to the subtle differences in meanings and in sentence construction that could have significance.

presented and individuals were asked to role-play situations. These were video-taped and their communication practices critiqued and evaluated. The company has been very satisfied with the improvement in the attendees' communication-effectiveness skills.

SOURCE: N. Patricia Freston and Judy E. Lease, "Communication Skills, Training for Selected Supervisors," *Training and Development Journal* (July 1987), pp. 67–70.

The instructor is leading a skill-building exercise during a seminar in the Questar "Communication Skills Training for Selected Supervisors," program. (Courtesy Questar Corporation)

VOICE TONE AND INFLECTION

Voice tone is that quality of voice that gives us some indication of the speaker's attitude. Voice tones can be assertive, bashful, aggressive, angry, passive, and so forth. Inflection is a change in tone and adds to our knowledge of attitudes. Tone and inflection are vital elements of effective communication, especially for managers. A tentative tone on the part of a manager who must reprimand a disruptive employee will undermine his or her message.

SPEED AND VOLUME

Rapid communication is appropriate for some messages and not for others. Important points are normally better made slowly. Less important points can be moved over quickly. Speed also indicates attitude. Nervous people usually talk more rapidly than those who are confident. Thus, varying the speed of speech and paying attention to the speed of others' words can assist your communication efforts. Volume can be employed to stress certain points. Sometimes high volume shows the importance of a subject. But sometimes a manager can capture a listener's attention most effectively by almost whispering the most important points. Unvarying volume or speed becomes monotonous; both are better varied throughout a conversation or presentation if understanding is to be achieved.

SILENCE

Silence communicates. Pauses, nonresponse, blank stares—all communicate. If someone pauses just before he or she wants to make a point, it tends to attract

Managers must learn to be effective listeners. This presentation is especially important to the managers assembled here. A total competitor analysis is being presented. If a manager misses an important part of the presentation, he may not be able to formulate strategy in the most appropriate way. (SOURCE © Robert Reichert)

the listener's attention. If a speaker pauses before he or she speaks, it seems to lend importance to what that person is about to say. Not responding to someone may communicate disagreement or lack of respect.

Listening

Listening is not just hearing; it's more than that. Effective **listening** involves the interpretation, understanding, and action phases of communication. Effective listening requires hard work and self-discipline. Becoming a good listener requires patience, practice, and persistence. Studies suggest that we spend as much as 80 percent of our time in communication and 45 percent of that time is listening. As a student, you probably spend 60 to 70 percent of your class time listening, so learning how to listen is very important. Unfortunately, most of us are inefficient listeners. Controlled research studies reveal that most people cannot recall more than half of what they have heard within a few minutes of having heard it.[20] The cost of poor listening to an organization is staggering. The cost to you may be staggering, as well. The good news is that effective listening can be learned.

If you want to listen effectively, you must be motivated to listen. Why might a manager want to listen? He or she may just solve a problem or get promoted or get a raise or make a friend of a subordinate or find that other people will listen. These are pretty good reasons for listening. Mike McCormack, the extremely successful professional sports agent, feels strongly about the importance of listening. He claims that if he listens for the first few minutes he spends with a new acquaintance, he can learn enough about that person's personality to enable him to formulate a strategy for working and negotiating with that person.[21]

The Sperry Corporation (now part of UNISYS) became concerned about communication among its members and with its various constituents. It was concerned that its customers' needs were not being heard, and that insufficient listening was lowering productivity and might be having a negative effect on the company's climate and culture. Sperry's top managers decided to solve the problems they had observed. They did something about listening: they started their now well-known listening program. How good a listener are you? The Manage Yourself on page 563 at the end of the chapter contains Sperry's quick quiz on listening, so test yourself and find out. You should probably do this now because the information that follows here might bias your answers.

Now that you have tested yourself on your listening skills, you are probably wondering what you can do to improve them. The keys to effective listening found in Table 16.2, which are part of the Sperry listening program, provide some keen insights into what it takes to be an effective listener.

WRITTEN COMMUNICATION

Because of the absence of tone, inflection, speed, volume, and silence, the effectiveness of **written communication** is almost totally a function of the words chosen and the structuring of sentences and paragraphs. Managers must communicate to their audiences in writing. No matter how simple an idea may seem to you, it may not be so simple to the people to whom you are writing. One way to test the effectiveness of a written communication is to ask yourself: If I knew nothing about what I have just written, would I understand it?

Written communications pose serious problems for organizations today. The widespread decline in the ability to use language effectively and to write it

GLOBAL MANAGEMENT CHALLENGE

Problems of Succeeding in Japan

Most US firms find it extremely difficult to gain entrance into Japanese markets. There are indeed, many artificial barriers placed in their path. But, a few firms manage to not only enter the Japanese market, but also find significant success in it. These firms include the Coca-Cola Company and IBM, to name a few. One of the reasons these firms succeed is that they are willing to work hard to understand the Japanese culture, including its language. They are therefore able to communicate the important features of their products and services to the Japanese market.

SOURCE: Carla Rapaport, "Understanding How Japan Works," *Fortune* (Pacific Rim Special Issue, 1990), pp. 14–18.

understandably has led many organizations to conduct special classes to teach their managers and others how to write and use other forms of communication. People who have been trained in such specialties as engineering and accounting often have difficulty communicating in any language other than mathematics.

Table 16.2. Ten Keys to Effective Listening

These keys are a positive guideline to better listening. In fact, they're at the heart of developing better listening habits that could last a lifetime.

Keys to Effective Listening	The Bad Listener	The Good Listener
1. Find areas of interest	Tunes out dry subjects	Opportunitizes: asks "What's in it for me?"
2. Judge content, not delivery	Tunes out if delivery is poor	Judges content, skips over delivery errors
3. Hold your fire	Tends to enter into argument	Doesn't judge until comprehension is complete
4. Listen for ideas	Listens for facts	Listens for central themes
5. Be flexible	Takes intensive notes, using only one system	Takes fewer notes. Uses 4–5 different systems, depending on speaker
6. Work at listening	Shows no energy output. Fakes attention.	Works hard, exhibits active body state
7. Resist distractions	Is easily distracted	Fights or avoids distractions, tolerates bad habits, knows how to concentrate
8. Exercise your mind	Resists difficult expository material; seeks light, recreational material	Uses heavier material as exercise for the mind
9. Keep your mind open	Reacts to emotional words	Interprets color words; does not get hung up on them
10. Capitalize on the fact that *thought* is faster than *speech*	Tends to daydream with slow speakers	Challenges, anticipates, mentally summarizes, weighs the evidence, listens between the lines to tone of voice

SOURCE: "Your Personal Listening Profile," Sperry Corporation, 1980. p. 9. Reprinted by permission. Courtesy of Sperry Corporation.

They, too, are often trained in communication by the organizations that employ them. The Global Management Challenge suggests the importance of learning the language when conducting business with the Japanese.

Nonverbal Communication

Although in written communications the words stand alone, oral communications are often accompanied by nonverbal forms of communication, such as body language. Many types of nonverbal communication also stand alone, however. We need to be aware of these forms of communication if we are to function fully in our world.

We all learn to read the subtleties in another person's body language, but few of us are as aware of this nonverbal form of communication as we should be. In addition to body language (primarily facial expressions, eye contact, hand gestures, and body postures), the physical distance between people (proxemics) and their attitudes toward time (chronemics) are important types of nonverbal communication. Status symbols, touching, and clothing also communicate quite clearly their intended messages. Other forms of nonverbal communication include the visual arts and music.

BODY LANGUAGE

In interactions between people, body language may take various forms and have various meanings. But interpreting those meanings is important even though there are no easy definitions applicable to all types of body language in all situations.[22] However, if you know people fairly well, you should be able to detect the meanings of their **body language**—their various facial expressions, postures, and gestures, and their use or avoidance of eye contact. Holiday Inns, Inc., teaches its employees to read body language in order to improve customer satisfaction.[23]

Some gestures have commonly accepted meanings within most cultures, but other gestures vary from culture to culture. For example, the gesture that we commonly use to indicate "come here"—hand upright, palm inward, fingers curled—means "goodbye" in many Latin American countries. The meanings of body language are very much affected by culture. Hence, when we communicate with people of other cultures, or even of subcultures within our own country, confusion may result. In fact, most body language indicators have different meanings in other cultures. Table 16.3 lists a number of forms of body language and how they are interpreted in the United States.

Body language is more readily interpreted when its four major components— facial expressions, eye contact, gestures, and body postures—occur in combination. For example, when someone stands with arms crossed, lips pursed, and eyes narrowed; maintains steady eye contact; and leans forward toward another person, what message is being conveyed? Body language is also best interpreted within the context of the situation: who is involved, what has happened, what is about to happen?

If you want to see just how important body language can be, tune in to your favorite television show, turn off the sound, and see if you can determine the plot of the story. It is less difficult than you might think because verbal and nonverbal messages usually reinforce each other.

Body language provides clues to the real meaning of a speaker's words. As Norman Sigband, a communication expert, has noted, when nonverbal messages conflict with verbal messages, most of the time you should probably believe the nonverbal ones.[24] Some teachers often receive clear body-language messages indicating boredom, such as yawns, slouching, closed eyes, and nodding heads.

AT A. L. WILLIAMS:
One of the advantages of television is that it allows for several forms of communication to occur at once: verbal, paralanguage, and nonverbal body language.

Table 16.3. Commonly Accepted Interpretations of Various Forms of Body Language in the United States

Body Language	Interpretation
Facial expressions	
Frown	Displeasure, unhappiness
Smile	Friendliness, happiness
Raised eyebrows	Disbelief, amazement
Narrowed eyes, pursed lips	Anger
Eye contact	
Glancing	Interest
Steady	Active listening, interest, seduction
Gestures	
Pointing finger	Authority, displeasure, lecturing
Folded arms	Not open to change, preparing to speak
Arms at side	Open to suggestions, relaxed
Hands uplifted outward	Disbelief, puzzlement, uncertainty
Body postures	
Fidgeting, doodling	Boredom
Hands on hips	Anger, defensiveness
Shrugging shoulders	Indifference
Squared stance or shoulders	Problem solving, concerned, listening
Fidgeting, biting lip, shifting, jingling money	Nervousness
Sitting on edge of chair	Listening, great interest
Slouching in chair	Boredom, lack of interest

THE USE OF SPACE

In some organizations status significantly determines having a corner office or an office along a corridor, having a large office or a smaller one, an office with a window or one without a window. These are just some of the ways space conveys messages about status.

Think of conversations you have recently observed. How close did the speakers stand to each other? Why did one person stand closer to some people than to others? Who sits at the head of the table at important organization meetings? Why does someone stand up when he or she wants the person already standing to view him or her as an equal? These questions are related to using space to define territory. **Proxemics** is the study of the use of interpersonal space. Look around you right now. What uses of space do you see? If someone moved the furniture, would someone else be very upset? Must everything be in its place, or is your current environment less structured?

We are territorial animals. We all try to stake claims to territory and to defend it against unwanted intrusion. Our territory may range from many acres of land to the foot or two of space with which we try to surround ourselves in a crowd. We allow some people to be closer to us than others. Edward T. Hall distinguishes four interpersonal space zones: intimate distance from physical contact, eighteen inches; personal distance, from eighteen inches to four feet; social consultive distance, from four to eight feet; and public distance, from eight to twelve feet or more.[25] The amount of space between two people reveals quite accurately the degree of intimacy of their conversation, their status, and the respect they accord each other. The intimacy involved decreases as the space between them increases. But a distance that indicates intimacy to us would not necessarily indicate intimacy to an Arab, who is likely to seek much closer contact with other people than most of us prefer. The use of space varies by country, sex, and certain cultural factors. Knowing these various preferences will become ever more important in a global economy.

If you want to test just how important space can be, invade someone's space, move the furniture, stand when others are sitting, or occupy the power position at the table. All of these violations of someone else's territory will show you just how important space can be. Space can be used to manipulate others. One manager in a steel plant constantly violated other people's territory and intimidated them by doing so. He would always stand right up next to someone when he spoke. He usually got his way, partly because of his use of space. This is not to suggest that you should manipulate others, only to show you just how important an awareness of space can be to you.

Companies communicate their respect and concern for their employees by their use of space. The larger, more nicely appointed offices, and those on upper floors, usually go to top managers.

During the 1970s many companies adopted the open-office concept, with partitions and open doorways. Such offices were designed to save costs and promote "an open atmosphere for communication." Westinghouse's Turbine Generator Division adopted this concept expressly to encourage openness.[26] But today with productivity declining, many companies consider "open" to mean "noisy." Xerox, for one, has reversed its position and is moving toward more traditional settings. It has found that noise was not the only problem; so was a lack of privacy.[27]

As a student, you too, should be interested in space—not only to learn to use it to communicate and to understand what others are communicating, but also because space is related to grades. Abner Eisenberg has shown that the classroom space students choose is directly correlated with participation in discussions. The students who sit in the middle of the row at the front of the room participate more than those in other seating positions.[28] If you were taking a course such as business policy, which requires a high degree of participation, you might raise your grade by sitting in one of those seats, and of course, by participating.

THE USE OF TIME
When was the last time you were late for an appointment with your boss or your professor? What happened? Or have you been late to a meeting lately? You probably received many dirty looks from friends or associates. Or maybe you missed an airplane because you were late. All of these events reveal the importance of your use of time. The study of the use of time, **chronemics,** can help you in your studies, your career, and your life.

Most of our interest in time in this chapter is focused on arrivals and departure and on how time is structured during meetings. People communicate disrespect, lack of concern, and lack of interest when they are late. The chronically late person also communicates a lack of organization in his or her life.

In the United States, Canada, and parts of Western Europe, "time is money." The more efficiently you use time, presumably the more money you can make. But in other parts of the world, other uses of time are more important. Norman Sigband notes that in Ethiopia, for example, lower-level bureaucrats take a disproportionately long time to make simple decisions in order to enhance their apparent importance in the eyes of the people who are waiting for those decisions.[29] An American radiator manufacturing firm headquartered in Alabama recently found that the Japanese like to have documents signed and sealed when they are ready to leave, even if the final negotiations are not complete. Although the American firm expected to meet again, the Japanese had only allocated a certain amount of time to the negotiations. That was it. Either the deal was made or it was not, but no more time could be spent on it.[30]

STATUS SYMBOLS

Many employers use **status symbols** as a reward system. Organizations use many status symbols, which can become almost as important as life itself to some people, probably because status symbols enhance their self-image and the esteem in which others hold them. Common organizational status symbols include the size, location, and furnishings of offices, first class versus tourist air travel, titles, reserved parking spaces, executive lunchrooms and bathrooms, country club memberships, private chauffeurs, and one's name on the door.

Status symbols also play important roles outside the organization: the type of car one drives, the social organization to which one belongs, the kind of home or neighborhood one lives in, the size of one's salary, the schools one attends, the vacations one takes, and the clothes one wears.

TOUCHING

Touching and avoiding touching play important roles in communication. A handshake, a backslap, a tender touch on the arm or body, holding hands, an embrace—all convey messages. In some organizations touching is strictly forbidden; in others it is not. If you work (or have worked), what is/was your organization's climate with respect to touching? What does/did it mean with respect to your organization's concern for people?

CLOTHING AND APPEARANCE AS COMMUNICATION

"Clothes make the man," the old saying goes—and the woman, too. What impact does clothing have? Several books stress the importance of **clothing and appearance as means of communication**.[31] The claim is that they have a great impact on success in the business world. For years the rule in many firms was that men could wear suits of any color as long as it was gray or black. Now navy blue appears to be the color of power and prestige. Look at what you are wearing. What messages are you conveying? If you want to make sure you don't get a white-collar job, just go to a job interview dressed in jeans and a T-shirt and see what happens. What message does such an appearance convey? Your clothing is only part of your appearance; your hair, your teeth, and your physical fitness convey various messages to others. What about the appearance of your office desk, home, and study area—what messages do they convey?

AESTHETIC FORMS OF COMMUNICATION

Art, poetry, music, dance, religious symbols, plays, and movies are **aesthetic forms of communication**. The symbols used may not be commonly recognizable, and they may not even be thought of as communication, but of course they are. And the message communicated by the symbol may vary with context.

Communicating in Organizations

Within the organization, there is formal and informal communication.

Formal Communication

Formal communication occurs through official channels and is sanctioned by the organization. Memos, policies, procedures, and reports of committee meetings are types of formal communication. There are three principal types of

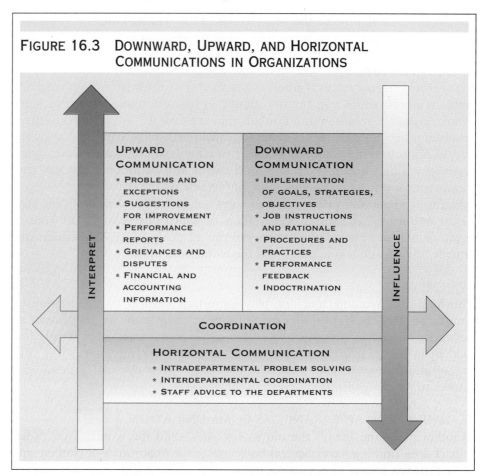

FIGURE 16.3 DOWNWARD, UPWARD, AND HORIZONTAL COMMUNICATIONS IN ORGANIZATIONS

INTERPRET

UPWARD COMMUNICATION
* PROBLEMS AND EXCEPTIONS
* SUGGESTIONS FOR IMPROVEMENT
* PERFORMANCE REPORTS
* GRIEVANCES AND DISPUTES
* FINANCIAL AND ACCOUNTING INFORMATION

DOWNWARD COMMUNICATION
* IMPLEMENTATION OF GOALS, STRATEGIES, OBJECTIVES
* JOB INSTRUCTIONS AND RATIONALE
* PROCEDURES AND PRACTICES
* PERFORMANCE FEEDBACK
* INDOCTRINATION

INFLUENCE

COORDINATION

HORIZONTAL COMMUNICATION
* INTRADEPARTMENTAL PROBLEM SOLVING
* INTERDEPARTMENTAL COORDINATION
* STAFF ADVICE TO THE DEPARTMENTS

SOURCE: ADAPTED FROM <u>ORGANIZATIONS: A MICRO/MACRO APPROACH</u> BY RICHARD L. DAFT AND RICHARD M. STEERS, P. 538. COPYRIGHT © 1986 BY SCOTT, FORESMAN AND COMPANY. USED BY PERMISSION OF HARPERCOLLINS PUBLISHERS.

Tandy's emphasis on communications makes their employees more effective. This manager and his subordinate benefit from the constant communication coming from corporate headquarters. So does the customer. (SOURCE © Charles Thatcher/Woodfin Camp & Associates)

formal communication: downward communication, upward communication, and horizontal communication. The principal components of each appear in Figure 16.3. Managers must learn to communicate in each of these directions. In a recent study by the consulting firm The Hay Group, a survey of 250 firms showed that 54 to 67 percent of employees see top-down communication as positive, but only 30 to 42 percent see bottom-up listening programs as positive.[32] This implies that companies are better at telling employees facts than at listening to them. In another survey of 48,000 employees by Opinion Research Corporation, a division of Arthur D. Little consulting company, it was determined that "downward communication, measured by employees rating their company on letting them know what is going on, is rated favorably by fewer than half the employees in all groups."[33] This implies that companies may not even be very good at telling employees facts. Of course, every company differs. Some companies, such as Tandy Computers, a California-based computer manufacturer, work hard at communication. In one recent year, the company staged six hundred hours of meetings in which executives from the various functional areas—operations and finance, for example—explained the company's strategy to employees.[34]

Informal Communication

Chapter 14 discussed the informal organization in detail. **Informal communication** occurs outside formal channels. It occurs continuously in the organization and includes impromptu discussions of new work procedures and bull sessions among friends. The manager must be attuned to the grapevine, the nature of the communication, the amount of information flowing, and the accuracy of the information. Often the manager can learn important pieces of information from the grapevine—such as the potential for employee relations problems. Informal communication is usually accurate but tends to become more inaccurate when emotional issues are involved.[35] Managers can best counter or head off negative rumors traveling through the grapevine by providing the facts.

Common Barriers to Communication

Many problems may interfere with a smooth transmission of thought from one communicator to another that stem from the characteristics of the sender and receiver. Many stem from the nature of the organization. Many stem simply from our culture. In the culturally diverse work world of the 1990s, each becomes more challenging.

Language Limitations

Language limits virtually all communication. The symbols chosen are abstractions of thought, feelings, and concepts. It is impossible to communicate every single sensed aspect of life, or even all of the most important ones. Rather, our languages enable us to communicate the aspects we perceive to be most important. Because the words we use are abstractions, other people may not interpret them the same way we do.

Speaking and Listening Habits

If we form good speaking and listening habits, our efforts at communication are likely to be effective. Few of us know how to speak properly in every situation, and most of us are simply not good listeners. Speaking too quickly or too slowly, failing to use the appropriate tone of voice, and failing to make eye contact are bound to lead to ineffective communication. Similarly, a person who does not listen well is not going to be of much assistance in the communication process.

Physical and Social Differences

Physical and social differences can create barriers to effective communication. For example, barriers may exist between managerial employees and first-line employees, between men and women, between Blacks and whites, between the people in the plant and those in the home office five hundred miles away. Meanings can be misinterpreted when such factors cause noise in the process. Even if interpretation is accurate, these problems may still interfere with understanding.

Timing

Communication must be well timed. Managerial communications such as instructions to change product lines, to set up new operations, or to delay payments must be issued when the need arises.

Wordiness

Wordiness should be avoided in written communications as well as in oral communications. The receiver can grasp the meaning of a message much more quickly and accurately if the sender keeps the message simple. Remember the KISS technique: *Keep It Simple, Stupid.* Companies can do much to improve communication by keeping down wordiness. Loew's, Inc., the conglomerate with interests in tobacco, hotels, financial services, broadcasting, watches, has gone so far as to eliminate written memos in an attempt to reduce bureaucracy.[36]

Characteristics of the Sender and Receiver: Personality, Role, Status, Perception, and Self-image

Personality plays an important role in communication. Each individual behaves in a unique manner. Behaviors stem from attitudes developed by experience. Attitudes help give meaning to reality through the perceptual process. Although people with similar experiences develop similar perceptual sets, enough differences remain to require us to be attuned to others' perceptions.

Two other sender/receiver characteristics that greatly influence the communication process are an individual's role and status. Because someone is fulfilling the role of mother, she may communicate in a certain way, either as sender or as receiver. She may send authoritative messages to little children in certain instances but may listen nurturingly under other circumstances. The doctor sends certain communications because of the role he or she plays in life; so do the lawyer, the dentist, the accountant, the carpenter, the engineer, the manager, the subordinate, the friend, the child, the parent, the professor, and the student. Roles affect virtually all stages of the communication process. Differences in status create barriers that affect communication. When sender and receiver do not have the same status, their perceptions differ. We must remain alert to and adjust for the consequences of these factors in our communications.

Sometimes we hear or see what we want to, rather than what is really there. Accurate interpretation becomes difficult and often impossible. A good part of life and therefore a good part of communication is involved in protecting our self-image. Thus, not only may we hear what we want to hear, but our own messages may be distorted to protect our self-image. This is one reason that maintaining or raising a subordinate's self-image is a vital managerial activity.

As noted in Chapter 13, the entire managerial-influence process, as described in the Motivation Performance Cycle, depends for its continuation (stage 10) on the perceived impact on the subordinate's self-image. Generally, where the process has a negative impact on someone's self-image, the process will not continue in the same way, and motivation will decline. Positive impacts may or may not alter the process, but motivation will remain the same or increase.

While hearing what we want to hear implies an intentionally personal interpretation, unintentional perceptual problems also lead to problems in interpretation. When we speak with someone whose mother tongue is not English, and when we realize that some of the words we use have as many as fifteen or twenty different definitions, the difficulty of accurate interpretation becomes all too obvious. Then when we consider all of the other variables involved in verbal and nonverbal communication, we must realize that we are lucky to get half of the message right.

Overload

Information **overload,** too much information, often boggles the mind. Today's managers are frequently swamped by too much information, resulting from too much communication.[37] We must constantly guard against creating paper for paper's sake. We also should be careful not to call too many meetings or invite everyone to the ones we have. The objective of any information system should be to provide only what is needed and usable.

Coping with Barriers to Communication

Make no mistake about it: coping with barriers to communication requires hard work. We human beings have a well-programmed tendency to do things the way we have always done them. Improving communication requires practicing proper communication. We must give thought to the need to take appropriate actions, we must decide what the appropriate actions are in various situations, and we must then practice these behaviors so that when a difficult situation occurs, we can handle it well. First we must decide that we want to.

This may sound like the old joke about going to the doctor and saying, "Doctor, it hurts when I do this," and the doctor replies, "So don't do that." The truth is that if anything you have been doing hurts your communication, then indeed you should stop doing it. Role playing provides experience in handling various types of situations. But practice alone is not enough. We must always realize the following:

1. We can never rehearse every possible situation, so learning general guidelines on how to determine appropriate behavior on the spot is important.

2. Our emotions may overcome our rational approach to problem solving and thus we may not resolve every situation satisfactorily.

There are no simple answers, obviously. Changing human behavior—here communication behavior—is never easy.

When sending a communication, be as open with the other person as possible. Be direct and honest. Maintain eye contact and provide a positive environment. Select words carefully and keep the language simple. Use repetition and as many channels or media as necessary to get your message across. Be aware of your receivers' situation and keep from putting them on the defensive. Have empathy with them. State your position on issues, including your feelings.

The receiver needs to listen actively, to hear what is said and what is not said. The receiver must try to understand the other person's position, provide feedback to make certain that his or her decodings are appropriate, learn to filter out noise, be attentive, maintain eye contact, and provide the proper climate. The receiver should try not to evaluate what is said until the other person has finished speaking. The receiver needs to remain nondefensive.

Within the organization, you will often meet obstacles to communication that seem to be insurmountable. They're not. One supervisor in a trucking company found it necessary to break the rules to communicate with his subordinates, all members of the Teamster's Union. The union contract specified, for example, that management would not communicate information on profitability to union members. The company was afraid that such information could be used by the union to justify demands for increased wages. The supervisor posted the firm's profit-and-loss figures on the bulletin board. By such actions he helped to lift his district out of the red and make it profitable.[38]

The manager must learn specific communication skills, such as assertiveness and active listening. **Active listening**[39] is a program designed to teach individuals to listen not only to the content of what is being said but also to the emotional aspects of that content and to feed back that information to the other individual in the communication situation. Active listening is an important means of helping someone work through a problem. You listen to what they have to say. You then summarize the content and tell them what you have heard. But perhaps more importantly, you tell them what feelings they are expressing about that content. Many times they will not be aware of their feelings. You do not, however, offer solutions. You let them arrive at those for themselves. **Assertiveness training** is a program of communication designed to teach people to communicate with respect for other people's rights. Assertiveness differs from passiveness, in which the individual allows other people to overcome their rights. As a manager, it is extremely important not only to give adherence to your own rights, but to the rights of others.[40]

Organizational Communication

If the organization is to have sound, positive communication with its employees, it must strive to create the proper communication climate. The proper climate exists when management recognizes that employees have rights to certain information, and certain other rights as well. When the organization keeps employees informed of actions that affect their jobs, treats them with respect, provides feedback on performance, and communicates relevant objectives; and when the organization recognizes employees' rights to fair and equitable treatment, to question policy, and to a reasonable amount of participation in decision making, the resulting satisfaction is normally going to have a positive effect on production.

Organizations can do a lot to improve communication and, hence, improve productivity, by means of either structural or informational approaches. Structural approaches attempt to change the organization's structure in order to improve communication. The two basic elements of organizational structure are jobs and authority. Structural approaches improve communication either by changing the nature of job content, by creating new or different jobs, by changing the way jobs are grouped, or by altering the amount of authority distribution within the organization. Improved communication systems usually call for increased delegation of authority, power equalization, and participation by subordinates in the decision-making processes of the organization. Much of the structural approach is implemented through the use of various personnel practices.

Structural Approaches

There are numerous ways in which structure can be altered. Chapters 8, 9, 10, and 11 addressed two of the most important of them, participation and organizational culture. Chapter 17 discusses appraisal systems. Here we shall briefly review several less comprehensive programs that have been instituted in an effort to improve organizational communication.[41]

EMPLOYEE ACTION PROGRAMS, ACTION LINES, AND COUNSELING
Monsanto calls them employee action lines, and many firms call them counseling programs.[42] What are they? They are attempts to help employees solve problems both related to and unrelated to the job. Many firms employ psychologists both full- and part-time to counsel employees on their problems. General American's action line focuses primarily on job-related problems; Monsanto's employee action program focuses on personal problems; many other firms fall between these two ends of a continuum of concern for people's needs. Sometimes employers must be creative in order to have employees fully utilize such programs, as Management Challenge 16.2 suggests.

GRIEVANCE PROCEDURES
Grievance procedures are formalized ways for employees to have their grievance against the organization and its managers addressed. Not all organizations have them. Not all such programs are perceived as being fair or effective in solving employees' complaints. If they are not effective, what do employees do as a result? The odds are that they decrease their productivity somehow—by absenteeism, shoddy work, tardiness, balking at orders, and more. That's why improving grievance procedures is so vital from the corporate viewpoint.

ATTITUDE SURVEYS
Surveys, questionnaires, and interviews with employees have recently grown in popularity as a way of keeping tabs on employees' needs and perceptions of the organization, as well as on potential problem areas. Frederick Starke and Thomas Ferratt propose that organizations develop a "behavioral information system," partly based on surveys. The system would enable management to remain aware, at least periodically, of employees' perceptions of major factors within the organization.[43] IBM has added another step to determining the attitudes among a particular manager's subordinates. The manager is encouraged to use "instrumented group process." This process involves manager and sub-

The Golden Nugget's 24 hour hot-line helped improve employee quality of life and productivity. (SOURCE © Craig Aurness/Woodfin Camp & Associates)

ordinates in open communication for the purpose of revealing the manager's weaknesses and building subordinates' confidence and reducing their fears. Although it is in limited use to date, this program has proved quite successful.[44] Tupperware found, as have many others, that the first companywide attitude survey often turns up some bad news. But the key is to react and let employees know what actions have been taken to solve problems.[45]

OMBUDSMEN

Have you ever worked for an organization where there was no one to turn to with questions or complaints? Then you know why so many organizations have created a position or department to handle employee questions, complaints, and problems. Usually the person in this position, often called an ombudsman, reports directly to the head of the organization, keeping communications with employees confidential. The ombudsman must have the capability to motivate the line function managers to take action on employee problems; otherwise this function will simply become a dead end and employees will cease to use it. Frederick W. Smith, chairman of Federal Express, spends every Tuesday handling employee complaints. He believes it is that important. His efforts are just part of an overall grievance system costing the company over $2 million a year. But the program results in many benefits, including improved morale and reduced legal problems.[46]

OPEN-DOOR POLICIES

Managers who keep "open doors" indicate to their subordinates that they are available to listen to problems and complaints at any time. The open door indicates a willingness to establish communication and an atmosphere of trust. Managers may have open doors as official policy, but unfortunately many managers do not make the commitment this practice requires. Many subordinates are reluctant to take advantage of the open door because they hesitate to bypass

A. L. Williams isn't the only firm broadcasting messages to its employees. These Domino's pizza employees are listening to Don Vleck, distribution vice-president, on improving customer service. (SOURCE © Peter Yates/Picture Group)

other managers in the chain of command. Only if the organization's climate is one of trust can such problems be overcome.

SUGGESTION PROGRAMS

Suggestion programs can make significant contributions to an organization. They provide a channel for employees to contribute their ideas. After all, who knows the job better than the person who does it? But suggestion programs do have their problems. After a while, all of the practical suggestions seem to have been offered, and when further suggestions are not accepted, problems may arise. Overall, though, such programs can be effective.

McDonnell Douglas Astronautics Company of St. Louis, the third largest component of McDonnell Douglas Corporation, is just one of many firms that asks employees (18,000) how the organization can cut costs, improve effectiveness and efficiency, raise morale, and improve job satisfaction, organizational climate and working conditions. The firm's goal is to improve its turnaround time to 30 days. As late as 1984, the time had been 415 days, but by April 1986 it had been reduced to 46 days. The company tracks suggestions on a computer. Monetary rewards from $25 to $25,000 are given to people whose suggestions save the company money. The company believes suggestions saved it $4 million in 1986.[47]

Informational Approaches

Informational approaches attempt to improve organizational communication primarily by disseminating information. Occasionally new jobs are created within the organization in this process, but usually already established positions merely expand their information functions. Several means of disseminating information beyond those ordinarily included in a firm's information-distribution system are available: periodic meetings with employees, television broadcasts, in-house publications (including newsletters, bulletin boards, and magazines), athletic programs, company manuals, and periodic performance reviews.

PERIODIC MEETINGS WITH EMPLOYEES

Whether meetings with employees are held daily, weekly, monthly, quarterly, semiannually, or annually, they are extremely important. Meetings between managers and employees give employees a chance to learn what the organization is all about, what it is accomplishing, and what it hopes to accomplish. Employees, and lower-level managers especially, often feel that they are the "last to know." Management that keeps its employees informed about an organization's situation can expect more interested, dedicated, concerned, and loyal employees.

Pitney-Bowes, an international manufacturer of office equipment, stresses informative, open communication with its employees. Its belief is that "informed employees are the best employees." It encourages employee participation in the system. Each month all employees meet with their supervisors to discuss problems and policies. The process of discussion moves upward in the organization through elected representatives until all problems are resolved.[48]

TELEVISION BROADCASTS

One of the problems associated with relaying information to employees is that not all of them may receive the same words at the same time. And when newspapers and newsletters are distributed, not all may receive the same words at the same time. And when newspapers and newsletters are distributed, not all may read the same meanings into the words. One way to alleviate such problems (but not to eliminate them totally) is to broadcast information to employees on television.

Television can also be used to reduce the costs and fatigue of travel. Ford Motor Company, for example, has eliminated the need for its sales force to gather in one place for its national sales meeting by installing television broadcasting and reception equipment at thirty sites around the country. Atlantic Richfield and TRW, a major diversified manufacturing firm, are among hundreds of other national firms that now conduct conferences by television.[49] Domino's Pizza, Federal Express, and Empire Savings Bank of America are just a few of the firms using television to get their company's messages across to employees.[50]

PUBLICATIONS AND BULLETIN BOARDS

Management can make employees feel that they are important simply by putting their names in print in company newsletters and newspapers. This form of recognition is relatively inexpensive but has proved to be effective for many firms. In large organizations, the key seems to be in personalizing the medium used. Employees do want to know about the company as a whole, but they especially want to know about their plant, their office, their friends, their acquaintances, and most important, on occasion, themselves. The video bulletin board using television monitors is becoming popular.[51]

ATHLETIC PROGRAMS

Organizational athletic programs communicate quite positive messages to employees. Such programs say, "We are a team. We need to stick together. The organization cares for your health and friendship activities. The company that plays together stays together. This is just one more benefit of belonging to the organization. This is something to do in your spare time that is safe and fun."

ORGANIZATIONAL RULES, REGULATIONS, POLICIES, PROCEDURES, MEMOS, AND HANDBOOKS

Any form of written communication with employees obviously communicates. But just what does it communicate? If it is poorly written in a "bureaucratese" that is not understandable by the average employee or if it communicates a lack of concern, the employee is not likely to be concerned for the organization that produced it.

One soft-drink bottler's retirement program was so complex that even its company lawyer had difficulty understanding it. Most employees could not comprehend it and wondered if the company wasn't trying to pull a fast one. Finally, after realizing the effect on morale, the firm ordered a simple interpre-

CEO Frederick Smith of Federal Express spends every Tuesday responding to employee complaints. His efforts convey the message that employee complaints are important. (SOURCE © George Lange/Outline Press)

tation of the program to be written. After much difficulty, one that could be understood by virtually all employees was completed, distributed, and explained. No one thinks the company is trying to pull a fast one any more.

John Mackay, founder and CEO of Whole Foods Market, headquartered in Austin, Texas, uses a handbook to tell employees what the company is all about. It doesn't contain the typical do's and don't's but rather discusses history, philosophy, and purpose. Mackey keeps his employees informed on strategy and other important issues through this handbook.[52]

The Portable Manager: Technology Changes Communication

Technology is changing the way managers communicate. Fax machines, laptop computers, video conferencing, cellular phones, and voice mail are causing managers—as well as salespeople, clerks, operative employees, and others—to change the way they communicate. More and more workers are working at home. Fax machines mean instant transmission of visual material between two locations at a very reasonable cost, and voice mail enables managers to distribute information to a large number of employees with minimal effort.[53] Management Challenge 16.3 illustrates how the new technology has changed communication at Westinghouse, which Chapter 19 discusses in more detail.

Paul Lego believes strongly in electronic communications. He believes that they have raised his personal productivity and that of the company significantly. (SOURCE © Lynn Johnson/Black Star)

MANAGEMENT CHALLENGE 16.3

At Westinghouse Electronic Mail Is the Answer

Faced with the need to improve its information flow, to improve customer relations, to improve productivity, and to cut costs, Westinghouse Electric Corporation adopted E-Mail, electronic mail. Some 6,000 personal computers connect 10,700 of the company's managers and employees along with about 1,000 customers. E-Mail links operations in the United States with offices in thirty-seven foreign countries. Telephone tag is no longer necessary because electronic-mail and voice-mail systems allow respondents to reply without ever talking to the other person.

President Paul E. Lego logs fifteen hours on his IBM PC AT using E-Mail from his home and office. He can respond to queries from Tokyo and the manager there can have the return message the next day. Similarly, he can ask someone in Brazil for information and he will have it the next day. This avoids a lot of the problems of overlapping work hours—or nonoverlapping work hours—that exist, for example, between the United States and Tokyo. In Lego's opinion the electronic communication used at Westinghouse has contributed fully one-third of the company's 60 percent annual increases in white-collar productivity in recent years. The company feels that the ability to transfer information so quickly gives them a competitive edge.

SOURCE: Gregory L. Miles, "At Westinghouse E-Mail Makes the World Go Around," *Business Week* (October 10, 1988), p. 110.

Communication as a Problem-Solving Exercise

This chapter does not contain the usual figure describing the topic of that chapter as a problem-solving exercise because virtually every single issue discussed involves decision making in all its phases: choosing how to code messages; what channels to use—whether downward or upward—and how; what particular skills to use; whether to train in communication; and how to interpret nonverbal communication, for example.

The Management Challenges Identified

1. The cultural diversity of the work force and changing expectations and demographics
2. The global nature of business
3. Accelerated rates of change
4. Increasing levels of competition
5. Increasing levels of technology

Some Solutions Noted in the Chapter

1. Increased levels of training in communication skills
2. Increased understanding of others
3. Increased levels of communication
4. Increased organizational use of communication systems

Summary

1. Communication has four major functions: to express emotions, to activate motivation, to inform, and to control.
2. Communication consists of seven major steps: ideation, encoding, transmission, receiving, decoding, understanding and action, and feedback.
3. Communication takes place in every managerial interaction with others. If you can communicate effectively, you will be well along the road toward sound management practices.
4. Communication may be verbal or nonverbal. Verbal communication consists of oral and written words. Nonverbal communication (paralanguage) consists of body language, the use of space, the use of time, status symbols, touching, clothing and appearance, and aesthetics.
5. Among the barriers to communication are language limitations, poor speaking and listening habits, physical and social differences, timing, and wordiness.

6. Listening is of critical importance to successful oral communication. The best way to develop it is to practice.

7. Organizations may take both structural and informational approaches in their efforts to improve communication. Structural approaches include junior boards, employee action programs, grievance procedures, communication audits, attitude surveys, deep sensing, ombudsmen, discussion sessions, open-door policies, and suggestions programs. Information approaches include periodic meetings with employees, television broadcasts, publications and bulletin boards, athletic programs, and organizational rules and other written communications.

8. Managers can learn very specific skills—such as listening, active listening, assertiveness, and transactional analysis—in order to be more effective.

9. Communication is changing in the age of technology, through the use of fax machines, computers, television, and cellular phones.

Thinking About Management

1. What are the four major functions of communication? Give examples of each.
2. Think of a recent communication you have had with someone. Follow the communication process through each of its steps.
3. Give examples of various types of verbal and nonverbal communication.
4. How many different meanings can you give to the statement, "You should not have done that" by varying tone, inflection, speed, and volume and using silence?
5. Describe how perception affects communication.
6. Discuss the electronic communication revolution.
7. Discuss how you cope with barriers to communication.

CASE

Communicating with Employees at McDonnell Douglas

Chairman John McDonnell had just completed a gut-wrenching restructuring of the aerospace giant, McDonnell Douglas. Many top managers and middle managers had been terminated or retired early in order to trim the firm's expenses and make it more competitive, and to meet the changing nature of relationships with the federal government. For that sizeable portion of their business based on contracts with the government, they faced a changing payment methodology. The government was moving from a cost-plus-profit contract to a fixed-price contract. High costs actually benefited the firm under a cost-plus environment because profits were usually granted as a percentage of costs. Under the fixed-price system, profits had to be extracted from the agreed-upon contract-fee amount, regardless of expenses. Costs also needed to be cut in other divisions as well, simply to meet competition.

As a consequence of the restructuring, overall profit problems and a lack of new products, morale was low. John McDonnell wanted to communicate with employees to assure them the firm was taking action, making progress, and in good condition. He also wanted to create a feeling of community among the fifty thousand employees spread over numerous locations. He considered several options. He could use a newsletter, but somehow that seemed to lack pizzazz. He could try a satellite TV hookup, but his advisors indicated that, for a while at least, it was not a sound option because of the number of locations and the difficulty of getting so many people tuned in at once. Finally, McDonnell decided that maybe a video tape could be distributed to employees on the company's periodic actions.

DISCUSSION QUESTIONS
1. What types of topics should or could be included?
2. How would you go about making the theme upbeat?
3. What problems might result over the long term with such a project?

MANAGERS AT WORK

Deciphering Communication

Mike had worked at Weldon Manufacturing Company for six years. He and his coworkers had enjoyed a solid relationship. Several of them bowled together in the same league, and they often got together for parties. Everyone was elated when Mike was promoted to be supervisor of the unit. Things went smoothly for several weeks, but then Mike began to detect a change in the attitudes of his old friends. They weren't quite as eager to talk with him. And he had dropped out of the bowling league, feeling that a manager should not be so close with his subordinates.

Mike sensed that something was wrong, but he wasn't quite sure what. He reflected on his management style. He made sure that everyone knew what their jobs were, what their objectives were. He checked periodically on everyone's work. He tried to be friendly but did not always have a chance to pat everyone on the back, as he would like to. He thought about a recent incident with David, who had been a close friend before Mike has been promoted. Mike was approaching him from the side, and David caught a view of him from the corner of his eye. Mike knew that David intentionally turned slightly, to keep from having to talk to him. But Mike began a conversation with David anyway. He had to because David was not doing his job right, and Mike felt he had to set him straight. David had not been receptive and Mike sensed a little anger in David's voice.

Then there was the incident with Julie. Julie had always been a good employee, but her work had fallen off lately. Mike had counseled her on her performance, but she had not responded favorably. She had used the new assembly process as an excuse, but Mike knew better. Something was bothering her. She seemed—that was the only way he could express how he knew—to be nervous. A couple of other incidents came to mind. Many managers might have blamed their subordinates inability to cope with a friend becoming their manager as the problem. But Mike was perceptive and understanding enough of the situation to realize that he might be part, maybe even a major part, of the problem. He wondered what steps to take next. He contemplated talking with his boss, the personnel director, and asking for advice. And he considered just having a meeting with his subordinates to air people's feelings.

DISCUSSION QUESTIONS
1. One of the most difficult problems all managers face is to determine what is on an employee's mind. It may take a while for a manager to realize that something is wrong. Some are so inner-directed that they never realize something is amiss. What clues did Mike have, as noted here? What other types of clues might he have had?
2. How does nonverbal communication provide clues to such problem situations? Are men or women, on the average, better at reading nonverbal behavior?
3. Should Mike go to his boss, the personnel director, or directly to his subordinates? Why?

MANAGE YOURSELF

LISTENING

AS A LISTENER, HOW OFTEN DO YOU FIND YOURSELF ENGAGING IN THESE 10 BAD LISTENING HABITS? FIRST, CHECK THE APPROPRIATE COLUMNS. THEN TABULATE YOUR SCORE USING THE KEY BELOW.

LISTENING HABIT	FREQUENCY					SCORE
	ALMOST ALWAYS	USUALLY	SOME-TIMES	SELDOM	ALMOST NEVER	
1. CALLING THE SUBJECT UNINTERESTING						
2. CRITICIZING THE SPEAKER'S DELIVERY OR MANNERISMS						
3. GETTING OVER-STIMULATED BY SOMETHING THE SPEAKER SAYS						
4. LISTENING PRIMARILY FOR FACTS						
5. TRYING TO OUTLINE EVERYTHING						
6. FAKING ATTENTION TO THE SPEAKER						
7. ALLOWING INTERFERING DISTRACTIONS						
8. AVOIDING DIFFICULT MATERIAL						
9. LETTING EMOTION-LADEN WORDS AROUSE PERSONAL ANTAGONISM						
10. WASTING THE ADVANTAGE OF THOUGHT SPEED (DAYDREAMING)						

KEY:
FOR EVERY "ALMOST ALWAYS" CHECKED, GIVE YOURSELF A SCORE OF 2
FOR EVERY "USUALLY" CHECKED, GIVE YOURSELF A SCORE OF 4
FOR EVERY "SOMETIMES" CHECKED, GIVE YOURSELF A SCORE OF 6
FOR EVERY "SELDOM" CHECKED, GIVE YOURSELF A SCORE OF 8
FOR EVERY "ALMOST NEVER" CHECKED, GIVE YOURSELF A SCORE OF 10

TOTAL SCORE

THE AVERAGE SCORE IS 62. OF COURSE THE BEST WAY TO FIND OUT JUST HOW GOOD A LISTENER YOU ARE IS TO HAVE SOMEONE WHO KNOWS YOU WELL RATE YOU ON THESE ITEMS.

SOURCE: "YOUR PERSONAL LISTENING PROFILE," SPERRY CORPORATION, 1980, P. 7. REPRINTED WITH PERMISSION.

CHAPTER SEVENTEEN

Controlling Performance: Strategic, Tactical, and Operational Control

CHAPTER OBJECTIVES

By the time you complete this chapter you should be able to

1. Define the control process and enumerate its steps.
2. Indicate why controlling is important.
3. Discuss the relationship of planning to control.
4. Indicate the relationships between control and management style.
5. Describe the characteristics of effective control systems.
6. List the dysfunctional aspects of control.
7. Identify the types of controls by various factors.
8. Discuss current trends in control management.

CHAPTER OUTLINE

Control
    The Importance of Control
Steps in the Control Process
    Establishing Performance Standards
        and Methods for Measuring
        Performance
    Measuring Actual Performance
    Comparing the Actual Performance
        Against the Standard
    Taking Necessary Action
Characteristics of the Control Process
The Interrelationships of Planning
and Control
Management Styles of Control
    Market Control
    Bureaucratic Control
    Clan Control
Choosing a Management
    Control Style
Designing Effective Control Systems
Dysfunctional Consequences
of Control
Types of Control
    Control as Defined by Timing
        Relative to the Transformation
        Process
    Control as Defined by the Level
        of Plan
    Control of the Economic Functions
    Control of the Management
        Functions
Control and the Changing
Environment
Control as a Problem-Solving Endeavor
    The Management Challenges
        Identified
    Some Solutions Noted in the Chapter

The Challenger Tragedy

Seventy-three seconds after launch on January 28, 1986, the space shuttle Challenger was destroyed along with its seven occupants—six astronauts and one civilian passenger, Christa McAuliffe. In the months that followed, the presidential commission formed to investigate this tragedy, headed by former Secretary of State William Rogers, uncovered mismanagement throughout all of NASA, not just at the Kennedy Space Center. The decision to launch the Challenger was not only a bad decision, it was a bad decision that was inevitable in a system gone awry. The focal point of this mismanagement was the control process.

First, NASA's top management had become isolated. Information from control reporting systems often failed to reach them. The agency's leaders had become preoccupied with raising money. They spent far too much time in Washington and far too little time managing the agency and the individual centers they were in charge of—the Marshall, Kennedy, and Johnson space centers.

Second, there were clear indications of violation of safety control processes. On the evening of January 27, Allan McDonald, who was the senior engineer present at the launch site for Morton Thiokol, the manufacturer of the booster rocket, refused to sign off on the launch, even after a lengthy argument with Lawrence Mulloy, rocket-booster manager at Huntsville, who was at the Cape for the launch. In a classic violation of appropriate safety procedures, Mulloy went over their heads and received permission from Joe Kilminster, Thiokol vice-president for their space boosters program in Utah, to sign the launch go-ahead. He did so shortly before midnight.

Third, there were several communications problems. For example, physical inspection of the vehicle before the launch turned up extremely cold spots on the skin of the right booster, but for some reason, this information was not fed back to Launch Control.

The Rogers Commission discovered that even on a day-to-day basis, information was not shared within or among the three centers. Even when information was made available, it was often lost in a morass of paperwork. This paperwork had been put in place in an attempt to establish control over a decentralized organization in the absence of management. Furthermore, this red tape tended to cover up, rather than identify problems.

Fourth, the defect in the O-ring, to which the crash was ultimately attributed, had been documented in NASA's written information systems since 1978. Budget cuts and demands to meet impossible flight schedules helped push the issue aside.

Fifth, it became evident during the investigation that the decision to launch was a political, as well as an economic decision. There were millions of school kids waiting to watch a teacher conduct class from space. The delayed launch would indicate failure to politicians, and politicians don't like failures, especially nationally televised ones.

Finally, the commission also found that safety standards had been sacrificed in not just one, but numerous areas of the launch program in order to meet deadlines. As one key official commented to his subordinates, "Safety is like caviar, a little bit is good but too much of it makes you sick."

SOURCES: Ed Magnesun, "Fixing NASA" (June 9, 1986), pp. 14–27; "Questions Get Tougher," *Time* (March 3, 1986), pp. 14–16; Michael Brody, "NASA's Challenge: Ending Isolation at the Top," *Fortune* (May 12, 1986); David Bailey, "NASA's Ace Space Boss," *Florida Trend* (January 1988), pp. 47–52; Tim Smart, "Rogers: NASA Came Close to a Cover-Up," *Orlando Sentinel* 11 May 1986, pp. A-1, A-18; and "After the Challenger—How NASA Struggled to Put Itself Back Together," *Newsweek*, (October 10, 1988), pp. 28–38.

In every company, minimizing waste and efficiency is *everyone's* job.

David Henry
Handbook of Cost Reduction Techniques

Control's managerial role has often been mistakenly considered to be synonymous with financial control.

Giovanni Giglioni and Arthur G. Bedeian
Researchers of control practices

The Challenger disaster was inevitable, given the circumstances, but it could have been prevented if the appropriate control systems and mechanisms had been in place, and if approved control procedures had been followed. Probably no event in recent history more vividly illustrates the need for appropriate levels, types, and degrees of control. With millions of Americans and others around the world watching, a series of control failures erupted into a national disaster. Ultimately, political and economic factors led to an expedient choice in a decentralized management system, over which top management failed to exercise proper control.

Every day in the newspaper other examples appear of the failure to exercise properly management control: Irangate—the illegal sale of arms to Iran, the Defense Department bribery scandals, the October 1987 collapse of the stock market, Eastern Airlines' alleged violation of safety laws in order to put planes in the air on time,[1] the failure of the numerous corporations that file bankruptcy,

The seven members of the crew of the space shuttle *Challenger*, who lost their lives in the disaster. (SOURCE © NASA/Black Star)

Eastern Airlines allegedly knowingly violated safety laws in order to keep their planes in the air and better meet their schedules. (SOURCE © Gerald Davis)

and the financial statements of firms that failed to control their cost and competitive strategies. In all these cases managers failed to exercise proper control.

The Challenger disaster exemplifies the key points of this chapter. The chapter begins by defining control and indicating its importance. Then it examines the stages of the control process. The general characteristics of the process are noted, the interrelationships of planning and control described, and the types of management control strategies and styles described. Next, the types of control and the characteristics of effective control systems are reviewed. The problems of controlling in a changing environment are noted. Finally, control as a problem-solving process is discussed.

Control

Control is the systematic process by which managers assure that the organization is reaching its objectives and carrying out the associated plans in an effective and efficient manner.[2] Robert J. Mockler describes the essential parts of this control process: "Management control is a systematic effort to set performance standards for planning objectives, to design information feedback systems, to compare actual performance with today's predetermined standards, to determine whether there are any deviations and to measure their significance, and to take any action required to assure that all corporate resources are being used in the most effective and efficient manner as possible in achieving corporate objectives."[3]

The term *control* finds its roots in recent years as far back as Frederick W. Taylor's *Scientific Management*. In fact, control was the "central idea" of scientific management.[4] Even as late as the early 1970s, it was generally agreed that control was still very neglected and not particularly well understood.[5] The issues of control and how the types of control mechanisms used should differ

> **AT NASA:** *NASA's Challenger experience occurred because the decision process itself was out of control, and because the control process—for example, quality control—was not being controlled.*

according to the situation have only recently been seen as being of major importance.[6] Control remains a major problem in many organizations, as you learned from NASA's Challenger experience. Controlling large organizations is often a complex process involving not just simple control systems, but organization structures, leadership styles, and the objectives and plans that are the driving force of organizations. Not only must planning, organizing, and leading be controlled, but so must control. Finally, the decision process itself must be controlled.

The Importance of Control

Control is the fourth major function of management. It is the concluding phase in the management cycle: planning, organizing, leading, and controlling. Appropriate control leads to the attainment of objectives and the fulfillment of plans in the economic functions and in the management functions. Planning and control are closely interdependent, as will be discussed in more detail shortly. The repercussions of the failure to exercise control can be horrendous. Another dramatic example is the failure of the United States to control illegal drug usage.[7] Drugs have destroyed millions of lives, and the hundreds of billions of dollars spent on illegal drugs have made billionaires out of criminals. The drug problem is further compounded by the fact that the objectives of the containment program are unclear. Given the tremendous level of illegal drug use in the United States, it is not even clear that its people want such drugs to remain illegal.[8]

In the medical field, software "bugs" can literally kill patients. Radiation machines may give lethal doses, pacemakers may stop unexpectedly, and computer-produced medicines may be hazardous to the user's health.[9] In business organizations, especially those in manufacturing, failure to control can lead not only to a loss of profits, but ultimately to bankruptcy. Japanese and other Pacific rim firms have put many U.S. businesses out of business through their ability to provide superior product quality. Quality control has become a critical weapon in the efforts of U.S. firms to be competitive.[10]

Control is also important because it helps cope with uncertainty, with complex environments, and with human limitations in the ability to carry out plans to reach objectives. Control helps to cope with uncertainty and complexity because managers and their subordinates must continually be checking to determine what progress is being made in uncertain and complex environments. This often means changing plans that no longer fit environmental circumstances. Managers must be flexible. Control helps overcome the problems of human limitations, especially through the delegation of authority, by checking continuously either through self-management or from management above to ascertain how objectives are being reached and plans carried out.

> AT NASA: *Had NASA exercised appropriate control, seven people would not have died. NASA would not have experienced a two-and-a-half-year delay in shuttle launchings, and thousands of people would not have been furloughed from work.*

> AT NASA: *This aspect of control, controlling the problem of human limitations, was noticeably absent at NASA.*

Steps in the Control Process

There are four essential steps in the control process:

1. Establishing performance objectives and standards.
2. Measuring actual performance.
3. Comparing actual performance to objectives and standards.
4. Taking necessary action based on the results of the comparison.[11]

The relationships of the steps are shown in Figure 17.1.

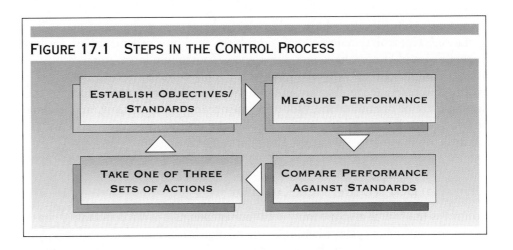

FIGURE 17.1 STEPS IN THE CONTROL PROCESS

ESTABLISH OBJECTIVES/
STANDARDS

MEASURE PERFORMANCE

TAKE ONE OF THREE
SETS OF ACTIONS

COMPARE PERFORMANCE
AGAINST STANDARDS

Establishing Performance Standards and Methods for Measuring Performance

The first step in control involves establishing performance standards and methods for measuring performance. Performance standards state organizational objectives and subunit objectives, which provide readily identifiable targets for individuals and groups to achieve and against which actual performance may be compared. Involving those whose performance is to be measured in developing standards provides more positive attitudes toward meeting those standards. A highly refined management by objectives, results, and rewards program includes standards for every job from maintenance engineer to company president. Sometimes standards are difficult to establish properly or are not changed to fit new circumstances. British radar on board the British frigate *Sheffield* was designed to detect Soviet bloc missiles. When dispatched to the Falkland Islands, the frigate was attacked by Argentinian Exocet missiles supplied by French arms makers. Because the frigate was unable to detect this type of in-bound missile, it was sunk, killing twenty sailors.[12]

Methods for measuring performance must be designed for each and every standard established. Whether it is measuring the number of patients per hour, sales per month, rejects per day, calls per hour, or productivity for a year, the standards and ways of measuring performance against those standards must be determined. Sometimes establishment of standards is difficult for service jobs, where specific objectives may not be readily identifiable. For example, what are the objectives of a grocery store checkout clerk? To put through X units of sales per hour? To keep the customer happy? Similarly, is a psychologist's standard of performance to see a certain number of patients per day or to cure a certain number of patients per year? Despite the difficulties involved in defining standards, to the extent possible, specific standards of performance must be identified for every job, and ways of measuring performance against these standards must be determined. Furthermore, these standards must be accepted by those who are to use them and they must be utilized.

Measuring Actual Performance

Once systems have been designed to measure performance against standards, individual, group, or department performance must be calculated. It is necessary to achieve a balance in the control process between too much information and too little. The typical cost information provided in manufacturing and service operations, which is principally used for controlling the efficient use of labor

AT NASA: The standard of performance tolerance for the O-ring was continually ignored by the individuals involved in the launch decision process. Thus though standards were defined, they were not used.

These Genentech researchers are shown celebrating the development of their new heart drug. Unfortunately, however, sales were not nearly as high as had been forecasted. (SOURCE © Robert Holmgren)

and machinery, has not provided the information necessary to make strategic decisions—for example, whether to delete product lines. So, while the organization may be performing efficiently from one standard, its performance from another standard perspective, such as meeting the needs of the market, may not be measured and may be in conflict with the aims of the existing cost system.[13]

Comparing the Actual Performance Against the Standard

Comparing actual performance against the standards for performance can help determine whether objectives have been achieved. A football coach, for example, continuously compares a player's performance against his expectations for blocking, tackling, running, passing, or scoring. He is in turn evaluated by the number of victories his team has during a season, season after season.

Taking Necessary Action

Once actual performance has been compared to performance standards, the manager is left with three choices of action:

1. If performance is less than the standards require, the manager must take corrective actions. The manager must first determine if performance is the problem. If so, efforts to improve performance must take place. Another corrective action may be to change the standards, as they may have been too high to begin with. This happened to then high-flying Genentech, the leading biotech firm in 1988. Estimates of sales for its new heart drug far exceeded actual sales, causing the company's stock to plunge. Revised sales forecasts became necessary.[14]

2. If performance is less than standard, or anticipated performance is less than standard, the manager must take preventive action to assure that the problem will not recur. This goes beyond merely taking corrective actions.[15] As management author William Greenwood has observed, it is insufficient simply to correct problems. Rather, the manager must take actions to make certain these problems do not occur again.[16]

3. If performance is greater than or equal to standards, then the manager may choose to reinforce the behaviors that led to achieving the standard.

Corrective actions are relatively easy in most cases. Something is wrong, so you fix it. But complex situations often defy rational solution. Political, economic, and social relationships must be adjusted, often to no one's satisfaction, as Management Challenge 17.1 reveals.

Characteristics of the Control Process

Several characteristics of the control process should be noted.

1. As seen in Figure 17.1, the control process is cyclical. Standards are established; performance is measured against standards; deviations from the standards lead to action; and the cycle begins again. Every time Eaton Corporation, a diversified manufacturer, makes one of its many products—for example, a hydraulic motor or a Golf Pride golf club hand grip—it goes through this cycle.[17]

ings resulted. Employees who had invested in Milken deals, often with spectacular results and millions in personal gains, demanded indemnity from Drexel, and they got it. The cash drain on the firm was tremendous, and there was no one controlling Joseph's actions.

Ironically, just a few days prior to declaring bankruptcy, Joseph had opted to take all of his 1989 bonus of $2.5 million in Drexel stock.

SOURCES: Laurie P. Cohen, "The Final Days: Drexel Itself Made Firm's Sudden Demise All but Inevitable," *Wall Street Journal* 26 February 1990, pp. A1, A4; and "After Drexel," *Business Week* (February 26, 1990), pp. 36–40.

Michael Milken declines further comment on his case. (SOURCE © Nina Berman/ SIPA Press)

2. Control tends to be viewed as a negative endeavor, but the process results in an extremely positive contribution to organizational success. For example, it has only been as U.S. firms began to emphasize product quality, that they have become competitive with Japanese firms. The trend toward self-control, as opposed to control imposed by others, should help satisfy the increasing needs of individuals for autonomy and should help lead to a more positive perspective of the control process.

3. Control is anticipatory as well as retrospective. The typical control process described here views control from an after-the-fact viewpoint, but control can be anticipatory.[18] Preliminary analysis and analysis of processes in progress help prevent deviations from the standards. This is especially important in some industries—for example, in steel. Molten metal must be constantly monitored not to get too hot, nor to cool too long. Otherwise, the whole batch could be lost.

4. Finally, control must occur throughout the organization. Although many organizations tend to rely on financial controls because they provide a common denominator by which to measure success, true control cannot be achieved unless all of the factors leading to those numbers are controlled as well—for example, quality, inventory levels, service, and theft.

From the total organizational perspective, control must occur at those critical points where performance can be matched against plans.[19] Unfortunately, no set of control points or standards is suitable for every manager because of the differences in organizations and departments, the variety of products and services to be controlled, the types of behaviors involved, and the various types of plans to be evaluated.[20] However, standards tend to fall into one of eight types, as Table 17.1 reveals.

Table 17.1 Eight Principal Types of Standards

1. Physical Standards: Nonmonetary measurements are common at the operating level—for example, units of production per machine hour.
2. Cost Standards: Monetary measurements are also common at the operating level—for example, costs per plane reservation.
3. Capital Standards: The application of monetary measurements is made to physical items. These are concerned with the capital invested in the company and its utilization—for example, the desired ratio of return on investment.
4. Revenue Standards: Monetary standards are relative to sales—for example, sales per capita.
5. Program Standards: The successful implementation of plans involved in a program may be used as a standard of performance—for example, the successful development of a new product.
6. Intangible Standards: Where job performance is difficult to describe, intangible standards are often employed—for example, customer loyalty.
7. Objectives Standards: Many companies are now moving to specific objectives for virtually every job—for example, salespeople trained per year for a personnel training specialist.
8. Strategic Plans: Control points are used for strategic control—for example, checking at each stage of action to see if a strategy is successful.

SOURCE: Harold Koontz and Heinz Weihrich, *Management*, 9th ed. (New York: McGraw-Hill, 1988), pp. 493–494.

However, although these may suffice for examining the total organization, each subunit, each department, and each individual must determine relevant control points for its assigned task. As discussed earlier, each organization is an input–transformation–output system. This is true for each subunit of the organization—for each group, for each individual. Thus, there must be control points for inputs, for various phases of transformation, and for the resultant outputs. Whether the process being controlled results in a physical product, a service, or an idea, standards must be established, performance measured and then compared to standards, and action taken where necessary for each of the control points established. McDonalds establishes control points for its franchises in such areas as housekeeping, quality, timeliness, and employee appearance. When it inspects franchise facilities, the control cycle is followed for each of these.

The Interrelationships
of Planning and Control

As can be seen in Figure 17.2, planning and control are intimately related. Planning begins the management cycle and control concludes it. Control is concerned with whether the objectives and plans established in the planning system have been achieved and carried out. In fact, control is defined in terms of determining whether the objectives established by planning have been accomplished and whether the plans established by planning have been carried out. As plans become increasingly flexible, control processes and standards must also. A major part of strategic planning is an "early warning system," a control system that "alerts management to potential opportunities and problems before they affect the financial statements."[21] GTE's Diversified Products Division, with

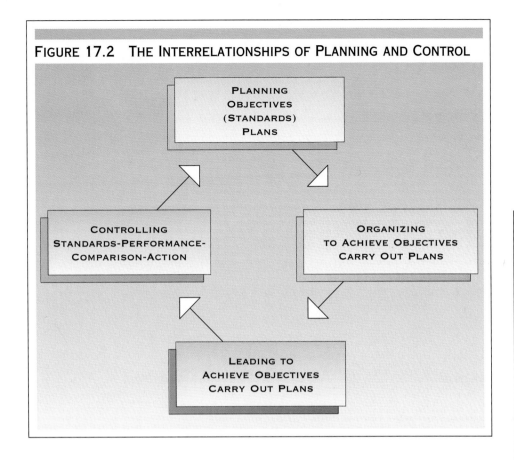

FIGURE 17.2   THE INTERRELATIONSHIPS OF PLANNING AND CONTROL

PLANNING
OBJECTIVES
(STANDARDS)
PLANS

CONTROLLING
STANDARDS-PERFORMANCE-
COMPARISON-ACTION

ORGANIZING
TO ACHIEVE OBJECTIVES
CARRY OUT PLANS

LEADING TO
ACHIEVE OBJECTIVES
CARRY OUT PLANS

AT NASA: Those who were charged with implementing top managements' plans to reach these objectives and those who were charged with controlling performance relative to achieving those objectives, often failed to communicate with top management. Worse, even when they did communicate, lower-level communications were ignored by upper-level management. And in the complex contractor-space agency relationship, the contractor's employees were ignored by space-agency top management. Finally, NASA's top managers were not aware of decisions made either at the levels just below them or at the front lines.

some 60,000 employees in 107 countries, continuously tracks the progress it is making toward accomplishing its objectives through its sophisticated Strategic Tracking System. This system is designed to provide an early warning of problems.[22] Typically, those who plan and those who control are different; thus, communication between the two is critical.[23]

Types of control may even be plans—strategies. As discussed in Chapter 6, for example, Michael E. Porter identifies taking the low-cost position relative to one's competitors as one of the three key strategies in which organizations can engage.[24] Additionally, high levels of quality, achieved through rigorous control efforts, have been identified as a key way of providing differentiation in the marketplace. If the quality of a firm's products or services is perceived by the consumer as higher than the quality of its competitors, then it has successfully differentiated its products or services.[25]

Management Styles of Control

William G. Ouchi, who introduced many U.S. managers to Japanese management, has identified three principal control strategies, or styles, that managers may choose to employ when designing and managing control systems: market control, bureaucratic control, and clan control.[26] These three styles are based on the belief that cooperation between the subunits of a firm is a function of

FIGURE 17.3 COMPONENTS OF THREE PRINCIPAL MANAGEMENT CONTROL STRATEGIES

TYPE OF CONTROL	HOW ENACTED
MARKET	PRICES, COMPETITION, MARKET EXCHANGES, MARKET MECHANISMS.
BUREAUCRACY	BUDGETS, RULES, POLICIES, PROCEDURES, HIERARCHIES, MANAGEMENT CONTROL SYSTEMS, SELECTION AND TRAINING, TECHNOLOGY.
CLAN	TRADITION, SHARED VALUES, TRUST, PEER GROUPS, SELECTION AND SOCIALIZATION.

SOURCE: WILLIAM G. OUCHI, "A CONCEPTUAL FRAMEWORK FOR THE DESIGN OF ORGANIZATIONAL CONTROL MECHANISMS," MANAGEMENT SCIENCE, 1979, PP. 833–838; "MARKETS, BUREAUCRACIES, AND CLANS," ADMINISTRATIVE SCIENCE QUARTERLY, NO. 1, 1980, P. 130

the exchanges taking place between those subunits and between individuals in the organization. For example, individuals exchange their labor and time for money, security, and job satisfaction. Organizations exchange materials, outputs, services, and products to achieve some objective or purpose. All three types of control may be in use simultaneously in an organization because each serves a different purpose. Exchanges have a cost associated with them that Ouchi calls a transaction cost—"any activity which is engaged in to satisfy each party to an exchange that the value given and received is in accord with his or her expectations."[27] The components of these three control styles are identified in Figure 17.3.

Market Control

Market control strategy allows market mechanisms such as competition to establish the standards of the control system. This strategy assumes that market mechanisms are most efficient in setting the prices or costs identified with certain transactions. This style of control relies on external forces to control behavior within the firm. It is a very quantitatively oriented control strategy. There must be an identifiable product or service whose contributions can be measured. Typically, divisions of the company become profit centers—their contributions to the company are measured by the profits they generate.[28] For example, the Walt Disney Companies have seven major divisions, each run virtually as a separate business: theme parks, movies, consumer products, cable television, Disney Development (real estate), hotels, and imagineering (creative designs).

Bureaucratic Control

Sometimes market control is inadequate, especially where there is little or no competition or one subunit is very powerful. In such cases bureaucratic control is a reasonable approach. **Bureaucratic control** is based on control by authority through the use of rules, regulations, and policies. It is based on compliance rather than commitment. This system is highly dependent on well-defined job descriptions and standards. Standardization of activities to achieve highly refined standards is at the core of this system. Any well-managed assembly line, for example, depends on repetition of activity according to highly refined specification for its success. Hierarchy, formalized control systems, computerized reporting systems, and other internally derived methods of control are utilized. The emphasis is on someone else controlling the individual.

In bureaucratically controlled organizations, decision making, the core management function, is depersonalized. The "rules" determine what is to be done, and you often hear people say, "You can't go against the rules," or "That's company policy." Large American organizations, such as Xerox and American Airlines, often use both market and bureaucratic control systems.

Clan Control

The **clan control style** relies on peoples' social needs—the desire to belong to a group. Control is established largely through cultural artifacts such as rituals and myths. Rituals, such as traditional Christmas bonuses, and myths, such as "being a team player is how you get ahead here," are examples. Ouchi suggests that clan control occurs most frequently "where teamwork is common, technologies change often, and therefore individual performance is highly ambiguous."[29] Clan control is often employed when the other two systems are inappropriate—when competition is lacking or powerful subunits exist, and when performance is too ambiguous to be defined in advance through standards and standardization. However, the Japanese have successfully employed clan control in many highly competitive situations.

Bureaucratic control has been characteristic of American businesses, while clan, or cultural, control has characterized Japanese businesses.[30] While most U.S. firms attempt to apply market control and bureaucratic methods following some type of management by objectives—such as results and rewards programs—Japanese firms follow clan control. The Japanese many times allow individuals to set their own objectives and pursue a cooperative effort. Many people point to clan, or cultural, control as one reason the Japanese have been so efficient in production and have had such high quality in their products. However, it is also recognized that the lack of planning in a clan-controlled organization may not promote innovative technology or allow management to handle radical changes as well as some bureaucratically controlled organizations.[31]

The clan style is becoming much more popular in America as organizations recognize two critical factors: first, the individual seeks more self-control and, second, the management of organizational culture can lead to more efficient and effective organizations. Many organizations are switching from dominant market and bureaucratic to a mixed bureaucratic, market, and clan-controlled management style. The opening incident in this book, in Chapter 1, discussed the efforts of Ford Motor Company to incorporate more clan control by becoming more team oriented.

Choosing a Management Control Style

Each of these three strategies uses a different approach to control. Each can be effective, given a certain situation. When neither a market nor a bureaucratic control style will suffice, clan control is recommended.[32] At the operating level, the choice is really between bureaucratic types of control and clan types of control. Market control is more of a strategic form of control imposed upon lower-level managers.

Cortlandt Cammann and David A. Nadler suggest that most managers really have only two types of management control style between which to choose: an internal motivation style, in which employees control themselves, similar to the clan style; and an external control strategy, in which rules, regulations, procedures, and external authority are used to control the employee, similar to bureaucratic control (with some elements of the market control strategy).[33,34] Certain situations may call for a mixture of the two strategies. Managers should ask themselves a series of four questions in choosing one of the two:

1. In general, what kind of managerial style do I have—participative or directive?
2. In general, what kind of culture, structure, and reward systems does my organization have—participative or nonparticipative?
3. How accurate and reliable are the measures of key areas of subordinate performance—accurate or inaccurate?
4. Do my subordinates desire to participate and respond well to opportunities to take responsibility for decision making and performance—high desire to participate, low desire to participate?[35]

In answering these four questions, managers should follow the chart presented in Figure 17.4; it will guide them in choosing an appropriate style for the circumstances. In general, when the manager is participative, the culture is participative, and the subordinate's desire to participate is high, the internal motivation—or clan strategy—should be employed. Where the manager is directive, the culture is nonparticipative, and subordinates do not desire to participate, the external control strategy—or bureaucratic strategy—should be employed. An interesting switch in control styles is observed in Management Challenge 17.2.

Designing Effective Control Systems

A number of authors have identified the following characteristics for incorporation into the design of control systems in order to make them effective:[36]

1. **Strategy, tactics, and operations.** There should be control measures at each level of the planning process. Importantly, control should be linked to strategy. It should measure performance against where the organization is headed, rather than against what has been acceptable behavior in the past. In the future, for example, innovation is going to be much more critical in most firms than it has been in the past. Control systems should not continue to emphasize efficiency, but innovation as well.

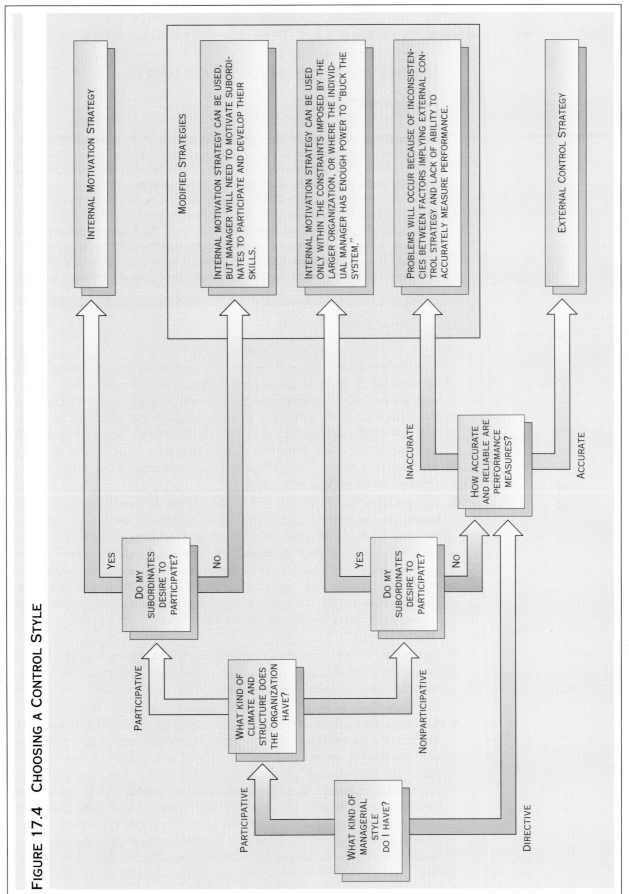

FIGURE 17.4 CHOOSING A CONTROL STYLE

INTERNAL MOTIVATION STRATEGY

MODIFIED STRATEGIES

INTERNAL MOTIVATION STRATEGY CAN BE USED, BUT MANAGER WILL NEED TO MOTIVATE SUBORDINATES TO PARTICIPATE AND DEVELOP THEIR SKILLS.

INTERNAL MOTIVATION STRATEGY CAN BE USED ONLY WITHIN THE CONSTRAINTS IMPOSED BY THE LARGER ORGANIZATION, OR WHERE THE INDIVIDUAL MANAGER HAS ENOUGH POWER TO "BUCK THE SYSTEM."

PROBLEMS WILL OCCUR BECAUSE OF INCONSISTENCIES BETWEEN FACTORS IMPLYING EXTERNAL CONTROL STRATEGY AND LACK OF ABILITY TO ACCURATELY MEASURE PERFORMANCE.

EXTERNAL CONTROL STRATEGY

YES

DO MY SUBORDINATES DESIRE TO PARTICIPATE?

NO

YES

DO MY SUBORDINATES DESIRE TO PARTICIPATE?

NO

INACCURATE

HOW ACCURATE AND RELIABLE ARE PERFORMANCE MEASURES?

ACCURATE

PARTICIPATIVE

WHAT KIND OF CLIMATE AND STRUCTURE DOES THE ORGANIZATION HAVE?

NONPARTICIPATIVE

PARTICIPATIVE

WHAT KIND OF MANAGERIAL STYLE DO I HAVE?

DIRECTIVE

SOURCE: PERMISSION OF THE HARVARD BUSINESS REVIEW FROM "FIT CONTROL SYSTEMS TO YOUR MANAGERIAL STYLE" BY CORTLANDT CAMMANN AND DAVID A. NADLER (JANUARY–FEBRUARY 1976), P. 71. COPYRIGHT © 1976 BY THE PRESIDENT AND FELLOWS OF HARVARD COLLEGE. ALL RIGHTS RESERVED.

Overcoming the Problems at Kennedy

As a consequence of the shuttle tragedy, the investigation by the committee, and subsequent layoffs as the result of the eventual two-and-a-half-year delay in program launches, morale at the Kennedy Space Center was terrible. Several obvious problems had to be solved, as at least fifty major problems in rocket design were uncovered. Thrust into the middle of this situation was retired Air Force General Forrest McCartney, who assumed direct control of the Kennedy Space Center in September 1987. He was the first military head of the Space Center, and many feared he would destroy the open and creative environment necessary to move forward. The skeptics were wrong. He brought with him a folksy, low-key but very demanding style—more demanding than his predecessor's. He restored morale

While efficiency will still need to be measured, but it should not be emphasized as much in the control system. For example, more than one cost system may be necessary. Typical cost systems focus on labor and materials inputs, the efficiency of their use, and the potential for substitutions—such as technology for labor. But they don't help managers make decisions about other important factors, such as gaining market share and retaining customers. Thus, additional management systems aimed at these types of decisions will be necessary.[37]

2. **Acceptability by those who will enforce them.** If those who must implement management's decisions are not in agreement with them, there will be dysfunctional consequences. This is an extension of Barnard's acceptance theory of authority discussed in Chapter 8. Methods of control have varying degrees of acceptance.[38] Clan control, for example, depends on trust, cooperation, and commitment for its success, whereas bureaucratic control relies on the acceptance of authority. Sometimes people simply choose to ignore controls, as the Global Management Challenge for this chapter reveals.

3. **Flexibility.** The environment of organizations is changing at an accelerating rate. Consequently, goals, strategic objectives, strategies, and related subobjectives and subplans are changing. The control systems and methods employed must be flexible enough to adapt to changing circumstances.

4. **Accuracy.** Any information system must provide accurate and timely information. Control is no different. Proper decisions cannot be made unless the information upon which they are based is accurate. In any business, inaccurate information can have disastrous results. For example, in the health care industry, inaccurate information regarding PAP smears can have disastrous results. Unfortunately, pressures to cut costs and to improve productivity have led to an increase in inaccurate PAP smear reports. This has led some patients to believe they had cancer when they didn't or, worse, led others to believe they didn't have cancer when they actually did.[39]

5. **Timeliness.** A decision made too late is a decision that will be ineffective.

and confidence by paying close attention to the details. He worked with workers and showed them he cared about every problem, especially theirs, rather than fly off to Washington to lobby for funds. He practiced management by wandering around and talking to people. He was hands on, as opposed to his predecessor's hands-off approach. He held daily 7:30 A.M. meetings for the whole staff; his predecessor had held meetings only every two weeks. He supervised the rewriting of 100,000 pages of documentation for instructions outlining how to perform shuttle-related work. He demanded accountability, and he set the example of leadership. He acted to aid workers to improve their situation. The other space centers viewed Kennedy Center workers as incompetent. McCartney had all the workers retrained and involved in the other centers in reformulating a program of action. Prior to McCartney's coming, safety personnel had been following the normal chain of command. They are now outside the chain of command, and the Kennedy safety director reports directly to McCartney. McCartney has worked hard to build relationships with the other centers and aid in a solution process.

SOURCE: David Bailey, "NASA's Ace Space Boss," *Florida Trend* (January 1988), pp. 47–52.

Information must be provided in time for managers to make an appropriate decision. Ironically, although the Japanese employ clan control methods, a study of control information among air conditioner manufacturers in Japan found that Japanese managers receive control information twice as fast as their American counterparts; the responses of Japanese management are also quicker than those of their American counterparts.[40]

6. **Cost effectiveness.** The cost of maintaining control should be no greater than, and at least equal to, the benefits derived from keeping control. Most added controls add costs.

7. **Understandability.** If the employee charged with the control effort or the individual who is being controlled cannot understand the control system, it is likely to have an adverse effect.

8. **Objectivity and, where appropriate, subjectivity.** Effective control systems balance the requirements for information that is factual and objective and subjective information. For example, a bureaucratic control strategy would typically require more objective information than a clan control strategy, which would typically require more subjective information.

9. **Other factors.** Other factors that have been identified as characteristics of effective control systems include the following. Effective control systems are coordinated with planning and other elements of management and the organization, is realistic, related to the work flow, and justifiable.

Dysfunctional Consequences of Control

If control systems do not possess the effective characteristics indicated here— or even if they do—sometimes certain dysfunctional consequences may occur. The following are among them:

Moscow's Problems with Control at Chernobyl

For a country known for bureaucratic, often harsh control, the revelations about Russia's Chernobyl accident provide important lessons about the role of the human element in the control process. Moscow was quite surprising in its candor over a public failure, blaming "gross" human error for the world's most serious nuclear accident. In an official report to the International Atomic Energy Agency, Moscow detailed six key violations of operating procedures that led to the Chernobyl catastrophe. The six blunders occurred as the plant's operators began reducing the Chernobyl reactor's power level so they could perform a turbine test. Each action was a violation of a rule, and if any one of the violations had not occurred, the accident would have been prevented. Against all odds, all six took place. These six actions were as follows:

1. The emergency cooling system was turned off to conduct the test.
2. The reactor power output was inadvertently lowered too much, making it more difficult to control.
3. All water circulation pumps were turned on, exceeding recommended flow rates.
4. The automatic signal, which shuts down the reactors if the turbines stop, was blocked.
5. The safety devices that shut down the reactor if steam pressure or water levels become abnormal were turned off.

GAME PLAYING

Some people will always view control systems as a challenge, as something to be beaten.[41] Some, for example, might figure out how to try to pad their budgets in order not to be controlled by them. Others might try to figure out ways of stealing from the company when excessive rules are placed over corporate materials inventories.

RESISTANCE TO CONTROL

There are many reasons for resistance to control, perhaps the most common reason is excessive control. When an organization tends to control too much, people will resist such efforts.

INACCURATE INFORMATION

There are clear indications that managers will pass inaccurate information upward in the chain of command in order to make themselves look better.[42] Even the Boy Scouts of America has suffered from such a circumstance. When top management brought pressure on local and regional managers to bring in substantial new members, the managers reported significantly larger numbers of new members than actually existed.[43]

6. Almost all control rods were pulled from the core.

The Soviet's nuclear reactors are generally considered to be of an older, unsafe type, one not approved in the United States nor Europe. Soviet authorities defended their technology, citing only human error as responsible. Soviet response to the catastrophe was immediate, as the site had to be cleaned up and the reactor encased in concrete. For the long term, the Soviets felt the need not so much to change control policies and procedures, as to ensure better that such human error would not occur again.

SOURCE: "Anatomy of a Catastrophe," *Time* (September 1, 1986), pp. 26–29.

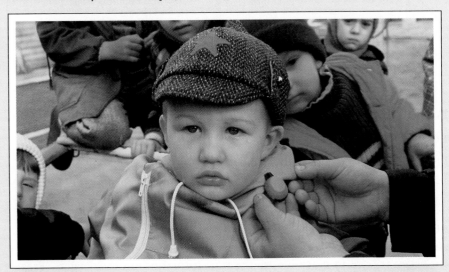

Soviet citizens in the Chernobyl area had to wear radiation detectors such as the one shown being placed on this child. (SOURCE © Wojtek Laski/SIPA Press)

RIGID BUREAUCRATIC BEHAVIOR
People will tend to obey a rule beyond a reasonable level themselves. For example, if you as a customer request additional bread when eating at a restaurant, but the waiter refuses to give you more without charge because it's against the rules, his behavior is to the detriment of the restaurant. Rather than save it money, the rule may cost it money—you may not return.

Types of Control

There are four different types of control.

1. Those defined according to the timing of the control process relative to the transformation process: preaction control, concurrent control, and postaction control.
2. Those defined according to the planning level involved: strategic, tactical, and operational control.
3. Those defined according to economic function: marketing, finance, operations, human resource management, information management.
4. Those defined according to the management function involved: problem solving, planning, organizing, leading, and controlling.

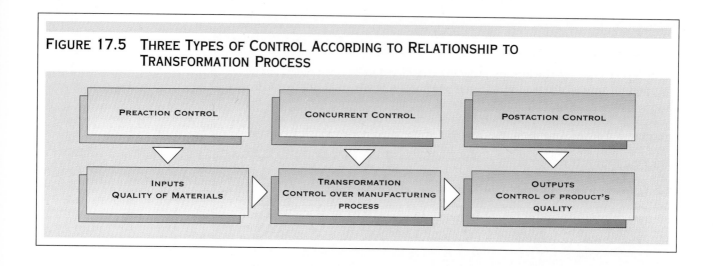

FIGURE 17.5   THREE TYPES OF CONTROL ACCORDING TO RELATIONSHIP TO TRANSFORMATION PROCESS

Control as Defined by Timing Relative to the Transformation Process

As shown in Figure 17.5, there are three principal types of control according to where each would be used in the input-transformation-output process: preaction, concurrent, and postaction control.[44]

PREACTION CONTROL

Preaction control is used to assure that the human, material, and financial resources necessary are in place before the transformation process begins. Preaction controls—sometimes referred to as preventive controls, precontrols, or feedforward controls—ensure that not only enough resources are available, but that the quality of these is sufficiently high to prevent problems once the transformation process is underway. Preaction controls recognize and identify potential problems before they occur.

Preaction controls have received significant attention in the manufacturing process in recent years. Historically, U.S. manufacturing firms relied on statistical sampling to ensure that an "acceptable" rate of defects resulted from the process. But with the attempt to make every product perfect, every input must therefore also be perfect. U.S. firms typically accepted a significant number of imperfect inputs from their suppliers, but they are no longer able to do so, under current high-quality management performance standards.[45]

Very close attention also is paid to organizational human resource inputs. The human resource department often spends exhaustive amounts of human and financial resources to select the best people to fill jobs. Undoubtedly one of the most exhaustive selection processes in the United States occurs at Toyota's auto assembly plant in Kentucky. Literally hundreds of applicants will be sifted through before each of the 3,000 jobs in the plant is filled.[46] American firms are becoming more and more concerned about the people they employ. Ironically, such efforts must be honed in a future environment in the 1990s that indicates a demand for skilled labor greater than the available labor supply.[47]

CONCURRENT CONTROLS

Concurrent controls assess ongoing activities. They are designed to detect variances from standards, leading to corrective action before a series of actions is completed.[48] Concurrent controls are often referred to as steering controls. This term derives from the analogy of steering an automobile. Before the automobile

AT NASA: *NASA actually had preaction controls. It had concerns about the value of the O-ring before the first launch was ever made, but budget cuts overrode the concerns of the engineers.*

reaches its destination, the driver will change direction many times, even if only minutely, to make certain that the automobile reaches predetermined objectives.

In a power generating plant, for example, engineers constantly monitor hundreds of gauges to ensure that all is going well and that there will not be a power shortage. Similarly, in a brewery, the brewmaster periodically checks the composition of each batch of beer to ensure that it meets standards. Finally, a dentist continuously checks his or her progress in performing a root canal operation. He or she checks for accomplishments at each stage of the surgical procedure. Control begins with prescribed standards of performance.

One particular type of concurrent control is the yes/no control. Although it is most frequently found in a concurrent area, it may also be found in the preaction control area. **Yes/no controls** are used on some specific action or series of actions that must be accomplished before the overall process may continue. Airplane pilots, for example, go down a checklist of items as they prepare for takeoff and landing. Neither process can continue until each item is satisfied.

The ability to control ongoing activities is critical, as Management Challenge 17.3 indicates.

MANAGEMENT CHALLENGE **17.3**

Concurrent Control at S-K-I

S-K-I Limited, which owns the two biggest ski resorts in New England—Killington and Mount Snow—takes a technological approach to concurrently controlling what is naturally a seasonal business. Many operators don't know whether they make a profit until the season is over, but S-K-I knows where it stands at the end of every day. Founder Preston Smith didn't see why he had to wait until the end of the season to find out where he was, because he knew computers could track his daily progress. S-K-I uses 370 computer terminals to track such factors as the number of tickets sold, restaurant sales, ski-lift usage, hotel bookings, and other key variables. S-K-I budgets for every single day of the season for each major part of the business—restaurants, ski school, snow making, and ski lifts. The results have been impressive. Since 1981 profits have grown at an annual rate of 21 percent, while revenues have climbed 19 percent a year.

SOURCE: Sara Smith, "Companies to Watch: SKI Limited," *Fortune* (March 28, 1988), p. 79.

Concurrent control measures allow S-K-I to know where it stands at the end of each and every ski day, thus allowing it to better serve both its customers and its owners. (SOURCE © Bob Perry)

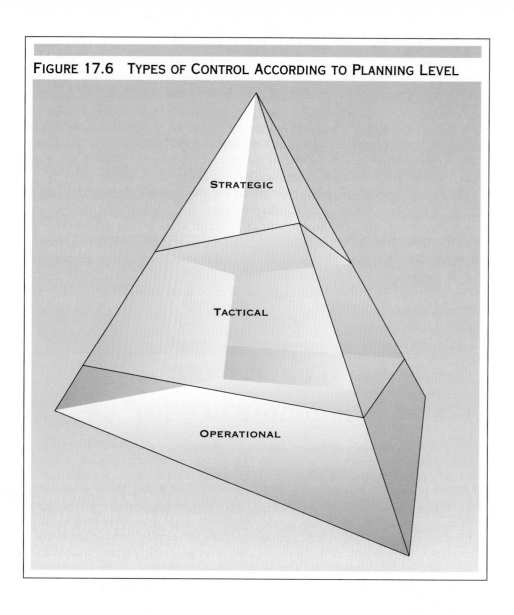

FIGURE 17.6 TYPES OF CONTROL ACCORDING TO PLANNING LEVEL

POSTACTION CONTROLS

Once a series of actions to reach an objective is completed, an effort must be made to determine whether the objective was reached. **Postaction controls** control for the results of completed action. By the time Bank of America discovered that they had a series of problems, they were faced with a financial crisis. Bad loans to Third World countries and high-risk real estate loans combined with inferior product services and poor technology, for example, a late entry into the ATM (automatic teller machines) market, left it with losses of $337 million in 1985, $518 million in 1986, and $985 million in 1987.[49] Nonetheless, without the controls it did have, Bank of America may not have discovered its problems for several more weeks or months. Many organizations use multiple types of control systems. More preaction and concurrent controls will be used in the future as the environment becomes more complex and more turbulent.

Control as Defined by the Level of Plan

There are three principal types of controls according to the level of plan: strategic, tactical, and operational, as shown in Figure 17.6.[50]

STRATEGIC CONTROL

Strategic control is concerned with the evaluation of strategy once it has been formulated or once it has been implemented. Prior to implementation, strategic control focuses on asking a series of questions about strategy and its consistency with other factors. For example, is the strategy consistent with internal strengths and weaknesses? Does it exploit external opportunities and mitigate threats? Is it timely? Additional external factors to be considered include constituent demand, suppliers, customers, internal, consistency with resources, and level of risk. Implementability must also be considered.[51]

TACTICAL CONTROL

Tactical control (often called management control) focuses on accomplishing the objectives of the various subplans between strategies and operational plans. As noted in Chapter 6, from the viewpoint of a multiple strategic business unit firm such as Martin Marietta, the sales and profitability levels of each of its SBUs would be control points. However, from the perspective of each of the SBUs, that information would be used for strategic control.

OPERATIONAL CONTROL

Operational control is designed to ensure that operational actions are consistent with established plans and objectives at that level. It is concerned with individual or group performance appraisals, and perhaps even project performance appraisals. These appraisals typically incorporate specific standards for an individual's or group's job performance, such as quantity and quality levels. Most operational controls are concerned with daily, weekly, monthly, quarterly, or yearly activities. More and more companies are taking control seriously at the operational level, as Management Challenge 17.4 suggests.

Control of the Economic Functions

The performance of the economic functions of marketing, operations, finance, human resource management, and information management must all be controlled.

MARKETING CONTROLS

Most efforts to control marketing are concerned with sales and service. Sales volume certainly has to be the major concern, but there is an increasing concern for service, as well. Marketing controls may also be concerned with providing information on competitor efforts, various factors in the marketplace—such as customer preferences—and margins, profits, returns, and the like—not just sales.

Marketing controls function at every level of planning—strategic, tactical, and operational. Much of the information about sales volume and service is dependent upon the performance of individual sales staff members. It is usually summarized for groups or departments in tactical and strategic terms. For example, a strategic objective of a sales increase of 5 percent for a year might result in a growing region's increase of 8 percent, and an increase of 3 percent in a less dynamic region. Individual sales goals might range from a 1 to 2 percent increase to a 10 to 12 percent increase. Performance would then be compared to these and control action steps taken.

FINANCIAL CONTROL

Many people believe that control is almost totally financial in nature. This is not true, but it is emphasized more than any other type of control in most organizations. Top management is certainly interested in "the numbers."

Turning Griping Customers into Loyal Customers

For years companies have viewed complaining customers as a nuisance. Many, if not most, still do. But more and more companies are trying to turn complainers into loyal customers. The financial evidence indicates that it's worth it. Companies such as GE, Johnson & Johnson, Coca-Cola, British Airways, and others are getting returns of well over 100 percent on the money they invest to handle complaints. Just listening is important, but more creative ways of responding have proven extremely effective. British Airways has installed video booths at Heathrow airport in London. Customers can complain immediately upon debarkation from a flight. These videotaped complaints are reviewed by service managers, and customers are responded to almost immediately. British Airways has in four years gone from one of the biggest money losers in the industry to one of the most profitable. Most of the turnaround is attributed to CEO Sir Colin Marshall's fixation with customer service.

SOURCE: Patricia Sellers, "How to Handle Customer's Gripes," *Fortune* (October 24, 1988), pp. 88–97.

British Airways video booths allow customers to immediately air their gripes. These booths are just one of numerous efforts by British Airways to improve customer service, and hence, improve corporate profits. (SOURCE © Graham Finlayson)

Bottom-line results are what most investors, analysts, and managers use to determine whether results were accomplished. Marketing, operations, human resources, and information management decisions must all be translated eventually into financial results. Much of the next chapter is concerned with discussing types of financial-control reports—such as profits, balance sheets, income statements, ratio analysis, and others.

OPERATIONS CONTROL

Firms such as IBM consider operations management controls essential components for production and service operations differentiation and cost strategies. The focal issues in recent years have been efficiency and quality. Purchasing, scheduling, and materials controls have also been emphasized, and just-in-time inventory programs have been viewed as increasingly important in order to be able to compete effectively with foreign competition, especially the Japanese and other Pacific rim countries. Operational control occurs in service and manufacturing operations, and the issues involved are essentially the same. Inputs, transformation, and outputs merely change forms and contents. The inputs differ, the process of transformation differs, and the outputs differ, but in each situation, control points must be determined, performance measured and compared against the standard, and corrective actions taken. Chapter 19 discusses in more detail the critical issues of operations control.[52]

HRM CONTROLS

Control of human resources occurs throughout the organization in marketing, in finance, in operations, in the information department, and even in the human resources department. The HRM department focuses on issues such as recruitment, selection, training and development, compensation and benefits, safety and health, EEO, labor relations, and employee evaluation and control. Frontline supervision is primarily responsible for administering policies, rules, and procedures. All managers are involved to some degree, however, and the key concerns include productivity levels, quality, service to the customer, absenteeism, turnovers, and tardiness.

INFORMATION MANAGEMENT CONTROL

Control of information management is largely dependent on the design of control points in the management information system. The primary issues include whether the managers are getting the right information, at the right time, in order to make effective decisions. Information system audits and control reports are important ways of controlling information management. More and more organizations are building decision support systems to aid managers in all areas of the firm. These have built-in information control points and are discussed in more detail in Chapter 19.

Control of the Management Functions

At every level of the organization, planning, organizing, leading, controlling, and problem solving must be controlled. The objectives established for each of these must be assured completion. The key concepts of the related control issues have been discussed in Chapters 1 and 4. Figure 1.6 portrays the management matrix and indicates these interdependent relationships. The problems that may result from failure to control these functions are revealed by the lessons from Irangate.

Colonel Oliver North, here shown testifying about Irangate, was one of the principal players in that political drama. One lesson from Irangate was clear—you cannot abdicate responsibility and expect control to exist. (SOURCE © John Ficara/Woodfin Camp & Associates)

LESSONS IN MANAGEMENT FUNCTION CONTROL FROM IRANGATE
President Reagan had been touted as a model manager, delegating to his subordinates many of the mundane chores, freeing himself for the really important issues. He was highly regarded for not spending eighty or ninety hours a week at work, as his predecessor, Jimmy Carter, had. Reagan did not get involved in details. He let others handle those. But he was also guilty of a major control oversight. He apparently forgot to control his subordinates' actions. Delegation requires greater accountability and tighter control than does a more authoritarian management style. Reagan confused delegation with the abdication of responsibility. The two issues are opposite sides of the same coin, but they are not the same thing. Thus, his subordinates used "illegal" sales of arms to Iran to foster Reagan's Central American policy objectives. While Reagan knew that certain objectives were being accomplished, he allegedly didn't know how, and the "how" was out of control.[53]

Control and the Changing Environment

The future holds increasing levels of uncertainty and complexity for most organizations. The control systems, methods, and types described in this chapter have, for the most part, been functioning in environments that were reasonably stable and often not very complex. New control models will be necessary for the future. The clan system, for example, seems to work well in certain types of changeful environments, as well as in those that are more stable and less complex. We can expect more use of the clan system and self-control, or variations of them, as we move toward the twenty-first century. Conversely, there are companies that have been able to employ technology to allow them to continue to use the bureaucratic type of control systems many would say would not work in highly changeful, highly complex environments.[54] Thus, there is evidence that indicates that we should move forward toward more individual control—more self-control in complex situations. Yet, conversely, there is also evidence to indicate that bureaucratic control, with quick response times provided by a computer, might be even more satisfactory.[55]

Control as a Problem-Solving Endeavor

As can be seen in Figure 17.7, controlling is a problem-solving endeavor—as were planning, organizing, and leading–paralleling the problem-solving process discussed throughout the text. The primary difference is that the control model uses simplified stages of the problem-solving process. Those stages are represented collectively in the four stages of the control model. All types of control and all methods of control are involved in all stages of the problem-solving process. Managers would make control-style choices at all points in the problem-solving process, but the essential consequences tend to be associated mostly with the establishment of standards, measuring performance, and the actions taken to control differences between standards and performance.

A manager, operating in a changing environment, might make control decisions that follow those in Figure 17.7. He or she would use planning as the basis from which the failure to reach standards or exceed objectives would both help him or her recognize and then identify a problem. After a problem was identified, a manager would make assumptions and then take actions to correct the difference between standards and performance. The style of control, the characteristics of the available control systems, and several other factors identified would affect all of the manager's problem-solving actions.

The Management Challenges Identified

1. Global competitors who excel at the control function
2. Control in complex and uncertain environments
3. Continual changes in plans, control standards

Some Solutions Noted in the Chapter

1. Emphasis on quality control by U.S. firms
2. Flexibility in control processes and standards

FIGURE 17.7 CONTROL AS PROBLEM SOLVING

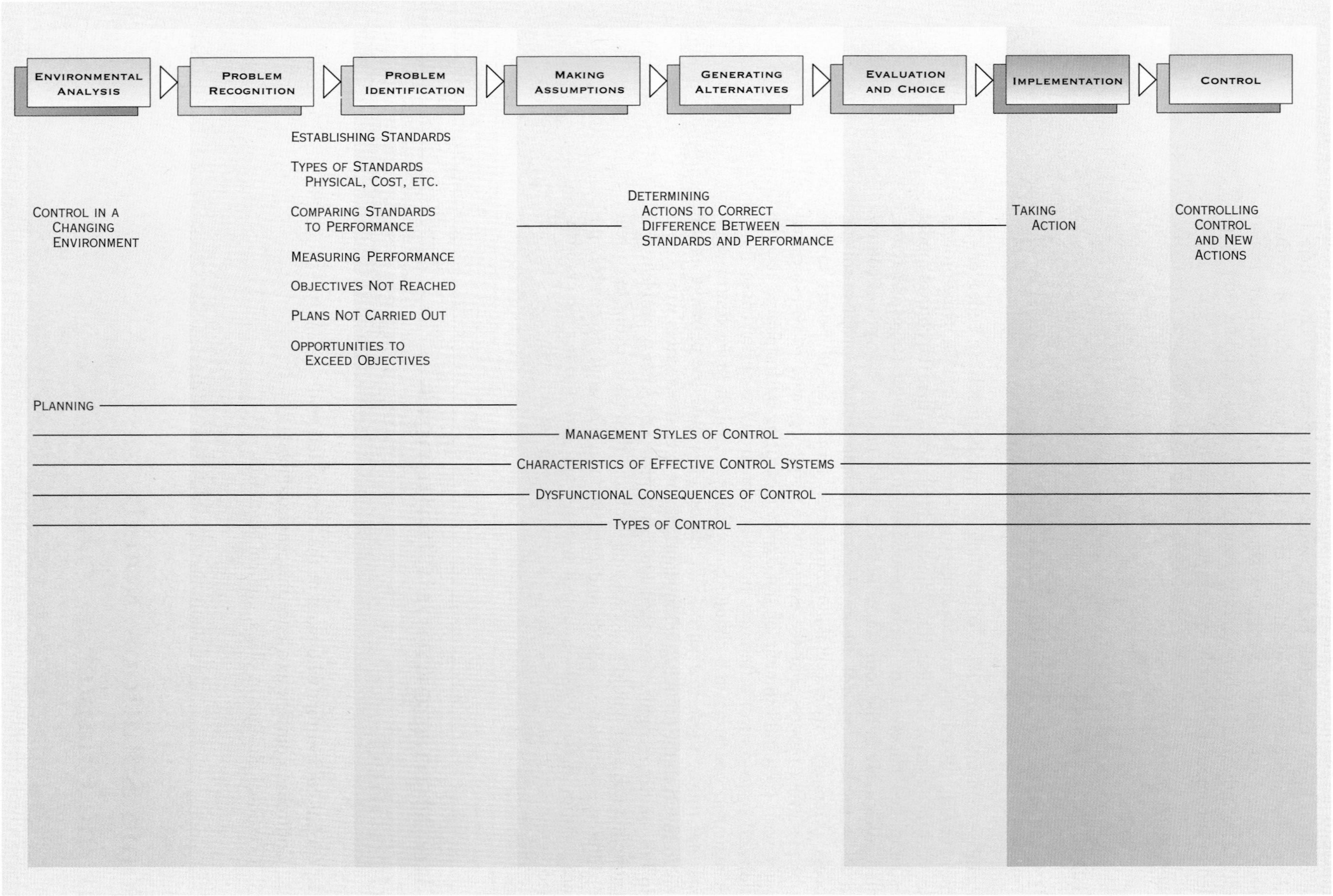

| ENVIRONMENTAL ANALYSIS | PROBLEM RECOGNITION | PROBLEM IDENTIFICATION | MAKING ASSUMPTIONS | GENERATING ALTERNATIVES | EVALUATION AND CHOICE | IMPLEMENTATION | CONTROL |

ESTABLISHING STANDARDS

TYPES OF STANDARDS PHYSICAL, COST, ETC.

COMPARING STANDARDS TO PERFORMANCE

MEASURING PERFORMANCE

OBJECTIVES NOT REACHED

PLANS NOT CARRIED OUT

OPPORTUNITIES TO EXCEED OBJECTIVES

DETERMINING ACTIONS TO CORRECT DIFFERENCE BETWEEN STANDARDS AND PERFORMANCE

TAKING ACTION

CONTROLLING CONTROL AND NEW ACTIONS

CONTROL IN A CHANGING ENVIRONMENT

PLANNING

MANAGEMENT STYLES OF CONTROL

CHARACTERISTICS OF EFFECTIVE CONTROL SYSTEMS

DYSFUNCTIONAL CONSEQUENCES OF CONTROL

TYPES OF CONTROL

3. More clan control
4. Change control styles
5. More preaction and concurrent control efforts
6. Increased use of technology—especially computers—to assist in the process.

Summary

1. Control is the systematic process by which managers assure that the organization is reaching its objectives and carrying out the associated plans in an effective and efficient manner. Its four steps include establishing performance objectives and standards, measuring actual performance, comparing actual performance to objectives and standards, and taking necessary action based on the results of the comparison.
2. Controlling is important because it helps lead to the attainment of objectives, cope with uncertainty in complex environments, and overcome the problems of human limitations.
3. Planning and control are extremely interdependent because controlling depends on the standards that result from the objectives established in planning. Planning in turn depends on the results of control when new objectives are established.
4. There are three main types of control based on management style: market control, bureaucratic control, and clan control.
5. Effective control systems have these characteristics: measures at each level of the planning process, acceptance by those who will enforce them, flexibility, accuracy, timeliness, cost effectiveness, understandability, objectiveness/where necessary subjectiveness.
6. The dysfunctional aspects of control include game playing, resistance, inaccurate information, and rigid bureaucratic behavior.
7. Control types include those for time relative to the process, management level, economic function, and management function.
8. The primary trends in control are toward self-management and the increasing use of clan control. Computers are also affecting the way control can be carried out.

Thinking About Management

1. Discuss the importance of control as a management function.
2. Describe the stages in the control process and discuss their use in some organization with which you are familiar.
3. Describe how control relates to the other management functions of planning, organizing, and leading.
4. Discuss how control might differ in marketing, finance, operations, HRM, and information management.
5. How does the perspective of control differ in preaction, concurrent, and postaction control?
6. What would be different about what was controlled by management level at strategic, tactical, and operational levels?
7. Describe the differences between market, bureaucratic, and clan control. When might each be used?
8. Discuss the dysfunctional aspects of control you have seen personally.
9. Discuss why organizational control systems will change in the future and describe some of those potential changes.

E. F. Hutton Loses Money the Old-Fashioned Way — They Don't Control It

In 1985 the E. F. Hutton Group Incorporated's Securities Unit pleaded guilty to two thousand counts of fraud related to check overdrafting. Within the next year, a series of additional events indicated that the company seemed to have a major control problem.

The Hutton Group lost $12.2 million in the fourth quarter of 1985. It suffered a 17 percent earnings drop per year while other firms were making record profits. The fourth-quarter loss was largely due to a $26.3 million reserve for a bad loan, a $14 million set-aside for losses in mortgage-backed securities, and a $7 million bond trading loss accumulated during one of the largest bond rallies in the history of the market.

In February 1986 Hutton's security unit received unpleasant notoriety. One of its former brokers, Leslie Roberts, was arrested for mail fraud by the FBI.

In March 1986 Hutton Group's Delaware Trust Company came under investigation by Delaware banking authorities after a former officer of the group testified that, among other things, Hutton brokers were unnecessarily trading stocks in the trust portfolio, to inflate their commissions. Additional allegations against Hutton also sprang up on other issues. There was a possibility, for example, that during the investigation of the check overdrafting scheme, some company officials may have obstructed justice by withholding information or destroying documents. Hutton denies intentionally withholding and destroying documents, but admits that it did inadvertently overlook some files.

The Hutton Group had undergone rapid growth in virtually all its business areas. Problems of controlling during such growth, while profound, are easy to overlook, especially during high-flying periods of the stock market. But faced with massive control problems, Hutton had to determine how to overcome the problem of control in the corporation.

DISCUSSION QUESTIONS

1. Recognizing that you don't know what existing systems were in place, what actions would you take to improve control within this firm based on what you read above?

2. How do you control behavior and make it more ethical in a company such as this?

SOURCE: Scott McMurray and Andy Paztor, "Growing Problems: Hutton Group Suffers a Series of Reverses in Wake of Overdrafts," *Wall Street Journal* 9 April 1986, pp. 1, 26.

Controlling Paperwork Reveals Other Areas in Need of Control

Doug was an industrial engineer with a very large manufacturing organization. Due to increased competition and other industry factors, the firm felt that it had to cut costs. Someone in top management had recognized that there was an excess amount of paperwork at all levels of the organization. Doug was assigned the task of heading up a seven-person task force to assess the situation and make recommendations to solve whatever problems were uncovered.

The task force determined to survey each and every manager at and below middle level. Managers were asked to complete a form indicating the reports they filled out, how long they took to complete them, and to whom they were sent. Similarly, they were asked to complete another form indicating what reports they received and of what use they were. No such analysis of the firm's reporting systems had ever been undertaken. An elaborate computer program was designed to help tabulate the results for the firm's two thousand managers involved.

DISCUSSION QUESTIONS

1. What are some of the results you might expect from such a survey? Why?
2. The survey discovered that, on average, 30 percent of a manager's time was made up of writing reports, only 15 percent of which were ever used by anyone. What are the implications for control? For cost cutting?
3. How do firms get in such shape?

What Is Cheating?

MANAGE
YOURSELF

Cheating is a problem in many universities and colleges. Many schools have honor codes, and codes of ethics to which students are expected to adhere. Consequently, they often sign an oath on their tests, papers, and other graded materials such as projects. Such an oath might be stated as follows: "I have neither received nor given help in creating the specifics of this paper (or test). I swear that this is my own work." The student then signs his or her name in testimony to this oath. Usually a student honor council would be designated to handle cases of suspected cheating.

Unfortunately, the above often is not enough. Some students will still cheat. Your instructor will divide the class into small groups. These groups will be asked to devise the best system of control for cheating in this class, and for your university or college overall. After a period of time, groups will be asked to report their findings back to the entire class. One very important issue to define before you get too far along is—what is cheating?

CHAPTER EIGHTEEN

Management Control Systems

CHAPTER OBJECTIVES

By the time you complete this chapter you should be able to

1. Discuss the importance of control systems and techniques to the control process.
2. Review the core control systems according to the Daft/Macintosh model.
3. Indicate the differences between strategic, tactical, and operational control systems.
4. Describe the various types of budgets.
5. Identify the role played by each of the various responsibility centers and discuss how control differs in each.
6. Indicate how each of the following financial statements might be used in the control process: balance sheet, income statement, and funds flow analysis.
7. Discuss the use of ratio analysis and return on investment.
8. List the various uses of cost analysis.
9. Describe how financial audits might be used in control.
10. Discuss the use of performance appraisals in control.
11. Indicate how each of the following is used in control: management by objectives-type systems, disciplinary systems, quality control, and operations controls.

CHAPTER OUTLINE

Core Control Elements
Strategic Control Systems
  Financial Analysis
  Ratio Analysis
  Return on Investment (ROI)
  Shareholder Value
  Cost Accounting
  Financial Audits
Tactical, or Middle-Management, Control Systems
  Budgets
  Responsibility Center Management
  Types of Budgets
  The Budgeting Process
  Departmental Budgets
  Zero-Based Budgeting
  Strengths and Weaknesses
    of Budgeting
  Performance Appraisals
Operational Control
  Disciplinary Systems
  Operations Management Control
    Mechanisms
Control in a Changing Environment
Control Systems as Part of the
  Problem-Solving Process
The Management Challenges Identified
Some Solutions Noted in the Chapter

Universal Studios: "Deep Pockets" No More

Like all movie studios, MCA Inc.'s Universal Studios was confronted with budgetary problems. For example, it faced a declining TV market because prime-time television markets were being eaten away by cable channels. The studio also faced drastically rising labor costs, declining syndication opportunities because of reduced advertising, and its own trend to allow producers to spend virtually as much money as they wanted to on production, hence becoming known as "Deep Pockets."

Top management's solution was to exercise more control over all the key factors that had caused budget overruns of about 13 percent in fiscal year 1986. As the result of these increased controls, the deficit had been reduced to approximately zero by March 1987. The "Suits," as the button-down, number-crunching executives from their headquarters in the "black tower" are known, often confronted producers over costs associated with various TV shows or movies. In a major 1986 announcement, executives from the "tower" warned 150 of their TV producers to cut costs by reducing shooting days and simplifying scripts, or else. "Or else" meant that they wouldn't be retained on the payroll. Many didn't take it seriously in 1986, but they did in 1987.

It was obvious that MCA was determined to cut costs even on such typically glamorous shows as "Miami Vice," "Murder She Wrote," and "Magnum P.I." They were limiting expensive action scenes such as car chases to, for example, one per segment for "Miami Vice." In the last days of "Magnum P.I." shooting schedules were on a seven-day cycle instead of eight. Costs were cut significantly by eliminating a lot of the expensive outside shooting of Hawaii's more exhilarating scenery. Programs were even shifted to Canada in order to cut costs. Twenty-four new episodes of "Airwolf," for example, were shot by a Canadian company. Each episode cost about $400,000, compared to the $1.5 million per episode when they were made at Universal Studios in Los Angeles.

Universal also built studios in Orlando, Florida, in order to acquire cheaper labor, especially writers and other production personnel, whose salaries had been rising at the rate of 10 percent per year for the past few years, principally because of union contracts. Studios in Florida provided a largely non-union environment in which such contracts could be avoided.

Critics of the cost-cutting process say that it hurts creativity and that the resulting product is not sufficiently sophisticated for the very demanding American market. Nonetheless the trend is likely to continue. There is concern by MCA's executives over quality, and upon occasion they will return finished products to producers asking them to spend a little more money on them. These occasions are rare, however.

SOURCE: Michael Cieply, "Universal Problem: MCA Is in Front Line of Hollywood's Fight to Reign in Costs," *Wall Street Journal* 6 March 1987, pp. 1, 18.

Nearly $100 billion in deposits are gone, with no one but the public to pay. (Actual loss is nearly $500 billion.)

Jane Bryant Quinn, Editor
U.S. News & World Report
(Commenting on the savings and loan catastrophe)

In today's environment, we don't think the numbers really tell the story.

Patrick S. Parker
Chairman, Parker Hannifin Corp.

U niversal Studios corraled its costs by employing formal control systems. Tight budgets were set, schedules trimmed, and ceiling costs per project installed. Universal used bureaucratic control systems to end its "deep pockets" era. Control systems exist for all three control strategies discussed in the previous chapter: market, bureaucratic, and clan control strategies. This chapter focuses principally on the formal bureaucratic management control systems found in organizations—those used to control performance toward organizational goals and objectives at various levels in the organization. This chapter revolves around the six core bureaucratic control systems involved at each of the several levels of the organization. It also reviews associated secondary systems that can be employed at each of these levels.

Even such high-flying series as "Miami Vice" had their budgets cut. Expensive-to-make scenes, such as the one being shot here, were reduced in number. Universal's "suits" had to educate directors to understand that while movie and television production is an art, it is also a business. (SOURCE © Globe Photos)

FIGURE 18.1   CORE CONTROL ELEMENTS

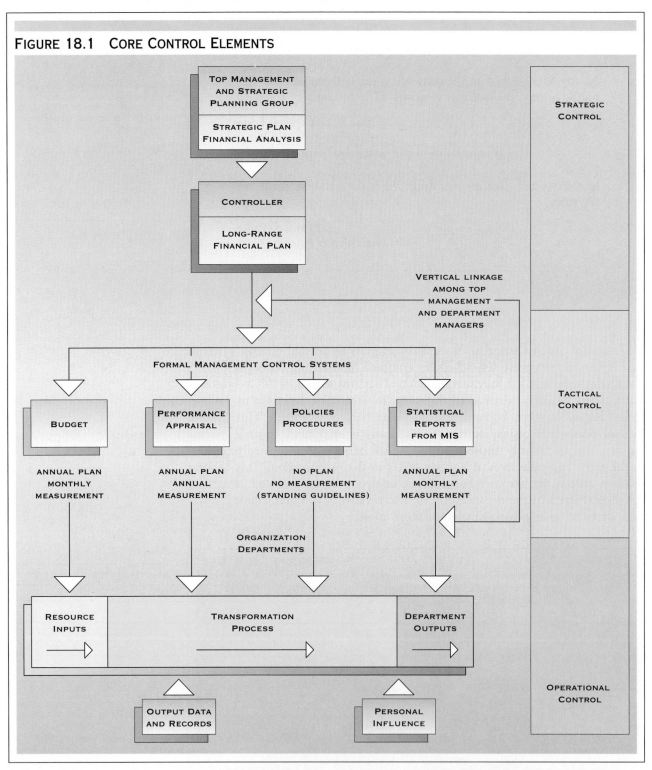

SOURCE: RICHARD L. DAFT AND NORMAN D. MACINTOSH, "THE NATURE AND USE OF FORMAL CONTROL SYSTEMS FOR MANAGEMENT CONTROL AND STRATEGY IMPLEMENTATION," JOURNAL OF MANAGEMENT, NO. 1, 1984, PP. 60, ADAPTED BY PERMISSION.

Core Control Elements

Six core formal management control systems exist for top- and middle-level management in organizations, as shown in Figure 18.1. At the strategic level, the strategic plan, financial analysis, and the long-range financial plan are used by top managers for strategy formulation. The operating budget, statistical reports, performance appraisal systems, and policies and procedures are used by middle managers for department control and strategy implementation.[1] The latter four core elements may also be used in the transformation process at the operational level.[2] But a study by William G. Ouchi and M. A. Maguire suggests that, at the operational level, control is usually accomplished through personal influence and surveillance or through output data and records—a results orientation, as shown in Figure 18.1.[3]

1. Strategic Plan: The **strategic plan** is the business unit's principal competitive strategy. It contains major objectives and plans to reach those objectives. The term *strategic plan* is actually somewhat of a misnomer. There may be several strategic objectives and several strategies included within the realm of the term as used here. From a control perspective, it is the objectives of these strategies that are the principal plan control mechanisms. As discussed in Chapter 5, key objectives might include profits, sales, margins on sales, and growth rates. Furthermore, financial analysis, which may result in the determination of such figures as return on investment, profit margins, and earnings per share, may be a dominant form of control at the strategic level. As strategies and objectives become more flexible, so must the control of these.

2. The Long-Range Financial Plan: The **long-range financial plan** is essentially a one- to five-year forecast of the anticipated financial performance of the organization if the strategy is followed and if the strategy is successful to the degree believed necessary.[4] "Pro forma" or forecasted financial income statements, balance sheets, and cash flows are the principal components of this long-range financial plan. Departmental breakouts may be part of this plan. Virtually all major companies use both strategies and a financial forecast for strategic control purposes.

3. The Operating Budget: The **operating budget** is typically an annual financial statement of the operating plan for the forthcoming year, matching revenues and expenses and calculating anticipated profits or losses. Sometimes operating budgets may be for a period of eighteen months or two years. Most organizations have a series of sub-budgets that combine to yield the operating budget. The budget is usually monitored on a monthly, or at least quarterly, basis by most organizations.

4. Performance Appraisals: **Performance appraisals** are the organization's way of formally evaluating the performance of its employees, including managers. Many companies use some type of management by objectives, results, and rewards system (MBORR) as a basis for their performance appraisal.

5. Statistical Reports: **Statistical reports** make available information used to manage both the transformation process and the interrelationships of the units. Examples of the information in such reports are labor efficiency rates, attendance figures, quality control rejects, bookings, accounts payable, accounts receivable, sales reports, the amount of scrap generated in the process, the quality of inputs, and team productivity. This information is found in the organization's MIS, to be discussed in more detail in Chapter 19.

6. Policies and Procedures: **Policies** are general guidelines for taking action. **Procedures** are a set of specific steps to perform a job. Both are used by managers to ensure that workers perform in the best way possible. Normally each job has procedures developed for it. Policies guide managerial actions so that managers won't have to make decisions in recurring situations. The decision to be made is indicated by the policy.

Creativity Stifled in Japan by Overcontrol

Japan's regimentation has been a clear asset in its rush to industrial success. But future industrial success may depend on loosening the reins and allowing more creativity. Basic laboratory research in Japan has lagged when compared to that in the United States. The Japanese have historically imitated, borrowed, bought, or stolen innovative products from the United States and learned how to make them cheaper and with higher quality, in turn selling them to the world's market. But they have never been skilled at creating products. Their rigid society simply won't allow it.

Yoshihide Tsujimoto, a molecular biologist, left Japan for the freedom of American laboratories. At thirty-four, he supervises five researchers, has his own grants, and does what he wants. But he could never have done this in Japan; there he would still be working for a full professor on that professor's pet project. He complains that the Japanese scientific establishment "idolizes seniority, loathes individualism, and muzzles debate."

But more and more of Japan's upper-level managers in organizations as well as government are beginning to realize that something must change in order for Japan to continue to progress industrially. Planners at the Ministry of International Trade and Industry state that the West will not continue to provide Japan with the fruits of its research for free. Japan must move forward to instill more creativity. The government is furiously originating programs to foster creativity and change the centuries-old habits of the scientific establishment. But change won't come easily. Some of the revered Japanese practices, such as lifelong employment, stifle creativity. There is little travel, there are few grants, and there is little chance for

There seems to be a distinct difference between information used at upper levels and information used at departmental levels to control the organization. At the upper levels, control information is primarily financial, and at middle and lower levels, it is primarily nonfinancial.[5] Performance appraisals, procedures and performance-related measures such as quality and efficiency are examined. The budget, which is financial, is used to allocate resources to departments, but the other three tactical control systems are normally based on nonfinancial data, although statistical reports occasionally use financial figures. Operational control is also principally nonfinancial, focusing on output measurements and day-to-day interpersonal relations. Virtually all of the control mechanisms will have to change as the situations in which control is necessary become more complex and more turbulent.

Strategic Control Systems

From a control perspective, the primary concerns at the strategic level are achieving the objectives of the strategic plan and the use of the financial resources allocated by the long-range financial plan. Most frequently the results associated with accomplishing organizational objectives will be expressed in financial terms and reported in an organization's financial statements: the balance sheet, income statement, and funds flow analysis. Financial audits test the validity of these

advancement, impelling a brain-drain from Japan. It is clear that Japan has a long way to go to change its scientific establishment. Unless Japan can change its cultural control systems to allow greater creativity, it may find itself unable to continue its economic growth.

SOURCE: Stephen Kreider Yoder, "Stifled Scholars: Japan's Scientists Find Pure Research Suffers Under Rigid Lifestyle," *Wall Street Journal* 31 October 1988, pp. A1, A6.

These Japanese rock musicians are typical of the many Japanese who are rebelling against the regimentation of their society. Many observers believe that only through such rebellion, especially that against overly bureaucratized research and development programs, can Japan become sufficiently innovative to lead global product developments. (SOURCE © Patrick Frilet/SIPA Press)

statements. There will also be related analyses of these results that typically focus on ratio analysis or other types of financial analysis. Combinations of various line items from these statements are used—for example, return on investment. Occasionally cost analysis of operations plays a major role in strategic control. Cost analysis is especially important when a low-cost strategy is being used.[6] For example, Japanese automobile manufacturers have competed in the United States on the basis of low cost and high quality. In the late 1980s, the value of the yen became significantly higher, relative to the value of the dollar. Consequently, the Japanese engaged in major cost-cutting programs in manufacturing in order to maintain their cost advantage. Key results are often expressed in terms of factors such as market share, new product developments, and other similar measures. A few firms examine themselves from an externally focused, environmentally based strategic perspective. Using social audits or stakeholder audits, for instance, a company might examine its impact on environmental pollution.

Strategic control as practiced in the West is largely bureaucratic and formal. By contrast, the Japanese control strategy through clan or cultural mechanisms.[7] Sometimes, however, clan controls can be as "bureaucratic" in effect as bureaucratic controls, as this chapter's Global Management Challenge suggests.

More and more computer-based strategic control and decision support systems intended for use by executives are being made available.[8] For example, at Kraft Inc.'s Grocery Products Group, top managers used to face an information nightmare—500 products and 15 separate brands, in 33,000 grocery stores. At

AT UNIVERSAL STUDIOS: *The income statement clearly indicated that production expenses were too high. This resulted in a tighter budget and in more day-to-day control of costs.*

Part of Georgia-Pacific Corporation's success lies in its ability to manage large-scale capital equipment successfully. (SOURCE © 1990 Louis Psihoyos/Matrix)

3:00 P.M. each day, executives would receive stacks of paper from which to determine the previous day's sales performance. Now that information is available on the computer at 8:30 A.M., sorted by product line and geographic region.[9] The use of information systems in control will be discussed more in Chapter 19.

Financial Analysis

Financial analysis is based largely on examining the organization's financial statements and the various ratios derived from information from its balance sheet and income statement.[10] The **balance sheet** reveals the condition of the company at a given point in time. The **income statement** shows the condition of the company for a period of time. The balance sheet looks at assets, liabilities, and equities. The income statement looks at revenues, expenses, and profits or losses. Examples of these statements for the Georgia-Pacific Corporation, a paper products company, are contained in Figures 18.2 and 18.3.

On the balance sheet, the amount of total assets of any company equals the total amount of its liabilities and owner's equity. Assets are typically divided into current and long-term or fixed categories. Liabilities are typically divided into short-term and long-term categories. Various types of equities may be listed, but the most frequently found types are common stock and retained earnings.

Income statements typically begin with revenue figures. Revenues, mainly sales, are offset by various types of expenses. Next on the statement comes the operating income results. Taxes are then deducted from that income to yield net income, the so-called bottom line. When managers speak of taking a "bottom line" orientation, it is this particular number they are discussing. The implication is that all actions taken by organizations should be taken to increase net income after taxes, at least in the long term.

A third statement that assists in controlling organizational operations and finances is the **cash flow statement.** It indicates the sources and uses of cash. Typical sources of cash include operations income, depreciation, increased lia-

FIGURE 18.2 STATEMENTS OF INCOME

GEORGIA-PACIFIC CORPORATION AND SUBSIDIARIES

| | YEAR ENDED DECEMBER 31 | | |
(MILLIONS. EXCEPT PER SHARE AMOUNTS)	1989	1988	1987
NET SALES	$10,171	$9,509	$8,603
COSTS AND EXPENSES			
COST OF SALES	7,621	7,452	6,777
SELLING, GENERAL AND ADMINISTRATIVE	689	632	583
DEPRECIATION AND DEPLETION	514	450	387
INTEREST	260	197	124
TOTAL COSTS AND EXPENSES	9,084	8,731	7,871
INCOME BEFORE UNUSUAL ITEM AND INCOME TAXES	1,087	778	732
UNUSUAL ITEM	—	—	66
INCOME BEFORE INCOME TAXES	1,087	778	798
PROVISION FOR INCOME TAXES	426	311	340
NET INCOME	$ 661	$ 467	$ 458
EARNINGS PER SHARE	$ 7.42	$ 4.76	$ 4.23
AVERAGE NUMBER OF SHARES OUTSTANDING	89.1	98.1	107.5

bilities, and financing activities. Typical uses include increases in current assets—inventories and receivables, and purchases of capital assets. Monitoring cash flows is very important to a firm's continued operations. For example, because revenues typically come in after expenses to produce them have already been made, firms may find themselves short of cash. Or, firms may not generate enough cash from revenues from sales to finance planned expansions, so they have to borrow. Thus, forecasting cash flows becomes critical.

Ratio Analysis

By examining ratios of various numbers identified on the income statement and the balance sheet, managers or other analysts may be able to discern better the organization's financial condition. There are four principal types of ratios: liquidity, leverage, activity, and profitability. Each type of ratio will have several associated ratios. Table 18.1 identifies one of the most common ratios used, for each of these four types of ratios, their formulas, a typical calculation, an industry average, and the evaluation of that ratio relative to the industry average. The following paragraphs discuss briefly each of these four major types of ratios.

LIQUIDITY

Liquidity ratios are concerned with the organization's ability to meet its current debt. A key ratio is the current ratio.

Current Ratio. The current ratio measures the liquidity of the firm—that is, its ability to handle short-term debts and liabilities. It is found by dividing current assets by current liabilities. The result shows how many dollars of current assets exist per dollar of current liabilities. A rule of thumb for manufacturing firms is to maintain a current ratio of at least 2:1 (assets to liabilities), but each firm must compare its position with the industry average. Service firms require a lower ratio because they have no inventories.[11]

FIGURE 18.3 BALANCE SHEETS

GEORGIA-PACIFIC CORPORATION AND SUBSIDIARIES

(MILLIONS, EXCEPT SHARES AND PER SHARE AMOUNTS)	DECEMBER 31 1989	1988
ASSETS		
CURRENT ASSETS		
CASH	$ 23	$ 62
RECEIVABLES, LESS ALLOWANCES OF $30 AND $29	890	905
INVENTORIES		
RAW MATERIALS	299	288
FINISHED GOODS	644	653
SUPPLIES	102	101
LIFO RESERVE	(169)	(150)
TOTAL INVENTORIES	876	892
OTHER CURRENT ASSETS	40	33
TOTAL CURRENT ASSETS	1,829	1,892
TIMBER AND TIMBERLANDS, NET	1,246	1,289
PROPERTY, PLANT AND EQUIPMENT		
LAND AND IMPROVEMENTS	151	152
BUILDINGS	688	669
MACHINERY AND EQUIPMENT	6,016	5,698
CONSTRUCTION IN PROGRESS	140	165
	6,995	6,684
ACCUMULATED DEPRECIATION	(3,304)	(2,961)
PROPERTY, PLANT AND EQUIPMENT, NET	3,691	3,723
OTHER ASSETS	290	211
TOTAL ASSETS	$ 7,056	$ 7,115
LIABILITIES AND SHAREHOLDERS' EQUITY		
CURRENT LIABILITIES		
BANK OVERDRAFTS, NET	$ 100	$ 138
COMMERCIAL PAPER AND OTHER SHORT-TERM NOTES	79	148
CURRENT PORTION OF LONG-TERM DEBT	31	32
ACCOUNTS PAYABLE	394	404
ACCRUED COMPENSATION	111	103
ACCRUED INTEREST	58	58
OTHER CURRENT LIABILITIES	151	130
TOTAL CURRENT LIABILITIES	924	1,013
LONG-TERM DEBT, EXCLUDING CURRENT PORTION	2,336	2,514
DEFERRED INCOME TAXES	841	788
OTHER LONG-TERM LIABILITIES	238	165
SHAREHOLDERS' EQUITY		
COMMON STOCK, PAR VALUE $.80; AUTHORIZED 150,000,000 SHARES; 86,664,000 AND 94,967,000 SHARES ISSUED	69	76
ADDITIONAL PAID-IN CAPITAL	1,009	1,046
RETAINED EARNINGS	1,713	1,533
LESS—COMMON STOCK HELD IN TREASURY, AT COST; 139,000 SHARES IN 1988	—	(4)
LONG-TERM INCENTIVE PLAN DEFERRED COMPENSATION	(56)	(11)
ACCUMULATED TRANSLATION ADJUSTMENTS	(18)	(5)
TOTAL SHAREHOLDERS' EQUITY	2,717	2,635
TOTAL LIABILITIES AND SHAREHOLDERS' EQUITY	$7,056	$7,115

LEVERAGE

The leverage ratios are concerned with a firm's utilization of debt, the relationship of its debt to total assets, and the firm's ability to pay its interest charges.

Debt to Total Assets. The debt-to-total-assets ratio equals total debt divided by total assets. It is represented as a percentage. Thus, a ratio of 0.50 means that the firm's debt equals 50 percent of the value of the firm's assets. Generally, the lower this percentage, the better, because a high ratio could mean that the firm has little ability to withstand losses. A low ratio indicates that the firm has a buffer of funds available to creditors should it become insolvent.

Table 18.1 Selected Financial Ratio Analysis

Ratio	Formula for Calculation	Calculation	Industry Average	Evaluation
Liquidity Current	$\dfrac{\text{Current assets}}{\text{Current liabilities}}$	$\dfrac{\$\ 700,000}{\$\ 300,000}$ = 2.3 times	2.5 times	Satisfactory
Leverage Debt to total assets	$\dfrac{\text{Total debt}}{\text{Total assets}}$	$\dfrac{\$1,000,000}{\$2,000,000}$ = 50 percent	33 percent	Poor
Activity Inventory turnover	$\dfrac{\text{Sales}}{\text{Inventory}}$	$\dfrac{\$3,000,000}{\$\ 300,000}$ = 10 times	9 times	Satisfactory
Profitability Return on total assets	$\dfrac{\text{Net profit after taxes}}{\text{Total assets}}$	$\dfrac{\$\ 120,000}{\$2,000,000}$ = 6.0 percent	10 percent	Poor

SOURCE: Adapted from J. Fred Weston and Thomas E. Copeland, *Managerial Finance,* 8th ed. (Hinsdale, Ill.: CBS College Publishing, 1986), pp. 190–191.

ACTIVITY

The principal concern of activity ratios is to determine how well assets are being utilized.

Inventory Turnover. Dividing sales by inventory will indicate how many times per year the firm has been able to sell its inventory. A general average for U.S. companies is nine times, but this figure can vary. More expensive items—such as autos, major appliances, and jewelry—normally have lower turnover rates than less expensive items.

PROFITABILITY

The principal concern of profitability ratios is the success of the firm in earning profits, as measured by several tests.

Return on Total Assets. The return on total assets (return on investment) is a percentage determined by dividing net profit after taxes by total assets. This percentage is compared with the industry average and, when used in conjunction with the firm's profit margin, is an indicator of earning power. It shows the rate of return the firm is getting per dollar invested in assets.

Return on Investment (ROI)

Return on investment is a ratio that indicates the income after taxes, relative to the organization's total assets. This provides the firm, the manager, or other analyst with a *short-term* measure of how well the organization is performing. It shows how well the company has used its assets to produce income. As shown in Figure 18.4, return on investment itself derives from two ratios, each of which consists of several inputs, that can be analyzed in more detail to determine their impacts on ROI. By analyzing each of these component contributors to ROI, the organization can determine why the operation is effective or ineffective. For example, a consultant found that a company he was examining showed a substantially reduced profit on sales ratio in one year. In further examining this ratio, it became obvious that net income was reduced because cost of sales was high as a result of extremely high operating expenses in comparison to previous

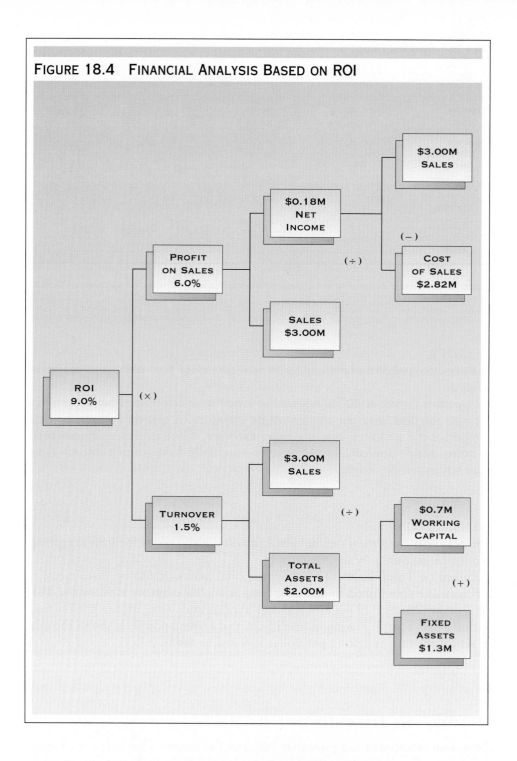

FIGURE 18.4   FINANCIAL ANALYSIS BASED ON ROI

years. Just before that operating period, the production manager had quit and he had not been replaced. The owner was very sales-oriented and had had no trouble selling products, but with no one managing the production area, expenses ran out of control. The owner didn't realize how important production management was, and hence quibbled over salary with several potential plant managers. His desire to save $5,000 in salary probably cost him $200,000 in lost profits. Once a new production manager was hired, operating expenses returned to their former lower levels and ROI improved. This decision to hire a manager was prompted by the analysis of ROI. A number of strategic problems, as well as operating decisions and policies, affect ROI and the accounts that go into its composition. For example, the decision to grow rapidly, or to cut costs, can greatly affect ROI. Managers must keep the effect of their decisions on ROI in mind.

Shareholder Value

Of increasing concern in recent years has been the concept of **shareholder value,** the belief that a company's performance should be measured in terms of how much shareholders gain from what the business does. The company's stock price, for example, is often used to reflect this value. Other, more complicated measures exist. One of the reasons that corporate raiders were prominent in the 1980s was that shareholders were not significantly benefiting under current management. Raiders often took over a company, improved its performance, and saw stock prices rise dramatically, as a consequence. Most measures of corporate performance, such as ROI, are historically accounting oriented. Shareholder value measurements often are too, but they also can be designed to cause CEOs and other top managers to look to the future.[12]

Cost Accounting

One of the objectives of any organization is the efficient use of resources. Cost accounting—cost analysis—allows organizations to achieve that objective. It is almost impossible to make pertinent decisions on issues such as pricing and whether to take on a product line or project without accurate cost information. Product costing is important for determining efficiency, for allocating resources, for pricing production, for long-range capacity decisions, for investment decisions, for budgeting, and for measuring divisional performance. The linkages between planning and cost control are critical. Managers can't determine if plans are successfully implemented without knowing the costs of the operation. Similarly, they can't plan if they don't know what costs may be. Management Challenge 18.1 reveals just how important controlling costs can be.

Historically, a major use of cost information was to value inventory for financial and tax statements, but cost systems designed to provide this kind of information are not providing the manager with the type of information they need to ensure operating efficiencies and measure product cost.[13] Companies have attempted to change their existing systems somehow to provide additional information, but this has not been sufficient. More and more companies are realizing that they need two, perhaps even three, cost control systems in an organization.[14] Especially important in today's highly competitive market environment is that organizations achieve high levels of operational cost control.

In order to be cost competitive, it is also important that companies be able to determine future product costs to know the long-term advisability of launching a product. Consequently, a few firms have begun to develop whole new cost accounting systems. Traditionally, for example, organizations would automate in order to cut costs, but now they can make different investment decisions in order to keep customers and perhaps win new ones. This type of decision making requires a whole new approach to cost accounting and includes examining variables outside the organization. Investment decisions may be made not just to save on labor, but to improve quality, reduce inventory levels, add flexibility, cut lead times, and generally provide more customer services.[15] Firms such as

Waterford Shows a Few Cracks

Failure to control costs and strategy properly is not just an issue in securing a profit. Controlling costs and strategy may be important in maintaining control of a company, as Ireland's Waterford Glass Group PLC found out. In 1986 the firm took the chivalrous action of acquiring Wedgwood, the British china manufacturer, to save the firm from an unfriendly takeover. This effort stretched the firm's resources, but its real problems lay in Waterford's marketplace and its factory. Younger buyers spurned the firm's heavy crystal, and sales declined by 11 percent in 1986, and 19 percent in 1987. The firm lost $85 million on sales of $404 million in 1987, despite an operating profit of $40 million for Wedgwood.

Chairman J. Patrick "Paddy" Hayes declared that the worst was over, but he was wrong. The firm had become dependent on the American market, which continued to decline as the dollar plummeted in value. The firm barely broke even in 1988, despite stringent efforts at cost control and substantial investment in cost-saving capital equipment.

What happened? Sloppy accounting resulted in the obscuring of higher costs until nearly year end. On the cost side, production costs were higher than expected partly because too many experienced glassblowers took advantage of an early retirement program aimed at lowering labor costs. Those left behind were unable to produce at the same levels as those who had retired. And the firm's workers had yet to become fully productive on the new equipment.

One result was that the company's stock plunged and takeover rumors began to abound. Several likely predators emerged, including an Irish investment firm.

SOURCE: "Waterford Is Showing a Few Cracks," *Business Week* (February 20, 1989), pp. 60, 61.

Waterford Crystal makes a fine product, but being a white knight has proven to have some drawbacks. It has had to learn to make these fine products more efficiently in order to continue to prosper. (SOURCE © Ted Morrison)

Parker-Hannifin Corporation, a major manufacturer of motion controls such as hydraulics and pneumatics, have significantly changed their cost accounting systems in order to make better strategic, competitive decisions. Consulting firms, such as Computer-Aided Manufacturing International, Inc., are promoting new accounting systems that some say may revolutionize the way companies figure costs.[16]

Financial Audits

Financial audits examine the organization's financial records and accounting systems.[17] There are two principal types of audits: internal and external. An **internal audit** is performed by members of the organization. Large organizations—such as the U.S. Air Force, Lockheed Corporation, the Denver Post, John Deere Companies, Boise Cascade, and Boeing—typically have a staff of individuals who audit the organization's statements of financial condition. **External audits** are conducted by individuals outside the organization, typically certified public accountants (CPAs) or CPA firms—such as Arthur Andersen, Arthur Young, and Kleinveld, Peat, Marwick, Goerdeler.

Only a selected percentage of transactions are examined in detail. Audits focus on major accounts, major areas of decision making, and areas where history indicates the potential for error or intentional falsification.[18]

Tactical, or Middle-Management, Control Systems

Whereas strategic control systems focus largely on total organization performance, tactical control systems focus largely on controlling tactical plans or the budget for the entire organization. There are four principal tactical/middle-management control systems: budgets, performance appraisals, statistical reports, and rules and procedures.

Budgets

The financial resource allocation process focuses on budgets and responsibility centers. **Budgets** are quantitative, usually financial statements of plans that allocate resources to various units of the organization. Budgets are normally operating plans, but they may also be drafted for longer-range plans. Budgets help define the boundaries between strategic and tactical, and tactical and operational plans. Budgets tend to cover one year or eighteen months in duration. Budgets typically

1. are stated in monetary terms.
2. are for a specific time period.
3. indicate some level of management commitment.
4. are based on some type of proposal typically submitted by lower-level managers and reviewed and approved by upper-level managers.
5. should be modified only under certain extenuating circumstances, such as a dramatic increase or decrease in sales or costs.[19]

Budgets generally have three common purposes: They help to refine organizational objectives; allocate resources in the most effective manner; and promote the efficient use of resources.

Responsibility Center Management

The financial resource allocation process ties performance not only to accomplishment of objectives, but also to their accomplishment within financial constraints identified by the long-term financial plan or shorter-term operating budget. Many larger organizations and some smaller ones establish responsibility centers to facilitate long-term financial planning, to identify responsibility accurately, to motivate subordinates to a greater extent, to aid in the budgetary process, and to provide better control of organizational performance. Responsibility centers are organizational subunits normally comprised of departments or divisions that are allocated resources to obtain specific objectives. There are four basic types of responsibility centers: revenue centers; cost, or expense, centers; profit centers; and investment centers.

REVENUE CENTERS
Revenue centers are responsibility centers controlled on the basis of their sales of products or services. Most revenue centers are found in the sales or marketing departments of their respective organizations. No attempt is made to measure the inputs, or expenses, of such centers. Rather, only outputs or revenues are measured and the budget is based on those. For example, a convention sales department of a major hotel will have its budget based on the anticipated amount of revenue it will generate. Typically this revenue is based on the estimated number of customer contacts.

COST CENTERS/EXPENSE CENTERS
Cost, or expense, centers are responsibility centers controlled on the basis of their costs/expenses generated. Their budget is based on the cost of inputs utilized in operations. A typical cost center might be a manufacturing plant for a boat manufacturer or a programming staff for a software company.

PROFIT CENTERS
Profit centers are responsibility centers controlled on the basis of the difference between revenues and expenses—profit. The principal focus is on the amount of profit contribution made to the overall organization. Large organizations such as General Electric may have as many as three hundred profit centers. More and more organizations are attempting to create profit centers to encourage internal entrepreneurship, known as intrapreneurship, in a belief that this will spur competitiveness.[20] Intrapreneurship will be discussed in more detail in Chapter 22.

INVESTMENT CENTERS
Investment centers are responsibility centers controlled on the basis not only of profit but also on the amount of capital investment made to produce the profit. The most common control measurement for investment centers is return on investment, obtained by dividing net profits by total assets. Strategic business units, as defined in Chapter 5, are typical investment centers and would include a company's major businesses, such as the Turbine Generator Division of Westinghouse. They might also include less distinct businesses, such as the trust division of First Denver Bank.

Types of Budgets

There are numerous types of budgets. Most organizations have at least the following types: a master, or summary, budget for the entire organization; revenue and expense budgets; capital expenditure budgets; cash budgets; and nonmonetary input budgets.

AT UNIVERSAL STUDIOS: *Universal Studios uses a budget as a key way of controlling the efforts of its producers. With over one hundred fifty investment centers— that is, films and TV shows—in operation at any one time, the organization must be able to control by the use of these centers. Each center will have certain identifiable investments, revenues, and costs.*

Mike McGrath, of the Pentagon Staff, has helped institute a number of innovative procurement controls and cost-saving activities for the Pentagon. (SOURCE © Katherine Lambert)

THE MASTER BUDGET

The **master budget** summarizes all budgets of the organization. It portrays sales, revenues, expenses, profits, capital employment, return on investment, and the relationships of these and other items to each other. The master budget is used to control the entire organization. It is the integration of the various revenue and expense budgets and capital expenditure budgets. Cash budgets are often derived from this, and nonmonetary resource input budgets are often used in compiling it. Master budgets often cover periods of one year to eighteen months but may be created for a period of a few years.

REVENUE AND EXPENSE BUDGETS

Revenue and expense budgets itemize the revenue and expenses for the revenue and expense responsibility centers. The most common budgets used are revenue and expense budgets; by far the most common of these are expense budgets. Virtually every operating unit of the organization has an expense budget. Only revenue centers, profit centers, and investment centers would have revenue budgets, but virtually every unit of the organization is a cost center to some degree.

CAPITAL EXPENDITURE BUDGETS

Capital expenditure budgets include capital expenditures for major capital purchases, such as plant and equipment, inventories, and development costs. Normally some capital expenditures occur each year. A capital expense budget may cover a period of several years, with the current years being integrated into the master budget. Capital budgets are critical because of the relatively large amounts of dollars expended over, normally, a long period of time, but with the decision being made in a short period of time.

Controlling procurement of capital equipment can be especially difficult in large, highly complex organizations—for example, the military. The Pentagon has recently adopted innovative procurement controls and shared cost savings with contractors in an effort to cut costs, as well as modernize defense contractor plants.[21]

CASH BUDGET

The **cash budget** is a forecast of cash receipts and disbursements. This budget is extremely important because it identifies the ability of the organization to meet financial obligations that require payment of cash. This budget also identifies the availability of excess cash to use for other purposes.

NONMONETARY RESOURCE INPUT BUDGET

The **nonmonetary resource input budget** budgets items such as man hours, units of product, and units of raw material. Eventually these are converted into expense, or revenue, budgets. At some point in time it must be a budget of dollars as well as the units involved. For example, the manufacturing unit of Eli Lilly Pharmaceuticals would first determine the units of materials needed to manufacture the product scheduled for the year. It would then cost these out, which would result in part of an expense budget.

The Budgeting Process

Conceptually, the budgeting process begins with a revenue forecast. This forecast will then be used as a basis for allocating funds to various responsibility centers. These centers will in turn develop budgets within constraints identified by the revenue forecast. In virtually all ongoing organizations, however, various responsibility centers will identify their costs, and in some cases their revenues, long before the revenue forecast is prepared. The reason for this is the time it takes to prepare the cost estimates. Cost and revenue budgets are then summarized into major types of organizational budgets—into cash budgets, expense budgets, and revenue budgets, as seen in Figure 18.5—and matched against the total revenue forecast. Because only one or a few responsibility centers will usually have a revenue forecast, it takes much less time to develop this forecast. Therefore, the lead time for developing cost and expenses for this portion of the budgetary process is longer. Furthermore, when new projects or programs are introduced, they may have their own individual budgets, based on the estimated revenue.

Departmental Budgets

At the departmental level, a preliminary budget is developed. It is then sent forward to upper-level management for a review process. Upper-level management returns it with recommended changes, and a final budget is prepared.

In preparing departmental budgets, managers typically use budget information from previous years to estimate how much will be necessary in the future. They factor in any major changes of which they are aware; some may add a "fudge factor" in order to be able to obtain the funds they feel are necessary. Understanding the budgeting process requires understanding the behavior involved. In virtually all organizations, when upper management reviews depart-

FIGURE 18.5 THE BUDGET

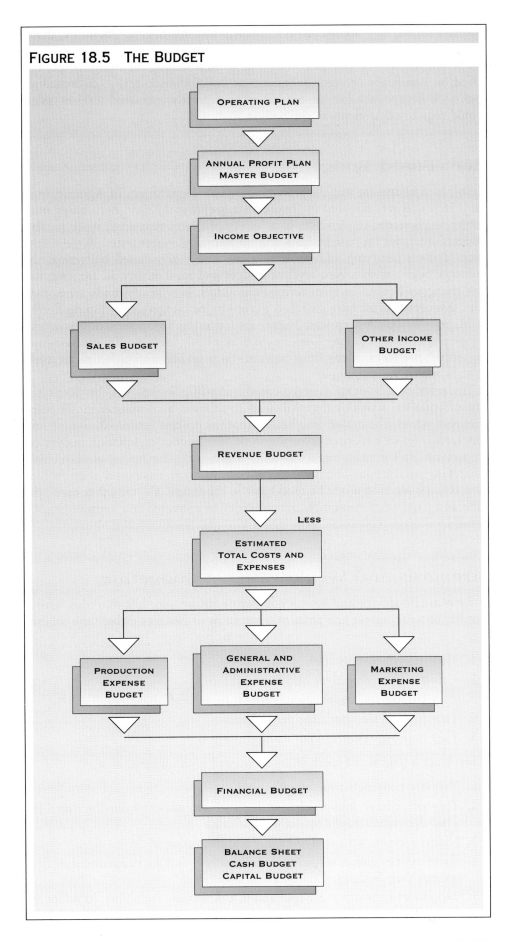

mental budgets, they almost always cut them to some degree. Therefore, many lower-level managers pad their budgets in order to obtain the funds they need.

The budget may be changed from time to time during the budgeted period, based on significant changes in environmental circumstances. A circumstance such as failing to achieve desired sales, or a greatly increased level of sales, would require adjustments in the budget.

Zero-Based Budgeting

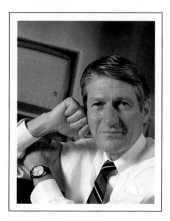

David Kearns, CEO of Xerox, is a firm believer in tight controls. His firm utilizes many varied control techniques, among them zero-based budgeting. Kearns keeps a personal computer on his desk and uses it constantly. Kearns spends at least an hour a day scanning company data bases for trends. (SOURCE © Claudio Edinger/Gamma Liaison)

Zero-based budgeting was pioneered at the U.S. Department of Agriculture in the 1960s and was adopted by Texas Instruments in 1970.[22] Zero-based budgeting was designed to eliminate some of the problems that occur when present budgets are based on past budgets and the manager concentrates on the differences and on justifying additional funding. Under **zero-based budgeting,** the manager begins with a zero level of budget and must justify all funding, not just changes—hence, the term zero-based budget. Last year's funds are not secure. Numerous firms have switched to zero-based budgeting, including Xerox, Ford, and Playboy Enterprises. Numerous federal and state agencies have also adopted the process. Jimmy Carter used it as a basis for payroll budgets during his term as president. Many firms attribute large savings and higher profit levels to their use of the technique.[23]

The primary advantage to zero-based budgeting is that it helps focus the organization on activities that will lead to mission accomplishment. It helps eliminate waste. The major drawback is that the process is time consuming and generates a lot of paperwork. Furthermore, the politics of inflating budget estimates can still appear in zero-based budgeting.[24] The future of zero-based budgeting is uncertain. The drive to cut costs in many businesses suggests that zero-based budgeting might be used more in the future. On the other hand, the time and paperwork it requires are a barrier to increased use because organizations will have to become more responsive and flexible in the future.[25]

Strengths and Weaknesses of Budgeting

Budgets are important and have a number of advantages, but they also have a number of weaknesses. The particular strengths of budgets include the following:

1. They are effective as control mechanisms.
2. They translate objectives into financial terms.
3. They coordinate organizational efforts to achieve objectives.
4. They provide standards for performance.
5. They improve resource allocation.

There are a number of weaknesses associated with budgets, as well:

1. They are extremely time consuming.
2. They often have bad results, such as when political behavior overrides what the budget might conceptually dictate.
3. Budget requests are often overstated, and inflationary.
4. There can be conflict between the departments and the budgeting staff that reviews their budgets.[26]
5. Budgets can restrict the organization's flexibility, its ability to adapt to change, and its ability to be innovative.

In an ever-changing and more complex operating environment, the budget as we know it may not survive. Because organizations must change, innovate, and adapt to their environments quickly, many may find budgets too difficult and time consuming to work with. On the other hand, the use of computers and the ability to change budgets almost instantaneously, or at least to examine them in a "what if" format, may allow budgets to remain an important part of the control process.[27] At the Lord Corporation, a privately held medium-sized manufacturing and research firm located in Erie, Pennsylvania, computerized budgeting has enabled major changes in a matter of hours instead of weeks.[28] Furthermore, firms can take certain steps to make sure their budgeting process is successful:

1. Be serious about budgeting, generate commitments to budgeting.
2. Build linkages to connect the firm's long-, medium-, and short-range plans.
3. Adapt detailed and comprehensive procedures to prepare budgets.
4. Analyze budget variances and deviations from standards, and take corrective action.[29]

Performance Appraisals

Most organizations have some type of formal appraisal system in place. **Performance appraisal** is the practice of determining whether an employee is performing his or her job effectively and efficiently. By definition performance appraisals should compare performance against the standards for that job. Because of EEO law, employees must be notified in advance of what constitutes the expected performance.[30] This legal requirement almost seems to beg for some type of management by objectives (MBO) system, but not all organizations interpret the requirement this way. A wide variety of appraisal systems exists and virtually no single system can adequately accomplish all the purposes for which it is intended.

PURPOSES OF PERFORMANCE APPRAISAL SYSTEMS

Performance appraisals are given for the following reasons: controlling performance, employee development, rewarding performance, motivation, legal compliance, personnel and employment planning, compensation, and communications, and for administrative purposes such as validating test selection.[31]

Controlling Performance. The primary purpose of performance appraisal is to make certain that employees are performing to standards. If they are not, then action must be taken to improve their performance. Standards assist in deciding who should be let go in a layoff and who should be terminated. If standards are inadequate, then "performance" may suffer, as Management Challenge 18.2 suggests.

DEVELOPMENTAL PURPOSES

Performance appraisals help indicate those who need higher levels of job proficiency and who therefore might need more training. They may also be used to indicate the results of training or to encourage supervisors to work more closely with subordinates to improve their performance. An interesting look at development of one's boss is examined in Management Challenge 18.3.

REWARDING PERFORMANCE

Appraisals assist in determining who should receive pay raises and promotions.

When Performance Appraisal Criteria Are Inadequate, Trouble Follows

Coach Barry Switzer was one of the most successful football coaches in the United States. His winning percentage of .844 had brought three national championships to the University of Oklahoma—in 1974, 1975, and 1985. By most measures of success, Switzer was at the top of his profession. But winning isn't the only criterion for coaching, and it became apparent that Switzer had failed to control his football program adequately and that perhaps the university's president had failed to control Switzer adequately. In 1988 and 1989 some rather revealing facts about the Oklahoma football program became known:

1. On September 4, 1988, former University of Oklahoma linebacker Brian "the Boz" Bosworth published an autobiography in which he detailed payoffs he received from Oklahoma boosters. He also described a football program with almost no control, one in which football players would horse around with Uzi machine guns and where steroids were as common as aspirin.

2. On December 19, 1988, the NCAA placed a three-year probation on the University of Oklahoma for paying players, an unethical recruiting practice, and for reselling football tickets. The Oklahoma Sooners were banned from postseason bowl games for two seasons and blocked from live television coverage for one season. Football scholarships and recruiting were cut severely. The NCAA cited Switzer for failure to "exercise supervisory control."

3. On December 26, 1988, through January 2, 1989, while in Orlando, Florida, for the Citrus Bowl, a few Sooner coaches and players destroyed property at a country club and hotel where they were staying.

4. On January 13, 1989, one team member was arrested for shooting another.

5. On January 21, 1989, three team members were arrested and charged with the rape of a 20-year-old woman in the players-only dorm.

6. On February 13, 1989, another player was arrested and charged with selling 17 grams of cocaine to an FBI undercover agent.

In Bosworth's book he says that Switzer doesn't cheat and he doesn't set up a slush fund, he simply turns his back and lets players fend for themselves. When they do, of course, there are plenty of alumni willing to make payments to them.

As a consequence of all these activities in the University of Oklahoma football program, Oklahoma Governor Henry Bellmon stated at a press conference that

MOTIVATION

Knowing that performance will be measured tends to stimulate employees to perform at higher levels. It develops a sense of responsibility and encourages initiative. Where rewards are based on performance, motivation is generally enhanced.[32]

LEGAL COMPLIANCE

Properly designed and administered performance appraisals enable the company or manager to help justify important decisions relating to pay, promotion, transfer, termination, and layoff.

"some fundamental changes need to be made." Furthermore, the state's board of regents issued five pages of recommendations. Eventually Barry Switzer had to resign from his coaching position. Oklahoma football survived. Other football programs have been less fortunate. Southern Methodist University received the death penalty: two years of banishment from intercollegiate football for similar offenses. The faculty completely revamped the program and seized control to make certain that the violations committed would not occur again.

SOURCE: Ron Givens, "Oklahoma Is Not OK," *Newsweek* (February 27, 1989), p. 80.

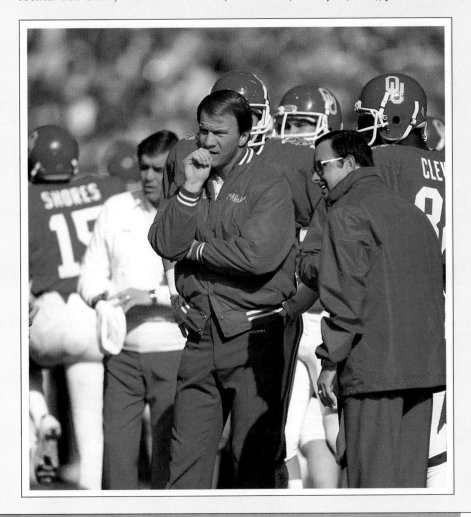

Barry Switzer was one of the winningest coaches in college football for many years, but he and others apparently forgot that winning wasn't the only criteria by which he could and should be judged. (SOURCE © John McDonough/Focus on Sports)

PERSONNEL AND EMPLOYMENT PLANNING PURPOSES
Personnel can help determine the skills available in the work force, and those who have them, thus aiding personnel planning.

COMPENSATION
Appraisals help determine who should receive rewards and help determine payroll and equitable monetary amounts.

COMMUNICATION
Appraisals help the organization communicate objectives and help improve communication between superiors and subordinates.

PERSONNEL/HRM RESEARCH PURPOSES

Appraisals can be used to validate selection tools or tests. The EEO Commission views the performance appraisal itself as a test.

TYPES OF APPRAISALS

Given the number of purposes and requirements, it is no wonder that no single performance appraisal system satisfies everyone. Chapter 11 reviews the types of appraisals in more detail.

Operational Control

Performance measurements and leadership/personal influence are the cornerstones of operational control. These mechanisms were discussed earlier, in Chapters 11, 13, 14, 15, and 16. Those systems used in middle management—especially MBORR and performance appraisal, statistical reports, and rules and procedures—also play important roles at the operational level. Virtually every facet of the organization normally has and should have operational control mechanisms. The disciplinary system was discussed in Chapter 11 as an HRM tool, but it is also a key operational control system that cuts across all organizational levels.

John Endee encourages honest appraisals by employees. He himself has weathered a negative comment or two and feels that other managers need to do so to be as effective as possible. Endee stresses that it takes a very trusting environment, a very positive and nonfearful environment, for this system to work.

SOURCE: Berkeley Rice, "Reversing Performance Reviews," *Psychology Today* (March 1984), p. 80.

At Photo Circuits, a manager and a subordinate often develop closer relationships than they might otherwise, due to the unique evaluation of managers by their subordinates. (SOURCE © Courtesy Photo Circuits)

Disciplinary Systems

Most organizations use some system for administering discipline. Companies have these systems in order to control four principal types of troublesome employee behaviors:

1. Ineffective employees: Individuals whose performances fall below their capabilities or the expectations of the organization, or who have motivational problems.
2. Alcoholic or drug-addicted employees: Employees whose drinking or drug abuse interferes with their performance on the job.
3. Participants in illegal acts: Employees who steal from the company or in some other way break the law.
4. Rule violators: Individuals who have been counseled but continue to engage in behaviors identified as undesirable.[33]

AT UNIVERSAL STUDIOS: *Producers were warned in 1986 to cut costs. The consequence of failing to adhere to warnings was the withdrawal of a producer's right to produce for Universal.*

Operations Management
Control Mechanisms

In Chapter 20 a number of mechanisms designed to control performance in the operations area, especially in the manufacturing area of the organization, are reviewed in more detail. Among these are systems for materials control, quality control, the statistical control of various manufacturing operations, and charting mechanisms for reviewing performance against planned objectives, especially on a time basis.

These controls work well in such isolated environments as a small factory, but imagine the difficulties of the U.S. federal government attempting to control procurement. Think, for example, of the costs involved and the potential for bribery. A major investigation, begun in the summer of 1988, uncovered the "Pentagate" scandal. Investigators found that information on business competitors could be acquired all too easily at the Pentagon, and that "classified" documents were passed around like playing cards. The close-knit culture of military procurement helped create these problems.[34] Or, imagine the difficulties in controlling federal expenditures for health care, as Management Challenge 18.4 portrays.

Control in a Changing Environment

One of the major problems experienced by managers in rapidly changing environments is that the control systems they use may have been designed to function in circumstances that no longer exist, to control factors that no longer need controlling. Worse, they may not be designed to control factors that do need controlling. A case in point is the financial services industry. Deregulation and consolidation have led to unparalleled change in many facets of the industry. Consequently, control systems are antiquated. Major impacts have resulted internally on budgets, profit center responsibilities, transfer pricing between divisions, revenue sharing, and compensation.[35]

Externally, government has failed to control adequately for fraud and just plain bad management in the industry, leaving the industry, especially the banking segment, badly in need of bailout.[36] The stocks and bonds portion of the financial services industry has also suffered from a lack of proper control sys-

Other elaborate schemes involve "runners," people whose job it is to steer patients to a doctor's office. Plays may be enacted between the "runners" and their "patients," whom they often find in bars. Sometimes these patients will fake injuries for which doctors can then make claims and for which the patients receive kickbacks. And even when individuals are caught running scams, if the scams are not totally illegal but are simply due to inflated pricing, shutting off payments does little good. Those running the scam change ID numbers and go into business as somebody else.

Insurance companies are setting up special investigating units, tightening up procedures, and trying to improve contracts among various companies to identify fraudulent claims. They are working closely with federal and local law enforcement agencies and attempting to use various laws to help prosecute, but the problem remains a complex one.

SOURCE: Glenn Ruffenach, "Scams on the Rise in Health Insurance," *Wall Street Journal* 22 June 1988, p. 27.

tems. Insider trading and only partly legal junk bonds have run rampant. Throughout the industry, growth and new offerings make a complex situation less controllable.[37] The bottom line for managers is that they must continually assess the appropriateness of control systems and redesign them when necessary.

Control Systems as Part of the Problem-Solving Process

Control is a problem-solving process. Control systems serve throughout that process by providing information. The environment is analyzed for information to indicate that performance is different than expected. Management then must

One of the ultimate consequences of failure, one of the control mechanisms of economics, and of lenders, is bankruptcy. Here the assets of a failed savings and loan are being disposed of at auction to help return savings to depositors. (SOURCE © Don Ford Connolly/Picture Group)

identify the real problem, to make certain that performance is not suffering for some reason other than the most obvious ones. Next, assumptions about the key factors in the situation must be made. Management then generates alternative ways to "fix" the problem. Among the assumptions made are those related to the success of potential solutions once they are generated. When the solution is implemented, that effort itself is controlled. And, of course, control is the eighth step in decision making; therefore, it is involved by definition in planning, organizing, leading, controlling, and problem solving. Most of the factors discussed in this chapter affect many of the steps in the entire decision process, which is why a figure showing the process is not provided here.

The Management Challenges Identified

1. Flexible strategies and their objectives
2. Changing nature of controlled situations
3. Global competitors who excel at quality control
4. Strategic decision use of cost information

Some Solutions Noted in the Chapter

1. Flexible control processes
2. More emphasis on control in U.S. firms
3. New cost accounting systems
4. Budget flexibility

Summary

1. Normally, control systems provide managers with the information necessary to determine whether the organization has reached its objectives. Various techniques are used to analyze performance. Without information and analysis, control would not be effectively accomplished.

2. The six core control systems are the strategic plan, the long-range financial plan, the operating budget, performance appraisals, statistical reports supplied through the organization's MIS, and policies and procedures.

3. Strategic control systems focus on total organizational performance. Tactical control systems focus largely on middle-level management activities and the budget; operational control systems focus on the achievement of front-line organizational objectives.

4. The master budget summarizes all the organization's budgets. Various revenue and expense budgets account for those items. Capital expenditure budgets identify major capital costs. The cash budget reviews cash flows for the year. Nonmonetary resource budgets are the source of much budget information.

5. Revenue centers are responsibility centers controlled on the basis of their sales of products or services. Cost centers/expense centers are responsibility centers that are controlled on the basis of their expenses, or costs, generated. Profit centers are

responsibility centers controlled on the basis of the difference between revenues and expenses—profit. Investment centers are responsibility centers controlled on the basis not only of profit, but also on the amount of capital investment made to produce those profits.

6. A balance sheet is principally used to determine the financial condition of an organization at some point in time. An income statement is used primarily to examine the performance of an organization over a period of time. The funds flow analysis examines the use of funds over a period of time.

7. Ratio analysis enables the manager or other analyst to discern better a firm's financial condition. Return on investment gives the manager a single figure that indicates the firm's financial condition for a specific period of time.

8. Cost systems serve three principal functions: inventory valuation, operational control, and individual product cost measurement. Increasingly, systems are being designed to enhance strategic marketing decisions.

9. Financial audits help assure that a firm's financial statements are accurate and that its accounting systems are functioning properly.

10. Performance appraisals help ensure that individual contributions to organizational objectives occur as expected. They also serve to motivate, to communicate, to assist in planning, to develop employees, and for legal compliance; they are used for compensation, in personnel and employment planning, and for administrative purposes.

11. MBO type systems, disciplinary systems, quality control, and operations control serve to provide control over specific areas: individual performance in pursuit of objectives, behavior relative to rules and procedures, product or service quality, and manufacturing or service operations respectively.

Thinking About Management

1. Discuss the control systems utilized in a current or past work organization, or some other organization to which you belong or have belonged.

2. Evaluate the effectiveness of the control systems you discussed in question 1.

3. Describe the control systems used in the organization you discussed in question 1 as either market, bureaucratic, or clan. Indicate why you believe it is such.

4. Describe the grading process used in this class as a control system, indicating how each step in the control process occurs.

CASE

Solving Cyanamid's Problems with Performance Appraisals

American Cyanamid Company had been employing a performance appraisal system entitled "Progress Review" for more than ten years when it decided it needed to examine the system because employees were dissatisfied with it. This evaluation also grew out of an effort launched by CEO George J. Sella, Jr., who wanted to change the company's culture to make it more innovative and more people oriented.

Cyanamid's old system rated salaried individuals on a ten-point scale divided into three classifications: outstanding, excellent, and achieving expected results. The guideline adhered to was 20 percent outstanding, 40 percent excellent, and 40 percent achieving expected results. Those in outstanding categories received the highest level of raises, but raises tended to even out over time across outstanding and excellent ratings because the largest salary increases went to those in the lowest pay grades, and pay grades had ceilings. The 20-40-40 guideline was not effectively implement-

CASE (Cont.)

able where members of a work unit were all outstanding but could not be rated as such.

When asked about the old program, scientists in Cyanamid's medical research division offered various caustic comments, including these:

> The progress reviews do illustrate some aspects of my performance but I know damn well that it is also influenced by quotas.
> My work could be outstanding year in and year out, but if one other person in my group was outstanding, I would be denied a raise.
> I don't take it seriously. It is a Mickey Mouse numbers game. My superior and I just laugh at it and we get through it as quickly as we can.

Cyanamid's personnel department decided that something had to be done. A system had to be designed that would reward excellent performance but not penalize the average person, especially the typical high performer in scientific areas.

DISCUSSION QUESTIONS
1. What are the problems with the existing system?
2. What solutions would you recommend?
3. What might a new system you would design be like?

SOURCE: Saul W. Gellerman and William G. Hodgson, "Cyanamid's New Take on Performance Appraisal," *Harvard Business Review* (May–June 1988), pp. 36–40.

MANAGERS AT WORK

Getting a Grasp on a New Business

Charles Brandon, part owner and manager of the Winter Park Brewery, a combination restaurant, beer and wine bar, and mini-brewery, was trying to get a grasp on the operation. He knew his food costs. He knew his margins on each item, but he didn't have a complete cost system which combined everything. And, he had never managed before. He had found that managing minimum wage workers was not as easy as it looked. Customers had complained about poor service. And working with food service managers to whom he had licensed the restaurant portion of the operation, had not been easy either.

Charles had begun the Brewery because he wanted to own his own business, had always liked beer and brewing, and saw it as a way to combine a hobby with a business. He began the operation with the vision that the restaurant would be a family restaurant, serving only beer and wine so that it might even become sort of a neighborhood pub. About half way through the first year, he realized that that was not the image that had been established. He liked blues and jazz and saw offering such to the community as a way of increasing business, which had fallen off.

Thursday night became blues night, and bands were scheduled on Fridays and Saturdays after 9:00 PM. The Brewery had no trouble selling all of the beer it could make. Capacity had been doubled, and aging time had been cut in half in order to meet demand. But the overall operation was not making money. In this its tenth month, it finally reached breakeven on cash flow, but had not yet shown a profit.

DISCUSSION QUESTIONS
1. Identify the various types of control problems revealed in the above.
2. Indicate how the control systems discussed in this chapter could be used to help solve these problems.
3. Discuss how strategy and marketing are issues in making a profit as shown in this case.

Computing Financial Ratios

Examine Table 18.1. Now compute each of the four financial ratios in the table for Georgia-Pacific for 1989, using the information provided in Figures 18.2 and 18.3. Compare these to the following industry averages:

Calculated for Georgia-Pacific	Industry Average* Evaluation
Liquidity	
Current	1.4 times
Leverage	
Debt to total assets	46%
Activity	
Inventory turnover	10 times
Profitability	
Return on total assets	5.4%

Almanac of Business and Industrial Financial Ratios, (Englewood Cliffs, NJ: Prentice-Hall, 1989), p 79. Manufacturing: Paper and Allied Products, Table II Corporation with Net Income, 1989 (over $250 million in assets). Based on these ratios, what is your evaluation of the financial condition of Georgia-Pacific?

CHAPTER NINETEEN

Management Information Systems and Control

CHAPTER OBJECTIVES

By the time you complete this chapter you should be able to

1. Define information and information systems and indicate the role of information as an organizational resource.
2. Describe the purpose of management information systems (MIS).
3. Relate the evolution of MISs.
4. Indicate how MISs are designed.
5. Describe how the company and/or manager should use an MIS.
6. Describe the functions of a chief information officer (CIO).
7. Identify how microcomputers have affected the manager's use of MISs.
8. Identify the impacts of artificial intelligence (AI), decision support systems (DSSs), networking, and expert systems (ESs) on management.
9. Indicate how an MIS affects the organization.
10. Describe knowledge-based organizations of the future.

CHAPTER OUTLINE

Management Information Systems (MISs)
    Characteristics of Quality Information
    The Information Needed by Managers
    MISs Defined
    The Evolution of MISs
    MIS Components
MIS Design
Using an MIS
    The Internal and External Environmental Information Needed
    Information Requirements in a Rapidly Changing World
    Strategic Use of Information
The MIS Director
    The Role of the CIO
The Changing Role of the MIS Function
Telecommunications and the MIS
Decision Support Systems (DSSs) and Expert Systems (ESs)
    DSSs
    ESs and Artificial Intelligence (AI)
    Executive Information Systems
Protecting the Information System
How an MIS Affects the Organization
Knowledge-Based Organizations and Their Management
Managing Information as a Problem-Solving Process
Management Challenges Identified
Some Solutions Noted in the Chapter

Mrs. Fields' Secret Ingredient

Mrs. Fields' Cookies of Park City, Utah, grew from one store, in 1978, to almost six hundred stores in thirty-seven states and five foreign countries by 1988. They earned 18.5 percent on sales of $87 million in 1987. Faced with phenomenal growth, Randy and Debbi both wanted to create a company that could be managed with one thousand stores, just as they had managed the company when it had only thirty stores. Randy focused on information systems as a way of maintaining the "feel" of a small company. He wanted the information system to perform two principal duties: to provide control and to aid managers in decision making.

The personal computer is really the key to Mrs. Fields' management systems. For example, at the beginning of each work day, Richard Lui, who runs the Pier 39 Mrs. Fields' in San Francisco, after unlocking the store, calls up the Day Planner program on his Tandy computer. He enters that day's sales projections (which are based on figures adjusted earlier for growth) and then answers a few questions that the program asks him: for example, the day of the week, type of day—normal day, sale day, school day, holiday, and so on. The computer then reviews the last three days of the type he indicates and gives him the projection of sales he is expected to make for that day. Hour by hour, it tells him how many batches to mix and when to mix them, in order to meet demand and minimize leftovers. Lui keeps the computer informed of the store's progress each hour. In fact, in some stores the information is automatically fed to the computer by new types of cash registers. The computer then, in turn, revises hourly projections and makes suggestions, depending upon the number and types of cookies sold. It also offers suggestions for improving sales, and other operating issues, perhaps suggesting that one of the crew should do sampling and give away free cookies up and down Pier 39. The computer also provides the headquarters' staff with virtual real-time information about all operations—that is, information available as something happens, not later.

Each day Lui checks his computerized PhoneMail messages and often hears from Debbi. If Lui has something to say to Debbi, he uses the computer. He calls up the PhoneMail program, types up his message, and the next morning it is on Debbi's desk. He will receive a reply from her or from someone on her staff within forty-eight hours.

In addition to the daily planning program, Lui's computer also helps him schedule crews, interview new applicants, and help with personnel, administration, and maintenance.

The computer helps keep Debbi in constant contact with all store managers. Managers report a great deal of information, but more importantly that information comes back to them in a way that they can use. For example, the computer can be used to generate supply orders, saving a manager's time.

Unfortunately, their information system had been used largely for internal control and not for external strategic surveillance and decision making. In late 1988, after losing $15 million in the first half of the year, Mrs. Fields' was preparing to close about one hundred stores. They had oversaturated their markets in some areas and had not been very careful about site selection in others.

SOURCE: Buck Brown, "How the Cookie Crumbled at Mrs. Fields'," *Wall Street Journal* 26 January 1989, p. B1; and Tom Richman, "Mrs. Fields' Secret Ingredient," *Inc.* (October 1987), pp. 65–72

The productivity of knowledge has already become the key to productivity, competitive strength, and economic achievement. Knowledge has already become the primary industry, the industry that supplies the economy, the essential and central resource of production.

Peter F. Drucker

Over the next thirty years, advances in computer-based technology will revolutionize the way in which we think about organizations. The very nature of organizations is being transformed from an emphasis on working with materials to an emphasis on working with knowledge.

C. W. Holsapple and Andrew B. Whinston
authors of *Expert Systems*

Debbi and Randy Fields know that information is one of the most important ingredients in helping make a company successful. They know that information should enable managers to make better decisions and realize that, without information, managers are shooting in the dark. Their experiences also reveal, however, that information systems are needed not just for operations, but for strategic planning and other functions, as well. This design feature was lacking in their information system and it cost them millions of dollars.

The core function of management is problem solving. Current and relevant knowledge about the environment and about the variables in the decision situation is necessary for sound decision making. The decision maker must be able to follow the steps of the decision process in a knowledgeable way. Organizational effectiveness is, in fact, often at the mercy of the information available to its managers.[1] Information systems have become so sophisticated that mangers can be assisted by decision support systems in addressing major issues. More and more frequently, information systems are being designed to do just that. Some information systems can even offer proposed solutions. Business is in the middle of an information revolution, and that revolution is changing the way the world does business. For example, American Hospital Supply Corp., which distributes products from 8,500 manufacturers to more than 100,000 healthcare providers, watched its market share soar after it established computer links to customers and suppliers. These links enabled the company to reduce inventories, improve customer service, and secure volume discounts for customers from suppliers. More importantly, these links locked out competitors who were not linked to customer computers.

American Airlines' Sabre reservation system is used by approximately 48 percent of some 24,000 travel agents in the United States, giving American Airlines an advantage in reaching agents and booking flights. Because each reservation made for other carriers costs $1.75, Sabre earned American Airlines about $170 million before taxes in 1985.[2] Information even enables Nissenbaum's auto junkyard in Somerville, Massachusetts, to improve customer service in the "looking for parts" business. Such sales have increased 75 percent since Nis-

Debbi and Randy Fields have plenty of reason to jump for joy. Their cookie operation is extremely successful, due in part to a sophisticated information system that allows them to control internal operations as they occur. (SOURCE © Jeanne Strongin)

The Sabre reservation system not only originally gave American Airlines a competitive edge, but now provides substantial revenues to the firm as competitors and travel agencies use its services. (SOURCE © Ken Kerbs)

senbaum's began using a satellite dish–PC system to find automobile engines and other parts across the country. Nissenbaum connects with six hundred similarly equipped junkyards and parts stores and is able to check for an inventory of needed items that could not be checked before. Similarly, McKesson Corporation, a San Francisco wholesaler, is linked by computer to drugstores. Such links cut costs, increase productivity, and make customers so dependent on McKesson they rarely switch distributors. For example, McKesson supplies computerized scanners to its customer drugstore managers, allowing them to process inventory needs automatically. McKesson not only ships the materials almost instantaneously, but adds pricing stickers with designated profit margins.[3] Electronic Data Interchange (EDI), in which company data bases are linked, connects Seminole Manufacturing Company with Wal-Mart, allowing it to cut its delivery time of men's slacks to Wal-Mart by 50 percent. That resulted in increased sales of 31 percent over nine months.[4] Finally, Merrill Lynch has established a global communications network linking all of its major offices via a communications satellite. This allows it not only to compete, but to control its global corporate operations.[5]

This chapter examines the role of information and information systems in decision making and control. It also discusses management information systems (MIS) specifically designed for use by management, common MIS mistakes, and the appropriate use of MIS. The role of the personal computer in managerial decision making and the role of the chief information officer are noted. The impact of artificial intelligence, expert systems, and decision support systems, as well as networking on the decision process, is reviewed. The role of MIS in the organization, and more importantly the role of information in a knowledge-based organization of the future, is discussed.

Management Information Systems (MISs)[6]

Information "is data that have been put into a meaningful and useful context and communicated to a recipient who uses it to make decisions."[7] By definition, managers need information on the environment in order to be able to recognize and identify problems, make assumptions about solutions, generate alternatives, choose alternatives, and implement and control their choices. Indeed, we have evolved into an information society in which a majority of employees work with or produce information rather than physical goods.[8] **Data** are raw, unanalyzed facts. Information then becomes data that have been meaningfully altered for use in decision making.[9] For example, lists of competitors' sales are data, but when the trends in those sales are compared to the ones in the firm analyzing them, information exists. One of the ways to assess a manager's information needs is through a checklist such as is shown in Table 19.1. Information is the lifeblood of organizations.

Table 19.1 Checklist for Manager's Information Needs

1. What types of decisions do you make regularly?
2. What types of information do you need to make those decisions?
3. What types of information do you regularly get?
4. What types of information would you like to get that you are not now getting?
5. What information would you want daily, weekly, monthly, yearly?
6. What types of data analysis programs would you like to see made available?

SOURCE: Adapted from Philip Kotler, *Principles of Marketing*, 3rd ed. (Englewood Cliffs, N.J.: Prentice-Hall, 1986).

Characteristics of Quality Information

Quality information has three critical attributes: accuracy, timeliness, and relevancy. **Accuracy** means that the information is free from mistakes and errors, that it is clear, and that it reflects the meaning on which the data are based. **Timely** means that decision makers have the information necessary within the relevant time frame. **Relevancy** means that the information specifically answers for the recipient the what, why, where, when, who, and how of the issue.[10] To be relevant, the information must be complete. The need for quality information is increasing dramatically. In complex, volatile environments the problem solver's decisions depend on his or her ability to obtain accurate, timely, and relevant information. Successfully selling automobiles, providing healthcare at a profit, or using personal computers or software in the business market requires more information now than at any time in history.[11]

The Information Needed by Managers

The information needed by managers varies principally by the level of the manager and his or her economic function. Figure 19.1 examines the various characteristics of jobs by levels of organization—top management, middle management, and operating management.[12] It is obvious from this figure that the information requirements in the various levels do differ significantly. Top management is principally focused on planning and on broad environmental concerns. Middle management focuses very heavily on control, functional areas,

FIGURE 19.1   THE INFORMATION NEEDED BY LEVEL OF ORGANIZATION

CHARACTERISTIC	TOP MANAGEMENT	MIDDLE MANAGEMENT	OPERATING MANAGEMENT
1. FOCUS ON PLANNING	HEAVY	MODERATE	MINIMUM
2. FOCUS ON CONTROL	MODERATE	HEAVY	HEAVY
3. TIME FRAME	ONE TO THREE YEARS	UP TO A YEAR	DAY TO DAY
4. SCOPE OF ACTIVITY	EXTREMELY BROAD	ENTIRE FUNCTIONAL AREA	SINGLE SUBFUNCTION OR SUBTASK
5. NATURE OF ACTIVITY	RELATIVELY UNSTRUCTURED	MODERATELY STRUCTURED	HIGHLY STRUCTURED
6. LEVEL OF COMPLEXITY	VERY COMPLEX, MANY VARIABLES	LESS COMPLEX, BETTER DEFINED VARIABLES	STRAIGHTFORWARD
7. JOB MEASUREMENT	DIFFICULT	LESS DIFFICULT	RELATIVELY EASY
8. RESULT OF ACTIVITY	VISIONS, GOALS, LONG-TERM OBJECTIVES, AND STRATEGIES	IMPLEMENTATION SCHEDULES, PERFORMANCE YARDSTICKS	END PRODUCT
9. TYPE OF INFORMATION UTILIZED	EXTERNAL, INTERNAL, UNCERTAIN ACCURACY	MOSTLY INTERNAL, REASONABLE ACCURACY	INTERNAL HISTORICAL, HIGH LEVEL OF ACCURACY
10.* MENTAL ATTRIBUTES	CREATIVE, INNOVATIVE, AS WELL AS ANALYTICAL	RESPONSIBLE, PERSUASIVE, ADMINISTRATIVE	EFFICIENT, EFFECTIVE
11. NUMBER OF PEOPLE INVOLVED	FEW	MODERATE NUMBER	MANY
12. DEPARTMENT/ DIVISIONAL INTERACTION	INTRA-DIVISION	INTRA-DEPARTMENT	INTER-DEPARTMENT

*THIS AREA NEEDS INCREASING INNOVATION AT ALL LEVELS

SOURCE: ADAPTED FROM JEROME KANTER, MANAGEMENT INFORMATION SYSTEMS, 3RD ED. (ENGLEWOOD CLIFFS, NJ: PRENTICE HALL, 1984), P. 6.

AT MRS. FIELDS' COOKIES: *Debbi and Randy understood very well the information needed for the operations functions of the organization, but they failed to incorporate necessary strategic information. This oversight cost them millions of dollars.*

and performance. Operating management is principally concerned with performance, effectiveness, and efficiency. Each of these perspectives requires different information in order to make sound decisions.

As Figure 19.1 suggests, the information needed by managers also varies by their function within the organization. Those in marketing need information on facts related to issues such as sales, advertising expenses, sales personnel, sales volume, market penetration, product quality and service, and service cost. Those involved in finance need information about stock prices, tax rates, interest rates, the state of the economy, financial performance within the organization, and depreciation policies. Those in operations need information related to such issues as efficiency rates, productivity, scrap problems, material utilization rates, labor utilization rates, and labor union contracts. Those involved in HRM need information on such issues as the availability of personnel within a work force to satisfy organizational labor requirements, comparative compensation rates, federal regulations related to occupational safety and health or EEO, and the evaluations of employees' performance. Those involved in information functions need information on such issues as utilization of reports, computer time availability, expert systems being developed or currently available, and information system user rates.

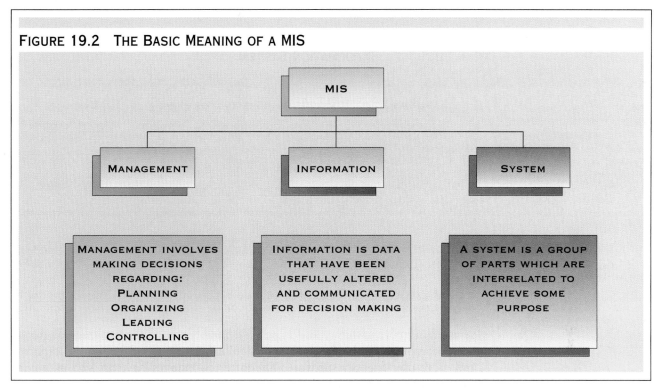

FIGURE 19.2   THE BASIC MEANING OF A MIS

MIS

MANAGEMENT

INFORMATION

SYSTEM

MANAGEMENT INVOLVES MAKING DECISIONS REGARDING: PLANNING ORGANIZING LEADING CONTROLLING

INFORMATION IS DATA THAT HAVE BEEN USEFULLY ALTERED AND COMMUNICATED FOR DECISION MAKING

A SYSTEM IS A GROUP OF PARTS WHICH ARE INTERRELATED TO ACHIEVE SOME PURPOSE

SOURCE: ROBERT G. MURDICK AND JOEL E. ROSS, INTRODUCTION TO MANAGEMENT INFORMATION SYSTEMS (ENGLEWOOD CLIFFS, NJ: PRENTICE HALL, INC., 1977), P. 8. ADAPTED BY PERMISSION.

MISs Defined

The MIS links three key words, as described in Figure 19.2: management, information, and systems. An MIS is created to provide information to managers so that they can make better decisions.

An MIS aids management in making decisions by collecting, organizing, and distributing information.[13] The MIS must facilitate the problem-solving process in all four of the major functions of management: planning, organizing, leading, and controlling. The MIS is a formal system of information gathering and analysis. It may be computerized or not. The manager must also be alert to available informal systems of gathering, receiving, evaluating, and distributing information.

The Evolution of MISs

All organizations have some type of MIS. Organizations have always had them, even though they may not have been defined as such. Historically, most information systems have been built around financial—and to some extent marketing—information. Only with the advent of the computer has information on other areas of the organization been extensively collected, analyzed, and distributed. Many people were disappointed with computers and information systems in the 1960s because they failed to deliver many of the expectations that people had of them.[14] Once computers and the necessary related software became more reliable and hardware memories increased substantially, along with the user friendliness of software, the computer's tremendous capacity for supplying information was realized and MISs were developed on a more formal basis. MISs have evolved in four principal stages according to their level of sophistication: electronic data processing, management information systems,

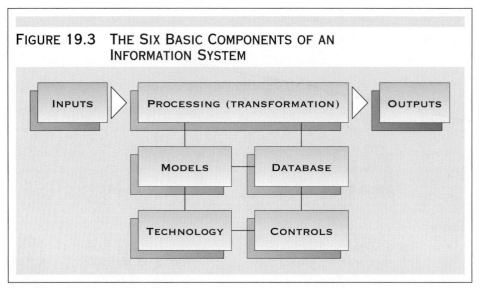

FIGURE 19.3 THE SIX BASIC COMPONENTS OF AN INFORMATION SYSTEM

SOURCE: ADAPTED FROM JOHN G. BURCH AND GARY GRUDNITSKI, INFORMATION SYSTEMS: THEORY AND PRACTICE, 4TH ED. (NEW YORK: WILEY, 1986), P. 36, BY PERMISSION OF JOHN WILEY & SONS, INC.

decision support systems, and expert systems. Each of these phases of development represents the increased availability of increased computer capacity and more user-friendly software. The latter two stages have an MIS as a core component.

ELECTRONIC DATA PROCESSING (EDP)

In the 1960s and early 1970s, mainframe computers processed information for a limited number of functions—for example, accounting, purchasing, and accounts payable. The machines were large and often temperamental. For example, they had to be kept at 72 degrees F, plus or minus a degree or two, or they would run the risk of shutting down. Their high cost and complexity made a centralized EDP office mandatory. Information from various departments was processed by the central department and reports were distributed to various managers. EDP was designed to process large numbers of transactions. It was based on scheduled computer runs, with integrated files for related jobs. Summary reports were prepared for management. It was data focused. It was not a true MIS.

MISs

EDP departments expanded in the 1970s as the cost of information declined and the size of mainframes increased rapidly. This increased capacity led **EDP** departments to expand services to more users. Production, engineering, and development became more frequent users of the system. As management information was actually "managed," the development and refinement of MISs became more widespread.[15] The focus was thus on information, not data; there were structured information flows; there was integration of **EDP** jobs by business functions; and there were inquiry and report generation capabilities.

DECISION SUPPORT SYSTEMS (DSSs)

Decision support systems are computer-based MISs that provide managers with easily accessible information and models that support decision making in an interactive manner.[16] This was the next logical step in the process. Managers had information they could manipulate in order to make better decisions; the focus was on decision making; and there was an emphasis on flexibility and adaptability. A **DSS** is user initiated and controlled.

EXPERT SYSTEMS (ESs)

Expert systems are MISs that actually provide guidance to managers. They use decision heuristics based on the knowledge and experience of "experts" in a given field to provide suggested alternative decisions. Both DSSs and ESs are discussed in more detail later in this chapter.

MIS Components

All information systems, whether computerized or not, have six basic components, as shown in Figure 19.3.[17] If we think of information as a resource and of the information system as representative of the systems model discussed in Chapter 2, then the inputs, processing (transformation), and outputs model used there applies to information, as well. When discussing an information system, processing, (transformation) should be broken into four building blocks: models, data base, technology, and controls. The six components of an information system are input, models, technology, database, control, and output.

INPUT

Inputs "are all the data, text, voice, and images entering the information system and the methods and media by which they are captured and entered."[18] The most common means of entering transactions for a text are bar-code/laser readers and via the computer keyboard. Voice input is also possible and will become more common as we move toward the twenty-first century.[19]

MODELS

The **models** component "consists of a combination of procedural, logical, and mathematical models that manipulate input and store data in a variety of ways, to produce the desired results or output."[20] Models may be very simple and simply update a file as a consequence of a transaction, or they may be extremely complex and simulate an entire organizational and environmental process—for example, a model of the U.S. economy.

TECHNOLOGY

Technology "is the 'toolbox' of information systems work. It captures the input, drives the models, stores and accesses data, produces and transmits output, and helps control the total system."[21] Technology has three principal components: technicians, hardware, and software. Technicians are those people who work with the technology, understand it, and make it work. Software programs enable the computer hardware to do the processes required by the models. Hardware consists principally of a variety of computers—large mainframe computers, mini-computers, and personal computers. Each of these may be accompanied by various input, central processing, and output devices, as well as storage devices.

DATABASE

The **database** "is where all the data necessary to serve the needs of all users are stored."[22] Data may be a combination of text, numbers, voice, and images. Databases may or may not be computerized. Managing databases is becoming ever more significant, as various users will need different parts of the database. Databases may exist on personnel, parts, services, competitors, inventories, customers, and numerous other pieces of information.

CONTROL

Every computer system has or should have control systems designed to protect it from a number of hazards—natural disasters, such as fire, and human dis-

This bar code reader, being used in a department store, allows the store's managers to not only know sales, but inventory levels as well. The input information and devices, bar codes and bar code readers, respectively, have totally transformed the inventory management process in recent years. (SOURCE © Ken Kerbs)

asters, such as fraud, sabotage, or competitor intelligence efforts. In most cases, however, control devices are principally designed to overcome inadequate operational procedures, incompetent employees, or poor management. Typical controls include records management systems, accounting controls, and personnel procedures.

OUTPUT

Output is the product of the information system. It is quality information for all levels of management and other users, both inside and outside the organization. It is the desired output that causes the models, other building blocks, and other components of the information system to be designed as they are. The output of a system can only be as good as the input and models upon which it is based.

MIS Design

The designers of information systems must contend with ten primary design forces acting on the eventual design of any MIS: integration, user/system interface, competitive forces, information quality and reusability, systems requirements, data processing requirements, organizational factors, cost-effectiveness requirements, human factors, and feasibility requirements.[23] A brief description of each of these ten forces is contained in Table 19.2. Designers must assess the relevance of each of these factors to the eventual design. Figure 19.4 portrays these forces as they impact on the MIS. Sometimes the requirements of one factor will be in conflict with the requirements of another. For example, when competition is very strong, the company must design the system to identify competitor actions quickly. As a result it might not sufficiently provide for human factors—the system users.

Table 19.2 Ten Primary Design Forces Impacting an MIS

Integration: Information systems must be designed to couple internal organizational units tightly. Manufacturing, marketing, personnel, and finance must be able to network with each other. Furthermore, in the future there will be much more integration with customer systems in order to provide better service.*

User/System Interface: The system must be designed to make sure the user has ready access to the system and can use it with as few obstructions as possible.

Competitive Forces: The MIS must be designed to improve the organization's competitiveness and domestic and global market situation in a world of rapid and accelerating change.

Information Quality and Useability: Quality is defined by the user. It is user needs that ultimately determine how a system will be designed. Many times, unfortunately, various users' needs will be in conflict, and many users depending on the same MIS will want different types of information and want to massage it in different ways.

Systems Requirements: The inherent operational requirements of the MIS include reliability, availability, flexibility, installation schedule, life expectancy and growth potential, and maintainability.

Data Processing Requirements: There are four categories of data processing requirements that are the detail work of the system: the volume of data involved, the complexity of data processing information, processing time constraints, and computational demands.

Organizational Factors: There are five key organizational factors that affect the kind of information required. They include the nature of the organization, its primary organizational structure, its size, its management style, and whether it is a functional organization, a divisional organization, or a matrix organization.

Cost-Effectiveness Requirements: Cost and benefits should be identified before spending a large amount of money to develop an MIS.

Human Factors: Any time technology is introduced into a work situation, the human factor becomes a key element and must be considered in the design of the system. People often fear and resist change.

Feasibility Requirements: Technical, economic, and legal operational and scheduling feasibility must be considered in the design of the system.

SOURCE: John G. Burch and Gary Grudnitski, *Information Systems: Theory and Practice,* 4th ed. (New York: Wiley, 1986), p. 3, by permission of John Wiley & Sons, Inc.
*See "Information Power," *Business Week* (October 14, 1985), pp. 108–114; and David Wessell, "Marketing Tool: Computer Finds a Role in Buying and Selling, Reshaping Businesses," *Wall Street Journal* 18 March 1987, pp. 1, 22.

FIGURE 19.4 FORCES IMPACTING ON THE MIS COMPONENTS

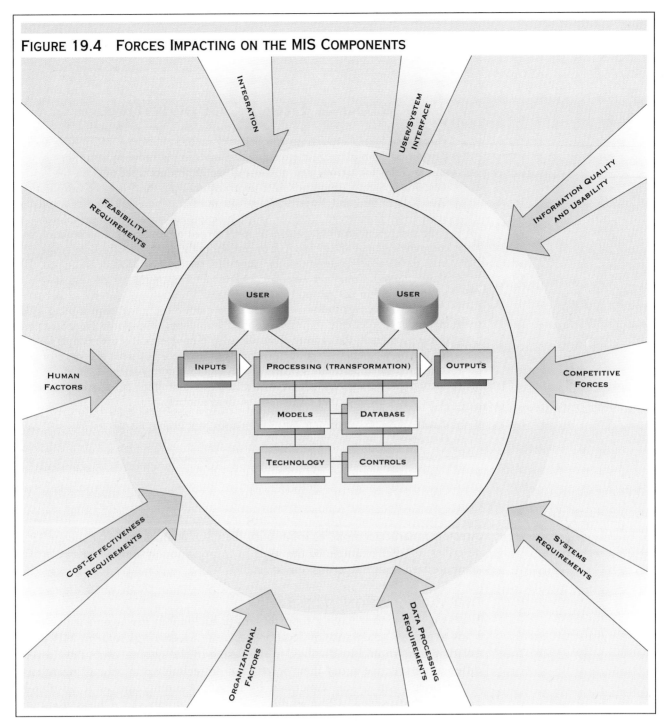

INTEGRATION

USER/SYSTEM INTERFACE

INFORMATION QUALITY AND USABILITY

FEASIBILITY REQUIREMENTS

HUMAN FACTORS

COMPETITIVE FORCES

USER   USER

INPUTS   PROCESSING (TRANSFORMATION)   OUTPUTS

MODELS   DATABASE

TECHNOLOGY   CONTROLS

COST-EFFECTIVENESS REQUIREMENTS

SYSTEMS REQUIREMENTS

ORGANIZATIONAL FACTORS

DATA PROCESSING REQUIREMENTS

SOURCE: ADAPTED WITH PERMISSION FROM JOHN G. BURCH AND GARY GRUDNITSKI, INFORMATION SYSTEMS: THEORY AND PRACTICE, 4TH ED. (NEW YORK: WILEY, 1986), P. 42. REPRINTED BY PERMISSION OF JOHN WILEY & SONS, INC.

Using an MIS

Once the MIS has been designed and put into place, there must be ongoing management of its various components, there must be controls in place, and there must be system policy and planning. Various projects and changes that occur throughout the system must be managed. In short there must be planning, organizing, leading, controlling, and decision making, relative to the information system itself. Much of the responsibility for that process lies with the MIS

Tuscaloosa Steel Corporation

Tuscaloosa Steel Corporation is a majority owned subsidiary of Tippins, Inc., a Pittsburgh, Pennsylvania, company that manufactures and installs turnkey rolling mill facilities for ferrous and nonferrous metal producers throughout the world. Tuscaloosa Steel Corporation is a joint venture with British Steel Corporation, O'Neal Steel Inc., and American Cast Iron and Pipe Company. Tippins wanted to build a mill that would compete with Japanese steel manufacturing facilities.

To compete with the Japanese, Tippins turned to almost total automation and computerized manufacturing. The operations in the plant are to be fully automated from the moment a part enters the plant until the finished product is shipped. The plant employs Computer Integrated Manufacturing (CIM), a process in which computers aid in design and manufacturing.

A telecommunications link connects the plant's computer with on-line order inquiry and order-entry terminals in the Birmingham offices of O'Neal Steel, one of the partners in the venture. This allows salespeople to access the database and tell instantly whether a specific product is in inventory or what the stage of production is for a customer's order. The company's computer also schedules production and reviews the progress of a customer's projects, using a computerized version of PERT, so that customers' needs are anticipated.

SOURCE: "Total Commitment to Automation Molds New Outlook for the Steel Industry," *Data Management* (June 1986), pp. 30–32, 45.

director; in larger companies it lies with the CIO. Management Challenge 19.1 describes another example of this type of information system and its role in a computerized manufacturing operation.

USER PARTICIPATION IN DESIGN
Just as it is true that having subordinates participate in management decisions leads to greater acceptance of decisions, there is a recurring theme in MIS practice that users should be involved in the design of the system. Users have a very different perspective about their needs than do technicians.[24] The growing customer orientation of the American business community makes it absolutely necessary that users—MIS customers—should be involved.[25] Unless users are involved, they may be overwhelmed by useless information or not receive the information they need. Unfortunately, if users do not participate with technicians in designing the system, serious line/staff conflicts may result.[26]

The Internal and External Environmental Information Needed

Figure 19.5 identifies the types of internal and external environmental information an MIS should provide. As seen in this figure, an information system may be both formal and informal and should collect extensive amounts of information so that it can be distributed to users and analyzed.

AT MRS. FIELDS' COOKIES: *They overlooked several of the external information needs of the organization. This meant that they could not do strategy properly. Conversely, their internal control system functioned well.*

This Tuscaloosa Steel plant contains an integrated manufacturing and information system that allows the firm to improve quality, productivity, and customer satisfaction. (Courtesy Tippins Corporation)

Information Requirements in a Rapidly Changing World

In Chapter 12 we discussed John Naisbitt's ten megatrends for the 1980s, which are affecting our society and are expected to have an ongoing impact throughout the twentieth century as well as his ten megatrends for the year 2000. All of the megatrends for the 1980s have been borne out by the events of the past few years, and the implications for business are tremendous. For example, the migration of the population from the northern United States to the southern and western parts of the country affects distribution systems, manufacturing locations, the needs for capital and personnel, and the need to train new labor forces. The trend toward decentralization in organizations directly affects the amount of authority to be distributed. The move from a national to a global economy impels business to think and act in global terms. The information requirements of such changes are staggering.[27]

Some of his megatrends for the year 2000 are already beginning to occur. For example, our global society is everywhere evident—on the evening news, in the supermarket, at the department store. The importance of the individual is ever increasing—in Eastern Europe people are embracing democracy and in the United States, companies are embracing cultural diversity. Finally, a decade of new global economic highs appears likely.

If you combine these megatrends with those areas of major change identified by Tom Peters and listed in Table 12.2 in Chapter 12, p. 412 and with the ten management challenges identified in Chapter 1 in this text, p. 23, you will see that the environmental information system for organizations must change con-

FIGURE 19.5 MANAGEMENT INFORMATION SYSTEMS

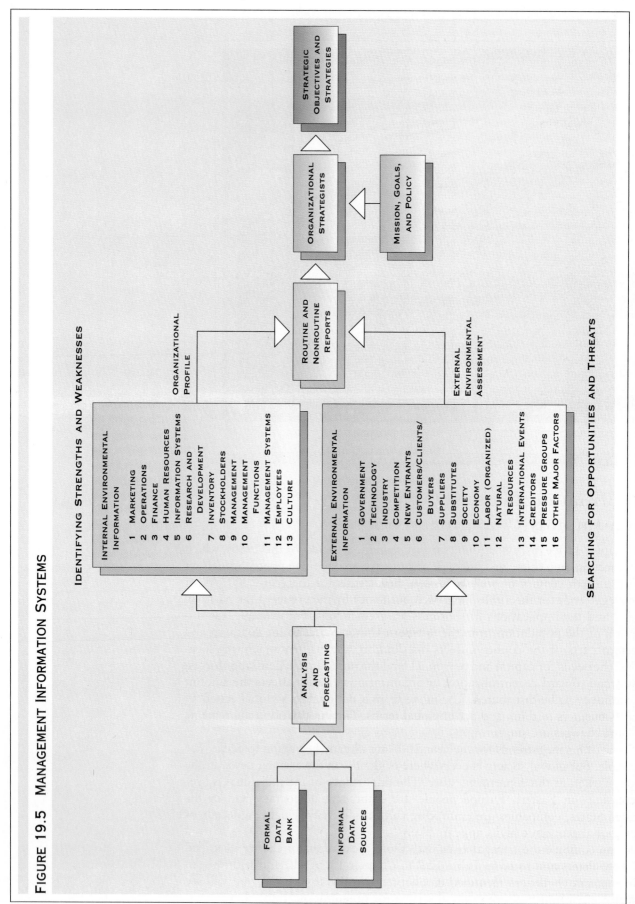

SOURCE: FIGURES FROM *STRATEGIC MANAGEMENT, TEXT AND CASES* BY J. HIGGINS AND J. VINCZE, COPYRIGHT © 1989 BY THE DRYDEN PRESS, INC., A DIVISION OF HOLT, RINEHART AND WINSTON, INC., REPRINTED BY PERMISSION OF THE PUBLISHER.

GLOBAL MANAGEMENT CHALLENGE

Managing Information Systems at Multinationals

Managing information systems at multinationals is a very complex task, especially for the extremely large corporation, such as 185-year-old E. I. Du Pont de Nemours & Company. This chemical giant generates one-third of its $27 billion in revenue overseas, where it employs 35,000 people in some 150 plants and offices. "When remote corporate clients as far apart as Rio, Tokyo, or Rome get 'gobbledygook' on their PCs, the situation is especially frustrating," comments Lee Foote, manager of Du Pont's Electronic Exchange Section at Wilmington, Delaware. "There are many misconceptions about what this right stuff—information—actually is," he adds.

The key to getting the "right stuff," is to get your data and information house in order. A worldwide manufacturing or service company cannot be successful if it hasn't done so. Two keys seem to be Electronic Data Interchange (EDI) and Structured Query Language (SQL). EDI "describes the standardized way of using computers to transmit and receive business documents such as purchase orders." SQL "is a standard means of accessing database management systems that are shared by different architectures."

Du Pont's customers in the United States and throughout the world can use EDI to conduct more of their business activities with the company electronically. "We pretty much had to educate the vendors, lead them by the nose," comments George Higgins, a data resource management consultant for Du Pont. The point that both he and Foote make is that the vendor sees technology as an end unto itself, but the user company needs the technology to accomplish something. You have "to show them what the end is." Part of the problem is that the technology promised by some of the major manufacturers, in particular IBM, simply won't be available to make the system work as well as they would like until the early 1990s, especially the SQL system.

Much work had to be done to convince vendors, customers, and corporate management at Du Pont, that EDI and SQL are the ways to go, but that has been done. Customers, in particular, have found it to be an extremely effective way of conducting business.

SOURCE: Ralph Emmett Carlisle, "Managing IS at Internationals," *Datamation* (March 1, 1988), pp. 54–63.

stantly to keep up with the rapidly changing internal and external environments. As an example, consider the requirements posed by global business, an issue addressed by both Naisbitt and Peters. Developing information systems for a global business is complex, as the Global Management Challenge suggests.

Strategic Use of Information

Information has become such an important resource, that the firm that is able to gather and process information more rapidly and utilize it more effectively gains a strategic advantage over its competitors. Michael E. Porter and Victor E. Miller suggest ways that information can be used to give a firm a competitive advantage. Quality strategic information will enable a firm to cut costs and/or differentiate its products better than its competitors. For example, Caesar's Palace, in Las Vegas, was able to cut its budget for complimentary services to "high rollers" by 20 percent by scientifically tracking high rollers on its computers. American Express was able to differentiate its travel services from those of other companies by tracking costs and obtaining the lowest fares and rates for its customers via information available on its computer system. Porter and Miller suggest that information, if used properly, can give an organization a very significant strategic advantage. They suggest that the following five steps should be used by strategists in devising an information strategy:

1. Assess information intensity or use.
2. Determine the role of information technology and industry structure.
3. Identify and rank the ways in which information technology might create competitive advantage.
4. Investigate how information technology might spawn new businesses.
5. Develop a plan for taking advantage of information technology.[28]

In the modern organization this means that the manager must have an **MIS** at his disposal—"computers and software that tell managers what is going on in their companies and help them coordinate activities."[29]

Transition to using information as a competitive tool rather than a way of simply processing transactions and developing costs has enabled organizations to take the offensive.[30] The ability to react—the ability to make decisions quickly—is in itself a competitive edge.[31] The MIS user must be comfortable with technology and with the communication linkages computers now have. Information will be much more instantaneous in the future, and the decision

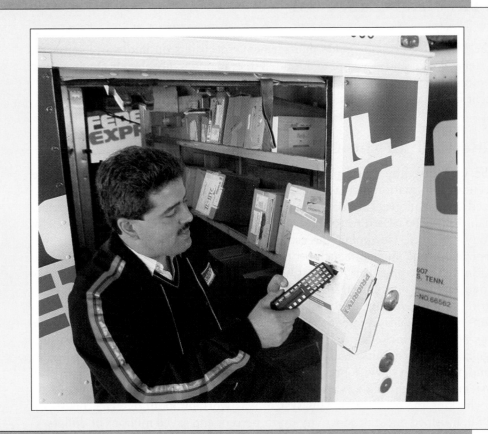

Federal Express used its COSMOS program as a major strategic weapon against other overnight delivery services. Using the transmission of bar codes over a telecommunications network, the company can tell a customer the location of a customer's package at any point in the delivery process. (SOURCE © John Abbott)

support systems that accompany MIS will provide much more guidance to decision makers. Management Challenge 19.2 portrays a use of information systems to gain a competitive edge through customer service.

More and more organizations are striving to develop a strategic MIS system, one that supports or shapes the business unit's competitive strategy.[32] A strategic MIS offers the organization new competitive opportunities by directly increasing the productivity, flexibility, and responsiveness to customers for an entire organization.[33] An MIS can be used competitively in many ways, for example, by

1. Creating barriers to competitor's entrance into the market, such as through the use of an on-line reservations system.

2. Building customer switching costs and/or operational dependence to discourage their changing suppliers, for example, as with the use of automated order-entry systems.

3. Completely changing the basis of information by offering new services, or products not offered by competitors.

4. Changing the organization's operations in such ways as to change the nature and environment of the business.

5. Partitioning a business process, such as pricing, that allows the firm to choose an optimal pricing strategy for products and services.[34]

One of the major issues in global competitiveness is the ability of the Japanese to analyze their competition, to know them almost better than they know themselves. Competitor analysis is a major focus of strategic planning.[35] But to do competitor analysis, the organization manager must have an information system that provides that type of information, and at present few do.

The MIS Director

The MIS director helps guide management's decisions on hardware, software, systems design and development, and system maintenance. He or she leads the professional MIS staff. The director plans, organizes, and controls the management information function.[36]

The Role of the CIO

The CIO currently exists principally in larger corporations. However, as the need for information increases, CIOs will become more prominent in medium-sized organizations. The role of the CIO is more encompassing, more strategic, than that of the MIS director. He or she is responsible for managing, especially from a strategic viewpoint, the use of information and systems within the organization. The impact of such people is exemplified in the actions of Lawrence T. Burden, vice-president for information services, of Firestore Tire and Rubber Company. An internal Firestone study revealed that the company's manufacturing process was out of date. It also showed that managers often made decisions based on guesses rather than information—for example, how much rubber was needed to make a production run to fill an order. Top management recognized that something had to be done to save money and time. Burden, in conjunction with the vice-president for U.S. tire operations, designed a computer system to track virtually every step in manufacturing a tire, from raw materials to checking the final tread. This system was working in all five U.S. plants by 1988. It helped boost productivity by 15 percent and saved millions of dollars.[37]

The Changing Role of the MIS Function

The MIS function is changing in most organizations.[38] Technological changes that allow PCs to have significant power and memory have also enabled managers to manage more information themselves. This has reduced the need in many organizations for the services a centralized MIS or data processing office might provide. Personal computers can be networked among departments where database information is important. This also increases the need for large, centralized databases that can be downloaded into various areas.

Another important change is the development of managerial work stations—"systems that serve the manager in the same way that engineering work stations contribute to the productivity of technical personnel."[39] Some of the following functions can be included in a managerial work station:

1. Spreadsheet processing with a program such as Lotus 1-2-3.
2. Word processing for preparing memos and reports.
3. Database management and a file system for setting up simple personal applications.
4. Presentation graphics for meetings.
5. Electronic mail.
6. Access to external databases such as Dun and Bradstreet and Dow Jones.
7. Connection with various networks to share data and programs.[40]
8. An increased level of computational power.

Telecommunications and the MIS

Telecommunications consist of a series of technologically based communication techniques and processes that assist in the management decision process. Telecommunications are important accessories to the MIS because they expand its capabilities. Probably the best known of the telecommunications techniques is electronic mail. This and several other important telecommunication technologies are discussed subsequently.

ELECTRONIC MAIL

Electronic mail uses electronic circuitry to transmit written messages instantaneously. One of its best features is that messages can be sent to those within the same geographic location or around the world via satellite. The message resides in the receiver's terminal until the individual turns it on. He or she may then respond. This avoids the problem of "telephone tag." Electronic mail is cheaper than long-distance telephone rates and much faster than a typical letter or even express mail. It is extremely useful for communicating with a large number of individuals at once.

As an example of how vital electronic mail can be in a competitive situation, consider these two TV channels. The "Discovery Channel" is very similar to the "Arts and Entertainment Channel" but uses 40 percent fewer employees to acquire, produce, and transmit two hundred television programs a month to four million homes in the United States. With its 105 staff members constantly traveling, the key to its success has been electronic mail. Discovery President Ruth Otte receives an average of one hundred electronic memos a day either in her Landover, Maryland, headquarters—or anywhere she can plug in her laptop PC. She says she is never out of the office.[41]

COMPUTER CONFERENCING

Computer conferencing is a multiparty extension of electronic mail. Numerous individuals at terminals can communicate with each other at the same time, sending and receiving messages.

FAX

Fax machines use electronic circuitry and telephone cabling to transmit visual images, much as electronic mail transmits written messages. Fax mail has the same benefits as electronic mail. The cost is cheaper than a long-distance phone call. It can be done instantaneously and in the same geographic area or globally. It is faster than a letter or express mail. Fax machines are being used at a significantly increasing rate.[42] By 1991 it is estimated that Fax machines will be installed in about half of all offices in the United States.[43]

CELLULAR PHONES

Managers can keep in touch with the office, call back important clients, and call subordinates and their managers with a cellular phone. The explosion in this industry has allowed executives to utilize better than thirty minutes to an hour or longer of commuting time between home and office, or between job locations in such industries as construction. Nonmanagerial personnel such as sales staff can also use their commuting time much more effectively.[44]

VOICE MAIL

In voice mail the computer acts as an answering machine. It takes messages and gives out messages.[45]

AT MRS. FIELDS' COOKIES: *Debbi and her managers often use electronic mail. This has saved her and her managers many thousands of hours of potential telephone tag time. Debbi routinely sends all of her managers many of the same messages.*

At this deli, as in many restaurants nationwide, you can fax in your order and it will be waiting for you when you arrive. (SOURCE © John Abbott)

ELECTRONIC BULLETIN BOARDS

Electronic bulletin boards are computerized systems for distributing routine memos throughout an organization, typically job openings, fringe benefits, and other information. Electronic bulletin boards are used not only for distributing current information, but corporate policies, rules, regulations, and procedures, as well. The bulletin board can become an electronic library. The North American Case Research Association, for example, uses an electronic bulletin board system, based at Rollins College in Winter Park, Florida, to distribute cases to its members.

VIDEO CONFERENCING

Video conferencing employs live television in a conference format. Most often, but not always, people with multiple sites receiving the video program are able to see one another. The Federal Judicial Center, the training research and systems development arm of the judicial branch of the federal government, uses video conferencing quite extensively. Its training clientele numbers over 17,000 persons, including judges serving in more than one hundred federal trial and appellate courts in the United States and its territories. Video conferencing has helped reduce the difficulty of delivering training quickly and efficiently on time-sensitive issues, such as recent court rulings, which might affect cases elsewhere. A number of video conferences have been held using 430 receiving sites, most with audiences of 150 to more than 2,000 people.[46]

ELECTRONIC DATA INTERCHANGE

Electronic data interchange (EDI) involves matching company and client database systems among companies, customers, and suppliers. Such programs provide a tremendous strategic advantage. Many programs link not only their databases, but all of their electronic telecommunications, to provide better service. Roger Milliken, head of Milliken and Company, the $2-billion-a-year textile-based firm, claims that this electronic pipeline is "the beginning of a revolution in our industry." It enables his firm and others to compete with their Asian rivals by making it easier for retailers to work with U.S. suppliers.[47]

Bernie E. Beleskey, marketing director for Investment Center Financial Corporation of Canada, a seller of financial services, has specially designed his own office on wheels. He logs some 3,700 miles a month in his van equipped with fax, cellular phone, and portable personal computer. He believes in the power and use of information and telecommunications so strongly, that he is trying to convince his 180-person sales force to use a similar system. (SOURCE © Peter Sibbald)

LAPTOP PERSONAL COMPUTERS

Laptop PCs assist an MIS when they can be used in conjunction with telecommunications—for example, to receive voice mail, teleconferencing, or electronic mail. They are most often used by salespeople to access databases and are often used by anyone preparing reports away from the office.

Decision Support Systems (DSSs) and Expert Systems (ESs)[48]

Many organizations are now turning to decision support systems (DSSs) to aid their managers in making decisions. These are simply systems designed to support a decision.[49] Break-even analysis is an example of a simple DSS. A very sophisticated DSS would include an integrated system of spreadsheets, graphics, and databases. All DSSs are MISs, but because they do more than simply provide management information, not all MISs are DSSs. Similarly, all expert systems (ESs) are MISs, but they are not DSSs—nor are all MISs expert systems. An ES provides solutions and is thereby different from a DSS. The following paragraphs outline the major differences between these three systems and identify present and future major issues for each.

DSSs

DSSs are conceived of as supporting, not replacing, managerial judgment.[50] DSSs are widely used. One recent survey of managers indicated that 32 percent were using DSSs either directly or indirectly to some degree.[51] DSSs have been applied in a wide variety of organizational functions and in a wide variety of organizations.

One successful DSS, which combines traditional MIS functioning and a DSS, has been extremely helpful to senior executives at Lockheed for a number of years. It helps these executives in the following ways:

1. Areas requiring information are identified and the relevant information is provided to the manager upon request.

2. Communications with various constituencies are improved significantly by sharing information—for example, among vendors, customers, legislators, and executives.

3. As the management information and decision support system has evolved, executives have identified additional areas where information is necessary, or have identified formats that might improve their decision making.

4. The present system is a testing ground for future improvements.

5. Cost savings have resulted because the system produces graphs, charts, and reports that were previously created by hand.[52]

Most authorities in the field believe that the use of DSS will increase significantly in the future, and that more and more user-friendly software will be available to make them easier to use.

ESs and Artificial Intelligence (AI)

T. H. Winston defines **artificial intelligence (AI)** as "the study of ideas which enable computers to do the things that make people seem intelligent."[53] AI attempts to get at human reasoning by working with qualitative as well as quantitative information. It often provides rules of thumb that may not give optimal solutions but yield good solutions. It allows its users to deal with "fuzzy" reasoning where decisions aren't based totally on rational analysis but must involve intuition. Among the areas in which AI currently appears to have promising potential near-term applications are robotics, natural language understanding, and ESs.[54]

ESs are those systems that "can be used to preserve and disseminate scarce expertise by encoding the relevant experience of an expert and making this expertise available as a resource to the less experienced person."[55] One of the most important ways in which **expert systems** differ from DSSs and MISs is in their use of heuristic reasoning. DSSs and MISs typically employ algorithms—that is, precise rules that always lead to a correct conclusion. ESs are used on more complex problems, where a "correct" conclusion is not always possible—such as in forecasting the weather or diagnosing a disease.[56] In summary then, ESs differ from MISs and DSSs in the following ways:

1. They contain facts and additional knowledge that an expert would use to solve a problem.[57]

2. They explain the reasons for the conclusion upon request.

3. They are designed to imitate the human decision-making process.

4. They are normally designed to solve a problem by asking questions, rather than by just accepting given input, as DSS and MIS typically do.[58]

5. They sometimes learn by experience.[59]

An ES can be quite expensive to develop. For example, the medical expert system—the INTERNIST—took twenty-six man years for development. However, this comprehensive ES provides doctors with an extremely accurate diagnosis of numerous diseases.[60] Expert systems have the potential to save hundreds of thousands and perhaps millions of dollars in certain applications. Arthur Andersen created a driver's license processing system for the state of Pennsylvania in only twenty work days. The system handles 90 percent of all the license processing for the state. This ES replaced a system that took four hundred work days to create but could handle only 25 percent of the processing.[61] A number

AT MRS. FIELDS' COOKIES: *An ES was used to help managers run the store by determining how many cookies to bake hour by hour, deciding when to run special promotions, and when and how much raw material to order. Much of Mrs. Fields' operational success is attributed to this ES, which freed a manager's time to manage other aspects of the business.*

United Uses Expert Systems to Reduce Delays at Hubs

United Airlines was confronted by aggravating delays in its hubs in Chicago and Denver. Part of its problem was that gate controllers had a huge amount of information to process and made assignments based largely on memory and rules of thumb. To solve this problem, United turned to an expert system titled "Gate Assignment Display System" (GADS). GADS was designed to reduce flight delays related to ground operations. This artificial intelligence program was created by drawing on the experience and knowledge of United's main controllers and systems analysts, through a process known as knowledge engineering transfer. The program uses Texas Instruments' Explorer Symbolic Processing Work Stations for working on such problems. The program uses high-resolution multicolor graphics representations.

GADS receives on-line, real-time information (simultaneously with the event) from United's central flight information data system, which contains information on current, past, and future United flights. GADS incorporates the knowledge and reasoning of the experts who had been assigning flights to help make gate assignments before. The system has eliminated the need for the time-consuming gate boards previously used to process gate assignments. GADS's video graphics presentation provides for overhead displays of aircraft and their gates. They indicate such important factors as times for arrival and departure and airplane numbers. The system also allows the gate controller to try out different aircraft gate combinations before changing gate plans. GADS automatically adjusts the gate plan as the controller moves a plane from one gate to another. In short, the controller has the ability to play "what if" games with gate plans.

SOURCE: Carole A. Shifrin, "Gate Assignment Expert System Reduces Delays at United's Hubs," *Aviation Week and Space Technology* (January 25, 1988), pp. 112–113.

United Airlines GADS expert system helps reduce the number of delays due to ground operations. Unfortunately, efficiency by ground crews doesn't always help relieve the problems caused by overcrowding of the airlines as demonstrated in this "stack-up" at Chicago's O'Hare airport. (SOURCE © Kevin Horan/Picture Group)

of ESs have been developed in accounting that enable accounting firms to improve productivity significantly. Among these are AUDITOR, TAX ADVISER, TAX MAN, CORP TAX, PLAN POWER.[62] Five hundred to 1,000 percent increases in productivity are typical when ESs are used.[63] To some extent ESs will not only aid decision makers, but will replace many of them.[64] It may very well be that middle management will disappear as top management uses more and more ESs.[65] Management Challenge 19.3 describes one very successful expert system in some detail.

Executive Information Systems

Executive information systems include all information systems tailored to the specific needs of executives. Thus, portions of the MIS, such as the strategic information system, decision support systems, and expert systems would all be included. Executive information systems are increasingly becoming available in user-friendly formats. Executives have tended to shy away from using personal computers, at least partly because of the time needed to learn how to use software that was not user friendly. But that is all changing now. Many of the most

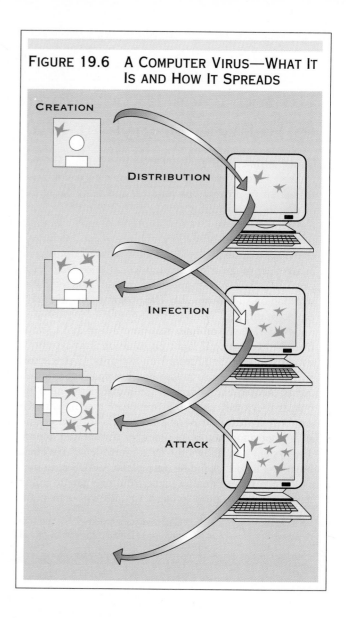

FIGURE 19.6   A COMPUTER VIRUS—WHAT IT IS AND HOW IT SPREADS

CREATION

DISTRIBUTION

INFECTION

ATTACK

recent executive systems have been user-friendly expert systems. As with other managers, an executive's productivity can be greatly increased through the use of PCs.

Protecting the Information System

The MIS is subject to any number of classic control problems: controlling the performance of knowledge technicians, controlling the capability of the performance of the hardware and the software, and controlling the design of the system, for example. Total loss of information may occur as the result of an earthquake or other natural disaster. Disaster protection systems include database duplicates. In recent months one of the most important factors in controlling an MIS is controlling invasion by a virus. A **virus** is a small unit of computer code written by a programmer that can attach itself to other programs, alter them, or destroy data kept on a computer disk.[66] Viruses are capable of reproducing themselves and attaching themselves to other programs stored in the same computer. Typically, a virus is attached to a normal software program that becomes its "Trojan Horse." The virus spreads and the owner of the Trojan Horse exchanges software with other computer users, typically through an electronic bulletin board or through the exchange of floppy disks. The more programs that are exchanged, the more the virus spreads, but people may not be aware of it for several months because the code may not instruct the virus to take effect until later. Eventually the virus activates itself, usually according to some internal clock in the computer. At this point the virus strikes, often wreaking havoc with the computers and programs that have come into contact with it. This process of creation, distribution, infection, and attack is illustrated in Figure 19.6.

Robert Woodhead, originator of Virex, is shown here with the introductory screen to his virus-hunting program "Virex." (SOURCE © Mike Okoniewski/Gamma Liaison)

To demonstrate the pervasiveness of viruses and how quickly they can be spread because of the constant interchange of computer enthusiasts, Richard R. Brandow, a twenty-four-year-old publisher of a Montreal computer magazine, and his co-worker, Pierre N. Zovile, created a benign virus to show the pervasiveness of software power. In two months, illegal copying apparently transferred the virus to more than 350,000 Macintoshes around the world. When the internal clocks of the infected machines hit, on March 2, each machine displayed the message "Universal Message of Peace to All Macintosh Users." Although the virus was meant to be innocuous, it was not. People claimed that it caused their computers to crash and that it infected other disks. Mark Kanter, president of a small Chicago software publisher, indicated that an infected disk he gave to software producer Aldus Inc., of Seattle, caused them to print disks of one of their software programs for three days with the virus attached. The disks were recalled, but not before some customers received them.

Solving this security problem is tricky. Alert employees are the first line of defense. They should not use software and disks from an unknown source. There are also a lot of "vaccines," that is, software programs that can track down viruses. Security software can be placed on large mainframe computers. In 1982 only 10 percent of IBM mainframes had such security software; in 1988, 35 percent did. Computer users can also use dial back systems on computers to ensure that incoming phone calls come only from authorized sources.[67] Companies are spending large amounts of money for protection against viruses, and the costs can be staggering.

How an MIS Affects the Organization

As with any type of technology, MIS arouses a number of somewhat predictable responses from among an organization's members. Resistance to change is one. Other key factors resulting from MIS include the restructuring of the organization; the elimination of many middle-management jobs, as well as certain staff positions; and the creation of technostress—stress from the introduction and increased use of technology.[68,69] The MIS also changes basic business documents because they have to be tailored to the needs and abilities of the computer.[70] The MIS also changes the basic way in which individuals make decisions. Because the computer does most of the number crunching, the individual is freer to do more creative thinking. And finally, MIS may change an organization's entire culture, as it moves toward knowledge as its future basis.

Knowledge-Based Organizations and Their Management[71]

C. W. Holsapple and A. B. Whinston observe: "In a most fundamental sense, organizations will increasingly be regarded as joint human-computer knowledge-processing systems. Human participants in these systems, from most highly skilled to least skilled positions, can be regarded as knowledge workers. Collectively they will work with many types of knowledge, in a variety of ways, and with various objectives. Their knowledge management efforts will be aided and supported by computers. Not only will these computer co-workers relieve us of the menial, routine, and repetitive, they will also actively recognize needs, stimulate insights, and offer advice. They will highly leverage an organization's uniquely human skills of intuition, creative imagination, value-judgment, the cultivation of effective interpersonal relationships, and so forth."[72]

The organization of the future portrayed in the preceding paragraph is dynamically different from the majority of organizations in existence today. It is not so different, however, from several that do exist, such as Bell Labs and Allen Bradley Corporation's manufacturing plant in Milwaukee. The overall implication for management is at least twofold. First, the new organization presents challenges to change management style. Management systems and methodologies for a whole new type of organization will come into existence. Second, it presents opportunities to make those who function in the organization more effective and efficient.

The **knowledge workers** "are concerned with procuring, storing, organizing, maintaining, reading, analyzing, presenting, distributing, and employing knowledge in order to meet an organization's goals."[73] Some workers will perform all these functions and work with all different types of knowledge; others will perform only with some. Increasing technological advances in both hardware and software will enable the knowledge worker to bring different types of tools to bear on problems than have been used in the past.

Training the knowledge worker will be critical. A rudimentary computer literacy will be necessary but not sufficient for a worker in a truly knowledge-based organization. Workers will have to learn about knowledge itself—how it is organized, the learning process, the types of representation techniques—and they will have to be extremely skilled in using computers to manipulate that knowledge. Cooperation and knowledge sharing among workers will also be extremely important in knowledge-based organizations.

Workers of the future, these knowledge workers, will be largely self-managed problem solvers, thus causing the entire nature and scope of management to change. As opposed to resting in the hands of a few, management will rest in the hands of many. Virtually millions of people will be required to plan, organize, lead, and control themselves as they solve problems at their work stations. The traditional role of "the manager" will change dramatically, and there will be fewer of them.[74]

Managing Information as a Problem-Solving Process

Because information is the basis for problem solving, virtually all the items identified in this chapter apply to almost all problem-solving stages. Therefore, the standard problem-solving model is not included in this chapter.

The Management Challenges Identified

1. Increasing amounts of information and change
2. Information needs in a rapidly changing environment
3. Formation of a knowledge organization

Some Solutions Noted in the Chapter

1. Increasing use of computers to solve problems
2. Management information systems, decision support systems, expert systems, executive information systems
3. Learning to manage the knowlege organization
4. Strategic MIS

Summary

1. Information is data that have been put into a meaningful and useful context and communicated to a recipient who uses it to make decisions. An MIS aids management in making periodic controlling decisions by collecting, organizing, and distributing information. Information is a vital organizational resource because it aids in decision making. It may even be a strategic advantage when used properly.

2. The MIS should facilitate problem solving.

3. Information systems have evolved largely from financial systems to all functional areas of the organization. They have evolved from hand-calculated systems, to electronic data processing, to formal MISs, to DSSs, to ESs.

4. MISs are designed around six components: inputs, models, technology, databases, controls, and outputs. Designers of these systems take into account ten key factors: integration, user/system interface, competitive forces, information quality and reuseability, systems requirements, data processing requirements, organizational factors, cost-effectiveness requirements, human factors, and feasibility requirements.

5. There must be an ongoing management of an MIS—of its various components, controls in place, and system policy and planning. There must be management of the changes that occur.

6. The CIO essentially looks for and develops strategic uses of information.

7. PCs and other microcomputers have enabled managers to do much more managing of information than they have in the past. This has caused the information management function to be more widely disbursed, with the central department becoming more in charge of databases.

8. In general, technology has enabled the manager to make better, more rational decisions, based on greater analysis of information, and more recently, with advice on solutions.

9. MIS can lead to resistance to change, to technostress, to restructuring, to changes in the way decision making occurs, to improved decision making, to changing the entire organizational culture, and to freeing people to be more creative.

10. The knowledge-based organization of the future will feature knowledge workers, working at work stations, utilizing support centers, communication paths, and knowledge storehouses to make decisions—that is, to solve problems.

Thinking About Management

1. Research and discuss the MISs used in the college or university at which you are taking this course. Discuss them in terms of their types, their impacts on the organization, their ability to provide the right information, their designs, and how well they are controlled.
2. Discuss the computer virus phenomenon and the various ways in which organizations can prevent it from occurring or damaging their disks and software programs.
3. Describe the knowledge-based organization of the future.
4. Describe how expert systems will help people manage in the future.
5. Discuss why virtually everyone in business needs to know how to use computers.
6. Discuss the development of MISs for the coming age of increased change, global competitiveness, and other management challenges.

CASE

Northern Telecom Changes Its Strategy

In 1985 Northern Telecom Inc., headquartered in Nashville, Tennessee (it is a subsidiary of Canada's Northern Telecom Limited), found itself faced with increasing levels of competition and rapid changes in technology and customer requirements. The firm employed 22,000 people at 13 separate manufacturing facilities, 14 R&D centers, and numerous sales and service facilities throughout the United States. After much strategic analysis, the firm determined that it had to change corporate strategy totally, rather than attempt short run improvements in the old strategy. The firm chose to compete on the basis of time—to reduce the time it took to introduce new products and product enhancements, and to improve its overall response time in meeting other customer needs.

Three strategic objectives were established for 1990. First, overall customer satisfaction, as measured by an annual survey of customers, had to increase 20 percent. Second, the company had to reduce manufacturing overhead as a percent of sales by one-half. Third, the company had to cut inventory days by 50 percent. The fundamental thrust was to double throughput velocity without increasing overhead—while cutting inventories and increasing customer satisfaction. The consequences for manufacturing strategy were substantial. Manufacturing had to be rethought totally because much of the time involved had to be cut from the time required to manufacture. One of the first actions taken was to use cross-functional teams. That put engineering and manufacturing in concert much sooner in the R&D product development/manufacturing cycle. This helped eliminate manufacturing problems created by the design process. This speeded up product development significantly. Additional actions included working with suppliers to improve quality and delivery, allowing for just-in-time inventory approaches. A "total quality control" program was initiated. Outside of manufacturing strategy, several additional issues had to be addressed.

Employees, including managers, were comfortable with the existing strategy. Thus, education as to the need for change had to take place. Many meetings, seminars, and training and development programs were initiated to change the organizational culture, to inform employees about strategic and operational changes and the need for those changes, and to develop and implement new systems, such as compensation and information systems.

DISCUSSION QUESTIONS
The preceding strategy proved to be effective, and by 1989 a high percentage of each of the three strategic objectives set out had been achieved. Instrumental to that end were the development of new designs and uses of MISs and of computers.

1. How might the MIS be redesigned to help accomplish this strategy of time?
2. What specific uses of computers might assist the design process?
3. How might the financial reporting system be changed to assist in the time strategy?
4. How might capital budgeting be changed to support the strategy?

SOURCE: Roy Merrills, "How Northern Telecom Competes on Time," *Harvard Business Review* (July–August 1989), pp. 108–114.

Gathering Competitive Information

Bob was an engineering manager for the workstation division of a multinational computer corporation headquartered in the United States. The workstation division was one of 15 different businesses of the parent company. The $10-billion-a-year-in-sales parent had always followed a strategy of taking someone else's basic technology and building products at lower cost than their competitors. But for the first time in the company's history, one of the firm's divisions, the workstation division, had developed proprietary technology which was leading the industry in this particular type of workstation. This technology allowed the firm to charge a higher price, even though it also had a fairly low cost position in the industry.

The workstation division was headquartered in the southeast. The firm's major competitor was headquartered in San Diego, California. The division president had asked Bob to draw up a plan for gaining information about what the strategy of this competitor was. Little was known about the firm in Bob's division. A recent computer magazine story on this type of workstation had indicated that the two firms were neck and neck in technology, and that the other firms in this segment had inferior products. The main competitor had over 25 percent of the market. Bob's firm had just 20 percent. With the total market size expected to be $6 billion in five years. Bob's manager wanted to insure that the firm had a major part of this market.

A major change in the market's structure was to occur in the next few months, as the primary users of the workstation were expected to change from engineers to managers of all types as new software would make the workstation more user friendly. Bob's boss wanted to know how far along their main competitor was in developing this software and what their overall strategy was for the next five years.

DISCUSSION QUESTIONS
1. You are Bob. What types of information do you need to gather?
2. How would you go about gathering that information?
3. What would be the design of the information system into which this information would be fed?

Developing an Executive Information System

Your instructor will divide the class into small groups. Each group will be asked to develop the components of an executive information system for a 500-person manufacturing or service firm. Key features should be noted, as well as the major pieces of information needed. After a few minutes, the instructor will ask for the groups to report their findings back to the entire class.

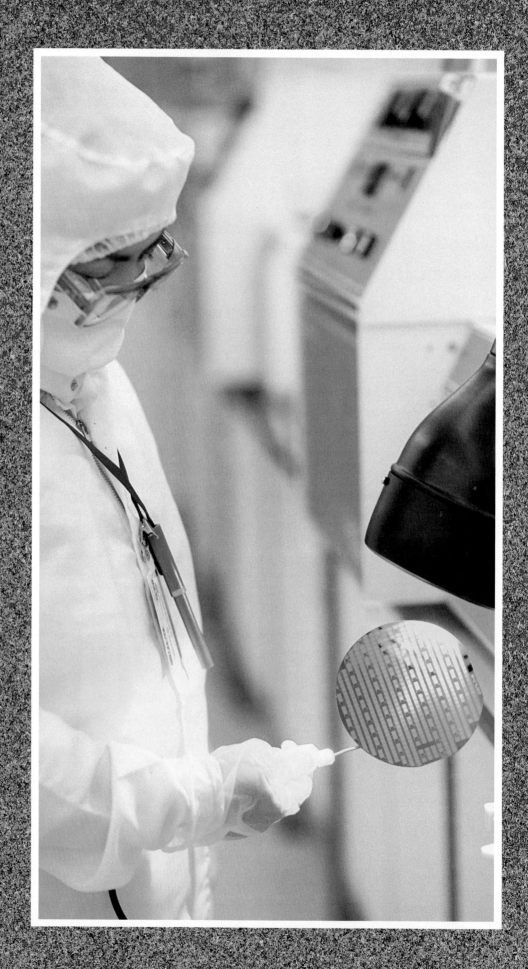

CHAPTER TWENTY

Operations Management

CHAPTER OBJECTIVES

By the time you finish studying this chapter, you should be able to

1. Describe the operations management function in manufacturing and service industries.
2. Relate why operations management has become so critical in recent years.
3. Discuss each of the principal strategic, tactical, and operational decisions in operations management.
4. Describe operations as a strategic competitive weapon.
5. Identify the impact of the globalization of business on the operations function.
6. Indicate why the Japanese have been so successful at operations management.
7. Describe the importance of inventory to manufacturing.
8. Discuss the importance of quality in manufacturing and service as it relates to successful business strategy.
9. Describe the factory of the future.
10. Indicate how productivity can be improved.

CHAPTER OUTLINE

Operations Management in Manufacturing and Service Organizations
    Operations Management as Decision Making
Operations' Strategic Importance
Strategic Operations Decisions
    Positioning the Operations System
    Focused Factories
    Product/Service Design and Process Planning
    Allocation of Resources to Strategic Alternatives
    Facility Capacity, Location, and Plant Layout
    Production Technology
    Work Force Management
    Total Quality Strategy
Tactical Operations Decision: Planning Production to Meet Demands
    Production Planning Systems
    The Control of Inventory and the Planning Process
    Material Requirements Planning (MRP)
    Materials Management and Purchasing
Planning and Controlling Day-to-Day Operations
    Scheduling and Shop Floor Planning and Control
    Workers and Productivity
    Quality Control
    Quality According to W. Edwards Deming
    Project Management: Planning and Controlling Projects
    Maintenance Management and Reliability
The Factory of the Future
Productivity Management
    How to Improve Productivity
Operations Management as Problem Solving
The Management Challenges Identified
Some Solutions Noted in the Chapter

Westinghouse Plans Productivity Gains

In the late 1960s and early 1970s, Westinghouse diversified into such differing businesses as mail order, watchmaking, and low-income housing—none of which seemed to complement its heavy manufacturing base. Profits began to lag, and individual companies began to have difficulties in their respective markets. R. E. Kirby, elected chairman in 1975, began to sell off a number of them. His successor, Douglas B. Danforth (1983), even more dramatically restructured the firm, selling off dozens of companies and eliminating 23,000 workers. Before long, the company was outpacing its competitors in earnings growth.

Once the major restructuring was over and Danforth had stepped aside, Westinghouse's two new leaders, Chairman John C. Marous and President Paul E. Lego (1988), managed a different situation. While their predecessors increased profits by cutting costs, widening margins, and eliminating companies, they had to make the existing businesses grow and occasionally either acquire or divest. Their plan is simple: "Pay close attention to quality and productivity, build new business through small acquisitions or by nurturing promising technology, then if a business doesn't show the superior profitability they demand, it will be eliminated."

Marous and Lego are intent on improving productivity. This task is coordinated by the company's Productivity and Quality Center, a SWAT team of some 130 computer gurus, consultants, and engineers. The center's objective is to help business units "do the right things right the first time." This center develops very innovative approaches to managing productivity in both manufacturing and in the office. The company's approach to managing productivity, often spearheaded by Marous and Lego as junior executives, has resulted in net income per employee more than doubling—from $3,100 in 1982 to $6,600 in 1987.

One of the primary tools used by the center is to chart the steps in making a product or delivering a service. Costs and time at each step are identified, enabling managers to address ways of cutting costs and time. Typically Westinghouse uses advanced automated factories, focused factories, just-in-time inventories (JIT, in place at two-thirds of Westinghouse plants), and expert systems that provide decision advice, electronic mail, and electronic data interchange with customers and suppliers. One of the key ingredients to the latter is their management information system, the Westinghouse Integrated Network (WIN). It links six hundred locations and is used by more than 90,000 people to help speed the flow not just of information, but of inputs, products and services, and processes. Business units can ask for Total Quality Fitness Reviews, in which the unit's training, processes, and products, as well as customer satisfaction, are measured. The manager is given a scorecard, and teams are established to fix problems.

A typical example of how the productivity center has helped comes from the Sumter, South Carolina, plant, which makes a broad range of products—for example, switchboards that protect electricity flow in buildings. In 1983 the plant was running at full capacity, generating $24 million in sales. This sounds good, but the productivity center didn't think it was good enough. The company installed semiautomated machinery, formed quality circles, retrained employees to make them capable of performing more tasks in smaller work areas, and reorganized the work flow. By 1988 the plant was filling orders faster, had 14 percent of its space left for expansion, and was generating $48 million in sales—same plant, same people, different productivity management.

SOURCE: Thomas A. Stewart, "Westinghouse Gets Respect at Last," *Fortune* (July 3, 1989), pp. 92–98; William R. Ruffin, "Wired for Speed," *Business Month* (January 1990), pp. 56–58; Vinoid K. Kapoor, "Just-in-Time and the Focused Factory: A Case History at Westinghouse," *Manufacturing System* (December 1989), pp. 47–49; and Gregory L. Marlows and David Griffiths, "How Westinghouse Is Revv'ing Up After the Rebound," *Business Week* (March 28, 1988), pp. 46–52.

Being good just isn't good enough any more. We must be better.

R. E. Heckert, chairman
E. I. duPont

When you aim for perfection, you discover it's a moving target.

Motorola Corporation
"Power of Belief"

In recent years, American businesses have accepted the crucial importance of operations management to competing in the global marketplace. Their fiercest competitors, primarily those from the Pacific rim countries and especially those from Japan and more recently Korea, have become masters of the operations process, particularly in manufacturing but also more recently in service. They have been able to produce high-quality, low-cost products not only because of lower labor costs, but also because they have made a commitment to their manufacturing processes and have taken the time and effort to perfect them. Westinghouse's efforts to improve its manufacturing processes are typical of the transition American firms are making in operations management today. In order for U.S. and Canadian firms to compete in a global marketplace, they must produce high-quality, low-cost products and services. Without dramatic improvements in their operations processes, many, if not most of these firms will no longer be globally competitive. Both the United States and Canada may no longer be competitive and may lose millions of high-paying manufacturing and service jobs as a result.[1] More and more U.S. companies are becoming religious in their devotion to product quality and low cost.[2]

Paul E. Lego not only believes in keeping Westinghouse fit and trim, but himself as well. (SOURCE © Ken Kerbs)

For the first few years after World War II, Japanese products were known for their inferiority to American products. The Japanese have come a long way since those days, partly because they hired American consultants in the late 1950s and early 1960s to teach them better manufacturing methods. Today the Japanese are considered superior to American manufacturers in many industries. Those consultants introduced the concepts and techniques of quality control. The two most prominent American control experts on the Japanese scene for years have been William Edwards Deming and Joseph M. Juran.[3] A third quality guru emerged in the 1980s, Phil Crosby, who advocated "zero defects" as a way of managing.

Furthermore, through the writings of other Americans, such as Douglas McGregor,[4] the Japanese recognized that traditional authority relationships, symbolized in hierarchical pyramids, were not suited to achieving the highest levels of productivity. They adopted group-based participative management systems, which fit into their culture very naturally.

This combination of a high-quality orientation and participative management systems in manufacturing quickly propelled the Japanese to world leadership in low cost and high quality in numerous major products, such as automobiles, electronics, cameras, and steel. More recently, a host of Pacific rim countries have followed those strategies, putting tremendous cost pressures on Japanese firms because most other Pacific rim countries have much lower wage rates than Japan.[5] Korean firms, and firms in Taiwan, Singapore, and Hong Kong, have made tremendous inroads into American markets, many of which were only recently captured by Japanese firms. They have even made progress into Japanese markets. Hyundai, in automobiles, and Daewoo, in electronics and automobiles, are examples.

In this chapter we will explore how the operations process occurs in both manufacturing and service organizations, how operations can be used to gain strategic advantage for companies, and the major trends in operations management. Much of the focus of the chapter is on operations management in manufacturing, primarily because so little is known about the service operations' function. But many points of the discussion are relevant to service, and they are noted.[6]

It is becoming imperative in most industries in most countries to have a high-quality, low-cost product regardless of the targeted market segment. Quality in manufacturing has become the table stakes, the price of entry in most industries. The contents of this chapter reflect the challenge of accomplishing those ends. While this chapter introduces you to operations management, it also offers insight into what will be necessary to compete in the future.

Operations Management in Manufacturing and Service Organizations[7]

Operations managers, whether they work in manufacturing or service organizations, are confronted with very similar problems. All organizations take inputs and transform them into outputs, as suggested by Figure 20.1. This is particularly clear in the manufacturing process, where a tangible product is produced; however, the same transformation occurs in service organizations. Labor is the principal input in service organizations, whereas raw materials, subcomponent parts, and labor are the major inputs of manufacturing operations. Put simply,

FIGURE 20.1 OPERATIONS DECISIONS

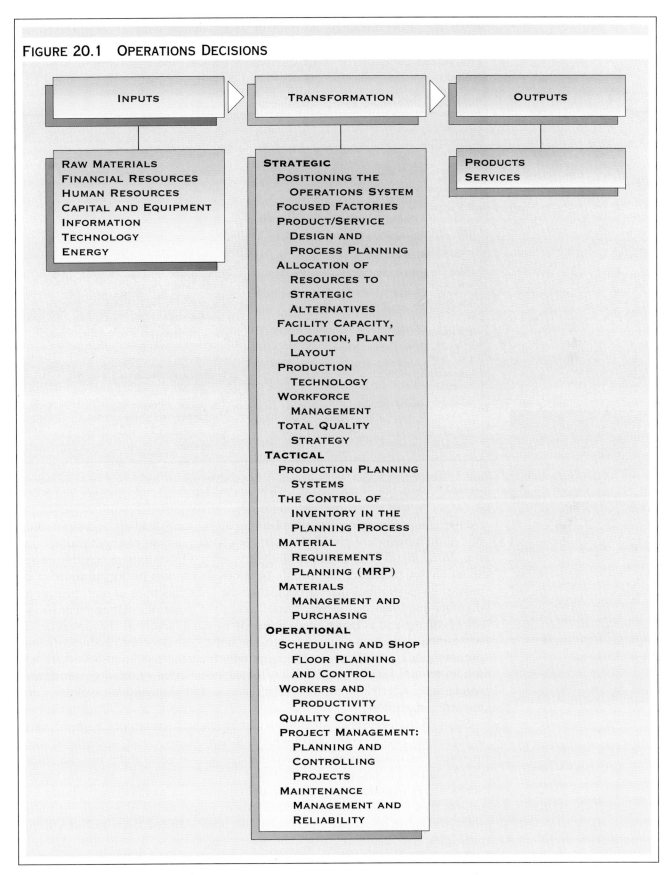

INPUTS

RAW MATERIALS
FINANCIAL RESOURCES
HUMAN RESOURCES
CAPITAL AND EQUIPMENT
INFORMATION
TECHNOLOGY
ENERGY

TRANSFORMATION

STRATEGIC
POSITIONING THE
   OPERATIONS SYSTEM
FOCUSED FACTORIES
PRODUCT/SERVICE
   DESIGN AND
   PROCESS PLANNING
ALLOCATION OF
   RESOURCES TO
   STRATEGIC
   ALTERNATIVES
FACILITY CAPACITY,
   LOCATION, PLANT
   LAYOUT
PRODUCTION
   TECHNOLOGY
WORKFORCE
   MANAGEMENT
TOTAL QUALITY
   STRATEGY
TACTICAL
PRODUCTION PLANNING
   SYSTEMS
THE CONTROL OF
   INVENTORY IN THE
   PLANNING PROCESS
MATERIAL
   REQUIREMENTS
   PLANNING (MRP)
MATERIALS
   MANAGEMENT AND
   PURCHASING
OPERATIONAL
SCHEDULING AND SHOP
   FLOOR PLANNING
   AND CONTROL
WORKERS AND
   PRODUCTIVITY
QUALITY CONTROL
PROJECT MANAGEMENT:
   PLANNING AND
   CONTROLLING
   PROJECTS
MAINTENANCE
   MANAGEMENT AND
   RELIABILITY

OUTPUTS

PRODUCTS
SERVICES

a manufacturing organization transforms inputs into physical outputs, or products, and a **service organization** transforms inputs into nonphysical outputs, or services, that usually cannot be inventoried and that involve customer interaction. Mixed organizations do both. In fact, a whole continuum of mixed organizations exists between pure manufacturing and pure service.[8] Table 20.1 enumerates some of the other differences between the two types of organizations.

Table 20.1 Differences Between Manufacturing and Service

Manufacturing	Service
The product is tangible	The service is intangible
Ownership is transferred at the time of purchase	Ownership is generally not transferred
The product can be resold	No resale is possible
The product can be demonstrated before purchase	The product does not exist before purchase
The product can be stored in inventory	The product cannot be stored
Production precedes consumption	Production and consumption are simultaneous
Production and consumption can be spatially separated	Production and consumption must occur at the same location
The product can be transported	The product cannot be transported (though producers can be)
The seller produces	The buyer takes part directly in the production process and can indeed perform part of the production
Indirect contact is possible between the company and the customer	In most cases direct contact is needed
The product can be exported	The service cannot normally be exported, but the service delivery system can be
Business is organized by functions, with sales and production separated	Sales and production cannot be separated functionally

SOURCE: Adapted from Richard Normann, *Service Management: Strategy and Leadership in the Service Business,* copyright © 1984 by John Wiley & Sons Ltd., Chichester, England. Reprinted by permission of John Wiley & Sons, Ltd.

Operations management is the planning, organizing, leading, and controlling of "all the activities of productive systems—those portions of organizations that transform inputs into products and services."[9] **Operations managers** are responsible for producing the supply of goods or services in organizations.[10] In most ways, operations managers practice the same functions of management as do other managers, but in very distinct ways.[11] Operations management is rapidly evolving and is being affected greatly by such factors as the globalization of business, high-tech manufacturing, the impact of Japanese productivity and product quality, fluctuation of international financial conditions, workers' attitudes toward factories and work, problems of service systems, governmental regulations, scarcity of productive resources, and changing societal attitudes toward competition.

Many of the forerunners of modern management discussed in Chapter 2, such as Frederick Taylor, Frank and Lillian Gilbreth, Henry Gantt, and others, were involved in manufacturing, and their management theories and principles reflect this background. Today, however, fewer than 25 percent of jobs in the United States are in manufacturing. Service operations have increased in importance, but we have not seen the kind of analysis of them that they deserve. Much of what we know of service operations has been adapted from manufacturing principles.

Table 20.2 identifies several typical operations systems, indicating the type of system, the primary inputs, conversion activities, and outputs. The inputs may be complex, as shown in Figure 20.2. Although we tend to think of the primary **inputs** as comprised of materials, supplies, and personnel, other inputs also

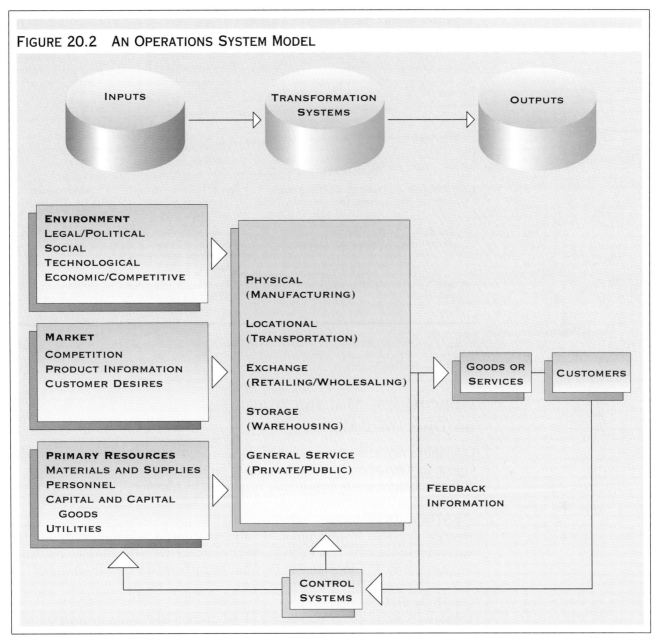

FIGURE 20.2 AN OPERATIONS SYSTEM MODEL

INPUTS

TRANSFORMATION SYSTEMS

OUTPUTS

ENVIRONMENT
LEGAL/POLITICAL
SOCIAL
TECHNOLOGICAL
ECONOMIC/COMPETITIVE

MARKET
COMPETITION
PRODUCT INFORMATION
CUSTOMER DESIRES

PRIMARY RESOURCES
MATERIALS AND SUPPLIES
PERSONNEL
CAPITAL AND CAPITAL
  GOODS
UTILITIES

PHYSICAL
(MANUFACTURING)

LOCATIONAL
(TRANSPORTATION)

EXCHANGE
(RETAILING/WHOLESALING)

STORAGE
(WAREHOUSING)

GENERAL SERVICE
(PRIVATE/PUBLIC)

GOODS OR SERVICES

CUSTOMERS

FEEDBACK INFORMATION

CONTROL SYSTEMS

SOURCE: FIGURES FROM PRODUCTION AND OPERATIONS MANAGEMENT: A PROBLEM SOLVING AND DECISION MAKING APPROACH, THIRD EDITION BY NORMAN GAITHER, COPYRIGHT © 1987 BY THE DRYDEN PRESS, INC., A DIVISION OF HOLT, RINEHART AND WINSTON, INC., REPRINTED BY PERMISSION OF THE PUBLISHER.

include environmental factors, such as legal requirements and technological abilities, and market considerations, such as competitors' actions. All of these factors and more affect the transformation process. The **transformation systems** are similarly complex and may include physical, locational, exchange, storage, or general service. Finally, the **outputs** are as varied as the kinds of companies, products, and services in the world. Although they may tend to be lumped into categories such as airlines or cameras, virtually no two products or services are ever truly identical.

The control system in Figure 20.2 is extremely important to overall operations. It provides information about the performance of the operations process and about customer reaction to the company's goods or services. This information helps enable decision makers to change inputs and conversion systems in order to ensure more appropriate outputs. Parts of this control system include, for example, product quality control efforts and surveys of customer satisfaction.

Table 20.2 Some Typical Operations Systems

Operations System	Primary Inputs	Transformation Subsystem	Outputs
1. Pet food factory	Grain, water, fish meal, personnel, tools, machines, paper bags, cans, buildings, utilities	Converts raw materials into finished goods (physical)	Pet food products
2. Trucking firm	Trucks, personnel, buildings, fuel, goods to be shipped, packaging supplies, truck parts, utilities	Packages and transports goods from sources to destinations (location)	Delivered goods
3. Department store	Buildings, displays, shopping carts, machines, stock goods, personnel, supplies, utilities	Attracts customers, stores goods, sells products (exchange)	Marketed goods
4. College or university	Students, books, supplies, personnel, buildings, utilities	Transmits information and develops skills and knowledge (private/public service)	Educated persons
5. Mini warehouses	Facilities, personnel	Takes space and converts it into storage space for personal goods	Rental space

SOURCE: Figures from *Production and Operations Management: A Problem Solving and Decision Making Approach,* Third Edition by Norman Gaither, copyright © 1987 by The Dryden Press, Inc., a division of Holt, Rinehart and Winston, Inc., reprinted by permission of the publisher.

Operations Management as Decision Making

Operations management is based on decision making as is all of management. Operations management decisions tend to fall into one of three categories, paralelling the three levels of planning introduced in Chapter 5.[12]

STRATEGIC DECISIONS
Strategic decisions involve products to make, process selection, and facilities expansion or location. These decisions concern operations strategies and have long-term (3 to 5 years planning horizon) importance for the organization.

TACTICAL DECISIONS
Tactical decisions about planning and production are made to meet annual demand. These decisions, such as building inventory before the selling season, are necessary for the ongoing production of goods and services to satisfy the seasonal demands of the market and provide profits for the company.

OPERATIONAL DECISIONS
Optional decisions are daily decisions about planning and controlling ongoing operations. They concern assigning workers to jobs, the quality of products and services, scheduling production overhead costs, and maintaining machines.

Operations' Strategic Importance

Operations strategies derive directly from business strategies aimed at achieving corporate objectives. Operations strategies are among the several strategies organizations employ in functional areas—for example, marketing, finance, human resources, and information. Operations strategies must support the other strategies, principally the marketing strategy of the business. As indicated in Chapter 6, two "generic" competitive strategies exist: relative differentiation and relative low cost. One of the major differentiation factors of the 1980s has been high quality. Low cost has also been critical in capturing market share and will continue to be in the 1990s. Manufacturing is obviously instrumental in achieving both differentiation and low cost.[13] Table 20.3 shows some of the major relationships between operations strategies and these two marketing strategies. This table reveals how the choice of marketing strategies directly affects how the manufacturing operation is designed. For example, low-cost strategy leads to manufacturing that emphasizes technology, processes, statistical process control, tight inventory control, mass distribution, and so on. Conversely, a product-innovation (differentiation) based marketing strategy favors flexibility, new product teams, fast reaction to changes, and selective distribution. Those firms seeking both low cost and product innovation—such as Hewlett-Packard, Mazda, and Philips—face an extremely difficult task integrating what appear to be conflicting manufacturing systems requirements. Special efforts, such as cross-functional teams of marketers, manufacturers, human resources staff, and often customers, are necessary to achieve both ends simultaneously.[14]

> AT WESTINGHOUSE: *Westinghouse realized that it had to improve operations. It had to cut costs and improve quality in order to be competitive. Operations became strategically important.*

Table 20.3 Strategic Alternatives

Business Strategy	Strategy A Low-Cost Producer	Strategy B Product Innovator
Market conditions	Price-sensitive Mature market High volume Standardization	Product-features sensitive Emerging market Low volume Customized products
Operations mission	Emphasize low cost while maintaining acceptable quality and delivery	Emphasize flexibility while maintaining reasonable cost, quality, and delivery
Distinctive competence operations	Low cost through superior process technology and vertical integration	Fast and reliable new-product introduction through product teams and flexible automation
Operations policies	Superior processes Statistical process control Central location Economy of scale Tight inventory control Low-skill work force Highly automated	Superior products Flexible automation Fast reaction to changes Economies of scope Use of product teams Skilled workers Low automation
Marketing strategies	Mass distribution Repeat sales Maximizing of sales opportunities National sales force Low-cost advertising	Selective distribution New-market development Product design Sales made through agents High-cost advertising
Finance strategies	High capital needed Low risk Low profit margins	Low capital needed Higher risks Higher profit margins

SOURCE: Roger G. Schroeder, *Operations Management: Decision Making in the Operations Function*, 3rd ed. (New York: McGraw-Hill, 1989), p. 33.

The amount of business strategy input contributed by operations varies with the firm and its situation, from no involvement to initiating actions that yield competitive advantage.[15] For example, many traditional firms consider manufacturing to be simply the making of products, but firms such as Briggs & Stratten, Allen-Bradley, and Ford Motor Company expect manufacturing to prepare strategies, assist in designing products, and to problem solve.

Federal Express Goes Global

Federal Express earned $188 million on revenues of $3.9 billion for the fiscal year ending May 31, 1988. Its income would have been substantially higher, except that it lost millions of dollars on its international business, a total of $74 million in the period from 1985–1988. Although not everything that Frederick Smith, founder and CEO of Federal Express Corporation, has attempted has turned to gold, just about everything has, except for the overseas operation. Increased competition at home—from United Parcel Service, the U.S. Post Office, and FAX mail—had eroded Federal Express's domestic profit margins, making the international operation even more important.

Smith decided to help solve his problem by purchasing, for $880 million, Tiger International, Incorporated, the world's largest heavy cargo airline and holding company for Flying Tiger Air Freight service. Smith claims that the merger represents an important step toward his goal of making Federal Express "the largest and best transportation company in the world." Smith gained two important competitive advantages in acquiring Tiger. First, it allowed him to use his own planes for package delivery overseas because he can now fly Tiger routes. Before, he had to lease planes from other airlines. Second, he could use Tiger's large, long-range fleet to move to a dominant position in the international heavy freight business. This diversified Federal Express's overall company portfolio—something he said he would never do but has obviously changed his mind about.

SOURCE: "Mr. Smith Goes Global," *Business Week* (February 13, 1989), pp. 66–72.

Strategic Operations Decisions

Strategic operations decisions concern products, processes, and facilities and their relationships to each other. More specifically these decisions include positioning the operations system; focusing the factories; product/service design and process planning; allocating resources to strategic alternatives; determining facility capacity, location, and layout; production technology; and quality.[16]

Positioning the Operations System

Positioning the operations system involves selecting for each major product line in the business plan:

1. The type of product design.
2. The type of production process.
3. The finished goods inventory policy.[17]

STRATEGIC POSITIONS DECISIONS
IN THE SERVICE INDUSTRY
Firms in service industries must also make strategic decisions related to "positioning the operations system," but because manufacturing is not involved, the issues are different. In the service industry, distribution as well as transformation

As this night delivery in Shanghai proves, Federal Express goes to all corners of the globe at all hours of the day and night to provide reliable, fast service to its customers. (Courtesy of Federal Express Corporation)

may play an important part in the process. Much of the conversion process in a service industry is the result of human interaction between customer and service provider. It thus becomes a human resource management function. Distribution may mean changing ways the product is distributed, requiring alterations in distribution channels. For example, Frederick W. Smith, CEO of Federal Express, had been experiencing problems with the distribution of his firm's services internationally, and decided to take strategic action for better "positioning the operations system," as the above Global Management Challenge reveals.

Focused Factories

Many experts believe that factories perform better in terms of efficiency and effectiveness if they are focused upon some particular product/market-niche.[18] As was discussed in Chapter 8 on organizing, Outboard Marine has dedicated each of its factories to various specific tasks in the manufacturing process. Its Spruce Pine, North Carolina, plant, for instance, casts engine blocks using their rare "lost-form" technique that yields more powerful, yet less expensive engines than conventional methods. Other plants add pistons, fuel systems, and other parts to the engine.[19] Conversely, marketing-oriented experts such as Thomas J. Peters believe that factories in the future will have to be more flexible and less focused and have to be capable of turning out products for what are known as "mass-customized" markets.[20] Although the term seems self-contradictory, his point and that of others is that the organization must be able to respond to small niches that are sizable and need particular products unique to their segment of the market. To be able to respond to these, the corporation's manufacturing or service operations area must be able to produce the product or service in a flexible fashion.[21]

Product/Service Design and Process Planning

Additional important operations strategy decisions are related to the design of products/services and the operations processes chosen to produce them. Product design is important to competitiveness—for example, in creating features that attract customers and that differentiate an organization's product or service from that of its competition. In addition, product designs that can be produced cheaply will be more competitive with low-cost producers, such as the Japanese and others in the Pacific rim. Historically, design engineers have translated new technology into product innovation with little marketing input. More recently firms have moved to involve marketing personnel actively in the design process, using integrators, cross-functional teams, or product/process design departments to determine design.[22] The **integrator** works with designers on producibility issues, serving as a liaison with manufacturing. For example, if marketing seeks a product that has an extremely low manufacturing cost, the integrator might work with engineering personnel to design a very simple product with few parts. **Cross-functional teams** consist of design, manufacturing, and often marketing personnel who jointly design the product. Milliken, the textile giant, uses such teams, often with customer members, to improve not only manufacturability, but customer satisfaction, as well.[23] The product process design department oversees both areas.

As cost and quality have become more critical competitive features, the manufacturing process has had to meet their demands, in many cases by simplifying product design. This means designing products simple enough so that manufacturing can be efficient and the product will have high quality, even if there are fluctuations in the production process, such as controlling for temperature in moulding plastics. Using what its conceptualizer, Genichi Taguchi, refers to as "robust design" (often called designing to manufacture), many firms are becoming more efficient.[24] IBM, for example, has chosen not only to automate, but to simplify product design, in order to beat its Pacific rim competition.[25] As Management Challenge 20.1 reveals, IBM was able to take over a Japanese-dominated market through simplification and automation.

Service industry jobs, often the service provided, may also be simplified. Most retail stores have redefined the service process, reducing the number of clerks, allowing customers to roam at will, and placing clerks only in specialty areas—such as perfumes, expensive clothing, or sporting goods. And in the university setting, larger universities have reduced the number of course preparations for professors, thus simplifying their particular jobs by asking them to learn fewer materials.

Process planning is also a critical strategic choice. **Process planning** determines how the process or service will be produced at the desired quality, in the required quantity, and at the budgeted cost. It is obviously highly interdependent with other operations management activities—for example, product design, facility layout, capital plant and equipment acquisitions, human resources utilization, facility capacity, job design, building design, quality control, forecasted demand for the product, and the allocation of operation management resources.[26]

IBM Simplifies and Automates to Beat Asian Rivals

In 1979 IBM established the strategic objective of becoming the world's lowest-cost producer of computers and related equipment. To do that it had to change its manufacturing strategies. And while it attacked all of the major issues relevant to operations strategies, two of the most critical ones it addressed were product design and the manufacturing process.

Typical of the competition IBM faced were the Japanese firms that had modified American personal computer printers—using technology developed by IBM—making them more efficient, and had given customers higher quality and more reliability. IBM chose to compete on both a cost and a quality basis against the Japanese firms.

To do so it opened a plant in Charlotte, North Carolina, to build its "Pro-Printer" series, and focused on simplifying the product and automating the plant. IBM also trimmed its product line in order to achieve greater efficiency and reliability in its products. The Pro-Printer has received rave reviews for its low cost, reliability, and quality. Within a couple of years, IBM seized 80 percent of a $2 billion retail market formerly dominated by the Japanese.

Even IBM's famous Selectric typewriter has been simplified. The labor time for each machine has been cut by 75 percent as a consequence of robotization. The number of product options, such as colors, was reduced in a strategy similar to Ford's "black" Model-T approach. An additional bonus of this simplified product design is that inventory requirements are lower.

SOURCE: John Marcom, Jr., "Slimming Down: IBM Is Automating, Simplifying Products to Beat Asian Rivals," *Wall Street Journal* April 14, 1986, pp. 1, 20.

Allocation of Resources to Strategic Alternatives

Giant firms such as IBM and GM seem to have almost infinite amounts of capital resources. Most firms, however, have limited levels of strategic resources that must be divided among several businesses, product, or functional uses within the organization. Consequently, those resources, available in any year or period of years, must somehow be allocated to maximize the objectives of the overall business strategy—and in this particular situation, of the operations strategy. Most organizations have highly complex capital budgeting allocation programs with stages of review for each major proposed capital purchase. The budgeting process typically is used to allocate resources, as well. Not infrequently, managers must defend their requirements in the presence of their peer managers. This is a common technique at Dana Corporation, a manufacturer of automobile subassemblies, such as axles, in what is known as "Hell Week." Each major division manager is required to make a brief presentation on his or her budget and to defend it in front of some two hundred plus key managers in the company.[27] In some organizations, this process becomes politicized.

Much of the financial, material, human, and information resource allocation process can be accomplished at least in the preliminary stages, using some of the quantitative methods and techniques discussed in Chapter 7. For example, linear programming can be used to aid in such key decisions as allocating fixed resources over a number of operating divisions, to determine the mix of products that best satisfies operating objectives, or to determine the production plan for the number of products and services from various operating facilities. Linear programming can also be used for less strategic and more operational decisions—such as the mix of ingredients for a particular product or the assignment of personnel, overhead, or labor to various operations divisions.[28]

Facility Capacity, Location, and Plant Layout

FACILITY CAPACITY

Deciding how much production or service capacity is needed to meet demand is critical to any organization. Enormous amounts of capital investment are usually required to increase production capacity. Land, plant, and equipment must be purchased or built and related technologies developed. As shown in Table 20.4, there are several ways of changing long-range capacity. These capacity changes also may be modified by actions taken with either technology or human resources. For example, by running more than one shift in a plant, by using existing facilities to manufacture perhaps sixteen or twenty-four hours a day as opposed to eight, it may not be necessary to build another plant. In terms of reduction of capacity, workers can work fewer than eight hours a day or fewer than five days a week, but sometimes organizations will have to sell plants and equipment.

Table 20.4 Ways of Changing Long-Range Capacity

Type of Capacity Change	Ways of Accommodating Long-Range Capacity Changes
Expansion	1. Subcontract with other companies to become suppliers of the expanding firm's components or entire products. 2. Acquire other companies, facilities, or resources. 3. Develop sites, build buildings, buy equipment. 4. Expand, update, or modify existing facilities. 5. Reactivate facilities on standby status.
Reduction	1. Sell off existing facilities, sell inventories, and lay off or transfer employees. 2. Mothball facilities and place on standby status, sell inventories, and lay off or transfer employees. 3. Develop and phase in new products as other products decline.

SOURCE: Figure from *Production and Operations Management: A Problem Solving and Decision Making Approach*, Third Edition by Norman Gaither, copyright © 1987 by The Dryden Press, Inc., a division of Holt, Rinehart and Winston, Inc., reprinted by permission of the publisher.

In the 1980s all three major firms in the American automobile industry made the decision to reduce long-range plant capacity—Chrysler and Ford first, in the 1979–1983 period, and General Motors in 1987 and 1988. Literally billions of dollars were involved.[29] The enormity of this decision can be understood best if you recognize that General Motors', Ford's, and Chrysler's actions indicated that they had conceded their lost market share to foreign competition. General Motors' plant closings came after the company had spent about $40 billion, from 1979 to 1986, building six new assembly plants and modernizing twelve others, only to emerge with an overcapacity of an estimated one million cars and trucks a year.[30] Due to increased sales, Chrysler acquired American Motors in 1987, to increase its capacity, after having reduced capacity earlier in the decade.[31] Ford, too, faced the agonizing decision of capacity expansion when sales boomed in the late 1980s.[32]

FACILITY LOCATION

Facility location decisions are very important in certain industries where nearness to customers or raw materials, or where production factors, such as cost of utilities, may be critical and vary significantly with location. Facilities location decisions begin with a choice of countries. Then region, community, and site locations follow. The principal factors involved in each of these particular location decisions are indicated in Figure 20.3. Locational factors are more or less important to members of various industries. In a warehousing business, for example, it would be important to be near customers, as it would be in retailing. But location near customers is not so important in heavy manufacturing. On the other hand, it might be extremely important for a firm in heavy manufacturing to be near its supply of raw materials. This is not so important in retailing and warehousing. A firm must strike a balance among the various requirements.

The globalization of business has made facility location extremely complex. Events such as those unfolding in Europe for 1992, when the European Economic Community (EEC) becomes a true single market, change how the game is played. Avery International, a $1.5 billion office supply firm, for example, has reduced the number of its European warehouses from one for each country (fourteen) to five regional warehouses, as the European market unites.[33] Many U.S. firms have located manufacturing plants outside the country to take advantage of significantly lower wage rates in places such as Mexico. Some have found that manufacturing "offshore"—that is, outside the United States—has definite limitations, such as the labor cost advantage often being offset by other disadvantages.[34]

FACILITY LAYOUT

Facility layout means "planning for the location of all machines, utilities, employee work stations, customer service areas, materials, aisles, restrooms, lunchrooms, drinking fountains, internal walls, offices, and computer rooms, and for the flow patterns of materials and people around, into, and within buildings."[35] Facilities layout is an extremely complex problem, consisting of a large number of interrelated decisions. In manufacturing, focal issues include plant capacity for that period of time; the size and number of machines that are necessary; the technology involved to achieve production levels; the requirements of keeping workers motivated, safe, and healthy; building and site constraints; the organization's growth trends; and finally the size, strength, and characteristics of the materials involved.

There are four basic types of layouts for manufacturing facilities: process, product, group technology, and fixed position. **Process layouts** are designed to accommodate a large number of product designs and processing steps. These are often associated with job shops that manufacture a variety of products. **Product layouts** accommodate only a few product and process designs and are associated with assembly lines that make a product in a fixed sequence of steps. In the **group technology** process, a group of machines acts like a product layout for a family of similar products within a larger processing layout design. Group technology will probably be used more in the future because it allows for more flexible manufacturing. In the **fixed position** layout, the product remains in a fixed position and workers, parts, and machines move to and from the product. This type of layout is typical in aircraft assembly, bridge building, and ship construction.

FIGURE 20.3 THE FACILITY LOCATION DECISION

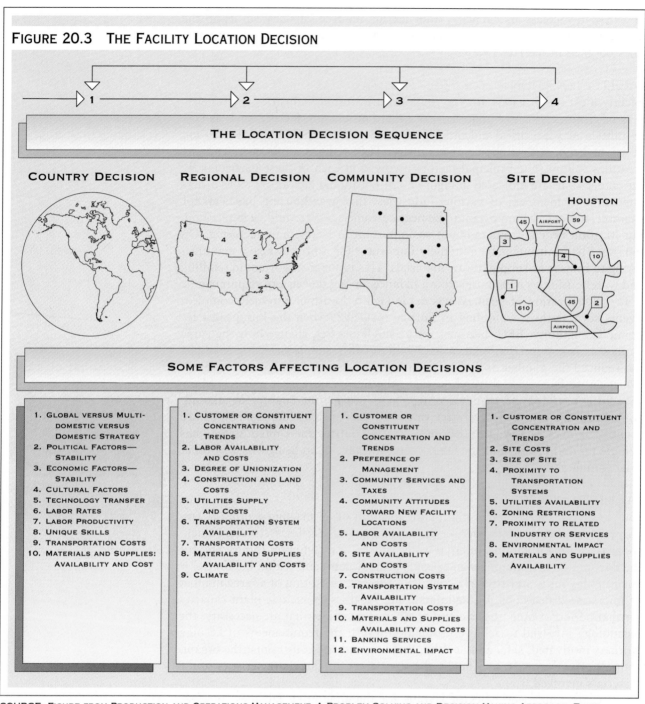

THE LOCATION DECISION SEQUENCE

COUNTRY DECISION   **REGIONAL DECISION**   **COMMUNITY DECISION**   **SITE DECISION**

HOUSTON

SOME FACTORS AFFECTING LOCATION DECISIONS

1. GLOBAL VERSUS MULTI-DOMESTIC VERSUS DOMESTIC STRATEGY 2. POLITICAL FACTORS—STABILITY 3. ECONOMIC FACTORS—STABILITY 4. CULTURAL FACTORS 5. TECHNOLOGY TRANSFER 6. LABOR RATES 7. LABOR PRODUCTIVITY 8. UNIQUE SKILLS 9. TRANSPORTATION COSTS 10. MATERIALS AND SUPPLIES: AVAILABILITY AND COST	1. CUSTOMER OR CONSTITUENT CONCENTRATIONS AND TRENDS 2. LABOR AVAILABILITY AND COSTS 3. DEGREE OF UNIONIZATION 4. CONSTRUCTION AND LAND COSTS 5. UTILITIES SUPPLY AND COSTS 6. TRANSPORTATION SYSTEM AVAILABILITY 7. TRANSPORTATION COSTS 8. MATERIALS AND SUPPLIES AVAILABILITY AND COSTS 9. CLIMATE	1. CUSTOMER OR CONSTITUENT CONCENTRATION AND TRENDS 2. PREFERENCE OF MANAGEMENT 3. COMMUNITY SERVICES AND TAXES 4. COMMUNITY ATTITUDES TOWARD NEW FACILITY LOCATIONS 5. LABOR AVAILABILITY AND COSTS 6. SITE AVAILABILITY AND COSTS 7. CONSTRUCTION COSTS 8. TRANSPORTATION SYSTEM AVAILABILITY 9. TRANSPORTATION COSTS 10. MATERIALS AND SUPPLIES AVAILABILITY AND COSTS 11. BANKING SERVICES 12. ENVIRONMENTAL IMPACT	1. CUSTOMER OR CONSTITUENT CONCENTRATION AND TRENDS 2. SITE COSTS 3. SIZE OF SITE 4. PROXIMITY TO TRANSPORTATION SYSTEMS 5. UTILITIES AVAILABILITY 6. ZONING RESTRICTIONS 7. PROXIMITY TO RELATED INDUSTRY OR SERVICES 8. ENVIRONMENTAL IMPACT 9. MATERIALS AND SUPPLIES AVAILABILITY

SOURCE: FIGURE FROM PRODUCTION AND OPERATIONS MANAGEMENT: A PROBLEM SOLVING AND DECISION MAKING APPROACH, THIRD EDITION BY NORMAN GAITHER, COPYRIGHT © 1987 BY THE DRYDEN PRESS, INC., A DIVISION OF HOLT, RINEHART AND WINSTON, INC., REPRINTED BY PERMISSION OF THE PUBLISHER.

The trend in U.S. manufacturing is toward the Japanese model. Richard Schonberger, who has studied Japanese techniques, suggests that there are two fundamentals to the Japanese success story in manufacturing: productivity and quality. The "just-in-time inventory" (JIT) approach underlies their high productivity. Commitment to "total quality control" procedures is how they achieve high levels of quality.[36] Thus, there is more emphasis on efficiency and quality, and to the extent that facility layouts can help this process, layouts are being changed. For example, layouts are being redesigned so that workers can see the entire layout and move quickly between work stations. Open work areas with fewer walls and partitions are becoming more common. Factories tend to be getting smaller, with distances between machines decreasing, as efficiency objectives become more critical. There is less and less space being provided for inventories, as organizations move to JIT manufacturing. Layouts are becoming increasingly more flexible and group technology more prominent as shorter production runs are anticipated. In addition, workers are being trained at more than one job, to allow flexibility in manufacturing. Schonberger urges that companies focus on simplicity—in product design and in the production process. He believes that Japanese manufacturing management and systems are transportable to the United States and other countries.[37]

SERVICE FACILITY LAYOUTS

Unlike manufacturing layouts, service layouts are designed to bring large numbers of customers into the organization. Service layouts are designed either to meet customer service requirements or to facilitate technological, materials handling, or production efficiency aspects of an operation.[38] A grocery store is very customer oriented and tends to keep the length of lines as short as possible, moving clerks in and out as customer numbers increase and decrease. Conversely, a discount merchandiser, where customers order from inventory after picking items from a showroom, is designed more for efficiency than service. Firms tend to use a mix of these layouts—for example, fast food restaurants emphasize technology, whereas an exclusive gourmet restaurant will emphasize customer service functions.

Most service organization facilities are designed to enable ready access for customers. In a bank, for example, there are few walls or partitions, so that customers can see when a loan officer or a clerk is available. There are well-lit and expansive parking areas, as well as wide sidewalks, so customers are able to move to and from the service area. In hospitals, the emphasis is more on locating technology and then bringing the patient to it. Thus, elevators are large and aisles are wide, to accommodate moving patients about.

Production Technology

Organizations must determine the amount and type of technology they want to employ. The trend in both manufacturing and service is toward increased use of technology. Important technology features include automation, computer integrated manufacturing, computer aided design, computer aided manufacturing, flexible manufacturing, automatic storage and retrieval systems, and robotics.

Within the broad categories of product, process, group technology, or fixed position factory layouts, a critical strategic decision is the amount of **automation**—the replacement of human effort with machine effort—that must take place. The amount of automation varies in four stages, based on the degree to which the machines perform simple, random tasks or complex processes: mechanized aids, numerically controlled machines, robots, and computer integrated manufacturing (CIM).[39] Automation, in particular the use of robots and computer integrated manufacturing, has met with mixed levels of success. At one time robotization and CIM were predicted for virtually all of American industry. Automation, robotization, and CIM have been shown to be very effective in improving productivity, even where production of just a few units at a time is occurring.[40] But the often-cited experience of General Motors at its NUMMI plant in Fremont, California, has revealed that proper usage of human resources, in combination with moderate amounts of automation but not necessarily robotization and CIM, often lead to superior productivity over totally robotized and CIM plants.[41]

This engineer is getting help from a computer-aided-design (CAD) system in designing new plastic products. (SOURCE © John Maher/Stock Market)

Computer integrated manufacturing (CIM) is a broad label applied to the use of computers in design and manufacturing processes, the use of just-in-time (JIT) inventories (in which the firm keeps zero, or near zero, inventories), flexible manufacturing, robotics, high levels of automation, and automatic storage and retrieval systems.[42]

Computer aided design (CAD) includes specialized hardware and software to assist engineers in performing designs on a computer terminal. General Electric, Texas Instruments, Exxon, Eastman Kodak, Boeing, and Caterpillar Tractor are just a few of the firms possessing this capability.[43]

Computer aided manufacturing (CAM) encompasses specialized computer systems that translate the CAD design information into instructions for automated manufacturing. The hardware is readily available for CAM, but the software is still limited in many industries.

Flexible manufacturing systems (FMS) are clusters of automated machinery controlled by computers that have the flexibility to produce a wide variety of products in medium, small, or even large production runs, with the same efficiency levels. General Electric and Westinghouse, among others, have plants with such capability. Tremendous strategic advantage may be gained by using such systems.[44]

Automated storage and retrieval systems (ASRS) are computer controlled automated warehouses that include automatic placement and retrieval of parts into and from the warehouse. Parts are ordered and retrieved as needed, according to computer control. Automatic transportation of parts occurs on self-guided carts.

Robotics involves the use of robots to perform a manufacturing or service function.

Work Force Management[45]

Organizations are changing their structures to provide workers with more challenging jobs. More decision making is being designed into jobs. Labor is increasingly viewed as a partner rather than as an antagonist. One of the key ingredients in the Japanese manufacturing success story has been the way in which they manage people. Table 20.5 indicates the more humanistic approach to management of Japanese firms (Type J) than American firms (Type A). There are American firms that closely resemble Japanese firms. Ouchi has labeled these Type Z.[46] The work group orientation of Japanese manufacturing management, and management in general, when combined with the participative aspects of allowing workers to solve problems as they arise, has enabled Japan to create a very effective operating system. It has major strategic impacts on their ability to reduce costs and increase quality, when compared to most American firms. Many U.S. firms are moving more in the direction of Theory Z management. One of the most successful efforts has been General Motors' NUMMI plant in Fremont, California. The introduction of Theory Z management into the plant changed it from one of GM's worst plants into its best, in terms of productivity.[47]

AT WESTINGHOUSE: *Quality is a religion. Everybody is responsible.*

Table 20.5 Theory A, J, and Z Management

Type J Firms (Japanese Firms)	Type A Firms (American Firms)	Theory Z Firms (American Firms Operating Similarly to Japanese Firms)
Lifetime employment (for men)	Short-term employment	Long-term employment
Slow process of evaluation and promotion	Rapid evaluation and promotion	Slow evaluation and promotion
Nonspecialized career	Specialized career planning	Moderate career planning
Consensual decision making	Individual decision making	Consensual decision making
Collective responsibility	Individual responsibility	Individual responsibility
Implicit/subtle control	Explicit/formal control	Informal, implicit control with explicit measures available
Holistic concern for employees	Segmented concern for employees	Holistic concern for employees

SOURCE: William J. Ouchi, *Theory Z: How American Business Can Meet the Japanese Challenge* (Reading, Mass.: Addison-Wesley, 1981), p. 38. Reprinted with permission of the publisher.

Total Quality Strategy

One of the major issues in any organization's strategic, as well as operational activities is the total quality control concept.[48] Total quality commitment should lead to a concerted effort on the part of all employees to be error-free in their activities, to seek ways to improve quality, and to strive constantly for quality. On the other hand, quality is what you say it is—that is, the appropriate level of quality can be designed into the product for the market for which the product or service is aimed.[49] But the reality is that most people want "high-quality" products and services. The Japanese have emphasized quality much more than their American competitors and have been able to capture large market shares in major industries such as autos, steel, and electronics, as a consequence. But many American firms are fighting back, as Management Challenge 20.2 reveals.[50]

Hewlett-Packard's Total Quality Control Program

Hewlett-Packard's CEO, John Young, recognized, in the late 1970s, that Japanese firms were entering his firm's markets and would not only continue to do so in the future, but would become more competitive in the computer field. He also recognized that while Hewlett-Packard was often touted as the industry leader in computer quality, Hewlett had to do something to head off the Japanese onslaught. To prepare Hewlett-Packard, he ordered a tenfold increase in quality. His employees thought he was crazy, but he had seen the handwriting on the wall (and it was written in Japanese). Hewlett's total quality control program was designed with the intent of changing the way the company did things.

At the core of the program was a measurement-range system that ensured that quality was measured and approved at every stage of every process, in every part of the organization. The foundation upon which the program was built was an ingenious method involving everyone. All individuals who worked for the company, regardless of their jobs, were to see themselves as customers and suppliers. As customers, people went to their suppliers and made sure that they received good service; as suppliers, they had to provide their customers with good service. By making all employees "customers and suppliers," each one became an individual business person. Dramatic savings resulted. Hewlett-Packard saved $542 million in manufacturing and inventory costs from 1979 to 1988, and total quality control has saved dramatic amounts of money in mundane areas like accounts receivable. Total quality control starts with the following six steps:

1. "Find something you can win at. Pick one product and set out to be the best in quality or service.
2. Analyze how you make the product (or deliver the service); break it down into sets of processes, and identify all the 'customers' and 'suppliers'.
3. Have your people as 'customers' measure the service they are getting.
4. Create high standards of improvement for your people, and let them know you believe they can attain them. Build the achievement of quality goals into your compensation system.
5. Improve your processes and chart your progress on the wall for all to see.
6. Set new goals. There is always room for improvement."

SOURCE: Robert H. Waterman, Jr., "Start Your Own Quality Revolution," *Success* (April 1988), p. 16.

Tactical Operations Decisions: Planning Production to Meet Demands

Tactical operations decisions are intermediate-range decisions between strategic decisions about products, processes, and facilities and operating decisions of planning and controlling the day-to-day operation. They include decisions to be

Each of the individuals on this assembly line at Hewlett-Packard knows exactly who his or her customers are, the service he or she provides, and the objectives to be accomplished in several performance categories. (SOURCE © Ed Kashi)

made about production planning systems, independent demand inventory systems, resource requirement planning systems, and materials management and purchasing.

Production Planning Systems

While determining capacity is a strategic decision, meeting anticipated demand is a tactical, often short-term decision. There must be a master production schedule derived to indicate what will be produced and when—within the next

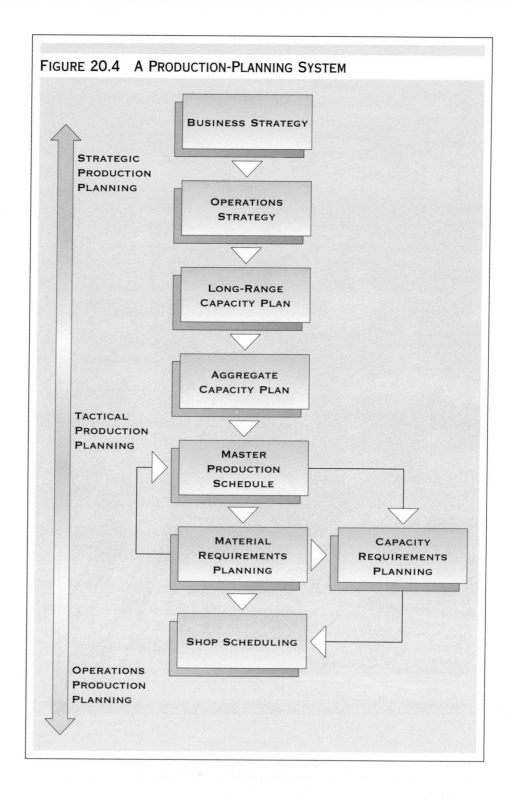

FIGURE 20.4   A PRODUCTION-PLANNING SYSTEM

operating period or periods. There must be sufficient capacity to satisfy market demand and keep production at top levels. Figure 20.4 provides an in-depth look at the relationships between strategic (long-range), tactical (intermediate-range), and operational (short-range) plans in the production planning system. The first step is to develop a long-range capacity plan dependent on sales forecasts for each product for each production period—either weeks, months, quarters, or years. These are then totaled until aggregate demand is translated into the requirements for workers, materials, machines, inventory, and facilities.

Shorter-term resource allocation plans are then developed, the result of which is a master production schedule. Linear programming is an excellent tool for assisting in determining these plans. A number of simulations are also available to assist in this planning process. Materials requirement planning, capacity requirements planning, and shop scheduling will follow.

The Control of Inventory and the Planning Process

Inventory is the supply of goods kept on hand for the production process, or as the result of it. There are three principal types of inventory: finished goods, work-in-process, and raw materials. Supplies are a fourth type of inventory used throughout the organization. Each has its own purpose, and each represents a financial investment on the part of the company. Table 20.6 indicates why each type of inventory is necessary.

Table 20.6 Why Are Inventories Necessary?

Type of Inventory	Reasons
Finished goods	1. Variation in customer demand from period to period rules out planning flows of products in to exactly match flows of products out. 2. It is more economical to hold inventory than constantly to place emergency orders to meet customers' demands. 3. It is physically impossible to instantaneously produce or acquire products when demanded by customers. 4. Backlogging of customers' orders may be unacceptable. 5. Allows efficient scheduling of production. This refers both to economic production runs and to stable production levels that may not match seasonal or other erratic demand patterns. 6. Allows the display of products to customers.
In-process	1. Production rates of processing steps are uneven. 2. Allows the uncoupling of operations. Each operation is then somewhat independent of other operations. This allows flexibility in planning each operation. 3. Allows large batches of materials to be moved at one time between operations, particularly with process layouts. This reduces materials-handling costs.
Raw materials	1. It is physically impossible and economically infeasible to instantaneously supply raw materials and supplies when demanded by operations. 2. Variation in demand for raw materials by operations from period to period and variation in delivery times of materials rule out planning flows of materials in that exactly match flows of materials out. 3. Allows favorable unit prices through volume buying. 4. Allows reduction of incoming unit freight costs through larger shipments. 5. Allows more efficient materials handling through larger loads.

SOURCE: Figures from *Production and Operations Management: A Problem Solving and Decision Making Approach,* Third Edition by Norman Gaither, copyright © 1987 by The Dryden Press, Inc., a division of Holt, Rinehart and Winston, Inc., reprinted by permission of the publisher.

ECONOMIC ORDER QUANTITY (EOQ)
Historically, companies have assumed that inventories should be held at certain levels. The purpose of the EOQ model is to determine the proper reorder point for inventory, either for the purchase of raw materials or the manufacture of inventory to produce final products, to satisfy customer needs. The **EOQ** is that amount of inventory to be ordered that will minimize the holding and ordering costs. The storage, management, and financing costs associated with holding inventory must be counterbalanced against the possible loss of customer sales, plus the cost of lost production time, plus the costs of ordering. Formulas can be developed to determine the EOQ. These depend upon product supply and

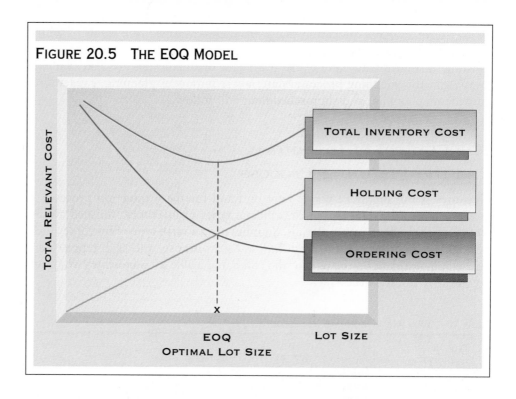

FIGURE 20.5   THE EOQ MODEL

demand and the associated cost of holding inventory and ordering costs. In most cases companies do not know the actual demand for their products, so forecasts must be made. To help maintain inventories at optimal levels, numerous mathematical models and computer simulations have been developed. Figure 20.5 portrays a typical EOQ model. The EOQ always occurs at the point at which total inventory cost is minimized, the lowest point on the curve in Figure 20.5. This corresponds in this case to the intersection of the ordering cost and holding cost curves shown in the figure. Ordering costs decrease as the lot size of inventory ordered increases because fewer orders are placed during the period; holding costs increase as lot size increases.

FACTORS FAVORING LARGE AND SMALL INVENTORIES

There are advantages to both large and small inventories. Factors favoring large inventories include fear of running out of stock; anticipation of possible jumps in demand; desire to keep ordering, shipping, and production costs low; desire to take advantage of favorable prices and quantity discounts; desire to have a hedge against inflation; fear of unexpected events, such as strikes, embargoes, and natural disasters. Factors favoring small inventories include the desire to minimize working capital tied up in inventory; the desire to minimize storage costs; limitations on storage capacity; the desire to keep insurance and tax expenses down; fear of obsolescence; and the danger of spoilage.[51]

JUST-IN-TIME INVENTORY (JIT)

More recently, firms have begun to move away from holding large inventories of raw materials and finished goods. It is an inventory system in which the firm maintains virtually a near-zero level of inventory. The economic order quantity approaches (one day's inventory) as the production process grows more efficient. Suppliers are required to provide just enough inventory for that day's operation or operations for some other given time period.

The JIT system, which American firms learned from the Japanese, has several

AT WESTINGHOUSE:
One of the cornerstones of Westinghouse's success has been the use of JIT inventories. These are used in two-thirds of their plants.

benefits. First, it reduces inventory carrying costs and financing and management costs, but these are only possible with a reduction in ordering or setup costs. JIT supports the company's efforts to be flexible and responsive to customer demand, and it helps improve quality. In the typical American inventory control system, workers simply throw away scrap pieces and defective parts as they come to them; these are written off as part of the manufacturing process. The JIT system requires high quality inputs.

Kanban. **Kanban** is a (low-cost) method for controlling inventory and product movement. Kanban literally means "card" in Japanese. The Kanban, or its equivalent, is an essential communication device in Japanese JIT. The "card" is used to signal that a worker's inventory is depleted; only when it is depleted can he or she trade the Kanban for additional inventory.[52]

In the Japanese system, quality is paramount because the next individual cannot complete his or her job until the previous worker has given him or her a perfect part. Thus, quality is built into the JIT system. By using JIT organizations not only improve quality, but also reduce their costs and improve their productivity. JIT is really a forced system of problem solving. Problems with the production process itself cannot be hidden by buffer zones of inventories. Problems must be solved when they arise.[53]

The relationships with suppliers tend to be few in number and long term, and suppliers must be willing to provide just-in-time inventory deliveries. Suppliers for major corporations, with large contracts involved, are motivated to make changes in delivery practices. Suppliers for smaller companies may not feel so inclined. Furthermore, even with large firms, some suppliers resist because of the effort involved on their part and therefore use warehouses or intermediaries to make JIT deliveries.

The JIT program is not as easy to manage as it might seem. Oftentimes not only must raw materials or component inventories arrive just in time; numerous parts must be shipped or stored in exactly the proper order. While some companies treat JIT as simply a way of getting suppliers to hold their inventories and cut costs, others work with their suppliers to make the process smoother, treating JIT as a philosophy of productivity improvement. Customers must help their suppliers by giving them plenty of advance notice about what is due, when, and in what order, as Management Challenge 20.3 suggests.[54] Unions often oppose JIT and some of the newer manufacturing processes because they perceive them as a threat to union objectives.

Richard Love, a general manager with Hewlett-Packard, examines a Kanban status board in one of the company's manufacturing plants. (SOURCE © Robert Holmgren)

Material Requirements Planning

Materials requirements planning (MRP) is a computer-based inventory planning and control system that examines the master planning schedule for required input resources—raw materials, parts, subassemblies and assemblies—for each time period of the planning horizon. It then examines the existing inventory materials levels and materials requirements and develops a schedule for ordering the necessary materials for arrival as needed on the planning horizon.[55]

This system has been seen as a way of managing extremely complex assembly processes with large numbers of components, assemblies, and subassemblies. Weapons systems manufacturing companies—for example, those making missiles and submarines—are important users of the system. Martin Marietta has spent millions of dollars and thousands of man-hours in developing its MRP II system to help manage its defense contracts.[56]

Having a Hard Time with JIT

Xerox found itself having great difficulties with JIT inventory when it first began to use the system. It attempted simply to push its inventory holding requirements onto its suppliers. It cut the number of suppliers from over five thousand to just three hundred and rewarded them with long-term contracts of two and three years. But Xerox management failed to recognize that its suppliers couldn't simply make the system work by themselves.

Xerox examined the situation and decided that it should make efforts not only to improve relationships with suppliers, but to help them with the JIT process, and they did. They firmed up order schedules so that suppliers could plan better. They held classes for suppliers so they could train their employees in the JIT process. Now the company has firmed up its order schedules and improved production planning to help suppliers meet its demands.

SOURCE: Dexter Hutchins, "Having a Hard Time with Just-In-Time," *Fortune* (June 9, 1986), pp. 64–66.

Materials Management and Purchasing

Decisions about the entire materials management system, from the purchasing of inventories to dispatching the final product, are so critical that most manufacturing organizations have someone in charge of overseeing the entire materials process: purchasing, internal logistics, and warehousing.

Planning and Controlling Day-to-Day Operations

Day-to-day operations management decisions involve the following issues: scheduling and shop floor planning and control, workers and their productivity, implementation of quality control, planning and control for each project, and maintenance management and reliability.

Scheduling and Shop Floor Planning and Control

This process is involved with tactical and short-range decisions regarding what to produce and when to produce it for each work area. How these problems are resolved depends partly on whether a plant is product layout or process layout. Scheduling is much easier in product layouts than in process layouts. In either the operations manager moves from the master production schedule to the capacity requirement plan to the MRP or other resources plan to determine day-to-day scheduling and shop floor decisions. Priorities and sequencing order must be determined. In process layouts which machine and which worker will do which order also must be determined. Efforts must be coordinated among the various work areas.

American Airlines' Fixer of Broken Schedules

Robert S. Norman is one of the most important customer service people at American Airlines. He is their manager of current schedules. He and his team of six analysts not only develop new schedules aimed at implementing ambitious expansion plans, but they also fix broken schedules, and that is where the real challenge comes. A typical day begins at 8:00 A.M., with a daily briefing by operations analysts at American. Thunderstorms diverted fifteen flights from American's Chicago hub and delayed others. Mechanical difficulties, a change of planes, and a delay waiting for a new crew resulted in a three-hour delay for a flight from Chicago to Manchester, England. A passenger on a plane on its way to Norfolk, Virginia, locked herself in the lavatory, took off all her clothes, and crammed them in the toilet, causing problems for the plane upon landing. These are the kinds of incidents that drive people like Robert Norman crazy, anger passengers, and provoke ripples throughout the system. Norman believes that you have to figure out what needs to be fixed and then whether it is fixable. Passenger "misconduct," such as that on the Norfolk flight, can't be corrected and can cause reverberations throughout the system all day. According to Norman the goal is to "reduce delays to the point where any delays are beyond our control." Because the federal government now publishes monthly statistics on flight time arrivals and on-time percentages, being on time is important, but it must be done safely. Every change has an impact on one, and usually on many more, flight schedules.

Walter J. Aue, Norman's boss, comments that "Scheduling aircraft is like working a jigsaw puzzle, except that every day you come in, someone has changed the shape of the pieces."

American Airlines has five major hubs, serves 150 airports, has 420 planes, and 2,140 daily flights, yet for seven straight months, in 1988, American was number one on the government's on-time statistics list. In April 1988 Delta supplanted it for the first time. As other airlines learn some of the tricks that American has used, such as adding an average of eight minutes to every flight, American's advantage in the future will depend pretty much on Robert Norman and his staff.

Staff must analyze reams of data every day, much of it supplied internally. For example, American publishes a 400-page monthly report that dissects every American flight, comparing all aspects of performance. But often one must depend on information from the outside. For example, when Los Angeles closed one of its runways, American schedulers knew in advance and were able to schedule around the change. However, in the summer of 1987, the city of Chicago closed a runway at O'Hare for repairs and didn't tell anybody. As a result, some American flights were late getting into the airport and out.

SOURCE: Robert L. Rose, "American Airlines' Fixer of Broken Schedules," *Wall Street Journal*, 28 June, 1988, p. 35.

Robert S. Norman controls the schedules of these planes and hundreds of others like them. Consequently, he controls the arrivals and departures of passengers, an important component of passenger perceptions of airline service. (SOURCE © Jim Knowles/ Picture Group)

Gantt charts, assembly charts, work process charts, and other scheduling devices are utilized. Labor must be assigned, dispatching orders must be given, and inventory must be withdrawn or made available. Literally hundreds of minute decisions must be made.

Operations planning and control and scheduling are important in service industries, as well as in manufacturing, as Management Challenge 20.4 plainly reveals.

At this General Motors plant, acceptable levels of tolerance on body parts are so minute, that computers must be used to determine whether parts meet these standards or not. (Courtesy New United Motor Manufacturing, Inc.)

Workers and Productivity

Moving from such strategic decisions as which type of structure and leadership style to employ across a company, to decisions involving everyday management, front-line operations managers must determine the most appropriate way to lead employees. This often includes decisions about job design, as well as leadership style. Teamwork is a focal point, as quality circles and similar team concepts are used by hundreds of major manufacturers in the United States.[57] The effects on productivity have been generally positive.[58] Quality circles are being used effectively in service industries. Other team-oriented approaches developed in Japan—for such "individualistic" actions as computer programming—have further demonstrated that teamwork can be more effective in service areas.

Quality Control and Kaizen

Achieving overall quality requires the commitment of the entire organization. Total quality control means that everyone is responsible. It involves establishing policies, standards, and procedures; quality control training; the design of products or services; assistance from suppliers; control of the production process itself; and control of purchasing, logistics, and warehousing distribution/sales, to be aided by JIT inventory systems. Employees must participate in bolstering quality if improvements are to be fully effective. Each worker now possesses the authority to stop the assembly line at Ford Motor Company. Some say Henry Ford would turn over in his grave if he knew this had happened.[59] The use of statistical sampling procedures has increased in most firms, but sampling items to ensure quality has given way in many firms to inspecting all items. Computers are being used more and more in quality control. Errors are reduced through computer-guided manufacturing systems. Computers also monitor for acceptable levels of tolerance.

Kaizen, or constant improvement, is an important part of the Japanese quality success story. They strive to continually improve products and processes incrementally. This allows them then to be continually ahead of their competitors, especially U.S. firms which make fewer improvements.[60] Many U.S. firms are now adopting this concept.

Quality According to W. Edwards Deming

William Edwards Deming is the father of quality control in Japan and, until recently, was a prophet no one would listen to in his own country.[61] W. Edwards Deming introduced statistical quality control concepts to Japan in 1950. Deming's "fourteen points" for improving quality are presented in Figure 20.6. Deming is generally recognized as having been responsible for transforming Japanese manufacturing from producing low-quality products to producing high-quality products. More recently, U.S. firms, having begun to recognize the importance of quality, have hired Deming, and others, to help them improve quality.

QUALITY CONTROL IN SERVICES

Quality control in services is often much more difficult to manage than it is in manufacturing; yet, it can mean the difference between success and failure.[62] Although it may not be difficult to control quality in some service organizations, such as McDonald's hamburger restaurants, which are almost manufacturing operations, it is difficult in others, such as health care, banking, airlines, and grocery stores. Often, surveys of customer satisfaction are undertaken. Other measures of quality control probably need to be utilized. For example, perhaps physicians, nurses, and health-care facilities should be rated on the basis of the product they put out. Maybe it is necessary, for example, to indicate the number of operations performed by particular physicians and their success and failure rates.

> AT WESTINGHOUSE:
> *Quality is critical at Westinghouse. It is one of the ways in which Chairman Marcus and President Lego believe they can help the company increase profits and compete successfully in the future. Combined with productivity efforts, the company believes that it can compete by listening to customers and by providing high levels of service and quality.*

Project Management: Planning and Controlling Projects

Just as with the ongoing planning and control of organizational operations, **project management**, the planning and control of projects, must occur. PERT and CPM, discussed in Chapter 7, are usually used to plan and control projects. Computerized versions of these and similar program planners are available.

Maintenance Management and Reliability

Maintenance management is extremely important, and malfunctions in manufacturing and service operations can lead to several problems: loss of production capacity, increased costs, product or service quality, danger for employees, or customer dissatisfaction. Two types of principal maintenance approaches exist, repairs and preventive maintenance.

Preventive maintenance in JIT inventory manufacturing operations is critical. No downtime can be allowed because there are no inventories to provide buffers between the various segments of the company. As soon as one work area has downtime, the rest of the plant will have downtime. This is, of course, one of the dangers of JIT inventory systems, and one reason why buffer inventories have historically been part of the manufacturing process.

The Factory of the Future

The so-called "factory of the future" is almost upon us, and in many cases is already here. The principal characteristics of **the factory of the future** include automated machinery and all the aspects of computer integrated manufacturing (CIM) we have discussed in this chapter.

FIGURE 20.6 DEMING'S 14 POINTS

1. CREATE CONSTANCY OF PURPOSE TOWARD IMPROVEMENT OF PRODUCT AND SERVICE, WITH THE AIM OF BECOMING COMPETITIVE TO STAY IN BUSINESS AND TO PROVIDE JOBS.

2. ADOPT THE NEW PHILOSOPHY: WE ARE IN A NEW ECONOMIC AGE, CREATED BY JAPAN. TRANSFORMATION OF WESTERN STYLE OF MANAGEMENT IS NECESSARY TO HALT THE CONTINUED DECLINE OF INDUSTRY.

3. CEASE DEPENDENCE ON MASS INSPECTION TO ACHIEVE QUALITY. ELIMINATE THE NEED FOR INSPECTION ON A MASS BASIS BY BUILDING QUALITY INTO THE PRODUCT IN THE FIRST PLACE.

4. END THE PRACTICE OF AWARDING BUSINESS ON THE BASIS OF PRICE TAG. PURCHASING MUST BE COMBINED WITH DESIGN OF PRODUCT, MANUFACTURING WITH SALES, TO WORK WITH THE CHOSEN SUPPLIER. THE AIM IS TO MINIMIZE TOTAL COST, NOT MERELY INITIAL COST.

5. IMPROVE CONSTANTLY AND FOREVER EVERY ACTIVITY IN THE COMPANY, TO IMPROVE QUALITY AND PRODUCTIVITY AND THUS CONSTANTLY DECREASE COSTS.

6. INSTITUTE TRAINING AND EDUCATION ON THE JOB, INCLUDING MANAGEMENT.

7. INSTITUTE SUPERVISION. THE AIM OF SUPERVISION SHOULD BE TO HELP PEOPLE AND MACHINES AND GADGETS DO A BETTER JOB.

8. DRIVE OUT FEAR, SO THAT EVERYONE MAY WORK EFFECTIVELY FOR THE COMPANY.

9. BREAK DOWN BARRIERS BETWEEN DEPARTMENTS. PEOPLE IN RESEARCH, DESIGN, SALES, AND PRODUCTION MUST WORK AS A TEAM, TO FORESEE PROBLEMS OF PRODUCTION AND IN USE THAT MAY BE ENCOUNTERED WITH THE PRODUCT OR SERVICE.

10. ELIMINATE SLOGANS, EXHORTATIONS, AND TARGETS FOR THE WORK FORCE ASKING FOR ZERO DEFECTS AND NEW LEVELS OF PRODUCTIVITY. SUCH EXHORTATIONS ONLY CREATE ADVERSARIAL RELATIONSHIPS, SINCE THE BULK OF THE CAUSES OF LOW PRODUCTIVITY LIE BEYOND THE POWER OF THE WORK FORCE.

11. ELIMINATE WORK STANDARDS THAT PRESCRIBE NUMERICAL QUOTAS FOR THE DAY. SUBSTITUTE AIDS AND HELPFUL SUPERVISION.

12A. REMOVE THE BARRIERS THAT ROB THE HOURLY WORKER OF HIS PRIDE OF WORKMANSHIP. THE RESPONSIBILITY OF SUPERVISORS MUST BE CHANGED FROM SHEER NUMBERS TO QUALITY.

12B. REMOVE THE BARRIERS THAT ROB PEOPLE IN MANAGEMENT AND IN ENGINEERING OF THEIR RIGHT TO PRIDE OF WORKMANSHIP. THIS MEANS ABOLISHMENT OF THE ANNUAL OR MERIT RATING AND OF MANAGEMENT BY OBJECTIVES.

13. INSTITUTE A VIGOROUS PROGRAM OF EDUCATION AND RETRAINING. NEW SKILLS ARE REQUIRED FOR CHANGES IN TECHNIQUES, MATERIALS, AND SERVICE.

14. PUT EVERYBODY IN THE COMPANY TO WORK IN TEAMS TO ACCOMPLISH THE TRANSFORMATION.

SOURCE: REPRINTED FROM OUT OF CRISIS BY W. EDWARDS DEMING BY PERMISSION OF MIT AND W. EDWARDS DEMING. PUBLISHED BY MIT, CENTER FOR ADVANCED ENGINEERING STUDY, CAMBRIDGE, MA 02139. COPYRIGHT 1986 BY W. EDWARDS DEMING.

Most such factories will include fewer workers, but the workers who remain will be more highly skilled. Most will be involved in quality control and distribution and troubleshooting and maintenance, as opposed to the actual physical manufacturing of the product—which for the most part will be accomplished by computer controlled machines. This complex interaction of people, machines, and ideas requires a new type of organizational structure and philosophy. Organizations will need to focus more on cross-functional teams and change capital budgeting and accounting to make them more strategically oriented, for example.[63]

Foreign competition is providing the impetus for such factories.[64] The United States cannot compete effectively against the lower wage rates and superior manufacturing processes of many foreign countries. The factory of the future must be able to provide perfect quality at very, very low cost, with little inventory, and virtually no waste.[65] Management Challenge 20.5 portrays a factory of the future that is in operation today.

Productivity Management

Productivity is the organization's output of goods and services divided by its inputs. High productivity is indicated by a large value for the ratio, whereas productivity is low if the ratio is small.[66] One of the important reasons that concern for productivity has been so great recently is that in the past few years America, while still leading productivity among the major industrialized nations, has seen its rate of productivity growth fall behind, often far behind, that of other major industrialized countries, especially Japan. As these other countries try to catch up with the United States, they may not only reach, but surpass, the U.S. rate, if the United States does not increase its levels of productivity.

How to Improve Productivity

Productivity can best be improved by either increasing the use of technology or by making better use of our human resources. Related measures for increasing productivity include more R&D, downsizing, restructuring, mergers, better equipment, and breaking conglomerate companies into component companies. Actions were taken in virtually all these areas in the mid-1980s, and as a consequence, in 1987 productivity increases in goods-producing industries rose to an average of 3.9 percent, up from a mere 1.4 percent for the period 1973 to 1979. Despite this increase in its growth rate, the United States still lags behind Japan, Britain, and France in productivity growth.[67] Some people question whether there are upper limits to productivity. Significantly higher rates of productivity growth may not be possible, as there may be physical limits to people and machines.

Technology and Productivity

It is clear that one of the major strategies of U.S. firms for counteracting Japanese productivity levels is to automate, to become more advanced technologi-

AT WESTINGHOUSE:
One of the major keys to Westinghouse's future is productivity gains. Its Productivity and Quality Center has made excellent progress in moving the company forward. Chairman Marous and President Lego believe that the future rides on the ability of the company to increase its profits partly, if not largely, through increases in productivity both in the factory and in the office. The actions taken at its Sumter, South Carolina, plant indicate the kinds of actions that Westinghouse will continue to take in the future.

Allen-Bradley's Factory of the Future

The Allen-Bradley Corporation's specialty is industrial controls. In the mid-1980s, it was faced with increasing levels of competition from Europe and Japan, especially in its electric motor control business. Because contactors and relays are major components in these controls, and European and Japanese models cost less and were smaller, the company had to make the decision either to protect its core electric motor control business by making European style contactors and relays, or miss out on the growing market and possibly lose some of its core business.

The company first explored the possibility of offshore manufacturing. However, after adjusting for the additional costs of nonautomated factories in order to hire low-cost labor—at $1 an hour in Mexico—it determined that total costs of supporting an individual foreign laborer would be an additional $12 per hour, for a total of $13 per hour, $2 short of the $15 cost of hiring in Milwaukee. The company therefore decided to build the most modern CIM line possible. They invested $15 million and now have what is considered to be the most advanced factory in the United States, possibly in the world. The computer analyzes the various orders, the various materials requirements, and determines the schedule for each day. It then informs the totally robotized CIM assembly line on what is to be produced and when and where it is to be shipped, the materials being employed, and from where the materials are to be drawn. Bar coding allows the computer to keep track of the production process, as all inputs, outputs, and process areas are bar coded. The line is so sophisticated it can make different products of different sized lots, even down to a single unit, at assembly line speeds.

Admittedly, manufacturing contactors and relays is not as complex as manufacturing automobiles or other highly sophisticated and numerous subassembly type products, but the subassemblies could be manufactured and put together in a similar way, using the same principles. Many other manufacturers have studied the Allen-Bradley plant and are intending to use similar technological applications in their plants.

SOURCE: John S. DeMott, "American Scene: In Old Milwaukee: Tomorrow's Factory Today," *Time* (June 16, 1986), pp. 66–67; and Gene Bylinski, "Breakthrough in Automating the Assembly Line," *Fortune* (May 26, 1986), pp. 64–66.

cally.[68] While technology offers a great deal of promise for manufacturing, it is not clear that it offers the same promise for services. Services productivity output for all measurements shows clearly that there has been virtually no gain in services productivity since 1980, but there has been a dramatic gain in output per hour in manufacturing, for the reasons previously mentioned.[69] Although there are some indications that technology, such as office automation, does pay off for services, the gains have not been impressive. The acquisition of technology must be aimed at a very specific goal, and where it has and where results are constantly monitored, there have been productivity gains.[70] For example, the Japanese have begun to move forward, as have others in automating software development, and these actions have produced positive results.[71]

This is the control room in Allen Bradley's factory of the future. Notice how the worker's role has changed from one of physical to one of mental labor. (SOURCE © Mark Jenkinson)

Operations Management as Problem Solving

Operations management is problem solving. Because this is an overview chapter, the details inherent in each of the problems identified are not presented. That is, the problems managers must solve have been presented without a detailed problem-solving model. Texts on operations management discuss issues such as recognizing and identifying problems and generating alternatives for these kinds of operations problems.

The Management Challenges Identified

1. Global competition
2. Increased levels of competition
3. Changing customer needs
4. Quality

Some Solutions Noted in the Chapter

1. Focusing on production strategy
2. Cross-functional design teams
3. Increased usage of technology, CIM
4. Employee participation in related decision making
5. Flexible manufacturing
6. Robust design, design to manufacture
7. Changing distribution systems
8. Adaptation of Japanese production and management systems and JIT

Summary

1. Operations management in manufacturing and service industries involves essentially the same three processes: inputs, transformation, and outputs. One of the primary differences between the two is that in service organizations the primary input is labor, whereas in manufacturing there may also be raw materials and subcomponent parts. The transformation processes are distinctly different, as the figures and tables in the chapter show.

2. Operations management has become critical in recent years because of foreign competition, principally from the Japanese and other countries on the Pacific rim, but also from other areas of the world. U.S. and Canadian firms have had to improve their operations management skills and processes to remain competitive. As the business environment has become more global, the ability to compete globally has become more critical.

3a. Strategic operations decisions include decisions concerning products, processes, and facilities. More specifically, these include positioning the operations system; focusing the factory's; product/service design and process planning; allocating resources to strategic alternatives; and determining facility capacity location and layout, production technology, and quality.

b. Tactical operations decisions are those intermediate decisions between strategic decisions and operating decisions. They include decisions about production planning systems, independent demand inventory systems, resource requirement planning systems, scheduling shop floor planning and control, and materials management and purchasing.

c. Operational level operations management decisions are related to workers and their productivity; implementation of quality control; planning control for each project; and maintenance management and reliability.

4. Operations is a strategic weapon because it can be used to provide products with the characteristics that will make them competitive in the marketplace. Most recently, these have focused on low cost and high quality.

5. The globalization of business has affected operations functioning significantly, especially in the United States and Canada. Protected home markets and pent-up demand after World War II were sufficient to sustain these economies throughout the mid-1970s, and interest in the operations function dwindled as we moved toward a service economy. The globalization of business and the penetration of U.S. markets by foreign competitors has focused attention on the operations function.

6. The Japanese have been successful in operations management for a number of reasons. Among them are their attention to quality and low-cost participation in decisions by their workers, flexibility, simplification, JIT inventory, and quality circles.

7. Inventory has traditionally been used to build in buffer zones for problems in the manufacturing process—when a problem occurred, inventories at various stages could be used to continue manufacturing while the problem at some other stage was fixed. But JIT inventory systems allow no buffer zones. The manufacturing process itself must be perfect. This helps in increasing quality and cutting costs.

8. One of the two key reasons the Japanese have been so successful is that they have provided a high-quality product, something most American companies in most industries had not been doing. Thus, the Japanese were able to penetrate American markets rapidly and take a significant amount of business away from many U.S. and Canadian firms, in many cases driving those firms out of business.

9. The factory of the future will be based on CIM incorporating computer aided design, computer aided manufacturing, flexible manufacturing systems, and automated storage and retrieval systems.

10. Productivity can be improved in two principal ways: by using more technology and by better using human resources.

Thinking About Management

1. Examine a major U.S. manufacturing company for its actions to become more competitive on a global basis.
2. Discuss how quality can be better obtained in manufacturing and service companies.
3. Describe the factors leading to Japanese firms' manufacturing success.
4. Discuss examples of how operations differ for various types of service and manufacturing firms.
5. Discuss the interrelationships between strategic, tactical, and operational level operations management decisions.
6. Describe the relationships between marketing strategies and operations strategies.
7. Describe the importance of product simplification to competitiveness.
8. Review the major facility location factors.
9. How does management of human resources affect operations management success?
10. Relate quality strategy to everyday quality management.

Quality Control at Spectrum Control, Inc.

Spectrum Control, Inc., is headquartered in Pennsylvania. It was founded in 1968 by Thomas L. Venable, Glen L. Warnshuis, and John R. Lane, three engineers who had met when they were employed with Erie Technological Products, Inc. Between 1968 and 1985, the company grew from a $300,000 start-up to a $22 million public company. It had four manufacturing plants and some 1,500 customers, including IBM and Hewlett-Packard. It was an extremely successful company with aftertax returns of about 10 percent on sales.

In the early days of the company, quality was not an issue. Warnshuis designed and built their principal products and oversaw manufacturing. But as the company grew, this hands-on approach to quality fell by the wayside. It was replaced by the more traditional, standard quality-control techniques, which indicated when there were acceptable quality levels. Control charts were used to make certain that the items shipped had acceptable levels of quality, with only a certain amount of defects. Statistical sampling was the basis for their control charts.

Slowly, however, Spectrum's market began to change. A Japanese company, Marata Manufacturing Company, purchased Erie, the three founders' former employer and a major competitor for Spectrum. Soon Spectrum's customers, including Hewlett-Packard and IBM, began to indicate that they wanted more quality in their products. The implication was, decrease the number of defects or lose your business to your Japanese competitor.

DISCUSSION QUESTIONS

1. Formulate a quality strategy for this company, indicating key components.
2. What type of cultural changes will be necessary? How do you handle those?
3. Why didn't management anticipate demands for better quality?

SOURCE: Craig R. Waters, "Quality Begins at Home," *Inc.* (August, 1985), pp. 68–71.

MANAGERS AT WORK

Groups May Be the Answer

Martin Marietta's plant in Orlando, Florida, had landed major defense contracts through expert salesmanship. But as the company began to build the products, it discovered that it was not manufacturing as efficiently as it would have liked. Top operations managers, spearheaded by the efforts of Charles Hardin and Bob Jones, set out to determine ways in which to improve productivity.

Charles Hardin had been exposed to the quality circle concept in his MBA classes. He knew the value of such groups, but culture at Martin Marietta was too authoritarian to allow participative quality circles. Furthermore, the company wanted a solution that would work primarily to raise the levels of efficiency in production. Charles Hardin, Bob Jones, and others set out to examine all alternatives, but with the goal in mind of somehow using groups to improve productivity. Some 1,500 operations employees would be involved in any solution they derived.

DISCUSSION QUESTIONS

1. Design a group situation that would fit the needs of Martin Marietta.
2. What types of implementation problems would you foresee, given the authoritarian culture described?

Deming's 14 Points

Test your understanding of Deming's fourteen points by using the college educational process as the illustration. The raw materials are entering students, knowledge, knowledge dissemination technology. The operative employees are professors, for the purpose of this exercise. The end product is the student who has completed an educational process, such as a course. For example, Deming's third point deals with building quality into the product in the first place, as opposed to testing at the end of the process. How could this be accomplished in the educational setting? Is this a matter of education or motivation? Perform a similar analysis of all fourteen points, either as individuals, or in small groups as assigned by your professor. This exercise will help you see how to apply the fourteen points, not just in manufacturing, but in service industries, as well.

CHAPTER TWENTY-ONE

Managing in an Ever-Changing Global Environment

CHAPTER OBJECTIVES

By the time you complete studying this chapter you should be able to

1. Describe what is meant by the globalization of business and give some examples of its occurrence.

2. Identify the triad of key markets and enumerate important factors for each.

3. Discuss the Japanese as competitors.

4. Review the strengths of the Asian Four Tigers from the Pacific rim.

5. Describe what will happen in Europe in 1992 and its possible impact on North American firms.

6. Discuss the implications of East-West integration.

7. Describe how managers should manage in a global environment, identifying the varying impacts of the four environmental forces: economic, political/legal, sociocultural, and technological.

8. Describe the difficulty involved in applying management practices used in one country to management situations in another country.

9. Identify the various stages of strategic activities in global businesses.

10. Describe typical macro organizational structures for global corporations.

11. Describe leadership in global situations.

12. Describe control in the global situation.

13. Identify the unique problems in managing multinational corporations.

CHAPTER OUTLINE

The Globalization of Business
The Triad of Key Markets
  Japan
  Europe—Europe 1992, East-West Economic Integration
  North America
Management and the Global Environment
  The Four Environmental Factors and the Global Environment
  Impacts of the Four Factors on Management Functions
  Impacts on Economic Functions
  A Three-Dimensional View of Managing in Multidomestic and Global Situations
Applying Management Practices Abroad
  Applying Japanese Management Practices Abroad
Unique Problems for Multinational Corporations
  Political Instability
  Terrorism
  Host Government Conflicts
  Human Rights
  Monetary Translations
The Management Challenges Identified
Some Solutions Noted in the Chapter

GE Appliance Moves to Become
a Global Competitor

In 1988 General Electric had $40 billion in sales, about $5 billion of it coming from its major appliance business. While GE has a major European presence in aircraft engines, plastics and mechnical diagnostics, it has never been a major player in Europe in major appliances since the 1960s, when it had a small Italian appliance manufacturing operation. Until recently, GE Chairman John F. Welch, Jr., saw no urgent need to get back on the continent in major appliances. But the events of recent years, and movement toward the unification of Europe into one true common market in 1992, have made Welch and his strategists aware of the necessity for a presence in major appliances in Europe. Within the past year, GE's appliance competitors, Whirlpool Corporation and Maytag Corporation, have both gone global with strategic alliances that would give them more power to compete. In addition, Stockholm-based Electrolux, the world's largest manufacturer of home appliances with sales of over $10 billion, has continued to expand globally.

While Welch and his staff were not concerned about a "fortress Europe" as a consequence of 1992, the possibility existed that Europeans could pass laws to keep Americans and others out of their markets. Because of the high stakes and the high costs involved in entering the European market, Welch, and others, in particular Lawrence Bossidy, GE's vice-chairman, sensed an urgency to create alliances before the better alternatives were gobbled up by others. Bossidy, in a speech to the Strategic Management Society in Boston in October 1987, had observed that the major partnerships for most of the rest of the century would be determined in the next few years, alluding to the globalization efforts and 1992.

Therefore, in mid-January 1989, GE acquired for $575 million a 50 percent ownership in Britain's General Electric Company,

PLC (GEC's profitable $800-million-a-year European appliance business). They also entered into another joint venture covering both parties' European electrical distribution and control business. No other alliances between the two companies were struck. The deal helped solve pressing problems for both parties: global competitiveness in appliances for GE and a takeover threat from Plessey Company for GEC—GE served as a kind of white knight in helping GEC overcome that threat. GE's search for an alliance had not been easy. It had attempted earlier to acquire part of Netherland's Phillips appliance business, but Phillips eventually sold it to Whirlpool. GEC's president, Lord Arnold Weinstock, had earlier looked for other partners, including the West German firm Siemens.

Some $100 million in GE sales and $1 billion in GEC sales are covered by the agreement. GEC will manage the appliance business, at least in the early stages of the alliance while GE will manage the electrical distribution and control business. The partners are jointly looking for additional acquisition candidates, especially major appliance businesses. Anticipating a shakeout in the industry in Europe, the GE-GEC alliance wants to acquire the best of the smaller firms, in order to have a significant European presence.

GE's action in the appliance industry is just part of an overall GE program to have a major presence in Europe. For example, it spent $2.3 billion in 1987, to acquire Borg-Warner's world-wide chemical operations, and in December 1988 announced that it would build a $2.5 billion Spanish plastics plant in Spain.

SOURCE: James R. Norman, "Why GE Took a European Bride," *Business Week* (January 30, 1989); Lawrence H. Bossidy, address to the Strategic Management Society, Boston (October 13, 1987); "Reshaping Europe: 1992 and Beyond," *Business Week* (December 12, 1988), p. 55; and Frederick H. Katayama, "GE and GEC," *Fortune* (February 13, 1989), p. 8.

Clearly, Japan has replaced the United States as the world's financial leader.

R. Taggart Murphy
Chase Manhattan Asia Limited

Our government has done a very poor job of bilateral negotiation on trade. We've got to get Japan to accept reciprocity.

Edward Hennessy, Jr., CEO
Allied-Signode Corporation

The single most significant global economic event since the formation of OPEC has already begun to occur and will culminate in 1992 when the twelve nations of the European Economic Community (EEC) become one market. The ramifications of this event for companies in countries all around the world, but especially for United States, Canadian, and Japanese firms, are significant and could even prove to be tumultuous. Large companies such as General Electric recognize the need to become global players. To do so, they are forming alliances with European firms, to be positioned for the events of 1992 and beyond. Firms such as IBM and Ford are already entrenched in Europe but are continuing to position themselves for the events of 1992. Ford, for example, plans to spend $7.5 billion in Europe between 1989 and 1994, to continue its modernization program.[1] Other firms, such as AT&T, are following GE's lead in establishing alliances.[2]

CFM International is a 50/50 joint venture between General Electric of the United States and SNECMA of France. This worker is helping to manufacture jet engines in Evendale, Ohio. (Courtesy General Electric Company)

But Europe in 1992 is only one part, albeit a a major part, of the global business story. The potential for East-West economic integration, begun in 1989, the reunification of Germany, the still hoped-for resurgence of capitalism in China, and the emergence of Brazil as a major economic entity are but a few of the events changing management on a global basis. For example, over 80 percent of Coca-Cola Company's 1989 profits came from the profit contributions of its foreign subsidiary, with more profit being made in Japan than in the United States.[3] And the Japanese have for years been successfully penetrating U.S. markets in automobiles, electronics, steel, and other manufactured goods. Thousands of Americans daily purchase shoes from Reebok, a British company that manufactures in Korea. The British annually purchase thousands of automobiles from an American company, Ford, that have been assembled in England with parts manufactured in thirteen different European countries. Finally, many U.S. firms have moved some of their manufacturing facilities to Mexico in order to employ cheap labor. This globalization of business is having a significant impact on the practice of management. This chapter addresses the key issues of how management is changing and will have to change to adapt to this changing situation.

The Globalization of Business

A "brave new world" is emerging in which there will be almost borderless trade, particularly with Eastern and Western Europe. Hybrid products lacking clear nationality will emerge. Joint ventures, mergers, acquisitions, and other forms of alliances will characterize the business world in the future. Ford Motor Company's new compact car, the Probe, was designed in Detroit, engineered in Hiroshima by equity partner Mazda, and assembled in Michigan. Similarly, Mitsubishi and Chrysler jointly produced two versions of an almost identical car, the Mitsubishi Eclipse and the Plymouth Laser, engineered and manufactured in the United States. Hewlett-Packard and Canada's Northern Telecom pooled their know-how to tap the enormous new market for corporation information systems. A leather processing subsidiary of Tata, the Indian conglomerate, is teaming up with France-based TFR to compete with Italians in marketing upscale leather goods. And Caterpillar and Mitsubishi are teaming up to make giant earth movers.[4]

Thomas J. Peters and John Naisbitt have both identified the move toward global business as one of the ten key changes of the present and the near future.[5] Naisbitt sees the change occurring as one from national to global business. Peters sees it as one in which U.S. firms are getting serious about being global competitors. The change Peters sees is that U.S. firms won't just take products designed and manufactured in the U.S. and sell them abroad, but rather will create new markets and new products abroad and will finance and manufacture them there. He feels it is especially important for CEOs to have international experience and to learn to speak languages other than English. The *Wall Street Journal*, in describing the CEO of the next century, makes it clear that he or she will be experienced abroad and may very well be someone from abroad.[6]

CHANGES IN GLOBAL BUSINESS
A fundamental change is occurring in the nature of business. Firms are moving from the point where they accept the possibility of international opportunities and threats, to a point where they recognize that global considerations must be part of the overall game plan. The fundamentals of the game are also changing.

A key change is that non-U.S.-based firms are gaining more relative power. For example, nine of the world's ten largest banks are Japanese, as shown in Table 21.1. In 1980 only one of the world's ten largest banks was Japanese.[7] Whether measured by the size of deposits or assets, only one U.S. bank made it into the top twenty-five in 1988—Citicorp. Japanese-owned banks supplied more than 20 percent of all credit granted in the state of California in 1988.[8] In 1988 nine of the world's twenty-five largest industrial companies were American, eleven European, four Japanese, and one Korean.[9] In 1980 only five of the fifty largest industrial companies were Japanese; none were Korean. Table 21.2 shows the twenty-five largest industrial corporations in 1988.

Table 21.1 World's 25 Largest Banks, 1988

Rank		Headquarters	Assets	Deposits
1988			$ Million	$ Million
1	Dai-Ichi Kangyo Bank	Tokyo	379,322.8	283,185.4
2	Sumitomo Bank	Osaka	363,232.6	267,995.2
3	Fuji Bank	Tokyo	360,529.8	258,574.7
4	Mitsubishi Bank	Tokyo	348,999.0	251,146.9
5	Sanwa Bank	Osaka	330,705.4	246,625.5
6	Industrial Bank of Japan	Tokyo	272,918.3	216,615.9
7	Norinchukin Bank	Tokyo	235,944.3	214,256.7
8	Tokai Bank	Nagoya	227,644.3	172,072.5
9	Mitsui Bank	Tokyo	211,358.6	152,698.9
10	Crédit Agricole	Paris	210,566.3	167,103.5
11	Mitsubishi Trust & Banking	Tokyo	208,341.7	178,030.5
12	Citicorp	New York	207,666.0	124,072.0
13	Banque Nationale de Paris	Paris	196,922.3	169,887.1
14	Barclays Bank	London	189,250.5	157,401.0
15	Bank of Tokyo	Tokyo	185,428.8	129,368.4
16	Long-Term Credit Bank of Japan	Tokyo	184,752.9	147,167.6
17	Sumitomo Trust & Banking	Osaka	182,529.1	162,201.0
18	Crédit Lyonnais	Paris	178,848.1	153,745.4
19	National Westminster Bank	London	178,394.1	153,688.1
20	Taiyo Kobe Bank	Kobe	175,470.4	131,757.8
21	Mitsui Trust & Banking	Tokyo	174,943.5	151,352.7
22	Deutsche Bank	Frankfurt	172,142.5	154,824.6
23	Yasuda Trust & Banking	Tokyo	167,125.4	126,845.0
24	Société Générale	Paris	155,457.3	134,494.6
25	Daiwa Bank	Osaka	150,733.7	76,790.4

SOURCE: Adapted from "The World's Biggest Commercial Banks," *Fortune* (July 31, 1989), p. 286. © 1989 The Time Inc. Magazine Company. All rights reserved.

The United States ran foreign trade deficits of $100 billion a year or greater for five consecutive years, 1984–1988 ($155 billion in 1987).[10] Much of this trade deficit occurred with Japan and other Pacific rim countries. As a consequence of these deficits, Japanese banks have become large and powerful. These deficits are also one of the reasons that the Japanese have a tremendous ability to affect the world's capital markets. Correlated with this, the United States went from the world's largest lending nation in 1980, with a surplus of $106 billion, to the world's largest debtor nation in a period of fewer than ten years, with a debt of $368 billion in 1987.[11] Consequently, Japanese banks wield great

Table 21.2 World's 25 Biggest Industrial Corporations in 1988

Rank 1988	Rank '87	Company	Headquarters	Industry	Sales $ Millions	Profits $ Millions
1	1	General Motors	Detroit	Motor Vehicles	121,085.4	4,856.3
2	4	Ford Motor	Dearborn, Mich.	Motor Vehicles	92,445.6	5,300.2
3	3	Exxon	New York	Petroleum Refining	79,557.0	5,260.0
4	2	Royal Dutch/Shell Group	London/The Hague	Petroleum Refining	78,381.1	5,238.7
5	5	International Business Machines	Armonk, N.Y.	Computers	59,681.0	5,806.0
6	8	Toyota Motor	Toyota City (Japan)	Motor Vehicles	50,789.9	2,314.6
7	10	General Electric	Fairfield, Conn.	Electronics	49,414.0	3,386.0
8	6	Mobil	New York	Petroleum Refining	48,198.0	2,087.0
9	7	British Petroleum	London	Petroleum Refining	46,174.0	2,155.3
10	9	IRI	Rome	Metals	45,521.5	921.9
11	11	Daimler-Benz	Stuttgart	Motor Vehicles	41,817.9	953.1
12	16	Hitachi	Tokyo	Electronics	41,330.7	989.0
13	21	Chrysler	Highland Park, Mich.	Motor Vehicles	35,472.7	1,050.2
14	18	Siemens	Munich	Electronics	34,129.4	757.0
15	17	Fiat	Turin	Motor Vehicles	34,039.3	2,324.7
16	19	Matsushita Electric Industrial	Osaka	Electronics	33,922.5	1,177.2
17	15	Volkswagen	Wolfsburg (W. Ger.)	Motor Vehicles	33,696.2	420.1
18	12	Texaco	White Plains, N.Y.	Petroleum Refining	33,544.0	1,304.0
19	14	E.I. DuPont de Nemours	Wilmington, Del.	Chemicals	32,514.0	2,190.0
20	20	Unilever	London/Rotterdam	Food	30,488.2	1,485.6
21	24	Nissan Motor	Tokyo	Motor Vehicles	29,097.1	463.0
22	22	Philips' Gloeilampen- fabrieken	Eindhoven (Netherlands)	Electronics	28,370.5	477.1
23	27	Nestlé	Vevey (Switzerland)	Food	27,803.0	1,392.7
24	32	Samsung	Seoul	Electronics	27,386.1	464.3
25	25	Renault	Paris	Motor Vehicles	27,109.7	1,496.7

■ U.S. ■ Europe ■ Asia ■ Latin America ■ Middle East • Not On Last Year's List

SOURCE: "The World's Biggest Industrial Corporations," *Fortune* (July 31, 1989), p. 282.

power to influence both debt structure and American firms' capability to expand because they hold much of that debt.[12]

European firms (members of the EEC) in 1992 will have a home market of 320 million people. U.S. firms will possess a home market of 240 million, and Japanese firms will have a home market of 120 million people. For the first time in history, European firms will have a consumer base large enough to enable them to be true global competitors.

There is also an international debt crisis, unfortunately tending to affect American banks more than any others. U.S. banks hold nearly $50 billion in potentially bad foreign loans.[13] It is also becoming clear that the United States' leadership role in the world, especially in the world of business, is being challenged.[14] Yet, for all its difficulties, it is likely to retain its overall global leadership based on its strengths, principally its consumer base and its military power. However, with the world changing so rapidly and with the role of military power diminishing so rapidly, it is difficult to tell what will happen in a few years in the global situation.[15]

The Triad of Key Markets

Kenichi Ohmae, senior partner for the consulting firm McKinsey & Company in Tokyo, has identified a triad of key global business markets: Japan, Europe, and North America.[16] Any corporate player on a global basis must be able to compete in each of those markets. Table 21.3 indicates important financial dimensions of the members of this triad, as well as information on the Soviet Union and China. The following sections examine each of the major players in the triad.

Table 21.3 A Comparison of Superpower Contenders*

	United States	Soviet Union	Japan	European Community	China
Population (in millions)	243.8	284.0	122.0	323.6	1,074.0
GNP (in billions of 1987 U.S. dollars*)	$4,436.1	$2,375.0	$1,607.7	$3,782.0	$293.5
Per capita GNP (1987 U.S. dollars†)	$18,200	$8,360	$13,180	$11,690	$270
GNP Growth Rate 1981–85 (annual average)	3.0%	1.8%	3.9%	1.5%	9.2%
1987	2.9%	0.5%	4.2%	2.9%	9.4%
Inflation (change in consumer prices)	3.7%	−0.9%	0.1%	3.1%	9.2%
Total Labor Force (in millions)	121.6	154.8	60.3	143.0	512.8
Agricultural	3.4	33.9	4.6	11.9	313.1
Nonagricultural	118.2	120.9	55.7	131.1	199.7
Unemployment rate	6.1%	N.A.	2.8%	11.0%	N.A.
Foreign Trade Exports (in billions of U.S. dollars)	$250.4	$107.7	$213.2	$953.5††	$44.9
Imports (in billions of U.S. dollars)	$424.1	$96.0	$150.8	$955.1**	$40.2
Balance (in billions of U.S. dollars)	−$173.7	$11.7	$80.4	−$1.6	$4.7
Energy Consumption (in billions of barrels of oil equivalent per capita)	55.6	37.3	22.7	24.4	4.8
Military Active armed forces	2,163,200	5,096,000	245,000	2,483,400	3,200,000
Ready reserves	1,637,900	6,217,000	46,000	4,565,800	1,200,000
Defense expenditures Share of GNP	6.5%	15–25%	1.6%	3.3%	4–5%

SOURCE: Taken from Karen Elliott House, "The 90s and Beyond: For All Its Difficulties, the U.S. Stands to Retain Its Global Leadership," *Wall Street Journal,* January 23, 1989, p. A10. Reprinted by permission of *Wall Street Journal,* © 1989 Dow Jones & Company, Inc. All Rights Reserved Worldwide.
*The data presented here, with a few exceptions, are for 1987, the latest year for which comparable data are available for all countries.
†Data were converted at U.S. purchasing power equivalents.
N.A. = Not available
**Data include trade among EEC members.

Japan

To use an analogy from the Western world, the Japanese economy has proven to be a phoenix, rising from the ashes of World War II to unparalleled heights. The following paragraphs discuss what makes the Japanese so successful and then review some of the changes affecting their potential for continued success.

WHAT MAKES JAPANESE FIRMS SUCCESSFUL

The official view of the Keidanren, the powerful federation of Japanese businesses, is that Japanese success results from a complex interaction of macro and micro variables involving government, capital, labor, and technology, as shown in Table 21.4. Items 3 and 4 in the exhibit—macro and micro labor factors—are essentially the same factors William G. Ouchi identified in his research on the relationship of Japanese management practice to Japanese success.[17] In addition, factors such as a highly educated work force, government policy, and a high savings rate are important. A survey of Japanese business executives indicated that the simple majority of them believe cultural factors to be the predominant cause of Japanese business success.[18] U.S. experts attribute much of Japan's success to restrictive trade barriers against foreign products and services.[19]

At the firm level, the individual Japanese corporation attempts to establish a "winner's competitive cycle."[20] The cycle begins with growth: Japanese companies believe they must grow faster than their competitors; they must increase their market share so that their volume of business will increase at a greater

Table 21.4 Factors Contributing to the Success of Japanese Economy

1. Macro Capital Factors:
   - high savings rate
   - effective industrial financing through the banking system
   - industrial grouping, such as the large trading companies
   - government industrial policy

2. Micro Capital Factors:
   - modern management: ownership and management are separated
   - middle and long-term gains, emphasizing the long-term view
   - capital investment by individual corporations
   - fund raising made easy through excellent access to sources

3. Macro Labor Factors:
   - high educational levels of the workforce
   - flexible manpower supply moving from declining to growth industries
   - good labor-management cooperation; only 32% unionized
   - wages are kept within productivity

4. Micro Labor Factors:
   - an employment system characterized by three elements: (1) life-time employment, (2) promotion system based on seniority, to which wages are tied, and (3) incentives for training employees
   - deciding by consensus, popularly called "bottom-up management"
   - labor transfers within the company: given employment security, employees are most willing to move

5. Macro Technology Factors:
   - Japan has aggressively imported overseas technology, and integrated and improved that technology
   - development of production technology
   - effective research and development that, while low, is helped by the government's implementation of policy

6. Micro Technology Factors:
   - TQC—total quality control system
   - workers' suggestions
   - parts availability through small business
   - highly competitive technologically; i.e., keeping abreast of and using new technology

SOURCE: Adapted from Masaya Miyoshi, managing director, Kendron, Tokyo, as printed in Norman Coates, "Determinants of Japan's Business Success: Some Japanese Executives' Views," *Academy of Management Executive* (January 1988), p. 70.

rate than their competitors. This in turn depends on a higher rate of investment, which can take many forms, including price cutting, capacity expansion, advertising, and product development.

The individual Japanese firm carries out this strategy within the framework suggested. Failure to do so leads ultimately to failure in the Japanese system.

CHANGES IN THE JAPANESE SUCCESS FORMULA

As with virtually every economy that has progressed from one of subsistence to one of success, the underlying needs and values of the individuals in that economy eventually change. While it seems clear that by the year 2000 the Japanese will probably be second only to the United States in overall economic power, it is uncertain how Japan intends to reach that level of economic performance. A national consensus is no longer evident.[21] Furthermore, a number of fundamental, underlying cultural as well as economic and historical factors seem to be leading to problems for the Japanese.[22]

The Japanese work ethic appears to be eroding, especially among younger Japanese. That generation is becoming restless, more westernized, and less willing to work long, hard hours. These *shinjinrui,* as Japanese young people are known, are indeed "new human beings"—the term's literal translation—who prefer playing to working.

The role of women in Japan is changing slowly but surely, to allow them a greater participation in the economic system.[23]

The Japanese educational system is viewed as too rigid for the twenty-first century. More innovation will be needed to be competitive, and the Japanese educational system stifles creativity. Japan's development as one of the world's financial capitals is threatened by overregulation by the Japanese government.

Japan has been a great imitator but is not yet a great inventor, a skill that may be necessary for the future, as Western countries are not likely to continue to give them technology as they have in the past.[24] Unemployment will rise as the use of technology increases.

Japan will be the target of many international firms. Those on the Pacific rim and in other developing areas will have distinct labor cost advantages.[25] The price the Japanese pay for their economic success has been horrendous, in terms of family life and personal sacrifice. Alcoholism, emotional breakdowns, and suicide are increasing, and wives are growing more resentful of their executive spouses' devotion to work.[26] Japan's population is aging, and its work force is decreasing in size. The aging work force will soon turn into social security recipients and occupants of nursing homes, using up huge portions of the GNP.

Employee loyalty is waning, as employees begins to switch firms for better work and pay.[27]

The Japanese have some internal political problems that lead to "pork barrel" distributions of money and political decisions, not unlike those sometimes experienced in the United States.

Despite its faults and challenges, the Japanese are still the dominant financial power in the world and could eventually replace the United States as the number one economic power.

Japan is building a new economic power base across Asia and the Pacific. It is moving rapidly ahead in Thailand, the Philippines, Indonesia, Malaysia, and China and is beginning to work closely to develop ties in Taiwan, Korea, Singapore, and Hong Kong. It seems certain that Japan will replace the United States as the most powerful economic influence in Asia.[28] Furthermore, because there has been little reduction in the trade deficit of the United States, it is likely that Japan's financial strength, relative to others in the world, will continue to grow. Finally, the Japanese are already beginning to move to dominate key

These *shinjinrui* have adopted a life style and values very different from those of their parents and of the generation of Japanese that has made Japan so economically successful. (SOURCE © Patrick Frilet/SIPA Press)

These bicycles are being sold in a shop in New Jersey, but they were manufactured in Taiwan. (SOURCE © Ken Kerbs)

science technologies for the twenty-first century—super conductivity, biotechnology, and microelectronics—and are taking great pains to improve their research capability.[29]

ASIA'S FOUR TIGERS
South Korea, Taiwan, Hong Kong, and Singapore—especially South Korea and Taiwan—have been rewarded for their hard work, competitive spirit, and free enterprise economy with increasing prosperity. Unfortunately for the United States, these Four Tigers also accounted for more than 22 percent of the 1987 trade deficit. Despite increasing American pressure, the Four Tigers have resisted attempts to open up trade barriers. Taiwan is the least resistant and has a "buy American" policy that seems to be working, favoring U.S. companies for major purchases and projects. For example, Japanese companies are not being allowed to bid on Taipei's new subway but American firms are. Hong Kong and Singapore have pegged their currencies to the American dollar, and hence we will have continuing deficits with those countries. Finally, South Korea has essentially balked at opening its borders to U.S. firms and is not offering much hope for compromise.[30] Furthermore, in 1999 Hong Kong will revert to Chinese rule, and this will have a substantial impact on its future.

Europe—Europe 1992, East-West Economic Integration

Europe, the second member of the Triad, is potentially the most economically significant, depending on the outcome of the 1992 Common Market landmark event and the potential for East-West economic integration that began in 1989.

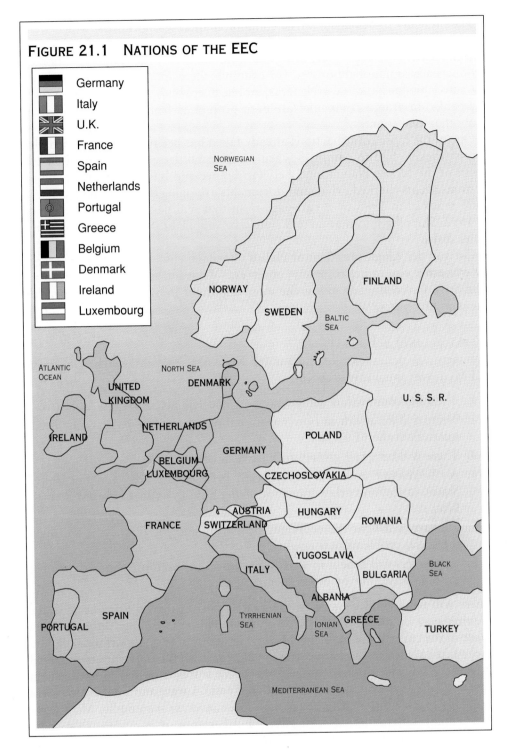

FIGURE 21.1   NATIONS OF THE EEC

Legend:
- Germany
- Italy
- U.K.
- France
- Spain
- Netherlands
- Portugal
- Greece
- Belgium
- Denmark
- Ireland
- Luxembourg

Map labels: NORWEGIAN SEA, NORWAY, SWEDEN, FINLAND, BALTIC SEA, ATLANTIC OCEAN, NORTH SEA, DENMARK, U.S.S.R., UNITED KINGDOM, IRELAND, NETHERLANDS, POLAND, GERMANY, BELGIUM, LUXEMBOURG, CZECHOSLOVAKIA, AUSTRIA, HUNGARY, ROMANIA, FRANCE, SWITZERLAND, YUGOSLAVIA, ITALY, BULGARIA, BLACK SEA, ALBANIA, TYRRHENIAN SEA, IONIAN SEA, GREECE, TURKEY, SPAIN, PORTUGAL, MEDITERRANEAN SEA

EUROPE 1992

This integrated market concept for firms in the EEC extends to much of the rest of Europe, as well. Firms in Scandinavian countries—such as Skopbank, in Finland—are planning strategies to ensure their preparedness.[31] This integration of markets for the first time gives European firms the ability to compete on a global basis with a home-sized market large enough to test a product with which it can then go global. It will help to eliminate, but not totally eliminate, the need for specialized products for various regions of Europe and make commerce and industry much easier to conduct. The EEC countries are shown in Figure 21.1.

AT GE: *The globalization of business caused GE to form an alliance with GEC. GE did not fear a "fortress" Europe but wanted to be positioned to take advantage of 1992 opportunities, and meet the challenge of its global competitors.*

The difficulty of achieving a true common market wasn't tariffs, which were abolished years ago, but rather eliminating the numerous local regulations that encumber virtually every facet of business, but especially the standardization of products across national borders. For example, there are no common standards for auto emissions, radio wavelengths, mobile telephones, or capitalization rules for banks. Insurance companies are even prohibited from selling insurance in more than one country.[32]

One of the most critical actions already taken has been to replace the lengthy forms truckers had to complete when crossing borders. Trucks would sit for hours at the Monte Blanc tunnel between France and Italy, for example, while customs agents checked exhaustive documents averaging thirty-five pages. These were replaced in 1988 by a two-page form that will be abandoned altogether in 1992. Shipping information will simply be supplied to governments on computer disks.

Cor van der Klugt, president of Philips Gloeilampenfabrieken, Europe's largest consumer electronics company, observes, "What Europe is doing is gigantic. The drive for economic unity is the most important thing that will happen for the next fifty years."[33]

WHAT IS LIKELY TO HAPPEN

Lammert deVries, senior consultant for Klynvold, Peat, Marwick, Gourdeler (KPMG), sees this likely scenario:

1. The EEC commission will get support and will achieve major objectives.
2. There will be a shift in power from national ministries to Brussels (headquarters of the EEC).
3. There will be a fast growth of European companies.
4. An "economic cold war" may begin between the EEC and the United States, Japan, and other countries, as the EEC attempts to protest its markets.
5. Industry will fight the economic problems, and the politicians will fight the social problems that result.
6. Consumers will benefit in some ways (lower prices, more choices) and lose in some ways (maybe more unemployment).[34]

There will be obvious changes in the strategies of European firms because the requirements of success in this new environment will be quite different from those in the current environment. Marketing will be a very important skill, and those firms skilled in marketing may be able to seize the opportunities created by 1992 in advance of their competitors. There will be a tremendous change in cost structures and widespread efforts to cut costs. Larger and smaller firms will probably be able to compete better than those stuck in the middle. Most firms will employ differentiation strategies.[35] Furthermore, it is evident that some countries will obtain advantages due to such factors as lower wage rates. Spain and southern Italy are especially likely to benefit from these.

The responses to 1992 will vary by country. The West Germans, for example, have not been particularly receptive to mergers, acquisitions, and alliances, but the Dutch have.[36] It is anticipated that Spain, Portugal, southern France, Italy, and Greece will become a European "sunbelt," and, just as in the United States, the population will move south. The cultural problems associated with European integration will be far greater than those experienced in the United States. It is highly likely that one currency may evolve. There most assuredly will be a period of bank consolidation, creating a significant shift of banking power among European banks.[37]

AT GE: *Because the GE-GEC alliance principally involves operations already in existence, the alliance can be expected to follow several of these strategies.*

A TYPICAL STRATEGY FOR AN EEC-BASED FIRM

A number of changes will be necessary for those firms already operating in EEC countries. For example, Avery International, a U.S.-based office supply firm with $1.5 billion in sales in 1988 (one-third of those sales came from its European subsidiary), has substantially altered its European strategy. G. J. van den Akker, head of Avery Europe, outlined the strategies they have followed:

1. Moved to a service-oriented strategy that will provide the product to any customer in Europe within twenty-four hours
2. Cut the number of distribution warehouses from one for each country to five regional warehouses
3. Reduced inventories
4. Reduced transportation and administrative costs
5. Moved to an integrated data network
6. Increased emphasis on quality
7. Eliminated nonvalue adding work
8. Tracked common product lines to ascertain characteristics of products needed in 1992
9. Reexamined price and quality competitiveness in the firm[38]

A TYPICAL STRATEGY FOR A NON-EEC-BASED FIRM

Firms that are not currently operating in the countries to be affected by the EEC will have to change strategies to become competitive: For example, Ford of Europe is the car manufacturer with the broadest scope of operations in Europe. It has twenty-two plants in fifteen countries. However, it is also positioning itself as an EEC-based company, through the following actions:

1. Increasing its investment in Spain
2. Considering a European credit operation
3. Planning to invest $7.5 billion from 1989 to 1994 to modernize plants and equipment and to redesign their European product line
4. Tailoring marketing and design to local tastes
5. Standardizing components to cut costs

Many believe that North American and Japanese firms may be locked out of this new market. At best the rules of the game will be changed significantly. Firms such as Philips, KLM, KPMG, Avery International, Ford Motor Company, General Motors, GE, and Mazda, among hundreds, have formulated strategies for 1992 as the countdown continues.

By the middle of 1990, 285 directives covering economic and legal issues related to the establishment of the common market were proposed, and more than 120 were passed. Though several major critical issues remain, it now seems apparent that the directives will pass.[39]

THE POTENTIAL FOR EAST-WEST ECONOMIC INTEGRATION

In 1989 a series of changes in political and economic structure began in Eastern Europe that could have the potential to surpass those of Europe 1992, in terms of economic significance. It is not immediately clear what the impacts will be, only that they will be significant. In the immediate future, Poland, Czechoslovakia, Hungary, and East Germany seem the most likely candidates to benefit from easing of economic and political constraints. But all nations in Eastern Europe and the Soviet Union will eventually benefit from these changes. The reunification in Germany may even slow progress toward 1992.

AT GE: *GE, which did not have a substantial position in Europe, took actions that were necessary for a non-EEC-based company: (1) engaging in a $580 million joint venture with Britain's General Electric company, (2) investing $1.7 billion in a plant to make plastics in Cartagena, Spain, (3) seeking other alliances, such as the attempted, but unsuccessful, takeover of the British firm Plessey, with the German firm, and Siemens; (4) acquiring Borg-Warner's European chemical operations for $2.3 billion.*

This Soviet militiaman gets his first taste of a hamburger as he stands on duty in front of Moscow's first McDonald's restaurant on January 31, 1990. (SOURCE © Reuters/Bettmann Newsphotos)

MANAGEMENT CHALLENGE 21.1

Cat Acts Like a Tiger

As of 1982 Caterpillar Inc had experienced fifty consecutive years of profits, with annual returns on owner's equity as high as 27 percent. For decades this Peoria, Illinois-based company had seemed almost as invincible as the earthmoving machinery it produced—it could literally crush or roll over just about anything that got in its way. Then in 1982, as George Schaefer, Caterpillar's chairman and CEO, recalls, "almost overnight the whole world changed for us." Construction markets around the world collapsed. Commodity prices plunged, killing the demand for the mining, logging, and pipe-laying equipment the company produced. As the dollar rose in value, Japanese firms—especially Komatsu—began to attack Caterpillar markets. In the midst of this gloomy situation, Caterpillar's blue-collar workers went on strike for seven months. Caterpillar's profits plummeted from $579 million in 1981, to three straight years of red ink totalling $953 million.

Caterpillar began its comeback strategy with planned cost reductions beginning in 1982. It closed seven plants in 1986, and in 1988 it announced plans to close two more. It cut its work force by about 40 percent, eliminating more than 33,000 positions. In contrast to the American automobile firms competing with the Japanese, Caterpillar already had the highest-quality product in the industry; yet, it strove to raise that quality. Unlike American automakers, it met Komatsu's price cutting head-on, in order to retain market share; it engaged in joint ventures with a South Korean firm to give it additional cost advantages. As the U.S. dollar began to decline in value, Caterpillar chose not to raise prices, as did members of the American automobile industry. Perhaps most critically, it chose to take innovative

North America

The principal economic powers in North America are the United States and Canada. The two signed a trade pact which took effect on January 1, 1989, calling for the abolishment of all tariffs over the next ten years. It has had significant impact on some firms, such as Harley-Davidson, which saw its "hog" cycle drop by an average of $1,250 per bike from 1988 prices, when the law went into effect in Canada. It is hoped that this trade pact will cause an increased number of big deals between firms in the two countries and enable them to grow and be sizeable enough to compete in Europe and Asia.[40]

DECLINING U.S. COMPETITIVENESS

Perhaps the most significant feature of the North American members of the triad is their declining global competitiveness. The United States has found itself with a competitive disadvantage on a global basis in both manufacturing and service industries for a number of reasons. Among them are the transition from a manufacturing to a service economy, declining investment in heavy manufacturing, disadvantageous wage rates and benefit structures, technological transfer from the United States to foreign competitors, and a short-term perspective with regard to the returns expected from an organization—ROI-based financial controls, strategic portfolio management concepts used to buy and sell businesses, and lack of quality of U.S. products.[41] Factors cited more recently include diversification strategies, the subsequent adoption of decentralized organizational approaches, first moving into new markets and then employing new technologies in what Caterpillar labels PWAF, "Plant with a Future." It has engaged in a six-year, $1.2 billion plan to modernize all 36 million square feet of its factory space. This is in addition to the $850 million the company will spend on normal machine replacement during that time. Part of the plant modernization program will involve cutting inventory costs, which will save a cumulative $850 million. From 1981 to 1988 the actual selling price of Caterpillar's equipment rose only 9.5 percent, while Komatsu's prices jumped as much as 20 percent. The company has changed plant layouts in order to improve efficiency and has moved to team management approaches. It believes it is important to use new technology, but not for the sake only of technology, as it believes General Motors did. Rather it is counting on low-risk computerized machine tools, laser-reading bar code systems, and automated carrier systems.

Caterpillar's turnaround has also occurred partly because of Schaefer's people skills. He has improved relations with the UAW, and Caterpillar's last two contract negotiations went on without strikes. Management has also enlisted the shop floor experts in helping it shape up its suppliers, redesign its plant, and provide comments on product engineering and quality improvement. "Five years ago the foreman wouldn't even listen to you, never mind the general foreman or the plant supervisor. Now everyone will listen," says Gary Hatmaker, a thirty-seven-year-old assembly-line worker in a Caterpillar factory. Finally, Caterpillar has also learned to use niche strategies and to increase its international sales. The turnaround has been extremely successful. Caterpillar sold a record $10.5 billion worth of products in 1988 and made record profits of $616 million.

SOURCE: Ronald Henkoff, "The Cat Is Acting Like A Tiger," *Fortune* (December 19, 1988), pp. 70–76; "Going for the Lion's Share," *Business Week* (July 18, 1988), pp. 70–71; and "The Fortune 500: Largest Industrial Corporations," *Fortune* (April 24, 1989), p. 354.

George Schaefer, CEO of Caterpillar Incorporated, holds a model of one of the company's main products. He had plenty to smile about when this photo was taken as Caterpillar had successfully countered its competitor Komatsu's gains in most of their marketplaces. (SOURCE © 1988 Bob Sacha)

structures, and evolutionary changes in the nature of the capital market.[42] The principal consequence of the impact of several of these items has been the reduction of investment in long-term product/market development. Innovation has been short changed both by the short-term perspective and by the absence of funds for investment in organizations that take a long-term perspective. In fact, it has been argued very strongly that U.S. competitiveness has declined principally because of a declining innovation effort.[43] Those firms that have survived, and that remain competitive on an international basis, have had to change how they think. A perfect example is Caterpillar, as Management Challenge 21.1 reveals.

Potential for Other Global Change

The Soviet Union, under Mikhail Gorbachev, is attempting, through the policies of *perestroika* and *glasnost*, to improve the well-being of its populace. The possibility exists that economic change even greater than that in Europe may occur in the Soviet Union and China, despite China's political setback in the summer of 1989, with both moving toward capitalism. Thus, two of the world's largest markets may suddenly open up for European, Japanese, and American competitors alike.[44] Furthermore, it seems very likely that Eastern Europe is definitely turning capitalist as major changes in all countries have occurred.

Management and the Global Environment

Global management is the performance of management activities on a truly global basis. Global management embodies the concept of a product sold in numerous countries, even though it may have to be tailored somewhat to the demands of the customer's needs in those countries. It requires a degree of coordination among activities not experienced in multidomestic/international operations.[45] **Multidomestic** firms are organizations that operate across national boundaries but treat each country as a separate market, and products are developed solely for that market.[46] Firms such as AT&T, Apple Computer, and Federal Express have been multidomestic, not designing a product for a global market but taking a product that worked in the United States and selling it in another country. They operate without a highly coordinated international manufacturing/service operation in conjunction with marketing, finance, and human resources. Firms such as Ford Motor Company, General Motors, Unilever, Mazda, Matsushita Electric Company, Sony, and GE are global companies. They produce products for global markets. However, even within these large corporations, especially GE and General Motors, there may be major divisions that still operate essentially in a multidomestic fashion. Both global and multidomestic companies are multinational corporations. A **multinational corporation** (MNC) is simply a firm that has significant operations in more than one country. MNCs may also be **multinational enterprises**—a group of corporations with businesses in several different countries but with one control headquarters.[47]

Most organizations don't become multinational or global overnight. Typically they start as domestic organizations and move through a series of stages, reach-

Table 21.5 Five Degrees of Internationalization

	Stage 1 First-Degree Internationalization	Stage 2 Second-Degree Internationalization	Stage 3 Third-Degree Internationalization	Stage 4 Fourth-Degree Internationalization	Stage 5 Fifth-Degree Internationalization
Nature of contact with foreign markets	Indirect, passive	Direct, active	Direct, active	Direct, active	Direct, active
Focus of international operations	Domestic	Domestic	Domestic and international	Domestic and international	International
Orientation of company	Domestic	Domestic	Primarily domestic	Multinational (domestic operations viewed as part of the whole)	Global (with domestic modifications)
Type of international activity	Foreign trade of goods and services	Foreign trade of goods and services	Foreign trade, foreign assistance contracts, foreign direct investment	Foreign trade, foreign assistance contracts, foreign direct investment	Foreign trade, foreign assistance contracts, foreign direct investment
Organizational structure	Traditional domestic	International department	International division	Global structure	Global structure

SOURCE: Adapted from Christopher M. Korth, *International Business, Environment of Management*, 2nd ed. (Englewood Cliffs, N.J.: Prentice-Hall, 1985), p. 7; Neil H. Jacoby, "The Multinational Corporation," *The Center Magazine* (May 1970), pp. 37–55.

ing multidomestic, and in some cases global, stages of multinationalization. Neil H. Jacoby and Christopher M. Korth have each identified a series of stages through which organizations pass on their way to becoming multinational.[48] Korth's model of these stages is depicted in Table 21.5; Jacoby's materials are integrated into this model. A fifth stage has been added, to reflect the concept of global competition. In examining Table 21.5, realize that not all organizations reach either the fourth or fifth stage, and some may reach them and subsequently withdraw. When Renault sold American Motors Corporation to Chrysler in 1987, it retreated to a multidomestic strategy from a global one.

One of the major changes in moving from stage 1 to stage 5 is that products designed for the domestic market are first sold overseas. In later stages manufacturing and financing may occur in foreign countries. And in the fifth stage, the organization becomes totally global, designing products for more than one national market and using coordinated manufacturing, financing, human resources, and information management to manage the global competitive situation. This five-stage evolutionary process has been shown to be typical of U.S. firms.[49]

The following paragraphs examine management in multinational environments, analyzing how the four environmental forces are different and their impact on the economic and management functions of an organization.

The Four Environmental Factors and the Global Environment

In Chapters 1 and 4, four fundamental environmental forces affecting organizations and their management were identified: economic/competitive, political/legal, sociocultural, and technological. Each of the four is impacted significantly by the change from domestic to multinational operations.

THE ECONOMIC/COMPETITIVE FACTORS

Organizations operating multinationally will be confronted with a myriad of different economic and competitive environmental factors. They will face different monetary systems; they will be operating in countries that are going through different stages of economic development; they may even be confronted with different economic systems, such as a moderate form of socialism in Great Britain, new capitalistic socialism in Hungary, a modified form of communism in China, a capitalist/socialistic approach in France, or pure capitalism in Canada. There will be fierce global competitors, powerful or weak customers and suppliers, new entrants, and an increased number of substitutes.

POLITICAL/LEGAL FACTORS

Similarly, the multinational corporation faces widely varying political/legal systems. In much of Europe government takes an active role in business, frequently changing monetary and fiscal policy and taxation programs, as well as offering various incentives for plant location or industrial development. Similarly, in Japan the government provides R&D funds, steers its country's firms toward selected industries, and generally has close ties to its multinationals. In Europe, prior to 1992, organizations were faced with at least twelve different sets of laws, controls, and policies, a situation that will continue to some extent after 1992. Throughout the world, property rights and laws governing the operation of business differ. Very few "free trade" countries exist, and import and export controls are common.

Yukari Yamaguchi works at Nikko Securities Company in Japan. Shown here among her male colleagues, she is the only professional woman in her section. Her plans to attend Harvard Business School is a first for the women in her company. (SOURCE © R. Wallis/SIPA Press)

R. Hall Mason notes that host countries—that is, countries hosting multinational corporations—often impose restrictive policies on the actions of MNCs. Some of the more important of these restrictions include required shared ownership with the host country or with its nationals, reservation of certain management and technical jobs for local people, profit and fee ceilings, contract renegotiations, external debt capital, development of the host country's personnel and export market, and a preference for technology-based industries over extractive industries—those that take raw materials from the country.[50]

SOCIOCULTURAL FACTORS

Multinational corporations must learn to operate in a widely varying context of culture and language. Educational systems, for example, vary widely from country to country. Stefan Robock and Kenneth Simmonds identify at least four distinct **cultural differences**: assumptions and attitudes; personal beliefs, aspirations and motivations; interpersonal relations; and social structure.[51] With respect to assumptions and attitudes, U.S. and Canadian management systems have been greatly influenced by their societies' belief in self-determination. But in many other countries, the belief is much more fatalistic—human beings really cannot control their own future. Other problems may arise, as well—for example, with respect to time. Being "on time" is very important in most Western societies but is of little importance in China. In fact, being late is more common there than being on time.

With respect to personal beliefs, aspirations, and motivations, the need to achieve is much less significant outside Western/capitalistic/Protestant countries—for example, in India and Peru. Underlying beliefs about authority also affect how management functions. In Japan teamwork is more readily accepted than in the United States or in Europe, although both are moving toward more teamwork in managing. The status of women in the workplace varies throughout the world. In the Middle East they are second-class citizens. In Europe there are varying degrees of acceptance of women in organizations. Scandinavian countries accept them wholeheartedly, while Spain tends to be much more resistant to integrating them into the work force in managerial and professional areas. In the United States women are a major part of the work force at all levels. In Japan they play almost no part in the organization other than as front-line workers, although, with the passage of an equal employment opportunity act in 1987, women are slowly beginning to be accepted in management and professional positions.

Finally, with respect to social structure, social status and interclass mobility play important roles in other cultures. Britain still has a very strong class structure, whereas Canada and the United States do not. The Japanese focus much of their energy on a group-oriented, patriarchical organization structure. In summary, sociocultural factors can have a very significant impact on management. Managers must learn to operate within the nuances of each individual country. Then, of course, there are the differences that exist in communication. Language, body language, the use of space, symbols and so forth, all vary and these must be learned if management is to occur appropriately.

TECHNOLOGICAL FACTORS

Within the triad nations, technology is easily transported and is waning as a source of competitive advantage. Organizations must be prepared to reformulate products and services quickly, improving upon technologies in order to maintain competitive advantages. In the future it may be the Japanese and Europeans who will be in the forefront of providing new technology, in a bid to overcome existing U.S. technological advantages. In the developing countries, multinationals will find different levels of technology and will have to function within those various levels or bring in advanced technology of their own.

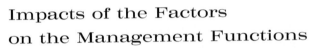

Impacts of the Factors on the Management Functions

Managers must adapt to the effects of these four environmental forces. The enactment of the five principal functions of management will vary in multinational situations. Managers must not only adapt to the differences in the way the functions are performed in the country in which they are operating, but they must also learn how to transfer good management practices to another culture and adapt them to the other environmental factors operating in that situation. However, sometimes management practices dominant in one country are simply not transferable to others.

> AT GE: *U.S. managers working in Europe and European managers working in the U.S. will have to adapt to new situations.*

PROBLEM SOLVING

While the basic stages must be followed regardless of country, the way decisions are made may differ by the degree of creativity applied in the decision process. Firms in several European countries, such as Phillips, are much more innovation oriented than most firms in the United States, and by comparison the level of creativity in U.S. firms in product development is generally higher than in Japanese firms.[52] By contrast, on the average, the Japanese engage in participative decision making much more than most American firms, which in turn surpass most European firms. The ability to use rational analytical processes in decision making in today's society often depends on the availability of computers, and in this respect American and Japanese managers are far ahead of the rest of the world. The Soviet Union, for example, has fallen far behind in its ability to analyze complex problems because of the shortage of personal computers.[53]

Finally, there is the issue of who controls decision making. In most organizations in most countries, strategic decisions are still made at the top of the organization, although there may be varying degrees of participation in relevant decisions at lower levels.

PLANNING

Planning is more acceptable in some societies than in others. For example, the Chinese are much less interested in strategic planning than the Japanese.[54] But for most of the developed nations, strategic planning and planning in general are acceptable. Strategic planning is the aspect of planning that is of most concern to multinationals. Strategic plans for multinationals will be concerned with such issues as how and to what extent a company should enter into or expand within a country or countries; whether to be a multidomestic or global competitor; and how to proceed through the various stages of growth toward global competition, as shown in Table 21.5.

Donald A. Ball and Wendell H. McCulloch, Jr., suggest that the various reasons for going international are either aggressive or defensive.[55]

Aggressive Reasons	Defensive Reasons
1. Seek new markets	1. Protect home markets
2. Yield higher profits/cut costs	2. Protect other markets
3. Obtain additional products for other markets	3. Guarantee raw-material supply
4. Satisfy top management's desire to expand	4. Acquire technology
	5. Diversify geographically
	6. Obtain bases for new operations

Stages to Global Strategy Table 21.5 clearly shows the various stages through which an organization may pass on its path to global strategy. Three important decisions are when to take such actions, upon what basis to take them, and what countries to enter.

The Decision: Domestic, Multidomestic, or Global? Not all products or services transfer well to other nations, but in an increasingly homogenous international environment, more and more products are being accepted from one country to another. Organizations typically move to overseas locations for the reasons outlined by Ball and McCulloch. The decision whether to be multidomestic or global depends on a large number of variables, but principally upon size and the changing nature of the industry in which firms compete. Most authorities believe, for example, that companies competing in the automobile industry must be able to compete globally.[56] The belief in the need to be global, for example, has caused Ford to revise its strategy to build a platform (underbody) for a world car.[57] But in other industries, such as fast food, it may be possible to take the existing domestic product and sell it globally without altering or creating a world product. This has certainly been the case with McDonald's hamburger chain. Thus, while they may obtain raw materials, and in a sense "manufacture" the product in various countries, McDonald's really has not had to tailor its product to other countries in most cases.[58]

How to Enter the Country Most firms enter a country first on a marketing or manufacturing basis. From a marketing perspective, firms may choose to import or export, to license, to set up direct investment, or to enter joint ventures. Joint ventures are becoming increasingly important for global conpetitiveness. Kenichi Ohmae and Howard V. Perlmutter and David A. Heenan argue that global alliances are vital to compete globally. Global companies incur and must defray immense fixed costs to compete globally. Ohmae argues that you need partners. Ohmae and Perlmutter and Heenan provide criteria for successful alliances.[59]

A perspective on joint ventures is provided in Management Challenge 21.2. Much of the thrust of U.S. firms' joint ventures have been with Japanese or

AT GE: *GE has already made the decision to be a global company. It has primarily chosen direct investment by acquisition as its primary means of entering foreign markets, but it also has some joint ventures.*

McDonald's has done an outstanding job of transferring its management practices and systems to the various cultures in which it does business. However, it often must make rather significant changes in its management practices in faraway places such as Tokyo. (SOURCE © Patrick Frilet/SIPA Press)

European allies, but the H. J. Heinz Company has attempted to solve the problem of slow growth in its industry by joint venturing with developing countries.

Which Countries to Enter? Analysts must examine all of the major factors to determine which countries to enter. In recent years, political risk has been especially closely examined.[60] All four of the forces must be assessed: economic, political/legal, sociocultural, and technological.

ORGANIZING

Managers must learn differing structural relationships in various countries. For the most part, macro structures are similar, but the exact amount of authority delegated varies significantly from country to country, even region to region of the same country. And, as in the U.S., authority relationships vary considerably from company to company, even department by department within a company. Furthermore, micro structures, work group and one on one boss-subordinate relationships, will vary significantly. Some countries are not actively using team approaches, for example, while others are.

LEADING

Appropriate leadership behaviors for managers vary greatly from country to country. Using the TRRAP model from Chapter 15 as the basis of discussion, the following paragraph reviews the major issues involved using various countries as examples. Firms in some countries, such as Japan, do not stress specific objectives for subordinate performance, while firms in other countries such as the United States, do. Rewards for performance are stressed in very few countries, but more so in the U.S., for example, than in heavily unionized countries such as France. Manager/subordinate relationships are important in countries such as Finland, but much less so in Germany. Participation is highly developed in Japan, but not so in Spain. A concern for attitudes while performing the leadership behaviors discussed above, varies greatly around the globe.

H. J. Heinz's Approach
to Joint Ventures
in Developing Nations

Anthony J. F. O'Reilly, CEO and chairman of H. J. Heinz Company, a U.S.-based firm, is an Irishman with a law degree from an Irish university and a Ph.D in agricultural marketing from the University of Bradford, England. In discussing several successful joint ventures in developing nations, O'Reilly observed that Heinz realized that its potential for growth was limited because projected food industry growth rates in the United States and Europe were approximately 1 percent. A research study conducted by the company indicated that 85 percent of the world's population had not even been exposed to Heinz. It became obvious to the firm that it needed to develop markets in developing nations rather than in already developed nations. In particular, O'Reilly mentioned the prospects for future growth in Pacific rim countries, whose combined GNP is growing at a remarkable rate of $3 billion a week.

The company determined that the best way for it to expand its business geographically was through joint venture. It established six key criteria for a joint venture partner:

1. A company whose field is, or is closely related to, the food business
2. A company staffed by nationals and not reliant on expatriates
3. A company of sufficient size to serve as a continental base for expansion within the country and the region
4. A company not heavily dependent on imported raw materials
5. A company not dependent on exports and with a ready market for its products within its own country
6. A company with good profit potential to justify the greater risk of investment in the Third World

The company chose not to invest in Malaysia because of what it considered to be restrictions on its investment, but did invest successfully in joint ventures in

CONTROLLING

While the more sophisticated countries will have similar information and control systems, what is controlled may vary significantly. Firms in Great Britain for example, tend to be very concerned about managing assets and liabilities, while firms in the U.S. are more concerned about controlling income and expenses. In Japan, group performance is controlled, as opposed to individual performance in Canada.

Global Competitiveness

Michael Porter, strategic consultant, author, researcher, and academic, having thoroughly analyzed the nature of global competition, suggests that whether or

Zimbabwe (after looking at Nigeria, the Ivory Coast, Kenya, and Cameroon), in the People's Republic of China, and in Thailand.

O'Reilly cautions, "Establishing successful joint ventures in developing nations is no easy task. It requires caution and care. But it can be done, and with great impact on the local market and the global corporation. Eight years ago 85 percent of the world's population was unfamiliar with the Heinz brand. Since then we have gained access to 20 percent of that global populace in China alone. Africa now makes a decided contribution to our company's total profits . . . and Asia has opened its doors to us. . . . My message to the leaders of developing countries is a very clear one: Open up your countries to capital and expertise and you will give your entire population better, cheaper, more exciting, more diversified, and more convenient food."

SOURCE: Anthony J. F. O'Reilly, "Establishing Successful Joint Ventures in Developing Nations: A CEO's Perspective," *The Columbia Journal of World Business* (Spring 1988), pp. 65–71.

When its prospects for future growth looked dim in the United States and Europe, Heinz went looking for joint venture partners in developing countries. (SOURCE © Andy Freeberg)

not a firm will be competitive globally depends on the four key factors identified in Figure 21.2: factor conditions; demand conditions; related and supporting industries; and company strategy, structure, and rivalry.

Factor conditions are a nation's abilities to turn the basics—natural resources, education, and infrastructure—into a specialized advantage. **Demand conditions** are the number and sophistication of domestic customers for the industry's product or service. **Related and supporting industries,** or the company a company keeps, include suppliers and competition in supportive industries. Finally, **company strategy, structure, and rivalry**—the latter being the conditions governing a nation's businesses, especially competition—completes the dynamic diamond Porter envisioned.[61]

What Porter's work suggests is that fierce competition domestically is one of the most significant factors in being competitive globally. Furthermore, the notion that a simple resource or special advantage can make you competitive globally just does not hold. The more of the four points of the diamond that

FIGURE 21.2 PORTER'S DYNAMIC DIAMOND

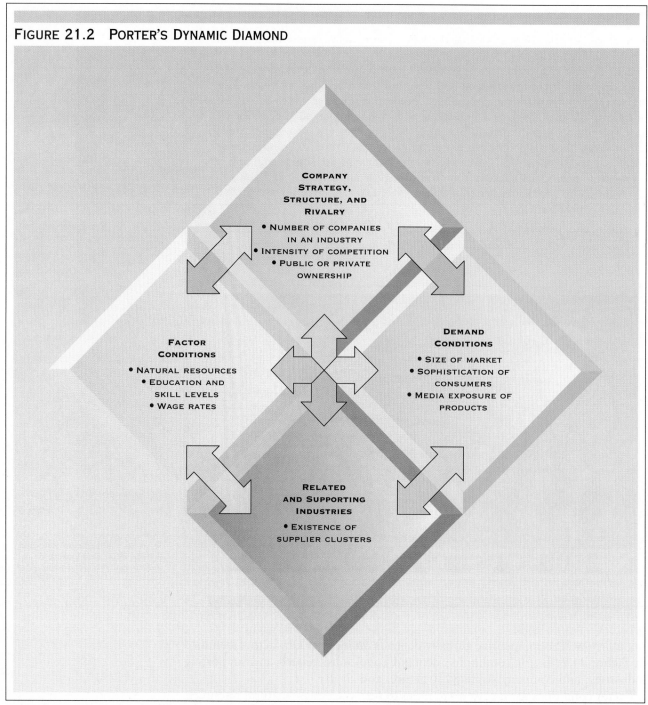

COMPANY STRATEGY, STRUCTURE, AND RIVALRY
- NUMBER OF COMPANIES IN AN INDUSTRY
- INTENSITY OF COMPETITION
- PUBLIC OR PRIVATE OWNERSHIP

FACTOR CONDITIONS
- NATURAL RESOURCES
- EDUCATION AND SKILL LEVELS
- WAGE RATES

DEMAND CONDITIONS
- SIZE OF MARKET
- SOPHISTICATION OF CONSUMERS
- MEDIA EXPOSURE OF PRODUCTS

RELATED AND SUPPORTING INDUSTRIES
- EXISTENCE OF SUPPLIER CLUSTERS

are positive for a firm, the better and more likely it is that the firm will have a sustainable competitive advantage. Porter proposes, for example, that in comparing Japanese and United States firms, Japanese firms are more likely to have sustainable competitive advantages because they have intense domestic competition and U.S. firms do not; the Japanese education system is superior; Japanese firms have strong supportive industries; and there is strong consumer demand for many products in Japan. Porter also identifies chance and government as two factors that influence a firm's success. Chance is outside a firm's influence, but not government. Again, Japanese firms have closer ties in general to government than do U.S. firms. Porter emphasizes that innovation is critical to competitiveness.

Impacts on Economic Functions

Managing in the multinational or global arena has major implications for each of the organization's economic functions: marketing, finance, operations, human resources, and information. For example, products and advertising must be formulated to local consumer preferences. Financing arrangements, terms, and the like vary from country to country. Firms may choose to place operations in different countries to take advantage of wage rates and skills. Human resources practices vary widely from country to country. And information systems may be sophisticated in one country, but nonexistent in another.

AT GE: One of the more complex problems facing the GE-GEC joint venture will be the creation of an information system for the operation. British firms and U.S. firms do not stress the same kinds of information in their existing system.

Applying Management Practices Internationally

The management practices of one country may have some applicability to other countries, but generally speaking, they have not been shown to be universally convertible to situations in other countries.[62]

Geert Hofstede, a Dutch scholar and international consultant, has shown that the values of various societies differ substantially on several basic dimensions: power distance, uncertainty avoidance, individualism and collectivism, and masculinity.[63] The **power distance** dimension is concerned with the degree to which the culture accepts any variances in power in organizational relationships, specifically superiors and subordinate relationships. Low power distance countries, such as Austria, Israel, and New Zealand, have small power variances, which means that there is very little difference between the power of boss and subordinate. Large power distance countries, such as the Philippines, Mexico, and India, have tremendous differences in authority between individuals. The **uncertainty avoidance** dimension is the degree to which a culture dislikes uncertainty or risk and therefore tries to reduce or avoid it. Countries weak in avoidance of uncertainty include Singapore, Denmark, Great Britain, and the United States. Those strong in avoidance of uncertainty include Greece, Japan, and France. Weak avoidance countries generally accept and tolerate uncertainty, whereas strong avoidance countries are unwilling or unable to tolerate it.

The **individualism and collectivism** dimension indicates the degree to which a culture is either individualistic or socially group oriented. Individualistic countries include the United States, Canada, and the Netherlands. Collectivist countries include Venezuela, Pakistan, and Taiwan. The fourth dimension of **masculinity** is concerned with characteristics that most cultures would attribute to men: acquisition of money, possessions, pursuit of advancement, and assertiveness. Some of the more masculine countries are Japan, Austria, and Italy. Some of the more **feminine** countries—those which show a preference for relationships caring for the weak, modesty, and the quality of life—include Sweden, Norway, and Switzerland. The United States ranks fairly high, thirty-sixth of the fifty nations studied, on the masculine end of the scale.

The consequences of these differences are significant, and there are important differences within some countries. Managers from one country will have some degree of difficulty transferring their management styles to foreign countries.

Conversely though, as nations grow more similar through globalization, it is likely that the variances in the dimensions will diminish, but this will require many years of cultural assimilation.

Applying Japanese Management Practices Abroad

Theory Z management asserts that there is a high degree of applicability of Japanese management styles to other cultures. Indeed, many of the characteristics of Japanese management style have been transferred to American organizations. The result is the Theory Z type of management system, which combines Japanese and American management styles but predominantly uses a style very similar to Japanese management, as discussed in Chapter 20.

Theory Z and Japanese type management styles have been transferred to Europe, as well. Jaguar and Ford and Ford of Europe have directly copied many of the Japanese management systems, especially those related to consensual decision making, long-term employment, and less specialized careers.[64]

Unique Problems for Multinational Corporations

Organizations doing business overseas face several unique situations: political instability, terrorism, host government conflicts, monetary transactions, and human rights issues.

Table 21.6 Political Risk of Investment in Foreign Countries

Sources of Political Risk	Groups Through Which Political Risk Can Be Generated	Political Risk Effects: Types of Influences on International Business Operations
Competing political philosophies (nationalism, socialism, communism)	Government in power and its operating agencies	Confiscation: Loss of assets without compensations
Social unrest and disorder	Nonparliamentary opposition groups (e.g., anarchist or guerrilla movement working from within or outside of country)	Expropriation with compensation: Loss of freedom to operate
Vested interests of local business groups		Operational restrictions: Market shares, product characteristics, employment policies, locally shared ownership
Recent and impending political independence	Nonorganized common interest groups: students, workers, peasants, minorities	Loss of transfer freedom: Financial (dividends, interest payments), goods, personnel, or ownership rights
Armed conflicts and internal rebellions for political power	Foreign governments or intergovernmental agencies, such as the EEC	Breaches or unilateral revisions in contracts and agreements
New international alliances	Foreign governments willing to enter into armed conflict or to support internal rebellion	Discrimination (taxes, compulsory subcontracting)
		Damage to property or personnel from riots, insurrections, revolutions, and wars

SOURCE: Stefan H. Robock and Kenneth Simmonds, *International Business and Multinational Enterprise*, 3rd ed. (Richard D. Irwin, 1983), p. 342, reprinted by permission.

Political Instability

When doing business in developing nations, political instability can be a major problem. Governments may rise and fall rather quickly in developing nations because of economic instability and outside political forces. Organizations obviously prefer to license, joint venture, or export, rather than invest, in countries with high levels of political risk. However, in many cases, the desirability of investment is so high, political risk must be taken. Table 21.6 indicates several sources of political risk and relevant factors and their effects on the international business operation.

Terrorism

For multinational corporate personnel operating overseas, especially in developing countries, but also in Europe, terrorism, kidnapping, and extortion are major problems. Furthermore, the physical plants of many companies are often targets for terrorists. In one incident in 1986, the American Express Company office in Lyons, France, was bombed. Consequently, many firms invest heavily in security fencing and guard forces. Body guards are often in demand for Americans and other foreigners.

Host Government Conflicts

Host country governments, as was discussed earlier, often place restrictions on multinational corporations operating within their geographic territories. Regardless of the country involved, organizations can take steps to reduce the potential for conflict.

Monetary Transactions

The value of currencies fluctuates tremendously. In the early 1980s, U.S. currency was very strong, and U.S. firms, which were actually making money in overseas operations in other countries' currency, were losing money on the exchange of those currencies back into American dollars. By contrast, in the late 1980s, the devaluation of the dollar enabled American firms to reap substantial benefits because they had overseas income that translated into more dollars when exchanges were made. It is almost impossible to factor in the appropriate figures for currency exchange in long-term strategic planning because of the high levels of fluctuation.

Human Rights

In developing countries, and even in some "developed" countries, human rights are often neglected, or not treated in the same way they are in the United States and Canada. In recent years South Africa has been a major human rights trouble spot on the globe. Many American companies have been caught up in the ethical dilemma of whether to remain in South Africa. Many of them employed principally black Africans, who, if the companies were to leave, would be unemployed, or perhaps treated less well by new owners. Yet, by staying, the companies appear to be supporting the South African government's apartheid policies. To withdraw, for all practical purposes, would mean they could not return to South Africa, a sizeable market, experiencing a major loss on their

This bottling plant in Johannesburg was divested by Coca-Cola in 1986 in response to protest against South Africa's policies of apartheid.
(SOURCE © J. Kuus/SIPA Press)

capital investments. Furthermore, many American companies have been under pressure from groups in the United States to take a stand on South Africa and to pull out. Pressures have been applied by stockholders of principally "social responsibility" investment funds and universities, and to some extent the federal government and various antiapartheid groups. Many firms have chosen to withdraw or in some way lessen their exposure in South Africa in order to reduce the negative publicity associated with remaining.[65]

Firms must develop strategies for coping with such complex situations. Some guiding principles are available for these situations, but in many cases organizations are alone in attempting to determine appropriate ethical courses of action, balancing many complex variables. South Africa is not the only country in which human rights have been violated. In much of the Eastern bloc, in Tibet, in countries in South and Central America, and in some Pacific rim nations, there are significant violations of human rights. Businesses typically have tried not to get involved in such internal issues as human rights, but in many cases, as in South Africa, they have been forced to become involved.

The Management
Challenges Identified

1. Increasing competition—Europe 1992, East-West economic integration; the changing dynamics of competition
2. Accelerating rates of change in economics—political and social arenas in Europe and Asia especially
3. The globalization of business
4. Declining U.S. competitiveness
5. Rapidly changing technology

Some Solutions Noted in the Text

1. Flexible strategic planning
2. Increased competitor intelligence
3. Improved strategic planning
4. Changes in the practice of the functions of management and the economic functions of business

Summary

1. Globalization of business means that organizations are creating a common, but tailored product for a number of markets in a number of different countries.
2. The triad of key markets is North America, Europe, and Japan. The more important factors for each include population—Europe, 320 million; United States, 243 million; and Japan, 120 million. GNP—United States, $4.4 billion; Japan, $1.6 billion; and EEC, $3.8 billion. GNP growth rates, 1987—United States, 2.9 percent; Japan, 4.2 percent; and EEC, 3.9 percent. Balance of trade in billions of U.S. dollars, 1987—United States, -174; Japan, $+80$; and EEC, -1.6.
3. The Japanese as competitors seek to grow faster than their competitors, to increase their market shares so that their volume of business will increase at a greater rate. Increased volume means decreased costs, and decreased costs mean more profitability and financial strength, and the whole cycle begins again.
4. The Four Tigers' principal strengths are their cheap labor rates and their ability to adapt foreign technology quickly for their own purposes.
5. In 1992 the EEC will become one true common market with essentially all major barriers to free trade eliminated. North American firms may be frozen out of that market. The more likely scenario is that it will be very difficult for them to enter; and therefore, they should begin entering that market before 1992 by arranging for mergers, alliances, acquisitions, and joint ventures, or by exploring other ways in which to have a presence in Europe.
6. The potential of East-West integration may surpass even that of Europe 1992; the changes there will greatly affect 1992, especially if German reunification occurs before then.
7. It is clear that managers must change the way they work in different environments, even though, as business becomes more globalized, each country will become more like another. Both economic and management functions are modified by differing economic, political/legal, socio/cultural, and technological forces.
8. It is often difficult to apply the management techniques used in one country in another country. Research has shown that underlying cultural dimensions in countries vary significantly—for example, masculinity.
9. Countries may export or license, they may move to become multidomestic, or they may become entirely global in their enterprises.
10. Global organizations have, in one way or another, essentially the same organizational structures as others, but you will seldom see functional or client-based structures. Most typically, global organizations begin with multiproduct structures and eventually have a divisional structure either by country or major region, depending on a number of variables.
11. Leadership varies according to the country of operation. Leadership styles that function well in Japan, for example, may not function well in Argentina or the Middle East. Most of the countries in the triad of key markets are moving toward more teamwork—that is, greater sharing of decision-making authority. But even within similar markets, leadership style may need to differ significantly.
12. Control in a global situation depends very much on the ability to develop strategic information systems.

13. Some of the unique problems that arise in managing in multinational situations include political instability, human rights violations, terrorism, host country conflicts, and currency fluctuations.

Thinking About Management

1. Describe how management, while becoming more complex, is also becoming more interesting because of the globalization of business.
2. Describe the major changes occurring in the globalization of business in 1990–1991, and more currently, if applicable. Indicate their impact on the functions of management.
3. Based on Porter's dynamic diamond, what must U.S. firms do to overcome their difficult competitive situations? How will Europe 1992 help European global firms be better competitors?
4. Enumerate the reasons that Japanese firms have been so successful in global competition.
5. Describe the actions necessary for EEC-based firms and non-EEC-based firms to respond to Europe 1992.
6. What problems does Japan face in the future, primarily internally, that may cause it to be less globally competitive?
7. Why are joint ventures and acquisitions so popular in global competition, in Europe especially?

CASE

To Invest or Not to Invest?

Phillip Knight was the CEO of a $200-million-a-year paper manufacturing subsidiary of a U.S. conglomerate headquartered in New York City. Knight had recently completed a five-year turnaround of the firm, moving it from losses of over $30 million in 1985, to profits of $26 million in 1989. Headquarters had then made him the leader of a task force to study business investment in the paper and related industries in Europe, principally Eastern Europe.

As part of that endeavor, Knight and two company analysts had made a fifteen-day trip to Europe, with stopovers in Italy, Hungary, Poland, and Turkey. In each case the trio toured existing plants and facilities, with the aim of determining which one or more, if any, of four companies the parent company would purchase. Knight had ruled out the Turkish company immediately, based on the age of plant and equipment and on cultural problems, relative to productivity. The Hungarian-owned plant posed its own set of problems, although the owners and the state had been more than willing to deal. This, too, he rejected.

Knight and the analysts believed that both the Italian and Polish companies could be turned into highly profitable operations within a few years. Because both were similar in function, design, and age, and because excess capacity would exist if both were acquired, a choice had to be made between the two. The financing was similar, so it was the soft issues upon which this decision had to be made. Knight and the analysts considered factors such as national infrastructure, existing and potential management styles, employee motivation, cultural differences, and political risk. Much of what they knew was subjective. They had to do a considerable amount of political, social, cultural, and economic forecasting. Other factors had to be considered as well, such as the desire on the part of top corporate management to be positioned in both EEC countries and in Eastern Europe.

DISCUSSION QUESTIONS

1. Examine the factors Knight has to consider and discuss their possible contrasting conditions in the two countries. Recognizing that factual knowledge may not be available readily, try simply to isolate the potential types of differences that might exist.
2. What other factors might Knight need to consider?
3. What are the potential problems of not investing in each of the two countries?

Skopbank

Timo Santalainen, executive vice-president for strategic planning and human resources of Skopbank, Finland's largest savings bank, pondered the situation his bank was facing. In 1988, four years away from Europe 1992, Skopbank, with assets of over $25 billion, operated in a country that was not a member of the EEC. Neither were Sweden and Norway. A large number of Finns and Finnish firms had been making investments in the EEC, especially Spain, in anticipation of 1992. Santalainen, the company's CEO, and other top leaders were anxious to establish a position as quickly as possible within the European community. They had already determined to be a global competitor. They wondered how best to go about positioning themselves for 1992. Santalainen and his staff set out to examine the various alternatives. Among the strategies they considered were

1. Joint ventures, to split expense and gain expertise, as well as entry.
2. Acquisitions, to gain entry and expertise.
3. Simply opening offices in various EEC countries.
4. Diversifying into other fields besides savings banks to help spread the risk.

Other issues of concern were how to fit the 1992 strategy into a global strategy and whether to invest conservatively or heavily in EEC countries.

DISCUSSION QUESTIONS

1. Based on the strategies noted in the case, discuss the various options available to the banks and their pros and cons.
2. What would you recommend doing and why? How would you fit 1992 into a global strategy?
3. What implications are there for HRM? For example, restructuring?
4. If restructuring to cut costs were to occur, how could the bank overcome any negative aspects?

Factors to Consider

Your professor will ask the class to break up into groups to discuss the following situation. You have received a job offer with your current U.S.-based firm for a position in management in a foreign subsidiary in Paris. You jump at the opportunity and accept the job. Your employer wants you to go to Paris to talk with personnel there before you formally accept the job. You speak only a minimal amount of French and would have to become conversationally skilled in the language as well as read it. But for you, that poses no problem. However, because you will be in management, and because you will have to adjust to a new culture, there are factors, you now realize, that you need to consider. What are those factors and how might you adapt to each?

CHAPTER TWENTY-TWO

Entrepreneurship, Small Business Management, and Innovation

CHAPTER OBJECTIVES

By the time you complete studying this chapter you should be able to

1. Define entrepreneurship and distinguish it from small business management.
2. Discuss several reasons why entrepreneurship is of major interest at this time in the United States and Canada.
3. Discuss the stages of growth model and how growth affects entrepreneurship and small business management.
4. Discuss the transition from an entrepreneurship to a larger firm and the changes in management it demands.
5. Review current trends in entrepreneurship.
6. Discuss the relationships between competitiveness, innovation, and entrepreneurship.
7. Discuss the management of innovation.

CHAPTER OUTLINE

Definitions of Entrepreneur
The Entrepreneurial Mystique
Entrepreneurship and Innovation
Entrepreneurship and Small Business Management
   How the U.S. Small Business Administration Defines Small Business
Managing the Entrepreneurship/Small Business
   Planning
   Organizing
   Leading
   Controlling
   Problem Solving/Decision Making
Preserving Entrepreneurship
Trends in Entrepreneurship
   Campus Capitalists
   More Kids Are Staying in the Family Business
   Many Leave the Large Corporation for the Small Business
   More Women Are Becoming Entrepreneurs Than Ever Before
   International Entrepreneurship
   Intrapreneurship: Major Corporations Seek Entrepreneurship
   Additional Views of Intrapreneurship
Succession
The Management of Innovation
The Management Challenges Identified
Some Solutions Noted in the Chapter

America's Most Successful Entrepreneur

Kenneth Harry Olsen, an engineer by trade, learned to manage by running a Sunday school and, according to *Fortune,* was arguably America's most successful entrepreneur in the 1970s and 1980s. In twenty-nine short years, he took Digital Equipment Corporation (DEC) from start-up to sales of $7.6 billion in 1986. At that time DEC was bigger, adjusting for inflation, than Ford Motor Company when Henry Ford died, U.S. Steel when Andrew Carnegie sold out, and Standard Oil when John D. Rockefeller stepped aside. While others may have amassed more wealth for themselves or their shareholders, no one has built a more formidable industrial enterprise than DEC. That is why *Fortune* rated Olson America's most successful entrepreneur.

DEC's minicomputers changed the way people use computers. Prior to DEC, computers were mainframes housed in large, special centers available only for certain selected tasks. DEC created a rugged minicomputer that could be used by virtually anybody, anywhere, and hence helped spur the use of the computer. DEC, in 1985 and 1986, experienced a resurgence in sales and profits when most firms in the industry were losing money. It had back-to-back years with 20 percent revenue gains. Olson's successful 1986 strategy for DEC, emphasizing technological leadership and computer networking, had been farsightedly adopted fifteen years previously. As a consequence, DEC grabbed $2 billion worth of sales from IBM in 1986 and was viewed by most analysts as IBM's most serious challenger.

Olson did not succumb to the problems that many entrepreneurs face. He learned to delegate responsibility, he devised a decentralized organization, he kept learning, and he kept changing, even abandoning the decentralized organization when he found it unsuitable to the needs of the company.

Even successful entrepreneurs sometimes face problems. By the early 1980s, it was apparent that DEC's computer technology was evolving faster than the rest of the company. In 1979 the company bet billions of dollars on a new generation of DEC super minis. Olson recognized that the decentralized control given product managers was no longer effective. It took five years of cajoling, hounding, and prodding to dismantle the product line organization and replace it with a functional one, but it worked.

Perhaps what separates Olson most from the average entrepreneur is that he learned how to manage. He declares, "A good manager never has to make any decisions at all." Olson delegates and seldom gives direct orders. But he is quick to punish those who are remiss. He believes strongly in committees and decision by consensus. In grueling review sessions, consensus is eventually reached. He solicits ideas and tosses out a few of his own. He does have one weakness, though. He publicly ridicules subordinates, avoiding one-on-one confrontations. He does so most often through the electronic mail system. He also employs what he calls "pulse management," in which he probes deeply into an area of the company that catches his attention. For example, he once personally spent numerous hours on a workbench designing a new standardized electrical plug for DEC equipment. But, overall, the company is creative, is open to exploiting opportunity, and sponsors innovation.

SOURCE: Peter Petre, "America's Most Successful Entrepreneur," *Fortune* (October 27, 1986), pp. 24–32.

The reasonable man adapts himself to the world: the unreasonable one persists in trying to adapt the world to himself, therefore, all progress depends on the unreasonable man.

George Bernard Shaw

The entrepreneurs sustain the world. In their careers there is little of optimizing calculation, nothing of delicate balance in markets. They overthrow establishments rather than establish equilibria. They are the heroes of economic life.

George Gilder
The Spirit of Enterprise

Ken Olson of DEC, Steven Jobs and Stephen Wozniak of Apple Computer, Mary Kay Ash of Mary Kay Cosmetics, Ray Kroc of MacDonald's, Sam Walton of Wal-Mart, An Wang of Wang Laboratories, Debbi and Randy Fields of Mrs. Fields' Cookies, H. Ross Perot of Electronic Data Systems, Carlo DeBenedetti of Olivetti, Akio Morita of Sony, and hundreds of thousands of others share a very important characteristic: they are successful entrepreneurs. Because he learned how to manage, Ken Olson is perhaps America's most successful entrepreneur. He learned to manage, not always as the textbooks might teach it, and he learned to delegate, to control, and to plan. He developed strategies and the related organization structures that proved to be just right for his company in its varying situations.

Recently there has been a significant increase in interest in entrepreneurship. Many people think that entrepreneurship makes America great. Much of this reverence for the phenomenon comes as a consequence of the realization that small entrepreneurial firms contribute very significantly to the well-being of the national economy—and did so especially in the ten-year period from 1977 to 1987. In fact, most of the jobs created in that ten-year period came not from major corporations, but from start-up operations of small businesses. From 1977 to 1987, seventeen million new jobs were created in small businesses, compared to a net loss of 3.1 million jobs among the Fortune 500 companies.[1] New corporations formed per year reached 700,000 for the first time in 1986.[2]

David Birch, of MIT's Program of Neighborhood and Regional Change, suggests that while the impact of entrepreneurship on the national economy is very significant, entrepreneurship can have an even greater impact on a small or regional section of the country. In California, for example, 70 percent of the state's employment results from small-scale entrepreneurs.[3] In another example, many entrepreneurs are emerging from the declining "rustbelt," those areas of the Northeast and Midwest where heavy industry has failed. What is unique about the situation that occurred in the rustbelt in the mid- to late 1980s was that the entrepreneurship that occurred resulted from massive layoffs, as rustbelt firms collapsed one after another. Furthermore, many of these entrepreneurships were founded by blue-collar workers.[4]

A manager's style can be revealed in his or her leisure activities as well as on the job behavior. Ken Olson prefers canoes to yachts, and as an outdoorsman, likes to explore the wilderness areas of Canada. He is more the adventuresome entrepreneur than the corporate mogul. (SOURCE © George Lange/Outline Press)

This chapter explores entrepreneurship and small business, beginning by defining them and distinguishing between them. Managing the small business/entrepreneurship is then discussed, with each of the management functions viewed from that perspective. Ways of preserving entrepreneurship are reviewed, and major trends in the process are noted. Finally, a brief discussion of managing innovations occurs.

Definitions of Entrepreneur[5]

Identifying exactly what entrepreneurship is has been a difficult task. Historically, entrepreneurship has been conceptualized partially as an economic function. In the early eighteenth century, Richard Cantillon observed that an entrepreneur was one who bore the risk of buying and selling.[6] Economists Adam Smith and Jean Baptiste Say suggested that an entrepreneur was someone who brought together the factors of production.[7] Austrian economist Joseph Schumpeter (1883–1950) later added innovation and the exploiting of opportunity as actions by the entrepreneur.[8] Some have suggested that the creation of new enterprises is entrepreneurship.[9] More recently Howard H. Stevenson and William H. Sahlman point out, however, that entrepreneurs can be identified who did not purchase or sell, who did not bring together the factors of production, who were not innovators but followers, and who did not create businesses, but managed the work of others.[10]

Today, entrepreneurship is recognized to be as much an attitude as it is a role, practiced in small and large organizations.[11] Stevenson and Jose Carlos Jarillo-Mossi's broad definition, added to here, defines an entrepreneur as "a person who perceives opportunity; finds the pursuit of opportunity desirable in the context of his (or her) life situation; and believes that success is possible."[12] It is also clear that an entrepreneur is one who initiates changes.

Note that it is their approach to problem solving that is the key difference between entrepreneurs and others. They look for opportunities. They are risk takers. They are not merely solving problems, they are not just reacting to problems, they are looking for opportunities. This view of the opportunity aspect of entrepreneurship was noted in 1964 by Peter Drucker, who indicated that "Resources, to produce results, must be allocated to opportunities, rather than to problems . . . maximization of opportunities is a meaningful, indeed a precise definition of the entrepreneurial job."[13] Later, in 1974, Drucker repeated this theme: "an entrepreneur . . . has to redirect resources from areas of low or diminishing results to areas of high or increasing results. He [or she] has to slough off yesterday and to render obsolete what already exists and is already known. He [or she] has to create tomorrow."[14] Entrepreneurship is also about change. Entrepreneurs initiate change.[15] They may initiate changes in all aspects of organizational functioning—marketing, finance, operations, human resources, and information. Drucker later combined his views of the opportunistic nature of entrepreneurs with this aspect of change, "the entrepreneur always searches for change, responds to it, and exploits it as an opportunity."[16] Fred Smith, founder of Federal Express, was just such an entrepreneur. He saw an opportunity and seized it.

In seeking to understand entrepreneurship, others have searched to identify the personal characteristics of entrepreneurs. Several commonly accepted characteristics include the need for achievement, the need for control, intuitive orientation, and a risk-taking propensity. Other commonly discussed, but not universally accepted factors include childhood deprivation, minority group membership, and early adolescent economic experiences.[17]

Elliott Hoffman, founder and owner of Just Desserts, a chain of specialty bakeries in San Francisco, experiences both the advantages and disadvantages of entrepreneurship, but on balance, he loves it. (SOURCE © Ed Kashi)

Many people claim that entrepreneurs and entrepreneurships are one of the major ways in which U.S. firms are able to compete with foreign firms—that is, principally because of innovation.[18] Not all agree, however. George Gilder suggests that entrepreneurs often sell out to foreign competitors, posing problems for the economy by giving away our technology.[19] He also points out that only large firms have the staying power necessary to compete in many industries, thus reducing the importance of entrepreneurships. Nonetheless, most would agree that entrepreneurs better enable the United States to compete successfully internationally because they have introduced literally hundreds of thousands of new products. It is clear that they are helping to create an export boom and thereby helping to reduce the U.S. trade deficit.[20]

The Entrepreneurial Mystique[21]

There definitely is something exciting about being an entrepreneur. It offers several psychological payoffs: a chance to be your own boss, initiate change, do it your way, take advantage of opportunities, and be at the forefront of change. There are also disadvantages—long hours, hard work, and risk. Most small businesses end in failure.

There are also several characteristics of entrepreneurs that are very different from those of other managers. Several surveys identify these characteristics. A

FIGURE 22.1 COMPARATIVE CHARACTERISTICS OF FORTUNE 500 EXECUTIVES, ENTREPRENEURS, AND SMALL BUSINESS EXECUTIVES

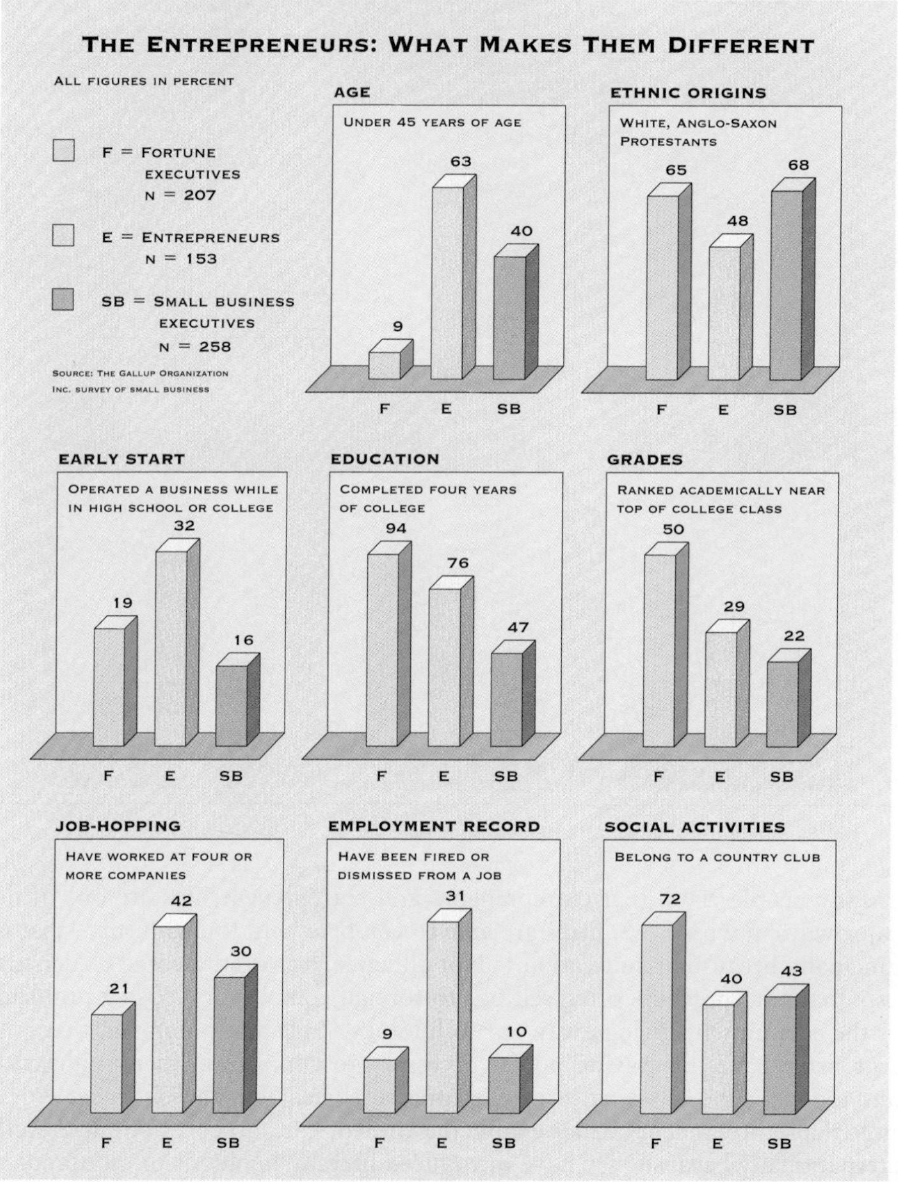
THE ENTREPRENEURS: WHAT MAKES THEM DIFFERENT
ALL FIGURES IN PERCENT
F = FORTUNE EXECUTIVES N = 207
E = ENTREPRENEURS N = 153
SB = SMALL BUSINESS EXECUTIVES N = 258
SOURCE: THE GALLUP ORGANIZATION INC. SURVEY OF SMALL BUSINESS
AGE
UNDER 45 YEARS OF AGE
9
63
40
F E SB
ETHNIC ORIGINS
WHITE, ANGLO-SAXON PROTESTANTS
65
48
68
F E SB
EARLY START
OPERATED A BUSINESS WHILE IN HIGH SCHOOL OR COLLEGE
19
32
16
F E SB
EDUCATION
COMPLETED FOUR YEARS OF COLLEGE
94
76
47
F E SB
GRADES
RANKED ACADEMICALLY NEAR TOP OF COLLEGE CLASS
50
29
22
F E SB
JOB-HOPPING
HAVE WORKED AT FOUR OR MORE COMPANIES
21
42
30
F E SB
EMPLOYMENT RECORD
HAVE BEEN FIRED OR DISMISSED FROM A JOB
9
31
10
F E SB
SOCIAL ACTIVITIES
BELONG TO A COUNTRY CLUB
72
40
43
F E SB

SOURCE: ELLEN GRAHAM, "THE ENTERPRENEURIAL MYSTIQUE," WALL STREET JOURNAL, SPECIAL REPORT ON SMALL BUSINESS, MAY 30, 1985, SECTION 3, PP. 1, 4, 6–7. REPRINTED BY PERMISSION OF WALL STREET JOURNAL, © 1985 DOW JONES & COMPANY, INC. ALL RIGHTS RESERVED WORLDWIDE.

AT DEC: *Ken Olson in many ways exemplifies the mystique associated with entrepreneurs. He started with nothing, he struggled, and he made DEC very successful. He has many of the personality characteristics that have been identified as common among entrepreneurs. Perhaps most important is the way he has learned to manage—for example, by using his pulse management technique.*

recent survey comparing entrepreneurs to Fortune 500 executives and small business executives is typical.[22] The *Wall Street Journal*/Gallup survey suggested that entrepreneurs tend to be mavericks, dreamers, and loners. They have rough edges, are uncompromising, and need to do it their own way. They are not particularly good students, are more likely to be expelled from school than others, and are less likely to graduate from college. They also are likely to take charge at an earlier age, are fired more frequently, and jump from job to job more often. See Figures 22.1 and 22.2.

But Fortune 500 executives, entrepreneurs, and small business executives all shared some common factors, as well. They all showed an early inclination to

FIGURE 22.2   ADDITIONAL COMPARATIVE CHARACTERISTICS OF FORTUNE 500 EXECUTIVES, ENTREPRENEURS, AND SMALL BUSINESS EXECUTIVES

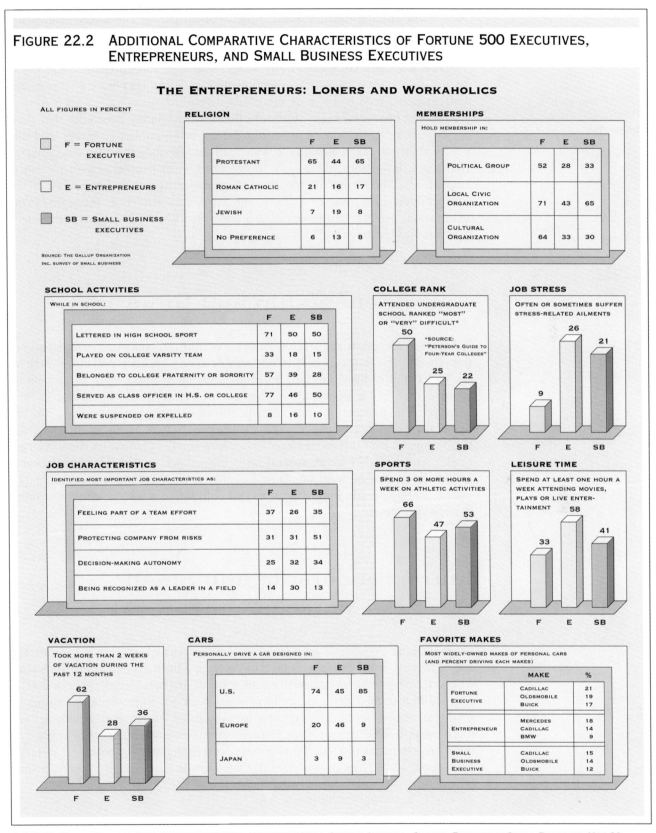

THE ENTREPRENEURS: LONERS AND WORKAHOLICS

ALL FIGURES IN PERCENT

☐ F = FORTUNE EXECUTIVES

☐ E = ENTREPRENEURS

▨ SB = SMALL BUSINESS EXECUTIVES

SOURCE: THE GALLUP ORGANIZATION INC. SURVEY OF SMALL BUSINESS

RELIGION

	F	E	SB
PROTESTANT	65	44	65
ROMAN CATHOLIC	21	16	17
JEWISH	7	19	8
NO PREFERENCE	6	13	8

MEMBERSHIPS

HOLD MEMBERSHIP IN:

	F	E	SB
POLITICAL GROUP	52	28	33
LOCAL CIVIC ORGANIZATION	71	43	65
CULTURAL ORGANIZATION	64	33	30

SCHOOL ACTIVITIES

WHILE IN SCHOOL:

	F	E	SB
LETTERED IN HIGH SCHOOL SPORT	71	50	50
PLAYED ON COLLEGE VARSITY TEAM	33	18	15
BELONGED TO COLLEGE FRATERNITY OR SORORITY	57	39	28
SERVED AS CLASS OFFICER IN H.S. OR COLLEGE	77	46	50
WERE SUSPENDED OR EXPELLED	8	16	10

COLLEGE RANK

ATTENDED UNDERGRADUATE SCHOOL RANKED "MOST" OR "VERY" DIFFICULT*

*SOURCE: "PETERSON'S GUIDE TO FOUR-YEAR COLLEGES"

50 F
25 E
22 SB

JOB STRESS

OFTEN OR SOMETIMES SUFFER STRESS-RELATED AILMENTS

9   F
26 E
21 SB

JOB CHARACTERISTICS

IDENTIFIED MOST IMPORTANT JOB CHARACTERISTICS AS:

	F	E	SB
FEELING PART OF A TEAM EFFORT	37	26	35
PROTECTING COMPANY FROM RISKS	31	31	51
DECISION-MAKING AUTONOMY	25	32	34
BEING RECOGNIZED AS A LEADER IN A FIELD	14	30	13

SPORTS

SPEND 3 OR MORE HOURS A WEEK ON ATHLETIC ACTIVITIES

66 F
47 E
53 SB

LEISURE TIME

SPEND AT LEAST ONE HOUR A WEEK ATTENDING MOVIES, PLAYS OR LIVE ENTERTAINMENT

33 F
58 E
41 SB

VACATION

TOOK MORE THAN 2 WEEKS OF VACATION DURING THE PAST 12 MONTHS

62 F
28 E
36 SB

CARS

PERSONALLY DRIVE A CAR DESIGNED IN:

	F	E	SB
U.S.	74	45	85
EUROPE	20	46	9
JAPAN	3	9	3

FAVORITE MAKES

MOST WIDELY-OWNED MAKES OF PERSONAL CARS (AND PERCENT DRIVING EACH MAKES)

	MAKE	%
FORTUNE EXECUTIVE	CADILLAC	21
	OLDSMOBILE	19
	BUICK	17
ENTREPRENEUR	MERCEDES	18
	CADILLAC	14
	BMW	9
SMALL BUSINESS EXECUTIVE	CADILLAC	15
	OLDSMOBILE	14
	BUICK	12

SOURCE: ELLEN GRAHAM, "THE ENTREPRENEURIAL MYSTIQUE," WALL STREET JOURNAL, SPECIAL REPORT ON SMALL BUSINESS, MAY 30, 1985, SECTION 3, PP. 1, 4, 6–7. REPRINTED BY PERMISSION OF WALL STREET JOURNAL, © 1985 DOW JONES & COMPANY, INC. ALL RIGHTS RESERVED WORLDWIDE.

hard work and high achievement. Most worked before age fifteen and earned about half of their college tuition. At least two-thirds of these three groups work sixty or more hours per week. Corporate officers tend to be more outstanding students and have completed more years of college. Entrepreneurs tend not to be joiners or team players, something necessary for corporate management. Entrepreneurs tend to be more ethnically diverse.

A review of several other studies by John A. Hornaday concludes that there are common characteristics of entrepreneurs: self-confidence, energy and diligence, ability to take calculated risks, creativity, flexibility, positive response to challenges, leadership, the ability to get along with people, responsiveness to suggestions, knowledge of the market, perseverance and determination, resourcefulness, the need to achieve, initiative, independence, foresight, profit orientation, perceptiveness, optimism, and versatility of knowledge, especially as related to technology.[23]

Entrepreneurship and Innovation

Whether practiced in the large organization (intrapreneurship) or in small entrepreneurships, innovation depends almost singly on entrepreneurial activity for its existence. By definition, an **innovation** is an application of something creative that has a significant impact on an organization, an industry, or a society.[24] The process of innovation is one of change. Entrepreneurs, not bureaucrats, promulgate change.[25] Not surprisingly, two recent studies of innovation suggest that it is more likely to occur in smaller companies than in larger ones.[26] On the other hand, several large firms, such as 3M, Hewlett-Packard, Miliken, Johnson & Johnson, Dow-Corning and others, have mastered innovation, largely by adopting structures and cultures that resemble those in small entrepreneurships.[27]

Entrepreneurship and Small Business Management[28]

Distinguishing between a small business and an entrepreneurship is relatively easy. The term *small business* is used to describe a business according to its size, whereas *entrepreneurship* describes an attitude or behavioral process that is engaged in a small-, medium-, or large-sized business. Entrepreneurs run many small businesses, but not all, perhaps not even most. Many small businesses are run by people who do not have entrepreneurial leanings and do not engage in the entrepreneurial process. Furthermore, entrepreneurs can be found in large businesses as well. The most frequently cited definition of small business is that provided by the Small Business Administration (SBA).

How the U.S. Small Business Administration Defines Small Business

To qualify for a loan from the SBA, a small business must have three principal characteristics:

1. It does not dominate its industry.
2. It has less than $10 million in annual sales.
3. It has fewer than 1,000 employees.[29]

However, there are some additional qualifications:

1. It must be independently owned and operated.
2. If in manufacturing, it should employ no more than 250 employees or be a relatively small size within a specific industry. In certain industries 1,500 employees is considered small.
3. If in wholesaling, it has annual sales no greater than $9.5 to $22 million, depending on the industry.
4. If in retailing or service, its annual sales are no greater than $2 to $8 million, depending on the industry.
5. If in construction, its annual receipts cannot exceed $9.5 million for the three most recently completed fiscal years for general construction. In special trade construction, its annual receipts cannot exceed $1 to $2 million for the same time frame, depending on the industry.
6. If in agriculture, its annual receipts cannot be greater than $1 million. The SBA uses these characteristics as guidelines. They are not hard-and-fast rules.

Numerous other definitions of what constitutes a small business can be found. For example, if it is family-owned, if it is owned and operated by a small group of investors, if it is a franchise, if it operates locally, if it has fewer than one hundred employees, and so forth.

Regardless of the criteria chosen, it is clear that the number of small businesses far exceeds the number of large businesses. As shown in Table 22.1, more than 99 percent of this country's 14 million businesses are small. These 14 million businesses include farms, franchises, and professional organizations.

Table 22.1 Small Businesses Classified by Size

Percentage of Business	Number of Employees
88.9%	Fewer than 10 persons
94.7%	Fewer than 20 persons
99.2%	Fewer than 100 persons
99.9%	Fewer than 500 persons

SOURCE: "The State of Small Business: A Report to the President" (Washington, D.C.: U.S. Government Printing Office, 1985), based on a population of 14 million business firms.
SOURCE: Ellen Graham, "The Entrepreneurial Mystique," *Wall Street Journal*, Special Report on Small Business, May 30, 1985, Section 3, pp. 1, 4, 6–7. Reprinted by permission of Wall Street Journal, © 1985 Dow Jones & Company, Inc. All Rights Reserved Worldwide.

Managing the Entrepreneurship/ Small Business

In Chapter 9 we examined some models that suggested that as organizations grow they pass through a series of stages. The first stage might be called growth through creation. But it is often followed by a crisis of leadership. In this crisis

An entrepreneur must learn to manage. This often involves learning to be a leader of a small group of people, and learning to delegate to those people. (SOURCE © 1987 Mark Ferri)

the entrepreneur or small business manager arrives at a point at which he or she can no longer run the business properly. He or she needs either to become a professional manager or to hire one or more to manage the business. He or she may also need to structure the organization on an economic basis, dividing job tasks among several different people. The entrepreneur can no longer do it alone. Research makes it clear though that the style and the intentions of the entrepreneur will remain and will significantly affect the firm's future. Some find it impossible ever to let go.[30]

Problem solving in the areas of planning, organizing, leading, and controlling occur in entrepreneurships and small businesses much as they would in larger organizations, with the exception that these processes tend to be less formalized and often nonexistent, except for what is implied. It is this essence of transition to formalized professional management that is usually necessary to save an entrepreneurship in the long term.

Planning

Perhaps the most important aspect of managing a small business is learning how to plan. Even in the start-up stages of an entrepreneurship, it is critical to develop a business plan. A business plan typically contains specific objectives and plans to reach those objectives across the organization's major economic functions. Special attention is paid to target markets; product development, pricing, distribution, and promotion strategies; and the ability of the organization to finance marketing and operations.

Developing a business plan includes at least the following information:

1. An overview of the business, which helps define the organization's mission and functional parts.
2. A specific set of objectives against which performance can be measured both for the organization and employees.
3. A plan by which capital may be raised. Most banks, for example, require a detailed business plan before they will loan money on a new enterprise or an ongoing smaller one.
4. A marketing plan by which to run the organization.
5. A plan by which personnel may be recruited, an operations plan, and a materials purchasing plan.

About 85 percent of all new businesses will fail within ten years of their start-up, so planning to avoid such failure is critical.[31] Businesses fail for many reasons besides poor planning—for example, a lack of capital—but failing to set objectives and to develop plans and budgets can only lead to failure. Performing a SWOT analysis (strengths, weaknesses, opportunities, and threats) of the firm enables the manager to prepare better strategic and operating plans. The budget enables managers to predict potential cash shortages and to take necessary offsetting actions. Now that simulation models are available for personal computers, such as Lotus 1-2-3, virtually any small business can calculate pro forma financial statements (income statement, balance sheets, and cash flow) and should thereby better understand the internal operations of their organizations. Just as with any major organization, the entrepreneur/small business manager must ask him- or herself three questions and provide in-depth answers:

1. Where are we now?
2. Where do we want to be?
3. How do we get there?

Organizing

Most of the crises identified in organizing are growth-related structural problems. For example, once an organization has a functional structure, there eventually is a crisis of authority, as managers in charge of economic functional areas are yet to be delegated sufficient authority by the entrepreneur/small business owner manager. Later, once such authority has been delegated, comes the question of how to control this delegation of authority. New structures may be necessary to solve this problem.[32]

Furthermore, as organizations grow they typically change their structure—from functional to product to strategic business unit, for example. As pointed out in Chapters 8, 9, and 10, one of the major factors in making organizations more efficient today is structuring in such a way that more authority is delegated to lower-level positions. Thus, middle-level management and staff positions are eliminated as much as possible. These actions make the organization more efficient and also more responsive to the external environment. Entrepreneurs typically have a high need for achievement and a high need for power.[33] It is often difficult for them to delegate, especially to front-line employees. Unfortunately, many small entrepreneurs and small business owners are unable to make this transition to delegation, and their organizations fail.

AT DEC: *Ken Olson was able to delegate early in his entrepreneurial career and thereby enable his firm to grow. When he found that the decentralized structure was no longer appropriate, he made a major change to a more centralized structure in the mid-1980s. This was done to become more market driven.*

Leading

Entrepreneurs and small business managers must become the leaders as well as the managers of their organizations. They must provide vision, mission, goals, and objectives. They must also be responsive to the needs of their subordinates. Leadership in the small business organization tends to be extremely personal because about 90 percent of all registered business organizations have fewer than twenty employees.[34] As with any management skill, entrepreneurs must learn how to lead, although a few may be naturally born to the task. Some are natural visionaries and some are natural dynamic group leaders, but most are not. Entrepreneurs and small business managers must instill shared values among their employees. They must help satisfy their employees' needs—in short, they must become coaches. These are characteristics that are often not part of a high achiever's makeup. It is difficult for an individual who is a high achiever to want to be a coach.[35] Sometimes entrepreneurs and small business managers need to do things a little differently, as Management Challenge 22.1 suggests.

Controlling

Planning, organizing, and leading are insufficient without control. Many entrepreneurs and small business managers have difficulty learning how properly to control. Part of that deficiency results from poor planning. They don't set sufficiently detailed objectives with appropriate time frames. Sometimes entrepreneurs, such as Patrick McGovern, aren't concerned about control because they are interested in ideas and in creating wealth, but not in managing. Once the idea is launched, implementation and the related details bore them.

Properly controlling an organization depends on information. With the advent of PCs, there is no excuse for most small organizations not to have information available with which to control. There is an old saw about planning that says, "If you don't know where you are going, any road will get you there." An appropriate one for controlling might be "If you don't know where you have gotten to, you are not likely to get there again." Perhaps the most critical control component for the small business is the budget. It helps establish not only objectives and standards, but also something against which performance can be compared.

As discussed in Chapter 6, organizations tend to compete on the basis of their ability to differentiate or be a low-cost producer.[36] Therefore, from a competitive viewpoint, cost control is absolutely mandatory. Controlling costs is not only vital to control, but also to the ability to be strategically viable. Controlling is also difficult for many of these individuals because many of them start with some technical knowledge—engineering, medicine, computer programming, or sales—but have little knowledge of proper management techniques. They have an idea and they want to see it to its end. The company grows, but then they don't know what to do next.

Problem Solving/Decision Making

Entrepreneurs focus on opportunities. Therefore, they may not be adept at discerning problems or solving them. They may not even be interested in them if the problems deal with the mundane, everyday world. Management is not often of concern to them. While some small business managers may be more management oriented than typical entrepreneurs, nonetheless they too may need assistance in learning how to solve problems more scientifically, more rationally, as well as more intuitively.

Table 22.2 provides an overview of most of the major differences between entrepreneurs and professional managers (or administrators), with respect to how they might manage.

Preserving Entrepreneurship

As entrepreneurs and small business managers learn how to manage, what often happens is that the entrepreneurial orientation may be lost. Howard H. Stevenson and Jose Carlos Jarrillo-Mossi suggest that several actions must be taken to keep an organization entrepreneurial.[37] The entrepreneur or small business manager must increase the perception of the opportunity of entrepreneurship, build the desire to pursue that opportunity, and make people believe that they can succeed.

As companies grow there are certain questions that must be asked of them, answered by them, and defined in terms of remaining entrepreneurial:

1. What is the appropriate concept of control?
2. How does one emphasize the individual sense of responsibility, not authority?
3. What kind of failures is the company willing to accept?
4. How can teams be created and nurtured?
5. How does the company promote functional excellence in all positions?
6. How can the company assure continuous adaptive organizational change?

Trends in Entrepreneurship

In addition to the increased level of interest in the process, several trends are identifiable in entrepreneurship:

Table 22.2 The Entrepreneurial Culture vs. The Administrative Culture

		Entrepreneurial Focus		Administrative Focus	
		Characteristics	Pressures	Characteristics	Pressures
A	Strategic orientation	Driven by perception of opportunity	Diminishing opportunities Rapidly changing technology, consumer economics, social values, and political rules	Driven by controlled resources	Social contracts Performance measurement criteria Planning systems and cycles
B	Commitment to seize opportunities	Revolutionary, with short duration	Action orientation Narrow decision windows Acceptance of reasonable risks Few decision constituencies	Evolutionary, with long duration	Acknowledgment of multiple constituencies Negotiation about strategic course Risk reduction Coordination with existing resource base
C	Commitment of resources	Many stages, with minimal exposure at each stage	Lack of predictable resource needs Lack of control over the environment Social demands for appropriate use of resources Foreign competition Demands for more efficient resource use	A single stage, with complete commitment out of decision	Need to reduce risk Incentive compensation Turnover in managers Capital budgeting systems Formal planning systems
D	Control of resources	Episodic use or rent of required resources	Increased resource specialization Long resource life compared with need Risk of obsolescence Risk inherent in the identified opportunity Inflexibility of permanent commitment to resources	Ownership or employment of required resources	Power, status, and financial rewards Coordination of activity Efficiency measures Inertia and cost of change Industry structures
E	Management structure	Flat, with multiple informal networks	Coordination of key noncontrolled resources Challenge to hierarchy Employees' desire for independence	Hierarchy	Need for clearly defined authority and responsibility Organizational culture Reward systems Management theory

SOURCE: Howard H. Stevenson and David E. Gumpert, "The Heart of Entrepreneurship," *Harvard Business Review* (March–April 1985). Copyright © 1985 by the President and Fellows of Harvard College, all rights reserved.

AT DEC: *Ken Olson has been very careful to make sure that DEC has kept its opportunistic perspective. He has encouraged people to seek out opportunities and has rewarded people for them. He has let them know they can succeed.*

1. There is an increasing number of campus capitalists.
2. More and more kids are working in the family business.
3. More and more managers are leaving large corporations to start their own businesses.
4. There is an increasing number of female entrepreneurs in what has historically been mostly an all-male activity.
5. The level of international entrepreneurship is increasing.
6. Large organizations are attempting to put more entrepreneurship into their modes of operation.

Campus Capitalists[38]

In the mid-1980s, a major "craze" on college campuses was starting one's own business. There were only six entrepreneurial clubs on campuses in 1983, but two hundred fifty in 1985. In these clubs, nineteen- and twenty-year-olds learn

These attendees at a young entrepreneur's conference seem to be saying, "power to the entrepreneur." (SOURCE © Charles Thatcher)

lessons from successful entrepreneurs, many just a few years older than themselves. The businesses they engage in run from printing student calendars and writing software to opening pizza parlors. Undergraduate entrepreneur courses are jammed full, and conventional business schools are offering more and more entrepreneurial courses. The 1984 collegiate entrepreneurs' conference in Dallas was attended by seven hundred student entrepreneurs representing more than two hundred universities and seven foreign countries.

Typical of the entrepreneurs is Mark David McKee, who founded Pyramid Pizza in Lawrence, Kansas. In a matter of months, he had four locations and was searching for a fifth. Another is Brett Kingstone, a graduate of Stanford University, who has already started several successful businesses, including a publishing company, a fiber optics manufacturing firm, and an investment firm. Another is Rayvon Reynolds. He began with Teddy's Tuck-In Service, a college student pampering service, and moved on to steel fabrication, trash transit, and light construction and is now president of Advantage International Marketing and Chemical Manufacturing Company. With a partner, he owns the nation's third-largest roast beef sandwich franchise, Sir Beef.

Then consider Jimmy Enriquez. When he returned home to Corpus Christi after his first year at the University of Texas, he couldn't find a summer job. So he established a construction site cleaning firm that netted $30,000 in three months. Using $2,000 from that venture, he and a younger brother began leasing table soccer games to restaurants, building demand by setting up competitive leagues. This venture soon produced revenues of $60,000. After graduation, he co-founded a financial firm and is involved in several projects for reconstructing decayed housing. Then there is Kim Merritt, who began selling chocolate at age eleven when she decided she could make better chocolate than the local candy store. She created her own recipe and people liked it. She now sells chocolates in her own retail stores. Kim had just turned seventeen.

More Kids Are Staying in the Family Business[39]

It used to be that sons and daughters of entrepreneurs would opt for large corporate environments or management consulting rather than return to the family business. But that is changing for a number of reasons.

Jimmy Enriquez has enjoyed the entrepreneurial experience. Having already founded more than one successful venture, he seems hooked for life. (SOURCE © Charles Thatcher)

Kim Merritt, successful chocolateur, is shown here with some samples of her products. (SOURCE © Charles Thatcher)

Even though these children of entrepreneurs did not found the family business, it still offers them the opportunity to be an entrepreneur, something of great interest today. Because small businesses are growing rapidly, there are often opportunities for success and advancement that are absent in large firms. In a small company, decisions can be made quickly, with a minimum of red tape. In addition, many of the baby boom generation are uncomfortable in the highly competitive environment of a large corporation. The family business can offer a gentler life-style and the security and joy of working with people you have known your whole life.

There seems to be a sense of responsibility along with the sense of freedom that typifies those who stay with the family business. Carole F. Bitter, president of Freedman Supermarkets, a seven-unit chain with headquarters in Butler, Pennsylvania, comments, "I don't have a life of my own, but I'm my own boss." Most of these people would rather work hard for themselves and their own goals than at the whim of "the big company."

Not all stay with the family company, however. Joseph A. Hardy, Jr., senior vice-president of 84 Lumber, works for his father, whom he describes as driven and intimidating. But Hardy's younger son, Paul, left the company, rather than compete for his father's attention.

Many Leave the Larger Corporation for the Small Business[40]

More and more executives are leaving the large corporation and going into business for themselves. Typical of these is Austin Furst. In October 1985 Austin Furst sold 15 percent of his Vestron Video Corporation to the public for $70 million. Furst had given up a ten-year career at Time, Inc., to start his own company just a few years earlier. He comments that he didn't start Vestron or take it public for the money. What he wanted was control over his own life. "The corporate world rewards you economically and psychologically, but corporations tend to impose conformity attitudes, and form becomes more important than content."

Furst became an entrepreneur in 1981, when Time, Inc., lost interest in Time Life Films because of the division's continuing losses. Furst, who was president of this subsidiary, bought up the home video rights of the films that Time had. To do so, he had to take out a second mortgage on his house and use all his personal savings. But he hit the market at just the right time, as consumers wanted movies for their new VCRs. His big break came when he, and after months of coaxing California producers, landed Michael Jackson's "Thriller" video, and distributed a million copies of that tape for sale at $29.00.

John Styles was a senior vice-president of operations for LifeMark, a Houston-based hospital management firm, but he could see that it wasn't going to grow, and he wasn't going to be able to leapfrog them. So he chucked his ten-year career, and with the aid of venture capital, started his own company, Ambulatory Hospitals, which he expected to break even in a year. Typical of entrepreneurs, he became bored running the business, and hired someone else as CEO. Now he spends his time charting the company's future course.

L. J. Seven started Mostek in 1969, leaving Texas Instruments to be on his own and "make a lot more money." After his company was purchased in 1980 by United Technologies, he decided to move on because he quickly grew tired of the drudgery of working for a large company again. There was too much control, too many reports to be handed in. He wanted control of his own life.

Anna Marks (left) and owner/ entrepreneur Frada Silver run the Seltzer Sisters, a South San Francisco firm that delivers bottles of seltzer to customer's homes. (SOURCE © Ed Kashi)

So in 1981 he co-founded a venture capital firm that has proven immensely successful, founding, among others, Lotus Development Corporation.

The underlying theme expressed by these and other entrepreneurially oriented executives seems to be the desire to be independent and to be able to take risks. But these people aren't the only ones leaving the big company environment for their version of greener pastures. As part of the restructuring of major corporations, many firms are selling off their subsidiaries to their current managements. For example, the leveraged buyout of Playtex by then president Joel E. Smilow helped save Playtex from floundering sales under two different conglomerate owners in less than two years. Similarly, another former Beatrice subsidiary, Meadow Gold, prospered when bought by Borden. They prospered, according to President Jay I. Johnson, because of Borden's focus on dairy products, which was only one of the many Beatrice subsidiaries.

Similarly, Diamond International left the Diamond Shamrock conglomerate after its breakup in 1986. Purchase of the firm by the management group allowed the company to become extremely profitable. Under its former conglomerate owners, it had been on a downward slide. The thrill of ownership, the renewed interest of employees, and some unique motivation programs combined to aid the company in its efforts. Entrepreneurship again was the key.[41] Collectively, these managers reveal that they were able to manage their businesses better because they were free of bureaucracy. Each made a former corporate subsidiary a successful entrepreneurial endeavor.

More Women Are Becoming Entrepreneurs Than Ever Before

A record number of women are becoming entrepreneurs.[42] *Inc.* magazine's entrepreneur of the year for 1987 was a woman, Betsy Tabac, who runs her policy research and writing firm out of her Cleveland home.[43] One reason suggested for this rise in feminine entrepreneurship is that many feel they reach an impasse on the way to the top in corporate America. So they strike out on their own.[44] The "typical" female entrepreneur is the first-born child of middle-class parents. Her father was often self-employed. She has a degree in liberal arts, is married, and has children. She begins her business venture when she is between the ages of thirty-five and forty-five.[45]

Female entrepreneur, Joan Barnes, founded Gymboree, a preschool exercise program, as an outgrowth of a part-time job. This Burlingame, California business was so successful, that she sold several hundred franchises, licensed the name for clothing and accessory items, and opened her own retail stores. (SOURCE © Robert Holmgren)

How Signode Fosters Intrapreneurs

Signode Industries, Inc., is a privately held corporation, formed by a leveraged buyout. Based in Glenview, Illinois, it employs about six thousand people worldwide, sells its products in more than one hundred countries, and has annual sales of nearly $750 million. It is the leading manufacturer of steel and plastic strapping systems for use in packaging and handling systems. Its other businesses include construction products, fastening tools, and bar coding systems. Signode wanted to foster intrapreneurship as a "big" company. It sought ways to create new products and act like a "small" entrepreneurial company. How did it go about it?

Signode developed a nine-step process it has found successful in developing new ventures, all revolving around venture teams.

1. *Define company strengths and weaknesses.*
2. *Define your likes and dislikes.*
3. *Select the venture topic.*
4. *Form the venture team.* Pick your best people. The profiles for venture team members at Signode include such characteristics as being a doer, a decision maker, a risk taker, a "big picture" thinker, able to work in an unstructured environment, creative, and open-minded and having interpersonal skills, the

International Entrepreneurship

All over the world, especially in Europe and the Pacific rim, entrepreneurship is gaining popularity. In the United States, entrepreneurs are helping to overcome a large international trade deficit.[46] In France, as a consequence of their recognition of America's success in creating jobs from entrepreneurship, many Frenchmen are going into business and the government is getting out of business.[47] This is true in Great Britain, as well.[48] Even in Japan, where entrepreneurship has been discouraged by the loss of face incurred by leaving a company, entrepreneurship is increasing significantly.[49] And finally, even in the People's Republic of China, entrepreneurship and capitalism were on the rise and were being encouraged by the government prior to its 1989 crackdown on freedom.[50]

Intrapreneurship: Major Corporations Seek Entrepreneurship

An **intrapreneur** is a company employee who is allowed to act like an entrepreneur but does so for the company, rather than strike out on his or her own. The company subsidizes and encourages intrapreneurs to develop and implement their ideas. Gordon Pinchot developed the concept of intrapreneurship after realizing the frustration and discontent shared by many managers and employees in large organizations. Pinchot comments that "the problem is that organizations hire people for their intelligence and imagination and then tell them what to imagine." Pinchot continues, "Entrepreneurs are people driven

ability to communicate, good general business skills, tolerance for the creative thinking process and for failure, and problem-solving abilities.

5. *Launch the team.* Signode gives its people at least six months to prepare a proposal.

6. *Send the team to the marketplace.* The team should talk to potential customers, suppliers, and competitors. Most of Signode's teams conduct more than two thousand interviews per project. It is in researching the marketplace that teams often come up with the best idea.

7. *Funnel the ideas.* The idea development process starts with many ideas and ends with a few—a funneling process. Signode focuses on selecting the best, rather than eliminating the worst. Ideas are combined, changed, modified, and eliminated.

8. *Present to management.* The team presents a preliminary business plan to top management, addressing issues such as competitive advantage and cash flow. Signode's usual hurdle rate for ventures is 15 percent ROI, after taxes.

9. *Launch the venture.* When a new venture is launched, the business is usually formed around several of the team's core members who become directors of the new business. Signode uses a very ambitious incentive plan to encourage and reward performance.

Signode's adventure teams have proven so profitable that it expects 25 percent of its 1990 profits to be derived from new ventures created in the last three years.

SOURCE: Robert J. Schaffhauser, "How a Mature Firm Fosters Intrapreneurs," *Planning Review* (March 1986), pp. 6–11.

by a need to see their visions become real; intrapreneurs share that need. Intrapreneurs are people with entrepreneurial personalities. Intrapreneurs, like entrepreneurs, are always self-starting and both cannot be primarily motivated by money. Instead they are motivated by visions. To them, money is just a way of keeping score."[51] Intrapreneurs are best rewarded by the organization in programs in which results lead to compensation, much as an entrepreneur would be rewarded by his or her success by the financial rewards of the marketplace. The 3-M Company has been especially good at fostering intrapreneurship.

Companies buy books such as *In Search of Excellence* and *Intrapreneuring*[52] for their managers because they want them to emulate the successes detailed in those books. Recognizing that success depends on innovation and the seizing of opportunity, more and more major corporations are attempting to incorporate entrepreneurship into their cultures. This attempt at encouraging intrapreneurship in large companies could not come at a better time for major U.S. corporations, as they see many of their best employees leaving their firms to become entrepreneurs. These large organizations discover that these entrepreneurs develop many new products that often compete directly with the parent firm. How do firms go about fostering intrapreneurship? Global Management Challenge tells how Signode Industries achieves this end.

IBM's personal computer was developed using the intrapreneurial approach. IBM established a separate division, located in Fort Lauderdale, Florida, far away from its Armonk, New York, headquarters and far away from any other major IBM division. This division was uniquely allowed to act as an independent subsidiary. It was largely because of this independence that the PC was developed as quickly as it was and was a major market success. Gordon Pinchot says

David Glass is a chip off the old CEO, Sam Walton. Corporate succession is often a problem, but especially so in entrepreneurships where drive and vision are so critical to success. (SOURCE © Jim Knowles/Picture Group)

of it, "Perhaps most importantly intrapreneurship makes corporations highly responsive, and top management will be able to turn the corporation on a dime to respond to changes in the market."[53] United Airlines, IBM, 3M, Texas Instruments, Northwestern Bell, and Kodak all have extensive intrapreneurship programs.[54]

ENTREPRENEURSHIP AND RESTRUCTURING

Much of the concept of restructuring discussed in Chapters 8 and 9 is aimed at increasing the independence of strategic business unit managers or new product managers, enabling them to act as if they were entrepreneurs. As intrapreneurs, corporate employees are allowed to take risks, their projects are funded, and they are allowed to turn creations and inventions into innovations.

Thomas J. Peters argues in *Thriving on Chaos*[55] that the future faced by most organizations will be one of constant accelerating rates of change, with each change being more significant than the previous one. This has been echoed by a number of authorities, including Alvin Toffler in *Future Shock*,[56] and Michael Naylor, executive in charge of strategic planning at General Motors.[57] Peters argues that because of these increasing changes and their increasing magnitude, organizations must be restructured into smaller units in order to be responsive to the demands of the changing marketplace. Responsiveness usually requires innovation. A new type of organizational culture is required to be able to be successful economically in the future. Honda is often used as a model of the future organization. It has, for example, been able to reduce the amount of time it takes from design to production of an automobile to one year, while the typical American firm takes seven years.[58] Peters sees pursuing fast-paced innovation as one of the five key steps for surviving in this chaotic environment and an entire intrapreneurial orientation as one way to achieve innovation.[59]

Succession

One of the major problems entrepreneurs face is the issue of succession: who will follow them as head of the organization. The entrepreneur must choose a successor if he or she expects the organization to continue to be well run. If investors are involved, their needs must also be recognized. Typically they seek a smooth transition from one top manager to another. The entrepreneur must establish criteria for his or her successor. Sam Walton picked someone much like himself, when he decided to become less active in Wal-Mart, as Management Challenge 22.2 describes.

The Management of Innovation

An **innovation** is something creative that has a significant impact on an organization, a society, or an industry. There are three principal types of innovation: product, process, and marketing.[60] **Product innovation** results in new products or services or enhancements to old products or services. **Process innovation** is that which results in improved processes in the organization—for example, operations, HRM or financing. **Marketing innovation** is related to the marketing functions of promotion, pricing, and distribution, as well as to the product function other than product development, for example, packaging or advertising.

Managing innovation is no easy task. It involves a strategy to innovate and a total organizational commitment to the task. It is clear that a certain type of organizational culture must exist to be successful at innovation. Among the major characteristics of this culture are encouragement of creativity, rewards for creativity, encouragement of risk taking, open communication, allowance for errors, participative climate, structural mechanisms that aid creativity, training in creative processes, and flexibility.[61] The individual manager must pursue a leadership style that possesses these same types of characteristics. Finally, the individuals involved in innovation need to be certain that they can, in fact, be innovative and understand and be able to use the creative techniques and processes. They do not have to be uniquely creative. Everyone is creative to some degree, and the innovative organization and manager will bring it out.[62] Individuals can learn many processes to enhance their creativity. Brainstorming and storyboarding, described in Chapter 3, are two of more than fifty major processes. Innovation is considered to be so important to the future of U.S. competitiveness that *Business Week* devoted an entire special issue to this topic in June 1989 and again in June, 1990.[63]

The Management Challenges Identified

1. Change
2. Increasing competition, especially foreign

Some Solutions Noted in the Chapter

1. Entrepreneurship
2. Innovation

Summary

1. An entrepreneur is someone who perceives and pursues an opportunity, believes that success is possible, and initiates change. His or her business is an entrepreneurship and is defined without regard to the resources controlled. A small business is defined by its financial or other operating characteristics and not by the process by which it is run. Some small businesses are entrepreneurial and others are not.

2. There are several reasons that entrepreneurship is of major interest at this point in America's history: Most new jobs in the last ten years have been created by small businesses—small businesses have a higher return on investment than larger businesses, and they tend to be more innovative than large businesses. Finally, there is a certain mystique and high level of psychological satisfaction in being an entrepreneur or in running your own small business.

3. As organizations grow, preserving entrepreneurship is critical. To retain the entrepreneurial spirit, organizations must increase the perception of opportunity, build the desire to pursue opportunity, and make people believe that they can succeed.

4. One of the key responsibilities of an entrepreneur as the organization grows is to learn how to manage—problem solving in planning, organizing, leading, and controlling. The central thrust of maintaining entrepreneurship is maintaining the difference in the approach to decision making and problem solving for that taken in nonentrepreneurial organizations.

5. Current trends in entrepreneurship include more kids staying in the family business, an increase in campus capitalists, many individuals leaving large corporations to start their own businesses, an increase in the number of female entrepreneurs, and an increase in the level of entrepreneurship (intrapreneurship) in the larger corporations.

6. Organizations face more chaotic environments than ever before. Restructuring to intrapreneurial arrangements is perceived by many experts as absolutely mandatory to future success for large organizations. Competitiveness and innovation have both been increased by such entrepreneurial (intrapreneurial) arrangements.

7. There are three principal types of innovation which must be managed: product, process, and marketing. Managing innovation properly requires a certain organizational culture, and leadership style. Individuals must be taught how to use creative processes.

Thinking About Management

1. Discuss why you would or would not want to be an entrepreneur.
2. Indicate why you think you might be an entrepreneur, or not.
3. Describe the major reasons that entrepreneurship has been important in America's recent economic history.
4. Review the topics of entrepreneurship and intrapreneurship and their relationship to competitiveness and innovation.
5. Indicate how an entrepreneur would
   A. Plan
   B. Organize
   C. Lead

D. Control

E. Make decisions

6. Discuss the current trends in entrepreneurship.

Stew's Dairy

Stew's family had been in the dairy business for many years, but the family dairy was virtually wiped out by a road expansion. It was at that time that Stew had some serious choices to make. The dairy business had been declining, so perhaps the road expansion was a blessing in disguise. People didn't buy home delivered milk much anymore, they bought it at the grocery store. The supply of milk was vanishing, too, because dairy farms in the area were being sold for real estate development. Stew really didn't have a dairy business to go back to, and funds were limited. But Stew persevered. He decided to offer a limited line of groceries in his dairy store, creating sort of a mini-market. He wondered how to compete with all of the other similar stores. He was almost out of money. A bank finally agreed to give him the necessary loan. His family was tired and anxious, as was he. After many hours of pondering, he decided to add some fun to the store as a differentiating factor. He also wanted to provide the best service he could to customers.

DISCUSSION QUESTIONS

1. How do you differentiate a small grocery and dairy from other small grocery stores—that is, provide fun? Here's a hint: be creative.

2. How could you provide more service than your competition? Here's a hint: be creative.

3. What kind of work ethic will Stew and his family need to make this endeavor a success? What sacrifices will they have to make?

Why Work for Someone Else?

Jack and his two partners had slowly but surely built their real estate business into a successful one. In the 11 years that they had worked together, their individual profit distribution had risen from $25,000 per year to just over $100,000 per year. This did not include the appreciation of properties they owned, including the company's building.

In early 1989 they had been approached by a national real estate group seeking to move in to their market area, which was interested in purchasing their firm. Eventually their offer became too good to turn down. They retained ownership in their building and received a five-year lease from the national firm. Jack and his partners each received handsome salaries, but were asked to sign an non-competitive contract for one year.

At first, Jack loved the arrangement. He didn't have to work as he had in the past, he had no responsibility, and he could take it easy. But as the year went by, he began to think about going back into business for himself again. He missed the excitement, the challenge, the rewards of seeing his business grow. He thought that when the year was up, he would start anew.

DISCUSSION QUESTIONS

1. Why would Jack want to give up such an easy job that paid him so well?

2. How does Jack fit the mold of the entrepreneur?

3. What are the rewards Jack will receive from his decision?

Entrepreneurial Profile

This Entrepreneurial Profile was created by the Center for Entrepreneurial Management, a 2,500-member private organization whose purpose is to provide educational and informational services to its members and others. The profile focuses on twenty-six characteristics that seem to differentiate its members from others. Read each question and select the answer that best seems to describe you or what you would do. After you have completed it, your instructor will tell you how to score it and will help you interpret the results.

1. How were your parents employed?
   a. Both worked and were self-employed for most of their working lives.
   b. Both worked and were self-employed for some part of their working lives.
   c. One parent was self-employed for most of his or her working life.
   d. One parent was self-employed at some point in his or her working life.
   e. Neither parent was ever self-employed.

2. Have you ever been fired from a job?
   a. Yes, more than once.
   b. Yes, once.
   c. No.

3. Are you an immigrant, or were your parents or grandparents immigrants?
   a. I was born outside of the United States.
   b. One or both of my parents were born outside of the United States.
   c. At least one of my grandparents was born outside of the United States.
   d. Does not apply.

4. Your work career has been:
   a. Primarily in small business (under 100 employees).
   b. Primarily in medium-sized business (100 to 500 employees).
   c. Primarily in big business (over 500 employees).

5. Did you operate any business before you were twenty?
   a. Many.
   b. A few.
   c. None.

6. What is your present age?
   a. 21–30.
   b. 31–40.
   c. 41–50.
   d. 51 or over.

7. You are the _____ child in the family.
   a. Oldest.
   b. Middle.
   c. Youngest.
   d. Other.

8. You are:
   a. Married.
   b. Divorced.
   c. Single.

9. Your highest level of formal education is:
   a. Some high school.
   b. High school diploma.
   c. Bachelor's degree.
   d. Master's degree.
   e. Doctor's degree.

10. What is your primary motivation in starting a business?
   a. To make money.
   b. I don't like working for someone else.
   c. To be famous.
   d. As an outlet for excess energy.

11. Your relationship to the parent who provided most of the family's income was:
   a. Strained.
   b. Comfortable.
   c. Competitive.
   d. Nonexistent.

12. If you could choose between working hard and working smart, you would:
   a. Work hard.
   b. Work smart.
   c. Both.

13. On whom do you rely for critical management advice?
   a. Internal management teams.
   b. External management professionals.
   c. External financial professionals.
   d. No one except myself.

14. If you were at the racetrack, which of these would you bet on?
   a. The daily double—a chance to make a killing.
   b. A 10-to-1 shot.
   c. A 3-to-1 shot.
   d. The 2-to-1 favorite.

15. The only ingredient that is both necessary and sufficient for starting a business is:
   a. Money.
   b. Customers.
   c. An idea or product.
   d. Motivation and hard work.

16. If you were an advanced tennis player and had a chance to play Boris Becker, you would:
   a. Turn it down because he could easily beat you.
   b. Accept the challenge, but not bet any money on it.
   c. Bet a week's pay that you would win.
   d. Get odds, bet a fortune, and try for an upset.

17. You tend to "fall in love" too quickly with:
   a. New product ideas.
   b. New employees.
   c. New manufacturing ideas.
   d. New financial plans.
   e. All of the above.

18. Which of the following personality types is best suited to be your right-hand person?
   a. Bright and energetic.
   b. Bright and lazy.
   c. Dumb and energetic.

19. You accomplish tasks better because:
   a. You are always on time.
   b. You are super-organized.
   c. You keep good records.

20. You hate to discuss:
   a. Problems involving employees.
   b. Signing expense accounts.
   c. New management practices.
   d. The future of the business.

21. Given a choice, you would prefer:
   a. Rolling dice with a 1-in-3 chance of winning.
   b. Working on a problem with a 1-in-3 chance of solving it in the allocated time.

22. If you could choose between the following competitive professions, it would be:
   a. Professional golf.
   b. Sales.
   c. Personnel counseling.
   d. Teaching.

23. If you had to choose between working with a partner who is a close friend and working with a stranger who is an expert in your field, you would choose:
   a. The close friend.
   b. The expert.

24. You enjoy being with people:
   a. When you have something meaningful to do.
   b. When you can do something new and different.
   c. Even when you have nothing planned.

25. In business situations that demand action, clarifying who is in charge will help produce results.
   a. Agree.
   b. Agree, with reservations.
   c. Disagree.

26. In playing a competitive game, you are concerned with:
   a. How well you play.
   b. Winning or losing.
   c. Both of the above.
   d. Neither of the above.

SOURCE: J. R. Mancuso, "The Entrepreneur's Quiz," Joseph Mancuso, The Center for Entrepreneurial Management, Inc., 180 Varick Street, Penthouse, New York, NY 10014. (212) 633-0060.

Careers and Management

CHAPTER OBJECTIVES

By the time you complete studying this chapter you should be able to

1. Understand the important aspects of managing your career.
2. Describe how you would go about establishing a realistic career plan.
3. Identify the major stages in the human life cycle.
4. Indicate major career choices.
5. Discuss the interview process.
6. Discuss the four stages of a career in management.
7. Review how stress enters into a manager's career.
8. Review how stress can be managed.
9. Describe some of the challenges in career management caused by the changing nature of management.

CHAPTER OUTLINE

Managing Your Career
    Life's Stages
    Major Career Choices
    The Interview and You
    Special Issues in Career Planning
Careers in Management
    Stages in Management Careers
    Management Development Programs
    Stress and the Manager
The Manager in the Twenty-First Century
The Management Challenges Identified
Some Solutions Noted in the Chapter

Thirty Something

A baby boomer with a high need for achievement, Stacy Jackson wanted it all. At thirty, she was one of three regional vice-presidents for a savings and loan. She had been with the firm for five years, when restructuring to avoid collapse meant that the two men above her in the hierarchy were removed, and she was promoted to her current position. That was two years ago. She hadn't really known whether she would like banking when she graduated from college. But she thought she would, and she did. She hadn't been sure that she would like management when she was promoted after two years on the job. She had loved it and the challenges it provided. The promotion to an executive position in charge of twenty branches and some 130 people had been even more interesting and demanding. But she could see the handwriting on the wall.

Her salary was only half of what one of her predecessors had been making, and the bank was struggling. The original bank she had worked for had recently been acquired by another bank, from another region of the state. The entire bank was facing a potential financial collapse. According to the federal government, it was only a matter of time before the bank would be put on the list of three hundred savings banks with financial problems and would probably become insolvent. In fact, it was now rated as number 326. And she was getting anxious to improve her situation. Several headhunters had contacted her. She was interested in advancement to another position in some other financial institution, but her undergraduate degree in psychology, while helpful in managing, really didn't appeal to a lot of banks, despite her obvious success record.

Stacy had considered getting an MBA. Her work hours were long, but she had managed to cut them by delegating to others. Recently divorced, she was concerned about spending the time away from her son that would be necessary to complete her degree. And she didn't know if she could handle the quantitative courses involved. But she felt almost as if she had no choice. The MBA would make her marketable in fields other than banking. She wondered, too, how long the bank would survive, and whether her region would be sold off, jeopardizing her position. She had considered complaining about sex discrimination because of her low pay, but felt that it would be a losing proposition in the long term, no matter what the immediate results — the best of which would be a higher salary. It might, after all, be possible to eliminate her position altogether. She wanted some kind of guarantee from the bank to support her MBA program expenses. Tuition was high at the local private college, but she felt she had to improve her situation. She received a verbal promise of support from her boss. She really wasn't sure, but she just didn't feel she could move to another job and get what she wanted as far as position and salary without the MBA. She applied to the school for admission.

> One measure of a person is the questions he raises, and another is the goals for which he uses his powers and talents.
>
> Sidney Jourard
> Psychologist and author

> In a fast-changing, global business world, the old lockstep, one-track career is a relic.
>
> Gunter David, *Wall Street Journal*

Stacy is typical of many people in the work force today. She is a single parent. She is a baby-boomer. She is at the point of making a career choice, and she has assessed her situation and determined a weakness she wants to correct in order to move ahead. She is concerned about her career, and her career is in management.

There are two principal concerns regarding careers and management:

1. Managing your career regardless of what your job function is
2. Careers in management

This chapter explores the major issues involved in managing your career regardless of your career area. Among the issues are the career planning process; drawing up realistic career plans; life's stages and their impact on careers; major career choices, such as industry and career area; the interview as an important part of career moves; and special issues in managing careers. The chapter also discusses careers in management—including career stages, advice for beginning managers, career plateaus, and stress and the manager. Finally, the chapter reviews the impacts on management careers of the twenty-first century environment.

The executive business woman must be prepared to manage her career, and if a parent, balance her career with her family life. (SOURCE © Robert Reichert)

Managing Your Career

Planning your career is a major part of planning and managing your life. It is ironic that most of us spend a great deal of time planning weekend outings, vacations, weddings, birthday parties, and so on, and yet spend little, if any, time planning our lives. Biographies of successful people reveal that virtually all of them possessed certain objectives that became burning desires.[1] Similarly, successful leaders and managers have been shown to have a concern for objectives and plans to reach those objectives.[2] Most successful organizations make plans.[3] So why can't you?

Planning for your career is just one part of planning for your life, albeit for most, a major part. Other facets of your life you might want to plan for include family, leisure, mental development, physical condition, psychological well-being, religious understanding, social life, societal concerns, and aesthetic interests.[4] Regardless of which area of your life you are planning, the process involved is essentially the same as shown in Figure 23.1.

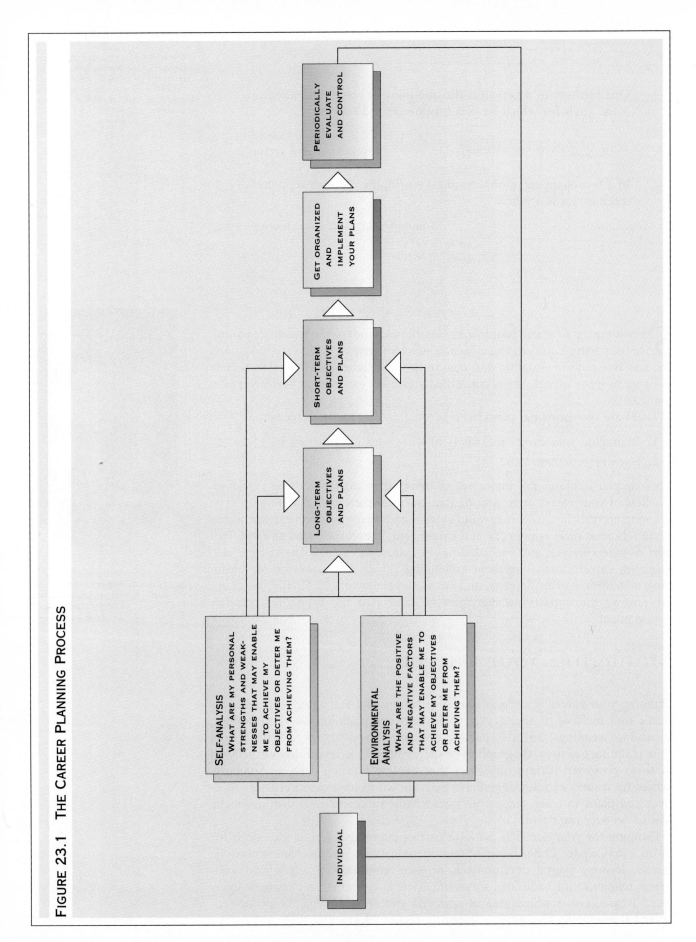

FIGURE 23.1   THE CAREER PLANNING PROCESS

INDIVIDUAL

SELF-ANALYSIS
WHAT ARE MY PERSONAL STRENGTHS AND WEAKNESSES THAT MAY ENABLE ME TO ACHIEVE MY OBJECTIVES OR DETER ME FROM ACHIEVING THEM?

ENVIRONMENTAL ANALYSIS
WHAT ARE THE POSITIVE AND NEGATIVE FACTORS THAT MAY ENABLE ME TO ACHIEVE MY OBJECTIVES OR DETER ME FROM ACHIEVING THEM?

LONG-TERM OBJECTIVES AND PLANS

SHORT-TERM OBJECTIVES AND PLANS

GET ORGANIZED AND IMPLEMENT YOUR PLANS

PERIODICALLY EVALUATE AND CONTROL

1. Individuals assess themselves and their environments to determine their strengths and weaknesses and to balance these against the threats and opportunities perceived externally.

2. They establish long-term and short-term objectives and plans to reach those career objectives.

3. The individual must get organized and implement his or her plans.

4. The process is repeated periodically to determine whether objectives have been reached and if not, why not, and what actions to take.[5]

This process is essentially the same as a corporation would follow in determining its strategic plans for the next few years. Career planning for the individual is analogous. Victor Kiam, CEO and owner of Remington Industries, goes through this process for himself every six months and attributes much of his success to it.[6] Linnet Deily, head of Interstate Bank's Los Angeles North Division, and one of only three female executive vice-presidents in the nation's ten largest banks, reports that she, too, periodically sets career objectives and plans for medium- and long-term situations.[7] Table 23.1 contains typical strengths, weaknesses, opportunities, and threats for a college senior in accounting.

THIRTY SOMETHING: *Stacy assessed her situation. She realized that her lack of a business degree would hurt her career. She recognized opportunities with other firms and obstacles in her own firm due to potential financial problems.*

Victor Kiam, here shown with some of his entrepreneurial trappings, attributes much of his success to his semi-annual self-assessment and life planning activities. (SOURCE © Ken Kerbs)

Table 23.1 Self- and Environmental Analysis of a Hypothetical Senior Majoring in Accounting

Self-Analysis	
Personal Strengths	**Personal Weaknesses**
Self-concept, understanding self	Lack of direction
Need to be successful	No master's degree
Like business subjects	Little experience
Ambition	Not sure what firm to go with
Bachelor's degree	Not sure how to lead others
Good communication skills	Sometimes let others make decisions
Father and mother have important contacts	
Quick learner	
Good at planning	
Knowledge of Lotus 1-2-3	

Environmental Analysis	
Opportunities	**Threats or Obstacles**
Employers seeking my degree area	They want experience, if possible.
High salaries in my degree area	Travel is required about 50% of the time.
Rapid turnover, quick advancement	Entry-level positions are often boring.
Two companies have good cultures	Job skills quickly become obsolete.
Highly respected profession	Only a few progress to high levels.
Demand outweighs supply	
Best jobs in urban areas	

The objectives and plans you establish now must remain flexible. Most of us change jobs several times in our lives, especially when we are young. But many people are now changing their careers in midlife, partly because they have come to question the appropriateness of their earlier decisions. An interesting book to use in arriving at your career plan is Richard Nelson Bolles, *What Color Is Your Parachute?*[8] The book offers numerous self-examination exercises, analysis techniques, and information and is interestingly written and illustrated. The *College Edition of the National Business Employment Weekly*, printed quarterly, provides a discussion of current issues in career management.[9]

REALISTIC CAREER PLANS

Allen N. Schoonmaker offers a nine-step career planning strategy and sound advice in formulating your career strategies.[10] He takes into account both an organization's perspective and that of the individual career planner. His nine steps follow:

1. **Accept the fact that there are some inescapable and irreconcilable conflicts between you and your organization.** Most organizations do not have a career planning program, although many do. Furthermore, virtually every organization must assure the satisfaction of its needs, sometimes to the detriment of its employees' needs. You don't want to be disloyal to the company, but you must always pay attention to satisfying your interests. If you are going to have a career plan, you must assume responsibility for it. Most organizations do not have career planning programs, but some companies are taking a more active concern for employees, as Management Challenge 23.1 suggests.

2. **Accept the fact that most of your superiors are essentially indifferent to your career ambitions.** In most organizations managers are responsible for assuring that the organization's needs are satisfied first. Subordinates' needs come second and most often third, behind the manager's needs. Managers can only do so much to improve your career possibilities.

3. **Analyze your own goals.** Your career is not merely made up of a series of promotions. If you want a real career, you must achieve the goals that you feel are important.

4. **Analyze your assets and liabilities.** Your strengths and weaknesses determine your ability to achieve your goals. If you cannot overcome your weaknesses and you do not have the appropriate strengths, you should not be pursuing goals that are out of reach. You should take advantage of your strengths to overcome external threats and take advantage of opportunities.

5. **Analyze your opportunities.** You should systematically evaluate the opportunities available to you, both inside and outside an organization. Many sources of information about such opportunities exist, including professional placement services (headhunters), professional trade associations, colleagues, and personal observation.

6. **Learn the rules of company politics.** There are definite dos and don'ts in organizations, and it is important to learn them. It is also important to learn how an organization really functions, relative to the distribution of power—that is, its politics. It is also important to identify people who will be crucial in helping you accomplish certain tasks; in return it is important to help them accomplish theirs. Networking—building working relationships within (and outside) the organization—is very critical.

7. **Plan your career.** As the process described in Figure 23.1 suggests, it is not enough just to establish objectives; you must also determine how you are going to achieve them. Your plans must be flexible. Having them will enable you to move in the direction of your objectives. Not having them will hinder your movements because you may tend to drift.

8. **Carry out your plan.** As suggested in Figure 23.1, you must implement whatever action your plans call for, be it asking for a promotion, a raise, or finding a job in another company.

9. **Chart your progress.** You must control and evaluate your progress. If you have not reached your objectives by the time you planned to do so, you must ask yourself why not and take corrective action. If you are ahead of

This woman is the customer service manager for Citicorp's Fifth Avenue Manhattan Branch. She is very much aware that she has to manage her career just as she manages this office. (SOURCE © Dilip Mehta/Woodfin Camp & Associates)

schedule, you must choose to change your plan in order to take advantage of new opportunities. Plans must be changed periodically to remain relevant to your current situation.

MANAGEMENT CHALLENGE **23.1**

Blue Cross & Blue Shield Improve Career Planning

Historically, Blue Cross & Blue Shield United of Wisconsin had relied on job postings to provide candidates for promotions for its 550 professional employees. All of those who applied as a result of seeing the postings were interviewed and one of them was promoted into the open position. Ann Steinmetz Harris, who was in charge of developing employees' careers for the health insurance company felt that "This was too random. There was no guarantee that the postings would attract the most qualified people."

The company therefore developed a new approach. Every employee, excluding the secretarial staff, began being required to meet periodically with their department manager to discuss their career objectives. Each manager then filed a report that was fed into a central computer. The result was a data base that indicated not only who was interested in what type of job, but also who was qualified. Now, whenever a department head has an opening, he or she can query the data base to determine who is interested in that opening, including people not currently working in that field. Thus, Blue Cross & Blue Shield was able to better utilize the talents of its people, stimulate employees to think in career terms, and improve morale.

SOURCE: "Helping Employees Shape Their Careers," *Success* (March 1986), p. 28.

Life's Stages

Career decisions may be quite appropriate at the time they are made, but become less appropriate over time. Why? The answer, at least partly, is because people change. A number of authorities on the **individual life-cycle process,** including Erik Erikson, Roger Gould, and Gail Sheehy,[11] have reported that people pass through various stages in their lives, what Sheehy refers to as "passages." Each of these stages has a significant potential impact on the individual's career and career choices. Each stage revolves around a crisis—not a catastrophe, but a turning point. Sheehy's passages are defined briefly below. Her stages are similar to those identified by others who have studied the life cycle, but her sample group was composed mostly of professionals, somewhat limiting the applicability of her findings to the general population.

> **Pulling up roots:** After age eighteen, the message is clear. We must get away from our parents' domination. Sometimes attachment to a strong "other" results. Usually this is not a good solution, and divorce is not infrequent in such cases.
>
> **The trying twenties:** During these years we work things out. We see if we can come to grips with the reality of the social and work worlds. These years are dominated by "doing what we should." Life patterns are established here, and career choices are important among them.
>
> **Catch thirty:** In the late twenties and early thirties, people begin to question the decisions they made earlier. Not infrequently, the result is a destruction of the life made in the early twenties. Reflection is the watchword. New choices are made, and divorce is common. Career choices are questioned.
>
> **Rooting and extending:** The early to midthirties are characterized by a turning inward to the family and by career commitment—commitment to "making it."
>
> **The deadline decade:** The midthirties to midforties foretell the end. Time squeezes us. We realize that we are getting older. Values, careers, and life objectives are reexamined. The push to make it may become too intense. Many people start second careers. Women seem to begin this stage earlier than men.
>
> **Renewal or resignation:** The last crisis comes from the mid-forties onward. Most people experience a mellowing, an acceptance of their situation. For others, the crisis may last forever. Life's cycle must be accepted. Some people never do accept it. (This is not to say that we must surrender physically or mentally. Quite the contrary. We can still exercise and we can still expand our minds.)

We all go through these stages, not always at the same times, but generally within the time spans indicated. Some people may reach stages later than others because of the time that career choices take. Some elements of one stage may overlap those of another. But we are all faced with these basic situations. And career planning must be sufficiently flexible to accommodate them. What are some of the major career issues that you must decide?

Major Career Choices

Some of the major issues you will confront during your career follow. At this point you may not be able to answer or even relate to all of them. You may have too little experience to go by. But look at them now and reflect on them again later in your career. Use those that are applicable now and the others later.

THIRTY SOMETHING: *Women tend to enter the deadline decade before men. Stacy is already questioning what to do, what changes are necessary, and how to start another career.*

This female manager has chosen to be a job site supervisor for PS&G. Industry and career field choices are extremely important decisions. If you make the wrong ones, it is often difficult to change them without extensively changing your whole life situation. They must be considered carefully. (SOURCE © Robert Reichert)

Career field: What skill area are you going to enter, remain in, or change to? A typical progression seems to be from a skilled area into management. Upward movement occasionally involves a change in skill area, although not necessarily a radical change. For example, an auditor might become a cost specialist, or a personnel specialist might switch from selection to training.

Industry: What industry do you wish to enter, remain in, or change to?[12] Not all industries pay the same. Because a lower-level employee's pay is usually a percentage of top management's pay, you may wish to pick an industry, all else being equal, on the basis of potential pay. Industries become obsolete, as do individuals. Do not remain in an industry becoming obsolete unless you are ready for retirement.

Obsolescence: Are you obsolete? What skills do you need—technical, human relations, conceptual—that will make you more marketable?

Life stage: In what life stage do you find yourself, and what is the impact of this stage on your career decisions?

Management: Do you want to move into management? What are the pluses and minuses? Are you ready for the responsibilities?

Mobility: Are you mobile? If not, why not? Have you been in your current job three years or more without a raise or promotion? If the answer is yes, maybe you should move on, or improve your performance.

Match: What is the match between you and your current and proposed future organization? Does it have the proper climate? How does it treat people? How do you want to be treated? Can you adjust to this climate?

Impacts: What are the impacts of a career decision on family and friends? Will relocation be necessary? Where? Is this location acceptable?

Value: Of what value are you to this organization? What indications do you have of this value? Are you likely to be promoted soon? What are your strengths and weaknesses?

Experience: What kinds of work experience have you liked and disliked?

THIRTY SOMETHING: *Stacy is beginning to question industry obsolescence and maybe even careers. She wants to remain mobile. The organization of choice is also an issue.*

Motivation: Do you have the burning desire that it takes to improve your career position?

Organization: Do you need to leave your organization and find another? Why, or why not?

Geographic location: Salaries, the cost of living, and opportunities typically vary widely by geographic location: nonjob-related factors are also important in choosing a location.

These and other major issues arise whenever a career decision is made.

The items to be examined in both personal and environmental areas remain relatively stable whether long-term or short-term objectives and plans are being established. Major career skill areas are changed only rarely, but changes do occur. Industry is changed fairly frequently. Life stage changes occur only periodically. But the rest of the items could occur on any planning horizon, long-term or short-term.

The Interview and You

When you graduate, most of you will be involved in seeking employment. All stages of the job search process—writing a résumé, company identification, interview, and choice—are important, but because the interview is such a key part of a successful job search, it is examined in more detail here. You are likely to have interviews with potential employers, including your prospective immediate supervisor. Most companies still place great weight on the interview in making their selection decisions, even though it has questionable predictive validity. It does not necessarily do what it is supposed to—that is, to predict the future job success of the people interviewed. There are two basic types of interviews that you will encounter: a preliminary screening interview and one or more comprehensive interviews. The ground rules are essentially the same, but the comprehensive interviews are the most significant hurdles.

The interview is a much-studied phenomenon, and you should gain personally from what we know about it. Here are some suggestions for improving your performance in the interview.

1. The **interview** is an interpersonal, applicant selection process. It is an exercise in human relations, usually between two people but occasionally involving a group of interviewers and one interviewee.

2. Study after study has shown that the single most important action you can take with respect to the interview is to make certain that your appearance is flawless. Hair, clothing, and shoes should all be appropriate to the job for which you are applying. Conservative fashion is recommended. I am reminded of one student who did not follow recommended practices. He came to me to complain after failing a job interview. His appearance was totally nonprofessional. His hair was greasy, his jacket was plaid and his pants were striped, and he wore a string tie that had been out of style for twenty years. Numerous studies indicate that interviewers form an immediate, though usually subconscious, first impression of you on the basis of your appearance and your actions in the first five minutes of the interview. They seek information throughout the interview to confirm this first impression, be it good or bad. Be neat and dress appropriately.

3. Verbal (and obviously nonverbal) communication has been shown to be particularly important. Researchers report that the appropriateness of the

content of your responses to the interviewer's questions (conciseness, cooperation, complete but not too verbose answers, keeping to the subject, stating your opinions when relevant, and fluency of speech) and your manner of speaking (spontaneity, word use, and articulation) are the two most critical factors in interviewer decisions. Other important factors are maintaining eye contact, using a clear and appropriately loud voice, having erect posture, supplementing verbal messages, corresponding with nonverbal communication, and your personal appearance and composure.

4. Your perceived personality will play an important role in your interviews. Presumably the interviewers have read your résumé. They know what you have accomplished; now they want to know what you are like. Be positive and friendly. Most interviewers follow a pattern. They ask the same basic questions of everyone (a sample of these questions is presented in Table 23.2). Sometimes they are probing for confirmation of weaknesses that appear on your résumé. Sometimes they are gathering information. Sometimes they may want to test your composure by berating, badgering, or startling you.

5. Role playing is important. Sit down with a friend and practice the interview. Practice answering and asking questions. Practice on common interview problems. For example, the badgering tactic, where the interviewer fires questions in rapid succession or otherwise tries to fluster you, is fairly common, so you need to practice handling it.

6. Studies show clearly that honesty is the best policy. If you lie to get a job, your stay is likely to be shorter than if you find an organization with which you are really happy. Honesty is the best policy for the employer, as well, although some still paint too rosy a picture of what the job and company can offer.

7. You want to appear enthusiastic, intelligent, rational, motivated, and interested in the organization and what it has to offer. You do not want to deceive, but do show genuine interest.

8. You should be knowledgeable about the potential employer. Do your homework. Read company reports, analyze its position in the market, and so forth. A study by John D. Shingleton and L. Patrick Sheetz indicates that knowledge about the job and company or business is an extremely important selection criterion.[13]

9. Be on time. In fact, be early. This will allow you to adjust to the situation. Sometimes you will have to wait. Take something to read or study. It makes use of your time and may impress the interviewer.

10. Ask questions. You should be prepared to find out what you need to know. Table 23.2 also lists common questions you might want to ask. Don't be afraid to ask questions, but do not monopolize the conversation.

11. The interview characteristically begins with polite conversation. The interviewer usually will give a brief presentation about the organization, and then begin asking you questions. You can expect the interviewer's talk to consume most of the opening portions of the interview, anywhere from 60 to 80 percent of it. Once the interviewer's questions have been asked and answered, the interview is usually thrown open for questions from the interviewee.

12. Listen attentively to the interviewer and pick up on nonverbal messages. Is the interviewer leading you? If so, where? Does the interviewer seem interested in hiring you, or not? How should you respond in either case?

13. Always be polite and courteous. One Ph.D in psychology with a strong résumé failed to be selected for a faculty position in a school of business because of his rude, almost hostile behavior. If anyone should have known how to behave, it was he. But he did not act appropriately.

14. Show your strong points. Not all interviewers are skilled at interviewing. Make sure the interviewer learns just how good you are.

15. All interviews come to an end. The interviewer is on a schedule and ordinarily must conclude the interview at a certain point. When the end draws near, you do not want to appear overly anxious. A decision is usually not made until all candidates have been interviewed and you will have to wait for a decision. Close on as positive a note as you can.

Table 23.2 Preparing for an Interview: Have You Thought About These Questions?

Questions Employers Often Ask

1. What was your overall grade-point average all through college?
2. What was your grade-point average in your major field of study?
3. What courses did you enjoy while in college? What courses did you enjoy least?
4. What do you know about our organization?
5. What qualifications do you have that make you feel that you will be successful in your field?
6. How did you happen to apply for this position with our organization?
7. Have you had any part-time or summer employment?
8. What have you learned from some of the jobs you have held?
9. Have you participated in any volunteer or community work?
10. How did previous employers treat you?
11. Do you like routine work?
12. What are your future vocational plans?
13. In what type of position are you most interested?
14. Are you willing to travel?
15. If you could write your ticket, what kind of job would you like to have?
16. What have you done that shows initiative and willingness to work?
17. Tell me about your extracurricular activities.
18. Did you hold any positions of leadership while at school?
19. Do you have any special skills, and where did you acquire them?
20. Have you had any special accomplishments in your lifetime that you would like to speak of?
21. Why did you leave a given job?
22. Do you have any geographical restrictions? (or preferences?)
23. How do you spend your spare time? What are your hobbies?
24. What are your salary requirements?
25. Do you have a girlfriend (or boyfriend)? Is it serious?
26. Why do you think you would like this particular company?
27. Tell me about your home life during the time you were growing up.
28. Have you ever changed your major field of interest while in college? Why?
29. Why did you choose your particular major?
30. What percentage of your college expenses did you earn? How?
31. Do you feel you did the best scholastic work you could?
32. What do you consider your strengths and weaknesses?
33. Is it an effort for you to be tolerant of persons with backgrounds and interests different from your own?
34. What types of people seem to "rub you the wrong way"?
35. Were you in the armed services? If so, what did you do?
36. What have you been doing since your last job (or since you got out of school)?
37. What books have you read recently?
38. If you were fired, what was the reason?
39. If you went to graduate school, what were your purposes and reasons for going?
40. When can you start work?
41. When can you visit our headquarters for further interviews?

Questions You May Want to Ask the Employer

1. Who was the last person on this job and what is he or she doing now?
2. Why was someone not promoted from within the organization to this vacancy?
3. Who will be my immediate supervisor and will I have a chance to speak to that person personally before being hired?
4. What is the growth potential of your organization?
5. What is the organizational pattern, and where do I fit into it?
6. What is the nature of the job?
7. Is there a job description of my job?
8. How long can I expect to be at the location in which I start?
9. Is it anticipated that I will have extended travel?
10. How much time will be spent away from home?
11. What is the normal progression of salary increases? (This should not be an early question.)
12. What are the housing arrangements and conditions in the general area?

SOURCE: From *Business Today,* second edition, by David J. Rachman and Michael H. Mescon. Copyright © 1976, 1979, 1982, 1985 by Random House, Inc. Reprinted by permission.

Special Issues in Career Planning

Career planning is difficult enough as it is, but for some people it becomes even more difficult because of their special situation. The following paragraphs examine three such special situations: minorities and women, dual-career families, and career plateauing.

MINORITIES AND WOMEN

Both minorities and women complain of "glass ceilings," invisible roofs above which they cannot be promoted in the good-old-boy network of most major organizations. Plus, the social-cultural phenomenon of a largely white, male-dominated upper level of the hierarchy poses challenges for those seeking membership in this "club." Minorities and women must learn to adapt. For example, they need to find "mentors," sponsors, to help them climb the corporate ladder. These mentors are senior managers who can provide guidance about managing one's career. Mentors show their protégés the ropes, how things are done in the company. Some companies assign mentors, but most individuals have to seek out their own.[14] Minorities and women also need to learn how to network and to use the political system. They also need to learn how to cope with co-worker feelings and problems of discrimination.

DUAL-CAREER COUPLES

When both partners are employed full time, extra effort must be made to balance the situation's demands. As we move toward the twenty-first century, this is becoming an ever-increasing problem. It has been estimated that by the year 2000, the number of dual-career families will move to 75 percent of married couples, up from its current level of 60 percent.[15] Couples must respect each other's rights, needs, and desires. Accommodations are often necessary. Day to day, each will need the other's support. Occasionally, major decision issues will arise. For example, in order for one of the partners to take advantage of a promotion opportunity in another geographic location, the other may have to decide whether the partnership or the career is more important.[16]

"MOMMY TRACK"

The term *mommy track* refers to an alternative career path for women who want to balance raising a family with having a career.[17] Normally this implies a slower career pace. It often involves working at home, a flexible work schedule, or part-time work. Such programs will become more necessary in the future, as the percentage of dual-career families increases and a labor shortage develops.[18] While accommodating the needs of working women is important, some see mommy tracks as providing a sort of second-class-citizen status for working women with kids. However, as demographics change, it seems clear that such programs will be necessary, and the prejudice against people in them will lessen.[19]

CAREER PLATEAUS

A **career plateau** is "that point in a career where the likelihood of additional hierarchical promotion is very low."[20] Few people ever reach the top of the corporate hierarchy in their careers. At some point, perhaps even at the first level, people will not be promoted or are not likely to be promoted. Career plateauing is an organizational reality; it is one reason many people leave one organization and move to another.

Being part of a dual-career family means sharing traditionally male and female roles. This father is dropping the children off at the day care center because his wife's job requires her to travel quite frequently. (SOURCE © Rick Friedman/Black Star)

As the restructuring of organizations continues, there will be fewer and fewer management positions, and plateauing will be a much more common occurrence. Furthermore, most large organizations have slowed in their growth and many have, in fact, retracted in size and personnel. Those seeking more growth opportunities and more promotion opportunities must, therefore, move to high-growth firms, which are relatively small. Fortunately, there are a large number of these in the United States, but the transition can be difficult. Firms in foreign countries are also having to learn how to cope with mass pleateauing, as the Global Management Challenge suggests. Many organizations have an up-or-out policy. Others allow managers to remain in positions because they can't be promoted, which then holds back those beneath them, as well. How an organization manages this career plateau problem often determines its ability to be successful. Although the term *career plateau* has a negative connotation, it in fact refers to everyone at one time or another and should be viewed merely as a part of organizational life, even though some people plateau faster than others.

Careers in Management

A number of issues are involved in management careers. The following sections examine the stages that management careers go through, management development programs, stress and the manager, and the anticipated impact of the future on careers in management.

Career Plateauing in a Japanese Firm

Wacoal Corporation of Japan is a leading manufacturer and marketer of women's apparel. Like most Japanese firms, this five-thousand-employee firm was faced with a large number of middle- and front-line managers with no place to go. Promotion was based almost entirely on seniority. The lengthening careers of senior management due to a higher mandatory retirement age and a bulge of middle managers born after World War II posed an extensive problem. Managers had been rotated within departments every three years. But changing societal values, with respect to promotion, and increased levels of competition prompted the company to examine this practice and seek alternative ways of determining who was rotated, and where.

The company enlisted the assistance of the U.S.-based consulting firm Assessment Design International. A comprehensive evaluation and management plan resulted. It called for an integration of existing training programs, a self-assessment process for career planning, and a company assessment of employee competencies. AD International adapted assessment center processes to Japanese culture because some concepts used in the United States simply did not translate well. For example, a recent survey of Japanese managers indicated that 21.5 percent valued effort more than performance results and that only 32.3 percent viewed performance appraisal as a useful tool. One result was that ADI's assessment appraisal system was made much more structured for the Japanese environment.

SOURCE: Craig Taylor and Federic Frank, "Assessment Centers in Japan," *Training & Development Journal* (February 1988), pp. 54–57.

Stages in Management Careers

All careers go through stages. Gene W. Dalton, Paul H. Thompson, and Raymond L. Price suggest that there are four stages through which professional management careers proceed.[21] An individual may choose to stay within the same company for a long period of time or may move from company to company. Either way, he or she may eventually wind up in management and proceed upward through the three principal levels: supervision, middle management, and top management.

STAGE 1
College graduates most typically take entry-level positions in an organization. They have some degree of technical competence but lack an overall ability to manage. Some college graduates are fortunate enough, or unfortunate enough, depending on the results, to be selected for management positions as they leave college. However, most will wait one or more years until they are ready to advance to stage 2 and enter management. Management development programs and presupervisory seminars are useful in assisting people to move to stage 2.

STAGE 2
As the college graduate proves him- or herself, he or she is given more independence on the job. Eventually, within a year, or two, or three, the individual may be chosen for a first-line or middle-level management position. The selec-

GE's New Manager's Programs

In Chapter 12, GE's Management Development Institute in Croton-on-Ossining, New York, was highlighted in a management challenge for its efforts to help mold GE's new culture. One of the focal points of that initiative is the New Manager's Programs. GE Chairman Jack Welch recognized that new managers weren't fully prepared for the rigors of managing. To that end a three-step program was initiated:

1. On or near their first day in the program, new managers receive a "starter kit" that helps them through the first six months. It contains audiocassettes with messages from GE's chairman and other experienced managers; several booklets on GE systems, procedures, and employee situations; and a calendar with tips for their first weeks and months as managers. The company encourages new managers to use the new manager assimilation process, which eases them into the work unit through a third-party processor.

2. GE believes a "teachable" time for new managers is between the sixth and twelfth month after they begin the program, a period when they attend the key six-day course that focuses on the critical skills and knowledge needed by new managers and the values of the company's culture.

tion into management often is made on the basis of technical competence, so it is extremely important that the individual work hard at entry-level positions, even though sometimes they may seem boring. Table 23.3 provides some important advice for new managers. The transition to being a manager from being a first-line operative employee is so critical that several major companies, such as GE, are developing special programs to help develop a new manager's skills. Management Challenge 23.2 reviews some of the key points in the GE New Manager's Programs.

STAGE 3

Individuals who show success at first-level and middle-level management are promoted to even higher levels. They assume more and more responsibility. The importance of their decisions increases. At this stage of management, and often even in stages 1 and 2 of professional growth, managers experience psychological stress. Upper-level managers are expected to interact more frequently with clients and suppliers.

THIRTY SOMETHING: *Stacy has already reached stage 2 here.*

STAGE 4

Only a few managers reach stage 4. At this level of the firm, the top level of managers shapes the strategy and the future of the firm. Managers at this level should no longer be specialists but generalists and be able to direct any of the organization's various functions.

Progressing through these four stages would typically require a minimum of ten to fifteen years, unless an individual starts his or her own company, in which case he or she may move from stage 1 to stage 4 overnight. In most large bureaucratic organizations, it may take thirty to forty years to reach stage 4. In such organizations most people never reach stage 4, which is one reason they do start their own companies, as we discussed in the last chapter, on entrepreneurship. Figure 23.2 relates career stages to life's stages, using the two models discussed in this chapter.

3. Trainees attend a follow-up communications skill-building course that is based on behavioral modeling concepts.

As the course progresses through cases, exercises, discussions, and lectures, participants learn how to

—Create and lead competitive work teams.
—Communicate candidly and effectively.
—Design work and apply proven work-planning techniques.
—Build networks outside their immediate work unit.
—Solve problems.
—Exhibit leadership.
—Create ownership of employee performance.
—Appraise differential contribution.
—Coach, counsel, and provide constructive feedback.
—Apply key corporate values in the workplace and in the marketplace.
—Manifest excellence and integrity.

The course also improves new managers' ability to implement specific corporate polices and practices in performance appraisals, staff development, compliance, and supplier-customer competitive relationships.

SOURCE: A. Nicholas Komaneck, "Developing New Managers at GE," *Training and Development Journal* (June 1988), pp. 62–64.

Table 23.3 Some Advice for Beginning Managers

Remember that good performance that pleases your superiors is the basic foundation of success, but recognize that not all good performance is easily measured. Determine the real criteria by which you are evaluated and be rigorously honest in evaluating your own performance against these criteria.

Manage your career, be active in influencing decisions, because pure effort is not necessarily rewarded.

Strive for positions that have high visibility and exposure, where you can be a hero observed by higher officials. Check to see that the organization has a formal system of keeping track of young people. Remember that high-risk line jobs tend to offer more visibility than staff positions like corporate planning or personnel, but also that visibility can sometimes be achieved by off-job community activities.

Develop relations with a mobile senior executive who can be your sponsor. Become a complementary crucial subordinate with different skills than your superior.

Learn your job as quickly as possible and train a replacement so you can be available to move and broaden your background in different functions.

Nominate yourself for other positions; modesty is not necessarily a virtue. However, change jobs for more power and influence, not primarily for status or pay. The latter could be a substitute for real opportunity to make things happen.

Before taking a position, rigorously assess your strengths and weaknesses, what you like and don't like. Don't accept a promotion if it draws on your weaknesses and entails mainly activities that you don't like.

Leave at your convenience but on good terms, without parting criticism of the organization. Do not stay under an immobile superior who is not promoted in three to five years.

Don't be trapped by formal, narrow job descriptions. Move outside them and probe the limits of your influence.

Accept that responsibility will always somewhat exceed authority and that organizational politics are inevitable. Establish alliances and fight necessary battles, minimizing upward ones to very important issues.

Get out of management, if you can't stand being dependent on others and having them dependent on you.

Recognize that you will face ethical dilemmas no matter how moral you try to be. No evidence exists that unethical managers are more successful than ethical ones, but it may well be that those who move faster are less socially conscious. Therefore, from time to time you must examine your personal values and question how much you will sacrifice for the organization.

Don't automatically accept all tales of managerial perversity that you hear. Attributing others' success to unethical behavior is often an excuse for one's own personal inadequacies. Most of all, don't commit an act that you know to be wrong in the hope that your supervisor will see it as loyalty and reward you for it. Sometimes he will, but he may also sacrifice you when the organization is criticized.

SOURCE: Ross A. Webber, "Career Problems of Young Managers," *California Management Review* (Summer 1976), p. 29. Copyright 1976 by the Regents of the University of California. Reprinted from the *California Management Review*, Vol. 18, No. 4 by permission of The Regents.

Linda Crosby is president of Charkit Chemical. She has reached the fourth stage of a management career. Few managers do. (SOURCE © Ken Kerbs)

Management Development Programs

Earlier, Allen Schoonmaker was cited as suggesting that you must take charge of your own career. One reason is that so few firms have career development programs. For example, in a survey of a random sample of U.S. firms with at least one thousand employees, fewer than one-third reported having management development programs. This same survey reported a number of different approaches and components being used in management development programs. They included: formal training/education, task force participation, mentoring, job rotation, career planning, and coverage of such topics as managing people, marketing, finance, ethics, and computers.[22]

Stress and the Manager

Many people suffer from stress. Researchers and authors Michael Matteson and John Ivancevich report that from 60 to 80 percent of doctors' patients have stress-related health problems.[23] Managers are no exception. Not all managers suffer from stress, but virtually all management jobs contain elements that can lead to stress.[24] Solving the problems created by stress for all employees is important to an organization's success because ineffective work behavior may result if no action is taken. Even worse, employees may have ulcers, heart attacks, cancer, or less serious health problems such as colds or flu due to stress or, more accurately, the individual's inability to cope with stressors. Learning how to avoid stressors and to cope with those you encounter is critical to your success in any career, but especially in management.

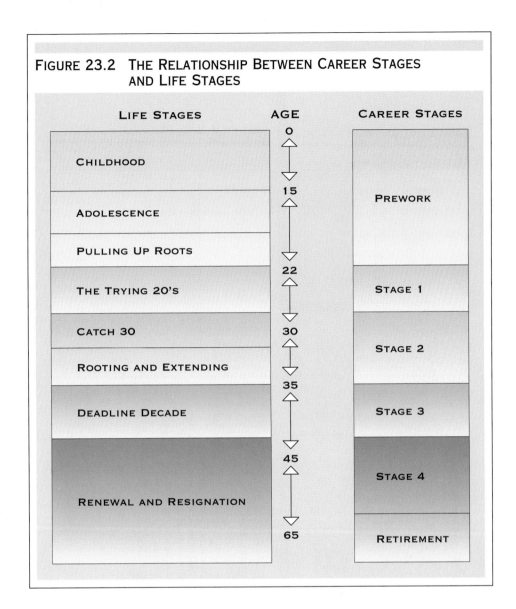

FIGURE 23.2 THE RELATIONSHIP BETWEEN CAREER STAGES AND LIFE STAGES

LIFE STAGES	AGE	CAREER STAGES
CHILDHOOD	0	PREWORK
ADOLESCENCE	15	
PULLING UP ROOTS		
THE TRYING 20'S	22	STAGE 1
CATCH 30	30	STAGE 2
ROOTING AND EXTENDING	35	
DEADLINE DECADE		STAGE 3
RENEWAL AND RESIGNATION	45	STAGE 4
	65	RETIREMENT

WHAT IS STRESS?

Stress is a physical and psychological condition resulting from attempts to adapt to one's environment. Figure 23.3 notes that stressors—various work-related and nonwork-related factors, such as your boss's personality, the time pressure of a job, or your and your spouse's relationship—impinge upon individuals. Depending on the individual's ability to cope with these stressors, he or she will then have some relative degree of stress, either high or low or somewhere in between. The impacts of adapting to stress can be either positive or negative. As can be seen in the diagram, the techniques for reducing stress work on either reducing the number and/or intensity of the stressors, improving the individual's psychological capacity for coping with stressors, improving the individual's psychological state, or overcoming the aftereffects of stress.

STRESSORS

Because most of the work-related and other stressors identified in Figure 23.3 are self-explanatory, they will not be covered here in depth. Rather, you can recall from previous discussions in this book how each of these might cause stress. One item not covered in any detail in previous chapters is the factor called Control of Decisions. Studies have shown that where an individual has

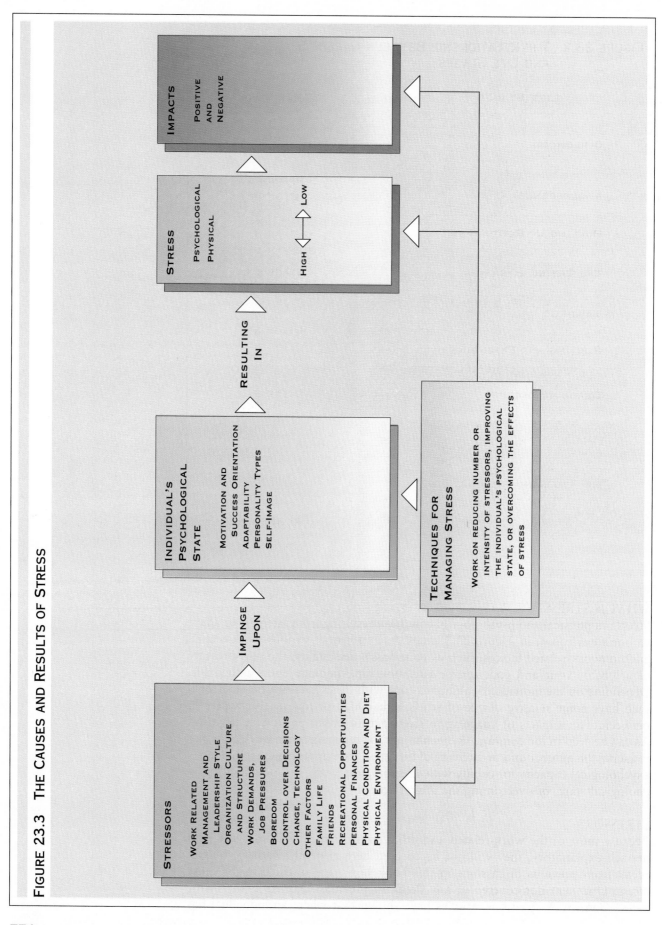

FIGURE 23.3 THE CAUSES AND RESULTS OF STRESS

IMPACTS

POSITIVE
AND
NEGATIVE

STRESS

PSYCHOLOGICAL
PHYSICAL

HIGH ⇕ LOW

RESULTING IN

**INDIVIDUAL'S
PSYCHOLOGICAL
STATE**

MOTIVATION AND
SUCCESS ORIENTATION
ADAPTABILITY
PERSONALITY TYPES
SELF-IMAGE

IMPINGE UPON

STRESSORS

WORK RELATED
MANAGEMENT AND
LEADERSHIP STYLE
ORGANIZATION CULTURE
AND STRUCTURE
WORK DEMANDS,
JOB PRESSURES
BOREDOM
CONTROL OVER DECISIONS
CHANGE, TECHNOLOGY
OTHER FACTORS
FAMILY LIFE
FRIENDS
RECREATIONAL OPPORTUNITIES
PERSONAL FINANCES
PHYSICAL CONDITION AND DIET
PHYSICAL ENVIRONMENT

**TECHNIQUES FOR
MANAGING STRESS**

WORK ON REDUCING NUMBER OR
INTENSITY OF STRESSORS, IMPROVING
THE INDIVIDUAL'S PSYCHOLOGICAL
STATE, OR OVERCOMING THE EFFECTS
OF STRESS

FIGURE 23.4   STRESSFUL LIFE EVENTS

LIFE EVENT	VALUE	YOUR SCORE	LIFE EVENT	VALUE	YOUR SCORE
1. DEATH OF SPOUSE	100	_____	24. TROUBLE WITH IN-LAWS	29	_____
2. DIVORCE	73	_____	25. OUTSTANDING PERSONAL ACHIEVEMENT	28	_____
3. MARITAL SEPARATION	65	_____	26. SPOUSE BEGINS OR STOPS WORK	26	_____
4. JAIL TERM	63	_____	27. STARTING OR FINISHING SCHOOL	26	_____
5. DEATH OF CLOSE FAMILY MEMBER	63	_____	28. CHANGE IN LIVING CONDITIONS	25	_____
6. PERSONAL INJURY OR ILLNESS	53	_____	29. REVISION OF PERSONAL HABITS	24	_____
7. MARRIAGE	50	_____	30. TROUBLE WITH BOSS	23	_____
8. FIRED AT WORK	47	_____	31. CHANGE IN WORK HOURS, CONDITIONS	20	_____
9. MARITAL RECONCILIATION	45	_____	32. CHANGE IN RESIDENCE	20	_____
10. RETIREMENT	45	_____	33. CHANGE IN SCHOOLS	20	_____
11. CHANGE IN FAMILY MEMBER'S HEALTH	44	_____	34. CHANGE IN RECREATION	19	_____
12. PREGNANCY	40	_____	35. CHANGE IN CHURCH ACTIVITIES	19	_____
13. SEX DIFFICULTIES	39	_____	36. CHANGE IN SOCIAL ACTIVITIES	18	_____
14. ADDITION TO FAMILY	39	_____	37. MORTGAGE OR LOAN UNDER $10,000*	17	_____
15. BUSINESS READJUSTMENT	39	_____	38. CHANGE IN SLEEPING HABITS	16	_____
16. CHANGE IN FINANCIAL STATE	38	_____	39. CHANGE IN NUMBER OF FAMILY GET-TOGETHERS	15	_____
17. DEATH OF CLOSE FRIEND	37	_____	40. CHANGE IN EATING HABITS	15	_____
18. CHANGE TO DIFFERENT LINE OF WORK	36	_____	41. VACATION	13	_____
19. CHANGE IN NUMBER OF ARGUMENTS WITH SPOUSE	35	_____	42. CHRISTMAS	12	_____
20. MORTGAGE OVER $10,000*	31	_____	43. MINOR VIOLATIONS OF LAW	11	_____
21. FORECLOSURE OF MORTGAGE OR LOAN	30	_____			
22. CHANGE IN WORK RESPONSIBILITIES	29	_____		TOTAL	_____
23. SON OR DAUGHTER LEAVING HOME	29	_____			

WHAT IT MEANS

CHECK EACH EVENT WHICH OCCURRED TO YOU IN THE LAST YEAR. THEN TOTAL YOUR SCORES FOR ALL EVENTS. A TOTAL OF 0–150 INDICATES A 37% LIKELIHOOD OF DEVELOPING AN ILLNESS IN THE NEXT TWO YEARS. A SCORE OF 150–300 INDICATES A 51% PROBABILITY OF ILLNESS. A SCORE OVER 300 AND YOU ARE RUNNING AN 80% CHANCE OF DEVELOPING AN ILLNESS IN THE NEXT TWO YEARS. THESE ARE MAJOR ILLNESSES AND INCLUDE CANCER, HEART ATTACKS, AND PSYCHOSIS.

*I SUGGEST YOU SUBSTITUTE $50,000 FOR $10,000 IN ORDER TO BRING THESE FIGURES UP TO MORE CURRENT AMOUNTS.

SOURCE: THOMAS H. HOLMES AND RICHARD H. RAHE, "THE SOCIAL READJUSTMENT RATING SCALE," JOURNAL OF PSYCHOSO-MATIC RESEARCH 11:213–218. REPRINTED WITH PERMISSION FROM PERGAMON PRESS, LTD., COPYRIGHT 1967.

little control over the decisions that affect his or her job, and when the job has a high psychological demand—for example, for a fireman, telephone operator, or cashier—this tends to increase the level of stress.[25] A second factor that needs some explanation is the idea of change. Research has clearly shown that the more change in an individual's life, the greater the degree of potential stress and the more he or she will suffer physical and mental illnesses. Change would include the loss of the life of a spouse or other close relative, to celebrating Christmas or taking a vacation.[26] To get an idea of how change may be affecting your life, take the questionnaire in Figure 23.4.

THE INDIVIDUAL'S PSYCHOLOGICAL STATE

Four key factors have been identified with the ability to cope with the stressors that impinge upon an individual's psychological state.

1. **Motivation.** The higher the level of individual motivation and success orientation, the more likely the individual is to be involved in a large number of complex, often competitive processes that may lead to increased stress levels.

2. **Change.** Similarly, the more complex or changeful an individual's situation is—for example, a job—the more important it is that the individual be adaptable.

3. **Personality types.** In the 1970s, a series of studies indicated that a personality type known as Type A would result in more heart attacks than another personality type known as Type B. The person with a Type A personality was characterized as being extremely competitive, taking on more work than he or she could possibly handle, extremely aggressive and hostile with other people, thinking of more than one thing at a time, impatient with others—especially with people who tended to be slow—and could be described as having a sort of "hurry sickness," trying to do more, faster, and faster. The Type B person was essentially described as the opposite—much more relaxed, less competitive, and less time-oriented.[27] Since that time, it has been discovered that numerous other factors enter into personality equations, and that Type A and Type B are not as accurate indicators of the propensity for heart attacks as was once thought.

   Furthermore, Dr. Robert S. Elliott, head of cardiology at the University of Nebraska, himself a heart attack victim, has uncovered an underlying personality characteristic known as "hot reactor." This is a person who exhibits "extreme cardiovascular reactions to standardized stress tests."[28] This reaction involves extreme biological responses, but not always behavioral ones, to external stressors. Thus, while many Type B personalities appear calm on the surface, they may be seething underneath. This helps explain the large number of heart attacks that Dr. Eliott found for Type B individuals. Research by Redford Williams, Jr., of the Duke University Medical School, has produced parallel findings to Elliott's. Williams found that hostility is probably the only characteristic of Type A people that accurately predicts heart attacks, and that the other characteristics probably don't result in heart attacks. Furthermore, cynicism seemed to be an important predictor as well.[29]

4. **Self-image.** Finally, self-image appears to be an important component of the ability to handle stress. Those with a lower degree of self-image tend not to handle stress as well as those with a high degree.

STRESS

Depending on the individual's psychological state and the ability to cope with stressors, some degree of psychological and physical stress will result. The body goes through a rather predictable series of stages when stressors are encountered. But the degree to which these may affect the individual will vary because of his or her psychological state.[30] The body will emit various chemicals, such as adrenaline, and these must be handled by the body if it is to function properly. Additionally, the mind will react to the stressors in a certain way.

Stress passes through three stages: alarm, resistance, and exhaustion. In the alarm state, immediate physiological and psychological impacts occur. In the resistance stage, over a period of time the body still reacts to the stressor, but not at the same high level: if the stressor continues and the body continues to react to it, the body may collapse in exhaustion. It is the prolonged period of resistance that eventually causes a phenomenon such as **burnout,** in which human beings are no longer able to react satisfactorily to their environment. It is a state of fatigue or exhaustion or frustration that is characterized by "not caring and not caring that you do not care." The manager must be alert to his own condition relative to stress and burnout and to that of his or her employees.

THE IMPACTS OF STRESS

Stress actually can have some positive impacts. A certain amount of stress will actually induce increased motivation and performance. But beyond some point, stress results in reduced performance.[31] The negative impacts of stress are essentially of two types: physical and psychological. Physically it is clear that health can be endangered by continual stress. Psychologically we have already indicated that psychosomatic illnesses abound and mental illness may result from stress over a long period of time. One of the consequences is, of course, burnout. The impacts of stress also depend upon the individual's physical condition and habits. Smoking, overeating, high blood pressure, high serum cholesterol levels, exercise or the lack thereof, and diet are all major factors in whether stress is having a major physical impact.

TECHNIQUES FOR MANAGING STRESS

Techniques for managing stress focus on reducing either the number or intensity of stressors, improving the individual's psychological state, and reducing the afteraffects of stress. Techniques that may reduce the number of stressors or their intensity include training to improve management and leadership styles and changing the organizational culture or structure to increase levels of participation or doing away with very negative norms. They may include resolving role conflicts; increasing participation to give people more control over decisions; reducing the number of changes in an organization; or providing education and participation in such changes as increasing technology.

Stress management courses teach individuals how to cope with stress. They include stress training or counseling, programs to improve self-image, and teaching people how to cope with their personality types. Those programs aimed at reducing the effects of stress include such activities as relaxation response, in which an individual learns a technique for relaxing and reducing the aftereffects of stress; and physical fitness programs, to deal with the blood sugar, adrenaline, and oxygen levels that the body uses up throughout the day because of stessors. Firms such as Levi Strauss & Company and Blue Cross & Blue Shield of Minnesota have established employee support groups to help cope with the effects of stress.[32] We know that stress can be managed and we know that managers must manage that stress for themselves and their subordinates.

The Manager in the Twenty-first Century

One of the principal focuses of this book has been the increased levels of change and the types of change being made in the general environment of business, as well as in the competitive environment. Such factors as technology, the economy, the political/legal arena, the society, and culture have created changes in management. Chapter 1 identified several major forces of change. They are repeated here:

One way of relieving stress is through physical activity. These Nissan employees enjoy a break by playing table tennis, which also helps them relieve the stress of their very demanding assembly line jobs. (SOURCE © Karen Kasmauski/Woodfin Camp & Associates)

1. Changing employee expectations of how they should be managed
2. Global economy
3. Shift from industrial based economy to information based economy
4. Accelerated rates of change
5. Increased levels of competition
6. Changing technology, especially computers
7. Improved problem solving requiring more creative approaches
8. Cultural diversity
9. Increasing demands of constituents
10. Changing demographics

As managers progress toward the twenty-first century, these factors will play a more prominent role in shaping a manager's career. In most of the chapters in this book, the changes in these factors and how they affect the management issues discussed in each chapter have been identified. A number of recent articles suggest that managers in the future will need to be more global and strategic in orientation; conversant with computer technology; able to make quick decisions; generalists rather than specialists; fluent in more than one language; and more participative in management style.[33]

Furthermore, these changes in management itself are intertwined with complex structural changes in the organization.[34] Networking and lateral relationships are becoming more important. Managers have less authority. Vertical relationships are becoming less important. There are cross-functional teams and teams with customers and suppliers, even joint ventures with competitors. Layers of management are being eliminated. Consequently, career planning is more difficult. There are fewer positions in the hierarchy for managers. At the same time, job holders at all levels of most major organizations will find themselves with more autonomy. Career plans will have to be flexible, and so will you.

Are you prepared for this type of future?

Summary

1. Managing your career involves self-assessment, and an assessment of the opportunities and obstacles in the environment. You must determine objectives and plans for reaching them. You must consider life's stages and major career choices in making career plans.

2. Allen N. Schoonmaker offers a nine-step career planning strategy: accept the fact that there are some inescapable and irreconcilable conflicts between you and your organization; accept the fact that your superiors are essentially indifferent to your career ambitions; analyze your own goals; analyze your assets and liabilities; analyze your opportunities; learn the rules of company politics; plan your career; carry out your plan; and chart your progress.

3. According to Gail Sheehy, life's stages for professionals after the age of eighteen consist of pulling up roots. She describes those stages as the trying twenties; catch-thirty; rooting and extending; the deadline decade; and renewal or resignation.

4. Major career choices include career field, industry, obsolescence, life-stage relevance, whether to enter management, mobility, match, the impacts of your decisions on others, your value to the organization, work experience—what you like and dislike—the organization, and geographic location.

5. The interview is critical to virtually all selection processes in virtually all organizations. But it is full of potential problems. You need to be well prepared, well rehearsed, and very knowledgeable for an interview. You need to pay attention to your appearance and how you communicate. A list of actions you should take is provided in the chapter.

6. Careers in management seem to follow four distinct stages: stage 1—entry-level position; stage 2—entry level of middle-level management position; stage 3—middle- and upper-level management position; stage 4—top-level management. Only a few reach stage 3 and even fewer reach stage 4.

7. Stress is a part of all managers' jobs. Stressors impinge upon an individual's psychological state, and depending upon his or her ability to cope with them, stress will result in some degree, either physically or psychologically. The impacts may be either positive or negative.

8. Stress can be managed by working on reducing the number or intensity of stressors, improving the individual's psychological state, or overcoming the effects of stress.

9. Management is changing. What managers need to be capable of doing is also changing. The number of available positions for managers is being reduced in most organizations. The predicability of career paths is being lessened in the era of the new management. Career plans must be more flexible.

The Management Challenges Identified

1. Increasing rates of change in careers, career opportunities
2. Stress

Some Solutions Noted in the Chapter

1. Career management, life planning
2. Stress management
3. Changes in management style

Thinking About Management

1. What is implied by the term *career,* as used in this book, that is not implied by the word *job*? When might you want a job as opposed to a career?
2. Have you ever established a career plan? Do you know anyone who has? Have you or they benefited from this planning?
3. What is meant by devising a "realistic" career plan, as opposed to simply drawing up a career plan?
4. According to Sheehy's life-stages model, the stages of catch-thirty and the deadline decade often involve changes in careers. Why do you suppose this is true?
5. What real need is there for career planning if all the changes taking place as we move toward the twenty-first century and the new management are making career planning more difficult?
6. Relate your experiences with job interviews. Were you sufficiently prepared? How well prepared was the interviewer? What types of possible problems associated with the interview were the one(s) you experienced?
7. Discuss the pros and cons of the advice given to new managers in Table 23.3.
8. Discuss your experiences with stressors—how you coped, how you failed to cope. Discuss people you have witnessed who failed to cope. To what would you attribute their inability to cope? For example, was it the tremendous pressure of stressors or the individuals' psychological state?

CASE

Squibb Pharmaceuticals

Squibb Pharmaceuticals Corp., one of the nation's leading pharmaceutical companies, considers management development and career planning to be major parts of its operating philosophy. The company promotes a participative management style. As part of that participation program in the specific area of management development, a survey of managers revealed that they felt they needed more development in interpersonal skills. They were concerned, for example, about their ability to communicate, to make the right leadership choices, to offer the right need satisfiers, to work with groups, and to build teams. As a result, the company established an "Insights" program, a series of workshops designed to improve managers' interpersonal skills.

DISCUSSION QUESTIONS

If you were put in charge of such a program:

1. What factors would you need to consider relative to its design—for example, existing abilities? (Think in terms of this chapter's material and the interpersonal skills discussed earlier.)
2. How might a manager's life-cycle stage affect his or her need for these skills?
3. How might a manager's career stage affect his or her needs for these skills?
4. What do you think is meant by "insights"? How does a person develop them?

SOURCE: William H. Wagel, "Developing Productive Leadership at Squibb," *Personnel* (May 1987), pp. 4–8.

Todd & Associates

Shirley Todd, at age forty-three, had been a sales representative for Xerox Corporation for seven years when she and her husband divorced. She had done well in her career at a time when women were just beginning to be accepted in the work force. But her divorce and the need to be home more with her nine-year-old son, coupled with a desire to be on her own, led her to start an insurance agency. Times were tough for her and her young son, but she persevered. Slowly, surely, she built the agency to its current level of revenues, revenues sufficient to provide her with a substantial income. Three agents and a secretary now work for her.

In the past two years, she has reduced her work load to only forty hours a week. She has taken her running more seriously, entering several marathons, and is running many 10K races. However, her income has dropped about $20,000 from its previous high, when she was working fifty to sixty hours a week. Todd is at a decision point. She can put in grueling hours and raise her sales to the point where her income would be $250,000 in three more years; she can sell the business for about $500,000; or she can stay right where she is in terms of income. But she is bored. She has been teaching for several years as an adjunct for a local community college and a local college. She likes teaching, but she knows she needs a Ph.D to become a full-time academician. She has spent several days thinking about her situation, off and on over a six-month period. She has had an offer from a potential buyer for her firm. She really doesn't look forward to working sixty-hour work weeks again. It's time for her to make a decision.

DISCUSSION QUESTIONS
1. How are life's stages affecting Todd's decision?
2. What career choices must she make?
3. How will her needs and values influence her choices?
4. What do you think her decision will be? Why?

Formulating A Career Plan

MANAGE YOURSELF

Most of you taking this course are college sophomores and juniors. Almost half of you will be working full time and going to college part time. The rest will be full-time students. For all of you—in your first full-time job or for those of you already working full time—making a decision about whether to stay with your current employer or to move on is an important one. To that end, complete the following exercise by identifying your

Strengths: Opportunities:
Weaknesses: Obstacles or threats:

Now think carefully through each of the career choice issues:

Career field	Mobility	Motivation
Industry	Match	Organization
Obsolescence	Impacts	Geographic location
Life stage and its impacts	Value	
Management	Experience	

Now, establish five-year objectives and plans for reaching those objectives for your career.
Objectives

Plans to reach those objectives

Glossary

Accelerated Rates of Change: All the evidence indicates that the rate of change in our society is accelerating.

Acceptance of Authority: Chester Barnard saw authority as deriving from the acceptance or rejection of authority by the subordinate—a bottom-up approach. For Chester Barnard, a "zone of indifference" exists within which each person would obey orders without questioning the authority of those who gave them. Once an order exceeded that zone of indifference, however, the person would have to choose whether to accept or reject that authority.

Acceptance Theory of Authority: States that a manager's authority is authority only if the subordinate chooses to accept the manager's formal authority as real authority.

Accommodative Social Response: The company has accepted its economic, legal, and ethical responsibilities, although sometimes it does so under pressure.

Achievement Motivation: Another major contribution to our understanding of human needs was made by researchers David C. McClelland and J. W. Atkinson. They found that a small percentage of people have an unusually high need for achievement (principally economic achievement) or "nAch."

Achievement-Oriented Leadership: The leader emphasizes the achievement of difficult tasks, emphasizes the importance of excellence of performance, and simultaneously shows confidence that subordinates will perform well. It entails setting challenging goals.

Active Recruitment: Involves placing advertisements in various media—newspapers, radio, TV, trade journals, and the like; visiting high schools, colleges, and other places where applicants may be found; and making contacts with people who seek applicants for the organization—

for example, employment agencies; or union hiring agents.

Activity Ratios: Determine how well assets are being utilized. *See also* Ratio Analysis.

Adhocracy (Mintzberg): Both a complex and nonstandardized organization.

Alderfer's Hierarchy: C. P. Alderfer identified these needs—growth, relatedness, and existence.

Alternative Generation: Once a manager has recognized a problem, identified the underlying cause, or causes, and made assumptions, he or she must generate alternatives to solve it and related problems.

Alternatives, Evaluating and Choosing: After generating a series of alternative solutions, the manager must then choose one or more alternatives that will meet the criteria for a successful solution.

Annual Operating Plan: The one-year plan of action to implement strategy.

Anticipated Problems: Good managers anticipate the problems that may occur as a result of most, if not all, of their actions and decisions.

Application Blank: The cornerstone document for both recruitment and selection is the job application blank. The application blank may be given to all applicants, or it may be given only to those who pass a preliminary screening process.

Artificial Intelligence (AI): T. H. Winston defines artificial intelligence (AI) as "the study of ideas which enable computers to do the things that make people seem intelligent."

Asia's Four Tigers: South Korea, Taiwan, Hong Kong, and Singapore.

Assessment Centers: Usually a two- or three-day program consisting of simulation exercises, various tests, interviews, and problem-solving assignments that are used to measure the potential for promo-

tion or assignment to some specific job for which the assessment center has been designed as a comprehensive test.

Attribution Theory: One of the most critical factors in determining future motivation is to whom the individual attributes success or failure, or to whom his or her manager attributes subordinate success or failure. In formulating his attribution theory, psychologist A. Bandura has shown that individuals tend to attribute success to themselves and failures to variables themselves outside. Conversely, managers tend to attribute the failure of subordinates to the subordinate and successes to outside factors.

Automated Storage and Retrieval Systems (ASRS): Computer-controlled automated warehouses that include automatic placement and retrieval of parts into and from the warehouse. Parts are ordered and retrieved as needed, according to computer control. Automatic transportation of parts occurs on self-guided carts.

Autonomous Work Teams: Applying job enrichment to groups, in the sense of increasing depth—autonomy in decision making—creates what are known as autonomous work teams.

Autonomy: The extent to which employees have substantial freedom and independence and a major say in scheduling their work, selecting the equipment they will use, and deciding on procedures to be followed.

Balance Sheet: Reveals the condition of the company at a given point in time.

Barriers to Communication: Typical barriers to communication include language limitations, speaking and listening habits, physical and social differences, timing, wordiness, characteristics of the sender and receiver, and information overload.

Behavioral Approach to Management: An approach concerned with increasing pro-

G-1

ductivity by focusing on understanding the human element of an organization—individuals and groups and how they can be combined, both effectively and efficiently, in a larger organization.

Behaviorally Anchored Rating Scale (BARS): A checklist identifying a series of behavioral activities that should be undertaken in any one job. It then provides verbal descriptions of several levels of performance for each behavioral activity.

Bet-Your-Company Culture: The bet-your-company culture results from decisions where feedback is slow, but risks are high. Large financial investments are made in highly competitive environments where payoffs take a while to develop. *See also* Deal & Kennedy's Culture Types.

Body Language: A form of nonverbal communication which has four major components—facial expressions, eye contact, gestures, and body postures.

Boston Consulting Group (BCG) Portfolio Matrix: This matrix is used by strategists to plot each business' relative competitive position (horizontal axis) as expressed by relative market share against the business's growth rate (vertical axis)—the industry growth rate.

Brainstorming: A group creative problem-solving process that focuses on the following procedures: No negative feedback is allowed on any suggested alternative until all alternatives have been generated. Piggybacking on others' ideas is encouraged. Quantity of ideas, not quality, is the key. Evaluation comes later. Freethinking is pursued. Let the "wild and crazy" ideas flow.

Break-even Analysis: Whenever new products or services are launched, whenever any projects are engaged in, whenever managers consider enacting an annual operating plan, in most cases, the plan will involve a point at which the revenue generated from the project, product, or service, from the year's or project's efforts, is going to equal the cost of generating that revenue—the break-even point.

Budget: The annual operating plan, with revenues and expenses determined for the actions necessary according to the annual operating plan.

Budgeting Process: Begins with a revenue forecast. This forecast will then be used as a basis for allocating funds to various responsibility centers. These centers will in turn develop budgets within constraints identified by the revenue forecast. Cost and revenue budgets are then summarized into major types of organization budgets—into cash budgets, expense budgets, and revenue budgets—and matched against the total revenue forecasts.

Budgets: Budgets are quantitative, usually financial statements of plans that allocate resources to various units of organization. Budgets are normally operating plans, but they may also be drafted for longer-range plans. Budgets tend to cover one year or eighteen months in duration. Budgets typically (1) are stated in monetary terms; (2) are for a specific time period; (3) indicate

some level of management commitment; (4) are based on some type of proposal typically submitted by lower-level managers and reviewed and approved by upper-level managers; (5) should be modified only under certain extenuating circumstances, such as a dramatic increase or decrease in sales or costs.

Building and Maintenance Roles (of Groups): Members of groups should build group-centeredness by performing actions that tend to maintain the group.

Bureaucracy: "The ideal or pure form of organization" according to Max Weber, but more lately, often negatively perceived as a cumbersome structural design.

Bureaucratic Control: Based on control by authority through the use of rules, regulations, and policies. It is based on compliance rather than commitment.

Business Plan: Typically contains specific objectives and plans to reach those objectives across the organization's major economic functions. Special attention is paid to target markets; product development, pricing, distribution, and promotion strategies; and the ability of the organization to finance marketing and operations.

Business Strategy: A strategic plan that indicates how an organization competes in a particular business.

Campus Capitalists: In the mid-1980s, a major "craze" on college campuses was starting one's own business.

Capital Expenditure Budgets: Include capital expenditures for major capital purchases, such as plant and equipment, inventories, and development costs.

Career Choices: Major choices include career field, industry, obsolescence, life stages, management, mobility, match, impacts, value, experience, motivation, organization, and geographic location.

Career Planning Process: The individual performs a self-analysis and an environmental analysis, then sets long-term objectives and plans, then sets short-term objectives and plans, then gets organized and implements plans, and then periodically evaluates and controls.

Career Plans, Realistic: Allen N. Schoonmaker offers a nine-step career planning strategy and sound advice in formulating your career strategies. He takes into account both an organization's perspective and that of the individual career planner.

Career Plateaus: That point in a career where the likelihood of additional hierarchical promotion is very low.

Cash Budget: A forecast of cash receipts and disbursements.

Cash Flow Statement: Indicates the sources and uses of cash.

Causal Forecasting Techniques: The two principal types of causal models are regression analysis and the econometric model.

Cellular Phones: Managers can keep in touch with the office, call back important clients, and call subordinates and their managers with a cellular phone.

Centralized Organization: Authority is not widely delegated.

Certainty, Problem-Solving Conditions of: Certainty exists in a problem-solving environment when a decision maker can predict the results of implementing each of the alternatives with 100 percent certainty.

Change, Management (HRM): The HRM department, now more than ever, has been assigned the central responsibility for aiding the organization in planning for and managing change. Of special concern is the management of the organization's culture, or shared values.

Changing Managerial Process: Many forces for change greatly affect managers and the management process. These forces, these management challenges, are changing the nature of the management process functions, the skills required of managers, and the roles that are necessary. They are also changing the relative mix of management functions, as well as how they are performed.

Chief Information Officer (CIO): Currently exists principally in larger corporations. However, as the need for information increases, CIOs will become more prominent in medium-sized organizations. The role of the CIO is more encompassing, more strategic, than that of the MIS director. He or she is responsible for managing, especially from a strategic viewpoint, the use of information and systems within the organization.

Clan Control: This style of control relies on people's social needs—the desire to belong to a group. Control is established largely through cultural artifacts such as rituals and myths.

Classical Approaches to Management: These were developed early in the twentieth century. There were two primary thrusts, scientific management and organization and administration. They focused primarily on improving work methods and formulating principles to understand how to administer and structure organizations, respectively.

Closed System: Does not interact with its environment.

Coercive Power: Depends on the ability to punish others for its effectiveness. Fear is a motivator, but fear does not highly motivate very many people for long.

Cohesiveness of a Group: The tendency of members to want to belong to the group, as opposed to wanting to leave it.

Combination Strategy: Often, organizations invoke some combination of the various basic action strategies.

Communicating: Transferring information from one communicator to another.

Communication: The transfer of information from one communicator to another through the use of symbols. For communication to be complete, both parties must understand what has been transferred.

Communication, Basic Model of: Ideation, encoding, transmission, receiving, decoding, understanding and action, feedback, noise, and barriers.

Communication, Functions of: William G. Scott and Terrence R. Mitchell, management authors, have identified four major functions of communication within the organization: the emotive, motivation, information, and control functions.

Communication Channels: Managers may choose from a variety of channels over which to communicate to subordinates, managers, and others in the organization. Memos, telephone, face-to-face conversation, and interactive video programs are but a few choices available.

Communication Process: The communication process begins when the sender, whether a person, a group, or an organization, has a thought, feeling, idea, or concept that the sender wishes to share with another entity, the receiver.

Company Strategy, Structure, and Rivalry: The conditions governing a nation's businesses, especially competition—completes the dynamic diamond Porter envisioned. See also Dynamic Diamond.

Compensation and Benefit Programs: Aimed at influencing motivation. Such programs define the limits within which individual managers can influence motivation using compensation or benefits. The classic method of influencing employee motivation is to offer financial-need satisfiers.

Competition, Increased Levels of: On an international basis, we face increased levels of competition. Competition is dramatically increased within our own country as well.

Competitive Advantage: Whatever it is that enables a firm to beat its competition in the marketplace.

Competitive Environment: This is comprised of those elements that form its competitive situation. Its major components include customers, competitors, suppliers, substitutes, and new entrants. See also External Environment.

Competitiveness, Declining U.S.: Perhaps the most significant feature of the North American members of the triad is their declining global competitiveness. The United States has found itself with a competitive disadvantage on a global basis in both manufacturing and service industries for a number of reasons. Among them are the transition from a manufacturing to a service economy, declining investment in heavy manufacturing, disadvantageous wage rates and benefit structures, technological transfer from the United States to foreign competitors, and a short-term perspective with regard to the returns expected from an organization—ROI-based financial controls, strategic portfolio management concepts used to buy and sell businesses, and lack of quality of U.S. products. Factors cited more recently include diversification strategies, the subsequent adoption of decentralized organizational structures, and evolutionary changes in the nature of the capital market. The principal consequence of the impact of several of these items has been the reduction of investment in long-term product/market development. Innovation has been short changed both by the short-term perspective and by the absence of funds for investment in organizations that take a long-term perspective.

Competitors: Competitors are other organizations that market similar products or services to the same set of customers. See also Competitive Environment.

Complex Environments: These usually have a large number of products, a large number of geographic locations, a change in consumers or their nature, and they often involve complex technology.

Complexity of Structures: Refers to the number of different jobs and different departments a structure incorporates.

Compressed Work Week: A work week in which forty hours of work are scheduled to be completed in fewer than the traditional five days.

Computer Aided Design (CAD): Includes specialized hardware and software to assist engineers in performing designs on a computer terminal.

Computer Aided Manufacturing (CAM): Encompasses specialized computer systems that translate the CAD design information into instructions for automated manufacturing.

Computer Conferencing: A multiparty extension of electronic mail. Numerous individuals at terminals can communicate with each other at the same time, sending and receiving messages.

Computer Integrated Manufacturing (CIM): A broad label applied to the use of computers in design and manufacturing processes, the use of just-in-time inventories, flexible manufacturing, robotics, high levels of automation, and automatic storage and retrieval systems.

Computer Virus: A small unit of computer code written by a programmer that can attach itself to other programs, alter them, or destroy data kept on a computer disk. Viruses are capable of reproducing themselves and attaching themselves to other programs stored in the same computer. Typically, a virus is attached to a normal software program that becomes its "Trojan horse." The virus spreads and the owner of the Trojan horse exchanges software with other computer users, typically through an electronic bulletin board or through the exchange of floppy disks.

Concentration Strategy: Organizations may concentrate on a single product or product lines.

Conceptual Skill: Ability to see the organization as a whole and solve problems to benefit the total system.

Concurrent Authority: The concept which states that the organization may require that all decisions be concurred with by the staff.

Concurrent Controls: They assess ongoing activities. They are designed to detect variances from standards, leading to corrective action before a series of actions is completed. Concurrent controls are often referred to as steering controls.

Conditions Under Which Decisions Are Made: The conditions under which managers make decisions have a tremendous impact on their choices of alternatives. The less routine, the less anticipated the problem, the more complex the problem, the more uncertain the environment usually.

Conflict Management: Conflict is inevitable in any organization. Unless it is managed effectively, it can destroy both sides of the controversy. Conflict has historically been viewed as undesirable, something to be avoided. The contemporary view is that conflict cannot always be avoided, but it can be managed.

Contemporary Management: This is a synthesis of the seven approaches to management discussed in Chapter 2.

Contextual Dimensions: Contextual dimensions that help define a job include interpersonal relations, authority and responsibility for goal setting, communication patterns.

Contingency Approach to Management: Portrays that a manager's actions should be contingent on the condition of various key elements in a given situation.

Contingency Theories (of Leadership): Propose that for any given situation there is a best way to manage.

Continuum of Leadership Behavior: Developed by Robert Tannenbaum and Warren H. Schmidt, presents seven alternative ways for managers to approach decision making, depending on how much participation they want to allow subordinates in the decision-making process.

Control: Is the systematic process by which managers assure that the organization is reaching its objectives and carrying out the associated plans in an effective and efficient manner. Control is the fourth major mission function of management. It is the concluding phase in the management cycle: planning, organizing, leading, and controlling.

Control, Dysfunctional Consequences of: If control systems do not possess the effective characteristics indicated here—or even if they do—sometimes certain dysfunctional consequences may occur. Among them are game playing, resistance to control, inaccurate information, rigid bureaucratic behavior.

Control, Management Styles of: William G. Ouchi, who introduced many U.S. managers to Japanese management, has identified three principal control strategies, or styles, that managers may choose to employ when designing and managing control systems: market control, bureaucratic control, and clan control.

Control, Types of: There are four different types of control: (1) those defined according to the timing of the control process relative to the transformation process: preaction control, concurrent control, and postaction control; (2) those defined according to the planning level involved: strategic, tactical, and operational control; (3) those defined according to economic function: marketing, finance, operations, human resource management, information management; (4) those defined according to the management function involved: problem solving, planning, organizing, leading, and controlling.

Control in the Creative Problem-Solving Process: Once the decision has been implemented, its success must be evaluated.

Control Function (of Communication): Reports, policies, and plans function to control the behaviors of an organization's members. They define roles; clarify duties, authority, and responsibilities; and provide organization structure (defined as jobs and the authority to do them).

Control Process, Characteristics of: (1) The control process is cyclical. (2) Control tends to be viewed as a negative endeavor, but the process results in an extremely positive contribution to organizational success. (3) Control is anticipatory as well as retrospective. (4) Finally, control must occur throughout the organization.

Control Process, Steps in: There are four essential steps in the control process: establishing performance objectives and standards, measuring actual performance, comparing actual performance to objectives and standards, taking necessary action based on the results of the comparison.

Control Systems, Effective: A number of authors have identified the following characteristics for incorporation into the design of control systems in order to make them effective: strategy, tactics, and operations; acceptability; flexibility; accuracy; timeliness; cost effectiveness; understandability; objectivity; and other factors.

Controlling: Controlling is the process of ascertaining whether organizational objectives have been achieved; if not, why not; and determining what actions should then be taken to achieve objectives better in the future.

Coordinating: Acting to ensure understanding. Viewed as part of organizing in this book.

Coordination: The process of integrating the efforts of individuals and departments in the organization to achieve organizational purpose.

Coordination (per Mary Park Follett): For Follett, coordination involved the sharing of responsibility by all people involved in an organization and was a means of relating all factors in a situation to each other.

Core Control Elements: Six core formal management control systems exist for top- and middle-level management in organizations. At the strategic level, the strategic plan, financial analysis, and the long-range financial plan are used by top managers for strategy formulation. The operating budget, statistical reports, performance appraisal systems, and policies and procedures are used by middle managers for

department control and strategy implementation. The last four core elements may also be used in the transformation process at the operational level. But a study by William G. Ouchi and M. A. Maguire suggests that at the operational level, control is usually accomplished through personal influence and surveillance or through output data and records—a results orientation.

Core Function: The core function of management is creative problem solving because it occurs during and is used in every other function of management to achieve those functions.

Core Job Dimensions: As identified by management researchers J. Richard Hackman and Greg R. Oldham they are skill variety, task identity, task significance, autonomy, feedback.

Corporate Myths and Sagas: Corporate myths and sagas tell us important historical facts about organizational behavior, including pioneer people and products; past triumphs and failures; and those visionaries who have transformed the company.

Corporate Social Policy Process: The organization institutionalizes the social responsibility needs and wants of society within the policy framework of the organization. Social responsibility is improved by business ethics, corporate social responsibility, and corporate social responsiveness.

Corporate Strategy: A strategic plan that identifies the business or businesses in which an organization will engage and how it will fundamentally conduct that business or those businesses.

Cost Accounting: Allows organizations to achieve efficient use of resources.

Cost Centers/Expense Centers: Are responsibility centers controlled on the basis of their costs/expenses generated. *See also* Responsibility Center Management.

Cost Leadership: Having the lowest cost possible.

Creative Problem Solving: Creative problem solving is the process of practicing ongoing environmental analysis, recognizing and identifying a problem, making assumptions about the decision environment, generating creative alternatives to solve the identified problem, deciding among those alternatives, acting to implement the chosen alternative(s), and controlling for results. There is strong evidence that the person who is intuitive as well as rational is a far superior decision maker than one who is simply rational and analytical.

Creativity, The Four Ps of: Product, possibilities, processes, and the person.

Creativity, The Possibilities for: The possibilities for creativity include a certain type of organizational culture, a supportive management style, and the right combination of societal characteristics.

Criteria (Decision): As part of the identification stage, problem solvers must establish criteria for a successful solution.

Critical Incidents: Type of performance appraisal—raters identify critical positive and negative employee performance.

Critical Path: The sequence of activities that leads from the starting circle to the finishing circle, in terms of the longest amount of time in PERT or CPM.

Cross-functional Teams: Consist of design, manufacturing, and often marketing personnel who jointly design the product.

Current Ratio: The current ratio measures the liquidity of the firm—that is, its ability to handle short-term debts and liabilities. It is found by dividing current assets by current liabilities. *See also* Ratio Analysis and Liquidity Ratios.

Customers: Customers consume the organization's product or service and include people or organizations.

Deal & Kennedy's Culture Types: Terrence R. Deal and Allan A. Kennedy, researchers of and consultants on corporate culture, suggest that the relationship between strategy and culture is very pronounced and results in the four readily identifiable cultural categories: tough-guy, macho culture; bet-your-company culture; work hard/play hard culture; and process culture. These are based on combinations of the speed of the feedback given on strategic performance and the degree of risk taken in the strategic decisions being made.

Debt-to-Total Assets Ratio: Equals total debt divided by total assets. It is represented as a percentage. *See also* Ratio Analysis and Leverage Ratio.

Decentralized Organization: Authority is widely delegated to subordinates.

Decision: A decision is a choice among alternatives. A "CKD" is a choice among alternatives. Decision making encompasses only the third through the sixth parts of the creative problem solving model. Problem identification, making assumptions, alternative generation, and choice.

Decision Makers Making Assumptions About the Future: Decision makers, after analyzing the environment and recognizing and identifying the problem or problems, must make assumptions about the future, assumptions about the conditions of various elements in the decision situation.

Decision Making, Administrative Model of: The administrative model of decision making has these realities: (1) Objectives of the decision are often vague, conflicting, and not agreed upon. (2) Often managers do not recognize that a problem exists. (3) Managers often do not go through the identification process and therefore solve the wrong conceptualization of the problem (what academician Ian Mitroff calls "Making an error of the third kind"). (4) Decision makers and problem solvers solve models of their world. (5) Only a few of the possible alternatives are considered. (6) As a core part of bounded rationality, few managers search to find the best possible alternative. (7) Managers base decisions on rules of thumb and frequently won't even evaluate alternatives according to criteria. Past experience is often the basis for making decisions. (8) The decision-making process, especially in the higher levels of the organization, is greatly affected by social relationships. (9) Decisions often occur in a series of small steps.

Decision Making, Economic Model of: The economic model of decision making has these assumptions: (1) Objectives are known and agreed upon. (2) The existence of the problem is recognized and its nature has been identified. (3) The consequences of implementing each alternative are certain, or a probability may be assigned to each. (4) Criteria for the best decision are known and agreed upon. Decision makers will seek to maximize their situation by choosing the "best alternative" indicated by these criteria. (5) Managers are rational. They can assign values, order preferences, and make the decision that will optimize the attainment of the decision's objectives. (6) Managers have complete knowledge of the situation.

Decision Support Systems (DSS): Computer-based MIS that provide managers with easily accessible information and models that support decision making in an interactive manner.

Decision Tree: A visual representation of the decision alternatives available to the decision maker, their interconnectedness in the environment—events (the states of nature)—and their consequences.

Decoding (Communication): The sensory information that arrives from the sender must undergo decoding—that is, interpretation by the receiver.

Defensive Social Responsibility: Occurs when the company admits that it made a mistake but defends its position as having been caught up in circumstances beyond its control; it may even take minor actions to attempt to offset its errors.

Delphi Groups: Utilizes a series of questionnaires administered by a central individual to experts who never meet face-to-face. As the respondents reply, their questionnaires are summarized, and a new questionnaire, based on their responses to the first, is developed and sent to them. This repeating process continues until a group consensus on the problem is reached.

Demand Conditions: For Michael Porter, the number and sophistication of domestic customers for the industry's product or service. *See also* Dynamic Diamond.

Deming's 14 Points: William Edwards Deming has identified 14 points that should guide quality control.

Departmental Plans: Typically, but not necessarily, a department's annual operating plan.

Departmentation: The grouping of jobs under the authority of (usually) a single manager, according to some common, rational basis, for the purposes of planning, coordination, and control.

Descriptive Statistics: This describes a situation as it exists currently. Inferential, or predictive, statistics are used by man-

agers to attempt to predict what will happen in a situation in the future.

Differentiation: Requires somehow distinguishing the product or service from that of other firms.

Differentiation (Structural): Each organization, and each department of that organization, adapts its subcomponents, including structure, processes, and member behaviors, to meet the constraints of its respective, specific environment.

DINKs (Double Income, No Kids): A dual wage earner family with no kids is sometimes called DINKs.

Directive Autocrat: Makes decisions unilaterally and closely supervises the activities of subordinates.

Directive Democrat: Wants full participation but closely supervises subordinate activity.

Directive Leadership: The leader explains what the performance goal is and provides specific guidance rules and regulations.

Disciplinary Programs: In conjunction with the labor agreement, if one exists, many organizations typically have a routine program of discipline normally consisting of a series of five steps: verbal warning, written warning, one-day suspension, three-day suspension, termination.

Disciplinary Systems: Most organizations use some system for administering discipline. Companies have these systems in order to control four principal types of troublesome employee behaviors: (1) ineffective employees, (2) alcoholic or drug-addicted employees, (3) participants in illegal acts, (4) rule violators.

Disposable Employee: Contingent workers make up about 25 percent of the U.S. labor force now in 1990. The benefits to the corporation are obvious. By having individuals only work part time, or for short periods of time, wages are usually less, benefit packages can be scaled way down, and the cost of the worker to the employer is significantly less.

Dissolution Stage of Group Development: Eventually, all groups dissolve.

Division of Labor: The subdivision of objectives and plans into smaller and smaller units until they reach the task level. Work is so divided based on the principle of specialization of labor.

Divisional Plans: Plans for the major divisions of an organization.

Divisionalized Form (Mintzberg): Characterizes the multiproduct or multibusiness organization.

Dual-Career Couples: When both partners are employed full time, extra effort must be made to balance the situation's demands.

Dynamic Diamond: Contains Michael Porter's four factors for global competitiveness: factor conditions; demand conditions; related and supporting industries; company strategy, structure, and rivalry.

East-West Economic Integration: Trend toward free market economics and democracies begun in 1989.

Econometric Models: Use a complex series of interdependent regression equations, combining both theory and applied research, to predict the performance of some dependent variable, often the national economy.

Economic Functional Structure: The most common basis for the overall organization structure—its "macro structure"—is economic functional activity.

Economic Order Quantity (EOQ): That amount of inventory to be ordered that will minimize the holding and ordering costs.

Economy: Economy element includes the general economic condition of the country or countries, region or regions, in which the organization functions.

Effectiveness: Describes whether objectives are accomplished.

Efficiency: Describes the relative amount of resources used in obtaining effectiveness.

Electronic Bulletin Boards: Computerized systems for distributing routine memos throughout an organization, typically job openings, fringe benefits, and other information.

Electronic Data Interchange: Involves matching company and client database systems among companies, customers, and suppliers.

Electronic Data Processing (EDP): In the 1960s and early 1970s, mainframe computers processed information for a limited number of functions—for example, accounting, purchasing, and accounts payable.

Electronic Mail: Uses electronic circuitry to transmit written messages instantaneously.

Emotive Function (of Communication): Is oriented toward feelings.

Employee Expectations, Changing: The evidence strongly suggests that the needs of today's employees are much different from what they were twenty years ago.

Employee Health and Safety: Major concerns of most managers.

Employee Transitions: A number of employee transitions must be managed for those who quit, receive promotions and demotions, are laid off or transferred, retire, die, or are fired.

Employment Testing: Some companies use testing devices to help them make employment decisions. Typical tests include those for job skills, such as typing. Psychological tests are given for people in certain occupations, such as sales and management. Testing may also include such devices as performance appraisals, where promotions are being considered.

Encoding: The person, group, or organization that wishes to communicate must place the message in some transmittable language, either verbal or nonverbal. The essence of encoding is to put ideas into symbols that others will understand.

Entering a Country: Most firms enter a country first on a marketing or manufacturing basis. From a marketing perspective, firms may choose to import or export, to license, to set up direct investment, or to enter joint ventures.

Entrepreneurial Mystique: There definitely is something exciting about being an entrepreneur. It offers several psychological payoffs: a chance to be your own boss, initiate change, do it your way, take advantage of opportunities, and be at the forefront of change. There are also disadvantages—long hours, hard work, and risk. Most small businesses end in failure.

Environmental Analysis: Problem solvers must be constantly scanning their ever-changing environments for signs of problems or the potential of opportunities.

Equal Employment Opportunity (EEO): An externally imposed requirement that affects each and every HRM practice in virtually all organizations (those with fifteen or more employees, in most cases). EEO laws prohibit the making of human resource management practice decisions on the basis of race, color, sex, religion, national origin, physical and mental handicap, pregnancy, age, or veteran status.

Equity Theory: In concert with the decisions relative to expectancies and the valences of outcomes, the individual also assesses the degree to which the potential rewards will be equitably distributed. J. Stacy Adams contends in his equity theory that people will seek rewards only if they perceive that the rewards will be equitably distributed. The term "equity" implies that a person is being treated equally or fairly when compared to the treatment of others who behave in a similar way.

Essay: Type of performance appraisal—raters describe employee performances in an essay format.

Ethical Behavior: Behavior that is acceptable and considered appropriate according to society, the company, the individual, and/or the profession. Unethical behavior is outside the norms of society. *See also* Ethical Responsibility.

Ethical Dilemma: A situation in which the ethical answer is not obvious and where the available choices all have negative aspects.

Ethical Responsibility: Includes behaviors that fit within the norms of society, the organization, the individual, and the profession that have not necessarily been made into law. *See also* Social Responsibility, Levels of.

Ethics: Simply the rules that say what is right and wrong.

Ethics Guidelines: According to Laura L. Nash: (1) Have you defined the problem correctly? (2) How would you define the problem if you stood on the other side of the fence? (3) How did this situation occur in the first place? (4) To whom and to what do you give your loyalty as a person and as an employee? (5) What is your intention in making this decision? (6) How does this intention compare with the probable result? (7) Whom could your decision or action injure? (8) Can you discuss the problem with the affected parties before you

make your decision? (9) Are you confident your decision will be as valid over a long period of time as it seems now? (10) Could you disclose without qualm your decision or action to your supervisor, your CEO, your board of directors, your family, and society as a whole? (11) What is the symbolic potential of your action if understood? If misunderstood? (12) Under what conditions would you allow exceptions to your stand?

Europe 1992: In 1992, the EEC becomes a true common market. The scenario for this: (1) The EEC commission will get support and will achieve major objectives. (2) There will be shift in power from national ministries to Brussels (headquarters of the EEC). (3) There will be a fast growth of European companies. (4) An "economic cold war" may begin between the EEC and the United States, Japan, and other countries, as the EEC attempts to protect its markets. (5) Industry will fight the economic problems, and the politicians will fight the social problems that result. (6) Consumers will benefit in some ways (lower prices, more choices) and lose in some ways (maybe more unemployment).

European Economic Community (EEC): Belgium, Denmark, France, Great Britain, Greece, Ireland, Italy, Luxembourg, Netherlands, Portugal, Spain, and West Germany.

Excellence, The Simple Scheme of: Care of customers, constant innovation, leadership (MBWA), people. (Thomas J. Peters and Nancy K. Austin).

Excellence Approach to Management: Includes for Thomas J. Peters and Robert H. Waterman, Jr., and Nancy K. Austin, a Bias for action; closeness to the customer; autonomy and entrepreneurship (innovation); productivity through people; hands-on and value driven; sticking to the knitting; simple form and lean staff; simultaneous loose-tight properties; and leadership.

Executive Information Systems: Include all information systems tailored to the specific needs of executives. Thus, portions of the MIS, such as the strategic information system, decision support systems, and expert systems would all be included. Executive information systems are increasingly becoming available in user-friendly formats.

Expectancy Theory: Victor Vroom and others have proposed in expectancy theory that when the individual goes through the motivational process, he or she contemplates the consequences of personal actions in choosing alternatives to satisfy his or her needs. In the organizational context, this translates into the individual's perception of the situation: (1) Can I do the job? (2) If I do the job, what is the probability that I will receive the need satisfier? (3) If I get the need satisfier, what is it worth to me?

Expert Power: Depends on special skill or knowledge. Think of someone where you work who is very good at what he or she does. Does this person have followers because of this skill? In most circumstances

the answer will be yes. In many college business administration programs, student computer experts have many followers because people who are less skilled at computers need their help.

Expert Systems (ES): MIS that actually provide guidance to managers. They use decision heuristics based on the knowledge and experience of "experts" in a given field to provide suggested alternative decisions.

External Audits: Conducted by individuals outside the organization, typically certified public accountants (CPAs) or CPA firms. *See also* Financial Audits.

External Environment: Contains four principal external forces: economic, competitive, technological, political-legal, and societal.

Facility Capacity: Deciding how much product or service capacity is needed to meet demand is critical to any organization.

Facility Layout: Means "planning for the location of all machines, utilities, employee work stations, customer service areas, materials, aisles, restrooms, lunchrooms, drinking fountains, internal walls, offices, and computer rooms, and for the flow patterns of materials and people around, into, and within buildings.

Facility Location: Facility location decisions are very important in certain industries where nearness to customers or raw materials, or where production factors, such as cost of utilities, may be critical and vary significantly with location. Facilities location decisions begin with a choice of countries. Then region, community, and site locations follow.

Factor Conditions: According to Michael Porter, national resources, education and skills level of work force, wage rates. *See also* Dynamic Diamond.

Factory of the Future: The so called "factory of the future" is almost upon us, and in many cases is already here. The principal characteristics of the factory of the future include automated machinery and all the aspects of computer integrated manufacturing.

Fax: Uses electronic circuitry and telephone cabling to transmit visual images, much as electronic mail transmits written messages.

Fayol's 14 Principles of Management: Specify rules for successfully managing and structuring an organization: Division of work, authority and responsibility, discipline, unity of command, unity of direction, subordination of individual interest to the general interest, remuneration of personnel, centralization, scalar chain, order, equity, stability of tenure for personnel, initiative, esprit de corps.

Feedback: The degree to which employees receive, in the course of their work, information that reveals how well they are performing the job.

Feedback (Communication): A message sent by the receiver to the sender during a communication.

Fiedler's Contingency Model: Leadership is effective when the leader's style is appropriate to the situation, as determined by three principal factors: the relations between leader and followers, the structure of the task, and the power inherent in the leader's position.

Financial Analysis: This is based largely on examining the organization's financial statements and the various ratios derived from information from its balance sheet and income statement.

Financial Audits: Examine the organization's financial records and accounting systems. There are two principal types of audits: internal and external.

Flat Organizations: Reflecting larger spans of control, fewer levels in the chain of command, and more decentralization than in a centralized organization.

Flexible Manufacturing Systems (FMS): Clusters of automated machinery controlled by computers that have the flexibility to produce a wide variety of products in medium, small, or even large production runs, with the same efficiency levels.

Focus: The firm serves a particular target market extremely well.

Focused Factories: Many experts believe that factories perform better in terms of efficiency and effectiveness if they are focused upon some particular product/market-niche.

For-Profit Organizations: Operate in a market-dominated economic function.

Force-Field Analysis: A concept developed by Kurt Lewin, a pioneer in the study of change. He suggests that change results from the relative strengths of competing driving and restraining forces. The driving forces push the organization toward change; the restraining forces push against change. The actual change that emerges is a consequence of the interaction of the two sets of forces.

Forced Choice: Type of performance appraisal—requires the evaluator to choose among descriptions of employee behavior. These are then scored according to a key.

Forecasting: A number of techniques exist that enable a manager to make predictions about the future. They are made largely on the basis of past experience.

Formal Communication: Occurs through office channels and is sanctioned by the organization. Memos, policies, procedures, and reports of committee meetings are types of formal communication. There are three principal types of formal communication: downward communication, upward communication, and horizontal communication.

Formal Structure: This consists of that structure sanctioned by the organization.

Formalization: The extent to which written documentation occurs within an organization. It focuses on objectives and related job descriptions but also includes policies, strategies, procedures, and systems manuals, for example.

Forming Stage of Group Development: A group becomes acquainted.

Fringe Group: The fringe group or secondary group consists of people who have lesser status and fewer group privileges but who still have greater acceptance than people the group does not recognize at all.

Functional Authority: Gives a person, work group, or department line authority over decisions related to their areas of expertise in other departments.

Functional Managers: Are responsible for an economic function of the organization or some part thereof.

Functional Strategy: A strategic plan that addresses the issue of how an organization can use its resources most effectively and efficiently to carry out corporate and business strategy.

Future Shock: Alvin Toffler's *Future Shock* sounded an alarm about our future—it will be dominated by change that would increase at an accelerating rate.

Gantt Chart: A simple, yet effective way to allow managers to schedule work forces across a series of tasks.

GE Stoplight Portfolio Matrix: Employs the use of different colored cells in a nine-cell matrix to indicate which strategies it should follow for various businesses. SBUs or products are located on the grid based on an evaluation of the attractiveness of the industry in which they are found and upon GE's strengths in that business.

General Environment: Includes those elements—such as society, technology, the economy, and legal/political factors—that have less daily contact with the organization than those in the competitive environment, but which occasionally influence it or can be influenced by it in a significant way. *See also* External Environment.

General Managers: The general manager's task is to take a total organizational viewpoint.

Generic Strategies: Some experts believe that organizations should follow very specific strategies at the business level in order to be successful. Substrategies are labeled generic.

Glasnost: Movement to openness of society in the Soviet Union.

Global Economy: Today, three primary trading zones exist: Europe, North America, and the Pacific Rim. To be successful on a large scale means that you have to be able to compete in all three zones.

Global Management: The performance of management activities on a truly global basis. Global management embodies the concept of a product sold in numerous countries, even though it may have to be tailored somewhat to the demands of the customer's needs in those countries. It requires a degree of coordination among activities not experienced in multidomestic/international operations.

Globalization of Business: A "brave new world" is emerging in which there will be almost borderless trade.

Goals: Are broadly stated, further refinements of organizational mission. They are more specific than mission and address

key issues within the organization, such as market standing, innovation, productivity, physical and financial resources, profitability, management performance and development, worker performance and attitude, public responsibility, treatment of employees, growth, efficiency, treatment of customers, returns to owners, and so on.

Grand Strategy: The strategy from which virtually all other strategies and plans derive. This is the driving force of an organization. It may be growth, diversification of any number of factors. Grand strategies may be corporate, business, or functional.

Grapevine: Communication within the organization that exists outside the formal channels.

Graphic Rating Scales: Type of performance appraisal—employees are rated on a scale, usually from 1 to 10, on traits and/or behavior such as intelligent, neatness, and quantity of work accomplished.

Grievance Procedure: The organization often provides a system for employees to air their grievances.

Group Composition: Group members have varying personalities, work styles and motivations, backgrounds, sexes, races, religions, and so on. The composition of a group can greatly affect its productivity.

Group Decision Process: Characterized by a large number of inputs from each individual member upon which other members may build.

Group Development, Stages of: When a new group is formed, it passes through a series of stages of development. Several studies have identified various stages of group development, but they are all essentially similar. From a decision-making perspective, those stages identified by J. Steven Heinen and Eugene Jackson are most appropriate: forming, storming, initial integration, and total integration. A final state of dissolution will also eventually occur.

Group Plans: Plans for a work group—typically, but not necessarily, the group's intended actions as their part in the annual operating plan.

Group Size: Groups can function adequately in various sizes, but the optimum size appears to be between five and seven members when problem solving is involved and frequent small group communication must occur.

Group Structure: In the 1940s J. L. Moreno, a sociologist, developed an approach to the structure of groups known as sociometry. He identified group structure as consisting of a leader, a primary group, a fringe group, and an out-group.

Group Think: A condition that exists in a group when "concurrence seeking becomes so dumb that in a cohesive in group it tends to override realistic appraisal and alternative course of action."

Groups, Context of: Groups operate within an organizational context. There are different types of groups—formal and informal—which are formed for various reasons. Regardless of the type of group, each operates within an organization that has purposes and strategies, structure, culture, and systems. The organization also functions within an external environment.

Groups, Friendship: Those that exist to satisfy social needs naturally arise from human interactions within the same and nearby work locations.

Groups, Informal: Informal groups form for one primary reason: to satisfy employee needs that the organization or manager does not satisfy.

Groups, Interest: Those formed on the basis of other common interests.

Groupware: Software for the team.

Growth Strategy: Organizations can choose to grow or not.

Growth Needs (and Job Design): J. Richard Hackman, Greg R. Oldham, Robert Janson, and Kenneth Purdy identify the associated critical psychological states that result from the existence of various core job characteristic dimensions. These have an impact on the effectiveness of job enrichment.

Hall's Competitiveness Model: Professor William K. Hall, after researching a number of firms, concluded that there were really two primary generic strategies—high differentiation relative to your competition, and a low-cost position relative to your competition. Combinations of these form various degrees of competitiveness.

Hawthorne Effect: When a secondary factor, such as the attention given the workers in these experiments, produces a result that could have come from the phenomenon being studied. *See also* Hawthorne Studies.

Hawthorne Studies: The Hawthorne studies (conducted at the Western Electric Plant in Hawthorne [Chicago], Illinois) consisted of three parts: the illumination experiments, experiments in the relay-assembly test room, and experiments in the bank wiring observation room. The primary contribution of the Hawthorne studies was to reveal the effect of behavioral factors on productivity—specifically social systems within a work group—and the existence of the informal group.

Hersey-Blanchard Contingency Theory: The Hersey-Blanchard contingency theory is based on task and relationship behaviors. Each of these dimensions of leadership behavior is represented on an axis of a two-dimensional grid. The underlying assumption of this model is that the most important factor in determining appropriate leadership behavior is the subordinate's (group's) perceived level of maturity. The manager should match his or her style to this maturity level. Maturity has two components: (1) job skill and knowledge and (2) psychological maturity.

Herzberg's Theory: According to Frederick Herzberg, there are two basic types of need satisfiers: hygiene factors and motivators. He views hygiene factors as extrinsic to the job. They include pay and supervision. He views motivators as intrinsic to the job. They include achievement and recognition for performance.

Hierarchy of Needs: Most experts feel that needs are ordered in a hierarchy of importance. There are two principal hierarchy of needs theories. The first was formulated by psychologist Abraham Maslow, the second by C. P. Alderfer.

Human Resource Audit: A systematic inventory of personnel.

Human Resource Inventory Database: Results from a human resource audit. It provides information on promotability, the need for training and development, and the need for replacement where weaknesses continue to exist.

Human Resource Management: The process of first placing employees in jobs determined in the planning and organizing processes, and then managing those employees, from an organizational point of view, once they are placed. HRM is the process of putting the right people with the right skills in the right place at the right time with the right motivation in order to accomplish strategy. Staffing describes the individual manager's role in the HRM process.

Human Resource Management Practices: Whether they are part of the individual manager's staffing activities or performed by the HRM department, these practices can be broken into two principal types: those concerned with placing the employee in the job position and those concerned with the organizational/employee relationship once the individual assumes that position.

Human Resource Planning: Often referred to as personnel planning, this is the process of determining the staffing requirements necessary to carry out an organization's strategy in order to achieve its strategic objectives. It is part of implementing strategy.

Human Skill: Ability to work effectively in interpersonal relationships.

Ideation (Communication): The conception of an idea or a thought is known as ideation.

Identifiable Value Systems and Behavioral Norms (Organizational Culture): Identifiable value systems and behavioral norms are reflected in strategy, structure, systems, style, staffing, corporate skills, policies, rules, procedures, and what is rewarded and what is not. Very importantly, they are passed on in informal communications.

Implementation: The actions taken to carry out a decision.

Income Statement: Shows the financial condition of the company for a period of time.

Increased Demands of Constituents: The 1990s will see an ever-increasing series of demands by constituents/stakeholders.

Individual Plans: Plans by an individual to contribute to the organization's accomplishment of objectives—typically, but not necessarily, his or her contribution to achievement of the annual operating plan.

Individual Roles (in Groups): Most groups have some members who are playing individual roles in the group setting, in an effort to satisfy their own needs rather than those of the group.

Individualism Dimension: According to Geert Hofstede, indicates the degree to which a culture is either individualistic or socially group oriented.

Industry Competition, Forces Driving: Threat of new entrants, bargaining power of suppliers, bargaining power of buyers, threat of substitute products or services, and rivalry among existing firms.

Industry Life Cycles: Are important to strategy formulation. There are four primary stages to these cycles: introduction, growth, maturity, and decline.

Industry Structure: This is indicated in Michael Porter's analysis by the strength and nature of existing competition, the threat of potential entrants, the threat of substitutes, the bargaining power of suppliers, and the bargaining power of buyers.

Informal Communication: Occurs outside the formal channels.

Informal Structure: Informal relationships develop among individuals while they are working, and when they get together away from work. Such groups develop on the basis of friendships or common interests. These relationships are not typically sanctioned by the formal organization, although it is usually aware of them.

Information Function (of Communication): Decision making depends on information. The organizational objective of this communication function is to provide the information necessary for decision making. The information involved is often technical.

Information-Based Economy: A number of authorities have pointed out that we are shifting from an industrially based economy to an information-based economy.

Informational Approaches to Improving Communication: Periodic meetings with employees; television broadcasts; publications and bulletin boards; athletic programs; organizational rules, regulations, policies, procedures, memos, and handbooks.

Initial Integration of Group Development: In this stage the group begins to function cooperatively. This stage is sometimes referred to as the "norming" stage because members are establishing the rules of acceptable conduct, or norms, for the group.

Innovation: Something creative that has a significant impact on an organization, a society, or an industry. There are three principal types of innovation: product, process, and marketing.

Integration (Structure): The directing of differentiated subunit efforts toward the fulfillment of an organization's central purposes.

Integrator: Works with designers on producibility issues, serving as a liaison with manufacturing.

Interacting Groups: Meet face-to-face with open interchange.

Intermediate Plans: Plans that help translate strategy into operations. These plans normally commit far fewer resources than do strategies.

Internal Audit: Is performed by members of the organization. *See also* Financial Audits.

Internal Environment: Includes people—owners, board members, general management, organized labor, nonorganized workers, informal leaders, and so on. Includes all of the elements within the organization's boundaries—corporate culture, current employees, stockholders, management, leadership style, organizational structure, and other similar factors.

Intrapreneur: When managers become entrepreneurs within the organization they are intrapreneurs.

Intrapreneurship: A company employee who is allowed to act like an entrepreneur but does so for the company, rather than strike out on his or her own.

Intuitive Thinkers: Are especially good at keeping track of many variables, which may defy ordinary analytical techniques.

Inventory Models: Several models exist that can forecast how much inventory to order and when.

Inventory Turnover: Dividing sales by inventory will indicate how many times per year the firm has been able to sell its inventory. *See also,* Ratio Analysis and Activity Ratios.

Investment Centers: Are responsibility centers controlled on the basis not only of profit but also on the amount of capital investment made to produce the profit. *See also* Responsibility Center Management.

Investment Reduction Strategy: Organizations may choose to cut costs and/or sell off assets.

Japanese Management: Practices focus on participative management, job design, quantitative methods, effectiveness and efficiency, the group and how to increase productivity through group decision making, holistic treatment of employees by treating them as individuals rather than as interchangeable parts, seeking cooperation and harmony in the workplace.

Japanese Success Factors: The official view of the Keidanren, the powerful federation of Japanese businesses, is that Japanese success results from a complex interaction of macro and micro variables involving government, capital, labor, and technology. Many U.S. experts cite restrictive trade barriers as another reason for their success.

Job Analysis: Consists of several steps leading to the job design process. Job analysis begins with an examination of the job and its fit in the organization. It continues with an in-depth analysis of the job using standard techniques. Job analysis concludes by producing a job description, which describes the job and its responsibilities and duties, and a job specification, which indicates the kind of person to perform the job depicted in the job description, in terms of skills, knowledge, and abilities.

Job Description: Describes the job and its responsibilities and duties.

Job Design: The process that determines the contents of a job, including the associated authority. Job design is situational. Environmental factors, organizational factors, and individual characteristics impact on the contents of any job—its primary dimensions—and on performance and other outcomes expected from its satisfactory completion.

Job Design, A Situational Model or Contingency of: The outcomes of a job, such as performance and satisfaction, are a function of four major factors: environmental factors, organizational factors, individual characteristics of the job holder, the primary job dimensions.

Job Enlargement: According to Kae H. Chung and Monica F. Ross, "involves reversing the work simplification or specialization process somewhat. Job enlargement embodies five basic components, any one or several of which might constitute job enlargement: task variety, a meaningful work module, performance feedback, ability utilization, worker-paced control.

Job Enrichment: According to Kae H. Chung and Monica F. Ross, job enrichment is "the provision for nonmanagerial employees to perform those functions previously restricted to managerial and supervisory personnel (in essence, increased depth)." They view job enrichment as encompassing employee participation, goal internalization, autonomy, and group management.

Job Evaluation: The systematic determination of the relative worth of a job in an organization.

Job Interviews: Part of the selection process using face-to-face question and answer discussions.

Job Posting: Advertising job openings in company media, usually bulletin boards.

Job Previews: The firm needs to present a realistic job preview, clearly indicating expectations, requirements, culture, leadership style, and so on.

Job Redesign (at the Group Level): Two very important job redesign efforts at the group level are autonomous work teams and quality circles.

Job Rotation: In job rotation an employee moves from one job to another.

Job Selection Process: When a pool of applicants has been chosen, the organization must decide who best matches the job specification—that is, who is most qualified to fill the position. This process is known as selection and consists of the following steps: completion of the application blank or some biographical data form; an employment interview/ongoing interviews; testing; reference checks; recommendations; a physical exam; and choice/selection.

Job Sharing: A form of alternative work scheduling. Typically, two individuals split the day in half, although the sharing could be done on alternating days as well.

Job Specification: Indicates the kind of person to perform the job depicted in the job description, in terms of skills, knowledge, and abilities.

Joint Ventures: Essentially partnerships between corporations.

Just-in-Time Inventory (JIT): Firms have begun to move away from holding large inventories of raw materials and finished goods. It is an inventory system in which the firm maintains virtually one or a near-zero level of inventory. The economic order quantity approaches zero as the production process grows more efficient. Where only enough inventory for one day's manufacturing is kept in work-in-process and raw materials inventories.

Kaizen: Japanese philosophy of constant improvement.

Kanban: A (low-cost) method for controlling inventory and product movement. Kanban literally means "card" in Japanese. The Kanban, or its equivalent, is an essential communication device in Japanese JIT, the "card" being used to signal that a worker's inventory is depleted. Only when inventory is depleted can the worker trade Kanban for additional supplies.

Knowledge-Based Organizations: C. W. Holsapple and A. B. Whinston observe: "In a most fundamental sense, organizations will increasingly be regarded as joint human-computer knowledge-processing systems. Human participants in these systems, from most highly skilled to least skilled positions, can be regarded as knowledge workers. Collectively they will work with many types of knowledge, in a variety of ways, and with various objectives. Their knowledge management efforts will be aided and supported by computers. Not only will these computer co-workers relieve us of the menial, routine, and repetitive, they will also actively recognize needs, stimulate insights, and offer advice. They will highly leverage an organization's uniquely human skills of intuition, creative imagination, value-judgment, the cultivation of effective interpersonal relationships, and so forth.

Language: Is communication by manipulation of recognizable symbols. It varies by country, culture, social class, age, sex, and other factors.

Language Systems and Metaphors (Organizational Culture): Used in organizations—often indicate shared values.

Laptop Personal Computers: Assist a MIS when they can be used in conjunction with telecommunications—for example, to receive voice mail, teleconferencing, or electronic mail. They are most often used by salespeople to access databases and are often used by anyone preparing reports away from the office.

Law of Effect: According to E. L. Thorndike, "Of several responses to the same situation, those that are accompanied or closely followed by satisfaction . . . will be more likely to recur; those which are accompanied or closely followed by discomfort . . . will be less likely to occur."

Leading: The process of making decisions about how to treat people and then carrying out those decisions to influence behavior.

Legal-Political: Legal-political segment includes laws and regulations at local, state, federal, and international levels, as well as those individuals and organizations that attempt to influence the legal environment, such as lobbyists and numerous protests groups.

Legitimate Power: Or authority, results from a person's position in the organization. The leader who simply depends on this type of power for success may suffer in the long run. Ordinarily, followers will follow a leader only as long as their needs are reasonably well satisfied. Much of the ongoing process of the organization depends on this type of power.

Leverage Ratio: Concerned with a firm's utilization of debts, the relationship of its debt to total assets, and the firm's ability to pay its interest charges. *See also* Ratio Analysis.

Life's Stages: According to Gail Sheehy include pulling up roots, the trying twenties, catch thirty, rooting and extending, the deadline decade, and renewal or resignation.

Line Authority: Authority within the chain of command of a given unit.

Line Managers: Those directly concerned with accomplishing the objectives of a particular organization.

Linear Programming: A technique that uses a sequence of steps leading to an optimum solution in a problem characterized by a single goal and objectives, a number of constraints, a number of variables, and a linear relationship among the variables.

Linking Pin: The manager of each work unit is a linking pin between at least three groups: the group that he or she leads and manages (a), the group of which he or she is a subordinate peer manager (b), and the group of managers higher in the organizational hierarchy (c), of which the manager's boss is a member.

Liquidity Ratios: Are concerned with the organization's ability to meet its current debt. A key liquidity ratio is the current ratio. *See also* Ratio Analysis.

Listening: Listening is not just hearing; it's more than that. Effective listening involves the interpretation, understanding, and action phases of communication. Effective listening requires hard work and self-discipline.

Litigation Audit: Determines potential corporate exposure to litigation.

Long-Range Financial Plan: Essentially a one- to five-year forecast of the anticipated financial performance of the organization

if the strategy is followed and if the strategy is successful to the degree believed necessary.

Lower-Level Managers: Supervisors, team leaders, and foremen are common titles in lower-level management.

Machine Bureaucracy (Mintzberg): The configuration most used in mass-production industries.

Management: The creative problem-solving process of planning, organizing, leading, and controlling an organization's resources to achieve its mission and objectives.

Management Challenges: Changing employee expectations of how they should be managed. The global economy. Shift from an industrially based economy to an information-based economy. Accelerated rates of change. Increased levels of competition. Changing technology, especially computers. Finding a more creative approach to improve problem solving. Emphasis on managing organizational culture. Increased demands of constituents. Changing demographics: the cultural diversity of the work force.

Management in the Future: As other approaches to management emerge, the contemporary synthesis will be fine tuned and perhaps even revolutionized. There may even be a revolution occurring now.

Management History: You need to know it and learn from it, but not be its prisoner.

Management Information Systems (MIS): Information "is data that have been put into a meaningful and useful context and communicated to a recipient who uses it to make decisions." The MIS links three key words: management, information, and systems. An MIS is created to provide information to managers so that they can make better decisions.

Management Matrix: The management functions of problem solving, planning, organizing, leading, and controlling are applicable to each of the economic functions of an organization, which include marketing, finance, operations, human resources, information management, and R&D. Managers must also manage each of the management functions. They have to plan planning, organize planning, lead planning, control planning, and so on, for all of the management functions. The management matrix shows that managers manage both economic and management functions.

Management by Objectives, Results, and Rewards (MBORR): An advanced form of MBO that measures results and distributes rewards based on these results.

Management Philosophy: Management may at any time, and at any level of the organization, determine that it wants a particular type of structure to achieve some chosen end or express its philosophy about management.

Management Process: Consists of creative problem solving in planning, organizing, leading, and controlling.

Management Science: An extremely broad term that encompasses virtually all

the rational approaches to managerial problem solving that are based upon scientific methods.

Management-Science Approach to Management: Often called operations research, or quantitative analysis, employs mathematical techniques to solve problems. Has four primary characteristics: (1) a focus on problem solving, (2) a rational orientation, (3) the use of mathematical models and techniques to solve problems, (4) an emphasis on computers in decision support systems.

Management Systems: Operational planning systems; integrative planning and controlling systems; organizational leadership, motivation, and communication systems; and the management of human resources from a system perspective are all critical to successful implementation.

Manager as a Creative Problem Solver: The increased complexity of the decision environment, the changing personalities and expectations of organizational members, and all the other factors noted in Chapter 1 are changing the way that problems must be solved. Managers are not only moving toward increased participation, but are also responding to the increased need for the decision maker, the problem solver, to be more creative. Most individuals in our organizations are confronted with an environment that demands increased levels of problem-solving creativity for four key reasons: (1) an accelerated rate of change, (2) increased levels of competition, (3) the requirements of decision making in the computer age, (4) the edge that those who are intuitive as well as rational have over those who use only rational approaches to decision making.

Managerial Grid: Robert Blake and Jane Mouton developed a model that, like most leadership models, focused on the task and relationship orientations uncovered in the Ohio State and Michigan leadership-behavior studies. Blake and Mouton created a 9 × 9 grid based on managers' concern for both people (relationships) and production (tasks).

Managerial Skills: An ability to translate action into results involving these three skills: technical, human, conceptual.

Managing Change: The individual and organization develop plans to influence change, implement it, and control its performance, as opposed to just letting change happen.

Managing by Objectives: A relatively simple planning and control process consisting of just a few steps at each level of management: (1) Objectives are determined. Objectives are then distributed to the next level of management. (2) Actions plans are formulated. (3) Some degree of participation occurs in the settling of objectives and the formation of plans. (4) Implementation occurs.

Market Control: Market control strategy allows market mechanisms such as competition to establish the standards of the control system. This strategy assumes that market mechanisms are most efficient in setting the prices or costs identified with certain transactions. This style of control relies on external forces to control behavior within the firm. It is a very quantitatively oriented control strategy. There must be an identifiable product or service whose contributions can be measured.

Marketing Innovation: Related to the marketing functions of promotion, pricing, and distribution, as well as to products in addition to product development, for example, packaging.

Masculinity: According to Geert Hofstede, is concerned with characteristics that most cultures would attribute to men: acquisition of money, possessions, pursuit of advancement, and assertiveness.

Maslow's Hierarchy: After a number of years researching the problems of his patients, Abraham Maslow concluded that people's needs are ordered in a hierarchy of prepotency. These needs are self-actualization, esteem, social, security, and physiological.

Master Budget: Summarizes all budgets of the organization.

Material Requirements Planning (MRP): A computer-based inventory planning and control system that examines the master planning schedule for required input resources—raw materials, parts, subassemblies and assemblies—for each time period of the planning horizon. It then examines the existing inventory materials level and materials requirements and develops a schedule for ordering the necessary materials for arrival as needed on the planning horizon.

Matrix Structure: Characterized by simultaneous authority over line and/or staff by project and by economic function.

McKinsey Seven Ss: Strategy, structure, systems, style, staff, skills, shared values.

Mechanistic Model: Focuses on hierarchical relationships and tends to be rigid in the worst sense of the word "bureaucratic."

Mechanistic Model of Structure: Embodies the concepts of classic bureaucracy. It focuses on hierarchical relationships and tends to be rigid in the worst sense of "bureaucratic."

Middle Managers: Middle managers include department heads, division managers, deans, plant managers, personnel directors, sales managers, and so on. They occupy the second and often third, fourth, fifth, sixth, or seventh layers of management in a large organization.

Mintzberg's Five Types of Organizational Design: The strategic apex is at the top of the organization and consists of the organization's strategists. The operating core is comprised of those who perform the basic work functions. The middle line is that group of management between the executives in the strategic apex and the operating core. The technostructure consists of the staff analysts, who design systems for the planning and control of work.

The support staff provide indirect services to the rest of the organization.

Mintzberg's Managerial Roles: Interpersonal (figurehead, leader, liaison), informational (monitor, disseminator, spokesperson), decisional (entrepreneur, disturbance handler, resource allocator, negotiator).

MIS Components: Input, models, technology, database, control, and output.

MIS Director: Helps guide management's decisions on hardware, software, systems design and development, and system maintenance. He or she leads for professional MIS staff. The director plans, organizes, and controls the management information function.

Mission Functions: Activities directly associated with accomplishing an organization's mission. They include planning, organizing, leading, and controlling.

Mission Statement: The primary thrust of a mission statement is external: it focuses on customers, markets, and fields of endeavor. The exact nature of mission statements varies from organization to organization. Many mission statements reveal not simply purpose, but philosophy.

Mommy Track: The term mommy track refers to an alternative career path for women who want to balance raising a family with having a career.

Motion and Time Studies: Careful studies of the work motions of various types of employees and their analysis of the time it took to perform those motions.

Motivation: The internal drive to satisfy an unsatisfied need. While motivation is internal to the individual, its strength and direction may be influenced by forces outside the individual. One of the manager's most important jobs is to influence the motivation of others in the direction of achieving organizational objectives in an effective and efficient manner.

Motivation Cycle: Begins with unsatisfied needs. It ends after the individual assesses the consequences of attempting to satisfy those needs. The six stages in this cyclical process are (1) An individual has an unsatisfied need. (2) Because the individual is driven to attempt to satisfy this need he or she searches for alternatives and satisfiers. (3) The individual chooses the "best" way to satisfy the need. (4) The individual is motivated to take action to obtain the need satisfier. (5) The individual reexamines the situation, contemplating what has transpired. (6) Depending on the outcomes of these efforts, the individual may or may not be motivated again by the same type of need satisfiers.

Motivation Function (of Communication): In this context, motivation is influence, the ability or process of affecting the behavior of others. Communication concerned with motivation is designed to elicit commitment to the organization's objectives.

Motivation and Performance: The manager and the organization are not just concerned with motivation. They must ensure that motivated effort results in

performance—the effective and efficient accomplishment of objectives. To ensure that motivated effort results in performance, managers and the organization must assure that the individual knows the objectives that must be achieved, knows the tasks necessary to achieve the objectives, and has the abilities, skills, and tools to accomplish the necessary tasks.

Motivation Performance Cycle: Ten stage model showing how managers can influence individual motivation cycles.

Mottos: A good motto should meet the following criteria: (1) It should convey and promote a core philosophy of the organization. (2) It should have an emotional appeal rather than a rational and intellectual appeal. (3) It should not be a direct exhortation for loyalty, productivity, quality, and any other organizational objective; otherwise, it will not have an emotional impact on the employee. (4) It should be mysterious to the public but not to organizational members. This allows insiders to understand it, but not others.

Muczyk-Reimann Model: Jan P. Muczyk and Bernard C. Reimann suggest that "participation" behavior is concerned with the degree to which subordinates are allowed to be involved in decision making. They separate this from "direction" which they view as the degree of supervision exercised in the execution of the tasks associated with carrying out the decision. Other authors either combine "direction" with "task," or with "participation." Thus, the major issue in adapting style to the situation, they believe, is related to delegation, as applied in both participation and direction. *See also* Directive Autocrat, Permissive Autocrat, Directive Democrat, Permissive Democrat.

Multidomestic Firms: Organizations that operate across national boundaries but treat each country as a separate market, and products are developed solely for each market.

Multinational Corporation (MNC): A firm that has significant operations in more than one country.

Multiple Business Corporate Strategy: Managing a series of businesses strategically is principally concerned with portfolio strategies.

Multiple Products Strategy: An organization can seek multiple products or product lines.

Myers-Briggs–Type Indicators (MBTI): Responses to over one hundred questions are used to indicate how an individual would be classified more at one or the other end of four dimensions: (1) social interaction—introvert or extrovert; (2) preference for gathering data—intuitive or sensor; (3) preference for decision making—feeling or thinking; (4) style of making decisions—perceptive or judgmental.

Negotiating: Bargaining with various parties to reach agreement. A type of conflict management approach.

Network Models: Building upon the Gantt techniques, large complex tasks are broken into small segments that can be managed independently. The two most prominent models are PERT (Program Evaluation Review Technique) and CPM (Critical Path Method) networking models used to plan and coordinate large-scale projects.

New Entrants, Threat of: Firms must be concerned about the threat of new entrants into the industry because these often greatly affect its ability to compete successfully. *See also* Competitive Environment.

Niche Strategy: Seeking a niche in which there isn't any real head-on competition.

Nominal Group: A nominal group is more structured than an interactive one. It intentionally eliminates much of the interpersonal exchange of the interacting group in order to preclude the influence of a dominant personality.

Nonmonetary Resource Input Budget: Budgets items such as man hours, units of product, and units of raw material.

Nonverbal Communication: The subtleties of a person's body language, the physical distance between people (proxemics), and their attitudes toward time (chronemics) are important types of nonverbal communication. Status symbols, touching, and clothing also communicate quite clearly their intended messages. Other forms of nonverbal communication include the visual arts and music.

Norms, Group: Norms are standards of performance or other conduct established by a group.

Not-for-Profit Organizations: Operate in more politically influenced environments, where clients are often not the source of funds. Instead, different external sources, be they resource contributors, legislators, or other political or activist groups, greatly influence incentives, constraints, and values.

Objectives: Are specific statements of results anticipated. They further define the organization's goals. Typically, each goal will be subdivided into a set of very specific objectives.

Objectives, Characteristics of Sound: (1) The goal area or attribute sought, (2) an index for matching progress toward the attribute, (3) a target to be achieved or hurdle to be overcome, (4) a time frame within which the target or hurdle is to be achieved.

Objectives as Motivators: People are goal-striving animals, and therefore objectives may be used to influence their motivation. Both Maslow's and Alderfer's hierarchies are goal-striving needs hierarchies.

Occupational Safety and Health Act of 1970: Requires employers to make their work areas safe and eliminate environmental hazards.

Open System: Interacts with its environment.

Operating Plans: Plans that deal with day-to-day operations, typically for a time frame of less than one year. They commit far fewer resources than strategies or intermediate plans.

Operational Control: Performance measurements and leadership/personal influence are the cornerstones of operational control. Designed to ensure that operational actions are consistent with established plans and objectives at that level. It is concerned with individual or group performance appraisals, and perhaps even project performance appraisals.

Operations Management: The planning, organizing, leading, and controlling of "all the activities of productive systems—those portions of organizations that transform inputs into products and services." *See also* Operations Managers.

Operations Management as Decision Making: Tend to fall into one of three categories, paralleling the three levels of planning introduced in Chapter 5: strategic, tactical, operational.

Operations Managers: Responsible for producing the supply of goods or services in organizations. *See also* Operations Management.

Operations Strategies: Derive directly from business strategies aimed at achieving corporate objectives. Operations strategies are among the several strategies organizations employ in functional areas—for example, maketing, finance, human resources, and information. Operations strategies must support the other strategies, principally the marketing strategy of the business.

Operations System, Positioning the: Involves selecting for each major product line in the business plan: (1) the type of product design, (2) the type of production process, (3) the finished goods inventory policy.

Opportunity: When there is potential for exceeding the established objectives.

Oral Communication: Speaking and listening.

Organic Organizations: Are characterized essentially by openness, responsiveness, and a lack of hierarchy of authority.

Organization: A group of people working together to achieve a common purpose.

Organization Chart: A pictorial representation of an organization's formal structure.

Organizational Climate: Indicates the desirability of the work and social environment of an organization. How people communicate, make decisions, establish objectives, lead, and carry out control are all indications of this desirability. Climate is a critical component of organizational culture, but there are many more values in culture than just those related to the desirability of the work and social environment.

Organizational Culture: That pattern of shared values and norms that distinguishes an organization from all others.

Organizational Culture, Managing: Studies of successful organizations provide evidence that managing culture, the organization's shared values, is a way of improving productivity and employee job satisfaction. The key to managing culture is the managers' leadership ability.

Organizational Design: The process of determining the best overall, macro organizational structure for the organization and its major subcomponents, and the subsequent characteristics of the division of labor, delegation of authority, and the other structural elements.

Organizational Development: Any planned program for managing change. Wendell French and Cecil Bell have provided us with a very widely accepted definition of organizational development—"a long-range effort to improve an organization's problem-solving and renewal processes, particularly through a more effective and collaborative management of organizational culture, with special emphasis on the culture of formal work teams, with the assistance of a change agent or catalyst, and the use of the theory and technology of applied behavioral science, including action research."

Organizational Planning: Problem solving for the future in a changing environment.

Organizational Purpose: A hierarchy, from the most general and greatest scope, to the most specific and narrowest scope, would include vision, mission, goals, and objectives. What an organization intends to accomplish. *See also* Organizational Planning.

Organizational Structure—Three Types: The hierarchical pyramid, the matrix, and the team.

Organizing: The process of determining how resources are allocated and prepared for accomplishing an organization's mission.

Orientation: Introduces the employee to the organization—to the requirements of the job, to the social situation in which he or she is about to be thrust, and to its norms and culture.

Other Functions of Management: Representing, staffing, negotiating, coordinating, and supervising.

Out-Group: Consists of people who have no membership, no privileges, and no interest in the group under discussion. These people may belong to many other groups, but not to this one.

Parity Principle: States that if you assign someone the responsibility for achieving an objective, you should also give that person the authority to achieve it.

Participative Leadership: The leader consults with subordinates about work, task goals, and paths to resource goals. It involves sharing information, as well as consulting with subordinates before making decisions.

Passive Recruitment: The organization waits for applicants to walk in and apply for the available jobs.

Path-Goal Theory: Robert J. House and Terrence R. Mitchell propose that leaders can be effective—that is, effect the satisfaction, motivation, and performance of group members, in several ways. The first is by making rewards contingent on the accomplishment of organizational goals—objectives as we have defined them in this text. Second, the leader can aid group members in attaining rewards that are valued by clarifying the paths to those goals and by removing obstacles to performance.

Perestroika: Movement toward free market conditions in the Soviet Union.

Performance: The effective and efficient accomplishment of objectives.

Performance Appraisal: The practice of determining whether an employee is performing his or her job effectively and efficiently.

Performance Appraisals: Instruments used to appraise employee performance.

Performance Standards (in the Control Process): State organizational objectives and subunit objectives, which provide readily identifiable targets for individuals and groups to achieve and against which actual performance may be compared.

Permissive Autocrat: Makes decisions unilaterally but allows subordinates a great deal of latitude in execution.

Permissive Democrat: Allows high participation in decision making and in execution.

PERT/CPM: Networking models used to plan and coordinate large-scale projects.

Plan: The intended set of actions to achieve an objective, goal, mission, or vision. Planning is not concerned with future decisions, but rather with the future impact of the decisions made today.

Planning: The process of determining objectives and how those objectives are to be accomplished in an uncertain future.

Planning, Limitations of: Environmental events cannot always be controlled. Internal resistance. Planning is expensive. Current crises. Failure to understand the weaknesses of the planning premises. Planning is difficult.

Planning, Reasons for Failures: Lack of commitment to planning. Failure to develop and implement sound strategies. Lack of meaningful objectives or goals. Failure to see planning as both a rational and creative process. Excessive reliance on experience. Failure to use the principle of limiting factor. Lack of clear delegation. Lack of adequate control techniques and information results. Resistance to change.

Planning Premises: Certain assumptions about the future condition of these and other environmental conditions.

Policies: Plans that provide general guidance to action.

Portable Manager: Fax machines, laptop computers, video conferencing, cellular phones, and voice mail are all making the concept of a "portable manager" a reality.

Porter's Generic Strategies: Cost leadership, differentiation, and focus.

Portfolio Matrix: Characteristics of market and industry are plotted against the characteristics of the firm, forming a matrix.

Portfolio Strategies: Strategies for managing a group (portfolio) of SBUs.

Postaction Controls: Once a series of actions to reach an objective is completed, an effort must be made to determine whether the objective was reached. Postaction controls control the results of completed action.

Power: The ability to influence others to carry out orders or to do something they would not have done otherwise, in order to achieve desired outcomes.

Power, Bases of: Legitimate power, reward power, coercive power, expert power, and referent power.

Power Distance Dimension: According to Geert Hofstede, this is concerned with the degree to which the culture accepts any variances in power in organizational relationships, specifically superior and subordinate relationships.

Preaction Control: Preaction control is used to assure that the human, material, and financial resources necessary are in place before the transformation process begins. Preaction control—sometimes referred to as preventive controls, precontrols, or feed-forward control—ensures that not only enough resources are available, but that the quality of these is sufficiently high to prevent problems once the transformation process is underway. Preaction controls recognize and identify potential problems before they occur.

Primary Group: Also popularly known as the in-group, consists of the group members of highest status—active members and members accorded all of the group's rights and responsibilities.

Primary Job Dimensions: Skill variety, task identity, task significance, autonomy, feedback, interpersonal relations, authority and responsibility for goal setting, and communication patterns.

Proactive Social Response: A firm goes beyond what is legally and ethically required. It leads the industry, seeking ways to improve communities.

Problem: When a level of performance is less than the established objectives.

Problem Identification: In this stage, the creative problem solver seeks to determine what the real problem is or the real problems are.

Problem-Solving Groups: There are three major types of problem-solving groups: the interacting group, the nominal group, and the Delphi group.

Problem-Solving Styles: Include systematic thinkers and intuitive thinkers.

Problems or Opportunities, Recognition of: In the recognition stage, problem solvers depend on formal and informal information systems, and often on their intuition, to alert them to a possible problem. In the recognition stage, problems are not precisely defined. Rather, the problem solver often has a vague feeling that something is amiss or that a tremendous opportunity exists.

Procedures: Plans that describe the exact series of actions to be taken in a given situation.

Process Culture: Evolves from situations in which the feedback is slow and the risk is low. Organizations with this culture typically include government agencies, insurance companies, and public utilities. *See also* Deal & Kennedy's Culture Types.

Process Innovation: Results in improved processes in the organization—for example, operations, HRM, or financing.

Product Innovation: Results in new products or services or enhancements to old products or services.

Product Plans: Cover the activities related to a product for some set period of time, often a year.

Product/Service Design: Is important to competitiveness—for example, in creating features that attract customers and that differentiate an organization's product or service from that of its competition. In addition, product designs that can be produced cheaply will be more competitive with low-cost producers, such as the Japanese and others in the Pacific Rim.

Product Structure: At some point in time, an organization will have a sufficient number of products in its product line so that it becomes necessary to change from a functional structure to a product structure.

Productivity: The organization's output of goods and services divided by its inputs.

Professional Bureaucracy (Mintzberg): The structure of the professional organization.

Profit Centers: Are responsibility centers controlled on the basis of the difference between revenues and expenses—profit. The principal focus is on the amount of profit contribution made to the overall organization. *See also* Responsibility Center Management.

Profitability Ratios: Indicate the success of the firm in earning profits, as measured by several tests. *See also* Ratio Analysis.

Program: Covers a large set of activities.

Project: Usually a subset of a program; the term is sometimes used as a substitute for program.

Project Structure: A functionally based, temporary organizational structure. It is disassembled in parts as each stage of the project is completed.

Qualitative Forecasting Methods: Judgments and opinions used in forecasting.

Quality Circles: Formal groups of employees that meet periodically during work hours to solve company problems.

Quality Control According to W. Edwards Deming: William Edwards Deming is the "father of quality control" in Japan and, until recently, was a prophet no one would listen to in his own country. W. Edwards Deming introduced statistical quality control concepts in Japan in 1950.

Quality of Work Life (QWL): The term has come to be defined in several ways but essentially means improving the satisfaction of individual needs in the workplace.

Quantitative Methods: Group of techniques for improving problem solving by making it a more rational, analytical process.

Queueing Theory: Describes how to determine the number of service units that will minimize both customer waiting time and cost of service.

Ratio Analysis: By examining ratios of various numbers identified on the income statement and the balance sheet, managers or other analysts may be able to discern better the organization's financial condition. There are four principal types of ratio: liquidity, leverage, activity, and profitability.

Reactive Social Responsibility: Means that the organization "fights all the way" against taking responsibility for its actions.

Receiving (Communication): The various senses must work in combination to detect the message and subsequently report it to the brain.

Recruitment: Consists of a series of activities intended to attract a qualified pool of job applicants.

Referent Power: That which depends on appeal, magnetism, and charisma. John Kennedy and Martin Luther King, Jr., had this kind of power.

Regression Analysis: One method for forecasting is regression analysis. It helps indicate relationships among two or more variables. Once a relationship has been defined historically, projections of it for the future can be made.

Reinforcement, Continuous: A reinforcement follows every behavior.

Reinforcement of Effort: This theory suggests that behavior that results in rewarding consequences is likely to be repeated, whereas behavior that results in no rewards or in punishing consequences is less likely to be repeated. These are not absolutes.

Reinforcement, Extinction: No positive or negative reinforcement is given. Behavior is ignored.

Reinforcement, Intermittent: A reinforcement follows some responses but not others. There are four types of intermittent reinforcement: fixed interval, variable interval, fixed ratio, and variable ratio.

Reinforcement, Negative: Something negative is taken away when the desired behavior occurs.

Reinforcement, Positive: Something positive is given after the behavior occurs.

Reinforcement, Punishment: Often used by managers to discourage undesirable behavior.

Reinforcement, Schedule of: The degree to which rewards are tied to performance is also critical. These two fundamental types of reinforcement schedules: continuous and intermittent. In continuous reinforcement a reinforcement follows every behavior. In intermittent reinforcement a reinforcement follows some responses but not others. There are four types of intermittent reinforcement: fixed interval, variable interval, fixed ratio, and variable ratio.

Reinforcement, Types of: Positive reinforcement, negative reinforcement, punishment, extinction.

Related and Supporting Industries: According to Michael Porter, the company a company keeps. Includes suppliers and competition in supportive industries. *See also* Dynamic Diamond.

Representing: Interacting with external constituents, often referred to as stakeholders.

Resistance to Change: OD is but one type of change management. Regardless of which program is used to manage change, the manager making the changes will invariably be faced with resistance to change.

Responsibility Center Management: The financial resource allocation process ties performance not only to accomplishment of objectives, but also to their accomplishment within financial constraints identified by the long-term financial plan or short-term operating budget. Many larger organizations and some smaller ones establish responsibility centers to facilitate long-term financial planning, to identify responsibility accurately, to motivate subordinates to a greater extent, to aid in the budgetary process, and to provide better control of organizational performance.

Responsibility Centers: There are four basic types of responsibility centers: revenue centers; cost, or expense, centers; profit centers; and investment centers. *See also* Responsibility Center Management.

Return on Investment (ROI) (ROA): Is a ratio that indicates the income after taxes, relative to the organization's total assets.

Return on Total Assets (ROA) (ROI): A percentage determined by dividing net profit after taxes by total assets.

Revenue and Expense Budgets: Itemize the revenues and expenses for the revenue and expense responsibility centers.

Reward Power: Depends on the leader's ability to control the rewards given to other people. Studies have shown that when leaders are not longer able to satisfy their followers' needs, the followers cease to follow. A good leader is able to provide rewards.

Risk, Problem Solving Under Conditions of: Under conditions of risk, problem solvers do not have complete certainty about the outcomes of their actions, but neither are they completely uncertain about what might result.

Risk Propensity: The willingness to undertake risk for possible gain.

Risky Shift: Propensity of groups to endorse a riskier position.

Robotics: Involves the use of robots to perform a manufacturing or service function.

Role Motivation: John Miner has formulated a very relevant theory of human needs known as role motivation. His research indicates that certain individuals enjoy the managerial role and seek it out. He has principally examined the managerial role and has developed a set of char-

acteristics of those who like to play that role. There is no reason to believe though that others—teachers, lawyers, doctors, and dentists—do not also feel the need to fulfill their particular roles, as well.

Rules and Regulations: Plans that describe exactly how one particular situation is to be handled.

Sales Forecasting: The process of predicting future sales.

Sampling Theory: Samples of populations to be used for a number of processes, such as quality control and marketing research, can be statistically determined through sampling theory.

Scalar Chain of Command: The formal distribution of organizational authority in a hierarchical fashion.

Scheduling and Shop Floor Planning: This process is involved with tactical and short-range decisions regarding what to produce and when to produce it for each work area.

Scientific Management: Sought to find "the one best way" to do the job. Scientific management had four underlying principles: the development of a true science of management; the scientific selection of the individual to fill each job; the scientific education and development of each employee, so that he or she would be able to do his job properly; cooperation between management and workers. *See also* Classical Approaches to Management.

Seven Steps of Socialization: Richard T. Pascale, after examining numerous corporate cultures, proposed that organizations fit employees into the company culture through a seven-step process that he calls the "Seven Steps of Socialization."

Shareholder Value: The belief that a company's performance should be measured in terms of how much shareholders gain from what the business does.

Simple Environments: Have few products, few competitors, few locations, and simple technology.

Simple Ranking: Type of performance appraisal—raters simply rank their subordinates from best to worst on their perceived performances.

Simple Structure (Mintzberg): The simple structure is, in a word, simple. It has virtually no support staff, no technostructure, and almost no middle line. It consists principally of a manager, normally an entrepreneur, and a group of subordinates.

Simulation: A model of a real-world situation that can be altered to understand how changes in its various components affect other parts of the model.

Single Business Corporate Strategy: At the single business unit (SBU) level, the firm begins by asking itself: (1) Is there some business in which the organization has a natural strategic advantage or an innate interest, and if already in that business, does that advantage or interest still exist? (2) Does the company want to compete directly or find a niche where there isn't any head-on competition? (3) Does the company want or need to concentrate in one specific business line or in multiple product lines (or multiple businesses)? (4) Once the company has answered these questions, its basic action-strategy choices are to grow, stabilize, engage in investment reduction, defend against a takeover or seek one, turn around company fortunes, or some combination of these.

Single-Use Plans: Plans that are used once, and then discarded. There are three types of single-use plans: strategies, intermediate plans, and operational plans.

Situational Factors for Creative Problem Solving: Before making assumptions, before generating alternatives, the key situational variables must be identified.

Situational Management: Suggests that the manager must review the key factors in a situation and then determine what action to take based on past experience and knowledge.

Skill Variety: The degree to which a job requires employees to perform a wide range of operations or to use a variety of procedures in their work.

Small Business: The size necessary to qualify as a small business depends on who is doing the defining—generally it is 500–1,000 people or fewer.

Social Audit: Is necessary to measure the performance of organizations in order to ascertain whether they have achieved corporate social responsiveness.

Social Power/Social Responsibility Concept: Suggests that business has a certain social responsibility because of the power that it wields

Social Responsibility: May be defined as the obligation of an organization to solve problems and take actions which further the best interests of both society and of the company.

Social Responsibility, Categories of: Product line; marketing practices; employee education and training; corporate philanthropy; environmental control; external relations; employee relations, benefits, and satisfaction with work; employment and advancement and minorities and women; employee safety and health.

Social Responsibility, Levels of: Social responsibility consists of four principal components: economic, legal, ethical, and discretionary responsibility.

Socially Contributive Actions: Many people feel a great need to contribute to society. Many teachers, nurses, doctors, and others feel that they are giving themselves to society in their particular occupations. Environmentalists and those who support social causes have a similar need.

Society and Culture: Societal/cultural element of the general environment includes the social, cultural, and demographic characteristics of the society(ies) within which an organization operates.

Span of Control: The number of people a manager directs.

Specialization of Labor: Dictates that work be divided into smaller and smaller subunits until it can be repeated easily and successfully by an individual or group of individuals.

Stabilization Strategy: Firms may choose to stabilize, perhaps to consolidate, until further growth is advisable.

Staff Authority: Authority which is advisory and comes from outside the chain of command of that unit.

Staff Managers: Are in charge of units that provide support to the line units.

Staffing: Recruiting, selecting, training, evaluating, and performing other functions relative to utilizing human resources. Viewed as part of organizing in this book.

Stakeholder Concept: Suggests that management must account for its impact on its stakeholders when it makes decisions, and it must take their interests into account.

Stakeholders: All those who are directly or indirectly affected by the decisions of the organization.

Standing Plans: Are used to guide activities that recur over a period of time. There are three principal types of standing plans: policies, procedures, and rules and regulations.

Statistical Analysis: The technique most frequently cited as used in business. Statistics are data that are assembled and clarified in some meaningful way.

Statistical Decision Theory: Characteristics in models, based on probabilities, can be determined through statistical decision theory.

Storming Stage of Group Development: Characterized as a period of high emotions. Cliques and coalitions of subgroups may occur and these are often accompanied by tension. Members learn further about their expected objectives and roles and about how their needs may be satisfied. Conflict may occur as each member seeks to have his or her agenda adopted by the group.

Storyboarding: A structured, but flexible brainstorming process that focuses on identifying major issues and then brainstorming each of them. Storyboarding allows for a complete picture (story) of the problem to be placed before participants, usually on some type of wallboard.

Strategic Alliances: Agreements to cooperate between two corporations.

Strategic Business Unit: The designation given each business serving distinct customers and markets.

Strategic Control: Is concerned with the evaluation of strategy once it has been formulated or once it has been implemented. Prior to implementation, strategic control focuses on asking a series of questions about strategy and its consistency with other factors.

Strategic Control Systems: From a control perspective, the primary concerns at the strategic level are achieving the objectives of the strategic plan and the use of the financial resources allocated by the long-range financial plan.

Strategic Management: The process of managing the pursuit of organizational mission while managing the relationship of an organization to its environment. Strategic management is more encompassing than strategic planning. Strategic planning is part of strategic management.

Strategic Operations Decisions: Concern products, processes, and facilities and their relationships to each other. More specifically these decisions include positioning the operations system; focusing the factories; product/service design and process planning; allocating resources to strategic alternatives; determining facility capacity, location, and layout; production technology; and quality.

Strategic Planning: The problem-solving process of establishing strategic objectives and formulating strategic plans to accomplish those objectives. Strategic planning may occur in any major area of an organization, but the central focus is often the marketplace. It is principally concerned with long-term actions to achieve objectives, but it could also be a major short-term action. Any strategic plan is based on answering these three questions: (1) Where are we know? (2) Where do we want to be? (3) How do we get there?

Strategic Thinking: This means that strategists "think" through the strategic planning process.

Strategies: Major plans committing extensive resources to proposed actions to achieve an organization's major goals and objectives.

Strategists: There are four principal types of strategists in any organization: the single entrepreneurial-type leader who makes most or all of the strategic decisions; a coalition (informal group) of top managers; the professional planner; and, in an emerging role of importance, the division manager.

Strategy Formulation: Strategy formulation, whether corporate, business, or functional, follows these steps: (1) It commences with a review of organizational vision, mission, and goals. (2) Next, strategists perform an internal environmental analysis and an external environmental analysis. (3) These analyses are used to determine strengths, weaknesses, opportunities, and threats—SWOT. This SWOT analysis helps answer the strategic question "Where are we now?" (4) Next, planning premises must be developed. Premises are the assumptions upon which strategic objectives and related strategies will be based. Forecasts of the future states of both internal and external environments are involved in formulating premises. (5) Strategic objectives are determined. These define "Where do we want to be?" (6) Alternative strategies are derived. (7) Choices among those alternatives must be made. This answers the question "How do we get there?"

Strategy Implementation: Once strategy is formulated, it must be implemented. In fact strategy should be formulated with implementation considered as one of the SWOT factors. There are four key ingredients in successful implementation:

proper organizational structure, suitable management systems, appropriate leadership style, and astute management of organizational culture.

Stress: A physical and psychological condition resulting from attempts to adapt to one's environment.

Stress Management, Techniques for: Work on reducing number or intensity of stressors, improving the individual's psychological state, or overcoming the effects of stress.

Stress Stages: Alarm, resistance, and exhaustion.

Stressors: Include "work" related management and leadership style; organization culture and structure; work demands, job pressures; boredom; control over decisions; change, technology. Other factors: family life; friends; recreational opportunities; personal finances; physical condition and diet; physical environment.

Structural Approaches to Providing Organizational Communication: Here are a few: employee assistance programs, action lines, and counseling; grievance procedures; attitude surveys; ombudsmen; open-door policies; suggestion programs.

Structure: Defines (1) the relationships between tasks and authority for individuals and departments, (2) formal reporting relationships, the number of levels in the hierarchy of the organization, and the span of control, (3) the groupings of individuals into departments and departments into organizations, (4) the systems to effect coordination of effort in both vertical (authority) and horizontal (tasks) directions.

Structured Problems: Those that occur on a routine basis and have readily identifiable attributes—the factors involved and their interrelationships. They have standard, almost automatic solutions, often referred to as programmed decisions.

Substitutes: Substitutes include those products that have a similar function to a company's products. *See also* Competitive Environment.

Supervising: Close monitoring of employee activities across all functions of management.

Suppliers: Suppliers provide the organization with the materials it uses to produce outputs. These may be raw materials, subassemblies, labor, computer programs, energy, or a host of other factors the organization takes in as inputs and transforms into outputs. *See also* Competitive Environment.

Supportive Leadership: The leader displays his or her personal concern for the subordinate. This includes being friendly to subordinates and sensitive to their needs.

Surprises: Are those problems managers cannot realistically anticipate.

SWOT: A situational analysis of four factors: strengths, weaknesses, opportunities, and threats.

Symbols, Ceremonies, and Rituals (Organizational Culture): Tell what's important in an organization. Its logo, flag, and slogans convey the importance it places on certain ideas or events.

Synergy: Means that the combined and coordinated actions of the parts (subsystems) achieve more than all of the parts acting independently could have achieved.

Systematic Thinkers: Tend to "look for a method, make a plan for problem solving, be very conscious of their approach, defend the quality of the solution largely in terms of the method, define specific constraints of the problem early in the process, discard alternatives quickly, move through a process of increasing refinement of analysis, conduct an orderly search for additional information, and complete any discrete analysis that they begin.

Systems Approach to Management: Views the organization as a system that is interdependent with other systems in its environment.

Systems Theory: Maintains that everything is related to everything else.

Systems View of the Organization: Inputs, transformation process, outputs.

Tactical, or Middle-Management Control Systems: Focus largely on controlling tactical plans or the budget for the entire organization. There are four principal tactical/middle-management control systems: budgets, performance appraisals, statistical reports, and rules and procedures.

Tactical Control: Often called management control. Focuses on accomplishing the objectives of the various subplans between strategies and operational plans.

Tactical Operations Decisions: Intermediate-range decisions between strategic decisions about products, processes, and facilities and operating decisions of planning and controlling the day-to-day operation. They include decisions to be made about production planning systems, independent demand inventory systems, resource requirement planning systems, and materials management and purchasing.

Takeover Strategy: Some organizations, because of their particular financial condition or because of the inabilities of management, or both, make particularly attractive targets for takeover by other firms. Firms must prepare a defense against takeovers or find themselves in a crisis management situation.

Tall Organizations: Reflecting smaller spans of control, more levels in the chain of command, and more centralization, than in a decentralized organization.

Task Identity: The extent to which employees do a complete piece of work and can clearly identify the results of their efforts.

Task Force: A special type of temporary group that comes together to solve one specific problem or series of problems.

Task Roles in Groups: Relate to the task that the formal group is assigned or that the informal group has determined to undertake.

Task Significance: The extent to which employees perceive a significant impact upon others as a result of their efforts.

Task Structure: Department by task specialty typically occurs in extremely large organizations where many task-specialist positions exist.

Team: The team is a group, normally within the same department, that is designed to work together to identify and solve group-related work problems.

Team Structure: Describes an egalitarian, highly cooperative, close-knit work group striving to achieve a set of mutually desirable objectives.

Technical Skill: Ability to use tools, techniques, and specialized knowledge as related to a method, process, or procedure.

Technology: The technology element includes existing technology as well as advances in technology.

Technical, Changing: The increased use of technology, especially computers, has given managers more ability to obtain information both about their unit and their entire organization. This increased use of technology carries with it the necessity for changing the way managers make decisions.

Technology as a Factor in Organizational Design: Refers to the equipment, knowledge, materials, and experience employed performing tasks in an organization. Technology affects any type of job and any type of organization.

Theory Z Firms (American firms operating similarly to Japanese firms): Characterized by long-term employment; slow evaluation and promotion; moderate career planning; consensual decision making; individual responsibility; informal, implicit control with explicit measures available; holistic concern for employees.

Time Series Forecasting Techniques: The assumption of time series analysis is that there are four separate components that affect time series data: trend, cyclical, seasonal, and irregular or random.

Top Managers: Include chief operating officers (CEOs), presidents, and vice-presidents. Such managers direct their attention to the major issues affecting the organization, such as setting goals and objectives and devising strategies to meet them.

Total Integration Stage of Group Development: At last, the group becomes fully functioning. Productive decisions are arrived at. Members are well organized, concerned about the group and its results, and are able to deal with task accomplishment and conflict in rational and creative ways.

Total Quality Strategy: Should lead to a concerted effort on the part of all employees to be error-free in their activities, to seek ways to improve quality, and to strive constantly for quality.

Tough-Guy, Macho Culture: When strategic problem solvers commit large sums of money in highly competitive situations seeking a quick turnaround in sales, a tough-guy, macho culture dominates. *See also* Deal & Kennedy's Culture Types.

Training: Helps the employee gain the specific job-related skills that ensure effective performance. Development is the process of helping the employee to grow, principally in his or her career, but perhaps also as a human being outside of work as well.

Trait Approaches (to Leadership): Successful leaders are considered to possess common traits.

Transmission (in Communication): Once the sender has determined the content of the message, it is transmitted across one or more of the available channels—the method of transmission. Channels may include the spoken word, body movements, the written word, television, radio, and artist's paint, electronic mail—anything through which a message is transmitted.

Triad of Key Markets: Kenichi Ohmae, senior partner for the consulting firm McKinsey & Company in Tokyo, has identified a triad of key global business markets: Japan, Europe, and North America. Any corporate player on a global basis must be able to compete in each of those markets.

Truth, Beauty, and Justice as Needs: Maslow recognized certain needs that do not fit into his hierarchy: truth, beauty, and justice. These are not goal-striving needs, they are simply to be enjoyed.

Turnaround Strategy: Organizations in dire straits must seek to turn around their situations.

Type A Firms (American Firms): Characterized by short-term employment, rapid evaluation and promotion, specialized career planning, individual decision making, individual responsibility, explicit/formal control, segmented concern for employees.

Type J Firms (Japanese Firms): Characterized by lifetime employment (for men), slow process of evaluation and promotion, nonspecialized career, consensual decision making, collective responsibility, implicit/subtle control, holistic concern for employees.

Uncertain Environments, Problem Solving in: Uncertainty exists when managers cannot assign even a probability to the outcomes of the various alternatives that the problem-solving process generates.

Uncertainty Avoidance Dimension: According to Geert Hofstede, the degree to which a culture dislikes uncertainty or risk and therefore tries to reduce or avoid it.

Understanding and Action (in Communication): If all has gone well to this point, the receiver understands the message.

Universality of Management: The belief that management practices are applicable to all organizations.

Unstructured Problems: Are nonroutine, complex problems with difficult-to-identify attributes. They lead to unprogrammed decisions. Normally, unstructured problems have not been faced before.

Verbal Communication: Are transmitted by means of two primary channels, hearing (for oral communication) and sight (for written communication).

Video Conferencing: Employs live television in a conference format. Most often, but not always, people with multiple sites receiving the video program are able to see one another.

Vision: Nonspecific directional guidance normally provided to an organization by its CEO. It describes where the company is going conceptually in the most general of terms, but it must also provide emotional direction.

Visionary Thinking: Simply thinking about the environment and making plans for coping with it.

Voice Inflection: A change in tone adds to our knowledge of attitudes.

Voice Mail: The computer acts as an answering machine. It takes messages and gives out messages.

Voice Tone: That quality of voice that gives us some indication of the speaker's attitude. Voice tones can be assertive, bashful, aggressive, angry, passive, and so forth.

Vroom-Yetton Model: A decision-tree–based approach to determining when and–why subordinates should participate in decision making.

Weber's Bureaucracy: A division of labor in which authority and responsibility are clearly defined and legitimized. A hierarchy of authority resulting in a chain of command. Organizational members who are selected on the basis of their qualifications, either by examination or because of their training or education.

Wellness Programs: Comprehensive programs to improve employee health.

Whistleblowing: Occurs when an employee discloses an illegal, immoral, or unethical practice by members of an organization.

Woodward Studies: Much of the significant research on the relationship between technology and organization structure was carried out in the 1950s by Joan Woodward, a British industrial sociologist, and her colleagues.

Work at Home: One of the implications of personal computers is that many people can perform their jobs at home. Individuals whose jobs consist largely of data analysis or data processing, such as an insurance claim processor would have, can perform much of their work at home, receiving and transmitting data over telephone lines.

Work Force, Cultural Diversity of: The work force of the 1990s will be significantly different than that of the past.

Work Force Management: Organizations are changing their structures to provide workers with more challenging jobs. More decision making is being designed into jobs. Labor is increasingly viewed as a partner rather than as an antagonist.

Work Hard/Play Hard Culture: Merges the situation characterized by fast feedback but low risk. It is a fast-paced culture where fun is important and there is lots of action for everyone. This culture encourages creativity in problem solving. *See also* Deal & Kennedy's Culture Types.

Work Simplification: The job is reduced to a very narrow set of tasks, involving standardized procedures with little or no latitude for making decisions.

Worker Expectations: An important factor affecting job design is the expectation of the average employee with respect to his or her job.

Zero-Based Budgeting: This was designed to eliminate some of the problems that occur when present budgets are based on past budgets and the manager concentrates on the differences and on justifying additional funding. Under zero-based budgeting, the manager begins with a zero level of budget and must justify all funding, not just changes—hence, the term zero-based budget. Last year's funds are not secure.

References

CHAPTER ONE

1. For a discussion of some of the benefits of several such changes, see John J. Sherwood, "Creating Work Cultures with Competitive Advantages," *Organizational Dynamics* Winter (1988), pp. 5–26.

2. Thomas J. Peters and Robert H. Waterman, Jr., *In Search of Excellence* (New York: Harper & Row, 1982); Thomas J. Peters and Nancy K. Austin, *Passion for Excellence* (New York: Random House, 1985); and Thomas J. Peters, *Thriving on Chaos: Handbook of a Management Revolution* (New York: Knopf, 1987).

3. From a speech given by Thomas J. Peters to the American Hospital Association, the Arthur C. Backmeyer memorial address. American College of Hospital Administrators, 25th Congress on Hospital Administration, 1983.

4. Carl Icahn, "What Ails Corporate America—and What Should Be Done," *Business Week* (October 27, 1986), p. 101.

5. For a pointed review of management, see Steve Lohr, "Overhauling America's Business Management," *New York Times Magazine* (January 4, 1981), pp. 15ff.

6. Other themes of how managers work do exist. For example, see William Whitely, "Managerial Work Behavior: An Integration of Results from Two Major Approaches," *Academy of Management Journal* (June 1985), pp. 344–362; "How RPI Helps Locate Talent," *Business Week* (September 18, 1978), pp. 129–131.

7. For a review of their applicability to management and management education, see Stephen J. Carroll and Dennis J. Gillen, "Are the Classical Management Functions Useful in Describing Managerial Work?" *Academy of Management Review* (January 1985), pp. 38–51. Their conclusion was that the functional approach was still the best way to represent management work in educational situations.

8. For example, see Richard P. Nielson, "Changing Unethical Behavior," *Academy of Management Executives* (May 1989), pp. 123–130; Laura L. Nash, "Ethics Without the Sermon," *Harvard Business Review* (November–December 1981), pp. 79–90; and "Businesses Are Signing Up for Ethics 101," *Business Week* (February 15, 1988), pp. 56–57.

9. I wish to thank Leon A. Dale for the addition

of the term "uncertain future" to my original definition.

10. Author's conversation with Betty Mizek.

11. Frank C. Barnes, "Nucor," in James M. Higgins and Julian W. Vincze, *Strategic Management: Text and Cases*, 4th ed. (Hinsdale, Ill.: Dryden, 1989).

12. Richard Gibson, "Honeywell Says It Reorganized Control Lines," *The Wall Street Journal* 19 September, 1986, p. 4.

13. Peters and Waterman, op. cit., pp. 122, 244, and 245.

14. Stanley N. Wellborn, "Putting a Freeze on Freon," *U.S. News & World Report* (November 17, 1986), p. 72.

15. T. A. Mahoney, T. H. Jerdee, and S. J. Carroll, "The Job(s) of Management," *International Relations* (February 1965), pp. 102–110.

16. Henry Mintzberg, "The Manager's Job: Folklore and Fact," *Harvard Business Review* (July–August 1975), pp. 49–61; and Lance B. Kurke and Howard E. Aldrich, "Mintzberg Was Right!: A Replication and Extension of the Nature of Managerial Work," *Management Science* (August, 1983), pp. 975–984.

17. Mintzberg, ibid., p. 50.

18. Developed from "Skills of an Effective Administrator," by Robert L. Katz, *Harvard Business Review* (September–October 1974), Vol. 52, p. 94. Research on 2,000 managers by David McClelland and Richard Goyotzis uncovered four primary sets of skills: goal and action management, directing subordinates, human resources management, and leadership, as reported in Mark B. Roman, "Know Thyself," *Success* (May 1987), pp. 46–52.

19. For a discussion of the increasing importance of the top manager having broader experiences, see W. Walker Lewis, "The CEO and Corporate Strategies in the Eighties: Back to Basics," *Interfaces* (January–February 1984), pp. 3–9.

20. For example, see "After a Long Diet, Apple Bites Back," *U.S. News & World Report* (January 26, 1987), pp. 47–48.

21. For a review of the first-line manager's situation, see Steven Kerr, Kenneth D. Hill, and Laurie Broedling, "The First-Level Supervisor: Phasing Out or Here to Stay?" *Academy of Management Review* (1986), pp. 103–117; and Leonard A. Schlesinger and Janice A. Klein, "The First-Line Supervisor: Past, Present and Future," in Jay

W. Lorsch (ed.), *Handbook of Organizational Behavior* (Englewood Cliffs, N.J.: Prentice-Hall, 1987), pp. 370–382.

22. "GM Moves into a New Era," *BW* (July 16, 1984), pp. 48–54.

23. For a lengthy discussion of how the management process differs by level, see Jack Duncan, *Management* (New York: Random House, 1983).

24. Mahoney, Jerdee, and Carroll, op. cit., p. 109; Virginia R. Boehm, "What Do Managers Really Do?" Paper presented at the annual meeting of the AACSB Graduate Admissions Council, Toronto (June 1981); J. P. Kolter, "What Effective General Managers Really Do," *Harvard Business Review* (November–December 1982), pp. 156–167; and G. David Hughes and Charles H. Singler, *Strategic Sales Management* (Reading, Mass.: Addison-Wesley, 1984), pp. 43–45.

25. Mintzberg, op. cit., p. 50; Kurke and Aldrich, loc. cit.

26. M. W. McCall and C. A. Sequist, "In Pursuit of the Manager's Job: Building on Mintzberg" (Greensboro, N.C.: Center for Creative Development, 1980); A. W. Lau, A. R. Newman, and L. A. Broedling, "The Nature of Managerial Work in the Public Sector," *Public Management Forum* (1980), pp. 513–521; and Cynthia M. Parrett and Alan N. Lau, "Managerial Work: The Influence of Hierarchical Level and Functional Specialty," *Academy of Management Journal* (March 1983), pp. 170–177.

27. Virginia R. Boehm, "What Do Managers Really Do?" (Paper presented at the annual meeting of the AACSB Graduate Admission Council, Toronto, June 1981.)

28. Joel Dreyfuss, "John Sculley Rises in the West," *Fortune* (July 9, 1984), pp. 180–183.

29. "The Strike That Rained on Archie McCardell's Parade," *Fortune* (May 19, 1980), pp. 90–99.

30. Author's discussion with a city official.

31. Myron D. Fottler, "Is Management Really Generic?" *Academy of Management Review* (January 1981), pp. 1–12.

32. Ibid.

33. Ibid.

34. "HRM Update," *Personnel Administrator* (February 1985), p. 12.

35. G. W. Meyer and R. G. Stott, "Quality Circles: Panacea or Pandora's Box?" *Organizational Dynamics*, 1985, no. 4, pp. 34–50. They estimate

at least 500 U.S. firms were using them in 1985.

36. Thomas L. Wheelen and J. David Hunger, *Strategic Management and Business Policy*, 2nd ed. (Reading, Mass.: Addison-Wesley, 1986), p. 12.

37. Michael E. Porter, *Competitive Strategy* (New York: Free Press, 1980).

38. For a discussion of both perspectives, see Henry W. Boettinger, "Is Management Really an Art?" *Harvard Business Review* (January-February 1975), pp. 54–64; and Ronald Gibbons and Shelly Hunt, "Is Management a Science?" *Academy of Management Review* (January 1978), pp. 139–144.

39. Thomas M. Mulligan, "The Two Cultures in Business Education," *Academy of Management Review* (October 1987), p. 593.

40. Jeremy Main, "Waking Up AT&T: There's Life After Culture Shock," *Fortune* (December 24, 1984), pp. 66–74.

41. For a philosophical discussion of the situation, see Stanley Davis, *Future Perfect* (Reading, Mass.: Addison-Wesley, 1987), and John Naisbitt and Patricia Auberdeen, *Reinventing the Corporation* (New York: Warner, 1986). For a review of how management may have to change in response to all of these challenges, see Brian Dumaine, "What the Leaders of Tomorrow See," *Fortune* (July 3, 1989), pp. 48–62; "What the Future Holds," Centennial Edition, *Wall Street Journal* 23 June, 1989; "The 21st Century Executive," *U.S. News & World Report* (March 7, 1988), pp. 48–51; Peter Nulty, "How Managers Will Manage," *Fortune* (February 2, 1987), pp. 47–50; Andrew Kupfer, "Managing Now for the 1990s," *Fortune* (September 26, 1988), pp. 44–47; Wayne Wright, "Escape from Mediocrity," *Personnel Administrator* (September 1987), pp. 109–117; and "Management for the 1990s," *Newsweek* (April 25, 1988), pp. 47–48.

42. For a philosophical discussion, see L. L. Cummings, "The Logics of Management," *Academy of Management Review* (October 1983), pp. 532–538.

43. "Fast Track Kids," *Business Week* (November 10, 1986), pp. 40–92; Peters, *Thriving on Chaos*, loc. cit.

44. "Loyalty Ebbs at Many Companies as Employees Grow Disillusioned," *Wall Street Journal* 11 July, 1986, p. 11.

45. Richard M. Steers and Edwin L. Miller, "Management in the 1990's: The International Challenge," *Academy of Management Executive* (February 1988), pp. 21–22; and Tomatsu Yamaguchi, "The Challenge of Internationalization: Japan's Kokushia, *Academy of Management Executive* (February 1988), pp. 33–36.

46. John Naisbitt, *Megatrends* (New York: Warner, 1982), chap. 1.

47. John Naisbitt and Patricia Auberdeen, *Reinventing the Corporations* (New York: Warner, 1986), chap. 1.

48. Alvin Toffler, *Future Shock* (New York: Bantam, 1970), chap. 1.

49. Peters, *Thriving on Chaos*, loc. cit.

50. Charles W. L. Hills, Michael A. Hitt, and Robert B. Hoskimson, "Declining U.S. Competitiveness: Reflections on a Crisis," *Academy of Management Executive* (February 1988), pp. 51–62.

51. "Help Wanted: America Faces an Era of Worker-Scarcity That May Last to the Year 2000," *Business Week* (August 10, 1987), pp. 48–54.

52. Peter Nulty, "How Managers Will Manage," *Fortune* (February 2, 1987), pp. 47–50.

53. See, for example, Lynda M. Applegate, James T. Cash, Jr., and D. Quinn Mills, "Information Technology and Tomorrow's Manager," *Harvard Business Review* (November-December 1988), pp. 128–136.

54. Presentation to the Academy of Management meetings, Chicago, August 12, 1986.

55. Michael A. Guillen, "The Intuitive Edge,"

Psychology Today (August 1984), pp. 68–69; Dina Ingber, "Inside the Executive Mind," *Success* (1984), pp. 33–37; David Coleman, "Successful Executives Rely on Own Kind of Intelligence," *New York Times*, 13 July, 1984, pp. C1–2; and Henry A. Mintzberg, "Planning on the Left Side and Managing on the Right," *Harvard Business Review* (July-August 1976), pp. 49–58.

56. Peters and Waterman, loc. cit., Naisbitt and Auberdeen, loc. cit.; Lawrence M. Miller, *American Spirit: Visions of a New Corporate Culture* (New York: Morrow, 1984); and Richard Pascale, "Fitting New Employees Into the Corporate Culture," *Fortune* (May 28, 1984), pp. 28–42.

57. Naisbitt, *Megatrends*, loc. cit.

58. Ibid.; "Help Wanted," *Business Week* (August 10, 1987), pp. 48–53; and Martha Brannigan, "Help Wanted: A Shortage of Youths Brings Wide Changes to the Labor Market," *Wall Street Journal* 2 September, 1986, pp. 1, 20.

59. Wayne Wright has prepared an extensive model from the organizational viewpoint: "Escape from Mediocrity," *Personnel Administrator* (September 1987), pp. 109–118.

CHAPTER TWO

1. Much of the discussion in these paragraphs is taken from Alan M. Kantrow, "Why History Matters to Managers," *Harvard Business Review* (January–February), 1986, pp. 81–88.

2. These are condensed from the six approaches reported in Harold Koontz, "The Management Theory Jungle," *Journal of the Academy of Management* (December 1961), pp. 174–188; and the eleven reported in Harold Koontz, "The Management Theory Jungle Revisited," *Academy of Management Review* (April 1980), pp. 175–187.

3. Much of the discussion that follows on the evolution of management theory is derived from Daniel A. Wren, *The Evolution of Management Thought*, 2nd ed. (New York: Wiley, 1979); and Claude S. George, Jr., *The History of Management Thought*, 2nd ed. (Englewood Cliffs, N.J.: Prentice-Hall, 1972).

4. Wren, ibid., p. 3.

5. Ibid., chap. 22.

6. James D. Mooney and Alan C. Reiley, *The Principles of Organization* (New York: Harper & Row, 1947), pp. 1–34.

7. 1865 is somewhat of an arbitrary year, but official statistics report agriculture as providing only 48 percent of the jobs in that year, apparently the first time since records were kept that it accounted for less than half. The statistics are cited in Stanley M. Davis, *Future Perfect* (Reading, Mass.: Addison-Wesley, 1987), p. 97. Davis discussed this point in a paper presented to the Strategic Management Society, Boston, October 14, 1987.

8. Frederick W. Taylor, *The Principles of Scientific Management* (New York: Harper & Row, 1911), reissued as part of Frederick W. Taylor, *Scientific Management* (New York: Harper & Row, 1947). Both books have the same pagination.

9. Ibid., p. 130.

10. Ibid., p. 140.

11. Ibid., pp. 40–50.

12. Wallace Clark, *The Gantt Chart: Working Tool of Management* (New York, Ronald Press, 1922).

13. Henry L. Gantt, *Organizing for Work* (New York: Harcourt, Brace, 1919), p. 15.

14. Frank B. Gilbreth, Jr., and Ernestine Gilbreth Carrie, *Cheaper by the Dozen* (New York: Crowell, 1948).

15. See William R. Spriegel and Clark E. Meyers, *The Writings of the Gilbreths* (Homewood, Ill.: Irwin, 1953).

16. See Lillian M. Gilbreth, *The Psychology of Management* (New York: Sturgis and Walton, 1914).

17. Max Weber, *The Theory of Social and Economic Organization*, ed. and trans. by A. M. Henderson and Talcott Parsons (New York: Free Press, 1947), pp. 329–333, adapted. Note that Weber was concerned with public organizations, while our discussion has focused on business organizations.

18. Ibid.

19. Henry C. Metcalf and Lyndall Urwick, eds. "Dynamic Administration: The Collected Papers of Mary Parker Follett (New York: Harper & Row, 1940); and Mary Parker Follett, *Creative Experience* (London: Longmans, Green, 1924), chap. 5.

20. Mary Parker Follett, "The Process of Control," in L. Gulick and Lyndall Urwick, eds., *Papers on the Science of Administration* (New York: Institute of Public Administration, Columbia University, 1937), p. 161.

21. Metcalf and Urwick, op. cit., p. 262.

22. Chester I. Barnard, *The Functions of the Executive* (Cambridge, Mass.: Harvard University Press, 1938), p. 6.

23. Ibid., p. 4.

24. Ibid., p. 72.

25. Ibid., p. 115.

26. Ibid., p. 163.

27. Ibid., pp. 217–230.

28. Elton Mayo, *The Human Problems of an Industrial Civilization* (New York: Macmillan, 1933), pp. 71–72; also see Fritz J. Roethlisberger and W. J. Dickson, *Management and the Worker* (Cambridge, Mass.: Harvard University Press, 1939).

29. Ibid., p. 78.

30. Wren, op. cit., p. 290.

31. James R. Miller and Howard Feldman, "Management Science – Theory, Relevance, and Practice in the 1980s," *Interfaces* (October 1983), pp. 56–60.

32. Robert A. Gordon and James E. Howe, *Higher Education for Business* (New York: Columbia University Press, 1959).

33. Herbert A. Simon, *The New Science of Management Decisions* (New York: Harper & Row, 1960).

34. Fremont E. Kast and James E. Rosenzweig, "General Systems Theory: Applications for Organization and Management," *Academy of Management Journal* (December 1972), pp. 447–465.

35. See: Ludwig von Bertalanffy, Carl G. Hempel, Robert E. Bass, and Hans Jones, "General Systems Theory: A New Approach to Unity of Science," *Human Biology* (December 1951), pp. 302–361; Ludwig von Bertalanffy, "General Systems Theory – A Critical Review," Walter Buckley, ed. *Modern Systems Research for the Behavioral Scientists* (Chicago: Aldine, 1968), p. 13; Ludwig von Bertalanffy, *General Systems Theory: Foundations, Development, Applications* (New York: Brazillier, 1968); and Ludwig von Bertalanffy, *Organismic Psychology and Systems Theory* (Barre, Mass.: Clark University Press, 1968).

36. Kenneth E. Boulding, "General Systems Theory – The Skeleton of Science," *Management Science* (April 1956), pp. 197–208.

37. For an additional, more current view of systems theory, see J. Miller, *Living Systems* (New York: McGraw-Hill, 1978).

38. Kast and Rosenzweig, loc. cit.

39. For additional perspectives on how systems theory can be used, see Donde P. Ashmos and George P. Huber, "The Systems Paradigm in Organization Theory: Correcting the Record and Suggesting the Future," *Academy of Management Review* (October 1987), pp. 607–621.

40. Fred E. Fiedler, *A Theory of Leadership Effectiveness* (New York: McGraw-Hill, 1967), p. 147.

41. Paul Hersey and Kenneth H. Blanchard, *Management of Organizational Behavior: Utilizing Human Resources* (Englewood Cliffs, N.J.: Prentice-Hall, 1977). (First published in 1969 with earlier published materials preceding the book.)

42. Fred Luthans, "The Contingency Theory of Management: A Path Out of the Jungle," *Business Horizons* (June 1973), pp. 62–72.

43. Charles Hofer, *Academy of Management Journal* (December 1975), pp. 784–810.

44. Harold Koontz, "Management Theory Jungle Revisited," *Academy of Management Review* (Spring 1980), p. 175.

45. William G. Ouchi, *Theory Z: How American Business Can Meet the Japanese Challenge* (Reading, Mass.: Addison-Wesley, 1981); and Richard T. Pascale and Anthony G. Athos, *The Art of Japanese Management* (New York: Simon and Schuster, 1981).

46. "The Difference Japanese Management Makes," *Business Week* (July 14, 1986), pp. 47–50.

47. Jeremiah J. Sullivan, "A Critique of Theory Z," *Academy of Management Review* (January 1983), pp. 132–142; J. Bernard Keys and Thomas R. Miller, "The Japanese Management Theory Jungle," *Academy of Management Review* (April 1984), pp. 345–356; S. Prahash Sethi, Nobuaki Namiki, and Carl L. Swanson, *The Attack on Theory Z: The False Promise of the Japanese Miracle* (Marshfield, Mass.: Pitman, 1984); and Peter F. Drucker, "Behind Japan's Successes," *Harvard Business Review* (January–February 1981), pp. 83–90.

48. Peters and Waterman, loc. cit.

49. Ibid., chap. 3.

50. Thomas J. Peters, *Thriving on Chaos: Handbook for a Management Revolution* (New York: Knopf, 1987).

51. R. Duane Ireland and Michael A. Hitt, "Peters and Waterman Revisited: The Unended Quest for Excellence," *Academy of Management Executive* (May 1987), pp. 91–99; "Who's Excellent Now," *Business Week* (November 5, 1984), pp. 76–77; Daniel T. Carroll, "A Disappointing Search for Excellence," *Harvard Business Review* (November–December 1983), pp. 78–80; and Kenneth E. Aupperle, William Acar, David E. Booth, "An Empirical Critique of *In Search of Excellence*: How Excellent Are the Excellent Companies?" *Journal of Management* (December 1986), pp. 499–512.

52. Thomas J. Peters, *Thriving on Chaos: Handbook for a Management Revolution* (New York: Knopf, 1987); Robert H. Waterman, Jr., *The Renewal Factor* (New York: Bantam, 1987); Thomas J. Peters and Nancy K. Austin, *Passion for Excellence* (New York: Random House, 1986); Thomas J. Peters and Robert H. Waterman, Jr., *In Search of Excellence*, a television program aired on Public Broadcasting TV in 1985; and Thomas J. Peters and Robert H. Waterman, Jr., *In Search of Excellence* (New York: Harper & Row, 1982).

CHAPTER THREE

1. Virtually all of the sources cited in Chapter 1 relate to what managers do; those cited in Chapter 2 describe the history of management thinking—for example, Henri Fayol emphasized the role of decision making/problem solving. For an upper-level Ford manager's perspective, see J. S. Ninomiya, "Wagon Masters and Lesser Managers," *Harvard Business Review* (March–April 1988), pp. 84–90.

2. Based on George T. Huber, *Managerial Decision Making* (Chicago: Scott, Foresman, 1980), p. 8.

3. For a thorough discussion, see David A. Cowan, "Developing a Process Model of Problem Recognition," *Academy of Management Review* (October 1986), pp. 763–776.

4. W. F. Pounds, "The Process of Problem Finding," *Industrial Management Review* (Fall 1969), pp. 1–19; support for Pounds's research was found by C. E. Watson, "The Problem of Problem Finding," *Business Horizons* (August 1976), pp. 94–99.

5. Marjorie A. Lyles and Ian I. Mitroff, "Organizational Problem Formulation: An Empirical Study," *Administrative Science Quarterly* (March 1980), pp. 102–119.

6. Herbert Simon, *Administrative Behavior* (New York: Free Press, 1957).

7. Carol J. Loomis, "The Strike That Rained on Archie McCardell's Parade," *Fortune* (May 19, 1980), pp. 91–99.

8. "End of a Troubled Reign," *Fortune* (May 31, 1982), p. 7.

9. Peter F. Drucker, *Innovation and Entrepreneurship: The Practice and Principles* (New York: Harper & Row, 1985).

10. Howard H. Stevenson, "Defining Corporate Strengths and Weaknesses," *Sloan Management Review* (Spring 1976), pp. 51–66.

11. Harold E. Klein and Robert E. Linnenmorn, "Strategic Environmental Assessment: An Emerging Typology of Corporate Planning Practice," *Contribution of Theory and Research to the Practice of Management*, Dennis F. Ray, ed. *Proceedings*, Southern Management Association, New Orleans (November 1982), pp. 4–9.

12. For a discussion of the multiple purposes of the problem statement, see Roger J. Volkema, "Problem Formulation as Purposeful Activity," *Strategic Management Journal* (May–June 1986), pp. 267–279.

13. Allan R. Cohen, Stephen L. Fink, Herman Gadon, Robin D. Willits, *Effective Behavior in Organizations*, 4th ed. (Homewood, Ill.: Irwin, 1988), pp. 24–29.

14. Sara Kiesler and Lee Sproull, "Managerial Response to Changing Environments: Perspectives on Problem Sensing from Social Cognition," *Administrative Science Quarterly* (December 1982), pp. 548–570; and Hillel J. Einhorn and Robin M. Hogarth, "Decision Making in Reverse," *Harvard Business Review* (January–February 1987), pp. 66–70. Hillel J. Einhorn and Robin M. Hogarth also report problems with linking events—that is, misinterpreting causal relationships. Managers think they see relationships that don't exist, partly because they don't look long and hard enough for other relationships. Factors such as ego, prior attributions, and group processes can affect one's view of the cause of a problem. It may distort it. See Jeffrey D. Ford, "The Effects of Causal Attributions on Decision Makers' Responses to Performance Downturns," *Academy of Management Review* (October 1985), pp. 770–786.

15. Michael Simpson, "Opportunities for Innovation in the Metal Industry," *Journal of Business Strategy* (Summer 1986), pp. 84–87.

16. James M. Higgins, "The Leadership TRRAP," *Human Relations: Behavior at Work* (New York: Random House, 1987), pp. 206–210.

17. "Eureka: New Ideas for Boosting Creativity," *Success* (December 1985), p. 27.

18. Danny Miller, "Towards a Contingency Theory of Strategy Formulation," *Proceedings* (Academy of Management, 1975), pp. 64–66.

19. "Getting a Clearer View of Smog," *Business Week Special Issue on Innovation in America* (June 1989), p. 73.

20. André L. Delbecq and Andrew H. Van de Ven, "A Group Process Model for Problem Identification and Program Planning," *Journal of Applied Behavioral Science* (1971), pp. 466–492.

21. Based on, but not limited to, Lyle Sussman and Samuel D. Deep, *Comex: The Communication Experience in Human Relations* (Cincinnati: South-Western, 1980), p. 120; Norman R. F. Maier, "Assets and Liabilities in Group Problem Solving," *Psychological Review* (1967), pp. 239–249; and Gayle W. Hill, "Group Versus Individual Performance: Are N + 1 Heads Better Than One?" *Psychological Bulletin* (1982), pp. 517–539.

22. Maier, ibid.; Hill, ibid.

23. James A. F. Stoner, "Risky and Cautious Shifts in Group Decisions: The Influence of Widely Held Values," *Journal of Experimental Social Psychology* (1988), no. 4, pp. 442–459.

24. Herbert A. Simon, *Administrative Behavior* (New York: Free Press, 1957); James G. March and Herbert A. Simon, *Organizations* (New York: Wiley, 1958); D. W. Taylor, "Decision Making and Problem Solving," *Handbook of Organizations*, James G. March, ed. (Chicago: Rand McNally, 1965), pp. 48–68; Peer Sollberg, "Unprogrammed Decision Making," *Research Toward Development and the Management Thought*, Proceedings, Academy of Management, H. P. Hotenstein and R. W. Williams, eds. (1967), pp. 3–16; Marcus Alexis and Charles Z. Wilson, eds., *Organizational Decision Making* (Englewood Cliffs, N.J.: Prentice-Hall, 1967), pp. 76–78; C. E. Lindblom, "The Science of Muddling Through," *Public Administration Review* (Spring 1959), pp. 79–88; J. V. Baldridge, *Power and Conflict in the University* (New York: Wiley, 1971); E. E. Carter, "The Behavioral Theory of the Firm and the Top Level of Corporate Decision," *Administrative Science Quarterly* (December 1971), pp. 414–429; and H. Mintzberg, D. Raisinghani, and A. Theoret, "The Structure of Unstructured Decision Processes," *Administrative Science Quarterly* (June 1976), p. 58.

25. Anna Grandori, "A Prescriptive Contingency View of Organizational Decision Making," *Administrative Science Quarterly* (1984), pp. 192–209.

26. Pounds, loc. cit.; Drucker, loc. cit.

27. Ian Mitroff and Tom R. Featherington, "On Systematic Problem Solving and the Error of the Third Kind," *Behavioral Science* (September 1974), pp. 300–393.

28. Hillel J. Einhorn and Robin M. Hogarth, "Decision Making: Going Forward in Reverse," *Harvard Business Review* (January–February 1987), pp. 66–70; and John McCormick, "The Wisdom of Solomon," *Newsweek* (August 17, 1987), pp. 62–63.

29. John R. Schermerhorn, Jr., *Management for Productivity*, 2nd ed. (New York: Wiley, 1986), pp. 65–66.

30. "How IBM Made 'Junior' an Underachiever," *Business Week* (June 25, 1984), p. 106; "The Computer War's Casualties Pile Up," *U.S. News & World Report* (August 20, 1984), pp. 37–38; and John Marcous, Jr., "IBM's PCjr Computer is Fulfilling Its Promise After a Faltering Start," *Wall Street Journal* 13 December, 1984, p. 33.

31. Arie De Gues, presentation to the Strategic Management Society, Boston, October 15, 1987; Pierre Wack, "Scenarios: Uncharted Waters Ahead," *Harvard Business Review* (September–October 1985), pp. 73–89; and Pierre Wack, "Scenarios: Shooting the Rapids," *Harvard Business Review* (November–December 1985), pp. 139–150.

32. James L. McKenney and Peter G. W. Keen, "How Managers' Minds Work," *Harvard Business Review* (July–August 1974), pp. 79–90.

33. Ibid.

34. Ibid.

35. Isabel Briggs Myers, "An Introduction to Type" (Palo Alto, Calif.: Consulting Psychologists Press, 1980).

36. Victor H. Vroom and P. W. Yetton, *Leadership and Decision Making* (Pittsburgh: University of Pittsburgh Press, 1973).

37. Victor H. Vroom and Arthur G. Yago, *The New Leadership: Management Participation in Organizations* (Englewood Cliffs, N.J.: Prentice-Hall, 1988).

38. James M. Higgins, *Innovate or Evaporate*, book forthcoming.

39. "Hewlett Sounds Call for Engineering Creativity in MIT Graduate Speech," *Electronic Engineering Times* (June 23, 1986), p. 78.

40. Dina Ingber, "Inside the Executive Mind," *Success* (1984), pp. 33–37; Daniel Coleman, "Success for Executives Rely on Our Kind of Intelligence," *New York Times* 13 July, 1984, pp. C1, C2; Henry Mintzberg, "Planning on the Left

Side, Managing on the Right," *Harvard Business Review* (July–August 1976), pp. 49–58; and Weston Agor, "The Logic of Intuition: How Top Executives Make Important Decisions," *Organizational Dynamics* (Winter 1986), pp. 5–18.

41. "Masters of Innovation," *Business Week* (April 10, 1989), pp. 58–63.

42. "Milliken: Quality Leadership Through Research" (Spartanburg, S.C.: Milliken, 1986), p. 5.

43. For a discussion of processes, see Roger Von Oech, *A Whack on the Side of the Head* (New York: Warner, 1985).

44. Ibid., and Betty Edwards, *Drawing on the Right Side of the Brain* (Los Angeles: J. P. Tarcher, 1979), distributed by St. Martin's Press, New York.

45. Agor, loc. cit.

46. Mintzberg, loc. cit.; Henry A. Mintzberg, Duru Raisinghani, and André Theoret, "The Structure of 'Unstructured' Decision Processes," *Administrative Science Quarterly* (June 1976), pp. 246–275; and Coleman, loc. cit. The latter reports on the research of Dr. Siegfred Streufert of the Pennsylvania State College of Medicine on the decision techniques of executives.

CHAPTER FOUR

1. "What on Earth Are We Doing?" *Time* (January 2, 1989), pp. 22–39.

2. "The Global Greenhouse Finally Has Leaders Sweating," *Business Week* (August 1988), pp. 74–76; "Heatwaves," *Newsweek* (July 11, 1988), pp. 16–20; and Jerry E. Bishop, "Global Threat: New Culprit Is Indicated in Greenhouse Effect—Rising Methane Level," *Wall Street Journal* 24 October, 1988, pp. A1, A7.

3. "A Gaping Hole in the Sky," *Newsweek* (July 11, 1988), pp. 21–24; and Barry Meier, "Ozone Demise Quickens Despite '78 Ban on Spray Propellant; New Curbs Debated," *Wall Street Journal* 13 August, 1986, p. 25.

4. Michael H. Brown, "Toxic Wind," *Discover* (November 1987), pp. 42–49; and Douglas Staglin, "Seizing the Politics of Pollution," *U.S. News & World Report* (December 8, 1986), p. 45.

5. "Troubled Waters: The World's Oceans Can't Take Much More Abuse," *Business Week* (October 12, 1987), pp. 89–104.

6. ABC News, September 7, 1988; "Suddenly a Deathwatch on the Rhine," *Business Week* (November 24, 1986), p. 52.

7. Amal Kumar Naj, "Back to the Lab: Big Chemical Concerns Hasten to Develop Biodegradable Plastics," *Wall Street Journal* 21 July, 1988, pp. 1, 6.

8. Tom Waters, "Fall of the Rain Forest," *Discover* (January 1989), p. 40; "The Global Greenhouse Finally Has Leaders Sweating," loc. cit.

9. "A Long Summer of Smog," *Newsweek* (August 29, 1988), pp. 46–49.

10. Robert Johnson, John Koten, and Charles F. McCoy, "State of Shock: Anheuser-Busch Company Is Shaken by Its Probe of Improper Payments," *Wall Street Journal* 31 March, 1987, pp. 1, 31.

11. Eileen White, "In the Spotlight: Rash of Investigations Is Damaging Image of Northrop Corporation," *Wall Street Journal* 22 June, 1987, pp. 1, 23.

12. Edward T. Pound, "On the Take: Investigators Detect Pattern of Kickbacks for Defense Business," *Wall Street Journal* 14 November, 1985, pp. 1, 25.

13. Charles P. Alexander, "Crime in the Suites," *Time* (June 10, 1985), p. 56.

14. Charles P. Alexander, "General Dynamics Under Fire," *Time* (April 8, 1985), pp. 23–26.

15. Robert Guenther and Joanne Lipman, "Building Distrust: Construction Industry in New York Is Hotbed of Extortion and Bribery," *Wall Street Journal* 7 May, 1986, pp. 1, 22.

16. Andy Pasztor and Cathy Trost, "Bad Buys: Fraud Frequently Mars Government Contracts to Acquire Computers," *Wall Street Journal* 7 July, 1986, pp. 1, 9.

17. Sonja Steptoe and Francine Schwadel, "Ex-Manager at Shearson Firm, Six Others Indicted for Laundering Gambling Funds," *Wall Street Journal* 27 June, 1986, p. 5.

18. Theodore Levitt, "Editorial," *Harvard Business Review* (January–February 1988), p. 4.

19. Richard L. Daft, *Organization: Theory and Design*, 2nd ed. (St. Paul, Minn.: West, 1986), p. 18, 49.

20. Adapted from L. J. Bourgeois, "Strategy and Environment: A Conceptual Integration," *Academy of Management Review* (January 1980), pp. 25–39. His term *task environment* has been changed to *competitive environment*.

21. Thomas J. Peters and Robert H. Waterman, Jr., *In Search of Excellence* (New York: Harper & Row, 1982); Thomas J. Peters and Nancy K. Austin, *A Passion for Excellence* (New York: Random House, 1985); and Thomas J. Peters, *Thriving on Chaos* (New York: Knopf, 1987).

22. Discussion with Tupperware top management and their benefits counselor.

23. A. C. Cooper, et al., "Strategic Responses to Technological Threats," *Proceedings* (Academy of Management 1974).

24. Brian Dumaine, "How Managers Can Succeed Through Speed," *Fortune* (February 13, 1987), pp. 54–59.

25. Jeremy Main, "Here Comes the Big New Cleanup," *Fortune* (November 21, 1988), pp. 102–118.

26. "State Regulators Rush in Where Washington No Longer Treads," *Business Week* (September 19, 1983), pp. 124–131.

27. Tom Burns and G. M. Stalker, *The Management of Innovation* (London: Tavistock, 1961).

28. Ibid.

29. Author's observation.

30. Robert B. Duncan, "Characteristics of Perceived Environments and Perceived Environmental Uncertainty," *Administrative Science Quarterly* (1972), no. 3, pp. 313–327.

31. Sue Greenfield, Robert C. Winder, and Gregory Williams, "The CEO and the External Environment," *Business Horizons* (November–December 1988), pp. 20–26.

32. Laurie Hays, "Fighting Back: Chemical Firms Press Campaigns to Dispel Their 'Bad Guy' Image," *Wall Street Journal* 20 September, 1988, pp. 1, 30.

33. "Small Companies Show Muscle in Efforts to Influence Congress," *Wall Street Journal* 3 October, 1988, pp. B1, B2.

34. Guenther and Lipman, loc. cit.

35. Neil H. Jacoby, *Corporate Power and Social Responsibility* (New York: Macmillan, 1973).

36. Jerry W. Anderson, Jr., "Social Responsibility and the Corporation," *Business Horizons*, July–August, 1986, pp. 22–27; Keith Davis and William C. Frederick, *Business and Society: Management, Public Policy, and Ethics*, 5th ed. (New York: McGraw-Hill, 1984).

37. David J. Fritzche and Helmet Becker, "Linking Management Behavior to Ethical Philosophy—An Empirical Investigation," *Academy of Management Journal* (March 1984), pp. 156–175.

38. Archie Carroll, "A Three-Dimensional Conceptual Model of Corporate Performance," *Academy of Management Review* (October 1979), p. 499.

39. Milton Friedman, *Capitalism and Freedom* (Chicago: University of Chicago Press, 1962), p. 133; and Milton Friedman and Rose Friedman, *Free to Choose* (New York: Harcourt, Brace, Jovanovich, 1979).

40. R. Edward Freeman and David L. Reed, "Stockholders and Stakeholders: A New Perspective on Corporate Government," *California Management Review* (Spring 1983), pp. 88–106; and R. Edward Freeman, *Strategic Management: Stakeholder Approach* (Boston: Pitman, 1984).

41. William C. Frederick, Keith Davis, and James E. Post, *Business and Society: Corporate Strategy, Public Policy, Ethics*, 6th ed. (New York: McGraw-Hill, 1988), p. 36.

42. Carroll, op. cit., p. 499; for an empirical test of a similar, but three-stage model, see Kimberly B. Boal and Newman Perry, "The Cognitive Structure of Corporate Social Responsibility," *Journal of Management* (1989), no. 3, pp. 71–82.

43. Carroll, op. cit., p. 500.

44. Ibid.

45. Frederick, Davis, and Post, op. cit., p. 52.

46. "W. R. Grace, Massachusetts Water District Settle Suit," *Wall Street Journal* 12 January, 1987, p. 33; "U.S. Jury Fines Grace $100 Million in Trial Involving Bank Loan," *Wall Street Journal* 21 October, 1987, p. 4; and CBS television show "60 Minutes" some time during fall 1987. Also see "Why Business Is Watching This Pollution Case," *Business Week* (March 28, 1986), p. 39.

47 Jeffery A. Fadiman, "A Traveler's Guide to Gifts and Bribes," *Harvard Business Review* (July–August 1986), pp. 122–136.

48. Presentation by Donald Peterson, CEO and chairman of the board, Ford Motor Company, to the Academy of Management, Washington, D.C., August 14, 1989.

49. Jerry W. Anderson, Jr., "Social Responsibility in the Corporation," *Business Horizons* (July–August, 1986), pp. 22–27.

50. "Money Talks, Nobody Walks in Boston," *Business Week* (April 21, 1986), p. 51.

51. Carroll, op. cit., pp. 501–502; Carroll uses the terms first employed by Ian Wilson in "What One Company Is Doing About Today's Demands on Business," in George A. Steiner, ed., *Changing Business Society into Relationships* (Los Angeles: Graduate School of Management, UCLA, 1975). He also references related strategies to each of the philosophical positions presented by Terry W. McAdams in "How to Put Corporate Responsibility into Practice," *Business and Society Review/Innovation* (1973), no. 6, pp. 8–16.

52. Ian Wilson actually uses the term "reactive," but I have used Terry McAdams' description of this same stage. Both are authors cited by Carroll, loc. cit., as developers of responsiveness continuums. See Wilson, loc. cit., and McAdams, loc. cit.

53. "General Dynamics Under Fire," *Business Week* (March 25, 1985), p. 7.

54. Barry Meier, "Citizen Suits' Become a Popular Weapon in the Fight Against Industrial Polluters," *Wall Street Journal* 17 April, 1987, p. 19.

55. Hays, loc. cit.

56. "American Express: Public Responsibility—A Report of Recent Activities," (New York: American Express, 1988).

57. Ibid.

58. Edwin M. Epstein, "The Corporate Social Policy Process: Beyond Business Ethics, Corporate Social Responsibility, and Corporate Social Responsiveness," *California Management Review* (Spring 1987), pp. 99–114. A similar, earlier version of this process is described by Steven L. Wortex and Phyllis R. Cochrane, "The Evolution in the Corporate Social Performance Model," *Academy of Management Review* (1985), no. 4, pp. 758–769. In this model they described social corporate policy as a field examining social issues in management, including issue identification, issue analysis, and response developing. It is directed at minimizing surprises and determining effective corporate social policies.

59. Kathleen Black, address to the Academy of Management, Washington, D.C., August 14, 1989.

60. Theodore J. Kreps, "Measurement of the Social Performance of Businesses," in monograph no. 7, *An Investigation of Concentration of Economic Power for the Temporary National Economic Committee* (Washington, D.C.: U.S. GPO, 1940).

61. Archie B. Carroll and George W. Beilier, "Landmarks in the Evolution of the Social Au-

dit," *Academy of Management Journal* (September 1975), pp. 589–599.

62. James M. Higgins, "A Social Audit of Equal Opportunity Programs," *Human Resource Management* (Fall 1977), pp. 2–7.

63. David Silverstein, "The Litigation Audit: Preventative Legal Maintenance for Management," *Business Horizons* (November–December 1988), pp. 34–42.

64. Jean B. McGuire, Alison Sundgren, and Thomas Schneeweis, "Corporate Social Responsibility and Firm Financial Performance," *Academy of Management Journal* (December 1988), pp. 854–872. This article cites relevant authors from each of the three referenced perspectives.

65. Kenneth Aupperle, Archie P. Carroll, and John D. Hatfield, "An Empirical Examination of American Corporate Social Responsibility and Profitability," *Academy of Management Journal*, (1985), no. 2, pp. 446–463; Philip L. Cochrane and Robert A. Wood, "Corporate Social Responsibility and Financial Performance," *Academy of Management Journal* (March 1984), pp. 42–56; and A. Ullman, "Data in Search of a Theory: Critical Examination of the Relationships Among Social Performance, Social Disclosure, and Economic Performance," *Academy of Management Review* (July 1985), pp. 540–577.

66. McGuire, Sundgren, and Schneeweis, loc. cit.

67. Thomas M. Jones, "An Integrative Framework for Research in Business and Society: A Step Towards an Elusive Paradigm," *Academy of Management Review* (1983), no. 4, pp. 559–564.

68. LaRue Tone Hoemer, *The Ethics of Management* (Homewood, Ill.: Irwin, 1987), pp. 3–12.

69. Derek Bok, "Ethics, The University, and Society," *Harvard Magazine* (May–June 1988), pp. 39–50, contains an excellent discussion of what a university can do, how its curriculum can help, and what a professor can do philosophically to challenge students to think about ethical behavior.

70. Adrianne Cadbury, "Ethical Managers Make Their Own Rules," *Harvard Business Review* (September–October 1987), pp. 69–73.

71. Rick Wartzman, "Nature or Nurture? Study Blames Ethical Lapses on Corporate Goals," *Wall Street Journal* 9 October, 1987, sec. 2, p. 1.

72. Laura L. Nash, "Ethics Without the Sermon," *Harvard Business Review* (November–December 1981), pp. 79–90.

73. Arthur Bedeian, *Management*, 1st ed. (Hinsdale, Ill.: Dryden, 1986), p. 623.

74. Amanda Bennett, "Ethics Code Spread Despite Skepticism," *Wall Street Journal* 15 July, 1988, p. 19.

75. "Businesses Are Signing Up for Ethics 101," *Business Week* (February 15, 1988), pp. 56–67.

76. Donald Robin, Michael Grallomakis, Fred R. David, and Thomas E. Moritz, "A Different Look at Codes of Ethics," *Business Horizons* (January–February, 1989), pp. 66–73.

77. "Hertz Is Doing Some Body Work – On Itself," *Business Week* (February 15, 1988), p. 57.

78. Janet P. Near, "Whistle-Blowing: Encourage It!" *Business Horizons* (January–February 1989), pp. 2–6.

79. Marcia Parmalree Miceli and Janet P. Near, "The Relationship Among Beliefs, Organizational Positions, and Whistle-Blowing Status: A Discriminant Analysis," *Academy of Management Journal* (December 1984), pp. 687–705. They use the term "illegitimate," I use the term "unethical."

80. Joseph A. Raelin, "The Professional as the Executive's Aide-de-camp," *Academy of Management Executive* (August 1987), pp. 171–182.

CHAPTER FIVE

1. For a discussion, see Henry Mintzberg, "What Is Planning Anyway?" *Strategic Management Journal* (1981), pp. 319–324; and Neil H. Snyder, "What Is Planning Anyway?: A. Rejoinder," *Strategic Management Journal* (July–September 1982), pp. 265–267.

2. Leon Rineharth, H. Jack Shapiro, and Ernest A. Callman, *Practice of Planning: Strategic, Administrative, and Operational* (New York: VanNostrand Reinhold, 1981).

3. William A. Bossidy, address to the Strategic Management Society, Boston, October 13, 1987; and Michael M. Robert, *Strategic Thinking: Charting the Future of Your Organization*, 2nd ed. (Woburn, Mass.: Decision Process International, 1985).

4. Charles Hofer and Dan Schendel, *Strategy Formulation: Analytical Concepts* (St. Paul, Minn.: West, 1978).

5. "United Once More," *Time* (June 22, 1987), pp. 46–47.

6. "Georgia-Pacific Turns Paper into Gold," *Business Week* (August 15, 1988), pp. 71–72.

7. John Huey, "Wal-Mart: Will It Take Over the World?" *Fortune* (January 30, 1989), pp. 52–61.

8. Kenneth Labick, "The Big Comeback of British Airways," *Fortune* (December 5, 1988), pp. 163–174.

9. Marj Charlier, "Second String: In a World of Miller's and Buds, Coors Beer Has to Play Catch-Up," *Wall Street Journal* 3 November, 1988, pp. A1, A12.

10. Tom Richman, "Mrs. Field's Secret Ingredient," *Inc.* (October 1987), pp. 65–72.

11. "Numbers Don't Tell the Story," *Business Week* (June 6, 1988), p. 105.

12. Marc Bassin, "Teamwork at General Foods: New & Improved," *Personnel Journal* (May 1988), pp. 62–70.

13. Steve Kaufman, "Going for the Buck," *Success* (January–February 1988), pp. 38–41.

14. William J. Hampton and James R. Norman, "General Motors: What Went Wrong?" *Business Week* (March 16, 1987), pp. 102–110.

15. Raymond M. Kinnunen, "The John Hancock Mutual Life Insurance Company," in James M. Higgins and Julian W. Vincze, eds. *Strategic Management: Text and Cases*, 4th ed. (Chicago: Dryden, 1989), pp. 1017–1041.

16. Ken Wells and Carol Hymonitz, "Gulf's Managers Find Merger into Chevron Forces Many Changes," *Wall Street Journal* 5 December, 1984, pp. 1, 22.

17. "A Software Whiz-Kid Goes Retail," *Business Week* (May 9, 1983), p. 111.

18. *IBM Annual Report*, 1983, p. 3.

19. Author's discussion with IBM personnel.

20. William G. Ouchi, *Theory Z: How American Business Can Meet the Japanese Challenge* (Reading, Mass.: Addison-Wesley, 1981).

21. John Sculley, with John A. Vern, "Sculley's Lessons from Inside Apple," *Fortune* (September 14, 1987), p. 120. Excerpted from John Sculley with John A. Vern, *Odyssey: Pepsi to Apple* (New York: Harper & Row, 1987).

22. For a discussion of planning under changing conditions, see Dale D. McConkey, "Planning in a Changing Environment," *Business Horizons* (September–October 1988), pp. 64–72.

23. Author's conversation with IBM sales representative.

24. William M. Bulkeley, "Back on Line: Digital Equipment, Still Led by Founder, Regains Momentum," *Wall Street Journal* 3 April, 1986, pp. 1, 18.

25. Lawrence A. Bossidy, "Some Thoughts on Strategic Thinking," address to the Strategic Management Society, Boston, August 14, 1987; and Graham Turner, "Inside Europe's Giant Companies: Olivetti Goes Bear-Hunting," *Long Range Planning* (April 1986), pp. 13–20.

26. Neil C. Churchill, "Budget Choice: Planning vs. Control," *Harvard Business Review* (July–August 1984), pp. 150–164.

27. Peter Lorange and Declan Murphy, "Considerations in Implementing Strategic Control," *Journal of Business Strategy* (Spring 1984), pp. 27–35.

28. For a review of part of this process, see Howard H. Stevenson, "Defining Corporate Strengths and Weaknesses," *Sloan Management Review* (Spring 1976), pp. 51–66.

29. George A. Steiner, *Top Management Planning* (New York: Macmillan, 1969), pp. 81–82.

30. The author's personal experience as a consultant to this organization.

31. See comments in Chapter 3 on premises.

32. Lee Berton, "Bottom Line: Peat Accountants Are Rushing to Merge," *Wall Street Journal* 17 July, 1989, pp. A-1, A-7.

33. Based primarily on Harold Koontz, Cyril O'Donnell, and Heinz Weihrich, *Management*, 8th ed. (New York: McGraw-Hill, 1984), pp. 213–215.

34. For example, see Thomas J. Peters, *Thriving on Chaos: Handbook for Management Revolution* (New York: Knopf, 1987), pp. 398–408; Noel M. Tichy and Mary Anne DeVanna, *The Transformational Leader* (New York: Wiley, 1986), pp. viii, ix; chaps. 1 and 5; Robert H. Waterman, Jr., *The Renewal Factor* (New York: Bantam, 1987), pp. 222–225.

35. Tichy and DeVanna, op. cit., p. 130.

36. Thomas J. Peters, *Thriving on Chaos: Handbook for a Management Revolution* (New York: Knopf, 1987), p. 399.

37. Peters, op. cit., pp. 401–404.

38. Philip Kotler, *Marketing Management: Analysis, Planning, Control*, 5th ed. (Englewood Cliffs, N.J.: Prentice-Hall, 1986), pp. 50–54; and John A. Pearce, II, "The Company Mission as a Strategic Tool," *Sloan Management Review* (Spring 1982), p. 15.

39. John A. Pearce, II, and Fred David, "Corporate Mission Statements: The Bottom Line," *Academy of Management Executive* (May 1987), pp. 109–116.

40. Richard Brandt, "The Billion Dollar Whiz Kid," *Business Week* (April 13, 1987), pp. 68–69.

41. Pearce, op cit., p. 14.

42. J. T. Kendrick, as quoted in "How W. T. Grant Lost $175 Million Last Year," *Business Week* (February 24, 1975), p. 75.

43. Peter F. Drucker, *The Practice of Management* (New York: Harper & Row, 1954).

44. Charles W. Hofer and Dan Schendel, *Strategy Formulation Analytical Concepts* (St. Paul: West, 1979).

45. Max Richards, *Setting Strategic Goals and Objectives* (St. Paul: West, 1986), p. 22.

46. Adapted from and added to Edwin A. Locke and Gary P. Latham, *Goal Setting for Individuals, Groups, and Organizations* (Chicago: Science Research Associates, 1984).

47. Robert N. Anthony, John Dearden, and Norton M. Bedford, *Management Control Systems*, 5th ed. (Homewood, Ill.: Irwin, 1984), pp. 1–15.

48. Hofer and Schendel, op. cit.

49. Drucker, op. cit.

50. George S. Odiorne, *Management by Objectives* (New York: Pitman, 1965); *MBO II: A System of Managerial Leadership for the 80s* (Belmont, Calif.: Pitman, 1979).

51. For example, see Robert C. Ford, Frank S. McLaughlin, and James Nixdorf, "Ten Questions About MBO," *California Management Review* (Winter 1980), pp. 84–94; and Fred E. Schuster and Alva F. Kindall, "Management by Objectives – Where We Stand – A Survey of the Fortune 500," *Human Resource Management* (Spring 1974), pp. 8–11.

52. Heinz Weihrich, *Management Excellence: Productivity Through MBO* (New York: McGraw-Hill, 1985).

53. Gary P. Latham and Gary A. Yukl, "A Review of the Research on Application of Goal Setting in Organizations," *Academy of Management Journal* (December 1975), pp. 824–845.

54. For a review of the various aspects of goal setting, see ibid.

55. For a lengthy review of the effects of participation, see Edwin A. Locke and E. M. Schwerger, "Participation Is Decision Making: One More Look," in Barry M. Stone, ed., *Research in Organizational Behavior*, vol. 1 (Greenwich, Conn.: JAI, 1979), pp. 265–339; for a description of the two main types of participation-setting objectives, and formulating plans, see Jan P. Muczyk and Bernard C. Reimann, "The Case for Directive Leadership," *Academy of Management Executive*, November 1987, pp. 301–311.

56. For example, see Jack N. Kondrasuk, "Studies in MBO Effectiveness," *Academy of Management Review* (July 1981), pp. 419–430 for a review of 185 studies of MBO; also see Jan P. Muczyk, "Dynamics and Hazards of MBO Applications," *Personnel Administrator* (May 1979), p. 52; and Ford, McLaughlin, and Nixdorf, loc. cit.

57. Kondrasuk, loc. cit.; Muczyk, loc. cit.; Ford, McLaughlin, and Nixdorf, loc. cit.

58. James M. Higgins, *Human Relations: Behavior at Work*, 2nd ed. (New York: Random House, 1987), p. 288.

59. William J. Kearney, "Behaviorally Anchored Rating Scales – MBO's Missing Ingredient," *Personnel Journal* (January 1979), pp. 20–25.

60. Odiorne, *MBO, II*, op. cit., pp. 127–140, for example, argues that managers should set three types of objectives: routine, creative, and personal development.

CHAPTER SIX

1. For reviews of the relationship between strategy and financial performance, see John A. Pearce II, Elizabeth B. Freeman, and Richard B. Robinson, Jr., "The Tenuous Link Between Formal Strategic Planning and Financial Performance," *Academy of Management Review*, October 1987, pp. 658–695; John A. Pearce, II, D. Keith Robbins, and Richard B. Robinson, Jr., "The Impact of Grand Strategy and Planning Formality on Financial Performance," *Strategic Management Journal* (March–April 1987), pp. 125–134; Gordon E. Greenley, "Does Strategic Planning Improve Company Performance?" *Long Range Planning* (March–April) 1986, pp. 101–109; Lawrence C. Rhyne, "The Relationship of Strategic Planning to Financial Performance," *Journal of Strategic Management* (September–October 1986), pp. 423–436; Jeffrey S. Bracker and John W. Pearson, "Planning and Financial Performance of Small, Mature Firms," *Journal of Strategic Management* (November–December 1986), pp. 503–522; and Charles B. Shrader, Lew Taylor, and Dan R. Dalton, "Strategic Planning and Organizational Performance: A Critical Appraisal," *Journal of Management* (Summer 1984), pp. 149–171.

2. Charles Hofer and Dan Schendel, *Strategy Formulation: Analytical Concepts* (St. Paul, Minn.: West, 1978).

3. See John A. Pearce, II, "Selecting Among Alternative Grand Strategies," *California Management Review* (Spring 1982), pp. 23–31.

4. For a discussion, see Daniel Gilbert, Edwin Hartman, John Mauriel, and Edward Freeman, *A Logic for Strategy* (Boston: Ballinger, 1988).

5. Based largely on James M. Higgins and Julian W. Vincze, *Strategic Management: Text and Cases*, 4th ed. (New York: Dryden, 1989), chaps. 1–11.

6. Ibid., p. 2; also for a discussion, see Charles W. Hofer and Dan E. Schendel, eds, *Strategic Management: A New View of Business Policy and Planning* (Boston: Little, Brown, 1979).

7. Roger Evered, "So What *Is* Strategy?" *Long Range Planning* (June 1983), pp. 57–72.

8. Michael E. Naylor, a speech delivered to the Academy of Management, Chicago, August 14, 1986.

9. Author's discussion with Disney managers.

10. For a review of recent research, see Lain Fahey and H. Kurt Christensen, "Evaluating the Research in Strategy Content," in James G. Hunt and John D. Blair, eds., *Yearly Review of Management of the Journal of Management* (Summer 1986); and Anne S. Huff and Rhonda Kay Rezer, "A Review of Strategic Process Research," in James G. Hunt and John D. Blair, eds., *Year Review of Management of the Journal of Management* (Summer 1987), pp. 211–236.

11. William Bossidy, vice-chairman of GE, address to the Strategic Management Society, Boston, October 14, 1987; Arie DeGues, vice-president, Shell International, remarks in a seminar at the same meeting; and Elserino Piol, vice-president for Strategies and Development at Olivetti, quoted in Graham Turner, "Inside Europe's Giant Companies: Olivetti Goes Bear Hunting," *Long Range Planning* (1986), no. 2, pp. 13–20.

12. DeGues, loc. cit; Pierre Wach, "Scenarios: Uncharted Waters Ahead," *Harvard Business Review* (September–October 1985), pp. 73–89; and Pierre Wach, "Scenarios: Shooting the Rapids," *Harvard Business Review* (November–December 1985), pp. 139–150.

13. For a critical review of this process see Henry Mintzberg, "The Design School: Reconsidering the Basic Premises of Strategic Management," *Strategic Management Journal*, March–April, 1990, pp. 171–195.

14. For a look at differences in perception relative to SWOT at a strategic level, see R. Duane Ireland, Michael A. Hitt, Richard A. Bettis, and Deborah Auld DePorees, "Strategy Formulation Processes: Differences in Perception of Strength and Weakness Indicators and Environmental Uncertainty by Management Level," *Strategic Management Journal* (September–October 1987), pp. 469–485.

15. George Steiner addresses this issue more fully than anyone else I've read. See George A. Steiner, *Strategic Planning: What Every Manager Must Know* (New York: Free Press, 1979), pp. 18–20, 122–148.

16. Barnaby J. Feder, "GE's Costly Locomotive Gamble," *Wall Street Journal* 25 January, 1987, p. 4F.

17. George Russell, "Hollywood's Top Gun," *Time* (December 29, 1986), pp. 58–59.

18. John Taylor, "Project Fantasy: A Behind the Scenes Account of Disney: Desperate Battle Against the Raiders," *Manhattan* (November 1984).

19. Michael E. Porter suggests that other issues include restructuring of current and acquired businesses, the transfer of skills between companies, and the sharing of activities between companies, such as distribution or marketing. "From Competitive Advantage to Corporate Strategy," *Harvard Business Review* (May–June 1987), pp. 53–56.

20. Adapted from Peter Lorange, "Divisional Planning: Setting Effective Direction," *Sloan Management Review* (Fall 1975), pp. 85–87.

21. Agis Salpukas, "Greyhound Selling Its Bus Operations," *New York Times*, Business Day, 24 December, 1986, p. 29.

22. For a discussion of the matrix, see Barry Hedley, "A Fundamental Approach to Strategy Development," *Long Range Planning* (December 1976), pp. 2–11.

23. Donald C. Hambrich, Ian C. MacMillan, and Diane L. Day, "Strategic Attributes and Performance on the BCG Matrix – A PIMS Based Analysis of Industrial Product Business." *Academy of Management Journal* (September 1982), pp. 510–531.

24. Michael E. Porter, *Competitive Strategy* (New York: Free Press, 1980).

25. William E. Fulmer and Jack Goodwin argue that low cost is just one form of differentiation in "Differentiation: Begin with the Consumer," *Business Horizons* (September–October 1988), pp. 55–63.

26. Brian Dumaine, "How Managers Succeed Through Speed," *Fortune* (February 13, 1989), pp. 54–59; and Joseph L. Bowers and Thomas M. Hout, "Fast-Cycle Capability for Competitive Power," *Harvard Business Review* (November–December, 1988), pp. 110–118.

27. For a brief review see Higgins and Vincze, op. cit., p. 176.

28. William K. Hall, "Survival Strategies in a Hostile Environment," *Harvard Business Review* (September–October 1980), pp. 73–86.

29. Some additional research efforts support Hall's view; for example, see Alan I. Murray, "A Contingency View of Porter's Generic Strategies," *Academy of Management Review* (1988), no. 3, pp. 390–400; and Charles W. L. Hill, "Differentiation Versus Low Cost or Differentiation and Low Cost: A Contingency Framework," *Academy of Management Review* (1988), no. 3, pp. 401–412.

30. Raymond E. Miles and Charles C. Snow, *Organizational Strategy, Structure and Process* (New York: McGraw-Hill, 1978).

31. S. Schoeffler, R. D. Buzzell, and D. F. Heany, "The Impact of Strategic Planning on Profit Performance," *Harvard Business Review* (March–April 1974), pp. 137–145.

32. Higgins and Vincze, op. cit., pp. 121–122.

33. Michael E. Porter, *Competitive Advantage* (New York: Free Press, 1985).

34. Kevin P. Cogne, "Sustainable Competitive Advantage – What It Is, What It Isn't," *Business Horizons* (January–February 1986), pp. 54–61.

35. Charles W. L. Hill, Michael A. Hitt, and Robert E. Hoskisson, "Declining U.S. Competitiveness: Reflections on a Crisis," *Academy of Management Executive* (January 1988), pp. 51–60.

36. For a discussion, see Briance Mascarehas and David A. Aaker, "Strategy Over the Business Cycle," *Strategic Management Journal* (May–June 1989), pp. 199–210.

37. For example, see Harold W. Fox, "A Framework for Functional Coordination," *Atlanta Economic Review* (November–December 1973), pp. 6–15.

38. James M. Higgins, "The Personal Computer Industry," in Higgins and Vincze, op. cit., pp. 790–792.

39. For discussions of the coalition, see James Bryan Quinn, *Strategies for Change: Logical Incrementalism* (Homewood, Ill.: Irwin, 1980); L. J. Bourgeois, III, and J. V. Singh, "Organizational Slack and Political Behavior Among Top Management Teams," *Academy of Management Proceedings* (1983), pp. 43–47; and Henry A. Mintzberg, Duru Raisinghani, and André Theoret, "The Structure of Unstructured Decision Processes," *Administrative Science Quarterly* (June 1976), p. 258.

40. The New Breed of Strategic Planners," *Business Week* (September 17, 1984), pp. 62–68.

41. For example, see Lee Iacocca, *Iacocca: An Autobiography* (New York: Bantam, 1984), especially chap. V.

42. M. L. Hatten, "Strategic Management and Not-For-Profit Organizations," *Strategic Management Journal* (April–June 1982), pp. 89–104; Ellen L. Greenberg, "Competing for Scarce Resources," *Journal of Business Strategy* (Winter 1982), pp. 81–87; and "Budget Anguish: Reagan's Plans to Cut Deficit Draws Outcrys from Affected Groups," *Wall Street Journal* 26 December, 1984, pp. 1, 8.

43. For a sample lengthier discussion, see Charles R. Stoner and Fred L. Fry, *Strategic Planning in the Small Business* (Cincinnati: Southwestern, 1987).

44. Israel Unterman and Richard H. Davis, *Strategic Management for Not-For-Profit Organizations* (New York: Praeger, 1984); and M. L. Hatten, "Strategic Management in Not-for-Profit Organizations," *Strategic Management Journal* (April–June 1982), pp. 89–104.

45. Higgins and Vincze, op. cit., chap. 11.

46. Jamie C. Simpson, "United Way Turns to Small Business as Support Wanes at Some Big Firms," *Wall Street Journal* 8 January, 1987, p. 19.

47. Y. N. Cheng and F. Campos-Flores, *Business Policy and Strategy* (Santa Monica, Calif.: Goodyear, 1980), Chapter 17; and Yves L. Doz, "Strategic Management and Multinational Companies," *Sloan Management Review* (Winter 1980), pp. 27–46.

48. Naylor, loc. cit.

49. James M. Higgins and Timo Santalainen, "Strategies for Europe 1992," *Business Horizons* (July–August 1989), pp. 54–58.

50. For a fuller discussion, see Jay R. Galbraith and Robert K. Kazanjian, *Strategy Implementation: Structure, Systems, and Process* (St. Paul, Minn.: West, 1986).

51. Higgins and Vincze, op. cit., chap. 8. Note: What I call style here, they label as the individual manager's human resource management.

52. A. D. Chandler, *Strategy and Structure* (Cambridge, Mass.: MIT, 1962).

53. See: Donald C. Hambrick and Albert A. Channella, Jr., "Strategy Implementation as Substance and Selling," *Academy of Management Executive*, November 1989, pp. 278–289.

54. Robert H. Waterman, Jr., "The Seven Elements of Strategic Fit," *Journal of Business Strategy* (Winter 1982); also see Thomas J. Peters and Robert H. Waterman, Jr., *In Search of Excellence* (New York: Harper & Row, 1982).

55. See: David Ulrich and Margarethe F. Wiersema, "Gaining Strategic and Organizational Capability in a Turbulent Business Environment," *Academy of Management Executive*, May 1989, pp. 115–122; and Dale D. McConkey, "Planning in a Changing Environment," *Business Horizons*, September–October, 1988, pp. 64–72; Kathleen M. Eisenhardt, "Making Fast Strategic Decisions in High-Velocity Environments," *Academy of Management Journal*, September 1989, pp. 543–576.

56. For a discussion of decision analysis in strategy formulation, see Howard Thomas, "Strategic Decision Analysis: Applied Decision Analysis and Its Role in the Strategic Management Process," *Strategic Management Journal* (April–June 1984), pp. 139–156.

CHAPTER SEVEN

1. For a discussion of how quantitative methods can help managers better understand the problem, see Rick Hesse, "Management Science or Management/Science," *Interfaces* (February 1980), pp. 104–109; and Allen F. Grum and Rick Hesse, "It's the Process Not the Product (Most of the Time)," *Interfaces* (October 1983), pp. 89–93.

2. For a typical, more in-depth discussion of these problems, see K. Roscoe Davis, Patrick G. McKeown, and Terry Rakes, *Management Science*, 2nd ed. (Reading, Mass.: Addison-Wesley, 1986), chap. 1; and David R. Anderson, Dennis J. Sweeney, and Thomas A. Williams, *An Introduction to Management Science: Quantitative Approaches to Decision Making*, 4th ed. (St. Paul, Minn.: West, 1986), chap. 1.

3. "Mind Prober," brochure (Palo Alto, Calif.: Leading Edge Software, 1985).

4. For example, see Dennis Kneale, "Computer Caution: Linking of PC's Is Coming, But Plenty of Obstacles Remain," *Wall Street Journal* 28 January, 1986, pp. 1, 22.

5. Based on the discussion by Ricky W. Griffin, *Management*, 2nd ed. (Boston: Houghton Mifflin, 1984), pp. 253–284; and the discussion by Louis E. Boone and David L. Kurtz, *Principles of Management* (New York: Random House, 1984), pp. 180–182. Also see M. J. Lawrence, "An Exploration of Some Practical Issues in the Use of Quantitative Forecasting Models," *Journal of Forecasting* (April–June 1983), pp. 169–179.

6. James S. Moore and Alan K. Reichert, "A Multivariate Study of Firm Performance and the Use of Modern Analytical Tools and Financial Techniques," *Interfaces* (May–June 1989), pp. 79–87.

7. Chase Econometrics, The Wharton School, and the Michael Evans Group.

8. For example, see Henry Mintzberg, Duru Raisinghani, and André Theoret, "The Structure of Unstructured Decision Processes," *Administrative Science Quarterly*, June 1976, p. 258, Weston H. Agor ed., *Intuition in Organizations: Leading and Managing Proactively* (Newbury Park, CA: Sage Publications, 1989), pp. 145–170.

9. G. Thomas and J. DaCosta, "A Sample Survey of Corporate Operations Research," *Interfaces* (1979), no. 4, pp. 102–111.

10. Norman Gaither, "The Adoption of Operations Research Techniques by Manufacturing Organizations," *Decision Sciences* (1975), vol. 6, no. 4, pp. 797–813.

11. W. Ledbetter and J. Cox, "Are OR Techniques Being Used?" *Industrial Engineering*, vol. 9, no. 2, pp. 1921–1977.

12. Jerry Wind, Paul E. Green, Douglas Shifflett, and Marsha Scarbrough, "Courtyard by Marriott: Designing a Hotel Facility with Consumer-Based Marketing Models," *Interfaces* (January–February 1989), pp. 29–47.

13. Barry Lewis and Jan Bell, "Decisions Involving Sequential Events: Replications and Extensions," *Journal of Accounting Research* (Spring 1985), pp. 228–239.

14. Jacob W. Ulvila and Rex V. Brown, "Decision Analysis Comes of Age," *Harvard Business Review* (September–October 1982), pp. 130–141.

15. David Cohen, Stephen M. Haas, David L. Radloff, and Richard F. Yarrick, "Using Fire in Forest Management: Decision Making Under Uncertainty," *Interfaces* (September–October 1984), pp. 8–19.

16. Robert E. Luna and Richard A. Reid, "Mortgage Selection Using a Decision Tree Approach," *Interfaces* (May–June 1986), pp. 73–81; and Jinoos Hosseini, "Decision Analysis and Its Application in the Choice Between Wild Cat Oil Ventures," *Interfaces* (March–April 1986), pp. 75–85.

17. Norman Gaither, *Production and Operations Management: A Problem-Solving and Decision-Making Approach*, 3rd ed. (Chicago: Dryden, 1987), pp. 538–551.

18. Thomas J. Peters, "The Home-Team Advantage," *U.S. News & World Report* (March 31, 1986), p. 49.

19. Quantitative methods have even been used to help reduce the airline overbooking problem. Marvin Rothstein, "OR and the Airline Overbooking Problem," *Operations Research* (March–April 1985), pp. 237–248.

20. Richard C. Larson and Thomas F. Rich, "Travel Time Analysis of New York City Police Patrol Cars," *Interfaces* (March–April 1987), pp. 15–26.

21. Discussion of transportation procedures with a high-level executive in this firm.

22. For a discussion of various types, see Peter Holmes, "Business Outlook '86," *Nation's Business* (January 1986), pp. 22–28; and Spyros Makridakis and Steven C. Wheelwright, eds., *The Handbook of Forecasting* (New York: Wiley, 1982).

23. Author's discussion with park officials.

24. For a discussion of the assumptions issue and the difficulty of modeling econometrically, see "The Art of Crunching Numbers," *The Economist* (May 9, 1987), pp. 68–69; and "Where the Big Econometric Models Go Wrong," *Business Week* (March 30, 1987), pp. 70–73.

25. William J. Stevenson, *Production/Operations Management*, 2nd ed. (Homewood, Ill.: Irwin, 1986), p. 107.

26. Ibid., p. 108.

27. A one-unit change in the independent variable results in either an exact proportional or multiplicative change greater than one in the dependent variable.

28. Robert J. Lambrix and Surendra S. Singhavi, "How to Set Volume-Sensitive ROI Targets," *Harvard Business Review* (March–April 1981), pp. 174–179.

29. Stevenson, op. cit., p. 190.

30. See Edward Markowski and Carol Markowski, "Some Difficulties and Improvements in Applying Linear Programming Formulations to the Discriminant Problem," *Decision Sciences* (Summer 1985), pp. 233–247, for a lengthy discussion of the technique.

31. Thomas J. Holloran and Jensen E. Byrn, "United Airlines Station Manpower Planning System," *Interfaces* (January–February 1986), pp. 39–50.

32. Robert E. Marklin, *Topics in Management Science*, 2nd ed. (New York: Wiley, 1983).

33. James Gleick, "Breakthrough in Problem Solving," *New York Times* 15 November, 1984, p. A1.

34. Bajis Dodin, "Bounding the Project Completion Time in PERT Networks," *Operations Research* (July 1985), pp. 1–33.

35. Stevenson, op. cit., p. 630.

36. Gaither, op. cit., pp. 772–774.

37. Mark B. Rowan, "The Critical Path," *Success* (September 1987), pp. 56–57.

38. For a discussion, see Dodin, loc. cit.

39. Stevenson, op. cit., p. 653.

40. Author's conversation with Blount Construction managers.

41. For a discussion, see Warren J. Erickson and Owen P. Hall, *Computer Models for Management Science*, 2nd ed. (Reading, Mass.: Addison-Wesley, 1986).

42. For a discussion, see Sang M. Lee and Jung Shim, *Micro Management Science* (Dubuque, Iowa: Brown, 1986).

43. "Idea Generator," Gerard I. Nierenberg, Experience Software Inc., Berkeley, Calif., 1985.

44. Bayard W. Wynne, "A Domination Sequence—MSLOR, DSS, and the Fifth Generation," *Interfaces* (May–June 1984), pp. 51–58.

45. Stephen Rosenberg, "Flexibility in Installing a Larger Scale HRIS: New York City's Experience," *Personnel Administrator* (December 1985), pp. 39–46.

46. William G. Wild, Jr., and Otis Port, "This Video Game Is Saving Manufacturers Millions," *Business Week* (August 17, 1987), pp. 82–84.

47. Mark R. Lembersky and Uli H. Chi, "Weyerhaeuser Decision Simulator Improves Timber Profits," *Interfaces* (January–February 1986), pp. 6–15.

48. Asim Roy, Leon Lasdon, and Donald R. Plane, "End-Users Optimization with Spreadsheet Models," *European Journal of Operational Research* (1989), pp. 131–137; and Execucom Systems Corporation, "Optimizing Gas Strategies Reaps Big Rewards for Public Utility Company," *The Planner* (Spring 1988), pp. 3–5.

49. Gordon L. Baker, William A. Clark, Jr., Jonathan J. Frund, and Richard E. Wendell, "Production Planning and Cost Analysis on a Micro Computer," *Interfaces* (July–August 1987), pp. 53–60.

50. For a discussion of this latter point, see John C. Anderson and Thomas R. Hofman, "A Perspective on the Implementation of Management Science," *Academy of Management Review* (July 1978), pp. 563–571.

51. Alex Taylor, III, "Lee Iacocca's Production Whiz," *Fortune* (June 22, 1987), pp. 36–44; and Steven Flax, "Can Chrysler Keep Rolling Along?" *Fortune* (January 7, 1988), pp. 34–39.

CHAPTER EIGHT

1. For example, see Amanda Bennet, "Middle Managers Face Job Squeeze as Cutbacks and Caution Spread," *Wall Street Journal* 25 April, 1986, p. 29; Amanda Bennet, "Growing Small: As Big Firms Continue to Trim Their Staffs, Two-Tier Set-Up Emerges," *Wall Street Journal* 4 May, 1987, pp. 1, 12; "Shifting Strategies: Surge in Re-

structuring is Profoundly Altering Much of U.S. Industry," *Wall Street Journal* 12 August, 1985, pp. 1, 12–13; and Myron Magnet, "Restructuring Really Works," *Fortune* (March 2, 1987), pp. 38–45.

2. Walter Kiechel, III, "Corporate Strategy for the 1990s," *Fortune* (February 29, 1988), pp. 34–42.

3. Hospitals, for example, have undergone tremendous cost-cutting programs, many of them aimed at cutting positions and delegating authority.

4. Ian C. MacMillan and Patricia E. Jones, "Designing Organizations to Compete," *Journal of Business Strategy* (Spring 1984), pp. 22–26; Kiechel, loc. cit.

5. For a discussion of coordination, see John R. Schermerhorn, Jr., James G. Hunt, and Richard N. Osborn, *Managing Organizational Behavior* (New York: Wiley, 1988), pp. 328–330.

6. For a discussion, see Richard L. Daft, *Organization Theory and Design*, 2nd ed. (St. Paul, Minn.: West, 1986), p. 9. Daft more formally defines an organization as "a readily identifiable goal–directed social system working together in deliberately structured activity systems."

7. For example, see Roderick E. White, "Generic Business Strategies, Organizational Context and Performance: An Empirical Investigation," *Strategic Management Journal* (1986), pp. 217–231. For a review of the literature and synthesis of the two fields, see James W. Frederickson, "The Strategic Decision Process and Organizational Structure," *Academy of Management Review* (April 1986), pp. 280–297.

8. Based loosely on Ernest Dale, *Organization* (New York: American Management Association, 1967), pp. 8–10.

9. Paul R. Lawrence and John W. Lorsch, *Organization and Environment* (Boston, Mass.: Division of Research, Harvard Business School, 1967).

10. AM International, internal documents.

11. Daft, op. cit. p. 385; Robert A. Dahl, "The Concept of Power," *Behavioral Science* (1957), pp. 201–215; W. Graham Astley and Paramijt S. Sachdeva, "Structural Sources of Intraorganizational Power: A Theoretical Synthesis," *Academy of Management Review* (January 1984), pp. 104–113.

12. Chester I. Barnard, *Functions of an Executive* (Cambridge, MA: Harvard University Press, 1938), pp. 163–174.

13. For a recent discussion of the Lordstown experience, see Simon Caulkin, "The Human Factor in IT: Man and Machine," *Multinational Business* (Spring 1989), pp. 1–9; for an earlier discussion, see "Spread of GM's Lordstown Syndrome," *Business Week* (October 7, 1972), p. 72; "GM Efficiency Move That Backfired," *Business Week* (March 25, 1972), pp. 46–47; D. N. Williams and R. A. Wilson, "Lordstown Shootout: Cost-Cutters vs. New Labor," *Iron Age* (February 3, 1972), pp. 38–39; "New Breed Surfaces at Lordstown, Ohio," *Automotive Industry* (March 1, 1972), pp. 18–19; J. Geschelin, "Transformation at GM Lordstown," *Automotive Industry* (August 15, 1967), pp. 63–66; and "GM Figures Rebut Lordstown Project Critics," *Engineering News* (July 10, 1969), pp. 28–29. For an overview, see Schermerhorn, Hunt, and Osborn, op. cit., p. 276.

14. Author's personal experience as leader of the USAF Resources Audit Team that audits this colonel's operation.

15. Kenneth Labich, "Making Over Middle Managers," *Fortune* (May 8, 1989), pp. 58–64.

16. Waino Soujanen, *The Dynamics of Management* (New York: Holt, 1966).

17. Labich, loc. cit.

18. Tom Barnard and G. M. Stalker, *The Management of Innovation* (London: Tavistock, 1961).

19. Carrie Dolan, "Hewlett-Packard Corporate Revamping Seen; Adding of Operating Chief Expected," *Wall Street Journal* 16 July, 1984, p. 2; "Who's Excellent Now?" *Business Week* (November 5, 1984), pp. 76–88; Bro Utal, "Delays and Defection at Hewlett-Packard," *Fortune* (October 29, 1984), p. 62.

20. Andrew D. Szilagyi, Jr., and Marc J. Wallace, Jr., *Organizational Behavior and Performance*, 4th ed. (Glenview, Ill.: Scott, Foresman, 1987), p. 557.

21. Author's experience as an accountant for Lockheed, Georgia.

22. Douglas R. Sease, "Getting Smart: How U.S. Companies Devise Ways to Meet Challenge from Japan," *Wall Street Journal* 16 September, 1986, p. 1.

23. Thomas J. Peters and Robert H. Waterman, Jr., *In Search of Excellence* (New York: Harper & Row, 1982).

24. MacMillan and Jones, loc. cit.

25. Author's personal knowledge.

26. This is a rule of thumb only. The contingency factors determine appropriate spans of control. However, if the manager is to perform all the desired leadership behaviors (see Chapter 14), the number of subordinates cannot become too large.

27. Author's personal consulting experiences.

28. For a lengthy discussion of the span of control, see David D. VanFleet and Arthur G. Bedeian, "A History of the Span of Management," *Academy of Management Review* (July 1977), pp. 356–372; and David D. VanFleet, "Span of Management Research and Issues," *Academy of Management Review* (September 1983), pp. 546–552.

29. C. W. Barkdall, "Span of Control – A Method of Evaluation," *Michigan Business Review* (May 1963), pp. 27–29.

30. Based on James D. Mooney, *The Principles of Organization*, rev. ed. (New York: Hamber, 1947), p. 5; and on Daft, op. cit., chap. 6.

31. Author's discussion with Phil Crosby, Jr., and other staff in the firm.

32. Russell Mitchell, "GM Hasn't Bought Much Peace," *Business Week* (December 15, 1986), pp. 24–28; William J. Cook, "Perot's War with GM Ends in $743 Million Goodbye," *U.S. News & World Report* (December 15, 1986), pp. 52–54; Stuart Gaines, "Is What's Good for GM Good for EDS?" *Fortune* (November 10, 1986), p. 64; and Russell Mitchell, "How General Motors is Bringing Up Perot's Baby," *Business Week* (April 14, 1986), pp. 96–97.

33. Paul R. Lawrence and Jay W. Lorsch, *Organization and Environment: Managing Differentiation and Integration* (Homewood, Ill.: Irwin), 1967), pp. 8–10.

34. Lawrence and Lorsch, loc. cit.

35. Rensis Likert, *New Pattern of Management* (New York: McGraw-Hill, 1961), pp. 113–115.

36. Daft, loc. cit.

37. Edgar F. Huse and Thomas G. Cummings, *Organizational Development and Change*, 3rd ed. (St. Paul, Minn.: West, 1985), pp. 5, 84.

38. Author's knowledge of a consultant's efforts to place team management in a dairy in Georgia.

39. Stanley M. Davis and Paul L. Lawrence, *Matrix* (Reading, Mass.: Addison-Wesley, 1977), pp. 11–24.

40. These are common problems, related to me by many of my students, who work for Martin Marietta, which uses the matrix system. For a thorough review, see Eric W. Larson and David H. Gobeil, "Matrix Management: Contradictions and Insights," *California Management Review* (Summer 1987), pp. 126–138.

41. Graham Turner, "Inside Europe's Giant Companies: Olivetti Goes Bear-Hunting," *Long Range Planning* (April 1986), pp. 13–20.

42. Bill Saporito, "Are IBM and Sears Crazy?" *Fortune* (September 28, 1987), pp. 74–80.

43. James L. Gibson, John M. Ivancevich, and James H. Donnelly, Jr., *Organizations: Behavior, Structure, Processes*, 6th ed. (Plano, Tex.: Business Publications, 1988), p. 279.

44. For a theoretical research review of structuring as a decision process, see H. Randolph Bobbitt, Jr., and Jeffrey D. Ford, "Decision-Maker Choice as a Determinant of Organizational Structure," *Academy of Management Review* (January 1980), pp. 13–23.

45. Carrie Dolan, "Hewlett-Packard Corporate Revamping Seen: Adding of Operating Chief Expected," *Wall Street Journal* 16 July, 1984, p. 2; "Who's Excellent Now?" *Business Week* (November 5, 1984), pp. 76–88; and Utal, loc. cit.

CHAPTER NINE

1. G. Slutsher, "Some Call It Restructuring," *Forbes* (September 6, 1985), pp. 40–41.

2. Alfred D. Chandler, Jr., *Strategy and Structure* (Cambridge, Mass.: MIT Press, 1962).

3. For a review of these three, see J. C. Ford and John W. Slocum, "Size, Technology, Environment, and the Structure of Organizations," *Academy of Management Review* (October 1977), pp. 561–575.

4. A number of books make this point. Two very early books to do so were William G. Ouchi, *Theory Z: How American Business Can Meet the Japanese Challenge* (Reading, Mass.: Addison-Wesley, 1981); and Robert T. Pascale and Anthony G. Arthos, *The Art of Japanese Management: Applications for American Executives* (New York: Simon & Schuster, 1981).

5. John J. Morse and J. W. Lorsch, "Beyond Theory Y," *Harvard Business Review* (May–June 1970), pp. 61–68.

6. James H. Donnelly, Jr., James L. Gibson, and John M. Ivancevich, *Fundamentals of Management*, 6th ed. (Plano, Tex.: BPI), pp. 180–183.

7. For a discussion of contingency views on structure and on fitting structure to key situational factors, see W. Alan Randolph and Gregory G. Dess, "The Congruence Perspective of Organizational Design: A Conceptual Model and Multivariate Approach," *Academy of Management Review* (January 1984), pp. 114–127; Andrew Van de Ven and R. Drazin, "The Concept of Fit in Contingency Theory," in Larry Cummings and Barry Stavo, eds., *Research in Organizational Behavior* (Greenwich, Conn.: JAI Press, 1983), pp. 333–365; and Raymond E. Miles and Charles C. Snow," "Fit, Failure, and the Hall of Fame," *California Management Review* (Spring 1984), pp. 10–28.

8. David J. Hall and Maurice A. Saias, "Strategy Follows Structure," *Strategic Management Journal* (April–June 1980), pp. 149–165.

9. Michael Tushman and David Nadler, "Organizing for Innovation," *California Management Review* (Spring 1986), pp. 74–92, discuss the theoretical and research perspective; "Masters of Innovation," *Business Week* (April 10, 1989), pp. 58–63, discusses specific examples, principally 3-M.

10. An advertisement in the *Wall Street Journal* 23 September, 1987, p. 39.

11. Danny Miller, "Configurations of Strategy and Structure: Towards a Synthesis," *Strategic Management Journal* (May/June, 1986), pp. 233–249.

12. Henry A. Mintzberg, "Patterns in Strategy Formation," *Management Science* (May 1978), pp. 934–948.

13. Tom Burns and G. M. Stalker, *The Management of Innovation* (London: Tavistock, 1961).

14. For example, see Gerald Zaltman, Robert B. Duncan, and John Holbek, *Innovations and Organizations* (New York: Wiley, 1973).

15. Gary Cohn, "Classic Mistake: Eastern Air's Borman Badly Underestimated Obduracy of Old Foe," *Wall Street Journal* 25 February, 1986, pp. 1, 27; Leslie Wayne, "Frank Bowman's Most Difficult Days," *New York Times* 17 February, 1985; Gary Cohn, "Eastern Airlines Blasts Union Request for Revenue Share, Will Reinstate Cut," *Wall Street Journal* 6 February, 1985.

16. Robert B. Duncan, "Characteristics of Perceived Environments and Perceived Environmental Uncertainty," *Administrative Science Quarterly* (September 1972), pp. 313–327.
17. Henry A. Mintzberg, "Organization Design: Fashion or Fit?" *Harvard Business Review* (January–February 1981), pp. 103–117.
18. Ibid., pp. 103–116.
19. Paul R. Lawrence and J. W. Lorsch, "Differentiation and Integration in Complex Organizations," *Administrative Science Quarterly* (June 1967), pp. 1–47; and Paul R. Lawrence and J. W. Lorsch, *Organization and Environment* (Homewood, Ill.: Irwin, 1969).
20. Ibid., p. 16.
21. Lawrence and Lorsch, "Differentiation and Integration in Complex Organizations," pp. 3–4.
22. Ibid., p. 4.
23. Gordon L. Lippitt and Warren H. Schmidt, "Crises of a Developing Organization," *Harvard Business Review* (November–December 1967), pp. 101–109; Bruce R. Scott, "The Industrial State: Oldness and New Realities," *Harvard Business Review* (March–April 1973), pp. 133–149; Donald H. Thain, "Stages of Corporate Development," *Business Quarterly* (Summer 1969), pp. 32–45; J. R. Kimberly, "Organization Size and the Structureship Perspective: A Review, Critique and Proposal," *Administrative Science Quarterly* (December 1976), pp. 591–597.
24. In addition, Ian McMillan and Patricia E. Jones have identified several combinations of first-level and second-level groupings that further complicate the design problem: function to function; function to product; function to customer; product to product; product to function; product to customer; geographic area to customer; customer to function; and customer to product. See "Designing Organizations to Compete," *Journal of Business Strategy* (Spring 1984), pp. 22–26.
25. John R. Kimberly, Robert H. Miles, and associates, *The Organizational Life Cycle* (San Francisco: Jossey-Bass, 1980).
26. Mintzberg, loc. cit.
27. For a similar, but yet different series of stages, see Robert E. Quinn and Kim Cameron, "Organizational Life Cycles and Shifting Criteria of Effectiveness: Some Preliminary Evidence," *Management Science* (1983), pp. 33–51; see also Larry E. Greiner, "Evolution and Revolution as Organizations Grow," *Harvard Business Review* (July–August 1972), pp. 37–46.
28. Thomas J. Peters, "Doubting Thomas," *Inc.* (April 1989), pp. 82–92; and "Is Your Company Too Big?" *Business Week* (March 27, 1989), pp. 84–94; Peters and Waterman loc. cit.; "Getting Smart," *Wall Street Journal*, 16 September, 1986.
29. John Child, "Managerial and Organizational Factors Associated with Company Performance—Part II: A Contingency Analysis," *Journal of Management Studies* (February 1975), pp. 12–27.
30. For a review of the research, see Louis W. Fry, "Technology-Structure Research: Three Critical Issues," *Academy of Management Journal* (September 1982), pp. 532–552.
31. David F. Gillespie and Dennis S. Mileti, "Technology and the Study of Organizations: An Overview and Appraisal," *Academy of Management Review* (January 1977), p. 8.
32. For example, see Gareth Jones, "Task Visibility, Free Riding and Shirking: Explaining the Effect of Structure and Technology on Employee Behavior," *Academy of Management Review* (October 1984), pp. 684–695; and Nancy M. Carter, "Computerization as a Predominant Technology: Its Influence on the Structure of Newspaper Organizations," *Academy of Management Journal* (June 1984), pp. 247–270.
33. For a theory of the impact of information technology on organizational design see George P. Huber, "A Theory of the Effects of Advanced Information Technology on Organizational Design, Intelligence and Decision Making," *Academy of Management Review*, January 1990, pp. 47–71. Charles Perrow, *Complex Organizations: A Critical Essay*, 2nd. ed. (Glenview, IL: Scott, Foresman & Co., 1979).
34. Joan Woodward, *Industrial Organization: Theory and Practice* (London: Oxford University Press, 1965).
35. Ibid., p. 35.
36. For a review of the literature on technology and its methodological problems, see Lewis W. Fry, "Technology—Structure Research: Three Critical Issues," *Academy of Management Journal* (September 1982), pp. 532–552.
37. Lyman W. Porter, Edward E. Lawler, III, and Jay Richard Hackman, *Behavior in Organizations* (New York: McGraw-Hill, 1975), pp. 232–243.
38. For example, see D. S. Pugh, D. J. Hickson, C. R. Hinings, K. M. MacDonald, C. Turner, and T. Lupton, "A Conceptual Scheme for Organizational Analysis," *Administrative Science Quarterly* (June 1963), pp. 291–315; D. S. Pugh, D. J. Hickson, C. R. Hinings, and C. Turner, "The Context of Organizational Structures," *Administrative Science Quarterly* (1969), pp. 91–113.
39. Peter Drucker, "New Templates for Today's Organization," *Harvard Business Review* (January–February 1974), p. 51.
40. Thomas A. Stewart, "Westinghouse Gets Respect at Last," *Fortune* (July 3, 1989), pp. 92–98.
41. For a review of the literature, see Robert I. Sutton and Thomas D'Aunno, "Decreasing Organizational Size: Untangling the Effects of Money and People," *Academy of Management Review* (April 1989), pp. 192–212.
42. Richard Pascale, presentation to the Strategic Management Society, Boston, October 14, 1987.
43. Peter F. Drucker, "The Coming of the New Organization," *Harvard Business Review* (January–February, 1988), pp. 45–53.
44. Stanley Davis, presentation to the Strategic Management Society, Boston, October 15, 1987.
45. Sang M. Lee, Fred Luthans, and Davis L. Olson, "A Management Science Approach to Contingency Models of Organizational Structure," *Academy of Management Journal* (September 1982), pp. 553–566; W. Alan Randolph and Gregory G. Dess, "The Congruence Perspective of Organization Design: A Conceptual Model and Multivariate Research Approach," *Academy of Management Review* (January 1984), pp. 114–127.

CHAPTER TEN

1. David F. Smith, "The Functions of Work," *Omega* (1975) no. 4, pp. 383–393.
2. For example, see Frederick W. Herzberg, "One More Time—How Do You Motivate People?" *Harvard Business Review* (January–February 1968), pp. 53–62.
3. James M. Higgins, *Human Relations: Behavior at Work* (New York: Random House, 1987), pp. 298–299.
4. J. Richard Hackman and Greg R. Oldham, *Work Redesigned* (Reading, Mass.: Addison-Wesley, 1980), pp. 77–80.
5. See for example: Henry P. Sims, Jr., Andrew D. Szilagyi, and Robert T. Keller, "The Measurement of Job Characteristics," *Academy of Management Journal* (June 1976), p. 197; and Higgins, op. cit., Chapter 12 for a review.
6. Japan's labor price advantage is actually slipping in many industries and is now virtually gone in the auto industry.
7. Douglas R. Sease, "Getting Smart: How U.S. Companies Devise Ways to Meet Challenge from Japan," *Wall Street Journal* 16 September, 1986, pp. 1, 25.
8. Some feel that performance leads to satisfaction. Others feel that rewards lead to satisfaction and performance. Others believe that satisfaction and performance are reciprocally causal. For a review of the literature, see the collection of studies reported in Frederick W. Herzberg, *The Managerial Choice: To Be Efficient and to Be Human* (Homewood, Ill.: Dow Jones-Irwin, 1976). For criticisms, see Robert J. House and Lawrence A. Wigdor, "Herzberg's Dual-Factor Theory of Job Satisfaction and Motivation: A Review of the Evidence and a Criticism," *Personnel Psychology* (Winter 1967), pp. 369–389; Steven Kerr, Anne Harlan, and Ralph Stogdill, "Preference for Motivator and Hygiene Factors in a Hypothetical Interview Situation," *Personnel Psychology* (Winter 1974), pp. 109–124; Benedict Grigaliunas and Yoash Wiener, "Has the Research Challenge to Motivation-Hygiene Theory Been Conclusive? An Analysis of Critical Studies," *Human Relations* (1974), vol. 27, pp. 839–871; Charles N. Greene, "The Satisfaction-Performance Controversy," *Business Horizons* (October 1972), pp. 31–41; Charles N. Greene and Robert E. Craft, Jr., "The Satisfaction-Performance Controversy Revisited," in Kirk Downey, Don Hellriegel, and John Slocum, eds., *Organizational Behavior: A Reader* (St. Paul, Minn.: West, 1977), pp. 187–201; Arthur H. Brayfield and Walter H. Crockett, "Employee Attitudes and Employee Performance," *Psychological Bulletin* (1955), vol. 52, pp. 415–422; Donald P. Schwab and Larry L. Cummings, "Theories of Performance and Satisfaction," *Industrial Relations*, 1970, No. 4, pp. 408–430; and Victor H. Vroom, *Work and Motivation* (New York: Wiley, 1964).
9. See footnote 8.
10. Richard E. Kopelman, "Job Redesign and Productivity: A Review of the Evidence," *National Productivity Review* (Summer 1985), p. 239.
11. Richard E. Walton, "Quality of Work Life: What Is It?" *Sloan Management Review* (Fall 1973), pp. 11–21.
12. Vida Scarpello and John P. Campbell, "Job Satisfaction and the Fit Between Individual Needs and Organizational Rewards," *Journal of Occupational Psychology* (1983), pp. 315–328.
13. Chris Argyris, *Personality and Organization* (New York: Harper, 1957).
14. Douglas McGregor, *The Human Side of Enterprise* (New York: McGraw-Hill, 1960).
15. Frederick W. Herzberg, *Work and the Nature of Man* (New York: World), 1971.
16. Gene Bylinsky, "America's Best-Managed Factories," *Fortune* (May 28, 1984), pp. 16–27.
17. "Job Rotation Keeps Swissair Flying High," *Management Review* (August 1985), p. 10.
18. Harry C. Katz, Thomas A. Kochan, and Mark R. Weber, "Assessing the Effects of Industrial Relations Systems and Efforts to Improve the Quality of Working Life on Organizational Effectiveness," *Academy of Management Journal* (September 1985), pp. 514–515; and Lawrence Miller, "The Impact of Unity: Tearing Down the Barriers Between Management and Labor Leads to Increased Productivity and Greater Profits," *Management Review* (May 1984), pp. 8–15.
19. Lori Fitzgerald and Joseph Murphy, *Installing Quality Circles: A Strategic Approach* (San Diego: University Associates, 1982), p. 3.
20. Robert Wood, Frank Hoe, and Koya Azuni, "Evaluating Quality Circles: The American Application," *California Management Review* (Fall 1983), p. 43.
21. Frederick W. Herzberg, "The Wise Old Truck," *Harvard Business Review* (September–October 1974), pp. 70–80.
22. Kae H. Chung and Monica F. Ross, "Differences in Motivational Properties Between Job Enlargement and Job Enrichment," *Academy of Management Review* (January 1977), pp. 113–122.
23. Ibid.
24. Ibid.
25. Richard M. Roderick, "Redesigning an Ac-

counting Department for Corporate and Personal Goals," *Management Accounting* (February 1984), pp. 56–60.

26. David C. McClelland, *Human Motivation* (Glenview, Ill.: Scott, Foresman, 1989); and David C. McClelland, *The Achieving Society* (Princeton, N.J.: Van Nostrand, 1961).

27. Carey W. English, "Now It's Bosses Who Are Giving the Orders Again," *U.S. News & World Report* (February 11, 1985), pp 84–85; and "A Work Revolution in U.S. Industry," *Business Week* (May 16, 1983), pp. 100–110.

28. See J. K. White, "Individual Differences and the Job Quality–Worker Response Relationships: Review, Integration, Comments," *Academy of Management Review* (July 1978), pp. 267–280; Milton R. Blood and Charles L. Hulin, "Alienation, Environmental Characteristics and Worker Responses," *Journal of Applied Psychology* (1967), pp. 284–290; William T. Rutherford and James M. Higgins, "Democracy at Work or Only Away from Work?" *Atlanta Economic Review* (November–December 1974), p. 8; and William E. Reif and Fred Luthans, "Does Job Enrichment Really Pay Off?" *California Management Review* (Fall 1972), pp. 30–37.

29. Barbara Carson in *Wall Street Journal*.

30. Bernard J. White, "The Criteria for Job Satisfaction: Is Interesting Work Most Important?" *Monthly Labor Review* (May 1977), pp. 30–35.

31. William J. Hampton and James R. Norman, "General Motors: What Went Wrong," *Business Week* (March 16, 1987), pp. 106–107.

32. Adapted from Robert N. Ford, "Job Enrichment Lessons from AT&T," *Harvard Business Review* (January–February 1973), pp. 96–106.

33. Pradip M. Khandwalla, "Mass Output Orientation of Operations Technology and Organizational Structure," *Administrative Science Quarterly* (March 1974), p. 74.

34. E. Mesthene, *Technological Change: Its Impact on Man in Society* (Cambridge: Harvard University Press, 1970); also see David F. Gillespie and Dennis F. Galletti, "Technology and Study of Organizations: An Overview and Appraisal," *Academy of Management Review* (January 1977), p. 8.

35. Jon L. Pieru, "Job Design and Technology: A Sociotechnical Systems Perspective," *Journal of Occupational Behavior* (April 1984), pp. 147–154.

36. "High Tech: Blessing Occurs," *U.S. News & World Report* (January 16, 1984), p. 38.

37. "Factory Toils into Night Without People," *Orlando Sentinel* 22 December, 1985, p. F10.

38. Hampton and Norman, op. cit., p. 107.

39. "Where Robots Can't Yet Compete," *Fortune* (February 21, 1983), p. 64. Harlan S. Byrne, "Briggs & Stratton: Small-Engine Maker Revving Up for Recovery," *Barron's*, September 25, 1989, pp. 55–56; Phillip Burgert, "Briggs Build High Volume FMS," *Manufacturing Week*, March 7, 1988, pp. 1, 24.

40. "High Tech," op. cit., p. 43.

41. Carol Hymowitz, "Manufacturing Change: Automation Experts Explore the Promise and Problems of the Factory of the Future," *Wall Street Journal Special Report on Technology in the Workplace*, 16 September, 1985, pp. 10c, 13c; and Dale D. Buss, "Winners and Losers: On the Factory Floor, Technology Brings Challenge for Some, Drudgery for Others," *Wall Street Journal Special Report on Technology in the Workplace*," 16 September, 1985, pp. 16c, 20c.

42. Brenton R. Schlender, "New Software Beginning to Unlock the Power of Personal Computers," *Wall Street Journal* 16 November, 1987, p. 33.

43. Dennis Kenale, "Computer Caution: Linking of PCs Is Coming, but Plenty of Obstacles Remain," *Wall Street Journal* 28 January, 1986, pp. 1, 22.

44. For example, see "Computer Nut: How Personal Computers Change Managers' Lives," *Fortune* (September 3, 1984), p. 38.

45. James M. Higgins, *Escape from the Maze*, unpublished manuscript, chap. 1.

46. Michael W. Miller, "Computers Keep an Eye on Workers to See If They Perform Well," *Wall Street Journal* 3 June, 1985, pp. 1, 16.

47. "Office Automation Restructures Business," *Business Week* (October 8, 1984), pp. 118–125.

48. Timothy K. Smith, "Electronic Control of Households Arrive with Advantages," *Wall Street Journal* 11 November, 1985, p. 27; and Robert Johnson, "Rush to Cottage Computer Work Falters Despite Advent of New Technology," *Wall Street Journal* 29 June, 1983, pp. 37, 42.

49. Part of this increasing expectation is due to the fact that people are now better educated. In 1970 one in seven adult workers had a college degree; in 1985 nearly one in four adult workers had completed college. *Monthly Labor Review* (February 1985), p. 43.

50. For example, see Michael Brody, "Meet Today's Young American Worker," *Fortune* (November 11, 1985, pp. 90–98; "The New-Collar Blues," *U.S. News & World Report* (September 16, 1985), pp. 59–65.

51. Howard Hayghe, "Working Mothers Reach Record Numbers in 1984," *Monthly Labor Review* (December 1984), p. 31.

52. *Business Week* (January 28, 1985), p. 80.

53. Robert W. Goddard, "Work Force 2000," *Personnel Journal* (February 1989), pp. 64–71.

54. L. B. Russell, "The Baby Boom Generation and the Economy" (Washington, D.C.: Brookings Institution, 1982).

55. Daniel Yankelovich and Jay Immerwahr, *Putting the New Work Ethics to Work* (New York: Public Agenda Foundation, September 1983); and Daniel Yankelovich, "Work, Values, and the New Breed," in C. Kerr and J. M. Roson eds., *Work in America: The Decade Ahead* (New York: Van Nostrand, 1979), pp. 3–26.

56. As quoted by John Naisbitt, *Megatrends* (New York: Warner, 1982), p. 184.

57. Simcha Ronen, *Flexible Working Hours: An Innovation in the Quality of Work Life* (New York: McGraw-Hill, 1981); and Allan R. Cohen, and Herman A. Gadon, *Alternative Work Schedules: Integrating Individual and Organizational Needs* (Reading, Mass.: Addison-Wesley, 1978).

58. Michael A. Pollock and Erin Berstein, "The Disposable Employee Is Becoming a Fact of Corporate Life," *Business Week* (December 15, 1986), pp. 52–56.

59. Simcha Ronen and Sophia B. Primps, "The Compressed Work Week as Organizational Change: Behavioral and Attitudinal Outcomes," *Academy of Management Review* (January 1981), pp. 61–74.

60. John M. Ivancevich and Herbert C. Lyons, "The Shortened Work Week: A Field Experiment," *Journal of Applied Psychology* (February, 1977), pp. 34–37.

61. David Clutterbuck, "Why a Job Shared Is Not a Job Halved," *International Management* (October 1979), pp. 45–47; and Michael Frease and Robert A. Zawacki, "Job Sharing: An Answer to Productivity Problems," *The Personnel Administrator* (October 1979), pp. 35–38.

CHAPTER ELEVEN

1. Randall S. Schuler, Steven P. Galiente, and Susan E. Jackson, "Matching Effective Human Resource Practices with Competitive Strategy," *Personnel* (September 1987), pp. 18–27.

2. Thomas A. Mahoney and John R. Deckop, "Evolution of Concept and Practice in Personnel Administration/Human Resource Management (PA/HRM)," in James G. Hunt and John D. Blair, eds., *1986 Yearly Review of Management of The Journal of Management* (Summer 1986), pp. 223–242.

3. For a review of this issue, see Cynthia A.

Lengneck-Hall and Mark L. Lengneck-Hall, "Strategic Human Resources Management: A Review of the Literature and a Proposed Typology," *Academy of Management Review* (July 1988), pp. 454–470.

4. For example, see Stephen Wermeil, "High Court's Affirmative Action Milestones," *Wall Street Journal* 26 March, 1987, p. 3.

5. Roger Ricklefs, "Faced with Shortages of Unskilled Labor, Employers Hire More Retired Workers," *Wall Street Journal* 21 October, 1986, p. 39.

6. Mark A. Jones, "Job Descriptions Made Easy," *Personnel Journal* (May 1984), pp. 31–34.

7. *Dictionary of Occupational Titles*, 4th ed., U.S. Department of Labor, Washington D.C., 1977.

8. Frederick W. Herzberg, B. Mausner, and B. Snyderman, *Motivation to Work* (New York: Wiley, 1959).

9. J. Richard Hackman and R. G. Oldham, "Motivation Through Design of Work: Test of a Theory," *Organizational Behavior and Human Performance* (August 1976), pp. 250–279.

10. Robert W. Goddhard, "Work Force 2000," *Personnel Journal* (February 1989), pp. 64–71; Martha E. Ingleshoff, "Managing the New Work Force," *Inc.*, January 1990, pp. 78–83.

11. Morton E. Grossman, "The Growing Dependence on HRIS," *Personnel Journal* (September 1988), pp. 53–58, reports that 40 percent of those who subscribe to *Personnel Journal* reported using such systems, and their use is growing.

12. George Milkavich, Lee Dyer, and Thomas Mahoney, *HRM Planning*, "Human Resources in the 1980s," in Steven J. Caroll and Randall S. Schuer, eds. (Washington, D.C., Bureau of National Affairs, 1983), pp. 21–29.

13. Author's conversations with senior Disney human resource managers.

14. Ann Coil, "Job Matching Brings Out the Best in Employees," *Personnel Journal* (January 1984), pp. 61–64.

15. Donn L. Dennis, "Are Recruitment Efforts Designed to Fail?" *Personnel Journal* (September 1984), pp. 60–67.

16. E. D. Pursell, M. A. Campion, and S. R. Gaylord, "Structured Inverviewing: Avoiding Selection Problems," *Personnel Journal* (November 1980), pp. 904–912.

17. For a review see William L. Donoghy, *The Interview: Skills and Applications* (Glenview, Ill.: Scott, Foresman, 1984).

18. Schermerhorn, p. 251. Schermerhorn material is from the *ASPA Handbook of Personnel and Industrial Relations*, Dale Yoder and Herbert G. Henneman, eds., vol. 1 (Washington D.C., Bureau of National Affairs, 1974), pp. 152–154.

19. *Principles for the Validation and Use of Personnel Selection Procedures* (Berkeley, Calif.: Division of Industrial Psychology, American Psychological Association, 1986).

20. Robert M. Guion, *Personnel Testing* (New York: McGraw-Hill, 1965), pp. 29–31.

21. "Privacy," *Business Week* (March 28, 1988), pp. 61–68.

22. "A Special News Report on People and Their Jobs and Offices, Field and Factories Reference Checking," *Wall Street Journal* 5 May, 1987, p. 1.

23. Author's conversation with former personnel director for a large paper manufacturer.

24. Harvey MacKay, "Swim with the Sharks," *Success* (April 1988), p. 62.

25. J. P. Wanous, *Organizational Entry* (Reading, Mass.: Addison-Wesley, 1980), pp. 21–84; G. M. McEvoy and W. F. Cascio, "Strategies for Reducing Employee Turnover: A Meta-Analysis," *Journal of Applied Psychology* (1985), pp. 342–353; J. A. Breaugh, "Realistic Job Previews: A Critical Appraisal and Future Research Directions," *Academy of Management Review* (1983), pp. 612–619; S. L. Premack and J. P. Wanous, "A

Meta-Analysis of Realistic Job Preview Experiments," *Journal of Applied Psychology* (1985), pp. 706–718.

26. W. D. St. John, "The Complete Employee Orientation Program," *Personnel Journal* (May 1980), pp. 376–377.

27. See Harry B. Bernhard and Cynthia A. Ingols, "Six Lessons for the Corporate Classroom," *Harvard Business Review* (September–October 1988), pp. 40–48.

28. Bernhard and Ingols, op. cit.

29. Amanda Bennett, "Company School: As Pool of Skilled Help Tightens, Firms Move to Broaden Their Role," *Wall Street Journal* 8 May, 1989, pp. A1, A4; Janice C. Simpson, "Firm Steps: A Shallow Labor Pool Spurs Businesses to Act to Bolster Education," *Wall Street Journal* 28 September, 1987, pp. 1, 26.

30. Ricklefs, loc. cit.

31. Constance Mitchell, "Corporate Classes: Firms Broaden Scope of Their Education Programs," *Wall Street Journal* 28 September, 1987, p. a37.

32. "How Japan Inc. Profits from Our Low Labor Turnover," *Business Week* (November 7, 1987), p. 24.

33. Randy Ross, "Technology Tackles the Training Dilemma," *High Technology Business* (September 1988), pp. 18–23.

34. For a review of management development trends, see Bernard Keys and Joseph Wolfe, "Management Education and Development: Current Issues and Emerging Trends," *Journal of Management* (1988), no. 2, pp. 205–229.

35. Randall S. Schuler, "Matching Effective Human Resource Practices with Competitive Strategy," *Personnel* (September 1987), pp. 18–27; and Douglas T. Hall, "Human Resource Development and Organizational Effectiveness," ed. in Charles J. Fombrum, Noel M. Tichy, and Mary Ann Devanna, *Strategic Human Resource Management* (New York: Wiley, 1984), chap. 11.

36. "Schooling for Survival," *Time* (February 11, 1985), pp. 74–75

37. For a further discussion, see Lloyd L. Byars and Leslie W. Rue, *Human Resource and Personnel Management* (Homewood, Ill.: Irwin, 1987), chaps. 10, 11.

38. Morton E. Grossman and Margaret Magnus, "The Boom in Benefits," *Personnel Journal* (November 1988), pp. 50–55.

39. Ibid.

40. Bruce G. Posner, "Preventive Medicine," *Inc.* (March 1989), p. 131.

41. Douglas C. Harper, "Control Health Care Costs," *Personnel Journal* (October 1988), pp. 65–70; and "Benefits Shock," *U.S. News & World Report* (March 28, 1988), pp. 57–74.

42. Richard E. Johnson and Susan J. Velleman, "Section 89: Close the New Pandora's Box," *Personnel Journal* (November 1988), pp. 70–76.

43. Aaron Bernstein, "Comparable Worth: It's Already Happening," *Business Week* (April 28, 1986), pp. 52–54; and Cathy Trost, "Pay Equity, Born in Public Sector, Emerges as an Issue in Private Firms," *Wall Street Journal* 8 July, 1985, p. 15.

44. Bernstein, op. cit., p. 52.

45. D. J. Fellner and B. Sulzer-Azaroff, "Increasing Industrial Safety Practices and Conditions Through Personal Feedback," *Journal of Safety Research* (1984), January, pp. 7–21; R. S. Haynes, R. C. Pine, and H. G. Fitch, "Reducing Accident Rates with Organizational Behavior Modification," *Academy of Management Journal* (1982), vol. 25, pp. 407–416; R. A. Weber, J. A. Wallin, and J. S. Chokar, "Reducing Industrial Accidents: A Behavioral Experiment," *Industry Relations* (1984), vol. 23, pp. 119–125; J. Komaki, K. D. Farwick, and L. R. Scott, "The Behavioral Approach to Occupational Safety: Pinpointing and Reinforcing the Safe Performance in Food Manufacturing Plants," *Journal of Applied Psychology* (1978), vol. 63, pp. 434–435.

46. Clare Ansberry, "Risky Business: Workplace Injuries Proliferate as Concerns Push People to Produce," *Wall Street Journal* 16 June, 1989, pp. A1, A8.

47. John M. Ivancevich, Michael T. Matteson, and Edward Richards III, "Who's Liable for Stress on the Job?" *Harvard Business Review* March/April 1989; "Stress Claims are Making Business Jumpy," *Business Week*, October 14, 1985, pp. 152–153.

48. A. J. Brennan, "Worksite Health Promotion Can be Cost Effective," *Personnel Administrator* (1983), vol. 28, no. 4, pp. 39–46; and J. J. Hoffman, Jr., and C. J. Hobson, "Physical Fitness and Employee Effectiveness," *Personnel Administrator* (1984), vol. 29, no. 4, pp. 101–114.

49. "Coors Ends Lie-Detector Tests for Job Seekers, But Added Drug Testing," Labor Letter, *Wall Street Journal* 16 September, 1986, p. 1; and Ted Gest, "Using Drugs? You May Not Get Hired," *U.S. News & World Report* (December 23, 1985), p. 38.

50. For a review of major issues, see "Privacy," *Business Week* (March 28, 1988), pp. 61–68.

51. Janice Castro, "Battling Drugs on the Job," *Time* (January 27, 1986), p. 43.

52. Prakash Gandhi, "Blood Goes into Building Florida," *Orlando Sentinel* (November 22, 1987), pp. A-1, A-8.

53. For a review of the issues, see Herbert G. Heneman III, Donald P. Schwab, John A. Fossum, and Lee P. Dyer, *Personnel/Human Resource Management*, 4th ed. (Homewood, Ill.: Irwin, 1989), pp. 77–78.

54. James M. Schlesinger, "Going Local: Plant-Level Talks Rise Quickly in Importance; Big Issue: Work Rules," *Wall Street Journal* 16 March, 1987, pp. 1, 15; Clemons P. Work, "Making It Clear Who's Boss," *U.S. News & World Report* (September 8, 1986), pp. 43, 45; David Kirkpatrick, "What Givebacks Can Get You," *Fortune* (November 24, 1986), pp. 60–72; and Cathy Trost, "New-Collar Jobs: Unions Court People in Service-Type Work to Stem Fall in Ranks," *Wall Street Journal* 19 September, 1986, pp. 1, 19.

55. Richard T. Pascale, "Fitting New Employees into the Company's Culture," *Fortune* (May 28, 1984), pp. 28–42.

56. Wendell L. French and Cecil H. Bell, Jr., *Organizational Development: Behavioral Science Interventions for Organizational Improvement* (Englewood Cliffs, N.J.: Prentice-Hall), 1973, p. 15.

57. Author's conversation with Barry Morris, a member of Anheuser-Busch's internal organizational development consulting group.

58. The court held in *Brito* v. *Zia.*

59. "White People, Black People, Not Wanted Here?" *Business Week* (July 10, 1989), p. 31.

60. David Balkin and Luis Gomez-Mejia, *New Perspective on Compensation* (Englewood Cliffs, N.J.: Prentice-Hall, 1987).

61. Author's discussion with Disney managers.

62. Andrew L. Abrams and Gary L. Tidwell, "Affirmative Action," *Business & Economic Review*, October–December 1989, pp. 27–29.

CHAPTER TWELVE

1. Andrew Kupfer, "Bob Allen Rattles the Cages at AT&T," *Fortune* (June 19, 1989), pp. 58–66.

2. Peter Petre, "What Welch Has Wrought at GE," *Fortune* (July 7, 1986), pp. 43–47; John A. Byrne, "Culture Shock at Xerox," *Business Week* (June 22, 1987), pp. 106–108; "Changing a Corporate Culture," *Business Week* (May 14, 1984), pp. 130–138; Thomas J. Peters, *Thriving on Chaos* (New York: Knopf, 1987); and Alvin Toffler, *Future Shock* (New York: Random House, 1970).

3. A number of definitions of culture exist. This one seems to be representative of the principal elements in most of them. For example, see

Ralph H. Kilmann, Mary J. Saxton, and Roy Serpa, "Issues in Understanding and Changing Culture," *California Management Review* (Winter 1986), pp. 87–94; and Robert H. Waterman, Jr., "The Seven Elements of Strategic Fit," *Journal of Business Strategy* (Winter 1982), pp. 69–73.

4. For example, see William G. Ouchi, *Theory Z: How American Business Can Meet the Japanese Challenge* (Reading, Mass.: Addison-Wesley, 1981); and Richard T. Pascale and Anthony Athos, *The Art of Japanese Management* (New York: Warner Books, 1981).

5. Paul Shrivastava, "Integrating Strategy Formulation with Organizational Culture," *Journal of Business Strategy* (Winter 1985), pp. 103–111.

6. James M. Cole, "Put On a Happy Face You Managers," *Wall Street Journal* 15 October, 1984, p. 471; and Mary Kay Ash, *Mary Kay on People Management* (New York: Warner Books, 1984).

7. Russell Mitchell, "Jack Welch: How Good a Manager," *Business Week* (December 14, 1987), pp. 92–103; Jack Eagen, "The GE Record," *U.S. News & World Report* (November 23, 1987), pp. 48–49; and Peter Petre, "What Welch Has Wrought at GE," *Fortune* (July 7, 1986), pp. 43–48.

8. Terrence E. Deal and Allan A. Kennedy, *Corporate Cultures: Rites and Rituals of Corporate Life* (Reading, Mass.: Addison-Wesley), 1982; and P. M. Hirsch and Jay Andrews, "Ambush and Shoot Outs of Knights of the Round Table, The Language of Corporate Takeovers," in L. R. Pondy, P. J. Fost, G. Morgan, and T. C. Dandridge, eds. *Organizational Symbolism* (Greenwich, Conn.: JAI Press), pp. 145–146.

9. For a sizeable review of the entire topic of organizational symbolism, see Peter J. Foust, ed., *Organizational Symbolism*, A Special Issue of the *Journal of Management* (Summer 1985).

10. Walter Kiechel, III, "Celebrating a Corporate Triumph," *Fortune* (August 20, 1984), p. 259.

11. Betsy Morris, "RJR Plans to Leave Winston-Salem, North Carolina; Move to Atlanta Reflects Nabisco's Influence," *Wall Street Journal* 12 January, 1987, p. 6.

12. "In Search of Excellence," the film, available from Tom Peters Group Inc., Palo Alto, CA.

13. Robert Hershey, "Corporate Mottos: What They Are, What They Do," *Personnel* (February 1987), pp. 52–56.

14. Ibid., p. 53.

15. Ibid., p. 55.

16. Ford television advertisement, January 8, 1988.

17. For a discussion of how to compete on the basis of quality, see David A. Garvin, "Competing on the Eight Dimensions of Quality," *Harvard Business Review* (November–December, 1987), pp. 101–109; and Peters, loc. cit.

18. John Huey, "Empire Builders: Trammel Crow Company Flourishes by Fostering Risk-Reward Culture," *Wall Street Journal* 27 March, 1986, pp. 1, 21.

19. J. B. Barney, "Organizational Culture: Can It Be a Source of Sustained Competitive Advantage?" *Academy of Management Review* (July 1986), pp. 656–665; "Corporate Culture: The Hard to Change Values That Spell Success or Failure," *Business Week* (October 27, 1980), pp. 148–160; Thomas J. Peters and Robert H. Waterman, Jr., *In Search of Excellence* (New York: Harper & Row, 1982); Deal and Kennedy, loc. cit.; and Noel Tischy, *Managing Strategic Change: Technical, Political, and Cultural Dynamics* (New York: Wiley, 1983).

20. Ralph H. Kilmann, "Corporate Culture," *Psychology Today*, April 1985, pp. 62–65.

21. Deal and Kennedy, op. cit., pp.107–108. For additional typologies see: Bernard C. Reimann and Yoash Wiener, "Corporate Culture: Avoiding the Elitist Trap," *Business Horizons*, March–April, 1988, pp. 36–44; and Carol Hymowitz, "Which Corporate Culture Fits You?" *Wall Street Journal*, 17 July, 1989, p. B1.

22. Kenneth Labich, "Boeing Battles to Stay on Top," *Fortune* (September 28, 1987), pp. 64–72.

23. Joan O. C. Hamilton, "Biotech's First Superstar," *Business Week* (April 14, 1986), pp. 68–72.

24. IBM internal documents.

25. Company documents. Louis Kraar, "Roy Ash Is Having Fun at Addressogrief/Multigrief," *Fortune* (February 27, 1978), pp. 47–52; and Thomas J. Peters, "Symbols, Patterns, and Settings: Optimistic Case for Getting Things Done," *Organizational Dynamics* (Autumn 1978), pp. 3–23.

26. David E. Whiteside, "Roger Smith's Campaign to Change the GM Culture," *Business Week* (April 7, 1986), pp. 84–85.

27. Reported to the author by a recent recruit.

28. Richard T. Pascale, "Fitting New Employees into the Company Culture," *Fortune* (May 20, 1984), pp. 28–42; and Richard T. Pascale, "The Paradox of Corporate Culture: Reconciling Ourselves to Socialization," *California Management Review* (Winter 1985), pp. 26–41.

29. Dr. David Boles, senior vice-president the Hay Group, Los Angeles. Quoted in "Tailoring Culture to Fit the Times," *Electric World* (February 1987), p. 29.

30. W. Jack Duncan, "Organizational Culture: 'Getting a Fix' On an Elusive Concept," *Academy of Management Executive* (August 1989), pp. 229–236; and K. L. Gregory, "Native-View Paradigms: Multiple Cultures and Culture Conflicts in Organizations," *Administrative Science Quarterly* (September 1983), pp. 359–376.

31. Jolie Solomon, "Firms Address Workers' Cultural Variety: The Differences Celebrated, Not Suppressed," *Wall Street Journal* 10 February, 1989, p. B-1.

32. Robert W. Goddard, "Work Force 2000," *Personnel Journal* (February 1989), pp. 64–71; Stephen L. Guinn, "The Changing Work Force," *Training & Development Journal*, December 1989, pp. 36–39.

33. Barbara Walker, DEC's director of its cultural diversity program, presentation to the Academy of Management, Washington, D.C., August 13, 1989.

34. Robert C. Maddox and Douglas Short, "The Cultural Integrator," *Business Horizons* (November–December 1988), pp. 57–59.

35. K. L. Gregory, "Native-View Paradigms: Multiple Cultures and Culture Conflicts in Organizations," *Administrative Science Quarterly* (September 1983), pp. 359–376.

36. William J. Cook, "Perot's War with GM Ends in $743 Million Goodbye," *U.S. News and World Report* (December 15, 1986), pp. 52–53; and "How Ross Perot's Shock Troops Ran into Flack at GM," *Business Week* (February 11, 1985), pp. 118–119.

37. For a further discussion, see James M. Higgins, *Human Relations: Behavior at Work*, 2nd ed. (New York: Random House, 1987), pp. 332–334.

38. Rensis Likert, *New Patterns of Management* (New York: McGraw-Hill, 1961); Keith Davis, *Human Behavior at Work*, 5th ed. (New York: McGraw-Hill, 1977); George H. Litwin and Robert A. Stringer, Jr., *Motivation and Organizational Climate* (Boston: Division of Research, Graduate School of Business Administration, Harvard University, 1968); Garlie A. Forehand and B. Von Haller Gilmer, "Environmental Variation and Studies of Organizational Behavior," *Psychological Bulletin* (December 1964), pp. 361–382; and Andrew W. Halpin and D. B. Crofts, *The Organizational Climate of Schools* (Washington, D.C.: U.S. Department of Health, Education, and Welfare, July 1962).

39. William K. Dowling, "System Four Builds Performance and Products," *Organizational Dynamics* (Winter 1975), pp. 23–38.

40. Alvin Toffler, *Future Shock* (New York: Random House, 1970).

41. Thomas J. Peters, *Thriving on Chaos: Handbook for a Management Revolution* (New York: Knopf, 1987).

42. For a lengthy review of definitions and related conceptual issues, see Donald F. Harvey and Donald R. Brown, *An Experiential Approach to Organizational Development*, 2nd ed. (Englewood Cliffs, N.J.: Prentice-Hall, 1982), pp. 72–73; and Wendell L. French, Cecil H. Bell, Jr., and Robert A. Zowacki, *Organization Development: Theory, Practice, and Research* (Plano, Tex.: BPI, 1983), pp. 6–9.

43. Wendell L. French and Cecil H. Bell, Jr., *Organizational Development: Behavioral Science Interventions for Organization Improvement* (Englewood Cliffs, N.J.: Prentice-Hall, 1973), p. 15.

44. Author's conversation with one of the internal OD consultants at Anheuser-Busch.

45. Theodore Levitt, "In This Issue," *Harvard Business Review* (January–February 1988).

46. Kurt Lewin, *Field, Theory, and Social Science: Selected Theoretical Papers* (New York: Harper & Row, 1951).

47. Author's consultation with managers in this division.

48. Kurt Lewin, "Frontiers in Group Dynamics: Concept, Method, and Reality in Social Science," *Human Relations* (1947), pp. 5–41; Edgar H. Scheim, *Organizational Psychology*, 3rd ed. (Englewood Cliffs, N.J.: Prentice-Hall, 1980), pp. 243–247; and Edgar F. Huse and Thomas G. Cummings, *Organizational Development and Change*, 3rd ed. (St. Paul, Minn.: West Publishing, 1985), p. 20.

49. Paul R. Lawrence and L. R. Greiner, "How to Deal With Resistance to Change," in G. W. Dalton, Paul R. Lawrence, and L. R. Greiner, *Organizational Change and Development* (Homewood, Ill.: Irwin, 1970), pp. 189–197.

50. Lester Coch and John R. P. French, Jr., "Overcoming Resistance to Change," *Human Relations* (1948), pp. 512–532.

CHAPTER THIRTEEN

1. Terence R. Mitchell, "Motivation: New Directions for Theory, Research and Practice," *Academy of Management Review* (January 1982), pp. 80–88.

2. Lyman W. Porter and Edward E. Lawler, III, *Managerial Attitudes and Performance* (Homewood, Ill.: Irwin, 1968).

3. Based loosely on the integrative efforts discussed in Richard M. Steers and Lyman W. Porter, eds., *Motivation and Work Behavior*, 3rd ed. (New York: McGraw-Hill, 1983); John P. Campbell, Marvin D. Durnette, Edward E. Lawler, III, and Karl E. Weick, *Managerial Behavior, Performance and Effectiveness*, (New York: McGraw-Hill, 1970); Martin G. Evans, "Organizational Behavior: The Central Role of Motivation," *1986 Yearly Review of Management, The Journal of Management* (Summer 1986), pp. 203–222; the review in John B. Miner and H. Peter Dachler, "Personnel Attitudes and Motivation," *Annual Review of Psychology*, vol. 54, no. 1 (1970), pp. 31–41; and those cited subsequently, but especially Abraham Maslow, Victor H. Vroom, Terence R. Mitchell, J. Stacy Adams, E. L. Thorndike, B. F. Skinner, Edwin A. Locke, and A. Bandura. For a theoretical model based on control theory see, Howard J. Klein, "An Integrated Control Theory Model of Work Motivation," *Academy of Management Review*, April 1989, pp. 150–172.

4. Abraham H. Maslow, *Motivation and Personality*, 2nd ed. (New York: Harper & Row, 1970).

5. Mahmoud A. Wahba and Lawrence G. Bidwell, "Maslow Reconsidered: A Review of the Research on the Need Hierarchy Theory," *Organizational Behavior and Human Performance*, vol. 15 (1976), pp. 212–240.

6. Edwin C. Nevis, "Cultural Assumptions and Productivity: The United States and China," *Sloan Management Review* (Spring 1983), pp. 20–28.

7. Clayton P. Alderfer, *Existence, Relatedness, and Growth* (New York: Free Press, 1972); Clayton P. Alderfer and Richard Grizzo, "Life Expectancies and Adults' Enduring Strengths of Desires in Organizations," *Administrative Science Quarterly* (September 1979), pp. 347–361; John P. Wanovs and Abram Zwanis, "A Cross Sectional Test of Need Hierarchy Theory," *Organizational Behavior and Human Performance* (February 1977), pp. 78–97.

8. "Motivation 101 at Merrill Lynch," *Wall Street Journal* 14 June, 1984, p. 33.

9. David C. McClelland, *Human Motivation* (Glenview, Ill.: Scott, Foresman, 1985); David C. McClelland, *The Achieving Society* (Princeton, N.J.: Van Nostrand, 1961); John W. Atkinson and David Birch, *An Introduction to Motivation*, rev. ed. (New York: Van Nostrand Reinhold, 1978); and David C. McClelland, *The Achievement Motive* (New York: Appleton-Century Crofts, 1953).

10. David C. McClelland, "Power Is a Great Motivator," *Harvard Business Review* (March–April 1976), pp. 100–110.

11. "For Gorbachev, Perestroika II May Mean Survival," *Business Week* (September 25, 1989), pp. 60–62; and "The Risks of a New Revolution," *U.S. News & World Report* (October 19, 1987), pp. 31–58.

12. For a review of recent research, see Martin L. Maehr and Larry A. Braskamp, *The Motivation Factor: A Theory of Personal Investment* (Lexington, Mass.: Lexington Books, 1986), pp. 18–26.

13. Charles A. Garfield, *Peak Performance*, and Richard Trubo, "Peak Performance," *Success* (April 1983), pp. 30–33, 56.

14. John B. Miner, *Studies in Management Education* (Atlanta: Organizational Management Systems Press, 1975).

15. Maslow, op. cit., p. 51.

16. For example, see Robert Waterman, Jr., "The Pygmalion Effect," *Success* (October 1988), p. 8; Dov Eden, "Self-Fulfilling Prophecy as a Management Tool: Harnessing Pygmalion," *Academy of Management Review*, January 1984, pp. 67–73; and J. Sterling Livingston, "Pygmalion in Management," *Harvard Business Review* (July–August 1969).

17. For a review of how setting objectives is motivating, see Edwin A. Locke and Gary P. Latham, *Goal Setting: A Motivational Technique That Works* (Englewood Cliffs, N.J.: Prentice-Hall, 1984).

18. Maslow, op. cit., p. 51.

19. Walter Kiechel, III, "How to Manage Salespeople," *Fortune* (March 14, 1988), pp. 179–180.

20. Kenneth A. Kovach, "What Motivates Employees? Workers and Supervisors Give Different Answers," *Business Horizons* (September–October 1987), pp. 58–65.

21. "Home Is Where the Heart Is," *Time* (October 3, 1988), pp. 46–53.

22. Frederick Herzberg, *Work and the Nature of Man* (New York: World, 1971); Frederick Herzberg, Bernard Mausner, and Barbara Snyderman, *The Motivation to Work* (New York: Wiley, 1959); and Frederick Herzberg, "One More Time: How Do You Motivate Employees?" *Harvard Business Review* (January–February 1968), pp. 53–62.

23. Robert J. House and Lawrence A. Wigdor, "Herzberg's Dual Factors Theory of Job Satisfaction, Motivation: A Review of the Evidence and a Criticism," *Personnel Psychology* (September 20, 1967), pp. 369–389; and Joseph Schneider and Edwin Locke, "A Critique of Herzberg's Classification System and a Suggested Revision," *Organizational Behavior and Human Performance* (July 1971), pp. 441–458.

24. Victor H. Vroom, *Work and Motivation* (New York: Wiley, 1965); Terence R. Mitchell, "Expectancy Models of Job Satisfaction, Occupa-

tional Preference, and Its Effort: The Theoretical, Methodological, and Empirical Appraisal," *Psychological Bulletin*, no. 79 (1974), pp. 1053–1075.

25. David A. Nadler and Edward E. Lawler, III, "Motivation: A Diagnostic Approach," in J. Richard Hackman, Edward E. Lawler, and Lyman W. Porter, eds. *Perspectives on Behavior in Organizations*, 2nd ed. (New York: McGraw-Hill, 1983), pp. 67–78.

26. For a review of how expectancy can be used with goal setting and Pygmalion, see Dov Eden, "Pygmalion, Goal Setting, and Expectancy: Compatible Ways to Boost Productivity," *Academy of Management Review* (October 1988), pp. 639–652.

27. Joseph R. Mancuso, "Go for the Goals," *Success* (February 1986), p. 14.

28. Ibid.

29. For a discussion of how to use the expectancy theory in a management system, see Thomas L. Quick, "Expectancy Theory in Five Single Steps," *Training and Development Journal* (July 1988), pp. 30–32.

30. J. Stacy Adams, "Toward an Understanding of Inequity," *Journal of Abnormal and Social Psychology* (November 1963), pp. 422–436; Paul S. Goodman and A. Freedman, "An Examination of Adams' Theory of Inequity," *Administrative Science Quarterly* (December 1971), pp. 271–288; Michael R. Carroll and J. E. Dettrich, "Equity Theory: The Recent Literature, Methodological Considerations in New Directions," *Academy of Management Review* (April 1978), pp. 202–210; and Robert P. Vecchio, "Models of Psychological Inequity," *Organizational Behavior and Human Performance* (October 1984), pp. 266–282.

31. Robert P. Vecchio, "Predicting Worker Performance in Inequitable Settings," *Academy of Management Review* (January 1982), pp. 103–110.

32. Richard C. Huseman, John D. Hatfield, and Edward W. Miles, "A New Perspective on Equity Theory: The Equity Sensitivity Construct," *Academy of Management Review* (April 1987), pp. 222–234.

33. Ken Jennings and Earle Traynham, "The Wages of Two-Tier Pay Plans," *Personnel Journal*, March 1988, pp. 56–63; and James E. Martin and Melanie M. Peterson, "Two-Tier Wage Structures: Implications for Equity Theory," *Academy of Management Journal* (April 1987), pp. 297–315.

34. Edwin A. Locke, "Toward a Theory of Task Motivation and Incentives," *Organizational Behavior and Performance* (May 1968), pp. 157–189; and Edwin A. Locke, Karyll N. Shaw, Lise M. Saari, and Gary P. Latham, "Goal Setting and Task Performance: 1969–1980," *Psychological Bulletin* (July 1981).

35. James L. Gibson, John M. Ivancevich, and James H. Donnelly, Jr., *Organizations: Behavior, Structure, Process*, 5th ed. (Plano, Tex.: BPI, 1985), p. 164.

36. Ibid., pp. 164–169; and James M. Higgins, *Human Relations: Behavior at Work*, 2nd ed. (New York: Random House, 1987), p. 164.

37. Edwin A. Locke, Gary P. Latham, and Miriam Erez, "The Determinants of Goal Commitment," *Academy of Management Review* (January 1988), pp. 23–39.

38. Edward L. Thorndike, *Animal Intelligence: Experimental Studies* (New York: Hafner, 1965 [1911]), p. 244.

39. B. F. Skinner, *Beyond Freedom and Dignity* (New York: Knopf, 1971); see also, Fred Luthans and Robert Kreitner, "A Social Learning Approach to Behavioral Management: Radical Behavioralists 'Mellowing Out,'" *Organizational Dynamics* (August 1984), pp. 47–63.

40. For a lengthy discussion, see Fred Luthans and Robert Kreitner, *Organizational Behavior Modification and Beyond* (Glenview, Ill.: Scott, Foresman, 1985).

41. Fran Tarkenton with Tad Tuleja, *How to Motivate People* (New York: Harper & Row, 1986).

42. Edward J. Feeney, "Modifying Employee Behavior: Making Rewards Pay Off," *Supervisory Management* (December 1985), pp. 25–27.

43. Kirk O'Hara, C. Merle Johnson, and Jerry A. Beehr, "Organizational Behavior Management in the Private Sector: A Review of Empirical Research and Recommendation for Further Investigation," *Academy of Management Review* (October 1985), pp. 848–865.

44. "Grading Merit Pay," *Newsweek* 14 November, 1988, pp. 45–46.

45. "Labor Letter," *Wall Street Journal* 25 October, 1988, p. 1.

46. See for example Dennis W. Organ, "A Restatement of the Satisfaction-Performance Hypothesis," *Journal of Management*, 1988, No. 4; pp. 547–557; Dennis W. Organ, "A Reappraisal and Reinterpretation of the Satisfaction-Causes-Performance Hypothesis," *Academy of Management Review*, April 1977, pp. 46–53; A. H. Brayfield and W. H. Crockett, "Employee Attitudes and Employee Performance," *Psychological Bulletin*, 1955, pp. 396–424.

47. Richard DeCharms, *Personal Causation* (Reading, Mass.; Addison-Wesley, 1968); Abraham Korman, "Toward an Hypothesis of Work Behavior," *Journal of Applied Psychology*, vol. 54, no. 1 (1970), pp. 31–41; Maxwell Maltz, *Psycho-Cybernetics: The New Way to a Successful Life* (Englewood Cliffs, N.J.: Prentice-Hall, 1960); Robert A. Sutermeister, "The Employed Performance of Employee Need Satisfaction: Which Comes First?" *California Management Review*, vol. 13, no. 4 (1971), pp. 43–47; and a host of articles in the educational and psychological literature.

48. P. Tharenon, "Employee Self-esteem: A Review of the Literature," *Journal of Vocational Behavior* (1979), pp. 316–349.

49. Ibid.

50. A. Bandura, *Social Learning Theory* (Englewood Cliffs, N.J.: Prentice-Hall, 1977); Harold H. Kelly and John L. Michael, "Attribution Theory and Research," *The Annual Review of Psychology* (1980), pp. 457–501; also see Mark J. Martinko and William L. Gardner, "The Leader/Member Attribution Process," *Academy of Management Review* (April 1987), pp. 235–249 for a discussion of a dyadic model of leader-subordinate attributional behavior. See Daniel Sandowsky, "A Psychoanalytic Attributional Model for Subordinate Poor Performance," *Human Resource Management*, Spring 1989, pp. 125–139, for a series of recommended actions for managers to take to overcome problems with attribution.

CHAPTER FOURTEEN

1. Marvin E. Shaw, *Group Dynamics: The Psychology of Small Group Behavior*, 2nd ed. (New York: McGraw-Hill, 1976).

2. Deborah L. Gladstein, "Groups in Context: A Model of Task Group Effectiveness," *Administrative Science Quarterly* (December 1984), pp. 499–517.

3. T. M. Mills, *The Sociology of Small Groups* (Englewood Cliffs, N.J.: Prentice-Hall, 1967), p. 2.

4. Kenneth N. Wexley and Gary A. Yukl, *Organizational Behavior and Personnel Psychology* (Homewood, Ill.: Irwin, 1977).

5. See Edgar H. Schein, *Organizational Psychology*, 3rd ed. (Englewood Cliffs, N.J.: Prentice-Hall, 1980), pp. 146–153.

6. James L. Gibson, John M. Ivancevich, and James H. Donnelly identify two types of task groups: the problem-solving group and the training group. The latter seems to be a special case of a task group—that is, a problem-solving group—and no such distinction is made here. The reader should be alert to the fact that some differences do exist. See James L. Gibson, John M. Ivance-

vich, and James H. Donnelly, *Organizations: Behavior, Structure, and Processes* (Dallas: Business Publications, 1979), pp. 142–143.

7. David M. Herold, "The Effectiveness of Work Groups," in Steven Kerr, ed. *Organizational Behavior* (New York: Wiley, 1979), p. 95.

8. George Homans, *The Human Group* (New York: Harcourt, Brace, Jovanovich, 1950).

9. John A. Seeger, in "No Innate Phases in Group Problem Solving," *Academy of Management Review* (October 1983), demonstrates that such stages occur primarily only when subject groups have never met before.

10. For example, see Bernard Bass, *Organizational Psychology* (Boston: Allyn & Bacon, 1965), pp. 197–198; J. Steven Heinen and Eugene Jackson, "A Model of Task Group Development in Complex Organization and a Strategy of Implementation," *Academy of Management Review* (October 1976), pp. 98–111; and Connie J. G. Gersuh, "Time and Transition in Work Teams: Toward a New Model of Group Development," *Academy of Management Journal* (March 1988), pp. 9–41.

11. Not everyone agrees that problem-solving groups go through stages. For example, see John A. Seeger, "No Innate Phases in Group Problem Solving," *Academy of Management Review* (October 1983), pp. 683–689.

12. Kenneth D. Benne and Paul Sheats, "Functional Roles of Group Members," *Journal of Social Issues*, vol. 4, no. 2 (1948), p. 43.

13. "How Power Will be Balanced on Saturn's Shop Floor," *Business Week* (August 5, 1985), pp. 65–68.

14. Benne and Sheats, op. cit., pp. 45–47.

15. Ibid., pp. 44–49.

16. J. L. Moreno, *Foundations of Sociometry*, Sociometry Monographs, no. 4 (Boston: Beacon, 1943).

17. Keith David, "Cut Those Rumors Down to Size," *Supervisory Management* (June 1975), pp. 2–6; "The Care and Cultivation of the Corporate Grapevine," *Dun's Review* (July 1973), pp. 44–47; and "Management Communication and the Grapevine," *Harvard Business Review* (September–October 1953), pp. 43–49.

18. E. J. Thomas and C. F. Fink, "Effects of Group Size," in Larry L. Cummings and William E. Scott, eds., *Readings in Organizational and Human Performance* (Homewood, Ill.: Irwin, 1969), pp. 394–408.

19. R. Z. Gooding and J. A. Wagner, III, "A Meta-Analytical Review of the Relationship Between Size and Efficiency of Organizations and Their Subunits," *Administrative Science Quarterly* (December 1985), pp. 462–481.

20. "How Power Will be Balanced . . . ," *Business Week*, op. cit., p. 66.

21. Gooding and Wagner, loc. cit.

22. For a discussion of groups and size, see Rodney W. Napier and Matti K. Gershenfield, *Groups: Theory and Experience*, 4th ed. (Boston: Houghton Mifflin, 1987), pp. 38–39, 87.

23. J. R. Hackman, "Group Influence on Individuals," in *Handbook of Industrial and Organizational Psychology*, M. D. Dunnette, ed. (Chicago: Rand McNally, 1976), pp. 1455–1525.

24. Daniel C. Feldman, "The Development and Enforcement of Group Norms," *Academy of Management Review* (January 1984), pp. 47–53.

25. Daniel C. Feldman and Hugh J. Arnold, *Managing Individual and Group Behavior in Organizations* (New York: McGraw-Hill, 1983), pp. 447–448.

26. Irving Janis, *Victims of Group Think*, 2nd ed. (Boston: Houghton Mifflin, 1982). See also Carrie R. Leana, "A Partial Test of Janis' Group Think Model: Effects of Group Cohesiveness and Leader Behavior on Defective Decision Making," *Journal of Management*, no. 1 (1985), pp. 5–17, for a research study that partially supports Janis's theory. See also Barbara Tuchman, *The March of Folly* (New York: Knopf, 1984).

27. For a review of the research on cohesiveness, see Marvin E. Shaw, *Group Dynamics* (New York: McGraw-Hill, 1971), pp. 110–112, 192.

28. Dorwin Cartwright, "The Nature of Group Cohesiveness," in *Group Dynamics: Research and Theory*, 3rd ed. (New York: Harper & Row, 1968), pp. 98–103.

29. Frank Shipper, "Quality Circles Using Small Group Formation," *Training and Development Journal* (May 1983), p. 82.

30. Gayle W. Hill, "Group Versus Individual Performance: Are N + 1 Heads Better Than One?" *Psychological Bulletin* (1982), pp. 517–539.

31. J. H. Davis, *Group Performance* (Reading, Mass.: Addison-Wesley, 1969); A. Paul Hare, *Handbook of Small Group Research* (Glencoe, N.Y.: Free Press, 1962), p. 201; and C. G. Smith, "Scientific Performance and the Composition of Research Teams," *Administrative Science Quarterly* (December 1971), pp. 486–495.

32. One of the purposes of self-managed groups is to increase the quality of employee work life. See, for example, Henry Sims and Charles C. Manz, "Conversations Within Self-managed Work Groups," *National Productivity Review* (1982), pp. 261–269.

33. For a discussion, see J. Richard Hackman, "The Design of Work Teams," in Jay W. Lorsch, ed., *Handbook of Organizational Behavior* (Englewood Cliffs, N.J.: Prentice-Hall, 1987), pp. 343–357.

34. Barry M. Straw, "Organizational Psychology and the Pursuit of the Happy/Productive Worker," *California Management Review* (Spring 1987), p. 25.

35. Gregory P. Shea and Richard A. Guzzo, "Group Effectiveness: What Really Matters?" *Sloan Management Review* (Spring 1987), p. 25.

36. For a lengthy discussion of groups, see Marilyn E. Gist, Edwin A. Locke, and M. Susan Taylor, "Organizational Behavior: Group Structures, Process and Effectiveness," in J. D. Blair and J. G. Hunt, eds., *Yearly Review of Management of the Journal of Management* (1987), pp. 237–257.

37. W. W. George, "Task Teams for Rapid Growth," *Harvard Business Review* (January–February 1981), pp. 103–116.

38. Thomas J. Peters, *Thriving on Chaos: A Management Revolution* (New York: Knopf, 1987), p. 297.

39. Toby D. Wall, Nigel J. Kemp, Paul R. Jackson, and Chris W. Clegg, "Outcomes of Autonomous Work Groups: A Long Term Field Experiment," *Academy of Management Journal* (June 1986), pp. 280–304.

40. See William D. Dyer, *Team Building* (Reading, Mass.: Addison-Wesley, 1977).

41. Shipper, loc. cit.

42. Walt Thompson, "Getting the Organization Ready for Quality Circles," *Training and Development Journal* (December 1982), p. 116.

43. Robert Wood, Frank Hall, and Koya Azumi, "Evaluating Quality Circles: The American Application," *California Management Review* (Fall 1983), p. 43.

44. Laurie Fitzgerald and Joseph Murphy, *Installing Quality Circles: A Strategic Approach* (San Diego, Cal.: University Associates, 1982), p. 3.

45. Allan Halcrow, "Portfolio," *Personnel Journal* (January 1988), pp. 10–11.

46. Dan Lippe, "Quality Circles Roll into Hospitals," *Modern Health Care* (August 1982).

47. Edward E. Lawler, III, and Susan A. Mohrman, "Quality Circles: After the Honeymoon," *Organizational Dynamics* (Spring 1987), pp. 42–54.

48. Robert P. Steel, Anthony J. Mento, Benjamin L. Dilla, Nestor N. Ovalle, and Russell F. Lloyd, "Factors Influencing the Success and Failure of Two Quality Circles Programs," *Journal of Management* (Spring 1985), pp. 99–119.

49. Rickey W. Griffin, "Consequences of Quality Circles in an Industrial Setting: A Longitudinal Assessment," *Academy of Management Journal* (June 1988), pp. 338–358.

50. Wood, Hall, and Azumi, op. cit., p. 40.

51. Alexander C. Philip, "A Hidden Benefit of Quality Circles," *Personnel Journal* (February 1984), p. 54.

52. David N. Landon and Steven Moulton, "Quality Circles: What's in Them for Employees?" *Personnel Journal* (June 1986), pp. 23–25.

53. Note, however, that group failure could lead to lessened self-esteem. See Joel Brocker and Ted Less, "Self-Esteem and Task Performance in Quality Circles," *Academy of Management Journal* (September 1986), pp. 617–623.

CHAPTER FIFTEEN

1. We all know about Lee Iacocca. He made a difference. Plentiful supporting research, based on case studies, surveys, and interviews, is cited in references throughout this chapter. One longitudinal research study clearly revealed that leadership did make a difference in organizational performance: Jonathan E. Smith, Kenneth P. Carson, and Ralph H. Alexander, "Leadership: It Can Make a Difference," *Academy of Management Journal* (December 1984), pp. 765–776.

2. Gary Yukl, *Leadership in Action* (Englewood Cliffs, N.J.: Prentice-Hall, 1981), pp. 1–5.

3. For additional definitions, see ibid., pp. 2–3.

4. Abraham Zaleznik, "Managers and Leaders: Are They Different?" *Harvard Business Review* (May–June 1977), pp. 67–78; Ted Levitt, "Command and Consent," *Harvard Business Review* (July–August 1988), p. 5; and John P. Kotter, *The Leadership Factor* (New York: Free Press, 1987).

5. Jack Falvey, "Before Spending $3 Million on Leadership, Read This," *Wall Street Journal* 3 October, 1988, p. A26.

6. Noel M. Tichy and Mary Anne Devanna. *The Transformational Leader* (New York: Wiley, 1987).

7. Zaleznik, loc. cit.

8. Ibid.

9. Tichy and Devanna, loc. cit.

10. James M. Korzes and Barry Z. Posner, *The Leadership Challenge* (San Francisco: Jossey-Bass, 1987). Kenneth Labich provides a similar list in "The Seven Keys to Business Leadership," *Fortune* (October 24, 1988), pp. 58–66: 1. Trust your subordinates, 2. Develop a vision, 3. Keep your cool, 4. Encourage risk, 5. Be an expert, 6. Invite dissent, 7. Simplify.

11. Chester I. Barnard, *The Functions of the Executive* (Cambridge: Harvard University Press, 1938), pp. 160–175.

12. Jeffrey C. Barrow, "The Variables of Leadership: A Review and Conceptual Framework," *Academy of Management Review* (April 1977), pp. 233–234.

13. John R. P. French and Bertram H. Raven, "The Bases of Social Power," in Dorwin Cartwright, ed., *Studies in Social Power* (Ann Arbor: University of Michigan Press, 1959). For a discussion of uses of these powers see: Thomas A. Stewart, "New Ways to Exercise Power," *Fortune*, November 6, 1989, pp. 52–64.

14. Daniel C. Pelz, "Influence: Key to Effective Leadership on the First-Line Supervisor," *Personnel* (1952), pp. 209–217.

15. Dennis Waitley, "The Psychology of Winning" (Chicago: Nightingale–Connant Corp., 1978), cassette tape.

16. Hugh D. Menzies, "The Ten Toughest Bosses," *Fortune* (April 21, 1980), pp. 62–72; and Paul A. Gigot and Laurel Sirenson, "Bank on the Mend: Morale and Earnings Rise Under New Chairman," *Wall Street Journal* 27 May, 1981, pp. 1, 25.

17. This is also a familiar case in business, where the expert builds relationships, and has power based on favors.

18. Daniel Yankelovich & Associates, *Work and Human Values* (New York: Public Agenda Foundation, 1983), pp. 6–7.

19. United Technologies, "Let's Get Rid of Management," *Wall Street Journal*, ran in several different issues in 1987.

20. Jack C. Horn, "Sweet Revenge," *Psychology Today* (January 1984), p. 48.

21. Jack Falvey, "Before Spending $3 Million on Leadership, Read This," *Wall Street Journal* 3 October, 1988, p. A26.

22. Yukl, op. cit., pp. 68, 69, 90.

23. Ralph M. Stogdill, *Handbook of Leadership: A Survey of Theory and Research* (New York: Free Press, 1974); also see Bernard M. Bass, *Stogdill's Handbook of Leadership: Revised and Expanded Edition* (New York: Free Press, 1981), chap. 5.

24. Yukl, op. cit., p. 70.

25. For an interesting view of certain personalities and leadership styles, see Seth Allcorn, "Leadership Styles: The Psychological Picture," *Personnel* (April 1988), pp. 46–54.

26. Douglas T. McGregor, *The Human Side of Enterprise* (New York: McGraw-Hill, 1960), pp. 33–34, 47–48.

27. J. C. Taylor, "An Empirical Examination of a Four-Factor Theory of Leadership Using Smallest Space Analysis," *Organizational Behavior and Human Performance* 6 (1971), pp. 249–266.

28. Yukl, loc. cit.

29. Robert R. Blake and Jane S. Mouton, *The New Managerial Grid* (Houston: Gulf, 1978); also see Robert R. Blake and Jane S. Mouton, "How to Choose a Leadership Style," *Training and Development Journal* (February 1982), pp. 38–47.

30. Ibid., chap. 7.

31. One study with an extremely large sample size (16,000) found that high-achieving executives, about 13 percent of the total, cared about people and profits. Average achievers were concerned only about profits, and low achievers were obsessed only with their own security. Low achievers displayed a basic distrust of subordinates' abilities; high achievers viewed them optimistically. High achievers sought advice from underlings; low achievers didn't. High achievers were listeners; moderate achievers listened only to achievers, and low achievers avoided communication, relying on policy manuals. ("Nice Guys in High Corporate Positions Get the Best Results from Subordinates," *Wall Street Journal* 22 August, 1978, p. 1).

32. Robert Tannenbaum and Warren H. Schmidt, "How to Choose a Leadership Pattern," *Harvard Business Review* 36 (1958), pp. 95–101.

33. Jerome L. Franklin, "Down the Organization: Influence Processes Across Levels of Hierarchy," *Administrative Science Quarterly* (June 1975), pp. 153–165.

34. Fred E. Fiedler, *A Theory of Leadership Effectiveness* (New York: McGraw-Hill, 1967), pp. 10–37.

35. Robert Vecchio, "An Empirical Examination of Fiedler's Model," *Organizational Behavior and Human Performance* (June 1977), pp. 180–206; and Fred Fiedler, "The Contribution of Cognitive Resources and Behavior to Leadership Performance," paper presented to the Academy of Management, Boston, August 12, 1984.

36. Robert Hersey and Terrence R. Mitchell, "Path-Goal Theory of Leadership," *Journal of Contemporary Business* (Autumn 1974), pp. 81–97.

37. Steven Kerr and John Jermier, "Substitutes for Leadership: Their Meaning and Measurement," *Organizational Behavior and Human Performance* (1978), pp. 375–403; and Jon P. Howell and Peter W. Dorfman, "Leadership and Substitutes for Leadership Among Professional and Nonprofessional Workers," *Journal of Applied Behavioral Sciences* (November 1, 1986), pp. 29–46.

38. Paul Hersey and Kenneth R. Blanchard, *Management of Organizational Behavior: Uti-*

lizing Human Resources (Englewood Cliffs, N.J.: Prentice-Hall, 1977).
39. Victor Vroom and Arthur G. Yago, *The New Leadership: Managing Participation in Organizations* (Englewood Cliffs, N.J.: Prentice-Hall, 1988); and Victor Vroom and P. W. Yetton, *Leadership and Decision Making* (Pittsburgh: University of Pittsburgh Press, 1973).
40. Jan P. Muczyk and Bernard C. Reimann, "The Case for Directive Leadership," *Academy of Management Executive* (August 1987), pp. 301–311.
41. James M. Higgins, "The TRRAP Model," *Human Relations: Behavior at Work*, 2nd ed. (New York: Random House, 1987), pp. 200–209.
42. Mark J. Martinko and William L. Gardner, "The Leader/Member Attribution Process," *Academy of Management Review* (April 1987), pp. 235–249; also see Larry E. Penley and Brian Hawkins, "Studying Interpersonal Communication in Organizations: A Leadership Application," *Academy of Management Journal* (June 1985), pp. 309–326.
43. For a lengthy discussion, see F. M. Jablin, "Superior-Subordinate Communication: The State of the Art," *Psychological Bulletin* (1979), pp. 1201–1222; and for a review of related research and a critique of this aspect of communication, see Penley and Hawkins, loc. cit.
44. William V. Haney, *Communication and Interpersonal Relations: Text and Cases* (Homewood, Ill.: Irwin-Dorsey, 1979), pp. 12–15.
45. For a review of the research, see Karl W. Kuhnert and Philip Lewis, "Transactional and Transformational Leadership: A Constructive/Developmental Analysis," *Academy of Management Review* (October 1987), pp. 648–657.
46. James McGregor Burns, *Leadership* (New York: Harper & Row, 1978).
47. Ibid., p. 4.
48. Bernard M. Bass, *Leadership and Performance Beyond Expectations* (New York: Free Press, 1985); see also Bernard M. Bass, J. Avolio, and Laurie Goodheim, "Biography and the Assessment of Transformational Leadership at the World Class Level," *Journal of Management* (Spring 1987), pp. 7–19.
49. Bass, op. cit., p. 27.
50. Ibid., p. 17.
51. Bernard M. Bass, "Leadership: Good, Better, Best," *Organizational Dynamics* (Winter 1985), pp. 26–40.
52. Noel M. Tichy and David M. Ulrich, "The Leadership Challenge: A Call for Transformational Leaders," *Sloan Management Review* (Fall 1984), pp. 59–68.
53. Tichy and Devanna, loc. cit.

CHAPTER SIXTEEN

1. Fred Luthans and Janet K. Larsen, "How Managers Really Communicate," *Human Relations* 39 (1986), pp. 161–178; and Peter C. Gronn, "Talk as Work: The Accomplishments of School Administration," *Administrative Science Quarterly* (March 1983), pp. 1–21.
2. Larry E. Penley and Brian Hawkins, "Studying Interpersonal Communication in Organizations," *Academy of Management Journal* (June 1985), pp. 309–326.
3. Daniel R. Boyd, Stephen D. Lewis, and Grady L. Butler, "Getting Your Message Across," *Management Review* (July–August 1988), pp. 7–10.
4. William V. Haney, *Communication and Interpersonal Relations* (Homewood, Ill.: Irwin, 1979), p. 3.
5. Thomas J. Peters and Robert H. Waterman, Jr., *In Search of Excellence* (New York: Harper & Row, 1982), pp. 246–247.
6. William G. Scott and Terrence R. Mitchell, *Organization Theory: A Structural Behavioral Analysis* (Homewood, Ill.: Irwin, 1979), p. 3

7. Holiday Inns of America, Inc., *First Concern* (Memphis, Tenn., 1985).
8. This model is based on a number of similar sources. For example, see Norman B. Sigband and Arthur H. Bell, *Communication for Management and Business* (Glenview, Ill.: Scott, Foresman, 1986); and Couillard L. Bovee and John V. Thill, *Business Communications Today* (New York: Random House, 1986).
9. Lyman W. Porter and Karlene H. Roberts, "Communication in Organizations," in Marvin D. Dunnette, ed., *Handbook of Industrial and Occupational Psychology*, 2nd ed. (New York: Wiley, 1983), pp. 1553–1589.
10. Jolie Solomon, "Business Communications in the Fax Age," *Wall Street Journal* 27 October, 1988, p. B1.
11. Richard L. Daft and Robert H. Lengel, "Organizational Information Requirements, Media Richness and Structural Design," *Management Science* (March 1986), pp. 554–572; and Richard L. Daft and Robert H. Lengel, "Information Richness: A New Approach to Managerial Behavior and Organizational Design," in *Research and Organizational Behavior*, vol. 6, Barry Stoll and Larry L. Cummings, eds. (Greenwich, Conn.: JAI Press, 1984), pp. 191–233.
12. Richard L. Daft, Robert H. Lengel, and Linda Klebe Trevino, "The Relationship Among Message Equivocality, Media Selection, and Manager Performance: Implications for Information Support Systems," *MIS Quarterly* (September 1987), pp. 355–366.
13. Walter St. John, "In-House Communications Guidelines," *Personnel Journal* (November 1981), pp. 872–878.
14. Larry R. Smeltzer and John L. Waltman, *Managerial Communication: A Strategic Approach* (New York: Wiley, 1984), p. 4.
15. Bruce K. Blaylock, "Cognitive Styles and the Usefulness of Information," *Decision Sciences* (Winter 1984), pp. 74–91.
16. Linda L. Davidoff, *Introduction to Psychology*, 2nd ed. (New York: McGraw-Hill, 1980), p. 172.
17. Maxwell Maltz, *Psychocybernetics* (New York: Pocket Books, 1960), p. 22.
18. Sondra Thiederman, "Breaking Through to Foreign-Born Employees," *Management World* (May–June 1988), pp. 22–23.
19. Nancy Heckel, "Transcending Boundaries," *Training and Development Journal* (July 1987), pp. 72–73.
20. "Your Personal Listening Profile," Sperry Corporation, 1980, pp. 4–5.
21. Mark McCormack, *What They Don't Teach You at the Harvard Business School* (New York: Bantam, 1984), p. 13.
22. For a discussion, see David Givens, "What Body Language Can Tell You That Words Cannot," *U.S. News & World Report* (November 19, 1984), p. 100.
23. As told to the author by a Holiday Inns' franchisee.
24. Norman B. Sigband, *Communication for Management and Business* (Glenview, Ill.: Scott, Foresman, 1969), p. 19.
25. Edward T. Hall, *The Hidden Dimension* (New York: Doubleday, 1968).
26. Discussion with a senior vice-president for that division.
27. Timothy K. Smith, "Open Offices, the Idea of the 70s, Are Up Against the Wall in the 80s," *Wall Street Journal* 26 September, 1985, p. 38.
28. Abner M. Eisenberg, *Understanding Communication in Business and the Professions* (New York: Macmillan, 1978), p. 392.
29. Sigband, *Communication*, op. cit., p. 354.
30. Related to me by a vice-president of the American firm. This seems to be a version of the clever Japanese habit of making Americans wait until the last moment to talk business on a business trip.

31. John T. Molloy, *Dress for Success* (New York: Wyden, 1975).
32. "Labor Letter, Dialogues with Workers Gained Increased Employer Attention," *Wall Street Journal* 3 January, 1989, p. A1.
33. Walter Kiechell, III, "No Word from Up High," *Fortune* (January 6, 1986), pp. 125–126.
34. Ibid., p. 125.
35. For a discussion see Alan Zaremba, "Working with the Organizational Grapevine," *Personnel Journal*, July 1988, pp. 38–42.
36. Chris Lee, "Training at Loew's Corp.: If It's Not Broken . . . ," *Training* (April 1985), p. 43.
37. David Lindlum, "10 Tips for Survival in the 1990s," *Computer World*, December 25, 1989, January 1, 1990, pp. 14–15; Robert M. Losee, Jr., "Minimizing Information Overload: The Ranking of Electronic Messages," *Journal of Information Sciences: Principle and Practices*, 1989, no. 3, pp. 179–189. "Information Overload Is Here," *USA Today* (February 20, 1989), pp. B1, B2.
38. Peters and Waterman, *In Search of Excellence* (New York: Harper & Row, 1982), pp. 237–238.
39. Thomas Gordon, *Leadership Effectiveness Training* (New York: Wyden, 1977), pp. 27–48, 193.
40. Patricia Jakubowski and Arthur J. Lange, *The Assertiveness Option* (Champaign, Ill.: Research Press, 1977); and Manual J. Smith, *When I Say No I Feel Guilty* (New York: Dial, 1975).
41. For a review of the frequency of usage of several of these approaches, see Paul L. Blocklyn, "Employee Communications," *Personnel* (May 1987), pp. 62–66.
42. Also called "listening posts." See John R. Hundley, "Listening Posts," *Personnel* (July–August 1976), pp. 39–43.
43. Frederick A. Starke and Thomas W. Ferratt, "Behavioral Information Systems," *Journal of Systems Management* (March 1976), pp. 26–30.
44. Louis A. Mischkind, "No-Nonsense Surveys Improve Employee Morale," *Personnel Journal* (November 1983), pp. 906–914.
45. Susan G. Strother, "Workers Speak Up," 'Central Florida Business,' *Orlando Sentinel* 3 October, 1988, p. 5.
46. J. J. Yore, "Dealing with Complaints," *Venture* (July 1985), pp. 25–26.
47. George G. Rich, "Revamped Suggestion System Saves McDonnell Douglas Millions of Dollars Annually," *Personnel Journal* (January 1987), pp. 31–34.
48. Fred T. Allen, "Winning and Holding Employee Loyalty," *Nation's Business* (April 1977), pp. 40–44.
49. "Business' New Communication Tools," *Dun's Review* (February 1981), pp. 80–82.
50. "Broadcast News Inc.," *Newsweek* (January 4, 1988), pp. 34–35.
51. Blocklyn, loc. cit.
52. Bruce G. Posner, "The Best Little Handbook in Texas," *Inc.* (February 1989), pp. 84–87.
53. "The Portable Executive," *Business Week* (October 10, 1988), pp. 102–112.

CHAPTER SEVENTEEN

1. Janice Castro, "Questions About Eastern," *Time* (August 24, 1987), p. 41.
2. Kenneth A. Merchant, *Control in Business Organizations* (Marshfield, Mass: Pittman, 1985).
3. Robert J. Mockler, *The Management Control Process* (Englewood Cliffs, N.J.: Prentice-Hall, 1972), p. 2.
4. Frank B. Copley, *Frederick W. Taylor, Father of Scientific Management*, vol. 2 (New York: Harper, 1923), p. 358.
5. Giovanni Giglioni and Arthur G. Bedeian, "A Conspectus of Management Control Theory: 1900–1972," *Academy of Management Journal* (June 1974), pp. 292–305; and Mockler, loc. cit.
6. For example, see Ralph E. Drtina and Theo-

dore T. Herbert, "Strategic Control Systems: Definition and Identification of Significant Parameters in Business Usage," paper presented to the Strategic Management Society, Amsterdam, October 1988.

7. William M. Corley, "Losing Battle: U.S. Air War on Drugs So Far Fails to Stem Caribbean Smuggling," *Wall Street Journal* 20 October 1988, pp. A-1, A-12.

8. "Taking on the Legalizers," *Newsweek* (December 25, 1989), pp. 46–48.

9. Bob Davis, "Costly Bugs: As Complexity Rises, Tiny Flaws in Software Pose a Growing Threat," *Wall Street Journal* 27 January 1987, pp. 1, 18.

10. Thomas J. Peters, "The Race for Quality," *Florida Trend* (November 1987), pp. 105–111; Jeremy Main, "Under the Spell of the Quality Gurus," *Fortune* (August 18, 1986), pp. 30–34; and "Purchase for Quality," *Business Week* (June 8, 1987), pp. 130–140.

11. Mockler, loc. cit.

12. Davis, loc. cit.

13. Robert S. Kaplan, "One Cost System Isn't Enough," *Harvard Business Review* (January–February 1988), pp. 61–66.

14. Marilyn Chase, "Lost Euphoria: Genentech, Battered by Great Expectations, Is Tightening Its Belt," *Wall Street Journal* 11 October 1988, pp. A-1, 10.

15. Laurie McGinley, "Two Eastern Air Pilots Testify Carrier Pressured Them to Fly Unsafe Planes," *Wall Street Journal* 16 October 1987, p. 6; and "Report Calls Eastern Airlines Delays in Repairs a Misuse of Policy," *New York Times*, as reported in *The Orlando Sentinel* 29 November 1987, p. A-17.

16. William T. Greenwood, *Management and Organizational Behavior Theories* (Cincinnati: Southwestern, 1965).

17. Easton Corporation Annual Report, Cleveland, Ohio, 1988.

18. W. H. Koontz and R. W. Bradspies, "Managing Through Feedforward Control," *Business Horizons* (June 1972), pp. 25–36.

19. Harold Koontz and Heinz Weihrich, *Management*, 9th ed. (New York: McGraw-Hill, 1988), p. 492.

20. For a review of the different types of control, such as control results, control personnel, control specific actions or avoiding control problems, see Kenneth A. Merchant, "Control Function in Management," in Max D. Richards, ed., *Readings in Management*, 7th ed. (Cincinnati: Southwestern, 1986), pp. 285–301.

21. Jack Gray and Diane Matson, "Early Warning Systems," *Management Accounting* (August 1987), pp. 50–55.

22. Charles M. Jones, "GTE's Strategic Tracking System," *Planning Review* (September 1986), pp. 77–80.

23. Vijay Sathe, "The Controllers Role in Management," *Organizational Dynamics* (Winter 1983), pp. 31–48.

24. Michael E. Porter, *Competitive Strategy* (New York: Free Press, 1980).

25. "Quality: The Competitive Advantage," an advertisement *Fortune*, 1987.

26. William G. Ouchi, "A Conceptual Framework for the Design of Organizational Control Mechanisms," *Management Science* (August 1979), pp. 833–838.

27. William G. Ouchi, "Markets, Bureaucracies, and Clans," *Administrative Science Quarterly*, vol. 25, no. 1 (March 1980), p. 130, Overview, pp. 129–141.

28. Richard L. Daft, *Organization Theory and Design*, 2nd ed. (St. Paul: West, 1986) p. 318.

29. Ouchi, "Markets, Bureaucracies, and Clans," op. cit., p. 136.

30. Alfred M. Jaeger and B. R. Baliga, "Control Systems and Strategic Adaptations: Lessons from the Japanese," *Strategic Management Journal* (December 1985), pp. 115–134.

31. Ibid., p. 128.

32. Ouchi, "Markets, Bureaucracies, and Clans," loc. cit.

33. Cortlandt Cammann and David A. Nadler, "Fit Control Systems to Your Management Style," *Harvard Business Review* (January–February 1976), pp. 65–72.

34. Other control styles have been identified. For example, Gareth R. Jones identifies four dimensions of leader control behavior at the supervisory level: obtrusive vs. inobtrusive, situational vs. personal, professional vs. paternalistic, and process vs. output. "Forms of Control and Leader Behavior," *Journal of Management*, vol. 9, no. 2 (1983), pp. 159–172.

35. Cammann and Nadler, op. cit., p. 71.

36. William H. Newman, *Constructive Control* (Englewood Cliffs, N.J.: Prentice-Hall, 1975); Earl P. Strong and Robert D. Smith, *Management Control Models* (New York: Holt, Rinehart, 1968); Peter Lorange and Decland Murphy, "Considerations in Implementing Strategic Control," *Journal of Business Strategy* (Spring 1984), pp. 27–35; and Peter F. Drucker, *Management: Tasks, Responsibilities, Practices* (New York: Harper & Row, 1974), pp. 490–502.

37. Zachary Shiller, "Numbers Don't Tell the Story," *Business Week* (June 6, 1988), p. 105; and Kaplan, loc. cit.

38. Richard E. Walton, "From Control to Commitment in the Workplace," *Harvard Business Review* (March–April 1985), pp. 76–84.

39. Walt Bogdanovich, "Lax Laboratories: The PAP Test Misses Much Cervical Cancer Through Lab's Errors," *Wall Street Journal* 2 November 1987, p. 1.

40. David A. Garbin, "Quality on the Line," *Harvard Business Review* (September–October 1983), pp. 65–75.

41. R. L. Dunbar, "Designs for Organizational Control," in P. C. Nystrom and W. H. Starbuch, eds. *Handbook of Organizational Design II* (London: Oxford University Press, 1981).

42. W. H. Read, "Upward Communication in Industrial Hierarchies," *Human Relations* (February 1962), pp. 3–15.

43. David A. Garbin, "Quality on the Line," *Harvard Business Review* (September–October 1983), pp. 65–75.

44. This discussion is based partly on Newman, loc. cit.; and Koontz and Bradspies, loc. cit.

45. Main, loc. cit.; Keki B. Bhote, "Improving Supply Management," *Management Review* (August 1987), pp. 50–53; Peters, loc. cit.; Philip Crosby, "Eternal Success: Lead Your Employees to Quality," *Success* (June 1980), pp. 60–61; Martin R. Smith, "Improving Product Quality in American Industry," *Academy of Management Executive* (August 1987), pp. 245–247; "The Search for Quality," *Business Week* (June 8, 1987), pp. 130–140; and Main, loc. cit.

46. Richard Koenig, "Exacting Employer: Toyota Takes Pains and Time, Filling Jobs at Its Kentucky Plant," *Wall Street Journal* 1 December 1987, pp. 1, 31.

47. Robert W. Goddard, "Work Force 2000," *Personnel Journal* (February 1989), pp. 64–71.

48. Newman, op. cit., pp. 12–25.

49. Bank of America *Annual Report* 1987.

50. Peter Lorange, Michael F. Scott Morton, and Sumantra Ghosakl, *Strategic Control* (St. Paul: West, 1986), chap. 1.

51. James M. Higgins and Julian W. Vincze, *Strategic Management: Text and Cases*, 4th ed. (Chicago: Dryden, 1989), chap. 9.

52. Richard J. Schonberger, *Japanese Manufacturing Techniques: Nine Hidden Lessons in Simplicity* (New York: Free Press, 1982), contains an excellent discussion of operations management, including vital control issues.

53. Peter F. Drucker, "Management Lessons of Irangate," *Wall Street Journal* 24 March 1987, p. 19.

54. Kaufman, loc. cit.

55. Lynda M. Applegate, James I. Cash, Jr., and D. Quinn Mills, "Information Technology and Tomorrow's Manager," *Harvard Business Review* (November–December 1988), pp. 128–136.

CHAPTER EIGHTEEN

1. Richard L. Daft and Norman D. MacIntosh, "The Nature and Use of Formal Control Systems for Management Control and Strategy Implementation," *Journal of Management*, vol. 10, no. 1 (Spring 1984), p. 57. While I use their basic framework, I have adapted the financial resource allocation process to their model in a slightly different way than they describe it. I have also added terms to clarify and broaden some of the definitions they have used. I have also added financial analysis to the strategic plan element because such analysis occurs at the strategic level.

2. Ibid., p. 61.

3. William G. Ouchi and Mary Ann Maguire, "Organizational Control: Two Functions," *Administrative Science Quarterly*, vol. 20 (December 1975), pp. 559–569.

4. Richard L. Daft, *Management* (Hinsdale, Ill.: Dryden, 1988), p. 558.

5. Daft and MacIntosh, op. cit., p. 59.

6. Michael E. Porter, *Competitive Strategy* (New York: Free Press, 1980).

7. Alfred M. Jaego and B. R. Baliga, "Control Systems and Strategic Adaptations: Lessons from the Japanese Experience," *Strategic Management Journal* (April–June 1985), pp. 115–134.

8. Steven B. Seilheiner, "Current State of Decision Support Systems and Expert Systems Technology," *Journal of Systems Management* (August 1988), pp. 14–18.

9. "The Computer Age Dawns in the Corner Office," *Business Week* (June 27, 1988), pp. 84–85.

10. Eugene Brigham, *Fundamentals of Financial Management*, 4th ed. (Hinsdale, Ill.: Dryden, 1986), chap. 7.

11. For an in-depth analysis of a current ratio, see Mary M. K. Fleming, "Current Ratio Revisited," *Business Horizons* (May–June 1986), pp. 74–77.

12. For a discussion see Bernard C. Reimann, "Achieving Management Consensus Around Value-Creating Strategies," *Planning Review*, (September–October 1989), pp. 38–46; and David L. Wenner and Richard W. Le Ber, "Managing for Shareholder Value—From Top to Bottom," *Harvard Business Review* (November–December 1989), pp. 52–66.

13. Robert S. Kaplan, "One Cost System Isn't Enough," *Harvard Business Review* (January–February 1988), p. 66.

14. Kaplan, ibid.

15. "The Productivity Paradox," *Business Week* (June 6, 1988), p. 101. See the additional discussion on pp. 100–114.

16. Ibid., pp. 105, 112; and John P. Campi, "Total Cost Management at Parker-Hannifin," *Management Accounting* (January 1989), pp. 51–53.

17. Belverd E. Needles, Jr., Henry P. Anderson, and James C. Caldwell, *Principles of Accounting*, 4th ed. (Boston: Houghton Mifflin 1990), pp. 30–31.

18. Ibid., pp. 31, 329–334.

19. Robert N. Anthony, John Dearden, and Norton M. Bedford, *Management Control Systems*, 5th ed. (Homewood, Ill.: Irwin, 1984), pp. 443–444.

20. Gordon Pinchot, III, *Intrapreneuring* (New York: Harper & Row, 1985).

21. Peter Gwynne, "The Pentagon's War on Costs," *High Technology* (March 1987), pp. 31–35.

22. Peter Pyhrr, "Zero-Based Budgeting," *Harvard Business Review* (November–December 1970), pp. 11–12.

23. "What It Means to Build a Budget from Zero," *Business Week* (April 19, 1976), p. 160.

24. Mark Dirsmith and Steven Jablonsky, "Zero-Based Budgeting ... and Political Strategy," *Academy of Management Review* (October 1979), pp. 555–565.

25. For a review of zero-based budgeting, see Michael F. Duffy, "ZBB, MBO, PPB and Their Effectiveness Within the Planning/Marketing Process," *Strategic Management Journal* (January–February 1989), pp. 163–173.

26. Henry L. Tosi, Jr., "The Human Effects Budgeting Systems on Management," *MSU Business Topics* (Autumn 1974), pp. 56–57.

27. Fred A. Shelton and Jack C. Bartes, "How to Create an Electronic Spreadsheet Budget," *Management Accounting* (July 1986), pp. 40–47.

28. Keith C. Gourley and Thomas R. Blecki, "Computerized Budgeting at Lord Corporation," *Management Accounting* (August 1986), pp. 37–40.

29. Srinivasan Umapathy, "How Successful Firms Budget," *Management Accounting* (February 1987), pp. 25–27.

30. Ronald G. Wells, "Guidelines for Effective and Defensible Performance Appraisal System," *Personnel Journal* (October 1982), p. 781.

31. John M. Ivancevich and William F. Glueck, *Foundations of Personnel/Human Resource Management*, 3rd ed. (Plano, Tex.: Business Publications, 1986), p. 280; and Cristina G. Banks and Loriann Roberson, "Performance Appraisers as Test Developers," *Academy of Management Review*, no. 1 (January 1985), pp. 128–142.

32. See the discussion in Chapter 13.

33. Ivancevich and Glueck, op. cit., pp. 565–570.

34. "The Enemy Within," *U.S. News & World Report* (July 4, 1988), pp. 16–22.

35. J. Kendall Middaugh, II, "Management Control in the Financial Services Industry," *Business Horizons* (May–June 1988), pp. 79–86.

36. Alan Murray and Paulette Thomas, "Dinosaur Industry: Bush's New Solution for Problem of S&L's Could Kill Them Off," *Wall Street Journal* 7 February 1989, pp. A1, A4; and Jeff Bailey and Charles F. McCoy, "Tricky Ledgers: To Hide Huge Losses, Financial Officials Use Accounting Gimmicks," *Wall Street Journal* 12 January 1987, pp. 1, 19.

37. "Going After the Crooks," *Time* (December 1, 1986), pp. 47–56.

CHAPTER NINETEEN

1. D. Lynch, "MIS: Conceptual Framework Criticism in Major Requirements for Success," *Journal of Business Communication* (Winter 1984), pp. 19–31.

2. "Information Power," *Business Week* (October 14, 1985), pp. 108–114.

3. David Wessel, "Marketing Tool: Computer Finds a Role in Buying and Selling, Reshaping Businesses," *Wall Street Journal* 18 March 1987, pp. 1, 22.

4. "An Electronic Pipeline That Is Changing the Way America Does Business," *Business Week* (August 3, 1987).

5. "Scramble for Global Networks," *Business Week* (March 21, 1988), pp. 140–148.

6. For a brief, but very good history and a review of major issues in mid-1980, see Tom Lutz, "Information-Catalyst for Corporate Change," *Data Management* (June 1986), pp. 25–29.

7. John G. Burch and Gary Grudnitski, *Information Systems: Theory and Practice*, 4th ed. (New York: Wiley, 1986), p. 3; see also, James I. Cash, Jr., F. I. McFarlan, James L. McKenney, and Michael Arthur Titale, *Corporate Information Systems Management: Text and Cases*, 2nd ed. (Homewood, Ill.: Irwin, 1988), chap. 1, for a discussion of information systems; and Jerome Kanter, *Management Information Systems*, 3rd ed. (Englewood Cliffs, N.J.: Prentice-Hall, 1984), pp. 9–13.

8. John Naisbitt, *Megatrends* (New York: Warner, 1982), p. 12.

9. Steven L. Mandell, *Computers and Data Processing* (St. Paul: West, 1985).

10. Burch and Grudnitski, op. cit., pp. 5–6.

11. Thomas W. Malone, JoAnne Yates, and Robert L. Benjamin, "The Logic of Electronic Markets," *Harvard Business Review* (May–June 1989), pp. 166–170; and "An Electronic Pipeline," loc. cit.

12. Kanter, op. cit., p. 6.

13. Ibid., p. 1; and John P. Murray, *Managing Information Systems as a Corporate Resource* (Homewood, Ill.: Dow Jones-Irwin, 1984), chap. 1.

14. Henry C. Lucas, Jr., "Utilizing Information Technology: Guidelines for Managers," *Sloan Management Review* (Fall 1986), p. 39.

15. For a review of the concept, see Paul H. Chaney and Norman R. Lyons, "MIS Update," *Data Management* (October 1980), pp. 26–32.

16. Guisseppi A. Forgionne, "Building Effective Decision Support Systems," *Business* (January–March 1988), p. 19.

17. Burch and Grudnitski, op. cit., pp. 37–41.

18. Ibid., pp. 37–38.

19. "Computers of the '90s: A Brave New World," *Newsweek* (October 24, 1988), pp. 52–53.

20. Burch and Grudnitski, op. cit., p. 39.

21. Ibid.

22. Ibid., p. 40.

23. Ibid., p. 41. Much of this discussion is based on this reference.

24. Kate Kaiser and Ananth Srinivasan, "User-Analyst Differences: An Empirical Investigation of Attitudes Related to Systems Development," *Academy of Management Journal* (September 1982), pp. 630–646.

25. Arnold Barnett, "Preparing Management for MIS," *Journal of Systems Management* (January 1972), pp. 40–43.

26. Blake Ives and Margrethe H. Olson, "User Involvement and MIS Success: A Review of Research," *Management Science* (May 1984), pp. 586–603.

27. "Information Power," *Business Week* (October 14, 1985), pp. 108–114.

28. Michael E. Porter and Victor E. Miller, "How Information Gives You Competitive Advantage," *Harvard Business Review* (July–August 1985), pp. 149–160.

29. Paul Strassmann, "Computers and Software That Are Supposed to Tell Managers What Is Going on in Their Companies and Help Them Coordinate Activities," *Inc.* (March 1988), pp. 25–40.

30. Mark L. Gillenson and Robert Gofer, *Strategic Planning Systems Analysis and Data Base Design* (New York: Wiley, 1984).

31. Lutz, op. cit., p. 27.

32. C. Joseph Sass and Teresa A. Keefe, "MIS for Strategic Planning and the Competitive Edge," *Journal of Systems Management* (June 1988), p. 14.

33. Arnold E. Keller, *Info Systems* (June 1987), p. 22.

34. Sass and Keefe, op. cit., p. 15.

35. Michale E. Porter, *Competitive Strategy* (New York: Free Press, 1980).

36. Connie Winkler, "Battling for New Roles," *Datamation* (October 15, 1986), pp. 82–88.

37. "Management's Newest Star: Meet the Corporate Information Officer," *Business Week* (October 13, 1986), pp. 160–172; John G. Burch, "CIO: Indian or Chief?" *Information Strategy: The Executive's Journal* (Winter 1989), pp. 5–13; and "CIO Is Starting to Stand for 'Career Is Over,'" *Business Week* (February 26, 1990), pp. 78–79.

38. Lucas, loc. cit.

39. Ibid., p. 41.

40. Ibid.

41. "The Portable Executive," *Business Week* (October 10, 1988), p. 103.

42. "Will There Be a Fax in Every Foyer?" *Business Week* (August 3, 1987), p. 82; and ibid., but see specifically the chart on p. 105.

43. Cary Lu, "FAX Finding," *Inc.* (November 1988), p. 155.

44. "Portable Executive," loc. cit.

45. Ibid.

46. Markus B. Zimmer, "A Practical Guide to Video Conferencing," *Training and Development Journal* (May 1988), p. 84. This article gives a series of questions and answers for people getting ready to do their first video conference.

47. "An Electronic Pipeline Is Changing the Way America Does Business," *Business Week* (August 3, 1987), p. 8.

48. Much of the opening commentary in this section is based on an article by Steven B. Seilheiner, "Current State of Decision Support Systems and Expert Systems Technology," *Journal of Systems Management* (August 1988), pp. 14–19.

49. Ibid.

50. Peter G. W. Keen and Michael S. Scott Morton, *Decision Support Systems: An Organizational Perspective* (Reading, Mass.: Addison-Wesley, 1978), p. 1.

51. P. K. Hough and N. M. Duffy, "Top Management Perspectives on Decision Support Systems," *Information and Management* (January 1987), p. 22.

52. George Houdeshel and Hugh J. Watson, "Management Information and Decision Support (MIDS) Systems at Lockheed-Georgia," *MIS Quarterly* (March 1987), p. 136.

53. T. H. Winston, *Artificial Intelligence*, 2nd ed. (Reading, Mass.: Addison-Wesley, 1984), p. 1.

54. Fred L. Luconi, Thomas W. Malone, and Michael S. Scott Morton, "Expert Systems: The Next Challenge for Managers," *Sloan Management Review* (Summer 1986), p. 3.

55. Ibid.

56. Ibid.

57. William Larry Gordon and Jeffrey R. Key, "Artificial Intelligence in Support of Small Business Information Needs," *Journal of Systems Management* (January 1987), p. 26.

58. Robert Michaelsen and Donald Michie, "Prudent Expert Systems Applications in Providing Competitive Weapon," *Data Management* (July 1986), p. 31.

59. E. Robert Keller, "Expert Systems: Alive and Well," *Journal of Systems Management* (November 1988), p. 35.

60. Engining Lin, "Expert Systems for Business Applications: Potentials and Limitations," *Journal of Systems Management* (July 1986), p. 19.

61. David H. Freedman, "AI Meets the Corporate Mainframe," *Info Systems* (February 1987), p. 32.

62. Jae K. Shim and Jeffrey S. Rice, "Expert Systems Applications to Managerial Accounting," *Journal of Systems Management* (June 1988), p. 10.

63. Freedman, op. cit., p. 36.

64. Jody L. Ryan, "Expert Systems in the Future: The Redistribution of Power," *Journal of Systems Management* (April 1992), pp. 18–21.

65. James A. F. Stoner and Charles Wankel, *Management*, 3rd ed. (Englewood Cliffs, N.J.: Prentice-Hall, 1986), p. 314.

66. "Is Your Computer Secure?" *Business Week* (August 1988), pp. 64–72.

67. Ibid.

68. Ibid.

69. Lynda M. Applegate, James I. Cash, Jr., and D. Quinn Mills, "Information Technology and Tomorrow's Manager," *Harvard Business Review* (November–December 1988), pp. 128–136.

70. Paul B. Carroll, "Computers Bringing Changes to Basic Business Documents," *Wall Street Journal* 6 March 1987, p. 33.

71. Much of the knowledge in the organization section is taken from C. W. Holsapple and A. B.

Whinston, *Business Expert System* (New York: Irwin, 1987), chap. 13.

72. Ibid., p. 301.

73. Ibid.

74. These are my own observations and not those of Holsapple and Whinston.

CHAPTER TWENTY

1. For a discussion, see Stephen S. Cohen and John Zysman, "Why Manufacturing Matters: The Myth of the Post-Industrial Economy," *California Management Review* (Spring 1987), pp. 9–26.

2. Joel Dreyfuss, "Victories in the Quality Crusade," *Fortune* (October 10, 1988), pp. 80–88; and "America's Leanest and Meanest," *Business Week* (October 5, 1987), pp. 78–88.

3. "Dr. Deming's Cure for U.S. Management," *Wards Auto World* (November 1981), p. 16; W. Edwards Deming, "Roots and Quality Control," *Pacific Basin Quarterly* (Spring–Summer 1985), pp. 1–4; and Mark B. Roman, "Made in the U.S.A.," *Success* (March 1987), pp. 47–52. For a brief history of quality issues, see "The U.S. Tries to Catch Up," *Business Week* (November 1, 1982), pp. 66–68; and Jeremy Main, "Under the Spell of the Quality Gurus," *Fortune* (August 18, 1986), pp. 30–34, who discusses the efforts of W. Edwards Deming, Joseph M. Juran, and Phillip Crosby, among others.

4. Douglas McGregor, *The Human Side of Enterprise* (New York: McGraw-Hill, 1960).

5. Damon Darlin, "Trade Switch: Japan Is Getting a Dose of What It Gave U.S.: Low-Priced Imports," *Wall Street Journal* 20 July 1988, pp. 1, 6.

6. For a discussion of managing in services, see Roger W. Schmenner, "How Can Service Business Prosper and Survive?" *Sloan Management Review* (Spring 1986), pp. 21–32.

7. Much of this chapter is designed around the strategic, tactical, and operational segmentation of the process approach found in Norman Gaither, *Productions and Operations Management: A Problem Solving and Decision Making Approach* (Chicago: Dryden, 1987), combined with the five key issues approach used by Roger G. Schroeder, *Operations Management: Decision Making in the Operations Function*, 3rd ed. (New York: McGraw-Hill, 1989).

8. Richard B. Chase, "Where Does the Customer Fit in a Service Operation?" *Harvard Business Review* (November–December 1978), pp. 137–142; and Schroeder, op. cit., pp. 19–26.

9. Gaither, op. cit., p. 3.

10. Schroeder, op. cit., p. 4.

11. Gaither, op. cit., p. 4; and James A. Fitzsimmons and Robert S. Sullivan, *Service Operations Management* (New York: McGraw-Hill, 1982).

12. Adapted from Gaither, op. cit., p. 30.

13. For a discussion of manufacturing strategy, see Steven C. Wheelwright, "Manufacturing Strategy: Defining the Missing Link," *Strategic Management Journal* (1984), pp. 77–91.

14. For a discussion, see Robert R. Bell and John M. Burnham, "The Paradox of Manufacturing Productivity and Innovation," *Business Horizons* (September–October 1989), pp. 58–63.

15. Robert H. Hayes and Steven C. Wheelwright, *Restoring Our Competitive Edge: Competing Through Manufacturing* (New York: Wiley, 1984).

16. Gaither, op. cit., p. 128.

17. Ibid., p. 129.

18. Wickam Skinner, "The Focused Factory," *Harvard Business Review* (May–June 1974), p. 113.

19. Douglas R. Sease, "Getting Smart: How U.S. Companies Devise Ways to Meet the Challenge from Japan," *Wall Street Journal* 16 September 1986, pp. 1, 25.

20. See Robert H. Hayes and Steven C. Wheelwright, *Restoring Our Competitive Edge—Competing Through Manufacturing* (New York: Wiley, 1984); and Wickham Skinner, *Manufacturing: The Formidable Competitive Weapon* (Ypsilanti, Mich.: Riley, 1985), for discussion of the major issues in the process itself. Also see Stanley M. Davis, *Future Perfect* (Reading, Mass.: Addison-Wesley, 1987).

21. Thomas J. Peters, *Thriving on Chaos: Handbook for a Management Revolution* (New York: Knopf, 1988), pp. 16–34 and 47–190, with the discussion of flexible manufacturing on pp. 161, 163, and 203.

22. James W. Dean, Jr., and Gerald I. Susman, "Organizing for Manufacturable Design," *Harvard Business Review* (January–February 1989), pp. 28–36.

23. Thomas J. Peters, "The Home-Team Advantage," *U.S. News & World Report* (March 31, 1986), p. 49.

24. "How to Make It Right the First Time," *Business Week* (June 8, 1987), pp. 142–143; and "The Best-Engineered Part Is No Part at All," *Business Week* (May 8, 1989), p. 150.

25. John Marcom, Jr., "Slimming Down: IBM Is Automating, Simplifying Products to Beat Asian Rivals," *Wall Street Journal* 14 April, 1986, pp. 1–20.

26. Gaither, op. cit., p. 143.

27. Dana Corporation, internal documents.

28. Gaither, op. cit., pp. 197–200.

29. General Motors *Annual Report* (Detroit, Mich.: General Motors, 1987, 1988, 1989); and William J. Hampton, "Downsizing Detroit: The Big Three's Strategy for Survival," *Business Week* (April 14, 1986), pp. 86–88.

30. Paul Ingrassia, "Losing Control: Auto Industry in U.S. Is Sliding Relentlessly into Japanese Hands," *Wall Street Journal* 16 February 1990, pp. A-1, A-5; Paul Ingrassia and Joseph B. White, "Losing the Race: With Its Market Share Sliding, GM Scrambles to Avoid a Calamity," *Wall Street Journal* 14 December, 1989, pp. A-1, A-10; and Hampton, doc. cit.; and Robert J. Samuelson, "The Coming Car Crunch," *Newsweek* (October 16, 1989), p. 62.

31. Jacob M. Schlesinger and Amal Kuman Naj, "Chrysler to Buy Renault's Stake in AMC: Seeks Rest of Company," *Wall Street Journal* 10 March 1987, p. 3.

32. Paul Ingrassia and Bradley A. Stertz, "Problems of Success: Ford's Strong Sales Raise Agonizing Issue of Additional Plants," *Wall Street Journal* 26 October 1988, pp. A1, 16.

33. G. J. VandenAkker, CEO, Avery International Europe, presentation to the Strategic Management Society, Amsterdam, The Netherlands, October 18, 1988.

34. Brian O'Reilly, "Business Makes a Run for the Border," *Fortune* (August 18, 1986), pp. 70–76; Cynthia F. Mitchell, "Coming Home: Some Firms Resume Manufacturing in U.S. After Foreign Fiascoes," *Wall Street Journal* 14 October 1986, pp. 1, 29; and Constantine C. Markides and Norman Berg, "Manufacturing Offshore Is Bad Business," *Harvard Business Review* (September–October 1988), pp. 113–120.

35. Gaither, op. cit., p. 327.

36. Richard J. Schonberger, *Japanese Manufacturing Techniques* (New York: Free Press, 1982), p. viii.

37. Gaither, op. cit., p. 335.

38. Ibid., p. 338.

39. Ibid., p. 149.

40. Cynthia A. Lengnick-Hall, "Technology Advances in Batch Production and Improved Competitive Position," *Journal of Management* No. 1 (1986), pp. 75–90. James E. Ashton and Frank X. Cook, Jr. suggest that much more remains to be done, however: James E. Ashton and Frank X. Cook, Jr., "Time to Reform Job Shop Manufacturing," *Harvard Business Review* (March–April, 1989), pp. 106–111.

41. William J. Hampton and James R. Norman, "General Motors, What Went Wrong," *Business Week* (March 16, 1987), p. 107.

42. Frederick C. Weston, Jr., "Computer Integrated Manufacturing Systems: Fact or Fantasy," *Business Horizons* (July–August 1988), pp. 64–68.

43. Gaither, op. cit., p. 13, is used for this discussion of CAD, CAM, FMS, and ASRS.

44. Patricia L. Nemetz and Louis W. Fry, "Flexible Manufacturing Organizations: Implications for Strategy Formulation and Organizational Design," *Academy of Management Review* No. 4 (1988), pp. 627–638. For a review of usage of flexible systems in Europe, Japan, and North America, see Arnoud DeMeyer, Jinichiro Nakane, Jeffrey G. Miller, and Kasra Ferdows, "Flexibility: The Next Competitive Battle, The Manufacturing Futures Survey," *Strategic Management Journal* (1989), pp. 135–144.

45. Judith H. Dobrzynski and James B. Treece, "Management Discovers the Human Side of Automation," *Business Week* (September 29, 1986), pp. 70–82.

46. William G. Ouchi, *Theory Z: How American Business Can Meet the Japanese Challenge* (Reading, Mass.: Addison-Wesley, 1981).

47. Leopold S. Vansina, "Total Quality Control: An Overall Organizational Improvement Strategy," *National Productivity Review* (Winter 1989–1990), pp. 59–73; and Armand V. Feigenbaum, "How to Implement Total Quality Control," *Executive Excellence* (November 1989), pp. 15–16.

49. Philip Crosby, *Quality is Free* (New York: Mentor/New American Library, 1979).

50. For additional information on product quality, see Martin R. Smith, "Improving Product Quality in American Industry," *Academy of Management Executive* (August 1987), pp. 245–247; Otis Port, "The Push for Quality: A Special Report," *Business Week* (June 8, 1987), pp. 130–137; and "Quality: The Competitive Advantage," special advertisement section *Fortune* (September 28, 1987).

51. Robert Kreitner, *Management*, 3rd ed. (Boston: Houghton-Mifflin, 1986), p. 627.

52. There are actually two cards involved, but the essence of the system is as described.

53. Schonberger, op. cit., pp. 1–3.

54. For more information on JIT systems, see Robert J. Schonberger, "The Transfer of Japanese Manufacturing Management Techniques to U.S. Industry," *Academy of Management Review* (October 1982), pp. 479–487.

55. Gaither, op. cit.

56. Author's discussion with Martin Marietta officials, 1988. And for a detailed analysis, see Joseph Orlicky, *Materials Requirement Planning* (New York: McGraw-Hill, 1975).

57. Thomas R. Miller, "The Quality Circle Phenomenon: A Review and Appraisal," *Advanced Management Journal* (Winter 1989), pp. 4–7, 12.

58. Ibid.; and "Quality Circles: Do They Work?" *Incentive* (May 1989), pp. 71–77.

59. "What's Creating an Industrial Miracle at Ford?" *Business Week* (July 30, 1984), pp. 80–81.

60. Michael Brodie, "Can GM Manage It All?" *Fortune* (July 8, 1985), p. 26.

61. See "The Leading Light of Quality," *U.S. News & World Report* (November 28, 1988), pp. 53–56; Myron Tribus, "Deming's Way," *Mechanical Engineering* (January 1988), pp. 26–30; and Main, loc. cit.

62. Leonard L. Berry, A. Parasuraman, and Valerie A. Zeithami, "The Service-Quality Puzzle," *Business Horizons* (September–October 1988), pp. 35–43.

63. Robert H. Hayes and Ramchandran Jakumar, "Manufacturing's Crisis: New Technologies, Obsolete Organizations," *Harvard Business Review* (September–October 1988), pp. 77–85.

64. Elizabeth A. Haas, "Breakthrough Manufacturing," *Harvard Business Review* (March–April 1987), pp. 75–81.

65. For more information, see Stephen R. Rosenthal, "Progress Toward the Factory of the Fu-

ture," *Journal of Operations Management* (May 1984), pp. 203–229; and Jack R. Meredith, "The Strategic Advantages of the Factory of the Future," *California Management Review* (Spring 1987), pp. 27–41.

66. John W. Kenrick, *Understanding Productivity: An Introduction to the Dynamics of Productivity Change* (Baltimore: Johns Hopkins, 1977), p. 114.

67. "The Productivity Paradox," *Business Week* (June 6, 1988), p. 100.

68. Ibid., throughout, pp. 100–114; Catherine L. Harris, Johnathon Levine, James B. Treece, Francis Seghars, Jodi Brodt, and Russ Mitchell, "Office Automation: Making It Pay Off," *Business Week* (October 12, 1987), pp. 134–146; and Norman Jonas, "Can America Compete? Its Options Are a Surge in Productivity, or a Lasting Decline," *Business Week* (April 20, 1987), pp. 45–69.

69. Maureen F. Allyn, "Rising Factory Productivity Is Giving the Expansion Room to Run," *Fortune* (August 1, 1988), p. 25; and Joan Berger, "Productivity: Why It Is the Number One Underachiever," *Business Week* (April 20, 1987), p. 55.

70. "Office Automation: Making It Pay Off," loc. cit; and Dan Guttman, "The Automation Edge," *Success* (October 1987), pp. 30–38.

71. Otis Port, John W. Verity, Anne R. Field, Susan M. Gelfond, Keith H. Hammonds, "The Software Trap: Automate—Or Else," *Business Week* (May 9, 1988), pp. 142–154.

CHAPTER TWENTY-ONE

1. "Reshaping Europe: 1992 and Beyond," *Business Week* (December 12, 1988), p. 60.

2. Ibid., p. 55.

3. Michael J. McCarthy, "The Real Thing: As a Global Marketer, Coke Excels by Being Tough and Consistent," *Wall Street Journal* 19 December, 1989, pp. A-1, A-6.

4. "Business Without Borders," *U.S. News & World Report* (June 20, 1988), p. 48.

5. Thomas J. Peters, *Thriving on Chaos: Handbook for Management Revolution* (New York: Knopf, 1987); and John Naisbitt, *Megatrends* (New York: Warner, 1982).

6. Amanda Bennett, "Going Global: The Chief Executives in the Year 2000 Will Be Experienced Abroad," *Wall Street Journal* 27 February 1989, pp. A1, A9.

7. "The Fortune Directory of the 50 Largest Commercial-Banking Companies Outside the United States," *Fortune* (August 10, 1981), p. 220; and "The 50 Largest Commercial Banking Companies," *Fortune* (July 31, 1981), p. 117.

8. R. Taggart Murphy, "Power Without Purpose: The Crisis of Japan's Global Financial Dominance," *Harvard Business Review* (March–April 1989), pp. 71–94. This article describes the tremendous influence the Japanese have financially in the world.

9. "The World's Biggest Industrial Corporation," *Fortune* (July 31, 1989), p. 282.

10. "Will We Ever Close the Trade Gap?" *Business Week* (February 27, 1989), pp. 86–92.

11. "Fitting into a Global Economy," *U.S. News & World Report* (December 26, 1988), p. 80.

12. Murphy, loc. cit.

13. Peter Truell, "Third World Debt Proposal Should Benefit Some Banks," *Wall Street Journal* 16 March, 1989, p. A9; and Charles F. McCoy and Peter Truell, "Lending Imbroglio: Worries Deepen Again on Third World Debt as Brazil Stops Paying," *Wall Street Journal* 3 March 1987, pp. 1, 24.

14. Karen Elliott House, "The 90s & Beyond: As Power Is Disbursed Among Nations the Need for Leadership Grows," *Wall Street Journal* 21 February 1989, pp. A1, A10.

15. Karen Elliott House, "The 90s & Beyond: For All Its Difficulties, the U.S. Stands to Retain Its Global Leadership," *Wall Street Journal* 23 January 1989, pp. A1, A8; plus the events in Eastern Europe in November 1989, the opening of the Berlin Wall, and political and economic reforms in virtually all of Eastern Europe.

16. Kenichi Ohmae, *Triad Power* (New York: Free Press, 1985).

17. William G. Ouchi, *Theory Z: How American Business Can Meet the Japanese Challenge* (Reading, Mass.: Addison-Wesley, 1981).

18. Norman Coates, pp. 69–72.

19. Robert T. Green and Trina L. Larsen, "Only Retaliation Will Open Up Japan," *Harvard Business Review* (November–December 1987), pp. 22–28.

20. James C. Abegglen and George Stalk, Jr., "The Japanese Corporation As Competitor," *California Management Review* (Spring 1986), pp. 9–27.

21. "Japan's Troubled Future," *Fortune* (March 30, 1987), pp. 21–22.

22. Unless otherwise indicated, this list of factors is principally derived from Lee Smith, "Cracks in the Japanese Work Ethic," *Fortune* (May 14, 1984), pp. 162–168; Lee Smith, "Divisive Forces in an Inbred Nation," *Fortune* (March 30, 1987), pp. 24–28; Joel Dreyfuss, "Fear and Trembling in the Colossus," *Fortune* (March 30, 1987), pp. 30–38; Gene Bylinsky, "Trying to Transcend Copycat Science," *Fortune* (March 30, 1987), pp. 42–46; and "Hour of Power?," *Newsweek* (February 27, 1989), pp. 14–20. Where these sources are substantiated by other facts, additional footnotes will be indicated.

23. "Look Whose Sun Is Rising Now: Career Women," *Business Week* (August 25, 1986), p. 50.

24. Stephen Kreider Yoder, "Stifled Scholars: Japan's Scientists Find Pure Research Suffers Under Rigid Lifestyle," *Wall Street Journal* 31 October 1988, pp. A1, A6.

25. Damon Darlin, "Trade Switch: Japan Is Getting a Dose of What It Gave the U.S.: Low-Priced Imports," *Wall Street Journal* 20 July 1988, pp. A1, A6.

26. "The High Price Japanese Pay for Success," *Business Week* (April 7, 1988), pp. 52–54; and Kathryn Graven, "The Home Front: Japanese Housewives Grow More Resentful of Executive Spouses," *Wall Street Journal* (September 30, 1987), pp. A1, A25.

27. Masayoshi Kanabayashi, "Bucking Tradition: In Japan, Employees Are Switching Firms for Better Work, Pay," *Wall Street Journal* 11 October, 1988, pp. A1, A19.

28. "Japan Builds a New Power Base," *Business Week* (April 10, 1989), pp. 42–45.

29. "Battle for the Future," *Time* (January 16, 1989), pp. 42–43.

30. "Can Asia's Four Tigers Be Tamed?" *Business Week* (February 15, 1988), pp. 46–50.

31. James M. Higgins and Timo Santalainen, "Strategies for Europe 1992," *Business Horizons* (July–August 1989), pp. 54–58.

32. Shawn Tully, "Europe Gets Ready for 1992," *Fortune* (February 1988), p. 81.

33. Ibid., pp. 81, 83.

34. Lammert deVries, presentation to the Strategic Management Society, Amsterdam, The Netherlands, October 19, 1988.

35. Ibid.

36. Philip Revcin, "Treading Water: Rich and Comfortable, West Germany Is Also Ominously Stagnant," *Wall Street Journal* 1 August, 1988, pp. 1, 12.

37. Greg Forman, "Future Shock: Banks Face Shakeout as Europe Prepares for Unified Market," *Wall Street Journal* 4 April, 1988, pp. A1, A18; and "The Money Men Can't Wait for the Starting Gun," *Business Week* (December 12, 1988), pp. 72–73.

38. G. J. van der Akken, presentation to the Strategic Management Society, Amsterdam, The Netherlands, October 18, 1988.

39. Steven Tupper, barrister, presentation to the Strategic Management Society, Amsterdam, The Netherlands, October 19, 1988.

40. "Crossing the Line from Talk to Action," *Business Week* (January 9, 1989), pp. 54–55.

41. Robert H. Hayes and William J. Abernathy, "Managing Our Way to Economic Decline," *Harvard Business Review* (July–August 1980), pp. 67–77.

42. Charles W. L. Hill, Michael A. Hitt, and Robert E. Hoskisson, "Declining U.S. Competitiveness: Reflections on a Crisis," *The Academy of Management Executive* No. 1 (1988), pp. 51–60.

43. Ibid., p. 53.

44. "Is the Soviet Union Next?" *U.S. News & World Report* (January 15, 1990), pp. 31–38; also see "The Deal of the Decade May Get Done in Moscow," *Business Week* (February 27, 1989), pp. 54–55. This article details an agreement by which U.S. companies and the Soviets are nearing a significant breakthrough in East/West joint ventures.

45. Michael E. Porter, "Changing Patterns of International Competition," *California Management Review* (Winter 1986), pp. 9–40.

46. Michael E. Porter, *The Competitive Advantage of Nations and Their Firms* (New York: Free Press, 1989). For a discussion of the more technical parameters of the definition of global strategy, see Gary Hemel and C. K. Prahalad, "Do You Really Have a Global Strategy?" *Harvard Business Review* (July–August 1985), pp. 139–148.

47. Stefan H. Robock and Kenneth Simmonds, *International Business and Multi-National Enterprises*, 3rd ed. (Homewood, Ill.: Irwin, 1983), p. 7.

48. Christopher M. Korth, *International Business, Environment of Management*, 2nd ed. (Englewood Cliffs, N.J.: Prentice-Hall, 1985), p. 7; and Neil H. Jacoby, "The Multinational Corporation," *The Center Magazine* (May 1970), pp. 37–55.

49. *Wall Street Journal* 25 April, 1988, p. 26.

50. R. Hall Mason, "Conflicts Between Host Countries and a Multi-National Enterprise," *California Management Review* (Fall 1974), pp. 5–14.

51. Stefan H. Robock and Kenneth Simmonds, *International Business and Multi-National Enterprises* (Homewood, Ill.: Irwin, 1973), pp. 243–249.

52. Author's personal observations about Europe vs. United States. The Japanese admit the need to bolster their R&D efforts in basic research.

53. Daniel Seligman, "Great Soviet Computer Screw-Up," *Fortune* (June 8, 1985), pp. 32–36.

54. For an interesting study of differences between Japanese and U.K. companies, see Toyohiro Kono, "Long Range Planning of U.K. and Japanese Corporations—A Comparative Study," *Long Range Planning* No. 2 (1984), pp. 58–76.

55. Donald A. Ball and Wendell H. McCulloch, Jr. *International Business: Introduction in Essentials*, 2nd ed. (Plano, Tex.: Business Publications, 1985), pp. 39–48.

56. Alex Taylor, III, "Who's Ahead in the World Auto War?" *Fortune* (November 9, 1987), pp. 74–88.

57. James B. Treece, "Can Ford Stay on Top?" *Business Week* (September 28, 1987), pp. 78–86.

58. Kenneth Labich, "America's International Winners," *Fortune* (April 14, 1986), pp. 34–46.

59. Kenichi Ohmae, "The Global Logic of Strategic Alliances," *Harvard Business Review* (March–April 1989), pp. 143–154; and Howard Perlmutter and David Heenan, "Cooperate to Compete Globally," *Harvard Business Review* (March–April 1986), pp. 136–152. Perlmutter and Heenan designate these alliances as global strategic partnerships (GSPs).

60. For a lengthy discussion of factors involved in making this choice, see Derek F. Channon,

with Michael Jalland, *Multi-National Strategic Planning* (New York: Amacom, 1978), pp. 193–194.

61. Michael Porter, "Why Nations Triumph," *Fortune* (March 12, 1990), pp. 94–95; excerpted from Michael Porter, *The Competitive Advantage of Nations* (New York: Macmillan, 1990).

62. Geert Hofstede, "Motivation, Leadership, and Organization: Do American Theories Apply Abroad?" *Organizational Dynamics* (Summer 1980), pp. 42–63.

63. Geert Hofstede, *Culture's Consequences*, abridged ed. (Beverly Hills: Sage, 1984), pp. 72, 92, 132–133, 166–167.

64. See H. Landis Gabel and Anthony E. Hall, "Ford of Europe and Local Content Regulations," in James M. Higgins and Julian W. Vincze, eds. *Strategic Management: Text and Cases*, 4th ed. (Hinsdale, Ill.: Dryden, 1987), pp. 944–972.

65. "Pull Out Parade," *Time* (November 3, 1986), pp. 32–34; "All Roads Lead Out of South Africa," *Business Week* (November 3, 1986), pp. 24–25; and "Fighting Apartheid, American Style," *U.S. News & World Report* (October 22, 1986), pp. 45–46.

CHAPTER TWENTY-TWO

1. David L. Birch, "The Hidden Economy," *Wall Street Journal* 10 June, 1988, p. 23 R, part of a special section on small business.

2. Ibid.

3. Ibid.

4. Bill Richards, "Starting Up: Blue-Collar Worker Laborers Laid Off in Rustbelt Try to Run Own Firms," *Wall Street Journal* 8 September, 1986, p. 1.

5. For a recent review of the relevant research, see Murray B. Lou and Ian C. Macmillan, "Entrepreneurship: Past Research and Future Challenges," *Journal of Management* (June 1988), pp. 139–161; and Max S. Wortman, Jr., "Entrepreneurship: An Integrating Typology and Evaluation of the Empirical Research in the Field," *Journal of Management*, 1987, no. 2, pp. 259–279.

6. For a review of Cantillon's theory, see Joseph A. Schumpeter, *History of Economic Analysis* (New York: Oxford, 1954), pp. 215–223.

7. Robert C. Ronstadt, *Entrepreneurship: Text, Cases and Notes* (Dover, Mass.: Lord, 1984), p. 8.

8. Joseph A. Schumpeter, *The Theory of Economic Development* (Cambridge, Mass.: Harvard, 1934).

9. Low and Macmillan, op. cit., p. 141.

10. Howard H. Stevenson and William A. Sahlman, "Entrepreneurship: A Process, Not a Person," working paper, Division of Research, Harvard Business School, 1987, pp. 15–17.

11. Ronstadt, op. cit., pp. 21–22; and Stevenson and Sahlman, loc. cit.

12. Howard H. Stevenson and José Carlos Jarillo-Mossi, "Preserving Entrepreneurship as Companies Grow," *Journal of Business Strategy* (Summer 1986), p. 13.

13. Peter F. Drucker, *Managing for Results* (New York: Harper & Row, 1964), p. 5.

14. Peter F. Drucker, *Management, Tasks, Responsibilities, Practices* (New York: Harper & Row, 1974), p. 45.

15. Paul H. Wilken, *Entrepreneurship: A Comparative and Historical Study* (Norwood, N.J.: Ablex, 1979), p. 60.

16. Peter F. Drucker, *Innovation and Entrepreneurship* (New York: Harper & Row, 1986), p. 28.

17. Stevenson and Sahlman, loc. cit.

18. Birch, loc. cit.

19. George Gilder, "The Revitalization of Everything: The Law of the Microcosm," *Harvard Business Review* (March–April 1988), pp. 49–61; also see "Big vs. Small," *Time* (September 5, 1988), pp. 48–49.

20. "The Long Arm of Small Business," *Business Week* (February 29, 1988), pp. 62–66.

21. Peter Drucker, "The Entrepreneurial Mystique," *Inc.* (October 1985), pp. 34–44. Peter Drucker indicates that the whole concept of an entrepreneurial mystique is largely a mistake. He views entrepreneurship as any other discipline, such as management—he feels it can be learned and that there is no particular formula. It simply requires very hard work, in his opinion.

22. Ellen Graham, "The Entrepreneurial Mystique," *Wall Street Journal*, Special Report on Small Business, 30 May, 1985, sec. 3, pp. 1, 4, 6–7. Small businesses consist of 250 businesses with 20 or more employees with less than $50 million in sales. The entrepreneurs were 153 chief executives of companies identified by *Inc.*, as part of the 500 fastest growing companies in America. The Fortune executive group consisted of 207 CEOs from the Fortune 500 list. Almost all respondents were male.

23. John A. Hornaday, "Research About Living Entrepreneurs," in Calvin A. Kent, Donald L. Sexton, and Karl H. Vesper, eds., *Encyclopedia of Entrepreneurship* (Englewood Cliffs, N.J.: Prentice-Hall, 1982), p. 28.

24. The traditional view holds that an innovation is simply the application of an invention. See, for example, Edward B. Roberts, "Managing Innovation and Innovation," *Research Technology Management* (January–February 1988), pp. 1–19; and Jay R. Galbraith, "Designing the Innovative Organization," *Organizational Dynamics* (Winter 1982), pp. 5–15. I have added the requirement of significance.

25. For a discussion of this issue, see Rosabeth Moss Kanter, *The Change Masters* (New York: Simon and Schuster-Touchstone, 1983).

26. David Birth, *Job Creation Process* (Cambridge, Mass.: MIT Press, 1978); and Karl H. Vesper, *Entrepreneurship and National Policy* (Chicago: Heller Institute, 1983).

27. "Masters of Innovation," *Business Week* (April 10, 1989), pp. 58–63. This observation is based on the descriptions of characteristics of these firms contained in the article.

28. For a discussion of the relationship of these two topics, see Max Wortman, Jr., "A Unified Framework, Research Typologies, and Research Prospectuses for the Interface Between Entrepreneurship and Small Business," in Donald L. Saxton and Raymond M. Smilor, eds., *The Art and Science of Entrepreneurship* (Cambridge, Mass.: Ballinger, 1986), pp. 273–332.

29. U.S. Government Printing Office, "The State of Small Business: A Report to the President," Washington D.C., 1985.

30. Barbara Bird, "Implementing Entrepreneurial Ideas: The Case for Intention," *Academy of Management Review* No. 3 (1988), pp. 442–453. This first stage, as described, here takes its terminology from Larry Greiner, "Evolution and Revolution as Organizations Grow," *Harvard Business Review* (July–August 1972), pp. 37–46.

31. "Matters of Fact," *Inc.* (April 1985), p. 32.

32. Greiner, loc. cit.

33. David C. McClelland, *The Achieving Society* (Princeton, N.J.: VanNostrand, 1961); and J. W. Atkinson, *An Introduction to Motivation* (New York: American Book, 1964).

34. "Fact Sheet: The State of Small Business: A Report to the President," *SBA News*, Washington D.C., U.S. Small Business Administration, 1984.

35. This is my conclusion after reading McClelland, loc. cit.; Atkinson, loc. cit.

36. Michael E. Porter, *Competitive Strategy* (New York: Free Press, 1980); and William K. Hall, "Survival Strategies in a Hostile Environment," *Harvard Business Review* (September–October 1980), pp. 73–86.

37. Stevenson and Jarillo-Mossi, loc. cit.

38. William Tucker, "Campus Capitalists," *Success* (October 1985), pp. 42–49.

39. Irene Pave, "A Lot of Enterprises Are Staying in the Family These Days," *Business Week* (July 1, 1985), pp. 62–63.

40. Gale Bronson, "Hitting It Big by Going Out on Your Own," *U.S. News and World Report* (October 21, 1985), pp. 50–51.

41. "How Sweet It Is to Be Out from Under Beatrice's Thumb," *Business Week* (May 9, 1986), pp. 98–99.

42. Tom Richman, "The Hottest Entrepreneur in America," *Inc.* (February 1987), p. 54; and Steven P. Galante, "Composition of Delegates Reveals Rise of Women in Small Business," *Wall Street Journal* 8 August, 1986, p. 25.

43. Ibid.

44. Sarah Harderty and Nehama Jacobs, *Success & Betrayal: The Crisis of Women in Corporate America* (New York: Touchstone Books, 1987).

45. "What Do Women Want? A Company They Can Call Their Own," *Business Week* (December 22, 1986), p. 61.

46. "The Long Arm of Small Business," *Business Week* (February 29, 1988), pp. 63–66; and Christopher Knowlton, "The New Export Entrepreneur," *Fortune* (June 6, 1988), pp. 87–102.

47. "America's Hottest New Export," *U.S. News & World Report* (July 27, 1987), pp. 39–41; and "France Gets Set for a Capitalist Comeback," *Business Week* (March 31, 1986), pp. 42–43.

48. Jay Finnegan, "Britain's New Generation of Company Builders," *Inc.* (November 1988), pp. 93–100; and Victoria Schofield, "Leading the Change," *Success* (January–February 1989), p. 8.

49. "America's Hottest New Export," op. cit., p. 41.

50. "China's Reformers Say: Let a Thousand Businesses Begin," *Business Week* (April 11, 1988), pp. 70–71; and "China: New Lows March, New Revolution," *U.S. News & World Report* (September 8, 1986), pp. 26–32.

51. Gordon Pinchot III, *Intrapreneuring* (New York: Perennial Library/Harper & Row, 1985), p. 67.

52. Thomas J. Peters and Robert H. Waterman, Jr., *In Search of Excellence* (New York: Harper & Row, 1982); and Gordon Pinchot, *Intrapreneuring* (New York: Harper & Row, 1985).

53. "How Intrapreneuring Can Change the Face of North America," *Management World* (April 1983), p. 24.

54. Richard J. Ferris, "Capturing Corporate Creativity," *United* (January 1987), p. 7; John Naisbitt, "Helping Companies Hatch Offspring," *Success* (May 1987), p. 14; and Colby H. Chyandler, "Eastman Kodak Opens Windows of Opportunity," *Journal of Business Strategy* (Summer 1986), pp. 5–8.

55. Thomas J. Peters, *Thriving on Chaos: Handbook for Management Evolution* (New York: Knopf, 1987), chap. 1.

56. Alvin Toffler, *Future Shock* (New York: Random House, 1970).

57. Michael Naylor, "General Motors: A 21st Century Corporation," presentation to the Academy of Management, August 14, 1986, Chicago, Illinois.

58. Richard T. Pascale, "Perspective of Strategy: The Real Story Behind Honda's Success," *California Management Review* (Spring 1984), pp. 47–72.

59. Peters, op. cit., chap. 1 and 5, sec. 3, pp. 191–280.

60. Michael Porter, *Competitive Strategy* (New York: Free Press, 1980), pp. 177–178.

61. A number of sources identify similar characteristics. See, for example, Charles O'Reilly, "Corporations, Culture, and Commitment: Motivation and Social Control in Organizations," *California Management Review* (Summer 1989), pp. 7–25.

62. Roger VonOech, *Whack on the Side of the Head* (New York: Warner, 1983).

63. "Innovation: The Global Race," Special Edition *Business Week* (June 1990). "Innovation in America," Special Edition *Business Week* (June 1989).

CHAPTER TWENTY-THREE

1. Earl Nightingale, "What Makes Successful People Tick," and "The Common Denominator of Success" (Chicago: Nightingale-Connant, n.d.), cassette tape.

2. Dennis E. Waitley, "Psychology of Winning" (Chicago: Nightingale-Connant, 1978), cassette tape; and Daniel Goleman, "1528 Little Geniuses and How They Grew," *Psychology Today* (February 1980), pp. 28–55.

3. For a review, see James M. Higgins and Julian W. Vincze, *Strategic Management: Text and Cases*, 4th ed. (Hinsdale, Ill.: Dryden, 1989), p. 8.

4. See James M. Higgins, *Human Relations: Behavior at Work*, 2nd ed. (New York: Random House, 1987), chap. 18, for a description of the life-planning process.

5. For an in-depth look at this complex process, see William L. Mihal, Patricia A. Sorce, and Thomas E. Comte, "A Process Model of Individual Career Decision Making," *Academy of Management Review* (January 1984), pp. 95–103.

6. Victor Kiam, presentation to the Roy E. Crummer Graduate School of Business Corporate Council, Orlando, Florida, November 1987.

7. Richard G. Kemmer, "Smart Moves—Clear Vision," *Executive Financial Woman* (Winter 1989), pp. 9–11.

8. Richard Nelson Bolles, *What Color Is Your Parachute?* (Berkeley, Calif.: Ten Speed Press, 1988), revised annually.

9. For example, see, "Managing Your Career," *College Edition of the National Business Employment Weekly* (Spring 1990), for several articles on issues such as career flexibility, training programs, self-assessment, and résumé writing.

10. Allen N. Schoonmaker, *Executive Career Strategy* (New York: American Management Association, 1971), pp. 6–11.

11. Erik H. Erickson, *Childhood and Society* (New York: Norton, 1950); Roger Gould, "The Phases of Adult Life: A Study in Developmental Psychology," *American Journal of Psychiatry* (November 1972), pp. 521–531; and Gail Sheehy, *Passages* (New York: Bantam, 1977).

12. For a lengthy discussion of desirable career fields in the 1990s, see "Best Jobs for the Future," *U.S. News & World Report* (September 29, 1989), pp. 60–72.

13. John D. Shingleton and L. Patrick Sheetz, "Recruiting Trends," Michigan State University, 1977.

14. Kathy E. Kram, *Mentoring at Work: Developmental Relationships in Organizational Life* (Glencoe, Ill.: Scott, Foresman, 1985).

15. Stephen L. Guinn, "The Changing Workforce," *Training and Development Journal* (December 1989), p. 36; and Karen Greenblatt Keating, Diana Delmar, and Kerry L. Johnson, "Balancing Work and Home," *Life Association News* (March 1989), pp. 22–43.

16. For a discussion of how couples handle such issues, see Francine Hall and Douglas T. Hall, *The Two-Career Couple* (Reading, Mass.: Addison-Wesley, 1978).

17. Nancy J. Miller, *Executive Financial Woman* (Summer 1989), p. 29.

18. Guinn, op. cit., pp. 36–39.

19. Elizabeth Erlich, "The Mommy Track: Juggling Kids and Careers in Corporate America Takes a Controversial Turn," *Business Week* (March 20, 1989), pp. 126–134.

20. Shelby Stewman, "Demographic Models of Internal Labor Markets," *Administrative Science Quarterly* (June 1986), pp. 212–247; and Thomas P. Ference, James A. F. Stoner, and E. Kirby Warren, "Managing the Career Plateau," *Academy of Management Review* (October 1977), p. 602.

21. Gene W. Dalton, Paul H. Thompson, and Raymond L. Price, "The Four Stages of Professional Careers—A New Look at Performance by Professionals," *Organizational Dynamics* (Summer 1977), pp. 19–42.

22. Lise M. Saari, Terry R. Johnson, Steven D. McLaughlin, and Denise M. Zimmerle, "A Survey of Management Training and Education Practices in U.S. Companies," *Personnel Psychology* (Winter 1988), pp. 731–743.

23. Michael Matteson and John Ivancevich, "Straining Under Too Much Stress?" *Management World* (July 1979), pp. 5–6.

24. For a review of factors and related research, see Steven P. Glowinkowski and Gary L. Cooper, "Managers and Professionals in Business/Industrial Settings: The Research Evidence," *Journal of Organizational Behavioral Management* (Fall–Winter 1986), pp. 173–193.

25. Bryce Nelson, "Bosses Face Less Risk Than Bossed," *New York Times* 3 April, 1983, sec. 4.

26. Thomas H. Holmes and Richard H. Rahe, "The Social Readjustment Rating Scale," *Journal of Psychosomatic Research*, Vol. 11 (1967), pp. 213–218.

27. Meyer A. Friedman and Ray H. Rosenman, *Type A Behavior and Your Heart* (New York: Knopf, 1974).

28. Dr. Robert S. Elliott and Dennis S. Breo, *Is It Worth Dying For?* (New York: Bantam, 1984).

29. Joshua Fischman, "Type A on Trial," *Psychology Today* (February 1987), pp. 47–48.

30. Hans Selye, "The General Adaptation Syndrome and the Diseases of Adaptation," *The Journal of Clinical Endocrinology* (1946), pp. 117–130; and Hans Selye, *The Stress of Life* (New York: McGraw-Hill, 1956).

31. Bruce M. Maglino, "Stress and Performance: Are They Always Incompatible?" *Supervisory Management* (March 1977), p. 8.

32. Earl Hipp, "When Employees Promote a Cathartic Atmosphere, Everybody Wins," *Business & Health* (March 1988), pp. 42–43.

33. Carol Hymowitz, "Stable Cycles of Executive Careers Shattered by Upheaval in Business," *Wall Street Journal* 26 May, 1987, p. 29; "The 21st Century Executive," *U.S. News & World Report* (March 7, 1988), pp. 43–46; Amanda Bennett, "Going Global: Chief Executives in the Year 2000 Will Be Experienced Abroad," *Wall Street Journal* 27 February, 1989, pp. A1, A9; Teecher Nolte, "How Managers Will Manage," *Fortune* (February 2, 1987), pp. 47–50; and Andrew Kupfer, "Managing Now for the 1990s," *Fortune* (September 26, 1988), p. 4.

34. Rosabeth Moses Kanter, "The New Managerial Work," *Harvard Business Review* (November–December 1989), pp. 85–92.

Company Index

A & P, 430–431
Advanced Genetic Sciences, Inc., 482
Advantage International Marketing and Chemical Manufacturing Company, 743
AEG, 52
Aerojet General, 262
Aetna Life & Casualty Company, 370
AFL-CIO, 295
Aid Association for Lutherans (AAL), 464–465
Airbus Industries, 200
Akerman, Senterfitt & Eidson, 527
Aldus, Inc., 653
Allied-Signal Corporation, 699
Allstate Insurance Group, 174
AM International, 396
Ambulatory Hospitals, 744
American Airlines, 114, 148, 289, 441, 442–443, 577, 631, 685
American Cancer Society, 196
American Cast Iron and Pipe Company, 640
American Cyanamid Company, 625–626
American Express, 125, 496, 497, 499, 500, 503, 516, 723
American Home, 76–77
American Hospital Supply Corporation, 631
American Management Systems, Inc., 644
American Motors Corporation, 672, 713
America West Airlines, 255–256
Anheuser-Busch, 73, 107, 116, 146, 301, 376, 407, 409
Apple Computer, Inc., 15, 17, 110, 149, 184, 192, 206, 260, 261, 292, 333, 386, 387, 388, 390–391, 395, 398, 712, 731

Armco, Inc., 231
Arrow Shirts, 466
Arthur Anderson, 611, 650
Arthur Young, 611
Arts and Entertainment Channel, 647
Atlantic Richfield, 339, 558
AT&T, 247, 274, 371, 387, 400, 401, 699, 712
AT&T Information Systems, 22, 141
Avery Europe, 709
Avery International, 673, 709

Baldor, 194–195
Bank America, 279–280, 586
Bank of Boston, 246
Barnett Banks, 138, 139, 142, 149, 150, 159
Beacon Street, 403
Bell Labs, 654
BeniHana of Tokyo, 219
Bennigans, 403
Berol Corporation, 449
Bethlehem Steel Corporation, 124, 238, 288–289, 330
Blount Brothers Construction Company, 234
Blue Cross & Blue Shield of Minnesota, 777
Blue Cross & Blue Shield United of Wisconsin, 761
Boeing, 57, 200, 611, 676
Boise Cascade, 611
Booz, Allen & Hamilton, 232
Borden, 746
Borg-Warner, 698
Boston Consulting Group (BSG), 184–185
Boy Scouts of America, 582
Bradley, Allen, Corporation, 654, 667, 690
Briggs and Stratton, 332–333, 667
British Airways, 146, 588
British Steel Corporation, 640

Brotherhood of Electrical Workers, 253
Brunswick, 187
Burger King, 110, 156–157, 249, 403
Burlington Express, 68
Burlington Northern Railroad, 450
Burroughs, 183

Caesar's Palace, 644
Cardinal Industries, 19
Carnegie-Mellon University, 644
Castle, A.M., 76
Caterpillar Corporation, 676, 700, 710–711
Center for Decision Research, 88
Center for Social Research, University of Michigan, 404
Chase Econometrics, 228
Chase Manhattan Asia Limited, 699
Chemical Bank, 131
Chernobyl, 582–583
Chevron, 147–148, 250–251
Chrysler Corporation, 242, 462, 672–673, 700, 713
Cigna Corporation, 622
Citgo Petroleum Corporation, 210, 211, 221
Citibank, 336–337
Citicorp, 701
Coca-Cola Company, 205–206, 588, 700
Coldwell Banker Real Estate Group, 174
Compaq, 15, 110
Computer-Aided Manufacturing International Inc., 611
Conference Board, 131
Continental Illinois National Bank & Trust Company, 121
Coors, 146, 374, 449

Crocker Bank, 150
Crop Genetics International, 482
Crosby, Philip, and Associates, Inc., 268
Crotonville Management Development Institute, 400
Cypress Semiconductor Company, 147, 162, 164

Daewoo, 662
Daimler-Benz, 52
Dana Corporation, 671
Data Resources, 228
Dayton-Hudson, 121
Deere, John, Companies, 611
Delaware Trust Company, 594
Deloitte, Haskins, & Sells, 153
Delta Airlines, 57, 84, 246, 399, 400
Denver Post, 611
Diamond Fiber Products Company Inc., 424–425
Diamond International, 424, 746
Diamond Shamrock, 746
Digital Equipment Corporation (DEC), 70, 150, 253, 349, 402, 411, 730, 731, 734, 738, 739, 742
Discovery Channel, 647
Disney, Walt, Company, 86, 152, 178, 183, 262, 359, 378, 390, 576
Disney, Walt, Productions, 20–21
Disney, Walt, World, 226
Diversitech General, 262
Domino's Pizza, 532, 558
Dornier, 52
Dow Chemical Company, 124
Dow Jones, 646
Dow-Corning, 736
Drexel Burnham Lambert, 572–573
Dun & Bradstreet, 646

Du Pont de Nemours, E.I., and Company, 115, 232, 247, 286, 418, 450, 643

Easter Seal Society, 18
Eastern Airlines, 114, 247, 289, 387, 567
Eastman Kodak, 57, 84–85, 247, 284, 285, 292, 300, 302, 676, 748
Eaton Corporation, 220, 392, 572
84 Lumber, 744
Electronic Data Interchange (EDI), 632
Electronic Data Systems (EDS), 236–237, 268–269, 398, 402–403, 731
Eli Lilly Pharmaceuticals, 614
Emerson Electric, 194
Emery Air Freight, 447
Empire Savings Bank of America, 558
Erie Technological Products, Inc., 694
Evan's Group, 228
Everglades National Park, 124
Exxon, 104–105, 111, 114, 123, 124, 676

Federal Communications Commission (FCC), 18
Federal Express, 527, 532, 556, 558, 644, 668, 669, 712, 732
Federal Judicial Center, 648
Finnish Parliament, 216–217, 218
Firestone Tire and Rubber Company, 646
First Chicago Bank, 500–501
First Denver Bank, 612
First National Bank, 260
First Service Bank, 382
Florida Informanagement Systems (FIS), 64
Florida Power & Light Company (FPL), 124–125
Flying Tiger Air Freight, 668
Ford Motor Company, 4, 5–6, 7, 12–13, 14, 15, 20, 21, 22, 26, 28, 34, 121, 260, 332, 391, 400, 462, 502, 532, 558, 577, 616, 667, 672, 686, 699, 700, 709, 712, 716, 722, 730
Ford of Europe, 709, 722
Foremost-McKesson, 462
Freedman Supermarkets, 744
Fuji Photofilm Company, 284

Gannett Company, Inc., 126–127
Gear, L.A., 174
GenCorp, 262, 263
Genentech, 393, 395, 571
General American, 555
General Dynamics, 107, 116, 124, 339
General Electric Company, 68, 107, 124, 148, 150, 174, 178, 185–186, 187, 194, 199, 224–225, 247, 292, 318, 332, 387, 388, 390, 400–401, 588, 676, 698, 699, 707, 708, 709, 712, 715, 716, 721, 770–771
General Foods, 147, 321, 460,

461, 462, 464, 467, 468, 472, 475, 479, 483
General Mills, 131, 146
General Mills Restaurants, 31
General Motors, 15, 26, 34, 35, 38, 39, 43, 44, 47, 49, 60, 68, 147, 148, 178, 197, 236, 237, 247, 254, 267, 270, 286, 294, 319, 326, 330, 332, 402–403, 404, 462, 470, 475, 480, 502, 671, 672, 675, 677, 686, 709, 712
General Tire, 262
Georgia-Pacific Corporation, 146, 604, 605, 606
Gerber, 218
Godfather's Pizza, 403
Golden Nugget Casino, 556
Golf Pride, 572
Gore, W.L., and Associates, 268–269, 270, 289
Grace, W.R., 121
Grant, W.T., 158
Greyhound Corporation, 139, 184
GTE, 371, 574–575
GTEL, 480
Gulf, 147, 251
Gulfstream, 302

Hancock, John, 121, 147, 339
Harley-Davidson, 409, 410–411, 710
Hay Group, 551
Heart Fund, 196
Heath Company, 182
Heinz, H.J., Company, 716–717, 718–719
Helsinki University of Technology, 216
Hercules, Inc., 334
Hertz Car Rental Company, 131, 146
Hewlett-Packard, 5, 8, 22, 57, 95, 96, 148, 159, 187, 256, 276, 301, 331, 667, 678, 694, 700, 736
High Steel Structures, Inc., 330
Hilton, 146
Hitashi, Limited, 400
Holiday Inns, 170, 516, 534
Home Depot, 174, 419
Honda Motor Company, 289, 295, 296, 306, 748
Honeywell, 8, 220, 348, 349, 358, 360, 364, 365, 462, 492
Hospital Corporation of America, 449
Hudson Institute, 349
Hughes Supply Company, 222–223, 419
Human Edge Software, 422, 423, 427, 431, 438
Hutton, E.F., 107, 594
Hyatt, 462
Hyundai, 187, 662

I & R Company, 338, 339
IBM, 12–13, 15, 18, 22, 57, 63, 70, 89, 110, 148, 150, 182, 183, 192, 193, 238, 246, 247, 256, 257, 261, 264, 268, 275, 295, 321, 352, 359, 371, 386, 396, 398, 399, 401, 411, 434, 439, 440, 470–471, 555, 589,

653, 670, 671, 694, 699, 730, 747, 748
Ingersoll Rand, 236
Intel Corporation, 506–507
Internal Revenue Service, 183
International Atomic Energy Agency, 582
International Harvester, 17, 75, 83
International Multi-Foods Corporation, 367
Interstate Bank, 759
ITT, 68

Jaguar, 722
Jeno's, 403
Johnson & Johnson, 736
Johnson, S.C., and Sons, Inc., 131, 175, 387, 449, 588

K Mart Corporation, 158, 174, 175, 182
Kay, Mary, Cosmetics, 388, 395, 731
Keidanren, 704
Kennedy Space Center, 566, 580–581
Kentucky Fried Chicken, 110, 187
Kenwood, 302
Kimberly Clark Corporation, 364
KLM, 709
Klynvold, Peat, Marwick, Gourdeler (KPMG), 611, 708, 709
KMG Main Henderson, 153
Kodak. See Eastman Kodak
Komatsu, 710, 711
Konveyer, 152
KPMG, 153
Kraft Inc., 603–604
Kroger, 51, 175

Leading Edge Software, 213
Levi Strauss & Company, 189, 221, 777
Life Insurance Company of America, 400
LifeMark, 146
Lincoln Electric Company, 477
Lincoln National Corporation, 68
Little, Arthur D., 551
Lockheed, 232, 273, 462, 485, 611
Lockheed Georgia, 264
Loew's Inc., 552
Lord Corporation, 617
Los Angeles Times, 486
Lotus Development Corporation, 745, 746

M & M Mars, 322
McDonald's, 18, 57, 110, 174, 183, 249, 292, 294, 355–356, 574, 687, 716, 731
McDonnell Douglas, 200, 557, 561
MacKay Envelope Corporation, 368
McKesson Corporation, 632
McKinsey and Company, 163, 201, 387–388, 393, 399, 703
Macmillan, 263, 264

Macy's, 174
MADD (Mothers Against Drunk Drivers), 113
Magnavox, 68
Manville, John, 127
Marata Manufacturing Company, 694
March of Dimes, 249
Marietta, Martin, 273, 462, 492, 587, 683
Marshall's, 222–223
Matsushita Electric Company, 712
Maytag Corporation, 698
Mazak Corporation, 332
Mazda, 191, 667, 700, 709, 712
MCA Inc., 598
Meadow Gold, 746
Merck, 96
Merrill Lynch, 431, 532, 632
Metropolitan Life Insurance Company, 373–374
Metropolitan Museum of Art, 18–19
Microsoft, 148
Miller, Herman, Inc., 27, 78, 398–399
Miller Beer, 146, 187
Milliken and Company, Inc., 96, 189, 221, 648, 670
Ministry of International Trade and Industry, 602
Mitsubishi, 700
Monsanto Company, 115, 555
Montgomery Ward and Company, 174
Morehouse College, 498–499
Mostek, 744
Motorola Corporation, 343, 371, 661
Mrs. Fields Cookies, 146, 175, 630, 634, 640, 647, 650, 731
MTU, 52

Nabisco, 390
NASA, 294–295, 566, 568, 569, 570, 575, 584, 586
National Academy of Sciences (NAS), 46
National Association for the Advancement of Colored People (NAACP), 113
National Food Associates, 539
National Football League, 443
National Institute on Drug Abuse (NIDA), 134
NCR, 57
New Jersey Bell, 41, 43
Nissenbaum's, 631–632
North Atlantic Case Research Association, 648
Northern Research and Engineering Corporation, 236
Northern Telecom, Inc., 656–657
Northern Telecom Limited, 656, 700
Northrup Corporation, 107
Northwestern Bell, 748
Nucor Steel, 8, 455
NUMMI (New United Motor Manufacturing, Inc.), 44, 330, 332, 675, 677

Occidental Petroleum, 210
Ohio State University, 505–506
Olin Corporation, 124
Olivetti, 150, 178, 274, 731
O'Neal Steel Inc., 640
Opinion Research Corporation, 551
Outboard Marine, 264–265, 669
Owens-Corning, 310
Oxford University, 112–113

Pacific Bell, 122–123
PACs (Political Action Committees), 113, 116
Paramount Studios, 183
Parker-Hannifin Corporation, 147, 610
Peabody, Peter, and Company, 400
Peat Marwick, 153
Penney, J.C., 532
Pentagon, 614, 622
PepsiCo of America, 17, 86, 386
Philips Gloeilampenfabrieken, 708
Phillips, 667, 709, 715
Photo Circuits, 620–621
Pillsbury, 403
Pitney-Bowes, 558
Playboy Enterprises, 616
Playtex, 746
Plessy Company, 698
Polaroid Corporation, 237
Porsche, A.G., 73, 75, 76, 77, 78, 80
Price Waterhouse, 288
Procter & Gamble, 53, 54, 183, 262, 395, 399, 400
Program of Neighborhood and Regional Change, 731
Pru-Care, 8
Psych System, 422
Pyramid Pizza, 743

Quality College, 194
Questar Corporation, 542–543

Ralston Purina, 231
Rand Corporation, 86, 232
Random House, 183
Raytheon, 107
RCA, 199, 359, 388
Reebok, 174, 700
Regency Communications, 464
Reliance Electric, 194
Remington Industries, 759

Renault, 713
Retail Planning Associates, 538
Revlon, 174
Reynolds, R.J., 339, 390
Rich's, 174
RKO General, 262
Royal Dutch Shell, 89–90, 178
Rule Industries, Inc., 153

Saab, 314
Samsung USA Inc., 12
Scandinavian Airline Systems (SAS), 414–415
Scherer Brothers Lumber Company, 449
Sears, Roebuck & Company, 158, 174, 175, 176, 179, 182, 183, 192, 195, 275, 286
Security Pacific Corporation, 397
Seminole Manufacturing Company, 632
7-11 stores, 210
Shearson and Lehman Brothers, 107
Shearson Loeb Rhoades, 496
Sierra Club, 113, 124
Signode Industries, Inc., 746–747
Singer, 184
Sir Beef, 743
S-K-I Limited, 585
Skippy Peanut Butter, 322
Skopbank, 707
Small Business Administration (SBA), 736–737
SOHIO, 16
Sometown, Inc., 325–326
Sony, 712
Southern California Edison Company, 374
Southland Corporation, 210
Spectrum Control, Inc., 694
Speedball Corporation, 449
Sperry Corporation, 183, 544
Squibb Pharmaceuticals Corporation, 780
Stamos Yachts, 302
Standard Oil of New Jersey, 286, 730
Stanley, Morgan, 399
Steak and Ale, 403
Summit Bank, 68
Sun-Trust Banks, 86, 273

Tandy Computers, 551
Tata, 700
Teamsters Union, 148, 554

Teddy's Tuck-In Service, 743
Texas Instruments, 321, 616, 651, 676, 748
TFR, 700
Thiokol, Morton, Inc., 132, 566
Thomson, 198–199
3M, 57, 94–95, 96, 401, 736, 747, 748
Tiger International, Inc. 668
Time Inc., 744
Time Life Films, 744
Tippins, Inc., 640
Torrington Company, 236
Totino's, 403
Touche Ross & Company, 153
Toyota Motor Corporation, 34, 267, 330, 332, 362–363, 486, 584
Toys "R" Us, 174
Trade Development Bank, 496
Trammel Crow Company, 392
TransAmerica, 287
Trans-Species Unlimited, 134
Travelers Insurance Company, 334
TRW, 247, 558
Tupperware, 110, 556
Tuscaloosa Steel Corporation, 640
Tylenol, 84

Unilever, 712
Unisys, 183, 411
United Airlines, 146, 231, 651, 748
United Auto Workers, 17, 75, 294
United Food & Commercial Workers (UFCW), 430
United Hospitals, Inc., 484
United Parcel Service, 668
U.S. Air Force, 107, 183, 255, 265, 611
U.S. Army, 270
U.S. Chamber of Commerce, 737
U.S. Civil Service Commission, 359
U.S. Department of Agriculture, 148, 270, 616
U.S. Department of Defense, 148, 567
U.S. Department of Health and Human Services, 396
U.S. Marine Corps, 391, 478
U.S. Navy, 234
U.S. Navy Special Projects Office, 232

U.S. Postal Service, 107, 668
U.S. Steel, 730
United Technologies, 501, 744
United Way, 125, 196
Universal Studios, 598, 599, 603, 612, 621
University of Chicago, 88
University of Denver, 49
University of Michigan, 506
University of Oklahoma, 618–619
University of Virginia, 48–49
USA Today, 126–127
USX Corporation, 338

Van de Kamp, 403
Versitek, 390
Vestron Video Corporation, 744
Volvo, 314, 315, 316, 322, 326, 329–330, 334, 336

Wacoal Corporation of Japan, 769
Wal-Mart Stores, 146, 174, 175, 182, 533, 632, 731, 748, 749
Wang Laboratories, 371, 731
Waterford Glass Group PLC, 610
Wedgewood, 610
Wells Fargo and Company, 150
Wendy's, 110, 175, 249, 466
Western Electric Company, 45, 46, 47
Westin, 146
Westinghouse Electric Corporation, 548, 559, 612, 660, 675, 676, 682, 687, 689
Weyerhaeuser, 236
Wharton Econometric Forecasting Associates, 228
Whirlpool Corporation, 698
Whole Foods Market, 559
Williams, A.L., Insurance Company, 532, 534, 538, 540, 546, 558
Wilson Learning Corporation, 480
World Bank, 279

Xerox Corporation, 17, 30, 111, 131, 255, 371, 387, 390, 399, 480, 516, 548, 577, 616, 684

Zenith, 182–183

Name Index

Abboud, Robert, 500–501
Adams, J. Stacy, 440
Agor, Weston H., 96
Akers, John, 63, 246
Akker, G.J. van den, 709
Alderfer, Clayton P., 429, 434, 437
Anderson, Wendy, 113
Ansberry, Clare, 284
Argyris, Chris, 320
Arthur, Henry D., 129
Ash, Mary Kay, 388, 731
Atkinson, J.W., 432
Aulthouse, Dale, 330
Aupperle, Kenneth E., 128
Austin, Nancy K., 57, 59
Ave, Walter J., 685

Babbage, Charles, 37
Bailey, David, 566, 581
Ball, Donald A., 716
Bandura, A., 451
Barnard, Chester, 41, 43–45, 50, 56, 57, 60, 254, 500, 580
Baron, Peter, 333
Bass, Bernard, 524
Bass brothers, 20, 359
Bassin, Marc, 460
Baum, Laurie, 13
Beals, Vaughn, 410
Beam, Alex, 79
Beazley, Ernest, 289
Bedeian, Arthur G., 65, 130, 567
Behling, O., 448
Bell, Cecil, 407
Bellmon, Henry, 618–619
Benne, Kenneth D., 470, 471, 472
Bennett, Amanda, 251, 370
Bennis, Warren, 497
Bernstein, Aaron, 443
Bickmore, Lee S., 69
Birch, David, 731
Bitter, Carole, 744
Black, Kathleen, 126, 127

Black, Leon, 572
Blake, Robert R., 508–509
Blanchard, Kenneth H., 53, 514–516
Blicker, Allen, 131
Blumenthal, Michael, 183
Boehm, Virginia, 16
Boesky, Ivan, 107
Boisjoly, Roger, 132
Bolles, Richard Nelson, 759
Bonaparte, Napoleon, 533
Boreham, Roland, Jr., 194
Bossidy, William H., 698
Bosworth, Brian ("the Boz"), 618
Boulding, Kenneth, 52
Boyle, Daniel, 424
Brandow, Richard R., 653
Branitzki, Heinz, 76, 77, 78
Breitschwerdt, Werner, 52
Brennan, A., 174
Brennan, Bernard F., 174
Brody, Michael, 566
Brown, Buck, 630
Brown, Francis C., III, 443
Burch, John G., 636, 638, 639
Burden, Lawrence T., 529, 646
Burns, James McGregor, 524
Burns, Tom, 113, 114, 288, 289–290, 294, 295
Bush, George, 483
Bussey, John, 54
Byans, Lloyd L., 281
Bylinski, Gene, 690

Caldwell, Phillip, 4
Cammann, Cortlandt, 578, 579
Campbell, David P., 139
Campbell, Jeff, 156–157
Camus, Albert, 315
Cannon, J. Thomas, 175
Cantillon, Richard, 732
Carlisle, David P., 223
Carlisle, Ralph Emmett, 643
Carlzon, Jan, 414, 415
Carnegie, Andrew, 730

Carrie, Ernestine Gilbreth, 40
Carroll, Archie, 118, 119, 128
Carroll, Paul B., 63, 246, 740
Carroll, S.J., 9, 15
Carter, Jimmy, 590, 616
Castle, A.M., 76–77
Chandler, Alfred D., Jr., 286
Chandler, Colby H., 284
Chapman, James, 422
Charlier, Marj, 443
Chase, Marilyn, 104
Chermers, Martin M., 512
Chung, Kae H., 325
Cieply, Michael, 598
Clausen, A.W., 279
Coch, Lester, 413
Cochrane, Philip L., 128
Cohen, Laurie P., 573
Conlen, Dan, 338
Cook, Suzanne H., 383
Copeland, Thomas E., 607
Costle, Douglas M., 483
Cousins, Gregory T., 104
Cox, J., 215, 216
Crofts, D.B., 404
Crosby, Phil, 194, 662

Da Costa, J., 216
Daft, Richard L., 271, 538, 539, 550, 600
Dalkey, Norman, 86
Dalton, Gene W., 769
Danforth, Douglas B., 660
Daniels, Bill, 49
David, Fred R., 157, 158
Davis, Keith, 404, 473, 474
Davis, Stanley M., 274
Deal, Terrence E., 393, 394
DeBenedetti, Carlo, 731
Deily, Linnet, 759
Delbecq, André L., 86
Deming, William Edwards, 5, 57, 662, 687, 688
DeMott, John S., 690
DeVanna, Mary Anne, 157, 497, 499, 525

deVries, Lammert, 708
Dimmett, William D., 348
Divorkin, Peter, 261
Dobrzynski, Judith H., 401
Doermer, Richard K., 68, 87
Donnelly, James H., Jr., 318
Donovan, Priscilla, 97
Dowling, William F., 314
Dreyfuss, Joel, 246, 261, 386
Drucker, Henry, 113
Drucker, Peter, 75, 161, 247, 304–305, 306, 631, 732
Dryfack, Kenneth, 183
Dumas, Alexander, 461
Duncan, Amy, 748
Duncan, Robert B., 114, 115, 275, 290
Dyer, William, 493

Eisen, Mark, 538
Eisner, Michael, 20, 21, 183, 359
Eklund, Christopher S., 431
Elliott, Robert S., 776
Endee, John, 620, 621
Ends, Earl J., 465
Enriquez, Jimmy, 743
Epstein, Edwin M., 126
Eriksen, Michael, 122, 123
Erikson, Erik, 762
Estes, Elliott M., 34

Fallon, Walter A., 284, 285
Farley, Frank, 101
Farmham, Alan, 195
Fasun, D., 405
Fayol, Henri, 41–42, 45, 53, 248, 270, 503
Ferratt, Thomas, 555
Feston, N. Patricia, 543
Fiedler, Fred E., 53, 510–512
Fields, Randy and Debbi, 620, 631, 731
Finnegan, Jay, 483
Fitzgerald, Lori, 322
Flowers, Vincent S., 423

Flynn, Mary Kathleen, 644
Foegen, J.H., 319
Follett, Mary Parker, 41, 43, 44, 45, 57
Ford, Henry, 35, 301, 686, 730
Forehand, Garlie, 404
Foster, Badi, 370
Frank, Frederic, 769
Franklin, Jerome, 510
Freeman, R. Edward, 120, 128
French, John, 413, 500
French, Wendell, 407
Friedman, Milton, 118

Gabor, Adrea, 21
Gaither, Norm, 216, 665, 666, 672, 681
Gantt, Henry L., 38, 39, 211, 664
Garfield, Charles A., 433
Gates, Bill, 157
Geishecker, John, 153
Gellerman, Saul W., 626
Gibson, G.H., 314
Gibson, James L., 318
Giglioni, Giovanni, 567
Gilbreth, Frank and Lillian, 38, 40, 211, 503, 684
Gilder, George, 731, 733
Givens, Ron, 619
Glass, David D., 748
Goddard, Robert W., 476
Goehing, Robert, 364
Goizueta, Robert, 205–206
Gomez, Alain, 198
Goodenough, Dave, 123
Gorbachev, Mikhail, 517, 518, 711
Gordon, Robert A., 48, 49
Gore, William L., 268–269
Gould, Roger, 762
Graham, Ellen, 734, 735, 737
Graham, Gerald H., 257
Graicunas, V.A., 265–266
Greenfield, Meg, 104, 105, 134
Greenwood, William, 571
Griffiths, David, 660
Grove, Andrew, 506–507
Grudnitski, Gary, 636, 638, 639
Gumpert, David E., 742
Gunter, David, 757
Guyon, Janet, 401
Gyllenhammar, Peter G., 314

Hackman, J. Richard, 317, 327, 328, 475
Hafner, Katherine M., 261, 386
Hahn-O'Leary, Michelle, 104
Hall, David J., 287
Hall, Stewart, 419
Hall, William K., 190–191
Halpin, Andrew W., 404
Hamalainen, Raimo P., 216, 217
Hamilton, "Red Dog," 4, 6
Hampton, William J., 34, 267
Hansell, Steven, 138
Hardaker, Maurice, 471
Hardin, Charles, 492
Hardy, Joseph A., Jr., 744
Harvey, L. James, 355
Hatfield, John D., 128
Hatmaker, Gary, 711
Hawkins, Steve L., 21

Hayes, J. Patrick ("Paddy"), 610
Hazelwood, Joseph, 104
Heckert, R.E., 661
Hefner, Christie, 301
Heinen, J. Steven, 467
Heinisch, Roger P., 348
Helm, Leslie, 85
Helyar, John, 170
Henderson, Jim, 122
Henkoff, Ronald, 711
Hennessy, Edward, Jr., 699
Henry VIII, 112
Henry, David, 567
Henry, John, 482, 483
Hersey, Paul, 53, 514–516
Hershey, Robert, 391
Herzberg, Frederick W., 321, 324–325, 326, 358, 436
Hewlett, William P., 95
Hezberg, Theodore, 155
Higgins, James M., 177, 261, 351, 354, 399, 425, 426, 437, 474
Hill, Charles W., 261
Hitt, Michael A., 261
Hodgson, William G., 626
Hofer, Charles W., 53, 160
Hofstede, Geert, 721
Holmes, Thomas H., 775
Holsapple, C.W., 631, 654
Horkison, Robert E., 261
Hornaday, John A., 736
House, Karen Elliott, 703
House, Robert J., 512–514
Howe, James E., 48, 49
Hudson, Rock, 123
Hughes, Charles L., 423
Hunt, James G., 463
Hurlock, James, 85
Hutchins, Dexter, 684
Hymowitz, Carol, 289

Iacocca, Lee, 193, 195, 242, 301, 524
Icahn, Carl, 5
Israelite, Michael A., 622
Ivancevich, John M., 318, 772
Iverson, Ken, 455

Jackson, Eugene, 467
Jacobson, Allen (Jake), 94–95
Jacoby, Neil H., 713
Janis, Irving, 477–478
Janson, Robert, 327, 328
Jarillo-Mossi, Jose Carlos, 732, 741
Jerdee, T.H., 9, 15
Jobs, Steven, 333, 390, 395, 731
Johnson, F. Ross, 390
Johnson, Jay I., 746
Johnson, Jim, 422, 423
Johnson, Robert, 403
Johnson, Sam, 175
Jones, Bob, 492
Jones, Patricia E., 265, 285
Jonsson, Berth, 314
Joseph, Frederick, 572, 573
Jourard, Sidney, 757
Juran, Joseph M., 57, 662

Kanter, Jerome, 634
Kanter, Mark, 653
Kantrowitz, Barbara, 353

Kapoor, Vinoid K., 660
Kast, Fremont E., 52
Katayama, Frederick Hiroshi, 296, 698
Katz, Robert L., 11
Kaufman, Steve, 163
Kearns, David T., 30
Keen, Peter G.W., 90
Kelley, J.A., 232
Kelley, Paul S., 391
Kelly, Kevin, 748
Kennedy, Allan A., 393, 394
Kennedy, John, 501
Kepner, Charles H., 76, 77
Kerwin, Jerry K., 182
Kiam, Victor, 759
Killiam, Keith, 134
Kilmann, Ralph H., 393
Kilminster, Joe, 566
King, Martin Luther, Jr., 498, 501
Kingstone, Brett, 743
Kirby, R.E., 660
Kirp, David, 123
Kissick, John, 572
Kizilos, Tolly, 348
Klingman, Darwin, 210
Klugt, Cor van der, 708
Kobayashi, Noritake, 387
Koenig, Richard, 363
Koepp, Stephen, 296
Komaneck, A. Nicholas, 771
Koontz, Harold, 55–56, 574
Kopelman, Richard E., 319
Korth, Christopher M., 712, 713
Korzes, James M., 499
Kotler, Philip, 157, 633
Kotter, John P., 412
Kroc, Ray, 731
Kume, Tadashi, 296

LaHair, Bob, 64
Lank, Alden G., 314
Latham, Gary P., 161
Lawler, Edward E., III, 423
Lawrence, Paul R., 270, 274, 297–298
Lazzano, Victor, 333
Ledbetter, W., 215, 216
Lee, Hai Min, 12
Legendre, Robin J., 382
Lego, Paul E., 559, 660, 689
Lengel, Robert H., 538
Lese, Judy E., 543
Levitt, Theodore, 78–79, 105, 107
Lewin, Kurt, 411, 412, 461
Lewis, David S., 124
Likert, Rensis, 271, 404–406, 482
Litke, Ann, 227
Litwin, George, 404
Locke, Edwin A., 443
Lorsch, Jay W., 270, 297–298
Lyles, Marjorie A., 75

McAuliffe, Christa, 566
McCardell, Archie R., 17, 75
McCartney, Forrest, 580–581
McClelland, David C., 326, 432
McCormack, Mike, 544
McCoy, Charles, 104

McCulloch, Wendell H., Jr., 716
McDonald, Allan J., 132, 566
McDonnell, John, 561
McGovern, Patrick, 740
McGregor, Douglas, 56, 57, 60, 320, 504–505, 662
McGuire, Jean B., 128
MacIntosh, Norman D., 600
MacKay, Harvey, 368
MacKay, John, 559
McKee, Mark David, 743
McKenney, James L., 90
McKilbin, Lawrence E., 49
MacMillan, Ian C., 265, 285
McMurray, Scott, 594
McNutt, Thomas R., 430
Magnesun, Ed, 566
Maguire, M.A., 601
Mahoney, T.A., 9, 15
Main, Jeremy, 4, 49, 68, 527
Mancuso, Frank, 183
Mancuso, J.R., 753
Mansen, R. Joseph, Jr., 117
March, James G., 88
Marcom, John, Jr., 671
Markowich, M. Michael, 484
Marlows, Gregory L., 660
Marous, John C., 660, 689
Marshall, Colin, Sir, 588
Marshall, Jim, 443
Martin, William C., 527
Maslow, Abraham, 427–429, 434, 437, 438, 467, 504
Mason, R. Hall, 714
Matteson, Michael, 772
Mayo, Elton, 46
Mays, Benjamin, 498–499
Merrills, Roy, 657
Merritt, Kim, 743
Mescon, Michael H., 356, 766
Metzcus, Richard, 529
Might, Robert J., 233
Mikalachi, A., 314
Miles, Gregory L., 559
Miles, Raymond E., 191
Milken, Michael, 572, 573
Miller, Danny, 80
Miller, Joe, 418
Miller, Joseph, 227
Miller, Michael W., 246
Miller, Victor E., 643, 644
Milliken, Roger, 648
Mills, T.M., 464
Miner, John, 434
Mintzberg, Henry A., 10, 16, 26, 258, 288, 290–295, 297, 298
Mitchell, Terrence R., 512, 534
Mitroff, Ian I., 75
Miyoshi, Masaya, 704
Mizek, Betty, 8
Mockler, Robert J., 568
Moore, James S., 215, 216
Moore, Thomas, 365
Moreno, J.L., 472
Morgenthaller, Eric, 125
Morita, Akio, 731
Moses, Winfield, Jr., 68, 69, 76, 80, 83, 87, 90
Mouton, Jane S., 508–509
Muczyk, Jan P., 517
Mulligan, Thomas, 21
Mulloy, Lawrence, 566
Murdick, Robert G., 635

Murphy, Joseph, 322
Murphy, Thomas A., 34
Murray, Robert, 390
Myers, Isabel Briggs, 366

Nadler, David A., 247, 578, 579
Naisbitt, John, 26, 406, 641, 643, 700
Nanus, Burt, 497
Nash, Laura L., 130
Nathan, Arte, 556
Naylor, Michael E., 26, 177–178, 197, 748
Neimark, Jill, 422
Neuharth, Al, 126, 127
Nevis, Edwin C., 429
Newman, James W., 533
Newport, John Paul, Jr., 496
Nickerson, Kenneth S., 223
Nixon, Richard M., 477
Norman, James R., 34, 267, 698
Norman, Robert S., 685
Normann, Richard, 664

O'Boyle, Thomas F., 73
Odiorne, George, 161
Oelman, Bradford, 310
Ohmae, Kenich, 703
Okamoto, Michiko, 134
Oldham, Greg R., 317, 327, 328
Olson, Frank D., 131
Olson, Kenneth Harry, 730, 731, 734, 738, 739, 742
O'Reilly, Anthony J.F., 718, 719
Osborn, Richard N., 463
Otte, Ruth, 647
Ouchi, William G., 575, 576, 577, 601, 677, 704
Owen, Robert, 37, 46, 57

Pacioli, Luca, 37
Packard, David, 331–332
Pae, Peter, 284
Page, Curtis W., 465
Pal, Warren B., 223
Parker, Patrick S., 599
Pascale, Richard T., 296, 398–401
Pascarella, Perry, 348
Patton, George, 123
Paztor, Andy, 594
Peak, Daniel, 27
Pearce, John A., II, 157, 158
Penfield, Wilder, 541
Perelman, Ronald O., 174
Perot, H. Ross, 268, 403, 731
Peters, Thomas J., 5, 25, 57–58, 59, 60, 109, 189, 269, 387, 406–407, 408, 423, 484, 641, 643, 669, 700, 748–749
Petre, Peter, 225, 730
Pfister, Peter L., 243
Philips, Julian, 163
Phillips, Nancy, 210
Pinchot, Gordon, 746–747, 747–748
Ponder, Ron, 644
Port, Otis, 237
Porter, Lyman W., 49, 423, 456–457
Porter, Michael E., 187, 188,

190, 287, 575, 643, 644, 718–721
Posner, Barry Z., 499
Poulter, Steve, 123
Pounds, W.F., 75
Power, Christopher, 77
Price, Raymond L., 769
Probst, Steven B., 223
Purdy, Kenneth, 327

Quinn, Jane Bryant, 599

Rachman, David J., 356, 766
Rahe, Richard H., 775
Raider, Calvin, 246
Ramirez, Anthony, 200
Raven, Bertram, 500
Raymond, Lee, 104, 123, 124
Reagan, Ronald, 8, 84, 301, 590
Reberg, Arthur, 26
Reformat, Pete, 338
Reibstein, Larry, 365
Reichardt, Carl, 150
Reichert, Alan K., 216
Reimann, Bernard C., 517
Renier, Jim, 348
Reynolds, Ray von, 743
Rhodes, Cecil, 112
Rhodes, Lucien, 269
Riccio, Lucius C., 227
Rice, Berkeley, 621
Rice, Charles, 138
Richardson, Elliot L., 483
Richman, Louis S., 52, 481
Richman, Tom, 630
Ricks, Thomas E., 138, 149
Rivers, Tom, 4, 5–6, 7, 15
Roberts, Leslie, 594
Robinson, Jim, 496, 497, 500, 503, 516
Robock, Stefan, 714, 722
Rockefeller, John D., 730
Rodgers, T.J., 162
Rogers, John, 246
Rogers, William, 566
Roland, Ian M., 68, 87
Rose, Robert L., 685
Rosenblum, John, 48
Rosenzweig, James E., 52
Ross, Joel E., 635
Ross, Monica F., 325
Roth, Terrence, 330
Ruckelshaus, William D., 483
Rudolph, Denise, 223
Rue, Leslie W., 281
Ruffenach, Glenn, 623
Ruffin, William R., 660

Safra, Edmond. 496
Sahlman, William H., 732
Saias, Maurice A. 287
St. John, Walter, 239
Samper, J. Phillip, 284
Sampieri, Linda, 31
Sanders, Myrtel, 12
Santayana, George, 35
Say, Jean-Baptiste, 732
Schaefer, George, 710, 711
Schaffhauser, Robert J., 747
Scheffi, Yosef, 223
Schein, Edgar H., 469
Schermerhorn, John R., Jr., 463
Schlendor, Brenton R., 261
Schlesinger, Leonard A., 412

Schmeisser, Peter, 113
Schmidt, Warren H., 510, 511
Schneeweis, Thomas, 128
Schonberger, Richard, 674
Schoonmaker, Allen N., 722, 760
Schriesheim, C., 448
Schroeder, Roger G., 667
Schumpeter, Joseph, 732
Scott, William G., 534
Sculley, John, 15, 17, 206, 261, 301, 386, 387
Seamonds, Jack A., 267
Segers, George E., 336
Seigel, Steve, 134
Sella, George S., Jr., 625
Sellers, Patricia, 174, 588
Sergiovanni, Thomas J., 529
Seven, L.J., 744–745
Shaw, George Bernard, 731
Sheats, Paul, 470, 471, 472
Sheehy, Gail, 762
Sheets, Kenneth R., 267
Sheetz, L. Patrick, 765
Shewmaker, Jack, 748
Shifrin, Carol A., 651
Shingleton, John D., 765
Shuman, Harry, 64
Sigband, Norman, 546, 548
Silverstein, David, 127
Simmonds, Kenneth, 714, 722
Simon, Herbert A., 49, 69, 88
Skinner, B.F., 445
Smale, John, 54
Smart, Tim, 566
Smilow, Joel E., 746
Smith, Adam, 36, 37, 248, 732
Smith, Dwight, 49
Smith, Frederick W., 556, 668, 669, 732
Smith, Michael, 4
Smith, Preston, 585
Smith, Robert B., 15, 34, 403
Smith, Sara, 585
Snow, Charles C., 191
Socks, Laverne J., 333
Solomon, Jolie B., 54
Springen, Karen, 353
Stafford, John M., 403
Stalker, George M., 113, 114, 288, 289–290, 294, 295
Starke, Frederick, 555
Steers, Richard M., 290, 550
Stevenson, Howard H., 732, 741, 742
Stevenson, William J., 40, 233
Stewart, Thomas A., 660
Stieger, David, 210
Stimmett, William D., 492
Stogdill, Ralph, 503
Stoner, James A.F., 243, 411
Staw, Barry M., 481
Stringer, Robert, 404
Styles, John, 744
Sundgren, Alison, 128
Sutermeister, Robert A., 315
Switzer, Barry, 618, 619

Tabac, Betsy, 746
Taggart, R., 699
Tannenbaum, Robert, 510, 511
Taylor, Craig, 769
Taylor, Donna, 349
Taylor, Frederick W., 37–38, 57, 211, 503, 568, 664

Teeter, Robert M., 483
Teets, John W., 139
Thatcher, Margaret, 112
Thomas, G., 216
Thomas, Kenneth W., 488–489
Thompson, Paul H., 769
Thorndike, E.L., 445
Tichy, Noel M., 157, 497, 499, 525
Toffler, Alvin, 25, 406, 748
Tolliver, J., 448
Toufexis, Anastasia, 449
Trautlein, Donald H., 288, 289
Tregoe, Benjamin B., 76, 77
Tsujimoto, Voshihide, 602
Tushman, Michael L., 247

Ullmann, A., 128
Ulrich, David O., 525

Van de Ven, Andrew H., 86
VanHorn, William L., 348, 492
Vecchio, Robert, 511
Vincze, Julian W., 177, 261, 280, 354
Vologzhin, Valentin, 152, 153
Von Bertalanffy, Ludwig, 51–52
Von Haller Gilmer, B., 404
Vroom, Victor, 90, 91, 92, 93, 438

Wagel, William H., 348, 537, 780
Walker, Barbara, 402
Walters, Roy W., 337
Walton, Richard E., 319, 576
Walton, Sam, 533, 731, 748, 749
Wang, An, 731
Wankel, Charles, 243, 411
Ward, Byron K., 471
Waterman, Robert H., Jr., 57, 58, 109, 150, 201, 423, 678
Waters, Craig R., 694
Watson, Thomas, Jr., 352
Watson, Thomas J., Sr., 396
Wayne, John, 123
Webber, Ross A., 771
Weber, Max, 41, 42–43, 45
Weihrich, Heinz, 574
Weill, Sanford, 496
Weinstock, Arnold, Lord, 698
Welch, Jack, 770
Welch, John F., Jr., 388, 390, 400, 698
Wells, Frank, 20, 21, 359
Wells, Kim, 104
Wensky, Arnold H., 382
Wessell, David, 638
Weston, J. Fred, 607
Whinston, Andrew B., 631, 654
White, Bernard J., 327
Whiteside, David E., 34
Whitney, Eli, 37
Wilcox, Ross, 124
Wild, William G., Jr., 237
Williams, A.L., 533, 534, 538, 540
Williams, Art, 532
Williams, Linda, 499
Williams, Redford, Jr., 776
Williams, Walter F., 288, 289
Willis, Rod, 411

Wilson, Kemmons, 170
Winwick, Patricia, 335
Wolsey, Cardinal, 112
Wonder, Jacqueline, 97
Wood, Robert A., 128
Woodman, Chuck, 123

Woodward, Joan, 302–304, 305
Wozniak, Stephen, 386, 395, 731
Wren, Daniel A., 36, 37, 42
Wriston, Walter B., 35

Wynne, Bayard, 235

Yago, Arthur G., 93
Yankelovich, Daniel L., 336
Yetton, P.W., 90, 91, 92
Yoder, Stephen Kreider, 603

Young, John A., 5, 678
Young, Warren, 210
Yukl, Gary, 161, 504, 506–507

Zovile, Pierre N., 653

Subject Index

Acceptability, in control systems, 580
Acceptance theory of authority, 254
  Barnard and, 44
Accident-prevention programs, 373
Accommodation, as conflict resolution
  technique, 489
Accommodative social response, 124
Accuracy
  in control systems, 580
  of information, 633
Achievement motivation, 432–433
Achievement-oriented leadership, 513,
  514
Acquired Immune Deficiency Syndrome.
  See AIDS
Action, in communication process, 540
Action lines, organizational
  communication improved by, 555
Action plans, in managing by objectives,
  161
Active recruitment, 360
Activity ratios, 607
Adhocracy, 292, 295, 297, 300, 306
Administration. See Classical approaches
  to management
Administration Industrielle et Generale
  (Fayol), 41
Administrative model of decision
  making, 87, 88–89
Age, size and growth and. See
  Organizational design
Age Discrimination in Employment Act
  of 1967, 352
AI. See Artificial intelligence
AIDS, 367, 374–375
Alcohol, concern about, 374
Allocation of resources, as strategic
  operations decision, 671–672
Americans with Disabilities Act of 1969,
  352
Annual operating plan, 146
Appearance, in nonverbal
  communication, 549
Application blank, 361, 363
Art, management as, 21
Artifacts. See Organizational culture

Artificial intelligence (AI), expert
  systems and, 650, 651
ASRS. See Automated storage and
  retrieval systems
Assessment centers, managers selected
  by, 368
Athletic programs, organizational
  communication improved by, 558
Attitude, in TRRAP model, 519, 521–524
Attitude surveys, organizational
  communication improved by,
  555–556
Attribution theory, future motivation
  and, 451
Audit
  external, 611
  financial, 611
  internal, 611
  social, 123, 127, 128, 603
  stakeholder, 603
AUDITOR, 651
Authoritarianism, as conflict resolution
  technique, 488, 489
Authority, 253
  acceptance theory of, 44
  as conflict-resolution technique,
  488–489
  delegation of, see Structure
  in organization chart, 250
Automated storage and retrieval systems
  (ASRS), 676
Automation, 334
  in factory of the future, 687
  job design and, 331, 334
  as strategic operations decision,
  675–676
  see also Computer
Autonomous work teams, 322
  job redesign and, 324, 330

Babylonians, contributions to
  management by, 37
Balance sheet, 602, 604, 606
Bank wiring observation room
  experiments, in Hawthorne
  studies, 47

Banks, largest, 701–702
Bargaining, as conflict resolution
  technique, 488, 489
BARS. See Behaviorally anchored rating
  scale
BCG matrix, 184–185
Beauty, need for, 434
Behavioral approach to management,
  45–48
  see also Hawthorne studies; Leadership
Behavioral norms, organizational culture
  revealed by, 392–393
Behaviorally anchored rating scale
  (BARS), 164–165
Benefits, compensation and, 372–373
Bet-your-company culture, 393, 394, 395
Body language, in nonverbal
  communication, 546–547
Bona fide occupational qualification
  (BFOQ), 362
Brainstorming, as interactive creative
  group process, 85–86
Break-even analysis, 229–231, 238, 649
Budgets. See Control systems
Building and maintenance roles, in
  groups, 471–472
Bulletin boards, organizational
  communication improved by,
  558
Bureaucracy
  machine, 292, 293–294, 300
  professional, 292, 294, 300, 306
  Weber and, 42–43
Bureaucratic control, 576, 577, 578,
  580
Burnout, 777
  see also Stress
Business environment, 107–109
  internal, 108–109
  organizations interfacing with,
  114–116
  see also External environment
Business plan, for small business/
  entrepreneurship, 738
Business strategy. See Strategy
  formulation

CAD. *See* Computer aided design
CAM. *See* Computer aided manufacturing
Canada, global competitiveness and, 710
Capacity, as strategic operations decision, 672–673
Capital expenditure budgets, 613–614
Career plateaus, 767–768, 769
Careers, 755–781
  advice for beginning managers, 771
  dual-career couples, 767
  future and, 777–778
  interview, 364, 764–766
  life's stages and, 762
  major choices, 762–764
  management development programs, 772
  minorities and women, 767
  mommy track, 767
  planning for, 757–759
  plateaus, 767–768, 769
  realistic plans for, 760–761
  stages in, 769–771
  see also Stress
Cash budget, 613, 614
Cash cows, in BCG matrix, 185
Cash flow statement, 604–605
Catch thirty, as life stage, 762
Catholic church, contributions to management by, 37
Causal forecasting techniques, 226–228
Cellular phones, 559, 647
Centralized organization, authority in, 255
Ceremonies, organization's culture revealed by, 390
Certainty, creative problem solving and, 80, 81
Chain of command, scalar, 253–254
Challenger, 566, 567, 568, 569
Change, management and, 5, 23–26, 28
  accelerated rates of change and, 25
  careers and, 777–778
  changing technology and, 25–26
  creative problem solving and, 26
  diversity of work force and, 26
  employee expectations and, 24
  global economy and, 24
  increased competition levels and, 25
  interpersonal skills and, 26
  in management functions, 28
  in 1990s, 6
  organizational culture and, 26
  shift from industrially based to information-based economy, 24–25
Change, managing, 375–376, 406
  change process, 417–418
  creative problem solving and, 414
  organizational development and, 407, 409
  resistance to change, 409–414
Channel richness, 538, 539
Channels. *See* Communication channels
Cheaper by the Dozen (Gilbreth, Jr., and Carrie), 40
China
  economy, 711
  entrepreneurship in, 746
CIM. *See* Computer integrated manufacturing
CIO, 646
Civil Rights Act of 1964, 352, 373

Clan control, 576, 577, 578, 580, 581, 590
Classical approaches to management, 37–45
  administration and organization, 41–45
    Barnard, 41, 43–45
    Fayol, 41–42
    Follett, 41, 43
    Weber, 41, 42–43
  legacy of, 45
  scientific management, 37–40
    control and, 568
    Gantt, 39
    Gilbreths, 40
    Taylor, 38–39
Classification method, for job evaluation, 372
Client, departmentation by, 265
Client relationship, in job redesign, 328, 329
Climate. *See* Organizational climate
Closed system, organization as, 50, 107–108
Clothing, in nonverbal communication, 549
Coalition, 194
Code of ethics, 130–131
Coercive power, 500–501
Cohesiveness, of groups, 478–479
Collaboration, as conflict resolution technique, 488, 489
Collectivism dimension, management practices and, 721
College Edition of the National Business Employment Weekly, 759
College students, as entrepreneurs, 742–743
Combination, single business corporate strategy and, 184
Common Market. *See* European Economic Community
Communication, 531–563
  barriers to, 551–554
    coping with, 553–554
    language limits, 551
    overload, 553
    physical and social limits, 552
    sender and receiver characteristics, 552–553
    speaking and listening habits, 552
    timing, 552
    wordiness, 552
  definition, 533
  formal, 549–551
  functions, 534–535
  informal, 551
  leadership and, 517
  as management function, 8
  nonverbal, 546–549
    aesthetic forms, 549
    body language, 546–547
    clothing and appearance, 549
    space in, 547–548
    status symbols in, 549
    time in, 548–549
    touching, 549
  perception in, 540–541
  performance appraisal and, 619
  process, 535–540
    communication channels, 538–539
    decoding, 540
    encoding, 536–537, 540
    feedback, 540
    ideation, 536, 540
    receiving, 539

    transmission, 538, 540
    understanding and action, 540
  verbal, 541–546
    language, 542
    listening, 544, 545
    oral communication, 542
    silence, 543–544
    speed and volume, 543
    voice tone and inflection, 543
    written communication, 544, 546
  see also Organizational communication
Communication channels
  in communication process, 538–539
  in organization chart, 250
Company strategy, structure, and rivalry, global competitiveness and, 719, 720
Comparison method, for job evaluation, 372
Compensation, 372–373
  motivation and, 437, 438
  performance appraisal and, 619
Competition
  change and increased levels of, 25
  as conflict resolution technique, 489, 490
  generic strategies, 187–190
  in global environment, 25, 713, 718–721
Competitive advantage, 192
Competitive environment. *See* External environment
Competitors, in competitive environment, 110
Complex environment, 114, 115, 290, 291
Complexity, coordination and, 269–270
Comprehensive plans, 147
Compressed work week, 339
Computer, 108, 334
  in decision making and planning, 235–238
  job design and, 334
  laptop, 559, 649
  life cycles of, 25
  management and, 25–26
  management information systems and, 646
  in quality control, 686
  quantitative methods using, 213, 214
  work at home and, 334
  see also Automation
Computer aided design (CAD), 676
Computer aided manufacturing (CAM), 676
Computer conferencing, 647
Computer integrated manufacturing (CIM), 675, 676
  in factory of the future, 687
Concentration, as single business corporate strategy and, 183
Conceptual skills, of managers, 11, 12, 16
Concurrent authority, 258
Concurrent controls, 584–585
Confidential plan, 148
Conflict management, 487–490
  consequences of, 488
  resolving, 488–490
Consumer surveys, 228
Contemporary management. *See* History of management
Content theories, in Motivation/ Performance Cycle, 427

Contextual dimensions, of job, 317–318
Contingency approaches. *See* Leadership
Contingency model, of leadership, 510–512
Continuous reinforcement, 447, 448
Continuum of leadership behavior, 510, 511
Control, 8, 15, 565–595
  budgets, *see* Control systems
  changes in, 28
  changing environment and, 590–591
  as communication function, 535
  creative problem solving and, 71, 80, 591, 592
  definition, 568–569
  dysfunctional consequences of, 581–583
  of economic functions, 587, 589
    financial control for, 587, 589
    human resources management control for, 589
    information management control for, 589, *see also* Management information systems
    marketing controls for, 587
    operational control for, 589
  evaluation of employees and, *see* Human resources management
  importance of, 569
  by level of plan, 586–587, *see also* Control systems
    operational control, 587
    strategic control, 587
    tactical control, 587
  of management functions, 589–590
  as management information system component, 637–638
  management style of, 575–578, 579
    bureaucratic control, 576, 577, 578, 580
    choosing, 578, 579
    clan control, 576, 577, 578, 580, 581, 590
    market control, 576, 578
  planning interrelated with, 150–151, 574–575
  process, 569–579
    actual performance compared with standard in, 571
    actual performance measured in, 570–571
    characteristics of, 572
    necessary action taken in, 571–572
    performance standards and methods of measuring performance in, 570, 574
  of small business/entrepreneurship, 740–741
  by timing relative to transformation process, 584–586
    concurrent controls, 584–585
    postaction controls, 586
    preaction control, 584
  see also Control systems
Control subsystem, in operations systems, 665
Control systems, 578, 580–581, 597–627
  budgets, 146–147, 150–151, 602, 611–617
    capital expenditure, 613–614
    cash, 613, 614
    departmental, 614, 616
    master, 613
    nonmonetary resource input, 613, 614

  operating, 600, 601
  process, 614
  responsibility centers and, 612, 614
  revenue and expense, 613
  strengths and weaknesses of, 616–617
  zero-based, 616
  in changing environment, 622–623
  core control elements, 600–610
  as creative problem-solving process, 643–644
  operational control, 601, 602, 620–622, *see also* Operations management
    disciplinary systems, 621
    for manufacturing, 621–622
  ratio analysis, 603, 605–607
    activity ratios, 607
    current ratio, 605
    debt-to-total assets ratio, 606
    inventory turnover, 607
    leverage ratios, 606–607
    liquidity ratios, 605–606, 607
    profitability ratios, 607
    return on total assets, 607
  strategic, 600–601, 602–611, *see also* ratio analysis, *above*
    balance sheet, 604, 606
    cost accounting, 603, 609–611
    financial analysis, 600, 602–603, 604–605, 606
    financial audits, 611
    flow statement, 604–605
    income statement, 604, 605
    long-range financial plan, 600, 601
    return on investment, 603, 607–609
    shareholder value, 609
    strategic plan, 600, 601
  tactical, 611–620, *see also* budgets, *above*
    performance appraisals, 601, 602, 617–620
    policies and procedures, 601, 602
    statistical reports, 600–601
Coordination
  Follett and, 43
  as management function, 9
Coordination centers, in organization chart, 250
Core function of management, creative problem solving as, 7–8
Core job characteristics, 317, 318
  growth needs and, 327–330
Core management function. *See* Creative problem solving
CORP TAX, 651
Corporate culture. *See* Organizational culture
Corporate social policy process, social responsibility improved by, 125, 126–127
Corporate strategy. *See* Strategy formulation
Cost accounting (analysis), 603, 609–611
Cost centers, 612
Cost effectiveness, in control systems, 581
Cost leadership, as generic competitive strategy, 187
Counseling programs, organizational communication improved by, 555
CPM (Critical Path Method), 232–233, 234, 235
  for project management, 687
Creative problem solving, 15, 26, 27, 69–101

  certainty and, 80, 81
  changes in, 28
  computers in, 235–238
  control as, 591, 592
  control systems and, 643–644
  decision making versus, 70–71
  in global environment, 715
  human resources management and, 378–380
  importance of, 94–97
  job design and, 339–341
  leadership as, 518–524
  leading groups as, 487
  management science in, 238
  managing culture and change as, 414
  motivation as, 451–453
  operations management as, 691
  organizational design and, 306–308
  organizational development improving, 409
  organizing as, 276–279
  problems in
    anticipated, 83
    structured, 82, 83
    surprises, 83–84
    unstructured, 82–83
  process, 73–80
    alternative generation, 78
    assumptions about future, 78
    constant environmental analysis, 73
    control, 80
    evaluating alternatives, 78
    implementing choice, 79
    key situational variables determination, 77
    problem identification, 76
    problem recognition, 75
  risk and, 81
  for small business/entrepreneurship, 741
  strategic management and, 202
  structured problems, 82, 83
  styles and tendencies in, 89–90
  uncertainty and, 81–82
  see also Decision making; Quantitative methods
Creativity
  Japanese management style and, 602–603
  planning and, 148–149
  in problem solving, 94–97
Critical incidents, as performance appraisal, 376
Critical path, 233
Critical Path Method. *See* CPM
Cross-functional teams, 273
  for product design, 670
Culture, in general environment, 111
  See also Organizational culture
Current ratio, 605
Customer
  in competitive environment, 109–110
  departmentation by, 265
Cyclical variations, in time series analysis, 225, 226

Database, as management information system component, 637
Day-to-day operations, operational decisions for. *See* Operations management
Deadline decade, as life stage, 762
Debt crisis, international, 702–703
Debt-to-total-assets ratio, 606
Decentralization, 306

Decentralized organization, authority in, 255–256, 257
Decision authority, in organization chart, 251
Decision making
  behavioral aspects of, 87–89
    administrative model, 87, 88–89
    economic model, 87–88, 89
  computers in, 235–238
  creative problem solving versus, 70–71
  groups for, 84–87, 479
    Delphi, 84, 86
    evaluating, 87
    interacting, 84, 85–86
    nominal, 84, 86
  participation in, 90–93
  see also Creative problem solving
Decision support systems (DSSs), 235, 636, 649–650
Decision theory, 218–220
Decision trees, 218, 219–220
Decisional role, of manager, 10, 11
Decoding, in communication process, 540
Defensive social responsibility, 123–124
Delegation of authority. See Structure
Delphi groups, 84, 86–87
Delphi technique, 228
Demand conditions, global competitiveness and, 719, 720
Departmental budgets, 614, 616
Departmental plans, 147
Departmentation. See Structure
Depth
  of job design, 324
  of jobs, 317, 318
Descriptive statistics, 217
Development, organizational, 407, 409
  see also Training and development of employees
Dictionary of Occupational Titles, 358
Differentiation
  coordination and, 270
  division of labor and, 249
  as generic competitive strategy, 187
  Lawrence and Lorsch studies on, 297–298
DINKS (double income, no kids), 336
Directive leadership, 513, 514
Disciplinary programs, 377, 447
  employees needing, 621
Discretionary responsibilities, 121
Disposable employee, 355
Dissolution stage, of group development, 468
Distribution models, 222–223
Division of labor. See Structure
Divisional plans, 146
Divisionalized form of organization, 292, 294–295, 297, 300
Dogs, in BCG matrix, 184, 185
Downward communication, 550, 551
Drug-addicted employees, disciplinary systems for, 621
Drugs
  companies concerned about, 367, 374
  human resources management and, 367
DSSs. See Decision support systems
Dual wage earner family (DINKS), 336
Dual-career couples, 767

Econometric models, 228
Economic factors, in global environment, 713

Economic model of decision making, 87–88, 89
Economic order quantity (EOQ), 681–682
Economic responsibilities, of business, 119
Economy, in general environment, 111–112
EDI. See Electronic data interchange
EDP. See Electronic data processing
EEC. See European Economic Community
EEO. See Equal employment opportunity
Effective work group, 481, 482
Effectiveness, 13
Efficiency, 13
Effort, motivation to expend, 442
Effort-to-performance expectancy, 439
Egyptians, contributions to management by, 37
Electronic bulletin boards, 648
Electronic data interchange (EDI), 648
Electronic data processing (EDP), 636
Electronic mail, 647
Emotive function, of communication, 534
Employee action programs, organizational communication improved by, 555
Employee expectations, changing, 24
Employee health and safety, 373–375
Employee relations, 375
  see also Human resources management
Employee stress. See Stress
Employee transitions, dealing with, 378
Employment. See Careers; Human resources management
Employment decisions, 368
Employment testing, 364–367
Encoding, in communication process, 536–537, 540
Entrepreneurial-type manager, 193
Entrepreneurship, 730–736
  administrators versus, 741, 742
  characteristics of, 733–736
  definitions, 732–733
  innovation and, 736
  intrapreneurship, 194, 612, 736, 746–749
  managing, 737–741
    leading, 739–740
    organizing, 739
    planning, 738–739
  preserving, 741
  small business distinguished from, 736
  succession and, 749
  trends in, 741–749
    children in family business, 743–744
    college students as entrepreneurs, 742–743
    international entrepreneurship, 746
    intrapreneurship, 736, 746–749
    leaving corporation for small business, 744–745
    restructuring and, 748–749
    women as entrepreneurs, 745
  see also Small business management
Environment
  complexity and change and, 290, 291
  group influenced by, 467
  managerial, 19–21
  simple, 290, 291
  stable, 289
  unstable, 289

see also External environment; Global environment; Internal environment
Environmental analysis, creative problem-solving process needing, 73, 75
Environmental Protection Agency (EPA), 482
EOQ. See Economic order quantity
EPS (Environmental Planning Systems), 237
Equal employment opportunity (EEO), 350, 351–353
  compensation and, 373
  in job specifications, 359
  performance appraisal and, 377, 617, 620
  recruitment and, 360, 361–362
  selection and, 363, 366–368
Equal Employment Opportunity Act of 1978, 352
Equal Employment Opportunity Commission (EEOC), 350
Equal Pay Act of 1963, 352, 373
Equity theory, of employee motivation, 440–441
ESs. See Expert systems
Essay, as performance appraisal, 376
Ethical behavior, 121
Ethics, 107, 121, 129–132
  improving, 130–132
    code of ethics for, 130–132
    inculturation programs, 132
    ombudsmen, committees and task forces, 132
    whistleblowing, 131–132
  management and, 130
  see also Social responsibility
Europe, 703
  East-West economic integration and, 706–710
  entrepreneurship in, 746
  home market, 702
European Economic Community (EEC), 197, 388, 673, 699, 706–709
Evaluation and control of employees. See Human resources management
Excellence approach to management, 57–58
Executive, Barnard on functions of, 44
Executive information systems, 651–652
Executive opinion, 228
Expectancy theory
  of employee motivation, 438–440
  reinforcement theory and, 445
Expected value, 219
Expense centers, 612
Expert opinion, 228
Expert power, 501
Expert systems (ESs), 637, 649, 650–651
Extending, as life stage, 762
External audits, 611
External environment, 108
  competitive environment, 108, 109–110
    competitors, 110
    customers, 109–110
    new entrants, 110
    substitutes, 110
    suppliers, 110
  complex, 114, 115
  general environment, 108, 110–113
    economy, 111–112
    legal/political factors, 112–113
    society and culture, 111
    technology, 110–111

External environment (*Continued*)
stable, 113, 114, 115
strategy and, *see* Organizational design
unstable, 113, 114, 115
External environmental analysis, in SWOT analysis, 179
External environmental factors, 19, 20
Extinction, as reinforcement, 447
Extrinsic need satisfiers, 436–438

Factor conditions, global competitiveness and, 719, 720
Factories
focused, 669–670
of the future, 669, 687, 689, 690
see also Operations management
Family business, children staying in, 743–744
Fax machines, 559, 647
Feedback, in communication process, 540
Feedback channels, in job redesign, 328, 329
Feed-forward controls. *See* Preaction control
Feminine countries, management practices and, 721
Finance, in global environment, 721
Financial analysis, 600, 602–603, 604–605, 606
Financial audits, 602–603, 611
Financial control, 587, 589
Finished goods, as inventory type, 681
First-line management. *See* Lower-level managers
Five configurations approach, Mintzberg's, 290–295, 297, 299–300
Fixed position layout, 673
Fixed-interval reinforcement, 447, 448
Fixed-ratio reinforcement schedule, 447, 448
"Flat" organizations, 267
Flexibility, in control systems, 580
Flexible manufacturing systems (FMS), 676
Flexi-time, 338
FMS. *See* Flexible manufacturing systems
Focus, as generic competitive strategy, 187
Focused factories, 669
Forced choice, as performance appraisal, 376
Force-field analysis, resistance to change and, 410, 411
Forecasting, 215, 223–229
human resource requirements, 358
limits of, 228
qualitative, 228
quantitative techniques, 225–228
causal, 226–228
time series, 225–226
sales, 223–225
Formal communication, 549–551
Formal group, *See* Groups
Formal leader, of group, 479
Formal structure, 248
see also Structure
Formalization, coordination and, 268–269
Forming stage, of group development, 468
For-profit organization, management in, 18
Four Tigers, 706

Fourteen points, for improving quality, 687, 688
Friendship groups, 466, 467
Fringe group, 472, 473
Functional authority, 258
Functional departmentation, 259–260
Functional managers, 13, 14
Functional strategy, 146, 193
Functions of the Executive (Barnard), 44
Funds flow analysis, 602
Future
decision makers making assumptions about, 78
management in the, 60, 777–778
Future Shock (Toffler), 25, 406, 748

Gantt chart, 39, 40, 232
GE portfolio matrix, 185–186
GE spotlight portfolio matrix, 185–186
General environment. *See* External environment
General managers, 13, 14
Generic competitive strategies, 187–190
Generic strategies, in business strategy, 187
Geography
departmentation by, 261, 263–264
organizational design and, 304
Gestures. *See* Body language, in nonverbal communication
Glasnost, 711
Global environment, 197, 697–727, 712–713
China and, 711
competition and, 718–721
economic/competitive factors and, 713
economic functions and, 721
entering country and, 716–717
globalization of business and, 700–703
international entrepreneurship, 746
location decisions and, 673
management and, 712–713, 721–722
management changes and, 24
multinational corporations, 712–713, *see also* problems of, *below*
cultures in, 402
ethics and, 121
management information systems and, 643
operations management and, 664
planning and, 716–718
problem solving and, 715
problems of
host government conflicts, 723
human rights, 723–724
monetary transactions, 723
political instability, 713–714, 722, 723
terrorism, 723
sociocultural factors and, 714–715
Soviet Union and, 711
strategic planning in, 196–199
technological factors and, 715
triad of key markets, 703–711, *see also* Japan
Europe, 703, 706–710
Four Tigers, 12–13, 706
North America, 703, 710–711
Globalization of business, 700–703
see also Global environment
Goals, groups influenced by, 467
see also Organizational purpose
Government, business and, 120
Graicunas' theory, 265–266
Grand strategy, 175

Grapevine, 473–474
Graphic rating scales, as performance appraisal, 376
Greeks, contributions to management by, 37
Grievance procedures, 377–378
organizational communication improved by, 555
Group decision process, 479
Group plans, 147
Group technology process, 673
Group think, 476–478
Group-based participative management, 662
Groups, 459–487
cohesiveness of, 478–479
composition of, 480
comprehensive look at, 482–483
decision making in, 479
definition, 464
development, 467–470
effectiveness of, 480–482
Follett and, 43
formal, 463, 464, 465
formation of, 466
group think, 476–478
informal, 47, 276, 463, 464–465
formation of, 466–467
leader, 463, 479, *see also* Leadership
creative problem solving and, 487
formal, 479
informal, 479
managers in, 463
maturity, 469
norms, 475–476
organization shaping, 467
reason for studying, 461–463
roles in, 470–472
size, 474–475
structure, 472–474
task force, 132, 484
team, 272–273, 484, 485, 686
work groups, 368, 461, 464, 481–482
see also Quality circles
Growth
age and size and, *see* Organizational design
in generic competitive strategies, 187
as single business corporate strategy, 183
Growth needs, job design matched to individual, 327–330

Handbook of Leadership, The (Stogdill), 503
Handbooks, organizational communication improved by, 558–559
Hardware, as management information systems technology, 637
Harvard Business Review, 78–79
Hawthorne effect, 47
quality circles and, 486
Hawthorne studies, 45–48
bank wiring observation room, 47
illumination experiments, 45, 46
relay-assembly test room experiments, 46–47
Health and safety, of employees, 373–375
Hebrews, contributions to management by, 37
Hersey-Blanchard contingency theory, of leadership, 514–516
Heuristic programming, 216

Hierarchy of needs, 427–429, 437
   informal groups satisfying, 467
"Higher Education for Business" (Gordon and Howe), 48, 49
History of management, 33–66
   contemporary management, 55–60
      excellence approach, 57–58
      Japanese management, 56–57
      as synthesis, 55–56
   contingency approach, 53–54
   early, 36–37
   future and, 60
   management-science approach, 47, 48–49
   systems approach, 49–52
   see also Behavioral approach to management; Classical approaches to management
Home, computers and working at, 334
Hong Kong, economy, 706
Horizontal communication, 550, 551
Human relations skills, of managers, 11, 12, 16, 26
Human resource audit, 359
Human resource department, preaction control and, 584
Human resource inventory database, 359
Human resource planning. See Human resources management
Human resources management, 347–383
   change and, 375–376
   compensation and benefits, 372–373
   control and, 589
   creative problem solving and, 378–380
   employee evaluation and control and, 376–377
      disciplinary programs and, 377
      equal employment opportunity and, 377
      grievance procedures, 377–378
      performance appraisal, 376–377
   employee health and safety and, 373–375
      AIDS and, 367, 374–375
      alcohol and, 374
      drugs and, 367, 374
   employee relations, 375, see also Unions
   employee transitions and, 378
   in global environment, 721
   management practices and, 350, 351
   ongoing practices, 370
   organizational strategy and, 378
   orientation, 368–369
   performance appraisals and, 620
   placement, see orientation; planning; recruitment; training and development; herein
   planning, 353–359
      current trends in, 355–356
      forecasting future requirements, 358–359
      job analysis in, 357–358
      job design in, 358, 359
      manager's role in, 356–357
      performance planning and, 619
      process, 354–356, 357
   recruitment, 360–363
      active, 360
      equal employment opportunity and, 360, 361–362
      factors affecting, 360
      internal or external, 360
      job applicant sources, 361
      job applications, 361, 363

matching recruit with organization and, 360–361
      passive, 360
      recruiter, 361
   selection, 363–368
      application blank, 361, 363
      assessment centers for, 368
      employment decisions and, 368
      equal employment opportunity and, 363, 366–368
      interview in, 364–365
      job previews for, 368
      physical exams for, 367
      reference checks in, 367
   staffing and, 349
   training and development, 369–370
      continuing, 371
   see also Equal employment opportunity
Human rights, as problem of multinationals, 723–724
Human Side of Enterprise, The (McGregor), 504
Hygiene factors, as need satisfiers, 436, 437

"Idea Generator," 235
Ideation, in communication process, 536, 540
IFPS (Interactive Financial Planning Systems), 237
Illegal activities, organizations changing the environment by, 116
Illumination experiments, in Hawthorne studies, 45, 46
Implementation. See Strategy implementation
In Search of Excellence (Peters and Waterman), 5, 57, 747
In Search of Mediocrity, 5
Incentive compensation plan, in scientific management, 38–39
Income statement, 602, 604, 605
Inculturation programs, ethics improved with, 132
Individual plans, 147
Individual roles, in groups, 472
Individualism, management practices and, 721
Industry life cycle
   in business level strategy formulation, 192
   corporate strategy and, 186–187
Inferential statistics, 217, 218
Inflection, in communication, 543
Influence, leadership and, 500–502
Informal communication, 551
Informal group. See Groups
Informal leader, of group, 479
Informal organization, Barnard and, 44
Informal structure, 248, 251, 275–276
Information, in global environment, 721
   see also Management information systems
Information function, of communication, 535
Information management control, of economic functions, 589
   see also Management information systems
Informational role, of manager, 10, 11
Information-based economy, shift from industrially based economy to, 24, 25
In-group. See Primary group

Initial integration stage, of group development, 468
Innovation
   entrepreneurship and, 736
   management of, 749
   marketing, 749
   process, 749
   product, 749
Innovation and Entrepreneurship (Drucker), 75
Input
   as management information system component, 637
   in operations systems, 664
Integration
   coordination and, 270
   Lawrence and Lorsch studies on, 297–298
   for product design, 670
Interacting groups, 84, 85–86
Interest group, 467
Intermediate plans, 146
Intermittent reinforcement, 447
Internal audit, 611
Internal entrepreneurship. See Intrapreneurship
Internal environment, 19, 20–21, 108–109
   analysis of, in SWOT analysis, 179
International business. See Global environment
International debt crisis, 702–703
Internationalization. See Global environment
INTERNIST, 650
Interpersonal skills. See Human relations skills, of managers
Interview, for employment, 364, 764–766
Intrapreneurship, 747
Intrapreneurship, 194, 612, 736, 747–749
Intrinsic need satisfiers, 436–438
Intuition, for creative problem solving, 26, 96
Intuitive thinkers, problem-solving style of, 90
Inventory
   control, 681–683, see also just-in-time, below
      economic order quantity, 681–682
      finished goods, 681
      large and small inventories, 682
      raw materials, 681
      supplies, 681
      work-in-progress, 681
   just-in-time, 221, 674, 676, 682–683, 684, 686, 687
      Japan and, 674–675
      preventive maintenance in, 687
      total quality control and, 686
   models, 214, 221
   theory, 216
   turnover, 607
Investment centers, 612
Investment reduction, as single business corporate strategy, 183
Irangate, 590

Japan, 703
   automobile companies of, 25
   banks in, 701
   changes in, 705–706
   home market, 702
   Kanban, 683

Japan (*Continued*)
  management in, 56–57, 332
    applied abroad, 722
    clan control, 577, 581
    competitiveness, 720–721
    control, 603
    creativity, 602–603
    development, 22–23
    just-in-time inventory and, 682–683
    layouts for manufacturing in, 674
    operations management, 661, 662
    participation, 413
    participative decision making, 715
    product design, 670
    productivity, 686, 689, 690
    quality circles, 485–486
    quality control, 677, 687
    strategic information systems, 645
    work force management, 677
  reasons for success of economy of,
    704–705
  in U.S. market, 700
JIT (just-in-time inventory). *See*
  Inventory
Job analysis, in human resource planning
  process, 357–358
Job application, 361, 363
Job descriptions, 358
Job design, 313–345
  contextual job dimensions and,
    317–318
  core job dimensions and, 317, 327–330
  creative problem solving and, 339–341
  definition, 316
  depth and, 317, 318, 324
  in human resource planning, 358, 359
  motivation and, 437
  organizational design and, 285–286
  quality of work life and, 319–320
  range and, 317, 318, 324
  situational model of, 316–317
  technology and, 331–336
    office automation and, 331, 334
    robotics and, 331–333
  time and, 336, 338–339
    compressed work week, 339
    flexi-time, 338
    job sharing, 329
    part-time, 338–339
  worker expectations and, 334–336
  see also Job redesign
Job enlargement, 320–321
  job redesign and, 320–321, 324,
    325–326
Job enrichment, 320–321
  job redesign and, 320–321, 324–325,
    326–327, 330, 335–336
  quality circles as, 486
Job evaluation, wages determined by,
  372, 373
Job posting, 360, 361
Job previews, in recruitment process, 368
Job redesign, 320–331
  effects of other jobs, 331
  at group level, 322–323
    autonomous work teams, 322, 324,
      330
    quality circles, 322–323, 324, 330
  job design matched to growth needs
    for, 327–330
  job enlargement and, 320–321, 324,
    325–326
  job enrichment and, 320–321, 324–325,
    326–327, 330, 335–336
  job rotation and, 322, 324

method of, 324–331
  work simplification and, 321, 324
Job rotation, job redesign and, 322, 324
Job sharing, 339
Job specifications, equal employment
  opportunity and, 359
Job summary, 358
Joint ventures, 274–275, 716–717
Justice, need for, 434
Just-in-time inventory. *See* Inventory

Kanban, 683
KISS technique, for effective
  communication, 552
Knowledge workers, 654
Knowledge-based organizations, 654
Korea, 706
  operations process, 661
  management style, 12–13

Labor relations. *See* Employee relations;
  Human resources management
Language
  as barrier to communication, 551
  in verbal communication, 542
Language systems, organization's culture
  revealed by, 390
Laptop computers, 559, 649
Law. *See* Legal factors
Leader effectiveness and adaptability
  description (LEAD), 515
Leaders (Bennis and Nanus), 497
Leadership, 8, 15, 495–529
  authoritarian, 502
  behavioral approaches to, 505–509
    Managerial Grid,® 508–509
    Ohio State and Michigan leadership
      studies, 505–506
    Yukl studies, 506–507
  changes in, 28
  communication and, 517
  contingency approaches to, 53–54,
    509–517
    contingency model, 510–512
    continuum of leadership behavior,
      510, 511
    Hersey-Blanchard contingency
      theory, 514–516
    Muczyk-Reimann model, 517
    path-goal theory, 512–514
    Vroom-Yetton-Yago decision-tree
      model, 516
  as creative problem-solving process, 71,
    518–524
  definition, 497
  Fiedler on, 53
  Follett on, 43
  management distinct from, 498–499
  power and influence and, 500–502
  of small business/entrepreneurship,
    739–740
  strategy implementation and style of,
    200–201
  trait approaches to, 503–505
    Theory X and Theory Y, 504–505
  transactional, 524
  transformational, 524–525
  TRRAP model of, 519, 521–524
  see also Communication; Groups
Leadership Challenge, The (Korzes and
  Posner), 499
Leadership in Action (Yukl), 506
Legal factors, 119, 120, 121
  in general environment, 112–113
  in global environment, 713–714

Legitimate power, 500
Leverage ratios, 606–607
Life stages, career decisions and, 762, 773
Life-cycle theory. *See* Hersey-Blanchard
  contingency theory, of leadership
Line authority, 256–258
Line managers, 16
Linear programming (LP), 215, 216,
  231–233
  for production planning, 681
  for resource allocation, 672
Linking-pin concept
  coordination and, 270–271
  manager and, 471
Liquidity ratios, 605–606, 607
Listening, in communication, 544, 552
Litigation audit, social responsibility
  improved with, 127
Location decisions, 673, 674
Long-range financial plan, 600, 601
Lotus 1-2-3, 237, 238
Lower-level managers, 14, 15
  planning by, 142, 143, 144
LP. *See* Linear programming

"M" form structure. *See* Divisionalized
  form of organization
Machine bureaucracy, 292, 293–294, 297,
  300
Maintenance and building roles, in
  groups, 471–472
Maintenance management, 687
Management, 5
Management by objectives (MBO),
  161–163
  for performance appraisal, 601, 617
Management by objectives, results, and
  rewards (MBORR), 164, 165
  for performance appraisal, 376, 601
Management control systems. *See*
  Control systems
Management development, 21–22, 772
Management functions, 6–9
  core, *see* Creative problem solving
  Fayol on, 41–42
  by level, 15–17
  Mahoney, Jerdee and Carroll on, 9
  mission, 6–7, 15
  see also Control; Leadership;
    Organizing; Planning
Management information systems (MIS),
  629–657
  change in function of, 646
  components, 637–638
    control, 637–638
    database, 637
    inputs, 637
    models, 637
    output, 638
    technology, 637
  decision support systems, 649–650
  definition, 635
  design, 638–639
  director, 646
  evolution, 635–637
    decision support systems, 636
    electronic data processing, 636
    expert systems, 637
    management information systems,
      636
  executive information systems,
    651–652
  expert systems, 649
    artificial intelligence and, 650–651
    information needs and, 633–634

information provided by, 640–643
knowledge-based organizations and, 654
at multinationals, 643
organization affected by, 653
protecting, 652–653
quality information and, 633
strategic, 643–645
telecommunications and, 647–649
  cellular phones, 647
  computer conferencing, 647
  electronic bulletin boards, 648
  electronic data interchange, 648
  electronic mail, 647
  fax, 647
  laptop personal computers, 649
  video conferencing, 648
  voice mail, 647
using, 639–645
virus, 652–653
Management levels, 14–15
  line managers, 16–17
  lower-level managers, 14, 15
  management functions by, 15–17
  middle managers, 14, 15, 16
  in organization chart, 250
  staff managers, 16–17
  top managers, 14–15, 16
Management matrix, 22–23
Management philosophy, organizational design and, 301
Management science, 47, 48–49, 211, 212
  as decision support for problem solving, 238
  see also Quantitative methods
Management systems, strategy implementation and, 199
Managerial environment, 19–21
  see also External environment; Internal environment
Managerial Grid,® 508–509
Managerial roles, 10–11
  by level, 16
Managerial skills, 11–12
  by level, 16
Managerial span of control, 265–267
Managerial work station, 646
Managing change. See Change, management and
Managing for Results, 161
Manufacturing. See Operations management
Market control, 576, 578, 587
Marketing, in global environment, 721
Marketing innovation, 749
Marketing strategy, operations strategies related to, 667
Masculinity, management practices and, 721
Mass production, 302–303, 305
Master budget, 613
Materials requirement planning (MRP), 683
Matrix structure, 273–274, 275
MBO. See Management by objectives.
MBORR. See Management by objectives, results, and rewards
Mechanistic organizations, 113–114, 288–290
Megatrends (Naisbitt), 26
Memos, organizational communication improved by, 558–559
Mentors, for minorities and women in careers, 767

Metaphors, organization's culture revealed by, 390
Middle line
  Mintzberg's, 290–295, 297, 299–300
  of organization, 290, 291, 292
Middle managers, 14, 15
  planning by, 142, 143, 144
Middle-management (tactical) control systems. See Control systems
Minorities, career planning and, 767
MIS. See Management information systems
Mission
  group influenced by, 467
  as organizational purpose, 157–158
Mission functions, 6–7, 15
  see also Control; Leadership; Organizing; Planning
Mission statement, 157–158
MNCs (multinational corporations). See Global environment
Models, as management information system component, 637
Mommy track, 767
Monetary transactions, as problem of multinationals, 723
Motion and time studies, Gilbreths on, 40
Motivation, 421–457
  as communication function, 534–535
  compensation and benefits for, 372–373
  as creative problem solving, 451–453
  cycle, 424–425, 427
  definition, 423
  Herzberg on, 321
  informal groups satisfying needs and, 466–467
  performance appraisal and, 618
  stress and, 776
  see also Motivation/Performance Cycle
Motivation cycle, 424–425, 427
Motivation/hygiene model, 436–438
Motivation/Performance Cycle (MPC), 426–453
  content and process theories in, 427
  extrinsic and intrinsic need satisfiers in, 436–438
  future motivation determination in, 450–451
  guidelines for using, 453
  individual reassessing situation in, 450
  motivation to expend effort in, 442
  motivation turned into performance in, 442–444
    objective setting and, 443–444
  need satisfiers obtained or not in, 444,
    see also reinforcement, below
  needs and, 427–435
    achievement motivation, 432–433
    hierarchy of, 427–429, 437
    manager and, 435–436
    managerial implications, 431
    nature and strength of current, 430–431
    objectives as motivators, 434
    role motivation and, 434
    socially contributive actions, 434
    for truth, beauty, and justice, 434
  performance in, 444
  reinforcement and, 444, 445–450
    continuous, 447, 448
    extinction, 448
    fixed-interval, 447, 448
    fixed-ratio, 447, 448

intermittent, 447
  negative, 446
  positive, 446
  punishment, 446–447
  theory, 445
  variable-interval, 447, 448
searching for and choosing alternative to satisfy need in, 438–442
  equity theory and, 440–441
  expectancy theory and, 438–440
Motivators, as need satisfiers, 436, 437
Mottos, organization's culture revealed by, 391
MRP. See Materials requirements planning
Muczyk-Reimann model, of leadership, 517
Multinational corporations. See Global environment
Multinational enterprises, 712
  see also Global environment
Multiple business corporate strategy, 184–187
Multiple cultures, in organization, 402–403
Multiple products, as single business corporate strategy, 183
Music, in nonverbal communication, 549
Myers-Briggs type indicator (MBTI), 365, 366
Myths, organization culture and, 388, 390

Natural work units, in job redesign, 328, 329
Nature of Managerial Work, The (Mintzberg), 10
Needs, motivation and, 424
  see also Motivation/Performance Cycle
Negative reinforcement, 446
Negotiating, as management function, 9
Network models, 215, 232–234
Networking, for minorities and women, 767
New entrants, in competitive environment, 110
Niche strategy, in single business corporate strategy, 182
Noise, in communication, 540
Nominal group, 84, 86
Nonlinear programming, 216
Nonmonetary resource input budgets, 613, 614
Nonverbal communication. See Communication
Norming stage, of group development, 468
Norms
  of groups, 475–476
  organizational culture revealed by, 392–393
North America, economy, 703, 710–711
Not-for-profit organizations, 12, 13, 18
  strategic planning in, 195, 196

Objectives. See Organizational purpose
Objectivity, in control systems, 581
Occupational Safety and Health Act of 1970, 373
OD. See Organizational development
Office automation. See Automation
Offshore manufacturing, 673
Off-the-job training and development, 369

Ohio State and Michigan leadership studies, 505–506
Ombudsmen
  ethics improved with, 132
  organizational communication improved by, 556
One-day suspension, as discipline, 377
On-the-job training, 369
OPEC, 699
Open system, 50–51, 107
Open-door policies, organizational communication improved by, 556–557
Operating budget, 600, 601
Operating core
  Mintzberg's, 290–295, 297, 299–300
  of organization, 290, 291, 292, 306
Operational control, 587, 589
  see also Control systems
Operational plans, 146–147, 148
Operations, in control systems, 578, 580
Operations management, 658–695
  as creative problem solving, 691
  definition, 664
  factories of the future and, 669, 687, 689, 690
  in global environment, 721
  in manufacturing organizations, 662–668
  operational decisions, 666, 684–687
    maintenance management, 687
    project management, 687
    quality control, 686–687
    scheduling and shop floor planning and control, 684–685
    workers and productivity, 686
  operations strategies, 666–668
  productivity and, 689–690
    improving, 689
    services and, 690
    technology and, 689–690
    workers and, 686
  in service industry, 662–668
    capacity, 675
    layout, 675
    process planning, 670
    productivity and, 690
    quality control, 687
    service design, 670
    strategic operations decisions, 668–669
  strategic operations decisions, 666, 668–678
    facility capacity, 672–673
    facility layout, 673–675
    facility location, 673, 674
    focused factories, 669–670
    positioning the operations system, 668
    process planning, 670
    product/service design, 670
    production technology, 675–676
    service facility layout, 675
    in service industry, 668–669
    total quality control, 677–678
    work force management, 677
  tactical operations decisions, 666, 678–684
    materials management and purchasing, 684
    materials requirement planning, 683
    production planning systems, 679–681
  see also Inventory
Operations managers, 664

Operations research (OR). See Management science
Operations strategies, 666–668
Opportunities. See SWOT analysis
Opportunity, problem-solving skills needed for, 70
"Optimization" analysis, spreadsheets for, 238
Oral communication, in verbal communication, 542
Organic organizational design, 288–290
Organic organizations, 113, 114
Organization, 12–13, 248
  Barnard on sociology of, 44–45
  as closed system, 107–108
  informal, 44
  interfacing with environment, 114–116
  knowledge-based, 654
  management information system and, 653
  mechanistic, 113–114
  as open system, 107
  organic, 113–114
  see also Classical approaches to management; Not-for-profit organizations; Structure
Organization chart, 249–252
Organizational behavior modification (OBM), 445, 448–449
  as reinforcement, see Motivation/Performance Cycle
Organizational climate, 403–406
Organizational communication, 554–559
  informational approaches, 557–559
    athletic programs, 558
    organizational rules, 558–559
    periodic meetings, 557–558
    publications and bulletin boards, 558
    television broadcasts, 558
  structural approaches to, 555–557
    attitude surveys, 555–556
    counseling programs, 555
    grievance procedures, 555
    ombudsmen, 556
    open-door policies, 556–557
    suggestion programs, 557
  technology and, 559
  see also Communication
Organizational culture, 387–403
  artifacts revealing, 388–393
    language systems and metaphors, 390
    myths and sagas, 388, 390
    symbols, ceremonies, and rituals, 390–391
    value systems and behavioral norms, 392–393
  creative problem solving and, 414
  creativity and, 96
  employees fitting into, 398–403
  groups and, 462, 467
  indoctrination programs for employee on, 375–376
  management information system and, 653
  managing, 26, 401–402
  multiple, 402–403
  organizational climate, 403–406
  organizational development and, 409
  shared values and, 396–397
  strategy and, 393–396
    bet-your-company culture, 393, 394, 395
    implementation and, 201–202
    process culture, 394, 395–396

tough guy macho culture, 383, 394
work hard/play hard culture, 394, 395
Organizational design, 283–311, 315
  creative problem solving and, 306–308
  definition, 286
  future and, 305–306
  geographic dispersion and, 304
  management philosophy and, 301
  size, age and growth and, 298–301
    growth theories of the firm and, 299
    Mintzberg's five configurations theory and, 299–300
  strategy and external environment and, 287–298
    adhocracy, 292, 295, 297, 300, 306
    differentiation and integration and, 297–298
    divisionalized form, 292, 294–295, 297, 300
    environmental complexity and change and, 290, 291
    machine bureaucracy, 292, 293–294, 297, 300
    mechanistic structures, 288–290
    Mintzberg on, 290–295, 297
    organic structures, 288–290
    professional bureaucracy, 292, 294, 297, 300, 306
    simple structure, 292–293, 297, 300
  technology and, 301–304
  see also Job design
Organizational development (OD), 407, 409
  change and, 376
Organizational ethics, 121
Organizational purpose, 155–165
  goals, 159
  mission, 157–158
  objectives, 159–165
    alternatives to, 164–165
    characteristics, 160
    group influenced by, 467
    importance, 160
    management by objectives, results, and rewards, 164, 165
    managing by, 161–163
    motivation and, 434, 443–444
    personal, 165
  vision, 155–157
Organizational strategy, human resources management and, 378
Organizational structure, strategy implementation and, 198–199
Organizing, 8, 15
  changes in, 28
  creative problem-solving decisions relating to, 71
  definition, 247
  as problem solving, 276–277
  of small business/entrepreneurship, 739
  see also Structure
Orientation, in human resources management, 368
Out-group, 472, 473
Output
  as management information system component, 638
  in operations systems, 663, 665, 666
Overload, as barrier to communication, 553

Pacific Rim
  entrepreneurship in, 746

operating process and, 662
product design and, 670
see also Japan
Parity principle, 254–255
Participation
resistance to change and, 413
in TRRAP model, 519, 521–524
Participative leadership, 513, 514
Participative management, 662
group-based, 662
Part-time employees, 338–339
Passion for Excellence (Peters and
Austin), 5, 57, 58, 59
Passive recruitment, 360
Path-goal theory, of leadership, 512–514
PC. *See* Computer
Perception, in communication, 540–541,
553
Perestroika, 711
Performance
factors turning motivation into,
442–444
motivation and, 427, *see also*
Motivation/Performance Cycle
see also Control
Performance appraisals, 376–377, 601,
602, 617–620
Performance standards, 570, 574
actual performance compared against,
571
in control process, 570
Performance-to-outcome expectancy, 440
Permanent work groups, 464
Personal computer. *See* Computer
Personal ethics, 121
Personal power, 500–501
Personality, communication and, 552
Personality tests, in selection process,
364–367
Personality types, stress and, 776
Personnel planning (human resource
planning). *See* Human resources
management
PERT (Program Evaluation and Review
Technique), 39, 232, 234, 235
for project management, 687
PERT/CPM, 216
Physical exams, in selection process, 367
Plan, 139
see also Planning
PLAN POWER, 651
Planning, 8, 15, 137–155, 176
changes in, 28
control and, 150–151, 574–575
creative problem-solving decisions
relating to, 71
creativity and, 148–149
criteria for plans, 147–150
environment conducive to, 154–155
failures in, 154
in global environment, 716–718
human resource, *see* Human resources
management
importance of, 142
levels of, 142–144
limitations of, 151–154
single-use plans, 145–147
intermediate plans, 146
operational plans, 146–147, 148
strategies, 146
situational analysis for, 151, *see also*
SWOT analysis
for small business/entrepreneurship,
738–739
standing plans, 144–145

in strategy formulation, 179–180
see also Organizational purpose;
Quantitative methods; Strategic
planning
Point method, for job evaluation, 372
Policies, for control, 601
Politics
in general environment, 112–113
in global environment, 713–714, 723
organizations changing the
environment by, 116
Porter competitive strategies, 187–190
Portfolio management, 184
Portfolio matrix, 184–185
Position power, 500
Positioning the operations systems, 668
Positive reinforcement, 446
Postaction controls, 586
Postjobs, 331
Power, 253
authority and, *see* Structure
leadership and, 500–502
Power distance dimension, management
practices and, 721
Preaction control, 584
Precontrols. *See* Preaction control
Predictive statistics. *See* Inferential
statistics
Pregnancy Discrimination Act of 1978,
352
Prejobs, 331
Prevention controls. *See* Preaction
control
Preventive maintenance, 687
Primary group, 472, 473
Principles of management, Fayol and,
41–42
PRISE-Personnel Reporting and
Information System for Employers,
235
Proactive social response, 125
Problem identification, in creative
problem solving, 76
Problem solving. *See* Creative problem
solving
Procedures
for control, 601, 602
organizational communication
improved by, 558–559
Process culture, 394, 395–396
Process innovation, 749
Process layouts, 673
Process planning, as strategic operations
decision, 670
Process production, 302, 303, 305
Process theories, in Motivation/
Performance Cycle, 427
Product, departmentation by, 260–262
Product design, as strategic operations
decision, 670
Product innovation, 749
Product layouts, 673
Product life style
accelerating, 25
in business level strategy formulation,
192
corporate strategy and, 186–187
Product plans, 146
Production planning systems, 679–681
Production technology, as strategic
operations decision, 675–676
Productivity. *See* Operations
management
Professional bureaucracy, 293, 300, 306
Professional ethics, 121

Professional planner, 194
Profit centers, 612
Profitability, social responsibility and,
118, 127–128
Profitability ratios, 607
Program, 146
Program Evaluation and Review
Technique. *See* PERT
Project, 146
Project management, 687
Project structure, 272
Promotions, performance appraisals and,
617
Public relations, organizations changing
the environment by, 115
Publications, organizational
communication improved by, 558
Pulling up roots, as life stage, 762
Punishment, as reinforcement, 446–447
Purpose, 139
see also Organizational purpose
Pyramid, computers and, 334
Pyramidal structures, 265

Qualitative forecasting, 228
Quality circles, 18, 272, 322–323,
485–487
job redesign and, 322–323, 324, 330
productivity and, 686
Quality control, 662, 686–687
Deming on, 687, 688
in services, 687
total, 674, 677–678, 686
Quality of work life (QWL), 318–320
job design and, 319–320
job redesign and, 335–336
Quantitative methods, 209–243
advantages of, 213, 214
decision theory, 218–220
decision trees, 218, 219–220
expected value, 218, 219
disadvantages of, 214
distribution models, 222–223
foundations of, 212–213
fundamental, 214–216
inventory models, 214, 221
queueing models, 215, 216, 221–222
regression analysis, 215
sampling theory, 216
statistical decision theory, 216
for planning, *see also* Forecasting
break-even-analysis, 229–231, 238
computers for, 235–238
CPM, 232–233, 234, 235
linear programming, 215, 216,
231–233
network analysis, 215, 232–234
PERT, 232, 234, 235
simulations, 215, 216, 236–238
for resource allocation, 672
statistical analysis, 217–218
see also Forecasting; Operations
management
Question marks, in BCG matrix,
184–185
Queueing models, 215, 216, 221–222
Queueing theory, 215, 216
QWL. *See* Quality of work life

Raises, performance appraisals and, 617
Random variations, in time series
analysis, 225, 226
Range
job design, 324
of jobs, 317, 318

Ranking method, for job evaluation, 372
Ratio analysis. *See* Control systems
Raw materials, as inventory type, 681
Reactive social responsibility, 123
Reference checks, in selection process, 367
Reference power, 501
Regression analysis, 215, 226–227
Regulated businesses, strategic planning in, 198
Rehabilitation Act of 1973, 352, 374
Reinforcement theory, 445
Related and supporting industries, global competitiveness and, 719, 720
Relationship, in TRRAP model, 519, 521–524
Relay-assembly test room experiment, in Hawthorne studies, 46–47
Relevancy, of information, 633
Renewal, as life stage, 762
Renewal process, organizational development improving, 409
Representing, as management function, 8, 9
Resignation, as life stage, 762
Resource allocation process, as strategic operations decision, 671–672
Responsibility centers, 612, 614
Restructuring, entrepreneurship and, 748–749
Return on investment (ROI), 603, 607–609, 612
  break even analysis for, 231
Return on total assets, 607
Revenue and expense budgets, 613
Revenue centers, 612
Revenue forecast, for budgeting process, 614
Reward, in TRRAP model, 519, 521–524
Reward power, 500
Rewards system. *See* Management by objectives, results, and rewards
Risk
  creative problem solving and, 81
  Farley Test for Risk Takers and, 101
Rituals, organization's culture revealed by, 390
Robotics, 675, 676
  job design and, 331–333
ROI. *See* Return on investment
Role, communication and, 552–553
Role motivation, human needs and, 434
Role playing, for interview, 765
Romans, contributions to management by, 37
Rooting, as life stage, 762

Sagas, organization culture and, 388, 390
Sales force composites, 228
Sales forecasting, 223–225
Sampling, in quality control, 686
Sampling theory, 216
SBU. *See* Strategic business unit
Scalar chain of command, 253–254
Scheduling, operational decision for, 684–685
Service, management as, 21
Scientific management. *See* Classical approaches to management
Scientific Principles of Management, The (Taylor), 38
Seasonal variations, in time series analysis, 225, 226
Secondary group. *See* Fringe group

Selection. *See* Human resources management
Self-image
  communication and, 553
  stress and, 776
Service industry. *See* Operations management
Seven Elements of Strategic Fit (Seven S's), 201–202, 387–388, 393
"Seven Steps of Socialization," 398–401
Shareholder value, 609
Shop floor planning and control, operational decisions for, 684–685
Silence, in communication, 543–544
Simple ranking, as performance appraisal, 376
Simple structure, 292–293, 297, 300
Simulation, 215, 216
  computer for, 236–238
  for production planning, 681
Singapore, economy, 706
Single business corporate strategy, 180–184
Single-use plan. *See* Planning
Situational analysis, 151
  see also SWOT analysis
Situational factors, determining for creative problem solving, 77
Situational management, 54
Situational model, of job design, 316–317
Size, age and growth and. *See* Organizational design
Small batch production, 302, 303, 305
Small business management
  definition, 736–737
  entrepreneurship distinguished from, 736
  failures, 739
  managing, 737–741
    leading, 739–740
    organizing, 739
    planning, 738–739
  strategic planning and, 196
  see also Entrepreneurship
Smoothing, as conflict resolution technique, 489–490
Social audit, 603
  social responsibility improved with, 125, 127, 128
Social control, 128–129
Social power/social responsibility concept, 116, 118
Social responsibility, 104–107, 116–128
  arguments for and against, 117
  categories of, 107
  definition, 116–117
  Gantt and, 39
  improving, 125–127
    corporate social policy process for, 125, 126–127
    litigation audit for, 127
    social audit for, 125, 127, 128
  issues identified for, 122–123
  levels of
    discretionary, 121
    economic, 119
    ethical, 121
    legal, 119, 120, 121
  philosophy of, 123–125
    accommodative, 124
    defensive, 123–124
    proactive, 125
    reactive, 123
    profit concept of, 118
    profitability and, 127–128

social power and, 116, 118
  stakeholder concept of, 118
  see also Ethics
Socially contributive actions, need for, 434
Societal ethics, 121
Society, in general environment, 111
Sociocultural factors, in global environment, 714–715
Sociometry, 472
Software, as management information systems technology, 637
South Africa, human rights and, 723–724
South Korea. *See* Korea
Soviet Union
  decision making in, 715
  economy, 711
Space, in nonverbal communication, 547–548
Span of control
  managerial, 265–267
  in organization chart, 250
Specialization of labor, 248–249
  in organization chart, 250
  work simplification and, 321
Speed, in communication, 543
Spreadsheet programs, 237–238
Stabilization, as single business corporate strategy, 183
Stable environments, 113, 114, 115, 289
Staff authority, 256–258
Staff managers, 16–17
Staffing, 9, 349
  see also Human resources management
Stakeholder audits, 603
Stakeholder concept, of social responsibility, 118
Standards. *See* Performance standards
Standing plans, 144–145
Star Wars Defense Initiative (SDI), 148
Stars, in BCG matrix, 184, 185
Statistical analysis, 216, 217–218
Statistical decision theory, 216
Statistical reports, 600–601
Statistical sampling, in quality control, 686
Status, communication and, 553
Status symbols, in nonverbal communication, 549
Steady-state equilibrium, in environment, 51
Steering controls. *See* Concurrent controls
Stoplight strategy. *See* GE stoplight portfolio matrix
Storming stage, of group development, 468
Storyboarding, as interactive creative group process, 86
Strategic alliances, 274
Strategic apex
  Mintzberg's, 290–295, 297, 299–300
  of organization, 290, 291, 292
Strategic business unit (SBU), 146, 306, 612
  departmentation by, 261, 262–263
Strategic control, 587
  see also Control systems
Strategic management, 173–208
  creative problem solving and, 202
  definition, 177
  human behavior and, 194–195
  human resources management as part of, 354
  strategists, 193–194

see also Strategic planning; Strategy formulation; Strategy implementation
Strategic management information system, 643–645
Strategic operations decisions. See Operations management
Strategic planning, 44, 147, 148, 176, 177, 600, 601
  Barnard and, 44
  multinationals and, 196–199, 716
  in not-for-profits, 196
  organizations adapting to environment by, 114
  in regulated businesses, 198
  in small business, 196
  strategic thinking and, 178
Strategic thinking, 178
Strategies, 146, 393
  in control systems, 578, 580
  group influenced by, 467
  see also Organizational culture; Organizational design
Strategists, 193–194
Strategy formulation, 175, 178–194
  at business level, 146, 180, 187–193
    competitive advantage, 192
    generic strategies, 187–192
  at corporate level, 146, 180–197
    multiple business, 184–187
    single business, 180–184
  at functional level, 193
  steps, 178–180, see also SWOT analysis
    planning premises, 179–180
Strategy implementation, 198–202
  leadership style and, 200–201
  management systems and, 199
  organizational culture management, 201–202
  organizational structure and, 198–199
Strengths. See SWOT analysis
Stress, 772–777
  causes and results of, 774
  definition, 773
  eliminating, 373
  impacts of, 777
  managing, 777
  personality type and, 776
  psychological state and, 776
  stages of, 776–777
  stressful life events, 775
  stressors, 773, 775
Stressors, 773, 775
Structure, 244–282
  communication and, see Organizational communication
  coordination, 268–272
    complexity and, 269–270
    formalization and, 268–269
    integration and differentiation and, 270
    linking-pin concept and, 270–271
  delegation of authority, 253–258
    acceptance theory of authority and, 254
    in centralized organization, 255
    concurrent authority, 258
    in decentralized organization, 255–256, 257
    functional authority, 258
    line and staff authority, 256–258
    parity principle and, 254–255
    scalar chain of command and, 253–254

departmentation, 258–265
  client or customer as basis for, 265
  by economic function of organization, 259–260
  by geography, 261, 263–264
  in organization chart, 250
  by product, 260–262
  by strategic business unit, 261, 262–263
  by task specialty, 264–265
  time as basis for, 265
division of labor, 248–252
  differentiation and, 249
  organization chart and, 249–252
  specialization of labor, 248–249, 250
"flat" versus "tall," 267
formal, 248
group influenced by, 467
informal, 248, 251, 275–276
joint ventures, 274–275
managerial span of control, 265–267
matrix, 273–274, 275
project, 272
pyramidal, 265
strategic alliances, 274
team, 272–273
see also Organizational culture; Participation
Structured problems, 82, 83
Subjectivity, in control systems, 581
Substitutes, in competitive environment, 110
Subsystems, in systems, 50, 52
Succession, entrepreneurship and, 749
Suggestion programs, organizational communication improved by, 557
Sumerians, contributions to management by, 37
Superordinate goals, as conflict resolution technique, 488, 489
Supervising, as management function, 9
Suppliers, in competitive environment, 110
Supplies, as inventory type, 681
Support staff
  Mintzberg's, 290–295, 297, 299–300
  of organization, 290, 291, 292
Supportive leadership, 513, 514
Suspension warnings, as discipline, 377
SWOT analysis, 151, 198
  for small business/entrepreneurship, 739
  in strategy formulation, 179–180
  see also Strategy implementation
Symbols, organization's culture revealed by, 390
Synergy, systems having, 51
Synthesis of management, 60
  as contemporary management, 60, see also History of management
System 4, organizational climate assessed with, 404–406
Systematic thinkers, problem-solving style of, 90
Systems
  control, 578, 580–581
  group influenced by, 467
  for strategy implementation, 199
Systems approach to management, 49–52
Systems theory, 50

Tactical control, 587
  see also Control systems
Tactical operations decisions. See Operations management

Tactics, in control systems, 578, 580
Taiwan, economy, 706
Takeover, single business corporate strategy and, 183–184
"Tall" organizations, 267
Task, in TRRAP model, 519, 521–524
Task combination, in job redesign, 328, 329
Task force, 132, 484
Task group. See Work group
Task roles, in groups, 470–471
Task specialty, departmentation by, 264–265
TAX ADVISER, 651
TAX MAN, 651
Team, 484, 485
  productivity and, 686
  structure, 272–273
  see also Groups
Technical and Miscellaneous Revenue Act of 1989 (TAMRA), 372
Technical skills, of managers, 11, 16
Technicians, in management information systems, 637
Technological forecast, 228
Technology, 331
  in general environment, 110–111
  in global environment, 715
  management and, 25–26
  as management information system component, 637, 646
  organizational communication and, 559
  organizational design and, 301–304
  productivity and, 689–690
  as strategic operations decision, 675–676
  technological forecast for, 228
  see also Job design
Technostructure
  Mintzberg's, 290–295, 297, 299–300
  of organization, 290, 291, 292
Telecommunications. See Management information systems
Television broadcasts, organizational communication improved by, 558
Temporary work groups, 464
Termination, as discipline, 377
Terrorism, as problem of multinationals, 723
Testing, in selection process, 364–367
Theory X, 320, 504–505
Theory Y, 320, 504–505
Theory Z management, 677
  applied abroad, 722
Therbligs, 40
Threats. See SWOT analysis
Three-day suspension, as discipline, 377
Thriving on Chaos: Handbook for a Management Revolution (Peters), 5, 25, 57, 60, 748
Time, 336
  in nonverbal communication, 548–549
  see also Job design
Time series forecasting techniques, 225–226
Timeliness, in control systems, 580–581
Timely, information as, 633
Timing, as barrier to communication, 552
Top level managers, 14–15
  planning by, 142, 143, 144
Total integration stage, of group development, 468, 469
Total quality control, 674, 677–678, 686

Touching, in nonverbal communication, 549
Tough-guy macho culture, 393, 394
Trade associations, organizations changing the environment and, 116
Training and development of employees, 369–370
    continuing, 371
Trait approaches, to leadership, 503–505
Transactional leadership, 524
Transformation systems, in operations systems, 663, 665, 666
Transformational Leader, The (Tichy and Devanna), 497, 499
Transformational leadership, 524–525
Transmission, in communication process, 538, 540
TRRAP model, of leadership, 519, 521–524
Trends, in time series analysis, 225, 226
Truth, need for, 434
Trying twenties, as life stage, 762
Turnaround, as single business corporate strategy, 183
Type A firms, 677
Type A personality, 776
Type B personality, 776
Type J firms, 677

Uncertainty, creative problem solving and, 81
Uncertainty avoidance dimension, management practices and, 721
Understandability, in control systems, 581
Understanding, in communication process, 540
Unions, 375
    as formal group, 467
    grievance procedures and, 377
    rewards and performance and, 450
Unit production, 302, 303, 305

United States, global competitiveness and, 710–711
Universality of management, 17
Unskilled labor, shortages of, 355–356
Unstable environment, 113, 114, 115, 289
Unstructured problems, 82–83
Upward communication, 550–551

Valdez oil spill, 104–105, 108, 123
Values
    organizational culture revealed by, 392–393
    organizations sharing, 396–397
Variable-interval reinforcement schedule, 447, 448
Variable-ratio reinforcement schedule, 448
Venetians, contributions to management by, 37
Verbal communication. *See* Communication
Verbal warning, as discipline, 377
Vertical job loading, 325
    in job redesign, 328, 329
    see also Job enrichment
Video conferencing, 559, 648
Vietnam-Era Veteran's Readjustment Act of 1974, 352
Virus, management information system and, 652–653
Vision
    group influenced by, 467
    as organizational purpose, 155–157
Visual arts, in nonverbal communication, 549
Voice input, 637
Voice mail, 559, 647
Voice tone, in communication, 543
Volume, in communication, 543
Vroom-Yago model, for decision making, 93

Vroom-Yetton-Yago decision-tree model, of leadership, 516

Wages. *See* Compensation
Weaknesses. *See* SWOT analysis
Wealth of Nations, The (Smith), 36
Wellness programs, 373–374
What Color Is Your Paycheck? (Bolles), 759
Whistleblowing, 131–132
Women
    career planning and, 767
    as entrepreneurs, 745
    mommy track, 767
Wordiness, as barrier to communication, 552
Work force, diversity of, 26, 402
    needs and, 430–431
"Work Force 2000" (Hudson Institute), 349
Work group, 368, 461, 464, 481–482
    see also Groups
Work hard/play hard culture, 394, 395
Work simplification, job redesign and, 321, 324
Work station. *See* Managerial work station
Work teams
    autonomous, 322
    organizational development improving, 409
Worker expectations, job design and, 334–336
Work-in-process, as inventory type, 681
Written communication, 544, 546
Written warning, as discipline, 377

Yes/no control, 585
Yukl leadership studies, 506–507

Zero-based budgeting, 616
Zero defects, 662